CLEP CORE EXAMS
COLLEGE-LEVEL
EXAMINATION PROGRAM

 TestWare® Edition

College Composition
Dominic Marullo, M.A.
Rachelle Smith, Ph.D.
Ken Springer, Ph.D.

Humanities
Edited by Patricia Van Arnum, M.S.

College Mathematics
Mel Friedman, M.S.

Natural Sciences
Laurie Ann Callihan, Ph.D.
David Callihan, M.S.

Social Sciences & History
Scott Dittloff, Ph.D.

Research & Education Association
Visit our website at: www.rea.com

Research & Education Association
61 Ethel Road West
Piscataway, New Jersey 08854
E-mail: info@rea.com

CLEP Core Exams
College-Level Examination Program
With TestWare® on CD-ROM

Library of Congress Control Number 2011922830

ISBN-13: 978-0-7386-0487-9
ISBN-10: 0-7386-0487-9

CONTENTS

ABOUT RESEARCH & EDUCATION ASSOCIATION

Founded in 1959, Research & Education Association (REA) is dedicated to publishing the finest and most effective educational materials—including software, study guides, and test preps—for students in middle school, high school, college, graduate school, and beyond.

REA's Test Preparation series includes books and software for all academic levels in almost all disciplines. REA publishes test preps for students who have not yet entered high school, as well as high school students preparing to enter college. Students from countries around the world seeking to attend college in the United States will find the assistance they need in REA's publications. For college students seeking advanced degrees, REA publishes test preps for many major graduate school admission examinations in a wide variety of disciplines, including engineering, law, and medicine. Students at every level, in every field, with every ambition can find what they are looking for among REA's publications.

REA's series presents tests that accurately depict the official exams in both degree of difficulty and types of questions. REA's practice tests are always based upon the most recently administered exams, and include every type of question that can be expected on the actual exams.

REA's publications and educational materials are highly regarded and continually receive an unprecedented amount of praise from professionals, instructors, librarians, parents, and students. Our authors are as diverse as the subject matter represented in the books we publish. They are well known in their respective disciplines and serve on the faculties of prestigious colleges and universities throughout the United States and Canada.

Today REA's catalog is a leading resource for teachers, students, and professionals.

We invite you to visit us at *www.rea.com* to find out how "REA is making the world smarter."

ACKNOWLEDGMENTS

We would like to thank Larry B. Kling, Vice President, Editorial, for his overall guidance, which brought this publication to completion; Pam Weston, Publisher, for setting the quality standards for production integrity and managing the publication to completion; John Paul Cording, Vice President, Technology, for coordinating the design and development of REA's TestWare® software; Alice Leonard, Senior Editor, and Diane Goldschmidt, Managing Editor, for project management; Heena Patel and Amy Jamison, Software Project Managers, for their software creation and testing efforts; Chris Feldman, for editing the content, and the S4Carlisle team for typesetting this edition.

ABOUT THIS BOOK AND TESTWARE®

This book, along with the accompanying CD, provides you with complete preparation for the CLEP core exams. These exams are among the most popular in the CLEP program and correspond to the core courses required by most colleges. The book covers the following subjects: College Composition and College Composition Modular, Humanities, College Mathematics, Natural Sciences, and Social Sciences and History.

We give you customized practice tests for each subject, featuring content and formatting based on the official CLEP exams. Our practice tests contain every type of question that you can expect to encounter on the actual CLEP exam. Following each practice test you will find an answer key and detailed explanations designed to help you more completely understand the test material.

Each CLEP subject review in this book gives you concise coverage of the material you most need to know to pass the exam and get the college credit you're seeking. On our exclusive TestWare CD you will find two more unique practice tests for each subject.

As you start your preparation, we strongly recommend that you begin by taking your first practice test on CD, as a diagnostic tool. This will help you zero in on your strengths and weaknesses in each subject area and pinpoint areas in need of further study. It's also an excellent way to become familiar with the content and format of the computer-based CLEP exam. Our easy-to-use, interactive software provides the added benefits of instant scoring, performance feedback, and enforced time conditions.

ABOUT THE EXAM

Who Takes CLEP Exams and What Are They Used for?

CLEP examinations are typically taken by people who have acquired knowledge outside the classroom and who wish to bypass certain college courses and earn college credit. The CLEP program is designed to reward students for learning—no matter where or how that knowledge was acquired. The CLEP is the most widely accepted credit-by-examination program in North America.

CLEP exams are now available in more than 30 subjects and test the material commonly required in an introductory-level college course. Examinees can earn from three to twelve credits at more than 2,900 colleges and universities in the U.S. and Canada.

Although most CLEP examinees are adults returning to college, many graduating high school seniors, enrolled college students, military personnel, veterans, and international students also take the exams to earn college credit or to demonstrate their ability to perform at the college level. There are no prerequisites, such as age or educational status, for taking CLEP examinations. However, because policies on granting credits vary among colleges, you should contact the particular institution from which you wish to receive CLEP credit.

For a complete list of the CLEP subject examinations offered, visit the College Board website.

Who Administers the Exam?

The CLEP exams are developed by the College Board, administered by Educational Testing Service (ETS), and involve the assistance of educators throughout the United States. The test development process is designed and implemented to ensure that the content and difficulty level of the test are appropriate.

When and Where Are the Exams Given?

CLEP exams are administered year-round at more than 1,400 test centers in the United States and can be arranged for candidates abroad upon request. To find the test center nearest you and to register for the exam, you should obtain a copy of the free booklets *CLEP Colleges* and *CLEP Information for Candidates and Registration Form*. They are available at most colleges where CLEP credit is granted, or by contacting:

CLEP Services
P.O. Box 6600
Princeton, NJ 08541-6600
Phone: (800) 257-9558 (8 A.M. to 6 P.M. ET)
Fax: (609) 771-7088
Website: *www.collegeboard.com/clep*

CLEP Options for Military Personnel and Veterans

CLEP exams are available free of charge to eligible military personnel and eligible civilian employees. All the CLEP exams are available at test centers on college campuses and military bases. In addition, the College Board has developed a paper-based version of 14 high-volume/high-pass-rate CLEP tests for DANTES Test Centers. Contact the Educational Services Officer or Navy College Education Specialist for more information. Visit the College Board website for details about CLEP opportunities for military personnel.

Eligible U.S. veterans can claim reimbursement for CLEP exams and administration fees pursuant to provisions of the Veterans Benefits Improvement Act of 2004. For details on eligibility and submitting a claim for reimbursement, visit the U.S. Department of Veterans Affairs website at *www.gibill.va.gov/pamphlets/testing.htm*.

CLEP can be used in conjunction with the Post-9/11 GI Bill, which applies to veterans returning from the Iraq and Afghanistan theaters of operation. Because the GI Bill provides tuition for up to 36 months, racking up college credits by testing out of general introductory courses with CLEP exams expedites academic progress and degree completion within the funded timeframe.

SSD Accommodations for Candidates with Disabilities

Many test candidates qualify for extra time to take the CLEP exams, but you must make these arrangements in advance. For information, contact:

College Board Services for Students with Disabilities
P.O. Box 6226
Princeton, NJ 08541-6226
Phone: (609) 771-7137 (Monday through Friday, 8 A.M. to 6 P.M. ET)
TTY: (609) 882-4118
Fax: (609) 771-7944
E-mail: ssd@info.collegeboard.org

HOW TO USE THIS BOOK AND TESTWARE®

What Do I Study First?

To begin your studies, read over the introduction and test-taking suggestions for the CLEP exam(s) you are going to take. Take your first exam on CD-ROM to determine your strengths and weaknesses, and then study the course review material, focusing on your problem areas. The course review includes the information you need to know for that specific CLEP exam. Make sure to follow up your diagnostic work by taking the remaining practice exam on CD-ROM to become familiar with the format and feel of the CLEP exams. Finally, take the practice exam printed in this book for the subject for which you are studying.

When Should I Start Studying?

It is never too early to start studying for your CLEP exams. The earlier you begin, the more time you will have to sharpen your skills. Do not procrastinate! Cramming is not an effective way to study, since it does not allow you the time needed to learn the test material. The sooner you learn the format of the exam, the more time you will have to familiarize yourself with it.

ABOUT OUR SUBJECT REVIEWS

The subject reviews in this book provide you with a thorough review of the major topics found on the individual CLEP exams. The reviews will help reinforce the facts you have already learned while better shaping your understanding of the discipline as a whole. By using the review in conjunction with the practice tests, you should be well prepared to take the CLEP exams.

SCORING YOUR PRACTICE TESTS

How Do I Score My Practice Tests?

CLEP exams are scored on a scale of 20 to 80. To score your practice tests, count up the number of correct answers. This is your total raw score. Convert your raw score to a scaled score using the conversion table included with each subject review in this book. (Note: The conversion table provides only an estimate of your scaled score. Scaled scores can and do vary over time, and in no case should a sample test be taken as a precise predictor of test performance. Nonetheless, our scoring table allows you to judge your level of performance within a reasonable scoring range.)

When Will I Receive my Score Report?

The test administrator will print out a full Candidate Score Report for you immediately upon your completion of the exam (except for CLEP College Composition and College Composition Modular exams). Your scores are reported only to you, unless you ask to have them sent elsewhere. If you want your scores reported to a college or other institution, you must say so when you take the examination. Since your scores are kept on file for 20 years, you can also request transcripts from Educational Testing Service at a later date.

STUDYING FOR THE EXAM

It is very important for you to choose the time and place for studying that work best for you. Some students may set aside a certain number of hours every morning, while others may choose to study at night before going to sleep. Other students may study during the day, while waiting on a line, or even while eating lunch. Only you can determine when and where your study time will be most effective. But be consistent and use your time wisely. Work out a study routine and stick to it!

When you take the practice tests, try to make your testing conditions as much like the actual test as possible. Turn your television and radio off, and sit down at a quiet table free from distraction. Make sure to time yourself. Start off by setting a timer for the time that is allotted for each section, and be sure to reset the timer for the appropriate amount of time when you start a new section.

As you complete each practice test, score your test and thoroughly review the explanations to the questions you answered incorrectly; however, do not review too much at one time. Concentrate on one problem area at a time by reviewing the question and explanation, and by studying our review until you are confident that you completely understand the material.

TEST-TAKING TIPS

Although you may not be familiar with computer-based standardized tests, there are many ways to acquaint yourself with this type of examination and to help alleviate your test-taking anxieties. Listed below are ways to help you become accustomed to the CLEP, some of which may be applied to other standardized tests.

Know the format of the test. CLEP computer-based tests are not adaptive but rather fixed-length tests. In a sense, this makes them kin to the familiar paper-and-pencil exam in that you have the same flexibility to go back and review your work in each section.

Read all of the possible answers. Just because you think you have found the correct response, do not automatically assume that it is the best answer. Read through each choice to be sure that you are not making a mistake by jumping to conclusions.

Use the process of elimination. Go through each answer to a question and eliminate as many of the answer choices as possible. By eliminating just two answer choices, you give yourself a better chance of getting the item correct, since there will only be three choices left from which to make your guess. Remember, your score is based only on the number of questions you answer correctly.

Work quickly and steadily. Avoid focusing on any one question too long. You only have a certain amount of time to finish the exam. Taking the practice tests in this book and on our CD will help you learn to budget your time.

Acquaint yourself with the computer screen. Familiarize yourself with the CLEP computer screen beforehand by logging on to the College Board website. Waiting until test day to see what it looks like in the pretest tutorial risks injecting needless anxiety into your testing experience. Also, familiarizing yourself with the directions and format of the exam will save you valuable time on the day of the actual test.

Be sure that your answer registers before you go on to the next item. Look at the screen to see that your mouse-click causes the pointer to darken the proper oval. This takes less effort than darkening an oval on paper, but don't lull yourself into taking less care!

THE DAY OF THE EXAM

On the day of the test, you should wake up early (hopefully after a decent night's rest) and have a good breakfast. Make sure to dress comfortably, so that you are not distracted by being too hot or too cold while taking the test. Also plan to arrive at the test center early. This will allow you to collect your thoughts and relax before the test, and will also spare you the anxiety that comes with being late. As an added incentive to make sure you arrive early, keep in mind that no one will be allowed into the test session after the test has begun.

Before you leave for the test center, make sure that you have your admission form and another form of identification, which must contain a recent photograph, your name, and signature (i.e., driver's license, student identification card, or current alien registration card). You will not be admitted to the test center if you do not have proper identification.

If you would like, you may wear a watch to the test center. However, you may not wear one that makes noise, because it may disturb the other test-takers. No dictionaries, textbooks, notebooks, briefcases, or packages will be permitted and drinking, smoking, and eating are prohibited.

Good luck on your CLEP exams!

CHAPTER 1
College Composition/College Composition Modular

CLEP COLLEGE COMPOSITION INDEPENDENT STUDY SCHEDULE

The following suggestions provide a framework you can use when preparing for the CLEP College Composition exams. As part of your preparation, be sure to set aside time each day to study. This method will work better than trying to review everything at once. No matter which study techniques work best for you, the more time you spend studying, the more prepared and relaxed you will feel.

Step	Activity
1	Take Practice Test 2 for the College Composition or the College Composition Modular exam on CD. Review the explanations provided for the answers. This will help you identify areas that you will need to review.
2	Carefully read and study each topic in the College Composition review chapters.
3	While reading, highlight items in the text you want to remember.
4	Jot down points of emphasis in a notebook or on index cards as you read.
5	Take Practice Test 3 found on the CD and review the answer explanations.
6	Note which questions you answered incorrectly on the Practice Test, and focus on these areas during your follow-up review.
7	Read through the College Composition review chapters again, paying particular attention to the topics you struggled with while taking the two Practice Tests.
8	Take Practice Test 1 located at the end on this chapter for additional reinforcement and practice.

REVIEW OUTLINE

The following is the order in which the topics are covered in this review:

CONVENTIONS OF STANDARD WRITTEN ENGLISH

The Conventions of Standard Written English section tests knowledge of English grammar, usage, diction, and idiom. Each question in this section consists of a sentence with four underlined words or phrases. Your task is to choose the one underlined word or phrase out of the four that is ungrammatical or reflects some other error in the way it is written. If the sentence contains no errors, you can indicate that instead.

The skills tested in this section include knowledge of syntax, agreement, diction, modifiers, punctuation, idiom, and voice. The Revision Skills section also tests many of these skills; therefore, what you learn from each of these sections may be tested in either section of the CLEP College Composition/College Composition Modular exams.

Among the previously mentioned skills, idiom and voice are discussed in a later section. The other skills are discussed in this section, followed by guidance on how to approach Conventions of Standard Written English questions, and then some practice questions with answers and explanations.

SYNTAX

Syntax refers to the rules that govern sentence structure, particularly the order of words and phrases in sentences. For example, the rules of English syntax indicate that the first sentence in the following example is grammatically correct, whereas the second sentence is grammatically incorrect:

> I have gone to the store.

> I have to the store gone.

Each language has its own syntactic rules. In German, for example, the first sentence would be incorrect, whereas the second sentence would be correct.

Although the grammatically incorrect sentence *I have to the store gone* is more or less understandable, in the extreme case a syntactic error will change the sentence's intended meaning. For example, the following two sentences consist of exactly the same words, but the meanings of the sentences are different owing to a difference in their order:

> The cat bit the dog.

> The dog bit the cat.

Simple Sentences

In written English, sentences usually must consist of a **subject** and a **predicate**. The predicate, in turn, must include a **verb**. Thus, the sentence *Marianna arrived* is grammatically correct, because it consists of a subject (*Marianna*) and a verb (*arrived*). Sentences can be much longer and more elaborate than this one, of course.

A simple sentence consists of one subject and one predicate, as in the following examples:

> Cecilia likes dark chocolate.

> The jaguar fell asleep in the only remaining secluded area of this once mighty rainforest.

> At 6:00 a.m. the alarm went off.

Each of these sentences is a simple sentence because each contains one subject (*Cecilia*, *the jaguar*, and *the alarm*, respectively) and one predicate.

In any sentence, a subject and its predicate are referred to as a **clause**. A clause that functions as a complete sentence is an **independent clause**. Thus, by definition, a simple sentence consists of one independent clause. A clause that does not function by itself as a complete sentence is a **dependent clause** (also known as a **subordinate clause**). The following are some examples of dependent clauses:

> in the park beside the tallest elm tree

> because he believed what his uncle had told him

> after dinner, sitting in my chair

As you can see, none of these clauses function as a complete sentence.

Compound Sentences

A **compound sentence** contains two or more independent clauses typically linked by a coordinating conjunction. The following list provides examples of coordinating conjunctions:

and	for	or	yet
but	not	so	

Coordination refers to the combination of independent clauses to form a compound sentence. For example:

> John fell asleep, but Mary stayed up a little while longer.

In the previous sentence, *John fell asleep* is one independent clause, whereas *Mary stayed up a little while longer* is a second independent clause.

Punctuation can also be used between two independent clauses in some cases, as in the following examples:

> John fell asleep; Mary stayed up a little while longer.

> John fell asleep. Mary stayed up a little while longer.

Further details about punctuation are discussed throughout this section and in the section on punctuation.

Complex Sentences

A complex sentence consists of an independent clause and one or more dependent clauses, as in the following example:

> I disliked the dessert that he brought.

In the previous sentence, the clause *I disliked the dessert* is an independent clause. The clause *he brought* is a dependent clause. In this example, the word *that* connects the two clauses.

A dependent (subordinate) clause will provide additional information about the statement established by the independent clause. In the preceding example, the dependent clause *that he brought* simply helps identify which particular dessert the writer dislikes.

In general, two kinds of words can be used to link the independent and dependent clauses in a complex sentence.

First, relative pronouns such as *that*, *which*, *who*, and *whoever* can be used. For example:

> I am grateful to the person who invented pizza.

In this example, *I am grateful to the person* is the independent clause and *invented pizza* is the dependent clause.

Second, subordinate conjunctions can be used to link independent clauses to dependent clauses, as in the following example:

> He always gets drowsy after eating a large dinner.

In this example, the subordinate conjunction is *after*. Other commonly used subordinate conjunctions are as follows:

although	before	once	unless
as	how	since	whether
because	if	though	whenever

In the complex sentence examples given thus far, the independent clause precedes the dependent clause. However, it is also acceptable for the dependent clause to come first, as in the following revision of the previous sentence:

> After eating a large dinner, he always gets drowsy.

When a dependent clause precedes an independent clause, a comma will often be used to separate them. However, when the independent clause comes first, a comma may not be used.

In some complex sentences, the subject and predicate of the independent clause will be divided, as in the following example:

> The man who called yesterday is at the door now.

In this example, the word *who* links the dependent clause (*called yesterday*) to the independent clause *The man is at the door now*.

Notice that although the subject and predicate of the independent clause can be divided, the dependent clause cannot.

Compound–Complex Sentences

A compound–complex sentence consists of at least two independent clauses and one or more dependent clauses. For example:

> The tree that grew near the house fell over yesterday, but the house was unharmed.

In this example, the first independent clause is *The tree fell over yesterday* and the second independent clause is *the house was unharmed*. The dependent clause is *grew near the house*.

Sentence Boundaries

Ordinarily a sentence cannot be grammatically correct unless it contains a subject and a predicate, which in turn contains a verb. The absence of any of these elements usually results in a sentence fragment. For example, the following fragments lack a subject:

> Ran the race in brand new shoes.

> Overcoming obstacles, one at a time.

The next two examples are fragments because each lacks a main verb:

> The parrot who suddenly flew away.

> A math teacher who perplexed the class.

Although each of the two fragments contains a verb (*flew* and *perplexed*, respectively), these verbs are part of phrases that modify the subject. In other words, each fragment is actually a subject. *The parrot who suddenly flew away* is a subject that requires some sort of predicate, as in the following example:

> The parrot who suddenly flew away just returned.

In this example, *just returned* is the predicate associated with the subject *The parrot who suddenly flew away*.

Another approach to rendering the fragment about the parrot grammatically correct is to simply remove the word *who*, as follows:

> The parrot suddenly flew away.

In this grammatically correct sentence, the subject is *The parrot* and the predicate is *suddenly flew away*.

Finally, here are two examples that are fragments because each one lacks a subject and a main verb:

>After a delightful stroll down to the beach followed by a dip in the ocean.

>Because she asked me to wait before knocking.

These examples are fragments, even though each one contains nouns and verbs, because neither fragment contains a noun that functions as a subject or a verb that helps complete the idea. Neither one of these fragments could be made into a complete sentence by adding only a noun or a verb; rather, what is needed is an independent clause that contains both. This point is illustrated by the first example that follows. (The second example illustrates how narrowing the scope of the fragment can result in a complete sentence.)

>Because she had asked me to wait before knocking, I decided to wait.

>She asked me to wait before knocking.

Notice that in some cases the subject of a sentence will be implied rather than directly stated, as in the following sentence:

>Think about this issue carefully.

In this sentence, the subject is *you*. The sentence is grammatically correct even though the subject is implied rather than directly stated. In contrast, the following example is a fragment and thus grammatically incorrect because the subject is neither known nor implied:

>Thought about this issue carefully.

These examples illustrate the idea that sentence fragments are usually dependent clauses.

In many forms of writing, a sentence fragment may be acceptable when the structure and meaning of the complete sentence implied by the fragment is clear. For example, consider the following passage:

>Mr. Johnson was convinced that Smith had committed the crime. Absolutely certain.

In this passage, the second sentence is actually a sentence fragment, as it lacks a subject. However, it is clear from the context established by the first sentence that Mr. Johnson is the subject.

The second sentence in the previous example could have been rewritten as a complete sentence, as illustrated by the following revision:

>Mr. Johnson was convinced that Smith had committed the crime. Mr. Johnson was absolutely certain of Smith's guilt.

Although the second sentence is now grammatically correct, it lacks the punch of the original version (*Absolutely certain.*).

For the Conventions of Written English and Revision Skills sections of the CLEP College Composition and College Composition Modular exams, you should be careful not to assume that a sentence fragment is acceptable for stylistic reasons, even if the meaning is clear. For example, consider the following passage:

> Imran climbed the stairs leading up to the park's entrance and then paused. Because his girlfriend had asked him to wait before entering.

In this passage, the second sentence is a fragment because it lacks a subject. Although the meaning and grammatical structure are clear from the context, you should not consider this a grammatically correct sentence.

Run-on sentences occur when the writer joins two or more sentences within the same sentence without separating them appropriately. Consider the following example:

> Will admires the actor Meryl Streep, she is so talented.

Here two different independent clauses are joined by means of a comma, resulting in a grammatically incorrect run-on sentence referred to as a **comma splice**. In order to make the sentence grammatically correct, the writer could divide it into separate sentences, as follows:

> Will admires the actor Meryl Streep. She is so talented.

Alternatively, the writer could add an appropriate conjunction or form of punctuation between the clauses, as in the following examples:

> Will admires the actor Meryl Streep, because she is so talented.

> Will admires the actor Meryl Streep; she is so talented.

Not all conjunctions or forms of punctuation are acceptable, as illustrated by the following grammatically incorrect sentences:

> Will admires the actor Meryl Streep, whereas she is so talented.

> Will admires the actor Meryl Streep, she is so talented.

This section has provided you with some information about the "mechanics" or basic rules of syntax.

PARALLELISM

When words or phrases serve the same function in a sentence, they should reflect the same grammatical category. In such cases, **parallelism** is a requirement for grammatical correctness. Consider, for example, the following pair of sentences:

> Suddenly he opened the desk drawer, retrieved a sheet of paper, and began to write the letter.

> Suddenly he opened the desk drawer, pulled out a sheet of paper, and there was a pen at the bottom of the drawer.

In the first sentence, parallelism can be seen across the verbs *opened*, *retrieved*, and *began*. Because these verbs serve the same function in the sentence (i.e., to indicate a sequence of actions), they all reflect the same grammatical category (i.e., simple past tense), and thus the sentence is grammatically correct. In contrast, the second sentence is grammatically incorrect owing to the lack of parallelism between the final clause and those that preceded it.

The following pair of sentences illustrates the need for parallelism across nouns or noun phrases:

> When doing this job, you should consider not only the product but also the process.

> When doing this job, you should consider not only the product but also enjoying your work.

In the first sentence, parallelism can be seen across the nouns *product* and *process*. This parallelism is required by the *not only. . . . but also* construction. The second sentence is grammatically incorrect, because what follows the *but also* is not a noun or noun phrase.

Not only . . . but also is an example of a **correlative conjunction**. Other examples include the following:

both . . . and	neither . . . nor
either . . . or	the more . . . the more
just as . . . so	whether . . . or

The use of any of these correlative conjunctions will require parallelism in what gets modified. Thus, of the following sentences, the first one is grammatically incorrect, whereas the second one is correct:

> Either you will love this movie, or obtain a refund for your ticket.

> Either you will love this movie, or you will be refunded for your ticket.

AGREEMENT

Grammatical agreement refers to relationships between words and/or phrases that are marked by changes in particular words. For example, in the sentence *Harriet, Letitia, and John are leaving*, it is necessary to use the verb *are* rather than *is* because the subject of the sentence consists of more than one individual. This sentence illustrates agreement between subject and verb. If Harriet were the only person leaving, we would say that Harriet *is* leaving, so that we maintain subject–verb agreement in the sentence.

As you can see, agreement is not the same as parallelism. Parallelism requires that different words or phrases reflect the same grammatical category (e.g., in the previous example, the word that appears after *Harriet, Letitia, and . . .* should also be a proper noun or noun phrase). In contrast, agreement requires that whatever verb follows the list of people should take on plural form.

Agreement in Number

Agreement in number refers to the relationship between nouns, pronouns, verbs, and other parts of speech in a sentence according to whether the nouns are singular or plural. The general rule is that the pertinent words should agree in number. For example, consider the following pair of sentences:

> The bedroom was filled with toys.

> The bedrooms were filled with toys.

These sentences are grammatically correct, in part because in each sentence there is agreement in number between subject and verb. The first sentence pertains to a single bedroom and thus the verb *was* is appropriate. The second sentence refers to more than one bedroom, and thus the plural form *were* is needed.

There are several kinds of agreement in number. For example, in each of the following sentences, you can see agreement in number between pronouns that have the same reference:

> His anger was revealed by the way he threw plates against the wall.

> Their anger was revealed by the way they threw plates against the wall.

In the first sentence, *his* and *he* are singular, whereas in the second sentence, *their* and *they* are plural.

The following examples illustrate agreement in number between a quantifier and noun:

> I carried a box up the stairs.

> I carried some boxes up the stairs.

The following examples show agreement between nouns:

> Many families live in small houses.

> The students all sat down in their seats.

In practice, you may need to look closely in order to determine whether or not there is agreement in number. For example, consider the following sentence:

> Some dogs walk around in a small circle before lying down in their bed.

The previous sentence is grammatically incorrect, because the subject (*some dogs*) is plural but the final noun *bed* is singular.

Following is another sentence that is grammatically incorrect owing to a lack of agreement in number:

> If a person wants to do well in school, they should study hard.

In this sentence, *person* is singular, and thus a singular pronoun should be used, as in the following grammatically correct revision:

If a person wants to do well in school, he or she should study hard.

Particular caution is required in evaluating agreement when quantifiers such as the following are used:

all	every	little	most	no
each	few	many	much	some

For example, see if you can determine which of the following sentences is correct and which is incorrect:

All drivers should glance at their tires periodically.

Every driver should glance at their tires periodically.

The first sentence is grammatically correct, in part because the plural subject (*all drivers*) is in agreement with the pronoun (*their*). The second sentence is incorrect, because the subject (*every driver*) is singular, but the pronoun (*their*) is plural. Following is a grammatically correct revision of this sentence:

Every driver should glance at his or her tires periodically.

Words like *each*, *either*, *every*, and *everyone* seem to refer to more than one person, but they are in fact singular. Thus, the following sentence is grammatically correct in its use of the singular pronoun *his*:

Either John or Ricardo will be describing his science fair project at the end of class today.

Agreement in Gender

Writers are expected to use **gender-neutral language**, unless they are referring specifically to one gender. Thus, it is acceptable to write *All men should serve their country* if one specifically intends to target men. However, one should not write *Everyone in the United States should serve his country* if one happens to be referring to everyone of both sexes. In this case, one should choose a form or expression that reflects the gender-inclusiveness of the term *everyone*, as in the following examples:

Everyone should serve his or her country.

All people should serve their countries.

The previous two examples illustrate that agreement in gender is required between the subject of a sentence (*everyone* and *all people*, respectively) and the pronouns associated with the subject.

The requirement of gender neutrality can create grammatical difficulties in some cases. To return to an earlier example, suppose that a teacher informs a classroom of students that John may describe his science fair project at the end of class that day, but that if John is reluctant or does not appear to be ready, Mary may describe her science fair project at the end of the class instead. Each of the following descriptions of the situation is grammatically incorrect:

> Either John or Mary will be describing his science fair project at the end of class today.

> Either John or Mary will be describing her science fair project at the end of class today.

> Either John or Mary will be describing their science fair project at the end of class today.

> Either John or Mary will be describing his or her science fair project at the end of class today.

To describe this particular situation, the writer's only recourse is to use a different sentence structure, as in the following grammatically correct example:

> Either John will be describing his science fair project at the end of class today, or Mary will be describing her project at that time.

Agreement in Person

Agreement in person pertains to the relationship between pronouns and verbs that are used to convey first, second, or third person in either singular or plural form. Generally speaking, pronouns and verbs should agree in person.

The fact that a verb is being used to convey first, second, or third person is often signaled by the particular pronoun that is used. Thus, *I go* indicates first person singular and *you go* indicates second person singular. (Nouns are always third person.) The form of the verb may change, as in the following sentence, which illustrates first, second, and third person usage, respectively:

> I am American, you are English, and she is Australian.

In other cases, the form of the verb does not change, and it is the pronoun or noun that signals person. For example:

> We are Americans, you two are English, and they are Australian.

Regardless of how person is conveyed, pronouns or nouns and the verbs they are associated with must agree in person. Thus, the following sentence is grammatically incorrect:

> If a student wants to do well in this class, you have to know when to approach the teaching assistants for guidance.

In this sentence, the phrase *a student* is third person, and it fails to agree with *you*, which is second person. Each of the following is a grammatically correct revision of this sentence:

> If a student wants to do well in this class, he or she has to know when to approach the teaching assistants for guidance.

> If you want to do well in this class, you have to know when to approach the teaching assistants for guidance.

To determine whether agreement in person exists, you will need to determine which verb is associated with which pronoun or noun. Consider the following sentence:

The captain, like his soldiers, is nervous.

This sentence is grammatically correct. Although you might be tempted to say that *are* should be used in place of *is*, the subject of the sentence is a singular noun (*the captain*) and thus a third person singular form of the verb (*is*) must be used in order for the sentence to reflect agreement in person.

Agreement in Case

Case refers to the grammatical function of a pronoun or noun in a sentence. Three cases are typically marked in English sentences: **nominative**, **accusative/dative**, and **possessive**. **Agreement in case** refers to usage of the correct pronoun or noun form associated with each case.

In the nominative case, a pronoun or noun serves as the subject of a sentence, as illustrated by the words *I* and *we* in the following sentences:

I was paid by the curator.

We ate more mashed potatoes.

In the accusative/dative case, a pronoun or noun serves as the direct or indirect object in a sentence, as illustrated by the words *me* and *ourselves* in the following sentences:

The curator paid me for the statue.

We helped ourselves to more mashed potatoes.

In the possessive case, a pronoun or noun has a relationship of possession to another noun in the sentence, as illustrated by the words *my* and *our* in the following sentences:

The curator paid for my statue.

The waiter filled our plates with mashed potatoes.

In these examples, a different pronoun is used for each case. Nouns do not change across nominative and accusative cases, but their form changes in the possessive case. Usually, possessive case is created by adding an apostrophe followed by the letter *s* to the end of a noun. Thus, the following sentences are grammatically correct with respect to the proper noun *Nicky*:

Nicky owns a hybrid car. (nominative)

I bought Nicky a hybrid car. (accusative)

This is Nicky's hybrid car. (possessive)

In some sentences, particular caution is needed to determine whether the requirement of agreement in case has been met. For example, consider the following sentences:

Charlonda, Bethany, and I went to the store.

Kendra gave Charlonda, Bethany, and me a ride.

Charlonda, Bethany, and me went to the store.

Kendra gave Charlonda, Bethany, and I a ride.

The first sentence is grammatically correct because the subject of the sentence is *Charlonda, Bethany, and I* and the nominative form of the pronoun (*I*) is correctly used.

The second sentence is also grammatically correct. Here, *Charlonda, Bethany, and me* is the direct object, and the accusative form of the pronoun (*me*) is correctly used.

The third sentence is grammatically incorrect because the accusative form of the pronoun (*me*) is used, but this pronoun is part of the subject and should be expressed in nominative form (i.e., *I*). This sentence illustrates a lack of agreement between a pronoun and its grammatical case.

The fourth sentence is incorrect for an analogous reason: the accusative form of the pronoun (*I*) is used, but this pronoun is part of the direct object and should be expressed in accusative form (i.e., *me*).

If the first two sentences do not "feel" correct, and/or the last two sentences do not "feel" incorrect, try dropping all words from the subject or direct object except for the pronoun. The grammatical correctness or incorrectness of the sentences may seem clearer, as illustrated in the following examples:

Charlonda and I went to the store. (correct)

Kendra gave me a ride. (correct)

Charlonda and me went to the store. (incorrect)

Kendra gave I a ride. (incorrect)

Non-Agreement in Tense

The verbs used in a sentence should be consistent in tense, as in the following examples:

Ricky fell off the slide, skinned his knee, and bumped his head.

When you see him, tell him that I want an explanation.

Lily is here and she feels hungry.

In the first sentence, simple past tense is used for each verb (*fell*, *skinned*, and *bumped*), whereas in the second and third sentences, present tense is used for each verb (*see*, *tell*, *want*, *is*, and *feels*).

At the same time, verb tense will not always be consistent within sentences that are grammatically correct. Changes in tense typically occur *across* rather than *within* clauses, and there are many reasons why these changes are needed. For example, the writer may shift tenses simply because he or she is shifting focus to a different time period, as in the following sentences:

Ricky fell off the slide, skinned his knee, and bumped his head, and now the tears are flowing.

When you see him, tell him that I want an explanation for what happened yesterday.

Lily is full now but she will feel hungry soon.

Causal explanations sometimes require a shift in tense, as in the following examples:

Bob is in the living room because he had gotten tired of waiting in the hallway.

Lily will feel hungry soon because she has not eaten lunch.

Another reason for shifting tense is that the **infinitive form** of a verb will be used in present tense when combined with another verb, regardless of the tense of the other verb. For example:

Demetria saw Jim's new hat and began to laugh.

In this sentence, *saw* and *began* are simple past tense forms, but in the infinitive phrase, *laugh* appears in its present tense form.

In both scientific and narrative writing, a writer may use simple past tense when describing a sequence of events in chronological order, but switch to present tense when describing characteristics that are more generally true and not simply part of the chronology. Consider, for example, the following sentences:

The first time Karima visited Shanghai, she looked around and noticed that the architecture in this great city reflects Western influences.

The first time Karima visited Shanghai, she looked into a small mirror and noticed a pigeon reflected in the glass.

Both sentences relate an anecdote using simple past tense (*visited*, *looked*, *noticed*). However, in the first sentence, the present tense verb *reflects* is used because the characteristics of the architecture that suggest Western influence have always been part of that architecture. In other words, the architecture did not begin to reflect Western influences when Karima looked at it, only to lose those influences when she looked away. Rather, the architecture always reflects those influences. In the second sentence, however, the reflection of the pigeon is a momentary occurrence, and thus the past tense verb *reflected* is used. The pigeon is not always reflected in the glass. Rather, it was reflected for a moment, and the writer would indicate what happened next by means of other past tense verbs (e.g., *The pigeon then flapped its wings, rose into the air, and vanished.*).

DICTION

Diction refers to a writer's choice of words. For example, describing a particular person as a *criminal* as opposed to a *thief* reflects a difference in diction that may affect what the reader infers about the writer's attitudes. However, neither term is necessarily inaccurate. Diction is also important in the sense that the wrong word choice can render a sentence incorrect or ambiguous.

In many cases, a writer's diction will be incorrect because the writer has confused words that are similar in form and/or meaning. Following are some of the more common examples of words that are confused.

Effect vs. Affect

The word *effect* can be used as a noun or a verb. As a noun, it refers to an outcome, as in the following sentences:

> Adding fertilizer to the garden had a positive effect on the gardenias.

> The effects of Internet addiction on children's well-being is a topic that psychologists are beginning to study.

As a verb, *effect* refers to creation of a change, as in the following sentence:

> The prime minister attempted to effect a change in public attitudes toward his family.

The word *affect* can also be used as a noun or as a verb. As a verb, it refers to the cause of a particular outcome, as in the following sentences:

> Exhaustion began to affect the boxer's ability to defend himself.

> A well-made movie always affects me emotionally.

Most sentences can be expressed using either *effect* or *affect*, but the writer must be careful to use each term correctly. For example:

> Prior generations of flame retardants are known to affect endocrine system functioning.

> Prior generations of flame retardants are known to have an effect on endocrine system functioning.

Imply vs. Insinuate vs. Infer

To **imply** is to hint at something. To **insinuate** is to hint at something negative. To **infer** is to draw a conclusion about something based on evidence. Thus, the following sentences are grammatically correct:

> The policeman implied that Brenda had committed the crime.

> The policeman's remark implied that Brenda had committed the crime.

> The policeman insinuated that Brenda had committed the crime.

> John inferred from the policeman's remark that Brenda had committed the crime.

Farther vs. Further

Farther and *further* are both comparative terms, but their meanings are different and thus they are not interchangeable. **Farther** indicates a difference in physical distance, whereas **further** suggests a difference in quantity or extent. Thus, each of the following sentences is grammatically correct:

> Ruth consistently hit the ball farther than any other batter of his time.

> After finishing the lecture, Smith discussed auditory development further with her students.

> Brianna is further along in her studies than Bettina will ever be.

The term *further* can also be used to mean *foster* and *in addition*, as illustrated by the first and second uses of the term, respectively, in the following passage:

> One of the main purposes of a high-quality child care program is to further children's intellectual development; further, such programs are designed to promote children's physical, social, and emotional well-being.

Than vs. Then

Than is a conjunction that is used when making comparisons, as in the following sentences:

> Bolt has consistently run faster than any of his competitors.

> It is later than you think.

Than is always preceded by a **comparative adjective** or **adjectival phrase**. Often, the adjective has an *-er* suffix and immediately precedes *than*, as illustrated in each of the previous examples. However, in some cases neither condition is observed. In the following sentence, for example, the comparative adjective (*more*) does not have an *-er* suffix, and it does not immediately precede *than*.

> The governor seems more peaceful this year than she was last year.

Then is not used to make comparisons. It has four possible meanings, none of which is interchangeable with *than*. Specifically, *then* could mean *at that point in time*, *next*, *in addition*, or something roughly synonymous with *therefore*. Each of these four meanings is illustrated in turn by the second through fifth sentences in the following passage:

> The late 1960s were difficult years for him. He was a high school student then in the most academically rigorous prep school in the state. Each day we would suffer through his classes and then return home to the tedium of homework. And then there were the chores his mother pestered him to do. He felt that if she would just stop asking him to do so many chores, then he could have concentrated more on the homework and done a better job.

Who vs. That vs. Which

As relative pronouns, *who*, *that*, and *which* serve similar functions in sentences. However, *who* refers to people, whereas *that* and *which* refer to groups, events, and things, as in the following examples:

> Celia is a person who believes strongly in community development.

> DCP is an organization that promotes community development.

> DCP, which is the organization where Celia works, has long promoted community development.

As relative pronouns, *that* and *which* are used in a similar way. The key difference is that *that* is used with restrictive clauses, whereas *which* is used with nonrestrictive clauses.

A **restrictive clause** limits the identity of the subject to which it refers. For example, in the second sentence of the previous examples, the clause *that promotes community development* limits the identity of the referenced organization. DCP is not just any organization, in other words. According to this sentence, it is an organization that engages in a certain kind of activity (i.e., the promotion of community development).

A **nonrestrictive clause** provides further information about the subject to which it refers, but it does not provide essential, limiting information about the nature of the subject. In the third sentence of the previous examples, the clause *which is the organization where Celia works* tells us something about DCP, but this detail is not part of the organization's essential nature. The fact that Celia works there does not limit the identity of the organization—it does not clearly distinguish the organization from others. Deleting a restrictive clause makes the sentence vague or difficult to understand, whereas deleting a nonrestrictive clause does not undermine the understandability of the sentence.

The distinction between restrictive and nonrestrictive clauses is not always clear cut. In some cases the distinction reflects something about the writer's intentions. Consider the following two sentences that might be found near the beginning of a media article or essay:

> DCP is a community development organization that has been discussed frequently in the local news.

> DCP, which is the organization where Barack Obama worked before attending law school, has long promoted community development.

In the first sentence, the fact that DCP has been discussed frequently in the local news is not very limiting, as other organizations probably are as well. Thus, this part of the sentence says little about the nature of DCP. Moreover, by dropping what appears to be the restrictive clause (*has been discussed frequently in the local news*), the sentence is still meaningful and conveys something essential about the organization. However, if the writer's purpose in the essay is to describe the kinds of local media attention that DCP has received, then the clause in question does function in a restrictive way. Media attention is part of what distinguishes the organization, according to the journalist.

In the second sentence, the fact that Barack Obama worked for DCP is quite distinctive, given that Mr. Obama is a highly recognizable public figure. However, the fact that Mr. Obama worked for DCP prior to attending law school is not part of the essential nature of the organization. Presumably the main purpose of the organization—to promote community development—would have been carried out regardless of whether or not Mr. Obama had spent time leading the organization. Thus, the *which* clause in the second sentence merely provides interesting information about DCP rather than further details about the nature of the organization. Moreover, removing this clause does not prevent the sentence from being understandable. Thus, the clause in question is a nonrestrictive clause.

Who vs. Whom

Who and **whom** are both relative pronouns that refer to people. However, *who* is used in reference to a subject, whereas *whom* refers to an object. The distinction is illustrated in the following grammatically correct sentences:

> Cecilia is the person who I love the most.

> To whom did she send that last letter?

There are two simple tests that can be used to determine whether *who* or *whom* is the appropriate pronoun to use in a particular sentence. Both tests are based on the assumption that because *who* refers to a subject, it will be synonymous with a nominative pronoun (*he* or *she*). But because *whom* refers to an object, it will be synonymous with an accusative/dative pronoun (*him* or *her*).

The first test is that if the sentence is a statement, you can substitute *he* (or *she*) and then *him* (or *her*) for the pronoun and check which result is grammatically correct. For example:

> Cecilia is the person [who or whom?] I love the most.

> She is the person who I love the most.

> Her is the person who I love the most.

As you can see, the second sentence is grammatically correct but the third one is not. Because the grammatically correct substitution for *Cecilia* is *she*, the correct relative pronoun will be *who*.

The second test is that if the sentence is a question, you can imagine an answer in which *he* (or *she*) and then *him* (or *her*) is part of the answer, and then check which result is grammatically correct. For example:

> To [who or whom?] did she send that last letter?

> She sent that last letter to he.

> She sent that last letter to him.

This time, the third sentence is grammatically correct but the second one is not. Because the appropriate pronoun is *him* rather than *he*, the correct relative pronoun will be *whom*.

There vs. Their vs. They're

There, *their*, and *they're* have different meanings and are thus not interchangeable. The primary meaning of the noun *there* is *that place*. The pronoun *their* refers to something that belongs to or is in some way part of others. *They're* is a contraction that stands for *they are*. Thus, the following sentences are grammatically correct.

> We should go there tonight for dinner.

> We should go to their house tonight for dinner.

> We should go to their house tonight. They're serving dinner.

Lie vs. Lay

One meaning of the verb *lie* is to recline. One meaning of the verb **lay** is to put or place. Thus, the following sentences are grammatically correct:

I want to lie down on the bed.

I want to lay my coat on the bed.

Strictly speaking, it would be incorrect to use a sentence like *I want to lay down on the bed* or *I want to lie my coat on the bed*.

Confusion sometimes arises from the fact that the simple past tense of *lie* is *lay*, whereas the simple past tense of *lay* is *laid*. Thus, the following sentences are grammatically correct:

I lay on the bed.

I laid my coat on the bed.

As you can see, the sentence *I lay on the bed* means that, at some point in the past, I was reclining on the bed. It does not mean that I am now reclining on the bed. In order to indicate that I am now reclining on the bed, I must say *I lie on the bed*.

You can also see that the sentence *After work I lay my coat on the bed* does not mean that, at some specific point in the past, I placed my coat on the bed after work. Rather, it means that I generally do so. If I want to indicate that I placed my coat on the bed after work one day (e.g., last Monday), I must say *After work I laid my coat on the bed*.

The **present progressive** verb tense indicates ongoing action, as in the phrases *I am singing* or *She is still sleeping*. The present progressive form of *lie* is *lying*, whereas the present progressive form of *lay* is *laying*. Thus, the following sentences are grammatically correct:

Hank is lying in bed.

Hank is laying the coat on the bed.

The **past participle** tense indicates a previously completed action, as in the phrase *I have finished reading Bellow's last novel*. The past participle of *lie* is *lain*, whereas the past participle of *lay* is *laid*. Thus, the following sentences are grammatically correct:

I have lain in bed until noon more than once in my life.

I have laid the coat on the bed already.

Other Commonly Confused Terms

A number of terms are commonly confused because they are similar or identical in pronunciation. Following are some examples.

Accept means *to receive*, whereas **except** means *to exclude*. Thus, one could say that Juan invited all of his friends to his birthday party, and that everyone *accepted except* for Steve, who has to work on the evening of Juan's party.

The term *elicit* means *to draw out*, whereas the term *illicit* refers to something illegal. Thus, a teacher might speak very gently and carefully to a student in order to *elicit* information about *illicit* activities that have been carried out by one of the student's classmates.

The *capitol* is a building where a government is housed, whereas the *capital* is the place (e.g., the city) where the government resides. Thus, one could say that in Rhode Island, the *capitol* building is located near downtown Providence, which is the state *capital*.

To *flaunt* is to show off, whereas to *flout* means to show contempt. Thus, a middle school student who wishes to *flaunt* his toughness might talk back to a teacher and otherwise *flout* class rules.

The term *principal* refers to something or someone that is important, whereas a *principle* is an important abstract truth. Thus, one could claim that the fundamental *principle* of management is to determine who has the *principal* authority for making decisions about hiring and firing.

Stationary means *standing still*, whereas *stationery* refers to writing paper. Most people are *stationary* while writing something on *stationery*.

A *compliment* consists of verbal praise, whereas a *complement* is something that completes or enhances something else. Thus, one could speak of how Rachel *complimented* Matthias on his understanding of how white wine *complements* a good meal.

Altogether means *entirely* or *on the whole*, whereas *all together* means *gathered in one place*. Thus, one could say that *altogether*, John approves of the plan to bring the family *all together* at the restaurant next week.

Discreet means *tactful*, whereas *discrete* means *separate*. Thus, a psychiatrist who happens to encounter one of his patients in the grocery store will greet the patient *discreetly*, without referring to any of their private discussions in his office, because the psychiatrist is obligated to keep his professional interactions with patients *discrete* from any accidental personal contact with them.

A *disinterested* person is impartial, whereas an *uninterested* person is unengaged or bored. Thus, we hope that judges will be *disinterested* concerning the cases that they hear but not *uninterested* in those cases.

MODIFIERS

A **modifier** is any clause, phrase, or word in a sentence that provides descriptive information about another part of the sentence. Among individual words, the two main types of modifiers are adjectives and adverbs.

Adjectives

Adjectives are words that modify nouns and pronouns. Typically, adjectives answer the following questions: *What kind of? How many? Which?* For example, in the following sentence, *long*, *three*, and *final* are adjectives:

> By the end of our surprisingly long hike, my brother had three blisters and could only walk slowly up the final hill.

The rules for use of adjectives are generally straightforward. However, certain adjectives can only be used with either count or mass nouns.

Count nouns are those that can be counted, as the name suggests, and thus written in plural form. Examples include *house*, *birthday*, *cloud*, *person*, *dynasty*, and *idea*.

Mass nouns cannot be counted. Examples include *sand*, *grass*, *food*, *air*, *money*, and *peace*. Whereas you can speak of one house, two houses, and so on, you cannot speak of one grass, two grasses, and so on. Mass nouns can only be counted by means of some other noun that identifies a discrete unit. Thus, you can speak of one field of grass, two fields of grass, and so on.

Some adjectives, such as *some*, *any*, and *enough*, can be used to modify both count and mass nouns. Others can only be used with one type of noun. For example, *many* can only modify count nouns, whereas *much* can only modify mass nouns. Thus, the following sentences are grammatically correct:

> She keeps many horses in the barn.

> She keeps much hay in the barn too.

Likewise, *few* can only modify count nouns, whereas *little* can only modify mass nouns. Thus, the following sentences are grammatically correct as well:

> Her best friends only own a few horses.

> Her best friends keep very little hay in their barns.

Thus, it would be grammatically incorrect to refer to *much horses*, *many hays*, or *few hays*. Reference to *little horses* is grammatically acceptable only when referring to size rather than quantity.

Adverbs

Adverbs are words that modify verbs, other adverbs, adjectives, and entire clauses. Typically, adverbs answer the question: *How?* For example, in the following sentence, *surprisingly* and *slowly* are adverbs:

> By the end of our surprisingly long hike, my brother had three blisters and could only walk slowly up the final hill.

Adjectives and adverbs are not interchangeable, although in many cases an adverb can be formed by adding the suffix *-ly* to an adjective, as in the following examples:

> He is a quick learner." (adjectival form)

> He learns quickly." (adverbial form)

> The end of the music was unexpected. (adjectival form)

> The end of the music came unexpectedly. (adverbial form)

Not all adverbs end in -*ly*, of course. Compare the following two sentences:

The cat smells good.

The cat smells well.

In the first sentence, *good* is an adjective that modifies the noun *cat*. In the second sentence, *well* is an adverb that modifies the verb *smell*. The second sentence indicates (somewhat awkwardly) that the cat has a good sense of smell. These two sentences highlight the importance of recognizing what word or phrase in a sentence is being modified when distinguishing between adverbs and adjectives. To take another example, compare the following sentences:

I am sure he can cook the soup without making a mess in the kitchen.

Surely he can cook the soup without making a mess in the kitchen.

In the first sentence, *sure* is an adjective because it modifies the initial pronoun *I*. In the second sentence, *surely* is an adverb because it modifies the remainder of the sentence.

Misplaced Modifiers

The rules of syntax allow some flexibility in the location of a modifier in a sentence. For example, as you read the following sentences, notice how the location of the adjective *hot* changes in relation to the noun that it modifies (*summer*):

We had a hot summer this year.

The summer was hot this year.

How hot the summer was this year!

The following examples show flexibility in the location of an adverb (*quickly*) in relation to the verb that it modifies (*found*):

He found the missing keys quickly.

Quickly he found the missing keys.

He quickly found the missing keys.

Misplaced modifiers result in sentences that are misleading, ambiguous, or incoherent. Although syntactic rules allow some flexibility in the locations of modifiers, there are still many rules. A general rule is that modifiers should be close to what they modify. For example, consider the following sentence:

The weather forecast called for heavy rain yesterday.

This sentence appears to state that, according to some weather forecast, heavy rain was expected yesterday. However, if the writer meant that yesterday the weather forecast predicted heavy rain at some point in the future, then the modifier (*yesterday*) should be located closer to the subject, as in the following examples:

> Yesterday the weather forecast called for heavy rain.

> The weather forecast yesterday called for heavy rain.

> Yesterday's weather forecast called for heavy rain.

Even when a modifier is right next to the word it modifies, the meaning may be compromised if it is on the wrong side. For example, suppose that Johnson arrives at a party and then asks nearly everyone else in attendance for money. Compare the following two descriptions of this unpleasant situation:

> Johnson asked almost everyone at the party to borrow money.

> Johnson almost asked everyone at the party to borrow money.

Although both sentences are grammatically correct, the first sentence accurately conveys the situation. However, in the second sentence, the misplacement of the modifier *almost* suggests incorrectly that Johnson did not ask others for money. Rather, it suggests that he considered asking everyone for a loan, but chose not to, or was otherwise prevented from doing so.

Notice that misplaced modifiers could consist of entire phrases rather than just words. Consider the following sentence:

> I heard that the governor decided to run for re-election while I was at Fiona's apartment.

It is not clear whether the governor made the decision to run for re-election during the time when the writer was at Fiona's apartment, or whether the writer learned while at Fiona's apartment that the governor had made this decision at some earlier time. If the latter is the case, then the sentence should be reordered as follows:

> While I was at Fiona's apartment, I heard that the governor decided to run for re-election.

Squinting and Dangling Modifiers

A **squinting modifier** is misplaced in such a way that it could refer to the clause that precedes it or to the one that follows. For example:

> Running on concrete surfaces quickly leads to knee damage.

Owing to the squinting modifier *quickly*, this sentence could mean that running at a high rate of speed on concrete surfaces leads to knee damage, or that running on concrete surfaces will very soon lead to knee damage. The writer would need to choose between revisions such as the following:

> Running quickly on concrete surfaces leads to knee damage.

> Running on concrete surfaces will quickly lead to knee damage.

The misplaced and squinting modifiers discussed so far are problematic because they modify the wrong word or phrase, or because it is ambiguous as to what they modify. However, in each case the correct word or phrase is present in the sentence. When a sentence does not contain the word or phrase that should be modified, a **dangling modifier** can be used. For example:

Walking to school this morning, the mosquitoes were everywhere.

In this example, the phrase *walking to school this morning* tells us something about the person who was walking. However, that person is not identified in the sentence. As a result, the sentence seems to indicate that the mosquitoes were walking to school. An acceptable revision of the sentence would need to include an appropriate subject. For example:

Walking to school this morning, I noticed that the mosquitoes were everywhere.

As I walked to school this morning, I noticed that the mosquitoes were everywhere.

REFERENCE

Misplaced, squinting, and dangling modifiers illustrate the need for a writer to be clear about what is referred to by the modifiers that he or she uses. More generally, the writer must be clear about the reference of all words or phrases that are used to indicate some other word or phrase.

The particular type of reference discussed in this section is **pronoun reference**, or the use of pronouns to refer to nouns. In the following sentence, for example, it is clear that the pronoun *he* refers to the individual named *George*:

George rushed into the room, and he looked scared.

In the following sentence, however, the reference of *he* is unclear:

George was fighting with Quinton and he looked scared.

Unless there are contextual cues, the reader cannot tell whether *he* refers to George or Quinton. Assuming that George is the one who appeared to be scared, here are a few of the many possible ways to fix the sentence:

George was fighting with Quinton; George looked scared.

George, looking scared, was fighting with Quinton.

While fighting with Quinton, George looked scared.

Pronoun reference is important when using the **demonstratives** *this*, *that*, *these*, and *those*. As adjectives, demonstratives direct the reader's attention toward particular nouns, as in the following sentence:

This bird is a robin.

I plan to install two more of these applications.

As pronouns, demonstratives are used in place of nouns, as illustrated by the following examples:

> This is an outstanding translation of Goethe's *Faust*.

> That was quite a party!

Confusion sometimes occurs when beginning a sentence with a demonstrative pronoun, as illustrated by the following passage:

> The surface of the brain is compressed, highly wrinkled, and covered with layers of tissue such as the meninges. This makes it difficult to visually examine features just below the surface.

In this passage, the word *this* points to whatever it is that makes it difficult to examine certain features of the brain. However, it is unclear whether *this* refers to the layers of tissue such as the meninges, or whether it refers to all of the physical characteristics of the brain described in the first sentence. Assuming the latter, here are two more suitable versions of the passage:

> The surface of the brain is compressed, highly wrinkled, and covered with layers of tissue such as the meninges. These characteristics make it difficult to visually examine features just below the surface.

> The surface of the brain is compressed, highly wrinkled, and covered with layers of tissue such as the meninges. This set of characteristics makes it difficult to visually examine features just below the surface.

PUNCTUATION

Many different types of punctuation contribute to the form and grammatical meanings of sentences.

Periods, Exclamation Points, and Question Marks

The end of a sentence can be indicated by a period, an exclamation point, or a question mark.

Periods are used to end complete sentences. For example, consider the following passage:

> Johnson criticized Milton's politics. But esteemed his poetic works most highly. Especially *Paradise Lost*.

As the first sentence is complete, the period is appropriately placed. The second two sentences are fragments, and thus setting them off by means of periods is grammatically incorrect. Generally, periods should not be used at the end of dependent clauses. Following is one possible revision of the passage that would be grammatically correct:

> Johnson criticized Milton's politics, but esteemed his poetic works most highly. Johnson especially admired *Paradise Lost*.

Exclamation marks are used to emphasize ideas, or to convey strong attitudes or emotions such as admiration or astonishment. For example:

> You should never hitchhike!

> Afterwards, the truck nearly exploded!

> He worked on his first novel for 17 years!

Exclamation marks can also be used for exclamations and commands, as illustrated by the following:

> Extraordinary!

> Stop!

Question marks are used to convey both **direct questions** (e.g., *What should we do today?*) and **rhetorical questions** (e.g., *What have they ever done for me?*). However, questions can be formed without using question marks, as in the case of the **indirect question**. For example:

> I want to know when someone will stand up and address our concerns.

The direct form of this question would be: *I want to know: When will someone stand up and address our concerns?* Alternatively, the direct form of the question could be: *When will someone stand up and address our concerns?*

Semicolons and Colons

Two of the more common ways to divide a sentence are the semicolon and the colon.

Semicolons are used to separate independent clauses. Consider, for example, the following sentences:

> Shonte came to school today; Anna stayed home.

> I really enjoy chocolate ice cream for dessert; unfortunately, there was no ice cream left in my freezer.

In each of these sentences, what comes before the semicolon and what follows it each consists of an independent clause. As you can see, each sentence consists of exactly two independent clauses. Sentences that contain more than two independent clauses are usually divided by commas rather than semicolons.

A **colon** is used at the end of an independent clause. Several grammatically correct options can follow the colon, including lists, explanations, quotations, and so on.

First, the clause following a colon may be a list, as in the following example:

> For the lunch special, diners can choose among three entrees: pasta salad, fried fish, or steak.

Second, the clause following the colon may be an explanation or restatement of what preceded the colon. For example:

> The immunization program was a resounding success in the village: 100% of the children were immunized.

Third, the clause following the colon may consist of a lengthy quotation, as in the following example:

> Our society suffers from too much knowledge and not enough optimism about how that knowledge can be used. Camus stated this point in a sophisticated way: "The modern mind is in complete disarray. Knowledge has stretched itself to the point where neither the world nor our intelligence can find any foot-hold. It is a fact that we are suffering from nihilism."

Notice that in each of these examples, the clause preceding the colon is an independent clause and thus stands alone as a complete sentence. Thus, the following sentences are grammatically incorrect, because what precedes the colon is a dependent clause:

> My favorite foods are: pizza, chocolate, and fried cheese.

> All I know is: you can't take it with you!

In order to make either one of these previous sentences grammatically correct, the writer would need to either revise the clause preceding the colon so that it becomes an independent clause, or simply remove the colon, as in the following grammatically correct examples:

> My favorite foods are as follows: pizza, chocolate, and fried cheese.

> My favorite foods are pizza, chocolate, and fried cheese.

> All I know is this: you can't take it with you!

> All I know is that you can't take it with you!

Commas

The **comma** is the form of punctuation used most frequently within sentences. Following are four of the more important purposes that commas serve.

First, a comma is used to separate a sequence of two or more modifiers, as in the following sentences:

> The highway was long, dark, and surprisingly narrow.

> *Moby Dick* appeared to be a long, difficult book.

In sentences like these, the comma takes the place of the word *and*. For example, the second sentence indicates that the book appeared to be both long and difficult. Strictly speaking, the presence of the comma indicates that both adjectives modify the noun. The absence of a comma between a pair of modifiers indicates that the first modifier actually modifies the second one rather than the noun. Consider, for example, the following sentence:

> All day in the lab he was a cautious, quiet employee; in the evening, however, his wild side emerged, and he lived the life of a recklessly optimistic adolescent.

In the first clause, a comma is used between *cautious* and *quiet* because both words modify the noun *employee*. In the final clause, no comma is used between *recklessly* and *optimistic* because only *optimistic* modifies the noun *adolescent*. *Recklessly* is an adverb that modifies *optimistic*.

Second, commas are used to separate a nonrestrictive modifier from the rest of the sentence in which it appears. Following are some examples of nonrestrictive modifiers that are set off by the use of commas:

> The next document, dated November 14, clearly indicates the man's identity.

> Although he would be flying to Paris, the most romantic city in the world, the purpose of the trip was purely business.

In the first sentence, the phrase *dated November 14* modifies *document*. In the second sentence, the phrase *the most romantic city in the world* modifies *Paris*. This phrase is actually an **appositive**, a noun or noun phrase that renames or otherwise identifies an associated noun. Here is another example:

> On that morning his wife, Mrs. Jane Doe, checked into a downtown hotel and went straight to her room.

In this sentence, *Mrs. Jane Doe* is the appositive for *his wife*. Notice that this sentence can be rearranged as follows in order to make *his wife* the appositive:

> On that morning Mrs. Jane Doe, his wife, checked into a downtown hotel and went straight to her room.

In each of these sentences, commas are used to divide the noun from the appositive, and the appositive from the rest of the sentence. Notice, however, that not all appositives require commas. For example:

> It was Shaw's play *Major Barbara* that we saw together last spring.

In this sentence, the name of the play is the appositive for the noun *play*, but no commas are needed.

Third, when a sentence begins with a dependent clause, and the sentence is sufficiently long, a comma is used to divide the dependent clause from the rest of the sentence, as in the following examples:

> After a long and sleepless night, he roused himself and got ready for work.

> If you suspect that an insurance company is disreputable, you should avoid buying a policy from that company.

If there is more than one dependent clause, a comma is used to divide each one from the others. For example, the following sentence consists of three dependent clauses followed by an independent clause:

> If you visit the downtown area, tour the arts district, or swim in the lake, you should be careful.

Notice that for short sentences beginning with a dependent clause a comma may not be needed, as in the following examples:

> After church they went out for brunch.

> In time governments may gain more humanity.

Fourth, as noted earlier, a comma should be used in a compound sentence (i.e., one that consists of two or more independent clauses) in order to separate the independent clauses. For example:

> The violist stood and stretched, but she still felt a bit of stiffness in her back.

Recall that a semicolon can also be used to divide independent clauses. The difference is that a semicolon must be used if there is no conjunction between the clauses, whereas a comma must be used if a conjunction is present. Thus, one can write *The violist stood and stretched; she still felt a bit of stiffness in her back*. However, the following two sentences are grammatically *incorrect*:

> The violist stood and stretched, she still felt a bit of stiffness in her back.

> The violist stood and stretched; but she still felt a bit of stiffness in her back.

The grammatically correct version of this sentence (*The violist stood and stretched, but she still felt a bit of stiffness in her back.*) reflects a common type of sentence that consists of independent clause–comma–independent clause. Although a sentence consisting of dependent clause–comma–independent clause is also grammatically correct, a sentence consisting of independent clause–comma–dependent clause will typically be incorrect. Thus, the first sentence in the following examples is grammatically correct, but the second sentence is grammatically incorrect:

> After standing and stretching, the violist still felt a bit of stiffness in her back. (dependent clause–comma–independent clause—correct)

> The violist stood and stretched, but still felt a bit of stiffness in her back. (independent clause–comma–dependent clause—incorrect)

The second sentence can become grammatically correct if the word *she* is included in the dependent clause in order to make it an independent clause, or the comma is removed. These two grammatically correct versions of the sentence are illustrated below:

> The violist stood and stretched, but she still felt a bit of stiffness in her back.

> The violist stood and stretched but still felt a bit of stiffness in her back.

Finally, notice that the rules for using commas to separate independent clauses in compound sentences are the same when the sentences contain more than two independent clauses, as illustrated by the following sentence:

> The violist stood and stretched, but she still felt a bit of stiffness in her back, and her neck still ached after that evening's performance.

Apostrophes and Possessives

Apostrophes are used for two different purposes: to create contractions such as *don't*, *could've*, and *let's*, and to mark the possessive case, as shown in the following sentences:

> This is John's book.
>
> Nature's path is one of mystery and beauty.
>
> The administration's position on this matter is quite clear.

The possessive form of a singular noun is usually created by adding an apostrophe and then an *s* to the end of the noun, as in the previous examples. When a noun is plural, the possessive is created by adding the apostrophe after the *s*, as you can see in the following example:

> The performance of any team is ultimately the players' responsibility.

There are some exceptions to the rule for plurals. For example, *children* and *men* are both plural, but the possessive forms are created by adding an apostrophe and then an *s* to the end of each word (*children's*, *men's*) as if they were singular.

Possessive pronouns constitute an important exception to the rules concerning use of apostrophes and other changes to indicate possession. Possessive pronouns include the following:

my	yours	hers	their
mine	his	its	theirs
your	her	our	whose

When these pronouns are used as modifiers, they do not change. For example:

> Everyone wondered where she left her book.
>
> This is their first trip to Nicaragua.

The forms of most of these pronouns change when they are used on their own. For example:

> This is my book.
>
> This book is mine.
>
> My suitcase weighs nine pounds; how heavy is your suitcase?
>
> My suitcase weighs nine pounds; how heavy is yours?

As these examples illustrate, *my* becomes *mine* when used by itself, whereas *your* becomes *yours*. In addition, *her* becomes *hers* and *their* becomes *theirs*. *His* and *its* do not change.

Its and *it's* are commonly confused. *It's* is a contraction for *It is*. *Its* is the possessive pronoun. Compare the following two sentences:

> My old car still sounds ragged when I start it up, and so I think its time for me to look at it's carburetor.

> My old car still sounds ragged when I start it up, and so I think it's time for me to look at its carburetor.

Because the writer means to say that *it is* time to examine the car's carburetor, the first sentence contains two grammatical errors (*its* and *it's*), but the second sentence is grammatically correct.

HOW TO APPROACH CONVENTIONS OF STANDARD WRITTEN ENGLISH QUESTIONS

Types of Questions

All of the questions in the Conventions of Standard Written English section have the same format. These questions consist of individual, stand-alone sentences in which certain parts are underlined. For example:

A person <u>can become</u> very <u>susceptible to</u> colds if <u>they do</u> not get <u>enough</u> rest. <u>No error</u>
         A   B   C   D   E

Your task is to choose the underlined part of the sentence that is *incorrect* with respect to grammar and other aspects of language. If there is no mistake in the sentence, you should choose option E. In the previous sentence, the correct answer is C. The subject of the sentence (*a person*) is singular, and thus a singular form of the verb phrase (e.g., *he or she does*) should have been used. (You are not asked for revisions in the Conventions of Standard Written English section.)

The directions you can expect to see for the Conventions of Standard Written English section are reproduced here from the CLEP College Composition/College Composition Modular Examination Guide:

> The following sentences test your knowledge of grammar, usage, diction (choice of words), and idiom. Note that some sentences are correct, and no sentence contains more than one error.

> Read each sentence carefully, paying particular attention to the underlined portions. You will find that the error, if there is one, is underlined. Assume that elements of the sentence that are not underlined are correct and cannot be changed. In choosing answers, follow the requirements of standard written English.

> If there is an error, select the one underlined part that must be changed to make the sentence correct.

> If there is no error, select No error.

Thus, for Conventions of Standard Written English questions, your task is to look for errors. As you consider each underlined portion of the sentence in turn, you can rule out those that reflect correct grammar and usage. However, it may be best if you read the entire sentence first before ruling out options, as the correctness of some options cannot be determined without examining other parts of a sentence. You do not have unlimited time, of course. However, few of the sentences will be extremely lengthy, and in some cases you might even be able to spot an error as you read before systematically weighing each option.

Sample Questions

The questions provided in this section draw upon the skills discussed throughout this section. The format of the questions is exactly what you will find in the Conventions of Standard Written English section of the CLEP College Composition and College Composition Modular exams. Here we will work through the questions together.

Consider first this short and relatively simple sentence:

<u>On Tuesday</u> the German <u>army</u> advanced, <u>the</u> Russian army <u>retreated</u>. <u>No error</u>
   A   B   C   D   E

When you first encounter this sentence, option A might seem to be correct, but you should still read further to determine whether anything else in the sentence might call for a different opening. Option B does not seem to be incorrect either, regardless of what follows. As for option D, by the time you reach the end of the sentence it should be clear that this option is not a source of error. Option C is the correct answer. Because the first clause (*On Tuesday the German army advanced*) is an independent clause, it needs to be separated from the second clause by means of a semicolon or by the addition of a conjunction, as illustrated by the following sentences, each of which is grammatically correct:

> On Tuesday the German army advanced; the Russian army retreated.

> On Tuesday the German army advanced, but the Russian army retreated.

> On Tuesday the German army advanced while the Russian army retreated.

Next, consider this more elaborate sentence:

In order to <u>determine</u> whether someone <u>is eligible for</u> admission to <u>this</u> academy, our admissions
            A   B   C
officer will first check <u>their</u> credentials and administer several assessments. <u>No error</u>
                  D   E

As you read through this sentence, the only option that appears to reflect an error is option D. *Their* refers to the word *someone* in the previous clause. But because *someone* is singular, the pronoun *their* does not reflect agreement in case. Thus, D is the correct answer. The word *their* needs to be replaced by *his or her*, for example, in order for the sentence to be grammatically correct.

Now consider a somewhat longer sentence:

Picasso was indispensible to the emergence of cubism, and he <u>was</u> the cubist movement's
A

<u>principle advocate</u>, but the role of other artists in the <u>movement's</u> development should not be
B   C

downplayed simply because <u>they</u> were lesser geniuses than Picasso. <u>No error</u>
D   E

This sentence contains an error of diction rather than grammar. In option B, the word *principle* is used instead of *principal*, which would mean *main* or *primary*.

The next sentence is relatively simple:

Mary stayed in the car <u>while</u> John <u>went</u> to the door; <u>I</u> found <u>this</u> very confusing. <u>No error</u>
A   B   C   D   E

In this sentence the pronoun reference is unclear. *This* could refer to Mary's behavior, John's behavior, or the behavior of both individuals considered simultaneously. Thus, option D is the correct answer.

Finally, here is a somewhat challenging sentence:

Criticism of Cheever's short stories <u>is</u> misguided, in my view, as it stems from malicious
A

<u>insinuations</u> that <u>he</u> knew nothing of life <u>beyond the suburbs.</u> <u>No error</u>
B   C   D   E

The correct answer is option E. There are no errors in this sentence. Regarding option A, agreement is required between the verb *is* and *criticism*, not between *is* and *short stories*. Regarding option B, *insinuations* is an acceptable term here (as opposed to, say, *inferences*). Regarding option C, it is clear that *he* refers to *Cheever*. Likewise, there is nothing ungrammatical about option D. Thus, option E is the correct answer.

REVISION SKILLS

The Revision Skills section will test your understanding of how to revise sentences and passages. In the CLEP College Composition exam, all of the Revision Skills questions will refer to passages. In the CLEP College Composition Modular exam, most of the Revision Skills questions will refer to passages; however, some will refer to stand-alone sentences. In each exam, each Revision Skills question will ask you to choose the best revision to some part of a passage or sentence. All of the questions are multiple-choice and consist of five options.

The Revision Skills section is the longest of the four multiple-choice sections in the CLEP College Composition and College Composition Modular exams. To some extent, this section tests your ability to apply the skills tested in other sections of these exams. You will find that many of the skills tested in the Revision Skills section are also tested in the Conventions of Standard Written English and Rhetorical Analysis sections. Thus, you should expect that the material reviewed in any section of this book may be tested in any section of the CLEP exam.

The skills tested in this section are described in the College Composition/College Composition Modular Examination Guide as follows:

- Organization
- Evaluation of evidence
- Awareness of audience, tone, and purpose
- Level of detail
- Coherence between sentences and paragraphs
- Sentence variety and structure
- Main idea, thesis statements, and topic sentences
- Rhetorical effects and emphasis
- Use of language
- Evaluation of author's authority and appeal
- Evaluation of reasoning
- Consistency of point of view
- Transitions
- Sentence-level errors

The discussion of skills in this section will be followed by guidance on how to approach Revision Skills questions, and then some practice questions with answers and explanations.

ORGANIZATION

In writing, **organization** refers to the order in which information is presented. Several factors contribute to effective organization.

- By considering the nature of the audience (i.e., the likely readers), the writer can organize the information in a way that is consistent with the audience's interests and expertise.
- By arranging sentences and paragraphs in a logical order, the writer can organize the information in a coherent and understandable way.
- By clearly introducing and later summarizing key points and themes, the writer can help the reader follow the argument that is being developed.
- By providing transitions between topics and themes, the writer can prevent the reader from becoming confused.
- By sticking to a particular type of organization, the writer can provide the reader with expectations about how various details will be organized.

Most works of nonfiction use chronological, emphatic, generality, comparison, or cause–effect organization. This section includes a brief introduction to each type of organization, with emphasis on how each type can be recognized in passages.

Chronological Organization

Chronological organization consists of a sequence of events presented in order of occurrence. For example, readers should be able to quickly spot the chronological organization of the following passage:

> The United States became a free and sovereign nation following a number of inter-related events. First, European explorers discovered the North American continent while trying to find shorter trade routes to Asia. Then, as more and more Europeans immigrated to the New World, colonies began to form, and a desire to be self-governed increasingly took root among the populace. . . .

Chronological organization is suggested by the first sentence of the passage, and by key words such as *first* and *then*. Other terms that suggest chronological organization include *afterward*, *beginning with*, *later*, *next*, and so on. As you can see, someone reading a passage such as this one will almost immediately expect to see a chronology of events, and any significant departure from this form of organization will be potentially confusing. For example, in the following version of the passage, the third sentence (*Trade is one of the contributors to cultural interdependence*) is out of place, because it delves into a topic (i.e., causes of cultural interdependence) that is not relevant to the chronology of the passage. The writer needs to delete the third sentence in a revision of the passage:

> The United States became a free and sovereign nation following a number of inter-related events. First, European explorers discovered the North American continent while trying to find shorter trade routes to Asia. Trade is one of the contributors to cultural

interdependence. Then, as more and more Europeans immigrated to the New World, colonies began to form, and a desire to be self-governed increasingly took root among the populace. . . .

Emphatic Organization

Emphatic organization consists of information that is presented in order of importance from greatest to least importance (or vice versa). For example, readers should be able to quickly see that information in the following passage is organized in terms of greatest to least importance:

> The main reason that Jones and Yamaguchi obtained different results is that their experiments relied on slightly different methodologies for DNA sampling. The fact that Jones and Yamaguchi run different labs located in different parts of the world may have also played a role. . . .

Here the use of terms such as *main reason* and *also played a role* hint that emphatic organization is being used. The reader will be able to see that a methodological difference is the main reason the two scientists obtained different results, and that other information in the passage will cover lesser contributors and other minor details. Any departure from this organization will be confusing, because the opening sentence has already led the reader to expect that no other contributor to the difference in results will be as important. For example, in the following version of the passage, the final sentence is out of place, because its assertion about what is the most important contributor seems inconsistent with what is asserted in the first sentence. The writer would need to delete the final sentence in a revision of the passage.

> The main reason that Jones and Yamaguchi obtained different results is that their experiments relied on slightly different methodologies for DNA sampling. The fact that Jones and Yamaguchi run different labs located in different parts of the world may have also played a role. But the most important reason for the difference in results is the use of a different statistical procedure for analyzing the data.

In the preceding passage, the writer may have in mind a distinction between the *main reason* (first sentence) and the *most important reason* (final sentence), but in the absence of further information the final sentence is problematic because *main* and *most important* can be construed as synonymous.

Emphatic organization does not always present information from greatest to least importance. Following is a passage that presents details in order of increasing importance:

> In order to engage in formal debate, a debater must research the topic ahead of time and become familiar with pertinent facts. More importantly, the debater must understand how to use these facts to support his or her own position. Winning a debate, however, does not rely solely on how the debater makes use of his or her knowledge. Ninety percent of communication consists of body language and delivery. Most important to successful performance in a debate is the ability to express oneself by means of passionate, persuasive delivery.

Here the reader will only gradually realize that the information is being presented in order of increasing importance. Once the reader comes to this realization, departures from this least-to-greatest importance organization will make the passage more difficult to follow. For example, consider what happens when one word—the first word of the second sentence—is changed:

> In order to engage in formal debate, a debater must research the topic ahead of time and become familiar with pertinent facts. Most importantly, the debater must understand how to use these facts to support his or her own position. Winning a debate, however, does not rely solely on how the debater makes use of his or her knowledge. Ninety percent of communication consists of body language and delivery. Most important to successful performance in a debate is the ability to express oneself by means of passionate, persuasive delivery.

The passage is now confusing because the second sentence and the final sentence each point to a different factor as most important to successful debate performance. Given that the passage places so much emphasis on delivery, it seems clear that the writer means to say that delivery is the most important factor. Thus, the best revision to the passage would be to change the phrase *Most importantly* at the outset of the second sentence. The phrase could be changed back to *More importantly*, for example, or simply deleted altogether.

Generality Organization

Generality organization consists of information presented in order of specificity, either from general to specific, or from specific to general. For example, readers will quickly recognize that the following passage begins with a broad theme that becomes progressively narrower:

> Put simply, our legal system is in disarray. Criminal trials in particular drag on much longer than they should. *People v. Simpson* is a classic example. This most famous of trials began in Los Angeles County Superior Court on January 29 and lasted until October 3, 1995, a period of over seven months. . . .

Following a very general opening statement, each sentence in the previous passage provides a more specific discussion of the idea introduced in the prior sentence. By the end of the passage, the reader will be expecting to see more details about the actual trial.

Following is the same passage rewritten in order to reflect specific-to-general organization:

> On January 29, 2005, in Los Angeles County Superior Court, the most famous trial in American history got underway. This trial, *People v. Simpson*, lasted more than seven months and represents a classic example of how criminal trials in our country drag on much longer than they should. Our legal system, put simply, is in disarray.

Here, the organization of the passage suggests that the writer may continue with a discussion of certain problems that plague our legal system.

In writing that reflects either general-to-specific or specific-to-general organization, shifts away from the organizational structure can be confusing. For example, consider the following passages:

> Put simply, our legal system is in disarray. *People v. Simpson* is a classic example. Criminal trials drag on much longer than they should. This most famous of trials began in Los Angeles County Superior Court on January 29 and lasted until October 3, 1995, a period of over seven months. . . .

> Put simply, our legal system is in disarray. *People v. Simpson* is a classic example. Criminal trials such as this drag on much longer than they should. This most famous of trials began in Los Angeles County Superior Court on January 29 and lasted until October 3, 1995, a period of over seven months. . . .

In the first passage, the third sentence (*Criminal trials drag on much longer than they should*) is out of place, because it is a general statement that appears in the midst of an increasingly specific discussion. (It is also out of place because it interferes with reference of the pronoun *This* at the out-set of the fourth sentence to the subject *People v. Simpson* in the second sentence.) Thus, one way to revise this passage is to relocate the third sentence so that it comes after the first one.

In the second passage, the third sentence (*Criminal trials such as this drag on much longer than they should*) may still seem somewhat out of place owing to its generality, but its placement is not a glaring problem. The reader can still see a general-to-specific progression in the passage.

Comparison Organization

Comparison organization presents information about things or ideas in order to compare and contrast them. For example, readers will quickly spot the comparison drawn in the following passage:

> The most influential political leaders are articulate as well as passionate. Two such figures are John F. Kennedy and Fidel Castro. Although the two men differed greatly in the ideals they represented, both had the capacity to inspire and motivate the citizens of their respective countries through their speeches and other public appearances.

The organization of this particular passage suggests that the writer will go on to focus on similarities between the two men. Other uses of comparison organization may focus on differences. In either case, substantial departure from comparative discussions may undermine the coherence of the writing. For example:

> The most influential political leaders are articulate as well as passionate. Two such figures are John F. Kennedy and Fidel Castro. Castro is still alive but has stepped down as president of Cuba. Although the two men differed greatly in the ideals they represented, both had the capacity to inspire and motivate the citizens of their respective countries through their speeches and other public appearances.

In this passage, the third sentence (*Castro is still alive but has stepped down as president of Cuba*) is informative but out of place, because the purpose of the passage is to discuss similarities between the two men. The simplest and most effective revision of this passage is to simply remove the third sentence.

Cause–Effect Organization

Cause–effect organization presents information about the relationship between a cause or causes and the effects produced by the cause(s). The writer may identify some cause, such as a historical event, and then discuss its various effects, or the writer may identify some effect and focus on discussing various causes. For example:

> From April 6 through April 12, 1968, rioting broke out in the city of Baltimore. The immediate cause of the rioting was the assassination of Dr. Martin Luther King, Jr., in Memphis on April 4. However, it seems unlikely that the assassination of any one figure, no matter how beloved, would have spurred rioting had there not already been decades of frustration and outrage concerning race relations in the United States. The Baltimore Riot of 1968 reflected a sudden explosion of pent-up frustration, one that echoed rioting which had already taken place in other American cities by April 6.

In this passage, the effect is the Baltimore Riot, and the author discusses two causes (the assassination of Dr. King and deep frustration among citizens). The author also hints that rioting in other cities may have played a causal role.

The organization of this passage suggests that the author will describe and analyze causes of a particular historical event. Significant departure from this organizational structure could be confusing, as illustrated by the following version of the passage:

> From April 6 through April 12, 1968, rioting broke out in the city of Baltimore. Baltimore is the capital of Maryland and a prominent eastern city. The immediate cause of the rioting was the assassination of Dr. Martin Luther King, Jr., in Memphis on April 4. However, it seems unlikely that the assassination of any one figure, no matter how beloved, would have spurred rioting had there not already been decades of frustration and outrage concerning race relations in the United States. The Baltimore Riot of 1968 reflected a sudden explosion of pent-up frustration, one that echoed rioting which had already taken place in other American cities by April 6.

Here, the second sentence (*Baltimore is the capital of Maryland and a prominent eastern city.*) is somewhat out of place, because it provides a descriptive detail that does not contribute to an understanding of the causes of the Baltimore Riot of 1968. The best way for a writer to revise this passage is to remove this sentence.

AUDIENCE, PURPOSE, AND TONE

The **audience** consists of the individuals who will be reading a written work. Authors must keep their audience in mind when considering topic, depth of coverage, organization, word choice, and tone.

Purpose refers to the main reason for creating a written work. The author's purpose will be closely matched to the intended audience.

Tone refers to the author's underlying attitudes, which may or may not be detected by readers. An author's tone will be influenced by his or her purpose as well as the nature of the audience.

EVALUATION OF EVIDENCE

Evidence consists of observations, references to scholarly works, quotations, logical analysis, and other kinds of information that are used by writers to bolster their arguments. There are several different types of evidence.

Observations

One type of evidence consists of the **observations** that the writer himself or herself has made, as illustrated in the following passage:

> The effects of global warming are even apparent in regions that seem to experience very little by way of carbon emissions. Outside of Lhasa, for example, cliffs that were heavily forested as little as two decades ago are now barren and dusty, as I discovered on my return to the area last year.

In this passage, the writer is presenting his or her own observations of erosion in the cliffs as evidence of climate change. Observational evidence can be relatively informal and anecdotal, as in the previous example, or it can be formal, as in a scholarly paper in which a scientist reports the observations he or she made during a study.

In some contexts, scientific observations are preferable as evidence to informal, anecdotal observations. For example, compare the following passages:

> In my research I find that males who have been smoking for more than a decade were twice as likely to have developed cardiovascular disease than nonsmokers. Hence I discourage young people from taking up smoking.

> My uncle Rick smoked for almost 30 years and then had a heart attack one day, so I discourage young people from taking up smoking.

Assuming that the writer's goal is to provide evidence concerning the relationship between smoking and heart disease, and to then discourage people from taking up smoking, the first passage provides better evidence than the second one. The first passage describes scientific observations of numerous people, whereas the second passage describes an anecdote about one person.

However, combining the two passages does not automatically yield better evidence:

> In my research I find that males who have been smoking for more than a decade were twice as likely to have developed cardiovascular disease than nonsmokers. My uncle Rick smoked for almost 30 years and then had a heart attack one day. Hence, I discourage young people from taking up smoking.

In this passage, the writer's credibility is undermined somewhat by the anecdote, and by the ambiguity of the word *Hence* in the third sentence. *Hence* could mean that the writer's conclusion is based on his or her own research evidence as well as Uncle Rick's heart attack, or it could mean that the conclusion is based primarily on the demise of Uncle Rick. One way to improve the passage is to remove the reference to Uncle Rick. Another way to improve it is to clarify the relationship between the evidence and conclusion, as follows:

> In my research I find that males who have been smoking for more than a decade were twice as likely to have developed cardiovascular disease than nonsmokers. I can also tell you that my uncle Rick smoked for almost 30 years and then had a heart attack one day. Although Rick is just one person, the findings from my research are clear and lead me to discourage young people from taking up smoking.

Although scientific observation is preferred as a source of evidence about scientific topics, there are two reasons that it is not automatically preferred.

1. Scientific observation does not work well for supporting certain kinds of arguments. A writer who wishes to argue for the merits of a particular musician or genre of music, for example, is not likely to find much support for the argument in scientific research. The same could be said about arguments about the moral character of a particular public figure.

2. Scientific evidence is not infallible. The fact that evidence is scientific implies that it is grounded in systematic observation, but not that it is automatically accurate or unbiased.

Findings

Another form of evidence consists of **findings** by someone other than the writer. These findings may consist of **theoretical claims**, **observations**, or **statistics**. In order to use these findings as evidence, the writer will typically either paraphrase or quote the original source.

Statistics are often given great respect as a source of evidence, and indeed percentages and other kinds of statistical information may constitute good evidence for or against a particular argument. However, statistics are not infallible. Moreover, as a reader, you must be cautious about misuse of statistics as a form of evidence. Consider, for example, the following passage:

> In 2009 the dropout rate in our city was 67.7%. In 2008 the dropout rate was 62.1%, and the year before that it was exactly 60%. The dropout rate in our city is increasing, in other words, and it will continue to increase until someday soon commencement exercises all across the city will be cancelled because there aren't any graduates.

Although the statistics do show a rise in the dropout rate, it does not follow that the dropout rate will reach 100% *someday soon*. A suitable revision to this passage would qualify the final sentence in some way. For example:

> In 2009 the dropout rate in our city was 67.7%. In 2008 the dropout rate was 62.1%, and the year before that it was exactly 60%. The dropout rate in our city is increasing, in other words, and judging from the statistics we can expect it to continue to increase.

The next passage illustrates a number of fallacies that can occur when arguments are based on statistical information.

> Abstinence-only programs do not work. A recent study showed that when abstinence-only programs are available to high school students during freshmen year, only 48% of the students who participate remain abstinent throughout their remaining high school years. Thus, the best way to reduce the rate of teenage pregnancy is for school districts to shut down abstinence-only programs and focus on teaching high school students safe-sex practices.

Here are three fallacies in the passage that even non-statisticians can recognize:

1. The assertion that abstinence-only programs do not work is based on the finding that "only" 48% of students remain abstinent following participation in such programs during freshman year. Perhaps this statistic does show that abstinence-only programs do not work. We cannot be sure, however, because we do not know what the rate of abstinence would be if students had not participated in these programs. There is no comparison group, in other words. We need more statistical information. If roughly 48% of students who do not participate in abstinence-only programs actually remain abstinent, then we could conclude that the programs do not work. If the figure were 68% or 78%, we would have evidence of the programs' effectiveness.

2. Given that participation in abstinence-only programs appears to be optional, perhaps the statistical results are influenced by who chooses to participate or not to participate. Perhaps students who are quite convinced they will remain abstinent during high school see no reason to participate, whereas students who are experiencing inner conflict about the issue are more likely to participate. If this were true, then any effectiveness that the abstinence-only programs have would be underestimated owing to the fact that students who are more susceptible to engaging in sex participate in the programs in the first place.

3. Even if we did conclude that abstinence-only programs are ineffective, it does not follow that school districts should focus on teaching safe-sex practices. Perhaps they should develop better abstinence-only programs. Perhaps there is another solution. The only thing the statistics can tell us is whether the abstinence-only programs are effective. The statistics themselves do not suggest alternatives here.

Authority

A third type of evidence consists of **authority**, including the authority of experts, groups, organizations, scholarly works, and testimonials. For example, consider the following sentence:

> As the U.S. surgeon general has observed, alcohol should not be consumed during pregnancy.

Because the surgeon general is a highly respected source, the writer has used this particular health-related recommendation as evidence for the passage's recommendation. This is an appeal to authority that differs somewhat from an appeal to the evidence provided by an authority or authorities, as in the following example:

> Alcohol should not be consumed during pregnancy, owing to a substantial number of studies showing that even low levels of alcohol consumption can harm the developing fetus.

This sentence illustrates an appeal to findings rather than to authority per se, even though we assume the writer believes that the studies he or she is citing are authoritative.

Appeal to authority can constitute good evidence for an argument, so long as the reader understands that authorities are not infallible—and that sometimes their views are not accurately depicted by writers. Appeals to authority will be effective if a specific authority is identified, and if the reader recognizes the authority as an expert and credible source. Consider the following sentences:

> As the U.S. surgeon general has observed, chocolate milk should be avoided during pregnancy.

> As a reputable expert has observed, chocolate milk should be avoided during pregnancy.

> As my sister Clarissa has observed, chocolate milk should be avoided during pregnancy.

In the first sentence, the fact that the surgeon general is the source of the recommendation constitutes some evidence for that recommendation, for the reasons noted earlier.

In the second sentence, the source is described as *reputable* but is not named. The fact that the recommendation came from a *reputable expert* does not constitute strong evidence in favor of the recommendation. Thus, a good way to revise this sentence would be to identify the expert who has made this observation.

In the third sentence, the source is named but does not appear to be authoritative. Unless Clarissa happens to be the surgeon general or some other known expert, the fact that she advocates against drinking chocolate milk during pregnancy does not itself constitute strong evidence for the recommendation. Thus, the sentence requires some sort of revision. For example, evidence could be introduced into the sentence, and the distinction between the evidence and the anecdote about Clarissa could be made more clearly, as in the following example:

> Scientific studies show that chocolate milk should be avoided during pregnancy, as my sister Clarissa likes to recommend.

In the previous sentence, studies are cited as the main evidence for the recommendation, and Clarissa's views are simply described as consistent with the evidence.

The original sentence (*As my sister Clarissa has observed, chocolate milk should be avoided during pregnancy*) could also be revised to simply remove any hint that evidence is being presented. For example:

> My sister Clarissa and I believe that chocolate milk should be avoided during pregnancy.

Reasoning

In some cases, evidence consists of applications of **logic** in order to yield information that the reader may not have anticipated. The mere use of logic does not in itself provide much evidence. For example, consider the following recommendation:

> In spite of the fact that flame retardants are used in mattresses, one should not smoke in bed. If you smoke while reclining in bed, you may fall asleep, and the burning cigarette you drop may then cause the mattress to catch fire. A burning mattress will in turn have negative consequences.

The final sentence of the passage yields little evidence in favor of the writer's main thesis. Since all readers presumably know that it is undesirable for one's mattress to be on fire, the writer does not help advance his or her argument by drawing out that inference for us. Thus, a desirable revision to this passage would be to delete the final sentence (or to revise it in some way, such as including statistics on the rate of injury or death resulting from smokers' mattresses catching fire).

In other cases, the writer may apply logic in such a way that the information revealed constitutes evidence, because the reader may not have considered this information before. For example, consider the following revision of the previous passage:

> In spite of the fact that flame retardants are used in mattresses, one should not smoke in bed. If you smoke while reclining in bed, you may fall asleep, and the burning cigarette you drop may then cause the mattress to catch fire. Since you would be asleep at this point, your ability to escape from the fire will be somewhat diminished.

Here, the final sentence provides evidence in support of the writer's main thesis. Although the inference conveyed by this sentence is not deeply insightful or reflective of something that readers could not figure out on their own, it does present an observation that readers may not have been considering at that particular moment.

Another example of how logic can be used to yield evidence is in the use of **analogy**. A writer will sometimes make an assertion about a particular scenario, and then point out similarities between this scenario and another one as evidence for the assertion. For example:

> In a recent editorial, an anonymous writer called upon Americans to voluntarily reduce their energy consumption. This appeal, however laudable, will accomplish nothing. If you want people to reduce their energy consumption, simply asking them to do so will never work. It didn't work in the 1970s when President Carter presented the same appeal to the American people, and it will not work now.

In this example, the writer's sole evidence that the appeal to voluntarily reduce energy consumption will not accomplish anything is that the appeal did not accomplish anything on a prior occasion. As you can see, the strength of the evidence here rests on two assumptions: first, that the writer accurately portrayed the prior occasion accurately, and second, that the two situations are analogous. Arguably, they are not. For example, one could argue that attitudes toward energy consumption were much different in the 1970s than they are now. A suitable revision of this passage might consist of adding a sentence that contains additional evidence, as follows:

> In a recent editorial, an anonymous writer called upon Americans to voluntarily reduce their energy consumption. This appeal, however laudable, will accomplish nothing. If you want people to reduce their energy consumption, simply asking them to do so will never work. It didn't work in the 1970s when President Carter presented the same appeal to the American people, and it will not work now. Survey data suggest that contemporary Americans have the same sense of entitlement with respect to energy consumption that we did in the 1970s.

Dimensions of Evaluation

When a writer attempts to make a point or otherwise convey some idea, the reader should evaluate whatever evidence the writer presents in favor of the idea to ensure it is relevant and logical. Although wildly irrelevant statements may be relatively easy to spot, in some cases the reader will need to judge the relevance of particular evidence very carefully. For example, consider the following passage:

> The role of women in Chinese society has been explored at length in recent fiction by authors such as Amy Tan and Maxine Hong Kingston. For example, in *Woman Warrior*, Kingston writes about her mother's struggles as a Chinese immigrant in the United States.

Although the passage is sensible, it is not clear how the second sentence constitutes evidence for the first one. The struggles of a female immigrant may or may not reveal something about the role of women in the home country, depending on how the writer treats the topic. Thus, a revision is needed to the preceding passage in order to increase its coherence. For example:

> The experiences of women immigrants from China has been explored at length in recent fiction by authors such as Amy Tan and Maxine Hong Kingston. For example, in *Woman Warrior*, Kingston writes about her mother's struggles as a Chinese immigrant in the United States.

Finally, writers must develop logical connections between the evidence they present and the conclusions they draw. Although illogical statements may be easy to spot, in some cases the reader must evaluate the writer's logic carefully. For example, consider the following passage:

> Thomson argues that the laws against possession of recreational drugs should be made more lenient in order to reduce the burden on law enforcement and to help the legal system focus on rehabilitation rather than punishment. The problem with this point of view is that if we allow people to take recreational drugs without negative consequences, the rates of addiction in this country will skyrocket and we will see an epidemic of drug-related crime.

This passage illustrates a logical fallacy called a **straw man argument**, in which the writer distorts a particular point of view before criticizing it. The result is that the writer criticizes the *straw man* (i.e., the distorted view) rather than the actual view. As you can see from the first sentence in the previous passage, Thomson is not arguing that there should be no negative consequences for taking recreational drugs. Rather, the argument is that the negative consequences should be lessened.

However, the writer does not attack this claim. Rather, the attack focuses on the straw man claim that we should allow people to take recreational drugs without negative consequences whatsoever. This is an easier claim to attack than Thomson's actual claim. The second sentence of the passage requires revision. For example:

> Thomson argues that the laws against possession of recreational drugs should be made more lenient in order to reduce the burden on law enforcement and to help the legal system focus on rehabilitation rather than punishment. The problem with this point of view is that if we diminish the negative consequences for taking recreational drugs, the rates of addiction in this country will skyrocket and we will see an epidemic of drug-related crime.

This revision is not ideal, because the writer is making predictions (skyrocketing addiction rates and a drug-related crime epidemic) that are not supported by evidence. However, the writer has at least paraphrased Thomson's view appropriately rather than attacking a straw man.

Another kind of logical fallacy is the **circular argument**, in which a conclusion is assumed as part of its own premises. Thus, the conclusion is not suggested by evidence and reasoning; rather, the conclusion is already assumed. For example:

> Sir Winston Churchill is known as a mesmerizing speaker because his speeches to huge crowds in Whitehall and elsewhere had a riveting effect on the public.

In the previous sentence, evidence for the conclusion that Churchill was a mesmerizing speaker is that his speeches were riveting. In short, because *mesmerizing* and *riveting* are very similar in meaning, the writer is saying, in effect, that Churchill was mesmerizing because he was mesmerizing. This reflects a circular argument. The evidence presented in support of the conclusion actually reflects that very conclusion. The following is one of the many possible non-circular revisions of the preceding sentence:

> Sir Winston Churchill is known as a mesmerizing speaker because his speeches to huge crowds in Whitehall and elsewhere caused audiences to stare, slack-jawed, and then erupt in shouts and peals of applause.

A third type of logical fallacy is called the **false analogy**, because it characterizes an argument in which an analogy is drawn between elements that are not truly analogous, or analogous in a merely superficial or irrelevant way. For example:

> The CEO of a large industrial chemical company recently argued that his company's newest product should not have been banned by the EPA simply because of evidence that proper use of the chemical resulted in several fatalities. "According to that line of reasoning," the CEO scoffed, "the use of automobiles should be banned, because they cause fatalities too. Nobody in their right mind would suggest that we actually pass a law banning automobiles."

In this passage, the CEO presents the following argument:

1. Use of my company's new product results in fatalities.

2. Use of automobiles results in fatalities.

3. The new product is therefore analogous to automobiles.

4. Since automobiles should not be banned, the new product should not be banned.

The analogy between the product and automobiles can be considered a false analogy because the connection between them is not very relevant. The use of many things can potentially cause fatalities. However, the proper use of automobiles, according to some reasonable definition of the term *proper*, would not result in fatalities. In contrast, the company's product seems to do so even when used properly.

LEVEL OF DETAIL

The author of a written work must choose the **level of detail** that is appropriate to the interests and expertise of the passage's audience. This requirement pertains to the entire work. In addition, the author must convey specific points with enough detail that these points are understandable and persuasive. Missing details undermine the coherence of an argument. To take just one example, consider the following passage:

> Thomson argues that the laws against possession of recreational drugs should be made more lenient in order to reduce the burden on law enforcement and to help the legal system focus on rehabilitation rather than punishment. Thomson has presented this argument in six different scholarly publications and uncounted numbers of editorials and interviews. The problem with this point of view is that if we diminish the negative consequences for taking recreational drugs, the rates of addiction in this country will skyrocket and we will see an epidemic of drug-related crime.

This passage contains too much detail on one point and too little on another. The second sentence (*Thomson has presented this argument in six different scholarly publications and uncounted numbers of editorials and interviews*) may be accurate, but these details have no bearing on either the substance of Thomson's view or the substance of the writer's objections to that view. In a suitable revision of this passage, the second sentence would be removed.

Although too detailed about Thomson's publications and media activity, this passage is not detailed enough concerning the link between diminished consequences for drug use and changes in rates of addiction and drug-related crime. The addition of a sentence describing this link would be helpful, as in the following revision:

> Thomson argues that the laws against possession of recreational drugs should be made more lenient in order to reduce the burden on law enforcement and to help the legal system focus on rehabilitation rather than punishment. The problem with this point of view is that if we diminish the negative consequences for taking recreational drugs, drug use will rise because users will be less afraid of getting caught. As a result, the rates of addiction in this country will skyrocket and we will see an epidemic of drug-related crime.

Although the argument in this passage may still not be very strong, the addition of further details has now made it more explicit.

COHERENCE

Coherence refers to the clarity and connectedness of written information. Writing can be judged coherent when the reader is able to understand the individual elements (phrases, sentences, paragraphs, ideas, and themes) as well as the connections between these elements. For example, consider two of the factors that contribute to the coherence of a paragraph: the topical focus of the paragraph and the extent of connectedness between sentences.

Topical Focus

The coherence of a paragraph is determined in part by its **focus** on a single point or idea. Coherence is undermined when more than one point or idea is developed in a paragraph. Consider, for example, the following:

> The use of bottled water is irresponsible. Water is readily available from taps and public fountains. In addition, water from taps and fountains is free. Bottled water costs us time and money to purchase, and the plastic from discarded water bottles is a major source of environmental pollution. Studies now show that all kinds of plastics break down quickly in the ocean, resulting in microscopic particles that make their way into the food supply via plankton and other tiny creatures; fish eat the plankton, we eat the fish, and thus our health is imperiled.

In some respects this paragraph is quite coherent. The main point is conveyed in the opening sentence, and the remainder of the paragraph provides evidence in support of that point. Moreover, each individual sentence in the paragraph is understandable. In spite of these positive qualities, the coherence of the paragraph is diminished by the final sentence. The main point of the paragraph is that use of bottled water is irresponsible. However, the final sentence of the paragraph is concerned with a related but separate point (i.e., the impact of plastics pollution on human health). Removal of this sentence would increase the coherence of the passage.

Sentence-Level Connections

The extent of **connectedness** between individual sentences also contributes to the coherence of a paragraph. Coherence in this sense can be created by a number of methods.

First, repetition of a word across sentences can link the sentences together. Consider, for example, the following pairs of sentences:

> Marijuana has been praised for its relaxing and euphoric qualities. Users should also recognize that slower reaction times and moderately impaired judgment are possible.

> Marijuana has been praised for its relaxing and euphoric qualities. Users of marijuana should also recognize that slower reaction times and moderately impaired judgment are possible.

Although the first pair of sentences is understandable, the second pair is more closely interconnected owing to the repetition of the term *marijuana*.

Second, rather than literally repeating a word, the writer can use a synonym, antonym, or pronoun that refers to a word in the previous sentence and thereby links the sentences together. Words that are merely close in meaning rather than synonymous can also be effective in this way. Compare the following examples:

> Marijuana has been praised for its relaxing and euphoric qualities. Users of the nostrum should also recognize that slower reaction times and moderately impaired judgment are possible.

> Marijuana has been praised for its relaxing and euphoric qualities. Users of the drug should also recognize that slower reaction times and moderately impaired judgment are possible.

Here again, the first pair of sentences is understandable, because the reader will recognize that *nostrum* is a reference to marijuana, but the coherence of the second pair of sentences is greater owing to the clearer relationship in meaning between *drug* and *marijuana*.

Third, the writer can simply use a word that tends to be associated with a word in the previous sentence, and in this way link the sentences together. Consider the following passages:

> Through his binoculars Francis saw the lion rise to its feet. Suddenly he heard a loud sound.

> Through his binoculars Francis saw the lion rise to its feet. Suddenly he heard a loud roar.

The link between the sentences is clearer in the second passage, because of the association that readers naturally make between lions and roaring.

Fourth, the writer can use parallelism to connect sentences.

Fifth, transitions between sentences can help connect them.

SENTENCE VARIETY

In the earlier section on syntax, you read about different sentence structures, which include simple, compound, complex, and compound–complex. Writing that does not include a mix of these structures quickly becomes tedious. To illustrate, compare the following two passages:

> Joe DiMaggio is one of the most well-known celebrities in American history. Marilyn Monroe is one of America's most famous celebrities too. Joe was a great baseball player. Marilyn was an actress. Joe and Marilyn met in 1952. They got married in 1954. They divorced less than one year later. Journalists followed their marriage and divorce closely. Joe and Marilyn did not like having so much media attention on their marriage. They were patient about the extent of media attention they received.

> Joe DiMaggio and Marilyn Monroe are two of the most well-known celebrities in American history. Joe was a great baseball player, whereas Marilyn was an actress. The couple met in 1952. Married in 1954, they divorced less than one year later. Both disliked the fact that journalists followed their marriage and divorce very closely, but they were patient about the media attention they received.

The first passage seems stilted, or awkward, because every one of its sentences is a simple sentence. The second passage is an improvement over the first one, because there is more variety in sentence structure. Here is the passage again, accompanied by labels indicating each sentence's type:

> Joe DiMaggio and Marilyn Monroe are two of the most well-known celebrities in American history [simple sentence]. Joe was a great baseball player, whereas Marilyn was an actress [compound sentence]. The couple met in 1952 [simple sentence]. Married in 1954, they divorced less than one year later [complex sentence]. Both disliked the fact that journalists followed their marriage and divorce very closely, but they were patient about the media attention they received [compound–complex sentence].

MAIN IDEA, TOPIC SENTENCE, AND THESIS STATEMENT

The **main idea** is the most important point developed in a paragraph, passage, or work of writing in its entirety. The **thesis statement** is the author's opinion on a topic. Although all coherent written works have a main idea, not all writing contains a thesis statement. A description of a historical event, for example, will not contain a thesis statement if the author simply wishes to state the facts.

The main idea is developed by means of each sentence in the paragraph, and it is summarized in the **topic sentence**. In some cases, the topic sentence is the first sentence of the paragraph, whereas in other cases it is the final paragraph.

In the following description of a research study, you can see that the first sentence is the topic sentence, in that it captures the main idea of the study. The final sentence of the paragraph consists of a thesis statement.

> In this study we showed that parenting style has an impact on children's honesty. All 83 parents whose children attended a local Montessori school were observed during brief interactions with their preschoolers on the school playground. Based on these interactions, each parent was labeled as authoritative, authoritarian, permissive, or uninvolved. Ten parents representing each style were chosen to participate in the lab phase of the study. In the lab phase, each child played cards with an experimenter while the parent waited in a separate room. During the card game, the experimenter left the room for 10 minutes, placing his cards face down on the table before leaving. While he was gone, a hidden camera recorded whether or not the child cheated by looking at the cards. We found that the incidence of cheating was greatest among children with authoritarian parents but least among those with authoritative parents. Thus, we believe that parents who exhibit authoritarian styles should be encouraged to shift to a more warm and receptive style of parenting.

RHETORICAL EFFECTS

Rhetoric consists of the use of language in an effective and persuasive way. Following Aristotle, three general approaches to persuasion have been identified: ethos, pathos, and logos.

Ethos refers to an appeal to the writer's own authority. For example, a writer can increase his or her persuasiveness by claiming to be knowledgeable, being recognized by others as an authority, or simply being an honest and reliable person.

Pathos refers to an appeal to the audience's emotions. A writer can increase his or her persuasiveness by engaging readers' interest in a topic, by amusing readers, by eliciting a sense of moral outrage among readers, and so on.

Logos refers to an appeal to the audience's reason. A writer can increase his or her persuasiveness by getting readers to think about a topic, by presenting compelling evidence for an argument, by pointing out logical fallacies in an opposing argument, and so on.

The rhetorical approach that will be most effective depends on the audience as well as the writer's purpose. Although logos will tend to be most effective when presenting a scholarly theory to scholars, a writer presenting the same theory to the general public will need to make use of ethos (in order to convince the audience to trust his or her rendition of the theory) as well as pathos (to help maintain audience interest). At the same time, overreliance on logos is counterproductive if it makes the writer seem distant or it fails to capture audience interest. Typically, a combination of approaches is needed, for the following reasons:

1. Exclusive reliance on ethos will often be counterproductive, because the writer is asking the reader to accept a particular idea simply because the writer is smart and credible. At the same time, written works are often unpersuasive when readers doubt the writer's authority and credibility, and thus ethos is generally needed.

2. Exclusive reliance on pathos will be counterproductive if readers wonder about the writer's authority or feel they need some sort of rationale for what is being asserted. At the same time, written works are often unpersuasive when they lack any sort of emotional appeal.

3. As noted, exclusive reliance on logos can be counterproductive if the audience senses a lack of emotional engagement on the author's part, or if the writing is so dry and logical that the audience fails to connect with it.

USE OF LANGUAGE

A writer's **diction** (i.e., choice or words and phrases) has a powerful influence on the coherence and persuasiveness of his or her writing. Following are some uses of language that should be avoided.

First, writers should avoid diction that is overly formal, or not formal enough, for a particular audience. Consider the following passage:

> The assassination of Abraham Lincoln was a national tragedy. The loss of this great man was an unexpected blow to the spirit of a nation already wounded by a bloody civil war. Lincoln's family was upset too.

In this passage, the final sentence is much too informal given what preceded it. Deleting this sentence would improve the overall diction of the passage.

Second, writers should avoid jargon. For example:

> Jack made one unwise investment after another, and not one of these ventures paid off. As his assets quickly dwindled, his wife began to realize that she had married a bad ball hitter.

In the previous passage, the baseball term *bad ball hitter* is used to indicate that Jack pursues investments that are unlikely to pay off (in the manner of a hitter who swings at a ball that he is unlikely to hit). However, if it seems likely that the audience will not recognize this particular piece of jargon, the writer should replace *bad ball hitter* with a more understandable phrase, as in the following revision:

> Jack made one unwise investment after another, and not one of these ventures paid off. As his assets quickly dwindled, his wife began to realize that she had married an unwise or unlucky risk taker.

Third, writers should avoid slang. For example:

> Following his conviction for embezzlement, the embattled congressman was sentenced to three years in the slammer, with the possibility of parole after six months.

In this sentence, *the slammer* is overly slang and should be replaced by a term that suits the overall diction of the sentence, such as *prison*.

Finally, writers should avoid gender-biased diction.

TRANSITIONS

As discussed earlier, **transition** terms and phrases contribute to the organization and coherence of writing. Following are some examples of these terms and phrases organized by the purposes they serve.

Purpose	Examples
Adding to a Previous Statement	also, again, as well as, besides, coupled with, furthermore, in addition, likewise, moreover, similarly
Describing a Consequence of a Previous Statement	accordingly, as a result, consequently, for this reason, for this purpose, hence, otherwise, so then, subsequently, therefore, thus
Illustrating a Previous Statement	chiefly, especially, for example, for instance, including, in particular, markedly, namely, particularly, specifically, such as, to illustrate
Restating or Summarizing a Previous Statement	all in all, briefly, in conclusion, in essence in other words, namely, in short, in sum, in brief, on the whole, that is, to put it simply
Contrasting with a Previous Statement	at the same time, but, however, in contrast, instead, nevertheless, on the contrary, rather, similarly, yet

HOW TO APPROACH REVISION SKILLS QUESTIONS

Types of Questions

All of the Revision Skills questions on the CLEP College Composition exam and most of those on the College Composition Modular exam pertain to passages. Usually there are three to five questions per passage. These passages may concern virtually any topic. Each passage may represent an introduction or a conclusion, or it may represent the body of a piece of writing. Some of the passages will be factual, whereas others will be theoretical or speculative. Many of the passages will be expository, whereas others will primarily attempt to persuade the reader to adopt a particular point of view.

The directions you can expect to see for the Revision Skills section are reproduced here from the CLEP College Composition/College Composition Modular Examination Guide.

First, here are the instructions for passage-based questions.

The following passages are early drafts of essays.

Read each passage and then answer the questions that follow. Some questions refer to particular sentences or parts of sentences and ask you to improve sentence structure or diction (word choice). Other questions refer to the entire essay or parts of the essay and ask you to consider the essay's organization, development, or effectiveness of language. In selecting your answers, follow the conventions of standard written English.

Second, here are the instructions for the Improving Sentences questions that are included in the Revision Skills section of the College Composition Modular exam:

The following sentences test correctness and effectiveness of expression. In choosing your answers, follow the requirements of standard written English: that is, pay attention to grammar, diction (choice of words), sentence construction, and punctuation.

In each of the following sentences, part of the sentence or the entire sentence is underlined. Beneath each sentence you will find five versions of the underlined part. The first option repeats the original; the other four options present different versions.

Choose the option that best expresses the meaning of the original sentence. If you think the original is better than any of the alternatives, choose the first option; otherwise, choose one of the other options. Your choice should produce the most effective sentence—one that is clear and precise, without awkwardness or ambiguity.

Sample Questions

The questions provided in this section draw upon the skills discussed in this chapter. The format of the following questions closely matches what you will find in the Revision Skills section of the CLEP College Composition and Composition Modular exams. That is, the questions pertaining to passages are organized into sets of about three to five questions each. The sentences within each passage are numbered, in order to make it easier to identify them in the questions. Five answer options are given for each question, and you are asked to choose the best option. In addition, you will find some Improving Sentences questions of the sort that are included in the Revision Skills section of the CLEP College Composition Modular exam.

We will work through the first set of questions together, once you have read the following passage.

(1) Why do people voluntarily relocate to a large city? (2) First of all, a large city will offer a wide variety of job opportunities owing to the variety of its businesses. (3) Given that rural areas suffer from high unemployment, low wages, and the workers are not satisfied, more and more people are choosing to relocate to the large metropolis in search of work. (4) The populations of large cities have continued to grow in recent years, partly due to an influx of people from rural areas.

(5) The public services in cities are superior. (6) For example, because public transportation is plentiful and efficient, residents waste less time in transit between locations. (7) The A-line bus is the one I use most frequently. (8) Medical services are more plentiful and supported by the latest technological improvements, there is access to modern hospitals too. (9) Educational opportunities in large cities are also quite advanced. (10) Along with public schools, it is relatively easy to find private schools and charter schools in these cities.

First, consider the following question about sentence 1. As is often the case in the Revision Skills section, the sentence to which the question refers is reproduced in italics beneath the question.

In context, which of the following versions of sentence 1 (reproduced below) is best?

Why do people voluntarily relocate to a large city?

(A) Why do people voluntarily relocate to the large city?
(B) Why do people voluntarily relocate to the large cities?
(C) Why does a person voluntarily relocate to large cities?
(D) Why do people voluntarily relocate to large cities?
(E) Why does a person voluntarily relocate to the large cities?

Options A and B reflect a change in article from *a* to *the*, and thus both options are incorrect. Specifically, option A is incorrect because the passage concerns cities rather than one particular city. Option B is incorrect because a particular set of large cities has not been identified.

Options C and E reflect a change in noun from *people* to *person*. Both options are thus incorrect because of the lack of agreement between *person*, which is singular, and the plural *cities*.

Option D is correct. The article has been removed, and *people* agrees with *cities*.

The next question asks you to consider a revision to just one part of a sentence rather than the entire sentence.

Which of the following would be the best revision to the underlined portion of sentence 2 (reproduced below)?

> *First of all, a large city will offer a wide variety of job opportunities <u>owing to the variety of its businesses</u>.*

(A) Leave it as it is.
(B) Change *owing to* to *because of*.
(C) Change the phrase to *owing to a wide variety of its job market*.
(D) Change *owing to the* to *in the*.
(E) Delete it.

Sentence 2 reflects what is referred to in this chapter as circular reasoning. The sentence says, in effect, that the fact that a wide variety of jobs is available can be attributed to the fact that there are a wide variety of jobs. Thus, option A is incorrect. Option B doesn't fix the problem, because it simply replaces one word phrase indicating causality with another one. Option C is simply grammatically incorrect, whereas option D is incoherent. Option E is the correct answer. By simply deleting the underlined phrase, the circular reasoning is removed.

The next question is analogous to the previous one but concerns a grammatical problem rather than circularity:

Which of the following would be the best revision to the underlined portion of sentence 3 (reproduced below)?

> *Given that rural areas suffer from high unemployment, low wages, <u>and the workers are not satisfied</u>, more and more people are choosing to relocate to the large metropolis in search of work.*

(A) Leave it as it is.
(B) Change it to *and dissatisfied workers*.
(C) Change it to *and that the workers are not satisfied*.
(D) Change it to *and workers are not satisfied*.
(E) Delete it.

In sentence 3, the parallelism of *high unemployment* and *low wages* is not continued in the final phrase of the sentence. The sentence must be revised in some way to preserve this parallelism, and thus option A is incorrect. Likewise, options C and D do not make the final phrase parallel to the ones that preceded it. Option E would yield a sentence that is grammatically incorrect. Option B is the correct answer, because it replaces the underlined phrase with one that matches the parallelism of other phrases in the sentence.

The next question pertains to the organization of the passage and requires you to consider several sentences rather than just one.

Where would be the best place to relocate sentence 4?

(A) Before sentence 1
(B) Before sentence 2
(C) Before sentence 3
(D) Before sentence 6
(E) Before sentence 7

This passage reflects cause–effect organization. That is, the causes for people relocating to large cities is discussed. Sentence 4 is out of place because it introduces the effect in the midst of a discussion of causes. By moving this sentence to the beginning of the essay, it no longer disrupts the organization of the essay, and it provides a strong introduction. Thus, option A is correct.

The next question also requires you to compare several sentences rather than focusing on just one.

Deleting which of the following sentences would most improve the coherence of the passage?

(A) Sentence 3
(B) Sentence 5
(C) Sentence 7
(D) Sentence 9
(E) Sentence 11

Unless you have already spotted a sentence that clearly does not belong in the passage, the best approach to a question like this is to consider each option in turn.

Although the removal of sentence 3 would not substantially undermine the coherence of the passage, doing so would not improve the passage's coherence; thus, option A is incorrect.

The removal of sentence 5 would diminish the coherence of the passage, since it would be unclear what the *For example* in sentence 6 refers to, and thus option B is not correct.

Sentence 7 is out of place because it relates an anecdote that has no relevance to the writer's purpose (i.e., to explain why people relocate to large cities). Removing this sentence clearly improves the coherence of the passage, and thus option C is the correct answer.

When evaluating each option in turn, if you have any doubts about the option you have identified as correct, you should consider the remaining options. Here, an examination of options D and E will reinforce the choice of option C as the correct answer.

As with sentence 3, the removal of sentence 9 would not diminish the coherence of the passage, but its removal does not increase the passage's coherence, so option D is not correct.

Sentence 11, like sentences 3 and 9, could be deleted without undermining the coherence of the passage, but its removal would not improve the passage, so option E is not correct.

The next question pertains to transitions, but it requires you to think about the organization of the passage as well as the writer's purpose:

In context, which of the following is the best word or phrase to add to the beginning of sentence 5?

    (A) Clearly
    (B) However,
    (C) We all know
    (D) Second,
    (E) Occasionally

Option A is incorrect, because it is not immediately clear that public services in cities are superior. The word *clearly* would be appropriate here only if the writer had previously given evidence for the superiority of public services in cities, or if that superiority were immediately recognizable to all readers (which is unlikely).

Option B is incorrect, because the transition term *however* introduces a contrast or qualification that does not reflect the organization of the passage. The writer is engaged in describing causes for a particular effect. The assertion that public services in cities are superior is one more cause for the reader to consider. Thus, a transitional phrase like *In addition* would be more appropriate than *however*.

Option C is incorrect for essentially the same reasons that option A is incorrect.

Option D seems correct, because sentence 5 constitutes the second cause that the writer is discussing.

Option E is incorrect, because the term *occasionally* would introduce a qualification that undermines the writer's purpose. If public services in cities were only occasionally superior, it would be less clear why public services would be one of the reasons people relocate to cities.

In sum, we can be confident that option D is the correct answer.

The next question pertains to a comma splice in one of the sentences:

Which of the following revisions to sentence 8 (reproduced below) is best?

> *Medical services are more plentiful and supported by the latest technological improvements, there is access to modern hospitals too.*

    (A) Medical services are more plentiful and supported by the latest technological improvements, and access to modern hospitals.
    (B) Medical services are more plentiful and supported by the latest technological improvements; and there is access to modern hospitals too.
    (C) Medical services are more plentiful and supported by the latest technological improvements, and there is access to modern hospitals too.
    (D) Medical services are more plentiful and supported by the latest technological improvements, access to modern hospitals.
    (E) Medical services are more plentiful and supported by the latest technological improvements; access to modern hospitals there.

An independent clause is needed following the comma in sentence 8, and thus option A is incorrect.

Regarding option B, the conjunction *and* should not be used following the semicolon, and thus this option is incorrect too.

Option C is the right answer, because it is the only grammatically correct option.

Option D is incorrect because it has the same kind of comma splice as in the original sentence. That is, the comma separates an independent clause from the dependent clause that follows. As discussed in the previous chapter, the dependent clause would need to be independent in order for the sentence to be grammatically correct.

Option E is incorrect because the clause following the semicolon is dependent, and the reference for the term *there* is ambiguous.

The next question asks you to make an inference about diction, or word choice, in one of the sentences.

In context, which option is the best choice to do with the word *advanced* in sentence 9 (reproduced below)?

Educational opportunities in large cities are also quite <u>advanced</u>.

(A) Leave it as it is.
(B) Replace *advanced* with *large*.
(C) Replace *advanced* with *urban*.
(D) Replace *advanced* with *helpful*.
(E) Replace *advanced* with *plentiful*.

As you read sentences 8 through 10, it becomes clear that the writer's emphasis is on the quantity, diversity, and accessibility of public services (transportation, medical, and educational) available to residents of large cities. Since nothing is said about educational opportunities until sentence 9, the word *also* in this sentence provides a hint that what will be said about education here is similar to what has been said about other services. Thus, you can assume that the correct answer will be one that reflects something about the quantity, diversity, and/or accessibility of educational opportunities.

Advanced is a vague term in this context, and thus option A is incorrect.

Option B is incorrect simply because it would render the sentence grammatically incorrect. *Opportunities* cannot be said to be *large*.

Option C is incorrect because *urban* means *pertaining to cities*, and thus the term would not clearly contribute any information about educational opportunities in large cities.

Option D is incorrect because the observation that educational opportunities are *helpful* in some way would not be consistent with the writer's point which, as noted earlier, pertains to the quantity, diversity, and accessibility of public services.

Option E is correct. By replacing *advanced* with *plentiful*, the relationship between sentences 9 and 10 becomes clearer, and the word *also* in sentence 9 can be understood to indicate that not only are medical services plentiful (see sentence 8), but educational opportunities are plentiful too.

Next is a question that asks you to consider the meaning and purpose of the entire passage:

Which of the following would be the best sentence with which to end the passage?

    (A) In sum, the advantages of city life outweigh the disadvantages.
    (B) In sum, more jobs and better schools are the main reasons people prefer large cities.
    (C) In sum, the attractions of rural life cannot compete with the advantages of cities.
    (D) In sum, there are several reasons why people voluntarily relocate to large cities.
    (E) In sum, education is the primary reason that people choose to relocate to large cities.

Option A is incorrect because the writer did not discuss the disadvantages of city life. This passage is not a comparison essay, in other words.

Option B is incorrect because it only mentions two of the reasons that the writer discusses. Option B would be an acceptable closing sentence only if it also included reference to medical services.

Option C is incorrect because the attractions of rural life are not discussed in the passage. In fact, the only mention of rural life focuses on its relative disadvantages.

Option D seems correct, because it accurately summarizes the content of the passage. However, it would be best for you to examine all options before deciding which one would be best as a closing sentence.

Option E is incorrect because it is not indicated anywhere in the passage that education is the *primary* reason that people relocate to large cities. Rather, it is just one of three reasons discussed by the author. Thus, we can be confident that option D is the correct answer.

Finally, here is one more question that asks you to consider the meaning and purpose of the entire passage:

Which of the following would make the most logical title for the passage?

    (A) The Perils of Country Living
    (B) Relocation to the City
    (C) The Advantages of City Life
    (D) Employment in the Big City
    (E) Why People Relocate to Cities

After reading the passage, it should be clear that option E is the best choice of titles among the available options. None of the other options capture the main idea of the passage quite so accurately.

ABILITY TO USE SOURCE MATERIALS

The Ability to Use Source Materials section tests knowledge of basic reference and research skills through both passage-based and stand-alone questions. The skills tested in this section include documentation of sources, evaluation of sources, integration of resource materials, and use of reference materials. Each of these skills is discussed in the following text, followed by guidance on how to approach Ability to Use Source Materials questions, and then some practice questions with answers and explanations.

DOCUMENTATION OF SOURCES

The ability to evaluate nonfiction writing includes an understanding of why writers provide **documentation** for some of the statements they make. Three reasons for documenting the source of a statement are to **enhance the credibility and persuasiveness** of the statement, to **provide readers with additional resources**, and to **meet ethical requirements**.

Enhancing Credibility and Persuasiveness

To illustrate how the documentation of a source can enhance a writer's credibility and persuasiveness, consider the following passage:

> Currently about a fifth of the world's electricity comes from hydroelectric power generated by dams. The largest of these dams, the Three Gorges Dam in southern China, is expected to become fully operational in 2012. This is an exciting development. Hopefully greater reliance on energy sources such as dams will reduce our reliance on fossil fuels.

In this passage, the first two sentences convey facts, whereas the final two sentences convey the writer's personal reaction to the construction of the Three Gorges Dam and to the broader implications of reliance on hydroelectric power. No authority is needed to justify these last two sentences. If the writer claims to feel a certain way about hydroelectric power, the reader will probably accept this as an accurate description of the writer's feelings.

In contrast, the reader could question the accuracy of the factual information provided by the writer. Thus, in order to increase credibility and persuasiveness, the writer could provide evidence for the factual assertions. Not direct evidence, of course. The writer of the passage would not attempt to prove that the Three Gorges Dam is the largest dam in the world by flying readers from dam to dam in order to take measurements. However, the writer might choose to mention other writers who have taken such measurements, or who have at least collated the results of published measurements. For example:

> Currently about a fifth of the world's electricity comes from hydroelectric power generated by dams, according to John Smith in *Hydroelectric Power*.

Adding a reference to Smith's book increases the credibility and persuasiveness of the sentence, as it suggests that the writer of the passage is relying on an expert rather than simply guessing about the extent to which the world's electric power is generated by dams. The writer might even add some details about the source in order to directly promote its credibility, as in the following examples:

> Currently about a fifth of the world's electricity comes from hydroelectric power generated by dams, according to hydroelectric engineering expert John Smith in *Hydroelectric Power*.

> Currently about a fifth of the world's electricity comes from hydroelectric power generated by dams, according to John Smith in his authoritative classic *Hydroelectric Power*.

> Currently about a fifth of the world's electricity comes from hydroelectric power generated by dams, according to recent estimates provided by hydroelectric energy expert John Smith.

The reader must be cautious, of course. The mere fact that a writer has cited a source does not guarantee that the source is accurate, complete, or reputable, even if the writer has praised its authoritativeness. This notion is discussed further in the evaluation of sources section.

Providing Readers with Additional Resources

By documenting their sources, writers provide readers with a way of obtaining additional information about a topic. For example, in the passages at the end of the previous section, the reader is alerted to Dr. Smith's book as a resource for further information about hydroelectric power.

When referring to a source, the writer may choose to give the reader information about what can be found in the source, as in the following example:

> Currently about a fifth of the world's electricity comes from hydroelectric power generated by dams, according to John Smith in his authoritative classic *Hydroelectric Power*, which provides a comprehensive overview of the contribution of dams to the world's energy supply.

Alternatively, the writer may simply name a source, and the reader will understand that the source may be consulted for further information. Mentioning sources also allows the reader to verify the accuracy and completeness of what has been written, if the reader so chooses.

Specific information about how writers use bibliographic details to cite sources is given in the integration of resource materials section.

Ethical Requirements

Most nonfiction writing, whether in scholarly journals, popular magazines, or news media, has rules concerning the documentation of sources. The main reason that a writer is expected to document a source is to ensure that the source, rather than the writer, gets credit for particular statements or ideas. Moreover, documentation is needed because the use of a source without proper documentation is considered **plagiarism**, an unethical and in some circumstances illegal practice. Plagiarism is illustrated in the following passage:

> I believe that democracy is the most enduring form of government. Government of the people, by the people, and for the people will not perish from the earth, in my view.

The second sentence of the passage is copied almost verbatim from Abraham Lincoln's Gettysburg Address. By failing to attribute this sentence to Lincoln, the writer appears to be taking credit for having written the sentence himself, and he would therefore be guilty of plagiarism. The following shows one way to revise this passage so that it contains no plagiarism:

> I believe that democracy is the most enduring form of government. As Abraham Lincoln put it, "Government of the people, by the people, for the people, shall not perish from the earth."

Usually, any quotation included in a piece of writing must be indicated by quotation marks or italics and attributed to a source. Doing so ensures that credit for the quotation is properly attributed. Notice that changing a quotation slightly does not obviate the need to provide a source. For example, compare the two quotations below:

> ". . . government of the people, by the people, for the people, shall not perish from the earth."

> A government that is created from the people, by the people, and for those very people, will never perish from the earth.

The first passage is quoted verbatim from the Gettysburg Address. The second passage would be considered a **plagiaristic rendering**, if not attributed to Lincoln, even though some of the words are different.

In practice, it can be difficult to determine whether or not a quotation is being used in a plagiaristic way. If the writer assumes that a particular quotation is highly recognizable, the writer may not feel obligated to provide the source. In some cases, a statement is so obviously a quotation, and the source of the quotation is so well-known, that nobody would expect the writer to provide a source. For example:

> As a highly religious person and a holder of public office, I *do* believe that we are one nation under god.

In this passage, the phrase *one nation under god* is taken verbatim from the Pledge of Allegiance, but the writer would not be considered to have committed plagiarism. Because virtually every American has memorized the Pledge of Allegiance, virtually every American would recognize the Pledge rather than the writer as the origin of the phrase *one nation under god*. Moreover, by using the phrase *I do believe*, the writer implies that the concept of being one nation under god has already been proposed by someone else, and that the writer himself or herself chooses to embrace the concept.

In other cases, a writer will use a phrase or sentence that others may have used, but the phrase or sentence is so commonplace that no plagiarism can be said to have been committed. Following are some examples:

Barack Obama was born on August 4, 1961.

The blue whale is the largest animal in the world.

The weather today was lovely.

Children need our love and guidance.

These sentences are likely to have been used more than once already in written works, but using any one of them again would not constitute plagiarism. The first two sentences are simple statements of widely known facts. The second two sentences convey opinions, but they are not particularly distinctive opinions, and there are not many alternatives for expressing these opinions quite so succinctly. In contrast, consider the following:

The weather today was as lovely as an unspoiled lake at the foot of the Swiss alps.

If the previous sentence already appears in a published work somewhere, using it again without documenting the source would constitute plagiarism, because the expression is highly distinctive. Although many writers have described the weather as lovely, it is not commonplace to compare the weather to an alpine lake. Such expressions should be quoted with attribution to a source.

Documentation of sources is not only critical for quoted material, but must also be provided for ideas and facts. However, an idea or fact that is common knowledge, such as that Atlanta is the capital of Georgia, need not be attributed to a source. However, the writer might need to provide a source if he or she asserts that as of 2009, the population of Atlanta was 540,922.

Generally, documentation of sources will be required for three types of material. First, documentation of sources should be provided for ideas that are highly distinctive owing to their originality. Consider, for example, the following passage:

Human beings experience considerable internal conflict. The primitive urges of the id clash with the moral restraints of the superego, while the ego does the best it can to compromise between them.

A source is not needed for the first sentence of the passage, because this sentence does not convey a particularly distinctive idea. Although you may not agree with the idea, you would recognize it as a generalization that many people accept on some level depending on how the words *considerable* and *internal conflict* are interpreted. In contrast, the idea expressed in the second sentence should be attributed to its source, which happens to be the psychologist Sigmund Freud. Freud held that the human psyche consists of the id, the ego, and the superego, and that these three entities interrelate in the way described in the passage. As this is a very distinctive idea, it should be attributed to the individual who proposed it.

Second, documentation of sources is needed for ideas or facts that are not commonly known, as in the following example:

> There are more than 400,000 species of beetle, and this year 25 new species were found in oak trees in the south of Turkey.

In this example, the number of species of beetle may be "common" knowledge in the sense of being commonly reported in textbooks and other reference materials, but the discovery of 25 additional species is a new scientific development, and thus in most cases would require documentation of the source of information about this discovery. The documentation might consist of reference to a scholarly journal, a magazine article, a newspaper report, or some other source.

Third, documentation of sources is needed for ideas and facts that are difficult to verify, as in the following example:

> Parrot Jungle was one of the most popular tourist attractions in South Florida during much of the second half of the twentieth century, but it has since vanished without a trace.

In this example, the fact that the writer is discussing something that no longer exists calls for documentation of sources. In brief, the writer should indicate exactly where he or she has obtained information about this tourist attraction.

The need for documenting a source is not always as clear cut as in the previous examples. When an idea that was originally distinctive becomes widely accepted, or at least widely known, the source may or may not need to be identified. For example:

> Most bacteria die when exposed to antibiotics. However, a small number of bacteria have mutations that make them resistant to antibiotics. These bacteria survive and reproduce. Thus, through natural selection, the next generation of bacteria will be primarily antibiotic-resistant.

This passage refers to facts about bacteria that were discovered in the twentieth century and are now considered to be well-established. Although an undergraduate writing a term paper may be required to provide sources for these facts, a journalist writing a newspaper article may not have such a requirement. Editorial policy may or may not require the journalist to provide specific citation. Alternatively, the journalist may be able to refer to the sources in a general way (e.g., *Experts agree that most bacteria die when exposed to antibiotics*). An additional consideration is the journalist's own level of expertise. The need for a citation may be relaxed for a journalist who is a doctor, or writes regularly about scientific topics.

The previous passage also refers to natural selection, a distinctive concept formulated by Charles Darwin in the nineteenth century. In some cases, the writer of this passage would be required to cite Darwin. In other cases, natural selection could simply be mentioned without reference to a source. Although not everyone accepts the phenomenon of natural selection, the concept is widely assumed among scientists and taught as a core concept in biology classes. Here again, the expertise of the journalist may be taken into account.

EVALUATION OF SOURCES

In some cases a source may be inaccurate, unreliable, or used in a misleading way by a writer. Thus, the ability to evaluate nonfiction writing depends in turn on the ability to analyze and evaluate a writer's sources.

Readers can evaluate a source by examining it, or at least by examining bibliographic information given by the writer who cites the source. Some of the dimensions on which sources can be evaluated include date of publication, edition, type of source, credibility of source, credibility of author, relevance and scope of coverage, and objectivity of coverage.

Date of Publication

When evaluating a source, readers should consider the **date** when the source was published or created. For some topics, such as science, technology, and current events, up-to-date sources can be critical. Consider the following two passages written in 2010:

> The great philosopher Aristotle was born in Stageira in 384 B.C. (Jones, 1990).

> At present a silicon microprocessor chip may contain as many as a million transistors (Smith, 1990).

In each case, a publication from 1990 is cited as a source. The fact that the source is 20 years old does not seem problematic with respect to the biographical details of a famous philosopher. However, the age of the source does seem problematic as a basis for information about current microprocessor technology. The assertion made by Smith (1990) may have been accurate 20 years ago, but it is almost certainly inaccurate regarding the present state of the field, given the rapidity of scientific and technological change.

Edition

Another characteristic that contributes to a source's credibility and persuasiveness is its **edition**. The first edition of a source represents the original publication. If the source is revised in some way and then released again for publication, the revision will be referred to as a *revised edition* or *new edition*, or it will be referred to by number (e.g., *second edition*, *third edition*, and so on).

Later editions of a work are often considered more authoritative than earlier ones. The fact that a publisher chooses to produce further editions beyond the first one suggests that that work has been well-received. Moreover, with each successive edition the author will have the opportunity to correct mistakes, make improvements, incorporate new developments, and otherwise improve the quality of the work. However, not all subsequent editions contain substantial revisions.

Type of Source

To the greatest extent possible, the reader should identify and evaluate the **types** of sources that a writer provides. In particular, the reader should consider whether each source is primary or secondary, and peer reviewed or non-peer reviewed.

Primary sources consist of original findings, observations, ideas, or creations. Examples of primary sources include scientific reports in which the authors describe the findings of their research, eyewitness accounts of events, original theoretical statements, and authoritative documents (e.g., the U.S. Constitution).

Secondary sources consist of summaries, analyses, or commentaries regarding primary sources. Examples of secondary sources include literature reviews (i.e., reviews of research and/or theory on a particular topic), critical analyses, textbooks, and guides to particular works of scholarship or art. The purpose of a secondary source is to help readers understand, integrate, and/or judge a primary source or sources.

A primary source is a **firsthand account**. The author of a primary source may be inaccurate, biased, or incomplete in his or her assertions, but the author will be the most direct source of information about what he or she asserts. A secondary source can provide background information and analysis that makes a primary source clearer, or that helps the reader understand biases and other limitations of the primary source. However, the secondary source is one step removed from the primary source, and may reflect its own limitations and biases.

The importance of distinguishing primary from secondary sources can be illustrated by comparing an eyewitness account of a historical event to a later description of the event in which eyewitness accounts are summarized. The eyewitness is in a unique position as to how it feels to have experienced or observed an event. However, if the eyewitness does not happen to be a historian, he or she may not be the best source of information about the historical context for the event. Rather, the historian writing a secondary source may be a better source of information about historical developments leading up to the event. In short, an eyewitness account may be a good source to cite when describing what it was like to experience a particular event. A historical analysis might be a preferable source to cite for an analysis of the causes of the event.

Peer review refers to the process by which a small number of experts in a particular field review a manuscript and make a recommendation as to whether it should be published. Typically, an editor will then decide whether the manuscript should be published as is, published with revisions, or rejected. Although peer review does not guarantee that a source is accurate and complete, peer-reviewed publications are typically considered more reliable than those that are not peer reviewed, owing to the quality control provided by the review process. Thus, in discussing the causes of economic distress, a peer-reviewed journal article will be a more credible source than a blog or a letter to the editor of a local newspaper.

The distinction between peer-reviewed and non-peer-reviewed sources roughly corresponds to a distinction between scholarly and popular sources. However, not all scholarly publications are peer reviewed, and some popular sources do have a rigorous editorial process. Thus, the reader should also consider whether the intended audience of a source is primarily scholars, some other specialist group, or the general public.

Credibility of Source

For the reader who does not have expertise in a particular area, it can be difficult to ascertain the **credibility** of sources representing that area. Peer review confers some degree of credibility but does not guarantee that a source is accurate or complete. The same can be said for university presses and government agencies, whose publications are generally considered to be reputable but are by no means infallible. Type of source is nonetheless an important detail that the reader should consider when evaluating credibility.

As noted, scholarly sources tend to be considered more credible than popular sources. However, popular sources vary widely in this dimension. News sources such as *The New York Times* or *The Washington Post* are highly respected, for example. At the other end of the spectrum, a blog written by someone with an extreme political agenda is likely to be a less credible source of information.

Evaluation of credibility can be aided by locating critical reviews of the source through a reference work such as *Book Review Index, Book Review Digest,* or *Periodical Abstracts*. The reader can then determine whether reviews tend to be positive, whether the source is respected, whether the source includes points that are controversial or widely considered false, and whether the reviews point to other sources that are considered more authoritative.

An important consideration when evaluating credibility is the possibility of **bias**. The reader should consider who publishes the source and for what purpose. For example, a source published by a particular corporation may tend to reflect that corporation's interests. A source published by a group with a specific political or social agenda may reflect that agenda both in the range of topics covered and in the treatment of those topics.

In some cases, the possibility of bias will be evident from the name of a source. For example, the following (fictional) sources would probably be biased sources of information about the debate over gun control:

Proceedings of the Biennial Meeting of the Mandatory Gun Ownership Society

The Annual Newsletter of the Consortium for the Worldwide Banishment of Firearms

Judging from their titles, neither one of these fictional sources would be likely to provide an unbiased look at the gun control debate, although they may be useful sources of information about extreme positions in the debate.

In other cases, the reader may need to evaluate the possibility of bias by examining the contents of a source. Even without expertise in a particular area, the reader may be able to determine that only certain kinds of topics or perspectives are reflected in the source. This point is discussed further in the objectivity section.

Credibility of Author

When evaluating a source the reader should consider the author's credentials and institutional affiliation, as well as any evidence as to the author's area of expertise, publication record, and professional reputation. Whether or not the author has been paid for the work, or has a professional affiliation with the organization that publishes the work, should also be considered.

By **cross-referencing** information in a source with information from other sources, the reader can determine the extent of convergence between an author's views and that of others who have written about the same topic. The credibility of an author may be diminished if he or she disagrees with the majority on basic facts (although, of course, the majority is not always right). Certainly the author's credibility is undermined if he or she makes claims that are easily refuted through cross-referencing. For example, if an author claims that no studies have been conducted on a particular topic, but you discover studies on that topic, you should question whether the author's view of the topic can be trusted.

Information about authors can also be obtained from publications, Internet searches, and biographical sources such as *American Men and Women of Science* and *Contemporary Authors*. Although even the most well-connected and highly esteemed authors make mistakes and exhibit biases, generally speaking the more widely respected the author, the more credible and persuasive the source created by that author will tend to be.

Relevance of Coverage

When documenting a statement, the sources that a writer provides should support that particular statement. For example, suppose that a writer is discussing the characteristics of Arenal Volcano in Costa Rica and wishes to document the dates of significant eruptions since the outset of the twentieth century. A scholarly work on Arenal would be a credible source of information, but not if the work exclusively pertains to the formation of the volcano, the nature of seismological processes inside the volcano, or the economic impact of the volcano as a source of tourism. Rather, the writer would need a source that specifically discusses the recent history of Arenal's eruptions. Unless the reader is already familiar with a source, the main way of determining its relevance is to examine the source.

As this example suggests, the breadth of coverage in a source can impact its credibility and persuasiveness. Sources that focus on highly specific topics can enhance the credibility of specific statements about such topics, but they do not serve well to support broader statements. Sources that treat topics more broadly can provide stronger support for broad assertions. However, a source that is very broad, such as an introduction or an overview of a topic, may not be very authoritative if the content sacrifices depth for breadth.

Objectivity

The **objectivity** of the writing in a source has some impact on its credibility and persuasiveness. Even if the reader is not an expert on the topic discussed in the source, the reader may be able to evaluate objectivity if he or she is able to examine the source. The reader can look for evidence as to whether the writer's point of view is more or less impartial or biased. If the writer promotes a particular theory or takes a particular side in a debate, the reader can check whether the writer presents all sides of key arguments and acknowledges potential limitations to the views that he or she favors. The reader can check whether the writer has omitted key details—particularly those that do not seem to support the writer's own particular point of view. The reader can also evaluate the quality of argumentation and whether the source itself provides additional sources, if appropriate.

To illustrate how objectivity can be evaluated, even in the absence of expertise regarding a topic, consider the following passages:

Although numerous studies in which socioeconomic status (SES) is measured rely on single-item indicators of SES, SES is clearly a multidimensional construct, and different dimensions differentially affect families and children. For example, children's academic achievement is affected by parent education levels more strongly than by family income, regardless of some misguided claims to the contrary.

Although numerous studies in which socioeconomic status (SES) is measured rely on single-item indicators of SES, evidence indicates that SES is a multidimensional construct, and that different dimensions differentially affect families and children (Conger & Dogan, 2007). For example, recent studies show that children's academic achievement is affected by parent education levels more strongly than by family income, although not all studies support this contention.

Even without knowledge of this particular area of research, the careful reader can detect that the writing of the first passage is less objective than that of the second one. The writer's tone is quite definitive, and his or her use of the term *clearly* as well as the phrase *regardless of some misguided claims to the contrary* seem dismissive of alternative points of view. In contrast, the second passage conveys similar points with a greater degree of impartiality. Rather than stating that SES *is clearly* multidimensional, the writer notes that *evidence indicates* as much, and the writer then provides a reference to an additional source (work by Conger & Dongan, 2007). In the final sentence, the writer supports his or her point through reference to *recent studies* and acknowledges that not all studies support the point. On the whole, the second passage seems less biased, and thus constitutes a more credible source.

One of the most important clues to bias is **word choice**. When evaluating a source, the reader should be attentive to the particular words and phrases that are used, as they reveal something about the writer's attitudes. Certain words and phrases clearly indicate a biased perspective. For example, consider the following descriptions of the same individual:

The manager hired a short order cook who had been convicted previously of theft.

The manager hired a short order cook with a criminal record.

The manager hired a short order cook who was a hardened criminal.

The manager hired a short order cook who was not only a cook but a crook!

The manager hired a short order cook who had been persecuted for committing a crime.

In the first two sentences, the cook's criminal history is described in an impartial way. The writer of each sentence might turn out to be biased, of course, but no bias is revealed in these particular sentences (at least when considered out of context), because they are merely statements of fact. In context, the phrase *hardened* in the third sentence conveys a negative judgment. The possibility of bias is suggested by use of this phrase rather than a more factual description of the person. In the fourth sentence, reference to the cook with the slang phrase *crook* suggests even more strongly that the writer is negatively biased against the cook. Here, the writer seems more concerned with judging the cook unfavorably (and attempting to be witty by exploiting the similarity between *cook* and *crook*) than providing an accurate description of the person. Finally, the fifth sentence seems to reflect positive bias, in that the writer acknowledges that the cook had committed a crime but also indicates that the cook had been *persecuted* for the crime. Through the use of the term *persecuted*, the writer appears to be taking the cook's side, an impression that would not be conveyed if the writer had chosen a more neutral term such as *convicted*.

INTEGRATION OF RESOURCE MATERIALS

Citations

A **citation** references a specific source within the main text of a piece of writing. You have seen an example of a citation already in the following sentence from the previous section:

> Although numerous studies in which socioeconomic status (SES) is measured rely on single-item indicators of SES, evidence indicates that SES is a multidimensional construct, and that different dimensions differentially affect families and children (Conger & Dogan, 2007).

In this sentence, two authors whose last names are Conger and Dogan are cited. The context of the citation suggests that Conger and Dogan are scholars, and that the work cited is scholarly rather than a popular source. The reader cannot tell, however, whether the citation is a book, a journal article, or some other kind of publication. As discussed later in the references section, full bibliographic details will typically be provided to the reader, either in a footnote or in a separate reference list. By looking at that footnote or reference list, the reader will be able to find the details of what *Conger & Dogan, 2007* refers to.

Now consider again the following statement about hydroelectric power:

> Currently about a fifth of the world's electricity comes from hydroelectric power generated by dams.

Let us suppose that the writer wishes to cite a source for this particular fact. Suppose too that an internationally renowned expert on hydroelectric power named John Smith has published a book in 2007 entitled *Hydroelectric Power,* and that pages 342 and 343 of this book include detailed and highly credible information about how much of the world's electricity comes from hydroelectric power and other technologies. Following are just a few of the approaches that could be used to integrate Smith's work into this sentence by means of a citation:

> As John Smith observes in *Hydroelectric Power*, currently about a fifth of the world's electricity comes from hydroelectric power generated by dams.

Hydroelectric Power tells us that currently about a fifth of the world's electricity comes from hydroelectric power generated by dams.

Currently about a fifth of the world's electricity comes from hydroelectric power generated by dams, according to an authoritative source.

Currently about a fifth of the world's electricity comes from hydroelectric power generated by dams (Smith, 2007).

Smith (2007) indicates that currently about a fifth of the world's electricity comes from hydroelectric power generated by dams.

Smith indicates that currently about a fifth of the world's electricity comes from hydroelectric power generated by dams (342–343).

Currently about a fifth of the world's electricity comes from hydroelectric power generated by dams (Smith 342–343).

Currently about a fifth of the world's electricity comes from hydroelectric power generated by dams (Smith 2007, 342–343).

Currently about a fifth of the world's electricity comes from hydroelectric power generated by dams, according to John Smith.[2]

Writers do not haphazardly cite sources in a text, footnote, or reference section. Rather, they are expected to systematically adhere to a set of rules. Three of the most prominent sets of rules are referred to as **APA style**, **MLA style**, and **Chicago style**. As you will see, each of these styles embodies a large number of highly specific rules, all of which reflect a common purpose: to facilitate access to sources. That is, the rules for citing sources and providing bibliographic details all help ensure that readers have the information they need to readily locate those sources.

APA Style Citation

The American Psychological Association (APA) publishes a book entitled *Publication Manual of the American Psychological Association*. This book is widely used in the social sciences as a comprehensive guide to scientific writing, and thus writers are often required to conform to APA style (or APA format).

In APA style, sources are cited in the text of a piece of writing, and full bibliographic details are given in a separate reference section. Following are some of the rules for citations in APA style. (Rules governing reference lists are discussed later in the references section.)

First, citations in the text typically consist of the last name(s) of the author(s) of a source and the year of publication. For example:

Smith and Jones (2006) found that many students dislike homework.

It has been found that many students dislike homework (Smith & Jones, 2006).

The first sentence illustrates what is known as an **in-text citation**, whereas the second sentence contains a parenthetical citation of the same source. Notice that the word *and* is used to link author names in the in-text citation, whereas the use of an ampersand (&) is used to link their names in the parenthetical citation. This illustrates the great specificity of the rules in APA style (as can also be observed in the other two styles discussed here). This section does not provide a comprehensive list of rules, but rather concentrates on describing those rules that a reader would need to know in order to understand the information that is given in citations and reference lists.

When more than one source appears in a parenthetical citation, the sources are listed alphabetically by the first letter of the first author's last name, and each source is separated by semicolons, as in the following example:

> It has been found that many students dislike homework (Smith & Jones, 2006; Thomson, 2001; Yoon, Hong, Kwan, & Li, 2010).

In the previous example, three sources are mentioned. Smith and Jones (2006) is the first source, Thomson (2001) is the second source, and Yoon, Hong, Kwan, and Li (2010) is the third source.

When a source has three to six authors, the writer must cite all authors the first time the source is identified in the text. In later references to the source, the writer should cite the last name of the first author, followed by the phrase *et al.*, which is Latin for *and others*. For example, notice the two citations of a work by Lassiter, Rynor, and Kilbretz in the following passage:

> Lassiter, Rynor, and Kilbretz (1997) found that many students dislike math homework more than other types of homework. Williams (1995) obtained similar findings. Lassiter et al. (1997) also found that the difference between attitudes toward math homework versus other types is stronger among high school students as compared with their middle school peers.

When a source has more than six authors, the writer only needs to cite the first six authors when the source is first identified in the text. All subsequent identifications of the source can consist of the first author's last name followed by the phrase *et al.*

When a source is an organization rather than an individual or group of individuals, the writer should cite the organization name in the text, as illustrated in the following sentence:

> Reading research that relies on experimental or quasi-experimental designs continues to play a prominent role in the field (U.S. Department of Education, 2009).

When a source is quoted, the page number(s) from which the quotation is drawn should also be provided, as in the following examples:

> Many students recognize the importance of homework even though they dislike spending time on homework assignments (Brooks, 2004, p. 37).

> As Brooks (2004) points out, "Many students recognize the importance of homework even though they dislike spending time on homework assignments" (p. 37).

When a source within a source is cited, both are included in the citation, as in the following example.

> Khan (2005) found a greater percentage of oaks than elms in this particular region (as cited in Jerrison, 2001).

In this example, Khan (2005) is likely to be a primary source that is discussed in Jerrison (2001).

Other rules govern the citation of sources without authors, articles in non-scholarly sources such as newspapers and magazines, personal communications such as e-mails and letters, theses and dissertations, and non-print materials such as audio recordings and videotapes.

When a source is an Internet resource, the rules for citation in the text are generally the same as for print publications. That is, the citation will consist of the last name of the author(s) and the year of publication. However, in some cases a writer will cite a website but not a specific document on that website. In such cases, the writer should provide the Internet address, as in the following example:

> The Bureau of Ocean Energy Management, Regulation, and Enforcement is the federal agency that oversees development of energy and mineral resources on the outer continental shelf (http://www.boemre.gov/aboutBOEMRE).

MLA Style Citation

The Modern Language Association (MLA) publishes a book now entitled *The MLA Style Manual and Guide to Scholarly Publishing*. This book is widely used in the humanities as a comprehensive writing guide, and thus writers are often required to conform to MLA style. MLA style differs from APA style in the rules governing citation of sources in the main text.

First, citations in the main text typically consist of the last name of the author(s) and the page number(s), as in the following examples:

> Smith and Jones found that many students dislike homework (47–48).

> It has been found that many students dislike homework (Smith and Jones 47–48).

If reference is made to an entire source, page numbers need not be included. If page information is included and reference must be made to more than one page or sequence of pages, the page numbers are separated by commas, as in the following example:

> It has been found that many students dislike homework (Smith and Jones 47–48, 50, 52–54).

As with APA style, semicolons are used to separate sources when more than one source is included in a parenthetical citation. For example:

> It has been found that many students dislike homework (Smith and Jones 47–48; Thomson 22; Yoon, Hong, Kwan, & Li 33, 35–36).

When a source has more than three authors, MLA style allows the writer to either name all authors, or simply name the first three followed by the designation *et al*. When the source is an organization, the organization name is used along with the page number, if page information is needed. If the source is part of a multi-volume set, the volume number is also included in the citation in the text, separated from the page number(s) by a colon, as in the following example:

Boys tend to dislike homework more than girls do (Mattingly 2: 166).

In this example, page 166 of volume 2 in a multi-volume series is cited.

When a source within a source is cited, both are included in the citation, as in the following example:

Khan found a greater percentage of oaks than elms in this particular region (cited in Jerrison 67).

If the source within a source is quoted, the abbreviation *qtd*. is used, as follows:

According to Khan, "Oaks predominate in this particular region" (qtd. in Jerrison 67).

As with APA style, other rules govern the citation of sources without authors, articles in non-scholarly sources such as newspapers and magazines, personal communications such as e-mails, theses and dissertations, and non-print materials such as audio recordings and videotapes.

The MLA rules for citation of Internet sources are similar to those for print sources. The citation should include the first item that appears in the reference list (referred to as the Works Cited section). Often this will be the first author's last name, but it may be the name of an article or website. No page numbers are needed unless a separate article is downloaded. If citing a website, the entire URL is not needed. Rather, a domain name or some other phrase that will direct the reader to the correct entry in the Works Cited section will be acceptable.

Chicago Style Citation

The *Chicago Manual of Style* (CMS) is older than the APA and MLA manuals and, unlike those two manuals, was not created by a professional organization. It is, however, widely used as a guide to all aspects of writing, and thus writers are often required to conform to Chicago style.

Chicago style allows writers to choose between two different systems for citations and full bibliographic details. One system is referred to as **notes and bibliography**, whereas the other is called **author–date**. Scholars in the arts and humanities often use the notes and bibliography system, whereas scholars in the physical and social sciences often use the author–date system.

In the notes and bibliography system, each source cited in the text is marked by a superscript at the end of each sentence in which the source is mentioned, as in the following example:

Garcia also found that the amount of homework assigned by middle-school teachers varies widely from school to school, even within the same district.[1]

Full bibliographic details are then provided in a footnote or endnote, as discussed later in the references section.

In the author–date system, citations in the main text generally consist of author(s), date of publication, and page number(s), as in the following example:

> High-achieving students do not necessarily like homework more than their less accomplished peers do, but they seem to value it more (Smits and von Kaampen 2002, 354).

As with the APA and MLA styles, Chicago style includes other rules that govern the citation of sources without authors, articles in non-scholarly sources such as newspapers and magazines, personal communications such as e-mails and letters, theses and dissertations, non-print materials such as audio recordings and videotapes, and Internet resources.

References

In order to examine a source that has been cited, the reader will need the complete bibliographic details for the source. Along with names of author(s), date of publication, and title, the reader will also need to know the publisher and edition (if the source is a book), or the journal name and volume (if the source is a journal). If the source is obtained from a website, the reader will need the URL and possibly also the DOI, if available.

The **URL** or **Universal Resource Locator** is the Internet address that uniquely identifies an electronic resource such as the page of a website. An example of a URL would be the home page of *The New York Times*: http://www.nytimes.com.

The **DOI** or **Digital Object Identifier** is a character string that uniquely identifies an electronic resource. Although not all resources on the Internet have a DOI, for those that do, the particular DOI will be permanent. URLs, in contrast, may change.

APA Style References

APA style requires that the writer create a separate list of references that contain full bibliographic details for all works cited in the main text. The works cited will be listed in alphabetical order in the reference list according to the first letter of the (first) author's last name.

Along with alphabetization of sources, there are many other rules governing how bibliographic details are presented in the APA style reference list. As a writer, you would need to consult the most recent edition of the *Publication Manual of the American Psychological Association* in order to conform to APA style in creating a reference section. As a reader, what is critical is that you understand what kinds of information are available from each part of a full citation. Following are example citations for four of the most common types of scholarly sources, as would be found in an APA style reference section:

Springer, K. (2010). *Educational research: A contextual approach*. New Jersey: Wiley.

Springer, K. (1999). How a naive theory of biology is acquired. In M. Siegal & C. Peterson (Eds.), *Children's understanding of biology and health* (pp. 45–70). Cambridge: Cambridge University Press.

Springer, K. (2001). Perceptual boundedness and perceptual support in conceptual development. *Psychological Review, 108,* 691–708.

Springer, K. (1997). Conceptual coherence in children's understanding of kinship. Invited paper presented at the 7th annual meeting of the European Association for Research in Learning and Instruction, Athens, Greece.

The first source is a book. The author is Springer and the publication date is 2010. The title is given in italics, followed by the place of publication (New Jersey) and the name of the publisher (Wiley).

The second source is a chapter from an edited book published in 1999. The author of the chapter is Springer and the chapter title is "How a Naive Theory of Biology Is Acquired." This chapter appeared in a book edited by Siegal and Peterson entitled *Children's Understanding of Biology and Health.* The chapter occupies pages 45 through 70 of the edited book. The edited book was published in Cambridge by Cambridge University Press.

The third source is a journal article. The author is Springer, the publication date is 2001, and the title is given immediately following the publication date. The name of the journal is *Psychological Review.* The volume number of the journal is 108. The article occupies pages 691 through 708 in the journal.

The fourth source is a conference presentation. The author is Springer, the date of the conference is 1997, and the title is given immediately following the conference date. The type of presentation is invited paper (as opposed to symposium paper, poster, keynote address, etc.). The name of the conference is the 7th Annual Meeting of the European Association for Research in Learning and Instruction, and the conference location is Athens, Greece.

For sources with more than six authors, only the first six need to be included in the reference list, as in the following example:

Dolan, L., Kellam, S., Brown, C., Werthamer-Larsson, L., Rebok, G., Mayer, L., et al. (1993). The short-term impacts of two classroom-based preventive interventions on aggressive and shy behaviors and poor achievement. *Journal of Applied Developmental Psychology, 14,* 317–345.

Sources that are organizations are cited in the reference list in much the same way as publications by specific authors. For example:

National Assessment of Educational Progress. (1999). *Reading report card for the nation and state.* Washington, DC: National Center for Education Statistics, Office of Education Research and Improvement, U.S. Department of Education.

For sources other than books and articles, the type of source will be clearly identified in the reference section, as in the following examples:

Doe, J. M. (2010). *Family conflict and stress.* Unpublished manuscript.

Smith, P. M. (2005). *Compliance with style guides in the creation of reference lists: A mixed-methods study* (Doctoral Dissertation). University of Terner, Joliet, FL.

Most of the discussion thus far has focused on scholarly sources. APA style references for non-scholarly sources are similar but not identical. For example, the following is a reference list entry for a magazine article:

> King, R. D. (1997, April). Should English be the law? *Atlantic Monthly, 279,* 55–64.

For resources obtained from the Internet, a stable URL should be provided along with a DOI (if available). If the URL is not stable, the home page of the website from which the source was retrieved should be provided. The date should be given for the final version of a work that is dated, but if the work has no date or the date changes (as in the case of an electronic encyclopedia article), then the date that the source was retrieved should be provided. Following are some examples:

> Sanchez, D., & King-Toler, E. (2007). Addressing disparities consultation and outreach strategies for university settings. *Consulting Psychology Journal: Practice and Research, 59*(4), 286–295. doi:10.1037/1065–9293.59.4.286.

> Miller, B. M. (2003). Critical hours: After-school programs and educational success. Retrieved 14 June 2006, from http://www.nmefdn.org/CriticalHours.htm.

> Center for Prevention Research and Development. (2004). Teen REACH: Annual evaluation report. Retrieved from http://www.cprd.uiuc.edu/research/highrisk-pubs/TRAnnualReport04.pdf.

MLA and Chicago Style References

In MLA style, bibliographic information appears in a separate Works Cited section, similar to the reference section used in APA style.

As noted earlier, Chicago style allows writers to choose between the **author–date (A–D)** and the **notes and bibliography (NB)** systems for citations and references. In the A–D system, each source is cited in the text (as described in the Chicago style citations section), and full bibliographic details are given in a separate reference list similar to the reference section in APA style.

In the NB system, each source is cited in the text by means of a superscript number wherever the source is mentioned or quoted. Full bibliographic details are then provided by number in footnotes or endnotes. (Endnotes are a separate section located at the end of a chapter or document.)

The information provided for each source differs somewhat in content and order across the three styles. For example, here is how the same book would be referenced in APA, MLA, Chicago A–D, and Chicago NB styles:

> APA style: Springer, K. (2010). *Educational research: A contextual approach.* New Jersey: Wiley.

> MLA style: Springer, Ken. *Educational research: A contextual approach.* New Jersey: Wiley, 2010. Print.

> Chicago A–D style: Springer, Ken. 2010. *Educational research: A contextual approach.* New Jersey: Wiley.

Chicago NB style: Ken Springer, *Educational research: A contextual approach*. (New Jersey: Wiley, 2010).

Along with variability in order of information, further differences between styles can be illustrated with reference to this single-author book.

First, unlike the other styles, MLA style requires that the type of source (print, audiovisual, electronic, etc.) be specified. Thus, in the MLA reference in the previous examples, the word *Print* at the end of the reference indicates that the source is available through hard copy only.

Second, in Chicago NB style, if a source is cited more than once, each subsequent reference to the source after the first one can be abbreviated. For example, suppose that Springer's book referenced in the previous examples is cited in an article on pages 4 and 12. Recall that each citation will be given in the text by means of a superscript number. A footnote on page 4 will provide the full reference to Springer's book. However, the footnote on page 12 can simply consist of the following abbreviated reference: Springer, *Educational Research*.

Third, if the writer wishes to quote from or otherwise refer to a specific page or pages in a source, APA and MLA styles require the writer to give the page number(s) in the text. In Chicago NB style, the page number may be given at the end of the bibliographic entry, as in the following example:

First citation: Ken Springer, *Educational research: A contextual approach*. (New Jersey: Wiley, 2010), 27–28.

Subsequent citations: Springer, *Educational Research*, 27–28.

Other differences between the styles can be seen in the following references to the same scholarly journal article. (Note that *Fall, 1995* is part of the title of the article rather than the date of publication. The date of publication is 1997):

APA style: Brod, R., & Huber, B. J. (1997). Foreign language enrollments in United States institutions of higher education, Fall 1995. *ADFL Bulletin, 28*(2), 55–61.

MLA style: Brod, Richard, and Bettina J. Huber. "Foreign Language Enrollments in United States Institutions of Higher Education, Fall 1995." *ADFL Bulletin* 28.2 (1997): 55–61. Print.

Chicago A-D style: Brod, Richard, and Bettina J. Huber. 1997. "Foreign Language Enrollments in United States Institutions of Higher Education, Fall 1995." *ADFL Bulletin* 28: 55–61.

Chicago NB style: Richard Brod and Bettina J. Huber, "Foreign Language Enrollments in United States Institutions of Higher Education, Fall 1995," *ADFL Bulletin* 28 (1997): 55–61.

There are many other specific differences between these styles guiding the way reference lists, footnotes, and endnotes are written, and thus authors should consult the appropriate style manual for guidance. As a reader, however, this section should provide you with enough information to decipher most of the information you may encounter in reference lists, footnotes, or endnotes. However, you will also need to know the meanings of various abbreviations and acronyms that are used in bibliographic entries.

Abbreviations in Bibliographic Entries

Following are some of the abbreviations commonly used in bibliographic entries in one or more of the three styles discussed here. (Note that some of these abbreviations may be capitalized in an entry.)

chap.—Chapter

dir.—Director

diss.—Dissertation

doi—Digital Object Identifier, or DOI (As explained earlier, this acronym refers to the character string that uniquely identifies an electronic resource.)

ed.—Editor or edition

eds.—Editors

et al.—*Et alia*, a Latin phrase meaning, literally, *and others* (As explained earlier, this abbreviation is used to indicate additional authors.)

ibid.—*Ibidem,* a Latin term meaning, literally, *the same place* (This abbreviation (sometimes capitalized) is used to indicate that a citation refers to the previous source. Thus, in order to determine what *ibid.* refers to, you must look at the immediately preceding bibliographic entry.)

lib.—Library

n.d.—No date available for the source

n.p.—No publisher or place of publication available for the source

n.pag.—No page numbers available for the source

no.—Number, as in volume number, section number, and so on

p—Press; that is, a publishing house

para.—Paragraph

p.—Page

p.p. or pp.—Pages

prod.—Producer

pt.—Part

qtd.—Quoted

rep.—Report

rev.—Revision or Reviewer

rpt.—Reprint

sec.—Section

s.v.—*Sub voca*, a Latin phrase meaning, literally, *under the word* (This abbreviation is used to refer to a particular section of a bibliographic entry. For example, if the source is a discussion of thermodynamics in an encyclopedia, bibliographic details will be given for the encyclopedia, followed by *s.v. Thermodynamics*.)

trans.—Translator

U—University (For example, *U Texas P* stands for University of Texas Press.)

URL—Universal Resource Locator (As explained earlier, this is the Internet address that uniquely identifies an electronic resource.)

vol.—Volume

writ.—Writer

USE OF REFERENCE MATERIALS

Types of Reference Materials

Readers have access to many different kinds of **reference materials**, or sources of factual information. When the facts are in dispute, as for certain topics discussed in an encyclopedia, for example, the coverage will be balanced and objective. Following are some key examples of reference materials.

An **almanac** is a book that consists of useful factual information presented in the form of lists, facts, tables, charts, timelines, and so on. Almanacs may pertain to a particular field or to the entire world. The organization may be topical or chronological. The reader might consult an almanac for astronomical data such as the times of sunrise and sunset, meteorological data such as forecasts, agricultural data such as information for gardeners, cultural data such as the dates of religious holidays and festivals, political data such as chronologies of international events, and so on.

An **atlas** is a set of maps. A particular atlas may provide information about the layout of the solar system or the geographic features of a particular planet. An atlas may provide information about the physical geography of the entire world, one country, and/or one city. An atlas may identify boundaries that are economic, social, cultural, or natural. An atlas may consist of national or local transportation routes such as road maps. Although the main information in an atlas is graphic, presented in the form of maps, statistical information may also be included.

A **bibliography,** a list of writings organized by a particular topic or author, provides citation information for sources such as books and articles. The reader may consult the bibliography to find sources for a particular topic or sources created by a particular author. In an annotated bibliography, information about each source such as a **summary** or a **critical evaluation** will also be provided.

A **citation index** is a list of citations for known sources. The citation index contains bibliographic information for later sources that cite each particular earlier source. The reader will consult the citation index to identify later sources that cite a particular book, article, and/or author. In this way the reader can find out where that book, article, or author has been discussed.

A **concordance** is an alphabetical list of significant words used in a written work or set of works. The concordance includes information such as a page number indicating where each word is used. The reader will consult a concordance in order to determine all usages of a particular word in a source or set of sources that share a common element such as authorship. In a topical concordance, an alphabetical list of significant topics rather than words is presented.

A **dictionary** is an alphabetized list of words in a language that provides each word's definition. Information about pronunciation, part of speech, origin, alternative forms, and/or usage may also be provided. Special kinds of dictionaries include foreign language dictionaries, picture dictionaries, and dictionaries for particular topics such as literary terms, phrases used in a particular body of work, quotations, and so on. Further details about dictionaries are described later.

An **encyclopedia** is an alphabetically arranged set of entries covering a broad range of topics. Each entry provides an overview and summary of a topic. Encyclopedias may pertain to all areas of human knowledge, or focus on topics in one particular area such as science and technology. The reader will consult an encyclopedia in order to obtain an introduction to a particular topic.

A **thesaurus** is an alphabetized list of words in which synonyms are provided for each word. Homonyms and antonyms may be provided as well. The reader will consult a thesaurus in order to identify different terms that convey the same concept. Further details about the thesaurus are described later.

Use of Dictionaries and Thesauri

This section contains information about how to make use of dictionaries and thesauri. Following is an example of a dictionary entry:

> bi·as (bī′əs) *n.* 1. A line cutting diagonally across the grain of fabric. 2. Preference or inclination that inhibits impartiality; prejudice. *-adv.* On a diagonal; a slant. *-v.* **-ased** or **-assed, as·ing** or **as·sing**. To cause to have a bias; prejudice. [< OFr. biais, oblique.]

This entry provides information about pronunciation, part of speech, meanings, grammatical forms, and etymology. (**Etymology** refers to the history of a word, including its origins and important changes in usage and form over time.)

First, pronunciation is indicated by the two renderings of the word *bias* in the entry: "bi·as (bī′ əs)". The dot that divides the first rendering in half indicates a syllable break. The accent mark that divides the second rendering in half indicates that the first syllable is stressed. The sounds of the consonants and vowels in the word are given in the second rendering.

Next, part of speech is indicated by the italicized *n*, which tells the reader that the word is a noun.

Following the *n* is a description of two different meanings for the noun. As you can see, the first meaning is concrete, whereas the second meaning is abstract.

Information is also provided about different inflections such as *biased* and *biasing*. From this entry you can see, for example, that *biasing* is a verb, that *biassing* is an alternative spelling of the word, and that there is a syllable break between the *as* and the *ing*.

Finally, information is provided in brackets about the etymology of the word. Apparently the word *bias* originates from an Old French word *biais*.

In the previous example, the literal meanings of the word *bias* are provided. The literal meaning of a word is referred to as its **denotation**. In contrast, the **connotation** is the subjective, suggested meaning of a word. For example, the words *slim* and *scrawny* can both refer to a particular body type, but *slim* has a positive connotation whereas *scrawny* has a negative one. A dictionary will typically include the connotations of a word, if it has any, along with the denotation, as in the following example of an entry for the word *vixen*:

1. A female fox.

2. A woman regarded as quarrelsome, shrewish, or malicious.

In the previous example, the first meaning is the denotation, whereas the second conveys a connotation.

Following are two examples of thesaurus entries from the third edition of *Webster's New World Thesaurus*:

> **instigate**, *v.* - *Syn.* prompt, stimulate, induce, incite; see **incite, urge** 2. *See Synonym Study at* INCITE.

> **green**, *n.* **1**. [A color] - *Syn.* greenness, verdure, virescence, emerald, chlorophyll, verdantness, greenhood, viridity.

> **2**. [A grass plot] - *Syn.* lawn, field, park; see **grass 3 long green*, folding green***- *Syn.* bills, paper money, greenbacks; see **money** 1.

The entry for each word provides information about part of speech, synonyms, and where to look in the thesaurus for additional information about synonyms for the word. The entry for the second word (*green*) also provides information about different meanings of the word, as well as usage.

In the first entry, the italicized *v* indicates that the word *instigate* is a verb. The abbreviation *Syn.* indicates that what follows is a list of synonyms for the word.

The reader is also referred to two closely related sets of synonyms, one given in the entry for *incite*, and the other given in the second entry for *urge*. Finally, the reader is informed that additional information is given in a *Synonym Study* section under the entry for *incite*.

In the second entry, the italicized *n* indicates that *green* is a noun. Synonyms for two different meanings of *green* are provided—the first is *green* in the sense of green color and the second is *green* used in reference to a grass plot. Under the second set of synonyms, the asterisks indicate that the usage is slang, colloquial, archaic, or unusual in some other way.

Abbreviations for Parts of Speech

Following is a list of abbreviations often used in dictionaries and thesauri for identifying different parts of speech:

abbr.—Abbreviation

adj.—Adjective

adv.—Adverb

conj.—Conjunction

fem.—Feminine

interj.—Interjection

interrog.—Interrogative

modif.—Modifier (adjective or adverb)

n.—Noun (Also: neuter.)

prep.—Preposition

pron.—Pronoun

sb.—Substantive

Abbreviations for Grammatical Information

Following are a few of the abbreviations used in dictionaries and thesauri to provide information about the grammatical structure or usage of words:

acc.—Accusative

appos.—Appositive

comp.—Compound

compar.—Comparative

compl.—Complement

dat.—Dative

dem.—Demonstrative

der.—Derivation

dim.—Diminutive

fem.—Feminine

gen.—Genitive

imp.—Imperative

ind.—Indicative

inf.—Infinitive

intr.—Intransitive

irreg.—Irregular

m.—Masculine

nom.—Nominative

pa. t.—Past tense

poss.—Possessive

pple.—Participle

pf.—Perfect

pl.—Plural

pref.—Prefix

refl.—Reflexive

reg.—Regular

sing.—Singular

subj.—Subject

suff.—Suffix

superl.—Superlative

trans.—Transitive

Abbreviations for Usage and Etymology

Finally, here are a few of the abbreviations used in dictionaries to provide explanations for usage and etymological information:

Amer.—American

app.—Apparently

bef.—Before

Brit.—British

c.—Century (Also, "cent.")

ca.—*Circa*, a Latin term meaning, literally, *approximately* (This term is used in reference to dates. For example, *ca. 1945* means *around 1945*.)

cf.—Confer; that is, *compare* (For example, the phrase *cf. oak* in a particular entry would ask the reader to compare the current entry to the entry for *oak*.)

colloq.—Colloquial (A **colloquial** term is causal and/or conversational rather than used in formal speech and writing.)

def.—Definition

dial.—Dialect

Eng.—English

esp.—Especially

etym.—Etymology

euphem.—Euphemism (A **euphemism** is a polite phrase used in place of one that might be considered offensive. For example, *I need to go powder my nose* is a euphemism for *I need to use the toilet.*)

fig.—Figuratively

freq.—Frequently

gen.—Generally

Gr.—Greek

Heb.—Hebrew

hist.—Historical

IE—Indo-European

L—Latin

lang.—Language

lit.—Literally

ME.—Middle English

mod.—Modern

mythol.—In mythology

obs.—Obsolete

occas.—Occasionally

OE—Old English

opp.—Opposite

orig.—Originally

phr.—Phrase

poet.—Poetic

pop.—Popularly

pr.—Present

q.v.—*Quod vide*, a Latin phrase meaning, literally, *which see* (This abbreviation indicates that the reader should consult the source or entry just provided for additional information. The meaning is similar to *cf.* (Cf. *cf.* above.))

rel.—Related to

rev.—Revised

sp.—Spelling

spec.—Specifically

unkn.—Unknown

usu.—Usually

var.—Variant of

viz.—*Videlicit*, a Latin word meaning, literally, *it may be seen* (This abbreviation indicates that what follows adds to what preceded it by providing a clarification, an example, or an omitted term.)

wd.—Word

HOW TO APPROACH ABILITY TO USE SOURCE MATERIALS QUESTIONS

Types of Questions

Some of the questions in the Ability to Use Source Materials section will be stand-alone questions whereas others will be organized around passages. Some of the passage-based questions will test some skills that fall under the headings of Revision Skills and Rhetorical Analysis. For the most part, each question in the Ability to Use Source Materials section will test your knowledge of the four types of skills discussed in this section (documentation of sources, evaluation of sources, integration of resource material, and use of reference materials).

The directions you can expect to see for the Ability to Use Source Materials section are reproduced here from the CLEP College Composition/College Composition Modular Examination Guide:

The following questions test your familiarity with basic research, reference, and composition skills. Some questions refer to passages, while other questions are self-contained. For each question, choose the best answer.

Sample Questions

The questions provided in this section draw upon the skills discussed throughout this section. The format of the questions closely matches what you will find in the Ability to Use Source Materials section of the CLEP College Composition and Composition Modular exams. That is, the questions pertaining to passages are organized into sets of roughly three to five questions each. Five answer options are given for each question, and you are asked to choose the best option. We will work through these questions together.

The first three questions pertain to the following citation:

Caine, Franklyn. "How Not to Prepare for a Test." *Educators Monthly*: Sept. 2009. 112. Print.

Consider the following question about one detail given in the citation:

In the citation, what is *Educators Monthly*?

    (A) A book
    (B) A website
    (C) A journal
    (D) A newspaper
    (E) A database

For most multiple-choice questions, even if you believe you know the answer right away, you will need to read each option carefully before choosing your final answer. Based on the details of MLA style discussed in this section, you should be able to recognize that *Educators Monthly* is the name of a journal in which an article entitled "How Not to Prepare for a Test" appeared, and thus option C is the correct answer.

Here is another question about a detail in the citation:

How many pages in length is the source?

    (A) 1
    (B) 11
    (C) 112
    (D) 2009
    (E) Unknown

You can determine the answer on the basis of what you know about MLA style. Option A is the correct answer, because the source is one page in length. That is, the source will appear in its entirety on page 112 of the September 2009 volume of *Educators Monthly*.

Following is a third question about the citation:

Which of the following best describes the authorship of this source?

    (A) There is one author named Caine Franklyn.
    (B) There is one author named Franklyn Caine.
    (C) There are two authors, one named Caine and the other named Franklyn.
    (D) There are three or more authors, including Caine and Franklyn.
    (E) No author information is provided.

As per the requirements of MLA style, the first piece of information in a single-author source consists of the author's last name and then first name, with a comma separating the two names. Thus, option B is the correct answer.

The next two questions pertain to the following dictionary entry:

> Bear *n.* 1. any of a family (Ursidae of the order Carnivora) of large heavy mammals of America and Eurasia that have long shaggy hair, rudimentary tails, and plantigrade feet and feed largely on fruit, plant matter, and insects as well as on flesh. 2. a surly, uncouth, burly, or shambling person <a tall, friendly *bear* of a man> 3. [probably from

the proverb about *selling the bearskin before catching the bear*] : one that sells securities or commodities in expectation of a price decline. 4. something difficult to do or deal with <the oven is a *bear* to clean> Middle English *bere,* from Old English *bera;* akin to Old English *brūn* brown—First Known Use: before 12th century.

The following question pertains to the meaning of the word defined here:

Which of the following statements is NOT supported by the definition above?

(A) The word *bear* denotes a kind of mammal.
(B) The word *bear* has positive and negative connotations.
(C) The word *bear* has literal and figurative meanings.
(D) The word *bear* has an old English derivation.
(E) The word *bear* can refer to someone who sells securities.

A small number of questions in the CLEP College Composition/College Composition Modular exams will ask you to choose an option that does NOT meet some criterion. For example, in order to answer the previous question, you must reject options that *are* supported by the definition. This is tantamount to rejecting all of the options that consist of accurate statements.

Option A is supported by the definition, because denotation refers to the literal meaning of a word, and a bear is described here as a type of large mammal. Thus, option A can be rejected.

In contrast, option B is not fully supported by the definition. While some of the connotations of *bear* are clearly negative, none of them appear to be positive. Hence, B appears to be the correct answer. In order to be sure, you should evaluate the remaining options.

Option C is supported by the definition. The word *bear* refers in a literal way to a type of mammal, and in a metaphorical way to people and things. Thus, option C can be ruled out.

Option D is supported by the definition, in that an Old English derivation is mentioned near the end of the entry. Thus, option D can be ruled out.

Finally, option E is supported by the definition, as reflected by one of the meanings of the word *bear*. Thus, option E can be ruled out, and we can be sure that option B is the correct answer.

Following is another question that asks you to choose the one inaccurate option out of all options provided:

Information about each of the following is provided in the entry EXCEPT

(A) etymology.
(B) part of speech.
(C) usage.
(D) denotation.
(E) inflection.

Your task here is to reject options that are provided in the entry. Option A can be rejected because etymological information about the origin of the word *bear* is provided at the end of the entry. Option B can be rejected because the word is labeled as a noun by means of the italicized *n*.

Option C can be rejected as well because phrases such as *a tall, friendly bear of a man* are provided as examples of usage. Option D can be rejected because the denotation is provided. Option E is correct, however, because no information is given as to how the word can be inflected (e.g., by adding an *s* to the end in order to pluralize it).

The next three questions pertain to the following passage:

> (1) In 1931, during the Great Depression, the U.S. Congress passed the Davis–Bacon Act. (2) This Act required governmental contractors to pay "prevailing wages" on public works projects. (3) That is, contractors carrying out work for the government were required by the Act to pay workers at least as much as they would ordinarily be paid for comparable work on similar projects in the area. (4) More than 40 states then adopted "prevailing wage" laws. (5) Although later some states repealed these laws, at present many states continue to maintain them (Smith 1998). (6) There continue to be claims that these laws were originally motivated by the desire to exclude African American contractors. (7) Clearly, racism was not the only contributor to the passage of the Davis–Bacon Act.

The next two questions pertain to the one citation given in the passage:

Which of the following is cited in sentence 5?

- (A) A website
- (B) A newspaper
- (C) A journal article
- (D) A book
- (E) Cannot tell

In the absence of further information, you cannot be sure what *Smith 1998* refers to. For example, whether the author used APA, MLA, or Chicago style, *Smith 1998* could be a book, an article, or one of many other sources. Thus, option E is the correct answer.

What is the purpose of citing Smith in sentence 5?

- (A) To provide a source for quoted material
- (B) To refer the reader to page 1998 of a work by Smith
- (C) To provide a source for the facts given in the sentence
- (D) To provide a source for the statement in sentence 6
- (E) To present an overview of a debate

Since no material is quoted in the passage, option A is incorrect. Option B is incorrect because in styles such as APA, MLA, and Chicago, the *1998* would be the year of publication rather than the page number. Option C appears to be correct. However, you should look through all the options before choosing an answer. Option D is incorrect, because a citation will refer to the sentence in which it appears, if not also the preceding sentence(s), but it will not refer to a later sentence. Option E is incorrect because there is no reference to a debate in sentence 5. Thus, option C is indeed the correct answer. Smith has apparently published some sort of work in 1998 in which the facts described in sentence 5 are presented.

The next question pertains to the difference between fact and opinion:

Which sentence in the passage expresses an opinion?

    (A) Sentence 1
    (B) Sentence 3
    (C) Sentence 4
    (D) Sentence 6
    (E) Sentence 7

Option A is incorrect because sentence 1 consists of a simple statement of fact. Option B is incorrect because sentence 2 consists of a paraphrase of a previously stated fact. Option C is incorrect because sentence 4 consists of a simple statement of fact. Option D is incorrect for the same reason. Although an opinion is mentioned in sentence 6, the sentence itself does not convey an opinion. Rather, it consists of a statement that a certain opinion has been expressed. Option E is correct because sentence 7 presents an assertion about causal contributors to a historical event. Although the writer uses the term *clearly*, no evidence for the assertion presented in sentence 7 is given in the passage. As a result, the word *clearly* merely emphasizes the writer's confidence in the accuracy of his or her opinion.

Finally, here is a question about the documentation of sources:

Which of the following sentences most needs a citation?

    (A) Sentence 1
    (B) Sentence 2
    (C) Sentence 3
    (D) Sentence 4
    (E) Sentence 6

Although a citation could be provided for any of these sentences, sentences 1 through 4 present simple facts that can be easily verified, and thus it is not critical that a citation be provided. Sentence 6 also presents a simple fact, but since it refers to a difference of opinion, perhaps among historians, a citation is needed. A citation would support the contention that a controversy exists, and it would provide the reader with information about further reading.

The next set of questions pertains to the following passage:

> (1) Nikolai Gogol's story, "The Fair at Sorochintsy," begins with a dramatic and lovely description of the lush countryside in Little Russia. (2) The narrator's tone is reverent and awed; even insects are described as "sparks of emerald, topaz, and ruby." (3) The profound silence and stillness of the region, a magical place adorned with other-worldly flora and fauna, immediately conjures up an image of Eden in the reader's mind. (4) This prefatory section contrasts sharply with the rest of the story, which includes rough provincial humor, the activities of unruly but appealing riffraff at a local fair, and

most notably the mysterious and mischievous presence of the devil. (5) Thus, the story turns out to be a delightful recounting of devilish pranks in the Garden of Eden, contrary to the less favorable assessment of the story as "facile and unengaging" by a renowned critic (qtd. in Saronoff 334). (6) Moreover, the story can be thought of as a moving religious allegory rather than merely a fanciful account of life in rural Russia.

The following question pertains to the tone of the entire passage:

Which of the following best characterizes the writer's attitudes concerning Gogol's story?

(A) The writer likes the prefatory part of the story more than the remainder of the story.
(B) The writer has a generally negative impression of the story as a whole.
(C) The writer has a generally positive impression of the story as a whole.
(D) The writer describes most details of the story neutrally without conveying an opinion.
(E) The writer approves of Gogol's writing but not of the events of the story.

Option A is not clearly supported by the passage. The word *delightful* in sentence 5 suggests that the writer has a positive view of the remainder of the story after the devil makes an appearance.

Option B can be ruled out quite easily, in light of the writer's use of several positive descriptive terms in sentences 1, 2, and 5. For the same reason, option C appears to be correct. However, you should consider the remaining options.

Option D is not supported by the passage. Most of the factual details about the story provided by the writer are conveyed in a way that implies a positive opinion. For example, in sentence 1 the fact that Gogol describes the countryside of Little Russia in the opening part of the story is not conveyed neutrally. Rather, the writer refers to this description as *dramatic and lovely*.

Option E is not supported by the passage either. The writer does not explicitly judge the events in the story. If anything, his or her choice of words in some cases implies approval—as in the reference in sentence 4 to the riffraff as *appealing*. Hence, option C is clearly the correct answer.

The following question pertains to the quotation in sentence 2:

What information should be given in a parenthetical citation for the quoted material in sentence 2?

(A) Page number
(B) Author and page number
(C) Author, title, and year
(D) Author, year, and page number
(E) Author, translator, and page number

In context, the author and title are clear and need not be provided in the citation. Full bibliographic details will be provided separately in a footnote, endnote, reference list, or Works Cited list. The only other information the reader needs in order to locate the quote would be the page number, and thus option A is correct.

The next question pertains to the interpretation of sentence 3:

Which of the following best characterizes sentence 3?

(A) The author expresses an opinion without providing supporting evidence.
(B) The author presents a simple statement of fact in a neutral way.
(C) The author qualifies an opinion developed throughout the passage.
(D) The author presents an opinion supported by details given in sentences 2 and 3.
(E) The author presents key facts along with an analysis of those facts.

In sentence 3, the author provides some details about what Gogol describes in the first part of his story. However, the assertion that the reader will think of Eden when reading this part of the story reflects an opinion presented by the writer. This opinion is supported by some of the details that the writer provides, such as the description of the narrator's tone as *reverent* and the flora and fauna as *otherworldly*. Thus, option D is the correct answer. Option A is incorrect because supporting evidence is indeed provided. Option B is incorrect because impressions and interpretation rather than merely facts are presented. Option C is incorrect because the sentence contributes to, rather than qualifies, an opinion. Finally, option E is incorrect because the sentence does not primarily convey analysis of factual information.

The next question pertains to the citation in sentence 5:

Which of the following is NOT indicated by the citation given at the end of sentence 5?

(A) The quoted material appears in a work by Saronoff.
(B) Saronoff is the author of the source.
(C) Saronoff has written about Gogol's story.
(D) The source is a scholarly article written by Saronoff.
(E) The phrase *facile and unengaging* appears on page 334 of the source.

From the citation, you can tell that the phrase *facile and unengaging* is used on page 334 of a work written by Saronoff, a work that presumably concerns Gogol's story, at least in part. Thus, options A, B, C, and E are not correct, because each option describes information that can be gleaned from the citation. Option D is the correct answer because it is not clear that the source is an article, as opposed to a book or some other scholarly work.

Finally, here is a question about the assertion made in sentence 6:

Which of the following best characterizes sentence 6?

(A) It is a simple statement of fact.
(B) It is an opinion that is supported by very strong evidence.
(C) It is an opinion that is undermined by evidence given in the passage.
(D) It is an opinion that is presented without strong evidence.
(E) It is a factual statement asserted by Saronoff.

Option A is incorrect because the description of the story as *moving* and as something that *can be thought of as* an allegory all indicate that the writer is expressing an opinion.

Option B also seems to be incorrect because there is not strong evidence or analysis favoring an interpretation of the story as allegorical rather than literal.

Option C is incorrect because even though there is not strong evidence for the assertion that the story is an allegory, the writer does not provide evidence that contradicts this assertion.

Option E is incorrect because the statement is not attributed to Saronoff, nor does it appear from context that Saronoff would have made the statement.

Option D appears to be correct. Sentence 6 presents an opinion. The only *evidence* is the writer's own assertion in sentence 3 that the reader would think of Eden when reading the story, along with other details such as the reference in sentence 2 to the author's *reverent* tone.

RHETORICAL ANALYSIS

The Rhetorical Analysis section tests your ability to analyze writing through both passage-based and stand-alone questions. These questions measure critical thinking, as well as your understanding of organization, style, audience, purpose, tone, and rhetoric. Each of these skills is discussed in the following section, followed by guidance on how to approach Rhetorical Analysis questions, and finally some practice questions with answers and explanations.

CRITICAL THINKING

In order to apply critical thinking to the analysis of writing, one must be able to analyze facts and opinions, evaluate arguments, compare and synthesize details, and make inferences.

Analyzing Facts and Opinions

Rhetorical analysis includes the ability to identify key facts, distinguish between facts and opinions, and understand the source and purpose of the opinions that a writer presents.

A **fact,** a statement that is known to be true, can be verified or proven by means of evidence. For example, it is a fact that Providence is the capital of Rhode Island, because one can verify the statement by consulting the appropriate sources. In contrast, an **opinion** is a statement that someone thinks is true, but that has not been—or cannot be—proven through evidence. For example, the statement that Boston is a splendid place to live represents an opinion. One could find evidence in favor of the statement, but one could also find evidence that undermines the statement.

In some cases, the distinction between fact and opinion is clearly marked by the writer, as in the following example:

> Every year there are more than six million traffic accidents in the United States. I think that number is much too high.

In this example, the first sentence is a statement of fact, whereas the second sentence expresses an opinion. The statistic reported in the first sentence may or may not be correct, but it is presented as a fact. The phrase *I think* at the outset of the second sentence alerts the reader that an opinion will follow. The following sentences feature a few of the many phrases that writers use to explicitly signal opinions:

> *I believe* that it rained more than once yesterday morning.
>
> *It seems to me* that hard work ultimately pays off.
>
> Kindness is a virtue, *in my view*.
>
> *As I see it*, special interest groups exert an undue influence on national politics.
>
> *I would say that* teachers need to be committed to the well-being of their students.
>
> *My sense is* that the knee is sprained rather than fractured.

In some cases, writers do not make explicit distinctions between fact and opinion. In these passages, the reader must identify the distinction. For example, consider the following passage:

> In 2000, 15% of high school students in Sheffield County dropped out of school. By 2010, the dropout rate was 24%. The steady decline in percentage of Sheffield County students who graduate from high school is troubling. It's not easy to find a decent job without a high school degree.

In this passage, the first two sentences present facts, whereas the last two sentences present opinions. However, the final statement is so widely accepted that many readers will view it as a fact.

The reader should be aware that the "facts" a writer reports may be misleading, incorrect, and/or incomplete. For example, the previous passage contains reference to a *steady decline* in Sheffield County graduation rates. If the writer has seen the county's graduation statistics for each year from 2000 to 2010, he or she may be accurate in referring to a steady decline. However, if the writer has not seen those statistics, it may not be accurate to assume that the decline was *steady*. Perhaps the dropout rate was consistently around 15% from 2000 through 2009, with an abrupt increase to 24% in 2010.

The final sentence of the passage sounds like a fact. One could find evidence to support the assertion that it's not easy for people without a college degree to find a decent job. However, one could also find evidence that it's not easy for people with a college degree to find a decent job. The way one interprets such evidence depends on how one defines terms like *easy* and *decent*. Thus, the final sentence reflects more of a commonly held opinion than a fact.

The distinction between fact and opinion is not always clear cut. For example, writers will often make a factual assertion but acknowledge some degree of uncertainty or possibility of error, as in the following example.

> It appears that global average temperatures were higher during the first half of 2010 than during any other six-month period in modern history.

In the previous sentence, the writer states a fact about global temperatures but acknowledges by means of the phrase *It appears* that the fact may be incorrect. Thus, the writer's statement about global temperatures represents an opinion. The following sentences use other phrases that acknowledge some degree of uncertainty about factual assertions:

> Apparently, the batter felt bad about striking out with the bases loaded, as he ran back to the dugout with his head down.

> It is likely that this new legislation will be unsettling to almost everyone.

> The snow seems to have stopped falling.

> Evidence suggests that the level of radioactivity at Chernobyl has returned to normal levels.

> Surely the two vehicles made contact before the blue car skidded into the ditch.

Critical thinking allows the reader to not only recognize that opinions are expressed in these sentences, but also evaluate the accuracy and persuasiveness of those opinions. The first sentence, for example, suggests that the batter felt bad. Given the circumstances, the opinion is plausible. In contrast, the opinion outlined in the second sentence does not seem plausible without further evidence.

In some cases, by insisting on the certainty of a fact, the writer actually implies the possibility that the assertion is incorrect, as illustrated by the following example:

> I am convinced that the country's standard of living rose last year.

In this example, the fact that the writer is convinced indicates that he or she could have arrived at a different conclusion, implying the possibility that the country's standard of living did not rise during the previous year.

Finally, a distinction can be made between the opinion that someone expresses and the fact that he or she has expressed an opinion. For example, consider the content of the following sentence:

> After the Treaty of Paris was signed on November 20, 1815, and news of the treaty was made public, some French citizens stated pessimistically that France would never again be a dominant power in Europe.

In this sentence, the date of the Treaty of Paris is a fact. It is also a fact that some French citizens responded to the treaty pessimistically. However, their pessimism itself reflects an opinion. Their statement that France would never be a dominant power is an opinion about the future political development of the country.

Evaluating Arguments

Rhetorical analysis includes the ability to **understand and evaluate the arguments** that a writer presents. To evaluate an argument, you must be able to recognize the logic underlying the argument, as well as judge the strength of the evidence that the writer offers in support of the argument.

In some cases, it is relatively easy to spot the flaws in an argument. For example, in the following passage, the logical contradiction is clear:

> Newton was a peevish, suspicious, and relatively antisocial person who valued his work above all else. As director of the Royal Mint, he spent a great deal of time enjoying conversation with friends and colleagues.

In this passage, there is a direct and readily detected contradiction between the description of Newton as *peevish* and *antisocial* and the anecdote of him enjoying interactions with friends and colleagues. In other cases, weaknesses in the logic of an argument and/or the nature of evidence presented are not as readily perceived. For example, consider the following passage:

> I agree with Smith's contention that Hitchcock was a terribly overrated director. Smith was fond of pointing out that, although Hitchcock made movies for over half a century, he never won an Oscar.

The details provided in the second sentence of this passage are meant to support the opinion outlined in the first sentence. However, the logic of the argument is questionable. In order to claim that an artist's work is overrated, one must demonstrate—or at least assert—that the work is admired to a certain extent, and one must then argue that the quality of the work does not merit quite so much admiration. In this passage, no statements are made about the extent to which Hitchcock's work is admired. Arguably, this omission is forgivable, because Hitchcock happens to be a famous director. The writer seems to assume, as most readers would, that Hitchcock's work as a director is rated very highly. A more serious problem is that the passage contains no direct statement about the quality of Hitchcock's work. Rather, the writer simply notes that Hitchcock made movies over a long period of time but never received an Oscar.

One way to strengthen the argument is to explicitly state that the true quality of Hitchcock's work is reflected in the fact that he never won an Oscar. For example, consider the following revision of the passage:

> I agree with Smith's contention that Hitchcock was a terribly overrated director. Smith was fond of pointing out that although Hitchcock made critically acclaimed movies for over half a century, he never won an Oscar. I believe, as Smith does, that regardless of what critics say, a director's work is no good unless he or she has won an Oscar.

In this revised passage, the logic of the argument is clearer. There is a phrase implying that Hitchcock's work is admired (i.e., *critically acclaimed*) and there is a statement that the work is not worthy of such admiration (i.e., *a director's work is no good unless he or she has won an Oscar*).

Although the logic of the argument in the revised passage is clearer, one might still question the strength of the presented evidence. Smith's argument relies on the assumption that a director's work cannot be good unless he or she has won an Oscar.

This argument seems to imply a simplistic distinction between *good* and *no good*, and it presumes that winning an Oscar is the sole criterion for judging the quality of a director's work.

In sum, the argument that the writer develops is not very persuasive, because it depends on at least two questionable assumptions. This is not to say that the writer is wrong. It may be that all works of art can be judged as either good or no good, and it may be true that winning an Oscar should be the sole criterion for judging a director's work to be good. However, the writer presents no evidence in support of these assumptions. Since it seems likely that very few people would agree with those assumptions, the writer's argument is weak.

There are many types of potential flaws in the logic of an argument. The reader must analyze a writer's assertions carefully, as some of these flaws are more difficult to spot than others, and the writers themselves may not even be aware of the logical fallacies that undermine their arguments. Some fallacies pertain to the way evidence is used. For example, the writer may draw stronger links between causes and effects than the evidence warrants, as illustrated in the following passage:

> I've had the flu many times in my life. Last time I had it, I drank jasmine tea three times a day, and I recovered much more quickly than ever before. I'm convinced now that jasmine tea kills the flu virus.

In this passage, the writer asserts that jasmine tea kills the flu virus, because he recovered from the flu more quickly than usual after drinking the tea. One problem with this line of reasoning is that it fails to acknowledge other possible causes of the writer's speedy recovery besides the tea. Another problem with the writer's reasoning is that even if the tea was helpful, it does not follow that the tea kills the flu virus. Perhaps the tea merely alleviates flu symptoms. In sum, the causal connection between drinking tea and the demise of the flu virus has not been clearly established.

Another kind of misuse of evidence occurs when writers overstate their conclusions. **Overstatements** can occur when a merely probable outcome is treated as a matter of necessity. For example:

> Computer viruses are prevalent on the Internet. If you use the Internet, it is inevitable that your computer will be infected by one of these viruses someday.

The first sentence of this passage suggests that it is possible, or perhaps even probable, that continued use of the Internet will result in one's computer becoming infected by a virus. However, this outcome is not inevitable. *Prevalent* does not mean *everywhere at all times*. Moreover, computer users have access to antivirus software and other protective strategies which help ensure that even if their computers are exposed to viruses, the computers may not be infected.

Another type of overstatement occurs when the writer is not careful about **generalizing from known facts**, as in the following passage:

> Pickup trucks require much more gasoline than cars do. Thus, pickup trucks are consuming much more of the world's dwindling fuel supply.

The conclusion expressed in the second sentence may be true, but it does not follow necessarily from the first sentence. There are more cars on the road than pickup trucks. Thus, it may be that cars are consuming much more of the fuel supply.

Still another type of overstatement occurs when the writer assumes a series of **gradations** and concludes that a relatively extreme outcome will occur. For example:

> Last week the governor granted a pardon to a man who had been convicted of aggravated assault. Two months ago he pardoned another hardened criminal. At this rate, criminals will continue to be released from jail until the streets are filled with them and ordinary citizens can no longer feel safe in their own homes.

In this passage, the writer concludes without evidence that the governor will continue to issue pardons, and that the rate of pardons will be so great that the streets are *filled* with criminals. The writer predicts an escalation in the rate of pardons without considering whether the earlier pardons represent exceptional cases; in addition, the writer does not acknowledge that pardons are typically granted because the individual is presumed to be innocent or at least to no longer pose a threat.

In some cases, the problem is not that a conclusion is overstated, but rather that the writer distorts his or her argument in such a way that any conclusion would be fallacious, as in the following passage:

> If you're patriotic, you support the current military action. You're either with us or against us.

In this passage, the first sentence implies that all patriots support the current military action (i.e., that it is impossible to be patriotic unless one supports this action). This is a questionable assumption. Conceivably, there is a definition of patriotism according to which some people are patriots yet do not support any military action. The second sentence of the passage is problematic because it reduces all possible attitudes to either *for* or *against* the military action. This dichotomization excludes the possibility of mixed feelings or indifference. It also glosses over differences in degree of support: Some people who are *with us* concerning the military action may possess a much greater degree of commitment and certainty than others who would also describe themselves as supporters.

In the previous example, the problem is that no middle ground is permitted between extreme positions. A different sort of fallacy occurs when extreme positions are presented and it is implied that only some sort of middle ground is acceptable. For example:

> Some members of Congress are saying that these tariffs should be doubled. Others are saying the tariffs should not be changed. Clearly what would be best for the economy is to raise tariffs moderately.

In this example, the existence of extreme positions is used as evidence that a moderate position is best. However, economic data might show that one of the extreme positions is overwhelmingly superior to the middle ground. (To illustrate this point, imagine that two people who have just washed your car disagree on how much to charge you. One person asserts that the going rate is about $10 while the other claims that most people would charge about $190. Here, the middle ground is $100, but that is not reflective of a typical price for a car wash, nor could one make a very persuasive argument that it is an appropriate price.)

The preceding examples illustrate logical fallacies that are reflected in the structure of an argument. Other fallacies arise from the use of evidence or argumentation that is more or less irrelevant to the main thrust of the argument. For example, consider the following six versions of a passage written by someone who disagrees with the tax policies of a commentator named Smith:

1. Smith actually claims that lowering taxes by as little as 10% per capita would destroy the national economy. That is a ridiculous assertion.

2. Smith actually claims that lowering taxes by as little as 10% per capita would destroy the national economy. Nothing could be further from the truth. Economists agree that our country has the strongest economy in the world. A change in tax rates would not significantly alter the strength of our economy.

3. Smith actually claims that lowering taxes by as little as 10% per capita would destroy the national economy. I find Smith's objection to lowering taxes misguided, and somewhat surprising given the fact that he was convicted of tax evasion in 1997 and 2009.

4. Smith actually claims that lowering taxes by as little as 10% per capita would destroy the national economy. My concern about Smith's argument is not just that he is wrong, but that he is dangerous. What would destroy the national economy is for anyone to take his views seriously. I would hate to see my children begging on the street corner because of him.

5. Smith actually claims that lowering taxes by as little as 10% per capita would destroy the national economy. Nobody holds such a view anymore.

6. Smith actually claims that lowering taxes by as little as 10% per capita would destroy the national economy. Smith is wrong. The flaw in his argument was pointed out very clearly in an influential article written by the internationally renowned economist Jane Doe.

In the first passage, reference to Smith's opinion as *ridiculous* does not contribute in any substantive way to the assertion that Smith is wrong. Ridicule or praise do not in themselves contribute substantively to an argument. If anything, the fact that the writer refers to Smith's view as ridiculous but does not provide any evidence to that effect undermines the writer's own persuasiveness. That is, the reader of this passage is likely to think more poorly of the writer than of Smith.

In the second passage, the writer does provide evidence in favor of his or her objection to Smith's view, but the evidence is of questionable relevance. Even if the writer's country does have the strongest economy in the world, it does not follow that a particular change in the country's tax rates could not damage its economy. In addition, the phrase *Nothing could be further from the truth* is an example of **hyperbole**—an exaggerated statement—and like most hyperbolic statements it contributes nothing to the argument.

In the third passage, the writer introduces a personal attack apparently intended to undermine Smith's credibility. The writer gives no evidence that Smith's crime bears on his point of view. Without additional evidence, the fact that Smith was convicted of tax evasion is irrelevant to the question of whether his claim about taxes and the national economy is accurate.

In the fourth passage, the writer attempts to frighten the reader. Rather than presenting evidence that Smith is wrong, the writer focuses on describing what would happen if Smith is wrong but people take his views seriously. Thus, the writer attempts to distract the reader. If the writer believes that Smith is in error, the writer should present evidence to that effect. If the writer also wishes to assert that Smith's errors are dangerous, a separate argument, with evidence, is needed. In this passage the writer presents no evidence for any assertion.

In the fifth passage, the writer's evidence consists solely of an alleged lack of popularity. The assertion seems to be that because nobody holds the view that Smith espouses, Smith must be wrong. Arguably, the popularity of an opinion should play some role in how it is evaluated. However, the fact that an opinion is widely accepted does not guarantee that it is true, any more than lack of popularity for an opinion guarantees that it is false. The writer's argument in this passage is weak because he or she merely states, without evidence, that Smith's view is not widely accepted anymore.

In the final passage, the writer appeals to authority. The evidence that Smith is wrong consists of reference to an *influential* paper written by an *internationally renowned* expert. Certainly, the opinions of experts should be considered when evaluating an argument. But even assuming that an expert did directly refute Smith's view, the fact that she did so does not necessarily constitute strong evidence against Smith. The expert may be wrong. It may be that other experts support Smith's view. Smith himself may be an expert too. (The reader might ask whether an internationally renowned expert would take the trouble to attack Smith if Smith were not somewhat prominent himself.) In short, the weakness of the argument in this passage is not that the writer cites an authority, but that the sole focus is on the authority's conclusions rather than on the evidence that Smith is misguided.

Comparing and Synthesizing Details

Rhetorical analysis includes the ability to **compare** and **synthesize** various details that a writer presents. Synthesis is needed for many purposes. First, a writer's general theme can be determined by synthesizing pertinent information. Consider, for example, the details given in the following passage:

> Ben Franklin, born in Boston in 1706, grew up to become Philadelphia's most famous citizen. He moved to Philadelphia at the age of 17 and quickly became a successful writer, editor, and printer. During his long life he was a prolific inventor as well. Franklin invented the lightning rod, the Franklin stove, bifocals, and a musical instrument that he called the glass armonica. In addition, as one of the Founding Fathers, Franklin was an extraordinarily accomplished politician, holding a variety of political offices including President of the Supreme Executive Council of Pennsylvania, Speaker of the Pennsylvania Assembly, U.S. Postmaster General, U.S. Ambassador to France, and U.S. Ambassador to Sweden.

Many details are provided in the passage, but the writer does not explicitly state his or her theme. The reader will observe, however, that each detail in the passage consists of one of Franklin's accomplishments. Phrases such as *as well* and *In addition* hint that the writer is presenting a list. This list of accomplishments is relatively long, and when the items on the list are compared, the reader will notice that the items are very different from each other (i.e., they represent very different kinds of accomplishments). Thus, through synthesis the reader can determine that the theme pertains to the extent and diversity of Franklin's accomplishments. The theme of the passage is that during his life Franklin achieved success in many different kinds of endeavors.

A second use of synthesis is to collate details from different statements in a passage and identify missing information. For example, suppose that the following sentence were added to the end of the preceding passage:

> This concludes my brief introduction to the life of Benjamin Franklin.

By synthesizing the various details of the passage, including the final sentence, the reader can see that certain kinds of information are missing. All we can gather from the passage about Franklin's life other than a sense of the extraordinary breadth of his accomplishments is his birthplace, his age when he relocated to Philadelphia, his longevity, and the fact that success as a writer, editor, and printer predated some of his other achievements. Missing is the chronology of those achievements, as well as details of his personal life, his world view, and many other kinds of information.

Finally, when different points of view are presented, synthesis can help the reader identify key similarities and differences between views. For example, consider the following passage:

> According to a recent study, taking aspirin on a regular basis reduces the risk of certain kinds of cancer. The study followed a large sample of people over a period of 20 years. People who took aspirin regularly had a lower incidence of cancer as compared to those who did not take aspirin. However, doctors caution that regular use of aspirin can increase the risk of gastrointestinal bleeding.

A reasonable synthesis of the information presented in the previous passage is that taking aspirin regularly has potential benefits as well as potential risks to one's health. This illustrates the use of synthesis to identify a theme. At the same time, synthesis helps us recognize that whether we wish to understand the benefits or the risks of aspirin consumption, one key piece of information missing from this passage is a definition of *regular*.

Making Inferences

Rhetorical analysis includes the ability to make **inferences** about the meaning, purpose, and impact of what a writer presents. Broadly, there are two kinds of inference: deductive and inductive.

Deductive inferences yield conclusions that necessarily follow from premises. Here is a simple example of deductive reasoning:

1. A person who is alive has a heartbeat. (premise)

2. John P. has a heartbeat. (premise)

3. John P. is alive. (conclusion)

In the preceding example, the conclusion (*John P. is alive*) follows necessarily from the premises. If you accept the premises, you must accept the conclusion.

To illustrate how deductive inference can be used when analyzing a piece of writing, consider the following sentence:

> The witness said that she saw three men enter the bank.

From this sentence, we can deduce that the witness is female. Our reasoning can be reconstructed as follows:

1. Only females are referred to by the pronoun *she*. (premise)

2. The witness is referred to by the pronoun *she*. (premise)

3. The witness is female. (conclusion)

Inductive inferences yield conclusions that are only suggested by the premises. Thus, the conclusions cannot be drawn with total certainty. For example:

1. Everyone I have met in my life has a first and a last name. (premise)

2. I will meet new people tomorrow. (premise)

3. Everyone I meet tomorrow will have a first and a last name. (conclusion)

In the previous example, the conclusion (*Everyone I meet tomorrow will have a first and a last name*) is suggested by the premises, but it does not necessarily follow from those premises. It is possible (though unlikely) that I will meet someone tomorrow who only goes by one name.

To illustrate how inductive inference can be used when analyzing a piece of writing, consider the following sentence:

> The witness said that she saw the three men leave the bank carrying several bags of money.

From this sentence, we can inductively infer that the three men have robbed the bank, but we cannot be sure. Perhaps the three men are actually security guards bringing the money to an armored car, and the witness is being interviewed about what happened when the armored car was subsequently robbed. Thus, the sentence suggests that the three men are robbers, but it does not offer definitive proof for this conclusion.

Now consider some of the deductive and inductive inferences that can be drawn from the following passage:

> Bullying continues to be a major problem in American schools, and now Internet applications such as Facebook are being used by bullies to harass their victims. Online bullying is called *cyber bullying*, and it can be every bit as devastating to victims as traditional forms of bullying behavior. Parents and school administrators should be aware of the potential threats posed by cyber bullying activities. As Mary, a ninth-grade cyber bullying victim describes it, "The bullies who kept posting nasty comments about me on their Facebook pages made my life hell.

A number of important deductive inferences can be made from this passage. For example, we can infer from the first sentence that bullying is not a new problem in American schools. This inference is supported by the phrase *continues to be*. From the second sentence we can infer that traditional forms of bullying are harmful to victims. The phrase *every bit as* is key to this particular inference.

This passage also sustains some important inductive inferences about the writer's opinions about bullying and his or her purpose in writing this passage. From the third sentence we can infer that the writer considers bullying to be a serious problem. This inference is supported by the recommendation that parents and administrators be aware of the threats posed by cyber bullying. We can also infer that the purpose of the final sentence is to provide a concrete illustration of the writer's theme. The student's reference to life becoming *hell* as a result of cyber bullying is part of an anecdote that is consistent with the theme developed in each sentence of this passage.

One of the specific applications of inductive inference is identifying logical fallacies of the sort described in the evaluating arguments section. Another application is in determining the likely meaning of unfamiliar words. By looking at how the words are used in context, you may be able to infer something about their likely meaning.

In some cases, the meaning of the word can be inferred from a restatement of its essential meaning, as in the following sentence:

She gave me a lugubrious look, and her sad eyes filled with tears.

From this sentence, the reader can infer that *lugubrious* and *sad* are most probably synonymous. In other cases, the meaning of the word is not directly restated, but inferable from an elaboration of the meaning. For example:

The main character in this book is sometimes described as suffering from dipsomania, which is understandable given that he was never without a bottle of beer in his hand.

Here the reader can infer that dipsomania has something to do with consumption of beer, or perhaps alcohol more generally. Reference to the character *suffering* from dipsomania suggests that the term denotes a problematic condition. Thus, the reader may guess that *dipsomania* refers to alcoholism, or a craving for alcohol. The root *mania*, which appears in the word, is also a potential clue as to its meaning.

In still other cases, something about the meaning of a word can be inferred from evidence about what it does *not* mean, as in the following sentence:

The student was belligerent while the teacher was scolding him, but when the principal appeared, he suddenly became very well-behaved.

In this sentence, the meaning of *belligerent* appears to be something like the opposite of *well-behaved*.

UNDERSTANDING OF ORGANIZATION

Rhetorical analysis includes recognizing and evaluating the **organization** of information in a piece of writing. Organization can be thought of in terms of the order in which information is presented. Six types of organization characterize most nonfiction writing: chronological, emphatic, generality, comparison, cause–effect, and problem–solution.

Chronological Organization

Chronological organization presents information in order of occurrence. The information may consist of a sequence of events, as seen in the reconstruction of a historical event, the telling of a story, or the report of an eyewitness. Chronological organization is also used in scientific reports, in which a series of procedures is described, and in essays in which the writer describes the development over time in his or her own views about a topic. The following passage illustrates chronological organization:

> In order to create this type of transistor, engineers begin with a silicon wafer. A layer of oxide is deposited on the wafer. Next, photolithographic techniques are used to etch the wafer. Etching creates all of the key devices on the wafer's surface. Finally, the functionality of these devices is tested.

Emphatic Organization

Emphatic organization presents information in order of importance. In some cases, the writer begins with the most important point in hopes of capturing the reader's attention or persuading the reader of some idea before he or she loses interest or gets caught up in details. In other cases, the writer begins with the least important point and builds to a crescendo in hopes that the impact on the reader will increase as well. The following passage illustrates emphatic organization of the first type (most-to-least important):

> I have been a vegetarian since I was 18 years old, and I think that others should give up eating meat too. I believe it is unethical to raise and kill animals for food. That is a completely unfair and exploitative practice, and if you eat meat, you should pause for a moment to consider the moral implications. And although vegetarianism should be practiced for ethical reasons, you should also keep in mind that a vegetarian diet, if carefully chosen, is healthier than one that includes meat. Healthier, and cheaper as well.

Generality Organization

Generality organization presents information in order of specificity. In some cases, the writer begins with a general theme and then focuses in on a specific topic of interest. In other cases, the writer begins with a highly specific point that he or she subsequently broadens. There are also cases in which the level of specificity is manipulated in a more nuanced way, as in the *five-paragraph essay* that many students learn how to write in middle school and high school. The five-paragraph essay consists of three parts: introduction, body, and conclusion. The introduction begins with a general statement that is narrowed down to the writer's main thesis. The body of the essay contains a specific discussion of the thesis. The conclusion provides a summary of the specifics and then broadens the discussion.

In the following passage, generality organization is used to proceed from specific to general:

> In 2005 more than 300 people were crushed to death during a pilgrimage to Mecca. In 2010 more than 300 people died during a stampede at the Water Festival along the

Tonle Sap River. There are countless other stories of people being injured or killed by crowd crush at concerts, sporting events, and other events. What all of these stories have in common, besides the tragic loss of life, is evidence that the relevant authorities failed to provide adequate crowd control. The management of crowds during organized events is becoming increasingly critical across the globe.

Comparison Organization

Comparison organization presents information about two or more things, events, or ideas in order to compare and contrast them. In some cases, the writer's purpose is simply to document similarities and differences. The writer may wish to develop a system of classification, in which categories and subcategories are identified. Often, the writer's purpose is also evaluative, in that he or she asserts that one thing is more appealing, important, worrisome, or funny than another. The writer may conduct a comparison by discussing concepts simultaneously, or by largely focusing on one concept at a time. In the following passage, comparison organization is used to contrast two concepts in sequence rather than simultaneously.

> The critical importance of hydration is a fairly recent idea in high school athletics. Traditionally, coaches felt that too much water would be harmful to young athletes. Besides slowing the athletes down, coaches believed that offering athletes ready access to water would reduce their toughness. In some cases, water was even withheld as a form of discipline. During the past two decades, following the high-profile deaths of athletes resulting from dehydration or heat stroke, high school coaches have come to recognize the critical importance of keeping their athletes hydrated. These days, water and sports drinks are mandatory during practice and on game day.

Cause–Effect Organization

Cause–effect organization presents information about the causes of some known or likely outcome. The following passage illustrates cause–effect organization.

> One of the contributors to poor performance on standardized tests of math achievement is inadequate instruction. The math classes that many students take simply do not prepare them to do well on these tests. Exacerbating the problem is the fact that most parents are unaware of the poor quality of instruction, and thus they do not provide their children with additional support for math skills. A further contributor to poor achievement on test performance is math anxiety. Some students, regardless of actual mathematical skill, find math to be an unpleasant and anxiety-provoking subject, and so the prospect of taking a math test is positively terrifying to them.

Problem–Solution Organization

Problem–solution organization presents information about a problem, followed by a description of one or more solutions. The writer may briefly summarize the solutions, compare and contrast solutions, evaluate the solutions, and/or provide a recommendation as to the preferred solution. Problem–solution organization is illustrated in the following passage:

> Attention Deficit Hyperactivity Disorder (ADHD) poses significant academic challenges to students who suffer from the disorder. During lectures, and when receiving instructions about homework and other assignments, students with ADHD often miss key information because they "zone out" or act impulsively while the teacher is talking. During tests and other assessments, students with ADHD may not perform well for much the same reasons. In hopes of dealing with these and other challenges, parents of children with ADHD have two general options. The first is for the children to regularly use stimulant medicines. These medications, known by brand names such as Ritalin, Adderall, and Concerta, have been shown to be somewhat effective at diminishing ADHD symptoms. The second option is the regular application of behavioral management strategies that involve parents, teachers, and the students themselves. These strategies have also proven to be somewhat effective. Each of these approaches, medical and behavioral, has its strengths and weaknesses, and experts often recommend that they be carefully combined.

In descriptive writing, the information may not be presented in any particular order. Rather, the characteristics of some person, place, event, or thing may simply be described, as in the following passage:

> With an American father and a Chinese mother, New Year's Eve at my house is a startling mix of cultures. We drink eggnog and sing "Auld Lang Syne." We make resolutions. We also make *jiao zi*, which are dumplings filled with pork, cabbage, and other goodies, and when mom serves the chicken for our main course, it still has the head and feet on it. I think that represents togetherness. I'm not sure, because I always close my eyes and ears when her chicken appears.

Framing and Transitions

Each type of organization discussed in the previous section pertains to an entire piece of writing. However, rhetorical analysis also includes the ability to recognize and evaluate organizational strategies that are used within and across individual sentences. Two of the most important organizational strategies used at the sentence level are framing and transitions.

Framing refers to the way a writer lets readers know what will be discussed prior to the actual discussion. A framing statement may pertain to the entire piece of writing, to one passage, or to a single sentence. In each of the following sentences, the first several words provide the reader with some information about what will be discussed next.

> In this review I will describe three limitations of Smith's theory, and then describe a plausible alternative.

> Now let me explain why I referred to Faulkner as a "limited" novelist.

> There are two good reasons to purchase a hybrid vehicle.

> This next section focuses on some of the more specific contributors to Kahlo's distinctive style.

Framing statements are useful because they inform readers about the content as well as the organization of what they are about to read. In a similar way, transitions provide information about content and organization. A **transition** term informs readers that there will be some sort of change in the writing, thereby allowing what was previously expressed to be linked smoothly to what is expressed next. Examples of transition terms include *for example*, *however*, *in contrast*, *moreover*, *thus*, and others. For example, the term *however* typically alerts the reader that the next statement will qualify the previous one. Consider the following examples:

Lismont was fast; however, Rogers was faster.

Scientists agree that many factors influence IQ. However, there is no consensus as to which factor has the greatest influence.

Johnny claimed that he didn't eat the candy. I could tell, however, that he was lying.

In each example, the clause following the word *however* introduces a qualification to the previous clause. The previous clause is not actually denied in these sentences. Rather, the word *however* tells the reader in each case that the previous clause does not convey the whole story. Lismont was indeed fast, but someone else happened to be faster. Scientists agree that many factors influence IQ, but they don't agree about everything. And Johnny did in fact claim that he didn't eat the candy. It just so happens that he was lying, according to the writer.

Transition terms such as *however*, *but*, *nevertheless*, *all the same*, and *in contrast* mark some sort of contrast between the previous sentence or clause and what follows, as in the following examples:

Mary's mother asked her to speak more softly during the service, but the little girl was not old enough to remember to do so.

Sartre and Camus disagreed on many topics, both philosophical and artistic; nevertheless, they remained friends for quite some time.

The hiker knew that the path ahead was treacherous. All the same, she chose to forge ahead anyway.

English plurals are marked by morphological changes such as the addition of an *s* to the end of a word. Chinese, in contrast, does not mark pluralization through morphological changes.

The transition terms in the previous examples indicate a contrast between sentences or clauses. Other transition terms, such as *in the same way*, *similarly*, and *likewise* highlight similarities, as in the following examples:

Jini shouted at Lester, in much the same way that Lester had shouted at her earlier that evening.

By means of camouflage, flounder blend in with the sea floor; similarly, butterflies may be indistinguishable from the leaves on which they rest.

A man hopes that his future spouse will suit him perfectly. Likewise, women hope to find the perfect spouse.

Transition terms such as *as a result*, *consequently*, and sometimes *thus* indicate a causal relationship, as in the following examples.

Almost every evening that year, Jordan practiced basketball with his father. As a result, his skills improved significantly.

The intern showed up late for work four days in a row; consequently, he was fired.

Clarissa was standing on a stepstool when she dropped the bowl. Thus, the bowl shattered when it hit the kitchen floor.

In each of these examples, the action described in the clause directly preceding the transition term is a cause of the outcome noted following the transition term.

Transition terms such as *then*, *afterwards*, and *later* are used to indicate temporal sequence, as in the following examples:

He dropped his bat, amazed to have hit the ball. Then he scampered to first base.

On Saturday it rained in Houston from about 6 a.m. to 6 p.m. Afterwards, some of the downtown streets were flooded.

Garfield was assassinated shortly after taking office; later, McKinley and then Kennedy were assassinated as well.

Some transitional phrases, such as *in other words*, *that is to say*, and *to reiterate*, tell the reader that what follows is essentially a restatement of what preceded the phrase. Other transitional phrases, such as *in short*, *in sum*, or *to put it briefly*, indicate that what follows is a succinct summary of what preceded that phrase. Following are some examples:

I believe that a lack of caffeine undermines success; in other words, you pretty much have to drink coffee in order to be successful.

The downfall of many televangelists has been concupiscence; that is to say, lust.

The next step on the road to economic recovery is more responsible federal spending. To reiterate, greater responsibility in federal spending should be our immediate priority in strengthening the economy.

It is critical to the health of our society that every adult citizen exercise his or her right to vote; in short, you need to vote.

First he lost his keys, then his car wouldn't start, and when he finally did start the car he noticed that it was almost out of gas. In sum, he had a very trying morning.

Picasso had the uncanny ability to anticipate new developments in the visual arts and then modify his work so that it quickly moved to the forefront of those developments. To put it briefly, he was a most talented innovator.

Some transitional phrases, such as *for example*, *specifically*, and *in general*, tell the reader that what follows bears a more specific or more general connection to what preceded the phrase, as in the following examples:

> Most professional athletes are not successful when they attempt to change sports; for example, after his first retirement from professional basketball, Michael Jordan was unable to become a major league baseball player.

> Orcas show great patience when hunting young whales; specifically, they will chase young whales and their mothers for great distances, waiting until the pair grow tired before attempting to separate them prior to the kill.

> The nobility objected to the king's approach to foreign affairs, the merchants detested his tax increases, and the peasants chafed under his onerous penal code. In general, the populace was dissatisfied with the king's leadership.

Many other kinds of transition phrases inform the reader about the nature of the relationship between clauses or sentences. In some cases, the phrases indicate this relationship in a very specific way. For example, the phrase *for example* indicates a very specific kind of relationship between the previous statement and the information that follows. Other transition phrases provide the reader with somewhat less specific guidance as to how later details connect with earlier ones, as in the following examples:

> Yolanda was at the party, so Jimmy came too.

> Visitors must be careful when walking around the city at night. And they must be especially careful not to lose their way.

Finally, some transition terms can be used to indicate more than one kind of relationship. Consider, for example, the following uses of the word *thus*:

> The bowl was already cracked when Clarissa dropped it. Thus, it shattered instantly upon hitting the floor.

> Jackson grew up in Paris; thus, he speaks French quite fluently.

> After we finished quarreling, she kissed me one last time and left for good. I watched, expressionless. Thus, we ended a long and bittersweet relationship.

In the first passage, *thus* indicates a causal relationship and is synonymous with *as a result*. In the second passage, *thus* marks a logical relationship and is synonymous with *therefore*. In the third passage, *thus* summarizes the previous anecdote and is synonymous with *in this way*.

UNDERSTANDING OF STYLE

Style reflects choices a writer makes that affect the way information is communicated. Different topics and audiences call for different styles. A writer may develop a distinctive style that can be recognized across different pieces of writing. Some of the many contributors to style include diction, syntax, and point of view.

Diction

Diction refers to a writer's choice of words. There are many different ways to convey essentially the same idea. However, the particular words that a writer uses to express an idea will impact the meaning, appeal, and persuasiveness of the idea, as well as the reader's sense of the writer's attitudes. Consider, for example, the following three sentences:

> With respect to alcohol consumption, I suspect that she resembles her father in a tendency to overindulge.

> When it comes to drinking, I think she takes after her dad. They both seem to overdo it.

> She's a drunk, just like her dad.

All three sentences convey essentially the same idea. However, as a result of differences in word choice, each sentence will probably have a different impact on readers. For example, the first sentence is much more formal than the other two, to the point that in most contexts it would seem pretentious or stilted. The second and third sentences are quite informal.

Another difference in the diction of the three sentences is that the third sentence indicates considerable certainty that the girl and her father have an alcohol problem, whereas the first two sentences convey an element of uncertainty, or at least open-mindedness. The phrase *I suspect that* in the first sentence and the phrases *I think* and *seem to* in the second sentence all imply that the writer is open to the possibility of being wrong. In order to see this difference in certainty, notice how the first two sentences would read if these phrases were removed: *With respect to alcohol consumption, she resembles her father in a tendency to overindulge.* And: *When it comes to drinking, she takes after her dad. They both overdo it.* The sentences now indicate greater certainty on the writer's part.

A further difference is in what each sentence implies about the writers' attitudes. The first two sentences are fairly neutral. In each case, the writer is cautious about attributing an alcohol problem to the girl and her father, and no judgment is offered. In contrast, the use of the derogatory term *drunk* in the third sentence conveys a more negative appraisal. The writer clearly disapproves. (Although not strictly a matter of diction, the brevity and definitiveness of the third sentence also contribute to its negative tone.)

Following are some of the dimensions on which a writer's diction can be analyzed.

First, some words and phrases are more formal than others, as illustrated by the following sentences:

> The prince bestowed a fine ring upon his servant.

> The prince gave his servant a fine ring.

Second, some words and phrases are more specific than others, as illustrated by the following references to the same individual:

> He was born in New Haven, Connecticut.

> He was born in New England.

> He was born up north somewhere.

Third, some words and phrases are more direct than others, as illustrated by the following sentences:

> She died last year.

> She passed away last year.

> She left us last year.

Fourth, in a particular context, the meanings of some words and phrases will be clearer than others, as illustrated by the following sentences (arranged in order of decreasing clarity):

> He spent most of New Year's Day attempting to understand some of the recent events in his life.

> He spent most of New Year's Day attempting to process some of the recent happenings.

> He spent most of New Year's Day attempting to deal with things.

Fifth, in a particular context, some words and phrases will be relatively fresh, whereas others will sound more clichéd, as illustrated by the following:

> The child is so thin. She's as light as a breath.

> The child is so thin. She's as light as a feather.

> The child is so thin. She's as thin as a rail.

Sixth, some words and phrases are literal, whereas others are more figurative, as can be seen in the following examples (arranged in order of increasingly figurative usage):

> The boy had a timid look.

> The boy had a mousy look.

> The boy had a frightened rodent look in his eyes.

> The boy had a mousetrap-closing-on-me look in his feral eyes.

Seventh, some words are more or less concrete, whereas others are abstract, as illustrated by the following:

> Just then, an orange cat padded out from behind the forsythia bush.

> Just then, a creature padded out from behind the bush.

> Just then, something came out from behind the bush.

Eighth, in a particular context, some words will be more or less appropriate in emphasis, whereas others will be more hyperbolic, as in the following:

> Amidst smoke, flames, and a loud roar, the rocket climbed up into the sky.

> Amidst smoke, flames, and a deafening roar, the rocket blasted up into the sky.

Finally, some words are more conventional, whereas others represent jargon, colloquialisms, or slang.

> Owing to his difficult childhood, he became a criminal.

> Owing to his difficult childhood, he became a crook.

> Owing to his difficult childhood, he became a total thug.

As you can see from each of the examples in this section, a writer's diction will have an influence on the clarity and persuasiveness of his or her arguments. Diction that is clear and persuasive in one context may be confusing and unappealing in another.

Syntax

Rhetorical analysis includes attention to **syntax**, or the order of words in a sentence. The sentences that a writer uses will vary in length, complexity, and internal structure. Across sentences there will be a greater or lesser extent of grammatical variety. These differences in syntax contribute to the style and, in many cases, the meaning of the sentences.

Among the many syntactic rules governing English sentences, an important stylistic distinction can be made between active and passive voice, as illustrated by the following pair of sentences:

> The dog smashed the vase. (active voice)

> The vase was smashed by the dog. (passive voice)

These sentences both convey the same meaning and consist of almost the same words. However, the first sentence is written in active voice, whereas the second sentence reflects passive voice. **Active voice** means that the subject *carries out the action* indicated by the verb. **Passive voice** means that the subject *is the recipient of the action* indicated by the verb. In the first sentence, the subject is *The dog*, whereas in the second sentence, the subject is *The vase*. Because the dog carries out the action of smashing the vase, the first sentence reflects active voice. Because the vase is the recipient of the action of being smashed, the second sentence reflects passive voice.

Although writers are often encouraged to use active rather than passive voice, some authorities on style hold that passive voice is useful when the recipient of the action is of greater importance than whatever carried out the action. For example, consider the following questions:

> What was that noise?

> I cannot find my priceless seventeenth century Ming vase. Do you know where it is?

The answer to the first question should be expressed in active voice (*The dog smashed the vase.*). However, the answer to the second question should be expressed in passive voice (*The vase was smashed by the dog.*), because the vase and its destruction are much more important at the moment than the fact that a dog (as opposed to some other creature) was responsible for smashing it.

Writers vary their syntax in order to keep their writing more interesting to the reader. For example, compare the following descriptions of the same event:

> I got into my car this morning. I drove to school. I saw a peacock on the way to school. I saw the peacock standing on the corner of Larchmont Avenue. I pulled over to look at it for a moment. I guess it was someone's pet.

> This morning I got into my car and drove to school. On the way I saw a peacock standing on the corner of Larchmont Avenue. I pulled over to look at it for a moment. It was someone's pet, I guess.

Both passages recount the same event using almost exactly the same words. However, by varying the syntax, the second passage sounds more natural and interesting than the first one, and is more likely to hold the reader's attention. The contribution of syntax to style is illustrated in this third rendition of the peacock incident:

> Got into the car this morning, drove to school. Saw a peacock on the way. A peacock. Standing on the corner of Larchmont Avenue. Pulled over to look at it for a moment. Someone's pet, I guess. A peacock.

In this passage, the writer suspends some of the rules of syntax that apply in formal writing. As you can see, the result is very different stylistically from the first two versions of the passage. As syntactic structures become more complex, rhetorical analysis depends increasingly on determining what the writer is saying and how the different parts of a sentence contribute to the overall meaning. For example, consider the following, relatively elaborated sentence:

> Yesterday evening, the tiger that had terrorized the village last year made a reappearance, according to an elderly villager who commented that he had been sitting on his porch when he heard the tiger's distinctive, terrifying growl, prompting him to rush inside and phone the authorities.

From this sentence, the reader can glean several facts: (1) The village had been terrorized by a tiger during the previous year. (2) An elderly man reported that the tiger had been in the village on the previous evening. (3) The man had been sleeping when he heard the tiger. (4) The man phoned the authorities to say that he had heard a tiger.

Point of View

Rhetorical analysis includes attention to **point of view**, the perspective through which information is conveyed. The three main points of view are first person, second person, and third person.

First person point of view conveys information from the author's or narrator's own perspective. Pronouns such as *I* and *me* are used. In literature, the *I* who tells the story is the narrator, and the narrative voice may be that of the author or a fictional character. In nonfiction writing, the *I* is the author, as illustrated in the following sentence:

> I have found that rugby is more popular in southern France than in the north.

Second person point of view conveys information from the reader's perspective. Pronouns such as *you* are used, as in the following example:

> When you visit France, you find that rugby is more popular in the south than it is in the north.

Third person point of view conveys information without explicitly mentioning the author, narrator, or reader. Information is conveyed as if by an unseen observer through pronouns such as *he*, *she*, *it*, and *they*. For example:

> When people visit France, they find that rugby is more popular in the south than it is in the north.

Each point of view allows the writer to present a different extent of detail and topical emphasis. A writer's style is defined in part by the particular point of view, or mix of points of view, that he or she uses. Although mixing is common in a piece of writing, one point of view will often predominate.

Writing from an exclusively or predominately second person point of view is uncommon, owing in part to the potential ambiguity in who is being referred to in the writing. This ambiguity is illustrated by the following passage:

> True enough, you will quarrel with your spouse once you are married, but you will also appreciate the support of this special person who knows you best and loves you most, and so in the end you will find that the advantages of marriage far outweigh the disadvantages.

The persuasiveness of this passage is limited by uncertainty as to whether *you* refers to the individual reader, all readers, or everyone in society. The writer appears to be addressing everyone, but is it credible that everyone will have the sort of experience described in the passage? Conceivably, the reader is already married and has (1) never quarreled with his or her spouse, or (2) quarreled with the spouse so frequently that he or she has concluded that the disadvantages of marriage far outweigh the advantages. At the very least, the reader may know of others who would consider marriage a primarily disadvantageous arrangement, in which case it is unclear exactly who *you* is intended to be.

When a writer is describing something that he or she has done, thought, or felt, first person point of view may be most appropriate. However, first person is not preferable to third person in every situation. For one thing, constant use of pronouns such as *I* and *me* may seem intrusive and unnecessary to readers. When describing a tribal culture, for example, an anthropologist who has lived among the tribe need not constantly say *I saw* this and *I heard* that. Rather, the anthropologist can simply describe what he or she saw and heard using third person point of view, because the reader will understand that in each case the anthropologist was the observer. In such cases, third person writing will predominate, and first person may be used sparingly.

In some cases, first person is actually prohibited in scientific writing, under the assumption that science is an objective activity, and that scientific principles and findings exist independently of the scientific enterprise. At the same time, because many scholars agree that the personal biases of scientists cannot be completely expunged from scientific activity, and because it is individual scientists who engage in such activities, first person is sometimes accepted or even encouraged in scientific writing. To illustrate the relative merits of third and first person writing in science, consider the following procedural descriptions:

> The wafer was immersed in BOE and then rinsed with deionized water.

> I immersed the wafer in BOE and then rinsed it with deionized water.

The third person phrasing in the first sentence contributes to a sense of *objectivity*, but because this sentence reflects passive voice, it is not clear to the reader who immersed and rinsed the wafer (or whether it was even the same person in each case). In the second sentence, first person phrasing makes it clearer that one person, the writer, carried out both procedures. Note that the point of view that predominates in a piece of writing is often determined by editorial policy rather than the writer's own preference.

UNDERSTANDING OF AUDIENCE, PURPOSE, AND TONE

Audience

Audience refers to the person or people who are likely to read a piece of writing. Writers must consider their audience when making decisions about the style, length, and informativeness of what they write. Both the expertise and the interests of the audience will be relevant. For example, a description of a particular military battle will be very different depending on whether it is written for a group of army officers versus the general public versus the bereaved spouse of a soldier who committed an act of heroism during the battle. The description of the battle written for army officers is likely to be highly detailed, neutral in tone, and focused on specific military issues. The diction will probably be formal and replete with technical terms. The following passage might be part of such a description:

> Armed with handguns and a stolen M14, eight hostiles then proceeded north toward a disabled AMX-30 approximately one half klick from 3rd Platoon flank. Hostiles approached 3rd Platoon with weapons drawn. SFC Jones initially detected their advance and opened fire at once while simultaneously ordering nearby subordinates to take cover.

The description of the battle written for the general public (e.g., in the form of a magazine or newspaper article) will be less formal and technical than the description written for army officers. The syntax will not be overly complicated, and the choice of details as well as the diction will probably be intended to evoke some sort of emotional response among readers. Following is a passage that might be found in such a description:

> The insurgents were a rag-tag bunch, armed with nothing more than handguns and a rifle scavenged from a dead soldier. Moving quietly, they crept toward a burned-out tank only 300 yards from one side of the platoon where Sergeant Ron Jones was chatting with subordinates. Sergeant Jones was the first to spot the enemy. As the insurgents advanced on the platoon, brandishing their weapons, Jones wheeled and opened fire while shouting orders to the other men.

The description of the battle written for a bereaved spouse will be formal but not at all technical, with very carefully managed diction. The description will be vague on some points but more specific about details that convey the fallen soldier's heroism and service to his country.

> Sergeant First Class Jones was engaged in conversation with several of his men when eight insurgents approached them with the intention of attacking the platoon. Sergeant Jones was the first to detect their approach and opened fire while instructing his men to take cover. Sergeant Jones displayed quick thinking and admirable courage by opening fire immediately rather than taking cover himself. Moreover, Sergeant Jones' leadership skills and great concern for his men were evident in the fact that he was able to request that they seek cover while he simultaneously acted to protect them as well as the rest of the platoon.

Purpose

An author's **purpose** for writing is inextricably linked to his or her intended audience. The description of a military battle written for army officers is most likely to be created for the purpose of providing information, presenting an analysis, or advocating a theory, if not some combination of the three. A description of the battle written for the general public might also be written in order to inform or analyze, but it may serve some other purpose as well. Articles, blogs, essays, and works of fiction written for the general public are also meant to entertain, to stimulate public debate about important issues, to spark moral outrage, and so on. In contrast, a description of the battle presented to the bereaved spouse of a heroic soldier will have been written solely to inform the spouse of the soldier's heroism and subsequent demise.

Different types of writing can be defined according to their purpose. For example, **expository writing** can be defined as writing intended to describe or explain a topic. In brief, the purpose of expository writing is to inform the reader about something.

Various kinds of expository writing can be further distinguished based on their specific purposes. For example, the writer may wish to teach the reader how to do something (e.g., cook, do algebra, play guitar). The writer may wish to describe a phenomenon (e.g., photosynthesis, road rage, the most recent presidential election), compare different entities (e.g., sports teams, cities, nocturnal predators), or describe cause–effect relationships.

Expository writing can be evaluated in terms of its accuracy, completeness, and often persuasiveness (even if the purpose of the writing is not to persuade the reader to act or think in a certain way). Other types of writing that are sometimes distinguished from expository forms include narrative and persuasive writing, each of which tends to reflect a somewhat different purpose.

The purpose of **narrative writing** is to relate a story. Rhetorical analysis of narratives focuses on how writers create various kinds of effects on readers. In such analyses, the accuracy or truthfulness of the writing will not usually be evaluated (although the accuracy with which a narrative writer presents a technical description may be praised, just as inaccuracies that are unintended might be criticized as distractions to the effects that the writer intends to create). Typically, the persuasiveness of narrative writing is only evaluated in terms of how much the reader has been caught up in the story and is influenced by its rhetorical devices.

The purpose of **persuasive writing** is to convince the reader of something. In practice, the distinction between expository and persuasive writing is not always clear cut. For example, the scientist who is describing a new species is not just attempting to inform readers about a topic but also to persuade them of the accuracy of his or her distinctions. At the same time, the essayist who is advocating education reform may not just be attempting to persuade readers regarding his or her view, but also to provide them with details necessary for making an informed judgment. In each case, both the accuracy and the persuasiveness of the writer can be evaluated.

Tone

A writer's attitude is referred to as his or her **tone**. Tone can be inferred from the writer's diction, phrasing, choice of content, and stated opinions. For example, compare the following two passages:

> Smith's book is a highly appealing introduction to the art of baking bread. It contains some tidbits about the history of bread and the chemistry of baking, as well as numerous recipes for the breads that most people—including yours truly—dearly love. I tried out several of these recipes myself, and each time the results were fantastic!

> Smith's book is an interesting introduction to the art of baking bread. It contains information about the history of bread and the chemistry of baking, as well as numerous recipes for the breads that most people love. I tried out several of these recipes myself and found them easy to understand.

The tone of the first passage is positive and enthusiastic. This is evident from word choice (e.g., *highly appealing*) as well as from overt statements of praise (e.g., *the results were fantastic*). In contrast, the tone of the second passage is considerably less enthusiastic. Although some praise is offered, it is much fainter than that of the first passage (e.g., the book is described as *interesting* rather than *highly appealing*). The absence of certain information in the second passage is also telling. The writer of the second passage refers to breads that most people love, without indicating whether he or she is one of those people. In addition, the writer refers to how easy it is to understand the recipes, without noting whether the results were appealing. There are some hints here—not proof, but just some hints—that the writer of the second passage does not particularly like the book or its recipes.

In some cases, the tone of a passage will be at odds with its literal meaning. For example, **irony** can be detected when the literal meaning of a passage contradicts what must be the intended meaning. Consider the father's terse comment in the following passage:

> "Dad," said the little girl, "I accidentally spilled a whole glass of milk on your keyboard."

> "Great," he replied.

The fact that the father's reply was ironic is suggested by the obvious discrepancy between the situation (a possibly ruined keyboard) and the literal meaning of the father's comment. In the absence of any other information about the father, we can assume that he probably does not think it is great to have a whole glass of milk spilled on his keyboard. Thus, we infer that his comment was ironic. What he intended to say is that the situation is *not* great.

Among the many uses of irony is **satire**, a form of criticism in which people or practices are held up to ridicule. For example, in order to criticize the British treatment of the Irish poor during the eighteenth century, Jonathan Swift wrote an essay known as *A Modest Proposal* in which he suggested that the Irish would improve their economic situation by selling their children as food to the upper class British. Swift did not actually believe that the Irish should do so. Rather, as Swift's essay progresses, one realizes that he wished to call attention to the mistreatment of the Irish. After describing the plight of the Irish poor in serious and poignant terms, Swift suddenly launches into a startlingly cheerful description of this proposal:

> I have been assured by a very knowing American of my acquaintance in London, that a young healthy child well nursed is at a year old a most delicious, nourishing, and wholesome food, whether stewed, roasted, baked, or boiled; and I make no doubt that it will equally serve in a fricasie, or a ragout.

The outrageousness of the suggestion, combined with the level of detail concerning preparation (*stewed, roasted. . . .*), are among the clues that Swift's tone was satirical rather than literal.

Tone is related to purpose and audience. In *A Modest Proposal*, Swift was speaking to British citizens of his day, including the wealthy and powerful, in order to effect a change in their attitudes. Now consider again the description of a particular military battle written for different audiences. The tone of the description written for army officers is likely to be serious. In addition, the writer will either be neutral or openly favor some analytical perspective. The tone of the description written for a bereaved spouse will be equally serious, and admiration and gratitude for the soldier's heroism will be clearly conveyed. As for descriptions written for the general public, many kinds of tone are possible. The writer may be neutral, or the writer may choose to take a stand for or against some aspect of the military situation, if not military action more generally. The writer may be primarily concerned with expressing a particular moral perspective or emotional state (e.g., outrage) or the writer's concern may be more intellectual and focus on developing an idea.

UNDERSTANDING OF RHETORIC

Rhetoric refers to the use of language in an effective and persuasive way. Writers always hope to make an impact on their readers. Generally speaking, the goal of **persuasion** is to effect some sort of change in the reader.

Writers seek to change their readers in many different ways. In some cases, the writer wishes to change the reader's present or future behavior, as illustrated by the following sentence:

> In light of the many adverse health effects of smoking, not to mention the actual cost of cigarettes and other nicotine-delivery products, you owe it to yourself not to smoke— or if you do smoke, to give up the habit as soon as possible.

In some cases, the writer may wish to change the reader's attitudes about an issue of present or future importance. For example:

> John Doe may have won the last election by a landslide, but he has yet to fulfill any of his campaign promises, and his public statements on domestic spending, tax reform,

and environmental conservation reveal a politician who will say anything to please the audience before him. Think carefully before deciding who to vote for in the next election.

In some cases, the writer may wish to change the reader's views about an event from the past, as in the example of an *exposé* of a widely respected historical figure in which the writer places great emphasis on personal and professional flaws, or the example of a critic who argues that a particular work of art from the past deserves greater or lesser admiration than it currently receives.

In still other cases, the writer may simply wish to persuade the reader to feel a certain way for a moment—to remember, to honor, or perhaps even to scorn.

Traditionally, rhetorical effects were said to be produced by appealing to the reader's intellect, emotions, and/or beliefs about the writer's motives and character. The distinction between these three sources of rhetorical effects emphasizes the fact that writers have many tools for creating such effects.

Rhetorical Devices

A **rhetorical device** consists of anything that a writer does to increase the persuasiveness of a statement or passage. Scholars have distinguished among dozens of different rhetorical devices, many of which are ultimately a matter of diction (i.e., word choice).

Among the rhetorical devices that have not yet been discussed here, one of the most powerful and frequently used is a manipulation of syntax known as parallelism. **Parallelism** refers to any grammatical structure that balances similar elements. These elements could be virtually any part of speech, component of a sentence, or section of a passage. One of the simplest yet most effective examples of parallelism is G. K. Chesterton's pithy remark about change:

> New roads; new ruts.

Here the close similarity of the two nouns (*roads* and *ruts*) increases the impact of the remark, which seems to mean that as we embark on new activities in our lives (thereby breaking out of old ruts), we have a tendency to slip once again into routines (i.e., new ruts).

Several kinds of parallelism are illustrated by the following well-known passage from the U.S. Declaration of Independence:

> We hold these Truths to be self-evident, that all Men are created equal, that they are endowed by their Creator with certain unalienable Rights, that among these are Life, Liberty and the pursuit of Happiness.

Here there is a parallelism across three of the clauses (each marked by the word *that*), and in the final clause, there is a rough parallelism across the three abstract nouns (*Life, Liberty and the pursuit of Happiness*).

This excerpt from the Declaration of Independence also illustrates another rhetorical device, called **tricolon** or *the rule of three*, which holds that lists tend to be most effective when they contain three items. Not all lists of three are persuasive, however, and in some cases shorter or longer lists can be quite powerful, as in the following excerpt from John F. Kennedy's Inaugural Address:

> Let every nation know, whether it wishes us well or ill, that we shall pay any price, bear any burden, meet any hardship, support any friend, oppose any foe to assure the survival and the success of liberty.

In Kennedy's statement, the underlying message of American determination is conveyed in part by the repeated parallelism across clauses that are very similar in rhythm. The same message of strength is conveyed by the unadorned repetition of Julius Caesar's famous phrase, "I came, I saw, I conquered."

Parallelism can be carried out by directly balancing elements or by inverting them, as in this famous appeal that Kennedy made later in his address:

> Ask not what your country can do for you—ask what you can do for your country.

The sudden inversion in this statement is surprising the first time it is encountered, and the grammatical twist mirrors Kennedy's appeal for citizens to change the way they think about their relationship to their country.

Parallelism is sometimes used across rather than within sentences. Kennedy makes use of this device several times in his Inaugural Address, as does Martin Luther King in his famous "I Have a Dream" speech at the Lincoln Memorial. In this speech, which is quite powerful even in written form, King uses the refrain "I have a dream" to create these and other parallel sentences:

> I have a dream that one day this nation will rise up and live out the true meaning of its creed: "We hold these truths to be self-evident, that all men are created equal."

> I have a dream that one day on the red hills of Georgia, the sons of former slaves and the sons of former slave owners will be able to sit down together at the table of brotherhood.

> I have a dream that one day even the state of Mississippi, a state sweltering with the heat of injustice, sweltering with the heat of oppression, will be transformed into an oasis of freedom and justice. . . ."

Notice that several of King's individual sentences in this excerpt contain parallelisms. For example, the close similarity of elements in *the sons of former slaves and the sons of former slave owners* subtly reinforces King's message that these groups of individuals are brothers. The repetition of the *sweltering with the heat* phrases mirrors the heaviness of the injustice and oppression King is referring to. Within the same sentence, a further parallelism is introduced between the reference to sweltering and the image of an oasis.

This excerpt from King's speech illustrates two important points about parallelism. First, many instances of parallelism incorporate other rhetorical devices. One example discussed already is repetition. Another example is illustrated by the next line in King's speech:

> I have a dream that my four little children will one day live in a nation where they will not be judged by the color of their skin but by the content of their character.

If you read this sentence out loud or listen to a recording of Dr. King, you can hear the impact of the repeated hard *c* sounds in the parallelism at the end of the line. Repetition of sounds in this way is referred to as **alliteration**. Although alliteration is a rhetorical device of great importance in spoken language, it creates rhetorical effects in written text as well when we can "hear" the sounds as we read.

The excerpt from King's speech also illustrates that parallelism, even when relied on heavily, is not the only rhetorical device that will be used by a skilled communicator. For example, his quotation from the U.S. Declaration of Independence (*We hold these truths to be self-evident*) represents an appeal to authority, a common rhetorical device. Although in some cases it will be undesirable to appeal to authority rather than provide evidence, here the practice is effective given that the Declaration of Independence is familiar to Americans and embodies what most citizens consider to be the country's most cherished ideals. Here, King exhorts the audience to live up to the particular ideals reflected in the quotation.

Another set of widely used rhetorical devices that King makes effective use of in this excerpt is **figurative language**. The *red hills* of Georgia is not just a physical description and reference to a particular region of Georgia, but also a subtle allusion to blood that has been spilled. Metaphorical images such as a table of brotherhood or an oasis of freedom and justice contribute to the persuasiveness of King's message by capturing audience interest through their profound appeal.

Rhetorical Analysis

Rhetorical analysis includes the ability to recognize and evaluate rhetorical effects in a piece of writing. For example, consider the organization and diction of the following two passages:

> Reverend King was an eloquent and riveting speaker. Whether delivering a sermon to a small congregation or a speech to the entire nation, his words touched every heart with their passionate commitment to the possibility of human progress and the eventual brotherhood and sisterhood of all. These words continue to inspire people around the world with their powerful message of hope.

> Reverend King's speeches were eloquent and smooth. These words continue to inspire people with their message. Whether giving a sermon or some other public address, his speeches impacted listeners and hung the moon in terms of their commitment to human progress and equality.

The purpose of each passage is the same—to praise King's oratorical prowess—but the diction is more effective in the first passage than in the second one. For example, consider the word *riveting*. To *rivet* something means to drive a mechanical fastening device into it in order to hold it firmly in place. Thus, the word *riveting* in the first passage connotes an audience that has been rendered motionless, held in place by the power of King's words. Another example of an effective rhetorical device that distinguishes the first passage is the parallelism of *delivering a sermon to a small congregation or a speech to the entire nation*. The contrast here is more specific and interesting than the corresponding parallelism in the second passage.

In contrast, the second passage exhibits a number of rhetorical weaknesses. In terms of organization, the second sentence would be more effective if it were located at the end of the passage (as in the first passage). There are also at least four problems with the diction of the second passage.

First, the combination of *eloquent and smooth* in the second passage seems redundant, as eloquence would be expected to include an element of smoothness. Second, the phrase *Whether giving a sermon or a major speech* is flat. Compare this phrase to the more vivid diction of the first passage (*Whether delivering a sermon to a small congregation or a speech to the entire nation . . .*). Third, the phrase *impacted listeners* is awkward and vague. Fourth, the phrase *hung the moon* is clichéd, and its informality clashes with the more abstract and formal phrase that follows.

HOW TO APPROACH RHETORICAL ANALYSIS QUESTIONS

Types of Questions

Most of the questions in the Rhetorical Analysis section will be organized around passages. Usually there will be three to five questions per passage. These passages may concern virtually any topic. Each passage may represent an introduction or a conclusion, or it may represent the body of a piece of writing. Some of the passages will be factual, whereas others will be theoretical or speculative. Many of the passages will be expository, whereas others will primarily attempt to persuade the reader to adopt a particular point of view.

Each question in the Rhetorical Analysis section will ask you to do one of the following:

- Choose the best synonym for a word in a sentence.
- Choose the best description of a word's purpose in a sentence.
- Choose the best description of a sentence's purpose in the passage.
- Choose the best summary of a sentence's meaning in the passage.
- Choose the reordering of sentences that most improves the passage's coherence.
- Choose the best description of the author's primary purpose in writing the passage.
- Choose the best summary of the passage.
- Choose the best summary of the organization of the passage.

The directions you can expect to see for the Rhetorical Analysis section are reproduced here from the CLEP College Composition/College Composition Modular Examination Guide:

> The following questions test your ability to analyze writing. Some questions refer to passages, while other questions are self-contained. For each question, choose the best answer.

Sample Questions

The questions draw upon the skills discussed throughout this section. The format of the questions closely matches what you will find in the Rhetorical Analysis section of the CLEP College Composition and College Composition Modular exams. That is, the questions pertaining to passages are organized into sets of roughly three to five questions each. The sentences within each passage are numbered, so that they can be easily located. Five answer options are given for each question. You are asked to choose the best option.

We will work through the first set of questions together, once you have read the following passage.

(1) Michelangelo di Lodovico Buonarroti Simoni, commonly known as Michelangelo, was born in March of 1475 in the small village of Caprese, roughly 100 kilometers east of Florence. (2) Michelangelo's father was an important official with ties to the ruling Medici family, but the fame that Michelangelo achieved in his lifetime outstripped that of his father. (3) Centuries after Michelangelo's death, many still consider him to be the greatest painter and sculptor who ever lived. (4) By the age of 15, Michelangelo was already an accomplished artist and a favorite of Florence's leading citizens; by 30 he was the most prominent and sought-after artist in Europe. (5) At the time of his death in 1564, his most famous works, including the Pietá, the statue of David, and the ceiling of the Sistine Chapel, had already achieved their enduring and highly influential position in the canon of Western art.

Now consider the following question, which pertains to the purpose of one part of a sentence:

Which of the following best describes the main purpose of the underlined portion of sentence 1 (reproduced below)?

Michelangelo di Lodovico Buonarroti Simoni, commonly known as Michelangelo, was born in March of 1475 in the small village of Caprese.

(A) To show that people born in the fifteenth century often went by one name
(B) To make sure that the reader knows to whom the full name refers
(C) To create a short version of Michelangelo's full name for use in the passage
(D) To emphasize that Michelangelo can be referred to by more than one name
(E) To draw a contrast between formal and informal modes of address

As you read through the five options, you should notice that option A can be ruled out right away, because the passage does not state anything about how people born in the fifteenth century were named.

Option B may seem like the best answer, but for any question you should be sure to read through each of the options before making a decision.

Although option C is not entirely inaccurate, it is not the best answer. The writer did not "create" a short version of Michelangelo's name. Rather, the writer simply used the conventional name for the artist. Thus, you can rule out option C.

Regarding option D, although it is true that Michelangelo can be referred to by more than one name, the first sentence of the passage does not seem to emphasize this point. In fact, most people can be referred to by more than one name. Thus, you can rule out option D.

Finally, option E can be ruled out because the sentence does not concern the contrast between formal and informal modes of address.

It should be clear now that option B is the best answer. Sentence 1 serves an introductory function in the passage. By alerting the reader that the long name at the outset refers to Michelangelo, the writer helps ensure that the reader knows who the passage is about. This illustrates how a writer considers his or her audience when deciding on the level of informativeness.

Now consider a question about word meaning:

In context, the word *outstripped* in sentence 2 most nearly means

- (A) matched.
- (B) enhanced.
- (C) exceeded.
- (D) contradicted.
- (E) fell short of.

Option A can be ruled out because Michelangelo's father is not mentioned elsewhere in the passage, but the fame of Michelangelo himself is described in the next sentence. Option B is incorrect too, for essentially the same reason. Option D can be ruled out on the grounds of incoherence—one person's fame cannot be said to *contradict* someone else's. Option E is clearly incorrect because Michelangelo is depicted as more famous than his father. Option C is clearly the best answer. In this sentence, the transition word *but* indicates that something is about to be said that contrasts with the first part of the sentence, which includes reference to the importance of Michelangelo's father. The next sentence confirms that the contrast pertains to the extent of fame.

The next question pertains to the purpose of a particular word:

What is the purpose of the word *still* in sentence 3?

- (A) To emphasize that the fame Michelangelo achieved in his lifetime endured over time
- (B) To indicate that Michelangelo remains famous in spite of questions about his skill
- (C) To illustrate the fact that for geniuses like Michelangelo fame will be enduring
- (D) To question whether Michelangelo deserves the extent of fame he has achieved
- (E) To highlight the fact that opinions about Michelangelo have never changed

Given that the preceding sentence made reference to the fame that Michelangelo achieved in his lifetime, option A appears to be the best answer. Option B can certainly be ruled out, because the passage contains no references to questions about Michelangelo's skill. Likewise, options C, D, and E can be ruled out, because each one pertains to themes that are not mentioned in the passage. Although Michelangelo's biography may illustrate that the fame of geniuses is enduring, this is not a theme that the writer explores, and thus it does not reflect the purpose of the word *still* in sentence 3.

The next question pertains to organization:

Which option is the best choice to do with sentence 4?

    (A) Leave it where it is.
    (B) Relocate it after sentence 5.
    (C) Relocate it before sentence 2.
    (D) Relocate it before sentence 3.
    (E) Relocate it before sentence 1.

Because the organization of this passage is roughly chronological, sentence 4 seems out of place, and thus option A is incorrect. The chronology of the passage would not be improved through implementing either options B, C, or E. Option D is the best answer. By switching the order of sentences 3 and 4, the chronology of the passage becomes clearer.

Finally, here is a question about the writer's purpose:

Which of the following best summarizes the author's likely purpose in writing this passage?

    (A) To illustrate how Michelangelo's father influenced his art
    (B) To describe the influence of Michelangelo on society
    (C) To provide a brief introduction to the life of Michelangelo
    (D) To show why Michelangelo is held in such great esteem
    (E) To argue that Michelangelo's reputation is well-deserved

Here, option C is the best answer, because throughout the chronology of the passage the writer introduces some of the details of Michelangelo's biography. Options A, B, D, and E represent themes that are at most barely alluded to in the passage.

Now take a look at the following passage:

> (1) Fishermen love a challenge. (2) The northern pike, a popular species that even professional fishermen call a "prize fish," is one of those more challenging fish that makes a fly-fishing experience worthwhile. (3) Northern pike are rough fighters once they are hooked, often taking refuge in deep water and escaping inexperienced anglers. (4) Experienced fishermen usually catch them.

First, here is an organizational question:

Which of the following best describes the organization of the passage?

    (A) A cause–effect relationship is explored with great specificity.
    (B) Information is presented in order of decreasing importance.
    (C) Different approaches are compared and contrasted.
    (D) A general theme is illustrated by increasingly specific details.
    (E) A chronological sequence of events is described.

Options A, B, C, and E do not reflect the organization of the passage. Option D is best, because the general theme of sentence 1 is illustrated by specific details concerning the popularity of northern pike among fishermen, and then the specific challenges that these fish pose.

The next question pertains to the purpose of one particular word:

What purpose is served by the word *even* in sentence 2?

    (A) It provides evidence of the challenges presented by northern pike.
    (B) It maximizes the importance of attempting to fish for northern pike.
    (C) It helps emphasize the widespread popularity of the northern pike.
    (D) It stresses the differences between northern pike and other fish.
    (E) It calls attention to the discernment of professional fishermen.

Since the popularity of northern pike is already mentioned in this passage, the word *even* serves to mark the importance of their popularity among an especially expert or discriminating group—fishermen. Thus, option C is the correct answer. The other options do not reflect a purpose that is directly served by use of *even* in this context.

Here is a question about word meaning:

The word *anglers* in sentence 3 seems to refer to

    (A) northern pike.
    (B) fishermen.
    (C) fly-fishing rods.
    (D) observers.
    (E) fishing gear.

The preceding context, and the reference to fishermen in sentence 4, make it clear that *anglers* is roughly synonymous with *fishermen*, and thus option B is the correct answer.

The next question tests your transitional word skills:

If sentences 3 and 4 were combined, which of the following transition words or phrases would be most suitable to use at the beginning of what is now sentence 4?

    (A) In spite of
    (B) It goes without saying that
    (C) Although
    (D) And
    (E) In contrast

Option A is incorrect because the result would be ungrammatical. Although option B could be used to create a grammatically well-formed sentence, the meaning of the sentence would be problematic. The fact that experienced fishermen would usually catch the northern pike is not so obvious from the passage that it goes without saying. Option D is incorrect because it does not support the intended contrast. Option E would create a sentence that does not make sense. Thus, option C is the best answer.

Finally, this question is about what can be inferred from the author's tone:

Which of the following best characterizes the author's attitude toward northern pike?

    (A) Indifferent
    (B) Alarmed
    (C) Dismissive
    (D) Enthusiastic
    (E) Ambiguous

Option D is the best answer, in light of the author's diction in several places.

THE ESSAYS

PURPOSE OF THE CLEP COLLEGE COMPOSITION EXAMINATION AND THE COLLEGE COMPOSITION MODULAR EXAMINATION

The College Board developed the new CLEP College Composition Examination, with Modular option, so that people could receive college credit for freshman composition. The new College Composition examination has two parts: a multiple-choice section and an essay section. The multiple-choice section tests general writing skills, including rhetorical analysis (25%), use of sources (25%), revision (40%), and the conventions of standard written English (10%). The essay section asks candidates taking the test to apply these writing skills by producing two timed essays. The first essay asks candidates to take a position in regard to a specific topic. The second essay also asks candidates to take a position in regard to a specific topic, but includes excerpts (with bibliographic information) from two sources. In the second essay, candidates are asked to use the sources in their composition. The essays are then each scored by college faculty from across the nation using a scoring guide provided by CLEP. The two essay scores are combined into one, which is then weighted equally with the multiple-choice section to produce one weighted score between 20 and 80 (CLEP does not report the individual scores on the two sections, only the one weighted score).

In the CLEP College Composition Modular examination, individual colleges have more control over the essay portion of the exam. Colleges can design their own essay portion of the exam, as well as administer and/or score the essay portion themselves. This allows colleges to tailor the essay portion of the exam to better suit the needs of their program. The multiple-choice section, which CLEP scores, remains the same, as well as the percentages that each skill is weighted. **If you are taking the CLEP College Composition examination to receive college credit at a particular college, make sure you check with the college to see if they have chosen the Modular option**. If so, the college itself is the best source for how to prepare for the essay portion of the exam. Access the college's website to find contact information for the director of the freshman composition program, or simply call the college's main number and ask to be directed to someone who can speak about CLEP exams accepted by the college for credit.

STRUCTURE AND SCORING OF THE ESSAY PORTION OF THE COLLEGE COMPOSITION EXAMINATION

The College Board employs a national pool of experienced college faculty to score the essay portion of the CLEP exam. Each of the two timed essays has its own scoring guide which scorers use to assess the quality of each essay. Each essay is scored by two people to provide one combined score between 0 and 6, with 6 being the highest. The scoring guide for the first essay is similar to the scoring guide for the second essay, with the main difference being that the second scoring guide takes into account the use of sources in the composition of the essay.

A careful analysis of the two scoring guides allows candidates to recognize what constitutes a good essay, as well as what writing skills they need to brush up on in order to write a successful response. The scoring guide for the first essay places great emphasis on the development of ideas, or arguments, in the essay, specifically in regard to reasons, examples, and/or details. The scoring guide for the second essay also places great emphasis on the development of a position using reasons, examples, and/or details for support, but adds the use of the sources. The differences between a score of 6 and a score of 4 in terms of these criteria is only one of degree, as indicated by the terms *effectively* and *insightfully* for a score of 6, *consistently* and *appropriately* for a score of 5, and *competently* and *adequately* for a score of 4. The last three points of emphasis for each scoring guide address focus and organization, vocabulary and sentence variety, and grammar and usage. **It is important to note that even the highest score, 6, allows for some errors in grammar and usage**.

According to the CLEP scoring guide for the first essay, the highest score possible is a 6. Typically, an essay scoring a 6 addresses the topic with a clear and thought-provoking position, or **thesis statement**, as well as good supporting evidence in the form of examples and reasons that fit the position. In addition to this basic argument structure, an essay scoring a 6 depicts writing that is focused, organized, and contains a good vocabulary and sentence variety. Although the essay may have a few minor errors, overall an essay scoring a 6 demonstrates a good command of grammar and usage. Essays that score a 5 or 4 contain the same criteria, but with less and less skill in each area. With a score of 3, essays begin to show a lack of skill in these areas, with essays scoring a 2 or 1 showing a serious lack of ability in one or more areas. A score of 0 is reserved for responses that do not even attempt to address the writing task.

The CLEP scoring guide for the second essay is identical to the one for the first essay, except that it includes criteria relating to the use of sources. Typically, an essay scoring a 6 does everything a "6" essay does in the first scoring guide, but also cites the sources CLEP provides in such a way as to support the position. In effect, the author uses the sources as supporting evidence and/or examples for his or her thesis, or position statement. Again, scores of 5 or 4 contain the previous features, but with diminishing skill level. As in the first scoring guide, it is with a score of 3 that essays begin to show a serious lack of ability in one or more areas, especially in terms of sources. For example, essays that incorporate only one of the two sources CLEP provides will only score a 3, no matter how good the essay is otherwise. Essays with a score of 2 or 1 show a serious lack of skill in one or more area, with a score of 0 reserved for essays that do not attempt to address the writing task.

Based upon these two scoring guides, candidates should focus most of their efforts on improving the area of their writing most highly valued according to the criteria: the basic structure of an argument. For both scoring guides, scores from 6 to 4 must contain these elements. All arguments include a clearly stated position, supported by evidence in the form of reasons and examples. Without having something insightful to say, even the most grammatically correct essay will fail. The advice that follows, therefore, pays scant attention to the standards of written English (10%), while placing a great emphasis on rhetorical analysis (25%), use of sources (25%), and revision (40%).

BASIC WRITING STRATEGIES FOR PRODUCING HIGH-SCORING CLEP ESSAYS

The Basic Structure of a Written Argument Made Simple

All argumentative essays include, in their simplest form, the same basic features: a claim, reasons supporting the claim, evidence supporting the reasons, and refutation of counterarguments. The following sample essay is a good example of an argumentative essay that contains this basic structure.

The lack of available, affordable parking is a complaint heard on many college campuses. Let's suppose a group of students meet to construct a formal request for the school to do something about the problem. Their document might sound something like this:

> The parking situation on our campus is deplorable and needs to be improved. There are so few parking spaces near the dorms, many students are forced to park blocks away, on the other side of campus. This is very inconvenient, forcing students to lug books and any other heavy packages they may have long distances, often in the rain and snow. In addition to being inconvenient, it also poses a safety risk for students who have night class, or are returning late from a job or party. With the cost of campus room and board rising each year, students have the right to expect a parking space near where they reside, just like students who rent apartments off campus. While it's true that space on campus is very limited, the school should immediately investigate options to solve the problem, such as building a parking garage, or supplying students with transportation to and from distant parking lots.

This example contains the basic structure of an argument. The **claim**, or position the author is taking, is found in the first sentence: *The parking situation on our campus is deplorable and needs to be improved.* The claim clearly tells the reader what the topic is, as well as what stand the author is taking in regard to it.

This example also contains three specific **reasons** that support the claim: (1) The parking situation is inconvenient, (2) it is a safety risk, and (3) students pay for the right to park close to where they reside. These three reasons are each followed by **evidence**, or specific examples, facts, or statistics that support the reasons. Here, the evidence supplied consists of the following specific examples:

Reason 1: Inconvenience
- Walking long distances
- Carrying heavy books and packages
- Walking in rain and snow

Reason 2: Safety

- Walking late after night classes
- Walking late after a job
- Walking late after a party

Reason 3: Already pay for close parking

- Rising cost of room and board
- Off-campus students have close parking

The more specific evidence provided, the stronger the reasons, and therefore the stronger the argument.

The **counterargument**, or argument someone might make in response to the claim, is found in the phrase *while it's true that space on campus is very limited*, followed by the **refutation of the counterargument** in the rest of the sentence: *the school should immediately investigate options to solve the problem, such as building a parking garage, or supplying students with transportation to and from distant parking lots.* Good writers include counterarguments as a way to anticipate objections a reader might have upon reading the claim, evidence, and reasons, and immediately satisfy those objections by refuting the counterargument. High-scoring CLEP essays include this basic argument structure.

How to Use Your Imagination to Find Claims, Reasons, Evidence, and Counterarguments

Recognizing the basic features of any argument is a great help when preparing to take the essay portion of the CLEP College Composition examination, but it also takes practice using these features to write effective CLEP essays. Most candidates can identify with the previous example, even if they don't live on a college campus. There's no guarantee, however, that the essay prompts on the CLEP exam you take will include such familiar topics. No one can expect to be an expert on all the potential topics possible for inclusion on any specific exam. How then does one prepare? Through the use of imagination!

Take the following essay prompt as an example. Suppose an unmarried 17-year-old high school girl discovers she is pregnant. What should she do? You are asked to write an essay where you discuss, in specific, what the girl should do about the situation, and give reasons to support your position. The only other information you are provided is that she has been dating the father for two years, that they plan to eventually marry, and that they both come from stable families.

It may be easy to imagine what you would do in this situation, but would that yield the best reasons, evidence, and counterarguments? How might you expand upon the range of possible answers? One way is to use your imagination to shift subject positions. What if, instead of your own views about the situation, you considered the viewpoint of the girl's father or the boy's mother? What about the girl's pastor or the couple's high school counselor? Both sets of grandparents? The boy's college football recruiter? The girl's supervisor at work? By imaginatively placing yourself in another's position, you can come up with more reasons and evidence than you can by simply approaching the issue from your own knowledge and experience.

One claim that you can make from this scenario is that the couple should get married now. What reasons, evidence, counterarguments, and refutations can you present to support this claim? The girl's pastor might argue that this is the best choice from a religious perspective. The school counselor might suggest programs that support high school students who have children, yet wish to finish their degree. A grandparent might provide examples of how couples married young in earlier times, yet had successful marriages. The boy's father might worry about his college future if he marries now; the college football recruiter might reassure everyone with the information that married players are still eligible to play. We don't have to be all of these people in order to imagine how they might feel in this situation. From such speculations, many more ideas can be identified and used than simply those we consider from our own perspective.

How to Organize Your Essay

An additional advantage to knowing and using the basic features of an argument is that it provides a ready-made structure to organize your essay. A good strategy is to plan your essay in terms of a five-paragraph response where the first paragraph states your position; the second paragraph contains reason #1, supported by evidence; the third paragraph contains reason #2 with its supporting evidence; and the fourth paragraph contains reason #3, also supported by evidence. The fifth and final paragraph contains the counterargument and its refutation. This strategy would not work for most writing situations, not even if you were writing for an actual college freshman class. Most writing tasks require much more extensive development than a five-paragraph template can provide. In many testing situations, however, this five-paragraph strategy is both effective and easy to remember. The CLEP College Composition Examination is one of them.

Using Signal Verbs and Phrases to Help Integrate Sources

So far, all of the advice provided here has applied to both the first and second CLEP essays. Signal verbs and phrases, however, are designed specifically to help integrate source material within your own writing. The first CLEP essay asks candidates to construct arguments from their own knowledge and experience. The second CLEP essay, in contrast, provides candidates with two sources from which they are expected to take information that they will use to compose their essays. How well you integrate this source material is a big factor in how high your essay is scored.

Good writers use a **signal verb** and **signal phrases** to indicate to readers that a quotation is about to be introduced.

> In her article on teenage nutrition, *Sally Jones argues* "Pizza is a good nutritional choice" (14).

> *Charles Black claims* school lunch programs are responsible for the rise of childhood obesity: "Most school cafeterias serve children food that is high in fat and sugar" (247).

No doubt the most common signal phrase is *the author says*. There is nothing wrong with the use of this phrase. The problem comes when the writer must introduce the next quotation and again uses *the author says*. Pretty soon his or her essay is peppered with the same repetitious phrase, much to the annoyance of readers. Worse, in test situations like the CLEP essay exam, scorers might see this as a sign of a novice writer, someone whose vocabulary and skills are not at a college level.

Introducing a quotation by using the author's name, as in the previous example, is both clear and simple. Furthermore, by choosing a signal verb other than *says*, writers can also communicate their interpretation of the source, which enhances the scorer's view of the writer's ability. Remember that when using a signal verb, you should always refer to a source in the present tense—*Jones argues*, not *Jones argued*.

Here is a list of commonly used signal verbs:

advises	comments	disagrees	lists	reports
agrees	concludes	discusses	objects	reveals
asserts	considers	explains	observes	states
believes	criticizes	finds	opposes	suggests
charges	declares	illustrates	proposes	thinks
claims	describes	interprets	remarks	writes

How to Avoid the 10 Most Common Errors Made by First-Year College Students

Since grammar and usage account for only 10% of the CLEP scoring guide, the preparation you have already done for the multiple-choice section of the exam is sufficient for the essay portion. When writing essays, however, there are a few common errors that can significantly detract from your essays. It's not that these errors are inherently worse than other errors; it's just that they are so common that scorers are immediately aware of their presence. Here are the 10 most common errors college freshmen make when writing, along with advice on how to avoid them.

1. **alot**

   A lot is two words, not one.

2. **it's, its**

   It's is a contraction of it is, as in "**It's** a great book."
   Its is a possessive pronoun, as in "The dog wagged **its** tail."

3. **your, you're**

   You're is a contraction of "**you are**," as in "**You're** a nice person."
   Your indicates possession, as in "**Your** car is new."

4. **there, their, they're**

   There indicates place, as in "**There** is your hat."
   Their indicates possession, as in "**Their** house is green."
   They're is a contraction of "they are," as in "**They're** going home."

5. **comma splice**

Never join two independent clauses together with just a comma. Correct the error by linking the clauses with a semicolon, or with a comma and a coordinating conjunction (*and*, *but*, *or*, *nor*, *for*, *so*, or *yet*), or by making them into two separate sentences.

> **Incorrect**: The author claims the information is correct, it is from a reliable study.
>
> **Correct**: The author claims the information is correct; it is from a reliable study.
>
> **Correct**: The author claims the information is correct, for it is from a reliable study.
>
> **Correct**: The author claims the information is correct. It is from a reliable study.

6. **misuse of quotation marks**

Never place the concluding quotation mark before the period.

> **Incorrect**: The author argues that the study "is unreliable".
>
> **Correct**: The author argues that the study "is unreliable."

7. **compound subject/verb agreement**

Make sure compound subjects (connected by *and*) have plural verbs.

> **Incorrect**: A pencil, an answer sheet, and a test booklet was issued to each student.
>
> **Correct**: A pencil, an answer sheet, and a test booklet were issued to each student.

8. **using commas after introductory elements**

Make sure you use a comma after introductory elements in a sentence.

> **Incorrect**: Unfortunately the student lost his textbook.
>
> **Correct**: Unfortunately, the student lost his textbook.
>
> **Incorrect**: In one of her best games Jane scored three home runs.
>
> **Correct**: In one of her best games, Jane scored three home runs.

9. **using commas to separate items in a series**

Make sure you use commas after items in a series.

> **Incorrect**: The long boring confusing speech left us feeling sleepy.
>
> **Correct**: The long, boring, confusing speech left us feeling sleepy.

10. **capitalizing correctly**

Make sure you capitalize all proper names, ethnic groups, languages, religions, and religious terms.

Marilyn Monroe	Chinese
African Americans	Iraqi
Islam	an Islamic

Fifty Words First-Year Writers Frequently Misspell

Most of the writing done by college freshmen is argumentative, just like the kind of writing the CLEP exam requires. The following list features words commonly misspelled by college freshmen as they compose essays similar to the CLEP first and second essay. If you know the meanings of the following words, as well as how to spell them, you will be prepared to use them to your advantage when writing argumentative essays.

1. accept	14. conceive	27. manageable	40. suppress
2. accomplish	15. consistent	28. necessary	41. tangible
3. achievement	16. criticize	29. noticeable	42. tendency
4. against	17. decide	30. occasion	43. therefore
5. alleged	18. definitely	31. occurred	44. thorough
6. apparent	19. dependent	32. perceive	45. though
7. argument	20. develop	33. preferred	46. through
8. basically	21. environment	34. realize	47. truly
9. beginning	22. explanation	35. relevant	48. until
10. believe	23. financially	36. sense	49. whether
11. business	24. fulfill	37. separate	50. wherever
12. cannot	25. guarantee	38. successfully	
13. category	26. immediately	39. sufficient	

PRACTICE WRITING THE CLEP ARGUMENTATIVE ESSAYS

Sample Writing Prompts for the CLEP First Essay

Writing Prompt #1:

> Reality television shows, like MTV's *Jersey Shore* or Bravo's *Real Housewives of New York,* do not simply entertain, but in fact pose a threat to our cultural values.

> Write an essay where you agree or disagree with the previous statement. Support your position with specific reasons and evidence from your reading, experience, and/or observations.

The previous statement and directions are very similar to the kind of essay prompts you will encounter for the CLEP first essay. Note that there are no sources included that you must integrate within your essay. How then does one begin to compose an essay in response?

Take a few minutes to plan your response by composing a scratch outline using the basic features of an argument. For the claim, pick the side for which you can supply the most reasons and evidence in support. It doesn't matter if this represents your true feelings or not; what matters is that you can come up with a good argument. Next, pick a good counterargument that you can refute.

For example, say you choose to disagree with the previous statement and you come up with several reasons that support your position. Choose the best three and support them with specific examples:

Reason #1: Reality television shows promote positive behavior.

Evidence/examples, etc.

- The show *The Biggest Loser* depicts real overweight people learning how to exercise, diet, and deal with the emotional issues connected with losing weight.
- The show *The Nanny* teaches parents with even the most difficult children effective discipline techniques.
- A&E's *Intervention* profiles real addicts, providing them and their families with expert advice on how to treat drug and alcohol addiction.

Reason #2: Reality television shows help combat stereotypes and social bias.

Evidence/examples, etc.

- HGTV often profiles homosexual couples in their reality series that focuses on house hunting and remodeling.
- Shows like *Little Couple* shatter preconceived notions of what those who are physically challenged can do.
- Shows like *Extreme Makeover: Home Edition* prove that many poor families in need are deserving of help.

Reason #3: Reality television shows are inexpensive to produce, compared with scripted shows, and therefore allow for more variety.

Evidence/examples, etc.

- A wide variety of reality shows today focus on food, such as *Top Chef*, *Chopped*, and *Cake Wars*.
- Entertainment shows, such as *American Idol*, *Dancing with the Stars*, and *You've Got Talent*, provide audiences with wholesome enjoyment.
- Dramatic shows, such as *First 48*, *Cops*, and *Ice Road Truckers*, promote new professions and /or hobbies.

Now raise a counterargument and refute it.

Many people argue that reality television shows promote antisocial behavior, and it is certainly true that some—like MTV's Snooki on the show *Jersey Shore*—seem to glamorize such things as casual sex and drunkenness.

However, given the huge number and variety of reality television shows, the bad ones are in the minority.

Once you have an outline of the argument, it's not too hard to construct five paragraphs.

Sample Essay in Response to Writing Prompt #1
Earning a Score of 6

Using the same prompt and outline from the previous example, the following is a typical five-paragraph essay earning a score of 6.

Writing Prompt #1:

Reality television shows, like MTV's *Jersey Shore* or *Real Housewives of New York,* do not simply entertain, but in fact pose a threat to our cultural values.

Write an essay where you agree or disagree with the previous statement. Support your position with specific reasons and evidence from your reading, experience, and/or observations.

Reality television shows do seem to emphasize the most outrageous behavior, especially where the media is concerned. Of course the drunken antics of Snooki from *Jersey Shore* or the White House gate-crashers, Michaele and Tareq Salahi from *The Real Housewives of D.C.,* make the news. It is an exaggeration, however, to claim that all these unscripted programs profiling real people, rather than actors, are somehow posing a threat to our culture. Taken as a whole, these shows depict as many people doing positive things as they do people doing negative ones. In fact, reality television shows often help society by educating the viewing population.

For every reality show profiling socially deviant behavior, there are several promoting positive behavior. Take, for example, the show *The Biggest Loser* where real overweight people learn how to exercise, diet, and deal with the emotional issues connected with losing weight. This reality television show addresses the number one health concern today in America—obesity. Another show, *The Nanny,* teaches parents with even the most difficult children effective discipline techniques. Perhaps the best example, however, is A&E's award-winning *Intervention* which profiles real addicts, providing them and their families with expert advice on how to treat drug and alcohol addiction.

In addition to shows that promote positive social behavior, a number of reality television programs help combat negative social stereotypes and prejudice. HGTV often profiles homosexual couples in reality shows that focus on house hunting and remodeling. Programs like *Little Couple* shatter preconceived notions of what those who are physically challenged can accomplish. Shows like *Extreme Makeover: Home Edition* prove that many poor families aren't just slackers, but are deserving of help.

Those who worry about reality television need only remember that as unscripted programming, reality TV shows are inexpensive to produce. This allows for a wide variety of shows that not only shock, but also educate and entertain. Reality television shows like *American Idol*, *Dancing with the Stars*, and *You've Got Talent* provide audiences with wholesome enjoyment. Many shows, like *Top Chef* and *Ice Road Truckers*, promote new professions and/or hobbies.

It is certainly true that some reality television shows promote dangerous, antisocial behavior, such as the drunkenness and casual sex depicted on *Jersey Shore*. But given the huge number and variety of reality television shows, the good outweighs the bad.

This sample essay achieves a score of 6 because it has a clear and thoughtful thesis or position statement that includes reasons and examples that are both specific and relevant. It is focused and organized, and it uses a good command of grammar and usage. The essay contains paragraphs with short, declarative sentences, as well as compound sentences. The vocabulary is both clear and specific.

Sample Writing Prompts for the CLEP Second Essay

Writing Prompt #2:

Carefully read the two sources found below. Using both sources, write an essay where you agree or disagree that cyber bullying poses a greater threat to children than traditional bullying. Make sure you use and cite both sources in your essay.

Kowalski, Robin M. "Cyber Bullying: Recognizing and Treating Victim and Aggressor." *Psychiatric Times* 25.11 (2008): 45–56. Print.

The following is an excerpt from the Kowalski article.

More individuals are potential cyber bullies than potential schoolyard bullies. People will say and do more things anonymously that they would not say and do directly or in front of someone. This disinhibition effect increases not only the number of potential perpetrators of cyber bullying but also the magnitude of threats, taunts, and so on that they are willing to deliver. (1) This effect is further compounded by that, in the virtual world, interactants are not privy to one another's emotions. When people tease or bully face-to-face, they use off-record markers (winks, smiles, etc.) to indicate the intent behind their behavior. With the exception of emoticons (smiley faces to convey positive affect), such nonverbal accompaniments are not available in the virtual world. Thus, perpetrators cannot see the emotional toll that their cyber bullying may be taking on the target; similarly, targets cannot read the off-record markers accompanying the perpetrator's behavior. Thus, targets cannot know if the perpetrator really is "just kidding."

Bennett, Jessica. "From Lockers to Lockup." *Newsweek* 11 Oct. 2010: 38. Print.

The following is an excerpt from the Bennett article.

But forget, for the moment, the dozens of articles that have called bullying a "pandemic"—because the opposite is true. School bullying can be devastating, but social scientists say it is no more extreme, nor more prevalent, than it was half a century ago. In fact, says Dan Olweus, a leading bullying expert, new data shows rates of school bullying may even have gone down over the past decade. Today's world of cyber bullying is different, yes—far-reaching, more visually potent, and harder to wash away than comments scrawled on a bathroom wall. All of which can make it harder to combat. But it still happens a third less than traditional bullying, says Olweus.

The reality may be that while the incidence of bullying has remained relatively the same, it's our reaction to it that has changed: the helicopter parents who want to protect their kids from every stick and stone, the cable-news commentators who whip them into a frenzy, the insta-vigilantism of the Internet. When it comes down to it, bullying is not just a social ill; it's a "cottage-industry," says Suffolk Law School's David Yamada—complete with commentators and prevention experts and a new breed of legal scholars, all preparing to take on an enemy that's always been there. None of this is to say that bullying is not a serious problem, or that tackling it is not important. But like a stereo with the volume tuned too high, all the noise distorts the facts, making it nearly impossible to judge when a case is somehow criminal, or merely cruel.

The previous directions and excerpted sources are similar to the kind of essay prompts you will encounter for the CLEP second essay. Note that there are two sources included that you must integrate within your essay. How then does one begin to compose an essay in response?

Again, you should take a few minutes to plan your response by composing a scratch outline using the basic features of arguments and the information found in the previous sources. For the claim, pick the side for which you can supply the most reasons and evidence in support. It doesn't matter if this represents your true feelings or not; what matters is that you can come up with a good argument. Now, pick a good counterargument that you can refute.

For example, you may choose to agree with the previous statement and come up with several reasons that support your position. Choose the best three and support them with specific examples both from the sources provided and from your own knowledge and experience:

Reason #1: There are, potentially, more cyber bullies than traditional bullies with more victims.

Evidence/examples, etc.

- According to Kowalski, because technology allows cyber bullies to be anonymous, called the "disinhibition effect," more students will bully another than in traditional public bullying.
- Cyber bullies can increase the number of their victims more easily than traditional bullies.
- Cyber bullies generally have no witnesses to their actions and therefore run less risk of punishment.

Reason #2: Cyber bullying causes more harm to victims than traditional bullying.

> **Evidence/examples, etc.**
> - According to Kowalski, the "disinhibition effect" increases the "magnitude of threats, taunts, and so on, that they are willing to deliver."
> - Cyber bullying provides a greater variety of ways, thanks to existing technology, to hurt a victim—for example, the case of the gay teen who committed suicide after exposure by webcam.
> - Cyber bullying allows the effects of the cruelty to last far longer than traditional bullying.

Reason #3: Cyber bullying extends beyond classmates and the school grounds.

> **Evidence/examples, etc.**
> - Older siblings and even adults can join in with a cyber bully—for example, the case of the Missouri mom.
> - Cyber bullies have a greater audience than traditional bullies.
> - Cyber bullies can expose their victims to more dangerous, adult predators.

Now raise a counterargument, and refute it.

> According to Bennett, cyber bullying is just a new form of the same thing schools have always had to deal with, and therefore is nothing to be alarmed about. What is new, she argues, is the way the media is blowing the issue out of proportion thanks to the "frenzy" generated by "helicopter parents" and "cable-news commentators."

> It's true that kids have always bullied one another, but to say that the kind of behavior seen in recent years thanks to the advent of technology is just a more advanced form of the same thing is patently foolish. Adults are obliged to protect children from situations where they can endanger themselves and others.

Once you have an outline of the argument, it's not too hard to construct five paragraphs.

Sample Essay in Response to Writing Prompt #2
Earning a Score of 6

Using the same prompt and outline from the previous example, the following is a typical five-paragraph essay earning a score of 6.

Writing Prompt #2:

> Carefully read the two sources found below. Using both sources, write an essay where you agree or disagree that cyber bullying poses a greater threat to children than traditional bullying. Make sure you use and cite both sources in your essay.

Kowalski, Robin M. "Cyber Bullying: Recognizing and Treating Victim and Aggressor." *Psychiatric Times* 25.11 (2008): 45–56. Print.

The following is an excerpt from the Kowalski article.

More individuals are potential cyber bullies than potential schoolyard bullies. People will say and do more things anonymously that they would not say and do directly or in front of someone. This disinhibition effect increases not only the number of potential perpetrators of cyber bullying but also the magnitude of threats, taunts, and so on, that they are willing to deliver. (1) This effect is further compounded by that, in the virtual world, interactants are not privy to one another's emotions. When people tease or bully face-to-face, they use off-record markers (winks, smiles, etc.) to indicate the intent behind their behavior. 13 With the exception of emoticons (smiley faces to convey positive affect), such nonverbal accompaniments are not available in the virtual world. Thus, perpetrators cannot see the emotional toll that their cyber bullying may be taking on the target; similarly, targets cannot read the off-record markers accompanying the perpetrator's behavior. Thus, targets cannot know if the perpetrator really is "just kidding."

Bennett, Jessica. "From Lockers to Lockup." *Newsweek* 11 Oct. 2010: 38. Print.

The following is an excerpt from the Bennett article.

But forget, for the moment, the dozens of articles that have called bullying a "pandemic"—because the opposite is true. School bullying can be devastating, but social scientists say it is no more extreme, nor more prevalent, than it was half a century ago. In fact, says Dan Olweus, a leading bullying expert, new data shows rates of school bullying may even have gone down over the past decade. Today's world of cyber bullying is different, yes—far-reaching, more visually potent, and harder to wash away than comments scrawled on a bathroom wall. All of which can make it harder to combat. But it still happens a third less than traditional bullying, says Olweus.

The reality may be that while the incidence of bullying has remained relatively the same, it's our reaction to it that has changed: the helicopter parents who want to protect their kids from every stick and stone, the cable-news commentators who whip them into a frenzy, the insta-vigilantism of the Internet. When it comes down to it, bullying is not just a social ill; it's a "cottage-industry," says Suffolk Law School's David Yamada—complete with commentators and prevention experts and a new breed of legal scholars, all preparing to take on an enemy that's always been there. None of this is to say that bullying is not a serious problem, or that tackling it is not important. But like a stereo with the volume tuned too high, all the noise distorts the facts, making it nearly impossible to judge when a case is somehow criminal, or merely cruel.

Cyber bullying may be prompted, psychologically speaking, by the same childhood impulses as the traditional style of bullying we are so familiar with from our own childhoods, but that's where the similarity ends. The technology which allows the kind of behavior we have seen depicted by the media in recent years is much more complex and dangerous in scope than a typical schoolyard fight.

Thanks to recent technological advances, today we have, potentially, more cyber bullies than traditional bullies—and with more victims. According to Kowalski, because technology allows cyber bullies to be anonymous, called the "disinhibition effect," more students will bully others than would have with traditional public bullying. Cyber bullies find opportunities to taunt, insult, or threaten others through e-mail, by instant messaging, via web pages, or through sending texts and/or images via cell phones. Perpetrators can also increase the number of their victims more easily than traditional bullies, given the ease of new technology. With a simple click, a cyber bully can literally reach hundreds of people via the Internet. Since cyber bullies generally have no witnesses to their actions, they run less risk of punishment.

Cyber bullying should be a concern for all since it can cause more harm to victims than traditional bullying. The "disinhibition effect" also increases the "magnitude of threats, taunts, and so on" that cyber bullies "are willing to deliver," Kowalski argues. As with traditional bullying, cyber bullying can cause victims to suffer both physical and psychological harm. But the recent spate of teenage suicides has many concerned that cyber bullying is more dangerous than traditional bullying. In the case of Phoebe Prince, cyber bullying allegedly spilled over into actual sexual assault. Cyber bullying also provides a greater variety of ways to hurt a victim than does traditional bullying. On September 22, 2010, Tyler Clementi threw himself off a bridge when his roommate filmed him having sex with another male via webcam and streamed it live to other students in their dorm. Cyber bullying allows the effects of the cruelty to last far longer than traditional bullying. Calling a victim "gay" in the hall in front of one's peers is nothing compared to having an actual sex tape widely distributed on the Internet where it may crop up again and again for years.

The most frightening thing about cyber bullying, however, is that it extends beyond classmates and the school grounds. With the anonymity of the Internet, older siblings and even adults can join in with a cyber bully in targeting a victim. For example, Megan Meier committed suicide after cyber bullying by one of her classmate's mother. Cyber bullies have a greater audience than traditional bullies, enlisting a huge number of virtual bystanders that can make victims feel even more threatened and humiliated. Worse such practices by cyber bullies can expose their victims to more dangerous, adult predators.

According to Bennett, cyber bullying is just a new form of the same thing schools have always had to deal with, and therefore is nothing to be alarmed about. What is new, she argues, is the way the media is blowing the issue out of proportion thanks to the "frenzy" generated by "helicopter parents" and "cable-news commentators." It's true that kids have always bullied one another, and it's certainly true that the media have made much of recent cases of cyber bullying. But to say that the kind of behavior seen in recent years, thanks to the advent of technology, is just a more advanced form of the same thing is foolish. Adults are obliged to protect children from situations where they can endanger themselves and others. Cyber bullying is different from traditional bullying and should be taken seriously by everyone involved.

This sample essay achieves a score of 6 because it has a clear and thoughtful thesis or position statement that includes reasons and examples that are both specific and relevant. It includes references to both sources, is focused and organized, and uses a good command of grammar and usage. The essay contains paragraphs with short, declarative sentences, as well as compound sentences. The vocabulary is both clear and specific.

CLEP College Composition Practice Test 1

TIME: *50 Minutes*

CONVENTIONS OF STANDARD WRITTEN ENGLISH

DIRECTIONS: The following sentences test your knowledge of grammar, usage, diction (choice of words), and idioms. Note that some sentences are correct, and no sentence contains more than one error. Read each sentence carefully, paying particular attention to the underlined portions. You will find that the error, if there is one, is underlined. Assume that elements of the sentence that are not underlined are correct and cannot be changed. In choosing answers, follow the requirements of standard written English. If there is an error, select the one underlined part that must be changed to make the sentence correct. If there is no error, select "No error."

1. Violence, corruption, and pollution <u>are among</u> the problems <u>that undermine</u> quality of life in
                                   A   B
 industrialized societies, <u>particularly</u> those <u>having</u> autocratic forms of government. <u>No error</u>
                     C   D   E

2. <u>Although</u> many people consider Richard Burton <u>to be</u> a fine actor, he never won <u>no</u> Oscar
     A   B   C
 for <u>his</u> work. <u>No error</u>
     D   E

3. <u>Since</u> the early twentieth <u>century, significant</u> changes <u>have taken</u> place in educational practice
    A   B   C
 <u>as well as in</u> the field of educational research. <u>No error</u>
    D   E

4. An <u>astute and powerful</u> woman, Frances Smith <u>had been</u> a beauty-contest winner <u>before</u> she
         A   B   C
 became president of Smith Corporation, <u>on the</u> death of her husband. <u>No error</u>
                                   D   E

5. For years, citizens <u>concerned about</u> the environment have compiled statistics which <u>shows</u> that
                 A   B
 <u>many</u> species <u>are endangered</u>. <u>No error</u>
   C   D   E

REVISION SKILLS

DIRECTIONS: The following passages are early drafts of essays. Read each passage and then answer the questions that follow. Some questions refer to particular sentences or parts of sentences and ask you to improve sentence structure or diction. Other questions refer to the entire essay or parts of the essay and ask you to consider the essay's organization, development, or effectiveness of language. In selecting your answers, follow the conventions of standard written English.

Questions 1–5 are based on the following draft of an essay.

(1) The phrase *reading wars* refers to heated debates among educators about the most suitable method for teaching children how to read. (2) Some people argue that phonics-based methods are best for reading instruction. (3) In phonics-based methods, children are taught letter sounds as well as rules for sounding out words. (4) Phonics-based methods are widely used. (5) Phonics-based methods direct children's attention to the constituents of words like their letters and groups of letters. (6) Other educators argue that whole-word methods are preferable for reading instruction. (7) In whole-word methods, teachers involve children in meaningful reading and writing activities even before they can sound out words. (8) So phonics is different from whole-word. (9) However, most whole-word advocates agree that teachers should spend at least some time on phonics instruction. (10) These educators acknowledge that reading instruction should include phonics-based methods, but only in the context of meaningful reading activities. (11) At the same time, advocates of phonics-based methods do not deny the importance of meaningful reading and writing activities.

1. In context, which is the best replacement for *people* in sentence 2?

   (A) citizens
   (B) educators
   (C) researchers
   (D) individuals
   (E) children

2. Which of the following versions of the underlined portion of sentence 5 (reproduced below) is best?

   > *Phonics-based methods direct children's attention to the constituents of <u>words like their letters</u> and groups of letters.*

   (A) words, such as letters
   (B) words, like letters
   (C) words and their letters
   (D) words, with letters
   (E) words, as their letters

3. Which of the following is the best revision for sentence 8?

   (A) Thus, phonics-based methods are different from whole word.
   (B) Thus, phonics is different from whole word.
   (C) Thus, phonics differs from the whole word.
   (D) Thus, phonics-based methods and whole-word methods are very different.
   (E) Thus, there are differences between the methods of phonics and the whole word.

4. Deleting which of the following sentences would most improve the coherence of the passage?

   (A) Sentence 2
   (B) Sentence 4
   (C) Sentence 6
   (D) Sentence 7
   (E) Sentence 9

5. Which of the following is the best sentence with which to end the passage?

   (A) Thus, the *reading wars* are not really wars at all and should be completely abolished.
   (B) Thus, the *reading wars* reflect two distinct positions regarding the most suitable methods for reading instruction.
   (C) Thus, the *reading wars* reflect disagreements about which method of reading instruction should be emphasized rather than disagreements about which method to use.
   (D) Thus, the *reading wars* are based on the mistaken assumption that phonics-based and whole-word methods of reading instruction are actually separate methods.
   (E) Thus, the *reading wars* are based in subtle differences between methods that have escaped the notice of educators.

Questions 6–12 are based on the following draft of an essay.

(1) Santiago, the main character in Ernest Hemingway's novel *The Old Man and the Sea*, displays admirable courage and strength in his fight with a great marlin, which is very symbolic. (2) The old fisherman then suffers a painful loss when sharks devour his marlin, and they left him little more than a skeleton to lug home. (3) But the novel rises above suffering and loss to express and deliver an inspiring message about the greatness of the human spirit. (4) The nobility of Santiago's character is revealed not only in his remarkable battle with the marlin, but also in his patience during the days and hours leading to it. (5) After 84 days without catching a fish, Santiago remains optimistic. (6) On the day of the battle, he ventures out into deeper water, and when he hooks the marlin, he shows infinite patience in spite of his desperate situation. (7) He is rewarded with the capture of the great fish. (8) But the price of his success is great.

6. Which of the following is the best revision for the underlined portion of sentence 1 (reproduced below)?

   Santiago, the main character in Ernest Hemingway's novel The Old Man and the Sea, *displays admirable courage and strength <u>in his fight with a great marlin, which is very symbolic.</u>*

   (A) when fighting symbolically with a great marlin.
   (B) in his fight with a great marlin, a symbolic fight.
   (C) when he has his fight with a great marlin, which is symbolic.
   (D) in his fight with a symbolic marlin.
   (E) in his symbolic fight with a great marlin.

7. Which of the following is the best revision for the underlined portion of sentence 2 (reproduced below)?

   > *The old fisherman then suffers a painful loss when sharks devour his marlin, <u>and they left him little more than a skeleton to lug home.</u>*

   (A) and little more than a skeleton to lug home
   (B) they left him little more than a marlin to lug home
   (C) and it was little more than a skeleton he could lug home
   (D) leaving him little more than a skeleton to lug home
   (E) it left him little more than a skeleton to lug home

8. Which of the following sentences, if inserted between sentences 1 and 2, would make the passage more coherent?

   (A) At first, after he hooks the marlin, Santiago is not completely sure what kind of fish he has caught.
   (B) As he prepares to go fishing that morning, Santiago is hopeful that maybe today he will catch a great fish.
   (C) Although he tries not to be disturbed by the thought, Santiago knows it has been 84 days since he last caught a fish.
   (D) After a prolonged and intense struggle, Santiago finally lands the marlin and ties it to the side of his boat.
   (E) Slowly and carefully, Santiago guides his boat out into the deep ocean in search of a large fish, such as a marlin.

9. Which option is the best choice to do with sentence 3 (reproduced below)?

   > *But the novel rises above suffering and loss to express and deliver an inspiring message about the greatness of the human spirit.*

   (A) Leave it as is.
   (B) Delete *express and*.
   (C) Place a comma after *message*.
   (D) Replace *inspiring* with *major*.
   (E) Replace *rises* with *raises*.

10. Which of the following is the best replacement for *leading to it* at the end of sentence 4 (reproduced below)?

    > *The nobility of Santiago's character is revealed not only in his remarkable battle with the marlin, but also in his patience during the days and hours leading to it.*

    (A) leading up to the battle
    (B) leading him to this
    (C) leading there
    (D) leading to that remarkable battle
    (E) leading that way

11. Which of the following phrases, added immediately after *deeper water* in sentence 6 (reproduced below), would make the sentence more coherent?

> *On the day of the battle, he ventures out into deeper water, and when he hooks the marlin, he shows infinite patience in spite of his desperate situation.*

(A) in order to fish
(B) with his little boat
(C) as optimistically as he can
(D) than he ever had before
(E) with determination and skill

12. Which of the following is the best way to combine sentences 7 and 8 (reproduced below)?

> *He is rewarded with the capture of the great fish. But the price of his success is great.*

(A) He is rewarded with the capture of the great fish, the price of his success was great.
(B) He is rewarded with the capture of the great fish, if the price of his success was great.
(C) He is rewarded with the capture of the great fish, as the price of his success was great.
(D) He is rewarded with the capture of the great fish, thus the price of his success was great.
(E) He is rewarded with the capture of the great fish, but the price of his success was great.

Questions 13–20 are based on the following draft of an essay.

(1) Many people consider the motorcyclist a highway nuisance who makes other motorists nervous and he takes the joy out of driving. (2) It cannot be denied that some motorcyclists are egotists who assert the roadways were created for their exclusive use. (3) Admittedly, others are riders who take unnecessary risks. (4) Yet many motorcyclists are responsible drivers. (5) Motorcyclists should always drive with caution. (6) Moreover, any truly honest driver will admit that at times he has envied the freedom of the motorcycle rider.

(7) Motorcycles are much less expensive than other vehicles. (8) Motorcycles are easier to park. (9) And motorcyclists usually enjoy the luxury of low insurance premiums. (10) The main disadvantage of motorcycle riding are the accidents; they are often caused by the motorcyclists themselves. (11) In my opinion the risk of accidents is a little price for the many advantages of riding a motorcycle.

13. Which of the following is the best replacement for the underlined portion of sentence 1 (reproduced below)?

> *Many people consider the motorcyclist a highway nuisance who makes other motorists nervous <u>and he takes</u> the joy out of driving.*

(A) and then takes
(B) and so takes
(C) and takes
(D) and soon takes
(E) and it takes

14. Which option is the best choice to do with *assert* in sentence 2 (reproduced below)?

> *It cannot be denied that some motorcyclists are egotists who assert the roadways were created for their exclusive use.*

(A) Leave it as is.
(B) Replace *assert* with *assess*.
(C) Replace *assert* with *believe*.
(D) Replace *assert* with *explain*.
(E) Replace *assert* with *doubt*.

15. Which of the following revisions would contribute most strongly to the purpose of sentence 3 (reproduced below)?

> *Admittedly, others are riders who take unnecessary risks.*

(A) Admittedly, others are individuals who take unnecessary risks.
(B) Admittedly, others are skilled riders who take unnecessary risks.
(C) Admittedly, others are the ones who take unnecessary risks.
(D) Admittedly, others are cyclists who take unnecessary risks.
(E) Admittedly, others are daredevils who take unnecessary risks.

16. Which of the following represents the best combination of sentences 2 and 3 (reproduced below)?

> *It cannot be denied that some motorcyclists are egotists who assert the roadways were created for their exclusive use. Admittedly, others are riders who take unnecessary risks.*

(A) It cannot be denied that some motorcyclists are egotists who assert the roadways were created for their exclusive use; in addition, others are riders who take unnecessary risks.
(B) It cannot be denied that some motorcyclists are egotists who assert the roadways were created for their exclusive use, while others are riders who take unnecessary risks.
(C) It cannot be denied that some motorcyclists are egotists who assert the roadways were created for their exclusive use, but others are riders who take unnecessary risks.
(D) It cannot be denied that some motorcyclists are egotists who assert the roadways were created for their exclusive use, although others are riders who take unnecessary risks.
(E) It cannot be denied that some motorcyclists are egotists who assert the roadways were created for their exclusive use; however, others are riders who take unnecessary risks.

17. Deleting which of the following sentences would increase the coherence of the passage?

(A) Sentence 2
(B) Sentence 4
(C) Sentence 5
(D) Sentence 6
(E) Sentence 7

18. Which of the following is the best sentence with which to begin the second paragraph?

(A) There are many advantages to driving a motorcycle as opposed to some other type of vehicle.
(B) Motorcycles are quite beneficial to their owners if maintained appropriately.
(C) All things considered, motorcycles are far from an ideal form of transportation.
(D) Motorcycles are the preferred mode of transportation among a wide variety of people.
(E) Motorcycles have a number of disadvantages that offset their obvious strengths.

19. Which of the following is the best revision of sentence 10 (reproduced below)?

> *The main disadvantage of motorcycle riding are the accidents; they are often caused by the motorcyclists themselves.*

(A) The main disadvantage of motorcycle riding is the accidents; caused often by the motorcyclists themselves.
(B) The main disadvantage of motorcycle riding are the accidents, as often caused by the motorcyclists themselves.
(C) The main disadvantage of motorcycle riding is the accidents that are often caused by the motorcyclists themselves.
(D) The main disadvantage of motorcycle riding are the accidents, but they are often caused by the motorcyclists themselves.
(E) The main disadvantage of motorcycle riding is the accidents, which are often caused by the motorcyclists themselves.

20. Which of the following is the best revision of the underlined portion of sentence 11 (reproduced below)?

> *In my opinion the risk of accidents is a <u>little price</u> for the many advantages of riding a motorcycle.*

(A) tiny price
(B) very low price
(C) minimum cost
(D) small price to pay
(E) cheap substitute

ABILITY TO USE SOURCE MATERIALS

DIRECTIONS: The following questions test your familiarity with basic research, reference, and composition skills. Some questions refer to passages, whereas other questions are self-contained. For each question, choose the best answer.

Questions 1–7 refer to the following passage.

(1) Among the influences on both the quantity and importance of educational research in recent years are growing concerns about the academic achievement of American students (Springer, 2010, 3). (2) Since the beginning of public education, concerns about achievement have been voiced by parents, educators, researchers, and policymakers. (3) Fueling these concerns have been studies indicating that the American educational system is in trouble and, in the words of an influential report *A Nation at Risk*, is threatened by a "rising tide of mediocrity."

(4) The most recent responses to concerns about student achievement include federal legislation passed during the first few years of the new millennium. (5) Prominent among this new legislation is the No Child Left Behind Act, signed into law in 2002. (6) No Child Left Behind (NCLB) was designed to "improve student achievement and change the culture of America's schools" (U.S. Department of Education, 2002, 9). (7) NCLB requires that states conduct annual testing of student progress in grades 3–8, and at least once in grades 10–12. (8) Through NCLB, federal spending on schools is linked to the results of these new tests. (9) Federal spending is also linked to attempts to improve student progress through instructional and curricular changes that are scientifically based. (10) Through NCLB, federal support is targeted to educational programs that are informed by rigorous scientific research. (11) In this way, federal support targets educational programs that have a rigorous scientific basis.

References

Springer, K. 2010. *Educational Research: A Contextual Approach*. Hoboken, NJ: Wiley.

U.S. Department of Education. 2002. *No Child Left Behind: A Desktop Reference,* Washington, D.C., 20202.

1. Which of the following is cited in sentence 1?

   (A) A scientific journal
   (B) A book
   (C) A media report
   (D) A popular magazine
   (E) A website

2. Which of the following is missing from sentence 3?

   (A) Further details about the content of *A Nation at Risk*
   (B) A critique of the central thesis of *A Nation at Risk*
   (C) Citation information for *A Nation at Risk*
   (D) A note about the relationship between the previous citation and *A Nation at Risk*
   (E) Information about whether *A Nation at Risk* is a book or some other type of source

3. Which of the following best describes the purpose of sentence 5?

   (A) To qualify the statement made in sentence 4
   (B) To illustrate the assertions made in sentence 6
   (C) To include a citation for the assertion made in sentence 6
   (D) To provide an example of the statement made in sentence 4
   (E) All of the above

4. Which of the following best describes the purpose of the quotation in sentence 6?

   (A) To contrast NCLB with *A Nation at Risk*
   (B) To support the writer's thesis that the American educational system is in trouble
   (C) To provide a succinct critique of NCLB
   (D) To give some examples of how NCLB impacts educational practice
   (E) To briefly summarize why NCLB was created

5. Which of the following best describes the purpose of the second paragraph (sentences 4–11)?

(A) To describe one example of federal legislation created in response to concerns about the achievement of American students

(B) To qualify the argument that a variety of people are concerned about the achievement of American students

(C) To explain why parents, educators, researchers, and policymakers have been concerned about student achievement

(D) To critically analyze the role of the federal government in educational practice

(E) To raise questions about the extent to which federal legislation ultimately translates into effects on student achievement

6. In context, which option is the best choice to do with sentence 11 (reproduced below)?

In this way, federal support targets educational programs that have a rigorous scientific basis.

(A) Leave it as is.
(B) Revise the sentence so that it is more similar to sentence 10.
(C) Add a definition of *scientific*.
(D) Delete it.
(E) Replace *In this way* with *In sum*.

7. Which of the following pieces of information, if added to the second paragraph (sentences 4–11), would most effectively advance the main point of the paragraph?

(A) A historical example of NCLB-like federal legislation related to education

(B) A concrete example of NCLB-related federal support for educational programs

(C) A qualifying example that shows how NCLB impacts outcomes other than achievement

(D) A contrasting example of how NCLB influences noneducational programs

(E) A supplemental example of other purposes served by NCLB

Questions 8–10 refer to the following passage.

(1) The term *Native American* is somewhat misleading. (2) According to experts, what we call *Native Americans* or Indians migrated to our continent from many other places. (3) For example, the ancestors of the Anasazi, who once occupied what is now Colorado, New Mexico, Utah, and Arizona, probably migrated from the Asian continent about 25,000 years ago while the continental land bridge still existed. (4) Other archaeologists have suggested more recent migrations to what is now the United States among peoples from the north (e.g., the so-called *Eskimos*). (5) Likewise, many *Native Americans* originated from more southern regions (e.g., the Apaches). (6) This is partly why my best friend, a full-blooded Cherokee and an amateur archaeologist, likes to say that he is not Native American but rather Cherokee.

8. For which of the following sentences is a citation least necessary?

(A) Sentence 1
(B) Sentence 2
(C) Sentence 3
(D) Sentence 4
(E) Sentence 5

9. In context, which of the following is the best replacement for *experts* in sentence 2?

   (A) scholars
   (B) commentators
   (C) scientists
   (D) archaeologists
   (E) critics

10. In sentence 6, the author's reference to his or her best friend serves what purpose?

   (A) It provides an expert view on the main idea expressed in the passage.
   (B) It illustrates the main idea of the passage by means of an anecdote.
   (C) It qualifies the main idea discussed in the passage.
   (D) It contradicts the expert claims that are alluded to in the passage.
   (E) It extends the main idea developed in the passage.

Questions 11–12 refer to the following sentence.

> The U.S. government is based on the principle that elected individuals should represent the entire citizenry (e.g., as political scientists would say, our government is a representative democracy).

11. Which option is the best choice to do with *e.g.* in this sentence?

   (A) Leave it as is.
   (B) Delete it.
   (C) Replace it with *n.p.*
   (D) Replace it with *et al.*
   (E) Replace it with *i.e.*

12. In context, what does the information in parentheses convey?

   (A) It provides an example of how the U.S. government operates, according to political scientists.
   (B) On the basis of what political scientists would say, it qualifies the description of the government given in the main portion of the sentence.
   (C) On the basis of what political scientists would say, it extends the description of the government given in the main portion of the sentence.
   (D) It identifies the category of *government* represented by the U.S. government, according to political scientists.
   (E) On the basis of what political scientists would say, it corrects the description of the government given in the main portion of the sentence.

RHETORICAL ANALYSIS

DIRECTIONS: The following questions test your ability to analyze writing. Some questions refer to passages, whereas other questions are self-contained. For each question, choose the best answer.

Questions 1–7 refer to the following passage.

(1) There is a lively debate among musicologists, critics, and fans about what should be considered the first rock and roll recording. (2) Some candidates for the first rock and roll song include Elvis Presley's "That's All Right (Mama)" (1954), Big Joe Turner's "Shake, Rattle, and Roll" (1954), and Bill Haley's "Rock Around the Clock" (1955). (3) In my opinion, "Rock Around the Clock" is the first true rock and roll song. "That's All Right (Mama)" has a country feel distinctive of the rockabilly tradition from which it springs, while "Shake, Rattle, and Roll" is more of a blues tune. (4) Rockabilly and blues are two of the major sources for the early development of rock and roll, but it is the fusion of these and other sources that distinguishes rock as genre. (5) "Rock Around the Clock" is a perfect example. (6) Based on rockabilly-style melody set to a 12-bar blues progression, the driving rhythm and flamboyant guitar solo of Bill Haley's classic set it apart as a true rock and roll song.

1. Which of the following best describes sentence 1?

   (A) It summarizes the author's view in a particular debate about music history.
   (B) It explains why the history of rock and roll is an important topic.
   (C) It outlines different positions in the debate about the origins of a particular musical genre.
   (D) It provides a context for the topic addressed in the passage.
   (E) It provides insight into the author's opinion about the first rock and roll song.

2. In context, the word *lively* in sentence 1 emphasizes that the debate in question is

   (A) bitter.
   (B) unresolved.
   (C) superficial.
   (D) positive.
   (E) useless.

3. Which of the following best describes the purpose of describing the musical qualities of the two songs named in sentence 3?

   (A) To undermine the claim that they are true rock and roll songs
   (B) To contrast them with other songs from each genre
   (C) To praise their creativity and musical qualities
   (D) To analyze their contributions to rock and roll
   (E) To emphasize limitations in the debate noted in sentence 1

4. What purpose is served by the first clause of sentence 4 (reproduced below)?

    Rockabilly and blues are two of the major sources for the early development of rock and roll

    (A) To emphasize the differences between rock and roll, rockabilly, and blues
    (B) To highlight the author's opinions about what constitutes the first rock and roll song
    (C) To implicitly criticize established views about the history of rock and roll
    (D) To indicate a preference for certain genres among the sources of rock and roll
    (E) To acknowledge that rock and roll is not completely distinct from rockabilly and blues

5. In sentence 5, what is "Rock Around the Clock" supposed to be a perfect example of?

    (A) A source for the early development of rock and roll
    (B) A genre of rock and roll
    (C) A fusion of rockabilly and blues
    (D) A blues song
    (E) A rockabilly song

6. Which of the following transition words, if inserted at the beginning of sentence 6 (reproduced below),
   would increase the coherence of the sentence in the context of this passage?

    *Based on rockabilly-style melody set to a 12-bar blues progression, the driving rhythm and
    flamboyant guitar solo of Bill Haley's classic sets it apart as a true rock and roll song.*

    (A) Although
    (B) If
    (C) However
    (D) Nevertheless
    (E) Since

7. This passage is primarily concerned with

    (A) criticizing alternative views.
    (B) tracing a historical progression.
    (C) summarizing the positions of a debate.
    (D) expressing an opinion.
    (E) drawing connections between facts.

Questions 8–13 refer to the following passage.

(1) Published in 1925, F. Scott Fitzgerald's classic novel *The Great Gatsby* is both a reflection
of and a commentary on its time. (2) The great prosperity and rapid cultural change in America
during the 1920s invited the nickname *The Roaring Twenties*. (3) Not all Americans embraced
the new attitudes and lifestyles of the age. (4) The Roaring Twenties embodied a gigantic clash
between traditional and contemporary moral views. (5) Thus, Prohibition was established in the
midst of a party atmosphere internationally renowned for its flappers, jazz, and general indulgence. (6) *The Great Gatsby* embraces such contradictions. (7) Nick Carraway, the protagonist,
both idolizes and worries about the unrestrained excess of the age.

8. Which of the following best characterizes sentence 1?

   (A) It introduces a claim that is questioned in later sentences.
   (B) It describes a theory of the relationship between literature and history.
   (C) It summarizes the theme of the passage.
   (D) It presents a statement about a particular historical period.
   (E) It evaluates a critical claim about a work of literature.

9. Which of the following transition words, if inserted at the beginning of sentence 3 (reproduced below), would be most logical in the context of the passage?

   > *Not all Americans embraced the new attitudes and lifestyles of the age.*

   (A) But
   (B) Although
   (C) Since
   (D) Consequently
   (E) Thus

10. Which choice is the best option to do with the word *gigantic* in sentence 4 (reproduced below)?

    > *The Roaring Twenties embodied a gigantic clash between traditional and contemporary moral views.*

    (A) Leave it as is.
    (B) Delete it.
    (C) Replace *gigantic* with *enormous*.
    (D) Replace *gigantic* with *heavy*.
    (E) Replace *gigantic* with *magnificent*.

11. The purpose of sentence 5 is to

    (A) qualify the assertion made in sentence 3.
    (B) comment on the historical trend described in sentence 4.
    (C) illustrate the point raised in sentence 4.
    (D) outline evidence for the main thesis of the passage.
    (E) provide examples of the idea conveyed in sentence 6.

12. In context, a synonym for *embraces* in sentence 6 is

    (A) rejects.
    (B) advocates.
    (C) ignores.
    (D) encompasses.
    (E) questions.

13. Which of the following would be best to add after sentence 7?

    (A) An example of the "unrestrained excess" of the 1920s
    (B) A hypothesis about the real-life model for Nick Carraway
    (C) A comment on another novel written during the 1920s
    (D) A brief discussion of F. Scott Fitzgerald's life
    (E) An anecdote illustrating Nick Carraway's ambivalence

CLEP College Composition Practice Test 1

ANSWER KEY
CONVENTIONS OF STANDARD WRITTEN ENGLISH

1.	(D)	4.	(D)
2.	(C)	5.	(B)
3.	(E)		

REVISION SKILLS

1.	(B)	8.	(D)	15.	(E)
2.	(A)	9.	(B)	16.	(B)
3.	(D)	10.	(A)	17.	(C)
4.	(B)	11.	(D)	18.	(A)
5.	(C)	12.	(E)	19.	(E)
6.	(E)	13.	(C)	20.	(D)
7.	(D)	14.	(C)		

ABILITY TO USE SOURCE MATERIALS

1.	(B)	5.	(A)	9.	(D)
2.	(C)	6.	(D)	10.	(B)
3.	(D)	7.	(B)	11.	(E)
4.	(E)	8.	(A)	12.	(D)

RHETORICAL ANALYSIS

1.	(D)	6.	(A)	11.	(C)
2.	(B)	7.	(D)	12.	(D)
3.	(A)	8.	(C)	13.	(E)
4.	(E)	9.	(A)		
5.	(C)	10.	(B)		

DETAILED EXPLANATIONS OF ANSWERS PRACTICE TEST 1

CONVENTIONS OF STANDARD WRITTEN ENGLISH

1. **(D)** The correct phrase is *that have*.

2. **(C)** The correct word is *an*.

3. **(E)** This sentence contains no errors.

4. **(D)** The correct phrase is *following the*.

5. **(B)** The correct word is *show*.

REVISION SKILLS

1. **(B)** Sentences 2 and 6 introduce each side of the debate. *Educators* is the specific group referred to in sentence 6.

2. **(A)** Option A is the only grammatically correct option in which letters and groups of letters are depicted as constituents of words.

3. **(D)** Option D is the only option that reflects the way each instructional approach is named in the passage.

4. **(B)** In sentence 4, reference to the popularity of phonics-based methods does not fit the other content of the passage, which pertains to the nature of the two instructional methods.

5. **(C)** Option C is the only option that accurately reflects the meaning of the passage.

6. **(E)** Option E is the only option that is both coherent and grammatically correct.

7. **(D)** Option D is the only option that is both coherent and grammatically correct.

8. **(D)** In option D, the reference to Santiago's struggle points back to the courage and strength attributed to him in sentence 1, while also describing the landing of the marlin whose loss is noted in sentence 2.

9. **(B)** In context, the phrase *express and* is redundant.

10. **(A)** In option A, the reference is clearest.

11. **(D)** Option D is the only option that provides a comparative phrase for *deeper water*.

12. **(E)** Option E is the only option that is both coherent and grammatically correct.

13. **(C)** Option C is the only option that is both coherent and grammatically correct.

14. **(C)** Option C is the only option that is both coherent and grammatically correct.

15. **(E)** Since the emphasis here is on the risk-taking of other riders, reference to these riders as *daredevils* will convey the message of sentence 3 most clearly.

16. **(B)** Option B is the only option that is both coherent and grammatically correct.

17. **(C)** The admonition in sentence 5 does not fit the content of the passage.

18. **(A)** Option A reflects the theme of the second paragraph.

19. **(E)** Option E is the only option that is both coherent and grammatically correct.

20. **(D)** Option D is the only option that is both coherent and idiomatic.

ABILITY TO USE SOURCE MATERIALS

1. **(B)** Examination of the references reveals that the source is a book.

2. **(C)** Citation information is needed for *A Nation at Risk*.

3. **(D)** The first clause of sentence 5 indicates that what follows is an example of the statement made in sentence 4.

4. **(E)** Option E is the only accurate option.

5. **(A)** All of the second paragraph following sentence 1 describes NCLB, one example of the kind of federal legislation in question.

6. **(D)** In context, sentence 11 is redundant.

7. **(B)** Although sentences 9–11 indicate that NCLB enables federal support for educational programs, no examples are given.

8. **(A)** Unlike sentence 1, sentences 2–5 each assert specific facts and hypotheses.

9. **(D)** *Archaeologists* is the more specific term also used in sentence 4.

10. **(B)** Option B is the only accurate option.

11. **(E)** The information in parentheses clarifies the meaning of the main portion of the sentence, and thus *i.e.* is the appropriate phrase.

12. **(D)** Option D is the only accurate option.

RHETORICAL ANALYSIS

1. **(D)** Option D is the only accurate option.

2. **(B)** In context, *lively* implies that the debate is energetic—and, therefore, unresolved.

3. **(A)** Option A is the only accurate option.

4. **(E)** Option E is the only accurate option.

5. **(C)**   Sentence 5 refers back to sentence 4, and thus "Rock Around the Clock" is meant to be a perfect example of the fusion described in sentence 4.

6. **(A)**   *Although* is a necessary term, because the first clause of sentence 6 is meant to acknowledge the influences of rockabilly and blues on the song, whereas the second clause indicates that in spite of those influences, it represents a distinctive genre (rock and roll).

7. **(D)**   Option D is the only accurate option.

8. **(C)**   Option C is the only accurate option.

9. **(A)**   Sentence 3 is meant to qualify the characterization presented in sentence 2. Thus, *but* serves as an appropriate comparative term.

10. **(B)**   In context, the term *clash* is sufficient to describe the relationship between traditional and contemporary views. The term *gigantic* and the adjectives in options C–E are exaggerated and distracting.

11. **(C)**   Option C is the only accurate option.

12. **(D)**   In context, option D is the only accurate option.

13. **(E)**   Sentence 7 presents a general description that would be clearer if accompanied by a concrete example.

ESSAYS

TIME: *70 Minutes*

DIRECTIONS: You will have a total of 70 minutes to write two argumentative essays. You will have 30 minutes to complete the first essay, which is to be based on your own reading, experience, or observations, and 40 minutes to complete the second essay, which requires you to synthesize two sources that are provided. Although you are free to begin writing at any point, it is better to take the time you need to plan your essays and to do the required reading than it is to begin writing immediately.

FIRST ESSAY

DIRECTIONS: According to Mark Twain, "Clothes make the man." Write an essay in which you discuss what you think Twain meant by this sentence. Then, discuss whether you agree or disagree. Support your discussion with specific reasons and examples from your reading, experience, or observations.

Sample Essay

I think that Twain's comment, "Clothes make the man," is a concise way of saying that appearances play an important role in the impressions people make on others. In the ideal world, people would be judged on the basis of their inner merits. Whether we are deciding to offer someone a job, to be his or her friend, or to forgive a crime that he or she has committed, the ideal would be to know every detail of the person's heart and mind before making a judgment. After all, the person's potential as an employee, friend, or reformed criminal should not depend on his or her appearance. But we cannot see directly into peoples' hearts and minds, and in any case, our time is limited. In a job interview, at a party, or during a legal trial, we judge people on the basis of limited information available during a limited amount of time. Thus, our judgments must rely on appearances. We examine specific behaviors, for example. A person who does not look us in the eye will inspire less trust than a person who readily meets our gaze. Another aspect of a person's appearance is his or her clothing. Often we look at what a person is wearing and make inferences about what type of person he or she is. Here again, we make judgments on the basis of limited information (a particular outfit) available during a limited amount of time (a quick glance). In this sense, clothes do make the man (or woman). You are, to an extent, what you wear.

Although I agree with Twain's observation, I also feel that, like many other catchy phrases, it is too simplistic. Yes, clothes help make the man (or woman). This is inevitable, as I pointed out in the previous paragraph, and to some extent, it is desirable. During a 20-minute job interview, I do want to consider my potential employee's outfit. Clothing that is dirty, inappropriate, or garishly mismatched would be a clue that the person might not be a careful worker, or be sufficiently aware of his or her impact on others. However, I would also want to consider the person's qualifications. In the case of a supremely qualified applicant, I might be willing to forgive a small soup stain on the shirt or a magenta-colored tie. So, yes, clothes would make or break the man (or woman), but so would the person's inner qualities. Arguably, in some cases, the inner qualities are more important.

The limitations of Twain's comment are evident when we consider some of the leading entrepreneurs of computer technology over the past three decades. Bill Gates, the founder of Microsoft, Sergey Brin, the cofounder of Google, and Mark Zuckerberg, the founder of Facebook, all have something in common besides their colossal influence on electronic technology: All of them, at least early in their careers, dressed informally, regardless of who they were with. I have read that some of the more traditional members of the industry were startled, or took offense, when these individuals showed up at business meetings wearing t-shirts, jeans, and sneakers. However, their casual clothing did not limit the success of these three superstars. Each one of them had ideas that were innovative and insightful, and it was the quality of these ideas rather than the cut of their clothing that determined their success. For people like Gates, Brin, and Zuckerberg, brilliance makes the man, in spite of the clothes.

Commentary

Look back at the directions for this essay. You will see that the directions include three requests: 1. *Write an essay in which you discuss what you think Twain meant by this sentence.* 2. *Then, discuss whether you agree or disagree.* 3. *Support your discussion with specific reasons and examples, etc.*

The author of the essay addresses the first request in the essay's first paragraph. The discussion there is detailed, and the author shows some thoughtfulness by linking Twain's observation about clothes to appearances more generally, and by then distinguishing appearances from the underlying substance.

The author addresses the second request by agreeing with Twain's comment (paragraph 1) but then describing the limitations of that comment (paragraphs 2 and 3). The reasons for agreeing with Twain, and for finding his comment simplistic, are clearly explained and supported by examples.

The author addresses the third request by providing a rationale for each idea developed in the essay, and by providing general examples (paragraphs 1 and 2) as well as specific examples (paragraph 3) of these ideas.

Notice that the essay is clear, well-organized, grammatically varied, and free of errors. In the last sentence or two of each paragraph, the author shows good command of the language in playing with variants of Twain's comment.

SECOND ESSAY

DIRECTIONS: The following assignment requires you to write a coherent essay in which you synthesize the two sources provided. Synthesis refers to combining the sources and your position to form a cohesive, supported argument. You must develop a position and incorporate both sources. **You must cite the sources whether you are paraphrasing or quoting.** Refer to each source by the author's last name, or by any other means that adequately identifies it.

Introduction

Social networks like Facebook and MySpace have changed our educational system. Some observers consider the changes beneficial. These observers note that it is desirable for teachers to make use of social networks as a way of facilitating communication among learners, as well as among teachers and outside experts. Other observers are concerned that these changes undermine the learning process. They argue that pedagogy (i.e., the way teaching is carried out) should determine how teachers use social networks. In actual practice, however, social networks are influencing pedagogy, which is a concern because social networks are created for profit rather than for educational purposes.

Assignment

Read the following sources carefully. Then write an essay in which you develop a position on whether social networks should or should not be used in the classroom. Be sure to incorporate and cite both of the accompanying sources as you develop your position.

McIntosh, Ewan. Web. 15 Jan. 2008. http://www.economist.com/debate/days/view/127

Social networking in all its forms has already begun to transform the way teachers teach, learners learn, and education managers lead learning, and will continue to do so. Social networking has arrived in hundreds of thousands of classrooms and is attempting to show that technology in education is less about anonymous chips and bytes filling up our children with knowledge, less about teachers reinforcing a "chalk and talk" style with an interactive whiteboard, and less about death by PowerPoint bullets. It's more about helping learners become more world-aware, more communicative, learning from each other, and understanding firsthand what makes the world go around.

Bugeja, Michael. Web. 15 Jan. 2008. http://www.economist.com/debate/days/view/127

[Social networks] are programmed for revenue generation, especially the vending of marketing data and the advertising base that can be established because of that data. To do so, those networks rely on technology developed by military (to surveil) and industry (to sell). . . . [Technology has] altered education in every conceivable facet. I have seen it used as delivery system, then as content in the classroom, and finally as classroom, building, and campus itself, and in every case, pedagogy changed to accommodate the interface.

Shouldn't it be the other way around? Unless we impose that logic on social networks, they will align educational methods with corporate motives. . . .

Suggestions for Essay Development

A good place to begin is to read these quotes, to be sure you understand the similarities and differences between the positions that McIntosh and Bugeja express, and then to think about the position you will develop in your own essay. Will you side with one of the authors? Will you develop a position that represents a compromise between their positions? Or will you develop a third position that is to some extent separate from theirs?

The next step is to plan your essay. Although your time is limited, you should take a few minutes to create an informal outline that will guide your writing. The outline should identify key points and examples and indicate the order in which they will be discussed.

The following text provides an outline for one particular essay that could be written. This outline is based on the premise that while McIntosh and Bugeja each make good points, other points should be considered when judging the desirability of using social networks in educational settings. The conclusion will be that social networks should be incorporated into classroom instruction, but only if used carefully.

The following outline is relatively detailed and written in complete sentences so that you can follow the progression of ideas. An outline written during the actual test would not need to be as elaborate.

1. Social networks (SN) are here to stay, as McIntosh notes; we couldn't ban them from classrooms even if we wanted to.

2. SN have advantages and disadvantages as classroom tools.

   (a) Advantages: SN connect learners to each other and to more knowledgeable sources (McIntosh). And, SN are fast and powerful.

   (b) Disadvantages: SN are created by corporations that have profit motives, and these SN drive pedagogy rather than vice versa (Bugeja). In addition, SN can be a source of distraction.

3. No technology is perfect. However, a technology will be desirable if its advantages outweigh its disadvantages. Bugeja does not make a strong case against SN.

   (a) Bugeja is correct that SN are motivated by corporate interests, but so are other materials used in the classroom. Textbooks and other curricular materials are created for a profit. The same may be true of teacher training programs.

   (b) Bugeja is correct that pedagogy is altered by the use of SN, but is this really a bad thing? Shouldn't teachers be flexible when incorporating new tools into their instruction? And, isn't the way that SN are used in the classroom determined by teachers rather than controlled by the technology?

4. Since we can't ban SN from the classroom, we should consider how to maximize their advantages and minimize their disadvantages. McIntosh is correct about the advantages but does not acknowledge the disadvantages that Bugeja notes.

5. SN are a desirable part of the classroom if used carefully.

   (a) Teachers can help students recognize profit motives, and to understand that exposure to advertising and pressure to purchase applications are among the distractions that come with superior connectivity to other learners and experts.

   (b) Teachers can incorporate SN in a sensible and discriminating way into their classroom instruction rather than allowing SN to completely determine their pedagogical approach.

CLEP College Composition Modular Test 1

TIME: *90 Minutes*

CONVENTIONS OF STANDARD WRITTEN ENGLISH

DIRECTIONS: The following sentences test your knowledge of grammar, usage, diction (choice of words), and idiom. Note that some sentences are correct, and no sentence contains more than one error. Read each sentence carefully, paying particular attention to the underlined portions. You will find that the error, if there is one, is underlined. Assume that elements of the sentence that are not underlined are correct and cannot be changed. In choosing answers, follow the requirements of standard written English. If there is an error, select the one underlined part that must be changed to make the sentence correct. If there is no error, select "No error."

1. "What do I know?" <u>was</u> the motto of the influential French essayist Michel de <u>Montaigne, who</u>
              A   B
   was born <u>on</u> 1533 and <u>lived for</u> 59 years. <u>No error</u>
           C   D   E

2. John <u>Steinbeck more</u> than any other writer, <u>sparked</u> the young <u>author's</u> interest <u>in twentieth</u>-century
         A   B   C   D
   American literature. <u>No error</u>
                E

3. <u>As soon as</u> the boxing match <u>ended and</u> the referee <u>announced</u> the winner, the crowd began to
      A   B   C
   <u>quickly move</u> toward the exit. <u>No error</u>
      D   E

4. <u>Confronted with</u> the choice of either <u>cleaning up</u> his room or <u>cleaning out</u> the garage, the teenager
       A   B   C
   <u>became</u> angry with his parents. <u>No error</u>
     D   E

5. <u>Of all</u> the important contributions to history that he <u>might have made</u>, John Montagu, the Earl of
   A   B
   Sandwich, is <u>better</u> known for a lunch of meat inserted <u>between</u> two slices of bread. <u>No error</u>
           C   D   E

6. One reason <u>astronomers</u> study quasars is <u>because</u> these small, quasi-stellar objects <u>might</u> provide
            A   B   C
   <u>clues</u> to the origin of the universe. <u>No error</u>
    D   E

7. Jerry <u>found</u> it <u>more difficult</u> to <u>divide</u> exponents than <u>adding</u> exponents. <u>No error</u>
           A   B   C   D   E

8. The kindergarten teacher <u>was so tired</u> after her first day on the job <u>that</u> thoughts of sleep <u>was all</u>
   　　　　　　　　　　　　　　　A　　　　　　　　　　　　　　　　　　　　B　　　　　　　　　　　　C

   that <u>went</u> through her mind. <u>No error</u>
   　　　　D　　　　　　　　　　　　E

9. Ramon y Cajal's 1904 monograph <u>on</u> the human nervous system, <u>still</u> considered a seminal work
   　　　　　　　　　　　　　　　　　　　　A　　　　　　　　　　　　　　B

   in neurobiology, <u>infers</u> that neural connections <u>in the brain</u> are highly structured. <u>No error</u>
   　　　　　　　　　　C　　　　　　　　　　　　　　　D　　　　　　　　　　　　　　　　E

REVISION SKILLS

DIRECTIONS: The following passages are early drafts of essays. Read each passage and then answer the questions that follow. Some questions refer to particular sentences or parts of sentences and ask you to improve sentence structure or diction (word choice). Other questions refer to the entire essay or parts of the essay and ask you to consider the essay's organization, development, or effectiveness of language. In selecting your answers, follow the conventions of standard written English.

Questions 1–6 are based on the following draft of an essay.

(1) This year, paleontologists discovered two new species of dinosaurs in southern Utah, *Kosmoceratops richardsoni* and *Utahceratops gettyi*. (2) Paleontologists believe that the two rhino-sized dinosaurs are closely related to the Triceratops. (3) However, the Kosmoceratops had 15 horns on its head, the Utahceratops had 5 horns, in contrast to the three-horned Triceratops. (4) Each horn was about 6 to 12 inches in length. (5) The horns were used, according to paleontologists, to attract females and to intimidate rivals for females. (6) However, the females of these species also had horns. (7) Paleontologists speculate that females evolved horns to ward off predators. (8) Kosmoceratops and Utahceratops lived about 76 million years ago.

(9) Kosmoceratops and Utahceratops are two of the dinosaur species recently discovered in the Grand Staircase-Escalante National Monument. (10) Which occupies a large area in southern Utah. (11) This part of the country is rocky and arid now, it would have been a swamp during the time that Kosmoceratops and Utahceratops flourished. (12) The ongoing discovery of new dinosaur species in areas such as the Grand Staircase-Escalante National Monument shows that the fossil record is constantly emerging rather than fixed.

1. In context, which of the following words should be used to replace the second comma in sentence 3 (immediately following the word *head*)?

   (A) but
   (B) and
   (C) as
   (D) though
   (E) then

2. Which of the following is the best way to reorder sentence 5 (reproduced below)?

> *The horns were used, according to paleontologists, to attract females and to intimidate rivals for females.*

(A) The horns were, according to paleontologists, used to attract females and to intimidate rivals for females.

(B) The horns, according to paleontologists, were used to attract females and to intimidate rivals for females.

(C) According to paleontologists, the horns were used to attract females and to intimidate rivals for females.

(D) The horns were used to attract females and, according to paleontologists, to intimidate rivals for females.

(E) The horns were used to attract females and to intimidate rivals, according to paleontologists, for females.

3. Where would be the best place to relocate sentence 8?

(A) After sentence 1

(B) After sentence 2

(C) After sentence 3

(D) After sentence 10

(E) After sentence 12

4. In context, which of the following is the best way to combine sentences 9 and 10 (reproduced below)?

> *Kosmoceratops and Utahceratops are two of the dinosaur species recently discovered in the Grand Staircase-Escalante National Monument. Which occupies a large area in southern Utah.*

(A) Kosmoceratops and Utahceratops are two of the dinosaur species recently discovered in the Grand Staircase-Escalante National Monument; which does occupy a large area in southern Utah.

(B) Kosmoceratops and Utahceratops are two of the dinosaur species recently discovered in the Grand Staircase-Escalante National Monument, a large area in southern Utah.

(C) Kosmoceratops and Utahceratops are two of the dinosaur species recently discovered in the Grand Staircase-Escalante National Monument, a monument that occupies a large area in southern Utah.

(D) Kosmoceratops and Utahceratops are two of the dinosaur species recently discovered in the Grand Staircase-Escalante National Monument, and this occupies a large area in southern Utah.

(E) Kosmoceratops and Utahceratops are two of the dinosaur species recently discovered in the Grand Staircase-Escalante National Monument, occupying a large area in southern Utah.

5. Which of the following words, if added to the beginning of sentence 11, would make the sentence both grammatically correct as well as coherent?

(A) However

(B) Since

(C) Although

(D) Because

(E) As

6. In context, which of the following is the best replacement for *emerging* in sentence 12 (reproduced below)?

> *The ongoing discovery of new dinosaur species in areas such as the Grand Staircase-Escalante National Monument shows that the fossil record is constantly emerging rather than fixed.*

(A) scintillating
(B) vacillating
(C) translating
(D) adding
(E) growing

Questions 7–14 are based on the following draft of an essay.

> (1) Although most new homes are finished in brick in the United States, stucco is becoming an increasingly popular finish. (2) Stucco finishes are composed of sand, water, and a binding material. (3) Traditionally, the binding material was lime; cement is widely used. (4) The first coat or two is 3/8 of an inch thick, while the final coat is about 1/4 to 1/8 of an inch thick. (5) Stucco is applied with a trowel. (6) It is quick and easy.
>
> (7) Stucco has many advantages, one advantage being energy efficiency. (8) A waterproof, low-maintenance exterior is produced by coating the final application of stucco with a clear acrylic finish. (9) Because colors can be mixed into stucco finishes, home owners and designers can select a color. (10) Finally, stucco is lightweight and quite inexpensive, too.

7. In context, which of the following is the best way to reorder sentence 1 (reproduced below)?

> *Although most new homes are finished in brick in the United States, stucco is becoming an increasingly popular finish.*

(A) In the United States, although most new homes are finished in brick, stucco is becoming an increasingly popular finish.
(B) Although in the United States most new homes are finished in brick, stucco is becoming an increasingly popular finish.
(C) Although most new homes in the United States are finished in brick, stucco is becoming an increasingly popular finish.
(D) Although most new homes are, in the United States finished in brick, stucco is becoming an increasingly popular finish.
(E) Although most new homes are finished in the United States in brick, stucco is becoming an increasingly popular finish.

8. Which option is the best choice to do with sentence 3 (reproduced below)?

> *Traditionally, the binding material was lime; cement is widely used.*

(A) Leave it as is.
(B) Change *was* to *is*.
(C) Replace the semicolon with a comma.
(D) Add *nowadays* at the end of the sentence.
(E) Break it into two sentences.

9. In context, which of the following is the best way to relate sentences 4 and 5?

   (A) Reverse their order.
   (B) Combine them into a single sentence separated by a semicolon.
   (C) Place them both inside one set of parentheses.
   (D) Combine them using the word *and*.
   (E) Combine them using the word *but*.

10. Which of the following is the best revision of sentence 6 (reproduced below)?

    It is quick and easy.

    (A) Stucco is quick and easy.
    (B) It is a quick and easy thing.
    (C) Stucco: quick and easy.
    (D) Applying stucco is quick and easy.
    (E) It is quick and easy, the stucco.

11. Which of the following is the best revision of the underlined portion of sentence 7 (reproduced below)?

    Stucco has many advantages, <u>one advantage being</u> energy efficiency.

    (A) and one of those advantages is
    (B) including
    (C) like the
    (D) but
    (E) and one being

12. In context, which word or phrase, added to the beginning of sentence 8, makes the purpose of the sentence clearer?

    (A) However
    (B) In addition
    (C) But
    (D) Nevertheless
    (E) Even so

13. In context, which revision to the underlined portion of sentence 9 (reproduced below) would make the sentence more persuasive?

    Because colors can be mixed into stucco finishes, home owners and designers can select <u>a color</u>.

    (A) from a variety of colors
    (B) from at least one color
    (C) an interesting color
    (D) a preferred color
    (E) one color or more

14. For which of the following audiences is this passage most likely to have been written?

    (A) A person who owns a stucco house
    (B) A recently retired stucco manufacturer
    (C) A manufacturer of brick finish
    (D) A potential buyer of stucco finish
    (E) An architect who specializes in stucco materials

Improving Sentences

DIRECTIONS: The following sentences test correctness and effectiveness of expression. In choosing your answers, follow the requirements of standard written English: that is, pay attention to grammar, diction (choice of words), sentence construction, and punctuation. In each of the following sentences, part of the sentence or the entire sentence is underlined. Beneath each sentence you will find five versions of the underlined part. The first option repeats the original; the other four options present different versions. Choose the option that best expresses the meaning of the original sentence. If you think the original is better than any of the alternatives, choose the first option; otherwise, choose one of the other options. Your choice should produce the most effective sentence—one that is clear and precise.

15. The Arctic Ocean is the <u>smallest, but shallowest</u> of the world's five major oceans.

    (A) smallest, but shallowest
    (B) smallest and shallowest
    (C) smallest, and the shallowest
    (D) smallest shallowest
    (E) smallest, yet shallowest

16. <u>The</u> Great Chicago Fire of 1871 was one of the largest U.S. disasters of the nineteenth century, the reconstruction that took place afterward helped Chicago become one of the most prominent American cities.

    (A) The
    (B) Surely the
    (C) Knowing that the
    (D) Since the
    (E) Although the

17. Nobody was surprised when Sandra won the race, <u>given she</u> had won so many races in the past.

    (A) given she
    (B) given when she
    (C) given that she
    (D) given where she
    (E) given the knowledge she

18. Madeleine L'Engle, a prominent writer of young adult <u>fiction, was born</u> in New York City on November 29, 1918.

   (A) fiction, was born
   (B) fiction; born
   (C) fiction. She was born
   (D) fiction was born
   (E) fiction, born

19. Although most professional basketball coaches believe that their players desire to win, some coaches doubt whether <u>they have</u> the necessary skills.

   (A) they have
   (B) their team have
   (C) they do have
   (D) their players have
   (E) they will have

20. Finding a book on top of the desk, <u>it was placed on the shelf with the others by the librarian</u>.

   (A) it was placed on the shelf with the others by the librarian
   (B) it was placed with the others on the shelf by the librarian
   (C) the librarian placed it on the shelf with the others
   (D) and placing it on the shelf with the others was the librarian
   (E) the librarian placed it on the shelf, with the others

21. The musicians carried four instruments <u>which is needed for the musical program</u>.

   (A) which is needed for the musical program
   (B) that is needed for the musical program
   (C) as are needed for the musical program
   (D) they are needed for the musical program
   (E) that are needed for the musical program

22. In writing *A Tale of Two Cities*, <u>Dickens produced one of the best-sellers of the Victorian Period</u>.

   (A) Dickens produced one of the best-sellers of the Victorian Period
   (B) one of the best-sellers of the Victorian Period was produced
   (C) the Victorian Period witnessed the production of one of Dickens's best-sellers
   (D) Dickens in the Victorian Period produced one of its best-sellers
   (E) production of one of the best-sellers of the Victorian Period was created by Dickens

23. If a person needs to leave the testing area during the test, <u>they should obtain</u> verbal permission as well as a pass from the proctor.

   (A) they should obtain
   (B) he or she should obtain
   (C) you should obtain
   (D) they could obtain
   (E) you could obtain

24. In *The Music Man,* Robert Preston portrays a fast-talking salesman who comes to a small town in Iowa <u>inadvertently falling in love with</u> the librarian.

    (A) inadvertently falling in love with
    (B) and inadvertently falls in love with
    (C) and afterwards he inadvertently falls in love with
    (D) then falling inadvertently in love with
    (E) when he inadvertently falls in love with

25. Two-thirds of American 17-year-olds do not know that the Civil War <u>takes place</u> between 1850 and 1900.

    (A) takes place
    (B) have taken place
    (C) has taken place
    (D) took place
    (E) is taking place

26. Father Junipero Serra, a Franciscan missionary sent from Spain to Mexico, <u>where he taught and worked among the Indians</u> and then founded many missions in California that later became cities.

    (A) where he taught and worked among the Indians
    (B) there he taught and worked among the Indians
    (C) he taught and worked among the Indians
    (D) taught and worked among the Indians
    (E) teaching and working among the Indians

27. He went to the meeting eager to explain his point of view but <u>had fear of public speaking</u>.

    (A) had fear of public speaking
    (B) having fear of public speaking
    (C) having fear he would have to speak in public
    (D) fearing the public speaking
    (E) was afraid of public speaking

28. Reducing calories <u>are ways to lose weight</u>.

    (A) are ways to lose weight
    (B) is a way to lose weight
    (C) loses weight
    (D) weight is lost
    (E) is a loss of weight

29. After having written many books, <u>the author was made popular</u>.

    (A) the author was made popular
    (B) the author is popular
    (C) the author became a popular author
    (D) the author will become popular
    (E) the author became popular

30. Patricia noticed that <u>some</u> button on her shirt had popped off.

   (A) some
   (B) this
   (C) a
   (D) that
   (E) any

31. As she read through Plato's early dialogues, the philosophy student found Socrates <u>a</u> brilliant and intriguing character.

   (A) a
   (B) as a
   (C) the
   (D) to be a
   (E) to be the

32. Without warning, the sky darkened and <u>the rain</u>.

   (A) the rain
   (B) then the rain
   (C) it began to rain
   (D) came the rain
   (E) it was the rain

33. In 1905, Theodore Roosevelt played the role of mediator between Russia and Japan <u>during</u> negotiations that resulted in the Treaty of Portsmouth.

   (A) during
   (B) among
   (C) around
   (D) considering
   (E) overseeing

34. Walking down Main Street, <u>the trees</u> were especially lovely.

   (A) the trees
   (B) there were many trees
   (C) she considered the trees
   (D) he noticed that the trees
   (E) it was the trees

35. If <u>I'd have been</u> paying closer attention, I wouldn't have overcooked the soup.

   (A) I'd have been
   (B) I had been
   (C) I would have been
   (D) I'd've been
   (E) I been

36. Mary reached down to pick up the <u>pencil, that</u> had fallen underneath her desk.

    (A) pencil, that
    (B) pencil as
    (C) pencil, what
    (D) pencil which
    (E) pencil that

ABILITY TO USE SOURCE MATERIALS

DIRECTIONS: The following questions test your familiarity with basic research, reference, and composition skills. Some questions refer to passages, whereas other questions are self-contained. For each question, choose the best answer.

Questions 1–6 refer to the following passage.

(1) During his two terms as president of the United States, George Washington established a number of precedents that subsequent presidents are known to have followed. (2) For example, Washington decided that his official title should be "Mr. President," choosing this designation over more formal options that Congress had considered, such as "His Highness" and "His High Mightiness" (Ellis, 2004). (3) Washington also delivered an inaugural speech and refused to serve as president for more than two terms, a practice that was later made law by means of the Twenty-Second Amendment to the U.S. Constitution. (4) Other aspects of Washington's presidency were more idiosyncratic. (5) He did not belong to a political party, for example, and he advocated neutrality in foreign affairs (Grizzard, 2005). (6) Ellis (2004) and many other historians suggest that the precedents established by Washington, whether or not adopted by future presidents, all reflected Washington's commitment to the strength and well-being of the United States, as well as the characteristics of his own distinctive personality.

References

Ellis, J. 2004. *His Excellency: George Washington*. New York: Random House.

Grizzard, F. 2005. *George! A Guide to All Things Washington*. Buena Vista and Charlottesville, VA: Mariner Publishing.

1. Which option is the best choice to do with the underlined portion of sentence 1 (reproduced below)?

    During his two terms as president of the United States, George Washington established a number of precedents that subsequent presidents <u>are known to have followed</u>.

    (A) Leave it as is.
    (B) Delete *are known to*.
    (C) Replace it with *have clearly followed*.
    (D) Add *, according to scholars* at the end.
    (E) Replace it with *will follow*.

2. Must each of the quoted phrases in sentence 2 be attributed to a separate source?

   (A) No.
   (B) Yes, but only if the source was one of Washington's contemporaries.
   (C) Yes, but only if a primary source is cited.
   (D) Yes, but only if the source is a professional historian.
   (E) Yes, but only if the source is an expert on Washington.

3. Which of the following best describes the purpose of sentence 3?

   (A) To qualify an earlier statement
   (B) To establish an overarching theme
   (C) To summarize an idea expressed earlier
   (D) To provide concrete examples of an earlier point
   (E) To criticize a general assumption

4. The information in parentheses at the end of sentence 5 most clearly indicates that

   (A) the sentence is a quotation from a work by Grizzard.
   (B) Grizzard has written a work that focuses on political affiliation and foreign affairs.
   (C) Grizzard has written a work that includes information about Washington's views on political affiliation and foreign affairs.
   (D) Grizzard was a contemporary of Washington who wrote a work about Washington's views of political affiliation and foreign affairs.
   (E) details about Washington's views on political affiliation and foreign affairs can be found on page 2005 of a work by Grizzard.

5. In context, the reference to Ellis (2004) at the beginning of sentence 6 informs the reader that

   (A) Ellis is a famous historian who has written extensively about U.S. presidents.
   (B) Ellis is the most important historian who has expressed the idea summarized in sentence 6.
   (C) Ellis has a unique perspective on Washington's political views.
   (D) Ellis is a historian who does not agree with the idea summarized in sentence 6.
   (E) Ellis is one of numerous historians who have expressed the idea summarized in sentence 6.

6. Which of the following kinds of information, if added to the end of this passage, would increase the coherence of sentence 6?

   (A) A general analysis of how a leader's personality can influence his or her leadership style
   (B) A concrete example of how Washingtonian precedents reflected Washington's distinctive personality
   (C) A critique of the ways that Washington's personality impacted his key decisions as president
   (D) A theoretical discussion of how Washington might have conducted his presidency differently
   (E) An exhortation for scholars to pay greater attention to the role of each president's personality in policy decisions

Questions 7–8 refer to the following citation.

Bronfenbrenner, U. 1986. Ecology of the family as a context for human development: Research perspectives. *Developmental Psychology 22*: 723–742.

7. In the previous citation, what is *Developmental Psychology*?

    (A) The name of a book
    (B) The name of an edited volume
    (C) The name of a journal
    (D) The name of Bronfenbrenner's academic department
    (E) The name of a field of inquiry

8. In the previous citation, what is the *22*?

    (A) It is part of the name of the source.
    (B) It is the total page length of the work cited.
    (C) It is the ranking of the source in a professional database.
    (D) It is the number of publications contributed by the author.
    (E) It is the volume number of the source.

Questions 9–17 refer to the following passage.

(1) A tree is a perennial woody plant . . . that has many secondary branches supported clear of the ground on a single main stem or trunk with clear apical dominance. (2) A minimum height specification at maturity varying from 3 m to 6 m is cited by some authors; some authors set a minimum of 10 cm trunk diameter (30 cm girth). (3) Woody plants that do not meet these definitions by having multiple stems and/or small size are called shrubs. (4) Compared with most other plants, trees are long-lived, some reaching several thousand years old and growing to up to 115 m (379 ft) high.

(5) Trees are an important component of the natural landscape because of their prevention of erosion and the provision of a weather-sheltered ecosystem in and under their foliage. . . . (6) Wood from trees is a building material, as well as a primary energy source in many developing countries. (7) Trees also play a role in many of the world's mythologies (see trees in mythology).

Quoted from *Wikipedia: The Free Encyclopedia*. Wikimedia Foundation, Inc. Web. 27 Sept. 2010. http://en.wikipedia.org/wiki/Tree

9. What kind of information does sentence 1 provide?

    (A) A definition
    (B) A hypothesis
    (C) A theme
    (D) A theory
    (E) A synthesis

10. In sentence 1, which of the following is most likely indicated by the ellipsis immediately following *plant*?

    (A) Overt omission of factually incorrect information
    (B) Deliberate censorship of objectionable material
    (C) Accidental omission of a sentence
    (D) Inadvertent loss of text from original source
    (E) Intentional omission of words

11. Which of the following information, if inserted at the end of sentence 1, would increase the understand-ability of sentence 1?

    (A) A description of one particular species of tree
    (B) A contrast between the features of various types of plants
    (C) A definition of the phrase *apical dominance*
    (D) A citation for the details given in sentence 1
    (E) A summary of the information to come in sentence 2

12. How does sentence 2 appear to contribute to the passage?

    (A) It shows that certain dimensions of trees are not fully understood.
    (B) It describes two possible criteria for the definition of a tree.
    (C) It contrasts the relative dimensions of trees versus shrubs.
    (D) It illustrates controversies about how trees have been defined.
    (E) It reflects natural variability in the physical dimensions of trees.

13. In context, which of the following is most clearly implied by the two references to *some authors* in sentence 2?

    (A) Not all authors agree that trees are classifiable in terms of physical dimensions.
    (B) Not all authors who discuss trees provide a concrete definition for this category.
    (C) Not all authors consider physical dimensions among the criteria for being a tree.
    (D) Not all authors agree about all of the criteria for the definition of a tree.
    (E) Not all trees fit the definitional criteria for a tree described by some authors.

14. Which of the following is the best revision to the underlined portion of sentence 2 (reproduced below)?

    > *A minimum height specification at maturity varying from 3 m to 6 m is cited by some authors;*
    > <u>*some authors*</u> *set a minimum of 10 cm trunk diameter (30 cm girth).*

    (A) other authors
    (B) these authors
    (C) a few authors
    (D) as well as authors
    (E) the many authors

15. Which of the following is the best revision of sentence 3 (reproduced below)?

    Woody plants that do not meet these definitions by having multiple stems and/or small size are called shrubs.

    (A) Woody plants that have multiple stems and/or small size and therefore do not meet these definitions are called shrubs.
    (B) Woody plants that do not meet these definitional criteria owing to multiple stems and/or small size are called shrubs.
    (C) Woody plants that do not meet these definitions owing to their multiple stems and small size are called shrubs.
    (D) Woody plants that do not meet these definitional criteria by their having multiple stems and/or small size are called shrubs.
    (E) Woody plants having multiple stems and/or small size that do not meet these definitions are called shrubs.

16. What is the contribution of the second paragraph (sentences 5–7) to the passage?

    (A) It shows that the scientific definition of a tree is inadequate.
    (B) It describes some of the natural functions and cultural uses of trees.
    (C) It explains why trees are more important than shrubs.
    (D) It illustrates why the conservation and management of trees is controversial.
    (E) It analyzes the role of trees in human society.

17. In sentence 7, the underlined phrase (*trees in mythology*) is a hyperlink that will most probably lead to

    (A) an online book.
    (B) a hypermedia display concerning trees.
    (C) a separate Wikipedia entry.
    (D) a slideshow.
    (E) a Greek mythology website.

Questions 18–22 refer to the following passage.

> (1) There are 131 breeds of dog currently recognized by the American Kennel Club. (2) Dalmatians are a particularly interesting breed. (3) They are quite popular, and they have risen in popularity recently from twenty-fourth to nineteenth. (4) Although scholars are unsure of their exact origin, the breed may have originated in Dalmatia, a narrow strip of land along the Adriatic Sea that is populated mostly by Croatians. (5) Most scholars believe that when bands of gypsies migrated westward to settle in Yugoslavia, the dogs traveled with them. (6) Dog-lovers are grateful now that they did.

18. Which of the following information would be most appealing to the reader who wishes to know more about the facts presented in sentence 1?

    (A) The name of a classic book about Dalmatians
    (B) The website of the American Kennel Club
    (C) The name of a book of photography that concerns Dalmatians
    (D) The reference for a classic article about Dalmatian breeding
    (E) The name of an essay about the joys of Dalmatian ownership

19. Which of the following kinds of information would contribute most to the understandability of sentence 3?

   (A) A description of why Dalmatians are popular
   (B) An analysis of whether the difference between twenty-fourth and nineteenth is statistically meaningful
   (C) A summary of which dogs are greater than nineteenth in popularity
   (D) An explanation of how the popularity of different breeds is measured
   (E) A characterization of the typical Dalmatian owner

20. Which details of sentence 4 and/or sentence 5 are in greatest need of clarification?

   (A) The geographic location of the possible origins of Dalmatians
   (B) The reasons why Dalmatians would have accompanied the gypsies during a migration
   (C) The historical basis for the assertion that Dalmatians originated in Dalmatia
   (D) The alternative accounts of the origins of Dalmatians, as proposed by other scholars
   (E) The connections between gypsies and Croatians, and between Yugoslavia and Dalmatia

21. Sentence 6 best serves as a transition to a paragraph that

   (A) describes and praises the characteristics of Dalmatians.
   (B) analyzes the geographical origins of other breeds.
   (C) discusses the features of the Adriatic Sea.
   (D) summarizes key issues in the care of Dalmatians.
   (E) advocates for the humane treatment of Dalmatians and other animals.

22. Which sentence is least clearly in need of a citation?

   (A) Sentence 1
   (B) Sentence 2
   (C) Sentence 3
   (D) Sentence 4
   (E) Sentence 5

RHETORICAL ANALYSIS

DIRECTIONS: The following questions test your ability to analyze writing. Some questions refer to passages, whereas other questions are self-contained. For each question, choose the best answer.

Questions 1–6 refer to the following passage.

   (1) The return of peace did not bring contentment to the Americans. (2) Because Congress had no means of raising a revenue or enforcing its decrees, it was unable to make itself respected either at home or abroad. (3) For want of pay, the army became very troublesome. (4) In January 1781, there had been a mutiny of Pennsylvania and New Jersey troops, which at one moment looked very serious. (5) In March 1783, inflammatory appeals were made to the officers at the headquarters of the army at Newburgh. (6) In the spring of 1782 some of the officers, disgusted with the want of efficiency in the government, seem to have entertained a scheme for making Washington

king; but Washington met the suggestion with a stern rebuke. (7) It seems to have been intended that the army should overawe Congress and seize upon the government until the delinquent states should contribute the money needed for satisfying the soldiers and other public creditors. (8) Gates either originated this scheme or willingly lent himself to it, but an eloquent speech from Washington prevailed upon the officers to reject and condemn it. (John Fiske, *The War of Independence*. Boston: Houghton Mifflin and Company, 1889, pp. 182–183.)

1. The purpose of sentence 1 is to

   (A) introduce the general theme of the passage.
   (B) demonstrate the writer's authority on the subject of the passage.
   (C) describe an idea that the author refutes later in the passage.
   (D) undermine the central claim of the passage.
   (E) present the idea that peace equals contentment.

2. In context, which of the following revisions of sentence 2 (reproduced below) would be preferable?

   Because Congress had no means of raising a revenue or enforcing its decrees, it was unable to make itself respected either at home or abroad.

   (A) Because Congress had no means of enforcing its decrees, it was unable to make itself respected either at home or abroad.
   (B) Because Congress had no means of raising a revenue, it was unable to make itself respected either at home or abroad.
   (C) Because Congress had no means of enforcing its decrees, it was unable to make itself respected.
   (D) Because Congress had no means of raising a revenue, it was unable to make itself respected.
   (E) Congress was unable to make itself respected.

3. What does sentence 4 contribute to the passage?

   (A) It provides for a transition between sentences 3 and 5.
   (B) It provides an example of the statement made in sentence 3.
   (C) It qualifies the assertion made in sentence 3.
   (D) It provides background for sentence 5.
   (E) It contributes nothing to the passage.

4. In context, *want* in sentences 3 and 6 most nearly means

   (A) desire.
   (B) interest.
   (C) abundance.
   (D) standards.
   (E) lack.

5. Which of the following seems least clearly conveyed by the passage?

   (A) The reason for the army's discontent
   (B) Details of concerns about the government's efficiency
   (C) The nature of the events that occurred between 1781 and 1783
   (D) The potential for significant political instability
   (E) Washington's personal view on a proposed increase in the army's power

6. Which of the following most clearly summarizes the relationship between Washington and the army that is implied by this passage?

(A) Washington and the army had a perpetually adversarial relationship.
(B) The army did not respect Washington's authority.
(C) Washington had considerable influence over the army.
(D) The army regularly consulted with Washington about matters of national importance.
(E) Washington was not interested in the army's views of political matters.

Questions 7–13 refer to the following essay.

(1) Most teenagers do not get in trouble on a regular basis, and few of us actually commit crimes. (2) The news media should give teenagers the publicity we deserve, instead of just focusing on our bad behavior. (3) For example, in my home town recently, a local youth group visited a retirement home one day in order to sing songs and chat with the residents. (4) This story was only reported on the second page of the local paper. (5) Another example is the Eagle Scout project of a teenager named Jay Jones, who made beautiful signs for the city to denote locations of public buildings such as city hall, the library, and the police station. (6) Did anyone from the news show up for the dedication of the signs? (7) A reporter was across town that day gathering information on a traffic accident caused by a teen-aged driver. (8) The story of the accident made the front page of the newspaper, of course, while the Eagle Scout's signs were not mentioned anywhere. (9) These examples show that the news media is totally unfair and that adults don't respect teenagers. (10) Our good works are passed over. (11) Truly, we deserve recognition for our positive contributions to society.

7. Which of the following, if inserted between sentences 1 and 2, would increase the persuasiveness of the first paragraph?

(A) The crime rate among teenagers is actually pretty low.
(B) We are not all bad; in fact, some of us are good.
(C) At the same time, many of us do good works for which we receive little or no publicity.
(D) Moreover, it is rare to see a teenager convicted of a highly serious crime.
(E) We are trying our best every day to be good citizens.

8. In context, which of the following terms, inserted before the phrase *bad behavior* in sentence 2, would increase the coherence of the sentence?

(A) well-known
(B) occasional
(C) underreported
(D) frequent
(E) notoriously

9. Why do sentences 3 and 4 fail to help the author develop the main theme of the essay?

(A) The author does not acknowledge that the teenagers' visit might have been mandatory rather than voluntary.
(B) Since the teenagers' visit took place in the author's home town, the author might be biased.
(C) The fact that the teenagers' visit was reported on the second rather than first page of the newspaper suggests that they were ignored.
(D) It is difficult to understand why the teenagers' visit can be considered an example of good behavior.
(E) The fact that the teenagers' visit was reported in the newspaper seems to contradict the main theme of the passage.

10. Which of the following sentences could be deleted without affecting the coherence of the essay?

    (A) Sentence 2
    (B) Sentence 3
    (C) Sentence 4
    (D) Sentence 6
    (E) Sentence 8

11. In context, sentence 8 serves to

    (A) introduce a new theme into the essay.
    (B) indicate similarities in the way that the news media covers stories that involve teenagers.
    (C) juxtapose two anecdotes that cast teenagers in an unflattering light.
    (D) provide a concrete illustration of the idea discussed in the previous sentence.
    (E) emphasize differences in the way the news media covers desirable versus undesirable behavior on the part of teenagers.

12. What is the main shortcoming of sentence 9?

    (A) The conclusion it draws is much broader than warranted by the examples in the passage.
    (B) It fails to acknowledge any of the benefits of the news media noted in the passage.
    (C) The two assertions in it contradict each other.
    (D) It reflects a somewhat negative tone regarding the news media and adults in general.
    (E) It is inaccurate concerning the relationship between adults and teenagers.

13. Which of the following best describes the organization of the passage as a whole?

    (A) A problem is described and solutions are discussed.
    (B) An assertion is made and examples are provided.
    (C) A hypothesis is presented and challenged by available data.
    (D) Two theories are proposed and evidence in support of one theory is discussed.
    (E) A question is developed and answers are evaluated.

Questions 14–19 refer to the following essay.

(1) Born in Crete in 1541, Domenikos Theotokopoulos grew up to become one of the world's great painters. (2) Known as *El Greco,* meaning "The Greek," he moved to Spain around 1577 after several frustrating years in Venice and Rome and eventually became known as a Spanish painter. (3) El Greco's relocation to Toledo, Spain, was probably due to his inability to obtain important commissions in Italy. (4) However, at first he had no better luck in Spain. (5) Paintings were supposed to inspire prayer and teach religious doctrine, but El Greco did not always adhere to scripture. (6) For example, he painted three Marys in *The Disrobing of Christ,* set biblical scenes in Toledo, and depicted Roman soldiers in sixteenth-century armor. (7) As a result, he lost the patronage of the Toledo Cathedral. (8) Later, he was able to gain the respect and patronage of Toledo's intellectuals. (9) Support from this liberal audience probably allowed the artist more freedom in developing his own style, which is characterized by elongated forms, graceful lines, and metallic colors with white highlights.

14. Which of the following words, inserted at the beginning of sentence 2, smoothes the transition between the first two sentences?

    (A) Although
    (B) Clearly
    (C) Better
    (D) Therefore
    (E) Once

15. The purpose of sentence 3 is to

    (A) explain an action that was introduced in sentence 2.
    (B) evaluate a theory about the painter's life.
    (C) contrast two different points of view.
    (D) analyze the relationship between individual and society.
    (E) illustrate key influences on the painter's style.

16. Which of the following phrases, added to the beginning of sentence 5, most improves the clarity of the sentence?

    (A) According to some,
    (B) As often asserted,
    (C) Thus,
    (D) At that time,
    (E) Arguably,

17. Which of the following is not explained in the first six sentences?

    (A) Why the painter is called El Greco
    (B) Where the painter was born
    (C) Why the painter struggled to obtain commissions
    (D) Where the painter flourished
    (E) Why the painter did not adhere to scripture

18. Which of the following is most clearly implied by the term *probably* in sentences 3 and 9?

    (A) The author has not read biographical portraits of El Greco very closely.
    (B) El Greco experienced much uncertainty in his development as an artist.
    (C) Some details of El Greco's life and personal choices are not known with certainty.
    (D) El Greco rarely spoke definitively about his career as an artist.
    (E) The author does not wish to speak very decisively about the topic.

19. Sentence 9 is most likely to serve as a transition to

    (A) a description of late sixteenth-century Toledo.
    (B) a discussion of El Greco's paintings.
    (C) an analysis of the artist's role in society.
    (D) an account of El Greco's voyage from Italy to Spain.
    (E) a critique of religious influences on the visual arts.

Questions 20–23 refer to the following essay.

(1) Alexander the Great's boyhood was shaped by two strong parents. (2) Alexander's father, King Philip of Macedonia, was a consummate general whose armies conquered Greece and made Macedonia a powerful force in the ancient world. (3) Taught to read, sing, and debate in Greek before he was 10, Alexander was tutored by the philosopher Aristotle from ages 13 to 16.

(4) As a young man, Alexander was fearless and showed great promise. (5) He was evidently perceptive as well. (6) At age 13, he was given a horse that no one had been able to touch, much less ride. (7) After noticing that the horse shied every time it saw its own shadow, Alexander turned it toward the sun and was able to tame it. (8) He called the horse Bucephalus, meaning ox-head, and kept the horse for many years, riding him into numerous battles.

20. Which of the following is most critical to include in the first paragraph?

    (A) Discussion of what Alexander learned from Aristotle
    (B) Anecdotes about Macedonian culture
    (C) Information about Alexander's other strong parent
    (D) Commentary on Macedonia's role in the ancient world
    (E) Description of King Phillip's personality

21. In sentence 2, *consummate* most nearly means

    (A) hesitant.
    (B) overbearing.
    (C) modest.
    (D) skilled.
    (E) inexperienced.

22. Which of the following would most improve sentence 4?

    (A) A description of the areas in which Alexander showed promise
    (B) The use of a flashier adjective than *great*
    (C) Replacement of *young man* with *youth*
    (D) An explanation of what *fearless* means
    (E) The addition of *reportedly* after *was*

23. In sentence 5, what does the word *evidently* allude to?

    (A) The tutoring that Alexander received from Aristotle
    (B) The name that Alexander gave to his horse
    (C) The author's personal opinion of Alexander
    (D) The military talent of King Phillip
    (E) The anecdote described in sentences 6 and 7

CLEP College Composition Modular Test 1

ANSWER KEY

CONVENTIONS OF STANDARD WRITTEN ENGLISH

1.	(C)	4.	(E)	6.	(B)	8.	(C)
2.	(A)	5.	(C)	7.	(D)	9.	(C)
3.	(E)						

REVISION SKILLS

1.	(B)	10.	(D)	19.	(D)	28.	(B)
2.	(C)	11.	(B)	20.	(C)	29.	(E)
3.	(A)	12.	(B)	21.	(E)	30.	(C)
4.	(B)	13.	(A)	22.	(A)	31.	(D)
5.	(C)	14.	(D)	23.	(B)	32.	(C)
6.	(E)	15.	(B)	24.	(B)	33.	(A)
7.	(C)	16.	(E)	25.	(D)	34.	(D)
8.	(D)	17.	(C)	26.	(D)	35.	(B)
9.	(A)	18.	(A)	27.	(E)	36.	(E)

ABILITY TO USE SOURCE MATERIALS

1.	(B)	7.	(C)	13.	(D)	19.	(D)
2.	(A)	8.	(E)	14.	(A)	20.	(E)
3.	(D)	9.	(A)	15.	(B)	21.	(A)
4.	(C)	10.	(E)	16.	(B)	22.	(B)
5.	(E)	11.	(C)	17.	(C)		
6.	(B)	12.	(B)	18.	(B)		

RHETORICAL ANALYSIS

1.	(A)	7.	(C)	13.	(B)	19.	(B)
2.	(D)	8.	(B)	14.	(C)	20.	(C)
3.	(B)	9.	(E)	15.	(A)	21.	(D)
4.	(E)	10.	(D)	16.	(D)	22.	(A)
5.	(B)	11.	(E)	17.	(E)	23.	(E)
6.	(C)	12.	(A)	18.	(C)		

DETAILED EXPLANATIONS OF ANSWERS MODULAR TEST 1

CONVENTIONS OF STANDARD WRITTEN ENGLISH

1. **(C)** The correct word is *in*.

2. **(A)** A comma is needed after *Steinbeck* given that one already appears after *writer*.

3. **(E)** This sentence contains no errors.

4. **(E)** This sentence contains no errors.

5. **(C)** The correct word is *best*.

6. **(B)** The correct word is *that*.

7. **(D)** The correct phrase is *to add*.

8. **(C)** The correct phrase is *were all*.

9. **(C)** Authors can *imply*, *indicate*, or otherwise convey an idea. It is the reader who makes inferences.

REVISION SKILLS

1. **(B)** *And* is needed, since sentence 3 presents a contrast between the two recently discovered dinosaurs and Triceratops.

2. **(C)** Option C is the only option in which the entire statement about the horns and their functions are clearly attributed to paleontologists.

3. **(A)** The only place where sentence 8 fits into the passage without disrupting the narrative flow is after sentence 1.

4. **(B)** Option B is the only option that is both grammatically correct and stylistically desirable.

5. **(C)** *Although* emphasizes the contrast between the two clauses in sentence 11.

6. **(E)** In context, option E is the only option that makes sense.

7. **(C)** Option C is the only option that is both grammatically correct and stylistically desirable.

8. **(D)** Option D is the only option that is both grammatically correct and supportive of the contrast between the two parts of the sentence.

9. **(A)** Reversing the order allows the action of applying stucco to be mentioned before the thickness of the applied stucco is discussed.

10. **(D)** Option D is the only option that is both grammatically correct and coherent.

11. **(B)** Option B is the only option that is both grammatically correct and stylistically desirable.

12. **(B)** Option B is the only option that correctly indicates the relationship between sentence 8 and the preceding sentence.

13. **(A)** Reference to a *variety* of colors makes option A most persuasive concerning the merits of stucco.

14. **(D)** Since the passage extols the virtues of stucco finish, option D is the best choice.

15. **(B)** Option B is the only option that is grammatically correct.

16. **(E)** Option E is the only option that is both grammatically correct and coherent.

17. **(C)** Option C is the only option that is grammatically correct.

18. **(A)** Option A is the only option that is grammatically correct.

19. **(D)** Option D is the only option that is grammatically correct and unambiguous as to who has the necessary skills.

20. **(C)** Option C is the only option that is grammatically correct and makes use of active voice.

21. **(E)** Option E is the only option that is grammatically correct.

22. **(A)** Option A is the only option that is both grammatically correct and stylistically desirable.

23. **(B)** Option B is the only option that is grammatically correct.

24. **(B)** Option B is the only option that is grammatically correct.

25. **(D)** Option D is the only option that is grammatically correct.

26. **(D)** Option D is the only option that is grammatically correct.

27. **(E)** Option E is the only option that is both grammatically correct and stylistically desirable.

28. **(B)** Option B is the only option that is both grammatically correct and stylistically desirable.

29. **(E)** Option E is the only option that is both grammatically correct and stylistically desirable.

30. **(C)** Option C is the only option that is both grammatically correct and stylistically desirable.

31. **(D)** Option D is the only option that is both grammatically correct and stylistically desirable.

32. **(C)** Option C is the only option that is grammatically correct.

33. **(A)** Option A is the only option that is both grammatically correct and coherent.

34. **(D)** Option D is the only option that is grammatically correct.

35. **(B)** Option B is the only option that is grammatically correct.

36. **(E)** Option E is the only option that is grammatically correct.

ABILITY TO USE SOURCE MATERIALS

1. **(B)** *Are known to* does not contribute any information that is not already implicit in the sentence.

2. **(A)** The quoted phrases are evidently noted in Ellis (2004).

3. **(D)** Sentences 2 and 3 each provide examples of the statement made in sentence 1.

4. **(C)** Options A and E are inaccurate. Evidently, Grizzard discussed the two facts about Washington described in sentence 5, and thus option C is most likely to be accurate.

5. **(E)** Option E is the only accurate option.

6. **(B)** Although sentence 6 asserts that Washingtonian precedents were, in part, reflections of his personality, no examples are given.

7. **(C)** Given the citation format, it is evident that *Developmental Psychology* is a journal.

8. **(E)** Option E is the only accurate option.

9. **(A)** Option A is the only accurate option.

10. **(E)** Option E is the only accurate option.

11. **(C)** The phrase *apical dominance* is unlikely to be understood by anyone other than an expert reader.

12. **(B)** Option B is the only accurate option.

13. **(D)** Since each use of the word *some* refers to different authors, it is clear that not all authors agree about the physical dimensions that should be included in the definition of a tree.

14. **(A)** Use of the phrase *other authors* clarifies the fact that two sets of authors are compared.

15. **(B)** Option B is the only grammatically correct and sensible option.

16. **(B)** Option B is the only accurate option.

17. **(C)** In context, option C is most likely to be correct.

18. **(B)** Since the American Kennel Club is mentioned as the source of the information in sentence 1, the website of this organization would be most appealing to interested readers.

19. **(D)** No information about the definition or measurement of popularity is given in sentence 3.

20. **(E)** Relationships between gypsies and Croatians, and between Yugoslavia and Dalmatia, are hinted at in these sentences but not made clear.

21. **(A)** Option A seems most likely in light of the favorable allusion to Dalmatians in sentence 6.

22. **(B)** Sentence 2 presents a highly general opinion expressed by the author.

RHETORICAL ANALYSIS

1. **(A)** Option A is the only accurate option.

2. **(D)** The discussion that follows sentence 2 focuses on military unrest arising from lack of pay. Option D is preferable owing to its sole focus on revenue and on lack of respect for Congress at home.

3. **(B)** Option B is the only accurate option.

4. **(E)** In context, option E is the only accurate option.

5. **(B)** No information is provided about governmental efficiency.

6. **(C)** Support for option C can be found in sentences 6 and 8.

7. **(C)** Option C succinctly expresses the theme of the passage.

8. **(B)** Since the sentence appears to assert that the news media should focus on good behavior rather than just negative behavior, the assertion will be clearer if it is emphasized that the bad behavior is occasional.

9. **(E)** Option E is the only accurate option.

10. **(D)** Sentence 6 presents a rhetorical question that disrupts the narrative flow from sentence 5 to sentence 7.

11. **(E)** Option E is the only accurate option.

12. **(A)** In sentence 9, the description of the news media as *totally* unfair, and the reference to adults in general following a discussion that had been restricted to the news media, both render the conclusion of the sentence much too broad relative to the examples discussed in the passage.

13. **(B)** Option B is the only accurate option.

14. **(C)** Given that El Greco's original name is given in sentence 1, Option C is preferable.

15. **(A)** Option A is the only accurate option.

16. **(D)** Option D would make explicit the fact that the sentence pertains to El Greco's time, and would thus help the reader understand sentences 6 and 7.

17. **(E)** Option E is the only accurate option.

18. **(C)** Option C is the only option that can be safely inferred.

19. **(B)** Option B is most likely to be accurate, given the focus of sentence 9 on the details of El Greco's style.

20. **(C)** Since *two* strong parents are mentioned in sentence 1 but only one parent is described in the first paragraph, option C is correct.

21. **(D)** In context, option D is the only accurate option.

22. **(A)** Options B–E would contribute virtually nothing to the passage.

23. **(E)** Perceptiveness is implied by Alexander's behavior in the anecdote described in sentences 6 and 7.

ESSAYS

TIME: *70 Minutes*

> **DIRECTIONS:** You will have a total of 70 minutes to write two argumentative essays. You will have 30 minutes to complete the first essay, which is to be based on your own reading, experience, or observations, and 40 minutes to complete the second essay, which requires you to synthesize two sources that are provided. Although you are free to begin writing at any point, it is better to take the time you need to plan your essays and to do the required reading than it is to begin writing immediately.

FIRST ESSAY

> **DIRECTIONS:** The old saying, "Experience is the best teacher," suggests that people will benefit more from learning on the job or in the world than from formal education in the academic setting of the classroom. Write an essay in which you discuss the relative importance of academic and experiential learning. Support your discussion with examples from your reading, observations, or personal experience.

Sample Essay

Perhaps I am old-fashioned, but I believe that academic learning is essential to personal growth. Nothing can substitute for the information we obtain from the classroom. Our capacity to be informed, productive citizens relies on what we have learned in school, from basic reading and math skills acquired during the early years all the way up to sophisticated information about nature and society we learn in high school. Academic learning is not infallible, of course. When I was a child, I learned that there are nine planets. Now there are eight, according to astronomers. But the fact that there are nine or eight planets is not something one could learn by walking outside at night and looking up into the sky. We learn such facts in school, and we would need to attend school for many years before we could examine the sky with a telescope and formulate an experience-based opinion about the number of planets. Along the way, we would also need to learn how to use the telescope, how to make astronomical calculations, and how to do a number of other things we could not figure out on our own.

Although academic learning is critical, I believe that learning from experience is important, too. Each type of learning is important in a different way. School prepares us for life. It gives us the foundation for safe, happy, productive lives. But outside of the classroom, we must continue to learn about life as we live it, and a critical source of learning after graduation will be experience. We would not be able to function without experiential learning. My father is a typical example. He is a police officer, and he is fond of saying that he learned more in his first six days on the job than he did during his entire six months of training at the police academy. When he makes comments like this, he means to say that he has learned things on the street that he wasn't taught in the police academy. His point is that academic learning is insufficient. But it is still the foundation for what he does. He wouldn't deny the importance of his academic training.

Although experiential learning becomes the main source of learning once we finish school, there will continue to be opportunities to advance our knowledge that are more academic than experiential. When we read a book or consult with an experienced co-worker, for example, we are engaging in what might be called academic learning rather than just acquiring information through direct personal experience. These examples show that academic learning is not limited to classroom settings. I believe that becoming an informed, productive citizen depends on continuing to learn in the academic sense and not just experiential learning. Academic learning can enrich our personal experiences, just as our experiences can extend what we learn through academic methods.

Commentary

Look back at the directions for this essay. You will see that the directions include two requests: 1. *[D]iscuss the relative importance of experiential and academic learning.* 2. *Support your discussion with examples from your reading, observations, or personal experience.*

The author of this essay addresses the first request throughout the essay. Paragraph 1 describes the importance of academic learning. Paragraph 2 describes the separate importance of experiential learning. Paragraph 3 continues to contrast the two types of learning, and closes with a brief comment on how they are related.

The author addresses the second request by describing examples in each paragraph of the essay, including personal examples (paragraphs 1 and 2) as well as general examples (paragraph 3).

Notice that the essay is clear, well-organized, grammatically varied, and free of errors. The author shows good command of the language in the choice of words and phrases.

SECOND ESSAY

DIRECTIONS: The following assignment requires you to write a coherent essay in which you synthesize the two sources provided. Synthesis refers to combining the sources and your position to form a cohesive, supported argument. You must develop a position and incorporate both sources. **You must cite the sources whether you are paraphrasing or quoting.** Refer to each source by the author's last name, or by any other means that adequately identifies it.

Introduction

There are many different views on the meaning of patriotism (i.e., love of one's country). Some writers assert that patriotism is expressed by devotion and service to one's country. Other writers hold that patriotism is expressed in the form of dissent that inspires other citizens to question their beliefs and actions. Both views assume that patriotism is motivated by the desire to improve the moral strength of one's country; the views differ as to whether support or dissent tends to be the preferable means of improvement.

Assignment

Read the following quotations carefully. Then write an essay in which you develop a position on whether support or dissent is closer to the true meaning of patriotism. Be sure to incorporate and cite both of the accompanying quotations as you develop your position.

"He loves his country best who strives to make it best." —**Robert G. Ingersoll**

"Dissent is the highest form of patriotism." —**Howard Zinn**

Suggestions for Essay Development

A good place to begin is to read these quotes, to be sure you understand the similarities and differences between each point of view, and then to think about the position you will develop in your own essay. Will you side with one of the authors? Will you develop a position that represents a compromise between their views? Or will you develop a third position that is to some extent separate from theirs.

The next step is to plan your essay. Although your time is limited, you should take a few minutes to create an informal outline that will guide your writing. The outline should identify key points and examples and indicate the order in which they will be discussed.

The following text provides an outline for one particular essay that could be written. This outline is based on the premise that the points of view represented in the two quotations are not as inconsistent as they might seem at first glance.

The following outline is relatively detailed and written in complete sentences so that you can follow the progression of ideas. An outline written during the actual test would not need to be as elaborate.

1. Patriotism consists of more than just words. Anybody can talk the talk. True patriotism means serving one's country through action, as Ingersoll suggests.

2. At first glance, Ingersoll and Zinn seem to present opposing views: Ingersoll's patriot supports his or her country, while Zinn's patriot expresses dissent. For example, when the country is at war, Ingersoll's patriot would do extra work to support the war effort, while Zinn's patriot would openly question the rationale for war.

3. A deeper interpretation of Ingersoll's comment shows that the two writers do not necessarily have opposing views. What does it mean to *strive* to make one's country *best*? It could mean supporting the country's actions blindly, of course. But it could also mean promoting the country's interests through everything that one says and does. Arguably, the greatest good one can do for one's country is to dissent from mainstream views whenever possible, so that other citizens can question their assumptions and consider

whether to alter their behavior. Even if the dissenter does not change anything, dissent keeps other citizens thinking and amenable to ideas for improvement they may not have considered. In a time of war, for example, the dissenter helps other citizens question whether involvement in the war continues to be best for the country. Dissent in such cases can be effective if the dissenter is tactful, coherent, and persuasive.

4. In sum, Zinn can be thought of as describing a method (i.e., dissent) by which a person can meet Ingersoll's criterion for patriotism (i.e., striving to make one's country best). The true meaning of patriotism is striving to make one's country best by means of tactful, coherent, and persuasive dissent from mainstream views.

CHAPTER 2
Humanities

CLEP HUMANITIES INDEPENDENT STUDY SCHEDULE

The following suggestions provide a framework you can use when preparing for the CLEP Humanities exam. As part of your preparation, be sure to set aside time each day to study. This method will work better than trying to review everything at once. No matter which study techniques work best for you, the more time you spend studying, the more prepared and relaxed you will feel.

Step	Activity
1	Take Practice Test 2 for Humanities on the CD. Review the detailed explanations provided for the answers. This will help you identify areas that you will need to review.
2	Carefully read each topic in the Humanities section.
3	In your review, pay particular attention to boldfaced terms and phrases.
4	Use a highlighter or pencil to emphasize items in your text you want to remember.
5	Jot down points of emphasis in a notebook or on index cards as you read.
6	Take Practice Test 3 on the CD.
7	Review the Detailed Explanations of the answers. These will not only provide the correct answer, but also explain why the other options were incorrect.
8	Note which questions you answered incorrectly on the Practice Test, and focus on these areas during your follow-up review.
9	Read through the Humanities section in your book again, paying particular attention to the topics you struggled with while taking the two Practice Tests.
10	Take Practice Test 1 in the book for additional reinforcement.

REVIEW OUTLINE

The following is the order in which the topics are covered in this review:

ABOUT THIS CHAPTER

This chapter provides you with a targeted review of the CLEP Humanities exam. We also provide a practice test in the book, and two practice tests on the accompanying CD. All are based on the official CLEP Humanities exam, and contain every type of question found on the actual exam. Following the practice test is an answer key with detailed explanations designed to help you more completely understand the test material.

FORMAT AND CONTENT OF THE CLEP HUMANITIES EXAM

The CLEP Humanities exam tests general knowledge of literature, art, and music. The test covers all periods, from classical to contemporary and covers poetry, prose, philosophy, history of art, music, dance, and theater. The questions are drawn from the entire history of Western art and culture and are fairly evenly divided among the following periods: Classical, Medieval and Renaissance, seventeenth and eighteenth centuries, nineteenth century, and twentieth century. Some questions could be based on African and Asian cultures.

The exam consists of 140 multiple-choice questions, each with five possible answer choices, to be answered within 90 minutes. The approximate breakdown of topics is as follows:

50% Literature

    10%   Drama

    10–15% Poetry

    15–20% Fiction

    10%   Nonfiction (including philosophy)

50% Fine Arts

    20%   Visual arts (painting, sculpture, etc.)

    15%   Music

    10%   Performing arts (film, dance, etc.)

    5%   Architecture

SCORING YOUR PRACTICE TESTS

How Do I Score My Practice Tests?

The CLEP Humanities exam is scored on a scale of 20 to 80. To score your practice tests, count the number of correct answers. This is your total raw score. Convert your raw score to a scaled score using the conversion table on the following page. (**Note: The conversion table provides only an *estimate* of your scaled score. Scaled scores can and do vary over time, and in no case should a sample test be taken as a precise predictor of test performance.**)

Practice-Test Raw Score Conversion Table*

Raw Score	Scaled Score	Course Grade	Raw Score	Scaled Score	Course Grade
140	80	A	109	67	B
139	80	A	108	66	B
138	80	A	107	66	B
137	80	A	106	65	B
136	80	A	105	65	B
135	79	A	104	65	B
134	79	A	103	64	B
133	78	A	102	64	B
132	78	A	101	64	B
131	77	A	100	64	B
130	77	A	99	63	B
129	76	A	98	63	B
128	76	A	97	63	B
127	75	A	96	62	B
126	75	A	95	62	B
125	74	A	94	62	B
124	74	A	93	61	B
123	73	A	92	61	B
122	73	A	91	61	B
121	72	A	90	60	C
120	72	A	89	60	C
119	71	A	88	60	C
118	71	A	87	60	C
117	70	A	86	59	C
116	70	A	85	59	C
115	69	B	84	59	C
114	69	B	83	58	C
113	68	B	82	58	C
112	68	B	81	57	C
111	68	B	80	57	C
110	67	B	79	56	C

Raw Score	Scaled Score	Course Grade	Raw Score	Scaled Score	Course Grade
78	56	C	54	47	D
76	55	C	53	46	D
75	55	C	52	45	D
74	54	C	51	45	D
73	54	C	50	44	D
72	53	C	49	44	D
71	53	C	48	43	D
70	52	C	47	43	D
69	52	C	46	42	D
68	51	C	45	42	D
67	51	C	44	41	D
66	50	C	43	41	D
65	50	C	42	40	D
64	50	C	41	40	D
63	50	C	40	39	D
62	49	D	39	39	D
61	49	D	38	38	D
60	48	D	37	38	D
59	48	D	36	37	D
58	48	D	35	37	D
57	48	D	34	36	D
56	47	D	33	36	D
55	47	D	32	35	F

* This table is provided for scoring REA practice tests only. The American Council on Education recommends that colleges use a single across-the-board credit-granting score of 50 for all CLEP computer-based exams. Nonetheless, on account of the different skills being measured and the unique content requirements of each test, the actual number of correct answers needed to reach 50 will vary. A "50" is calibrated to equate with performance that would warrant the grade C in the corresponding introductory college course.

LITERATURE REVIEW

PROSE

General Rules and Ideas

Prose is what we write and speak most of the time in our everyday intercourse: unmetered, unrhymed language. This does not mean that prose does not have its own rhythms—language, whether written or spoken, has cadence and balance. Language is, after all, **phonic**.

1. Fiction and Nonfiction

Prose may be either **fiction** or **nonfiction**. A novel (like a short story) is fiction; an autobiography is nonfiction.

The **essay** presents a relatively straightforward account of the writer's opinion(s) on an endless array of topics. Depending upon the type of essay, the reader may become informed (expository), provoked (argumentative), persuaded, enlightened (critical), or, in the case of the narrative essay, better acquainted with the writer who wishes to illustrate a point with his story, whether it is autobiographical or fictitious.

2. Reading Prose

Readers of prose, like readers of poetry, seek aesthetic pleasure, entertainment, and knowledge, not necessarily in that order. Reading prose for the CLEP General Examination in English Composition is really no different from reading prose for your own purposes, except for the time constraints, of course! Becoming a competent reader is a result of practicing certain skills. Probably most important is acquiring a broad reading base. Read widely, eclectically, actively, and avidly. The idea is not that you might stumble onto a familiar prose selection on the CLEP and have an edge in writing about it; the idea is that your familiarity with many authors and works gives you a framework upon which to build your understanding of **whatever** prose selection you encounter on the CLEP General Examination in English Composition. So read, read, and read some more!

Reading Novels

Most literary handbooks will define a novel as an extended fictional prose narrative, derived from the Italian *novella*, meaning "tale, piece of news." The term *novelle,* meaning short tales, was applied to works such as Boccaccio's *The Decameron*, a collection of stories which had an impact on later works such as Chaucer's *Canterbury Tales*. In most European countries, the word for **novel** is **roman**, short for romance, which was applied to longer verse narratives which were later written in prose.

The novel has, over some 600 years, developed into many special forms: detective novel, psychological novel, historical novel, regional novel, picaresque novel, Gothic novel, stream-of-consciousness novel, epistolary novel, and so on. Furthermore, depending on the conventions of the author's time period, his style, and his outlook on life, his *mode* may be termed **Realism**, **Romanticism**, **Impressionism**, **Expressionism**, **Naturalism**, or **Neo-Classicism**.

1. Plots

Analyzing novels is a bit like asking the journalist's five questions: what? who? why? where? and how? The **what?** is the story, the narrative, the plot, and subplots. Most students are familiar with **Freytag's Pyramid**, originally designed to describe the structure of a five-act drama but now widely used to analyze fiction as well. The stages generally specified are **introduction** or **exposition**, **complication**, **rising action**, **climax**, **falling action**, and **denouement** or **conclusion**. As the novel's events are charted, the "change which structures the story" should emerge.

Subplots often parallel or serve as counterpoints to the main plot line, serving to enhance the central story. Sometimes the parallels involve reversals of characters and situations, creating similar yet distinct differences in the outcomes. Nevertheless, seeing the parallels makes understanding the major plot line less difficult.

Sometimes an author intentionally divides the novel into chapters, books, and/or parts. Readers should take their cue from these divisions. What causal or other relationships are there between sections and events? Some writers, such as Steinbeck in *The Grapes of Wrath*, use intercalary chapters, alternating between the "real" story (the Joads) and peripheral or parallel stories (the Okies and migrants in general).

2. Characters

Of course, plots cannot happen in isolation from characters, the **who?** element of a story. Both major and minor characters can be **static** or **dynamic**. Static characters do not change in significant ways. A character may die (i.e., change from alive to dead) and still be static, unless his death is central to the narrative. This makes the character dynamic. For instance, in Golding's *Lord of the Flies*, the boy with the mulberry birthmark apparently dies in a fire early in the novel. Momentous as any person's death is, this boy's death is not what the novel is about. This character is static. However, when Simon is killed, and later Piggy, the narrative is directly impacted because the reason for their deaths is central to the novel's theme regarding man's innate evil. These characters are dynamic. A dynamic character may change only slightly in his attitudes, but those changes may be the very ones upon which the narrative rests.

Major characters or "actors" in novels are **protagonists** or **antagonists**. The *protagonist* struggles **toward** or for someone or something; the *ant(i)agonist* struggles **against** someone or something. The possible conflicts are usually cited as man against himself, man against man, man against society, or man against nature.

A **stock** character exists because the plot demands it, such as the grizzled old police officer who is assigned to the hotshot rookie. A character can also be a **stereotype**, without individuating characteristics, such as the corrupt politician. Characters often serve as **foils** for other characters, enabling us to see one or more of them better. A classic example is Tom Sawyer, the romantic foil for Huck Finn's realism.

Sometimes characters are **allegorical**, standing for qualities or concepts rather than for actual personages. For instance, Jim Casey (initials "J. C.") in *The Grapes of Wrath* is often regarded as a Christ figure, pure and self-sacrificing in his aims for the migrant workers. Other characters are fully three-dimensional, "rounded," "mimetic" of humans in all their virtue, vice, hope, despair, strength, and weakness, creating characters who are credible and plausible.

3. Themes

The interplay of plot and characters determines in large part the **theme** of a work, the **why?** of the story. A **topic** is a phrase, such as "man's inhumanity to man"; or "the fickle nature of fate." A **theme**, however, turns a phrase into a **statement**: "Man's inhumanity to man is barely concealed by 'civilization,'" or "Man is a helpless pawn, at the mercy of fickle fate." Many writers may deal with the same topic, but their themes may vary widely.

To illustrate the relationship between plot, character, and theme, let's examine a familiar fairy tale. In "The Ugly Duckling," the structuring story line is "Once upon a time there was an ugly duckling, who in turn became a beautiful swan." In this case, the duckling did nothing to merit either his ugliness nor his eventual transformation; however, he did not curse fate. He only wept and waited, lonely and outcast. And when he became beautiful, he did not gloat; he eagerly joined the other members of his flock, who greatly admired him. The theme here essentially is: "Good things come to him who waits," or "Life is unfair—you don't get what you deserve, nor deserve what you get." What happens to the theme if the ugly duckling remains an ugly duckling: "Some guys just never get a break"?

4. Motifs

A **motif** is a detail or element of the story which is repeated throughout, and which may even become symbolic. Television shows are ready examples of the use of motifs. A medical show uses elements such as the half-masked surgeon whose brow is frequently mopped by the nurse; the gloved hand open-palmed to receive a scalpel, sponge, and so on; the various oscilloscopes giving read-outs of the patient's very fragile condition. These details help convince the viewer that this story occurs in a hospital, that the mood is pretty tense, and that the medical team is doing all it can.

Motifs can also become symbolic. The oscilloscope line quits blipping, levels out, and gives off the ominous hum. And the doctor's gloved hand sets down the scalpel and shuts off the oscilloscope. These elements signal "It's over, finished."

This example is very crude and mechanical, but motifs in the hands of a skillful writer are valuable devices. And in isolation, and often magnified, a single motif can become a controlling image with great significance. For instance, Emma Bovary's shoes signify her obsession with material things; and when her delicate slippers become soiled as she crosses the dewy grass to meet her lover, we sense the impurity of her act as well as its futility.

5. Settings in Novels

Setting involves the **where?** and **when?** elements of the story: place, atmosphere, time of day, time period, or year. The question for the reader is whether the setting is ultimately essential to the plot/theme, or whether it is incidental (i.e., could this story/theme have been told successfully in another time and/or place)? For instance, could the theme in *Lord of the Flies* be made manifest if the boys were not on an island? Could they have been isolated in some other place? Does it matter, in terms of the theme, whether the "war" which they are fleeing is WWII, WWIII, or some other conflict?

6. Style

The final question, **how?**, relates to an author's **style**: language (word choice), syntax (word order, sentence type, and length), the balance between narration and dialogue, the choice of narrative voice (first person participant, third person with limited omniscience), use of descriptive passages, and other aspects of the actual words on the page which are basically irrelevant to the first four elements (plot, character, theme, and setting). Jane Austen's style is very formal and mannered; Mark Twain's style is very casual and colloquial; William Faulkner's prose often spins on without punctuation or paragraphs far longer than the reader can hold either the thought or his breath; and Hemingway's dense but spare, pared-down style has earned the epithet, "Less is more."

Reading Short Stories

The modern short story emphasizes *showing* rather than *telling*. Gaining popularity in the nineteenth century, the **short story** generally was realistic, presenting detailed accounts of the lives of middle-class personages. Furthermore, the characters are human with recognizable human motivations, both social and psychological. Setting—time and place—is realistic rather than fantastic. And, as Poe stipulated, the elements of plot, character, setting, style, point of view, and theme all work toward a single *unified* effect. Modern writers have stretched these boundaries and have mixed in elements of nonrealism—such as the supernatural and the fantastic—sometimes switching back and forth between realism and nonrealism.

Unlike the novel, which has time and space to develop characters and interrelationships, the short story must rely on flashes of insight and revelation to develop plot and characters. The "slice of life" in a short story is of necessity much narrower than that in a novel; the time span is much shorter, the focus much tighter.

1. Point of View

Point of view indicates the perspective through which the story is told. A narrator in a story may be *objective*, presenting information without bias or comment. The third-person narrator may, however, be less objective in his presentation, directly revealing the thoughts and feelings of one or more of the characters. We say that such a narrator is fully or partially *omniscient*, depending on how complete his knowledge is of the characters' psychological and emotional makeup. The least objective narrator is the *first-person* narrator, who presents information from the perspective of a single character who is a participant in the action.

Reading Essays

1. Categories of Essays

Essays fall into four rough categories, which are neither exhaustive nor mutually exclusive: **speculative**, **argumentative**, **narrative**, and **expository**. Depending on the writer's purpose, his essay will fit more or less into one of these groupings.

The **speculative** essay is so named because it looks at ideas rather than explaining them. The writer deals with ideas in an associative manner, playing with ideas in a looser structure than he would in an expository or argumentative essay. This "flow" may even produce *intercalary* paragraphs, which present alternately a narrative of sorts and thoughtful responses to the events being recounted.

The **argumentative** essay, on the other hand, presents a point and provides evidence, which may be factual or anecdotal, to support it. The structure is usually very formal, as in a debate, with counterpositions and counterarguments.

Narrative and **expository** essays have elements of both the speculative and argumentative modes. The narrative essay may recount an incident or a series of incidents and is almost always autobiographical, in order to make a point. The informality of the storytelling makes the narrative essay less insistent than the argumentative essay, but more directed than the speculative essay.

Students are probably most familiar with the **expository** essay, the primary purpose of which is to explain and clarify ideas. Although the expository essay may have narrative elements, that aspect is minor and subservient to that of explanation. Furthermore, while nearly all essays have some element of persuasion, argumentation is incidental in the expository essay.

2. Elements of Essays

Voice in nonfiction essays is similar to the narrator's tone in fiction, but the major difference is in who is "speaking." In fiction, the author is not the speaker—the **narrator** is the speaker. In an essay, however, the author speaks directly to the reader, even if he is presenting ideas which he may not actually espouse personally—as in a satire. This directness creates the writer's **tone**, his attitude toward his subject.

Style in nonfiction derives from word choice, syntax, balance between dialogue and narration, voice, use of description—those things specifically related to words on the page. Generally speaking, an argumentative essay will be written in a more formal style than will a narrative essay, and a meditative essay will be less formal than an expository essay.

Structure and **thought** are so intertwined as to be inextricable. Changing the structure of an essay will alter its meaning. Writers signal structural shifts with alterations in focus, as well as with visual clues (spacing), verbal clues (*but*, *therefore*, *however*), or shifts in the kind of information being presented (personal, scientific, etc.).

Thought is perhaps the single element which most distinguishes nonfiction from fiction. Whether the essayist chooses the speculative, narrative, argumentative, or expository format, he has something on his mind that he wants to convey to his readers. And it is this idea which we are after when we analyze his essay.

Reading Satire

Satire, properly speaking, is not a genre at all, but rather a **mode**, elements of which can be found in any category of literature—from poetry and drama to novels and essays. Satire is a manifestation of authorial attitude (tone) and purpose.

Satire mainly exposes and ridicules. Although the satirist has many techniques at his disposal, there are basically only two types of satire: gentle or harsh, depending on the author's intent, his audience, and his methods.

1. Role of Satire

The terms *Romanticism*, *Realism*, and *Naturalism* can help us understand the role of *satire*. **Romanticism** sees the world idealistically, as perfectible if not perfect. **Realism** sees the world as it is, with healthy doses of both good and bad. **Naturalism** sees the world as imperfect, with evil often triumphing over good. The satirist is closer to the naturalist than he is to the romantic or realist, for both the satirist and the naturalist focus on what is wrong with the world, intending to expose the foibles of man and his society. The difference between them lies in their techniques. The naturalist is very direct and does not necessarily employ humor; the satirist is more subtle, and does.

2. Techniques of Satire

The satirist's techniques—his weapons—include **irony**, **parody**, **reversal** or **inversion**, **hyperbole**, **understatement**, **sarcasm**, **wit**, and **invective**. By exaggerating characteristics, by saying the opposite of what he means, by using his cleverness to make cutting or even cruel remarks at the expense of his subject, the writer of satire can call the reader's attention to those things he believes are repulsive, despicable, or destructive. Whether he uses more harsh (Juvenalian) or more gentle (Horatian) satire depends upon the writer's attitude and intent.

3. Poetic Satires

The basis of **irony** is inversion or reversal, doing or saying the opposite or the unexpected. Shakespeare's famous sonnet beginning "My mistress' eyes are nothing like the sun . . ." is an ironic tribute to the speaker's beloved, who, he finally declares, is "as rare/As any she belied with false compare." At the same time, Shakespeare is poking fun at the sonnet form as it was used by his contemporaries—himself included—to extol the virtues of their ladies. By selecting a woman who, by his own description, is physically unattractive in every way imaginable, and using the conventions of the love sonnet to present her many flaws, he has inverted the sonnet tradition. And then by asserting that she compares favorably with any of the other ladies whose poet-lovers have lied about their virtues, he presents us with the unexpected twist. Thus, he satirizes both the love sonnet form and its subject by using irony.

Other notable poetic satires include Koch's "Variations on a Theme by William Carlos Williams" and Nemerov's "Boom!"

4. Satire in Drama

Satire in drama is also common. Wilde's "The Importance of Being Earnest" is wonderfully funny in its constant word play (notably on the name *Ernest*) and its relentless ridiculing of the superficiality which Wilde saw as characteristic of British gentry. Barrie's "The Admirable Chrichton" has a similar theme, with the added assertion that it is the "lower" or servant class which is truly superior—again, the ironic reversal so common in satire. Both of these plays are mild in their ridicule; the authors do not expect or desire any change in society or in the viewer. The satire is gentle; the satirists are amused, or perhaps bemused at the society whose foibles they expose.

5. Satire in Classic Novels

Classic novels which employ satire include Swift's *Gulliver's Travels* and Voltaire's *Candide*, both of which fairly vigorously attack aspects of the religions, governments, and prevailing intellectual beliefs of their respective societies. A modern novel which uses satire is Heller's *Catch-22*, which is basically an attack on war and the government's bureaucratic bungling of men and material, specifically in WWII. But by extension, Heller is also viewing with contempt the unmotivated, illogical, capricious behavior of all institutions which operate by that basic law: "catch-22." Like Swift and Voltaire, Heller is angry. And although his work, like the other two, has humor, wit, exaggeration, and irony, his purpose is more than intellectual entertainment for his readers. Heller hopes for reform.

POETRY

It is hard to imagine that poetry was the "current language" for students growing up in the Elizabethan or Romantic eras. In our world information can be retrieved in a nanosecond, in those worlds, time was plentiful to sit down, clear the mind, and let poetry take over. Very often the meaning of a poem does not come across in a nanosecond; for the modern student, this proves very frustrating.

Reading Poetry for an Examination

People write **poetry** to convey an experience, an emotion, an insight, or an observation in a startling or satisfying way. But why wrap up that valuable insight in fancy words, rhyme, paradox, meter, allusion, symbolism, and all the other seeming mumbo-jumbo that explicators of poetry use? Why not just come right out and say it like "normal people" do? An easy answer to these questions is that poetry is not a vehicle for conveying meaning alone. Gerard Manley Hopkins, one of the great innovators of rhythm in poetry, claimed that poetry should be "heard for its own sake and interest even over and above its interest or meaning." One of the best ways of studying a poem is to consider it a jigsaw puzzle presented to you whole, an integral work of art, which can be taken apart piece by piece (word by word), analyzed scientifically, labelled, and put back together again into a whole, and then the meaning is complete.

Meanings in Poetry

One interpretation of a poem's "work" is that it changes us in some way. We see the world in a new way because of the way the poet has seen it and told us about it. Maybe one of the reasons people write poetry is to encourage us to *see* things in the first place. The poet captures a moment that we have all experienced. His magic is to make that moment new again.

If poets enhance our power of sight, they also awaken the other senses as powerfully. For example, we can hear Emily Dickinson's snake in the repeated "s" sound of the lines:

> His notice sudden is—
> The Grass divides as with a Comb—
> A spotted shaft is seen—

and because of the very present sense of sound, we experience the indrawn gasp of breath of fear when the snake appears.

More important than ideas and sense awakening is the poet's **appeal to the emotions**. This area disturbs a number of students, as our modern society tends to block out emotions. Poets write to overcome that blocking (very often it is their own blocking of emotion they seek to alleviate), but that is not to say that poetry immediately sets us laughing, crying, loving, or hating. The important fact about the emotional release in poetry is that poets help us explore our own emotions, sometimes by shocking us, sometimes by drawing attention to balance and pattern, and sometimes by cautioning us to move carefully in this inner world.

Reasons for Reading Poetry

Why read poetry? One might contend that a good drama, novel, or short story might provide the same emotional experience. However, a poem is much more accessible. Apart from the fact that poems are shorter than other genres, there is a unique directness to them which hinges purely on language. Poets can say in one or two lines what may take novelists and playwrights entire works to express. For example, Keats' lines—

> Beauty is truth, truth beauty,—that is all
> Ye know on earth, and all ye need to know—

studied, pondered, and opened to each reader's interpretations—linger in the memory with more emphasis than George Eliot's *Middlemarch*, or Ibsen's *The Wild Duck*, which endeavor to make the same point.

On reading a poem, the brain responds on several different levels: to the sounds, to the words themselves and their connotations, to the emotions, and to the insights or learning of the world being revealed. Poetry, perhaps the oldest art, surrounds us without our even realizing it. Today we listen to pop-song lyrics and find ourselves, sometimes despite ourselves, repeating certain rhythmic lines. Advertisements we chuckle over or say we hate have a way of repeating themselves as we use the catchy phrase or snappy repetition. Both lyricists and advertisers cleverly use language, playing on the reader's/listener's/watcher's ability to pick up on a repeated sound or engaging rhythm or inner rhyme. Think about nursery rhymes you learned as a child. Even though you probably had no idea of the meaning of the words ("Little Miss Muffet sat on a tuffet . . ." a tuffet?!) you responded to the sound, the pattern. Adults read poetry for that same sense of sound and pattern.

A poem can speak to the novice reader at a particular time and become an experience in itself. A student who recently lost her mother may read a poem like Elizabeth Jennings' "Happy Families" differently than someone who did not have a similar experience. The poem may help the student by allowing her to see death through another's eyes, reevaluate, and view a universal human response to grief as well as encourage her to deal with her own.

Preparation Tips for Reading Poetry

1. Make a list of poets and poems you remember; analyze poems you liked, disliked, loved, hated, and were indifferent to. Find the poems. Reread them and for each one analyze your *feelings,* first of all, about the poetry itself. Have your feelings changed? Then paraphrase the *meaning* of each poem.

2. Choose a poem at random from an anthology or one mentioned in this introduction. Read it a couple of times, preferably aloud, because the speaking voice will automatically grasp the rhythm and that will help the meaning. Do not become bogged down in individual word connotation or the meaning of the poem—let the poetry do its "work" on you.

3. Now take the poem apart. Look carefully at the title. Sometimes a straightforward title helps you focus. Sometimes a playful title helps you get an angle on the meaning.

4. Look carefully at the punctuation. Does the sense of a line carry from one to another? Does a particular mark of punctuation strike you as odd? Ask why that mark was used.

5. Look carefully at the words. Try to find the meaning of words with which you are not familiar within the context. Familiar words may be used differently: ask why the poet chose that particular use. If your memory bank of vocabulary leaves you at a loss, go to a dictionary. Once you have the *denotation* of the word, start wondering about the *connotation.* Put yourself in the poet's position and think why that word was used.

6. Look carefully at all the techniques being used. As soon as you come across a new idea—"caesura" perhaps—learn the word, see how it applies to poetry, and determine where it is used. Be on the lookout for it in other poetry. Ask yourself questions such as why the poet used alliteration here, why the rhythm changes there, why the poet uses a sonnet form, and which sonnet form is in use. Forcing yourself to ask and answer the *why* questions will train the brain to read more perceptively.

7. Look carefully at the speaker. Is the poet using another persona? Who is that persona? What is revealed about the speaker? Why use that particular voice?

8. Start putting all the pieces of the puzzle together. The rhythm helps the meaning. The word choice helps the imagery. The imagery adds to the meaning. Paraphrase the meaning. Ask yourself simple questions: What is the poet saying? How can I relate to what is being said? What does this poem mean to me? What does this poem contribute to human experience?

9. Find time to read about the great names in poetry. Locate people within time areas and analyze what those times entailed. For example, the Romantics (Wordsworth, Coleridge, Keats, Shelley, Byron) loved nature and saw God within nature. The Victorians (Tennyson, Blake), in contrast, saw nature as a threat to mankind and God, being replaced by the profit cash-nexus of the Industrial Age.

10. Write a poem of your own. Choose a particular style; use the sonnet form; parody a famous poem; express yourself in free verse on a crucial, personal aspect of your life. Then analyze your own poetry with the previously noted ideas.

Tips for Test-Taking

1. Internalize the reading—hear the reading in your head. Read through the poem two or three times following the absorbing procedure.

2. If the title and poet are supplied, analyze the title as before and determine the era of the poetry. Often this pushes you toward the meaning.

3. Look carefully at the questions, which should enable you to "tap into" your learning process. Answer the ones that are immediately clear to you: form, technique, language perhaps.

4. Go back for another reading for those questions that challenge you—theme or meaning perhaps—analyze the speaker or the voice at work—paraphrase the meaning—ask the simple question "What is the poet saying?"

5. If a question asks you about a specific line, metaphor, opening, or closing lines, mentally highlight or underline them to force your awareness of each crucial word. Internalize another reading, emphasizing the highlighted area—analyze again the options you have for your answers.

6. Do not waste time on an answer that eludes you. Move onto another section and let the poetry do its "work." Very often the brain will continue working on the problem on another level of consciousness. When you go back to the difficult question, it may well become clear.

7. If you still are not sure of the answer, choose the option that you *think* is the closest to correct.

Verse and Meter

1. Verse

In modern use we refer to poetry often as **verse** with the connotation of rhyme, rhythm, and meter; but we still recognize verse because of the positioning of lines on the page and the breaking of lines that distinguish verse from prose.

Stanzas are a grouping of lines with a metrical order and often a repeated rhyme which we know as the **rhyme scheme**. Such a scheme is shown by letters. Byron's "Stanzas" will help you recall the word, see the use of a definite rhyme, and note how to mark it:

"Stanzas"
(When a man hath no freedom to fight for at home)

When a man hath no freedom to fight for at home,	*a*
Let him combat for that of his neighbors;	*b*
Let him think of the glories of Greece and of Rome,	*a*
And get knocked on the head for his labors.	*b*
To do good to mankind is the chivalrous plan,	*c*
And is always as nobly requited;	*d*
Then battle for freedom wherever you can,	*c*
And, if not shot or hanged, you'll get knighted.	*d*

The rhyme scheme is simple—*abab*—and your first question should be "Why such a simple, almost sing-song rhyme?" The simplicity reinforces the **tone** of the poem: sarcastic, cryptic, and cynical. There is almost a sneer behind the words "And get knocked on the head for his labors."

2. Forms of Rhymes

Certain types of rhyme are worth learning. The most common is the **end rhyme**, which has the rhyming word at the end of the line, bringing the line to a definite stop but setting up for a rhyming word in another line later on, as in "Stanzas": home . . . Rome, a perfect rhyme. **Internal rhyme** includes at least one rhyming word within the line, often for the purpose of speeding the rhythm or making it linger. Look at the effect of Byron's internal rhymes mixed with half-rhymes: "combat . . . for that"; "Can/And . . . hanged" slowing the rhythm, making the reader dwell on the harsh long "a" sound, prolonging the sneer which almost becomes a snarl of anger. **Slant rhyme**, sometimes referred to as half, off, near, or approximate rhyme, often jolts a reader who expects a perfect rhyme; poets thus use such a rhyme to express disappointment or a deliberate let-down. **Masculine rhyme** uses one-syllable words or stresses the final syllable of polysyllabic words, giving the feeling of strength and impact. **Feminine rhyme** uses a rhyme of two or more syllables, the stress not falling upon the last syllable, giving a feeling of softness and lightness.

If the lines from "Stanzas" had been unrhymed and varying in metrical pattern, the verse would have been termed **free**, or to use the French term, *"Vers libre,"* not to be confused with **blank verse**, which is also unrhymed but has a strict rhythm. The Elizabethan poets Wyatt and Surrey introduced blank verse, which Shakespeare uses to such good effect in his plays. Free verse has become associated with "modern" poetry, often adding to its so-called obscurity because without rhyme and rhythm, poets often resort to complicated syntactical patterns, repeated phrases, awkward cadences, and parallelism.

3. Meter

Meter, from the Greek word *metron*, meaning *measure*, simply means the pattern or measure of stressed or accented words within a line of verse. When studying meter a student should note where stresses fall on syllables—that is why reading aloud is so important, because it catches the natural rhythm of the speaking voice—and if an absence of stressed syllables occurs there is always an explanation why. We "expect" stressed and unstressed syllables because that is what we use in everyday speech. We may stress one syllable over another for a certain effect; however, we usually use a rising and falling rhythm, known as **iambic rhythm**. A line of poetry that alternates stressed and unstressed syllables is said to have **iambic meter**. A line of poetry with 10 syllables of rising and falling stresses is known as **iambic pentameter**, best used by Shakespeare and Milton in their blank verse. The basic measuring unit in a line of poetry is called a **foot**. An **iambic foot** has one unstressed syllable followed by a stressed marked by u. Pentameter means "five-measure." Therefore, **iambic pentameter** has five groups of two syllables, or 10 beats, to the line. Read aloud the second and fourth, sixth and eighth lines of "Stanzas," tapping the beat on your desk or your palm, and the 10 beat becomes obvious. Read again with the stresses unstressed and stressed (or soft and loud, short or long, depending on what terminology works for you) and the iambic foot becomes clear.

Tapping out the other alternate lines in this poem, you will not find 10 beats but 12. The term for this line is **hexameter**, or six feet, rather than five. Other line-length names worth learning are:

monometer	one foot	**dimeter**	two feet
trimeter	three feet	**tetrameter**	four feet
heptameter	seven feet	**octameter**	eight feet

Other foot names worth learning are:

the **anapest**, marked u u /, the most famous anapestic line being:

```
 u u /   u u   / u u / u u /
```

"Twas the night before Christmas, when all through the house . . ."

the **trochee**, marked / u, the most memorable trochaic line being:

```
 / u   / u / u / u
```

"Double double toil and trouble . . ."

and the **dactyl**, marked / u u, the most often quoted dactylic line being:

```
 / u u / u u
```

"Take her up tenderly. . . ."

4. Accentual Meter

Old English poetry employs **accentual meter**, with four stresses to the line without attention to the unstressed syllables. Although contemporary poets tend not to use it, one of the greatest innovators in rhythm and meter, Gerard Manley Hopkins, used it as the "base line" for his counterpointed "Sprung Rhythm." One stanza from "The Caged Skylark" will show the method at work:

> As a dare-gale skylark scanted in a dull cage
> Man's mounting spirit in his bone-house, mean house, dwells—
> That bird beyond the remembering his free fells;
> This in drudgery, day-labouring-out life's age.

The stress on "That" and "This" works particularly well to draw attention to the two captives: the skylark and Man. The accentual meter in the second line reinforces the wretchedness of the human condition. No reader could possibly read that line quickly, nor fail to put the full length of the syllable on "dwells." The dash further stresses the length and the low pitch of the last word.

Many poets will "mix and match" their meter and your task as a student of poetry is to analyze why. If the poet abruptly changes the poem's pattern, there is a reason. If the poet is doing "a good job" as T. S. Eliot suggested, then the rhyme, rhythm, and meter should all work together in harmony to make the poem an integral whole.

Figurative Language and Poetic Devices

Perhaps what most distinguishes poetry from any other genre is the use of figurative language—figures of speech—used through the ages to convey the poet's own particular worldview in a unique way. Words have connotation and denotation, figurative and literal meanings. We can look in the dictionary for denotation and literal meaning, but figurative language works its own peculiar magic, tapping into shared experiences within the psyche. A simple example involves the word *home*. The denotation is quite straightforward: a house, apartment, or dwelling that provides shelter for an individual or family. However, depending on a person's past experiences, the word *home* might suggest words like comforting, scary, lonely, dark, creepy, safety, haven, or hell. Poets include in their skill various figures of speech to "plug into" the reader's experiences, to prompt the reader to say "I would have never thought of it in those terms but now I see!"

1. Metaphors and Similes

Metaphors compare two unlike things, feelings, or objects. **Similes** also compare two dissimilar things but always use the words *as if* (for a clause) or *like* (for a word or phrase). Metaphors suggest the comparison; the meaning is implicit. An easy way to distinguish between the two is the simple example of the camel. **Metaphor**: The camel is the ship of the desert. **Simile**: A camel is like a ship in the desert. Both conjure up the camel's almost sliding across the desert, storing up its water as a ship must do for survival for its passengers, and the notion of the vastness of the desert parallels the sea. The metaphor somehow crystallizes the image. Metaphors and similes can be *extended* so that an entire poem consists of them, or unfortunately they can be *mixed*. The latter rarely happens in poetry unless the poet is deliberately playing with his readers and provoking humor.

2. Personification

Personification is a much easier area than metaphor to detect in poetry. Usually the object that is being personified—referred to as a human with the personal pronoun sometimes, or possessing human attributes—is capitalized, as in this stanza from Thomas Gray's "Ode on a Distant Prospect of Eton College":

> Ambition this shall tempt to rise,
> Then whirl the wretch from high,
> To bitter Scorn a sacrifice,
> And grinning Infamy.
> The stings of Falsehood those shall try,
> And hard Unkindness' altered eye,
> That mocks the tear it forced to flow;
> And keen Remorse with blood defiled,
> And moody Madness laughing wild
> Amid severest woe.

As the poet watches the young Eton boys, he envisions what the years have to offer them, and the qualities he sees he gives human status. Thus, Ambition is not only capable of tempting, an amoral act, but also of "whirling," a physical act. Scorn is bitter, Infamy grinning, and so on.

3. Image

The word **image** brings us to another important aspect of figurative language. Not a figure of speech in itself, the image plays a large role in poetry because the reader is expected to **imagine** what the poet is evoking through the senses. The image can be **literal**, wherein the reader has little adjustment to make to see or touch or taste the image; a **figurative image** demands more from readers, almost as if they have to be inside the poet's imagination to understand the image. Very often this is where students of poetry, modern poetry particularly, find the greatest problems because the poetry of **imagism**, a term coined by Ezra Pound, is often intensely personal, delving into the mind of the poet for the comparison and connection with past memories that many readers cannot possibly share. Such an image is referred to as *free*, open to many interpretations. This concept suits the Post-Modern poet who feels that life is fragmented, open to multiple interpretations—there is no fixed order. Poets of the Elizabethan and Romantic eras saw the world as whole, steady, *fixed*, exactly the word used for their type of images. Readers of this poetry usually share the same response to the imagery.

4. Symbol

Image in figurative language inevitably leads to **symbol**. When an object, an image, or a feeling takes on a larger meaning outside of itself, then a poet is employing a symbol, something which stands for something greater. Because mankind has used symbols for so long, many have become **stock** or **conventional**: the rose standing for love, or the flag standing for patriotism. If you are not versed in the Christian tradition, it might be useful to read its symbols because the older poetry dwells on the church and the trials of loving God and loving Woman.

If the symbol is not conventional, then it may carry with it many interpretations, depending on the reader's insight. Some students "get carried away" with symbolism, seeing more in the words than the poets do! If the poet is "doing a good job," the poetry will steer you in the "right" direction of symbolism. Sometimes we are unable to say what "stands for" what, but simply that the symbol evokes a mood; it suggests an idea to you that is difficult to explain. The best way to approach symbolism is to understand a literal meaning first and then shift the focus, as with a different camera lens, and see if the poet is saying something even more meaningful.

5. Allusion

When using **allusion**, poets tap into previous areas of experience to relate their insights and to draw their readers into shared experiences. Poets will refer to history, myth, other older poems, plays, music, heroes, or famous people. Allusion is becoming more and more difficult for the modern student because reading is becoming more and more a lost art. Fortunately, modern poets are shifting their allusions so that contemporary readers can appreciate and join in with their background of knowledge. However, be aware that for the examination in poetry it will be useful to have a working knowledge of the traditional canon of literature. Think of areas of history that were landmarks: the burning of Carthage; Hannibal's elephants; Caesar's greatness; Alexander the Great; the First World War and its carnage of young men; the Second World War and the Holocaust. Think of the great Greek and Roman myths: the giving of fire to the world; the entrance of sin into the world;

the labyrinth; the names associated with certain myths (Daedalus, Hercules, the Medusa). You may never have a question on the areas you read but your background for well-rounded college study will already be formulated.

6. Additional Poetry Elements

Alliteration is the repetition of consonants at the beginning of words that are next to each other or close by. Always try to understand the reason for the alliteration. Does it speed or slow the rhythm? Is it there for emphasis? What does the poet want you to focus on? **Apostrophe** is the direct address of someone or something that is not present. Many odes begin this way. **Assonance** is the repetition of vowel sounds, usually internally rather than initially. **Bathos** is a deliberate anticlimax to make a definite point or draw attention to a falseness. The most famous example is from Pope's "Rape of the Lock": "Here thou, great Anna! whom three realms obey, /Dost sometimes counsel take—and sometimes tea." The humor in the bathos is the fact that Anna is the Queen of England— she holds meetings in the room Pope describes but also indulges in the venerable English custom of afternoon tea. The fact that <u>tea</u> should rhyme with <u>obey</u> doubles the humor as the elongated vowel of the upper-class laconic English social group is also mocked.

Caesura is the pause, marked by punctuation (/) or not within the line. Sometimes the caesura (sometimes spelled cesura) comes at an unexpected point in the rhythm and gives the reader pause for thought. **Conceits** are very elaborate comparisons between unlikely objects. The metaphysical poets such as John Donne were criticized for "yoking" together outrageous terms, describing lovers in terms of instruments or death in terms of battle. **Consonance** is similar to slant rhyme—the repetition of consonant sounds without the vowel sound repeated. **Diction** is the word for word choice. Is the poet using formal or informal language? Does the poetry hinge on slang or a dialect? If so what is the purpose? **Enjambment** is the running-on of one line of poetry into another. Usually the end of lines are rhymed so there is an end-stop. In more modern poetry, without rhyme, poets often use run-on lines to give a speedier flow, or to provide the sound of the speaking voice or a conversational tone.

Hyperbole is an obvious and intentional exaggeration. **Irony** plays an important role in voice or tone, inferring a discrepancy between what is said and what is meant. **Metonymy** is a figure of speech in which a term is used to evoke or stand for a related idea. For example: "The pen is mightier than the sword." *Pen* and *sword* are metonymical designations for (the artful use of) words and (engagement in) physical battle.

Onomatopoeia is a device in which the word captures the sound: the whiz of fireworks; the crashing of waves on the shore; the booming of water in an underground seacave. **Oxymoron** is a rhetorical device of epigrammatic form in which incongruous or contradictory terms are conjoined, such as "painful pleasure" or "sweet sorrow." **Paradox** is a situation, action, or statement that appears to be contradictory but that nevertheless holds true. **Pun** is a play on words often for humorous or sarcastic effect. The Elizabethans were very fond of them, and many of Shakespeare's comedies come from punning. **Sarcasm** occurs when verbal irony is too harsh. It is the "lowest form of wit" of course but can be used to good effect in the tone of a poem. Browning's **dramatic monologues** (poems that address another person who remains silent) make excellent use of the device.

Synecdoche occurs when a part of an object is used to represent the entire thing or vice versa. When we ask someone to give us a hand, we would be horrified if they cut off their hand; what we want is the person's help, from all of the body! **Syntax** is the ordering of words into a particular pattern. If a poet shifts words from the usual word order, you know you are dealing with an older style of poetry (Shakespeare, Milton) or a poet who wants to shift emphasis onto a particular word. **Tone** is the voice or attitude of the speaker. Remember that the voice need not be that of the poet's. He or she may be adopting a particular tone for a purpose. Your task is to analyze if the tone is angry, sad, conversational, abrupt, wheedling, cynical, affected, satiric, and so on.

Types of Poetry

1. Form

The pattern or design of a poem is known as **form**, and even the strangest, most experimental poetry will have some type of form to it. Knowing the form of poem may dictate certain areas of rhyme or meter and may enhance the meaning. **Closed form** will be immediately recognizable because lines can be counted and shape determined. The poet must keep to the recognized form, in number of lines, rhyme scheme, and/or meter. **Open form** in contrast, gives a freedom of pattern to the poet.

2. Sonnets

The most easily recognized closed form of poetry is the **sonnet**, sometimes referred to as a **fixed form**. The sonnet always has 14 lines, but there are two types of sonnets: the Petrarchan (or Italian) and the Shakespearean (or English). The word *sonnet*, in fact, comes from the Italian word *sonnetto*, meaning a "little song." Petrarch, the fourteenth century Italian poet, took the form to its peak. The Petrarchan sonnet is organized into two groups: eight lines and six—the **octave** and the **sestet**. Usually the rhyme scheme is *abbaabba-cdecde*, but the sestet can vary in its pattern. The octave may set up a problem or a proposition, and then the answer or resolution follows in the sestet after a turn or a shift. The Shakespearean sonnet organizes the lines into three groups of four lines: **quatrains** and a **couplet** (two rhyming lines). The rhyming scheme is always *abab cdcd efef gg*, and the turn or shift can happen at one of three places or leave the resolution or a "twist in the tail" at the end.

3. Couplets

The couplet is a two-line stanza that usually rhymes with an end rhyme. If the couplet is firmly end-stopped and written in iambic pentameter, it is known as an **heroic couplet**. Alexander Pope became a master of the heroic couplet, sometimes varying to the 12-syllable line from the old French poetry on Alexander the Great. The line became known as the **Alexandrine**. Pope gained fame first as a translator of the epics and then went on to write **mock-heroic** poems like "The Rape of the Lock," written totally in heroic couplets.

4. Epics

You may be confronted with an excerpt of an **epic** on an exam and will need to recognize the structure. The translation will usually be in couplets and the meter regular with equal line lengths, because originally these poems were sung aloud or chanted to the beat of drums. Repetition plays an important part. The subject deals with great deeds of heroes: Odysseus (Ulysses), Hector, and Aeneus, their adventures and their trials; the theme will be of human grief or pride, divided loyalties—but all "writ large." The one great English epic, *Paradise Lost*, is written by Milton and deals with the story of Adam and Eve and the Fall.

5. Ballads

A **ballad** is a story in a song, first sung as early as the fifteenth century. Usually the ballads are anonymous and simple in theme, having been composed by working folk who originally could not read or write. The stories revolve around love and hate and lust and murder, often rejected lovers, knights, and the supernatural. As with the epic, and for the same reason, repetition plays a strong part in the ballad; a repeated refrain often holds the entire poem together. The form gave rise to the **ballad stanza**, four lines rhyming *abcb* with lines 1 and 3 having eight syllables and lines 2 and 4 having six. Poets who later wrote what are known as **literary ballads** kept the same pattern.

6. Lyrics

Wordsworth and Coleridge marked a turning point by not only using "the language of men" in poetry but also by moving away from the narrative poem to the **lyric**. The word comes again from the Greek, meaning a story told with the poet playing upon a lyre.

Part of the lyric "family" is the **elegy**, a lament for someone's death or the passing of a love or concept. The most famous is Thomas Gray's "Elegy Written in a Country Churchyard," which mourns not only the passing of individuals but of a past age and the wasted potential within every human being. Often **ode** and elegy become synonymous, but an ode, also part of the lyric family, is usually longer, dealing with more profound areas of human life than simply death. Keats' odes are perhaps the most famous and most beloved in English poetry.

7. Specialized Types of Poetry

More specialized types of poetry need mentioning so that you may recognize and be able to explicate how the structure of the poem enhances the meaning or theme. For example, the **villanelle** is a courtly love poem structure from medieval times, built on five three-line stanzas known as **tercets**, with the rhyme scheme *aba*, followed by a four-line stanza, and a **quatrain** which ends the poem *abaa*. As if this were not pattern and order enough, the poem's first line appears again as the last line of the second and fourth tercets; *and* the third line appears again in the last line of the third and fifth tercets; *and* these two lines appear again as rhyming lines at the end of the poem! The most famous and arguably the best villanelle is Dylan Thomas' "Do not go gentle into that good night."

The most difficult of all closed forms is the **sestina**, also French, sung by medieval troubadours, a "song of sixes." The poet presents six six-line stanzas, with six end-words in a certain order, then repeats those six repeated words in any order in a closing tercet.

Perhaps at this stage an **epigram** might be more to your liking and time scale because it is short, even abrupt, a little cynical, and always to the point. The cynical Alexander Pope mastered the epigram, as did Oscar Wilde centuries later. Perhaps at some stage we have all written **doggerel**, rhyming poetry that becomes horribly distorted to fit the rhymes, not through skill but the opposite. In contrast, **limericks** are very skilled: five lines using the anapest meter with the rhyme scheme *aabba*. Unfortunately, they can deteriorate into types such as "There was a young lady from . . . ," but in artful hands such as Shakespeare's and Edward Lear's, limericks display fine poetry. Finally, if you are trying to learn all the different types of closed-form poetry, you might try an **aubade**—originally a song or piece of music sung or played at dawn—a poem written to the dawn or about lovers at dawn—the very time when poetic creation is extremely high!

Although the name might suggest open-form, **blank verse** is in fact closed-form poetry. As we saw earlier, lines written in blank verse are unrhymed and in iambic pentameter. Open-form poets can arrange words on the page in any order, not confined by any rhyme pattern or meter. The lines break at any point—the dash darts in and out—the poets are talking to the audience with all the "natural" breaks that the speaking voice will demonstrate. Open-form poets can employ rhyme, often internal rhyme, and is usually thought of as "modern," or at least post-World War I.

DRAMA AND THEATER

Theater, as a performed event, combines the talents and skills of numerous artists and craftspersons, but before the spectacle must come the playwright's work, the pages of words designating what the audience sees and hears. These words, the written script separate from the theatrical performance of them, is what we call *drama*, and the words give the spectacle its significance because without them the illusion has neither frame nor content.

Comparison of Drama to Prose and Poetry

Although drama is literature written to be performed, it closely resembles the other genres. Like fiction and narrative poetry, drama tells a tale—that is, it has plot, characters, and setting—but the author's voice is distant, heard only through the stage directions and perhaps some supplementary notes. With rare exceptions, dialogue dominates the script. Some drama is poetry, such as the works of Shakespeare and Molière, and all plays resemble poems as abstractions because both forms are highly condensed, figurative expressions.

A play contains conflict which can be enacted immediately on the stage without any alterations in the written word. **Enacted** means performed by an actor or actors free to use the entire stage and such theatrical devices as sets, costumes, makeup, special lighting, and props for support. This differs from the oral interpretation of prose or poetry. No matter how animated, the public reader is not acting. This is the primary distinction between drama and other literary forms. Their most obvious similarity is that any form of literature is a linguistic expression. There is, however, one other feature shared by all kinds of narratives: the pulsating energy which pushes the action along is generated by human imperfection. The most fundamental human truth is human frailty.

Although it can be argued that a play, like a musical composition, must be performed to be realized, the script's linguistic foundation always gives the work potential as a literary experience. Moreover, there is never a "definitive" interpretation. The script, in a sense, remains unfinished because it never stops inviting new variations. Lee J. Cobb and Dustin Hoffman both gave notable performances as Willy Loman from *Death of a Salesman*, despite their individual approaches to the part. The same could be said about the Willys created by the minds of the play's countless readers.

1. Mimesis

Drama's earliest great critic, Aristotle, believed art should create a **mimesis**, the Greek word for "imitation." For centuries this "mimetic theory" has asserted that a successful imitation is one which reproduces natural objects and actions in as realistic portrayal as possible. Later, this notion of imitation adopted what has been called the "expressive theory," a variation allowing the artist a freer, more individual stylized approach. Realistic imitation: captures experience as unadorned raw sense, the way it normally appears to be. As twentieth century drama moved toward examinations of people's inner consciousness as universal representations of some greater human predicament, new expressive styles emerged.

Plot Structure

1. Exposition

As with other narrative types, a play's **plot** is its sequence of events, its organized collection of incidents. Most plays condense and edit time much as novels do. Decades can be reduced to two hours. The plot includes **exposition**, the revealing of whatever information we need in order to understand the impending conflict. This exposed material should provide us with a sense of place and time (**setting**), the central participants, important prior incidents, and the play's overall mood.

In some plays, such as Shakespeare's, the exposition comes quickly. The plots in plays like *Oedipus Rex* and *Death of a Salesman*, in contrast, tend not to attack us head-on but rather to surround us and gradually close in, the circle made tighter by each deliberately released clue to a mysterious past.

2. Complication and Crisis

Conflict requires two opposing forces. Fairly soon in a play we must experience some incident that incites the fundamental conflict when placed against some previously presented incident or situation. In most plays, conflicts generate the actions which make the characters' worlds worse before they can get better. Any plot featuring only repetitive altercations, however, would soon become tiresome. Potentially, anything can happen in a conflict. The **complication** is whatever presents an element capable of altering the action's direction. The plot is not a series of similar events but rather a compilation of related events leading to a culmination, called a **crisis**.

3. Resolution

After the crisis comes the **resolution** (or **denouement**), which gives the play its concluding boundary. This does not mean that the play should offer us solutions for whatever human issues it raises. Rather, the playwright's obligation is to make the experience he presents to us seem filled within its own perimeters. Terms such as **exposition**, **complication**, **crisis**, and **resolution**, though helpful in identifying the conflict's currents and directions, at best only artificially define how a plot is molded.

Character

Essential to the plot's success are the characters who participate in it.

Antigone begins with two characters, Antigone and Ismene, on stage. They initiate the exposition through their individual reactions to a previous event, King Creon's edict following the battle in which Thebes defeated an invading army. Creon has proclaimed Eteocles and the others who recently died defending Thebes as heroes worthy of the highest burial honors; in addition, Creon has forbidden anyone, on penalty of death, from burying Polyneices and the others who fell attacking the city. Since Antigone, Ismene, Polyneices, and Eteocles are the children of Oedipus and Iocaste, the late king and queen, conflict over Creon's law seems imminent. These first two characters establish this inevitability. They also reveal much about themselves as individuals.

ANTIGONE: . . . now you must prove what you are:
A true sister, or a traitor to your family.

ISMENE: Antigone, are you mad! What could I possibly do?

ANTIGONE: You must decide whether you will help me or not.

ISMENE: I do not understand you. Help you in what?

ANTIGONE: Ismene, I am going to bury him. Will you come?

ISMENE: Bury him! You have just said the new law forbids it.

ANTIGONE: He is my brother. And he is your brother, too.

ISMENE: But think of the danger! Think what Creon will do!

ANTIGONE: Creon is not strong enough to stand in my way.

ISMENE: Ah sister!

Oedipus died, everyone hating him
For what his own search brought to light, his eyes
Ripped out by his own hand; and Iocaste died,
His mother and wife at once: she twisted the cords
That strangled her life; and our two brothers died,
Each killed by the other's sword. And we are left:

But oh, Antigone,
Think how much more terrible than these
Our own death would be if we should go against Creon
And do what he has forbidden! We are only women,
We cannot fight with men, Antigone!
The law is strong, we must give in to the law
In this thing, and in worse. I beg the Dead
To forgive me, but I am helpless: I must yield
To those in authority. And I think it is dangerous business
To be always meddling.

ANTIGONE: If that is what you think,
I should not want you, even if you asked to come.
You have made your choice, you can be what you want to be.
But I will bury him; and if I must die,
I say that this crime is holy: I shall lie down
With him in death, and I shall be as dear
To him as he to me.

It is the dead,
Not the living, who make the longest demands:
We die for ever . . .
You may do as you like,
Since apparently, the laws of the gods mean nothing to you.

ISMENE: They mean a great deal to me; but I have no strength
To break laws that were made for the public good.

ANTIGONE: That must be your excuse, I suppose. But as for me,
I will bury the brother I love.

ISMENE: Antigone, I am so afraid for you!

ANTIGONE: You need not be:
You have yourself to consider, after all.

ISMENE: But no one must hear of this, you must tell no one!
I will keep it a secret, I promise!

ANTIGONE: Oh tell it! Tell everyone!
Think how they'll hate you when it all comes out
If they learn that you knew about it all the time!

ISMENE: So fiery! You should be cold with fear.

ANTIGONE: Perhaps. But I am doing only what I must.

ISMENE: But can you do it? I say that you cannot.

ANTIGONE: Very well: when my strength gives out, I shall do no more.

ISMENE: Impossible things should not be tried at all.

ANTIGONE: Go away, Ismene:
I shall be hating you soon, and the dead will too,
For your words are hateful. Leave me my foolish plan:
I am not afraid of the danger; if it means death,
It will not be the worst of deaths—death without honor.

ISMENE: Go then, if you feel that you must.
You are unwise,
But a loyal friend to those who love you.

[Exit into the palace. ANTIGONE goes off . . .]

Reading the Play

All we know about Antigone and Ismene in this scene comes from what they say; therefore, we read their spoken words carefully. However, we must also remain attentive to dramatic characters' propensity for not revealing all they know and feel about a given issue. Often characters do not recognize all the implications in what they say. We might be helped by what one says about the other, yet these observations are not necessarily accurate or sincere. Even though the previous scene contains fewer ambiguities than some others in dramatic literature, we would be oversimplifying to say the conflict here is between one character who is "right" and another who is "wrong." Antigone comes out challenging, determined and unafraid, whereas Ismene immediately reacts fearfully. Antigone brims with the self-assured power of righteousness while Ismene expresses vulnerability. Yet Antigone's boast that "Creon is not strong enough to stand in my way" suggests a rash temperament. We might admire her courage, but we question her judgment. Meanwhile, Ismene can evoke our sympathies with her burden of family woes, at least until she confesses her helplessness and begs the Dead to forgive her, at which point we realize her objections stem from cowardice and not conscience.

What immediately strikes us about Antigone and Ismene is that each possesses a sense of self, a conscious awareness about her existence and her connection with forces greater than herself. This is why we can identify with them. As social creatures, a condition about which they have had no choice, both Antigone and Ismene have senses of self which are touched by their identification with others: each belongs to a family, and each belongs to a civil state. Indeed, much of the play's conflict focuses on which identification should be stronger. Another connection influences them as well—the unbreakable tie to truth. With Antigone, we see how her sense of self cannot be severed from its bonds to family obligations and certain moral principles.

1. Theme

Reading literary art is no passive experience; it requires active work. And since playwrights seldom help us decide *how* characters say what they do or interrupt to explain *why* they say what they do, what personal voice he gives through stage directions deserves special attention, because playwrights never tell as much as novelists; instead, they show. Prior to the nineteenth century, dramatists relied heavily on poetic diction to define their characters. Later playwrights provided stage directions which detail stage activities and modify dialogue. Modern writers usually give precise descriptions for the set and costume design and even prescribe particular background music. But no matter when a play was written or what its expressive style is, our role as readers and audience is to make judgments about characters in action, just as we make judgments about Antigone and Ismene the first time we see them. As we peer into the playwright's mirror, we seek among the populated reflections shadows of ourselves. This allows us to discover the **theme**, a commentary about life in general.

2. Types of Plays

Some readers believe all plays can be neatly categorized according to preconceived definitions, as though playwrights follow literary recipes. The notion is not entirely ridiculous, since audiences and readers can easily tell a serious play from a humorous one, and a play labeled "tragedy" or "comedy" will generate certain valid expectations from us all, regardless of whether we have read a word by Aristotle or any other literary critic.

All plays contain **thought**—its accumulated themes, arguments, and overall meaning of the action—together with a **mood** or **tone**, and we tend to categorize dramatic thought into three clusters: the **serious**, the **comic**, and the **seriocomic**. Thus, in our attempts to interpret life's complexities, it is tempting to place the art forms representing it in precise, fixed designations. From this can come critical practices which ascertain how well a work imitates life by how well it adheres to its designated form. It should become clear that there is a better way of explaining what a play's form should be—not so much fixed as organic. In other words, we should think of a play as similar to a plant's growing and taking shape according to its own design. This analogy works well because the plant is not a mechanical device constructed from a predetermined plan, yet every plant is a species and as such contains qualities which identify it with others. So just as Shakespeare could ridicule overly precise definitions for dramatic art, he could still write dramas which he clearly identified as tragedies, comedies, or histories, even though he would freely mix two or more of these together in the same play. For the purpose of understanding some of the different perspectives available to the playwright's examining eye, we will look at plays from different periods which follow the three main designations Shakespeare used, followed by a fourth which is indicative of modern American drama.

Comedy

1. Forms of Comedy

The primary aim of **comedy** is to amuse us with a happy ending, although comedies can vary according to the attitudes they project, which can be broadly identified as either **high** or **low**. **Farce** is low comedy intended to make us laugh by means of a series of exaggerated, unlikely situations that depend less on plot and character than on gross absurdities, sight gags, and coarse dialogue. The "higher" a comedy goes, the more natural the characters seem and the less boisterous their behavior. The plots become more sustained, and the dialogue shows more weighty thought. Comedies create deviations from accepted normalcy, presenting incongruities which we might or might not see as harmless. If these incongruities make us judgmental about the involved characters and events, the play takes on the features of **satire**, a rather high comic form implying that humanity and human institutions are in need of reform. If the action triggers our sympathy for the characters, we feel even less protected from the incongruities as the play tilts more in the direction of **tragi-comedy**. In other words, the action determines a figurative distance between the audience and the play. It is a rare play that can freely manipulate its audience back and forth along this plane and still maintain its unity. Shakespeare's *The Merchant of Venice* is one example.

2. Example of a Comedy

A more consistent play is Oscar Wilde's *The Importance of Being Earnest*, which opened in 1895.

It is full of exaggerations, in both the situation being discussed and the manner in which the characters, particularly Lady Bracknell, express their reactions to the situation. Under other circumstances a foundling would not be the focus of a comedy, but we are relieved from any concern for the child since the adult Jack is obviously secure, healthy, and, with one exception, carefree. Moreover, we laugh when Lady Bracknell exaggerates Jack's heritage by comparing it with the excesses of the French Revolution. On the other hand, at the core of their discussion is the deeply ingrained and oppressive notion of English class consciousness, a mentality so flawed it almost begs to be satirized. Could there be more there than light, witty entertainment?

Tragedy

1. Terms

The term *tragedy,* originating with Aristotle, when used to define a play has historically meant something very precise, not simply a drama which ends with unfortunate consequences. Comedy, as we have seen, shows us a progression from adversity to prosperity. Tragedy must show the reverse; moreover, this progression must be experienced by a certain kind of character, says Aristotle, someone whom we can designate as the **tragic hero**. This central figure must be basically good and noble: "good" because we will not be aroused to fear and pity over the misfortunes of a villain, and "noble" both by social position and moral stature because the fall to misfortune would not otherwise be great enough for tragic impact. These virtues do not make the tragic hero perfect, however, for he must also possess **hamartia**—a tragic flaw—the frailty which leads him to make an error in judgment which initiates the reversal in his fortunes, causing his death, the death of others, or both. These dire consequences become the hero's **catastrophe**. The most common tragic flaw is **hubris**, an excessive pride that adversely influences the protagonist's judgment.

Witnessing these events produces the emotional reaction Aristotle believed the audience should experience, the **catharsis**. Although tragedy must arouse our pity for the tragic hero as he endures his catastrophe and must frighten us as we witness the consequences of a flawed behavior which anyone could exhibit, there must also be a purgation, "a cleansing," of these emotions which should leave the audience feeling not depressed but relieved and almost elated. The assumption is that while the tragic hero endures a crushing reversal somehow he is not thoroughly defeated as he gains new stature through suffering and the knowledge that comes with suffering.

2. Example of a Tragedy

Sophocles' plays give us some of the clearest examples of Aristotle's definition of tragedy. Shakespeare's tragedies are more varied and more modern in their complexities. *Othello* is one of Shakespeare's most innovative and troublesome extensions of tragedy's boundaries. The title character commands the Venetian army and soon becomes acting governor of Cypress. He is also a Moor, a dark-skinned African whose secret marriage to the beautiful Desdemona has infuriated her father, a wealthy and influential Venetian, whose anger reveals a racist element in Venice which Othello tries to ignore. Iago hates Othello for granting a promotion to Cassio which Iago believes should rightfully be his. With unrelenting determination and malicious deception, Iago attempts to persuade Othello that Desdemona has committed adultery with Cassio.

Dramatically, for Iago's machinations to compel our interests we must perceive in Othello tragic proportions, both in his strengths and weaknesses; otherwise, *Othello* would slip into a malevolent tale about a rogue and his dupe. Much of the tension emanates from Othello's reluctance either to accept Iago's innuendos immediately or to dismiss them. This confusion places him on the rack of doubt, a torture made more severe because he questions his own desirability as a husband. Consequently, since Iago is not the "honest creature" he appears to be and Othello is unwilling to confront openly his own self-doubts, Iago becomes the dominant personality—a situation which a flawless Othello would never tolerate.

History

The playwright's raw data can spring from any source. A **passion play**, for instance, is a dramatic adaptation of the Crucifixion as told in the gospels. A **history play** is a dramatic perspective of some event or series of events identified with recognized historical figures. Among the earliest histories were the **chronicle plays** which flourished during Shakespeare's time. Similarly, Shakespeare's *Henry V* and *Henry VIII* emphasize national and religious chauvinism in their treatments of kings who, from a more objective historical perspective, appear less than nobly motivated. These plays resemble romantic comedies with each one's protagonist defeating some adversary and establishing national harmony through royal marriage. *King Lear* and *Macbeth*, on the other hand, movingly demonstrate Shakespeare's skill at turning historical figures into tragic heroes.

1. Example of a History Play

Ever since the sixteenth century history plays have seldom risen above the level of patriotic white-wash and political propaganda. Of course there are notable exceptions to this trend: Robert Bolt's *A Man for All Seasons* is one. The title character, Sir Thomas More, is beheaded at the play's conclusion, following his refusal to condone Henry VIII's break from the Roman Catholic Church and the king's establishment of the Church of England with the monarch as its head. Henry wants More to condone these actions because the Pope will not grant Henry a divorce from Queen Catherine so that he can marry Anne Boleyn, who the king believes will bear him the male heir he desperately wants. The central issue for us is not whether More's theology is valid but whether any person of conscience can act freely in a world dominated by others far less principled.

Bolt's imagination, funneled through the dramatist's obligation to tell an interesting story, presides over the historical data and dictates the play's projections of More, Henry, and the other participants. Thus, we do not have "history"; instead, we have a dramatic perception of history shaped, altered, and adorned by Robert Bolt, writing about sixteenth century figures from a 1960 vantage point. However, the characters' personalities are not simple reductions of what historical giants should be. Henry struts a royal self-assurance noticeably colored by vanity and frustration; yet although he lacks More's wit and intelligence, the king clearly is no fool. Likewise, as troubled as More is by the controversy before him, he projects a formidable power of his own. *A Man for All Seasons* succeeds dramatically because Bolt provides only enough historical verisimilitude to present a context for the characters' development while he allows the resultant thematic implications to touch all times, all seasons.

Modern Drama

1. Forms of Modern Drama

From the 1870s to the present, the theater has participated in the artistic movements reflecting accumulated theories of science, social science, and philosophy which attempt to define reality and the means we use to discern it. First caught in a pendulum of opposing views, modern drama eventually synthesized these perspectives into new forms, familiar in some ways and boldly original in others. Henrik Ibsen's plays began the modern era with their emphasis on **Realism**, a seeking of truth through direct observation using the five senses. As objectively depicted, contemporary life received a closer scrutiny than ever before, showing everyday people in everyday situations. Ibsen's work influenced many others, and from Realism came two main variations. The first, **Naturalism**, strove to push Realism toward a direct transformation of life on stage, a "slice of life" showing how the scientific principles of heredity and environment have shaped society, especially in depicting the plights of the lower classes. The second variation, **Expressionism**, moved in a different direction and actually denied Realism's premise that the real world could be objectively perceived; instead—influenced by Sigmund Freud's theories about human behavior's hidden, subconscious motivations and by other modernist trends in the arts, such as James Joyce's fiction and Picasso's paintings—Expressionism imitated a disconnected dream-like world filled with psychological images at odds with the tangible world surrounding it. While Naturalism attempts to imitate life directly, Expressionism is abstract and often relies on symbols.

No work of art is necessarily confined within a particular school of thought. It is quite possible that seemingly incongruent forms can appear in the same play and work well. *The Glass Menagerie*, *A Man for All Seasons*, and *Death of a Salesman* feature characters and dialogue indicative of realistic drama, but the sets described in the stage directions are expressionistic, offering either framed outlines of places or distorted representations. Conventions from classical drama are also available to the playwright. In short, anything is possible in modern drama, a quality which is wholly compatible with the diversity and unpredictability of twentieth century human experiences.

2. Example of a Modern Drama

Death of a Salesman challenges the classical definitions of tragedy by giving us a modern American, Willy Loman, who is indeed a "low man," a person of little social importance and limited moral fiber. His delusionary values have brought him at age 64 to failure and despair, yet more than ever he clings to his dreams and painted memories for solace and hope.

In Arthur Miller's stage directions for *Death of a Salesman*, the Loman house is outlined by simple framing with various floors represented by short elevated platforms. Outside the house the towering shapes of the city angle inward, presenting the crowded oppressiveness Willy complains about. First performed in 1949, the play continues to make a powerful commentary on modern American life. We see Willy as more desperate than angry about his condition, which he defines in ways as contradictory as his assessments of Biff. In his suffocating world so nebulously delineated, Willy gropes for peace while hiding from truth; and although his woes are uniquely American in some ways, they touch broader, more universal human problems as well.

VISUAL ARTS AND ARCHITECTURE REVIEW

CLASSICAL PERIOD

The **classical period** of architecture and art begins with, and is best represented by, the civilization of the ancient Greeks; the city-state of Athens being the most dominant. The Greeks of the classical period were fascinated by physical beauty: their Olympian gods were fashioned in the human image, and a universe of perfection, guided by a master plan, was re-created in their idealized and gracefully proportioned sculptures, architecture, and paintings.

The amazing innovations of classical Greek art had their origins in earlier "Greek" civilizations—the Minoans of Crete and the people of mainland Mycenae. The **Minoans** flourished about 2500–1400 B.C. and produced increasingly sophisticated terracotta and bronze figurines and painted vases. The **Mycenaeans** produced beautiful work in gold, such as face masks, and artistically adopted the Minoans' ritual animal, the bull, but with a more aggressive character. Much of their best ornamentation was reserved for weapons.

The earliest period of Greek city-state civilization, the **Archaic**, boasted exemplary art in the form of vase paintings, whose simple, precise, linear decoration evolved from the earlier, geometric style of the ninth and eighth centuries B.C.—zigzag, meandering, and triangular designs—to include, by the end of the eighth century, lively animals and humans. By the sixth century the dominant method of painting black figures as silhouettes on vases gave way to red figures with drawn-in details on a black background; pictured were heroes, athletes, feasts, weddings, and genre scenes. Contact with Egyptian culture in the mid-seventh century encouraged development of marble statuary in Greece. The emphasis on nakedness in the *kouros* led quickly to the virtuosic treatment of **naturalistic representation**. The elements that characterize the spirit of ancient Greek art include respect for and re-creation of visual reality; a love of beauty in itself; and the application of rules and formulas to achieve representations of ideal beauty. The philosopher Plato's emphasis on the existence, in the spiritual realm or mind of God, of ideal forms for everything on Earth was the basis of much artistic creativity in both art and architecture.

The Greek temple developed as a columnar structure, with sculptures on the **pediments** (triangular space just below the roof) and relief sculpture (usually of narrative action) on the rectangular panels of the **friezes** (metopes) that banded the buildings above the columns. The most perfect example of classical proportions is found in the great Greek temples on the Athenian Acropolis. In the Parthenon (fifth century B.C.), the architect Ictinus created a structure that represented the striving for perfection and ideal beauty in Athenian culture; refinement and perfect proportions are achieved by subtle curvatures in the relation of vertical elements and the tapering of the Doric columns. The style and elements of the Parthenon and other Greek buildings provided the forms—from the three major classical orders of columns (**Doric**, **Ionic**, and **Corinthian**) to pediments and sculptural friezes (relief sculptures in realistic narratives)—for two millennia of Western architecture. The turning point for Greek sculpture came with the preeminence of Athens, after that city's victory over the Persians in the early fifth century.

In the fourth century the Greek city-states warred upon one another, and Macedonia prevailed, first under Philip II, then under his son Alexander, who by 323 B.C. had expanded the Greek empire to include Persia. The art of this period is characterized by greater naturalism, a wider variety of poses and of emotional display, and the intricate play of drapery. Praxiteles (*Hermes and the Infant Dionysus,* c. 350–330 B.C.) was skilled in portraying the human body in a rhythmic curve; he produced the first free-standing lifesize female nude, *The Cnidian Aphrodite* (known from a marble copy; originally c. 350–330 B.C.). Scopus was known for his naturalistic portraiture, notably the statues on the tomb of Mausolos at Halicarnassus (c. 353 B.C.).

During the **Hellenistic period** (323–31 B.C.), Greek culture spread throughout the Mediterranean. Art was characterized by new freedoms, insistent naturalism, more genre subjects (not merely heroic figures, but old women, sportsmen, etc.), less symmetry, and emphasis on technical virtuosity and the depiction of movement. Few examples of Greek painting survive, but notable painters were Apelles and Nikias in the fourth century B.C.

The Romans adopted much of the art and architectural forms of ancient Greece. The culture of Rome excelled in engineering and building; the Romans built temples, roads, bath complexes, civic buildings, palaces, and aqueducts. The cult of individual prestige and power was of major significance in Roman culture, and thus many of the statues were personalized and realistic. Greek ideal beauty was replaced by monuments and portraiture exalting specific personalities. The decoration of homes and public places by paintings and mosaics reflects the importance of a leisure-oriented "consumer" lifestyle. The first-century development of the **dome**—a major engineering and artistic contribution to world architecture—for public buildings was important for the Renaissance and later periods, when the writings of the great Roman architect Vitruvius (first century B.C.) were widely studied. The Roman **basilica** (an oblong building ending in a semicircular apse) was the basis for church architecture during the early Christian and medieval periods (300–1300).

Roman art was heavily influenced by the Greeks, especially after the sack of Syracuse in 212 B.C., when Greek artistic treasures—including the artists themselves—began pouring into Rome. While Greek forms were adopted, Greek ideas of beauty and perfection were not: Roman art served to provide luxury, as status symbols, and to enhance social position. **Portraiture** became very important, and the Romans eagerly adopted the innovation of the portrait bust from the Etruscans. The decorative paintings at Pompeii, such as those at the House of the Vettii (before 79 A.D.), depict realistically modeled humans in convincing landscapes, portraits of real characters, and the Roman fondness for **trompe l'oeil**—painting intended to fool the eye into believing one is seeing real three-dimensional objects, architectural details, or natural vistas.

The major Roman artistic statements were related to monumental architecture and sculpture. The **Arch of Titus** (c. 81 A.D.) describes the emperor's triumph and the spoils of Jerusalem in deep relief sculpture, a narrative of real events with lively poses. **Trajan's Column** (98–117 A.D.) is unlike any previous carved record: its story of Trajan's campaigns against the Dacians winds unbroken for more than 650 feet up the shaft of the 125-foot-high marble column; in low relief, like most ancient sculpture it was originally heightened with color. The emperor Hadrian (reigned 117–138 A.D.), commissioned the rebuilding of the greatest achievement of Roman architecture, the **Pantheon** in Rome. The relatively plain exterior of this temple "of all the gods" belies the astonishing technical accomplishment and interior decorative details. Inside, the wall of the building's main circular section is characterized by rectangular niches and apses, small tabernacles, and a wealth of variously colored marble panels. A massive concrete dome is broken by a central oculus, or hole, that lets in an ever-moving shaft of light.

The **late classical era** overlaps the early Christian period. Beginning with the monuments in the age of Constantine—the first Roman emperor to embrace Christianity—a new emphasis can be seen, more on spiritual meaning and symbolism, less on the realistic depiction of the world and personal accomplishments. Similar de-emphasis of the real world and a burgeoning Christian iconography (salvation of souls, divine intervention, miracles) can be found in the art of the Catacombs, underground burial chambers outside Rome (200–400 A.D.).

MEDIEVAL AND RENAISSANCE PERIODS

During the Middle Ages, the Romans' cultural and artistic legacy lived on in the Byzantine empire, whose capital was the magnificent city of Constantinople (modern Istanbul, in Turkey). Perhaps the greatest of the Byzantine emperors was Justinian (527–565 A.D.), who reaffirmed the empire and made Ravenna, a northeast Italian city on the Adriatic coast, the government center of the West. The Byzantine style was meant to convey a supernatural, otherworldly effect.

During the **Dark Ages** (about the fifth to eighth centuries), Celtic artists of Ireland, Scotland, and northern Britain, especially in the monasteries, kept Western art alive in stone carvings and crosses with interlace patterns, and in magnificent illuminated manuscripts (Book of Durrow, Lindisfarne Gospels, Book of Kells), whose design was influenced by Celtic metalwork. The end of the Dark Ages was officially marked by the coronation of the Frankish king Charlemagne as Holy Roman Emperor by the pope on Christmas Day 800. Charlemagne, whose capital was at Achen (Aix-la-Chapelle), aspired to create an empire that rivaled the Roman empire as well as reviving classical culture and learning. He acquired ancient Roman sculptures, established schools, gathered around him the scholars Alcuin and Theodulf, and commissioned illuminated manuscripts (Utrecht Psalter, Ebbo Gospels,

Lorsch Gospels). The empire lapsed after Charlemagne but was revived by Otto the Great (after his 955 victory over the Hungarians). This period is marked by a revival of early Christian, Carolingian, and Byzantine art.

The **Romanesque** style of art and architecture was preeminent in the eleventh and twelfth centuries. By then many local styles, including the decorative arts of the Byzantines, the Near East, and the German and Celtic tribes, were contributing to European culture. Common features of Romanesque churches are round arches, vaulted ceilings, and heavy walls that are profusely decorated—primarily with symbolic figures of Christianity, the realism of which for its creators had become less and less important and was, instead, subordinate to the message. Sculpture, usually relief in stone, was an integral part of church architecture on portals (doorways) and capitals (column crowns). In France, prominent sculptural areas were around the door jambs and the semicircular area above the door, the tympanum.

Gothic art flourished in Europe from the twelfth through the fifteenth centuries and was primarily a French and northern European style. The cathedrals in this style are some of the purest expressions of an age: they combine a continued search for engineering and structural improvement with features that convey a relentless verticality, a reach toward heaven, and the unbridled adoration of God. Gothic art emphasized greater spirituality, as well as greater humanity and tenderness, than previous Christian art; its most important religious figure is the Virgin Mary. The style in sculpture displays grace and realism, and figures are often elongated to match the skyward-stretching form of the architecture.

The work of Nicholas of Verdun at the end of the twelfth century reveals a classical style; the awakening of the spirit of humanism in Gothic art led to a new interest in the natural world and a revival of the Classical tradition. The thirteenth and fourteenth centuries were a vital and exciting period that came to be considered both Gothic and proto-Renaissance. In northern Europe, life itself became more festive, the artisan and merchant classes achieved some status—all of which inspired the colorful and realistic paintings of the sumptuous books of hours (the Limbourg Brothers: *Les Très Riches Heures du Duc de Berry,* 1413–1416).

The Italian school of this period—from 1250 onward—provides the first glimmers of the **Renaissance**—in a new naturalism, plus an emphasis on wall decoration in fresco and the painting of alterpieces (panels—the forerunners of the easel paintings). Its notable painters were Cimabue (active 1272–1302) and Duccio (active 1278–1318). The work of Giotto (c. 1267–1337) is often regarded as the beginning of Renaissance art in Florence. His Arena Chapel paintings in Padua depict the life story of the Virgin and Christ in a series of independent but continuous narrative pictures, full of drama and psychological nuance. In the fourteenth century, Sienese painters were among the leaders in the new realism.

Lines were often blurred between the Gothic and the early Renaissance in sculpture. In Pisa, innovations were made in the thirteenth and fourteenth centuries by Nicola Pisano (active 1258–1284) and his son Giovanni. Nicola created the marble pulpit for the Baptistry at Pisa; Giovanni's Pisa Cathedral pulpit (1302–1310) merges Gothic and classical influences.

In fifteenth-century Florence, wealthy patrons, merchants, and nobles consciously revived classical art and philosophy. The technical discovery of **proportion** was used in architecture and art, and the great artists of the Renaissance often combined talents in all fields. Architecture, in the hands of Filippo Brunelleschi and Leon Battista Alberti, revived the Greco-Roman elements and took a scientific, ordered approach, one similarly expressed in painting with the emphasis on the calculated composition of figures in space known as perspective. Brunelleschi (1377–1440) invented single-vanishing-point perspective, and Alberti (1404–1472) wrote on the mathematics of perspective in *On Painting* (1435). Michelozzo (1396–1472) designed the first great Renaissance palace, the Palazzo Medici in Florence. In Rome, Donato Bramante (1444–1514) designed the first Renaissance building created in imitation of a circular Roman temple, which is vaulted by a hemispherical dome and encircled by classical columns. Andrea Palladio (1508–1580) wrote the most influential treatise on architecture for centuries *(The Four Books of Architecture)*.

The greatest of the early Renaissance sculptors was **Donatello** (1386–1466), whose work was not only classically inspired and realistic, but highly theatrical and full of psychological undertones. His *David,* one of the most famous Renaissance bronze sculptures, marks the revival of the classical free-standing nude male—sinuous in form, in an elegant, almost impish pose.

The first great painter of the Renaissance was **Masaccio** (1401–c. 1428). In the *Holy Trinity* fresco for the Church of Santa Maria Novella in Florence, he used perspective based on Brunelleschi's ideas; there is a clear light source that unifies the whole, plus classical details, such as the Corinthian pilasters framing Ionic columns. More than any other painter, **Botticelli** (c. 1445–1510) epitomized the spirit of the early Renaissance. A favorite of the Medicis, his work is intensely religious and allegorical and insistent on recalling the images of classical antiquity. He painted many Madonnas as well as humanist allegories of classical inspiration.

The three pillars of the High Renaissance of the early sixteenth century are **Leonardo da Vinci**, **Michelangelo**, and **Raphael**. Leonardo's intellectual curiosity led him to make scientific deductions (and sketch out inventions such as flying machines) based on observed reality; these he recorded in his famous **Notebooks**. In addition to *The Last Supper* (1495–1498) and the *Mona Lisa* (1503), he painted *The Virgin of the Rocks* (1483–1485), which epitomizes his artistic approach: strange and metaphysical, suffused with mysterious light, the picture uses the technique of sfumato, a smoky-shadowy way of modeling form.

Michelangelo, too, excelled in many fields: he was a poet, painter, sculptor, and architect. He redesigned St. Peter's in Rome, adding an enormous dome and completing the work previously planned by Bramante and Raphael. His sculptures seek to portray bodily perfection and convey a perfect synthesis of the human and the divine—the epitome of the **Neoplatonic** philosophy of the Renaissance (that is, the body expresses the spirit). The Sistine Chapel frescoes in the Vatican in Rome are his masterpieces: in painting a complex system of dynamic figures full of raw human power and divine spirit, Michelangelo created some of the world's most unforgettable artistic images. For centuries the paintings of Raphael (1483–1520) have been the measure of artistic perfection. Raphael's Madonnas are both spiritual ideals and clear personalities, set against a serene landscape, and represent perfect compositional balance.

Venetian and northern Italian painters worked in highly personal styles, leading toward the style called **Baroque**. The **Mannerists** of the first half of the sixteenth century (notably Parmigianino, Pontormo, and Bronzino) produced work full of exaggerations: floating angels, the confusion of illusion and reality, contorted and elongated figures, awkward spatial relationships, and strange lighting effects. Among the great Venetians were Bellini (the San Zaccaria Altarpiece) and Giorgione (an innovator in "mood painting"). The giant among the Venetians is Titian (active c. 1500–1576), whose brilliant color and dynamic brushwork made him one of the most admired artists of his time and made his name synonymous with great art through the succeeding centuries. Drawing ever closer to the Baroque spirit were two other Venetians: Veronese, who specialized in vast pageants unfolding in a single, grand painting, and Tintoretto, whose unique canvases team with vibrant life and dramatic incident.

The northern European Renaissance also displayed a renewed interest in the visible world, and works by Albrecht Dürer, Lucas Cranach, Matthias Grünewald, and Albrecht Altdorfer reveal an emphasis on the symbolism of minutely observed details and an accurate realism based on observation of reality rather than on prescribed rules. This unique northern emphasis can be seen as far back as the fifteenth century. Northern art, particularly in the Netherlands (later Flanders and Holland) and Germany, pursued a parallel course to that in Italy from the Gothic period to the Baroque era—but with a clear difference: the reawakening to the material world was less intellectual and less based on classical models than in the south. Rather, it was a realism based on the tastes of a rising wealthy merchant and middle class, delighting in their everyday lives.

In Germany the Renaissance produced many outstanding painters: Dürer, Grünewald, and Altdorfer, as well as Lucas Cranach, Hans Holbein, and Pieter Bruegel. By far the greatest of these was **Albrecht Dürer** (1471–1528), in many ways equal to Michelangelo in stature and innovation. Dürer traveled extensively and was influenced by the art of the Venetians; his scientific curiosity about the natural world was nearly equal to Leonardo's. Dürer's fame spread throughout Europe because of his prolific and groundbreaking work in the area of printmaking. One of the finest painters of the sixteenth century was Hans Holbein the Younger (1497–1543), who continued the northern emphasis on symbolic detail and highly finished realism, particularly in the area of portraiture.

THE SEVENTEENTH AND EIGHTEENTH CENTURIES

Presaged by the works of the Venetian artist Tintoretto (the radiating *Last Supper*) and El Greco in Spain (the visionary *Toledo; The Immaculate Conception*), the **Baroque** period of the seventeenth century produced artists who added heightened drama to the forms of Renaissance art. Bernini (1598–1680) was the giant of the style in Italy and enjoyed papal patronage, working in sculpture and architecture to create some of the most dynamic and personal statements of art, such as the Piazza of St. Peter's in Rome. Bernini's rival was Francesco Borromini, the other great Italian architect of the Baroque.

In France, Baroque splendor was carried to its grandest at **Versailles**, a complex supervised by Charles Le Brun. Vast terraces, water gardens, fountains, and the gallery of mirrors were all calculated to equate Louis XIV, the Sun King, with the god Apollo. In England, however, the seventeenth century marked the beginning of a new classicism, particularly through the influential writings of Palladio. The Palladian/classical "revival" in architecture—**Neo-Classicism**—continued throughout the eighteenth and early nineteenth centuries.

In painting, the most significant proponent of the Italian Baroque was Caravaggio (1571–1610), whose models were ordinary people, and whose use of contrasting shadow and light was revolutionary and made for works of bold drama. The Flemish masters Peter Paul Rubens (1577–1640) and Jacob Jordaens portrayed figures in constant motion, draperies of agitated angles, and effects of lighting and shadow that amplified emotional impact and mystery. In this spirit followed such painters of court life and middle-class portraiture as Velazquez (1599–1660) in Spain; Anthony Van Dyck in England; and in Holland, Frans Hals (1581–1666) and Rembrandt van Rijn. **Rembrandt** (1601–1669), one of the greatest artists of all time, used expressive brushwork and mysterious light contrasts to enliven religious and genre painting and portraiture, particularly of groups.

The art of the early eighteenth century is often called **Rococo**. Painters like Jean Antoine Watteau, Giambattista Tiepolo, François Boucher, and Jean Honoré Fragonard turned the agitated drama of the Baroque into light, pastel-toned, swirling compositions that seem placed in an idyllic land of a golden age. Rococo style in architecture is marked by a profusion of elegant and fantastic decorative elements, often employing representations of shells, scrolls, and leaves. The influence of Versailles, with its mirrors radiating light and theatricality, is seen in the stucco fantasies covering Rococo interiors like living organisms, the relentless vegetation often supported by floating cherubs.

In the seventeenth and eighteenth centuries, European artists also responded to middle-class life and everyday objects to create **genre paintings**. Such narrative art combined in the late eighteenth and early nineteenth centuries with romantic literature—Goethe, Byron, Shelley, Scott, Wordsworth, and others—and political events to produce works with a political point of view or a story to tell, in a variety of styles. Jacques Louis David (1748–1825) used a severe classical sculptural style (Neo-Classicism) in his paintings to revive antique art and ennoble images of the French Revolution and Napoleon's empire. The spiritual godfather of Neo-Classicism is Nicholas Poussin (1593–1665), whose paintings of the seventeenth century are perfectly balanced, severe, idealized, and sculptural models of pristine classicism. Neo-Classical sculpture in the late eighteenth century revived the aloof severity and perfection of form of ancient art. Leading sculptors were Jean Antoine Houdon, Antonio Canova, and Bertal Thorvaldsen. In England, the draughtsman and engraver John Flaxman produced engraved outline illustrations reminiscent of Greek vase paintings for illustrations to the *Iliad;* his work was the basis for the enduring style of Wedgwood pottery.

THE NINETEENTH CENTURY

In the late eighteenth century, there occurred a full-blown revival of Greek and Roman design. Another revival stressed the Gothic style, championed by architect Augustus Pugin and writer John Ruskin—inspiring numerous Victorian Gothic buildings in England and America.

Political and other national events were important subjects for the romantic-realist painters of the early nineteenth century. The Spanish painter Francisco de Goya commented powerfully on political events in his painting *May 3, 1808*. In France, Eugene Delacroix (1798–1863) and Theodore Gericault (1791–1824) imbued subjects from literature, the Bible, exotic lands, and current events with dramatic, heroic intensity. The grandeur and transcendence of nature, the emotional reaction to inner dreams, and metaphysical truths of romanticism are seen in the work of such mystical artists as England's William Blake (a master of innovative printmaking), Henry Fuseli, and John Martin, and America's Thomas Cole.

In the first half of the nineteenth century, **landscape painting** in England reached a zenith with the works of John Constable (1776–1837) and Joseph Mallord William Turner (1775–1851). Turner's awe-inspiring landscapes, revolutionary in their lighting effects achieved through bold, expressive brushwork, form a bridge between the spirit of romanticism and the expressionistic brushwork and realism of the Barbizon School in France, whose chief painters were Charles Daubigny and Jean Baptiste Camille Corot. Beginning with Barbizon, the French painters of the nineteenth century concentrated more and more on the reporter-like depiction of everyday life and the natural environment in a free, painterly (gestural brushwork) style. The realist pioneers paved the way for the stylistic and subject innovations of the Impressionists.

In **Impressionism**, traditional means of composing a picture were rejected in favor of an art that emphasized quickly observed and sketched moments from life, the relation of shapes and forms and colors, the effects of light, and the act of painting itself. Beginning with Edouard Manet in the 1860s, French artists continually blurred the boundaries of **realism** and **abstraction**. The great Impressionist painters included Claude Monet (1840–1926) and Auguste Renoir (1841–1919). Like Manet and many other French artists, Edgar Degas (1834–1917) was influenced by the compositional techniques of Japanese prints; he delighted in achieving spontaneity by depicting his subjects from unusual angles and with figures seemingly arbitrarily cut off at the edge. Degas specialized in scenes of Parisian life and horses, nudes, and dancers.

By the 1880s pure Impressionism gave way to the more experimental arrangements of form and color of the **Post-Impressionists**—Japanese prints held much allure for Paul Gauguin (1848–1903), who arbitrarily placed almost garish colors in compositions where design and shape took precedence over any sense of perspective or proportion. Vincent van Gogh (1853–1890) adopted Gauguin's harsh and unusual color schemes that were unrelated to the reality of a scene, and painted with an innovative, personal, expressive brushwork of thick swirling lines—which paved the way for twentieth-century **Expressionism**. Georges Seurat (1859–1891) produced noble and serene compositions in a style called **pointillism**, which allowed the viewer to visually mix the colors of a painting that had been applied in minute individual dots. Henri de Toulouse-Lautrec, more than any other French artist, concentrated on themes of night life and entertainment and employed thick outlines and the flatness of shapes and color of Japanese prints, especially in his many color lithographic posters. Paul Cézanne, considered by many to be the father of modern art, used the lessons of Impressionism to make the subjectivity of the artist paramount. He bent his subjects' shapes and contours away from realistic proportions and relationships, and assigned colors based on harmonious balance in the picture. Cézanne (1839–1906) was able to break apart and re-form reality, and make the act of painting itself significant, and in so doing he was able to usher in the achievements of twentieth-century **Cubism** and abstract art.

Other important groups in the last two decades of the nineteenth century that distorted reality and pursued sinewy forms or abstract patterning were the Nabis, the art nouveau artists, the early expressionists, and the Symbolists.

The most significant innovations in nineteenth-century architecture were related to technical accomplishment; the possibility of construction on a large scale in metal, iron, and glass allowed for revolutionary skeletal structures. The Crystal Palace, built for London's Great Exhibition in 1851 by Joseph Paxton, was 1,600 feet long, and basically a glass building. A famous metal monument of no apparent purpose other than to symbolize another world's fair (in Paris in 1889) was Gustave Eiffel's tower.

THE TWENTIETH CENTURY

Architecture in the twentieth century announced a clean break with the past, building upon the technical and structural innovations of such nineteenth-century masters as Joseph Paxton and Louis Sullivan. **Frank Lloyd Wright** (1867–1959), perhaps the new century's greatest innovator, transformed both commercial and residential architecture into structures that perfectly matched their surroundings, broke with the decorative language of the past, and offered functionalism in working and living spaces. In the 1920s, the **Bauhaus school of design** in Dessau, Germany, championed abstract art, geometric design, machine-age elements, and restricted ornament. The director was the important architect Walter Gropius, whose design for the Bauhaus school building featured glass facades— pure line and geometric shapes. In America, Miës van der Rohe's Seagram building in New York (1954–1958) is perhaps the most famous example of the trend of skyscraper glass rectangles. This style of technology-driven, unadorned, stripped-to-essentials architecture in the industrialized nations since the 1930s has been called **International Style** or simply **Modernism**. In the last 20 years, the austerity of Modernism has been redirected into a more decorative and humanistic style, often termed **Post-Modernism**, which incorporates cultural influences, imaginative decorative touches, and historical architectural elements into designs appropriate to modern technology and uses.

Sculpture and painting, from the beginning of the twentieth century, built upon the rejection of realistic proportions and naturalistic depiction, substituting a breakup of forms and a play of shape and color such as employed by Gauguin, Van Gogh, Cezanne, the Nabis, and others. The new freer form of art centered around the personality of the artist and celebrated personal style and the manipulation of two-dimensional pictorial elements. In the late nineteenth and early twentieth centuries this evolved in a number of directions. Some artists (**Symbolists**, **Expressionists**, and exponents of **art nouveau**) turned inward to explore mystical, symbolic, and psychological truths. The German Expressionists portrayed disturbing psychological truths through highly personal styles and disjointed compositions, and they frequently worked in woodcut. These German artists banded together from 1905 to 1913 in a group called **Die Brucke**; their aims were unabashedly revolutionary; their work was often meant to shock; and their compositions emphasized distortion, angular and contorted figures, sometimes screaming color, and outrageous themes. In the face of the horrors of World War I, shock value and humor were the artistic weapons of choice for the **Dada artists**, whose "antiart" or "nonart" works often assembled any materials available ("found objects"), from newspaper clippings and photographs to bicycle wheels.

Henri Matisse (1869–1954) was the leading figure of the **Fauves** (dubbed "wild beasts" because of their relentlessly unreal use of color). Matisse's most important works reduced a picture to its essentials—flat color and line (*The Dance; Le Luxe II*). The most revolutionary and far-reaching art movement of the twentieth century was **Cubism**—which, by its blatant visual decomposition and reassemblage of observed reality, seemed the most direct call for the total destruction of realistic depiction and for abstraction. The greatest Cubist artist and one of the most important figures in the history of art was Pablo Picasso (1881–1973).

In the first decades of the twentieth century, pure abstraction, with little or no relation to the outside world, was approached in the more emotional, expressionistic, and color-oriented paintings of Wassily Kandinsky (with Franz Marc, a proponent of the Blue Rider school), Robert Delaunay, and Paul Klee. More cerebral arrangements of abstract geometrical shapes and colors were the mark of Kasimir Malevich (his Suprematist compositions), Piet Mondrian, and the Bauhaus School of Design in Germany. The Bauhaus's simplified and usually geometric-oriented aesthetic influenced architecture, industrial and commercial design, sculpture, and the graphic arts for half a century.

Inspired by the psychoanalytic writings of Sigmund Freud and Carl Jung, the subconscious and the metaphysical became another important element in art, especially in the work of the **Surrealist** artists like Salvador Dali.

Obsession with self and with abstraction also led to the major American art movement after World War II, **Abstract Expressionism** (exemplified by Clyfford Still and Jackson Pollock). Other Americans took this movement into the area of color-field painting, a cooler, more reserved formalism of simple shapes and experimental color relationships.

Other important trends in American art in the twentieth century were reflective of a democratic and consumer society. The muralists and social realists during the first half of the century created art that was dynamically realistic—representative of a youthful and vigorous America—and whose subjects were accessible to the average person. John Sloan, George Bellows, Edward Hopper, Thomas Hart Benton, Grant Wood, and John Stuart Curry were among those who celebrated the American scene in paintings, and frequently in murals for public buildings and through widely available fine prints. The great Mexican muralists, who usually concentrated on political themes—Diego Rivera, José Clemente Orozco, and David Siqueiros—brought their work to the public both in Mexico and in the United States.

The icons of American popular culture found their way, in the movement known as **pop art**, into canvases by Andy Warhol, such as the multiplied silk-screened images of Campbell Soup cans and Marilyn Monroe. Other developments during the last 30 years include **kinetic art** (works that move or produce an illusion of movement) and **op art** (manipulation of abstract color and repetitive patterns to play tricks on the eye); **minimal art** (the work reduced to essentials) and **conceptual art** (the idea itself, rather than the technical accomplishment); and the actual movement of, or covering of, land and monuments on a massive scale.

PHILOSOPHY REVIEW

ANCIENT PHILOSOPHERS

All of the Greek philosophers before Socrates are known as the **pre-Socratics**.

Pythagoras	a sixth century B.C. pre-Socratic philosopher and mathematician, believed in the transmigration of souls.
Thales	Sometimes called "the father of Western philosophy," Thales, a sixth and fifth century B.C. pre-Socratic philosopher, held that the first principle, or substance, that everything in the universe is made out of is water.
Parmenides	a pre-Socratic philosopher in the fifth and fourth century B.C., denied the existence of time, plurality, and motion. He is considered the founder of metaphysics.
Heraclitus	a pre-Socratic philosopher in the fourth century B.C., was said to have believed that everything is in a continuous state of flux.
Zeno	a pre-Socratic philosopher in the fourth century B.C. and a disciple of Parmenides, was famous for a set of paradoxes showing that plurality and motion do not really exist.
Socrates	an Athenian fourth century B.C. philosopher, supposedly wrote down none of his views, because he believed writing distorted ideas. It is unclear to what extent the views attributed to Socrates' character in Plato's dialogues were the views of the actual historical Socrates.

Atomism is the belief that matter consists of atoms. Both Leucippus, a fourth century B.C. Greek philosopher, and Democritus, a fourth and third century B.C. Greek philosopher, were atomists.

Plato, a Greek philosopher who lived from 427 to 347 B.C., wrote dialogues that provided the starting point for many later developments in various areas—for example, ethics, the study of morals; epistemology, the study of knowledge; and metaphysics, the study of reality. Plato's best known theory is the **theory of Forms (or Ideas)**.

Aristotle, an extremely influential Greek philosopher who lived in the third century B.C., criticized Plato's theory of Forms. The Medieval study and development of Aristotle's philosophy is known as **Aristotelianism**.

PHILOSOPHERS OF THE FIRST MILLENNIUM

Neoplatonism was the dominant philosophy in Europe from 250 through 1250 A.D. Begun by Plotinus, a third century A.D. philosopher, Neoplatonism combined Plato's ideas with those of other philosophers, such as Aristotle and Pythagoras. Augustine, a fourth and fifth century bishop and philosopher, had a profound effect on Medieval religious thought.

St. Anselm	an eleventh century philosopher, was an Italian monk who became archbishop of Canterbury. He founded Scholasticism and was best known for his ontological argument for the existence of God.
St. Thomas Aquinas	a thirteenth century philosopher, was best known for his "**Five Ways**," five proofs of the existence of God. The philosophy of Aquinas and his followers is called **Thomism**. He is considered the greatest thinker of the Scholastic School. His ideas were made the official Catholic philosophy in 1879.
Ockham	a fourteenth century English philosopher and cleric, was famous for the dictum "Do not multiply entities beyond necessity."
Hobbes (1588–1679)	a British materialist, felt that a powerful absolute ruler is necessary because men are selfish by nature.

Rationalism is the view that knowledge of the external world can be derived from reason alone, without recourse to experience.

Descartes (1596–1650)	an extremely influential French philosopher, mathematician, and Rationalist, believed the mind and body are two distinct, though interactive, entities (**Cartesian dualism**). Descartes is famous for the statement "*cogito ergo sum*," or "I think; therefore, I am."
Blaise Pascal (1623–1662)	a French philosopher, mathematician, and theologian, is most famous for an argument called "**Pascal's Wager**," which provides prudent reasons for believing in God.
Benedict Spinoza (1632–1677)	a Dutch-born Rationalist philosopher, felt mind and body are aspects of a single substance, which he called God or Nature.
Gottfried Wilhelm von Leibniz (1646–1716)	was a German Rationalist philosopher who argued, in his *Theodicy*, that this is the best of all possible worlds.

Empiricism is the view that all knowledge is derived from experience.

John Locke (1632–1704)	an English philosopher, attempted to present an Empiricist account of the origins, nature, and limits of human reason.
Berkeley (1685–1753)	another Empiricist, was an Irish philosopher and an idealist. Idealism is the view that the so-called "external world" is actually a creation of the mind.
David Hume (1711–1776)	a Scots philosopher and empiricist, drew attention to the problem of induction.
Jean Jacques Rousseau (1712–1778)	a German born political philosopher and a philosopher of education who wrote *The Social Contract* (1762), emphasized man's natural goodness.
Adam Smith (1723–1790)	a Scots philosopher and political economist who wrote *The Wealth of Nations*, had an enormous impact on economics.
Immanuel Kant (1724–1804)	a German idealist philosopher, was most famous for the categorical imperative—"Act only on that maxim which you can at the same time will to become a universal law"—as a test of moral principles.
Jeremy Bentham (1748–1832)	a British philosopher and a lawyer, was one of the founders of **Utilitarianism**. He was a powerful reformer of the British legal, judicial, and prison system.
Georg Wilhelm Friedrich Hegel (1770–1831)	a German Idealist philosopher, is famous for his theory of the **dialectic**, a process of argument which proceeds from a thesis and its antithesis to a synthesis of the two.
James Mill (1773–1836)	a Scots philosopher and economist, was the father of the better-known philosopher J. S. Mill (1806–1873).
Arthur Schopenhauer (1788–1860)	a German philosopher, was a Kantian who believed that only art and contemplation could offer escape from determinism and pessimism.
J. S. Mill (1806–1873)	is best known both for his System of Logic and for his ethical writings, including Utilitarianism and On Liberty.
Søren Kierkegaard (1813–1855)	a Danish philosopher, was probably the first Existentialist. **Existentialism** is the view that the subject of philosophy is *being*, which cannot be made the subject of objective inquiry but can only be investigated by reflection on one's own existence. Sartre is another notable Existentialist.
Karl Marx (1818–1883)	a German social theorist, author of *Das Kapital*.
Engels (1820–1895)	Marx's collaborator, was a dialectical materialist. **Dialectical materialism** is the metaphysical doctrine that matter, rather than the mind, is primary.
Brentano (1838–1917)	a German philosopher and psychologist, is remembered for his "doctrine of intentionality."

Charles Peirce (1839–1914)	an American philosopher, was the founder of **Pragmatism**, a theory of meaning.
William James (1842–1910)	an American (Empiricist) philosopher and psychologist, used Pragmatism as a theory of truth according to which "ideas become true just so far as they help us get into satisfactory relations with other parts of our experience."
Friedrich Wilhelm Nietzsche (1844–1900)	a German philosopher, is best known for introducing the concept of the **Übermensch**, or the Overman.
Bradley (1846–1924)	an English philosopher and idealist, was known for his work *Appearance and Reality*.
Frege (1848–1925)	a German philosopher and mathematician, is considered the founding father of modern logic, philosophy of mathematics, and philosophy of language.
Edmund Husserl (1859–1938)	a German philosopher, developed **phenomenology**, a method of inquiry which begins with the scrupulous inspection of one's own conscious thought processes.
John Dewey (1859–1952)	an American Pragmatist philosopher and educational theorist, developed his own version of Pragmatism that emphasized the importance of inquiry into acquiring knowledge.
George Santayana (1863–1952)	an American Platonist philosopher, novelist, and poet, attempted to reconcile Platonism and materialism.
Bertrand Russell (1872–1970)	a British philosopher, was coauthor of the extremely influential *Principia Mathematica*. Russell argued that the structure of the world can be revealed by the proper analysis of language.
G. E. Moore (1873–1958)	a British philosopher, emphasized the common sense view of the reality of material objects.

Logical Positivism (logical Empiricism), a radical Empiricist position, states the meaning of a proposition consists in the method of its verification. A group of logical Positivists, known as the **Vienna Circle**, centered around the University of Vienna in the 1920s and 1930s.

Ludwig Wittgenstein (1889–1951)	a Viennese-born philosopher, wrote *Tractatus Logico-Philosophicus*, a defense of a picture theory of meaning. This work contains such often quoted aphorisms as "The world is everything that is the case."
Martin Heidegger (1889–1976)	a German philosopher, is commonly regarded, as an Existentialist. His own philosophy emphasized the need to understand "being."

(Continued)

Alfred Tarski (1902–1993)	a logician and mathematician, is famous for his definition of the concept of truth for formal logical languages.
Sir Karl Popper (1902–1994)	a philosopher of science, is best known for his claim that falsifiability is the hallmark of science.
Jean-Paul Sartre (1905–1980)	a French philosopher who helped found Marxism and Existentialism, believed man is condemned to be free and to bear the responsibility of making free choices.
Hempel (1905–1997)	a German Empiricist philosopher of science. His theories of confirmation and explanation have been extremely influential.
Goodman (1906–1998)	an American philosopher, was a Nominalist.
Merleau-Ponty (1908–1961)	was a French philosopher who worked on ethics and problems of consciousness.
Willard Van Orman Quine (1908–2000)	was an American Empiricist philosopher of language and a logician.
Sir Alfred Jules Ayer (1910–1989)	an English philosopher, is a logical Positivist and member of the Vienna Circle.
Austin (1911–1960)	a British philosopher of language, developed the speech act theory.
Davidson (1917–)	an American philosopher of language and the mind, holds a theory of the mind called **anomalous monism**.
Strawson (1919–)	a British philosopher of language and a metaphysician, is best known for arguing that some meaningful sentences have no truth value.
Rawls (1921–)	an American political philosopher, is best known for *A Theory of Justice*.
Noam Chomsky (1928–)	an influential American linguist and philosopher, argues that there is an innate universal grammar.
Kripke (1941–)	an American philosopher of language, philosopher of the mind, and logician. His causal theory of reference, in part, deals with the distinction between a statement's sense and its reference.

Music is the organization of sound in time. Each individual tone has four properties that give it a particular character: duration, frequency, intensity, and timbre. **Duration** refers to how long a sound or a silence lasts and the rate at which one sound succeeds another. **Rhythm** is based on this fundamental property of sound and is essential to our perception of time. Most of the music that we hear and all music to which we dance or march has a steady beat, a regular **pulse** that underlies the melody. Whereas the pulse is steady with an unchanging note value, melodic rhythm involves a variety of note values. Some beats have more than one melodic note to them and some melodic notes extend over several beats. For instance, in "Happy Birthday to You," both of the notes of "happy" occur on a single beat while "you" extends over two beats.

Tempo refers to the speed of the pulse. If the beats are in the range of our heartbeats, around 72 pulses a minute, the tempo is *moderato* (moderate). If the beats are faster than our heartbeats, the tempo is *vivace*, or if very much faster, it is *presto*. If the beats are slower than our heartbeats, the tempo is *lento* or *largo*. A fast tempo conveys a mood of energy and excitement; a slow tempo produces a more somber or thoughtful feeling.

Patterns are formed when some beats are regularly stronger than others. Music organized in this fashion is said to be **metric**. In order to have meter, there must be both a steady pulse and a pattern of accented and unaccented beats. Music that does not have a steady pulse (such as recitative in operas or some atonal music), or music that has a steady pulse but no accents at all (such as Gregorian chant) or has unpredictable accents that do not form a recognizable pattern (such as Stravinsky's *Rite of Spring*) is said to be **ametric**. Most of the music in the world, however, is metric.

Western music has only two basic patterns. A strong beat followed by a weak beat (ONE two, ONE two) or a strong beat followed by three weak beats (ONE two three four) is said to be **duple meter**. Almost all popular music is duple. The other pattern is **triple**, with a strong beat followed by two weak ones (ONE two three, ONE two three).

In notated music, each occurrence of the pattern constitutes a **measure** or **bar** and is set off by vertical bar lines. The meter itself is denoted by a **time signature** placed at the beginning of the music. This consists of two numbers positioned vertically. The upper number indicates how many beats are in a measure and the lower number identifies which kind of note gets the beat. For example, if the time signature is ¾, there are three beats per bar and each bar will have the equivalent of three quarter notes.

Duple and triple refer to how beats are joined together. Beats can also be subdivided, that is, a single beat may carry several melodic notes. If the beat is subdivided into two or multiples of two, the meter is said to be **simple**. Duple simple meter is counted 1 & 2 & / 1 & 2 &, and triple simple meter is counted 1 & 2 & 3 & / 1 & 2 & 3 &. Sometimes, however, there are three melodic notes evenly spread over a single beat. In this case, the meter is said to be **compound**. "Row, row, row your boat" is in duple compound meter, counted 1 & a 2 & a / 1 & a 2 & a. Compound triple meter, counted 1 & a 2 & a 3 & a, also exists, but is less common.

Sometimes there is a strong underlying meter, but the melodic accents come where you don't expect them—between the beats or on weak rather than strong beats, as in 1 & 2 **&**. This is called **syncopation** and is the means by which jazz conveys a feeling of swing. Meter in much of the rest of the world is more complex than it is in even the most sophisticated Western music.

Sound happens when something that is capable of vibrating, such as a taut string or a vocal cord, is set in motion by the movement of air. If the vibrations are irregular, the result is noise. If the vibrations are regular, the result is a tone that has the property of pitch. **Pitch** refers to how high or low the ear perceives the tone to be. Frequency determines pitch and measures the number of regular vibrations per second. These are too fast to see; 440 vibrations per second produces the pitch to which instrumentalists tune, which is the note "A." The higher the frequency, the more vibrations per second and the higher the pitch; fewer vibrations per second produce a lower pitch.

When the number of vibrations is doubled or halved, the pitch that is produced is the same, but in a different register. Since 440 vibrations per second produce a note called "A," 220 will also produce an "A" but in a lower register; 880 will produce an "A" but in a higher register, and so on. An **interval** is the distance between two pitches. The interval from one pitch to its next repetition, for example from A220 to A440, is called an **octave**.

There are several ways of dividing up the octave into smaller intervals. In Western music, the octave is divided into only 12 intervals of equal size, called **half steps**.

Pitches are named according to the alphabet, from A to G, at which point the pitches repeat. On a piano keyboard, pitch ascends as we move from left to right. Only the white keys are given alphabet names:

The white key between the pair of black keys is always D. The black keys are named according to their relationship to the white keys. When the black key is named in relationship to the white key on its left, it raises the pitch of that key a half step and is called a **sharp**. The symbol for a sharp is ♯. When the same black key is considered in relationship to the white key on its right, its pitch is a half step lower and is called a **flat**. The symbol for a flat is ♭. Thus, the same pitch may have two different names, depending on the context. For example, C♯ is the same pitch as D♭.

The arrangement of pitches within an octave is called a **scale**. A scale which contains all 12 half steps, that is, one that uses every key on the piano, is called a **chromatic** scale. A scale consisting only of whole steps is called a whole tone scale. Most scales, however, are a mixture of whole and half steps, and some have augmented seconds, which is an interval of three half steps.

Almost all Western music is based on **diatonic** scales, that is, scales that use each letter name only once, and thus have seven different pitches. Not all scales are diatonic. A **pentatonic** scale has only five different pitches and therefore skips some letter names. Using only the black keys on the piano, you can produce a pentatonic scale. Much Japanese, Indonesian, Scottish, and folk music is based on pentatonic scales, as is the well-known hymn "Amazing Grace." A **blues scale** has six different pitches, but one letter name is repeated and two are skipped: G B⊠ C C♮ D F G.

There are two forms of diatonic scales: **major** and **minor**. A major scale consists of half steps between the third and fourth notes and between the seventh and eighth notes. All other steps are whole steps. As long as this arrangement is kept intact: 1 - 2 - 3 4 - 5 - 6 - 7 8, a major scale can be built from any note.

The scale that a piece of music is built on is indicated in notated music by a **key signature** at the beginning of the music, just after the time signature. For example, in the scale built on D, the key signature would have two sharps, one on F and one on C.

A diatonic scale in the **minor** mode is found on the white keys beginning on A. Here the half steps are between 2 and 3 and between 5 and 6 to produce the arrangement: 1 - 2 3 - 4 - 5 6 - 7 - 8. It may seem like a small detail, whether the third note of the scale is two whole steps or a whole step and a half step above the starting pitch, but the difference in effect is big.

The note on which a diatonic scale is built is called the **tonic**. Music that uses a diatonic scale is said to be **in the key of** the tonic note upon which the scale is built. Thus, music that uses the white notes beginning on C is said to be **in the key of** C major. Music that uses the scale beginning on C but with half steps between 2 & 3 and 5 & 6 (C - D E⊠ - F - G A⊠ - B⊠ - C) is said to be **in the key of** C minor. In both cases, C is the tonic, the home note, the goal of the music. All the other notes of the diatonic scale are named in relation to this most important note. The note an interval of a fifth above the tonic (G in C major) is called the **dominant**. The note a fifth below the tonic (F in C major) is called the **subdominant**. The note between the tonic and the dominant (E in C major) is the **mediant**; that between the subdominant and the tonic is the **submediant**. The second step of the scale is the **supertonic**. And the note a half step below the tonic in a major scale is called the **leading tone**. The notes can also be identified by solfege syllables:

Tonic	Supertonic	Mediant	Subdominant	Dominant	Mediant	Leading Tone	Tonic
Do	Re	Mi	Fa	Sol	La	Ti	Do

When three or more notes are sounded simultaneously, the result is a **chord**. The most prevalent chord is a **triad**, a three-note chord comprised of alternating scale degrees. The tonic triad in C major is spelled C - E - G. C is the root of the triad, E is the third, and G the fifth of the triad. From C to E are two whole steps, which is called the interval of a **major 3rd (M3rd)**. From E to G are a whole step and a half step, an interval of a **minor 3rd (m3rd)**. The distance from the root to the fifth is three and a half steps, the interval of a **perfect 5th (P5th)**. This is the definition of a major triad: M3rd on bottom; m3rd on top; P5th from root to fifth. There are four possible kinds of triads, depending on the arrangement of major and minor thirds:

Quality of triad	MAJOR	MINOR	DIMINISHED	AUGMENTED
Root to Third	Major	Minor	Minor	Major
Third to Fifth	Minor	Major	Minor	Major
Root to Fifth	Perfect	Perfect	Diminished	Augmented

Triads may be built on each step of the scale. Their position and quality are identified by roman numerals: uppercase for major, lowercase for minor, a small circle for diminished, and a plus sign (+) for augmented.

	Tonic	Supertonic	Mediant	Subdominant	Dominant	Mediant	Leading Tone	Tonic
Major scale:	I	ii	iii	IV	V	vi	vii°	I
Minor scale:	i	ii°	III	iv	v	VI	VII	i

The most common triads are I, IV, and V. With only these three chords, many songs can be accompanied.

Chords are pitches that happen simultaneously, or vertically. Pitches that occur horizontally, that is, in succession over time, create **melody**, a succession of pitches in a particular rhythmic pattern.

Melodic direction refers to the shape of the arrangement of pitches: mostly ascending, mostly descending, curling around itself, or a mixture of all three. **Range** refers to how far the highest note is from the lowest note in a given melody.

Melodic motion is how a tune gets from one pitch to the next. If the melody moves by small steps, it is said to be using conjunct motion. If it moves by leaps, it is using disjunct motion. All of these factors together produce the mood of a melody.

A good melody has the right balance between repetition and contrast. The second and fourth phrases of "twinkle, twinkle, little star" are exactly like the first—repetition. The third is different—contrast. So the phrases of this simple tune could be diagrammed as: *a a b a*.

Texture refers to how melodies are presented. If there is only a single melody with no accompaniment at all, the texture is monophonic, such as the opening notes of Beethoven's fifth symphony, "ta ta ta dum." If two or more melodies are happening at the same time, seem to be of equal interest, and seem to be competing for the listener's attention, as happens when people sing a round beginning at different times, the texture is polyphonic. If there is a single melody in the foreground with subsidiary melodies or chords accompanying it in the background, the texture is homophonic. Most of the music in much of the non-Western world is monophonic, but in the West the most prevalent texture is homophony.

Intensity refers to the loudness or softness of a tone. The musical term for this is **dynamics**. As with tempo markings, the names for dynamics are in Italian. Ranging from softest to loudest they are:

pianissimo	*piano*	*mezzopiano*	*mezzoforte*	*forte*	*fortissimo*
pp	**p**	**mp**	**mf**	**f**	**ff**

Music can gradually go from loud to soft (*decrescendo*) or from soft to loud (*crescendo*). It can be in a *piano* dynamic and suddenly become loud (*subito forte*), or in a *forte* dynamic and suddenly get soft (*subito piano*).

Timbre refers to the source of the musical sound, whether instrument or voice. Timbre has to do with the physics of sound, specifically what overtones are present and in what proportions.

The earliest musical instrument was undoubtedly the human voice. The lowest male voice is a **bass**, the highest a **tenor**, and in between the two is the **baritone**. The comparable female voices are **alto**, **soprano**, and **mezzosoprano**.

One method for categorizing instruments is based on how the sound is produced. **Chordophones** (violins, pianos, harpsichords, guitars) produce sound when a taut string or chord is set in motion, by either bowing, hammering, or plucking. **Aerophones** (flutes, trumpets, whistles) are instruments that confine a column of air that is set in motion by breath. **Membranophones** (drums) produce sound when a membrane that is stretched across a hollow cavity is struck. **Idiophones** (bells, cymbals, rattles) are instruments that themselves vibrate when struck.

The second method classifies instruments according to families in a symphony orchestra and is appropriate only for Western music. The **string family** includes violins, violas, cellos, and double basses. The **wind family** includes flutes, single-reed instruments like the clarinet, and double-reed instruments like the oboe and bassoon. The **brass family** comprises trumpets, French horns, trombones, and tubas. The **percussion section** includes all drums and anything that is struck, such as the xylophone.

In Western music, harmony is treated in a sophisticated manner, while rhythm and melody remain relatively simple. In the music of Africa, rhythm is given a highly complex treatment, while harmony and melody are less developed. In the Arab world and India, both melody and rhythm are more intricate, but there is little, if any, harmony. And in China, the emphasis is placed on subtleties of timbre.

WESTERN MUSIC

The history of Western music is divided into six periods: Medieval, Renaissance, Baroque, Classical, Romantic, and Twentieth Century. The **Medieval** period began with the earliest music in Europe for which any notated music survives and ended around the year 1450. Gradually during this period, **musical notation** was developed. Over time, a more precise method was devised for fixing pitches: **noteheads** were placed on ledger lines, which numbered anywhere from two to ten before finally settling into today's five-line staff. **Clef signs** were designed to resemble letter names: the G clef is our soprano clef; the F clef our bass clef. There are also C clefs, which are used by voices and violas. Finally, late in the period, a method was devised for indicating durations of notes, thus allowing rhythmic variety. The only music that was notated was **liturgical chant**—that is, music that was performed as part of a religious service. Nomadic poet-musicians known as **troubadours** and **trouvères** sang songs of chivalric devotion and crusader feats as well as pilgrim songs, which were monophonic.

The liturgical music—called plainchant or, more commonly, **Gregorian chant**—was performed *a capella,* voices only with no instrumental accompaniment or doubling; and was monophonic. Beginning around the tenth century, Medieval polyphony gradually came about, laying the foundation for the development of harmony.

By the twelfth century, Paris produced the first named composers. **Leonin** (c. 1135–1201) composed the first complete annual cycle of chants for the mass in two parts. His successor, **Perotin** (fl. 1190–c. 1225), did the same in four parts.

Because of advances in musical notation in the fourteenth century, especially in the area of rhythm, music got enormously complex. Musicians of the time self-consciously called themselves *Ars Nova*, to set themselves apart from what they considered old-fashioned, conservative musical practices. The inevitable reaction against an excess of complexity led to the next stylistic musical period.

The **Renaissance** period in music began around 1450 and extended to 1600. The word literally means "rebirth." Renaissance musicians had a great reverence for the importance of text when combined with music. Unlike *Ars Nova* polyphony, all the voices are of equal value; none is relegated to drone status. This new kind of texture, called **imitative polyphony**, is the most characteristic feature of Renaissance music.

As the church had reformed itself, there was a renewed emphasis on sacred compositions. Renaissance composers concentrated on the Kyrie, Gloria, Credo, Sanctus and Benedictus, and Agnus Dei, mass elements that never vary from day to day. These, being sacred and for liturgical use, were in Latin, and were sung *a capella* in imitative polyphony. Free standing religious compositions, called **motets**, have the same characteristics as mass settings. Renaissance composers also wrote secular (non-religious) compositions called **madrigals**. They are similar to mass movements and motets, except they are in the vernacular—such as Italian or English—rather than Latin and tend to be in a livelier style. Composers like **Carlo Gesualdo** (c. 1561–1613) wrote madrigals that displayed daring harmonic dissonances, but had a precious, mannered approach to the text. The most outstanding composer of the Renaissance period was **Josquin Desprez** (1440–1521).

Giovanni Palestrina (c. 1525–1594) demonstrated to the cardinals at the Council of Trent during a reformation period that music could be polyphonic and yet be clearly understood with his Pope Marcellus Mass. Music written for the Roman Catholic church has been conservative ever since.

The **Baroque** period began around 1600 with the invention of **opera** and ended around 1750 with the death of Johann Sebastian Bach. In the last decade of the sixteenth century, a group of intellectuals in Italy called the **Florentine Camerata** once again looked back to classical Greek drama for inspiration to reform music, which led to the creation of **opera**.

In early opera, the ideal was a solo voice with a light instrumental accompaniment. A sustaining instrument such as a cello played the bass line while the harmony was improvised by a harpsichord or lute player. This was called **basso continuo** and is characteristic of almost all Baroque music. During this period, **functional tonal harmony** using major and minor diatonic scales was established.

Baroque music is strongly metrical. Once a rhythmical pattern is established, it often persists throughout the entire piece or movement, reflecting an urge toward cohesion and unity.

The first great opera composer was **Claudio Monteverdi** (1567–1643). But the most famous composer of Italian *opera seria* was **George Frideric Handel** (1685–1759). *Opera seria* deals with serious topics borrowed from Roman mythology or from ancient history. The elements of Italian opera are an instrumental overture, then alternating vocal recitative and arias. **Recitative** is like heightened speech and occurs in that part of the drama where action is carried forward. An **aria** is more akin to poetry and has a fuller orchestral accompaniment. Handel created unstaged opera in English using biblical stories as his subject matter and added the new ingredient of the chorus: the **oratorio**. His *Messiah* is one of the most beloved musical works of all time.

An exact contemporary of Handel's whose music is the epitome of the High Baroque style is **Johann Sebastian Bach** (1685–1750). Bach never wrote an opera, but he wrote **cantatas** and The St. John and St. Matthew **passions** for the Lutheran church that, like Handel's oratorios, have all the characteristics of opera.

During the Baroque period, instrumental music became as important as vocal music. **Absolute music** is abstract instrumental music that is not dependent on words or movement for its form.

Arcangelo Corelli (1653–1713), wrote exclusively for the violin in the genres of solo sonatas (one solo instrument plus continuo) and trio sonatas (two solo instruments plus continuo). In addition, **Antonio Vivaldi** (1678–1741) established the three-movement instrumental concerto (one or more solo instruments plus orchestra).

The harpsichord was essential to almost all Baroque music as part of the *basso continuo*, but was also used extensively as a solo instrument. Bach, the greatest organist of his day, wrote **fugues** for organ and harpsichord as well as for vocal chorus. "Fugue" comes from the Italian "*fuga*," meaning to chase. In the Baroque fugue, a single musical idea, called the fugue subject, appears throughout, first in the tonic, then in other key areas, and finally in the tonic again. The repetition of the fugue subject provides unity; its appearance in different keys provides contrast.

The **Classical** period, dating from the death of J. S. Bach in 1750 until the 1820s, saw the proliferation of public concerts, which anybody could attend for the price of a ticket. Music publishing flourished, meaning the latest compositions were quickly available for the amateur music market. Composers imbued their music with clarity, naturalness, and a pleasing variety, all hallmarks of the newly emerging Classical style.

Italian *opera seria* comprised three acts. In the first half of the eighteenth century, a two-act *opera buffa* (comic opera) was often inserted between the acts to entertain the audience. In time, *opera buffa* became so popular that it was detached from *opera seria* and became a genre in its own right.

Franz Josef Haydn (1732–1809) did much to develop two new Classical instrumental genres and **Wolfgang Amadeus Mozart** (1756–1791) further perfected them. The **symphony**, a work for full orchestra, and the **string quartet** (two violins, viola, and cello) are generally in four movements. The first movement is usually in **sonata** form, which is more of a dynamic process than a form. It comprises three sections that correspond to three acts of a drama. In the **exposition**, a musical idea is presented in the tonic key. There is then a transition to a new key area and, usually, contrasting thematic ideas. There is thus tension between the two key areas. In the **development** section, the plot thickens as material presented in the exposition is broken apart, combined in new ways, and taken to more distant key areas. The denouement in the **recapitulation** is brought about by repeating the exposition, but this time keeping everything in the tonic—the home key—to provide a resolution. The second movement of symphonies and quartets is often a slow movement. It might be in sonata form, or theme and variations, or ternary form. The latter has three parts diagrammed as A B A: the first is in the tonic, the middle section presents contrasting material in a different key, and the third is a repetition of the first. The third movement, paired dances that hark back to the Baroque suite, is also in ternary form, with the A sections being a minuet or scherzo and the contrasting B section a trio. The fourth movement is usually fast and may be in sonata form, theme and variations, or rondo-sonata. Rondo form, inherited from the Baroque period, is an extension of the ternary idea with several contrasting sections, each in a different key, alternating with the A section, which is always in the tonic, for example A B A C A D A. In rondo-sonata form, the D section is replaced by the B section, which is now resolved in the tonic.

The classical **concerto** for soloist and orchestra omits the fourth movement, but is otherwise organized in the same manner, as is the classical **piano sonata**, for which the number of movements is more variable. The *fortepiano* was invented around the middle of the eighteenth century. Because it was capable of producing a wide range of dynamics, the piano rapidly replaced the softer-voiced harpsichord as the keyboard instrument of choice for solos, concerti, and chamber music.

Unlike Haydn and Mozart, **Ludwig van Beethoven** (1770–1827) was born late enough to have been influenced by the French Revolution. His music expanded all the elements of the classical style and enlarged the range of expression. His dynamic range is wider, his rhythm more propulsive, and his harmonic resources greatly extended.

Composers of the **Romantic** period, which extended through the end of the nineteenth century, sought ambiguity. Rhythm became more complex through the use of shifting meters and *rubato*, a surging forward or holding back of the pulse. Tonal harmony was obscured through the increasing use of *chromaticism*, which is the inclusion of notes that are foreign to the key, and through a tendency to defer a sense of resolution by seeming to evade arrival at the tonic.

The pianist and composer **Franz Liszt** (1811–1886) and the violinist **Niccolo Paganini** (1782–1840) enjoyed the kind of adulation we associate with today's rock stars. **Program** music, instrumental music that depends for its inspiration and its understanding on something external to music, grew in importance during this period. One composer who resisted the trend was **Johannes Brahms** (1833–1897). His symphonies, concerti, and chamber music adhere to abstract musical principles.

Lieder, which is German for art songs, is poetry set to music for a solo singer with piano accompaniment. **Franz Schubert** (1797–1828) wrote hundreds of *lieder*, including one written when he was only 18. Like *lieder*, piano character pieces are one-movement miniatures that aim to set a mood in a brief space of time. **Frederic Chopin** (1810–1849) wrote polonaises, études, and impromptus exclusively for the piano.

Opera during the nineteenth century was dominated by two composers. The Italian **Giuseppe Verdi** (1813–1901) wrote 28 operas, including some of the most beloved in the repertoire. His exact German contemporary, **Richard Wagner** (1813–1883), wrote his own *libretti* drawing on German mythic legends.

By the end of the nineteenth century, composers experimented with new techniques of composition and explored new directions for their music. Music of the **twentieth century** is therefore not distinguished by a single style. Impressionist painters, such as Monet, fragmented the visual into its elements of color and shape. **Impressionism** in music tried to do the same thing by careful attention to tone color and the manipulation of melodic fragments. **Expressionist** painters and composers were influenced by the work of Sigmund Freud on the irrational subconscious. They depict the outer world through a sort of deranged subjectivity. **Primitivism** was influenced by the Spanish painter Pablo Picasso. Russian composer **Igor Stravinsky** (1882–1971) obsessively repeats fragments taken from Russian folk songs in his *ostinatos*.

In the 1920s, **Arnold Schönberg** devised a new method for organizing atonal music. He called it the *12-tone* method or *serialism*, whereby the composer makes a pre-compositional decision about the order in which the 12 notes of the chromatic scale will be heard. This was called the *tone row*. Once the composer sets the tone row, the pitches may only come in that order, although the row may be inverted (turned upside down) or played retrograde (backwards). Other composers, such as the American **Milton Babbitt** (b. 1916), took this even further and "serialized" duration and dynamic level as well as pitch.

Diametrically opposed to such total control was **chance music**, which also had parallels in the other arts such as participatory theater and art events known as "happenings." The ultimate example of this is *4′33″* by the American composer **John Cage** (1912–1992). With advances in technology, some composers experimented with computer-generated music, such as *poème électronique* of the French composer **Edgard Varèse** (1883–1965). **Minimalism**, a more recent movement, represents a return to tonality and meter, but with a minimum of musical ideas obsessively repeated, for example *Glassworks* by the American composer **Philip Glass** (b. 1937).

Jazz originated in American black culture around the beginning of the twentieth century. Some of its roots are found in the **call and response** of "field hollers," work songs where a leader sings a line and the others respond sympathetically; **blues** songs; **gospel** singing; and the **ragtime** piano style of black artists like **Scott Joplin** (1868–1917).

Jazz is more of a performer's than a composer's art since the music is improvised rather than read from a score or memorized. Syncopation—putting an accent where one doesn't expect it—is an important element in jazz. This happens at two levels: the rhythm section provides a steady "back-beat" (one TWO one TWO) over which the melody instruments move a fraction of a beat ahead or behind the pulse.

The earliest jazz style is **New Orleans** style, also called Dixieland. Small ensembles consisted of a rhythm section of drums, piano, and/or bass and two or more soloists on trumpet, saxophone, clarinet, trombone, or voice. **Louis Armstrong** (1900–1971) played trumpet and sang in a style called "scat," where the voice, singing syllables rather than words, is used as another instrument. During the Depression years of the early 1930s, solo piano came to the fore with **stride** and **boogie woogie**. In the late 1930s and early 1940s during World War II, **swing** or **big-band** jazz "crossed over" and became widely popular. Swing bands were large ensembles of 10 to 20 performers playing under the direction of a leader from written-out arrangements called "charts," which left less room for improvisation. One of the greatest of the swing band leaders was the pianist and composer **Duke Ellington** (1899–1974).

After the war years, jazz performers returned to the emphasis on improvisation afforded by smaller ensembles. But they did so with a new virtuosity and more sophisticated, complex harmonies in a style called **bebop**. Some of the outstanding performers of bebop were the alto saxophonist **Charlie Parker** (1920–1955) and the trumpeter **Miles Davis** (1926–1991). Bebop has been succeeded by many different jazz styles, such as the more laid back cool jazz, free jazz (total improvisation), and a blended style called **fusion**.

PERFORMING ARTS REVIEW

THEATER REVIEW

Theater in Greece

The earliest Greek plays were probably ritualistic performances that might involve, for instance, a conflict between winter and summer, and that would include a combat, a death, and a resurrection. These simple plays may have evolved into the **dithyramb**, a frenzied and impassioned hymn performed by a chorus of 50 men costumed in goatskins, which celebrated Dionysus, the god of the abundance of nature.

Thespis, a poet and actor from whose name we derive the word *thespian*, is known as the founder of classical **tragedy**. He is credited with inventing a new breed of performer, the actor, who would engage the audience by impersonating one or more characters between the dances of a chorus. Thespis also came up with the notion of a prologue to the choral narrative. With the creation of the actor to tell the story, the reaction of the chorus assumed greater importance, for it served to offer commentatary on the struggles of the narrative's hero.

Aeschylus further refined the form and content of the Greek tragedy by adding a second and third actor, which allowed for conflict between the characters. He also introduced the concept of choice, providing the hero with a decision he or she must make, which frequently leads to his or her downfall.

By the fifth century B.C., the form of Greek tragedy had taken on a recurring structure. Most plays began with a **prologue**, spoken by a single actor in iambic verse, which described the events leading up to the action of the play. This was usually followed by the entrance of the **chorus**, a body of 15 people who chanted in anapestic meter to introduce the action and to create the desired mood in the audience. This was followed by a series of alternating **episodes** (scenes of action) and **stasima** (lyric songs sung by the chorus). The play was concluded by the **exodos**, during which the chorus continued to chant as the characters departed.

The plays of **Sophocles** (496?–406 B.C.), such as *Oedipus Tyrannus*, *Antigone*, and *Electra*, deal with men and women whose flaws lead to suffering and destruction, but ultimately result in increased wisdom and divine retribution. **Euripides** (480?–406 B.C.), the author of 19 extant plays, is known for dramatic realism achieved by complex plots, increasingly natural speech, and the combination of good and evil found in all of his characters, be they human or divine.

Greek drama was a seasonal event. In addition to mastering tragedy, all dramatists were required to perfect at least one comic form. The **Old Comic** form probably employed three actors; contained burlesque, parody, and farce; and was wild and bawdy. Old Comedies always featured music, and frequently made use of fantastical subjects and settings. Old Comedy had a rigid structure similar to that of Classical Tragedy, combining lyrical, prosaic, and choral passages. Aristophanes (450–385 B.C.) is considered the father of Greek comedy.

Middle Comedy, the primary dramatic form between 400 and 338 B.C., was far less obscene than Old Comedy. **New Comedies** were usually comedies of manners designed for an educated leisure class. They involved a number of stock scenes and stock characters and followed a five-act structure. The only New Comedies that survive are those of Menander of Athens (c. 342–c. 292 B.C.), including *The Grouch*.

Greek tragic actors wore large masks that covered their whole faces and made them appear much taller than they actually were. Actors would wear several masks during a performance, to allow them to play a variety of roles. The weight and size of the masks contributed to an emphasis on the study of movement, which tended to be slow, graceful, and stately, and to emphasize a number of standard gestures. The costumes for comedy were more colorful and fantastic than those for tragedy, and tended to exaggerate certain parts of the actors' bodies. Comedians, too, wore masks; however, comedic masks portrayed a larger variety of characters than the tragic masks.

Theater in China

The first performances in China were recorded about 1500 B.C., during the Shang Dynasty. Dance, music, and ritual were important elements in Chinese life. The Han Dynasty (206 B.C.–A.D. 221) actively encouraged the arts and founded the **Imperial Office of Music** in 104 B.C., which functioned to organize entertainment and to promote dance and music. **Chinese Shadow Puppets** (c. 121 B.C.) were first used to materialize departed gods or souls, but later evolved into a source of entertainment. Marionettes, puppets moved by string or hand, were created between A.D. 265 and A.D. 420. Many festivals and plays continued to spread through China around A.D. 610.

Emperor Hsuan Tsung established "**The Pear Garden**," a school for dancers, singers, and various court entertainers. Storytelling using puppets became a popular dramatic form from A.D. 960–A.D. 1279.

Stage direction was practiced in Chinese theaters by the fourteenth century. The stage was usually stripped bare, with a door on either side for exits and entrances and an embroidered decorative wall hanging between the two doors as a backdrop.

Medieval Period

Medieval theater originally began as a springtime religious observance. However, religious theater was restricted by such elements as the liturgy, church calendar, and ecclesiastical dress. In England during the Middle Ages, pageant plays known as **cycles** were created using biblical and religious literature. The cycles were performed by a troupe of actors who traveled from town to town in wagons that also served as stages for performances. Morality plays were also performed during this time. After approximately 200 years, drama moved out of the church because the troupes were too restricted by the church's ruling.

The playwrights in the Medieval period wrote anonymously. Historians document that women never performed in Medieval plays for two reasons. First, male-dominated, rigidly hierarchical groups like clergy, craftsmen, and merchants predominated. Secondly, it was believed that boys with trained voices could produce more volume than women.

Elizabethan Theater in England

During the Elizabethan era in England, theater emerged as a commercial enterprise. The stage became lavish with detailed scenery and colorful costumes. There were two basic types of costumes: **Symbolic costumes**, worn to distinguish the important characters from the ordinary people, and **contemporary**.

Theater companies acquired new plays by request from freelancers and from actor/playwrights. Notable playwrights of the Elizabethan era include Christopher Marlowe (1564–1593) and Ben Jonson (1573–1637).

Theater in Italy

The Romans, borrowing architectural design from the Greeks, built amphitheaters of permanent stone for a variety of entertainment, such as dancing, acrobatics, and gladiatorial events.

Commedia dell'arte was a popular form of entertainment akin to street theater. The plays, performed by a number of traveling troupes, were largely improvisational, though their plots were usually limited to the misadventures of a set of stock characters whose actions were commented on by a chorus of clowns or *zannis*. Throughout Europe in the late fifteenth century, audiences were entertained between the acts of larger comedies by short dramatic and musical works known as **Intermezzi**.

Theater in Seventeenth Century France

French playwright/actor/director Jean Baptiste Poquelin (1622–1673), also known as Molière, wrote and acted in comedies that weigh follies of humanity against common good sense. Two other famous playwrights at this time were Pierre Corneille (1606–1684) and Jean Racine (1639–1699).

The first **proscenium** arch stage, which resembled a picture frame, was built in France in 1618 by Teatro Farnese. The proscenium was a wall with one large center opening that divided the theater-goers from the raised stage.

Restoration Period

During the **Interregnum period** in England (1649–1660), theater and acting were banned due to political upheavals at the command of Oliver Cromwell. Once theaters were reopened,

Charles II (1630–1685) marked the start of the modern proscenium playhouse, and repertory companies flourished.

The majority of the Restoration prose plays, referred to as a *comedy of manners*, were witty in dialogue and revolved around sexual intrigue.

Contemporary Theater

Successful playwrights who emerged from nineteenth century Europe introduced stage realism and naturalism, leading to contemporary theater.

In Russia, Konstantin Stanislavsky (1863–1938) developed an acting technique that came to be called "**The Method**" on account of its broad impact on the schooling of Western actors. In 1931 several method teachers formed the Group Theater in America, which consisted of actors and directors who provided actor-training workshops in New York City.

Playwright Eugene O'Neill brought a powerful insight into human passion and suffering to American drama. Other accomplished American playwrights of the twentieth century include Arthur Miller, Tennessee Williams, and Lillian Hellman.

In Britain, the **Fringe theatre** was considered equivalent to America's off-off Broadway theater, which was home to most experimental shows. **Mobile theater** (the Fun Bus) and **avant garde theater** brought the arts into urban communities and bridged the gap between nations and classes.

Significant off-off Broadway companies included La Mama theater, the Circle Repertory Company, the Manhattan Theatre Club, and the New York Shakespeare Festival Public Theatre.

In 1968, after censorship of British theatre was abolished, the rock musical *Hair*, which contained nudity and obscenity, was produced in London. Plays with homosexual themes were also performed. Meanwhile, U.S. musicals like *Oh, Calcutta*, which included various scenes involving nudity, and *Che!*, which displayed explicit sexual acts, challenged theater audiences.

DANCE REVIEW
Origins of Dance

Archaeologists have studied ancient drawings depicting dancing hunters costumed as animals wearing make-up and masks. Egyptian dance paintings were found that depict religious dancing in funeral processions. War dances, hunting dances, medicine dances, dances for health, and fertility dances were performed as a form of sympathetic magic or medicine. There were dances for death, birth, peace, and courtship.

The emergence of **dance** was evident in early Greek culture. The Greeks used dance as a communal activity, enjoyed as entertainment and religious ritual. For the Romans, dance was a vehicle for spectacle rather than for a classic dramatic presentation, and commonly included acrobatics.

Dancing was incorporated in Christian services until the twelfth century, at which time theologians decided that dancing was distracting and impious. Later, music and acting were banned by the church.

Forms of Dance

The first major **ballet** was choreographed by an Italian named Balthasar de Beaujoyeux (formerly Baldassari de Belgiojoso) in 1581.

In France, Louis XIV established a school in 1661 called the **Academie Royale de Danse** which produced the best and most experienced dance masters.

The establishment of the **five positions** of the feet became the foundation of ballet technique. In the first position, legs are turned out away from the hips and heels and knees touch each other. The feet are to be out so as to form a straight line. Similar to first position, the legs remain turned out away from the hips during the second position, but the heels must be approximately 10 to 12 inches apart. During the third position, the heel of the right foot is touching the middle of the left foot. The legs must be turned out away from the hips. In the fourth position, one foot is in front of the other with about eight inches separating the two feet. In the fifth position, the legs are turned out from the hips, and one foot is directly in front of the other. The heel of the front foot should also be placed at the joint to the toe of the rear foot. Correct weight and body balance, arm control, and attitude are essential in ballet.

Marius Petipa (1822–1910), often referred to as the father of classic ballet, transplanted the glory of the Romantic ballet from France to Russia, made Russia the leading country of ballet, and raised the standard of dance technique. Isadora Duncan (1878–1927) wanted to be free of the control of ballet and desired to let the body rather than the mind dictate movement. She took off her ballet slippers and danced barefoot, wearing loose-fitting clothing so her body was not restricted.

American dancer and choreographer Martha Graham's technique is based on breath rhythms and is recognized for sharpness and preciseness. In contrast, choreographer Doris Humphrey's movement technique was created from natural observations of human movement, specifically rhythms of breath, weight shifts, motion, and successional flow.

The bridge between classical ballet and modern dance was connected under Agnes de Mille's direction. She stressed the understanding that dance is movement, and the body is its instrument.

Jazz dancing is a controlled style of dancing characterized by parallel feet, flat-footed steps, undulating torso, body isolation, and syncopated rhythms.

Ballet troupes and opera houses were established in America, among them the New York City Ballet, the Metropolitan Opera, Lincoln Center for the Performing Arts, and the American Ballet Theater.

In the 1960s, Americans flocked to clubs and dance halls. **Ballroom dancing**, the **foxtrot**, the **samba**, and the **salsa** became popular. In the 1970s, choreographers added jazz to the most successful

American musicals, such as *West Side Story*, *Fiddler on the Roof*, *42nd Street*, *Chicago*, *A Chorus Line*, and *Evita*. A form of dance known as **body art** also became popular in the 1970s, which was used to demonstrate at political rallies. The artists were costumed or appeared nude and performed in galleries and small performance spaces.

American dancing has gone through many styles. Popular dances of the 1930s were the **Peabody** and the **foxtrot**. In the 1940s, they danced the **jitterbug**. The 1950s brought about the **stroll**, the **mashed potato**, and the **cha-cha**. The **salsa**, the **monkey**, and the **pony** were created in the 1960s. In the 1970s, two new types of dances were born—the **hustle** and the **boogie**, which became American favorites. In the 1980s, **breakdancing** emerged and faded away. With each new decade, dance styles change and vibrant new forms emerge.

FILM REVIEW
Origin of Film

The creation of film was the result of a centuries-old fascination with the control and capture of movement and a series of inventions and ideas, from Plato's shadows on the cave wall to magic lanterns and zoetropes. Around 1889, Thomas Alva Edison and his assistant, W. K. L. Dickinson, combined a number of existing inventions to create the **kinetoscope**, the original motion picture machine. To view the movie of an animal eating or a person dancing, one would look through a small peephole in the cabinet. The average film ran for one minute and was 50 feet in length. Louis and Auguste Lumière held the first public showing of motion pictures projected on a screen at the Grand Café in Paris.

Edison soon abandoned kinetoscopes to form his own production company to make films for theaters and founded the first motion picture studio. In the studio, **vaudeville** entertainers and celebrities performed for the camera. Notable actors of the time included Mme. Bertholdi, Annie Oakley, and Colonel William Cody, the original Buffalo Bill.

Cinema had consisted of mainly newsreel footage, but narrative form quickly entered. In 1895, the **Lumière brothers** produced their first experimental film. The brothers understood the profit to be made from narrative films, so they perfected their experiment. Their competitor was Georges Méliès, considered "the creator of cinematic spectacle." The first American motion picture theater, was called "The Electric." Because each show cost a nickel, movie theaters were nicknamed "**nickelodeons**."

Edison's determination to exploit the cinema for residuals led to his attempt to force competing filmmakers out of business by bringing lawsuits against them for violation of patents. Several companies, particularly Biograph, managed to survive by inventing cameras that differed from those Edison had patented.

In France, the progress of French cinema was becoming paralyzed at the time of World War I. In the 1920s, America, which did not experience the post–World War I depression as strongly as European countries, became dominant in film production. After 1912, old nickelodeons were outdated and new theaters were rapidly being built.

The Hollywood Era

After 1910, film companies began moving to a small town outside of Los Angeles, California, known as **Hollywood**. Filming in Hollywood had many advantages—the climate permitted year-round shooting, and California provided a great number of locations, from mountains to ocean to desert. The **Academy of Motion Picture Arts and Sciences (AMPAS)** was founded in 1927 by Louis B. Mayer and other film industry innovators to raise the educational, cultural, and technical standards of American movies. The main function of the AMPAS is the annual presentation of the Academy Awards, or "Oscars," for distinguished film achievement in the previous year.

Introduction of Sound in Film

Sound was introduced in 1926 with the release of *Don Juan*, a film with an orchestral accompaniment, sound effects, and a series of vaudeville shorts. Warner Brothers, in an attempt to promote the concept of films with sound, released *The Jazz Singer* (1927), a part sound/part silent film that was a huge success. In 1928, Walt Disney produced *Steamboat Willie*, his first musical cartoon, contributing to the sound film genre and introducing to the world the beloved character, Mickey Mouse. By 1930, most American theaters were wired for sound.

Introduction of Color

During the 1930s, color film became widely used for the first time. Although photographic color had been used in various forms since 1908, only a few films in the 1920s had **Technicolor** sequences, because the process was too expensive to use on a large-scale basis. However, by the mid-1930s, three-strip Technicolor proved to be economically feasible.

Television, Color, and Film

As Americans who owned television sets stayed home rather than go to the cinema, Hollywood fought back by exploiting the technological advantages which film possessed—the vast size of the images and the capacity to produce the images in color. As a result, Hollywood made a rapid conversion from black-and-white to color production between 1952 and 1955. The transition was made possible largely through a 1950 antitrust decree which disassembled the Technicolor Corporation's monopoly on color cinematography and ordered it to release its basic patents to all producers. By 1952, the Eastman Kodak Corporation had developed the Eastmancolor system.

Film in the 1950s and 1960s

Hollywood's mania for producing films on a large scale in the 1950s damaged the conventional dramatic film. First, the standard length of a feature film rose from 90 minutes to an average of three hours before settling at a more manageable two hours in the mid-1960s. Second, there was a tendency on behalf of the studios to package every A-class film as a dazzling, big-budget spectacle, whether or not this format suited the material of the film. From 1955 to 1965, new genres emerged, including **musicals**, **comedies**, **westerns**, **science fiction**, and **gangster** and **anti-communist** films. In the 1950s and 1960s, Hollywood abandoned original scripts in favor of successful stage plays. By the 1960s, the genre shifted to big-budget sex comedies concerned with strategies of seduction and to corporate comedies.

The heroic, idealized epic westerns of John Ford and his imitators remained popular in the 1950s but were gradually replaced by the adult western which concentrated on the psychological and moral conflicts of the hero in society.

Science fiction emerged as a distinct genre in the 1950s, typically featuring some form of a world-threatening crisis or the arrival of a dangerous creature from another planet. In the 1960s, low-budget monster films were replaced by medium-to-high budget science fiction films, including *The Time Machine* (1960) and *Planet of the Apes* (1967). Serious filmmakers, including Stanley Kubrick (*2001: A Space Odyssey*, 1968), became interested in science fiction.

Two types of gangster films appeared in the 1950s—the caper film, concentrated on a plan to pull off a big heist, and the anti-communist film, in which the criminal figure was a Communist spy and the syndicate was the international Communist conspiracy. The James Bond espionage thrillers maintained some of these themes.

Film in the 1970s and 1980s

The enormous success in 1970 of two conventional films, *Love Story* and *Airport*, restored Hollywood's faith in the big-budget feature. Between 1972 and 1977, the average production budget for a film increased by 178 percent. Profits were based on the film's success, so the financial risks of production multiplied. Consequently, fewer and fewer films were made every year, and there was a steady increase in the amount spent on advertising campaigns to ensure the success of the film. Often, the price for advertising would cost twice as much as the production cost of the film itself.

The 1970s could be considered a renaissance of creative talent, as a result of many young directors, such as **Francis Ford Coppola**, **George Lucas**, **Martin Scorsese**, **Steven Spielberg**, and **Brian DePalma**. Coppola's epic of organized crime in the United States, *The Godfather Parts I, II, and III,* is one of the most significant American cinematic achievements of the 1970s. Lucas's *Star Wars* and Spielberg's *Jaws* (1975) and *Close Encounters of the Third Kind* (1977) were historically important for their use of dazzling special effects. DePalma directed some of the most stylish horror films of the 1970s, including *Carrie* (1976), while Scorsese directed *Taxi Driver* (1976). Not only were these films critically acclaimed, but they were financially successful. *Star Wars* grossed over $200 million, *Jaws* over $130 million, and *Close Encounters of the Third Kind* over $83 million.

Film in the Present

In the 1980s Hollywood was again faced with technological advances that would affect box office sales. **Cable television** services and **video cassette recorders (VCRs)** brought theatrical movies into the home for a monthly subscription or rental fee, transforming the entire system of film distribution. This trend continued in the 1990s and twenty-first century with the development of DVDs and the increased ability to download feature films through the Internet. However, the speculation that movie theaters would become obsolete and that all films would one day be distributed through some form of home video technology remains a theory. People are still going to the movies in theaters and paying rising prices for tickets to experience the spectacle of the big screen. Directors like Quentin Tarantino, Spike Lee, and James Cameron have produced innovative work and introduced new film techniques.

CLEP Humanities Practice Test 1

(Answer sheets appear in the back of the book.)

TIME: *90 Minutes*
140 Questions

DIRECTIONS: Each of the following questions or incomplete statements is followed by five possible answers or completions. Select the BEST choice in each case and fill in the corresponding oval on the answer sheet.

1. In ancient Egyptian architecture, the large, sloping walls which flank the entrance to a temple complex are called

    (A) pyramids.
    (B) mastabas.
    (C) tombs.
    (D) pylons.
    (E) obelisks.

2. An improvised performance, usually held in churchyards or city squares, that was performed in a circle and involved playing the role of redeemers, by the act of scourging and whipping themselves, which made them move and gesture, was performed by

    (A) fools.
    (B) flagellants.
    (C) minnesingers.
    (D) mimes.
    (E) joculators.

3. An *a priori* truth is one that is known to be true

    (A) independently of experience.
    (B) after careful experimentation or observation.
    (C) as a result of mathematical calculation.
    (D) only by God.
    (E) because its denial is a contradiction.

4. The fourth degree of a major scale is given what name?

    (A) Tonic
    (B) Dominant
    (C) Leading tone
    (D) Subdominant
    (E) Mediant

5. A natural minor scale contains five whole steps and two half steps. Between which scale degrees do the half steps occur?

    (A) 2-3, 5-6
    (B) 3-4, 7-8
    (C) 1-2, 7-8
    (D) 2-3, 7-8
    (E) 3-4

6. An example of the use of Primitivism can be found in which musical selection?

    (A) "Prelude a l'après-midi d'un faune"
    (B) "Le Sacre du Printemps"
    (C) "Salome"
    (D) "Wozzeck"
    (E) "The Liberty Bell"

7. Which of the following is the earliest and clearest demonstration of the principles of Romanticism?

    (A) Pope's "The Rape of the Lock"
    (B) Rousseau's *The Social Contract*
    (C) Blake's *Songs of Innocence and Experience*
    (D) James' *Daisy Miller*
    (E) Shakespeare's *Romeo and Juliet*

8. Which of the following works is known for defining the parameters of Existentialism?

    (A) *L'Étranger*
    (B) *Le Morte D'Arthur*
    (C) *Candide*
    (D) *Saint Joan*
    (E) *Le Misanthrope*

9. Which American classic is known for its comprehensive description of frontier families' lives in the Midwest during the nineteenth century?

    (A) *The Last of the Mohicans*
    (B) *The History of the Dividing Line*
    (C) *On Plymouth Plantation*
    (D) *My Antonia*
    (E) *Huckleberry Finn*

10. Which of the following is a "coming of age" novel that utilizes the concept of the anti-hero?

    (A) *Tom Sawyer*
    (B) *Martin Chuzzlewit*
    (C) *Catcher in the Rye*
    (D) *The Great Gatsby*
    (E) *Sister Carrie*

11. Of the following poems, which is known as one of the most poignant elegies to President Abraham Lincoln?

    (A) "Elegy Written in a Country Churchyard"
    (B) "When Lilacs Last in the Dooryard Bloomed"
    (C) "After Death"
    (D) "Howl"
    (E) "Elegiac Stanzas"

Question 12 refers to the following.

12. Which of the following is an important feature of the building pictured above?

    (A) A dependence on rectilinear lines and angles
    (B) An emphasis on the structural framework of the building
    (C) An interplay of large and small geometric shapes
    (D) The use of curvilinear forms to suggest organic growth or motion
    (E) An orderly, classically inspired floor plan

Questions 13–15 refer to the following illustrations (A) through (E).

(A)

(B)

(C)

(D)

(E)

13. Which example is intent on a naturalistic rendering of an animal's anatomy?

14. Which example uses animals as a metaphor for human behavior?

15. In which example are animals seen in a magic or ritual context?

Question 16 refers to the following.

16. The example pictured on the previous page most likely presents which of the following?

    (A) A passage from a classical epic
    (B) A scene from a Wagnerian opera
    (C) An eighteenth century satire on human foibles
    (D) An episode from a Shakespearean drama
    (E) An incident from the French Revolution

17. Which of the following lines is an example of iambic pentameter?

    ∪ / ∪ / ∪ / ∪ /
    (A) Her deck/once red/with he/roes' blood/
    / ∪ / ∪ / ∪ /
    (B) Here goes/the try/I've al/ways know/
    / ∪ / ∪∪ / ∪∪
    (C) She loves the/way I hold/her hand/
    / / ∪ / / ∪ / /
    (D) Although I/knew the road/led home/
    ∪ / ∪ / / ∪ / /
    (E) As I lay/wait ing/for the/morn

Questions 18 and 19 refer to the following verses.

O God, do you hear it, this persecution,
These my sufferings from this hateful
Woman, this monster, murderess of children?
Still what I can do that I will do:
I will lament and cry upon heaven,
Calling the gods to bear me witness
How you have killed my boys to prevent me from
Touching their bodies or giving them burial.
I wish I never begot them to see them
Afterward slaughtered by you.

18. These lines are spoken by

    (A) the murderer.
    (B) the father of the dead children.
    (C) one of the gods.
    (D) a bystander.
    (E) a judge.

19. It can be inferred from this passage that

    (A) the woman had a right to kill her children.
    (B) the man deserved to lose his children.
    (C) the rites and ceremonies of burial are extremely important.
    (D) the gods decreed the death of the children.
    (E) the woman will get away with the murders.

Questions 20–22 refer to the following verses (A) through (E).

    (A) For shade to shade will come too drowsily,
        And drown the wakeful anguish of the soul.
    (B) Rocks, caves, lakes, fens, bogs, dens, and shades of death.
    (C) 'Twas brillig, and the slithy toves
        Did gyre and gimble in the wabe
    (D) Because I could not stop for Death—
        He kindly stopped for me—
    (E) . . . yet from these flames
        No light, but rather darkness visible

20. Which passage contains an oxymoron?

21. Which passage uses assonance?

22. Which passage is written in iambic pentameter?

23. Which of the following are African-American playwrights who won awards and critical recognition for their plays in the 1920s?

    (A) August Wilson and Lorraine Hansberry
    (B) Charles Gordone and Imamu Amiri Baraka
    (C) Ed Bullins and Sonia Sanchez
    (D) Zora Neale Hurston and Marita Bonner
    (E) Eugene O'Neill and Clifford Odets

24. A well-made play may have all of the following EXCEPT

    (A) a tight and logical construction.
    (B) a plot based on a withheld secret.
    (C) a misplaced letter and documents.
    (D) an obligatory scene.
    (E) an episodic structure.

25. Frank Lloyd Wright was the original architect/designer of which of the following twentieth century museums?

   (A) Solomon R. Guggenheim Museum, New York
   (B) East Wing, National Gallery of Art, Washington, D.C.
   (C) Museum of Architecture, Frankfurt-am-Main
   (D) The High Museum of Art, Atlanta
   (E) None of the above.

Questions 26–28 refer to the following ballet definitions.

   (A) Quick springing movement that resembles a cat walk by alternating feet.
   (B) Placing and applying body weight to one foot that is against the floor while sliding the other foot into fifth position.
   (C) Positioning one foot in front of the other while the feet remain one step apart.
   (D) Weight proportioned incorrectly, creating the body to shift and lean in that direction.
   (E) One left leg lifted at a 45-degree angle rotating from front to outer side, from back to inner side.

26. Which description describes glissade?

27. Which description describes improper balance?

28. Which description is fourth position crossed?

29. The predecessor of the modern-day piano is the

   (A) lute.
   (B) harpsichord.
   (C) synthesizer.
   (D) harp.
   (E) xylophone.

30. A poem set to music is a(n)

   (A) madrigal.
   (B) art song.
   (C) opera.
   (D) aria.
   (E) symphony.

31. A high male voice is classified as a(n)

   (A) soprano.
   (B) tenor.
   (C) bass.
   (D) baritone.
   (E) alto.

32. Which of the following well-known writers is famous for his verses about the struggle for Irish independence?

   (A) James Joyce
   (B) J. P. Donleavy
   (C) W. B. Yeats
   (D) G. B. Shaw
   (E) John O'Hara

33. The idea of evolution is propounded by which of the following English writers?

   (A) Alfred Lord Tennyson
   (B) Dr. Samuel Johnson
   (C) Charles Darwin
   (D) Robert Browning
   (E) Thomas Henry Huxley

34. Which of the following early American novels deals with the author's personal attempt to exorcise many of the negative aspects of his Puritan heritage?

   (A) Irving's *The History of New York*
   (B) Melville's *Moby Dick*
   (C) Brown's *Wieland*
   (D) Cooper's *The Pathfinder*
   (E) Hawthorne's *The Scarlet Letter*

35. Though condemned as indecent and controversial, this modern English autobiographical novel is now acclaimed for its originality.

   (A) *The Metamorphosis*
   (B) *Sons and Lovers*
   (C) *Time and Again*
   (D) *The Heart of Darkness*
   (E) *Ethan Frome*

36. Known for its Transcendentalist underpinnings, this early American work also emphasizes the importance of self-reliance.

    (A) *The Scarlet Letter*
    (B) *The Open Boat*
    (C) *Walden*
    (D) *The Last of the Mohicans*
    (E) *The Red Badge of Courage*

Questions 37–39 refer to illustrations (A) through (E).

(A)

(B)

(C)

(D)

(E)

37. Which example characterizes a culture which values logic and order?

38. In which example are architectural forms and materials used for a whimsical effect?

39. Which example best characterizes a culture which values technological precision and efficiency?

Question 40 refers to the following.

40. In the building pictured above, the cantilevered horizontal forms do all of the following EXCEPT

(A) echo the natural waterfall's rock ledge.
(B) emphasize the structural framework of the building.
(C) deny the mass and weight of the materials.
(D) integrate the building with the natural setting.
(E) rely on industrial construction materials.

Question 41 refers to the following.

41. The architect of the building pictured above probably relied primarily on which of the following?

(A) Steel
(B) Concrete
(C) Wood
(D) Stone masonry and mortar
(E) Sheet glass

Questions 42 and 43 refer to the following poem.

The Sick Rose
O Rose, thou art sick.
The invisible worm
That flies in the night
In the howling storm

Has found out thy bed
Of crimson joy,
And his dárk sécret love
Does thy life destroy.
—*William Blake*

42. The imagery in this poem is mainly

(A) religious.
(B) sexual.
(C) animal.
(D) light.
(E) darkness.

43. The word *life* in line 8 means

(A) passion.
(B) spirit.
(C) love.
(D) beauty.
(E) memory.

Questions 44–46 refer to the following poem.

Apparently with no surprise
To any happy flower
The Frost beheads it at its play
In accidental power.

The blonde Assassin passes on,
The Sun proceeds unmoved
To measure off another Day
For an Approving God.

44. Line 3 demonstrates

(A) alliteration.
(B) personification.
(C) onomatopoeia.
(D) assonance.
(E) conceit.

45. "The blonde Assassin" in line 5 refers to

(A) fate.
(B) disease.
(C) the frost.
(D) the sun.
(E) an approving god.

46. Which of the following best describes the meaning of the poem?

(A) The cruelty of God
(B) The inevitability of death
(C) The indifference of God
(D) The happiness of flowers
(E) The inevitability of winter

47. Poetic drama is best described as

(A) poetry in dialogue.
(B) a poem in dialogue written for performance.
(C) ancillary to action.
(D) a one-act play.
(E) a play with no well-defined scenes.

48. *The Three Penny Opera* is best described as

(A) an adaptation of John Gay's *The Beggar's Opera.*
(B) a melodrama.
(C) a comedy.
(D) an epic drama.
(E) historification.

49. The belief that a human being has an absolute power to choose his or her own destiny is a hallmark of

(A) Existentialism.
(B) Essentialism.
(C) Pragmatism.
(D) Marxism.
(E) Platonism.

50. *Cyclopean* is a term which is often used to refer to the masonry building of which of the following civilizations?

(A) Ancient Egyptian
(B) Mesopotamian
(C) Aztec
(D) Roman
(E) Mycenean

51. Descartes used his *cogito* argument ("I think; therefore, I am") to establish

(A) an indubitable foundation for knowledge.
(B) the basis of personal identity.
(C) metaphysics on a firm footing.
(D) the existence of God.
(E) the foundation of mathematics.

52. Which analysis represents a through-composed form?

(A) AB
(B) ABA
(C) ABCDE
(D) ABACA
(E) A

53. Which of the following can be a synonym for Gregorian chant?

(A) Plainchant
(B) Motet
(C) Canon
(D) Aria
(E) Fugue

54. Which composer is best known for his technique of weaving favorite melodies, often patriotic, into his compositions?

(A) Sousa
(B) Ives
(C) Bernstein
(D) Stravinsky
(E) Haydn

55. Which of the following is perhaps the most curious—even hilarious—novel written in the eighteenth century?

(A) *Tristram Shandy*
(B) *Don Quixote*
(C) *Candy*
(D) *Catch-22*
(E) *Where the Bee Sucks There Suck I*

56. Which Shakespeare play is considered by many critics to be the Bard's finest study of guilt and conscience following a crime?

(A) *Julius Caesar*
(B) *Macbeth*
(C) *Hamlet*
(D) *A Midsummer Night's Dream*
(E) *Love's Labor Lost*

57. In which of the following tales is a house presented as a personification of a family?

(A) *Anne of Green Gables*
(B) *The House of Morgan*
(C) *The Young Housewife*
(D) *The House of the Seven Gables*
(E) *An Angel on the Porch*

58. Which of the following is a twentieth century novel about the Wild West written in the tradition of the Realistic movement?

(A) *Huckleberry Finn*
(B) *The Bird Comes to Yellow Sky*
(C) *The Oxbow Incident*
(D) *The Occurrence at Owl Creek Bridge*
(E) *The Red Badge of Courage*

59. Which of the following poets is known as an American original who experimented with extensive works of detailed images and free verse?

(A) Alexander Pope
(B) Samuel Langhorne Clemens
(C) Walt Whitman
(D) Emily Dickinson
(E) Anne Bradstreet

Question 60 refers to the following.

60. The pose of the horse in the sculpture pictured on the previous page serves to express

    (A) physical aging and decay.
    (B) stability.
    (C) strength.
    (D) lightness and motion.
    (E) moral fortitude.

Question 61 refers to the following.

61. Which of the following best describes the example pictured above?

    (A) Monumental architecture dominates the scene.
    (B) The scene is viewed from the window of a passing train.
    (C) Human drama is the artist's main concern.
    (D) The composition has a dramatic central focus.
    (E) The scene is viewed as though from a second-story window.

Question 62 refers to the following.

62. Which of the following is probably true of the sculpture pictured on the previous page?

    (A) The artist modelled it with his hands.
    (B) The artist poured it into a mold.
    (C) The artist shaped his materials with a blowtorch and welding tools.
    (D) The artist shaped natural materials with a chisel.
    (E) The artist used industrial forms as he found them.

Question 63 refers to the following.

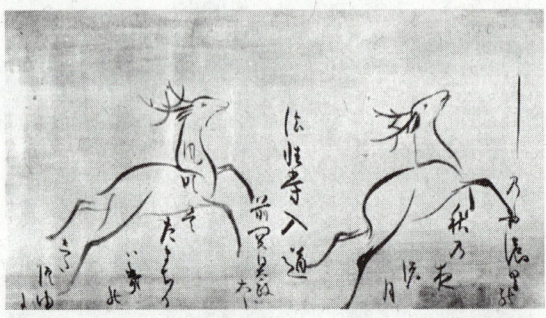

63. Which of the following is the most important artistic device in the example shown above?

    (A) Line
    (B) Tone
    (C) Perspective
    (D) Volume
    (E) Hue

Question 64 refers to the following.

64. Which of the following does NOT contribute to order and regularity in the example pictured on the previous page?

(A) The repeated second-story window design
(B) A facade which lacks deep recesses and voids
(C) The use of columns at the center and corners of the building
(D) A subtle use of the arch
(E) The balustrade running across the roof line

Questions 65 and 66 refer to the following stanza.

When my mother died I was very young
And my father sold me while yet my tongue
Could scarcely cry "weep! weep! weep! weep!"
So your chimneys I sweep, and in soot I sleep.

65. The above stanza was taken from a longer poem written by

(A) Shakespeare.
(B) Milton.
(C) Chaucer.
(D) Blake.
(E) Hardy.

66. Which of the following best explains the use of the word *weep!* in line 3 of the stanza?

(A) The child is so young he cannot yet pronounce the word.
(B) The child has a speech impediment because of neglect.
(C) The child is weeping because he was sold as a chimney sweep.
(D) The child wants to make you feel guilty about sweeping your chimneys.
(E) The child is so young he is upset at having to sweep chimneys.

Questions 67–71 refer to the following epic poem.

A whole days journey high but wide remote
From this Assyrian garden, where the Fiend
Saw undelighted all delight, all kind
Of living creatures new to sight and strange:
Two of far nobler shape erect and tall,
God-like erect, with native honor clad
In naked majesty seemed lords of all,
And worthy seemed, for in their looks divine
The image of their Maker shone,

. . .

For contemplation he and valor formed,
For softness she and sweet attractive grace,
He for God only, she for God in him:

67. The term *epic* refers to

(A) a long poem written in rhyming couplets about a hero.
(B) a long poem translated from Latin.
(C) a long poem written about heroic actions.
(D) a long poem written by Virgil.
(E) a long poem about death.

68. The above lines are from

(A) Dante's *Inferno.*
(B) Virgil's *Aeneid.*
(C) *The Iliad.*
(D) *The Arabian Nights.*
(E) *Paradise Lost.*

69. The viewpoint of the lines is

(A) Faust's.
(B) God's.
(C) Scheherazade's.
(D) Satan's.
(E) Dante's.

70. Which best describes the couple in lines 4–6?

(A) Beowulf and Grendel's mother before the crucial fight
(B) Grendel and Grendel's mother after the crucial fight
(C) Adam and Eve before "The Fall"
(D) Hector and his wife before the crucial battle
(E) Adam and Eve after "The Fall"

71. Which best describes the poet's views on the roles of men and women?

   (A) Men and women are equal.
   (B) Men are made for thoughtful action and women for beauty.
   (C) Women must be submissive to the god in men.
   (D) Men must be powerful and women soft.
   (E) Men are reasonable and strong and women soft and graceful.

72. Which of the following plays focuses on a marriage built on a lie and problems with eyesight?

   (A) *The Wild Duck*
   (B) *Oedipus*
   (C) *Electra*
   (D) *Antigone*
   (E) *Andromache*

73. *Tartuffe* is best described as a play about

   (A) the downfall of a noble king.
   (B) the problems of a marriage.
   (C) a man of considerable stature duped by a hypocrite.
   (D) individuals who wait and do not act.
   (E) children who are ingrates.

74. An *insula* refers to a(n)

   (A) Greek public meeting square.
   (B) multi-storied Roman apartment block.
   (C) western portion of a Carolingian church.
   (D) Greek cross plan.
   (E) vertical groove on the surface of a column.

75. Berkeley's famous dictum, "Esse est percipi" ("To be is to be perceived"), is associated most strongly with the outlook known as

   (A) Idealism.
   (B) Pragmatism.
   (C) Empiricism.
   (D) Rationalism.
   (E) Phenomenology.

76. Which jazz saxophonist was named "Bird"?

   (A) Charlie Parker
   (B) John Coltrane
   (C) Dizzy Gillespie
   (D) Paul Desmond
   (E) Stan Getz

77. Which jazz tenor saxophonist is famous for his *Giant Steps*?

   (A) Charlie Parker
   (B) Stan Getz
   (C) John Coltrane
   (D) Coleman Hawkins
   (E) Ornette Coleman

78. A collaboration between Aaron Copland and the dance-choreographer Agnes de Mille resulted in the creation of which ballet suite?

   (A) "West Side Story"
   (B) "Rodeo"
   (C) "Porgy and Bess"
   (D) "Phantom of the Opera"
   (E) "Salome"

79. Which of the following novels of adventure presents the most detailed picture of eighteenth century English manorial and city life?

   (A) *Great Expectations*
   (B) *Moby Dick*
   (C) *Jane Eyre*
   (D) *Tom Jones*
   (E) *Silas Marner*

80. Which of the following is among the most famous of English works by the group of writers called the "Decadents"?

   (A) Coleridge's "Rime of the Ancient Mariner"
   (B) Lawrence's *Sons and Lovers*
   (C) Fielding's *Joseph Andrews*
   (D) Wilde's *The Picture of Dorian Gray*
   (E) Joyce's *The Dubliners*

81. The important literary concept of the "pathetic fallacy" was first set forth in

   (A) Ruskin's *Modern Painters*.
   (B) Emerson's *Nature*.
   (C) Shakespeare's *As You Like It*.
   (D) Thomas Lodge's *Rosalynde*.
   (E) Samuel Johnson's *Dictionary*.

82. A reaction against Utilitarianism—the theory of ethics formulated in England in the eighteenth century—can be seen in nineteenth century literature, such as

   (A) Eliot's *Middlemarch*.
   (B) Dreiser's *Sister Carrie*.
   (C) Melville's *Billy Budd*.
   (D) James' *Washington Square*.
   (E) Dickens' *David Copperfield*.

83. Which of the following writers participated energetically in the Celtic Revival of the eighteenth century?

   (A) James Joyce
   (B) John O'Hara
   (C) J. P. Donleavy
   (D) James Macpherson
   (E) W. B. Yeats

Question 84 refers to the following.

84. In the painting illustrated on the previous page, all of the following are important compositional devices EXCEPT

    (A) the perspective grid of the checkerboard floor.
    (B) the strong highlighting of the foreground figures.
    (C) the arcade of arches in the background.
    (D) the vigorous movement of the main figure group.
    (E) the intersecting lines of the arms and the swords.

Question 85 refers to the following.

85. The building pictured above was produced in which of the following countries?

    (A) Japan
    (B) Indonesia
    (C) Easter Island
    (D) Greece
    (E) Nigeria

Questions 86–88 refer to the following illustrations (A) through (E).

(A)

(B)

(C)

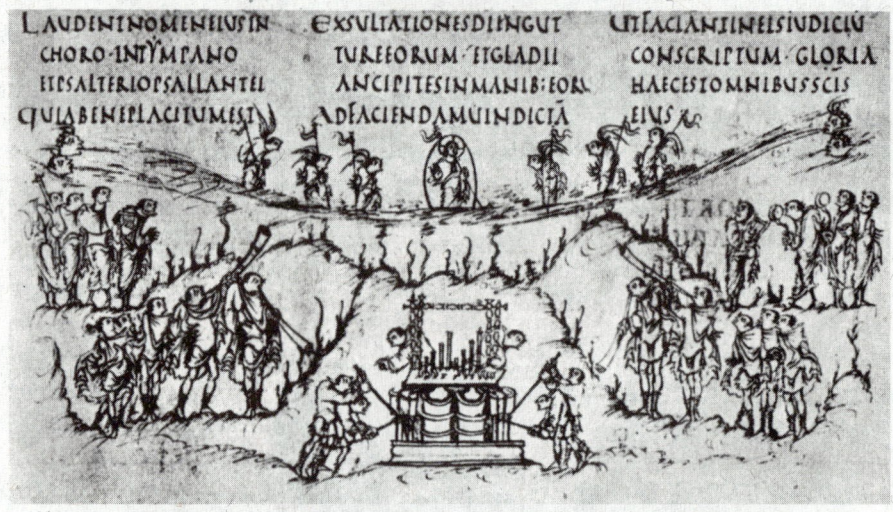

LAUDENTNOMENEIUSIN   EXSULTATIONESDIINGUT   UTFACIANTINELSIUDICIÚ
CHORO·INTYMPANO   TUREEORUM·ETGLADII   CONSCRIPTUM·GLORIA
ETPSALTERIOPSALLANTEI   ANCIPITESINMANIB·EOR·   HAECESTOMNIBUSSCIS
QUIABENEPLACITUMEST   ADFACIENDAMUINDICIA   EIUS·

(D)

(E)

86. Which example seeks to give a schematic representation of a ceremonial event?

87. In which example is the human figure most stylized and repeated in order to fit its container?

88. In which example do the figures show the greatest tendency toward rhythmic calligraphy?

Questions 89–91 refer to the following lines.

> As when in the sky the stars about the moon's shining
> are seen in all their glory, when the air has fallen to stillness.
> and all the high places of the hills are clear, and the shoulders out-jutting,
> and the deep ravines, as endless bright air spills from the heavens
> and all the stars are seen, to make glad the heart of the shepherd:
> such in their numbers blazed the watchfires the Trojans were burning
> between the waters of Xanthos and the ships, before Ilion.

89. The previous lines are an example of

   (A) a Homeric simile.
   (B) an extended metaphor.
   (C) Augustan couplets.
   (D) English heroic verse.
   (E) Miltonic free verse.

90. What is being described as what?

   (A) The stars are like hills.
   (B) The stars are like shepherds.
   (C) The stars are like rivers.
   (D) The Trojan fires are like the stars.
   (E) The Trojan ships are like the stars.

91. The shepherd is introduced in line 5 in order to

   (A) humanize the description.
   (B) give some humor to the description.
   (C) give some depth to the description.
   (D) give some gladness to the description.
   (E) glamorize the description.

Questions 92–95 refer to lines (A) through (E) below.

   (A) As soon as April pierces to the root
       The drought of March, and bathes each bud and shoot
       . . .

   (B) Of man's first disobedience, and the fruit
       Of that forbidden fruit whose mortal taste
       . . .

   (C) My heart leaps up when I behold
       A rainbow in the sky;
       . . .

   (D) I placed a jar in Tennessee,
       And round it was, upon a hill.

   (E) Because I could not stop for Death—
       He kindly stopped for me—

92. Which of these is written by a woman?

93. Which of these is written by Chaucer?

94. Which of these represents the Romantic period?

95. Which of these represents the epic?

96. As Gregor Samsa awoke one morning from an uneasy dream he found himself transformed into a gigantic insect.

   This opening line is

   (A) Genet's.
   (B) Sartre's.
   (C) Ionesco's.
   (D) Kafka's.
   (E) Tolstoy's.

97. The best definition for the original use of scapegoat is

   (A) a table ornament used when royalty was unable to appear.
   (B) a fur-bearing animal that was used to provide milk.
   (C) an animal tethered to lure animals terrorizing the village.
   (D) a victim, sacrificed for the redemption of the tribe, being driven into the wilderness.
   (E) a royal personage like Oedipus who went into exile.

98. Which of the following types of ancient Roman architecture most directly influenced the development of early Christian church planning?

    (A) Temple
    (B) Basilica
    (C) Bath
    (D) Forum
    (E) Villa

99. Dance was originated by

    (A) religious groups.
    (B) Egyptians.
    (C) Greeks.
    (D) Romans.
    (E) savage hunters.

100. The logical fallacy involved in concluding that the universe itself must have a cause because every event in the universe has cause is

    (A) the fallacy of composition.
    (B) the fallacy of division.
    (C) the slippery slope fallacy.
    (D) the *ad hominem* fallacy.
    (E) the fallacy of ignorance.

101. The themes of many musical compositions are often that of folk music. Which composer is most famous for his folk music settings for wind ensemble?

    (A) Sousa
    (B) Grainger
    (C) Beethoven
    (D) Strauss
    (E) Haydn

Questions 102–105 refer to the following musical notation.

102. What is the key of this excerpt?

    (A) B flat
    (B) F
    (C) C
    (D) D
    (E) A

103. The time signature for the previous excerpt is not noted. What should it be?

    (A) $\frac{4}{4}$
    (B) $\frac{2}{4}$
    (C) $\frac{6}{8}$
    (D) $\frac{3}{4}$
    (E) $\frac{12}{8}$

104. How many measures are present?

    (A) 1
    (B) 2
    (C) 3
    (D) 0
    (E) 5

105. What is the arrow pointing toward?

    (A) Key signature
    (B) Clef sign
    (C) Double bar
    (D) Repeat sign
    (E) Time signature

106. Which of the following is considered among the body of literature currently termed "American Ethnic"?

(A) James' *Daisy Miller*
(B) Poe's *Cask of Amontillado*
(C) Roth's *Goodbye Columbus*
(D) Updike's *Rabbit Redux*
(E) Hawthorne's *Scarlet Letter*

107. One of the most famous and prophetic descriptions of settlements in the young American nation was

(A) *The Journals of Lewis and Clark.*
(B) *Main Street.*
(C) *Letters From an American Farmer.*
(D) *The Last of the Mohicans.*
(E) *The Diary of Captain John Smith.*

108. Which of the following modern novels describes the difficulties faced by African-Americans in twentieth century America?

(A) *As I Lay Dying*
(B) *Ethan Frome*
(C) *Heart of Darkness*
(D) *The Metamorphosis*
(E) *The Invisible Man*

109. Which of the following nineteenth century novels was used as an accurate travel guide well into the twentieth century?

(A) *Journey to the Center of the Earth*
(B) *The Mysterious Island*
(C) *Robinson Crusoe*
(D) *20,000 Leagues Under the Sea*
(E) *Gulliver's Travels*

110. Which of the following novels recalls a time of Medieval chivalry?

(A) Eliot's *Middlemarch*
(B) Scott's *Ivanhoe*
(C) Poe's *The Fall of the House of Usher*
(D) King's *The Shining*
(E) West's *The Dreamlife of Balso Snell*

111. It has been said that Victorian poetry is essentially a continuation of the poetry of the Romantic movement. This can be seen in

(A) Hemingway's veneration for Eliot.
(B) Tennyson's veneration for Browning.
(C) Arnold's veneration for Wordsworth.
(D) Rossetti's veneration for Browning.
(E) Wordsworth's veneration for Scott.

112. Which of the following is one of the most hilarious stories in *Huckleberry Finn*—one which demonstrates both the accepting nature and eventual canniness of the heartland Americans?

(A) *The Duke and the Dauphin*
(B) Tom Sawyer and his painted fence
(C) Huck's escape from Pap
(D) Jim's escape to freedom
(E) Huck "lighting out for the territories"

Question 113 refers to the following.

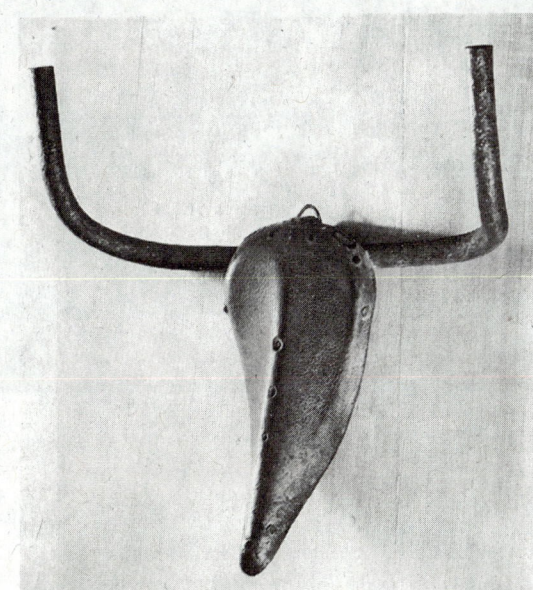

113. In combining found objects to make the sculpture shown above, the artist sought to create

(A) a contrast of line and tone.
(B) a religious symbol.
(C) a visual analogy to a living creature.
(D) a metaphor for human experience.
(E) a functional device.

Questions 114–116 refer to the following illustrations (A) through (E).

(A)

(B)

(C)

(D)

(E)

114. In which example do carefully rendered decorative details in the painting help to visually relate the main subject to the background?

115. In which example is an off-center subject cropped to produce the effect of a casual photograph?

116. In which example does the subject's off-center position lead the viewer's eye out of the picture?

Question 117 refers to the following.

117. The staircase in the Hotel van Eetvelde, designed by Victor Horta in 1895, illustrates which one of the following art historical styles?

   (A) Surrealism
   (B) Post-Modernism
   (C) Neo-Classicism
   (D) Post-Impressionsim
   (E) Art Nouveau

Questions 118 and 119 refer to the following illustrations (A) through (D).

(A)

(B)

(C)

(D)

118. Which of these buildings is Gothic?

    (A) Building (A)
    (B) Building (B)
    (C) Building (C)
    (D) Building (D)
    (E) None of the above.

119. Which of these buildings was NOT constructed as a place of religious worship?

    (A) Building (A)
    (B) Building (B)
    (C) Building (C)
    (D) Building (D)
    (E) None of the above.

Questions 120 and 121 refer to the following verse.

> On the one-ton temple bell
> a moonmoth, folded into sleep,
> sits still.

120. The above verse is an example of

    (A) hyperbole.
    (B) an ode.
    (C) haiku.
    (D) an epigram.
    (E) doggerel.

121. The original of the above verse was written in

    (A) French.
    (B) Japanese.
    (C) Chinese.
    (D) British English.
    (E) Persian.

122. Which of the following best defines the term *bathos*?

    (A) A gross exaggeration
    (B) A build to a climax
    (C) An abrupt fall from climax
    (D) An abrupt fall from the beautiful to the funny
    (E) An abrupt build to a climax

123. Which poet gave us the term *negative capability*?

(A) William Carlos Williams
(B) T. S. Eliot
(C) William Wordsworth
(D) e. e. cummings
(E) John Keats

124. If all tragedies are finished by death, and all comedies by a marriage, then which of the following is the best example of tragedy?

(A) *A Death of a Salesman*
(B) *A Midsummer's Night's Dream*
(C) *Oedipus*
(D) *The Tempest*
(E) *The Bad-Tempered Man*

Questions 125–127 refer to what happens when:

(A) misunderstandings are cleared up.
(B) action not intended by the main character takes place.
(C) the public is aided in its discovery of the villain.
(D) the main character whispers an "aside" to the audience.
(E) the hero's understanding of the true nature of the situation and the self changes.

125. Which of the choices best defines Anagnorisis, the Greek word for "recognition" or "discovery"?

126. Which choice best describes Mark Antony's intent in the public oration that he makes regarding Julius Caesar's death?

127. Which choice is best used to characterize Othello's description of himself as "one that loved not wisely, but too well"?

128. "So the whole ear of Denmark
Is by a forged process of my death
Rankly abused."

The speaker is

(A) the Royal Dane.
(B) King Lear.
(C) Puck.
(D) Falstaff.
(E) Caliban.

129. The unglazed opening in the center of the dome of the Pantheon in Rome is called a(n)

(A) window.
(B) oculus.
(C) splayed window.
(D) stained-glass window.
(E) clerestory.

130. Parallel feet, flat-footed steps, undulating torso, body isolation, and syncopated rhythms refer to

(A) beledi dance (abdominal dance).
(B) jazz dance.
(C) danse mora (Flamenco dance).
(D) tap dance.
(E) country dance.

131. Suppose two theories are equally powerful in explaining certain phenomena, but one of them (**X**) postulates a larger number of unobservable entities than the other (**Y**). Which is preferable and why?

(A) **Y**, because of Occam's Razor
(B) **Y**, because of the Principle of Plenitude
(C) **X**, because of the Open Question Argument
(D) **X**, because of Underdetermination
(E) **Y**, because of Scientific Realism

132. The hero of what nineteenth century novel states that ". . . vanity is a weakness indeed. But pride—where there is a real superiority of mind, pride will be always under good regulation."

(A) *Silas Marner*
(B) *Emma*
(C) *Gone with the Wind*
(D) *Pride and Prejudice*
(E) *Gulliver's Travels*

133. A trumpet can play different notes by adjusting the lip or by doing what?

(A) Pressing down a valve
(B) Striking a string
(C) Covering a hole
(D) Using an octave key
(E) Using a slide

Questions 134 and 135 refer to the following musical notation.

134. The diagram is an example of

  (A) hemiola.
  (B) paradiddle.
  (C) fermata.
  (D) crescendo.
  (E) glissando.

135. The C in measure 1 is a C sharp. Therefore, the C in measure 2 is a

  (A) C natural.
  (B) C sharp.
  (C) C flat.
  (D) B.
  (E) D.

136. What is another name for the bass clef?

  (A) F clef
  (B) G clef
  (C) Tenor clef
  (D) Treble clef
  (E) Alto clef

137. One of the greatest modern chronicles of a famous incident during the Civil War is

  (A) Hoover's *None Dare Call It Treason.*
  (B) Wouk's *Caine Mutiny.*
  (C) Mailer's *The Naked and the Dead.*
  (D) Catton's *A Stillness at Appomattox.*
  (E) Crane's *Red Badge of Courage.*

138. Which of the following is Edward Albee's memorable drama of the trials and tribulations of a university professor and his wife?

  (A) *Troilus and Cressida*
  (B) *Who's Afraid of Virginia Woolf*
  (C) *The American Dream*
  (D) *Brighton Beach Memoirs*
  (E) *A View from the Bridge*

139. One of the greatest diarists of the Restoration was

  (A) Sir Laurence Olivier.
  (B) Laurence Sterne.
  (C) O. E. Rolvaag.
  (D) Samuel Pepys.
  (E) Jonathan Swift.

140. In the early 1800s, which American minister and writer promoted the philosophical and literary movement called Transcendentalism?

  (A) Jonathan Edwards
  (B) Sir William Pitt
  (C) Ralph Waldo Emerson
  (D) Henry David Thoreau
  (E) Dr. Samuel Fuller

CLEP Humanities Practice Test 1

Answer Key

1.	(D)	36.	(C)	71.	(E)	106.	(C)
2.	(B)	37.	(A)	72.	(A)	107.	(C)
3.	(A)	38.	(D)	73.	(C)	108.	(E)
4.	(D)	39.	(B)	74.	(B)	109.	(A)
5.	(A)	40.	(B)	75.	(A)	110.	(B)
6.	(B)	41.	(D)	76.	(A)	111.	(C)
7.	(C)	42.	(B)	77.	(C)	112.	(A)
8.	(A)	43.	(D)	78.	(B)	113.	(C)
9.	(D)	44.	(B)	79.	(D)	114.	(B)
10.	(C)	45.	(C)	80.	(D)	115.	(C)
11.	(B)	46.	(B)	81.	(A)	116.	(D)
12.	(D)	47.	(B)	82.	(E)	117.	(E)
13.	(D)	48.	(D)	83.	(D)	118.	(C)
14.	(A)	49.	(A)	84.	(D)	119.	(A)
15.	(E)	50.	(E)	85.	(A)	120.	(C)
16.	(C)	51.	(A)	86.	(A)	121.	(B)
17.	(A)	52.	(C)	87.	(C)	122.	(D)
18.	(B)	53.	(A)	88.	(D)	123.	(E)
19.	(C)	54.	(B)	89.	(A)	124.	(A)
20.	(E)	55.	(A)	90.	(D)	125.	(E)
21.	(B)	56.	(B)	91.	(A)	126.	(C)
22.	(A)	57.	(D)	92.	(E)	127.	(E)
23.	(D)	58.	(C)	93.	(A)	128.	(A)
24.	(E)	59.	(C)	94.	(C)	129.	(B)
25.	(A)	60.	(C)	95.	(B)	130.	(B)
26.	(B)	61.	(E)	96.	(D)	131.	(A)
27.	(D)	62.	(C)	97.	(D)	132.	(D)
28.	(C)	63.	(A)	98.	(B)	133.	(A)
29.	(B)	64.	(D)	99.	(E)	134.	(A)
30.	(B)	65.	(D)	100.	(A)	135.	(A)
31.	(B)	66.	(A)	101.	(B)	136.	(A)
32.	(C)	67.	(C)	102.	(B)	137.	(D)
33.	(C)	68.	(E)	103.	(D)	138.	(B)
34.	(E)	69.	(D)	104.	(C)	139.	(D)
35.	(B)	70.	(C)	105.	(D)	140.	(C)

DETAILED EXPLANATIONS OF ANSWERS PRACTICE TEST 1

1. **(D)** Pylons serve as large "gates" to ancient Egyptian temple complexes. Pyramids (A), mastabas (B), and tombs (C) were burial sites and were not as a rule located near the entrances of temples. (E) Obelisks, while positioned near the entrance to many Egyptian temple complexes, are tall, narrow, vertical shafts, which are physically quite unlike wide, massive pylon walls.

2. **(B)** The group of performers who used such techniques for the purpose of displaying power were called flagellants. Fools used crude jokes and quick wit in their technique (A). Minnesingers were a group of entertainers who sang about war, political issues, and love (C). The mimes mimicked and acted out a situation without speech (D). Joculators were seen as actors and jesters, dancing mimes, acrobats, poets, and musicians (E).

3. **(A)** Although the definition of an *a priori* truth is not altogether clear, it is usually said that such truths are known independently of experience or "from the first." Thus, (B) cannot be correct. Mathematical calculation can count as a kind of experience, so (C) is incorrect. Human beings are believed to know truth "from the first" by many philosophers; thus, (D) is incorrect. A truth whose denial is a contradiction (E) is called an "analytic" truth.

4. **(D)** The fourth degree of a major scale is called the subdominant (D). Each degree is given a name to show its relation within the scale. The tonic (A) is the first step of a scale. The dominant (B) is the fifth degree of the scale. The leading tone (C) is the seventh degree of the scale. The mediant (E) is the third degree of a scale.

5. **(A)** A minor scale ascends from the tonic in the following pattern: w $\frac{1}{2}$ w w $\frac{1}{2}$ w w. Therefore, the half steps occur between the 2–3 and 5–6 scale degree, so choice (A) is correct. Half steps between steps 3–4 and 7–8 (B) are found in a major scale, w w 2 w w w 2. Half steps between steps 1–2 and 7–8 (C) and 2–3 and 7–8 (D) are not defined scales. A half step between the third and fourth degrees of a scale (E) is found in the blues scale.

6. **(B)** Stravinsky's "Le Sacre du Printemps" (B) is an example of the use of Primitivism—employing rhythms that are explosive and powerful. Debussy employs Impressionism for "Prelude a l'après-midi d'un faune" (A). "Salome" (C) is a tone poem by Richard Strauss which experiments with atonality. "Wozzeck" (D) is a 12-tone opera by Alban Berg. "The Liberty Bell" (E) is a march composed by John Phillip Sousa.

7. **(C)** William Blake (1757–1827) has been described as "the first clear voice of romanticism" and perhaps his greatest work was *Songs of Innocence and Experience* (C), in which many of the characteristics of romantic poetry can be seen: the poetry expresses the poet's personal feelings, not the actions of other men. Pope's (A) "hero-comical" poem from the seventeenth century demonstrates none of the above. *The Social Contract* (B) is a sociological and philosophical essay. *Romeo and Juliet* (E), while commonly understood to be a romance between two teenagers, is not "romantic," and predates Romanticism by 200 years. James' novel (D) belongs to the American Realist period.

8. **(A)** The titles presented here, of course, are mostly in French (except for (D) which is about a French historical figure)—the language of Albert Camus, the father of Existentialism. Camus' *L'Étranger (The Stranger)*—the story of an expatriate Frenchman in Algeria—presents many of the precepts of Existentialism: an emphasis on existence rather than essence, and the inadequacy of human reason to explain the enigma of the universe. *Le Morte D'Arthur* (B) was written in English by Tennyson; *Candide* (C) was by Voltaire and *Le Misanthrope* (E) was a comedy of the 1700s by Molière. While the latter title might indicate Existential estrangement, the work appears 200 years before the literary movement. *Saint Joan* (D), a dramatic tragedy by G. B. Shaw, is biographical.

9. **(D)** All of the writings listed here describe life on an American frontier—but only *My Antonia* (D) deals with frontier life in the Midwest during the nineteenth century. Cooper's famous work (A), while written during that century, refers to upstate New York during the eighteenth century. William Byrd's work (B) deals with defining the border between Virginia and North Carolina during the late eighteenth century. Bradford's diary (C) is a Pilgrim document written in colonial Massachusetts, and Twain's classic (E), while it tangentially involves Illinois and the shores of Iowa on the Mississippi River, does not deal with the Midwest per se.

10. **(C)** Salinger's work is recognized as a coming of age novel in which his main character, Holden Caulfield, is an "antihero"—a character whose appeal is that his flaws are dominant. *Tom Sawyer* (A) has always been viewed by critics as a children's novel, because Tom can be seen as the "All-American Boy," unlike Huck Finn, Twain's later, more complicated creation. Dickens' work (B) does not deal with coming of age. Dreiser's *Sister Carrie* (E), on the other hand, does concern itself with changes in the protagonist through time, but Carrie is more a classic heroine in her rigid self-reliance and conquest over adversity. Fitzgerald (D) creates a number of interesting figures—some, like Gatsby, who have anti-heroic qualities—but all have basically "come of age" before the summer in which the story takes place.

11. **(B)** Whitman's poem is one of four elegies, entitled "Memories of President Lincoln," which were made part of *Drum-Taps* after Lincoln's death in 1864. The Englishman Gray's "Elegy" (A) is of a much earlier vintage (late 1700s). Christina Rossetti's "After Death" (C) is not an elegy, nor is Allen Ginsburg's "Howl" (D). Wordsworth's work (E) deals with the death of Sir George Beaumont, the poet's patron.

12. **(D)** The design pictured carefully avoids all reminders of the symmetrical, balanced floor plans of Classical and Renaissance architecture. It also dispenses with a conventional structural framework and with the geometric forms and angles of traditional buildings. Instead, it exploits fully the potential of a new material—in this case, poured concrete—to create dynamic, curving forms whose arcs and spirals echo both the shape of growing organisms and the motion of wind and water.

13. **(D)** Answer choices (A), (B), and (E) each contain images of animals which are based to some degree on naturalistic observation. In each case, however, the animals are presented either as black-and-white line drawings or as schematic, two-dimensional renderings, with no attempt to model the forms of the animals; and in each case, the imagery functions in either a narrative or magical context and does not intend to explore anatomy. Answer choice (C) presents a basically

realistic, well-modelled animal, based on naturalistic observation and with close attention to detail, but the addition of the wings adds a fantastic touch and the animal as a whole is elegantly designed and positioned to act as the functional handle of a jar. Only answer choice (D) explores the expressive forms of the animal's musculature, here conveying a sense of untamed emotion and animal energy through the tensed, swelling muscles of the crouched jaguar.

14. **(A)**   Answer choices (B) and (E) each present somewhat schematic representations of animals, the first in order to document the character and activities of an Egyptian noble, and the second to fulfill a magical, ritual function. The animal in answer choice (C) exists solely as a decorative detail on a purely functional object. Answer choice (D) shows animal behavior which might be called analogous to human behavior (i.e., the violence of the strong over the weak) but the image itself does not intend to comment directly on human life. Only answer choice (A) uses animal imagery to directly caricature human behavior. In this case, the Japanese scroll employs monkeys, frogs, hares, and foxes to mimic Buddhist religious practices.

15. **(E)**   Answer choice (E) presents animal images with a high degree of naturalism in a sophisticated, abstract, almost "modern" style. The artist, however, despite his naturalism, was not concerned with perspective or with conventional pictorial space, and concentrated solely on the overlapping images of the animals, which have no narrative function. He has included a view of the animals ascending, possibly to indicate a magical essence of these animals. These paintings were executed on the walls of a cave in what appears to be a sacred precinct, and seem to function as magical images to ensure success in the hunt.

16. **(C)**   The example pictured, by the English painter William Hogarth, satirizes eighteenth century English life in a comic way. In telling the story of the human characters illustrated in the work, the picture uses a wealth of carefully chosen detail which the viewer is to "read" in a novelistic manner. The period details, therefore (as of dress, architecture, furnishings, etc.), and the attitudes and actions of the figures (the exasperated look, for instance, of the servant on the left) tell us that this is a human comedy set in the eighteenth century. Of the other answer choices, (A), (B), and (D) would be both historically anachronistic and weightier in subject matter. Answer choice (E) would fall roughly within the correct period, but it, too, would likely present a more dramatic content.

17. **(A)**   Choice (A) contains five iambic feet and is an example of iambic pentameter. The other examples have incorrectly marked accents and feet.

18. **(B)**   This passage comes from the Greek play *Medea* by Euripides. Medea, a woman who is being cast aside so her husband, Jason, can marry a princess, kills their two sons in retaliation. This passage shows Jason lamenting over the boys' deaths and invoking the gods to punish his ex-wife.

19. **(C)**   In the passage Jason mourns that Medea killed the boys "to prevent me from/Touching their bodies or giving them burial." In Greek society, the dead were honored by elaborate burial rites and ceremonies. To be buried without ceremony was considered to be dishonorable to the dead, especially when they were related to great warriors, such as Jason.

20. **(E)**   An oxymoron is an apparent contradiction in terms, such as "jumbo shrimp," "cruel kindness," or (as some would say) "military intelligence." Passage (E) contains an oxymoron because it mentions flames which give "No light, but rather darkness."

21. **(B)**   Assonance is the repetition of vowel sounds in a single line of poetry. Passage (B) contains three examples of assonance: the words *rocks* and *bogs,* the words *caves, lakes,* and *shades,* and the words *fens* and *dens.*

22. **(A)**   Iambic pentameter refers to the meter, or rhythm, of a line of poetry composed of five feet, each of which is an iamb, having one unstressed syllable followed by a stressed syllable. A line of poetry written in iambic pentameter is 10 syllables long. Passage (A) contains two lines of poetry written in iambic pentameter. When read aloud, the unstressed-stressed pattern emerges: "For SHADE to SHADE will COME too DROWsiLY, / And DROWN the WAKEful ANGuish OF the SOUL."

23. **(D)**   Zora Neale Hurston and Marita Bonner (D) won awards and recognition for their plays in the 1920s. Wilson and Hansberry (A) are of different generations; Wilson is a contemporary playwright and Hansberry wrote her plays between 1961 and 1964. Gordone and Baraka (B) were best known in the 1970s. Ed Bullins (C) was a novelist/poet who came to prominence in the late 1960s, too late for this question. Sonia Sanchez is a contemporary poet and is also too late to be considered as a correct answer for this question. O'Neill and Odets (E) are not African-American playwrights.

24. **(E)**   A well-made play is characterized by (A) tight and logical construction, (B) a plot based on a withheld secret, (C) misplaced letters or documents, and (D) an obligatory scene. (E) Episodic structure is antithetical and characterized by little more than a series of incidents and has little logical arrangement; therefore, (E) is the exception to the well-made play and is the best answer.

25. **(A)**   The Solomon R. Guggenheim Museum, New York (A), is the correct answer. The East Wing of the National Gallery of Art in Washington, D.C. (B), was designed by I. M. Pei. O. M. Ungers designed the Museum of Architecture in Frankfurt-am-Main (C). Richard Meier was the architect of the High Museum of Art in Atlanta (D).

26. **(B)**   To brush one foot against the floor is glissade. Pas de chat is a quick "cat-like" step (A), feet positioned in front of one another with a step separating them and legs turned out is fourth position crossed (C), body weight shifted incorrectly is improper balance (D), and a pointed foot and extended leg moving in a circular motion is a demi-rond de jambe (E).

27. **(D)**   Weight and body shifted incorrectly is improper balance. Choices pas de chat (A), glissade (B), fourth position crossed (C), and demi-rond de jambe (E) are specific ballet movements.

28. **(C)**   One foot in front of the other with a step separating them describes fourth position crossed. Pas de chat (A) and glissade (B) are steps in motion, improper balance is incorrect body alignment caused by uneven weight distribution (D), and demi-rond de jambe is a circular foot motion (E).

29. **(B)**   The harpsichord (B) is the predecessor of the piano. The harpsichord was widely used during the Baroque period. The lute (A) is similar to the guitar. The synthesizer (C) is an electronic keyboard using analog and/or digital technology to produce sound. The harp (D) is a stringed instrument that is plucked with the fingers. The xylophone (E) is a percussion instrument which is struck with a mallet.

30. **(B)** An art song (B), or *lieder*, is a poem set to music, for solo voice and piano. A madrigal (A) is verse set to music for two or more voices, which often follows a prescribed form. An opera (C) is a theatrical drama which is sung, often with instrumental accompaniment. An aria (D) is a solo for voice with accompaniment, occurring during a longer form such as an opera. A symphony (E) is a three or four movement work for orchestra.

31. **(B)** A tenor (B) is a high male voice. The range of voices is classified from high to low; that is, soprano, alto, tenor, baritone, bass. A soprano (A) is a high female voice. A bass (C) is the lowest male voice. A baritone (D) has a range between the tenor and the bass. An alto (E) is a medium female voice.

32. **(C)** W. B. Yeats (C), the famous Irish poet and essayist of the early twentieth century, is always remembered for his devotion to Irish nationalism. James Joyce (A) is known for his depiction of Irish life, and dramatist G. B. Shaw (D) is generally regarded more in a strictly literary and not political tradition. The other two choices—Donleavy (B) and O'Hara (E)—are modern American writers, whose literary interests tend more to romance and mystery than Irish nationalism and unification.

33. **(C)** Charles Darwin's *On the Origin of Species* (C) helped shape Victorian English thought as well as considerations of natural history throughout the world. Tennyson (A) referred to Darwin's theory of evolution in some of his major poems. English scientist and essayist Huxley (E) was a proponent of Darwin's theories. Dr. Johnson's (B) degree was not in science; his work as an essayist, commentator, and lexicographer remains an enormous contribution to arts and letters. Browning's (D) wonderful poetic monologues, while written during the Victorian Age, in no way represent a suitable answer to the question.

34. **(E)** *The Scarlet Letter.* Hawthorne, a descendant of Judge John Hathorne (no *w*), one of the three judges who presided over the Salem Witch Trial, believed that a curse existed on the male members of his family. He changed the spelling of his name and wrote *The Scarlet Letter* (E), in which Puritan justice is seen as harsh, overreactive, and heartless. In this and other ways, he hoped to atone for the cruelty of his ancestors. Irving (A) was an entertaining historian with no such worries. Melville (B) and Cooper (D) were great tale tellers, and Charles Brockden Brown's (C) main claim to fame is as the first American novelist.

35. **(B)** Lawrence's *Sons and Lovers* (B) shocked an entire generation of critics with its passionate prose and erotic evocations. Kafka's story (A) about a man who changes into an insect is dense with philosophy. Conrad's great work (D) is vivid in its natural descriptions, but hardly a novel to be "banned in Boston." Jack Finney's (C) modern novel of dimensional travel is also tame by any comparison, as most certainly is Edith Wharton's (E).

36. **(C)** Thoreau's *Walden* (C) most clearly engages his friend Emerson's precepts of rugged individualism which the minister set down in his essay "Self Reliance." Thoreau writes about his month-long sojourn living off the land in a cabin near Walden Pond in Massachusetts. Hawthorne's work (A), while written at about the same time, demonstrates few of these concerns. Crane's works (B) and (E) are brilliant descriptions of an accident and warfare, and great stories—as is Cooper's (D)—but none is based in Transcendentalist theory—a reliance on individual and conscience—and expressed powerfully through prose.

37. **(A)**   Answer choices (C), (D), and (E) illustrate buildings which employ arching, curving, cylindrical, and circular forms, often in elaborate, complex combinations, and suggest the play of emotion, fantasy, or romance, but do not seem founded on any general cultural need for logic and order. Choice (B) shows a modern building whose design certainly proceeds from logical precepts, but, of the principles offered in the answer choices, technological precision seems to best characterize this example. Example (A), however, the famous fifth century B.C. Parthenon in Athens, presents a building whose design reflects perfectly the logical philosophies which defined Classical Greek culture. The Parthenon's architects were careful to construct a building of simple, refined forms, methodically repeated according to calculated ratios of size and space. The result is an effect of perfect balance and order which would be undermined by altering any one of the building's essential components.

38. **(D)**   Choices (A) and (B) illustrate structures whose severe, regularized forms seem to deny the possibility of humor and whimsy. Choice (C), a Gothic cathedral interior, uses soaring arches and strong vertical thrust to express spirituality and religious fervor, while choice (E), an Italian Baroque church exterior, conveys a sense of intellectual, nervous agitation through a contrast of convex and concave curves and the use of an overabundance of ornamental detail. Only choice (D), a nineteenth century English pleasure pavilion, combines a fanciful assortment of playful, whimsical shapes—as in the "Islamic" domes and minarets—to create an effect of exotic fantasy and underscore its function as a place of recreation.

39. **(B)**   Example (B) pares its structural forms to an absolute minimum, stressing the industrial materials to achieve an effect of absolute structural logic and clarity. This "international style" architecture reflects the high cultural value placed on industrial and commercial efficiency in the modern urbanized society.

40. **(B)**   In the example, the 1939 "Falling Water" house by the American architect Frank Lloyd Wright, the horizontal forms which project dramatically over the small waterfall do not emphasize the building's structural framework but, rather, deny the presence of a structural support altogether and seem almost to defy gravity. All of the other observations offered in the answer choices are valid.

41. **(D)**   The building pictured in the example, the *Abbaye-aux Hommes at Caen*, is a good example of the Norman Romanesque style. The original building was wooden-roofed, but stone masonry is the most important element. All of the other materials listed in the answer choices are industrial-age materials which were unavailable to the Medieval architect.

42. **(B)**   The rose has, for centuries, been a symbol of virginal love and beauty. By calling the rose "sick," the poet is implying that somehow this virginal beauty has been lost. This is due to, as the poet states, an "invisible worm," that has found the rose's "bed/Of crimson joy."

43. **(D)**   Because of the "worm," the "rose" is "sick"; choice (D) is the best answer because it addresses the archetypical symbol of the rose as virginal love and beauty. Since the rose is "sick," this beauty is gone. Some of the other choices may adequately answer the question, but not as well as (D).

44. **(B)** Personification means an object or emotion has been made into a person with human attributes—here the frost is seen beheading as if in battle as a show of power. Easily detected, the personified word is frequently capitalized. Alliteration (A) is a device that repeats the initial consonants (or vowels) as in "crowing cocks" or "weeping widows." Onomatopoeia (C) uses verbs that sound like the action, as in "ooze" or "hiss" or "swish." Assonance repeats the vowel sounds in a line or sentence. Although present in lines 6–8, for the technique in line 3 (D) is incorrect. Conceit (E) is a term connected with the metaphysical poets like John Donne where outrageous comparisons are made between unlike objects. Here frost is referred to as a killer of flowers, not compared to a weed-whacker.

45. **(C)** The frost has already been described as a killer beheading the flowers in line 3; it is a clear connection to see frost as blonde or icy white and the whole point of the poem is the killing power as of an assassin. Fate (A) is part of the poem's *interpretation* but not the meaning of this particular line; disease (B) is not mentioned, rather, random acts of violence; the sun (D) follows the act of frost and is not involved in the killing; it is "unmoved." An approving god (E) watches but is not the assassin here. (C) is the best possible answer.

46. **(B)** Although the other choices have something to do with the meaning of the poem, the "best" meaning is that death comes to everyone; it cannot be planned for nor avoided. Certainly a cruelty is indicated in the frost's action but that is not (A) God's cruelty. God is shown not to be indifferent, but in fact approving, so (C) is incorrect. The flowers being happy (D) suggests that we put human experience into plants, but this is not the poem's central theme, nor is the fact that we know winter comes each year, so (E) is likewise an idea that is in the poem but is not the central point.

47. **(B)** Note that what is required here is both a knowledge of drama as well as an awareness of qualifying terms in both the question stem and answer. You are asked what poetic drama is "best" described as, while (A) asks for a value judgment; (B) is a full description incorporating both the fact that poetic drama is comprised of poetry and performance. (C) demonstrates value judgment; (D) is too limiting; so, too, is (E).

48. **(D)** Bertolt Brecht described his work as (D) epic drama, not (B) melodrama. It was based on (A) John Gay's *The Beggar's Opera*, but this is not the most important fact. The major characteristic of *The Three Penny Opera* is that Brecht's adaptation of it corresponds with his view of what drama should be. He thought that theaters should make things strange through (E) historification, the use of material drawn from other times and places, which allowed the audience to view the performance in a detached manner. This method of alienating the audience was the most important criterion for the development of an "epic" (meaning narrative, or non-dramatic) work. Since drama is antithetical to comedy, (C) should be eliminated immediately.

49. **(A)** Existentialism, a philosophy that arose in France and Germany in the late nineteenth century, claims that "existence precedes essence" or that what one becomes is a matter of choice and not something usually called "human nature" or "essence." Essentialism (B) is thus incorrect because it is the opposite of Existentialism. Pragmatism (C) is a distinctively American philosophy that the worth of an idea is its "cash value" or power to solve a problem. Marxism (D) depends on the supposition that humans have an essence or nature, as does Platonism (E). Platonists are clear examples of Essentialism.

50. **(E)** The ancient Greeks, upon viewing the massive masonry blocks used in much Mycenean construction, believed that they could only have been placed by giants; thus they are referred to as "cyclopean" after the giant Cyclopes of Greek mythology. Although ancient Egyptian (A), Mesopotamian (B), Aztec (C), and Roman (D) methods of construction often included the use of very large, heavy stone blocks, the term *cyclopean* is never used to identify them.

51. **(A)** The *cogito* resolves Descartes' methodological doubt and establishes a firm foundation for knowledge. He does not question the basis of personal identity (B) in the way that, say, Locke does. Descartes uses a separate argument to establish the existence of God (D). He then uses his proof of God's existence to put metaphysics (C) and mathematics (E) on firm foundations. The *cogito* is the foundation for his epistemology.

52. **(C)** Through-composed form is represented by ABCDE (C). This is because new music is created for each verse. AB (A) is binary form that starts in the tonic key and may modulate before the end. This is considered an open structure. ABA (B) is ternary form in which both A sections are in the tonic and the B section modulates and contains new material. ABACA (D) is a rondo form that contains multisections. These utilize modulations with new material and return to the tonic. A form of A (E) would only contain one musical idea.

53. **(A)** Gregorian chant, often referred to as plainchant, is monophonic vocal music, which was primarily used in church. A motet (B) is a polyphonic vocal composition used in church music for two or more voices. A canon (C) is imitated polyphonic vocal composition consisting of two or more voices. An aria (D) is a vocal solo with accompaniment found in a larger composition. A fugue (E) is imitative polyphony with variations.

54. **(B)** Charles Ives mastered the technique of weaving bits of patriotic melodies within his compositions. Sousa (A) popularized patriotic marches. Bernstein (C) worked in many genres using classical and jazz elements. Stravinsky (D) explored Primitivism and tonalities. Franz Joseph Haydn (E) was a composer of the classical period.

55. **(A)** *Tristram Shandy*, written by Laurence Sterne, was sometimes bawdy, often hilarious, and demonstrated an extraordinary playfulness with the language and with concepts of space and time in storytelling. Cervantes' (B) work was amusing, but the gentleman author was Spanish. *Candy* (C) is an American bawdy novel of the 1960s not to be confused with the French novel *Candide*. *Catch-22* (D) is at least as funny as the others, but is of the same vintage as the previous novel; and (E), though possessed of an amusing title, is a Shakespearean song.

56. **(B)** Shakespeare's *Macbeth* deals with the powerful influence of guilt and conscience after the fact of an illicit deed, the king's death. *Julius Caesar* (A) deals with many political themes including ambition—but conscience does not seem prominent. *Hamlet* (C) demonstrates the restraining power of conscience—even in the face of seeking revenge for a vile act. The fantasy (D) and the comedy (E) are artful treatments of happier themes.

57. **(D)** Hawthorne's famous work is well known for its personification of the fading fortunes of the Pyncheon family in the famous seven gabled structure still to be visited in Salem, Massachusetts. The imploding and collapse of the structure at the end of the novel represents the end of the family that had been cursed during the witchcraft trials 150 years before. (A) of course, is a

delightful children's book. (B), by Dos Passos, is a twentieth century description of the banking family. William Carlos Williams wrote the brief poem (C); and (E) was the first piece of fiction published by Thomas Wolfe, but does not deal with the subject in question.

58. **(C)**   The 1940 book *The Oxbow Incident* deals with a hanging in the fictional Western town of Bridger's Wells. While Realism was a nineteenth century movement, Clark employs Realistic techniques—accurate usage of concrete details to raise interest or create an effect—in relating his compelling story. Twain's famous story (A) had realistic elements in it, but was written during the nineteenth century—though only in one section can he be said to deal with the Wild West. Crane's work (B) was realistic and was about the Wild West, but was a short story also written in the nineteenth century. Bierce's tale (D)—though again in a similar tradition, and while it also deals with a hanging—also takes place during the Civil War.

59. **(C)**   Walt Whitman's poetry presented American critics with a new American voice: one not bounded by the constraints of rhyme schemes and meter. His long listing of examples of American characters and prototypes are so detailed that they provide us with an accurate picture of the mid-nineteenth century nation of Whitman's day. The Englishman Pope (A) does not qualify for reason of nationality alone. Clemens (B) is the novelist Mark Twain's real name. Emily Dickinson (D) is known for short, rhyming verse, and Anne Bradstreet (E)—perhaps our first American poet—wrote in traditional rhyme schemes and meter.

60. **(C)**   Donatello, one of the most representative sculptors of the early Renaissance, created the equestrian statue of Gattamelta, his first from Padua. It expresses strength, not lightness and motion or stability, and completely denies any suggestion of physical decay. Additionally, this sculpture does not allude in any specific way to moral fortitude.

61. **(E)**   This city view by the French Impressionist Camille Pissarro is one of many in which the artist painted the scenes he saw beneath his second- or third-story Paris hotel windows. The resulting composition lacks not only a central focal point, but any single focal point at all; likewise, the only architecture visible does not dominate the scene, but, rather, acts as incidental local detail. The anonymous figures in the crowds below the artist's window share this lack of focus: they are busy in normal daily activity, without the least suggestion of drama. Finally, the idea that this scene was recorded from the window of a train lacks evidence: the scene is distinctly urban, not rural, and it is unlikely that a train would either pass through the crowded centers of a city or that it would be elevated to this height.

62. **(C)**   In the work pictured, the American sculptor David Smith used power tools to cut, weld, and polish industrial-strength steel to create an ensemble in which the heavy, cubic forms balance in arrested motion. The sculptor obviously neither modelled the materials with his hands nor poured them into a mold: these forms have a rigid, machinelike, technological perfection to them and lack any such irregularities as those resulting from the molding action of human fingers. This same cubic perfection, and the gleaming, reflective surfaces, refute the idea of chisel work as well. And, finally, the erroneous suggestion that the artist merely joined ready-made industrial forms as he found them stems from this same sense of rigid, cubic perfection in the work's individual components.

63. **(A)** The seventeenth century Japanese ink-on-paper scroll painting shown in the example relies almost exclusively on the qualities of line to convey the graceful forms of two leaping deer. Gradations of tone are unimportant here, since the images are defined by black line on white, and volume, too, is absent, since these forms show no shading or modulation of tone. Perspective is not an issue here since this drawing does not attempt to reproduce a third dimension.

64. **(D)** The arch, whether rounded or pointed, is completely absent from the building pictured in the example, even though the alternating use of windows with rounded pediments in the lower story seems to suggest the presence of arches. Otherwise, all of the other features listed in the answer choices do help regularize the design of this seventeenth century English Renaissance structure.

65. **(D)** You may not have come across this poem by William Blake so you need to look at the language and the topic. Blake often writes about the ugliness and horror of the Industrial Revolution; the topic of child labor gives you an immediate clue. Shakespeare (A), Milton (B), and Chaucer (C) may be familiar, so you can see the difference in their rhyme schemes and language. This rhyme and meter suggest a more modern style than the older writers. Hardy (E) often uses a similar simple rhyme and rhythm but his topics were more of fate and destiny, war and lost loves. By such a process of elimination, you will come to (D) as the correct answer.

66. **(A)** The word *weep!* is cleverly used because it does suggest the child's weeping but the meaning of the line carries on from the opening line when he was sold before he could clearly say the chimney sweeper's cry for business: "Sweep! Sweep!"—not because of neglect (B), but because he is so young he still lisps on the "s" sound. The other suggestions all deal with emotions conjured up by the child's plight—of course he is upset at being sold (C); "the your" pronoun does make for guilt (D) but you are looking for the reason the poet chose this word, not the "message" of the poem. Of course he hates cleaning chimneys (E), but analyze the word's usage in the line itself and the best answer is (A).

67. **(C)** The epic is long and tells of heroes engaged in battles and actions involving valor. Look at the rhyme scheme and analyze. There are no rhyming couplets (A), epics are not all written in Latin (B), nor by Virgil (D), and although death (E) is usually featured, epics are not just about death.

68. **(E)** If you do not know *Paradise Lost* look at the context—the garden idea, the noble couple made in God's image. Dante would be describing Hell so (A) is incorrect. Virgil (B) deals with family and honor in Latinate verse; *The Iliad* (C) deals with battles and the Greek gods; and *The Arabian Nights* (D) tells fantastic stories, so none of these apply.

69. **(D)** The keyword here is viewpoint—not the one writing the poem or telling the main story. Even if you do not know *Paradise Lost*, you will no doubt have heard of the fiend—place that fiend in a garden and the answer is Satan; not Faust (A) which is another story; not God (B)—the fiend is watching God's creation; not Scheherazade (C) who tells of magical things, not people in a garden; and not Dante (E) who watches fiends in hell—he is not a fiend himself.

70. **(C)** The situation in the Garden is idyllic; the couple is naked—all such signs point to before the Fall. The references to God and "the image of their Maker" eliminate both (A) and (B); the fiend is not a Homeric character, so (D) is incorrect; as stated, the idyllic setting indicates that this is before the Fall, so (E) is also incorrect.

71. **(E)** The last three lines need to be carefully equated with each of the options: equality is not possible if she sees God in the man (A); women are not just made for beauty but softness and grace (B); and (C) and (D) tell only half the meaning of the lines.

72. **(A)** *The Wild Duck* is the correct answer. *Oedipus* (B) is also a play about a man who kills his father and blinds himself. In *The Wild Duck* Gregers returns home to find that Gina, who was once a maid in his family, is now married to Hjalmar. Gregers believes that Gina was impregnated by his father, Old Werle, who is slowly losing his eyesight. Gregers believes that Gina and Hjalmar's marriage is based on a lie. Old Werle's diminished eyesight may be read symbolically, but it does not hold the same significance as Oedipus' blinding. The eyesight motif joins *The Wild Duck* and *Oedipus* and makes it easier to eliminate the other three answer choices. Both Sophocles and Euripides wrote plays they titled *Electra;* Sophocles also wrote *Antigone* and Euripides, *Andromache.* Basically, these answers are meant to confuse; therefore, (C), (D), and (E) should be eliminated immediately.

73. **(C)** In *Tartuffe*, Orgon is rich, middle class, and middle-aged. He is duped by Tartuffe, who assumes a mask of religious piety. The answer is (C). This question is testing your ability to recognize the situation of each play. For example, (A) is too vague, as the downfall of a king is a frequent theme in plays. (B) is also vague, as are (D) and (E).

74. **(B)** A multi-storied Roman apartment block (B) is the correct answer. A Greek public meeting square (A) is called an *agora;* the western portion of a Carolingian church (C) is referred to as a *westwerk.* A Greek cross-plan (D) is that of a centrally planned church whose four arms are all of equal length. A vertical groove on the surface of a column (E) is called a *flute.*

75. **(A)** Berkeley held, in his famous dictum, that only ideas are real. Hence, the view expressed is known as Idealism (A). Pragmatism (B) is the view that ideas which work should be believed true. Empiricism (C) and Rationalism (D) are broad tendencies to answer a question about the source of knowledge either as in experience or in the mind itself. Phenomenology (E) is a position in metaphysics that takes a special view of experience.

76. **(A)** Charlie Parker (A) was nicknamed "Bird" due to his rapid alto saxophone Bebop figures. John Coltrane (B) was a master of the tenor and soprano saxophone. Dizzy Gillespie (C) was a master of the trumpet. Paul Desmond (D) was the alto saxophonist in the Dave Brubeck Quartet, which played classical jazz styles. Stan Getz (E) was a tenor saxophonist of the "cool" jazz style.

77. **(C)** John Coltrane (C) made a lasting impact on the jazz scene with his album *Giant Steps*. Charlie Parker (A) played alto, not tenor saxophone, and performed such works as "Ko-ko" and "YardBird Suite." Stan Getz (B) is the tenor saxophone player famous for his work on "The Girl from Ipanema." Coleman Hawkins (D) is considered the father of jazz tenor saxophone. Ornette Coleman (E) experimented with "free jazz" on the alto saxophone.

78. **(B)** "Rodeo" (B) is the result of a collaboration between Aaron Copland and Agnes de Mille that incorporated music with dance. "West Side Story" (A), a musical by Leonard Bernstein, is a modern-day version of "Romeo and Juliet." "Porgy and Bess" (C) is an opera with music by George Gershwin, portraying the struggles of black Americans in the South. "The Phantom

of the Opera" (D) is a novel by Gaston LeRoux that has been adapted for film, stage, and, most recently, a Broadway musical. "Salome" (E) was a composition of Strauss.

79. **(D)** *Tom Jones* (D), Henry Fielding's (1707–1754) wonderful and raucous novel, is the only one here both written in and about the eighteenth century. Tom's travels take him from the seat of manorial propriety to the very bawdiest of tumbletown inns. Known for its wanton character-ization and surprising turns of plot, it is considered by many to be one of the most picturesque of the Picaresque novels (defined as the "life story of a rascal of low degree . . . consisting of a series of thrilling incidents"). Dickens' work (A) is about England in the following century, as are Brontë's *Jane Eyre* (C) and George Eliot's *Silas Marner* (E). *Moby Dick* (B) is an American work by Melville.

80. **(D)** Oscar Wilde's famous work is in the well-known tradition of the Decadents—a group of writers in the late nineteenth and early twentieth century in France, England, and America. One of their major precepts was that the finest beauty was that of dying or deteriorating things. Thus, Dorian—a character of low virtues—ages grotesquely and supernaturally on a canvas, while the actual person seems to be forever young. The Mariner (A) may be aging, but the lengthy roman-tic poem is not in the Decadent tradition, nor written at that time. Fielding's work (C) may be about decadence, but was written 100 years earlier than the movement. The same might be said about Lawrence's mid-twentieth century work (B), and Joyce's *Dubliners* (E), which is even less a possibility.

81. **(A)** Ruskin in *Modern Painters* (A) actually introduced the phrase "pathetic fallacy" to denote a tendency of some poets and writers to credit nature with the emotions of human beings. Nowa-days it has come to mean writing that is false in its emotionalism—even if the topic considered is not nature. Emerson's work (B) is about the importance and reality of the natural world. Shakespeare's comedy (C) has nothing whatsoever to do with the topic, except that its plot does involve deception and falseness. Lodge's 1590 work (D) is considered a pastoral romance—in that it sets forth a romance in a beautiful natural setting. Johnson's *Dictionary* (E) could not have listed the term, as it was published over 50 years before Ruskin invented it.

82. **(E)** Dickens' *David Copperfield* is one of his many works that present an opposing argument to Utilitarianism—the powerful argument from the former century that defined utility in gov-ernment and society as "the greatest happiness for the greatest number." Eliot's *Middlemarch* world (A) is the antithesis—as is James' *Washington Square* (D). Dreiser (B) does write about the seedier side of nineteenth century American life, but does not seem to "take sides" as far as the economic system itself is concerned. *Billy Budd* (C), of course, is an adventure novel by Melville.

83. **(D)** While all of the writers suggested might claim Celtic origins, James Macpherson, the eighteenth century composer of the poems "Fingal" (1762), and "Temora" (1763), is the most likely candidate. Macpherson invented, recorded, and reinterpreted Gaelic pieces preserved in the Scottish Highlands and published translations of the great early Celtic poet Ossian. His works, along with those of Thomas Gray, influenced many minor poets of the late eighteenth century. Joyce (A) and Yeats (E) were Irishmen of the twentieth century. O'Hara (B) and Don-leavy (C) are contemporary American writers.

84. **(D)**   The late eighteenth century Neo-Classical painting shown in the example illustrates an episode from ancient Roman legend and attempts to simulate the static, balanced, monumental character of much Classical relief sculpture. The men in the main figure group, therefore, are represented in statuesque, absolutely motionless poses, and the correct answer choice here is (D). The compositional devices listed in all of the other answer choices are important to the painting. The figures stand within a shallow pictorial space, which is marked off by the arches in the background; these arches also serve to focus the man in the center. This shallow space, however, is modified somewhat by the checkerboard floor, which creates a slight perspective recession into the background and makes the figures' space seem logical and convincing. The strong highlighting on the foreground figures accentuates their static, sculptural quality, even as it pulls them to the absolute front of the picture. The intersecting lines of arms and swords establish the central focal point of the composition.

85. **(A)**   This question asks you to consider both geographical proximity and some general characteristics of Eastern architecture in order to logically determine who would have the most direct influence on Japanese style. Of the answer choices, Greece and Nigeria fall well outside the Asian sphere both in distance and in building styles, while Easter Island, a Pacific site, is not known for a distinctive native architecture. Indonesian temple buildings may share something of the exotic, heavily ornamented character of the structure pictured but the most representative Indonesian buildings are both much larger and are constructed of stone. The seventh century building pictured, in fact, illustrates the strong dependence of Japan on the arts of China. The Chinese character of the structure is visible in the distinctive silhouette of the roof, with its long sweeping pitch and upturned corners in the heavy tiled roof, and in the wealth of elaborate brackets which support the dramatically projecting eaves.

86. **(A)**   Three of the answer choices—(A), (C), and (D)—show groups of figures engaged in activities which might be interpreted as ceremonial. Choice (C) illustrated a column of soldiers marching across the midsection of a ceramic vessel; while they may be marching in a ceremonial function such as a parade or assembly, they are most likely intended to be shown advancing into battle, and, in any case, their primary function on this vase is decorative. Choice (D) shows figures engaged in music-making activities in formally arranged groups, but here, too, the illustrations serve the secondary purpose of amplifying the accompanying text. Only answer choice (A), an ancient Persian relief sculpture, uses a rigidly schematized, formal composition and style to record an actual ceremonial event. Here, the clear-cut, well-defined figures are strictly arranged in three horizontal tiers, and each carries an accessory or attribute which identifies his role within this state occasion.

87. **(C)**   Only answer choices (A) and (C) repeat the simplified forms of the human figure within a sculptural or ceramic context. Choice (A) appears to continually repeat a series of nearly identical figures arranged on three horizontal levels, but close inspection reveals several types of figures here, each marked by a variety of detail in posture, costume, accessories, and so on. Further, the figures are sculpted in a softly rounded, convincing style. The figures in choice (C), in contrast, are grouped in a horizontal sequence which appears to show variety and movement; close examination, however, shows that the artist here has simply repeated figures whose clothing, weapons, postures, positions, and facial features are identical. While this serves

to illustrate an anonymous mass of marching soldiers, it is even more important in helping the group of figures fit neatly, conveniently, and decoratively into its allotted space on the round "belly" of the vase.

88. **(D)** Calligraphy, or "fine writing," implies a two-dimensional or graphic format. Three of the possible answer choices—(A), (B), and (E)—are forms of sculpture or sculptural relief, and therefore contain no drawn, calligraphic elements. Choice (C) presents a flat, two-dimensional illustration painted in black and white and minimal color. However, the images here are rigidly formalized and static, and display none of the rhythmic curves or flourishes of artistic penmanship. Only choice (D), a ninth century manuscript illustration, links calligraphy with figure drawing in the same rhythmic, linear style. In this illustration of the Bible's Psalm 150, the text written in ink above accompanies the figures below. Each is drawn in the same bold, agitated black-and-white line, with a sketchy spontaneity that creates an animated, nervous tension.

89. **(A)** If you familiarize yourself with *The Iliad* and *The Odyssey*, you will see how Homer uses the simile with the long-extended idea clinched at the end—look out for the words *such* or *so* which signal the last clause of the simile. An extended metaphor (B) is close except that the metaphor never has the signal words *as when*, *as if*, or *like* (B); (C) is not an option as the verse is "free form" rather than rhymed couplets; the other options mix terms. Be on the lookout for terms that sound reasonable but, upon analysis, are gibberish.

90. **(D)** This is a case of working your way through the simile until you come to the signal word *such* which gives the image of the watchfires. The stars are not compared to hills (A), shepherds (B), rivers (C), or ships (E), so these are all incorrect choices.

91. **(A)** Again, the more familiar you become with Homer, the more you will see touches like this to humanize the lofty, godlike themes and characters, so the answer is (A). If this had been a Medieval English piece, humor of a coarse, ribald kind, especially in the drama, might have been the answer, but there is no humor here (B). Depth in Homer comes from the poetry itself rather than the people who feature in the poetry (C). Gladness (D) takes a back seat to the power of the simile and in any poetry shepherds never glamorize (E)!

92. **(E)** Questions such as these rely on identification of famous lines; read through anthologies and see the often repeated poems. If you do not recognize Emily Dickinson (the use of the long dash often gives her away—it is one of her "trademarks"), work your way through and eliminate. Obviously this is not Chaucerian, as the language is stark and modern (A); nor is the passage epic in its voice or theme: think of lofty topics and rhythm and rhyme—this is conversational and choppy in its rhythm (B). Wordsworth is taught in most high-school poetry classes and this opening line is much quoted—even if you do not recall the poem itself, you might recall that Wordsworth was not a woman (the Romantic males dominated the field of poetry), so the answer cannot be (C). The jar and Tennessee is unique and should immediately make you think of one of the most famous modern male American poets, Wallace Stevens, so (D) is incorrect.

93. **(A)** This is the famous opening line of *The Canterbury Tales*; it would be worth looking over the poem (this is in translation from the middle English language), as Chaucer is said to be the "father of English poetry." If you do not recognize the lines, look again at each of the answers

and, as for the previous explanation, eliminate. (B) sounds too modern and conversational, as does (C) and (E), so eliminate both those on voice alone. Tennessee (D) did not exist in Chaucer's time and is definitely not the answer.

94. **(C)** Even if you do not recognize Wordsworth, the idea of a love of nature would clue you to the Romantics who looked upon nature as a rejuvenating force for the human spirit. You are working your way through elimination, narrowing down your field through language and topic, so none of the other possibilities apply.

95. **(B)** If you recognize the opening of *Paradise Lost*, this is straightforward; if not, think of epics that you have read with the lofty, heroic subjects—none of the others fit this category.

96. **(D)** is the correct answer. In your reading, be very aware of opening and closing lines in whatever genre. Kafka's famous opener from *Metamorphosis* sets symbol and theme for the entire work. All the other possibilities involve striking writers, but Genet and Ionesco are primarily playwrights, and Sartre and Tolstoy have less dramatic starting points.

97. **(D)** is the correct answer. (A) refers to the coat of arms representing royal presence; (B) should be eliminated immediately because it is too vague; the same is true of (C). While (E) Oedipus did go into exile, he was not sacrificed for the redemption of the tribe.

98. **(B)** The basilica, a large, hall-like building with a minimum of internal supporting members, served a variety of public functions in the Roman era and was designed to accommodate large crowds. The basilican plan was thus an appropriate building type to contain large numbers of Christian worshippers. Roman temples (A) were not designed to regulate crowds, and, with their overt pagan associations, were not favored for use within a Christian context. Roman baths (C) consisted of several bathing rooms and facilities, and did not adhere to a specific type of plan. A Roman forum (D) is an open air, public city square, not a building type. A Roman villa (E) is a private domestic dwelling, composed of multiple rooms and courtyards, the design of which is inappropriate for the containment and regulation of communal worship.

99. **(E)** Dance began with the savage hunters (E). Religious groups (A), Egyptians (B), Greeks (C), and Romans (D) succeeded the savage hunters and created their own style of dance for self-expression, religious and political rituals, and entertainment.

100. **(A)** The fallacy of composition (A) consists in thinking that what is true of the parts of some-thing must be true of the whole composed by those parts. The fallacy of division (B) is just the opposite: what is true of the whole is incorrectly reasoned to be true of the parts. The slippery slope fallacy (C) is committed when one thinks small differences never add up to a significant difference, while the *ad hominem* fallacy (D) involves personal attacks. The fallacy of ignorance (E) is committed when one reasons that because something has not been proven false, it is true.

101. **(B)** Percy Grainger wrote extensively for wind ensemble. Most of his compositions were based on folk songs such as "Country Gardens" and "Ye Banks and Braes o' Bonnie Doon." Sousa (A) composed primarily for military band. Beethoven (C) composed many works, includ-ing symphonies for orchestra and piano concertos. Strauss (D) is famous for his tone poems. Franz Joseph Haydn (E) composed for the orchestra.

102. **(B)** The key signature of this excerpt is F major. It contains a B flat, which can be determined by using the Circle of Fifths and proceeding counterclockwise from C to the scale with one flat, F. The B flat scale (A) contains B flat and E flat. The key of C (C) contains no flats or sharps. The key of D (D) contains an F sharp and a C sharp. The key signature of A major (E) contains an F#, C#, and G#.

103. **(D)** The time signature of this excerpt should be $\frac{3}{4}$. The total number of beats in each measure is three, and a quarter note would equal one beat. A time signature of $\frac{4}{4}$ (A) would require four beats in each measure. A time signature of $\frac{2}{4}$ (B) would require two beats in each measure. A time signature of $\frac{6}{8}$ (C) would have six beats in each measure. A time signature of $\frac{12}{8}$ (E) would have 12 beats in each measure.

104. **(C)** The excerpt is divided into three measures. The measures are divided by the number of beats found in each and marked by a vertical line through the staff. One measure (A), two measures (B), and zero measures (D) are incorrect. Five measures (E) cannot be calculated from the material presented.

105. **(D)** The arrow is pointing at the repeat sign. This directs the musician to repeat the selection. The key signature (A) is the B flat symbol. The clef sign (B) is the G clef. The double bar (C) is a symbol which denotes the end of the music. The time signature (E) is not in the figure, but would be $\frac{4}{4}$.

106. **(C)** Philip Roth's *Goodbye Columbus* (C) was a big literary hit in the late 1950s and was both part of and ushered in the age of the American Ethnic novelist. James' (A) novel concerns a pre-"recent" immigrant America of 100 years ago. Hawthorne's work (E) concerns the earliest Pilgrim immigrants, but ethnic Pilgrim has long been recognized as "ruling class standard." Updike's novels (D) of midwest suburbia do not involve "ethnics" so much as the descendants of Hawthorne's folk—and Poe's famous short story (B) takes place in Italy, not America.

107. **(C)** Alexis de Tocqueville's *Letters From an American Farmer* (C) is considered one of the most perceptive and accurate portraits of the newly independent American nation. The Frenchman traveled widely and recorded his observations and perceptions. Lewis and Clark (A), the famed adventurers, explored the uninhabited West under orders from President Thomas Jefferson. Sinclair Lewis' novel (B) deals with the early decades of this century. Cooper's *Mohicans* (D) describes the frontier of New York State 200 years ago. Smith's *Diary* (E) predates the establishment of the United States by almost 200 years.

108. **(E)** Ralph Ellison's powerful novel defined for America of the 1950s the second-class status of African-Americans and is still referred to as a great work of literature that galvanized a nation at the height of the battle for civil rights. Faulkner's work (A), while it may have a seemingly appropriate title, does not deal with this subject—neither does Wharton's (B), about a white man in New England. Conrad's (C) powerful novel deals with Africa, and Kafka's (D) strange story superficially deals with a man's transformation into a bug.

109. **(A)** *Journey to the Center of the Earth* (A) by Jules Verne has a remarkable history. Though its subject deals with a phenomenon—a hollow Earth—that apparently does not exist, the description it gives of Iceland is so accurate that travelers there were urged to take the book with them

well into the 1950s. Stevenson's island (B) is invented, as is Defoe's (C). Verne's other work here (D) is not focused in its description of a single spot. Swift's "travel" novel (E) is not one at all, but rather a well-known political satire.

110. **(B)** Sir Walter Scott's famous nineteenth century romance *Ivanhoe* (B) deals with the thirteenth century. Until recently, this period was thought of as the flower of the Middle Ages, replete with knights in shining armor and damsels in distress. Eliot's work (A) is a picture of manorial England in the nineteenth century and Poe's (C) of a formerly wealthy family in America at approximately the same time. King's terrifying book (D) is modern and also American, as is West's hilarious short novel (E).

111. **(C)** Like many Victorian poets, Matthew Arnold venerated the works of Wordsworth (C). In Arnold's preface to the "Poems" of 1853, he pleads for poets to turn to the epic or drama—as epitomized, perhaps, by Wordsworth in lyrical ballads such as "The Ruined Cottage." The major problems with the other possible answers here is one of time sequence. Hemingway and Eliot (A) are modern, not Victorian. Tennyson and Browning (B) are Victorian contemporaries, as are Rossetti and Browning (D). Wordsworth and Scott (E) are Romantic contemporaries.

112. **(A)** In *The Duke and the Dauphin* (A), Twain relates the story of a bogus pretender to the French throne and his accompli who perform what they hope will pass as Shakespeare to frontier audiences. Initially taken by the idea, the settlers get wise to their scam and chase them out of town. The famous fence painting scene (B) took place in *Tom Sawyer*. Huck's escape from Pap (C) does not prove the quote; neither does Jim seeking freedom (D). At the end of the famous novel, Huck "lights out for the territories" (E). The West certainly represented a future of promise to Huck and Twain, but again, clearly does not prove the point.

113. **(C)** In the example shown, the *Bull's Head* of 1943, the Spanish artist Pablo Picasso joined a bicycle seat and a set of handlebars in a clever, unexpected combination to produce a sculptural analogy to an actual bull. Thus, the artist was concerned here with form and substance, not with a contrast of line and tone and, even though the resulting artwork resembles a hat- or coat-rack the sculptor's first purpose was not to produce a functional device. Likewise, even though the bull has mythological connotations and figures prominently in many ancient religions, the artist was intent not on creating a religious symbol, but in exploring the visual unity of common objects brought together in new ways. The result is a strictly visual, sculptural effect, and in no way provides a metaphor for human experience.

114. **(B)** Three of the answer choices—(A), (C), and (E)—illustrate Impressionist paintings, which tend to suppress or eliminate secondary or decorative detail in the search for a quick, spontaneous, and optically "true" impression of the subject. None can be said to concentrate on details pointedly. Choice (D) shows a work of exhaustive detail, in which each tree branch, leaf, and grass stem, and the details and textures of clothing, stand out with stark realism. The main figure subject, however, far from merging into the background detail, is dramatically set off against it, especially in the face, neck, and arms. Only choice (B), by the American James MacNeill Whistler, accentuates decorative detail at the expense of the subject. In this case, the details of tiny flowers running up the back of the woman's dress connect visually to the delicate floral details

in the wallpaper to the left, while the pale form of the woman's figure shades and merges into the background and almost reduces her to a flat pattern.

115. **(C)** Two of the answer choices crop, or cut off, the main subject, much as the arbitrary framing of a photograph might do. Choice (E), a study of two women and a child by the American Impressionist Mary Cassatt, pulls the figures to the very front of the picture plane, and cuts them off abruptly at the bottom edge and right side of the picture. The result seems to be an unposed, accidental image produced by a moment's glance. These figures, however, are firmly centered within the picture's borders, with a definite focal point in the image of the child with the book at center. Choice (C), by contrast, presents an extremely random composition in which the human subject is so far off-center and so dramatically cropped that she barely retains pictorial "presence" in the composition. This picture by the French Impressionist Edgar Degas produces an effect of seemingly unplanned, immediate realism which resembles a casually aimed photographic snapshot.

116. **(D)** Only two of the answer choices, (C) and (D), create their desired effect by positioning the primary subject noticeably off-center, thereby undermining the picture's formal visual balance. Choice (C), by the French painter Degas, shows a woman seated at a table on which rests an enormous bouquet of flowers. Even though the woman, apparently the main subject or sitter, glances out of the picture to the right and invites the viewer's gaze to follow, the huge bunch of flowers dominates the picture and calls the viewer's eye continually back to the painting's focal center. Answer choice (D), however, by the French Realist Bastien-Lepage, clearly positions the primary subject off-center, as she stares and steps to the right with her arm outstretched. The figure seems to have just left the empty center of the picture and is about to exit the painting at the right. Her glance, her pose, and her position create a strongly directional thrust which draws the viewer's eye out of the picture as the figure moves.

117. **(E)** Art Nouveau is distinguished by the extensive use of curvilinear, decorative details of interior design. Post-Modernism (B) is a later period in the history of architecture, and is not defined by such decorative elements. Neo-Classicism (C), a nineteenth century era of architecture, is charcterized by the use of classical Greek and Roman architectural details, which are more austere in nature. Post-Impressionism (D) and surrealism (A) are movements in painting that have no equivalents in the history of architectural design.

118. **(C)** The sheer verticality of the Reims Cathedral (ca. 1211–1260) twin towers, the overall upward movement, and the multitude of pinnacles are identifying characteristics of the Gothic style and would most clearly set Reims apart from the most closely related structure in this group, St. Peter's (D), a work of the late Renaissance in Rome. (A) The Taj Mahal, Agra, India (1630–1648), is incorrect because it is the most famous mausoleum of Islamic architecture. (B) The Parthenon, Acropolis, Athens (448–432 B.C.) is incorrect because it represents the classical phase of Greek architecture. (D) St. Peter's, Rome (1546–1564), by Michelangelo is incorrect because it is an example of the colossal order in Renaissance architecture. It has a symmetrical plan crowned by a central dome, very different from the longitudinal emphasis of the Gothic cathedral. St. Peter's basilica lacks the exterior ornamentation of Reims, but its monumental dome creates a dramatic exterior profile.

119. **(A)** The Taj Mahal was built by Shah Jahan, one of the Moslem rulers of India, as a home for his wife. She died before it was finished and so in its completion the Taj Mahal became a memorial to her. (B) is incorrect because the Parthenon has served as a place of worship for four different faiths. It was originally built by the Greeks to honor the Goddess Athena. In Christian times it became the first Byzantine church, then a Catholic cathedral, and, finally, under Turkish rule, a mosque. (C) is incorrect because the Reims Cathedral is a Catholic church. (D) is incorrect because St. Peter's is a Roman Catholic church. (E) is incorrect because (A) was not constructed as a place of worship.

120. **(C)** This is the short 17 syllable form called haiku (C) that is highly evocative. Hyperbole (A) is characterized by exaggeration, which is not present. Odes (B) honor or exalt a specific person or subject, also not present. An epigram (D) is usually a witty expression of a particular idea. A doggerel (E) describes loose, inferior verse.

121. **(B)** If you are not aware of the original language of the form, start discounting the others—French and Chinese would be more symbolic; British would not be so succinct and evocative; Persian would be on topics of love or religion.

122. **(D)** If you are not aware of the term *bathos*, it is a useful one to learn—Pope uses it frequently to attain humor. Eliminate the other terms by what you know: (A) is hyperbole; (B) is crescendo; (C) is anticlimax; and (E) is not related to the question. Analyze that a climax suggests a building toward or upward.

123. **(E)** As well as learning meter, rhyme, and rhythm, look into what poets themselves say about poetry. Keats had a lot to say, especially about the ways to read and the use of the imagination. Wordsworth and Coleridge did as well, but they frequently tied their comments into poetry being of and for the common man: this phrase often bemuses the "average" man so (C) is incorrect. T. S. Eliot wrote copiously on the art of writing poetry but his comments are not so easily captured in a phrase, except perhaps "objective correlative," but this phrase can only be fit into a long explanation—definitely not (B). If you are not aware of the term, think of the sorts of poetry the others write: Keats is the only one here who wants the mystery (of something like the "Grecian Urn" for example); neither William Carlos Williams nor e. e. cummings wanted mystery, preferring to have cryptic to-the-point statements about their art, so clearly neither (A) nor (D) are correct.

124. **(A)** is the correct answer. Though you may disagree with the quotation, you must make your selection based on the quotation. *A Midsummer Night's Dream* (B) is a comedy. *Oedipus* (C) is, indeed, a tragedy, but it does not fit the requirements for tragedy as established in the quotation. *Oedipus the King* is not completed by a death. Jocasta commits suicide, but Oedipus, the central character, remains within the walls of the city for many years before he is exiled. *Oedipus the King* is thus eliminated on the basis of this argument. Shakespeare's *The Tempest* (D) and Menander's *The Bad-Tempered Man* (E) should also be eliminated because both are comedies.

125. **(E)** is the correct answer. Anagnorisis means recognition or discovery. Therefore, when the hero's understanding of the true nature of the situation and the self is evident in drama or fiction, then this is an example of Anagnorisis. As a complete definition, this differs from (A), which is vague.

126. **(C)** is the correct answer. After the idealistic Brutus tells the people that he participated in Caesar's murder because he loved Rome more, he and the other conspirators make the mistake of allowing the wily Mark Antony to speak. Antony must aid the public or rabble in understanding the villainy of the murder of Caesar, no matter the motivation. Thus, the statement he makes is ironic as what he wishes to do is arouse the people to act against Caesar's murderers.

127. **(E)** is the correct answer. Othello's great weakness is his inability to recognize Iago's villainy and Desdemona's innocence. Iago is able to convince Othello that Desdemona is not the "chaste and heavenly true" wife she appears to be. Not until after he kills Desdemona does Othello understand the true nature of the situation and his own weakness.

128. **(A)** is the correct answer. Though all of the characters listed are from plays by Shakespeare, Dane and Denmark are the contextual clues here. One who comes from or resides in Denmark is called a Dane.

129. **(B)** Oculus, meaning "eye," refers to the round opening in the dome, which is without glass and thus open to the sky. The terms window (A), splayed window (C), and stained-glass window (D) are all defined as wall openings that are glazed in some form, which is not applicable here. A clerestory (E) refers to the upper portion of a building whose walls are pierced with windows and which emits light to the remainder of the building below; this type of construction refers to fenestrated walls only.

130. **(B)** The basic rules to jazz dance are parallel feet, flat-foot steps, undulating torso, body isolation, and syncopated rhythms. Beledi dance (abdominal dance) (A), danse mora (Flamenco dance) (C), tap dance (D), and country dance (E) each have their own different specific rules.

131. **(A)** Occam's Razor (A) contends that one should not multiply entities beyond necessity: since both theories are equally powerful, choose the simpler one. The Principle of Plenitude (B) says that the universe contains as many types of things as possible. The Open Question Argument (C) applies to claims about the nature of goodness, not theories in general. The Underdetermination Principle (D) involves the notion that a given set of facts is compatible with many theories. Scientific Realism (E) is the view that the entities postulated by science actually exist.

132. **(D)** Jane Austen's *Pride and Prejudice* is the source of this quote. The word *pride*, found in both the quote and the title, should give you a clue to the correct answer, even if you have not read these books. Austen's *Emma* (B) and Margaret Mitchell's *Gone with the Wind* (C) also deal with the issues of pride and vanity, although to a lesser extent than does *Pride and Prejudice*. However, neither of these is the source of the quote. In addition, Mitchell's novel, although set in the nineteenth century, was written in 1936. George Eliot's *Silas Marner* (A), written in 1861, is a story of an old linen-weaver and his adopted daughter. Jonathan Swift's *Gulliver's Travels* (E) describes the four voyages of Lemuel Gulliver; it was written in the 1720s.

133. **(A)** A trumpet can play different notes by pressing a valve down. A trumpet has three valves that, when combined in different prescribed combinations, help produce various notes. Violins and pianos use strings (B) to produce sound. By covering and uncovering holes (C), the clarinet can change notes. Saxophones use octave keys (D) to change octaves. Trombones use a slide (E) to change pitches.

134. **(A)**   The hemiola (A) is a rhythmic term that is used to define three notes of a given value occupying the space of two notes of the same value. It is also referred to as three against two. A paradiddle (B) is a percussion roll that follows a pattern such as RLRR LRLL. A fermata, [art] (C), directs a musician to hold the note until the conductor cuts it off. A crescendo, < (D), indicates to increase in volume. A glissando (E) is sliding through the pitches quickly.

135. **(A)**   The C in measure 1 is sharp because the accidental makes it sharp. This accidental affects all C's in the given measure. As a result, the C in measure 2 is C natural (A) because there are no accidentals before the note. Consequently, the C is not sharp (B), flat (C), or a B (D). A D would be located on the fourth line, so choice (E) is incorrect.

136. **(A)**   The bass clef is also referred to as the F clef (A). The symbol locates F below middle C, which is the fourth line. The G clef (B) and treble clef (D) locate the G above middle C. The tenor clef (C) is used for cello, bassoon, and trombone to locate middle C. The alto clef (E) is used primarily by the viola.

137. **(D)**   Catton's work about the surrender of Lee at Appomattox stands as one of the great Civil War accounts, though it was written almost 100 years after the incident. The temptation here is to respond with Crane's work (E), but *Red Badge* was written during the nineteenth century. Mailer's war novel (C) concerned WW II in the Pacific, as did Wouk's novel (B). That leaves Hoover's anti-Communist screed (A) written during the 1950s.

138. **(B)**   Albee's 1960 popular play was made into a movie, starring Richard Burton and Elizabeth Taylor as the university professor and his wife, who display their troubled marriage to a young faculty couple who they had invited to their home for a visit. Albee's *American Dream* (C) does not concern itself with this subject matter. Miller's work (E) concerns longshoremen and immigrants in Red Hook, Brooklyn. Neil Simon's reflective comedy (D) also relates the experience of growing up in a distinctly blue collar, immigrant world. (A) is a medieval play.

139. **(D)**   Pepys' diary, written during the restoration of the Stuarts and Charles II in 1660, is still compelling material, especially his account of the Great Fire of London. Many critics consider that Pepys pioneered the form as literature, though he was not the first by any means to keep a diary. The time factor alone eliminates from consideration the satirists Swift (E) and Sterne (B), who wrote in the 1700s. O. E. Rolvaag (C) is a twentieth century Swedish novelist. Sir Laurence (A), of course, is the recent star of stage, screen, and Shakespeare.

140. **(C)**   Ralph Waldo Emerson, Unitarian minister, writer, and philosopher, is generally considered the chief promoter of Transcendentalism. His influence was widely felt—on no less a personage than Henry David Thoreau (D)—with whom, eventually, Emerson had a falling out due to the inappropriate attentions Thoreau was said to have paid to Emerson's wife. Jonathan Edwards (A) was a New England minister of the early 1700s. Pitt (B) was a British parliamentarian of the American Revolutionary period. Dr. Samuel Fuller (E) was the only doctor to accompany the pilgrims to Massachusetts in 1620.

CHAPTER 3
Mathematics

CLEP COLLEGE MATHEMATICS INDEPENDENT STUDY SCHEDULE

The following suggestions provide a framework you can use when preparing for the CLEP College Mathematics exam. As part of your preparation, be sure to set aside time each day to study. This method will work better than trying to review everything at once. No matter which study techniques work best for you, the more time you spend studying, the more prepared and relaxed you will feel.

Step	Activity
1	Take Practice Test 2 for College Mathematics on the CD. Review the Detailed Explanations provided for the answers. This will help you identify areas that you need to review.
2	Carefully read each topic in the CLEP College Mathematics section.
3	In your review, pay particular attention to boldfaced terms and phrases.
4	Use a highlighter or pencil to emphasize items in your text you want to remember.
5	Jot down points of emphasis in a notebook or on index cards as you read.
6	Take Practice Test 3 found on the CD.
7	Review the Detailed Explanations of the answers. These will not only provide the correct answer, but also explain why the other options were incorrect.
8	Note which questions you answered incorrectly on the Practice Test, and focus on these areas during your follow-up review.
9	Read through the CLEP College Mathematics section in your book again, paying particular attention to the topics you struggled with while taking the two Practice Tests.
10	Take Practice Test 1 in the book for additional reinforcement.

The following is the order in which the topics are covered in this review:

PASSING THE CLEP COLLEGE MATHEMATICS EXAM

ABOUT THIS CHAPTER

This chapter provides you with a targeted review of the CLEP College Mathematics exam, as well as test-taking tips and strategies. We also provide three practice tests, one in the book and the other two on the CD. All feature content and formatting based on the official CLEP College Mathematics exam. Our practice tests contain every type of question found on the actual exam. Following the practice test is an answer key with detailed explanations designed to help you more completely understand the test material.

FORMAT AND CONTENT OF THE CLEP COLLEGE MATHEMATICS EXAM

The CLEP College Mathematics exam tests the material one would find in a college-level class for non-mathematics majors. The exam places little emphasis on arithmetic, and calculators are not allowed. A nongraphing calculator is provided to the test-taker during the examination as part of the testing software.

The exam consists of 60 questions, most with four possible answer choices, to be answered within 90 minutes. The approximate breakdown of topics is as follows:

- 10%   Sets
- 10%   Logic
- 20%   Real Number System
- 20%   Functions and Their Graphs
- 25%   Probability and Statistics
- 15%   Additional Topics from Algebra and Geometry

SCORING YOUR PRACTICE TESTS

How Do I Score My Practice Tests?

The CLEP College Mathematics exam is scored on a scale of 20 to 80. To score your practice test, count the number of correct answers. This is your total raw score. Convert your raw score to a scaled score using the conversion table on the following page. (**Note: The conversion table provides only an estimate of your scaled score. Scaled scores can and do vary over time, and in no case should a sample test be taken as a precise predictor of test performance.**)

Practice-Test Raw Score Conversion Table*

Raw Score	Scaled Score	Course Grade	Raw Score	Scaled Score	Course Grade
60	80	A	29	49	C
59	79	A	28	48	C
58	78	A	27	47	C
57	77	A	26	46	C
56	76	A	25	45	C
55	75	A	24	44	C
54	74	A	23	43	C
53	73	A	22	42	C
52	72	A	21	41	C
51	71	A	20	40	C
50	70	A	19	39	D
49	69	A	18	38	D
48	68	A	17	37	D
47	67	A	16	36	D
46	66	A	15	35	D
45	65	A	14	34	D
44	64	B	13	33	D
43	63	B	12	32	D
42	62	B	11	31	D
41	61	B	10	30	D
40	60	B	9	29	F
39	59	B	8	28	F
38	58	B	7	27	F
37	57	B	6	26	F
36	56	B	5	25	F
35	55	B	4	24	F
34	54	B	3	23	F
33	53	B	2	22	F
32	52	B	1	21	F
31	51	B	0	20	F
30	50	C			

* This table is provided for scoring REA practice tests only. The American Council on Education recommends that colleges use a single across-the-board credit-granting score of 50 for all CLEP computer-based exams. Nonetheless, on account of the different skills being measured and the unique content requirements of each test, the actual number of correct answers needed to reach 50 will vary. A "50" is calibrated to equate with performance that would warrant the grade C in the corresponding introductory college course.

SETS

Set theory is the basis for most of your mathematical and logical thought. This section introduces the Set theory vocabulary as well as such topics as Venn diagrams for the union and intersection of sets (used in logic), laws of set operations (similar to those for operations on the real number system), and Cartesian products (used in graphs of linear functions).

SETS

A **set** is a collection of items. Each individual item belonging to a set is called an **element** or **member** of that set. Sets are usually represented by capital letters, and elements by lowercase letters. If an item k belongs to a set A, we write $k \in A$ ("k is an element of A"). If k is not in A, we write $k \notin A$ ("k is not an element of A").

The order of the elements in a set does not matter:

$$\{1, 2, 3\} = \{3, 2, 1\} = \{1, 3, 2\}, \text{etc.}$$

A set can be described in two ways:

1. element by element.

2. a rule characterizing the elements.

For example, given the set A of the whole numbers starting with 1 and ending with 9, we can describe it either as $A = \{1, 2, 3, 4, 5, 6, 7, 8, 9\}$ or as $A = \{$whole numbers greater than 0 and less than 10$\}$. In both methods, the description is enclosed in brackets. Instead of writing out a complete sentence between the brackets, we can write instead

$$A = \{k \mid 0 < k < 10, k \text{ a whole number}\}$$

This is read as "the set of all elements k such that k is greater than 0 and less than 10, where k is a whole number."

A set not containing any members, called the **empty** or **null** set, is written either as ϕ or $\{\ \}$. A set is **finite** if the number of its elements can be counted.

The following list contains examples of sets.

- $\{2, 3, 4, 5\}$ is finite since it has four elements.
- $\{3, 6, 9, 12, \ldots, 300\}$ is finite since it has 100 elements.

> *Note*: The empty set, denoted by ϕ, is finite since we can count the number of elements it has, namely zero.

Any set that is not finite is called **infinite**.

- $\{1, 2, 3, 4, \ldots\}$
- $\{\ldots, -7, -6, -5, -4\}$
- $\{x \mid x$ is a real number between 4 and 5$\}$

SUBSETS

Given two sets A and B, A is said to be a **subset** of B if every member of set A is also a member of set B.

A is a *proper* subset of B if B contains at least one element not in A. We write $A \subseteq B$ if A is a subset of B, and $A \subset B$ if A is a proper subset of B.

Two sets are **equal** if they have exactly the same elements; in addition, if $A = B$, then $A \subseteq B$ and $B \subseteq A$.

Example: Let $A = \{1, 2, 3, 4, 5\}$

$$B = \{1, 2\}$$
$$C = \{1, 4, 2, 3, 5\}$$

1. A equals C, and A and C are subsets of each other, but not proper subsets.

2. $B \subseteq A, B \subseteq C, B \subset A, B \subset C$ (B is a subset of both A and C. In particular, B is a proper subset of A and C).

Two sets are **equivalent** if they have the same *number* of elements.

Example: $O = \{3, 7, 9, 12\}$ and $E = \{4, 7, 12, 19\}$. O and E are equivalent sets, since each one has four elements.

Example: $F = \{1, 3, 5, 7, \ldots, 99\}$ and $G = \{2, 4, 6, 8, \ldots, 100\}$. F and G are equivalent sets, since each one has 50 elements.

Note: If two sets are equal, they are automatically equivalent.

A **universal set** U is a set from which other sets draw their members. If A is a subset of U, then the complement of A, denoted A', is the set of all elements in the universal set that are not elements of A.

Example: If $U = \{1, 2, 3, 4, 5, 6, \ldots\}$ and $A = \{1, 2, 3\}$, then $A' = \{4, 5, 6, \ldots\}$.

Figure 1 illustrates this concept through the use of a simple **Venn diagram**.

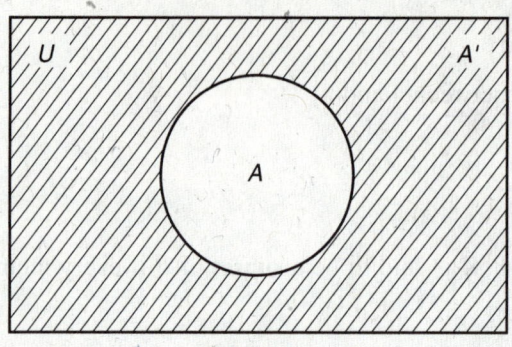

Figure 1

A Venn diagram shows the relationships among or between sets that share something in common. Usually, the Venn diagram consists of two or more overlapping circles, with each circle representing a set of elements, or members. If two circles overlap, the members in the overlap belong to both sets; if three circles overlap, the members in the overlap belong to all three sets. As shown in Figure 1, the circles are usually drawn inside a rectangle called the **universal set**, which is the set of all possible members in the universe being described.

Venn diagrams are used to organize similarities (overlaps) and differences (non-overlaps of circles) visually, and they can pertain to any subject. For example, if the universe is all animals, Circle A may represent all animals that live in the water, and Circle B may represent all mammals. Then whales would appear in the intersection of Circles A and B, but lobsters only in Circle A, humans only in Circle B, and scorpions in the part of the universe outside of Circles A and B. These relationships are shown in Figure 2.

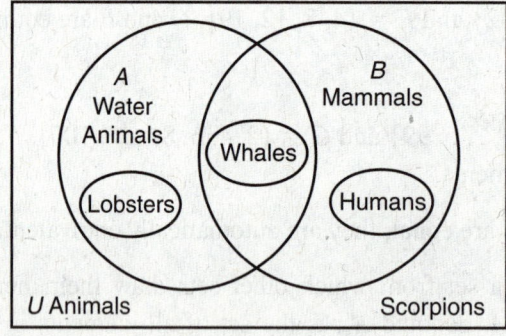

Figure 2

UNION AND INTERSECTION OF SETS

The **union** of two sets A and B, denoted $A \cup B$, is the set of all elements that are either in A or B or both. Figure 3 is a Venn diagram for $A \cup B$. The shaded area represents the given operation.

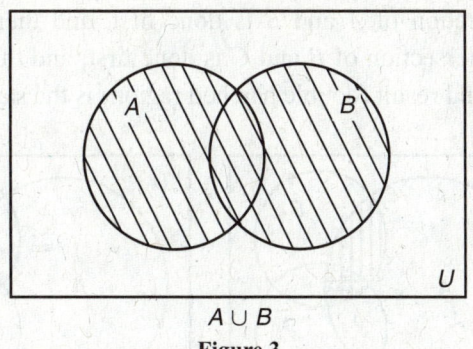

$A \cup B$

Figure 3

The **intersection** of two sets A and B, denoted $A \cap B$, is the set of all elements that belong to both A and B. Figure 4 is a Venn diagram for $A \cap B$. The shaded area represents the given operation.

If $A = \{1, 2, 3, 4, 5\}$ and $B = \{2, 3, 4, 5, 6\}$, then $A \cup B = \{1, 2, 3, 4, 5, 6\}$ and $A \cap B = \{2, 3, 4, 5\}$. If $A \cap B = \phi$, A and B are **disjoint**.

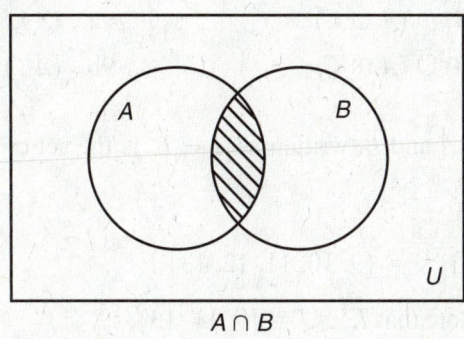

$A \cap B$

Figure 4

LAWS OF SET OPERATIONS

If U is the universal set, and A, B, and C are any subsets of U, then the following hold for union, intersection, and complement:

Identity Laws

1a. $A \cup \phi = A$
1b. $A \cap \phi = \phi$
2a. $A \cup U = U$
2b. $A \cap U = A$

Complement Laws

4a. $A \cup A' = U$
4b. $A \cap A' = \phi$
5a. $\phi' = U$
5b. $U' = \phi$

Associative Laws

7a. $(A \cup B) \cup C = A \cup (B \cup C)$
7b. $(A \cap B) \cap C = A \cap (B \cap C)$

Idempotent Laws

3a. $A \cup A = A$
3b. $A \cap A = A$

Commutative Laws

6a. $A \cup B = B \cup A$
6b. $A \cap B = B \cap A$

In Figure 5, the intersection of A and B is done first, and then the intersection of this result with C. In Figure 6, the intersection of B and C is done first, and then the intersection of this result with A. In both cases, the end result (double hatched region) is the same.

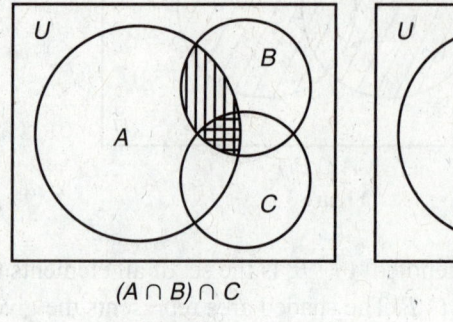

$(A \cap B) \cap C$ $A \cap (B \cap C)$

Figure 5   Figure 6

Distributive Laws

8a. $A \cup (B \cap C) = (A \cup B) \cap (A \cup C)$

8b. $A \cap (B \cup C) = (A \cap B) \cup (A \cap C)$

De Morgan's Laws

9a. $(A \cup B)' = A' \cap B'$

9b. $(A \cap B)' = A' \cup B'$

The **difference** of two sets, A and B, written as $A - B$, is the set of all elements that belong to A but do not belong to B.

Example: $J = \{10, 12, 14, 16\}$, $K = \{9, 10, 11, 12, 13\}$

$J - K = \{14, 16\}$. Note that $K - J = \{9, 11, 13\}$.

In general, $J - K \neq K - J$.

Example: $T = \{a, b, c\}$, $V = \{a, b, c, d, e, f\}$.

$T - V = \phi$, whereas $V - T = \{d, e, f\}$.

T is a proper subset of V. In general, whenever set A is a proper subset of set B, $A - B = \phi$.

If set P is any set, then $P - \phi = P$ and $\phi - P = \phi$. Also if P and Q are any sets, $P - Q = P \cap Q'$.

CARTESIAN PRODUCT

Given two sets M and N, the **Cartesian product**, denoted $M \times N$, is the set of all ordered pairs of elements in which the first component is a member of M and the second component is a member of N.

Often, the elements of the Cartesian product can be found by making a table with the elements of the first set as row headings and the elements of the second set as column headings; the elements of the table are the pairs formed from these elements.

Example: $M = \{1, 3, 5\}, N = \{2, 8\}$

The Cartesian product $M \times N = \{(1, 2), (1, 8), (3, 2), (3, 8), (5, 2), (5, 8)\}$. We can easily see that these are all of the elements of $M \times N$ and the only elements of $M \times N$ by looking at Table 1.

Table 1–$M \times N$

	2	8
1	1, 2	1, 8
3	3, 2	3, 8
5	5, 2	5, 8

In general, if the first set has x elements and the second set has y elements, the Cartesian product will have xy elements.

THE REAL NUMBER SYSTEM

Real numbers provide the basis for most precalculus mathematics topics. **Real numbers** are all of the numbers on the **number line** (see Figure 7). Real numbers include positives, negatives, square roots, π (pi), and just about any number you have ever encountered.

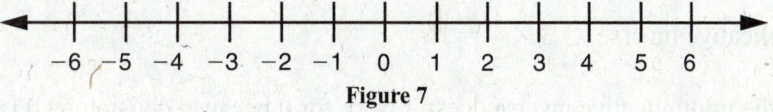

Figure 7

PROPERTIES OF REAL NUMBERS

Real numbers have several properties that you should know. The following list provides the names for these properties. The examples use the numbers 2, 3, and 4, but the rules apply to any real numbers.

Commutative Property

The numbers *commute*, or move:

Addition $\qquad 2 + 3 = 3 + 2$

Multiplication $\qquad 2 \times 3 = 3 \times 2$

Associative Property

The numbers can be grouped, or *associated*, in any order:

Addition $2 + (3 + 4) = (2 + 3) + 4$

Multiplication $2 \times (3 \times 4) = (2 \times 3) \times 4$

Distributive Property

The first number gets *distributed* to the ones in parentheses.

$$2 \times (3 + 4) = (2 \times 3) + (2 \times 4)$$

The following properties have to do with the special numbers 0 and 1.

Identity Property

Adding 0 or multiplying by 1 doesn't change the original value.

Addition $3 + 0 = 3$

Multiplication $3 \times 1 = 3$

Inverse Property

The *inverse* of addition is subtraction and the *inverse* of multiplication is division.

Additive Inverse $3 + (-3) = 0$

Multiplicative Inverse $3 \times \dfrac{1}{3} = 1$

Note that the multiplicative inverse doesn't work for 0 because division by 0 is not defined.

COMPONENTS OF REAL NUMBERS

The set of all real numbers (designated as R) has various components:

$N = \{1, 2, 3, \ldots\}$, the set of all **natural numbers**

$W = \{0, 1, 2, 3, \ldots\}$, the set of all **whole numbers**

$I = \{\ldots, -3, -2, -1, 0, 1, 2, 3, \ldots\}$, the set of all **integers**

$Q = \left[\dfrac{a}{b} \mid a, b \in I \text{ and } b \neq 0 \right]$, the set of all **rational numbers**

$S = \{x \mid x$ has a decimal that is nonterminating and does not have a repeating block$\}$, the set of all **irrational numbers**

It is obvious that $N \subseteq W$, $W \subseteq I$ and $I \subseteq Q$, but a similar relationship does not hold between Q and S. More specifically, the decimal names for elements of Q are either (1) terminating or (2) nonterminating with a repeating block.

Examples of rational numbers include $\frac{1}{2} = 0.5$ and $\frac{1}{3} = 0.333....$

This means that Q and S have no common elements.

Examples of irrational numbers include $0.101001000\ldots$, π, and $\sqrt{2}$.

All real numbers are normally represented by R and $R = Q \cup S$. This means that every real number is either rational or irrational.

FRACTIONS

All rational numbers can be displayed as **fractions**, which consist of a numerator (on the top) and a denominator (on the bottom). **Proper fractions** are numbers between -1 and $+1$; the numerator is less than the denominator. Examples of proper fractions are $\frac{1}{2}$, $\frac{3}{4}$, and $\frac{17}{19}$. **Improper fractions** are all other rational numbers; the numerator is greater than or equal to the denominator.

Improper fractions, also called mixed numbers, can be written as a whole number with a fractional part. Examples of improper fractions are $\frac{2}{1}$, $\frac{4}{3}$, and $\frac{19}{17}$. The first of these is actually a whole number (2); the others are equivalent to the mixed numbers $1\frac{1}{3}$ and $1\frac{2}{17}$, respectively.

ODD AND EVEN NUMBERS

When dealing with odd and even numbers keep in mind the following:

Adding

even + even = even

odd + odd = even

even + odd = odd

Multiplying

even × even = even

even × odd = even

odd × odd = odd

FACTORS AND DIVISIBILITY NUMBERS

Any counting number that divides into another number with no remainder is called a **factor** of that number. The factors of 20 are 1, 2, 4, 5, 10, and 20. Any number that can be divided by another number with no remainder is called a **multiple** of that number. Examples of multiples of 20 are 20, 40, 60, 80, and so on.

ABSOLUTE VALUE

The **absolute value** of a number is represented by two vertical lines around the number and is equal to the given number, regardless of sign. The absolute value of a real number A is defined as follows:

$$|A| = \begin{cases} A \text{ if } A \geq 0 \\ -A \text{ if } A < 0 \end{cases}$$

Absolute values follow the given rules:

1. $|-A| = |A|$

2. $|A| \geq 0$, equality holding only if $A = 0$

3. $\left|\dfrac{A}{B}\right| = \dfrac{|A|}{|B|}, B \neq 0$

4. $|AB| = |A| \times |B|$

5. $|A|^2 = A^2$

INTEGERS

There are various subsets of I, the set of all integers.

- **Negative integers** are the set of integers starting with -1 and decreasing, such as $\{-1, -2, -3, \ldots\}$.
- **Even integers** are the set of integers divisible by 2, such as $\{\ldots, -4, -2, 0, 2, 4, 6, \ldots\}$.
- **Odd integers** are the set of integers not divisible by 2, such as $\{\ldots, -3, -1, 1, 3, 5, 7, \ldots\}$.
- **Consecutive integers** are the set of integers that differ by 1, such as $\{n, n + 1, n + 2, \ldots\}$ ($n =$ an integer).
- **Prime numbers** are the set of positive integers greater than 1 that are divisible only by 1 and themselves, such as $\{2, 3, 5, 7, 11, \ldots\}$.
- **Composite numbers** are the set of positive integers, other than 1, that are not prime.

A number can be classified in different ways. For example, 3 is a real number, an odd number, and a rational number.

INEQUALITIES

If x and y are real numbers, then one and only one of the following statements is true.

$$x > y, x = y, \text{ or } x < y.$$

This is the **order property of real numbers**.

If a, b, and c are real numbers, the following statements are true:

If $a < b$ and $b < c$, then $a < c$.

If $a > b$ and $b > c$, then $a > c$.

This is the **transitive property of inequalities**.

If a, b, and c are real numbers and $a > b$, then $a + c > b + c$ and $a - c > b - c$. This is the **addition property of inequality**. An **inequality** is a statement in which the value of one quantity or expression is greater than ($>$), less than ($<$), greater than or equal to ($\geq$), less than or equal to ($\leq$), or not equal to ($\neq$) that of another. For example, the expression $5 > 4$ means that the value of 5 is greater than the value of 4.

The **graph of an inequality** in one variable is represented by either a ray or a line segment on the real number line.

The endpoint is not a solution if the variable is strictly less than or greater than a particular value. In those cases, the endpoint is indicated by an open circle. For example, if $x > 2$, the number line would appear as:

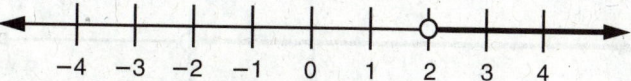

2 is not a solution and should be represented as shown.

The endpoint is a solution if the variable is either (1) less than or equal to or (2) greater than or equal to a particular value. In those cases, the endpoint is indicated by a closed circle. For example, if $5 > x \geq 2$, the number line would appear as:

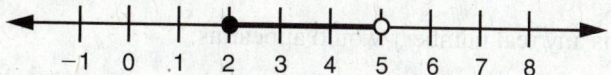

In this case, 2 is a solution and 5 is not a solution, and the solution should be represented as shown.

In the case of $x < 2$ or $x > 5$, neither 2 nor 5 is a solution. Thus, an open circle must be shown at $x = 2$ and at $x = 5$.

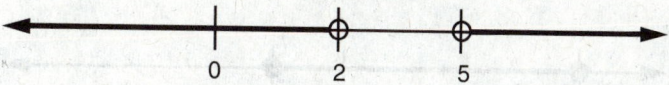

In the case of $x \leq 2$ and $x \geq 5$, there is no solution. It is impossible for a number to be both no greater than 2 and no less than 5.

In the case of $x \geq 2$ or $x \leq 5$, the solution is all real numbers. Any number *must* belong to at least one of these inequalities. Some numbers, such as 3, belong to both inequalities. If you graph these inequalities separately, you will notice two rays going in opposite directions and which overlap between 2 and 5, inclusive.

Intervals on the number line represent sets of points that satisfy the conditions of an inequality. An **open** interval does not include any endpoints. For example, the graph for $\{x \mid x > -3\}$, read as "the set of values x such that $x > -3$," would appear as:

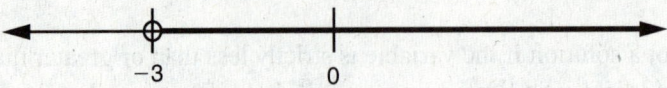

The graph for $\{x \mid x < 4\}$ would appear as:

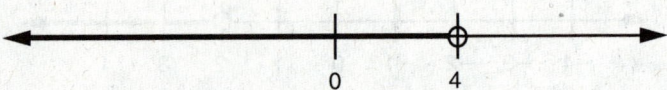

The graph for $\{x \mid 2 < x < 6\}$ would appear as:

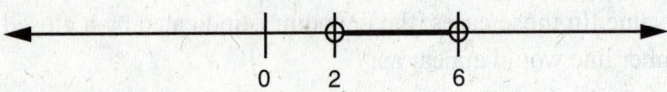

The graph for $\{x \mid x$ is any real number$\}$ would appear as:

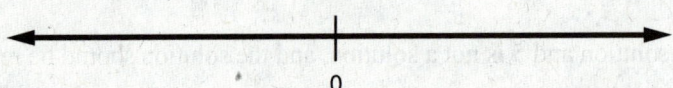

A **closed** interval includes two endpoints. For example, the graph for $\{x \mid -5 \le x \le 2\}$ would appear as:

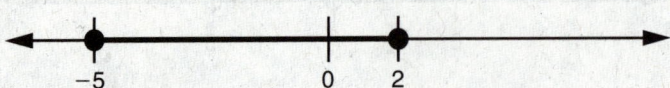

A **half-open** interval includes one endpoint. For example, the graph of $\{x \mid x \ge 3\}$ would appear as:

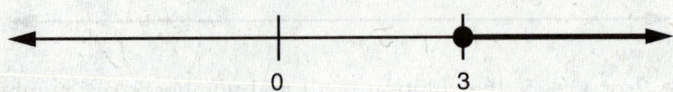

The graph of $\{x \mid x \le 6\}$ would appear as:

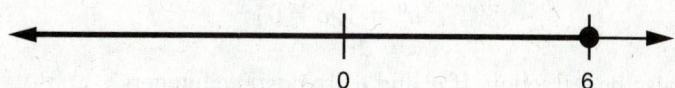

The graph of $\{x \mid -4 < x \le -1\}$ would appear as:

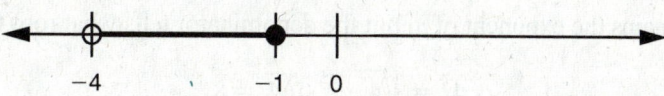

The graph of $\{x \mid -2 \le x < 1\}$ would appear as:

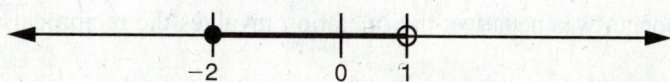

ALGEBRA TOPICS

EXPONENTS

When a number is multiplied by itself a specific number of times, it is said to be **raised to a power**. The way this is written is $a^n = b$, where a is the number or **base**; n is the **exponent** or **power** that indicates the number of times the base appears when multiplied by itself; and b is the **product** of this multiplication. In the expression 3^2, 3 is the base and 2 is the exponent. This means that 3 appears 2 times when multiplied by itself (3×3), and the product is 9.

An exponent can be either positive or negative. A negative exponent implies a fraction, such that if n is a negative integer

$$a^{-n} = \frac{1}{a^n}, a \ne 0$$

So, $2^{-4} = \frac{1}{2^4} = \frac{1}{16}$.

The **reciprocal** of a number is 1 divided by that number. The exception is 0, since $\frac{1}{0}$ is undefined. Essentially, any quantity raised to a negative exponent can be "flipped" to the other side of the fraction bar and its exponent changed to a positive exponent. For example,

$$4^{-3} = \frac{1}{4^3} = \frac{1}{64}$$

An exponent that is 0 gives a result of 1, assuming that the base itself is not equal to 0.

$$a^0 = 1, a \neq 0$$

An exponent can also be a fraction. If m and n are positive integers,

$$a^{\frac{m}{n}} = \sqrt[n]{a^m}$$

The numerator remains the exponent of a, but the denominator tells what root to take. For example,

$$4^{\frac{3}{2}} = \sqrt[2]{4^3} = \sqrt{64} = 8$$

$$3^{\frac{4}{2}} = \sqrt[2]{3^4} = \sqrt{81} = 9$$

If a fractional exponent was negative, the operation involves the reciprocal as well as the roots. For example,

$$27^{-\frac{2}{3}} = \frac{1}{27^{\frac{2}{3}}} = \frac{1}{\sqrt[3]{27^2}} = \frac{1}{\sqrt[3]{729}} = \frac{1}{9}$$

General Laws of Exponents

$a^p a^q = a^{p+q}$, bases must be the same.

$$4^2 4^3 = 4^{2+3} = 4^5 = 1,024$$

$(a^p)^q = a^{pq}$

$$(2^3)^2 = 2^6 = 64$$

$\dfrac{a^p}{a^q} = a^{p-q}$, bases must be the same, $a \neq 0$

$$\frac{3^6}{3^2} = 3^{6-2} = 3^4 = 81$$

$(ab)^p = a^p b^p$

$$(3 \times 2)^2 = 3^2 \times 2^2 = (9)(4) = 36$$

$\left(\dfrac{a}{b}\right)^p = \dfrac{a^p}{b^p}, b \neq 0$

$$\left(\frac{4}{5}\right)^2 = \frac{4^2}{5^2} = \frac{16}{25}$$

LOGARITHMS

An equation $y = b^x$, (with $b > 0$ and $b \neq 1$), is called an **exponential function**. Exponential functions with base b can be written as $y = f(x) = b^x$.

The inverse of an exponential function is the **logarithmic function**, $f^{-1}(x) = \log_b x$. Inverse is denoted by $f^{-1}(\ )$; this doesn't mean a negative exponent.

Logarithm Properties

If M, N, p, and b are positive numbers and $b \neq 1$, then

$$\log_b 1 = 0$$

$$\log_b b = 1$$

$$\log_b b^x = x$$

$$\log_b (MN) = \log_b M + \log_b N$$

$$\log_b (M/N) = \log_b M - \log_b N$$

$$\log_b M^p = p \log_b M$$

EQUATIONS

An **equation** is defined as a statement that two separate expressions are equal. A **solution** to an equation containing a single variable is a number that makes the equation true when it is substituted for the variable. For example, in the equation $3x = 18$, 6 is the solution since $3(6) = 18$. Depending on the equation, there can be more than one solution. Equations with the same solutions are said to be **equivalent equations**. An equation without a solution is said to have a solution set that is the **empty** or **null** set, represented by ϕ.

Suppose we are given the equation $3x + y + x + 2y = 15$. By combining like terms, we get $3x + y + x + 2y = 4x + 3y$. Since these two expressions are equivalent, we can substitute the simpler form into the equation to get $4x + 3y = 15$.

Performing the same operation to both sides of an equation will result in a new equation that is equivalent to the original equation.

Addition or Subtraction

In the equation $y + 6 = 10$, we can add (-6) to both sides.

$$y + 6 + (-6) = 10 + (-6)$$
$$y + 0 = 10 - 6 = 4$$

Multiplication or Division

In the equation $3x = 6$, we can divide both sides by 3.

$$\frac{3x}{3} = \frac{6}{3}$$

$$x = 2$$

So $3x = 6$ is equivalent to $x = 2$.

Linear Equations

A **linear equation** with one unknown can be put into the form $ax + b = 0$, where a and b are constants, and $a \neq 0$. To solve a linear equation means to transform it into the form $x = \dfrac{-b}{a}$.

A. If the equation has unknowns on both sides of the equality, it is convenient to put similar terms on the same sides. Refer to the following example.

$$4x + 3 = 2x + 9$$

$4x + 3 - 2x = 2x + 9 - 2x$	Add $-2x$ to both sides
$(4x - 2x) + 3 = (2x - 2x) + 9$	Commutative property
$2x + 3 = 0 + 9$	Additive inverse property
$2x + 3 - 3 = 0 + 9 - 3$	Add -3 to both sides
$2x = 6$	Additive inverse property
$\dfrac{2x}{2} = \dfrac{6}{2}$	Divide both sides by 2
$x = 3$	

B. If the equation appears in fractional form, it is necessary to transform it using cross-multiplication, and then repeat the same procedure as in (A). For example,

$$\frac{3x + 4}{3} = \frac{7x + 2}{5}$$

Cross-multiply as follows:

$$\frac{3x + 4}{3} \diagdown\!\!\!\!\diagup \frac{7x + 2}{5}$$

Your result, $3(7x + 2) = 5(3x + 4)$, is equivalent to $21x + 6 = 15x + 20$, which can be solved as in (A).

$21x + 6 = 15x + 20$	
$21x - 15x + 6 = 15x - 15x + 20$	Add $-15x$ to both sides
$6x + 6 - 6 = 20 - 6$	Combine like terms and add -6 to both sides
$6x = 14$	Combine like terms
$\dfrac{6x}{6} = \dfrac{14}{6}$	Divide both sides by 6
$x = \dfrac{7}{3}$	

Factor Theorem

If $x = c$ is a solution of the equation $f(x) = 0$, then $(x - c)$ is a **factor** of $f(x)$. For example, let $f(x) = 2x^2 - 5x - 3$. By inspection, we can determine that $2(3)^2 - (5)(3) - 3 = (2)(9) - (5)(3) - 3 = 0$. In this example, $c = 3$, so $(x - 3)$ is also a factor of $2x^2 - 5x - 3$.

Remainder Theorem

If a is any constant and if the polynomial $p(x)$ is divided by $(x - a)$, the **remainder** is $p(a)$. For example, given a polynomial $p(x) = 2x^3 - x^2 + x + 4$, divided by $x - 1$, the remainder is $P(1) = 2(1)^3 - (1)^2 + 1 + 4 = 6$. That is, $2x^3 - x^2 + x + 4 = q(x) + \dfrac{6}{(x-1)}$, where $q(x)$ is a polynomial.

Note that in this case $a = 1$. Also, by using long division, we get $q(x) = 2x^2 + x + 2$.

Simultaneous Linear Equations

Two or more equations of the form $ax + by = c$, where a, b, and c are constants and a, $b \neq 0$ are called **linear equations** with two unknown variables, or **simultaneous equations**. Equations with more than one unknown variable are solvable only if you have as many equations as unknown variables.

There are several ways to solve systems of linear equations with two variables. Three of the basic methods are:

Method 1: **Substitution**—Find the value of one unknown in terms of the other. Substitute this value in the other equation and solve.

Method 2: **Addition or subtraction**—If necessary, multiply the equations by numbers that will make the coefficients of one unknown in the resulting equations numerically equal. The result is one equation with one unknown; we solve it and substitute the value into the other equations to find the unknown that we first eliminated.

Method 3: **Graph**—Graph both equations. The point of intersection of the drawn lines is a simultaneous solution for the equations, and its coordinates correspond to the answer that would be found by substitution or addition/subtraction.

A system of linear equations is **consistent** if there is only one solution for the system. A system of linear equations is **inconsistent** if it does not have any solutions. Inconsistent equations represent parallel lines, which are discussed later in this section.

Dependent Equations

Dependent equations are equations that represent the same line; therefore, every point on the line of a dependent equation represents a solution. Since there are an infinite number of points on a line, there are an infinite number of simultaneous solutions. For example, the following equations are dependent.

$$2x + y = 8$$
$$4x + 2y = 16$$

Since they represent the same line, all points that satisfy either of the equations are solutions of the system.

Parallel Lines

Given two linear equations in x, y, their graphs are **parallel** lines if their slopes are equal. If the lines are parallel, they have no simultaneous solution. For example, suppose line l_1 is $2x - 7y = 14$ and line l_2 is $2x - 7y = 56$. In the slope-intercept form, the equation for l_1 is $y = \frac{2}{7}x - 2$ and the equation for l_2 is $y = \frac{2}{7}x - 8$. Each line has a slope of $\frac{2}{7}$.

Perpendicular Lines

If the slopes of the graphs of two lines are negative reciprocals of each other, the lines are **perpendicular** to each other. An example of two numbers that are negative reciprocals of each other are 2 and $-\frac{1}{2}$. (Remember: $2 = \frac{2}{1}$.)

Consider these equations:

$$l_3: 5x + 6y = 30, \quad l_4: 6x - 5y = 90$$

In the **slope-intercept form**, the equation for l_3 is $y = -\frac{5}{6}x + 5$ and the equation for l_4 is $y = \frac{6}{5}x - 18$. The slope of l_3, which is $-\frac{5}{6}$, is the negative reciprocal of the slope of l_4, which is $\frac{6}{5}$. Therefore, l_3 is perpendicular to l_4.

To summarize:

- Parallel lines have slopes that are equal.
- Perpendicular lines have slopes that are negative reciprocals of each other.

ABSOLUTE VALUE EQUATIONS

The **absolute value** of a, denoted $|a|$, is defined as

$|a| = a$ when $a > 0$,

$|a| = -a$ when $a < 0$,

$|a| = 0$ when $a = 0$.

When the definition of absolute value is applied to an equation, the quantity within the absolute value symbol may have two values. This value can be either positive or negative before the absolute value is taken. As a result, each absolute value equation actually contains two separate equations.

When evaluating equations containing absolute values, proceed as follows: $|5 - 3x| = 7$ is valid if either

$$5 - 3x = 7 \qquad \text{or} \qquad 5 - 3x = -7$$
$$-3x = 2 \qquad\qquad\qquad -3x = -12$$
$$x = -\frac{2}{3} \qquad\qquad\qquad x = 4$$

The solution set is therefore $x = \left(-\dfrac{2}{3}, 4\right)$

Remember, the absolute value of a number cannot be negative. Therefore, the equation $|5x + 4| = -3$ would have no solution.

INEQUALITIES

The solution of a given inequality in one variable x consists of all values of x for which the inequality is true. A **conditional inequality** is an inequality whose validity depends on the values of the variables in the sentence. That is, certain values of the variables will make the sentence true, and others will make it false. The sentence $3 - y > 3 + y$ is a conditional inequality for the set of real numbers, since it is true for any replacement less than 0 and false for all others, or $y < 0$ is the solution set.

An **absolute inequality** for the set of real numbers means that for *any* real value for the variable, x, the sentence is always true. The sentence $x + 5 > x + 2$ is an absolute inequality because the expression on the left is greater than the expression on the right.

A sentence is **inconsistent** if it is always false when its variables assume allowable values. The sentence $x + 10 < x + 5$ is inconsistent because the expression on the left side is always greater than the expression on the right side. The sentence $5y < 2y + y$ is inconsistent for the set of non-negative real numbers. For any y greater than or equal to 0, the sentence is always false.

Two inequalities are said to have the same **sense** if their signs of inequality point in the same direction. The sense of an inequality remains the same if both sides are multiplied or divided by the same *positive* real number. For the inequality $4 > 3$, if we multiply both sides by 5, we will obtain:

$$4 \times 5 > 3 \times 5$$
$$20 > 15$$

The sense of the inequality does not change.

If each side of an inequality is multiplied or divided by the same *negative* real number, however, the sense of an inequality becomes opposite. For the inequality $4 > 3$, if we multiply both sides by -5, we would obtain:

$$4 \times (-5) < 3 \times (-5)$$
$$-20 < -15$$

The sense of the inequality becomes opposite.

If $a > b$ and a, b, and n are positive real numbers, then

$$a^n > b^n \text{ and } a^{-n} < b^{-n}$$

If $x > y$ and $q > p$, then $x + q > y + p$.

If $x > y > 0$ and $q > p > 0$, then $xq > yp$.

Inequalities that have the same solution set are called **equivalent inequalities**.

COMPLEX NUMBERS

On occasion, real numbers by themselves are not enough to explain what is happening. As a result, complex numbers were developed. A **complex number** is a number that can be written in the form $a + bi$, where a and b are real numbers and $i = \sqrt{-1}$. The number a is the **real part**, and the number bi is the **imaginary part** of the complex number.

Returning momentarily to real numbers, the square of a real number cannot be negative. More specifically, the square of a positive real number is positive, the square of a negative real number is positive, and the square of 0 is 0.

i is defined to be a number with a property that $i^2 = -1$. Obviously, i is not a real number. C is then used to represent the set of all complex numbers: $C = \{a + bi \,|\, a \text{ and } b \text{ are real numbers}\}$.

Addition, Subtraction, and Multiplication of Complex Numbers

Suppose $x + yi$ and $z + wi$ are complex numbers. Then (remembering that $i^2 = -1$):

$$(x + yi) + (z + wi) = (x + z) + (y + w)i$$
$$(x + yi) - (z + wi) = (x - z) + (y - w)i$$
$$(x + yi) \times (z + wi) = (xz - wy) + (xw + yz)i$$

Division of Complex Numbers

Division of two complex numbers is usually accomplished with a special procedure that involves the **conjugate** of a complex number. The conjugate of $a + bi$ is denoted by $\overline{a + bi}$ and defined by $\overline{a + bi} = a - bi$.

Also, $(a + bi)(a - bi) = a^2 + b^2$. The usual procedure for division is to multiply and divide by the conjugate as shown below. Remember that multiplication and division by the same quantity leaves the original expression unchanged.

$$\frac{x + yi}{z + wi} = \frac{x + yi}{z + wi} \times \frac{z - wi}{z - wi}$$

$$= \frac{(xz + yw) + (-xw + yz)i}{z^2 + w^2}$$

$$= \frac{xz + yw}{z^2 + w^2} + \frac{-xw + yz}{z^2 + w^2}i$$

If a is a real number, then a can be expressed in the form $a = a + 0i$. Hence, every real number is a complex number and $R \subseteq C$. All the properties of real numbers carry over to complex numbers.

QUADRATIC EQUATIONS

Consider the polynomial $ax^2 + bx + c = 0$, where $a \neq 0$. This type of equation is called a **quadratic equation**. If the product of two factors is 0, either one or the other of the factors equals 0. The equation can be solved by setting each factor equal to 0. If you cannot see the factors right away, however, the quadratic formula, which is the last method presented, *always* works.

Solution by Factoring

We are looking for two binomials that, when multiplied together, give the quadratic trinomial $ax^2 + bx + c = 0$. This method works easily if $a = 1$ and you can find two numbers whose product equals c and sum equals b. The signs of b and c need to be considered:

- If c is positive, the factors are going to both have the same sign, which is b's sign.
- If c is negative, the factors are going to have opposite signs, with the larger factor having b's sign.

Once you have the two factors, insert them in the general factor format $(x + \_)(x + \_) = 0$.

To solve the quadratic equation, set each factor equal to 0 to yield the solution set for x. For example, to solve the quadratic equation $x^2 + 7x + 12 = 0$, we need two numbers whose product is $+12$ and sum is $+7$. They would be $+3$ and $+4$, and the quadratic equation would factor to $(x + 3)(x + 4) = 0$.

Therefore, $x + 3 = 0$ or $x + 4 = 0$ would yield the solutions, which are $x = -3, x = -4$.

Suppose the quadratic equation is similar to the previous example, but the sign of b is negative. To solve the quadratic equation $x^2 - 7x + 12 = 0$, we need two numbers whose product is $+12$ and sum is -7. They would be -3 and -4, and the quadratic would factor to $(x - 3)(x - 4) = 0$.

Therefore, $x - 3 = 0$ or $x - 4 = 0$ would yield the solutions, which are $x = 3, x = 4$.

As a final example, to solve the quadratic equation $x^2 + 4x - 12 = 0$, we need two numbers whose product is -12 and sum is $+4$. They would be $+6$ and -2 (note that the larger numeral gets the $+$ sign, the sign of b). The quadratic equation would factor to $(x + 6)(x - 2) = 0$.

Therefore, $x + 6 = 0$ or $x - 2 = 0$ would yield the solutions, which are $x = -6, x = 2$.

Sum of Two Squares

If the quadratic consists of the difference of only two terms of the form $ax^2 - c$, and you can recognize them as perfect squares, the factors are simply the sum and difference of the square roots of the two terms. Note that a is a perfect square, but not necessarily 1, for this method. To solve the quadratic equation $x^2 - 16 = 0$, realize that this is the difference of two perfect squares, x^2 and 16, whose square roots are x and 4. Therefore, the factors are $(x + 4)(x - 4) = 0$, and the solution is $x = \pm 4$.

Quadratic Formula

If the quadratic equation does not have obvious factors, the roots of the equation can always be determined by the **quadratic formula** in terms of the coefficients a, b, and c as shown below:

$$x = \frac{-b \pm \sqrt{b^2 - 4ac}}{2a}$$

where $(b^2 - 4ac)$ is called the **discriminant** of the quadratic equation.

- If the discriminant is less than zero ($b^2 - 4ac < 0$), the roots are complex numbers, since the discriminant appears under a radical and square roots of negatives are imaginary numbers. A real number added to an imaginary number yields a complex number.

- If the discriminant is equal to zero ($b^2 - 4ac = 0$), the roots are real and equal.

- If the discriminant is greater than zero ($b^2 - 4ac > 0$), then the roots are real and unequal. The roots are rational if and only if a and b are rational and ($b^2 - 4ac$) is a perfect square; otherwise, the roots are irrational.

ADVANCED ALGEBRAIC THEOREMS

A. Every polynomial equation $f(x) = 0$ of degree greater than zero has at least one root either real or complex. This is known as the **fundamental theorem of algebra**.

B. Every polynomial equation of degree n has exactly n roots.

C. If a polynomial equation $f(x) = 0$ with real coefficients has a root $a + bi$, then the conjugate of this complex number $a - bi$ is also a root of $f(x) = 0$.

D. If $a + \sqrt{b}$ is a root of polynomial equation $f(x) = 0$ with rational coefficients, then $a - \sqrt{b}$ is also a root, where a and b are rational and $\sqrt{b}$ is irrational.

E. If a rational fraction in lowest terms $\dfrac{b}{c}$ is a root of the equation $a_n x^n + a_{n-1} x^{n-1} + \ldots + a_1 x + a_0 = 0$, $a_0 \neq 0$, and the a_i are integers, then b is a factor of a_0 and c is a factor of a_n.

F. Any rational roots of the equation $x^n + q_1 x^{n-1} + q_2 x^{n-2} + \ldots + q_{n-1} x + q_n = 0$ must be integers and factors of q_n. Note that $q_1, q_2, \ldots, q_n$ are integers.

FUNCTIONS AND THEIR GRAPHS

ELEMENTARY FUNCTIONS

A **function** is any process that assigns a single value of y to each number of x. Because the value of x determines the value of y, y is called the **dependent variable** and x is called the **independent variable**. The set of all the values of x for which the function is defined is called the **domain** of the function. The set of corresponding values of y is called the **range** of the function.

Operations on Functions

Functions can be added, subtracted, multiplied, or divided to form new functions.

   a. $(f + g)(x) = f(x) + g(x)$

   b. $(f - g)(x) = f(x) - g(x)$

   c. $(f \times g)(x) = f(x)\,g(x)$

   d. $\left(\dfrac{f}{g}\right)(x) = \dfrac{f(x)}{g(x)}$

Composite Function

The **composite function** $f \circ g$ is defined $(f \circ g)(x) = f(g(x))$.

Inverse

The **inverse** of a function, f^{-1}, is obtained from f by interchanging the x and $y\ (= f(x))$ and then solving for y.

Two functions f and g are inverses of one another if $g \circ f = x$ and $f \circ g = x$. To find g when f is given, interchange x and g in the equation $y = f(x)$ and solve for $y = g(x)$.

TRANSLATIONS, REFLECTIONS, AND SYMMETRY OF FUNCTIONS

A **translation** of a function will move each point of the function a specific number of units left or right, then up or down.

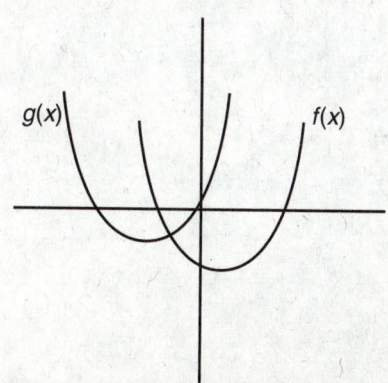

A 90° **rotation** of a function moves each point P to a new point P' so that $OP = OP'$ and $\overline{OP}$ is perpendicular to $\overline{OP'}$. The letter O represents the origin, which is located at $(0, 0)$. If the rotation is *counterclockwise*, each point (x, y) becomes $(-y, x)$. If the rotation is *clockwise*, each point (x, y) becomes $(y, -x)$.

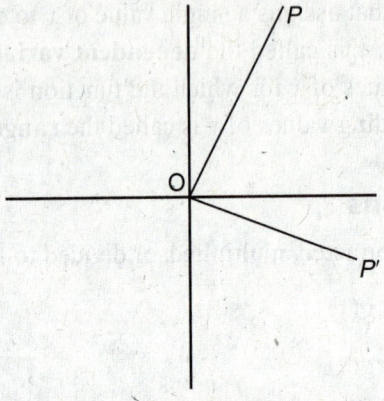

A **reflection** of a function is simply the mirror image of the function. A reflection about the x-axis changes point (x, y) into point $(x, -y)$. A reflection about the y-axis changes point (x, y) into point $(-x, y)$. A reflection about the line $y = x$ will move each point P to a new point P' so that the line $y = x$ is the perpendicular bisector of $\overline{PP'}$. Each point (x, y) becomes (y, x) after the reflection.

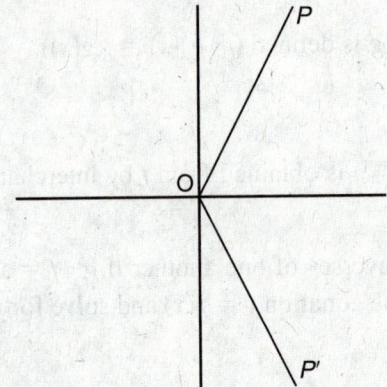

GEOMETRY TOPICS

Plane geometry refers to two-dimensional shapes (that is, shapes that can be drawn on a sheet of paper), such as triangles, parallelograms, trapezoids, and circles. Three-dimensional objects (that is, shapes with depth) are the subjects of solid geometry.

TRIANGLES

A closed three-sided geometric figure is called a **triangle**. The points of the intersection of the sides of a triangle are called the **vertices** of the triangle.

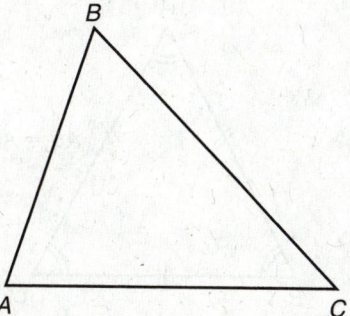

A **side** of a triangle is a line segment whose endpoints are the vertices of two angles of the triangle. The **perimeter** of a triangle is the sum of the measures of the sides of the triangle.

An **interior angle** of a triangle is an angle formed by two sides and includes the third side within its collection of points. The sum of the measures of the interior angles of a triangle is 180°.

A **scalene triangle** has no equal sides.

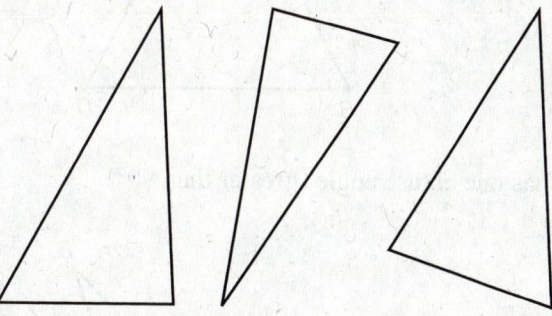

An **isosceles triangle** has at least two equal sides. The third side is called the **base** of the triangle, and the base angles (the angles opposite the equal sides) are equal.

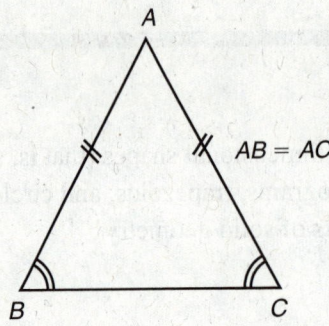

An **equilateral triangle** has all three sides equal. $\overline{AB} = \overline{AC} = \overline{BC}$. An equilateral triangle is also **equiangular**, with each angle equaling 60°.

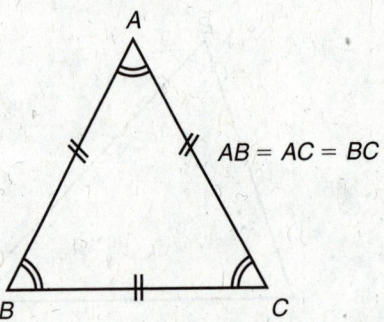

An **acute triangle** has three acute angles (less than 90°).

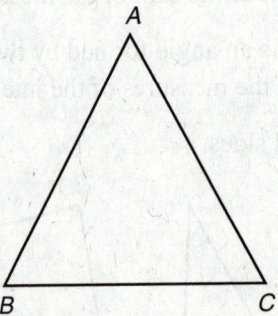

An **obtuse triangle** has one obtuse angle (greater than 90°).

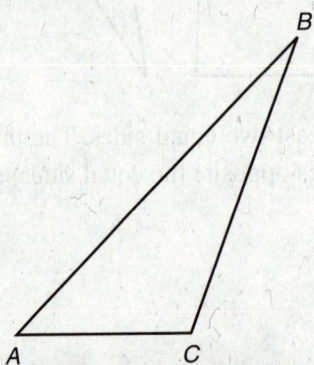

A **right triangle** has a right angle. The side opposite the right angle in a right triangle is called the **hypotenuse**. The other two sides are called the **legs** (or arms). By the **Pythagorean Theorem**, the lengths of the three sides of a right triangle are related by the formula $c^2 = a^2 + b^2$ where c is the hypotenuse and a and b are the other two sides (the legs).

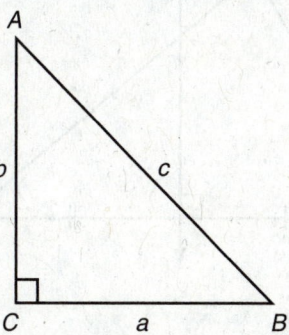

An **altitude**, or **height**, of a triangle is a line segment from a vertex of the triangle perpendicular to the opposite side. For an obtuse triangle, the altitude sometimes is drawn as a perpendicular line to an extension of the opposite side.

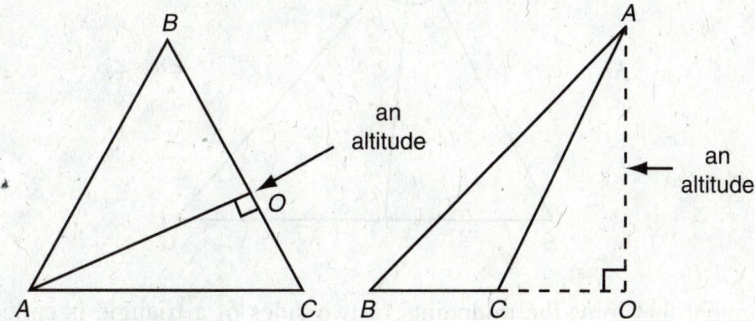

The **area** of a triangle is given by

$$A = \frac{1}{2}bh$$

where h is the altitude and b is the base to which the altitude is drawn.

A line segment connecting a vertex of a triangle and the midpoint of the opposite side is called a **median** of the triangle.

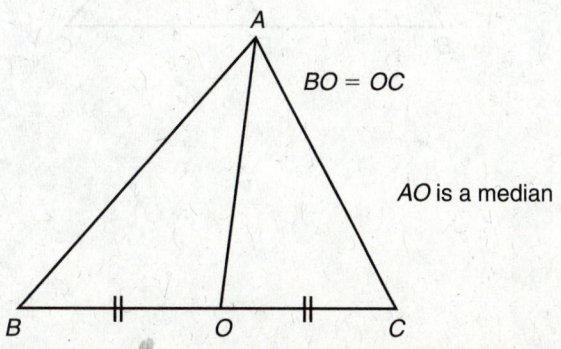

A line that bisects and is perpendicular to a side of a triangle is called a **perpendicular bisector** of that side.

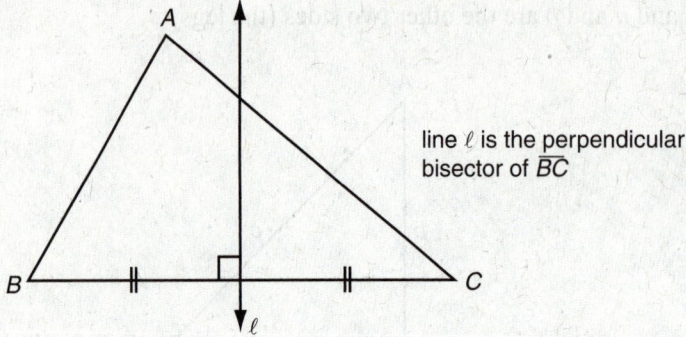

line ℓ is the perpendicular bisector of $\overline{BC}$

An **angle bisector** of a triangle is a line that bisects an angle and extends to the opposite side of the triangle.

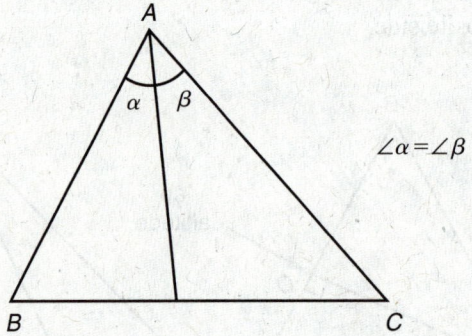

$\angle\alpha = \angle\beta$

The line segment that joins the midpoints of two sides of a triangle is called a **midline** of the triangle.

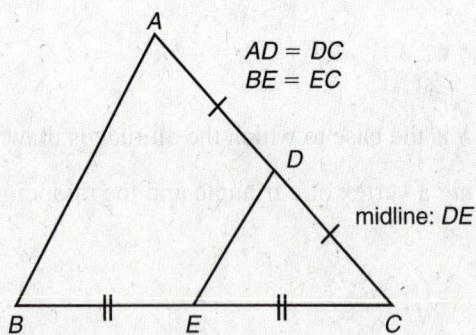

AD = DC
BE = EC

midline: DE

An **exterior angle** of a triangle is an angle formed outside a triangle by one side of the triangle and the extension of an adjacent side.

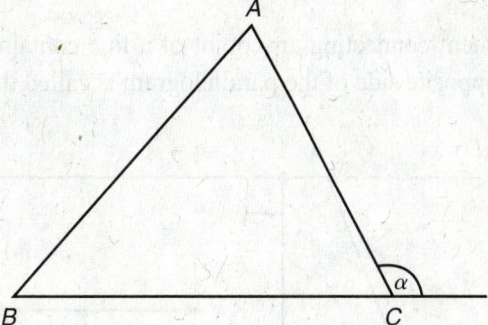

THE PYTHAGOREAN THEOREM

The **Pythagorean Theorem** pertains to a right triangle, which, as we saw, is a triangle that has one 90° angle. The Pythagorean Theorem tells you that the square of the hypotenuse of a right triangle is equal to the sum of the squares of the other two sides, or $c^2 = a^2 + b^2$.

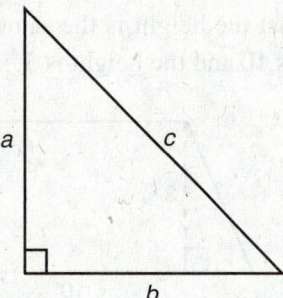

The Pythagorean Theorem is useful because if you know the length of any two sides of a right triangle, you can figure out the length of the third side.

QUADRILATERALS

A **polygon** is any closed figure with straight line segments as sides. A **quadrilateral** is any polygon with four sides. The points where the sides meet are called **vertices** (singular: **vertex**).

Parallelograms

A **parallelogram** is a quadrilateral whose opposite sides are parallel.

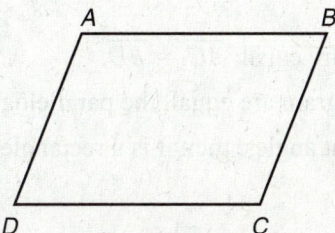

Two angles that have their vertices at the endpoints of the same side of a parallelogram are called **consecutive angles**. So $\angle A$ is consecutive to $\angle B$; $\angle B$ is consecutive to $\angle C$; $\angle C$ is consecutive to $\angle D$; and $\angle D$ is consecutive to $\angle A$.

The perpendicular segment connecting any point of a line containing one side of a parallelogram to the line containing the opposite side of the parallelogram is called the **altitude** of the parallelogram.

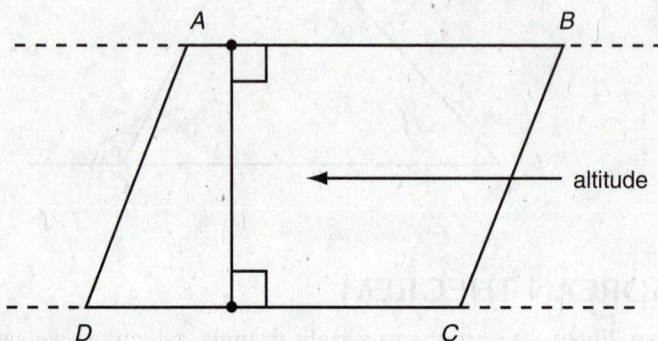

A **diagonal** of a polygon is a line segment joining any two nonconsecutive vertices. The area of a parallelogram is given by the formula $A = bh$, where b is the base and h is the height drawn perpendicular to that base. Note that the height is the same as the altitude of the parallelogram. In the parallelogram below, the base is 10 and the height is 3, so $A = bh = (10)(3) = 30$.

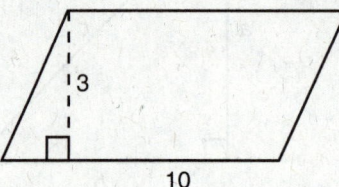

Rectangles

A **rectangle** is a parallelogram with right angles.

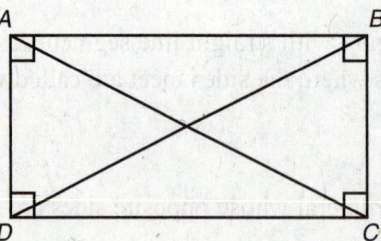

- The diagonals of a rectangle are equal, $\overline{AC} = \overline{BD}$.
- If the diagonals of a parallelogram are equal, the parallelogram is a rectangle.
- If a quadrilateral has four right angles, then it is a rectangle.

- The area of a rectangle is given by the formula $A = lw$, where l is the length and w is the width. For example, if a rectangle has a length of 4 and a width of 9, then $A = lw = (4)(9) = 36$.

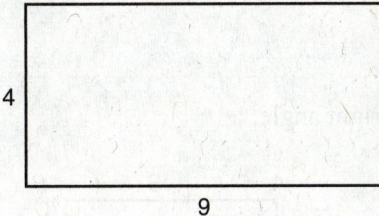

Rhombi

A **rhombus** (plural: **rhombi**) is a parallelogram that has two adjacent sides that are equal.

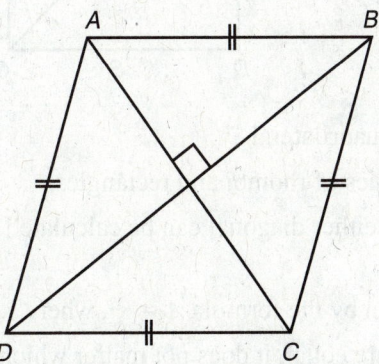

- All sides of a rhombus are equal.
- The diagonals of a rhombus are perpendicular bisectors of each other.
- The area of a rhombus can be found by the formula $A = \frac{1}{2}(d_1 \times d_2)$, where d_1 and d_2 are the diagonals.

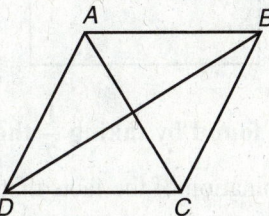

ABCD is a rhombus. $AC = 4$ and $BD = 7$. The area of the rhombus is

$$\left(\frac{1}{2}\right)(AC)(BD) = \left(\frac{1}{2}\right)(4)(7) = 14.$$

- The diagonals of a rhombus bisect the angles of the rhombus.
- If the diagonals of a parallelogram are perpendicular, the parallelogram is a rhombus.

- If a quadrilateral has four equal sides, then it is a rhombus.
- A parallelogram is a rhombus if either diagonal of the parallelogram bisects the angles of the vertices it joins.

Squares

A **square** is a rhombus with a right angle.

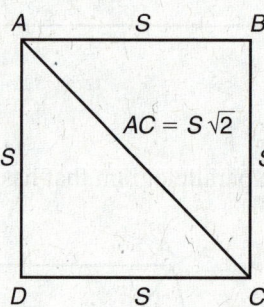

- A square is an equilateral quadrilateral.
- A square has all the properties of rhombi and rectangles.
- In a square, the measure of either diagonal can be calculated by multiplying the length of any side by the square root of 2.
- The area of a square is given by the formula $A = s^2$, where s is the side of the square.
- Since all sides of a square are equal, it does not matter which side is used. For example, if one side of a square is 6, then $A = s^2 = (6)^2 = 36$.

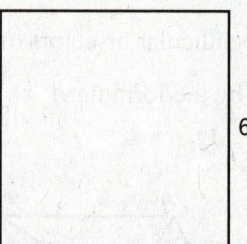

The area of a square can also be found by taking $\frac{1}{2}$ the product of the length of the diagonal squared. This comes from a combination of the facts that the area of a rhombus is $\left(\frac{1}{2}\right)d_1 d_2$ and that $d_1 = d_2$ for a square. For example, if the diagonal is 8, then $A = \frac{1}{2}d^2 = \frac{1}{2}(8)^2 = \frac{1}{2}(64) = 32$.

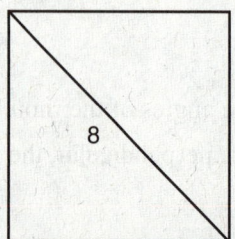

Trapezoids

A **trapezoid** is a quadrilateral with two and only two parallel sides. The parallel sides of a trapezoid are called the **bases**. The **median** of a trapezoid is the line joining the midpoints of the nonparallel sides.

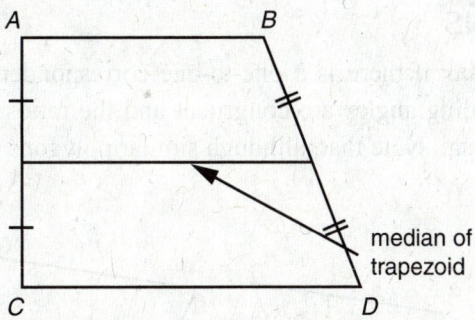

median of trapezoid

The perpendicular segment connecting any point in the line containing one base of the trapezoid to the line containing the other base is the **altitude** of the trapezoid.

A pair of angles including only one of the parallel sides is called a pair of **base angles**.

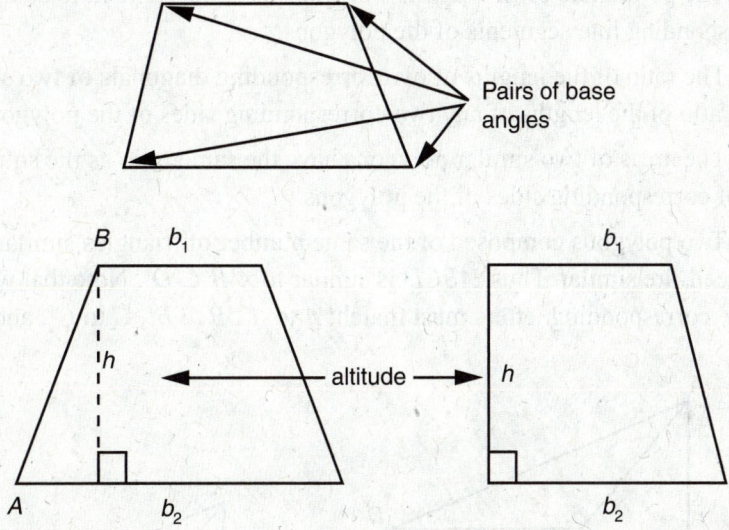

Pairs of base angles

- The median of a trapezoid is parallel to the bases and equal to one-half their sum.
- The area of a trapezoid equals one-half the altitude times the sum of the bases, or $\frac{1}{2}h(b_1 + b_2)$.
- An **isosceles trapezoid** is a trapezoid whose non-parallel sides are equal.

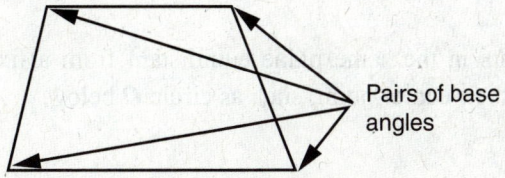

Pairs of base angles

- The base angles of an isosceles trapezoid are equal.
- The diagonals of an isosceles trapezoid are equal.
- The opposite angles of an isosceles trapezoid are supplementary.

SIMILAR POLYGONS

Two polygons are **similar** if there is a one-to-one correspondence between their vertices such that all pairs of corresponding angles are congruent and the ratios of the measures of all pairs of corresponding sides are equal. Note that, although similar polygons must have the same shape, they may have different sizes.

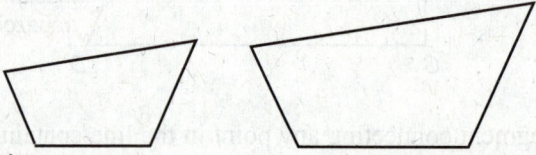

Theorems of Similar Polygons

- **Theorem 1.** The perimeters of two similar polygons have the same ratio as the measure of any pair of corresponding line segments of the polygons.
- **Theorem 2.** The ratio of the lengths of two corresponding diagonals of two similar polygons is equal to the ratio of the lengths of any two corresponding sides of the polygons.
- **Theorem 3.** The areas of two similar polygons have the same ratio as the square of the measures of any pair of corresponding sides of the polygons.
- **Theorem 4.** Two polygons composed of the same number of triangles similar to each, and similarly placed, are similar. Thus, $ABCD$ is similar to $A'B'C'D'$. Note that when naming similar polygons, the corresponding letters must match: A to A', B to B', C to C', and D to D'.

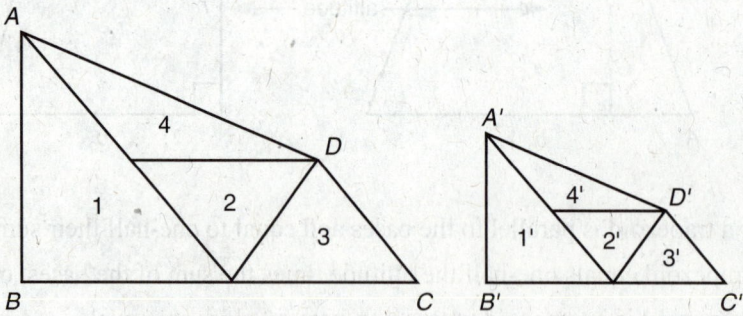

CIRCLES

A **circle** is a set of points in the same plane equidistant from a fixed point, called its **center**. Circles are often named by their center point, such as circle O below.

A **radius** of a circle is a line segment drawn from the center of the circle to any point on the circle.

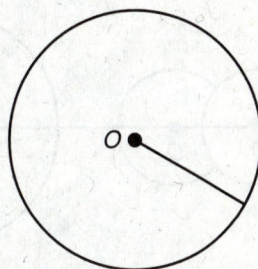

The **circumference** of a circle is the length of its outer edge, given by $C = \pi d = 2\pi r$, where r is the radius, d is the diameter, and π(pi) is a mathematical constant approximately equal to 3.14.

The **area** of a circle is given by $A = \pi r^2$.

A full circle is 360°. The measure of a semicircle (half a circle) is 180°.

A line that intersects a circle in two points is called a **secant**.

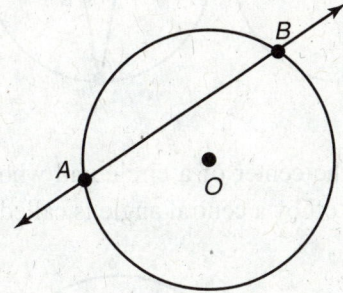

A line segment joining two points on a circle is called a **chord** of the circle.

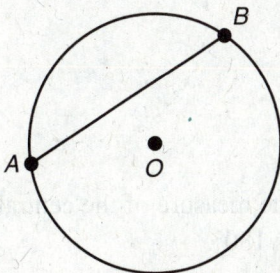

A chord that passes through the center of the circle is called a **diameter** of the circle. The length of the diameter is twice the length of the radius, $d = 2r$.

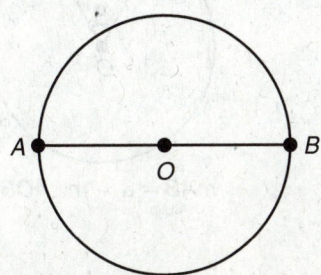

The line passing through the centers of two (or more) circles is called the **line of centers**.

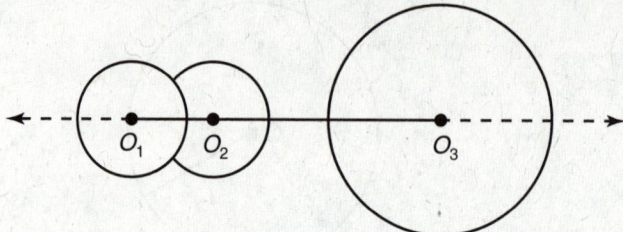

An angle whose vertex is on the circle and whose sides are chords of the circle is called an **inscribed angle** ($\angle BAC$ in the diagrams).

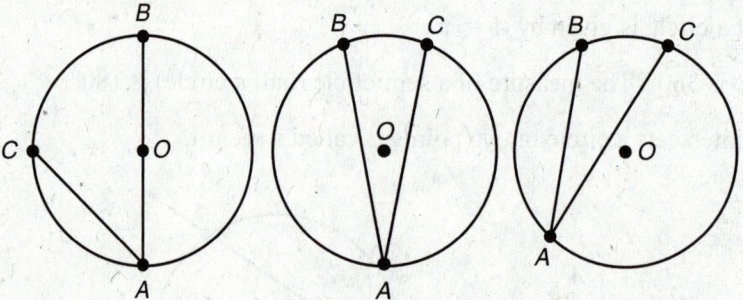

An angle whose vertex is at the center of a circle and whose sides are radii is called a **central angle**. The portion of a circle cut off by a central angle is called an **arc** of the circle.

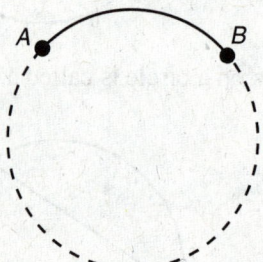

The measure of a minor arc is the measure of the central angle that intercepts that arc. The measure of a semicircle (half a circle) is 180°.

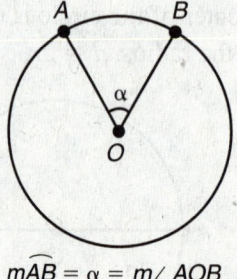

$$m\overset{\frown}{AB} = \alpha = m\angle AOB$$

The length of an arc intercepted by a central angle has the same ratio to the circle's circumference as the measure of the arc is to 360°, the full circle. Therefore, arc length is given by $\frac{n}{360} \times 2\pi r$, where $n =$ measure of the central angle.

A **sector** is the portion of a circle between two radii (sector *AOB* here). Its area is given by $A = \frac{n}{360} \times (\pi r^2)$, where n is the central angle formed by the radii.

The distance from an outside point *P* to a given circle is the distance from that point to the point where the circle intersects with a line segment with endpoints at the center of the circle and point *P*. The distance of point *P* to the diagrammed circle with center *O* is the line segment $\overline{PB}$, part of line segment $\overline{PO}$.

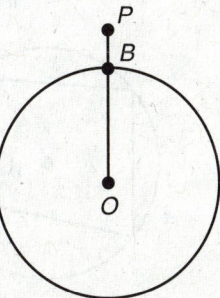

A line that has one and only one point of intersection with a circle is called a **tangent** to that circle, and their common point is called a **point of tangency**. In the diagram, *Q* and *P* are each points of tangency. A tangent is always perpendicular to the radius drawn to the point of tangency.

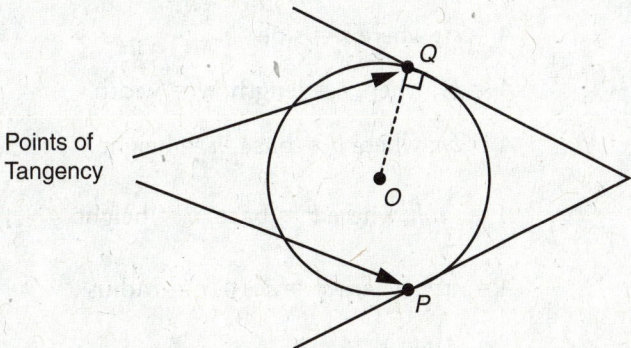

Congruent circles are circles whose radii are congruent.

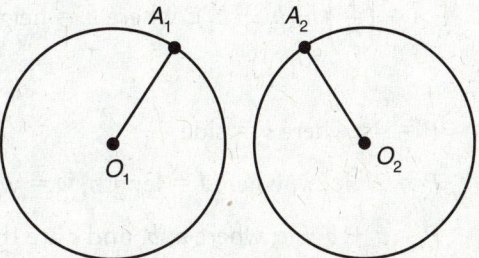

If $O_1A_1 \cong O_2A_2$, then $O_1 \cong O_2$.

Circles that have the same center and unequal radii are called **concentric circles**.

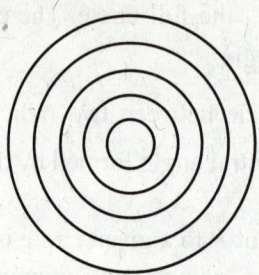

A **circumscribed circle** is a circle passing through all the vertices of a polygon. The polygon is said to be **inscribed** in the circle.

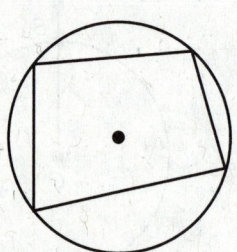

FORMULAS FOR AREA AND PERIMETER

Figures	Areas
Area (A) of a:	
square	$A = s^2$; where s = side
rectangle	$A = lw$; where l = length, w = width
parallelogram	$A = bh$; where b = base, h = height
triangle	$A = \dfrac{1}{2}bh$; where b = base, h = height
circle	$A = \pi r^2$; where π = 3.14, r = radius
sector	$A = \left(\dfrac{n}{360}\right)(\pi r^2)$, where n = central angle, r = radius, π = 3.14
trapezoid	$A = \left(\dfrac{1}{2}\right)(h)(b_1 + b_2)$; where h = height, b_1 and b_2 = bases
Perimeter (P) of a:	
square	$P = 4s$; where s = side
rectangle	$P = 2l + 2w$; where l = length, w = width
triangle	$P = a + b + c$; where a, b, and c are the sides
Circumference (C) of a circle	$C = \pi d$; where π = 3.14, d = diameter

THE FUNDAMENTAL COUNTING PRINCIPLE

The **fundamental counting principle** deals with identifying the number of outcomes of a given experiment and encompasses the **counting rule**: If one experiment can be performed in m ways, and a second experiment can be performed in n ways, then there are $m \times n$ distinct ways both experiments can be performed in this specified order. the counting principle can be applied to more than two experiments.

For example, if Niki's mother bought her five tops, three shorts, and two pairs of shoes for the summer, she will have 30 different outfit choices ($5 \times 3 \times 2$).

PERMUTATIONS

A **permutation** is an arrangement of specific objects in which order is of particular importance. To determine the number of possible permutations, the following formula can be used:

$$_nP_r = \frac{n!}{(n-r)!}$$

where n is the number of objects in the given set, r is the number of objects being chosen, and ! is the notation used for factorial. The **factorial** of a number is the product of that number and all the numbers less than it down to 1, or $n! = n \times (n-1) \times (n-2) \times \ldots \times 3 \times 2 \times 1$. For example, $5! = 5 \times 4 \times 3 \times 2 \times 1 = 120$.

The formula for permutations is a consequence of the counting rule described previously. In the permutation $_6P_2 = \dfrac{6!}{4!} = \dfrac{6 \times 5 \times 4 \times 3 \times 2 \times 1}{4 \times 3 \times 2 \times 1}$, note that 4! cancels out part of 6! and we are left with only $6 \times 5 = 30$. So you really don't have to do that much multiplication. Permutations cancel down to $n \times (n-1) \times (n-2) \times \ldots (n-r+1)$, so even a permutation with large numbers, such as $_{12}P_3$, becomes $12 \times 11 \times 10 = 1,320$.

COMBINATIONS

A **combination** is an arrangement of specific objects in which order is *not* of particular importance. To determine the number of possible combinations, use the formula $_nC_r = \dfrac{n!}{r!(n-r)!}$ where n is the number of objects in the given set, r is the number of objects being chosen, and ! is the notation used for factorial. Note that this formula is similar to the one for permutations, but since order is not important, we have to factor out all the duplications. In combinations, *ABC* is the same as *ACB*, *BAC*, *BCA*, *CAB*, and *CBA*. So we must divide the permutation by the duplications, which occur *r*! times.

As with permutations, we don't have to do too much calculation for combinations. After the cancellations, combinations reduce to a fraction in which the first *r* factors of *n*! are in the numerator and *r*! is in the denominator, and then further cancellations can take place. For example, $_8C_3 = \dfrac{8 \times 7 \times 6}{3 \times 2 \times 1}$, which cancels to $8 \times 7 = 56$. The final cancellations are always possible in combinations before multiplying to get the final answer, and the denominator *always* cancels out.

PROBABILITY

Before discussing the actual calculation of a probability, let's review the following probability facts:

1. Probabilities are values ranging from 0 to 1 inclusive: $0 \le P(E) \le 1$, where $P(E)$ means probability (P) of an event (E).

   a. Probabilities cannot be negative or greater than 1.

   b. A probability of 0 means that the event cannot or did not occur.

   c. A probability of 1 means that the event must occur or always occurred.

   d. A probability is expressed as a fraction or a decimal.

2. An experiment consists of all possible outcomes.

3. An event consists of one or more outcomes.

4. The sum of the probabilities of all possible outcomes in any given experiment is 1.

5. The notation used for the probability of an event E not happening is $P(E')$, where E' is read as "E complement."

6. Combining facts (4) and (5), we then see that $P(E) + P(E') = 1$. That is, the probability of an event happening or its complement happening is 1. This formula may also be applied in the following form: $P(E) = 1 - P(E')$, depending on the context of the problem.

An experiment consists of rolling an ordinary number cube once. Then, each of 1, 2, 3, 4, 5, and 6 are outcomes and $P(1) + P(2) + P(3) + P(4) + P(5) + P(6) = 1$. An example of an event E_1 would be the set of outcomes numbered below 3, then $E_1 = \{1, 2\}$. The complement of E_1, denoted as E'_1, consists of outcomes 3, 4, 5, 6; that is: $E'_1 = \{3, 4, 5, 6\}$.

The mathematical formula associated with the probability of a simple event is $P(E) = \dfrac{m}{n}$, where m is the number of favorable outcomes relative to event E, and n is the total number of possible outcomes.

Probability of A or B

If the probability of one event is not affected by the probability of another, then the probability of either one of them occurring in an experiment is the sum of their individual probabilities; however, one of the instances of both occurring has to be subtracted out to prevent counting twice the probability of both events. The mathematical formula that allows us to find the probability of obtaining either event A or event B is $P(A \text{ or } B) = P(A) + P(B) - P(A \text{ and } B)$.

For example, the probability of selecting a spade or an ace from a deck of cards would be the probability of a spade $\left(\dfrac{13}{52} = \dfrac{1}{4}\right)$ plus the probability of an ace $\left(\dfrac{4}{52} = \dfrac{1}{13}\right)$, but each of these probabilities includes the ace of spades, so we have to subtract one of the probabilities that the card is the ace of spades $\left(\dfrac{1}{52}\right)$. Therefore, the formula is:

$$P(\text{spade or ace}) = P(\text{spade}) + P(\text{ace}) - P(\text{ace of spades})$$

$$= \frac{1}{4} + \frac{1}{13} - \frac{1}{52} = \frac{16}{52}.$$

When you think about it, 16 (and not 17) of the cards in a deck are either a spade or an ace or both.

Note: If events A and B are mutually exclusive, $P(A \text{ and } B) = 0$, then the previous formula simplifies to $P(A \text{ or } B) = P(A) + P(B)$.

Probability of One of Two Exclusive Events

Given two events, A and B, if we want the probability that *exactly* one of these occurs, then the formula becomes: $P(\text{exactly one of } A \text{ or } B) = P(A) + P(B) - 2 \times P(A \text{ and } B)$.

The factor of 2 in this equation eliminates all possibility of both events taking place, since you want *exactly one* of events A or B to occur, not both. In the last example, it eliminates the probability of an ace and a spade (the ace of spades) when considering $P(\text{ace})$ plus the probability of a spade and an ace (also the ace of spades) when considering $P(\text{spade})$.

Conditional Probability

From the **conditional probability** formula $P(A \mid B) = \dfrac{P(A \text{ and } B)}{P(B)}$, where $P(A|B)$ means "the probability of A, given that B has occurred," we can derive the multiplication rule: $P(A \text{ and } B) = P(A|B) \times P(B)$. It is not necessary to fully understand what conditional probability is as long as you are able to apply the counting rules discussed earlier.

If the occurrence of event A in no way affects the occurrence or non-occurrence of event B, then events A and B are said to be **independent**. If events A and B are independent, then $P(A$ and $B) = P(A) \times P(B)$, according to the counting rule.

PROBABILITY WORD PROBLEMS

As with all prior real-world problems, the context of the problem can vary widely. A table or graph will provide the necessary information to calculate a single outcome, multiple outcomes, conditional probability, or an expected value.

Using Tables for Probability

Tables present data in an easy-to-read format. This table is a breakdown of the student vote for the winner of the election for student body president.

Student Votes for Student Body President

	Freshman	Sophomore	Junior	Senior
Male	9%	17%	10%	9%
Female	16%	13%	15%	11%

For example, to determine the probability of a randomly selected student not being a senior, we see that 20% of the students (9% male and 11% female) are in the senior column. Those that are not in the senior column total 80%. Thus, the probability of not being a senior is 0.80.

MEASURES OF CENTRAL TENDENCY

There are three ways to describe the tendency of a set of data, meaning what a "typical" value is: the mean, median, and mode. All three of these numbers are measures of **central tendency**. They describe the "middle" or "center" of the data.

Mean

The **mean**, the arithmetic average, is the sum of the variables divided by the total number of variables. For example, the mean of 4, 3, and 8 is $\dfrac{4 + 3 + 8}{3} = \dfrac{15}{3} = 5$.

Median

The **median** is the middle value in a set. The set of numbers first needs to be put in order, smallest to largest or vice versa. When there is an odd number of values in the set, the median is simply the middle value, and there is an equal number of values larger and smaller than the median. When the set has an even number of values, the average of the two middle values is the median. For example, the median of (2, 3, 5, 8, 9) is 5. However, the median of (2, 3, 5, 9, 10, 11) is $\frac{5+9}{2} = 7$.

Note that the median doesn't have to be an element of the set. In fact, with an even number of values, it often is not. Also note that these rules apply even if some numbers are repeated. For example, the median of (2, 3, 3, 4, 6, 8, 9) is 4.

Mode

The **mode** is the most frequently occurring value in the set of values. For example, the mode of (4, 5, 8, 3, 8, 2) would be 8, since it occurs twice, whereas the other values occur only once. There can be two modes (in which case the set is called **bimodal**), or in fact as many modes as you have values. The set 2, 2, 3, 3, 5, 5, 8, 8, 9, 9 has five modes, since each value is mentioned twice. If each number in a set of numbers appears only once, there is no mode. Of course, in this case the mode isn't a very useful measure of central tendency, and the mean or median would describe the data better.

Comparing the Mean, Median, and Mode in a Variety of Distributions

It is sometimes useful to make comparisons about the relative values of the mean, median, and mode. This section presents steps to do that without having to calculate the exact values of these measures.

Step 1: If a bar graph is not provided, sketch one from the information given in the problem. The graph will either be skewed to the left, skewed to the right, or approximately normal. A **skewed** distribution has one of its tails longer than the other.

- A graph skewed to the left will look like Figure 8; its left tail is longer. The order of the three measures is mean < median < mode (alphabetical order).

- A graph skewed to the right will look like Figure 9; its right tail is longer. The order of the three measures is mode < median < mean (reverse alphabetical order).

- A graph that is approximately **normal** (also called **bell-shaped**) will look like Figure 10, and the mean = median = mode.

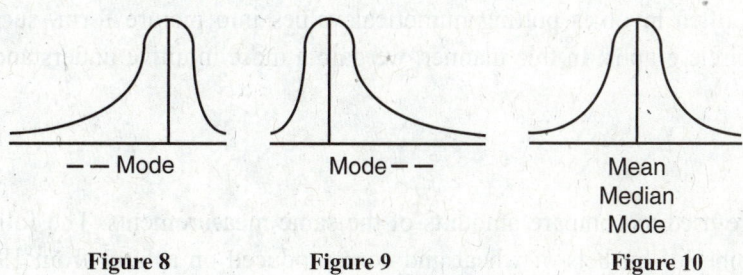

– – Mode	Mode – –	Mean Median Mode
Figure 8	**Figure 9**	**Figure 10**

Step 2: Write the word *mode* under the highest column of the bar graph, because the mode is the most frequent. If the graph is skewed right or left, the positioning of the mode establishes the order for the remaining two terms according to the information provided above. If the graph is approximately symmetrical, the values of all three terms are approximately equivalent.

MEASURES OF VARIABILITY

In addition to measures of central tendency, distributions need to be described with measures of **variability**, or spread. It is not enough to know where the middle of a distribution is, but also how spread out it is. A manufacturer of light bulbs would like small variability in the amount of hours the bulbs will likely burn. A track coach who needs to decide which athletes go on to the finals may want larger variability in heat times because it will be easier to decide who are truly the fastest runners.

The **range** of a data set is simply the difference between the maximum value and the minimum value. The range is rarely a good choice to represent the data set, especially because it can be affected by outliers.

For data that are fairly symmetric, the standard deviation and variance are useful measures of variability. The **variance** tells us how much variability exists in a distribution. It is the "average" of the squared differences between the data values and the mean. The variance is calculated with the formula $S^2 = \dfrac{1}{n-1}\sum\left(x_i - \overline{x}\right)^2$ where n is the number of data points, x_i represents each data value, and $\overline{x}$ is the mean.

The **standard deviation** is the square root of the variance. The formula for the standard deviation is therefore $S = \sqrt{\dfrac{1}{n-1}\sum\left(x_i - \overline{x}\right)^2}$.

The standard deviation is used for most applications in statistics. It can be thought of as the typical distance an observation lies from the mean.

DATA ANALYSIS

Data analysis often involves putting numerical values into picture form, such as bar graphs, line graphs, and circle graphs. In this manner, we gain a more intuitive understanding of the given information.

Bar Graphs

Bar graphs are used to compare amounts of the same measurements. The following bar graph compares the number of bushels of wheat and corn produced on a farm from 1975 to 1985. The horizontal axis for a bar graph consists of categories (e.g., years, ethnicity, marital status) rather than values, and the widths of the bars are uniform. The emphasis is on the height of the bars.

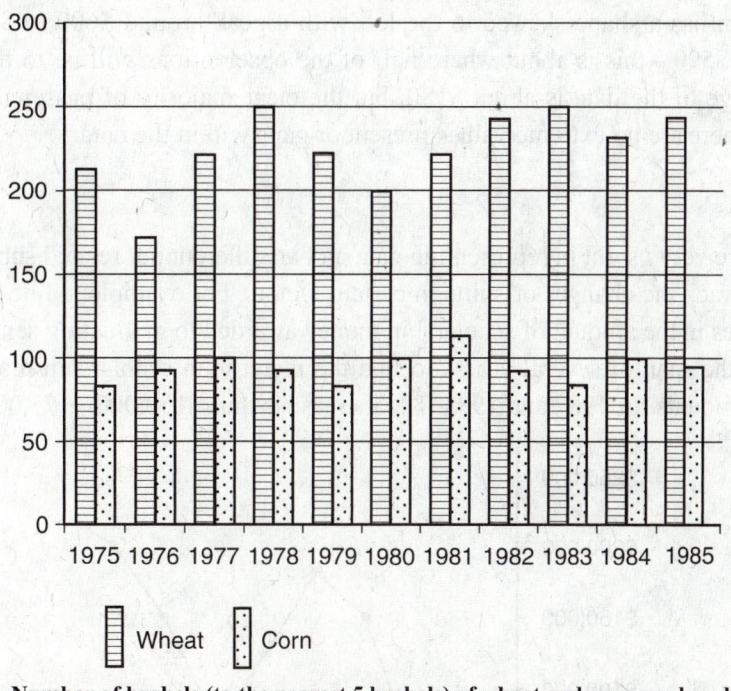

**Number of bushels (to the nearest 5 bushels) of wheat and corn produced
by Farm RQS, 1975–1985**

Histograms

A **histogram** is an appropriate display for quantitative data. It is used primarily for continuous data, but may be used for discrete data that have a wide spread. The horizontal axis is broken into intervals that do not have to be of uniform size. Histograms are also good for large data sets. The area of the bar denotes the value, not the height, as in a bar graph.

The following histogram shows the amount of money spent by passengers on a ship during a recent cruise to Alaska.

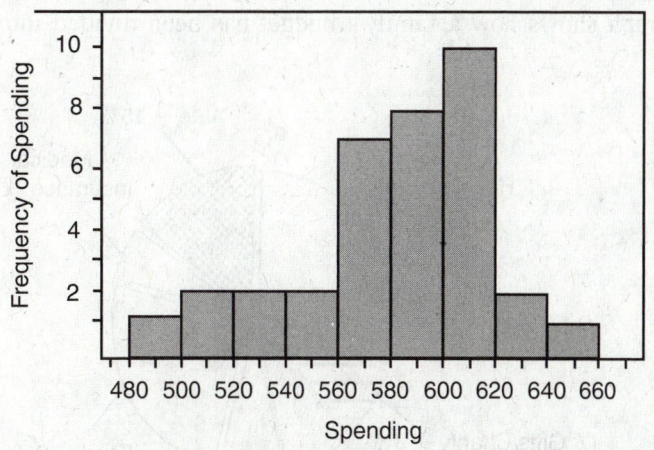

Passenger spending during cruise to Alaska

The intervals have widths of $20. One person spent between $480 and $500, two spent between $500 and $520, and so on. We cannot tell from the graph the precise amount each individual spent.

The distribution has a shape skewed to the left with a peak around $600 to $620. The data are centered at about $590—this is about where half of the observations will be to the left and half to the right. The range of the data is about $180, but the clear majority of passengers spent between $560 and $620. There are no extreme values present or gaps within the data.

Line Graphs

Line graphs are very useful in representing data on two different but related subjects. Line graphs are often used to track the changes or shifts in certain factors. For example, a line graph can be used to track the changes in the amount of scholarship money awarded to graduating seniors at a particular high school over the span of several years. To find the increase in scholarship money from 1987 to 1988, locate the amounts for 1987 and 1988. The increase is thus $150,000 − 75,000 = $75,000$.

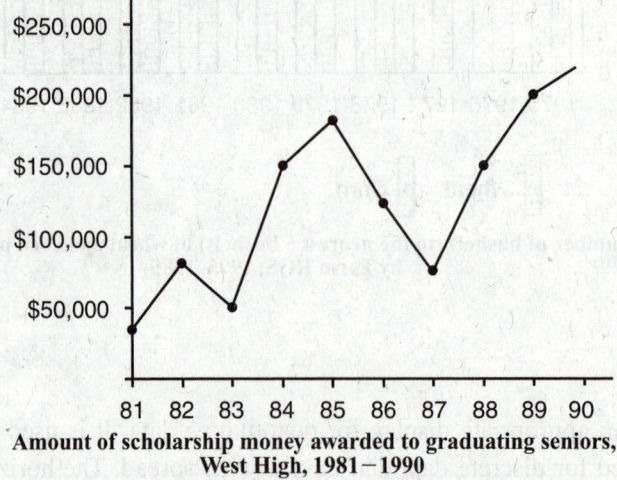

**Amount of scholarship money awarded to graduating seniors,
West High, 1981–1990**

Pie Charts

Circle graphs (or **pie charts**) are used to show the breakdown of a whole picture. When the circle graph is used to demonstrate this breakdown in terms of percents, the parts of the circle graph represent percentages of the total. When added together, these percentages add up to 100%. The following circle graph shows how a family's budget has been divided into different categories by using percentages.

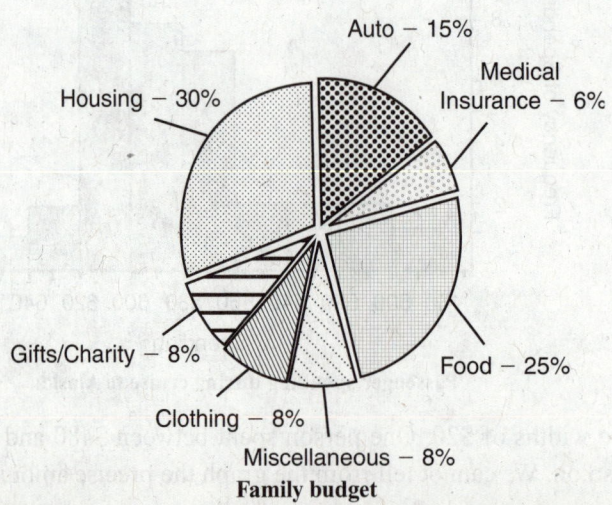

Family budget

Stemplots

A **stemplot**, also called a stem-and-leaf plot, can be used to display univariate data as well. It is good for small sets of data (about 50 or less) and forms a plot much like a histogram. This stemplot represents test scores for a class of 32 students.

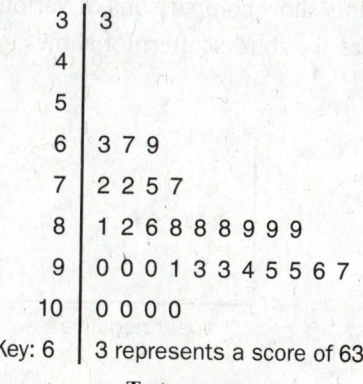

```
 3  | 3
 4  |
 5  |
 6  | 3 7 9
 7  | 2 2 5 7
 8  | 1 2 6 8 8 8 9 9 9
 9  | 0 0 0 1 3 3 4 5 5 6 7
10  | 0 0 0 0
```

Key: 6 | 3 represents a score of 63

Test scores

The values on the left of the vertical bar are called the stems; those on the right are called leaves. Stems and leaves need not be tens and ones—they may be hundreds and tens, ones and tenths, and so on. A good stemplot always includes a key for the reader so that the values may be interpreted correctly.

ANALYZING PATTERNS IN SCATTERPLOTS

Bivariate data consist of two variables. Typically, we are looking for an association between these two variables. The variables may be categorical or quantitative; in this section, we focus on quantitative bivariate data. **Scatterplots** are used to visualize quantitative bivariate data.

The two variables under study are referred to as the **explanatory variable** (x) and the **response variable** (y). The explanatory variable *explains* or *predicts* the response variable. The response variable measures the outcomes that have been observed.

Scatterplots can tell us if and how two variables are related. When we examined univariate data in the preceding sections, we described a distribution's shape, center, spread, and outliers/unusual features. In a scatterplot, we focus on its shape, direction, and strength, and we look for outliers and unusual features. Below is a scatterplot of the top 30 leading scorers in the history of the National Basketball Association (NBA). Each point represents 1 of the 30 players. Michael Jordan, who scored 32,292 points in 1,072 games, is noted.

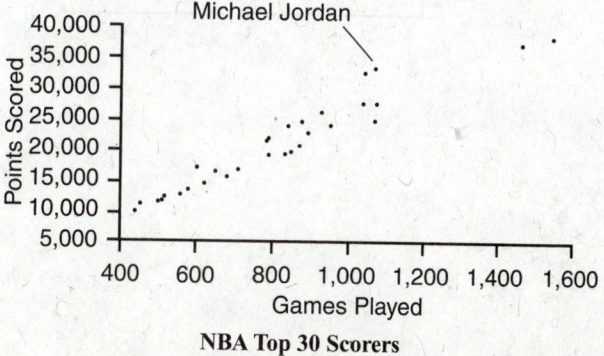

NBA Top 30 Scorers

The **shape** of a plot is usually classified as linear or nonlinear (curved). The **direction** of a scatterplot tells what happens to the response variables as the explanatory variable increases. This is the slope of the general pattern of the data. The **strength** describes how tight or spread out the points of a scatterplot are.

The following three scatterplots show comparisons of various directions of the data. The first two have a clear linear trend, whereas the third scatterplot shows a random type of distribution with no clear association among points.

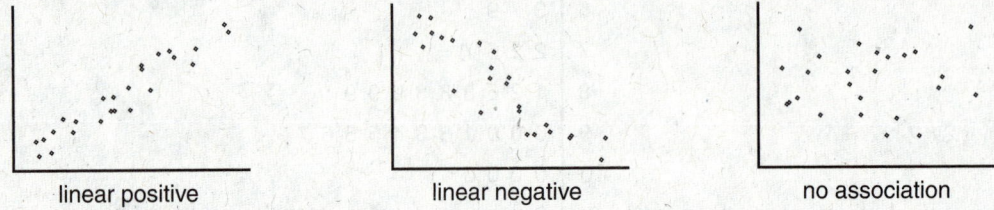

| linear positive | linear negative | no association |

When analyzing a scatterplot, it is also a good idea to look for outliers, clusters, or gaps in the data. The following scatterplot has an obvious gap. There is an overall positive, linear association, but we should find out the reason for the gap.

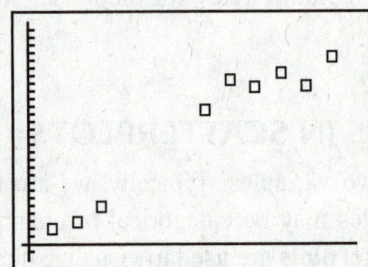

The following scatterplot has an obvious outlier that falls outside the general pattern of the data. There could be several possible reasons for the outlier, which merits investigation.

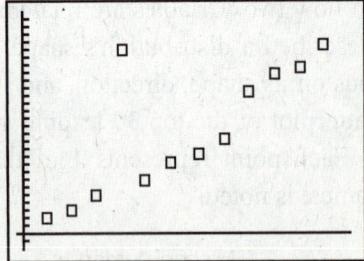

The topic of **logic** encompasses a wealth of subjects related to the principles of reasoning. This section is designed to familiarize you with the terminology you might be expected to know as well as thought processes that you can use in everyday life.

Sentential calculus is the "calculus of sentences," a field in which the truth or falseness of assertions is examined by using algebraic tools. We will approach logic from a "true" or "false" perspective here. This chapter contains many examples of sentences to illustrate the terms that are defined.

SENTENCES

A **sentence** is any expression that can be labeled either true or false. Expressions to which the terms true or false can be assigned include the following:

1. "It is raining where I am standing."

2. "My name is George."

3. "1 + 2 = 3"

Expressions to which the terms *true* or *false* cannot be assigned include the following:

1. "I will probably be healthier if I exercise."

2. "It will rain on this day, one year from now."

3. "What I am saying at this instant is a lie."

Sentences can be combined to form new sentences using the connectives **AND**, **OR**, **NOT**, and **IF-THEN**. For example, the sentences "John is tired" and "Mary is cooking" can be combined to form:

1. "John is tired AND Mary is cooking."

2. "John is tired OR Mary is cooking."

3. "John is NOT tired."

4. "IF John is tired, THEN Mary is cooking."

Logical Properties of Sentences

1. Consistency

A sentence is **consistent** if and only if it is *possible* that it is true. A sentence is **inconsistent** if and only if it is not consistent; that is, if and only if it is *impossible* that it is true. For example, "At least one odd number is not odd" is an inconsistent sentence.

2. Logical Truth

A sentence is **logically true** if and only if it is *impossible* for it to be false; that is, the denial of the sentence is inconsistent. For example, this sentence is logically true: Either Mars is a planet or Mars is not a planet.

3. Logical Falsity

A sentence is **logically false** if and only if it is *impossible* for it to be true; that is, the sentence is inconsistent. For example, this sentence is logically false: Mars is a planet and Mars is not a planet.

4. Logical Indeterminacy (Contingency)

A sentence is **logically indeterminate** (contingent) if and only if it is neither logically true nor logically false. For example, this sentence is logically indeterminate: Einstein was a physicist and Pauling was a chemist.

5. Logical Equivalent of Sentences

Two sentences are **logically equivalent** if and only if it is *impossible* for one of the sentences to be true while the other sentence is false; that is, if and only if it is impossible for the two sentences to have different truth values. "Chicago is in Illinois and Pittsburgh is in Pennsylvania" is logically equivalent to "Pittsburgh is in Pennsylvania and Chicago is in Illinois."

STATEMENTS

A **statement** is a sentence that is either true or false, but not both.

Conjunction

If a and b are statements, then a statement of the form "a and b" is called the **conjunction** of a and b, denoted by $a \wedge b$.

Disjunction

The **disjunction** of two statements a and b is shown by the compound statement "a or b," denoted by $a \vee b$.

Negation

The **negation** of a statement q is the statement "not q," denoted by $\sim q$.

Implication

The compound statement "if a, then b," denoted by $a \rightarrow b$, is called a **conditional statement** or an **implication**. "If a" is called the **hypothesis** or **premise** of the implication, "then b" is called the **conclusion** of the implication. Further, statement a is called the **antecedent** of the implication, and statement b is called the **consequent** of the implication.

Converse

The **converse** of $a \rightarrow b$ is $b \rightarrow a$.

Contrapositive

The **contrapositive** of $a \rightarrow b$ is $\sim b \rightarrow \sim a$.

Inverse

The **inverse** of $a \rightarrow b$ is $\sim a \rightarrow \sim b$.

Biconditional

The statement of the form "p if and only if q," denoted by $p \leftrightarrow q$, is called a **biconditional** statement.

Validity

An argument is **valid** if the truth of the premises means that the conclusions must also be true.

Intuition

Intuition is the process of making generalizations on insight.

BASIC PRINCIPLES, LAWS, AND THEOREMS

1. Any statement is either true or false. (The Law of the Excluded Middle)

2. A statement cannot be both true and false. (The Law of Contradiction)

3. The converse of a true statement is not necessarily true.

4. The converse of a definition is always true.

5. For a theorem to be true, it must be true for all cases.

6. A statement is false if one false instance of the statement exists.

7. The inverse of a true statement is not necessarily true.

8. The contrapositive of a true statement is true and the contrapositive of a false statement is false.

9. If the converse of a true statement is true, then the inverse is true. Likewise, if the converse is false, the inverse is false.

10. Statements that are either both true or both false are said to be **logically equivalent**.

NECESSARY AND SUFFICIENT CONDITIONS

Let P and Q represent statements. "If P, then Q" is a conditional statement in which P is a sufficient condition for Q, and similarly Q is a necessary condition for P. Consider the statement: "If it rains, then Jane will go to the movies." "If it rains" is a sufficient condition for Jane to go to the movies. "Jane will go to the movies" is a necessary condition for rain to have occurred.

Note that for the statement given, "If it rains" may not be the only condition for which Jane goes to the movies; however, it is a *sufficient* condition. Likewise, "Jane will go to the movies" will certainly not be the only result from a rainy weather condition (for example, "the ground will get wet" is another likely conclusion). However, knowing that Jane went to the movies is a *necessary* condition for rain to have occurred.

In the biconditional statement "*P* if and only if *Q*," *P* is a necessary and sufficient condition for *Q*, and vice versa. Consider the statement "Rick gets paid if and only if he works." "Rick gets paid" is both a sufficient and necessary condition for him to work. Also, Rick's working is a sufficient and necessary condition for him to get paid.

Thus, we have the following basic principles to add to our list of ten from the preceding section:

11. If a given statement and its converse are both true, then the conditions in the hypothesis of the statement are both necessary and sufficient for the conclusion of the statement.

12. If a given statement is true but its converse is false, then the conditions are sufficient but not necessary for the conclusion of the statement.

13. If a given statement and its converse are both false, then the conditions are neither sufficient nor necessary for the statement's conclusion.

DEDUCTIVE REASONING

An arrangement of statements that allow you to deduce the third one from the preceding two, called a **syllogism**, has three parts:

1. The first part is a general statement concerning a whole group. This is called the **major premise**.

2. The second part is a specific statement which indicates that a certain individual is a member of that group. This is called the **minor premise**.

3. The last part of a syllogism is a statement to the effect that the general statement which applies to the group also applies to the individual. This third statement of a syllogism is called a **deduction**. For example, this is an example of a properly deduced argument:

    A. Major Premise: All birds have feathers.
    B. Minor Premise: An eagle is a bird.
    C. Deduction: An eagle has feathers.

The technique of employing a syllogism to arrive at a conclusion is called **deductive reasoning**.

If a major premise that is true is followed by an appropriate minor premise that is true, a conclusion can be deduced that must be true, and the reasoning is valid. However, if a major premise that is true is followed by an *inappropriate* minor premise that is also true, a conclusion cannot be deduced. This is an example of an improperly deduced argument:

A. Major Premise: All people who vote are at least 18 years old.

B. Improper Minor Premise: Jane is at least 18.

C. Illogical Deduction: Jane votes.

The flaw in this argument is that the major premise in statement A makes a condition on people who vote, not on a person's age. If statements B and C are interchanged, the resulting three-part deduction would be logical.

In the following we will use capital letters $X, Y, Z, \ldots$ to represent sentences, and develop algebraic tools to represent new sentences formed by linking them with the previous connectives. Our connectives may be regarded as operations transforming one or more sentences into a new sentence. To describe them in greater detail, we introduce symbols to represent them. You will find that different symbols representing the same idea may appear in different references.

TRUTH TABLES AND BASIC LOGICAL OPERATIONS

The **truth table** for a sentence X is the exhaustive list of possible logical values of X. The **logical value** of a sentence X is *true* (or T) if X is true, and *false* (or F) if X is false.

Negation

If X is a sentence, then $\sim X$ represents the **negation**, the opposite, or the contradiction of X. Thus, the logical values of $\sim X$ are as shown in Table 2, where $\sim$ is called the **negation operation** on sentences. For example, for $X = $ "Jane is eating an apple," we have $\sim X = $ "Jane is *not* eating an apple."

Table 2–Truth Table for Negation

X	~X
T	F
F	T

The negation operation is called *unary*, transforming a sentence into a unique image sentence.

IFF

We use the symbol **IFF** to represent the expression "if and only if."

AND

For sentences X and Y, the conjunction "X AND Y," represented by $X \wedge Y$, is the sentence that is true IFF both X and Y are true. The truth table for $\wedge$ (or AND) is shown in Table 3, where $\wedge$ is called the **conjunction operator**.

Table 3–Truth Table for AND

X	Y	X ∧ Y
T	T	T
T	F	F
F	T	F
F	F	F

The conjunction $\wedge$ is a *binary* operation, transforming a pair of sentences into a unique image sentence. For X = "Jane is eating an apple" and Y = "All apples are sweet," we have $X \wedge Y$ = "Jane is eating an apple AND all apples are sweet."

AND/OR

For sentences X and Y, the disjunction "X AND/OR Y," represented by $X \vee Y$, denotes the sentence that is true if either or both X and Y are true. The truth table for $\vee$ is shown in Table 4, where $\vee$ is called the **disjunction operator**.

Table 4–Truth Table for AND/OR

X	Y	X ∨ Y
T	T	T
T	F	T
F	T	T
F	F	F

As with the conjunction operator, the disjunction is a *binary* operation, transforming the pair of sentences X, Y into a unique image sentence $X \vee Y$. For X = "Jane is eating the apple" and Y = "Marvin is running," we have $X \vee Y$ = "Jane is eating the apple AND/OR Marvin is running."

IF-THEN

For sentences X and Y, the **implication** $X \rightarrow Y$ represents the statement "IF X THEN Y." $X \rightarrow Y$ is false IFF X is true and Y is false; otherwise, it is true. The truth table for $\rightarrow$ is shown in Table 5. $\rightarrow$ is referred to as the **implication operator**.

Table 5–Truth Table for IF-THEN

X	Y	X → Y
T	T	T
T	F	F
F	T	T
F	F	T

Implication is a *binary* operation, transforming the pair of sentences X and Y into a unique image sentence $X \rightarrow Y$.

LOGICAL EQUIVALENCE

For sentences X and Y, the **logical equivalence** $X \leftrightarrow Y$ is true IFF X and Y have the same truth value; otherwise, it is false. The truth table for $\leftrightarrow$ is shown by Table 6, where $\leftrightarrow$ represents logical equivalence, "IFF."

Table 6–Truth Table for Equivalence

X	Y	$X \leftrightarrow Y$
T	T	T
T	F	F
F	T	F
F	F	T

For example, for X = "Jane eats apples" and Y = "apples are sweet," we have $X \leftrightarrow Y$ = "Jane eats apples IFF apples are sweet."

Equivalence is a *binary* operation, transforming pairs of sentences X and Y into a unique image sentence $X \leftrightarrow Y$. The two sentences X, Y for which $X \leftrightarrow Y$ are said to be logically equivalent.

Logical Equivalence versus "Meaning the Same"

Logical equivalence ($\leftrightarrow$) is not the same as an equivalence of meanings. Thus, if Jane is eating an apple and Barbara is frightened of mice, then for X = "Jane is eating an apple" and Y = "Barbara is frightened of mice," X and Y are logically equivalent, since both are correct. However, they do not have the same meaning. Statements having the same meaning are, for example, the double negative $\sim\sim X$ (not-not) and X itself.

1. THEOREM 1—Double Negation Equals Identity

For any sentence X, $\sim\sim X \leftrightarrow X$.

2. THEOREM 2—Properties of Conjunction Operation

For any sentences X, Y, Z, the following properties hold:

1. Commutativity: $X \wedge Y \leftrightarrow Y \wedge X$

2. Associativity: $X \wedge (Y \wedge Z) \leftrightarrow (X \wedge Y) \wedge Z$

3. THEOREM 3—Properties of Disjunction Operation

For any sentences X, Y, Z, the following properties hold:

1. Commutativity: $X \vee Y \leftrightarrow Y \vee X$

2. Associativity: $X \vee (Y \vee Z) \leftrightarrow (X \vee Y) \vee Z$

4. THEOREM 4—Distributive Laws

For any sentences X, Y, Z, the following laws hold:

1. $X \vee (Y \wedge Z) \leftrightarrow (X \vee Y) \wedge (X \vee Z)$

2. $X \wedge (Y \vee Z) \leftrightarrow (X \wedge Y) \vee (X \wedge Z)$

5. THEOREM 5—DeMorgan's Laws for Sentences

For any sentences X, Y, the following laws hold:

1. $\sim(X \wedge Y) \leftrightarrow (\sim X) \vee (\sim Y)$

2. $\sim(X \vee Y) \leftrightarrow (\sim X) \wedge (\sim Y)$

6. THEOREM 6—Two Logical Identities

For any sentences X, Y, the sentences X and $(X \wedge Y) \vee (X \wedge \sim Y)$ are logically equivalent. That is, $(X \wedge Y) \vee (X \wedge \sim Y) \leftrightarrow X$.

For any sentences X, Y, the sentences X and $X \vee (Y \wedge \sim Y)$ are logically equivalent, i.e., $X \vee (Y \wedge \sim Y) \leftrightarrow X$. For any sentences X, Y, $(X \rightarrow Y)$ and $(\sim X \vee Y)$ are logically equivalent.

7. THEOREM 7—Proof by Contradiction

For any sentences X, Y, the following holds: $X \rightarrow Y \leftrightarrow \sim Y \rightarrow \sim X$.

SENTENCES, LITERALS, AND FUNDAMENTAL CONJUNCTIONS

We have seen that logically equivalent sentences may be expressed in different ways, the simplest examples being that a sentence is equal to its double negation, $\sim\sim X \leftrightarrow X$, and by DeMorgan's theorem, $X \vee Y \leftrightarrow \sim(\sim X \wedge \sim Y)$.

The significance of sentential calculus and the algebra of logic is that it provides us with a method of producing a "standard" form for representing a statement in terms of the literals. This is indeed unique and, although usually the simplest representation, it does serve as a standard form for comparison and evaluation of sentences.

CLEP College Mathematics Practice Test 1

(Answer sheets appear in the back of this book.)

TIME: *90 Minutes*
60 Questions

DIRECTIONS: Solve each problem, using any available space on the page for scratch work. Then either enter the correct numerical answer in the box provided, or decide which answer choice is the best and fill in the corresponding oval on the answer sheet.

NOTES:

(1) Unless otherwise specified, the domain of any function f is assumed to be the set of all real numbers x for which $f(x)$ is a real number.

(2) i will be used to denote $\sqrt{-1}$.

(3) All figures lie in a plane and are drawn to scale unless otherwise indicated.

1. Which one of the following is equivalent to the negation of the statement "Cats are friendly and Bob has a hamster"?

   (A) If cats are friendly, then Bob does not have a hamster.

   (B) If Bob has a hamster, then cats are friendly.

   (C) If cats are not friendly, then Bob has a hamster.

   (D) If Bob does not have a hamster, then cats are not friendly.

2. If A is the set of odd integers, B is the set of multiples of 5, and C is the set of counting numbers, which of the following contains -7?

   (A) $A \cap B$

   (B) C

   (C) A

   (D) $B \cap C$

3. If x is an odd integer and y is even, then which of the following must be an even integer?

   I. $2x + 3y$

   II. xy

   III. $x + y - 1$

   (A) I only

   (B) II only

   (C) I, II, and III

   (D) II and III only

4. An ordinary six-sided cube, with its sides numbered 1 through 6, is rolled twice. The probability of rolling any of the six numbers is equally likely. What is the probability that, on two consecutive rolls of the cube, a number less than 3 appears on the first roll and the number 5 appears on the second roll?

5. Not counting the empty set, how many proper subsets are there for $R = \{2, 3, 4\}$?

   (A) 5

   (B) 6

   (C) 7

   (D) 8

6. If $f(x) = 2x + 4$ and $g(x) = x^2 - 2$, then $(f \circ g)(x)$, where $(f \circ g)(x)$ is a composition of functions, is

   (A) $2x^2 - 8$.

   (B) $2x^2 + 8$.

   (C) $2x^2$.

   (D) $2x^3 + 4x^2 - 4x - 8$.

7. Let P, Q, and R represent statements where P is true, Q is false, and R is false. Which one of the following is a true statement?

(A) (P and R) or Q
(B) (P implies Q) and Not R
(C) Not P or (Q and R)
(D) Not P implies (Q and R)

8. Given that $i = \sqrt{-1}$, what is the simplified expression for $3i^3 - 4i^2 + 5i$?

(A) $-2i - 4$
(B) $-2i + 4$
(C) $2i - 4$
(D) $2i + 4$

9. Consider the function $P(x) = \sqrt{1 - x^2}$ shown below. Which graph represents $P^{-1} \{-1 \leq x \leq 0\}$?

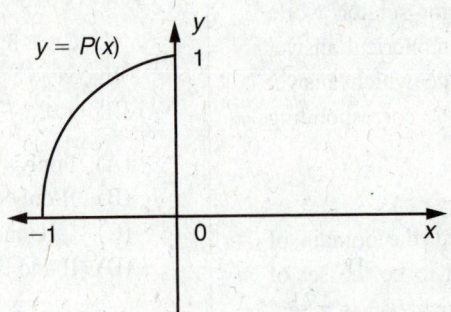

(A)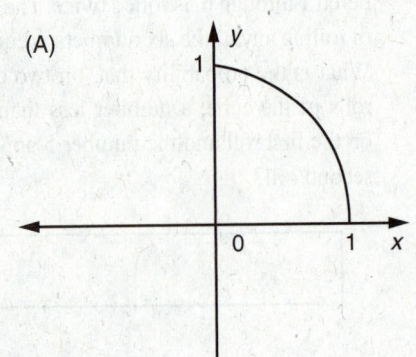

(C)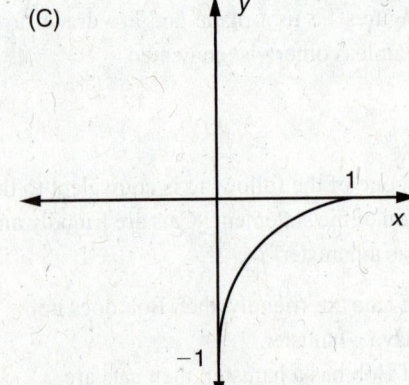

(B)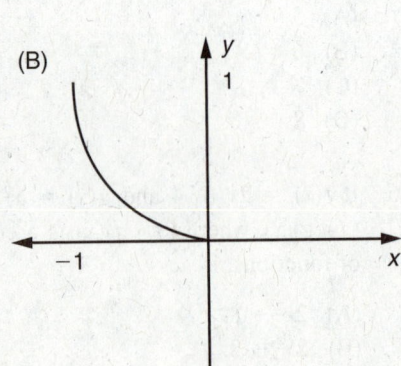

(D)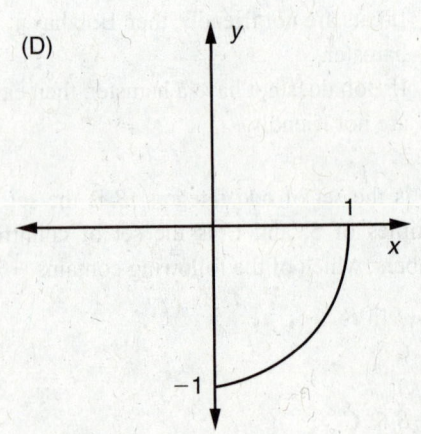

10. What is the range, R, of the function $f(x) = \dfrac{x}{|x|}$?

   (A) $R = \{1, 0\}$
   (B) $R = \{-1, 1\}$
   (C) $(1, -1, 0)$
   (D) All positive integers

11. The sum of three different prime numbers is 22. One of these numbers is 2. What is the largest possible value of either of the other numbers?

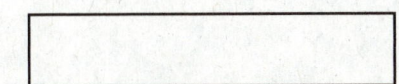

12. There are six knights of the Round Table. Given that Sir Lancelot must sit in a specific chair and that Sir Gawain must be directly on either side of him, in how many ways may the knights be seated?

   (A) 24
   (B) 120
   (C) 48
   (D) 25

13. If $m^x \cdot m^7 = m^{28}$ and $(m^5)^y = m^{15}$, what is the value of $x + y$?

   (A) 31
   (B) 24
   (C) 14
   (D) 12

14. Which one of the following is a factor of $2x^2 - x - 3$?

   (A) $2x - 3$
   (B) $2x + 1$
   (C) $x - 1$
   (D) $x + 3$

15. Suppose $S = \{5, 6, 9\}$ and $T = \{7, 8, 9\}$. Which one of the following ordered pairs is *NOT* in the Cartesian product of $T \times S$?

   (A) $(9, 9)$
   (B) $(8, 5)$
   (C) $(6, 8)$
   (D) $(7, 6)$

16. If $f(x) = \{(2, 5), (6, 9), (11, 2), (x, 4)\}$ is a function, what is the smallest value x may not have?

17. A fair coin is tossed five times. What is the probability of two heads occurring?

   (A) $\dfrac{1}{16}$
   (B) $\dfrac{5}{16}$
   (C) $\dfrac{5}{32}$
   (D) $\dfrac{1}{4}$

18. Given the following list of six numbers:

$$\pi, \sqrt{5}, \sqrt{\dfrac{4}{25}}, -0.212, 5\dfrac{2}{7}, \text{ and } 0.1\overline{8}$$

How many of these numbers are irrational?

19. The mean of Sheila's five exam scores is 78. She will be taking three more exams. Assuming that each exam is given the same weight, what must her mean score be on the remaining exams in order to attain a mean score of 84 on all eight exams?

   (A) 94
   (B) 92
   (C) 90
   (D) 88

20. Look at the following triangle.

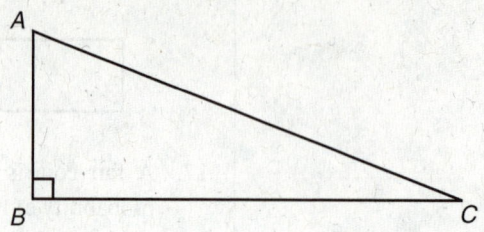

$\overline{AB}$ is perpendicular to $\overline{BC}$. $AB = 10$ and $AC = 26$. What is the area of the triangle?

(A) 260
(B) 240
(C) 130
(D) 120

21. Which graph does *NOT* represent a function ($y = f(x)$)?

(A)
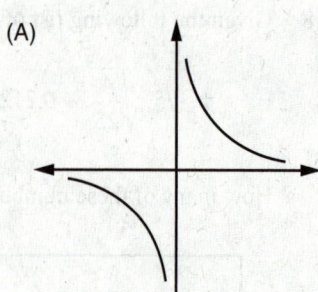

(C)
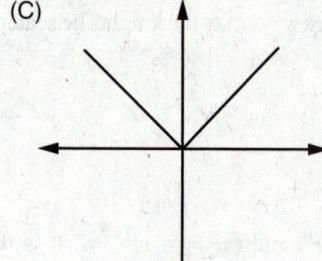

(B)
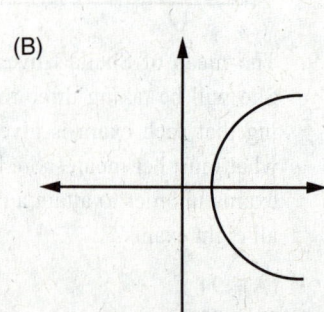

(D)
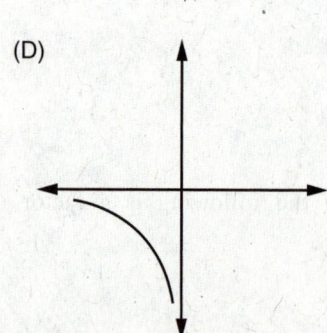

22. Find the minimum value of the function $f(x) = (x - 1)^2 + 3$.

(A) 0
(B) 1
(C) 2
(D) 3

23. Which one of the following has the lowest value?

(A) $|-8| - |3|$
(B) $-|-8 - 3|$
(C) $|-3 + 8| - |-8 + 3|$
(D) $-|3 - 8|$

24. Let $U = \{$cat, dog, frog, goat, horse, pig, tiger$\}$, $A = \{$dog, frog, horse, pig$\}$, and $B = \{$dog, goat, pig, tiger$\}$. Define A' as the elements in set U that are not in set A. Which of the following completely describes $A' \cap B$?

    (A) $\{$cat, goat, tiger$\}$
    (B) $\{$goat, tiger$\}$
    (C) $\{$dog, pig$\}$
    (D) $\{$dog, goat, pig$\}$

25. When a positive integer n is divided by 5, the remainder is 4. Which one of the following will yield a remainder of 2 when it is divided by 5?

    (A) $n + 1$
    (B) $n + 2$
    (C) $n + 3$
    (D) $n + 4$

26. Ten white balls and 19 red balls are in a box. If a ball is drawn from the box at random, what are the odds in favor of drawing a red ball?

    (A) $10 : 29$
    (B) $19 : 29$
    (C) $19 : 10$
    (D) $\dfrac{10}{19} : \dfrac{19}{29}$

27. If $A \subset C$ and $B \subset C$, which of the following statements is true?

    (A) The set $A \cup B$ is also a subset of C.
    (B) The complement of A is also a subset of C.
    (C) The complement of B is also a subset of C.
    (D) The union of $\overline{A}$ and $\overline{B}$ is also a subset of C.

28. Which one of the following is equivalent to the statement "If Joan sings, then I will play my guitar"?

    (A) Joan sings and I will play my guitar.
    (B) Joan does not sing and I will not play my guitar.
    (C) Joan sings or I will not play my guitar.
    (D) Joan does not sing or I will play my guitar.

29. The function $f(x)$ is divisible by $x + 5$ with no remainder. When $f(x)$ is divided by $x - 1$, the remainder is 3. Which one of the following statements is completely correct?

    (A) 5 is a solution to $f(x) = 0$ and $f(-1) = 3$.
    (B) -5 is a solution to $f(x) = 0$ and $f(1) = 3$.
    (C) 5 is a solution to $f(x) = 0$ and $f(1) = 3$.
    (D) -5 is a solution to $f(x) = 0$ and $f(-1) = 3$.

30. A floor that measures 10 feet by 20 feet is to be tiled with square tiles that are 36 square inches in area. How many tiles are needed to cover the entire floor?

    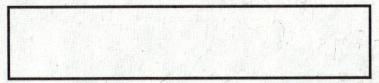

31. How many four-digit numbers are there such that the first digit is odd, the second is even, and there is no repetition of digits?

    (A) 1,200
    (B) 1,625
    (C) 200
    (D) 1,400

32. Which one of the following is the inverse of the statement "If animals could talk, then they would not reveal secrets"?

    (A) If animals could talk, then they would reveal secrets.
    (B) If animals could not talk, then they would reveal secrets.
    (C) If animals would not reveal secrets, then they could talk.
    (D) If animals would reveal secrets, then they could not talk.

33. What is the domain of the function given by $f(x) = \dfrac{x^3 + 1}{x + 3}$?

    (A) All numbers except -3
    (B) All numbers except -1
    (C) All numbers except 1
    (D) All numbers except 3

34. Look at the following graph

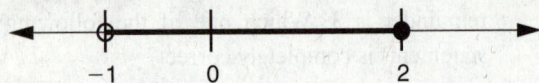

Which one of the following represents this graph?

(A) $x \leq 2$ or $x > -1$
(B) $-1 < x \leq 2$
(C) $x < -1$ or $x \geq 2$
(D) $-1 \leq x < 2$

35. What is the median of the following data?
2, 24, 7, 10, 15, 8

(A) 7.5
(B) 8.5
(C) 9
(D) 11

36. Which one of the following is a valid argument?

(A) All rainy days are cloudy.
Yesterday was not cloudy.
Yesterday was not rainy.
(B) All trees have brown leaves.
This plant has brown leaves.
This plant is a tree.
(C) Some wolves are vicious.
This animal is vicious.
This animal is a wolf.
(D) Some people have stocks and bonds.
Charles has stocks.
Charles has bonds.

37. The inverse of the function $y = \log_2 \dfrac{2x - 1}{2}$ is

(A) $y = \dfrac{4^x + 1}{2}$.

(B) $y = \dfrac{2^{x+1} + 1}{2}$.

(C) $y = \dfrac{2^{x+1}}{2}$.

(D) $y = 2^x$.

38. Which one of the following groups of data has exactly two modes?

(A) 1, 1, 3, 4, 4, 5, 5, 5
(B) 1, 1, 1, 2, 2, 2, 2
(C) 1, 2, 3, 3, 4, 4, 5, 5
(D) 1, 3, 3, 3, 4, 4, 4

39. If f is defined by $f(x) = \dfrac{5x - 8}{2}$ for each real number x, find the solution set for $f(x) > 2x$.

(A) $\{x \mid x > 6\}$
(B) $\{x \mid x > 8\}$
(C) $\{x \mid x < 8\}$
(D) $\{x \mid 6 < x < 8\}$

40. Look at the following Venn diagram, for which a Roman numeral has been assigned to each region.

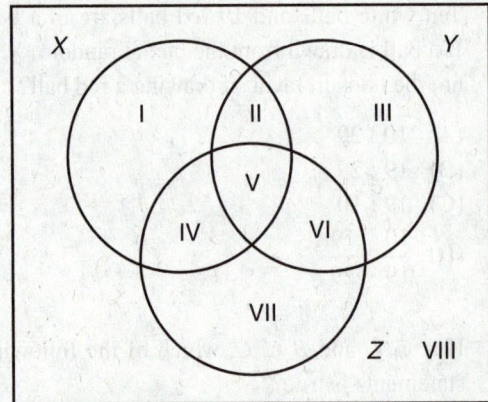

Which region(s) would include $(X \cup Y)'$?

(A) VII and VIII
(B) Only VII
(C) V, VII, and VIII
(D) Only VIII

41. The sample standard deviation, s, of a group of data is given by the formula

$$s = \sqrt{\dfrac{\sum_{i=1}^{n}(X_i - \bar{X})^2}{n - 1}},$$ where X_i represents

each data, $\bar{X}$ represents the mean, and n represents the number of data. What is the sample standard deviation for the following data? 4, 5, 6, 9, 11. (Round off your answer to the nearest hundredth).

```

```

42. A jar consists of ten marbles, of which seven are green, one is blue, and two are red. Two marbles will be randomly drawn from this jar, one at a time, without replacement. What is the probability of drawing a green marble followed by a red marble?

(A) $\dfrac{83}{90}$

(B) $\dfrac{19}{90}$

(C) $\dfrac{7}{45}$

(D) $\dfrac{7}{50}$

43. If g is a linear function such that $g(4) = 6$ and $g(10) = 21$, what is the value of $g(8)$?

(A) 19
(B) 18
(C) 16
(D) 10

44. Suppose that point K is reflected across the line $y = x$. If the original coordinates of K are $(-9, 3)$, what will be K's new coordinates?

(A) $(-9, -3)$
(B) $(-3, 9)$
(C) $(3, -9)$
(D) $(9, -3)$

45. A group of children share a package of cookies, each having six. If two more children join the group, they can each have four cookies. How many cookies were in the package, assuming none are left over?

(A) 8
(B) 10
(C) 16
(D) 24

46. If x and y are each odd numbers, which one of the following is also an odd number?

(A) $x + y$
(B) $4x - 6y$
(C) $(x)(y) + 10$
(D) $(x)(y) - 5$

47. A bike wheel has a radius of 12 inches. How many revolutions will it take to cover 1 mile? (Use 1 mile = 5,280 feet, and $\pi = \dfrac{22}{7}$.)

(A) 70
(B) 84
(C) 120
(D) 840

48. For which one of the following groups of data are the mean and median identical?

(A) 2, 2, 5, 6, 8, 8, 11
(B) 2, 3, 6, 6, 6, 8, 12
(C) 2, 4, 5, 6, 8, 11
(D) 2, 5, 5, 7, 8, 12

49. Which one of the following is an equation of a line containing the point $(2, -1)$ and is perpendicular to the graph of $x + 3y = 4$?

(A) $x + 3y = -1$
(B) $3x - y = 7$
(C) $3x + y = 5$
(D) $x - 3y = 5$

50. A quiz consists of five questions. Three of the questions are true-false, and the other two questions are each multiple-choice with four answer choices. In how many different ways can a student fill in the answers to these questions?

(A) 14
(B) 36
(C) 96
(D) 128

51. Including the number itself, which one of the following numbers has a total of 72 factors?

    (A) $2^2 \times 3^6 \times 5^6$
    (B) $2^2 \times 3^2 \times 67^2$
    (C) $2^2 \times 5^3 \times 17^1 \times 23^2$
    (D) $2^1 \times 5^{19} \times 11^2 \times 43^2$

52. The function $f(x)$ is defined as follows:

    $f(x) = 4x - 1$, if $x \leq -5$
    $ = 5x + 1$, if $x > -5$

    What is the value of $f(-7) + f(10)$?

53. Given a collection of nine books, in how many different ways can any four of them be placed on a shelf?

    (A) 262,144
    (B) 60,480
    (C) 6,561
    (D) 3,024

54. Which one of the following is true for any function?

    (A) A horizontal line may only intersect the graph of the function once.
    (B) The inverse must also be a function.
    (C) A vertical line may only intersect the graph of the function once.
    (D) The function must be defined for all real numbers.

55. Suppose that the point B, which is currently located at $(-4, 5)$, is translated three units to the left and two units up. What is B's new location?

    (A) $(-2, 2)$
    (B) $(-1, 7)$
    (C) $(-7, 7)$
    (D) $(-7, 2)$

56. At a social club, there are 20 women and 15 men. Half the women vote Republican and the rest vote Democratic. Only one-fifth of the men vote Republican and the rest vote Democratic. The names of all individuals who vote Republican are placed in a hat. One person's name will be drawn from this hat. What is the probability of drawing the name of a woman?

    (A) $\dfrac{10}{13}$
    (B) $\dfrac{20}{35}$
    (C) $\dfrac{13}{35}$
    (D) $\dfrac{10}{35}$

57. A rectangle and a square have the same perimeter. The side of the square is 9 and the length of the rectangle is 13. What is the width of the rectangle?

58. What is the domain of $f(x) = \sqrt{7 - x}$?

    (A) All numbers less than or equal to 7
    (B) All numbers greater than or equal to 7
    (C) All numbers less than or equal to -7
    (D) All numbers greater than or equal to -7

59. The number $0.\overline{8}$ is equivalent to what reduced fraction?

60. In a room of 20 people, if each person shakes hands with every other person, how many different handshakes are possible?

    (A) 40
    (B) 190
    (C) 380
    (D) 400

CLEP College Mathematics Practice Test 1

Answer Key

1.	(A)	16.	2	32.	(B)	48.	(A)
2.	(C)	17.	(B)	33.	(A)	49.	(B)
3.	(C)	18.	2	34.	(B)	50.	(D)
4.	$\frac{1}{18}$	19.	(A)	35.	(C)	51.	(C)
		20.	(D)	36.	(A)	52.	22
5.	(B)	21.	(B)	37.	(B)	53.	(D)
6.	(C)	22.	(D)	38.	(D)	54.	(C)
7.	(D)	23.	(B)	39.	(B)	55.	(C)
8.	(D)	24.	(B)	40.	(A)	56.	(A)
9.	(D)	25.	(C)	41.	2.92	57.	5
10.	(B)	26.	(C)	42.	(C)	58.	(A)
11.	17	27.	(A)	43.	(C)	59.	$\frac{8}{9}$
12.	(C)	28.	(D)	44.	(C)		
13.	(B)	29.	(B)	45.	(D)	60.	(B)
14.	(A)	30.	800	46.	(C)		
15.	(C)	31.	(D)	47.	(D)		

DETAILED EXPLANATIONS OF ANSWERS
PRACTICE TEST 1

1. **(A)** When a statement is in the form "If P, then Q," the equivalent statement is in the form "Not P or Q." The negation of "Not P or Q" is the statement "P and not Q." Let P represent the statement "Cats are friendly." Let "not Q" represent the statement "Bob has a hamster." Then the given statement in the stem of this question is written in the form "P and not Q," so the negation will be in the form "If P, then Q." Note that Q represents the statement "Bob does not have a hamster."

2. **(C)** To solve this problem we must know the meanings of the rules for the sets that have been stated.

    The set of odd integers is:

    $$A = \{\dots, -7, -5, -3, -1, 1, 3, 5, 7, \dots\}$$

    The set of multiples of 5 is:

    $$B = \{\dots, -10, -5, 0, 5, 10, \dots\}$$

    The set of counting numbers is:

    $$C = \{1, 2, 3, 4, 5, \dots\}$$

    We notice that -7 is an element of set A. $A \cap B = \{\dots, -25, -15, -5, 5, 15, 25, \dots\}$, so -7 is not an element of $A \cap B$. Set C does not contain any negative numbers, so -7 is not an element of set C. Finally, $B \cap C = \{5, 10, 15, 20, 25, \dots\}$, so -7 is not an element of $B \cap C$.

3. **(C)** I. An odd integer times two will become an even integer. An even integer times any number will remain even. The sum of two even numbers is also an even number. Therefore, $2x + 3y$ must be even.

    II. An even integer times any number will remain even. Therefore, xy must be even.

    III. The sum of an odd integer and an even integer is odd. An odd integer minus one will become even. Therefore, $x + y - 1$ must be even.

4. The correct answer is $\dfrac{1}{18}$. A number less than 3 means 1 or 2. The probability of 1 or 2 appearing on the first roll is $\dfrac{2}{6} = \dfrac{1}{3}$. The probability of 5 appearing on the second roll is $\dfrac{1}{6}$. Since these events are independent, the probability that both will occur is the product of these probabilities, which is $\dfrac{1}{3} \cdot \dfrac{1}{6} = \dfrac{1}{18}$.

5. **(B)** Given a set of n elements, the number of proper subsets is given by the expression $2^n - 1$. The set of proper subsets does not include the set itself. However, the expression $2^n - 1$ does include the empty set. Thus, the answer is $2^n - 2 = 2^3 - 2 = 6$.

6. **(C)** The definition of the composition of functions is $(f \circ g)(x) = f(x) \circ g(x) = f(g(x))$. For the functions given in this problem we have $2(g(x)) + 4 = 2(x^2 - 2) + 4 = 2x^2 - 4 + 4 = 2x^2$.

7. **(D)** Not P becomes false. Q and R is also false. A statement that reads: "False implies false" is always true. Answer choice (A) is wrong because P and R is false, so it reads "False or False." Answer choice (B) is wrong because P implies Q is false, so it reads "False and True" which is false. Answer choice (C) is wrong because Q and R is false, so it reads "False or False."

8. **(D)** $i^2 = -1$ and $i^3 = i^2(i) = (-1)(i) = -i$. So, $3i^3 - 4i^2 + 5i$

$$= (3)(-i) - (4)(-1) + 5i = 5i - 3i + 4 = 2i + 4.$$

9. **(D)** By reflecting $P(x)$ about the line $y = x$, we obtain $P^{-1}(x)$. Graph (D) is the result of such an operation and is therefore the correct choice.

10. **(B)** The variable x can be replaced in the formula $\dfrac{x}{|x|}$ with any real number except 0, so if x is negative, $\dfrac{x}{|x|} = -1$, and if x is positive, $x = 1$. Thus, there are only the two numbers -1 and 1 in the range of our function; $R = \{-1, 1\}$.

11. The correct answer is 17. The sum of the other two numbers must be 20. The possible pairs of integers for which both are prime are 7 and 13 or 3 and 17. Thus, 17 is the largest possible value. Note that 1 and 19 cannot be considered since 1 is not a prime.

12. **(C)** Since Sir Lancelot must sit in an assigned chair, and Sir Gawain on either side of him, there are 4! or 24 ways of seating the other four. For each of these arrangements, Sir Gawain can be in either of two seats, so the total number of ways of seating the knights is 24×2 or 48.

13. **(B)** For the first equation, $x + 7 = 28$, so $x = 21$. For the second equation, $5y = 15$, so $y = 3$. Then $x + y = 24$.

14. **(A)** In factored form, $2x^2 - x - 3 = (2x - 3)(x + 1)$. The other correct factor would be $x + 1$.

15. **(C)** The Cartesian product of $T \times S$ consists of all ordered pairs, where the first element is chosen from T and the second element is chosen from S. The correct answer choice (6, 8) is not a member of $T \times S$. It is a member of $S \times T$.

16. The answer is 2. If x is a function, then each member of the domain is mapped into one and only one member of the range. Hence, x may not be 2, 6, or 11; these numbers are already first components of ordered pairs in x.

17. **(B)** With each toss there are two possibilities, heads or tails. There are five tosses so there are $2^5 = 32$ possible outcomes. The number of ways to choose two heads from five tosses is

$$\binom{5}{2} = \frac{5!}{2!3!} = 10.$$

So the probability is

$$\frac{10}{32} = \frac{5}{16}.$$

18. The correct answer is 2. The irrational numbers are π and $\sqrt{5}$. Irrational numbers cannot be written as a quotient of two integers. The other four numbers can be written as a quotient of integers.

$$\sqrt{\frac{4}{25}} = \frac{2}{5}, -0.212 = -\frac{212}{1000}, 5\frac{2}{7} = \frac{37}{7}, \text{ and } 0.1\overline{8} = \frac{17}{90}.$$

19. **(A)** The total number of points on Sheila's five exams is $(5)(78) = 390$. In order to attain a mean score of 84 on all the exams, she will need a total of $(8)(84) = 672$ points. Thus, she needs a total of $672 - 390 = 282$ points on the next three exams. Finally $282 \div 3 = 94$.

20. **(D)** Using the Pythagorean Theorem, $AB^2 + BC^2 = AC^2$. By substitution, $10^2 + BC^2 = 26^2$. Then $BC^2 = 676 - 100 = 576$, so $BC = 24$. The area of the triangle is given by the formula $\left(\frac{1}{2}\right)(AB)(BC) = \left(\frac{1}{2}\right)(10)(24) = 120$.

21. **(B)** To determine whether or not a graph represents a function, it is possible to apply the "vertical line test." If any vertical line to the graph intersects it in more than one point, the graph is not a function. The only graph for which a vertical line passes through more than one point is (B). A relation is a function if for any x there is one and only one y.

22. **(D)** Since $(x - 1)^2 > 0$ for all x, the minimum value occurs when $(x - 1)^2 = 0$. Hence, $f(x) = 0 + 3 = 3$ is the minimum value. This conclusion can also be made by considering the graph of the function which is a parabola.

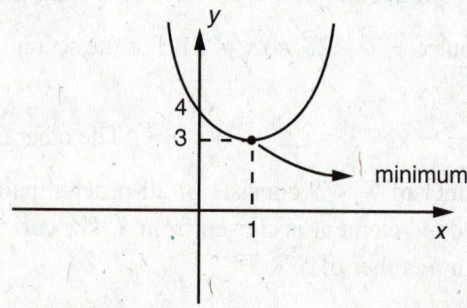

23. **(B)** $-|-8 - 3| = -|-11| = -11$. The values of answer choices (A), (C), and (D) are 5, 0, and -5, respectively.

24. **(B)** In this example, $A' = \{\text{cat, goat, tiger}\}$.
Then, $A' \cap B = \{\text{cat, goat, tiger}\} \cap \{\text{dog, goat, pig, tiger}\} = \{\text{goat, tiger}\}$.

25. **(C)** From the first sentence, we can deduce that when $n + 1$ is divided by 5, there is no remainder. To find an expression that would have a remainder of 2 when it is divided by 5, simply add 2 to $n + 1$. Then, $n + 1 + 2 = n + 3$.

26. **(C)** If an event can happen in p ways and fail to happen in q ways, then, if $p > q$, the odds are p to q in favor of the event happening.

   If $p < q$, then the odds are q to p against the event happening. In this case, $p = 19$ and $q = 10$, $p > q$. Thus, the odds in favor of the event of drawing a red ball are $19 : 10$.

27. **(A)** The set $A \cup B$ contains all elements which belong to either set A or set B. Since all elements which belong to set A or set B also belong to C, the set $A \cup B$ is a subset of C.

28. **(D)** Given a conditional statement in the form "If P then Q," an equivalent statement is in the form "Not P or Q." In this example, P is the statement "Joan sings" and Q is the statement "I will play my guitar."

29. **(B)** By the Factor Theorem, whenever $x - c$ is a factor of $f(x)$, the number c must be a solution to $f(x) = 0$. In this case, $c = -5$. Thus, -5 must be a solution to $f(x) = 0$. Also, by the Remainder Theorem, whenever a function $f(x)$ is divided by $x - c$, the remainder must be $f(c)$. In this case, $c = 1$, so that the remainder, which is 3, must be the value of $f(1)$.

30. The answer is 800. The floor that measures 10 feet by 20 feet has an area of $10 \times 20 = 200$ sq. ft. The tiles with 36 sq. in. of area must measure 6 in. by 6 in. or $\frac{1}{2}$ ft. by $\frac{1}{2}$ ft. for $\frac{1}{4}$ sq. ft. of area. Because it would take four tiles to cover 1 sq. ft., $4 \times (200 \text{ sq. ft.}) = 800$ tiles would be needed to cover the entire floor.

31. **(D)** There are five possibilities for the first $(1, 3, 5, 7, 9)$, five for the second $(0, 2, 4, 6, 8)$, eight possibilities for the third $(10 - 2)$, and seven for the fourth $(8 - 1) = 7$. We subtracted two possibilities on the third and three on the fourth because there is no repetition, as shown: $5 \times 5 \times (10 - 2)(8 - 1) = 5 \times 5 \times 8 \times 7 = 1{,}400$.

32. **(B)** Given a statement in the form "If P, then Q," the inverse is in the form "If not P, then not Q." In this example P is represented by "animals could talk" and Q is represented by "they would not reveal secrets."

33. **(A)** The domain refers to all allowable values of x. In this example, the only value(s) of x that are not allowed are those for which the denominator is zero. If $x + 3 = 0$, then $x = -3$. Thus, -3 is the only value that is not allowed in the domain.

34. **(B)** The shaded area lies between -1 and 2. Since there is a dot at 2, this number is included. Likewise, since there is an open circle at -1, this number is not included.

35. **(C)** To find the median, first arrange the data in ascending order. The data will then appear as follows: 2, 7, 8, 10, 15, 24. The median will be the average of the two middle numbers. Thus, the median is $\frac{(8 + 10)}{2} = 9$.

36. **(A)** An argument is valid if given that the premises are true, then the conclusion *must* be true. Only answer choice (A) would satisfy this definition. Answer choice (B) is wrong because other objects besides trees may have brown leaves. Answer choice (C) is wrong because animals other than wolves may be vicious. Answer choice (D) is wrong because people may own only stocks, only bonds, both stocks and bonds, or neither stocks nor bonds.

37. **(B)** To determine the inverse of a function, it is necessary to replace the variable y by x and x by y.

The function $y = \log_2 \dfrac{2x - 1}{2}$ becomes:

$$x = \log_2 \dfrac{2y - 1}{2}$$

$$2^x = \dfrac{2y + 1}{2}$$

$$2^x \cdot 2 = 2y - 1$$

$$2^{x+1} = 2y - 1$$

$$2^{x+1} + 1 = 2y$$

$$y = \dfrac{2^{x+1} + 1}{2}$$

38. **(D)** The correct answer (D) has exactly two modes, namely 3 and 4. Answer choice (A) has a single mode of 5. Answer choice (B) has a single mode of 2. Answer choice (C) has three modes, namely 3, 4, and 5.

39. **(B)** To find the solution set of $f(x) > 2x$, we proceed as follows:

$$\dfrac{5x - 8}{2} > 2x$$

$$5x - 8 > 4x$$

$$-8 > -x$$

which implies $x > 8$.

40. **(A)** $(X \cup Y)'$ means the regions that are *not* included by X, by Y, or by both X and Y. Note that answer choice (C) is wrong because it includes region V which is in all three of X, Y, and Z.

41. The correct answer is 2.92. The value of $\overline{X}$ is $(4 + 5 + 6 + 9 + 11) \div 5 = 7$.

The value of $\displaystyle\sum_{i=1}^{n} (X_i - \overline{X})^2$ can be found by computing

$$(4 - 7)^2 + (5 - 7)^2 + (6 - 7)^2 + (9 - 7)^2 + (11 - 7)^2$$

$$= 9 + 4 + 1 + 4 + 16 = 34.$$

Then $s = \sqrt{\dfrac{34}{4}} = \sqrt{8.5} \approx 2.92$

42. **(C)** The probability of drawing a green marble is $\dfrac{7}{10}$. Since the second marble is drawn from among the remaining nine marbles, the probability of drawing a red marble is $\dfrac{2}{9}$. The probability of both occurrences is $\left(\dfrac{7}{10}\right)\left(\dfrac{2}{9}\right) = \dfrac{7}{45}$.

43. **(C)** Since g is a linear function, the ratio of the change in $g(x)$ values to the change in x values between any two points on the graph is constant. For the two given points $(4, 6)$ and $(10, 21)$,

the constant ratio is $(21 - 6) \div (10 - 4) = 2.5$. Let $g(8) = k$. Combining this point with $(4, 6)$, we can state that $(k - 6) \div (8 - 4) = 2.5$. Simplifying, we get $\dfrac{k - 6}{4} = 2.5$. Then, multiplying both sides of the equation by 2.5, $k - 6 = 10$, so $k = 16$.

44. **(C)** When any point (x, y) is reflected across the line $y = x$, the coordinates are simply reversed so that the new coordinates become (y, x). Thus, $(-9, 3)$ becomes $(3, -9)$.

45. **(D)** Using some algebraic expressions to represent the unknown should help here. Let:

$$x = \text{the number of children in the original group}$$

$$6x = \text{the number of cookies in the package.}$$

When two more children join the group, the expressions are:

$$x + 2 = \text{the number of children}$$

$$4(x + 2) = \text{the number of cookies in the package.}$$

Notice that there are two expressions for "the number of cookies in the package." These are equivalent expressions, so set up an equation and solve for x.

$$6x = 4(x + 2)$$
$$6x = 4x + 8$$
$$2x = 8$$
$$x = 4$$

Then $6x = 24$, which is the number of cookies.

46. **(C)** The product of two odd numbers is an odd number. When an odd number is added to 10, the result is still an odd number. Each of answer choices (A), (B), and (D) results in an even number.

47. **(D)** The circumference of the wheel is:

$$C = 2\pi(1 \text{ ft.})$$

$$C = 2\left(\frac{22}{7}\right) = \frac{44}{7} \text{ ft.}$$

To find the number of revolutions the wheel takes, calculate:

$$5{,}280 \div \frac{44}{7} = 5{,}280 \times \frac{44}{7}$$

$$= 120 \times 7 = 840 \text{ revolutions}$$

48. **(A)** The mean and the median are each 6. For answer choice (B), the median is 6 but the mean is $\dfrac{43}{7}$. For answer choice (C), the mean is 6 but the median is 5.5. For answer choice (D), the median is 6 but the mean is 6.5.

49. **(B)** Rewriting $x + 3y = 4$ as $y = -\dfrac{1}{3}x + \dfrac{4}{3}$, we can identify the slope as $-\dfrac{1}{3}$. A line that is perpendicular to the graph of this line must have a slope that is the negative reciprocal

of $-\dfrac{1}{3}$, which is 3. When answer choice (B) is rewritten as $y = 3x - 7$, the slope can be identified as 3. Note also that $y = 3x - 7$ contains the point $(2, -1)$. The slopes for answer choices (A), (C), and (D) are $-\dfrac{1}{3}$, -3, and $\dfrac{1}{3}$, respectively.

50. **(D)** The number of different ways to answer the true-false questions is $2^3 = 8$. The number of different ways to answer the multiple-choice questions is $4^2 = 16$. Then the number of different ways to fill in all five answers is $(8)(16) = 128$.

51. **(C)** The total number of factors can be found as follows: After the given number is written in prime factorization form, add 1 to each exponent. Then take the product of these numbers. For answer choice (C), the computation would be $(2 + 1)(3 + 1)(1 + 1)(2 + 1) = (3)(4)(2)(3) = 72$. The total number of factors for answer choices (A), (B), and (D) are 147, 27, and 360, respectively.

52. The correct answer is 22. $f(-7) = (4)(-7) - 1 = -29$ and $f(10) = (5)(10) + 1 = 51$. Then $-29 + 51 = 22$.

53. **(D)** There are 9 selections for the first spot on the shelf, 8 selections for the second spot, 7 selections for the third spot, and 6 selections for the fourth spot. The number of different ways is $(9)(8)(7)(6) = 3{,}024$. This is a permutation of 9 items taken 4 at a time.

54. **(C)** Since each x value in the domain can only correspond to one y value in the range, any vertical line can intersect the graph at most once. Answer choice (A) is wrong because the same y value may correspond to two different x values. An example to show why answer choice (B) is wrong would be $f(x) = \{(1, 2), (2, 3), (4, 3)\}$. $f(x)$ is a function consisting of three points. Its inverse would be $\{(2, 1), (3, 2), (3, 4)\}$, which is not a function. An example to show why answer choice (D) is wrong would be $g(x) = \{(1, 5), (3, 7)\}$. $g(x)$ is only defined for $x = 1$ or $x = 3$.

55. **(C)** We need to subtract 3 from the first coordinate and add 2 to the second coordinate. The new location for point B is $(-4-3, 5+2) = (-7, 7)$.

56. **(A)** There are $\left(\dfrac{1}{2}\right)(20) = 10$ women who vote Republican, and there are $\left(\dfrac{1}{5}\right)(15) = 3$ men who vote Republican. Thus, there are a total of 13 people who vote Republican and whose names are in the hat. From these 13 names, 10 are women. Thus, the required probability is $\dfrac{10}{13}$.

57. The correct answer is 5. The perimeter of the square is $(4)(9) = 36$, which is the same as the perimeter of the rectangle. The perimeter of a rectangle is twice the length plus twice the width. Twice the length is 26, so twice the width must be 10. Thus, the width is 5.

58. **(A)** The domain is defined as all numbers for which $7 - x$ is at least zero. Solving $7 - x \geq 0$, we get $x \leq 7$.

59. The correct answer is $\dfrac{8}{9}$. Let $N = 0.\overline{8}$. Multiply both sides of the equation by 10 to get $10N = 8.\overline{8}$. Subtract $N = 0.\overline{8}$ from $10N = 8.\overline{8}$ to get $9N = 8$. Then $N = \dfrac{8}{9}$.

60. **(B)** Each handshake involves two people, so the number of handshakes for 20 people is given by the expression $_{20}C_2 = (20)(19) \div 2 = 190$.

CHAPTER 4
Natural Sciences

CLEP Natural Sciences Independent Study Schedule

The following suggestions provide a framework you can use when preparing for the CLEP Natural Sciences exam. As part of your preparation, be sure to set aside time each day to study. This method will work better than trying to review everything at once. No matter which study techniques work best for you, the more time you spend studying, the more prepared and relaxed you will feel.

Step	Activity
1	Take Practice Test 2 for Natural Sciences on the CD. This will help you identify areas that you need to review.
2	Carefully read each topic in the Natural Sciences section.
3	In your review, pay particular attention to boldfaced terms and phrases.
4	Use a highlighter or pencil to emphasize items in your text you want to remember.
5	Jot down points of emphasis in a notebook or on index cards as you read.
6	Take Practice Test 3 found on the CD.
7	Review the Detailed Explanations of the answers. These will not only provide the correct answer, but also explain why the other options were incorrect.
8	Note which questions you answered incorrectly on the Practice Test, and focus on these areas during your follow-up review.
9	Read through the Natural Sciences section in your book again, paying particular attention to the topics you struggled with while taking the two Practice Tests.
10	Take Practice Test 1 in the book for additional reinforcement.

Review Outline

The following is the order in which the topics are covered in this review:

PASSING THE **CLEP** NATURAL SCIENCES EXAM

ABOUT THIS CHAPTER

This chapter provides you with a targeted review of the CLEP Natural Sciences exam, as well as test-taking tips and strategies. We also provides a practice test in the book, and two practice tests on the CD. All are based on the official CLEP Natural Sciences exam, which contains every type of question found on the actual exam. Following the practice test is an answer key with detailed explanations designed to help you more completely understand the test material. Refer to CD practice tests.

FORMAT AND CONTENT OF THE CLEP NATURAL SCIENCES EXAM

The CLEP Natural Sciences exam covers the material one would find in a freshman or sophomore general science survey course covering biology and physical science. It is meant for students who are non-science majors. The exam stresses basic facts and principles, as well as general theoretical approaches used by scientists.

The exam consists of 120 multiple-choice questions, each with five possible answer choices, to be answered in 90 minutes. The approximate breakdown of topics is as follows:

50% Biological Science

10% Origin, evolution, and classification of life

10% Cell organization and division, gene regulation, bioenergetics, and biosynthesis

20% Structure, function, and development of organisms; heredity

10% Concepts of population biology and ecology

50% Physical Science

7% Atomic and nuclear structure, properties, and reactions; elementary particles

10% Chemical elements, compounds, reactions, molecular structure, and bonding

12% Heat, thermodynamics, states of matter; classical mechanics; relativity

4% Electricity and magnetism, waves, light, and sound

7% The universe: galaxies, stars, and the solar system

10% Earth: atmosphere, hydrosphere, structure features, geologic processes, and history

SCORING YOUR PRACTICE TESTS

How Do I Score My Practice Tests?

The CLEP Natural Sciences exam is scored on a scale of 20 to 80. To score your practice test, count the number of correct answers. This is your total raw score. Convert your raw score to a scaled score using the conversion table on the following page. (**Note: The conversion table provides only an *estimate* of your scaled score. Scaled scores can and do vary over time, and in no case should a sample test be taken as a precise predictor of test performance.**)

Practice-Test Raw Score Conversion Table*

Raw Score	Scaled Score	Course Grade	Raw Score	Scaled Score	Course Grade
120	80	A	111	79	A
119	80	A	110	78	A
118	80	A	109	78	A
117	80	A	108	78	A
116	80	A	107	77	A
115	80	A	106	77	A
114	79	A	105	77	A
113	79	A	104	77	A
112	79	A	103	76	A

Practice-Test Raw Score Conversion Table*

Raw Score	Scaled Score	Course Grade	Raw Score	Scaled Score	Course Grade
102	76	A	71	62	B
101	75	A	70	61	B
100	75	A	69	61	B
99	75	A	68	60	B
98	74	A	67	59	B
97	74	A	66	59	B
96	73	A	65	58	B
95	73	A	64	57	B
94	73	B	63	57	B
93	72	B	62	56	B
92	72	B	61	56	B
91	71	B	60	55	B
90	71	B	59	54	B
89	70	B	58	54	B
88	69	B	57	53	B
87	69	B	56	53	B
86	68	B	55	52	B
85	68	B	54	52	B
84	67	B	53	51	B
83	67	B	52	51	C
82	67	B	51	50	C
81	66	B	50	50	C
80	66	B	49	50	C
79	65	B	48	49	C
78	65	B	47	49	C
77	65	B	46	48	C
76	64	B	45	48	C
75	64	B	44	47	C
74	63	B	43	47	C
73	63	B	42	47	C
72	62	B	41	47	C

(Continued)

Practice-Test Raw Score Conversion Table* (*Continued*)

Raw Score	Scaled Score	Course Grade	Raw Score	Scaled Score	Course Grade
40	46	D	19	32	F
39	46	D	18	31	F
38	45	D	17	31	F
37	45	D	16	30	F
36	44	D	15	29	F
35	44	D	14	28	F
34	43	D	13	28	F
33	43	D	12	27	F
32	42	D	11	27	F
31	41	D	10	26	F
30	40	D	9	25	F
29	39	D	8	24	F
28	38	D	7	23	F
27	37	D	6	22	F
26	36	D	5	21	F
25	35	D	4	20	F
24	34	F	3	20	F
23	34	F	2	20	F
22	33	F	1	20	F
21	33	F	0	20	F
20	32	F			

* This table is provided for scoring REA practice tests only. The American Council on Education recommends that colleges use a single across-the-board credit-granting score of 50 for all CLEP computer-based exams. Nonetheless, on account of the different skills being measured and the unique content requirements of each test, the actual number of correct answers needed to reach 50 will vary. A "50" is calibrated to equate with performance that would warrant the grade C in the corresponding introductory college course.

HISTORY OF EVOLUTIONARY CONCEPTS

Evolution refers to the gradual change of characteristics within a population, producing a change in species over time that is driven by the process of **natural selection**. In his book *The Origin of Species by Means of Natural Selection, or The Preservation of Favoured Races in the Struggle for Life* (published in 1859), Charles Darwin first articulated natural selection as a driving force, even though scientists before Darwin had already promoted some of the ideas inherent in evolutionary biology.

Carolus Linnaeus, the well-known botanist, speculated on the origin of and relationships between groups of species in the mid-1700s. The French scientist Lamarek proposed that organisms acquire traits over their lifespan that equip them to survive within their environment and pass those traits on to their offspring. This Lamarckian theory of acquired characteristics has since been discredited.

Darwinian Concept of Natural Selection

Individuals within a species that are unable to acquire the minimum requirement of resources are unable to reproduce. The ecosystem can support only a limited number of organisms—known as the **carrying capacity** (usually designated by the letter K). Once the carrying capacity (K) is reached, a competition for resources ensues. Darwin considered this competition to be the basic *struggle for existence* and proposed that those individuals who win the competition for resources pass those successful traits on to their children.

Mechanisms of Evolution

All evolution is dependent upon genetic change. The entire collection of genes within a given population is known as its **gene pool**. Individuals in the population will have only one pair of alleles for a particular single-gene trait. Yet, the gene pool may contain dozens or hundreds of alleles for this trait. Evolution does not occur through changes from individual to individual, but rather as the gene pool changes through one of a number of possible mechanisms.

One mechanism that drives the changing of traits is **differential reproduction**. Differential reproduction proposes that those individuals within a population who are most adapted to the environment are also the most likely individuals to reproduce successfully. This increases the number of alleles for desirable traits in the gene pool, eventually producing a population where the desirable trait is dominant.

A **mutation** is a change in a gene's DNA sequence, resulting in a change of the trait. Although a mutation can cause a very swift change in the **genotype** (genetic code) and possibly **phenotype** (expressed trait) of the offspring, mutations do not necessarily produce a trait desirable for a particular environment. Mutation is a much more random occurrence than differential reproduction.

Although mutations occur quickly, the change in the gene pool is minimal, so change in the population occurs very slowly (over multiple generations). However, mutation does provide a vehicle of introducing new genetic possibilities.

A third mechanism that influences the evolution of new traits is **genetic drift**. Over time, a gene pool (particularly in a small population) may experience a change in frequency of particular genes simply due to chance fluctuations. The change of gene frequency may produce a small or a large change, depending on what traits are affected. The process of genetic drift, as opposed to mutation, actually causes a reduction in genetic variety.

Although genetic drift occurs within finite separated populations, an individual from an adjacent population of the same species may occasionally immigrate and breed with a member of the previously locally isolated group. The introduction of new genes from the immigrant results in a change of the gene pool, known as **gene migration**. Gene migration is also occasionally successful between members of different, but related, species.

In a situation where random mating is occurring within a population (which is in equilibrium with its environment), gene frequencies and genotype ratios will remain constant from generation to generation. This law is known as the **Hardy-Weinberg Law of Equilibrium**, named after the two men (G. H. Hardy and Wilhelm Weinberg, c. 1909) who first studied this principle in mathematical studies of genetics.

According to the Hardy-Weinberg Law, the sum of the frequencies of all possible alleles for a particular trait is 1. That is, $p + q = 1$, where the frequency of one allele is represented by **p** and the frequency of another is **q**. It then follows mathematically that the frequency of genotypes within a population can be represented by the equation $p^2 + 2pq + q^2 = 1$, where the frequency of homozygous dominant genotypes is represented by p^2, the homozygous recessive by q^2, and the heterozygous genotype by 2pq.

For instance, in humans the ability to taste the chemical phenylthiocarbamide (PTC) is a dominant inherited trait. If **T** represents the allele for tasting PTC and **t** represents the recessive trait (inability to taste PTC) then the possible genotypes in a population would be **TT**, **Tt**, and **tt**. If the frequency of non-tasters in a particular population is 4% or 0.04 (that is, $q^2 = 0.04$), then the frequency of the allele **t** equals the square root of 0.04, or 0.2. It is then possible to calculate the frequency of the dominant allele, **T**, in the population using the equation $p + 0.2 = 1$, so, $p = 0.8$.

The frequency of the allele for tasting PTC is 0.8. The frequency of the various possible genotypes (**TT**, **Tt**, and **tt**) in the population can also be calculated since the frequency of the homozygous dominant is p^2 or 0.64 or 64%. The frequency of the heterozygous genotype is 2pq.

$$2pq = 2(0.8)(0.2) = 0.32 = 32\%.$$

Frequency of TT = 64%, Tt = 32%, tt is 4% . . . totaling 100%

or $0.64 + 0.32 + 0.04 = 1$

In order for Hardy-Weinberg equilibrium to occur, **random mating** (no differential reproduction) must be taking place and no migration, mutation, selection, or genetic drift can be occurring.

Speciation

A **species** is an interbreeding population that shares a common gene pool and produces viable offspring. There are two mechanisms that produce separate species: allopatric speciation and sympatric speciation.

In order for a new species to develop, substantial genetic changes must occur between populations, which prohibit them from interbreeding. **Allopatric speciation** occurs when two populations are geographically isolated from each other, perhaps by a catastrophic event such as a volcanic eruption. Two populations (separated by the volcanic flow) continue to reproduce and experience genetic drift and/or mutation over time. Even if the geographic separation later is eliminated, the two populations have now experienced too much change to allow them to successfully interbreed again.

Speciation may also occur without a geographic separation when a population develops members with a genetic difference, which prevents successful reproduction with the original species. This process is called **sympatric speciation**.

As populations of an organism in a given area grow, some will move into new geographic areas looking for new resources or to escape predators. Over time the species will specially adapt to live more effectively in the new environment. Through this process, known as **adaptive radiation**, a single species can develop into several diverse species over time. Adaptive radiation is proven to have occurred when the species remerge and do not interbreed successfully.

All of these evolutionary mechanisms are dependent upon reproduction of organisms over a long period of time, a very gradual process. **Punctuated equilibrium**, in contrast, is a scientific model that states species undergo a long period of equilibrium, which at some point is upset by environmental forces causing a short period of quick mutation and change.

Scientists still do not agree on the degree to which gradualism, punctuated equilibrium, or a combination of these processes is responsible for speciation.

PLANT AND ANIMAL EVOLUTION

Evolution of the First Cells

Modern evolution theory assumes the earliest forms of life began approximately four billion years ago. The pre-life Earth environment would have been rich in water, ammonia, and methane, all compounds rich in hydrogen. In order for life to arise on Earth, organic molecules such as amino acids (the building blocks of proteins), sugars, acids, and bases would need to have formed from the available chemicals.

The **Oparin Hypothesis**, developed by a Russian scientist (A. I. Oparin) in 1924, proposed that Earth was formed approximately 4.6 billion years ago and that early Earth had a reducing atmosphere, meaning there was very little free oxygen present. Instead, there was an abundance of ammonia, hydrogen, methane, and steam (H_2O), all escaping from volcanoes. Earth was in the process of cooling down, so there was a great deal of heat energy available, as well as a pattern of recurring violent lightning storms providing another source of energy. During this cooling of Earth, much of the steam surrounding Earth would condense, forming hot seas. In the presence of abundant energy, the synthesis of simple organic molecules from the available chemicals became possible. These organic substances then collected in the hot, turbulent seas (sometimes referred to as the "**primordial soup**").

As the concentration of organic molecules became very high, they began forming into larger, charged, complex molecules. Oparin called these highly absorptive molecules "**coacervates**." Coacervates were also able to divide.

Stanley Miller provided support for Oparin's hypotheses in experiments where he recreated conditions as they were supposed to exist in early Earth history, and was successful in his attempts to produce complex organic molecules including amino acids under these conditions. Sidney Fox, a major evolution researcher of the 1960s, conducted experiments that proved ultraviolet light may induce the formation of dipeptides from amino acids. Further strides were made by researcher Cyril Ponnamperuma, who demonstrated that small amounts of guanine formed from the thermal polymerization of amino acids. He also proved the synthesis of adenine and ribose from long-term treatment of reducing atmospheric gases with electrical current.

Once organic compounds had been synthesized, primitive cells most likely developed that contained genetic material in the form of RNA, and that used energy derived from ATP. These primitive cells were prokaryotic and similar to some bacteria now found on Earth.

Plant Evolution

The evolution of plant species is considered to have begun with heterotrophic prokaryotic cells. Over time, some bacteria evolved the ability to carry on photosynthesis (**cyanobacteria**), thus becoming autotrophic, which in turn introduced significant amounts of oxygen into the atmosphere. As oxygen is poisonous to most anaerobic cells, a new niche opened up: cells able not only to survive in the presence of oxygen, but also to use it in metabolism.

Cyanobacteria were incorporated into larger aerobic cells, which then evolved into photosynthetic eukaryotic cells. Cellular organization increased, nuclei and membranes formed, and cell specialization occurred, leading to multicellular photosynthetic organisms (plants).

The earliest plants were aquatic, but as niches filled in marine and freshwater environments, plants began to move onto land. Anatomical changes occurred over time allowing plants to survive in a non-aqueous environment. Cell walls thickened, and tissues developed to carry water and nutrients. As plants continued to adapt to land conditions, differentiation of tissues continued, resulting in the evolution of stems, leaves, roots, and seeds. The development of the **seed** was a key factor in the survival of land plants. Asexual reproduction dominated in early species, but sexual reproduction developed over time, increasing the possibilities of diversity.

Animal Evolution

The evolution of animals is thought to have begun with **marine protists**. Fossilized burrows from multicellular organisms begin to appear in the geological record approximately 700 million years ago, during the **Precambrian period**. These multicellular animals had only soft parts.

During the **Cambrian period** (the first period of the Paleozoic Era), beginning about 570 million years ago, the fossil record begins to show multicellular organisms with hard parts, namely exoskeletons. This sudden appearance of multitudes of differentiated animal forms is known as the **Cambrian explosion**. At the end of the **Paleozoic Era**, the fossil record attests to several mass extinction events, resulting in the extinction of about 95% of animal species developed to that point.

The **Ordovician period**, which began approximately 505 million years ago and lasted until about 440 million years ago, was marked by diversification among species and the development of land plants. Early forms of fish that arose in the Cambrian, developed during the Ordovician, becoming the first vertebrates to be seen in the fossil record. Again, the end of the Ordovician is marked by vast extinctions, but these extinctions allowed the opening of ecological situations, which in turn encouraged adaptive radiation.

The **Silurian period** from 440 to 410 million years ago is marked by widespread colonization of landmasses by plants and animals. The mass movement onto land by formerly marine animals required adaptation in numerous areas including gas exchange, support (skeletal), water conservation, circulatory systems, and reproduction.

Structures that exist in two different species because they share a common ancestry are called **homologous**. **Analogous** structures are similar because of their common function, although they do not share a common ancestry. Analogous structures are the product of **convergent evolution**. Convergence occurs when a particular characteristic evolves in two unrelated populations. For example, wings of insects and birds are analogous structures (they are similar in function regardless of the lack of common ancestors).

It is presumed that species that face **extinction** have not been able to adapt appropriately to environmental changes. However, there have also been several "**extinction events**" that have wiped out up to 95% of the species of their time. These events served to open up massive ecological niches, encouraging evolution of multitudes of new species.

Human Evolution

Humans are thought to have evolved from primates who over time developed larger brains. A branch of bipedal primates gave rise to the first true hominids about 4.5 million years ago. The earliest known hominid fossils were found in Africa in the 1970s. The well-known "**Lucy**" skeleton, named *Australopithecus afarensis*, had a human-like jaw and teeth, but a skull that was more similar to that of a small ape. The arms were proportionately longer than humans, indicating the ability to still be motile in trees.

The fossilized skull of ***Homo erectus***, who is considered the oldest known fossil of the human genus, is thought to be about 1.8 million years old. *Homo erectus* was thought to walk upright, had a larger skull, and had facial features more closely resembling humans than apes. The oldest fossils to be designated *Homo sapiens* are also called **Cro-Magnon** man, with brain size and facial features essentially the same as modern humans. Cro-Magnon *Homo sapiens* are thought to have evolved in Africa and migrated to Europe and Asia approximately 100,000 years ago.

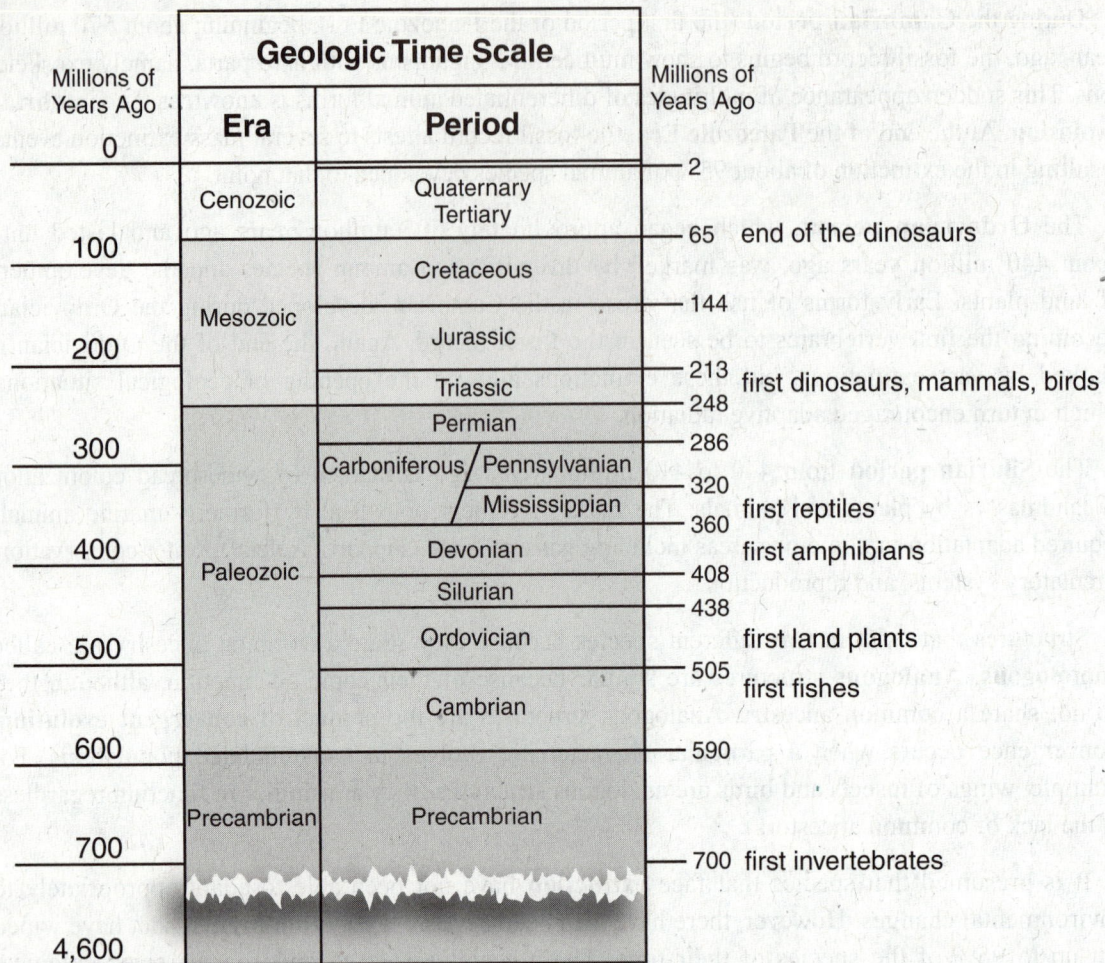

Millions of Years Ago			Millions of Years Ago	
Geologic Time Scale				
Era	**Period**			
0			2	
	Cenozoic	Quaternary		
		Tertiary	65	end of the dinosaurs
100		Cretaceous		
	Mesozoic		144	
200		Jurassic	213	first dinosaurs, mammals, birds
		Triassic	248	
		Permian	286	
300		Carboniferous / Pennsylvanian	320	
		Mississippian	360	first reptiles
400	Paleozoic	Devonian	408	first amphibians
		Silurian	438	
500		Ordovician	505	first land plants
		Cambrian		first fishes
600			590	
	Precambrian	Precambrian		
700			700	first invertebrates
4,600				

Evolutionary Ecology

Ecological circumstances affect (if not determine) the course of evolution of species in a particular area. The characteristics that differentiate these types of organisms are known collectively as **life history strategies**. There are two types of life history strategies: opportunistic and equilibreal.

Organisms with **opportunistic** life history strategies (also known as r-selected) possess traits that allow them to succeed in the long term, as well as traits that help make them succeed in a changing or new ecosystem. They tend to have short maturation times, short overall lifespans, and high mortality rates. Often reproduction is asexual, with high numbers of offspring. They find it easy to disperse over large areas. They do not parent their young. These are rapidly reproducing species that are also easily wiped out by more sophisticated populations that follow. For example, dandelions are an opportunistic species.

Species with **equilibreal** life strategies (also known as K-selected) are those organisms that overtake the opportunistic pioneer species. These tend to have long lifespans with a long maturation time and corresponding low mortality rate. They reproduce sexually and produce fewer (longer-living) offspring that they tend to parent. They tend to stay within their established borders rather than dispersing. These characteristics form the basis for particular species to dominate in varying ecosystems. For example, an oak tree is an equilibreal species.

Altruism (social behavior where organisms seem to place the needs of the community over their own need) may actually decrease the fitness of the individual with the trait (known as the cost of altruism), while it increases the fitness of the community (the benefit of altruism). In order for the traits of altruism to evolve some other factor must influence the preservation and proliferation of those traits.

Kin selection is the tendency of an individual to be altruistic toward a close relative, resulting in the preservation of its genetic traits. Close relatives have a greater likelihood of passing on identical traits to their offspring. Thus, those relatives are more likely to survive, and their genes are passed on to the offspring, thus preserving the altruistic trait in future generations.

Classification of Living Organisms

The study of **taxonomy** seeks to organize living things into groups based on morphology or, more recently, genetics. Carolus Linnaeus, who published his book *Systema Naturae* in 1735, first developed our current methods of taxonomy. Linnaeus based his taxonomic keys on the morphological (outward anatomical) differences seen among species. Linnaeus used two Latin-based categories—*genus* and *species*—to name each organism. Every genus name could include one or more types of species. We refer to this two-word naming of species as **binomial nomenclature** (literally meaning "two names" in Latin). For example, Linnaeus named humans *Homo sapiens* (literally "man who is wise"). *Homo* is the genus name and *sapiens* the species name.

Beyond genus and species, Linnaeus further categorized organisms in a total of seven levels. Every **species** also belongs to a **genus**, **family**, **order**, **class**, **phylum**, and **kingdom**. *Kingdom* is the most general category, *species* the most limited. Taxonomists now also add "sub" and "super" categories to give even more opportunity for grouping similar organisms, and have added categories even more general than kingdom (that is, **domains**).

Today, the classification system also serves to show relationships between organisms. When one constructs a **phylogenetic tree** (an evolutionary family tree of species) the result will generally show the same relationships represented with Linnaeus's taxonomy.

The most modern classification system contains three domains: the **Archaea**, the **Eubacteria**, and the **Eukaryota**. The organisms of the domain Archaea are prokaryotic, have unique RNA, and are able to live in the extreme ecosystems on Earth. The domain Eubacteria contains the prokaryotic organisms we call bacteria. *Note*: Some taxonomists still use a system including five kingdoms and no domains. In this case, the kingdom Monera would include organisms that are considered by other taxonomists to be included within the domains Archaea and Eubacteria.

The domain Eukaryota includes all organisms that possess eukaryotic cells, which make up the four kingdoms: **Protista, Fungi, Animalia,** and **Plantae.** The following chart gives the major features of the four kingdoms of the Eukaryota:

Kingdom	No. of Known Phyla/Species	Nutrition	Structure	Included Organisms
Protista	27/250,000 +	photosynthesis, some ingestion and absorption	large eukaryotic cells	algae & protozoa
Fungi	5/100,000 +	absorption	multicellular (eukaryotic) filaments	mold, mushrooms, yeast, smuts, mildew
Animalia	33/1,000,000 +	ingestion	multicellular, specialized eukaryotic motile cells	various worms, sponges, fish, insects, reptiles, amphibians, birds, and mammals
Plantae	10/250,000 +	photosynthesis	multicellular, specialized eukaryotic nonmotile cells	ferns, mosses, woody and non-woody flowering plants

There are nine major phyla within the **Kingdom Animalia.** (Each phylum is further broken down, but the focus here will be on the phylum Chordata.)

1. **Porifera**—the sponges

2. **Cnidaria**—jellyfish, sea anemones, hydra, etc.

3. **Platyhelminthes**—flatworms

4. **Nematoda**—roundworms

5. **Mollusca**—snails, clams, squid, etc.

6. **Annelida**—segmented worms (earthworms, leeches, etc.)

7. **Arthropoda**—crabs, spiders, lobster, millipedes, insects

8. **Echinodermata**—sea stars, sand dollars, etc.

9. **Chordata**—fish, amphibians, reptiles, birds, mammals, lampreys

Vertebrates are within the phylum Chordata, which is split into three subphyla, the **Urochordata** (animals with a tail cord such as tunicates), the **Cephalochordata** (animals with a head cord, such as lampreys), and **Vertebrata** (animals with a backbone).

The subphylum Vertebrata is divided into two **superclasses:** the **Aganatha** (animals with no jaws) and the **Gnathostomata** (animals with jaws). The Gnathostomata includes six classes with the following major characteristics:

a. **Chondrichthyes**—fish with a cartilaginous endoskeleton, two-chambered heart, 5–7 gill pairs, no swim bladder or lung, and internal fertilization (sharks, rays, etc.).

b. **Osteichthyes**—fish with a bony skeleton, numerous vertebrae, swim bladder (usually), two-chambered heart, gills with bony gill arches, and external fertilization (herring, carp, tuna).

c. **Amphibia**—animals with a bony skeleton, usually with four limbs having webbed feet with four toes, cold-blooded (ectothermic), large mouth with small teeth, three-chambered heart, separate sexes, internal or external fertilization, amniotic egg (salamanders, frogs, etc.).

d. **Reptilia**—horny epidermal scales, usually have paired limbs with five toes (except limbless snakes), bony skeleton, lungs, no gills, most have three-chambered heart, cold-blooded (ecothermic), internal fertilization, separate sexes, mostly egg-laying (oviparous), eggs contain extraembryonic membranes (snakes, lizards, alligators).

e. **Aves**—spindle-shaped body (with head, neck, trunk, and tail), long neck, paired limbs, most have wings for flying, four-toed foot, feathers, leg scales, bony skeleton, bones with air cavities, beak, no teeth, four-chambered heart, warm blooded (endothermic), lungs with thin air sacs, separate sexes, egg-laying, eggs have hard calcified shell (birds—ducks, sparrows, etc.).

f. **Mammalia**—body covered with hair, glands (sweat, scent, sebaceous, mammary), teeth, fleshy external ears, usually four limbs, four-chambered heart, lungs, larynx, highly developed brain, warm-blooded, internal fertilization, live birth (except for the egg-laying monotremes), milk producing (cows, humans, platypus, apes, etc.).

CELLULAR AND MOLECULAR BIOLOGY

THE STRUCTURE AND FUNCTION OF CELLS

The **cell** is the smallest and most basic unit of most living things (**organisms**). There are two main types of cells. **Prokaryotes** have no nucleus or any other membrane-bound **organelles** (cell components that perform particular functions). The DNA in prokaryotic cells usually forms a single chromosome, which floats within the cytoplasm. Prokaryotic organisms have only one cell and include all bacteria. Plant, fungi, and animal cells, as well as protozoa, are **eukaryotic**. Eukaryotic cells contain membrane-bound intracellular organelles, including a nucleus. The DNA within eukaryotes is organized into chromosomes.

A single organism can be *unicellular* (consisting of just one cell) or *multicellular* (consisting of many cells). A multicellular organism may have many different types of cells that differ in structure to serve different functions.

Viruses

Scientists do not agree as to whether **viruses** are actually alive. Although they can reproduce, they do not have the ability to conduct metabolic functions on their own. Virus structure consists of only a protein capsule, DNA, or RNA, and sometimes enzymes. Viruses survive and replicate by invading a living cell. The virus then utilizes the cell's mechanisms to reproduce itself, sometimes destroying the cell in the process.

Cell Organelles of Plants and Animals

All cells are enclosed within the **cell membrane** (or plasma membrane). Near the center of each eukaryotic cell is the **nucleus**, which contains the chromosomes. Between the nucleus and the cell membrane is a region called the **cytoplasm**. Since all of the organelles outside the nucleus but within the cell membrane exist within the cytoplasm, they are all called **cytoplasmic organelles**.

The shape and size of cells can vary widely. The longest nerve cells (neurons) may extend over a meter in length with an approximate diameter of only 4–100 micrometers (1 millimeter = 1,000 micrometers, μm). A human egg cell may be 100 micrometers in diameter. The average size of a bacterium is 0.5 to 2.0 micrometers. However, most cells are between 0.5 and 100 micrometers in diameter.

Animal Cells

The **cell membrane**, also called a plasma membrane, encloses the cell and separates it from the environment. This membrane is composed of a double layer (bilayer) of phospholipids with globular proteins embedded within the layers. The membrane is extremely thin (about 80 angstroms) and elastic. The combination of the lipid bilayer and the proteins embedded within it allow the cell to determine and regulate what molecules and ions can enter and leave the cell.

Endocytic vesicles allow the cell to absorb larger molecules than would be able to pass through the cell membrane, or that need to remain packaged within the cell.

Microvilli, projections of the cell extending from the cell membrane, increase the surface area of the cell membrane, increasing the area available to absorb nutrients. They also contain enzymes involved in digesting certain types of nutrients.

Microtubules are long, hollow, cylindrical protein filaments, which give structure to the cell. **Microfilaments** are double-stranded chains of proteins, which also serve to give structure to the cell. Together, they form the **cytoskeleton**, providing stability and structure. **Centrioles** are tubes constructed of a geometrical arrangement of microtubules in a pinwheel shape. Their function is primarily the formation of structural skeleton around which cells split during mitosis and meiosis. Basal bodies are structurally similar to centrioles, but their function is to anchor and aid in the movement of flagella or cilia.

Ribosomes, the site of protein synthesis within cells, are composed of certain protein molecules and RNA molecules (ribosomal RNAs, or rRNAs). **Free ribosomes** float unattached within the cytoplasm. The proteins synthesized by free ribosomes are made for use in the cytoplasm, not within membrane-bound organelles. **Attached ribosomes** are attached to the ER. Proteins made at the site of attached ribosomes are destined for use within the membrane-bound organelles.

The **endoplasmic reticulum**, a large organization of folded membranes, is responsible for the delivery of lipids and proteins to certain areas within the cytoplasm (a sort of cellular highway). **Rough endoplasmic reticulum** or **RER** has attached ribosomes. In addition to packaging and transport of materials within the cell, the RER is instrumental to protein synthesis. **Smooth endoplasmic reticulum** or **SER** is a network of membranous channels. Smooth endoplasmic reticulum does not have attached ribosomes. The endoplasmic reticulum is responsible for processing lipids, fats, and steroids, which are then packaged and dispersed by the Golgi apparatus.

The **Golgi apparatus** (also known as Golgi bodies, or the Golgi complex) is instrumental in the storing, packaging, and shipping of proteins. These packages are shipped (via the endoplasmic reticulum) to the part of the cell where they will be used, or to the cell membrane for secretion from the cell.

Secretory vesicles are packets of material packaged by either the Golgi apparatus or the endoplasmic reticulum that carry substances produced within the cell to the cell membrane. The vesicle membrane fuses with the cell membrane in a process called **exocytosis**, allowing the substance to escape the cell.

Lysosomes digest unused material within the cell, damaged organelles, or materials absorbed by the cell for use.

Mitochondria are centers of cellular respiration (the process of breaking up covalent bonds within sugar molecules with the intake of oxygen and release of ATP, adenosine triphosphate). Mitochondria (plural of mitochondrion) are more numerous in cells requiring more energy (muscle, etc.). Mitochondria are self-replicating, containing their own DNA, RNA, and ribosomes. Mitochondria have a double membrane; the internal membrane is folded. Cellular respiration reactions occur along the folds of the internal membrane (called **cristae**). Mitochondria are thought to be an evolved form of primitive bacteria (prokaryotic cells) that lived in a symbiotic relationship with eukaryotic cells more than two billion years ago. This concept, known as the **endosymbiont hypothesis**, is a plausible explanation of how mitochondria, which have many of the necessary components for life on their own, became an integral part of eukaryotic cells.

The **nucleus** is an organelle surrounded by two lipid bilayer membranes. The nucleus contains chromosomes, nuclear pores, nucleoplasm, and nucleoli. The **nucleolus** is a rounded area within the nucleus of the cell where ribosomal RNA is synthesized. Several nucleoli (plural of nucleolus) can exist within a nucleus. The **nuclear membrane**, the boundary between the nucleus and the cytoplasm, is actually a double membrane, which allows for the entrance and exit of certain molecules through the **nuclear pores**, points at which the double nuclear membrane fuses together, forming a passageway between the inside of the nucleus and the cytoplasm outside the nucleus. Nuclear pores allow the cell to selectively move molecules in and out of the nucleus.

Plant Cells

The structure of plant cells differs noticeably from animal cells with the addition of three organelles: the cell wall, the chloroplasts, and the central vacuole. Several organelles, such as the Golgi apparatus, mitochondria, rough endoplasmic reticulum, ribosome, nucleus, nucleolus, and smooth endoplasmic reticulum, function the same way in plant cells as in animal cells. However, other organelles do have distinct differences.

Cell walls surround plant cells. (Bacteria also have cell walls.) Cell walls are made of cellulose and lignin, making them strong and rigid (whereas the cell membrane is relatively weak and flexible). The cell wall encloses the cell membrane, providing strength and protection for the cell. The cell wall allows plant cells to store water under relatively high concentration. The combined strength of a plant's cell walls provides support for the whole organism. The structure of the cell wall allows substances to pass through it readily, so transport in and out of the cell is still regulated by the cell membrane.

The **cell membrane** functions in plant and animal cells in the same way. However, in some plant tissues, channels connect the cytoplasm of adjacent cells.

Chloroplasts are the site of photosynthesis within plant cells. **Chlorophyll** pigment molecules give the chloroplasts their green color. The body (or **stroma**) of the chloroplast contains embedded stacked, disk-like plates (called **grana**), which are the site of photosynthetic reactions.

The **central vacuole** takes up much of the volume of plant cells. It is a membrane-bound (this particular membrane is called the **tonoplast**), fluid-filled space, which stores water and soluble nutrients for the plant's use. The tendency of the central vacuole to absorb water provides for the rigid shape (turgidity) of some plant cells. (Animal cells may also contain vacuoles for varying purposes.)

Properties of Cell Membranes

The cell membrane is made up of a fluid phospholipid bilayer, proteins, and carbohydrates. Substances can cross the cell membrane by passive transport, facilitated diffusion, and active transport. During **passive transport**, substances freely pass across the membrane without the cell expending any energy. **Facilitated diffusion** does not require added energy, but it cannot occur without the help of specialized proteins. Transport requiring energy output from the cell is called **active transport**.

Diffusion, a type of passive transport, is the process whereby molecules and ions flow through the cell membrane from an area of higher concentration to an area of lower concentration (thus tending to equalize concentrations). Diffusion requires no added energy to propel substances through a membrane.

Another type of passive transport that only occurs with water molecules is **osmosis**. Osmosis does not require the addition of any energy, but occurs when the water concentration inside the cell differs from the concentration outside the cell. The water on the side of the membrane with the highest water concentration will move through the membrane until the concentration is equalized on both sides. When the water concentration is equal inside and outside the cell, it is called **isomotic** or **isotonic**.

Facilitated diffusion allows for transfer of substances across the cell membrane with the help of specialized proteins. These proteins, which are embedded in the cell membrane, are able to pick up specific molecules or ions and transport them through the membrane.

Active transport also requires membrane-bound proteins. Unlike facilitated diffusion, active transport uses energy obtained from ATP to move molecules across a cell membrane against a concentration gradient (in the opposite direction than they would go under normal diffusion circumstances).

Endocytosis is the process whereby large molecules (i.e., some sugars or proteins) are taken up into a pocket of membrane. The pocket pinches off, delivering the molecules, still inside a membrane sack, into the cytoplasm. **Exocytosis** is the reverse process, exporting substances from the cell.

Energy Transformations (Bioenergetics)

All living things require energy. Ultimately, the source of most energy for life on Earth is the sun. **Photosynthetic organisms** (plants, some protists, and some bacteria) are able to harvest solar energy and transform it into chemical energy eventually stored within covalent bonds of molecules (such as carbohydrates, fats, and proteins). These organisms are called **primary producers**. Consumers eat producers and utilize the chemical energy stored in them to carry on the functions of life. Other organisms then consume the consumers. In each of these steps along the food chain, some energy is lost as heat.

Cellular metabolism includes all types of energy transformation processes, including photosynthesis, respiration, growth, and movement. Energy transformations occur as chemicals are broken apart or synthesized within the cell. The process whereby cells build molecules and store energy (in the form of chemical bonds) is called **anabolism**. **Catabolism** is the process of breaking down molecules and releasing stored energy.

ATP

Photosynthetic organisms transform energy from the sun into chemical energy in the form of **ATP (adenosine triphosphate)**, the energy currency of cellular activity. ATP consists of a nitrogenous base (adenine), a simple sugar (ribose), and three phosphate groups. When a cellular process requires energy, a molecule of ATP can be broken down into **ADP (adenosine diphosphate)** plus a phosphate group. Even more energy is released when ATP is decomposed into **AMP (adenosine monophosphate)** and two phosphate groups. These energy-releasing reactions are then coupled with energy-absorbing reactions.

Photosynthesis

The process of **photosynthesis** converts the light energy of the sun into chemical energy usable by living things. Photosynthetic organisms carry out photosynthesis, use the converted energy for their own life processes, and also store energy that may be used by organisms that consume them.

Although the process of photosynthesis actually occurs through many small steps, the entire process can be summed up with the following equation:

$$6CO_2 + 6H_2O + \text{light energy} \rightarrow C_6H_{12}O_6 + 6O_2$$

$$(\text{carbon dioxide} + \text{water} \rightarrow \text{glucose} + \text{oxygen})$$

Chlorophyll is a green pigment (a pigment is a substance that absorbs light energy) that is able to absorb a photon of light. Photosynthesis can only occur where chlorophyll is present.

There are two phases of the photosynthetic process: the light reaction, or **photolysis**, and the dark reaction, or CO_2 **fixation**. During photolysis, the chlorophyll pigment absorbs a photon of light, leaving the chlorophyll in an excited (higher energy) state. The light reaction is a decomposition reaction, which separates water molecules into hydrogen and oxygen atoms utilizing the energy from the excited chlorophyll pigment. Oxygen, which is not needed by the cell, combines to form O_2 (gas) and is released into the environment. The free hydrogen is grabbed and held by a particular molecule (called the **hydrogen acceptor**) until it is needed. The excited chlorophyll also supplies energy to a series of reactions that produce ATP from ADP and inorganic phosphate (Pi).

The dark reaction (CO_2 fixation) then occurs in the stroma of the chloroplast. This second phase of photosynthesis does not require light; however, it does require the use of the products (hydrogen and ATP) of photolysis. In this phase, six CO_2 molecules are linked with hydrogen (produced in photolysis) forming glucose (a six-carbon sugar). Glucose molecules can link to form polysaccharides (starch or sugar), which are then stored in the cell.

Cellular Respiration

Respiration is the process that releases energy for use by the cell. **Glycolysis** is the breaking down of the six-carbon sugar (glucose) into smaller carbon-containing molecules yielding ATP (*glyco* = sugar, *lysis* = breakdown). Each molecule of glucose (six carbons) is broken down into two molecules of pyruvic acid (or pyruvate with three carbons each), two ATP molecules, and two hydrogen atoms (attached to NADH, nicotinamide adenine dinucleotide). This is an **anaerobic reaction**. After glycolysis has occurred, respiration will continue on one of two pathways, depending upon whether oxygen is present or not. The process of glycolysis is summarized by the following chemical equation:

$$\text{glucose (6 C)} + 2ADP + 2\,Pi + 2NAD^+ \rightarrow 2 \text{ pyruvic acid (3 C each)} + 2ATP + 2NADH + 2H^+$$

Aerobic Pathways

Aerobic respiration (in the presence of oxygen) begins with glycolysis and proceeds through two major steps. The first step, the **Krebs cycle** (also known as the citric acid cycle), occurs in the matrix of a cell's mitochondria and breaks down pyruvic acid molecules (three carbons each) into

CO_2 molecules, H^+ (protons), and 2 ATP molecules. The Krebs cycle also liberates electrons, which then enter the next step.

The second step occurs along the **electron transport** system, or ETS. The ETS is a series of **cytochromes**, which exist on the cristae of the mitochondria. They include a protein and a **heme** (iron containing) group. The iron in heme groups may be either oxidized (loses electron to form Fe^{+3}) or reduced (gains electron to form Fe^{+2}) as electrons are passed along the ETS. As electrons pass from one cytochrome to another, energy is given off. Some of this energy is lost as heat; the rest is stored in molecules of ATP. This process can produce the most ATP molecules per cycle, 32 ATPs per glucose molecule. The final step of the electron transport chain occurs when the last electron carrier transfers two electrons to an oxygen atom that simultaneously combines with two protons from the surrounding medium to produce water.

Anaerobic Pathways

If no oxygen is present within the cell, respiration will proceed anaerobically after glycolysis. Anaerobic respiration, also called **fermentation**, breaks down the two pyruvic acid molecules (three carbons each) into end products (such as ethyl alcohol, C_2H_6O, or lactic acid, $C_3H_6O_3$), plus carbon dioxide (CO_2). The net gain from anaerobic respiration is two ATP molecules per glucose molecule. Fermentation is not as efficient as aerobic respiration; it uses only a small part of the energy available in a glucose molecule.

CHEMICAL NATURE OF THE GENE

Watson and Crick were responsible for explaining the structure of the DNA molecule. Today, through the discoveries of these two scientists, and through the collaborative work of scientists worldwide, the study of chromosomes and genetic inheritance has proceeded to discover the intricacies of the **genomes** (sum total of genetic information) of many organisms, including humans.

A **gene** is a length of DNA that encodes a particular protein. Each protein the cell synthesizes performs a specific function in the cell, called a trait.

DNA Replication

In order to replicate, a portion of a DNA molecule unwinds, separating the two halves of the **double helix**. (This separation is aided by the enzyme helicase.) Another enzyme (DNA polymerase) binds to each strand and moves along them as it collects nucleotides using the original DNA strands as templates. The new strand is complementary to the original template and forms a new double helix with one of the parent strands. If no errors occur during DNA synthesis, the result is two identical double helix molecules of DNA.

This process is occasionally subject to a mistake known as a **mutation**. Mutations can also result from damage to DNA caused by exposure to certain chemicals, such as some solvents or the chemicals in cigarette smoke, or by radiation, such as ultraviolet radiation in sunlight or X-rays. A mutation expresses itself in a change (small or large) in the cell structure and function.

The DNA information for making a particular protein can be called the gene for that protein. Genetic traits are expressed, and specialization of cells occurs, as a result of the combination of proteins encoded by the DNA of a cell. Protein synthesis occurs in two steps called transcription and translation.

Transcription refers to the formation of an RNA molecule, which corresponds to a gene. The DNA strand "unzips" and replicates; individual RNA nucleotides are strung together to match the DNA sequence by the enzyme RNA polymerase. The new RNA strand (known as messenger RNA or **mRNA**) migrates from the nucleus to the cytoplasm, where it is modified in a process known as **post-transcriptional processing**. This processing prepares the mRNA for protein synthesis by removing the non-coding sequences. In the processed RNA, each unit of three nucleotides or **codon** encodes a particular amino acid.

The next phase of protein synthesis is called **translation**. In order for the protein synthesis process to continue, a second type of RNA is required. Transfer RNA or **tRNA** is the link between the "language" of nucleotides (codon and anticodon) and the "language" of amino acids (hence the word *translation*). Transfer RNA is a chain of about 80 nucleotides. At one point along the tRNA chain, there are three unattached bases, which are called the anticodon. This anticodon will line up with a corresponding codon during translation. Each tRNA molecule also has an attached, specific amino acid.

Translation occurs at the ribosomes. A **ribosome**, a structure composed of proteins and ribosomal RNA (rRNA), attaches to the mRNA strand at a particular codon known as the **start codon**. The ribosome continues to add tRNA whose anticodons make complementary bonds with the next codon on the mRNA string, forming a peptide bond between amino acids as each amino acid is held in place by a tRNA. At the end of the translation process, a **terminating codon** stops the synthesis process and the protein is released.

Structural and Regulatory Genes

Genes encode proteins of two varieties. **Structural genes** code proteins that form organs and structural characteristics. **Regulatory genes** code proteins that determine functional or physiological events, such as growth. These proteins regulate when other genes start or stop encoding proteins, which in turn produce specific traits.

1. Transduction and Transformation

Transduction is the transfer of genetic material (portions of a bacterial chromosome) from one bacterial cell to another, mediated by a **bacteriophage** (a virus that targets bacteria). Bacteria may also absorb and incorporate pieces of DNA from their environment (usually from dead bacterial cells), a process called **transformation**.

Cell Division

The process of cell reproduction, called **cell division**, centers on the replication and separation of strands of **DNA**.

Structure of Chromosomes

Chromosomes are long chains of subunits called **nucleosomes**, each composed of a short length of DNA wrapped around a core of small proteins called **histones**. The combination of DNA with histones is called **chromatin**. Each nucleosome is about 11 nm in diameter and contains a central core of eight histones with the DNA double helix wrapped around them. Each gene spans dozens of nucleosomes.

In a cell that is getting ready to divide, each strand of chromatin is duplicated. The two identical strands (called **chromatids**) remain attached to each other at a point called the **centromere**. During cell division, the chromatin strands become more tightly coiled and packed, forming a chromosome with an **X** shape.

Within the nucleus, each chromosome pairs with another of similar size and shape, called a **homolog**. Each set of homologous chromosomes has a similar genetic constitution, but the genes are not necessarily identical. Different forms of corresponding genes are called **alleles**.

Restriction Enzymes

Restriction enzymes (restriction endonucleases) cut sections of DNA molecules by cleaving the sugar-phosphate backbone at a particular nucleotide sequence. Restriction enzymes are made by bacteria and act to destroy foreign DNA (for example, viral DNA) that has entered the bacterial cell. Restriction enzymes are generally named after their host of origin, rather than the substrate upon which they act.

The Cell Cycle

A cell that is going to divide progresses through a particular sequence of events ending in cell division, which produces two daughter cells. This is known as the **cell cycle**. The time taken to progress through the cell cycle differs with different types of cells, but the sequence is the same.

There are two major periods within the cell cycle. **Interphase** is the period when the cell is active in carrying on its function. Interphase is divided into three phases. During the first phase, the **G₁ phase**, metabolism and protein synthesis are occurring at a high rate, and most of the cell growth occurs at this time. During the second phase, the **S phase**, the cell begins to prepare for cell division by replicating the DNA and proteins necessary to form a new set of chromosomes. In the final phase, the **G₂ phase**, more proteins are produced, which will be necessary for cell division, and the centrioles (which are integral to the division process) are replicated as well. Cell growth and function occur through all the stages of interphase.

Mitosis

Mitosis is the process by which a cell distributes its duplicated chromosomes so that each daughter cell has a full set of chromosomes. Mitosis progresses through four phases: prophase, metaphase, anaphase, and telophase.

During **prophase**, the chromatin condenses into chromosomes within the nucleus and becomes visible through a light microscope. The centrioles move to opposite ends of the cell, and **spindle fibers** begin to extend from the centromeres of each chromosome toward the center of the cell. During the second part of prophase, the nuclear membrane dissolves and the spindle fibers attach to the centromeres forming a junction called a **kinetochore**. The chromosomes then begin moving in preparation for the next step, metaphase.

During **metaphase**, the spindle fibers pull the chromosomes into alignment along the equatorial plane of the cell, creating the metaphase plate. This arrangement ensures that one copy of each chromosome is distributed to each daughter cell.

During **anaphase**, the chromatids are separated from each other when the centromere divides. Each former chromatid is now called a chromosome. The two identical chromosomes move along the spindle fibers to opposite ends of the cell. **Telophase** occurs as nuclear membranes form around the chromosomes. The chromosomes disperse through the new nucleoplasm and the spindle fibers disappear. After telophase, the process of **cytokinesis** produces two separate cells.

Cytokinesis differs somewhat in plants and animals. In animal cells, a ring made of the protein actin surrounds the center of the cell and contracts. As the actin ring contracts, it pinches the cytoplasm into two separate compartments. Each cell's plasma membrane seals, making two distinct daughter cells. In plant cells, a cell plate forms across the center of the cell and extends out toward the edges of the cell. When this plate reaches the edges, a cell wall forms on either side of the plate, and the original cell then splits into two.

Mitosis, then, produces two nearly identical daughter cells. Organisms (such as bacteria) that reproduce asexually do so through the process of mitosis.

Meiosis

Meiosis is the process of producing four daughter cells, each with single unduplicated chromosomes (**haploid**). The parent cell is **diploid**, that is, it has a normal set of paired chromosomes. Meiosis goes through a two-stage process resulting in four new cells, rather than two (as in mitosis). Each cell has half the chromosomes of the parent. Meiosis occurs in reproductive organs, and the resultant four haploid cells are called **gametes** (egg and sperm). When two haploid gametes fuse during the process of fertilization, the resultant cell has one chromosome set from each parent, and is diploid. This process allows for the huge genetic diversity available among species.

Two distinct nuclear divisions occur during meiosis: reduction (or meiosis 1) and division (or meiosis 2). **Reduction** affects the **ploidy** (referring to haploid or diploid) level, reducing it from 2n to n (i.e., diploid to haploid). **Division** then distributes the remaining set of chromosomes in a mitosis-like process.

As in mitosis, chromosome replication occurs before prophase; then during prophase 1, homologous chromosomes pair up and join at a point called a **synapse** (this happens only in meiosis). The attached chromosomes are now termed a tetrad, a dense four-stranded structure composed of the four chromatids from the original chromosomes. At this point, some portions of the chromatid may break off and reattach to another chromatid in the tetrad. This process, known as **crossing over**, results in an even wider array of final genetic possibilities.

In metaphase 1, the two chromosomes (a total of four chromatids per pair) align themselves along the cell's equatorial plane. Each homologous pair of chromosomes contains one chromosome from the mother and one from the father. When the homologous pairs orient at the cell's center in preparation for separating, the chromosomes randomly sort. The resulting cells from this meiotic division will have a mixture of chromosomes from each parent. This increases the possibilities for variety among descendent cells.

Anaphase 1 occurs next as the chromosomes move to separate ends of the cell. In telophase 1, the nuclear envelope may or may not form, depending on the type of organism. In either case, the cell then proceeds to meiosis 2.

The nuclear envelopes dissolve (if they have formed) during prophase 2 and spindle fibers form again. All else proceeds as in mitosis, through metaphase 2, anaphase 2, and telophase 2. Again, as in mitosis, each chromosome splits into two chromatids. The process ends with cytokinesis, forming four distinct gamete cells.

Biosynthesis

Biosynthesis, the process of producing chemical compounds by living things, takes reactant molecules and, with added energy (and often the action of enzymes), produces the products that are needed for cell or organism function.

Enzymes are protein molecules that act as catalysts for organic reactions. Enzymes do not make reactions possible that would not otherwise occur under the right energy conditions, but they lower the activation energy, which increases the rate of the reaction.

Enzymes are named ending with the letters *-ase*, and usually begin with a syllable describing the catalyzed reaction (i.e., hydrolase catalyzes hydrolysis reactions). Enzymes are effective catalysts because of their unique shapes. Each enzyme has a uniquely shaped area, called its **active site**. For each enzyme, there is a particular substance known as its **substrate**, which fits within the active site (like a hand in a glove). When the substrate is seated in the active site, the combination of two molecules is called the **enzyme-substrate complex**.

The operation of enzymes lowers the energy needed to initiate cellular reactions. However, the completion of the reaction may either require or release energy. Reactions requiring energy are called **endothermic reactions**. Reactions that release energy are called **exothermic reactions**. Endothermic reactions can take place in a cell by being coupled to the breakdown of ATP or a similar molecule. Exothermic reactions are coupled to the production of ATP or another molecule with high-energy chemical bonds.

Some enzymatic reactions require a non-protein substance called a **cofactor** that binds to the active site. This allows the substrate to fit into the active site. **Inorganic cofactors** include metal ions—for example, iron, copper, or zinc. **Organic cofactors** are also called **coenzymes**. Some coenzymes are not made by cells but must be obtained in the diet. Most vitamins are coenzymes (or precursors of coenzymes). **Prosthetic groups** are similar to cofactors; they also facilitate the enzyme reaction. However, prosthetic groups are bound to the enzyme, rather than being separate atoms or molecules.

If a substance, known as an **inhibitor**, attaches to an enzyme before a cofactor, the cellular reaction will not take place. Environmental conditions within the cell, such as high temperature or acidity, may also inhibit an enzymatic reaction. Enzyme control (or **regulation**) may occur when the product of the reaction is also an inhibitor to the reaction. This slows down the production rate as the concentration of the product increases. In other cases, a particular molecule serves as a regulator by changing the structure of the active site, making the enzyme more or less effective.

STRUCTURE AND FUNCTION OF PLANTS AND ANIMALS; GENETICS

PLANTS (BOTANY)

The plant kingdom is divided into several classifications according to physical characteristics. **Vascular** plants (tracheophytes) have tissue organized in such a way as to conduct food and water throughout their structure. These plants include some that produce seeds (such as corn or roses) as well as those that do not produce any seeds (such as ferns). **Nonvascular** plants (bryophytes), such as mosses, lack special tissue for conducting water or food.

Angiosperms are plants that produce flowers as reproductive organs. **Gymnosperms**, on the other hand, produce seeds without flowers. These include conifers (cone-bearers) and cycads.

Plants that survive only through a single growing season are known as **annuals**. Other plants are **biennial**; their life cycle spans two growing seasons. **Perennial** plants continue to grow year after year.

Plant Anatomy

Angiosperms and gymnosperms differ mostly in the structure of their stems and reproductive organs. Gymnosperms are mostly trees, with woody, instead of herbaceous stems. Gymnosperms do not produce flowers; instead they produce seeds in cones or cone-like structures.

Angiosperms

The shoot system of angiosperms includes the stem, leaves, flowers, and fruit, as well as growth structures such as nodes and buds. The signature structure of an angiosperm is the **flower**, the primary reproductive organ. Before the flower blooms, it is enclosed within the **sepals**, small, green, leaf-like structures, which fold back to reveal the flower **petals**. The petals attract insects and birds, to assist with pollination. The short branch of stem, which supports the flower, is called the **pedicel**.

Usually (but depending on the species), a single flower will have both male and female reproductive organs. The **pistil** is the female structure, and includes the stigma, style, ovary, and ovules. The **stigma** is a sticky surface at the top of the pistil which traps pollen grains. The stigma sits above a slender vase-like structure, the **style**, which encloses the ovary. The **ovary** is the hollow, bulb-shaped structure in the lower interior of the pistil. (After seeds have formed, the ovary will ripen and become fruit.) Within the ovary are the **ovules**, small round cases each containing one or more egg cells. (If the egg is fertilized, the ovule will become a seed.) In the process of meiosis in the ovule, an egg cell is produced, along with smaller bodies known as polar nuclei. The polar nuclei will develop into the endosperm of the seed when fertilized by sperm cells.

The male structure is the stamen, consisting of the **anther** atop the long, hollow **filament**. The anther has four lobes and contains cells (microspore mother cells) that become pollen. Some mature **pollen grains** are conveyed (usually by wind, birds, or insects) to a flower of a compatible species, where they stick to the stigma. The stigma produces chemicals, which stimulate the pollen to burrow into the style, forming a hollow **pollen tube**. This tube is produced by the tube **nucleus**, which has developed from a portion of the pollen grain. The pollen tube extends down toward the ovary. Behind the tube nucleus are two **sperm nuclei**. When the sperm nuclei reach the ovule, one will join with an egg cell, fertilizing it to become a zygote. The other sperm nucleus merges with the polar bodies forming the endosperm, which will feed the growing embryo.

The **shoot apex** is composed of **meristem** tissue (consisting of undifferentiated cells capable of quick growth and specialization), and is the region where elongation of the stem occurs. The **terminal bud** (the beginning of a new set of leaves) is also located at the shoot apex. Each year, as the plant continues to grow taller, a new terminal bud and shoot apex are produced. The spot where the previous year's terminal bud was located is then called a **terminal bud scar**.

Fruit is a matured ovary, which contains the seeds (mature fertilized ovules). The fruit provides protection for the seeds, as well as a method to disburse them. Fruits that develop from a single ripened ovary are known as **simple fruits** (e.g., apple, corn, olive, acorn, cucumber). **Compound fruits** develop from many separate ovaries. They may be an **aggregate fruit**, in which many ovaries of a single flower fuse together (e.g., raspberry), or a **multiple fruit**, which forms from the fusing of several ovaries of separate flowers during ripening (e.g., strawberry or pineapple).

Each **seed** contains a tiny embryonic plant, stored food, and a seed coat for protection. When the seed is exposed to proper moisture, temperature, and oxygen, it germinates (begins to sprout and grow into a new plant). Angiosperms are classified according to the structure of their cotyledons. Plants with two cotyledons in each seed are known as dicotyledons (**dicots**); those with only one are known as monocotyledons (**monocots**). The following chart outlines the major differences between monocots and dicots:

Dicots	Monocots
ex. oaks, flowers, vegetables	ex. grasses, lilies, palm trees
two cotyledons in seed	one cotyledon in seed
leaves have branched or networked veins	leaves have parallel veins
vascular bundles (collections of xylem and phloem tubes) are arranged in rings	stems have random arrangement of vascular bundles
taproot system with smaller secondary roots	fibrous roots
flowers with petals in multiples of four or five	flowers with petals in multiples of three

The **stem**, the plant's main support structure, produces leaves and lateral (parallel with the ground) branches. **Nodes** are the locations along the stem where new leaves sprout, and the space between nodes is the **internode**. New leaves begin as **lateral buds**, which can be seen on growing plants.

Most of the stem tissue is made up of **vascular tissue**, including two varieties. **Xylem** tissue is composed of long tubular cells, which transport water up from the ground to the branches and leaves. **Phloem** tissue, made of stacked cells connected by sieve plates (which allow nutrients to pass from cell to cell), transports food made in the leaves (by photosynthesis) to the rest of the plant.

The **leaf** is the primary site of photosynthesis in most plants. Most leaves are thin, flat, and joined to a branch or stem by a petiole (a small stem-like extension). The petiole houses vascular tissue, which connects the veins in the leaf with those in the stem.

The **cuticle**, which maintains the leaf's moisture balance, covers most leaf surfaces. The outermost layer, the **epidermis**, is generally one cell thick. It secretes the waxy cuticle and protects the leaf's inner tissue.

The mesophyll is composed of several layers of tissue between the upper and lower epidermis. The uppermost, the **palisade layer**, contains vertically aligned cells with numerous chloroplasts. Most photosynthesis occurs in this layer.

The sugars produced by photosynthesis are transported throughout the plant via the **vascular bundles** of xylem and phloem, which make up the veins in the leaf.

The next layer beneath the palisade cells is the **spongy layer**, a layer of parenchyma cells separated by large air spaces that allow for the exchange of gases (carbon dioxide and oxygen) for photosynthesis.

On the underside of the leaf there are openings ringed by **guard cells**. The openings are called **stomata** (or stomates). The stomata serve to allow moisture and gases (carbon dioxide and oxygen) to pass in and out of the leaf, thus facilitating photosynthesis.

The root system of a typical angiosperm includes the **primary roots**, which extend downward, and the **lateral roots**, which develop secondarily and extend horizontally, parallel with the ground surface. Roots function to provide water and needed nutrients to the plant. Roots are structured to provide a large surface area for absorption. The network of the root system also anchors the plant.

Roots have four major structural regions, which run vertically from bottom to top. The **root cap** is composed of dead, thick-walled cells, and covers the tip of the root, protecting it as the root pushes through soil. The **meristematic region** is just above the root cap. It consists of undifferentiated cells, which carry on mitosis, producing cells that grow to form the **elongation region**. In the elongation region, cells differentiate, large vacuoles are formed, and cells grow. As the cells differentiate into various root tissues, they become part of the **maturation region**.

A cross-section of root tissue above the maturation region would reveal several types of **primary root tissue**. In the maturation region, the epidermis produces **root hairs**, extensions of the cells, which reach between soil particles and retrieve water and minerals. The primary tissues include the outermost layer, the **epidermis**. The epidermis is one cell layer thick and serves to protect the internal root tissue and absorb nutrients and water.

Inside the epidermis is a ring known as the **cortex**, made up of large parenchyma cells, thin-walled cells loosely packed to allow for flow of gases and uptake of minerals.

Inside the cortex is a ring of **endodermis**, a single layer of cells, which are tightly connected so no substances can pass between cells. This feature allows the endodermis to act as a filter; all substances entering the vascular tissues from the root must pass through these cells. In the center of the root is the **vascular cylinder**, including xylem and phloem tissue.

Plant Physiology

1. Water and Mineral Absorption and Transport

Water is essential to all cells of all plants, so plants must have the ability to obtain water and transport water molecules throughout their structure. Most water is absorbed through the plant's root system, then makes its way in one of two pathways toward the xylem cells. The first pathway is for water to seep between the epidermal cells of the roots and between the parenchyma cells of the cortex. When water reaches the endodermal tissue, it enters the cells and is pushed through the vascular tissue toward the xylem. A second pathway is for the water to pass through the cell wall and plasma membrane. Water travels along this intracellular route through channels in the cell membranes (**plasmodesmata**) until it reaches the xylem.

Once water reaches the xylem, hydrogen bonding between water molecules (known as **cohesion**) causes tension that pulls water through the water column up through the stem and on to the leaves (known as the **cohesion-tension process**). Some water that has traveled up through the plant to the leaves is evaporated, a process known as **transpiration**. As water is evaporated, it causes a siphoning effect (like sucking on a straw), which continues to pull water up from the root xylem.

2. Food Translocation and Storage

Food molecules are transferred from the source cells to phloem tissue through active transport. Once in the phloem, the sugars begin to build up, causing osmosis to occur. The entrance of water into the phloem causes pressure, which pushes the water-sugar solution through **sieve plates** that join the cells. This pressure thrusts the water-sugar solution to all areas of the plant, making food available to all cells in the plant.

Plant Reproduction and Development

The reproductive cycle of plants occurs through the alternation of **haploid** (n) and **diploid** (2n) phases. Haploid cells have one complete set of chromosomes (n). Diploid cells have two sets of chromosomes (2n). Diploid and haploid stages are both capable of undergoing mitosis in plants. The diploid generation is known as a **sporophyte**. The reproductive organs of the sporophyte produce **gametophytes** through the process of meiosis. Gametophytes may be male or female and are haploid. The male gametophyte produces **sperm** (**male gamete**); the female produces an **egg cell** (**female gamete**). When a sperm cell **fertilizes** an egg cell (haploid cells join to form a diploid cell) they produce a **zygote**. The zygote will grow into an **embryo**, which resides within the growing seed.

Various phyla of plants have their own identifiable life cycles, which include an **alternation of generations**. Mosses and ferns alternate haploid and diploid phases, developing two distinct generations of the plant, each with its own recognizable form. One generation is haploid, the other diploid. The haploid phase is most prominent in mosses, while in ferns the diploid stage is most prominent.

1. Asexual Plant Reproduction

Some plants may also reproduce through **vegetative propagation**—an asexual process. Asexual reproduction occurs through mitosis only (it does not involve gametes), and produces offspring genetically identical to the parent. While sexual reproduction leads to genetic variation and adaptation, asexual reproduction of a plant with a desirable set of genetic traits preserves these intact in successive generations. Many plants reproduce through a combination of sexual and asexual reproduction, reaping the advantages of each.

Several types of plants produce structures specifically designed to carry on vegetative propagation. These are described in the following chart:

Reproductive Structure	Description of Structure	Plants with These Structures
tubers	underground storage stems, develop new shoots after dormant season	potatoes
rhizomes	underground runners that develop into new plants	irises
stolens	above-ground runners that grow roots of their own, then develop into new plant	strawberries
bulbs	underground storage units that grow into many new plants via division	amaryllis
corms	resemble bulbs but with enlarged, solid stem for food storage	gladiolus, crocus

Plant Growth and Development

Hormones are chemicals that regulate the growth, development, and function of an organism. Each type of hormone affects changes in particular cells known as target cells. Note the most common hormones and their functions in the following chart:

Hormone	Process Regulated or Influenced
gibberellins (65 hormones)	cell division & cell elongation
cytokinins	cell division & fruit development
abscisic acid	opening and closing of stomata (controlling water lost through transpiration and formation of winter buds that puts plant in dormant state)
ethylene	ripening of fruit (spoiling releases ethylene which stimulates ripening of surrounding fruit); metabolic activity (i.e., producing female flowers to increase fertilization)
auxins	growth factors (i.e., tropisms)

A **tropism** is an organism's involuntary response to an external stimulus such as light, water, gravity, or nutrients. For instance, plant stems are usually positively **phototropic** (they grow toward light), while plant roots are negatively phototropic (they grow away from light). Plant roots are positively

geotropic; they grow toward the center of the Earth, while stems are negatively geotropic, growing against gravity.

Other factors besides hormones influence plant growth and development. For instance, plants respond to relative periods of light and darkness, a characteristic known as **photoperiodicity**. Light-sensitive chemicals in the leaves trigger a response in the plant, which encourages growth, flowering, or other reactions. This trait causes flowering and growth of varying plants at different times of year.

ANIMALS (ZOOLOGY)

The animal kingdom includes a wide variety of phyla that have a range of body plans. Organisms in the animal kingdom share the following traits:

1. Animal cells do not have cell walls or plastids.

2. Adult animals are multicellular with specialized tissues and organs.

3. Animals are heterotrophic (they do not produce their own food).

4. Animal species are capable of sexual reproduction, although some are also capable of asexual reproduction (ex. hydra).

5. Animals develop from embryonic stages.

In addition to these traits, most adult animals have a symmetrical anatomy. Adult animals can have either **radial symmetry** (constituent parts are arranged radiating symmetrically about a center point) or **bilateral symmetry** (the body can be divided along a center plane into equal, mirror-image halves). While there is wide variation in the physical structure of animals, the animal kingdom is usually divided into two broad categories—invertebrates and vertebrates.

Invertebrates are those species having no internal backbone structure; **vertebrates** have internal backbones. Invertebrates include sponges and worms, which have no skeletal structure at all, and arthropods, mollusks, crustaceans, and so on, which have exoskeletons. In fact, there are many more phyla of invertebrates than vertebrates (about 950,000 phyla of invertebrates and only about 40,000 phyla of vertebrates).

Animal Anatomy

1. Tissues

There are eight major types of animal tissue:

1. **Epithelial tissue** consists of thin layers of cells which make up the layers of skin, line ducts and the intestine, and cover the inside of the body cavity. Epithelial tissue forms the barrier between the environment and the interior of the body.

2. **Connective tissue** covers internal organs and composes ligaments and tendons. This tissue holds tissues and organs together, stabilizing the body structure.

3. **Muscle tissue** is divided into three types—smooth, skeletal, and cardiac. **Smooth** muscle makes up the walls of internal organs and functions in involuntary movement (breathing, etc.). **Skeletal** muscle attaches bones of the skeleton to each other and surrounding tissues. Skeletal muscle's function is to enable voluntary movement. **Cardiac** muscle is the tissue forming the walls of the heart. Its strength and electrical properties are vital to the heart's ability to pump blood.

4. **Bone tissue** is found in the skeleton and provides support, protection for internal organs, and the ability to move as muscles pull against bones.

5. **Cartilage tissue** reduces friction between bones, and supports and connects them. For example, it is found at the ends of bones and in the ears and nose.

6. **Adipose tissue** is found beneath the skin and around organs providing cushioning, insulation, and fat storage.

7. **Nerve tissue** is found in the brain, spinal cord, nerves, and ganglion. It carries electrical and chemical impulses to and from organs and limbs to the brain. Nerve tissue in the brain receives these impulses and sustains mental activity.

8. **Blood tissue** consists of several cell types in a fluid called plasma. It flows through the blood vessels and heart, and is essential for carrying oxygen to cells, fighting infection, and carrying nutrients and wastes to and from cells. Blood also has clotting capabilities, which preserve the body's functions in case of injury.

Systems

Vertebrates are highly complex organisms with several systems working together to perform the functions necessary to life. These include the digestive, gas exchange, skeletal, nervous, circulatory, excretory, and immune systems.

1. Digestive System

The **digestive system** serves as a processing plant for ingested food. The digestive system in animals generally encompasses the processes of **ingestion** (food intake), **digestion** (breaking down of ingested particles into molecules that can be absorbed by the body), and **egestion** (the elimination of indigestible materials). In most vertebrates, the digestive organs are divided into two categories. The **alimentary canal**, also known as the **gastrointestinal** (or GI) **tract**, includes the mouth, pharynx, esophagus, stomach, small intestine, large intestine, rectum, and anus. The **accessory organs** include the teeth, tongue, salivary glands, liver, gallbladder, and pancreas.

The **mouth** (oral cavity) is the organ of ingestion and the first organ of digestion in the GI tract. Chewing is the initial step in breaking down food into particles of manageable size. Chewing also increases the surface area of the food and mixes it with saliva, which contains the starch-digesting enzyme amylase. Saliva is secreted by the **salivary glands**. Chewed food is then swallowed and moved toward the **stomach** by peristalsis (muscle contraction) of the **esophagus**. The stomach continues the mechanical and chemical breakdown of food particles begun by the chewing process. The stomach also secretes digestive enzymes and hydrochloric acid, which continue the digestive process to the point of producing a watery soup of nutrients, which then proceeds through the pyloric sphincter into the small intestine (the duodenum). The **pancreas** and **gallbladder** release more enzymes into the small intestine. The cells lining the **small intestine** have protrusions out into the lumen of the intestine called **villi**, which provide a large surface area for absorption of nutrients. Nutrients move into the capillaries through or between the cells making up the villi. The enriched blood travels to the **liver**, where some sugars are removed and stored. The indigestible food proceeds from the small intestine to the **large intestine** where water is absorbed back into the body. The waste (**feces**) is then passed through the **rectum** and excreted from the **anus**.

Many invertebrates, such as insects and earthworms, have digestive systems resembling those of vertebrates, including a mouth, esophagus, stomach, and intestines. Many of these species also have a **crop**, an organ that stores food until it is processed for absorption. Other animals have only a sac-like digestive cavity that performs the necessary functions of digestion.

2. Respiratory or Gas Exchange System

Also known as the **respiratory system**, the **gas exchange system** is responsible for the intake and processing of gases required by an organism, and for expelling gases produced as waste products. In humans, air is taken in primarily through the **nose** (although gases may be inhaled through the mouth, the nose is better at filtering out pollutants in the air). The **nasal passages** have a mucous lining to capture foreign particles. This lining is surrounded by epithelial tissue with embedded capillaries, which serve to warm the entering air. Air then passes through the **pharynx** and into the **trachea**. The trachea includes the windpipe or **larynx** in its upper portion, and the **glottis**, an opening allowing gases to pass into the two branches known as the bronchi. The glottis is guarded by a flap of tissue, the **epiglottis**, which prevents food particles from entering the bronchial tubes. The **bronchi** lead to the two **lungs** where they branch out in all directions into smaller tubules known as **bronchioles**. The bronchioles end in **alveoli**, thin-walled air sacs which are the site of gas exchange. At the alveoli, the carbon dioxide diffuses from the blood into the alveoli and oxygen diffuses from the alveoli into the blood. The oxygenated blood is carried away to tissues throughout the body.

Invertebrates such as the earthworm are able to absorb gases through their skin. Insects rely on the diffusion of gases through holes in the exoskeleton known as spiracles. In single-celled organisms such as the amoeba, diffusion of gases occurs directly through the plasma membrane.

3. Musculoskeletal System

The **musculoskeletal system** provides the body with structure, stability, and the ability to move. In humans, the musculoskeletal system is composed of joints, ligaments, cartilage, muscle groups, and 206 bones. Bones, in addition to providing structure, perform the important function of storing calcium and phosphates, and producing red blood cells within the bone marrow.

Skeletal muscles are voluntary—they are activated by command from the nervous system. **Smooth muscle** lines most internal organs, protecting their contents and function, and generally contract without conscious intent. **Cardiac muscle** is involuntary muscle unique to the heart which causes it to "beat" rhythmically. Cardiac muscle cells have branched endings that interlock with each other, keeping the muscle fibers from ripping apart during their strong contractions. In addition, electrical impulses travel in waves from cell to cell in cardiac muscle, causing the muscle to contract in a coordinated way with a rhythmic pace.

4. Nervous System

The **nervous system** is a communication network that connects the entire body of an organism and provides control over bodily functions and actions. Nerve tissue is composed of nerve cells known as **neurons**. Neurons carry impulses via electrochemical responses through their **cell body** and **axon** (long root-like appendage of the cell). Nerve cells exist in networks, with axons of neighbor neurons interacting across small spaces (**synapses**). Chemical neurotransmitters send messages along the nerve network causing responses specific to varying types of nerve tissue. The nervous system allows the body to sense stimuli and conditions in the environment and respond with necessary reactions. **Sensory organs**—skin, eyes, nose, ears, etc.—transmit signals in response to environmental stimuli to the **brain**, which then conveys messages via nerves to glands and muscles, which produce the necessary response.

The human nervous system (and that of many mammals) is anatomically divided into two systems: the central nervous system and the peripheral nervous system.

The two main components of the **central nervous system (CNS)**, the **brain** and **spinal cord**, control all other organs and systems of the body. The spinal cord is a continuation of the brainstem and acts as a conduit of nerve messages. The **peripheral nervous system (PNS)** is a network of nerves throughout the body consisting of two divisions. The **sensory division** contains the **visceral sensory nerves** (which carry impulses from body organs to the CNS) and the **somatic sensory nerves** (which carry impulses from the body surface to the CNS). The **motor division** contains the **somatic motor nerves** (which carry impulses to skeletal muscle from the CNS) and the **autonomic nerves**, which can be further broken down into the **sympathetic nervous system** (which carries impulses that stimulate organs) and the **parasympathetic nervous system** (which carries impulses back from the organs).

The brain of vertebrates has three major divisions: the forebrain, midbrain, and hindbrain. The **forebrain** is located most anterior, and contains the **olfactory lobes** (sense of smell) and **cerebrum** (controls sensory and motor responses, memory, speech, and most factors of intelligence), as well as the **thalamus** (integrates senses), **hypothalamus** (involved in hunger, thirst, blood pressure, body temperature, hostility, pain, pleasure, etc.), and **pituitary gland** (releases various hormones). The **midbrain** is between the forebrain and hindbrain and contains the **optic lobes** (visual center connected to the eyes by the optic nerves). The **hindbrain** consists of the **cerebellum** (controls balance, equilibrium, and muscle coordination) and the **medulla oblongata** (controls involuntary response such as breathing and heartbeat).

Within the brain, nerve tissue is grayish in color and is called **gray matter**. The nerve cells, which exist in the spinal cord and throughout the body, have insulation covering their axons. This insulation (called the **myelin sheath**) speeds electrochemical conduction within the axon of the nerve cell. Since the myelin sheath gives this tissue a white color, it is called **white matter**. The myelin sheath is made up of individual cells called Schwann cells.

5. Circulatory System

The **circulatory system** is the conduit for delivering nutrients and gases to all cells and for removing waste products from them.

In invertebrates, the circulatory system may consist entirely of diffusion in the gastrovascular cavity, or it may be an **open circulatory system** (where blood directly bathes the internal organs) or a **closed circulatory system** (where blood is confined to vessels).

Closed circulatory systems are also typical of vertebrates. In vertebrates, **blood** flows throughout the circulatory system within **vessels** (**arteries**, **veins**, and **capillaries**). The pumping action of the **heart** (a hollow, muscular organ) forces blood in one direction throughout the system. In large animals, valves within the heart, and some of the vessels in limbs, keep blood from flowing backwards (being pulled downward by gravity).

Blood carries many products to cells throughout the body, including minerals, infection-fighting white blood cells, nutrients, proteins, hormones, and metabolites. Blood also carries dissolved gases (particularly oxygen) to cells and waste gases (mainly carbon dioxide) away from cells.

Capillaries (tiny vessels) surround all tissues of the body and exchange carbon dioxide for oxygen. Oxygen is carried by **hemoglobin** (containing iron) in red blood cells. Oxygen enters the blood in the lungs and travels to the heart, then through **arteries** (larger vessels that carry blood away from the heart), then **arterioles** (small arteries), to capillaries. The blood picks up carbon dioxide waste from the cells and carries it through capillaries, then **venules** (small veins) and **veins** (vessels that carry blood toward the heart), back to the heart, and on to the lungs. Thus, blood is continually cycled.

6. Excretory System

The **excretory system** is responsible for collecting waste materials and transporting them to organs that expel them from the body. The primary excretory organs of most vertebrates are the kidneys. The **kidneys** filter metabolic wastes from the blood and excrete them as **urine** into the urinary tract. Urine is typically 95% water, and may contain urea (formed from breakdown of proteins), uric acid (formed from breaking down nucleic acids), creatinine (a byproduct of muscle contraction), and various minerals and hormones.

The **liver** produces **bile** from broken-down pigments and chemicals (often from pollutants and medications) and secretes it into the small intestine, where it proceeds to the large intestine and is expelled in the feces. The liver also breaks down some nitrogenous molecules (including some proteins), excreting them as urea.

The **lungs** are the sites of excretion for carbon dioxide. The **skin** is an accessory excretory organ; salts, urea, and other wastes are secreted with water from sweat glands in the skin.

7. Immune System

The **immune system** defends the body from infection by bacteria and viruses. The **lymphatic system** is the principal infection-fighting component of the immune system. **Lymph** is a collection of excess fluid that is absorbed from between cells into a special system of vessels, which circulates through the lymphatic system and finally dumps into the bloodstream.

Lymph nodes are small masses of lymph tissue whose function is to filter lymph and produce lymphocytes. **Lymphocytes** (B cells and T cells) begin in bone marrow as stem cells and are collected and distributed via the lymph nodes. **B cells** emerge from the bone marrow and produce **antibodies**, which enter the bloodstream. These antibodies find and attach themselves to foreign **antigens** (i.e., toxins, bacteria, foreign cells, etc.).

The **spleen**, located in the abdomen, filters larger volumes of lymph than nodes can handle. The **tonsils** are a group of lymph cells connected together and located in the throat.

The **thymus**, another mass of lymph tissue which is active only through the teen years, fights infection and produces T cells. **T cells** mature in the thymus gland. Some T cells (like B cells) patrol the blood for antigens, but T cells are also equipped to destroy antigens themselves. T cells also regulate the body's immune responses.

Homeostatic Mechanisms

When the conditions of an organism are within acceptable ranges to maintain survival of cells, tissues, and organs, it is said to be in **homeostasis**. Homeostasis is a state of dynamic equilibrium, which balances forces tending toward change with forces acceptable for life functions.

Homeostasis is achieved mostly by actions of the sympathetic and parasympathetic nervous systems by a process known as **feedback control**. Feedback control takes effect when any situation arises that may drive levels out of the normal acceptable range. In other words, the homeostatic mechanism is a reaction to a stimulus. This reaction, called a **feedback response**, is the production of some counterforce that levels the system.

1. Hormonal Control in Homeostasis and Reproduction

Hormones are chemicals produced in an organism's endocrine glands, which travel through the circulatory system and are taken up by specific targeted organs or tissues, where they modify metabolic activities. Hormones control many physiological functions, from digestion, to conscious responses and thinking, to reproduction.

Hormonal control occurs through one of two processes. The first is the **mobile receptor mechanism**. A hormone is manufactured in response to a particular **stimulus**. The hormone (for instance, a **steroid**) enters the bloodstream from one of the ductless endocrine glands that manufacture hormones. The steroid passes through the cell membrane of the targeted cell and enters the cytoplasm. The hormone combines with a particular protein known as a receptor, creating the **hormone-receptor complex**. This complex enters the nucleus and binds to a DNA molecule, causing a gene to be transcribed. The mRNA molecule leaves the nucleus for the endoplasmic reticulum, where it encodes a particular protein. The protein migrates to the site of the stimulus and counteracts the source of the stimulus. The result is homeostasis, a balance of the counterproductive forces.

The second process targets receptors on a cell's membrane. A particular **receptor** exists on the membrane when the cell is in a particular condition (for instance, containing an excess of glucose). When the hormone binds with the receptor on the membrane, the receptor changes its form. This triggers a chain of events within the cytoplasm resulting in the production or destruction of proteins, thus moderating the conditions.

Animal Reproduction and Development

Reproduction in multicellular animals is a complex process that generally proceeds through the steps of **gametogenesis** (gamete formation) and then **fertilization**.

Gametes are the sex cells formed in the reproductive organs—sperm and eggs. When a sperm of one individual combines with the egg cell of another, the resulting cell is known as a **zygote**, which then develops into a new individual. In the case of **spermatogenesis** (sperm formation), diploid **primary spermatocytes** are formed from special cells (**spermatogonia**) in the testes. The primary spermatocytes then undergo meiosis I, forming haploid **secondary spermatocytes** with a single chromosome set. The secondary spermatocytes go through meiosis II, forming **spermatids**, which are haploid. These spermatids then develop into the **sperm cells**.

In human female reproductive organs, egg cells are formed through a similar process known as **oogenesis**. **Primary oocytes** are typically present in great number in the female's ovaries at birth. Primary oocytes undergo meiosis I, forming one **secondary oocyte** and one smaller **polar body**. Both the secondary oocyte and the polar body undergo meiosis II; the polar body producing two polar bodies (not functional cells), and the oocyte producing one more polar body and one haploid **egg cell**. The egg cell is now ready for fertilization, and if there are sperm cells present, the egg may be fertilized, forming a diploid cell with a new combination of chromosomes, the zygote.

All multicellular organisms that reproduce sexually begin life as a zygote. The zygote then undergoes a series of cell divisions known as **cleavage**. After the first few divisions, the cluster of cells is called a morula. The **morula** then continues cell division, and the cluster begins to take shape as a thin layer of cells surrounding an internal cavity, the **blastula**. As cell division continues, the cells migrate and rearrange themselves, transforming the blastula into a two-layered cup shape, called the **gastrula** (a process known as **gastrulation**). As the gastrula develops, the cup shape reforms itself into a double-layered tube. The outer layer of the gastrula tube will become the **ectoderm**, which later will develop into the skin, some endocrine glands, and the nervous system. The inner layer of the tube will become the **endoderm**, the precursor of the gut lining and various accessory structures. With further development, a third layer, between the ectoderm and endoderm arises—the **mesoderm**. The mesoderm layer will eventually form muscles and organs of the skeletal, circulatory, respiratory, reproductive, and excretory systems. The ectoderm, mesoderm, and endoderm collectively are called the **germ layers**. As the germ layers develop, the embryo becomes recognizable, and differentiation continues until the organ systems are fully developed.

In addition to forming the tissues and organ systems of vertebrates, the germ layers also develop into **extraembryonic membranes** (i.e., membranes not part of the embryos themselves). The first of these membranes is the **chorion**. In egg-laying vertebrates, the chorion lies in contact with the innermost surface of the shell, while in other vertebrates it is the outermost membrane surrounding the **embryo** and in contact with the **uterus**. In both cases, the chorion functions in regulating the passage of gases and water from the embryo to its surrounding environment. In embryos without shells, the chorion also controls passage of nutrients and wastes between the embryo and the mother.

Within the chorion is the **amnion**, a fluid-filled (**amniotic fluid**) sac enclosing the embryo. The amniotic fluid cushions the embryo and helps keep temperatures constant. The fluid also keeps the amnionic membrane from sticking to the developing embryo.

The third membrane, the **allantois**, arises from the developing digestive tract. In humans and other vertebrates that bear live young, the allantois appears in the third week of development and becomes part of the **umbilical cord**. It contains blood vessels, which function to exchange gases and nutrients between the embryo and the mother. In egg-laying reptiles, the allantois is a reservoir for wastes. It fuses with the chorion, forming the **chorioallantoic membrane**, which regulates gas exchanges through the shell.

The **yolk sac membrane**, enclosing the **yolk sac**, also forms from the developing digestive tract and becomes part of the umbilical cord. The yolk sac stores nutrients for use by the embryo. The yolk sac cells also give rise to gametes, which develop in reproductive organs of the embryo.

In mammals, the outer cells of the embryo and the inner cells of the uterus combine to form the **placenta**, the site of transfer for nutrients, water, and wastes between mother and embryo. The embryo synthesizes its own blood that is kept separate from the mother's blood. In the placenta, the vessels (that connect the circulatory system of the embryo through the umbilical cord to the placenta) pass right next to the mother's blood vessels. Nutrients, water, and oxygen diffuse from the mother's blood to the embryo's blood, while wastes and carbon dioxide diffuse into the mother's blood supply.

PRINCIPLES OF HEREDITY (GENETICS)

The process by which characteristics pass from one generation to another is known as **inheritance**. The study of the principles of heredity (now called genetics) advanced greatly through the experimental work of **Gregor Mendel** (c. 1865).

Mendel systematically bred pea plants to determine how certain hereditary traits passed from generation to generation. First, he established true-breeding plants, which produce offspring with the same traits as the parents. Mendel named this first generation of true-breeding plants the parent or **P₁ generation**; he then bred the plant with yellow seeds and the plant with green seeds. Mendel called the first generation of offspring the **F₁ generation**.

Mendel continued his experiment by crossing two individuals of the **F₁** generation to produce an **F₂ generation**. In this generation, he found that some of the plants (one out of four) produced green seeds. Mendel performed hundreds of such crosses, studying some 10,000 pea plants, and was able to establish the rules of inheritance from them. The following are Mendel's main discoveries:

- Parents transmit hereditary factors (now called **genes**) to offspring. Genes then produce a characteristic, such as seed-coat color.

- Each individual carries two copies of a gene, and the copies may differ.

- The two genes an individual carries act independently, and the effect of one may mask the effect of the other. Mendel coined the terms geneticists still use: *dominant* and *recessive*.

Modern Genetics

We now know that **chromosomes** carry all the genetic information in most organisms. Most organisms have corresponding pairs of chromosomes that carry genes for the same traits. These pairs are known as **homologous chromosomes**. Genes that produce a given trait exist at the same position (or **locus**) on homologous chromosomes. Each gene may have different forms, known as **alleles**. A gene can have two or more alleles, which differ in their nucleotide sequence. That difference can translate into proteins that function differently, resulting in variations of the trait.

Sexual reproduction (meiosis) produces gamete cells with one-half the genetic information of the parents (paired chromosomes are separated and sorted independently). Therefore, each gamete may receive one of any number of combinations of each parent's chromosomes.

In addition, a trait may arise from one or more genes. If a trait is produced from a gene or genes with varying alleles, several possibilities for traits exist. The combination of alleles that make a particular trait is the **genotype**, while the trait expressed is the **phenotype**.

An allele is considered **dominant** if it masks the effect of its partner allele. The allele that does not produce its trait when present with a dominant allele is **recessive**. That is, when a dominant allele pairs with a recessive allele, the expressed trait is that of the dominant allele.

A **Punnett square** is a notation that allows us to easily predict the results of a genetic cross. In a Punnett square, a letter is assigned to each gene. Uppercase letters represent dominant traits, while lowercase letters represent recessive traits (a convention begun by Mendel). The possible alleles from each parent are noted across the top and side of a box diagram; then the possible offspring are represented within the internal boxes. If we assign the allele that produces yellow seeds the letter **Y**, and the allele that produces green seeds **y**, we can represent Mendel's first cross between pea plants (**YY** × **yy**) by the following Punnett square:

	Y	Y
y	Yy	Yy
y	Yy	Yy

One parent pea plant had green seeds (green seeds is its phenotype), so it must not have had any of the dominant genes for yellow seeds (**Y**); therefore, it must have the genotype **yy**. If the second parent had one allele for yellow and one for green, then some of the offspring would have inherited two genes for green. Since Mendel started with true-breeding plants, we may deduce that one parent had two genes for green seeds (**yy**) and the other two genes for yellow seeds (**YY**).

When both alleles for a given gene are the same in an individual (such as **YY** or **yy**), that individual is **homozygous** for that trait. Furthermore, the individual's genotype can be called homozygous. Both of the above parents (**P₁**) were homozygous. The children in the **F₁** generation all have one dominant gene (**Y**) and one recessive gene (**y**), their phenotype is yellow, and their genotype is **Yy**.

When the two alleles for a given gene are different in an individual (**Yy**), that individual is said to be **heterozygous** for that trait; its genotype is heterozygous.

Breeding two **F₁** offspring from the previous example produces the following Punnett square of a double heterozygous (both parents **Yy**) cross:

	Y	y
Y	YY	Yy
y	Yy	yy

Through this Punnett square, we can determine that three-fourths of the offspring will produce yellow seeds. This is consistent with Mendel's findings. However, there are two different genotypes represented among the yellow seed offspring. One-half of the offspring were heterozygous yellow (**Yy**), while one-fourth were homozygous yellow (**YY**).

The previous example shows a **monohybrid cross**—a cross between two individuals where only one trait is considered. Mendel also experimented with crossing two parents while considering two separate traits, a **dihybrid cross**.

The Law of Segregation

The first law of Mendelian genetics is the **law of segregation**, which states that traits are expressed from a pair of genes in the individual (on homologous chromosomes). Each parent provides one chromosome of every pair of homologous chromosomes. Paired chromosomes (and thus corresponding genes) separate and randomly recombine during gamete formation.

The Law of Dominance

Mendel determined that one gene was usually dominant over the other. This is the **law of dominance**, Mendel's second law of inheritance. In Mendel's experiments, the first generation produced no plants with green seeds, leading him to recognize the existence of genetic dominance. The yellow-seed allele was clearly dominant.

The Law of Independent Assortment

Mendel also investigated whether genes for one trait always were linked to genes for another. These dihybrid cross experiments demonstrated that most traits were independent of one another. In most cases, genes for traits randomly sort into pairs (although some genes lie close to others on a chromosome and can therefore be inherited together). Since homologous chromosomes separate and independently sort in gamete formation, alleles are also separated and independently sorted, an assertion known as the **law of independent assortment**.

The following Punnett square demonstrates independent assortment. **Y** stands for the allele for yellow color, **y** for the allele for green, **T** for the allele tall, and **t** for short:

	TY	Ty	tY	ty
TY	TTYY	TTYy	TtYY	TtYy
Ty	TTYy	TTyy	TtYy	Ttyy
tY	TtYY	TtYy	ttYY	ttYy
ty	TtYy	Ttyy	ttYy	ttyy

Incomplete Dominance

Some traits have no genes that are dominant and instead produce offspring that are a mix of the two parents. For instance, in snapdragons a plant with red flowers crossed with a plant with white flowers produces offspring with pink flowers. This is known as **incomplete dominance**. In incomplete dominance, the conventional way to symbolize the alleles is with a capital letter designating the trait (in this case **C** for color) and a superscript designating the allele choices (in this case ^{R} for red, ^{W} for white), making the possible alleles C^R and C^W. The following Punnett square represents the incomplete dominance of the allele for red flowers (C^R), the allele for white (C^W), and the combination resulting in pink ($C^R C^W$).

	C^R	C^R
C^W	$C^R C^W$	$C^R C^W$
C^W	$C^R C^W$	$C^R C^W$

In this case, two plants, one with white flowers, one with red, cross to form all pink flowers. If two of the heterozygous offspring of this cross are then bred, the outcome of this cross ($C^R C^W \times C^R C^W$) will be:

	C^R	C^W
C^R	$C^R C^R$	$C^R C^W$
C^W	$C^R C^W$	$C^W C^W$

One-fourth of the offspring will be red, one-half pink, and one-fourth white, a 1:2:1 ratio.

Multiple Alleles

In the previous instances, two possible alleles exist in a species, so the genotype will be a combination of those two alleles. There are some instances where more than two choices of alleles are present. For instance, for human blood types there is a dominant allele for type A blood, another dominant allele for type B blood, as well as a recessive allele for neither A nor B, known as O blood. There are three different alleles and they may combine in any way. In multiple-allele crosses, it is conventional to denote the chromosome by a letter (in this case **I** for dominant, **i** for recessive), with a subscript letter representing the allele types (in this case **A**, **B**, or **O**). The alleles for A and B blood are co-dominant, while the allele for O blood is recessive. The possible genotypes and phenotypes then are as follows:

Genotype	Phenotype
$I^A I^A$	Type A blood
$I^B I^B$	Type B blood
$I^B i^O$	Type B blood
$I^A i^O$	Type A blood
$I^A I^B$	Type AB blood
$i^O i^O$	Type O blood

Note: There is another gene responsible for the Rh factor that adds the + or − to the blood type.

Linkage

Traits that are inherited together are said to be **linked**. Genes are portions of chromosomes, so most traits produced by genes on the same chromosome are inherited together. (The chromosomes are independently sorted, not the individual genes.)

However, an exception to this rule complicates the issue. During metaphase of meiosis I, when homologous chromosomes line up along the center of the dividing cell, some pieces of the chromosomes break off and move from one chromosome to another (change places). This random breaking and reforming of homologous chromosomes allows genes to change the chromosome they are linked to, thus changing the genome of that chromosome. This process, known as **crossing over**, adds even more possibility of variation of traits among species. It is more likely for crossing over to occur between genes that do not lie close together on a chromosome than between those that lie close together.

Gender is determined in an organism by a particular homologous pair of chromosomes. The symbols **X** and **Y** denote the sex chromosomes. In mammals and many insects, the male has an **X** and **Y** chromosome (**XY**), while the female has two **X**'s (**XX**). Genes that are located on the gender chromosome **Y** will only be seen in males. It would be considered a **sex-limited trait**. An example of a sex-limited trait is bar coloring in chickens that occurs only in males.

Some traits are **sex-linked**. In sex-linked traits, more males (**XY**) develop the trait because males have only one copy of the **X** chromosome. Females have a second **X** gene, which may carry a gene coding for a functional protein for the trait in question that may counteract a recessive trait. These traits (for example, hemophilia and colorblindness) occur much more often in males than females.

Still other traits may be **sex-influenced**. In this case, the trait is known as autosomal—it only requires one recessive gene to be expressed if there is no counteracting dominant gene. A male with one recessive allele will develop the trait, whereas a female would require two recessive genes to develop it. An example of a sex-influenced trait is male-pattern baldness.

Polygenic Inheritance

While the best-studied genetic traits arise from alleles of a single gene, most traits, such as height and skin color, are produced from the expression of more than one set of genes. Traits produced from interaction of multiple sets of genes, known as **polygenic traits**, are difficult to map and difficult to predict because of the varied effects of the different genes for a specific trait.

ECOLOGY AND POPULATION BIOLOGY

ECOLOGY

Ecology is the study of how organisms interact with other organisms, and how they influence or are influenced by their physical **environment**. The word *ecology* is derived from the Greek term *oikos* (meaning "home" or "place to live") and *ology* (meaning "the study of").

The study of ecology centers on the **ecosystem**, a group of populations found within a given locality, plus the inanimate environment around those populations. A **population** is the total number of a single species of organism found in a given ecosystem. Typically, there are many populations of different species within a particular ecosystem. The term **organism** refers to an individual of a particular species. Each species is a distinct group of individuals that are able to interbreed (mate), producing viable offspring. Although species are defined by their ability to reproduce, they are usually described by their morphology (their anatomical features).

Populations that interact with each other in a particular ecosystem are collectively termed a **community**. For instance, a temperate forest community includes pine trees, oaks, shrubs, lichen, mosses, ferns, squirrels, deer, insects, owls, bacteria, fungi, and so on.

The **biosphere**, the part of Earth that includes all living things, includes the **atmosphere** (air), the **lithosphere** (ground), and the **hydrosphere** (water).

A **habitat** refers to the physical place where a species lives. A species' habitat must include all the factors that will support its life and reproduction. These factors may be **biotic** (i.e., living—food source, predators, etc.) and **abiotic** (i.e., nonliving—weather, temperature, soil features, etc.).

A species' **niche** is the role it plays within the ecosystem. It includes its physical requirements (such as light and water) and its biological activities (how it reproduces, how it acquires food, etc.). One important aspect of a species' niche is its place in the food chain.

Ecological Cycles

The **energy cycle** supports life throughout the environment. There are also several **biogeochemical cycles** (the water cycle, the carbon cycle, the nitrogen cycle, the phosphorous cycle, the rock cycle, etc.), which are also important to the health of ecosystems. A biogeochemical cycle is the system whereby the substances needed for life are recycled and transported throughout the environment.

Carbon, hydrogen, oxygen, phosphorous, and nitrogen are called macronutrients; they are used in large quantities by living things. Micronutrients—those elements utilized in trace quantities in organisms—include iodine, iron, zinc, and copper.

1. Energy Cycle (Food Chain)

On Earth, the sun provides the energy that is the basis of life in most ecosystems. (An exception is the hydrothermal vent communities that derive their energy from the heat of Earth's core.) Energy generally flows through the entire ecosystem in one direction—from producers to consumers and on to decomposers (consumers may also consume decomposers) through the **food chain.**

Photosynthetic organisms—such as plants, some protists, and some bacteria—are the first link in most food chains; they use the energy of sunlight to combine carbon dioxide and water into sugars, releasing oxygen gas (O_2). Photosynthetic organisms are called producers, since they synthesize sugar and starch molecules using the sun's energy to link the carbons in carbon dioxide. Primary consumers (also known as herbivores) are species that eat photosynthetic organisms. Consumers utilize sugars and starches stored in cells or tissues for energy. Secondary consumers feed on primary consumers, and on the chain goes, through tertiary, quarternary (etc.) consumers. Finally, decomposers (bacteria, fungi, some animals) are species that recycle the organic material found in dead plants and animals back into the food chain. The steps in the food chain are also known as **trophic levels**.

Animals that feed only on other animals are called **carnivores** (meat-eaters), whereas those that consume both photosynthetic organisms and other animals are known as **omnivores**.

Energy can neither be created nor destroyed. However, every use of energy is less than 100% efficient; about 10% is lost as heat.

Each trophic level is greater in biomass (total mass of organisms) than the level above it. Producers, the **first trophic level**, are also known as **autotrophs**, as they produce their own food (i.e., grass). Organisms in the **second trophic level** (i.e., grasshoppers) consume the producers, and are then consumed by organisms in the **third trophic level** (i.e., toads). Each trophic level is consumed by the next, until death, when the decomposers recycle the nutrients in the dead organism to be used by the first trophic level.

Within every ecosystem there may be numerous food chains interacting in varying ways to form a **food web**. Furthermore, all organisms produce waste products that feed decomposers. The food web represents the cycling and recycling of both energy and nutrients within the ecosystem.

2. Water Cycle

Water, a crucial need for all living things, is available in several ways. Its vapor circulates through the biosphere in a process called the **hydrologic cycle**. It is evaporated from oceans and the soil, released from vegetation by transpiration, flows through waterways (a process called runoff), and falls to Earth as precipitation.

The water cycle also has a profound effect on Earth's climate. Clouds reflect the sun's radiation away from Earth, causing cool weather. Water vapor in the air also acts as a **greenhouse gas**, reflecting radiation from Earth's surface back toward Earth, and therefore trapping heat. The water cycle also intersects nearly all the other cycles of elements and nutrients.

3. Nitrogen Cycle

Nitrogen, another substance essential to life processes, is a key component of amino acids (components of proteins) and nucleic acids. The nitrogen cycle recycles nitrogen, the most plentiful gas in the atmosphere (making up 78% of the air). However, neither photosynthetic organisms nor animals are able to use nitrogen gas (N_2), which does not readily react with other compounds, directly from the air. **Nitrogen fixing** is the process of combining nitrogen with either hydrogen or oxygen, mostly by **nitrogen-fixing bacteria**, or to a small degree by volcanoes and **lightning**, to make it absorbable by the roots of plants.

Nitrogen-fixing bacteria live in the soil and perform the task of combining gaseous nitrogen from the atmosphere with hydrogen, forming ammonium (NH_4^+ ions). (Some cyanobacteria, also called blue-green bacteria, are also active in this process.)

Some plants are unable to use ammonia; instead, they use **nitrates**. Some bacteria perform **nitrification**, a process which further breaks down ammonia into nitrites (NO_2^-), and yet again another bacteria converts nitrites into nitrates (NO_3^-).

When plants are consumed, the amino acids are recombined and used, a process that passes the nitrogen-containing molecules on through the food chain or web. Animal waste products, such as urine, release nitrogen compounds (primarily ammonia) back into the environment, yet another source of nitrogen. Finally, large amounts of nitrogen are returned to Earth by bacteria and fungi, which decompose dead plant and animal matter into ammonia (and other substances), a process known as **ammonification**.

Various species of bacteria and fungi are also responsible for breaking down excess nitrates, a process known as **denitrification**, which releases nitrogen gas back into the air. The nitrogen cycle involves cycling nitrogen through both living and nonliving entities.

4. Carbon Cycle

The **carbon cycle** is the route by which carbon is obtained, used, and recycled by living things. Earth's atmosphere contains large amounts of carbon in the form of carbon dioxide (CO_2). Most of the carbon within organisms is derived from the production of carbohydrates through photosynthesis. The process of photosynthesis also releases oxygen molecules (O_2), which are necessary to animal respiration. Animal respiration releases carbon dioxide back into the atmosphere in large quantities.

When animals and photosynthetic organisms die, decomposers, including the detritus feeders, bacteria, and fungi, break down the organic matter. **Detritus feeders** include worms, mites, insects, and crustaceans, which feed on dead organic matter, returning carbon to the cycle through chemical breakdown and respiration.

Finally, organic matter that is left to decay may, under conditions of heat and pressure, be transformed into coal, oil, or natural gas (the **fossil fuels**). When fossil fuels are burned for energy, the combustion process releases carbon dioxide back into the atmosphere, where it is available to plants for photosynthesis.

5. Phosphorous Cycle

Phosphorous is a key component in ATP, NADP (a molecule that, like ATP, stores energy in its chemical bonds), and many other molecular compounds essential to life. Phosphorous is found within rocks and is released by the process of erosion. Water dissolves phosphorous from rocks, and carries it into rivers and streams, creating phosphates. Phosphates are absorbed by photosynthetic organisms in and near the water and are used in the synthesis of organic molecules. As in the carbon and nitrogen cycles, phosphorous is then passed up the food chain and returned through animal wastes and organic decay. New phosphorous enters the cycle as undersea sedimentary rocks which are thrust up during the shifting of Earth's tectonic plates.

POPULATION GROWTH AND REGULATION

The population growth of a species is regulated by limiting factors that exist within the species' environment. A population's overall growth rate is affected by the population's birth rate (**natality**) and death rate (**mortality**). The rate of increase within a population is represented by the birth rate minus the death rate.

There are two models of population growth: the **exponential curve** (or J-curve) and the **logistic curve** (or the S-curve). The exponential curve represents populations in which there is no environmental or social limit on population size, so the rate of growth accelerates over time. Exponential population growth exists only during the initial population growth in a particular ecosystem, since as the population increases the limiting factors become more influential.

The logistic curve reflects the effects of limiting factors on population size, where growth accelerates to a point, then slows down. The logistic curve shows population growth over a longer period of time, and represents population growth under normal conditions.

Population growth is directly related to the life characteristics of the population such as the age at which an individual begins to reproduce, the age of death, the rate of growth, and so on. For instance, species that grow quickly, mature sexually at an early age, and live a long life would have a population growth rate that exceeds that of species with a short life span and short reproductive span.

Limiting Factors

Populations within an ecosystem will be affected by changes in the environment from **abiotic factors** (physical, nonliving factors such as fire, pollution, sunlight, soil, light, precipitation, availability of oxygen, water conditions, and temperature) and **biotic factors** (biological factors, including availability of food, competition, predator/prey relationships, symbiosis, and overpopulation). These biotic and abiotic factors are known as **limiting factors** since they will determine how much a particular population within a community will be able to grow. It may be stated that the establishment and survival of a particular organism in an area is dependent upon both (1) the availability of necessary elements in at least the minimum quantity, and (2) the controlled supply of those elements to keep it within the limits of tolerance.

Homeostasis, a dynamic balance achieved within an ecosystem functioning at its optimum level, is the tendency of the ecological community to stay the same. However, the balance of the ecosystem can be disturbed by the removal, or decrease, of a single factor or by the addition, or increase, of a factor.

Many factors interact to control population size. Changes in limiting factors have a domino effect in an ecosystem, as the change in population size of one species will change the dynamics of the entire community. The number of individuals of a particular species living in a particular area is called the population **density** (number of organisms per area).

Both **abiotic** and **biotic** limiting factors exist in a single community; however, one may be dominant over the other. Abiotic limiting factors are also known as **density-independent factors**. That is, they are independent of population density. Pollution, a major density-independent factor in the health of ecosystems, is usually a byproduct of human endeavors and affects the air or water quality of an ecosystem with secondary effects. In addition to producing pollution, humans may deliberately utilize chemicals such as pesticides or herbicides to limit growth of particular species. Such chemicals can damage the homeostatic mechanisms within a community, causing a long-term upset in the balance of an ecosystem.

In other situations, biotic factors, called **density-dependent factors**, may be the dominant influence on population in a given area. Density-dependent factors include population growth issues and interactions between species within a community.

Within a given area, there is a maximum level the population may reach at which it will continue to thrive, known as the **carrying capacity**. When an organism has reached the carrying capacity, the population growth rate will level off and show no net growth. Populations also occupy a particular geographic area with suitable conditions. This total area occupied by a species is known as the **range**. Typically, populations will have the greatest density in the center of their range, and lower density at the edges. The area outside the range is known as the area of intolerance for that species, since it is not able to survive there.

Over time, species may move in or out of a particular area, a process known as **dispersion**. Dispersion occurs in one of three ways—through **emigration** (permanent one way movement out of the original range), **immigration** (permanent one way movement into a new range), and **migration** (temporary movement out of one range into another, and back). Migration allows animals that might not survive year round in a particular ecosystem to temporarily relocate for a portion of the year. Therefore, migration gives the opportunity for greater diversity of species in an ecosystem.

Two or more species living within the same area and that overlap niches (their function in the food chain) are said to be in **competition** if the resource they both require is in limited supply. If the niche overlap is minimal (other sources of food are available), then both species may survive. In some cases, one of the species may be wiped out in an area due to competition, a situation called **competitive exclusion**.

A **predator** is simply an organism that eats another. The organism that is eaten is known as the **prey**. The **predator/prey** relationship is one of the most important features of an ecosystem. This relationship not only provides transfer of energy up the food chain, it also is a population control factor for the prey species.

When two species interact with each other within the same range it is known as **symbiosis**. **Amensalism** is one type of symbiosis where one species is neither helped nor harmed while it inhibits the growth of another species. **Mutualism** is another form of symbiosis where both species benefit. **Parasitism** is symbiosis in which one species benefits, but the other is harmed. (Parasites are not predators, since the parasitic action takes a long period of time and may not actually kill the host.)

When the entire population of a particular species is eliminated, it is known as **extinction**. The extinction of a single species may also cause a chain reaction of secondary extinctions if other species depend on the extinct species. Conversely, the introduction of a new species into an area can also have a profound effect on other populations within that area. This new species may compete for the niche of native population or upset a predator/prey balance.

Ultimately, the survival of a particular population is dependent on maintaining a **minimal viable population** size. When a population is significantly diminished in size, it becomes highly susceptible to breeding problems and environmental changes that may result in extinction.

Community Structure

Community structure refers to the characteristics of a specified community including the types of species that are dominant, major climatic trends of the region, and whether the community is open or closed. A **closed community** is one whose populations occupy essentially the same range with very similar distributions of density. These types of communities have sharp boundaries called **ecotones** (such as a pond aquatic ecosystem that ends at the shore). An **open community** has indefinite boundaries, and its populations have varying ranges and densities (such as a forest). In an open community, the species are more widely distributed and animals may actually travel in and out of the area. An open community is often more able to respond to calamity and may be therefore more resilient.

Communities do grow and change over time. When one community completely replaces another over time in a given area, it is called **succession**. Succession occurs both in terrestrial and aquatic biomes.

Succession may occur because of small changes over time in climate or conditions, the immigration of a new species, disease, or other slow-acting factors. It may also occur in direct response to cataclysmic events such as fire, flood, or human intervention (for example, clearing a forest for farmland). The first populations that move back into a disturbed ecosystem tend to be hardy species that can survive in bleak conditions. These are known as **pioneer communities**.

When succession ends in a stable community, the community is known as the **climax community**. The climax community is the one best suited to the climate and soil conditions, and one that achieves a homeostasis. Generally, the climax community will remain in an area until a catastrophic event (fire, flood, etc.) destroys it.

BIOMES

A **biome** is an ecosystem that is generally defined by its climate characteristics. Several major biomes have been identified by ecologists. There are two basic types of biome—terrestrial and aquatic. **Terrestrial biomes** are those that exist on land, **aquatic biomes** are within large bodies of water. The following table gives the name of the major biomes with their major characteristics:

Biome	Temperature	Precipitation Level	Features
Tropical Rain Forest	warm	high	dense forest, heavy rainfall, abundant vegetation, relatively poor soil
Savanna	warm	moderate	grassland, light seasonal rains
Chaparral	hot summer, temperate winter	low in summer, high in winter	trees, shrubs, small animals, prolonged summer
Temperate Grassland	moderate and seasonal	low for most of year	large land tracts of grassland, shrubs and annuals, rodents, and some larger carnivores
Desert	extreme hot or cold	very low	sandy or rocky terrain, sparse vegetation, mainly succulents, small animals, rodents, reptiles
Tundra	extreme cold	low	modified grassland, permafrost, short growing season w/ some plants and animals
Taiga	cold	moderate	snow most of year, thick coniferous forests, wide variety of animal life
Temperate Deciduous Forest	moderate, seasonal	moderate	many trees (that lose leaves in cold season), mosses, grasses, shrubs, abundant animal life
Marine Aquatic	varied	not applicable	large amounts of dissolved minerals (particularly salts) in the water, huge array of aquatic animal and plant life
Freshwater Aquatic	varied	not applicable	still or running water with little dissolved minerals, large array of aquatic plant and animal life

Island Biogeography

Biogeography is the study of how photosynthetic organisms and animals are distributed in a particular location, plus the history of their distribution in the past. **Island biogeography** is a subdiscipline that investigates the distribution of species in an island habitat.

Since islands are by nature separated from other land ecosystems, species of both photosynthetic organisms and animals found on a particular island usually have arrived there by natural **dispersal** processes (by air or sea). Dispersal to an island is dependent on geographic as well as historical factors. Obviously, the closer the island is to other land, the easier dispersal of species to that island will be. Prevailing winds and ocean currents are also geographic factors that will affect species introduction. Historical factors such as climate shifts (for instance, the shift to an ice age), drought, volcanic action, plate shifting (where the continental plates of Earth's crust move slowly), and so on, will also affect which species are able to travel to a given island. Species that inhabit a given ecosystem because humans transported them there are known as **introduced** species.

In some cases, new species develop from parents that were dispersed to the island. These new species are **native** to that island. Arrival of a species on an island, however, does not ensure that it will survive and thrive there. Ultimately, the species must be able to reproduce for many generations in its new setting, or it will not remain a part of the ecosystem. If the island contains a habitat suitable for the newly arrived species, then that species has a chance of survival in its new environment.

Islands may also develop new habitats over time as the climate and geology change. In general, the larger and older the island, the more species it will support. The one exception to this is an old island whose soil has eroded and lost its nutrients. In this case, its habitats may not be able to support life. Also, the harsher the climate (high or low temperature or water conditions) of the island, the fewer species it will have.

PRINCIPLES OF BEHAVIOR

The study of **ethology** involves studying how animals act and react within their environments. Behavior simply is what an organism does and how it does it. Behavioral characteristics of animals may include how they acquire food, how they seek out and relate to a mate, how they respond to danger, or how they care for young.

Some behaviors are extremely simple in nature; they are a response to an environmental stimulus. These basic behaviors are innate; they exist from birth and are genetic in origin (they are inherited). **Innate behaviors** are the actions in animals we call **instincts**. Innate behaviors are highly stereotyped; all individuals of a species perform these behaviors in the same way. **Stereotyped behaviors** are of four basic varieties:

- **taxes** (plural of taxis) are directional responses either toward or away from a stimulus,
- **kineses** are changes in speed of movement in response to stimuli,
- **reflexes** are an automatic movement of a body part in response to a stimulus, and
- **fixed action patterns (FAP)** are complex but stereotyped behaviors in response to a stimulus.

The fixed action pattern, the most complex of stereotyped behaviors, is a pre-programmed response to a particular stimulus known as a **releaser** or a **sign stimulus**. FAPs include courtship behaviors, circadian rhythms, and feeding of young. Organisms automatically perform FAPs without any prior experience (FAPs are not learned).

Learned behaviors may have some basis in genetics, but they also require learning. Generally, there are three types of learned behavior in animals: conditioning, habituation, and imprinting.

Conditioning involves learning to apply an old response to a new stimulus. The classic example of conditioning is that of Pavlov's dogs. The dogs were conditioned to produce an instinctive behavior (salivating) in response to a new stimulus (bell).

B. F. Skinner, another scientist who studied conditioning, started with the thesis that learning happens through changes in overt behavior. Skinner believed that when a particular behavior is rewarded, the individual is being conditioned to repeat that behavior.

Habituation is a learned behavior where the organism produces less and less response as a stimulus is repeated, without a subsequent negative or positive action. Habituation safeguards species from wasting energy on irrelevant stimuli.

Imprinting is a learned behavior that develops in a critical or sensitive period of the animal's lifespan. Konrad Lorenz (a behavioral scientist) was able to show that baby geese responded to their mother's physical appearance shortly after birth. However, if another object was exposed to the gosling during that critical period (immediately following hatching) the gosling would interpret the substituted object to be its mother.

Social Behavior

Some animal species demonstrate **social behavior**—behavior patterns that take into account other individuals. Animals will develop a **home range** (an area in which they spend most of their time). Animals may also develop an area of land as their **territory**, which lies within the home range, but is the area the individual will defend as his own. The establishment of a territory implies the recognition by one individual that other individuals exist; thus, it is a simple social behavior.

Sexual and mating behaviors often rely on complex interactions of the endocrine, nervous, and musculoskeletal systems. In many cases, an individual will compete with another for a particular mate.

In some species, social interactions are highly complex; for instance, an entire population may function as a hierarchy (or society), where individuals have specified roles and status. A **society** is an organization of individuals in a population in which tasks are divided, in order for the group to work together. Within a society, the individuals may be constantly growing, changing, and adapting, while the functions of the community remain the same over time.

While the social behavior of insects is more a question of division of labor, societies of primates are built around the idea of **dominance**. A hierarchy is formed through actual competitions among individuals. The community member(s) at the top of the hierarchy enjoy privileges related to their selection of food and mates. This hierarchy is challenged as individuals mature, causing a succession of leaders.

Social animals exhibit a characteristic known as **altruism**, that is, having traits that tend to serve the needs of the society as a whole in addition to its own individual needs.

SOCIAL BIOLOGY
Human Population Growth

Human population growth is a direct function of human birth and death rates (natality and mortality). People are able to reason around many of the limiting factors (for example, problems of food shortage or disease), making human population growth a much more complex situation. Furthermore, reproductive behaviors of humans are also subject to the reasoning process, unlike the instinctual mating behaviors of most animals.

The development of vaccines and antibiotics has greatly increased the life-span of people in recent history, decreasing the mortality rate. Infant mortality rates have steeply declined in the last 150 years, as safer birthing processes and infant care have been developed. On the other hand, the development of contraceptives has reduced the natality rate in many countries.

A theory known as **demographic transition** proposes that there are progressive demographic time periods of human population growth. In the first period, birth and death rates are approximately equal, allowing the population to be in equilibrium with the environment. **Social evolution** (i.e., ability to fight disease, mass produce food, etc.) causes the birth rate to overtake the death rate, in turn causing rapid population growth throughout another period. Agrarian lifestyles (where families have numerous children to "work the farm") become less common and children become a liability in urban society. However, **biomedical progress** of urban society causes a lowering of the infant mortality rate. Society then faces a period of dramatic population growth, most of it within cities. The final stage occurs as developed industrialized nations work to lower birth rates through contraceptive practices.

As the human population proceeds through demographic transition, the **age composition** (the relative numbers of individuals of specific ages within the population) changes. As birth rates increase, the population tends to shift toward youth, whereas medical advancements may increase the average age of the population. For instance, in 1900 approximately 40% of Americans were under 18; in 1960, 36%; and in 1996, only 26% of Americans were under 18. Demographic transition also has an effect on the population growth rate.

Meanwhile, **genetic engineering**, the intentional alteration of genetic material of a living organism, has produced plant species able to resist drought, disease, or other threats—providing for more abundant food production. Genetic engineering is also responsible for disease-fighting breakthroughs such as the production of human insulin to fight diabetes. (Insulin is produced industrially using genetically engineered bacteria that produce human insulin.)

Environmental pollution (the addition of contaminants to the air and water by human intervention and industry) has profoundly affected Earth's ecosystems. Most pollution has occurred in recent decades as industrialization has increased.

Progress has been made in the management of resources in the recent past. Careful resource management, including the active human intervention of recycling energy, water, nutrients, and chemicals, will encourage the natural cyclic processes within the biosphere to maintain a viable balance.

ATOMIC CHEMISTRY

STRUCTURE OF THE ATOM

The study of matter is known as **chemistry**. An **element** is a substance that cannot be broken down into any other substances. The simplest unit of an element that retains the element's characteristics is known as an **atom**. The properties of matter are a result of the structure of atoms and their interaction with each other. Each atom of a given element has a nucleus containing a unique number of **protons** and usually a similar number of **neutrons**. The nucleus is surrounded by **electrons**.

Elements are listed by atomic number on the **periodic table of the elements**. The **atomic number** is the number of protons found in the nucleus of an atom of that element. In an uncharged atom, the number of protons is equal to the number of electrons.

The **atomic mass** is calculated by adding up the masses of the protons and neutrons in an atom. For example, a helium atom consists of 2 protons and 2 electrons. It would have an atomic mass of 4 amu (atomic mass units—the mass of 1 proton or neutron).

Atoms with the same number of protons but different numbers of neutrons are called **isotopes** of one another. For example, carbon-12 and carbon-14 are the same element (carbon). The difference in the **mass numbers** indicates that carbon-12 has 6 neutrons, while carbon-14 has 8 neutrons. The average mass number takes into account the relative frequencies of the different isotopes. The average mass number is also called the **atomic weight**. This number is also the **molar mass** of the element, or the mass in grams of one mole of atoms. (6.02×10^{23} atoms constitute one mole of atoms.)

Electrons have a charge of -1, while protons have a charge of $+1$. Neutrons have no charge. The number of protons in the nucleus of an atom carries a positive charge equal to this number; that is, if an atom's nucleus contains 4 protons, the charge is $+4$. Since positive and negative charges attract, the positive charges of the nucleus attract an equal number of negatively charged electrons.

Electrons travel freely in a three-dimensional space that may be called an **electron cloud**, an **electron shell**, or an **orbital**. Current models of the atom follow the principles of **quantum mechanics**, which predict the probabilities of an electron being in a certain area at a certain time. Although the term *orbital* is used, electrons do not orbit the nucleus like a planet orbiting a sun.

Each shell has a particular amount of energy related to it, and is therefore also referred to as an **energy level**. Energy levels are named utilizing a *quantum number* and a *letter designation* (i.e., 1s, 2s, 2p, etc.). The quantum number of the energy level closest to the nucleus is 1, and progresses as the levels get farther from the nucleus (2, 3, etc.). The letter designation indicates the shape of that particular energy level. The energy level closest to the nucleus has the least energy related to it; the farthest has the most. Lower energy levels (closer to the nucleus) have less capacity for electrons than those farther from the nucleus.

Since electrons are attracted to the nucleus, electrons fill the electron shells closest to the nucleus (lowest energy levels) first. Once a given level is full, electrons start filling the next level out. The outermost occupied energy level of an element is called the **valence shell**. The number of electrons in the valence shell will determine the combinations that this atom will be likely to make with other atoms. Atoms are more stable when every electron is paired and are most stable when their valence

THE PERIODIC TABLE

KEY

Atomic Number → 4 / IVA / IVB

Group Classification

Symbol

$$\boxed{\begin{array}{c} 22 \\ Ti \\ 47.88 \end{array}}$$

Atomic Weight

( ) indicates most stable or best known isotope

METALS — NONMETALS

TRANSITIONAL METALS

1 IA	2 IIA	3 IIIB	4 IVB	5 VB	6 VIB	7 VIIB	8 VIII	9 VIII	10 VIII	11 IB	12 IIB	13 IIIA	14 IVA	15 VA	16 VIA	17 VIIA	18 0
1 H 1.008																	2 He 4.003
3 Li 6.941	4 Be 9.012											5 B 10.811	6 C 12.011	7 N 14.007	8 O 15.999	9 F 18.998	10 Ne 20.180
11 Na 22.990	12 Mg 24.305											13 Al 26.982	14 Si 28.086	15 P 30.974	16 S 32.066	17 Cl 35.453	18 Ar 39.948
19 K 39.098	20 Ca 40.078	21 Sc 44.956	22 Ti 47.88	23 V 50.942	24 Cr 51.996	25 Mn 54.938	26 Fe 55.847	27 Co 58.933	28 Ni 58.693	29 Cu 63.546	30 Zn 65.39	31 Ga 69.723	32 Ge 72.61	33 As 74.922	34 Se 78.96	35 Br 79.904	36 Kr 83.8
37 Rb 85.468	38 Sr 87.62	39 Y 88.906	40 Zr 91.224	41 Nb 92.906	42 Mo 95.94	43 Tc (97.907)	44 Ru 101.07	45 Rh 102.906	46 Pd 106.4	47 Ag 107.868	48 Cd 112.411	49 In 114.818	50 Sn 118.710	51 Sb 121.757	52 Te 127.60	53 I 126.905	54 Xe 131.29
55 Cs 132.905	56 Ba 137.327	57 La 138.906	72 Hf 178.49	73 Ta 180.948	74 W 183.84	75 Re 186.207	76 Os 190.23	77 Ir 192.22	78 Pt 195.08	79 Au 196.967	80 Hg 200.59	81 Tl 204.383	82 Pb 207.2	83 Bi 208.980	84 Po (208.982)	85 At (209.982)	86 Rn (222.018)
87 Fr (223.020)	88 Ra (226.025)	89 Ac (227.028)	104 Unq (261.11)	105 Unp (262.114)	106 Unh (263.118)	107 Uns (262.12)	108 Uno (265)	109 Une (266)	110 Uun (269)	111 Uuu (272.153)	112 Uub (277)						

Alkali Metals · Alkaline Earth Metals · Halogens · Noble Gases

LANTHANIDE SERIES

58 Ce 140.115	59 Pr 140.908	60 Nd 144.24	61 Pm (144.913)	62 Sm 150.36	63 Eu 151.965	64 Gd 157.25	65 Tb 158.925	66 Dy 162.50	67 Ho 164.930	68 Er 167.26	69 Tm 168.934	70 Yb 173.04	71 Lu 174.967

ACTINIDE SERIES

90 Th 232.038	91 Pa 231.036	92 U 238.029	93 Np (237.048)	94 Pu (244.064)	95 Am (243.061)	96 Cm (247.070)	97 Bk (247.070)	98 Cf (251.080)	99 Es (252.083)	100 Fm (257.095)	101 Md (258.1)	102 No (259.101)	103 Lr (262.11)

shell is full. The tendency for an atom toward stability means that elements having unpaired or partially filled valence shells will easily gain or lose electrons in order to obtain the most stable configuration.

Electrons give off energy in the form of **electromagnetic radiation** when they move from a higher level, or an excited state, to a lower level. The energy represented by light, using Planck's equation, represents the difference between the two energy levels of the electron. Atoms contain electromagnetic energy that is found in discrete bundles, expressed by the following equation:

$$E = hv \text{ or, since } c = v\lambda, \text{ then } E = \frac{hc}{\lambda}$$

where: E = Energy of the photon, J

h = Planck's constant, 6.63×10^{-34} J • sec

v = frequency of light, sec^{-1}

λ = wavelength of light, m

c = speed of light, 3.00×10^8 m/sec

The following table shows periodic trends relating to electromagnetic radiation.

	Moving Left to Right across a Period	Moving Down a Group from Top to Bottom
Atomic radii	decreases	increases
Ionization energy	increases	decreases
Electron affinity	increases	generally decreases
Electronegativity	increases	decreases

NUCLEAR REACTIONS AND EQUATIONS

Alpha decay occurs when the nucleus of an atom emits a package of 2 protons and 2 neutrons, called an *alpha particle* (α), which is equivalent to the nucleus of a helium atom. This usually occurs with elements that have a mass number greater than 60. Alpha decay causes the atom's atomic mass to decrease by four units and the atomic number by two units. For example:

$$^{238}_{92}U \rightarrow \alpha \text{ particle } (^{4}_{2}He) + ^{234}_{90}Th$$

Beta decay occurs when the nucleus emits a *beta particle* ($\beta-$) that degrades into an electron as it passes out of the atom. This usually occurs with elements that have a mass number greater than their atomic weight. Beta decay causes the mass number to remain the same but increases the atomic number by one. Beta decay converts a neutron into a proton. For example:

$$^{234}_{90}Th \rightarrow \beta^- \text{ particle } (^{0}_{-1}e) + ^{234}_{91}Pa$$

Positron decay occurs when the nucleus emits a particle that degrades into a *positron* as it passes out of the atom. This usually occurs with elements that have a mass number smaller than their atomic weight. Positron decay causes the mass number to remain the same but decreases the atomic number by one. Positron decay converts a proton into a neutron and a positron. For example:

$$^{13}_{7}N \rightarrow\ ^{0}_{+1}e +\ ^{13}_{6}C$$

Gamma radiation consists of *gamma rays* (γ), high-frequency, high-energy, electromagnetic radiation that is usually given off in combination with alpha and beta decay. Gamma decay can occur when a nucleus undergoes a transformation from a higher-energy state to a lower-energy state. The resulting atom may or may not be radioactive. Gamma rays are photons, which have neither mass nor charge.

RATE OF DECAY (HALF-LIFE)

Half-life is the time it takes for 50% of an isotope to decay. Nuclear decay represents a "first-order" reaction in that it depends on the amount of material and the rate constant.

CHEMISTRY OF REACTIONS

COMMON ELEMENTS

Properties of each element, such as mass, electronegativity, valence electrons, and so on, make a particular element fit for interaction with other elements in a variety of ways. The most common elements encountered in chemical reactions are found on the following table:

Atomic Number	Symbol	Common Name
1	H	Hydrogen
2	He	Helium
6	C	Carbon
7	N	Nitrogen
8	O	Oxygen
11	Na	Sodium
12	Mg	Magnesium
14	Si	Silicon
15	P	Phosphorus
16	S	Sulphur
17	Cl	Chlorine
19	K	Potassium

Atomic Number	Symbol	Common Name
20	Ca	Calcium
24	Cr	Chromium
26	Fe	Iron
29	Cu	Copper
30	Zn	Zinc
47	Ag	Silver
53	I	Iodine
79	Au	Gold
80	Hg	Mercury
82	Pb	Lead
88	Ra	Radium

Chemical Bonds

A **covalent bond** between atoms is formed when atoms *share* electrons. For instance, hydrogen has only one electron, which is unpaired, leaving the 1s valence shell one electron short of full. Oxygen has 6 electrons in the valence shell; it needs 2 more electrons in the valence shell for that shell to be full. It is easy for 2 hydrogen atoms to share their electrons with the oxygen, making the effective valence shells of each full.

A **molecule** is two or more atoms held together by shared electrons (covalent bonds). A **compound** is formed when two or more different atoms bond together chemically to form a unique substance (i.e., H_2O, CH_4).

Charged atoms are called **ions**. An atom that loses one or more electrons becomes a positively charged particle, a positive ion, or a **cation**. An atom that gains one or more electrons becomes a negative ion, or an **anion**. Positive and negative ions are attracted to each other in a bond called an **ionic bond**. An ionic bond is the strongest bond and is stronger than a covalent bond.

Molecules that have regions of partial charge are called **polar molecules**. For instance, water molecules (which have a net charge of 0) have a partial negative charge near the oxygen atom and a partial positive charge near each of the hydrogen atoms. The force of attraction between water molecules is called a **hydrogen bond**, a weak chemical bond between molecules.

Attractions between Molecules

A **polar intermolecular attraction** can exist between two polar molecules. The slightly positive end of one molecule forms an electrostatic attraction to the slightly negative end of another molecule.

Van der Waals forces are momentary forces of attraction that exist between molecules and are created by the chance movement of electrons in a system of atoms bonded together. The strength of attraction is proportional to the number of electrons in the molecule. These forces are weak relative to polar intermolecular forces, and they become apparent only if there are many electrons, or if the molecules come very close together.

Structure and Physical Properties

Physical properties of substances are related to the forces between atoms and molecules. Hardness, melting point, and boiling point are all measures of the strength of interatomic or intermolecular attraction holding the molecule together.

Network covalent crystals have the strongest attraction holding atoms together. They have the highest melting points and are the hardest of all crystals. **Ionic crystals** have strong electrostatic forces holding atoms together. They tend to have high melting and boiling points, and are poor conductors in the solid phase (because the electrons are in fixed positions). However, when ionic crystals are in an aqueous solution (dissolved in water), they are good conductors because the charge is mobile.

Nonpolar molecules, held together predominantly with van der Waals forces, are soft crystals, are easily deformed, and vaporize easily. They have much lower melting and boiling points than polar compounds of similar molar mass. Nonpolar molecules are poor conductors and tend to be more volatile because of their high vapor pressure.

Polar molecules have intermolecular attractions that are weaker than ionic forces but are much stronger than nonpolar dispersion forces. The melting and boiling points of polar compounds depend on the strength of the dipole moment (difference in charge between the poles) of the two compounds. The stronger the cumulative dipole moment, the greater the intermolecular attraction and the higher the melting and boiling points.

Hydrogen bonds have the strongest polar intermolecular attraction because the hydrogen atom has only one electron. When that electron leaves, the exposed proton of the hydrogen nucleus is strongly attracted to the slightly negative charge of the other molecule. Consequently, polar molecules with hydrogen bonds have higher melting and boiling points than polar molecules of similar molar mass that do not have hydrogen bonds.

> **Summary of strength of attraction:**
>
> Ionic > covalent > metallic > polar > intermolecular > nonpolar > intermolecular

Chemical Reactions

Chemical reactions occur when molecules interact with each other to form one or more molecules of another type. Those that occur within cells provide energy, nutrients, and other products that allow the organism to function.

Chemical reactions are symbolized by an equation where the reacting molecules (**reactants**) are shown on one side and the newly formed molecules (**products**) on the other, with an arrow between indicating the direction of the reaction. Some chemical reactions are simple, such as the breakdown of a compound into its components (a **decomposition** reaction):

$$AB \rightarrow A + B$$

A simple **combination** reaction is the reverse of decomposition:

$$A + B \rightarrow AB$$

When one compound breaks apart and forms a new compound with a free reactant, it is called a **replacement** reaction:

$$AB + C \rightarrow AC + B$$

Chemical reactions may require an input of energy (**endothermic**) or they may release energy (**exothermic**).

Properties of Water

Water is able to dissolve many types of organic and inorganic substances. This property promotes several biological processes such as muscle contraction, nerve stimulation, and transport across membranes (**permeability**).

Because water molecules are polar, certain types of chemicals dissociate in water. An **acid** is a chemical that donates protons (H+ ions) when dissolved in water. Acidity, then, is a measure of the concentration of H+ ions in a solution. A chemical that accepts protons (H+ ions) when dissolved in water is a **base**. The **pH** (standing for potential of hydrogen) scale is a measurement of H+ ions in solution. The pH of a substance can range from 0–14; a pH of 7 is neutral (as is pure water), a pH below 7 is acidic, and a pH above 7 is basic (or alkaline). Acids and bases neutralize each other when dissolved together in water. The neutralization of an acidic solution with a basic solution produces a salt (an ionic compound) and water.

Water also exhibits unique responses to temperature change. Most substances contract upon becoming a solid; however, water expands as it solidifies (a process we call freezing), forming a loose lattice structure (crystal). This crystalline form also makes frozen water (ice) less dense than liquid water. Water has a high specific heat; it resists changes in temperature. The presence of water in an environment will tend to moderate the effect of harsh temperature changes.

Chemical Structure of Organic Compounds

Organic compounds, the building blocks of all living things, are defined as those that contain carbon. Organic substances include many types of molecules active in biological processes (or biomolecules), such as carbohydrates, lipids, proteins, and nucleic acids.

1. Carbohydrates

Carbohydrates are made up of varying combinations of only carbon, hydrogen, and oxygen. The ratio of hydrogen to oxygen in carbohydrates is always 2:1, just as in water (H_2O)—thus, the name *carbo* (carbon) *hydrate* (plus water).

Sugars and **starches** are both forms of carbohydrates. The basic sugar unit is a **monosaccharide**, which usually contains 3 to 7 carbon atoms plus attached oxygen and hydrogen atoms. The most common monosaccharides, called **hexoses** (six-carbon sugars), are usually in a ring-shaped (or cyclic) structure.

Two monosaccharide molecules may join together, producing a **disaccharide** and liberating a molecule of water. Table sugar is a disaccharide of glucose and fructose (the most common monosaccharides). When three monosaccharides join together, the chain is then called a **trisaccharide**. When more than three monosaccharides merge, the resultant molecule is known as a **polysaccharide**.

Plants store energy by synthesizing polysaccharides known as **starches**, which are stored within the plant's cells until energy is needed. Plants also synthesize starches that provide structure to their cells; the most common is a plant fiber known as **cellulose** (a long chain of water-insoluble polysaccharides). **Glycogen** is a polysaccharide composed of many joined glucose units. Many animals use glycogen as a short-term storage molecule for energy. In mammals, glycogen is found in muscle and liver tissue.

2. Lipids

Lipids are organic compounds composed of carbon, hydrogen, and oxygen. The ratio of hydrogen to oxygen in lipids is always greater than 2:1. Lipids are hydrophobic (from the Greek for "water fearing") and will not dissolve in water. Some lipids form structural components of cell membranes (phospholipids), some provide moisture barriers (waxes), and others are primarily used to store energy (fats). Other lipids serve as vitamins or hormones.

Fats are highly efficient lipid molecules used for long-term energy storage. When an organism takes in more carbohydrates than are necessary for its current energy use, the excess energy is stored in chemical bonds between the atoms of lipid molecules. When these bonds are broken, energy is released. In addition to storing energy, fats also function in organisms to provide a protective layer that insulates internal organs and maintains heat within the body.

3. Proteins

Proteins are large unbranched chains of **amino acids**. Amino acids are single links (**monomers**) that join together to form linear chains with many links (**polymers**). There are 20 common amino acids that can combine in various sequences to form thousands of different proteins. Amino acids are connected into chains by a water-releasing (dehydration) reaction that forms peptide bonds. For this reason, proteins may also be called **polypeptides**.

Enzymes are special proteins that act as **catalysts** for reactions. A catalyst is a substance that changes the speed of a reaction without being affected itself. Enzyme names have the suffix -ase (such as polymerase, lactase).

4. Nucleic Acids

There are two groups of nucleic acids, deoxyribonucleic acid (**DNA**) and ribonucleic acid (**RNA**). Each type is composed of chains of nucleotides, the monomers that form nucleic acids, which are polymers. Each nucleotide has a sugar (from the pentose group) attached to a phosphate group and a nitrogenous base. The sugar and phosphate groups alternate in long chains forming the backbone of the DNA or RNA molecule. In DNA, the sugar molecule is deoxyribose; in RNA, it is ribose. RNA chains are generally single strands, but DNA strands pair up to form a shape like a twisted ladder. This **double-helix** structure of DNA was discovered and modeled by two scientists, James Watson and Francis Crick, in the 1950s. DNA and RNA structure is therefore known as the **Watson-Crick** model.

The nitrogen bases in DNA include **adenine**, **cytosine**, **guanine**, and **thymine** (A, C, G, and T). In RNA, thymine is replaced by the base **uracil** (U). The nucleic acid bases form complementary pairs, that is, cytosine (C) and guanine (G) pair together forming hydrogen bonds, while thymine (T - or uracil in RNA - U) pairs with adenine (A). [A sequence of GATTACA would then pair with the sequence CTAATGT, or with the RNA sequence CUAAUGU.] This pairing allows DNA and RNA strands to accurately duplicate themselves and to encode the order of amino acids in proteins.

PHYSICS

HEAT

Heat is energy that flows from a warm object to a cooler object. It is important to understand the difference between heat and temperature. **Temperature** is the measure of the **average kinetic energy** of a substance. The atoms and molecules of all substances are constantly in motion, and this energy is called its kinetic energy. Temperature is a measure of that energy. The faster the particles in a substance move (more energy), the higher the temperature.

The theoretical temperature at which particle motion stops is called *absolute zero* (or 0 Kelvin). This temperature has never been reached by any known substance.

When substances come in contact, the hotter (greater energy) substance transfers kinetic energy to the cooler (lower energy) one—heat has been expended. Heat is measured in calories or joules.

Energy (including heat) may be transferred from one object to another by three processes—radiation, conduction, and convection. **Radiation** is the transfer of energy via waves. Radiation can occur through matter, or without any matter present. **Convection** involves the movement of energy by the movement of matter, usually through currents. **Conduction** is movement of energy by transfer from particle to particle. Conduction can only occur when objects are touching.

Specific Heat

The measure of a substance's ability to retain energy is called **specific heat**. Specific heat is measured as the amount of heat needed to raise the temperature of one gram of a substance by one degree Celsius.

THE LAWS OF THERMODYNAMICS

The laws of thermodynamics explain the interaction between heat and work (energy) in the universe. The first law (the **Law of Conservation of Matter and Energy**) says that matter and energy can neither be created nor destroyed. The second law (the **Law of Entropy**) states that whenever energy is exchanged, some energy becomes unavailable for use (entropy increases). The third law (the **Law of Absolute Zero**) says that absolute zero cannot be attained in any system (that is, energy of motion of particles cannot be stopped). The *Zeroth Law of Thermodynamics* says that when two bodies are in contact that they will move toward a state of thermodynamic equilibrium—where both bodies eventually reach the same temperature.

STATES OF MATTER

All matter has physical properties that affect the way substances react with each other under various conditions. Physical properties include color, odor, taste, strength, hardness, density, and state.

Solids, Liquids, Gases, and Plasma

Matter exists in one of four states—solid, liquid, gas, or plasma. Under most conditions elements will be in the solid, liquid, or gas state. **Plasma** only exists in the case of extreme heat and ionization—in this state ions and electrons move about freely, giving plasma properties different from the other three states.

A **solid** has molecules in fixed positions, giving the substance a definite shape and a definite volume. In a solid the molecules are packed and bonded together. The strength of the bonds determines the strength of the solid and its melting point. When heat energy is applied to the bonds they break apart, the molecules can move about, and the substance becomes a liquid.

A **liquid** has definite volume but not definite shape since the molecules are loosely attracted. This allows the shape of the substance to mold to its surroundings. When a liquid is cooled the molecules become bonded and the substance becomes a solid. When heat energy is added to a liquid, the weak attractions holding the molecules together break apart, causing the molecules to move about randomly and the liquid becomes a gas.

A **gas** is a substance with relatively (relative to solids and liquids) large distances and little attraction between molecules. The molecules are free to move about randomly. Gases have no definite shape or volume since temperature and pressure can impact the density.

The following are some terms that are important to know related to substances and their states:

— **Melting point**—temperature at which a substance changes from solid to liquid form

— **Heat of fusion**—heat required to melt 1 kg of a solid at its melting point (also known as enthalpy of fusion)

— **Freezing point**—temperature at which a substance changes from liquid to solid

— **Boiling point**—temperature at which a substance changes from liquid to gas

— **Heat of vaporization**—amount of energy required to change 1 kg of liquid of a substance to a gas (also known as enthalpy of vaporization)

— **Evaporation**—escape of individual particles of a substance into gaseous form

— **Condensation**—change of a gaseous substance to liquid form

— **Diffusion**—mixing of particles in a gas or liquid

Density

The **density** of a substance is determined by measuring the mass of a substance and dividing it by the volume ($D = m/v$). It is important to understand that density is a function of mass (amount of matter), not weight (attraction of gravity on mass).

Pressure is a measure of the amount of force applied per unit of area. **Pascal's principle** states that the pressure exerted on any point of a confined fluid is transmitted unchanged throughout the fluid. Therefore, if you exert pressure on a liquid, it will exert that same pressure on its surroundings. **Archimedes's principle** states that when an object is placed in a fluid, the object will have a buoyant force equal to the weight of the displaced fluid. Archimedes's principle results in **buoyancy**, a decrease in the measured apparent weight of an object in a fluid due to the net upward force caused by the displaced fluid.

Gravity

The **mass** of an object refers to *the amount of matter* that is contained by the object; however, the **weight** of an object is *the force of gravity acting upon that object*. The mass of an object (measured in kg) will be the same no matter where in the universe the object is located. The amount of mass and the gravitational field of Earth (or the moon, etc.) imparts weight to an object. The weight, however, will vary according to where in the universe the object is.

All matter exerts a gravitational force on all other matter. The gravity on Earth is greater than the gravity on the moon, since Earth has much more matter or mass than the moon. The force of gravity on an object caused by the mass of Earth equals the mass of the object (m) times the acceleration caused by gravity (g). The equation is $F = mg$.

This acceleration caused by gravity on Earth, g (more commonly called the acceleration of gravity), equals 9.8 m/s^2 in the metric system and 32 ft/s^2 in the English system.

The weight of an object is the measurement of the force of gravity on that object. The equation is weight $= mg$.

The mass of the moon is less than the mass of Earth, so the acceleration of gravity (g) is less on the moon than Earth. If you put an object on the moon and weighed it, its weight would be 1/6 the weight on Earth. In other words, a 180-pound man would only weigh 30 pounds on the moon.

The fundamental units of measure used in the metric system are the **meter**, **kilogram**, and **second**, or *mks* system. To get the weight of an object in the metric system, you multiply the mass in kilograms by the acceleration of gravity (9.8 m/s^2), resulting in the units of kg-m/s^2 or *Newtons*.

The **universal gravitational law**, first described by Sir Isaac Newton, states that *the force of gravity between two objects is proportional to the product of the masses of the objects and inversely proportional to the square of the distance between them*—in simple English—as objects get further apart, the effect of gravity drops dramatically. The following equation shows this relationship . . . the mass of one body is designated as M, the mass of a second as m, and the distance between them is r; the force of attraction between the two bodies is F.

$$F = G\frac{Mm}{r^2}$$

where G is the universal gravitational constant $G = 6.67 \times 10^{-11}$ N(m²/kg²) (Newton-meter squared per kilogram squared).

Although a falling object will continue to accelerate until it is made to stop (when it hits the ground), air resistance will slow down that acceleration. Air resistance is approximately proportional to the square of the velocity, so as the object falls faster, the air resistance increases until it equals the force of gravity. The point at which these forces are equal is called its *terminal velocity*.

The acceleration of the force of gravity on falling bodies is *independent of the mass* of the falling object. In addition, gravity of the mass of an object is also *independent of the velocity* of the object parallel to the ground.

Since *force = mass × acceleration* ($F = ma$), the universal gravity equation implies that as objects are attracted and get closer together, the force increases and the acceleration between them also increases.

CLASSICAL MECHANICS

Mechanics is the study of things in motion. **Classical mechanics** involves particles bigger than atoms and slower than light. **Newton's laws of motion** are:

#1 Law of Inertia: A particle at rest will stay at rest and a particle in motion will stay in motion until acted upon by an outside force.

#2 Law of Force versus Mass: The rate of change of a particle is directly proportional to its mass and the force that is exerted on it, or

$$F = m \times a \text{ or } F = ma$$

(where F is force, m is mass, and a is acceleration).

#3 Law of Action and Reaction: Mutual interactions between bodies produce two forces that are equal in magnitude and opposite in direction; one body exerts a force on the second and the second body exerts an equal force on the first.

When studying relationships in classical mechanics, we usually identify quantities in terms of both their magnitude and direction. These mathematical quantities, called **vectors**, recognize both the size and direction of the dimension being considered. For example, velocity involves both a *speed* and a *direction* of the object. The formula for momentum (p) would then be written as $p = mv$, where p and v are both vector quantities, that is, they represent both a quantity of magnitude (or size) and a direction in which the object is moving. Vectors are identified with either bold letters or an arrow over the letter that indicates direction.

The following definitions and equations are those central to the general study of classical mechanics:

— **Work** is the movement of a mass over a distance:

$$\text{Work} = \text{Force} \times \text{Distance}$$
$$W = F \times d \text{ or } W = Fd$$

— **Speed** is the rate of change of an object's distance traveled.

$$s = \frac{d}{t}$$

— **Displacement** measures the change in position of an object, using the starting point and ending point and noting the direction.

— **Velocity** is the rate of change of displacement; it includes both speed and direction.

$$v = \frac{d}{t}$$

(where v is velocity and has a directional component of plus or minus; d is displacement, t is time)

— **Friction** is the rubbing force that acts against motion between two touching surfaces, which is dependent upon the surface attractions or the roughness or smoothness of the two surfaces. The measurement of the amount of friction between any two given objects can be determined experimentally and is designated by the Greek symbol mu, μ, called the *coefficient of friction*. If μ approaches zero, then there is very little friction. As the value for μ increases, it indicates that there is increasing friction between the objects.

— **Acceleration** is the *rate of change of velocity*; it can act in the direction of motion, at an angle, or opposite to the direction of motion.

$$a = \frac{v_2 - v_1}{t_2 - t_1}$$

— **Momentum** is the product of mass and velocity; the quantity of motion for an object.

$$p = mv$$

(where p = momentum)

— **Force** is the push or pull exerted on an object.

$$F = ma$$

$$F = \frac{W}{d}$$

It is also important to note measurements related to mechanics. In science, all measurements are recorded and reported in **metric** units, known as the Système Internationale (International System) or **SI** units:

Mass—measured in kilograms

Length—measured in meters

Time—measured in seconds

Volume—measured in liters

THEORY OF RELATIVITY

In 1905, Albert Einstein expanded on the work of Faraday, Lorentz, and Maxwell to propose his "**special theory of relativity**." In basic terms, Einstein's special relativity states that

- **The speed of light is a constant.**
- **The laws of physics are the same in all inertial (non-accelerating) reference frames.**

The famous equation that resulted from this theory is $E = mc^2$, where E is energy, m is the mass of an object, and c is the speed of light.

These two postulates logically say that if you measure the velocity of light c to have a particular value, then no matter which inertial (non-accelerated) reference frame you are moving in, you will always measure it to have the same value; this is an experimental fact.

Classical mechanics "works" because for objects at speeds not approaching the speed of light and at masses much greater than atomic particles, the equations are appropriate. However, Einstein postulated that the speed of light was the only true constant, and that time and distance would always be made relative in order to maintain the speed of light as a constant.

Einstein proposed several experiments to test his special theory of relativity which required equipment and technology unavailable during his time, but which have now been carried out and verified. In addition, the special theory of relativity has also added understanding to the field of *quantum mechanics*—the world of very small objects, namely subatomic particles. Scientists have long known through experimentation that subatomic particles did not follow the laws of classical mechanics, but rather have their own rules for motion.

ELECTRICITY AND MAGNETISM

Electrical charges consist of **electrons** (with their negative charge) gathered on the surface of an object. When the electrical charges are not moving, it is called *static electricity*. When a positively charged ion attracts the electron, a spark may occur, which is a transfer or discharge of the electrical charge.

Electrical charges may also move from atom to atom within substances that are called **conductors**. A flow of electrons through a conductor is an **electrical current**. Some elements are good conductors (such as metals); others are poor conductors (called **insulators**). Plastic, rubber, glass, and wood are insulators.

An electrical **circuit** is the path that an electric current follows. Every electric circuit has four parts:

1. a *source* of *voltage* [a battery, generator, or AC source],

2. a set of *conductors* [wires],

3. a *load* [light, meter, appliance, etc.], and

4. a *switch*.

A **closed circuit** is one that has a continuous path for electron flow (no interruptions). An **open circuit** has no flow of electrons because the pathway is interrupted (by a switch, disconnection, etc.).

Voltage refers to the *electromotive force* that pushes electrons through the circuit. **Amperage** is the measure of the amount of electron flow or current. **Resistance** is a hindrance to current due to objects that deter the current by their size, shape, or type of conductor.

Series and Parallel Circuits

In a *series circuit*, there is only one path along which the electrons may flow, moving around the circuit along this single pathway from the positive to the negative pole of the battery (source). The current flows through each component in succession. Linking this group of electric cells in a series means that the voltage of the circuit will be equal to the sum total of the voltages in each cell added together.

In a **parallel circuit**, the electrical devices are connected to provide two or more paths through which the current may flow. Linking electrical cells in parallel will increase the amperage of the circuit (the current of the circuit will equal the sum of the currents in each cell).

Magnetism

Magnetism is defined as the ability of a substance to produce a magnetic field. The magnetic field acts like point charges (in electricity) producing north (N) and south (S) poles. When magnets are placed in close proximity to each other, the similar poles repel, while opposite poles attract. **Permanent magnets** contain natural magnetic ore, such as iron, cobalt, or nickel, the three natural elements with magnetic properties. **Temporary magnets** can be induced to carry a magnetic field, but will not hold the magnetic field permanently. **Electromagnets** are electrically induced magnets usually created by wrapping coils of wire around an iron core.

WAVES: SOUND AND LIGHT

Many things in nature travel in waves, including sound, light, and water. A wave has no mass of its own; it is simply movement within a medium, a disturbance that does not cause the medium itself to move significantly.

Light and ocean waves travel in transverse waves. A **transverse wave** causes particles to move up and down while the wave moves forward (perpendicular to the wave motion). Sound and some earthquake waves travel as longitudinal (compression) waves. In a **longitudinal wave** the particles move back and forth but in the same direction as (parallel with) the wave motion.

The **wavelength** of a wave is defined as the distance from one crest (or top) of a wave to the next crest on the same side. The **frequency** of a wave is the number of wavelengths that pass a point in a second.

Wave **interference** can increase wave amplitude if the crests and troughs of the waves coincide. If the crest and trough of two waves coincide, they can also cancel each other or reduce the amplitude. Waves can also be **reflected** when they hit a surface.

The speed of a wave can be described by the equation: $v = f\lambda$; where v = the speed of the wave, f = frequency of the wave, and λ = wavelength of the wave.

Sound

Sound travels in longitudinal waves. Sound waves are made when an object vibrates and causes air molecules to take on a compression wave motion. This motion is picked up by our eardrums and translated in our brains into sounds. Changes in wavelength account for volume changes, while changes in frequency result in pitch changes.

The **Doppler effect** refers to the characteristic of sound to lower in pitch as its source moves away, as calculated by the equation:

$$f_0 = \frac{v}{\cancel{L}v - v_s\cancel{\lambda}}\, f_s$$

where the frequency of the detected sound will be f_0, v is the velocity of sound in air, v_s is the velocity of the source, and f_s is the frequency of the emitted sound wave from the source.

Light

Light is often considered to travel in waves, but also has characteristics indicative of a particle. It is important to understand the ways that light moves by reviewing the following terms:

Diffraction—the bending of a light wave around an obstacle

Reflection—the bouncing of a wave of light off an object

Refraction—the change of direction of a wave as it passes from one **medium to another**

The Light Spectrum—A spectrum is used to identify the arrangement of the components of a light wave according to wavelength. The visible spectrum of light is the arrangement of the visible wavelengths in a beam of light in the order red, orange, yellow, green, blue, indigo, violet.

Different kinds of light have different spectra. Fluorescent light has sharper bands than incandescent light (light bulb). Sunlight has more blue and violet in its spectrum.

THE UNIVERSE

ASTRONOMY

Galaxies

Scientists, beginning with Tycho Brahe, Johannes Kepler, and Isaac Newton, began proposing methods of how stars and planets move in the celestial sphere and worked out mathematical relationships in a discipline called **celestial mechanics** to clarify this movement. However, a complete understanding of these mechanics didn't occur until the early twentieth century.

Edwin Hubble (the famous space telescope is named for his work) identified a **redshift** in the light spectrum of velocities of galaxies that indicated that galaxies are moving away from one another. At the same time, Albert Einstein was still attempting to understand issues related to his theory of general relativity. With the distortion of space-time caused by the effects of gravity tending to pull the universe together, Einstein was concerned how it was kept from completely collapsing when described by his gravitational constant. The expanding universe seemed to be contradicting Einstein's observations. However, recent scientific speculations of "dark energy" are giving additional credibility to Einstein's gravitational constant.

The Big Bang

The expansion of the universe recognized by Hubble gives further support to the evidence of a *Big Bang* to explain the origin of the universe, speculated to have occurred nearly 13 billion years ago. The series of events from that initial moment to the present involved the cooling of elementary particles starting with very light things (electrons) expanding into stellar clouds, then converting to matter and energy to form galaxies and clusters of galaxies. Photons in the early universe combined to form the *cosmic microwave background* (CMB) that resulted in radio wavelengths that we observe today. Through further cooling, coalescence, and expansion, stars and galaxies formed under gravitational forces. Speculation and theory combine to attempt to explain this through complex physics.

Stars

The core of our sun, along with most stars, begins with hydrogen. With the core temperature of stars being over 10 million Kelvin, and the tremendous pressures they contain, protons can fuse together to produce helium, gamma ray energy, positrons, and neutrinos. These neutrinos are nearly massless and chargeless. They do not interact with other matter very much and flow almost unimpeded throughout the universe.

Stars are huge masses of plasma with colossal amounts of energy and gravity. Many stars are held in by magnetic fields, but particles slip through occasional holes in the fields. The atoms are so hot, the protons, neutrons, and electrons move rapidly and react with each other, thus releasing energy. This energy moves out from stars in electromagnetic waves producing heat and light.

The stars consist of incredible amounts of matter. Since we know all matter has gravity, stars have very large gravitational forces. Many stars have their own systems, like our solar system with planets, asteroids, and moons orbiting them.

The positions of stars have also assisted in navigation since biblical times; **Polaris, the North Star**, is a common reference point, as it sits directly over the North Pole.

The sun is our own star that Earth and the rest of the planets in our solar system orbit.

Sun

The **sun** is the source of light energy plants need to produce food for themselves and all living things on Earth. The sun is also our source of warmth and power. The sun is about 740 times greater in mass than all the rest of our solar system combined. Using scientific notation, we calculate the size of the sun as 1.989×10^{30} kilograms. This works out to be about 2 octillion metric tons. An octillion is a billion-billion-billion.

The sun releases incredible amounts of energy as protons interact with each other (*nuclear fusion*). The Earth's atmosphere protects us from much of the harmful effects of radiation from the sun.

Solar System

In 1919, the **International Astronomical Union (IAU)** was designated with the job of defining and naming planets and moons in our solar system. Our solar system consists of all of the common celestial bodies such as planets, moons, asteroids, and various types of space debris which orbit the sun. In 2006 and 2008, the IAU General Assembly introduced two new planetary categories to include *dwarf planets* and *plutoids*, respectively.

The sun is incredibly huge in relation to all the other objects in the solar system. With a diameter of 1.4 million kilometers (~110 times Earth's diameter), its enormous mass results in the gravitational forces that hold our eight planets and three dwarf planets, their moons, various asteroids, comets, plutoids, and other smaller space particles in its orbit.

The characteristics of the planets vary greatly because of their size, composition, and distance from the sun. Recent modifications to the names of the planets and dwarf planets are redefining old standards. The new scheme reclassifies Pluto as a "plutoid" along with Eris, Pluto's twin dwarf, and adds Ceres as a third unique dwarf planet in the solar system, just inside the asteroid belt. To learn about these new modifications, visit *www.nasa.gov* to regularly check for changes.

The IAU's latest description of a **planet** is "a celestial body that (a) is in orbit around the Sun, (b) has sufficient mass for its self-gravity to overcome rigid body forces so that it assumes a hydrostatic equilibrium (nearly round) shape and (c) has cleared the neighborhood around its orbit."

The new definition of a "**dwarf planet**" (introduced in 2006) is "a celestial body that (a) is in orbit around the Sun, (b) has sufficient mass for its self-gravity to overcome rigid body forces so that it assumes a hydrostatic equilibrium (nearly round) shape, (c) has not cleared the neighborhood around its orbit, and (d) is not a satellite."

"*Plutoids*" are now identified as small celestial bodies that "orbit the" sun at a semi-major axis greater than Neptune's which possess a sufficient mass for their self-gravity to overcome rigid body forces so that they assume a hydrostatic equilibrium (near-spherical) shape, and that have not cleared the neighborhood around their orbit." Thus, Pluto and Eris are identified as plutoids, along with a third one identified in July of 2008 as MakeMake.

Our calendar year is a measure of the time Earth takes in orbiting the sun. Each year Earth completes one trip around the sun in 365.2422 days, or about 365¼ days. The seasons we experience on Earth are a result of Earth's inclination on its axis. That is, if you drew a line through Earth's poles, this line is not perpendicular with its orbit around the Sun.

Earth's axis tilts at an angle of 23½ degrees with its orbit. The tilt means that the Northern Hemisphere will be tilted toward the sun for half the orbit, and the Southern Hemisphere will be tilted for the other half (half-a-year). The hemisphere tilted toward the sun absorbs more of the solar radiation during that half of the year and experiences summer. The hemisphere tilted away from the sun experiences winter.

The moon's orbit around Earth occurs approximately every 29 days. This is the origin of our months. A day is the time the Earth takes to rotate one time on its axis. An hour is simply a division of the rotation of the Earth (one day) obtained by taking the globe and dividing it into 24 time zones.

Moon

Our view of the moon is constantly changing as the moon orbits Earth and as Earth rotates on its axis. Our daily view of the moon changes as it moves around Earth along its regular orbital path. The changes we see in the moon's shape and location are regular in their occurrence because of the regular nature of the rotation and orbit. The moon orbits around Earth once approximately every 29 days (one lunar month). The moon's rotation on its axis is synchronous with its orbit, so we always see the same side of the moon reflecting the sunlight.

The moon does not emit any of its own light, but reflects the light from the sun. The phases that we see are a result of the angle between Earth, the moon, and the sun as viewed by us from Earth.

A *new moon* occurs when the moon is directly between Earth and the sun. At this point, the moon will rise at about 6:00 a.m. and set at about 6:00 p.m. (on standard, not daylight saving, time). The lighted side of the moon is toward the sun, so our view is of the dark side only (we don't see it at all).

Following the new moon, the moon (continuing its orbit) moves so that we see an increasing portion of the lit side each night. We call this the *waxing crescent moon*.

In about a week, the angle between Earth, the sun, and the moon is 90 degrees, allowing us to see half its lighted surface, the *first quarter*. This 90 degree angle means the moon rises halfway through the day at about noon, and sets at about midnight.

For the following week, we see more of the moon's surface each night (*waxing gibbous*) until the full moon, which marks the middle of the lunar orbit (and the lunar month).

During the *full moon*, the Earth/moon/sun angle is 180 degrees, meaning Earth is between the sun and the moon so we see the entire bright half of its surface. The full moon rises near sundown and sets near sunrise, opposite the sun.

During the remaining two weeks of the lunar month, the moon wanes through another gibbous moon to the *third quarter* (the other half of the moon's lit surface is visible rising around midnight and setting at noon). It wanes through another *crescent moon* and on until it returns to the beginning of the orbital—the new moon.

EARTH

Earth, home to over 6.5 billion people, is an oblate spheroid with a surface area of over 5.1×10^8 square kilometers (nearly 200 million square miles). Revolving around the sun at an average distance of 1.49×10^8 kilometers (93 million miles), it leans at an angle of 23.5 degrees to provide most of the inhabitants with four changing seasons. Its mass is approximately 6.0×10^{24} kilograms and a volume of 1.08 billion cubic kilometers (260 billion cubic miles).

ATMOSPHERE

Earth's **atmosphere** is an essential feature that allows our planet to sustain life. It extends approximately 560 km (350 miles) from Earth's surface, though the actual thickness varies from place to place. Our atmosphere makes Earth a habitable planet for people, plants, and animals by absorbing the sun's energy, recycling and preserving water and chemicals needed for life, and moderating our weather patterns. The atmosphere is attracted and maintained by the force of Earth's gravity.

Without the protection of our atmosphere, Earth would be subjected to the extreme freezing temperatures found in the vacuum of space. Our atmosphere is specifically formulated to provide us with an environment suited to our needs.

Earth's atmosphere is made up of about 78% nitrogen, 21% oxygen, slightly less than 1% argon, and the remaining fraction of 1% contains small amounts of other gases (including carbon dioxide, helium, hydrogen, krypton, methane, neon, nitrogen dioxide, nitrous oxide, ozone, sulfur dioxide, water vapor, and xenon).

We identify five distinct layers (called *strata*) of atmosphere: the troposphere, stratosphere, mesosphere, thermosphere, and exosphere. Four transition zones separate the four atmospheric layers: the tropopause, stratopause, mesopause, and thermopause.

The **troposphere**, the atmospheric layer closest to Earth's surface, extends to an altitude of approximately 8 to 15 kilometers (5 to 9 miles). The force of gravity is strongest nearest the Earth's surface; thus, the number of gas molecules per area (density) is greatest at the lowest altitudes. In addition, the density of gas molecules decreases as altitude increases. Therefore, the troposphere is the densest atmospheric layer, accounting for most of the atmosphere's mass.

The troposphere contains 99% of the water vapor found in the atmosphere. Water vapor in the air absorbs solar energy and absorbs heat that radiates back from Earth's surface. The water vapor concentration within the troposphere is greatest near the equator and lowest at the poles.

Nearly all weather phenomena experienced on Earth are caused by the interactions of gases (including water vapor) within the troposphere. The temperature of the troposphere decreases as altitude increases from about 16°C (60°F) nearest Earth's surface to −65°C (−85°F) at the tropopause. (Temperatures are averages of all the temperatures over Earth's surface and across all seasons.) For every kilometer in altitude above Earth, the temperature drops approximately 6°C within the troposphere.

The troposphere is separated from the next layer (the stratosphere) by the **tropopause**. The **stratosphere** located above the troposphere, extends from the tropopause (found approximately 14 km or 9 miles above Earth's surface) to approximately 48 km (30 miles) above Earth's surface. The stratosphere contains much less water vapor than the troposphere. The gases of the stratosphere are much less dense than in the troposphere as well.

The temperature within the lower stratosphere (up to about 25 km altitude) is mostly constant. In the upper stratosphere, the temperature rises gradually with increased altitude to a temperature of approximately 3°C. The rising temperatures are caused by the absorption of ultraviolet radiation from the sun by ozone molecules.

Ozone (O_3) molecules form the ozone layer at the upper ranges of the stratosphere. Ozone molecules absorb solar ultraviolet radiation, which is converted to kinetic energy (heat). This process accounts for the increased temperature levels as altitude increases within the stratosphere. The ozone layer also performs the crucial function of protecting organisms from the harmful effects of too much ultraviolet radiation.

The stratosphere is separated from the next atmospheric layer (the mesosphere) by the **stratopause**. The **mesosphere**, the atmospheric layer found at approximately 50 to 80 km altitude, is characterized by temperatures decreasing with increased altitude from about 3°C at the stratopause to −110°C at 80 km. The mesosphere has a low density of molecules with very little ozone or water vapor. The atmospheric gases of the upper mesosphere separate into layers of gases according to molecular mass.

This phenomenon is caused by the weakened effects of gravity on the gas molecules (because of distance from Earth). Lighter (low molecular mass) gases are found at the higher altitudes.

The **mesopause** separates the stratosphere from the next layer, the thermosphere. The **thermosphere** is found at altitudes of approximately 80 to 480 kilometers. Gas molecules of the thermosphere are widely separated, resulting in very low gas density. The absorption of solar radiation by oxygen molecules in the thermosphere causes the temperature to rise to approximately 1980°C at the upper levels of the thermosphere.

The final layer, the **exosphere**, extends from the **thermopause** at approximately 480 km to an altitude of 960 to 1000 kilometers. The exosphere, however, is difficult to define and is more of a transitional area between Earth and space than a distinct layer. The low gravitational forces at this altitude hold only the lightest molecules, mostly hydrogen and helium. Even these are at very low densities.

The troposphere and tropopause together are sometimes referred to as the *lower atmosphere*. The stratosphere and mesosphere are sometimes called the *middle atmosphere*, while the thermosphere and exosphere are together known as the *upper atmosphere*. Still other scientists call the troposphere, mesosphere, and stratosphere together as the *homosphere*, and the thermosphere and exosphere as the *heterosphere*.

The **ionosphere** includes portions of the mesosphere and thermosphere. The term *ionosphere* refers to the portion of the atmosphere where ultraviolet radiation causes excitation of atoms, resulting in extreme temperatures. Under extreme temperature conditions, electrons are actually separated from the atoms. The highly excited atoms are left with a positive charge. Charged atoms (ions) form layers within the thermosphere.

Solar flares create magnetic storms in the thermosphere near Earth's poles that temporarily strip electrons from atoms. When the electrons rejoin the atoms, brilliant light (in green and red) is emitted as they return to their normal state. These lights are called **auroras**, or the Northern and Southern lights.

The total weight of the atmosphere exerts a force on Earth known as **atmospheric pressure** that can be measured with a **barometer**.

EARTH'S LAYERS

The **geosphere**, Earth's solid or mineral part, consists of layers, from the outer crust down to the inner core separated according to density and temperature. There are two ways to classify the composition of the geosphere:

1. chemically, into crust, mantle, and core, or

2. functionally, into lithosphere and asthenosphere.

Crust, Mantle, and Core

Earth's density averages three times that of water. This density varies depending upon the layer of Earth being considered.

The **crust**, the outermost layer of the geosphere, is what we think of as "Earth." The crust is rich in oxygen, silicon, and aluminum, with lesser amounts of other elements like iron, nickel, and so on. It has low density (2.5 to 3.5 gm/cm^3), which allows it to float on the denser mantle. It is brittle, breaks relatively easily, and is made up mostly of sedimentary rocks resting on a base of igneous rocks. Several separate tectonic plates float beneath it on the surface of the mantle.

The **mantle**, the complex middle layer of the geosphere, is a broad layer of dense rock and metal oxides that lies between the molten core and the crust and extends to a depth of between 40 to 2,900 kilometers. It accounts for around 82% of Earth's volume and is thought to be made up mostly of iron, magnesium, silicon, and oxygen. Analysis of seismic waves shows that the material that makes up the mantle behaves as a plastic—a substance with the properties of a solid that flows under pressure. More precisely, the mantle consists of rigid and plastic zones.

The **core**, the innermost layer of the geosphere, is composed of mostly iron and nickel. It extends from a depth of about 2,900 kilometers to nearly 6,400 kilometers (1,800 to 3,900 miles). The core has two layers, the liquid **outer core**, and the solid iron **inner core** at Earth's center. Even with the high temperatures at the center (up to 7,500K, hotter than the sun's surface), this layer is solid due to the immense pressure of the overlying layers.

Another way to classify the layers is into the lithosphere and asthenosphere. The rigid outermost layer of the geosphere (from the Greek, *lithos*—stone) is called the **lithosphere**. The upper layer of the lithosphere is the crust. Beneath the crust is a layer of rigid mantle. The **asthenosphere** is the molten plastic outer mantle of hot silicate rock beneath the lithosphere (from the Greek, *asthenos*—devoid of force).

The Discontinuities

The **Mohorovicic** discontinuity or **Moho** is the sharp boundary between the crust and mantle. The **Gutenberg** discontinuity separates the mantle from the core.

The Hydrosphere

Earth is unique among planets in the solar system because of the large quantities of water that cover its surface. Two-thirds of the planet's surface are covered by water at an average ocean depth of 3.9 kilometers (12,795 feet). The water area is 3.6×10^8 square kilometers (nearly 140 million square miles).

The Magnetosphere

The magnetic field that surrounds Earth extends thousands of miles into outer space. The power of Earth's magnet is not very strong, being approximately 0.5 Gauss at Earth's surface.

The location of the North Magnetic Pole was determined in 1996 by a Canadian expedition and certified by magnetometer and theodolite at 78°35.7′N 104°11.9′W. In 2005, the location was at 82.7°N 114.4°W, slightly west of Ellesmere Island in Northern Canada. It is clear that the magnetic field moves over time.

The Geologic Column

Earth's estimated age is determined by radiometric dating and geological estimates to be about 4.6 billion years. The geologic column represents Earth's layers near the surface that contain fossils and various types of sediment. The geologic column is currently used as a tool of evolutionary uniformitarian scientists to display a "progression" of life from simple species in the deepest (oldest) layers to more complex species in the layers closer to the surface (younger). The layers are categorized into Eras, Periods, and Epochs.

Geologic Time Scale

Eon	Era	Period	Epoch	Age (my)
Phanerozoic (Visible Life)	Cenozoic *(Recent Life)* (Age of Mammals)	Quaternary	Holocene	0.01
			Pleistocene	1.6
		Tertiary	Pliocene	5.3
			Miocene	23.7
			Oligocene	36.6
			Eocene	57.8
			Paleocene	66.4
	Mesozoic *(Middle Life)* (Age of Reptiles)	Cretaceous		144
		Jurassic		208
		Triassiac		245
	Paleozoic *(Ancient Life)*	Permian		286
		Pennsylvanian		320
		Mississippian		360
		Devonian		408
		Silurian		438
		Ordovician		505
		Cambrian		570
Proterozoic (Early Life)	Oldest Known Life			2500
Archean	Oldest Known Rocks			3900
Hadean	Age of Earth			4600

CLEP Natural Sciences Practice Test 1

(Answer sheets appear in the back of this book.)

TIME: *90 Minutes*
120 Questions

DIRECTIONS: Each of the following groups of questions consists of five lettered terms followed by a list of numbered phrases or sentences. For each numbered phrase or sentence, select the one choice that is most clearly related to it. Each choice may be used once, more than once, or not at all.

Questions 1–5 _____

- (A) Mammalia
- (B) Amphibia
- (C) Reptilia
- (D) Aves
- (E) Chondrichthyes

____ 1. Cold-blooded animals with bony skeletons, webbed feet, and separate sexes

____ 2. Cold-blooded animals with horny scales and a bony skeleton that lay eggs

____ 3. Cartilaginous fish

____ 4. Warm-blooded animals, mostly with wings, that lay eggs

____ 5. Animals with a hairy body and highly developed brain that have live births (in most cases) and produce milk

Questions 6–10 _____

- (A) Secretory vesicle
- (B) Smooth endoplasmic reticulum
- (C) Microvilli
- (D) Nucleolus
- (E) Nuclear pore

____ 6. Communication channel between the cytoplasm and nucleoplasm

____ 7. Extensions that provide extra surface area for absorption

____ 8. Contain digestive enzymes

____ 9. Packets that carry substances (hormones, fats, etc.) synthesized within the cell

____ 10. Network of membranes that deliver lipids and proteins throughout the cytoplasm

Questions 11–13 _____

- (A) KCl
- (B) NaF
- (C) Cu
- (D) SiC
- (E) $HC_2H_3O_2$

____ 11. Atoms are held together with network covalent attraction.

____ 12. Atoms are held together with covalent attraction.

____ 13. Atoms are held together with metallic attraction.

Questions 14–18 _____

- (A) Nodes
- (B) Nonvascular plants
- (C) Angiosperms
- (D) Gymnosperms
- (E) Lateral buds

____ 14. Bryophytes

____ 15. Flowering plants

____ 16. Shoots and roots

____ 17. Produce seeds without flowers

____ 18. Conifers and cycads

Questions 19–21 _____

(A) Radiation
(B) Convection
(C) Irradiation
(D) Conduction
(E) Diffusion

_____ 19. An athlete with a sore shoulder places a warm compress on it to transfer energy to soothe the muscle.

_____ 20. On a cold February morning, a blower system in a car warms up after several minutes and blows air through vents in the floor, dashboard, and windshield. Eventually, the driver is able to unbutton his coat and stay warm when the outside temperature is still 23°F.

_____ 21. Getting ready for a fall cruise inspires a young lady to spend a couple of weeks going to a local spa and reclining under a tanning lamp. However, such practices might result in dangerous overexposure to ultraviolet rays that can lead to cancer or premature aging of the skin.

Questions 22–24 _____

(A) H_2
(B) $KMnO_4$
(C) MgO
(D) KCl
(E) Fe_2O_3

_____ 22. This substance is a very strong oxidizing agent.

_____ 23. The metal in this substance has an oxidation number of +2.

_____ 24. The oxidation potential of this substance is zero.

Questions 25–29 _____

(A) Natality
(B) J-curve
(C) Population rate of growth
(D) Mortality
(E) S-curve

_____ 25. Exponential population growth curve; population growth accelerates

_____ 26. Birth rate minus death rate

_____ 27. Death rate

_____ 28. Birth rate

_____ 29. Logistic population growth curve; population growth accelerates and then slows down because of limits

DIRECTIONS: Each of the following questions or incomplete statements is followed by five possible answers or completions. Select the best choice in each case and fill in the corresponding oval on the answer sheet.

30. The evolution of plant species is considered to have begun with

(A) autotrophic prokaryotic cells.
(B) heterotrophic eukaryotic cells.
(C) aerobic eukaryotic cells.
(D) pre-nucleic eukaryotic cells.
(E) aerobic prokaryotic cells.

31. What type of a wave is a sound wave?

(A) Compression
(B) Transverse
(C) Inverse
(D) Converse
(E) Convex

32. Salinity is a measure of dissolved solids in water. On average, 1,000 g of typical seawater contains 35 g of salt. The level of salinity is below average in areas where large amounts of fresh water enter the ocean and above average in hot, arid climates. The Mediterranean Sea and the Red Sea are adjacent to deserts. The water in these two seas would be expected to have

(A) above-average salinity.
(B) below-average salinity.
(C) average salinity.
(D) no salt content.
(E) cold temperatures.

33. According to the law of inertia, which of the following would offer the greatest resistance to a change in its motion?

    (A) A pellet of lead shot
    (B) A golf ball
    (C) A large watermelon
    (D) A feather
    (E) A sheet of notebook paper

34. The site of transfer for nutrients, water, and waste between a mammalian mother and embryo is the

    (A) yolk sac membrane.
    (B) uterus.
    (C) placenta.
    (D) umbilical membrane.
    (E) ovary.

35. The process of genetic inheritance was first investigated and explained by

    (A) Robert Hooke.
    (B) Dmitri Mendeleev.
    (C) Theodor Schwann.
    (D) Matthias Schleiden.
    (E) Gregor Mendel.

36. The first cells to evolve on Earth were most likely NOT

    (A) anaerobic.
    (B) specialized.
    (C) prokaryotic.
    (D) aquatic.
    (E) small.

37. Which of the following best represents the sequence of human evolution?

    (A) *Australopithecus afarensis*, Cro-Magnon, *Homo erectus*, *Homo sapiens*, Modern man
    (B) Cro-Magnon, *Australopithecus afarensis*, *Homo erectus*, *Homo sapiens*
    (C) *Homo sapiens*, *Australopithecus afarensis*, *Homo erectus*, Cro-Magnon
    (D) *Australopithecus afarensis*, *Homo erectus*, Cro-Magnon, Modern man
    (E) Cro-Magnon, *Homo erectus*, *Australopithecus afarensis*, Modern man

38. Which of the following demonstrates pi bonding?

    (A) OH^-
    (B) H^+
    (C) C_2H_2
    (D) H_2S
    (E) KCl

39. The sun crosses the celestial equator going north on March 21. This is known as the

    (A) solstice.
    (B) lunar eclipse.
    (C) solar eclipse.
    (D) spring equinox.
    (E) autumnal equinox.

40. Cells of eukaryotes have all of the following EXCEPT

    (A) membraned organelles.
    (B) DNA organized into chromosomes.
    (C) a nucleus.
    (D) DNA floating free in the cytoplasm.
    (E) ribosomes.

41. A small non-protein molecule such as iron that works with enzymes to promote catalysis is known as

    (A) a protein.
    (B) an inorganic cofactor.
    (C) a coenzyme.
    (D) a hormone.
    (E) a carbohydrate.

42. Which of the following will NOT inhibit enzymatic reactions?

    (A) Temperature
    (B) pH level
    (C) Particular chemical agents
    (D) Lack of substrate
    (E) Large amount of enzyme

For questions 43–46, identify the answer that corresponds with the correct functional group.

(A)
$$R - \underset{\underset{H}{|}}{\overset{\overset{H}{|}}{C}} - OH$$

(B)
$$R - \underset{\parallel}{\overset{}{C}} - H$$
$$O$$

with C double bonded to O

(C)
$$R - \underset{\parallel}{\overset{}{C}} - O - \underset{|}{\overset{H}{C}} - R$$
with first C double bonded to O and second C bonded to H

(D)
$$R - \underset{\parallel}{\overset{}{C}} - R$$
$$O$$

(E)
$$R - \underset{\parallel}{\overset{}{C}} - OH$$
$$O$$

____ 43. Ketone

____ 44. Alcohol

____ 45. Ester

____ 46. Aldehyde

47. The conversion of light energy into chemical energy is accomplished by

(A) catabolism.
(B) oxidative phosphorylation.
(C) metabolism.
(D) protein synthesis.
(E) photosynthesis.

48. Which of the following terms is defined as the increase in the statistical disorder of a physical system?

(A) Enthalpy
(B) Entropy
(C) Epathy
(D) Euprophy
(E) Empathy

49. Which of the following evolutionary developments is out of sequence?

(A) Formation of coacervates occurred in primordial seas.
(B) Development of eukaryotic cells took place.
(C) The process of photosynthesis was developed within single cells.
(D) Amphibians diversified into birds, then mammals.
(E) A branch of mammals developed into primates, the direct ancestors of man.

50. Energy flows through the food chain from

(A) producers to consumers to decomposers.
(B) producers to secondary consumers to primary consumers.
(C) decomposers to consumers to producers.
(D) secondary consumers to producers.
(E) consumers to producers.

51. If the moon completely covers the sun as seen by an earthbound observer, there is a

(A) total lunar eclipse.
(B) total solar eclipse.
(C) partial lunar eclipse.
(D) partial solar eclipse.
(E) parallax.

52. The projection of Earth's axis on the sky is the

(A) celestial equator.
(B) zenith.
(C) celestial poles.
(D) ecliptic.
(E) zodiac.

53. The process that releases energy for use by the cell is known as

 (A) photosynthesis.
 (B) aerobic metabolism.
 (C) anaerobic metabolism.
 (D) cellular respiration.
 (E) dark reaction.

54. Which of the following is NOT a step in the translation portion of protein synthesis?

 (A) tRNA anticodons line up with corresponding mRNA codons.
 (B) A ribosome attaches to the start codon on mRNA; ribosome adds tRNA whose anticodons complement the next codon on the mRNA string; and the process repeats to locate sequential amino acids.
 (C) Ribosomal enzymes also link the sequential amino acids into a protein chain.
 (D) As the protein chain is forming, rRNA moves along the sequence adding amino acids designated by codons on the mRNA.
 (E) Terminating codon stops the synthesis process and releases the newly formed protein.

55. Which of the following most closely represents the sequence leading to human evolution?

 (A) Coacervates, eukaryotes, plants, fish, amphibians, mammals, primates, man
 (B) Eukaryotes, plants, amphibians, fish, mammals, primates, man
 (C) Eukaryotes, coacervates, plants, fish, amphibians, mammals, primates, man
 (D) Coacervates, eukaryotes, plants, fish, amphibians, primates, mammals, man
 (E) Plants, eukaryotes, coacervates, fish, amphibians, mammals, primates, man

56. Water molecules are attracted to each other due to which of the following?

 (A) Polarity; partial positive charge near hydrogen atoms; partial negative charge near oxygen atoms
 (B) Inert properties of hydrogen and oxygen
 (C) Ionic bonds between hydrogen and oxygen
 (D) The crystal structure of ice
 (E) Brownian motion of hydrogen and oxygen atoms

57. The voltage across the terminal of a circuit containing a resistor is 12 V, and it contains a resistor connected to the circuit which reads 8 ohms. What is the amperage of the service?

 (A) 1.5 A
 (B) 48 A
 (C) 0.67 A
 (D) 15 A
 (E) 96 A

58. The percentage of Earth's surface that is water is

 (A) 10%.
 (B) 30%.
 (C) 50%.
 (D) 70%.
 (E) 90%.

59. Traits that are produced by the expression of more than one set of genes are known as

 (A) polygenic traits.
 (B) autosomal traits.
 (C) sex-limited traits.
 (D) monohybrid traits.
 (E) dihybrid crosses.

60. The major driving force of the evolution of species is known as

 (A) the Oparin Theory.
 (B) natural selection.
 (C) environmental determinism.
 (D) Hardy-Weinberg Equilibrium.
 (E) genetic drift.

61. Which of the following items found on a bicycle is NOT a simple machine?

(A) Tire
(B) Pedal mechanism
(C) Rear wheel gear mechanism
(D) Horn
(E) Kickstand

62. Which of the following sets of quantum numbers (listed in order of n, l, ml, ms) describe the highest energy valence electron of nitrogen in its ground state?

(A) 2, 0, 0, +½
(B) 2, 1, 1, −½
(C) 2, 1, 1, +½
(D) 2, 1, −1, −½
(E) 2, 1, −1, +½

63. The change of state from liquid to solid or solid to liquid involves a phase where the temperature remains constant. This phase is known as the

(A) transition phase.
(B) heat of fusion.
(C) heat of fission.
(D) specific heat.
(E) equilibrium.

64. Which of the following solid crystals has, on average, one atom per cubic unit cell?

(A) Face-centered
(B) Body-centered
(C) Rhombic
(D) All cubic crystals
(E) Simple cubic crystals only

65. Which of the following is part of the alimentary canal?

(A) Artery
(B) Sinus
(C) Vagus nerve
(D) Bronchus
(E) Esophagus

66. Which of the following experimental evidence was NOT considered supportive of the Oparin Hypothesis?

(A) Amino acids can be produced in the laboratory by exposing simple inorganic molecules to electrical charge.
(B) Guanine can be formed in the laboratory by thermal polymerization of amino acids.
(C) Ultraviolet light induces the formation of dipeptides from amino acids in laboratory experiments.
(D) In the laboratory, proteins are not useful as catalysts, indicating that early proteins were stable.
(E) Phosphoric acid increases the yield of polymers in the laboratory, simulating the role of ATP in protein synthesis.

Questions 67–71 _____

In snapdragons, a red flower crossed with a white flower produces a pink flower. In this illustration, R stands for red and W represents white. The Punnett square for a cross between a white snapdragon and a red snapdragon is shown here:

	R	R
W	RW	RW
W	RW	RW

67. The cross illustrated in this Punnett square is an example of

(A) a sex-linked trait.
(B) multiple alleles.
(C) incomplete dominance.
(D) a dihybrid cross.
(E) complete dominance.

68. The symbol *RW* represents which of the following?

(A) The allele for red
(B) The genotype for pink
(C) The phenotype for pink
(D) The allele for white
(E) The genotype for white

69. In this cross, both parents have genotypes that are

(A) heterozygous for color.
(B) homozygous for color.
(C) recessive for pink.
(D) dominant for pink.
(E) dominant for white.

70. Which of the following statements about this cross must be true?

(A) Both parents of the red snapdragon must have had the genotype *RR*.
(B) One of the parents of the red snapdragon must have had the genotype *RR*.
(C) Both parents of the red snapdragon must have been pink.
(D) Neither parent of the red snapdragon could be white.
(E) One parent of the red snapdragon could have been white.

71. If two of the heterozygous offspring (*RW*) of this cross are bred, what will be the ratio of phenotypes of the offspring?

(A) 0 red: 4 pink: 0 white
(B) 2 red: 2 pink: 0 white
(C) 1 red: 1 pink: 1 white
(D) 2 red: 0 pink: 2 white
(E) 1 red: 2 pink: 1 white

72. The physical place where a particular organism lives is called a

(A) niche.
(B) biosphere.
(C) lithosphere.
(D) habitat.
(E) ecosystem.

73. What is the most likely explanation for the fact that a sample of solid nickel is attracted into a magnetic field, but a sample of solid zinc chloride is not?

(A) There are unpaired outer electrons in nickel.
(B) There is some iron mixed in with the nickel.
(C) There are unpaired outer electrons in zinc.
(D) The presence of chlorine keeps zinc from being attracted to the magnet.
(E) Nickel does not produce a magnetic field to oppose the one that is attracting it.

74. The specific heat of water is 4.2 J/g°C. What mass of water will be heated by 10°C by 840 J?

(A) 0.5 g
(B) 10 g
(C) 20 g
(D) 4.2 g
(E) 840 g

75. A light-year represents the

(A) total amount of light energy that travels past a point on Earth in one year.
(B) total distance that an object travels in space at the speed of light in one year.
(C) total amount of time that a photon of light travels in order to reach a star, planet, or other extraterrestrial object.
(D) speed at which light travels in one year.
(E) speed of a photon in a vacuum when it collides with an x-ray.

76. The half-life of C-14 is 5,730 years. A piece of cypress is measured to have ¾ of the carbon to be C-12 and ¼ C-14. How many years old is this piece of wood likely to be?

(A) 5,730
(B) 2,865
(C) 4,297
(D) 11,460
(E) 1,435

77. Igneous rock forms are commonly called

    (A) marble.
    (B) limestone.
    (C) cement.
    (D) granite.
    (E) sandstone.

78. Which of the following statements is true?

    (A) Despite the contraction of space, galaxies appear to be static relative to each other when observed.
    (B) The expansion of space makes galaxies appear to be moving apart, causing the color of their spectral lines to shift when observed.
    (C) Galaxies themselves are moving apart from each other.
    (D) Hubble's law states that the redshift in light coming from a distant galaxy is inversely proportional to its distance from Earth.
    (E) The actual motion of galaxies is questionable due to variations in Hubble's constant.

79. All of the following are major structural regions of roots EXCEPT the

    (A) meristematic region.
    (B) elongation region.
    (C) root cap.
    (D) epistematic region.
    (E) maturation region.

80. When a yellow pea plant is crossed with a green pea plant, all the offspring are yellow. The law that best explains this is the law of

    (A) intolerance.
    (B) dominance.
    (C) interference.
    (D) relative genes.
    (E) codominance.

81. Which of the following statements is true about electrons?

    (A) Electrons have a positive charge.
    (B) Electrons have less mass than protons and neutrons.
    (C) Electrons are found within the nucleus of atoms.
    (D) The number of electrons is equal to the number of protons in an ion.
    (E) An atom's valence number is the number of electrons in its lowest energy level.

82. What is the energy-generating mechanism of the stars, including the sun?

    (A) Fission
    (B) Fusion
    (C) Spontaneous generation
    (D) Combustion
    (E) Stellar explosion

83. When measuring the flow of heat in a system, a natural process that starts at one equilibrium state and flows to another will go in what direction for an irreversible process which is impacted by the entropy of the system plus the environment?

    (A) Increase
    (B) Decrease
    (C) Remain static
    (D) Fluctuate between increases and decreases in a constant pattern
    (E) Increase steadily and then drop off, similar to the conservation of momentum in a closed system

84. What is the resistance of an electric can opener if it takes a current of 10 A when plugged into a 120 V service?

    (A) 1,200 ohms
    (B) 0.083 ohms
    (C) 130 ohms
    (D) 12 ohms
    (E) 1.2 ohms

85. Photosynthesis would NOT proceed without which of the following that allow moisture and gases to pass in and out of the leaf?

    (A) Surface hairs
    (B) Stomata
    (C) Cuticles
    (D) Epidermal cells
    (E) Cilia

86. In ferns, the individual we generally recognize as an adult fern is really which structure?

    (A) A mature gametophyte
    (B) A prothallus
    (C) A mature sporophyte
    (D) A young sporophyte
    (E) A young gametophyte

87. Which of the following is the least polar molecule?

    (A) H_2
    (B) H_2O
    (C) H_2S
    (D) C_2H_2
    (E) NaH

88. Which state of matter does NOT have a definite shape or a definite volume?

    (A) Solid
    (B) Liquid
    (C) Gas
    (D) Plasma
    (E) Both (C) and (D)

89. A person who has been exercising vigorously begins to sweat and breathe quickly. These reactions are involuntary responses known as

    (A) fight-or-flight responses.
    (B) homeostatic mechanisms.
    (C) equilibrium responses.
    (D) stimulus receptors.
    (E) hormone reactions.

90. The nervous system is an integrated circuit with many functions. Which of the following parts of the nervous system are matched with the wrong function?

    (A) Forebrain—controls olfactory lobes (smell)
    (B) Cerebrum—controls the function of involuntary muscles
    (C) Hypothalamus—controls hunger and thirst
    (D) Cerebellum—controls balance and muscle coordination
    (E) Midbrain—contains optic lobes and controls sight

91. Fog is

    (A) the same as smog.
    (B) caused when cold air moves over warm air.
    (C) a collection of minute water droplets.
    (D) associated with a tornado.
    (E) Both (C) and (D).

92. Land and sea (or lake) breezes form because of

    (A) uneven heating of coastal environments.
    (B) the pressure gradient force.
    (C) the difference in temperature between land and water surfaces.
    (D) solar radiation.
    (E) a variety of factors involving temperature, pressure, and geographical components.

93. An electric shock can restart a heart that has stopped beating. Which of the following statements is a valid reason for this fact?

    (A) Electric shock stimulates the nervous system.
    (B) Smooth muscle is affected by electric shock.
    (C) The electric shock pushes blood through the stopped heart.
    (D) Cardiac muscle of the heart responds to the electric shock.
    (E) Electric shock causes air to enter the lungs.

94. When a hamburger is consumed by an individual, it passes through all of the following organs EXCEPT the

    (A) mouth.
    (B) esophagus.
    (C) salivary glands.
    (D) stomach.
    (E) small intestine.

95. Each ecosystem can support a certain number of organisms—a number usually designated by the letter K and known as

    (A) ecodensity.
    (B) population.
    (C) carrying capacity.
    (D) a community.
    (E) the biosphere.

96. Which of the following parts of an atom is NOT a subatomic particle?

    (A) A quark
    (B) A boson
    (C) A neutrino
    (D) An electron
    (E) A positron

97. The function of the gallbladder and pancreas is to aid digestion by producing digestive enzymes and secreting them into the

    (A) small intestine.
    (B) large intestine.
    (C) stomach.
    (D) esophagus.
    (E) mouth.

98. Many insects have special respiratory organs known as

    (A) spiracles.
    (B) alveoli.
    (C) cephalothorax.
    (D) lungs.
    (E) gills.

99. Most of Earth's photosynthesis takes place in which one of the following biomes?

    (A) Oceans
    (B) Tundra
    (C) Deciduous forests
    (D) Deserts
    (E) Tropical rain forests

100. Which of the following chemical equations represents a replacement reaction?

    (A) $A + C \rightarrow AC + B$
    (B) $A + B \rightarrow AB$
    (C) $AB + C \rightarrow AC + B$
    (D) $AB \rightarrow A + B$
    (E) $AB + CD \rightarrow A + B + C + D$

101. The study of the interaction of organisms with their living space is known as

    (A) environmentalism.
    (B) habitology.
    (C) zoology.
    (D) ecology.
    (E) paleontology.

102. What is the name of a distinct group of individuals that are able to mate and produce viable offspring?

    (A) A class
    (B) A community
    (C) A phylum
    (D) A family
    (E) A species

103. Which of the following is true concerning Einstein's theory of relativity?

    (A) As energy increases, the speed of light increases and mass is constant.
    (B) As energy increases, mass increases and the speed of light is constant.
    (C) As energy increases, the speed of light decreases and mass is constant.
    (D) As energy increases, mass decreases and the speed of light is constant.
    (E) As energy increases, the speed of light and mass will increase.

104. Which of the following is an autotroph?

(A) *E. coli* bacteria
(B) A Portuguese man-of-war
(C) A portobello mushroom
(D) An asparagus fern
(E) A perch

105. The Michelson-Morley experiment in 1887 proved that the speed of light

(A) is the same in all directions.
(B) can slow down in a vacuum.
(C) is slower in air than in liquid.
(D) is different on the moon.
(E) continuously speeds up in a vacuum.

106. Which of the following is NOT a fundamental geological principle?

(A) The principle of original horizontality
(B) The principle of supererogation
(C) The principle of lateral continuity
(D) The principle of fossil succession
(E) The principle of uniformitarianism

107. Astronomers observing the redshift of light from a faraway star means that the star is

(A) moving away from us.
(B) moving toward us.
(C) ready to explode.
(D) a dwarf star.
(E) a giant nova.

108. The three most recent geological eras are

(A) Paleozoic, Proterozoic, Archean.
(B) Mesozoic, Paleozoic, Cenozoic.
(C) Cenozoic, Mesozoic, Paleozoic.
(D) Cenozoic, Archean, Paleozoic.
(E) Recent, Tertiary, Quaternary.

109. A form of symbiosis in which one species is benefited while the other is harmed is called

(A) parasitism.
(B) mutualism.
(C) amensalism.
(D) altruism.
(E) commensalism.

110. An axis is

(A) a connecting line at the equator.
(B) a connecting line between the poles.
(C) a connecting line between orbits.
(D) a pole.
(E) a connecting line at the tropical zones.

111. In order of magnitude, how many galaxies are there in the universe?

(A) Hundreds
(B) Thousands
(C) Millions
(D) Billions
(E) Trillions

112. An astronaut is traveling in a spacecraft that is slowing down. To the astronaut inside the spacecraft, the apparent force inside the craft is directed

(A) backward.
(B) forward.
(C) sideways.
(D) vertically only.
(E) nowhere because there is no force.

113. The cells of which of the following organisms are most likely to be prokaryotic?

(A) Mold
(B) Seaweed
(C) Blue-green algae
(D) Fern
(E) Hydra

114. The name for the imaginary object that centers on and surrounds Earth by which background stars are projected is called a(an)

(A) geodesic dome.
(B) celestial sphere.
(C) stellar ball.
(D) Cartesian coordinate system.
(E) equatorial coordinate system.

115. Why is stratospheric ozone depletion (destruction of the ozone layer) a serious concern?

    (A) It is a major cause of the "greenhouse effect."
    (B) It will increase the amount of ultraviolet radiation reaching the ground.
    (C) It causes acid rain.
    (D) It is really nothing to worry about.
    (E) It leads to global warming as more radiation enters through the hole in the atmosphere.

116. Mountain and valley breezes form because of

    (A) gravity and the pressure gradient force.
    (B) the pressure gradient force and heating.
    (C) gravity and heating.
    (D) the pressure gradient force and the Coriolis force.
    (E) high pressure forming near the top of the mountain due to warm air expansion forcing air up the mountain from the valley below.

117. As you go down the periodic table and to the left, which of the following traits increases?

    (A) Atomic radius
    (B) Electronegativity
    (C) Electron affinity
    (D) Ionization energy
    (E) Acidity of the oxides

118. According to Newton's laws of motion, the greater the mass of an object, the greater the force necessary to change its

    (A) position.
    (B) force.
    (C) state of motion.
    (D) shape.
    (E) density.

119. The top or peak of a sine wave is called the

    (A) crest.
    (B) trough.
    (C) amplitude.
    (D) period.
    (E) frequency.

120. A wave does not carry along the medium through which it travels. Thus, it follows that

    (A) molecules of water in the ocean are pushed to shore by waves.
    (B) the ocean's water molecules are thoroughly mixed each day by waves.
    (C) debris in the ocean is washed ashore by waves.
    (D) individual water molecules do not travel toward shore, but wave peaks do.
    (E) waves move water, not swimmers.

CLEP Natural Sciences Practice Test 1

Answer Key

1.	(B)	31.	(A)	61.	(D)	91.	(C)
2.	(C)	32.	(A)	62.	(C)	92.	(E)
3.	(E)	33.	(C)	63.	(B)	93.	(D)
4.	(D)	34.	(C)	64.	(E)	94.	(C)
5.	(A)	35.	(E)	65.	(E)	95.	(C)
6.	(E)	36.	(B)	66.	(D)	96.	(D)
7.	(C)	37.	(D)	67.	(C)	97.	(A)
8.	(C)	38.	(C)	68.	(B)	98.	(A)
9.	(A)	39.	(D)	69.	(B)	99.	(A)
10.	(B)	40.	(D)	70.	(D)	100.	(C)
11.	(D)	41.	(B)	71.	(E)	101.	(D)
12.	(E)	42.	(E)	72.	(D)	102.	(E)
13.	(C)	43.	(D)	73.	(A)	103.	(B)
14.	(B)	44.	(A)	74.	(C)	104.	(D)
15.	(C)	45.	(C)	75.	(D)	105.	(A)
16.	(C)	46.	(B)	76.	(D)	106.	(B)
17.	(D)	47.	(E)	77.	(D)	107.	(A)
18.	(D)	48.	(B)	78.	(B)	108.	(C)
19.	(D)	49.	(C)	79.	(D)	109.	(A)
20.	(B)	50.	(A)	80.	(B)	110.	(B)
21.	(A)	51.	(B)	81.	(B)	111.	(D)
22.	(B)	52.	(C)	82.	(B)	112.	(B)
23.	(C)	53.	(D)	83.	(A)	113.	(C)
24.	(A)	54.	(A)	84.	(D)	114.	(B)
25.	(B)	55.	(A)	85.	(B)	115.	(B)
26.	(C)	56.	(A)	86.	(C)	116.	(C)
27.	(D)	57.	(A)	87.	(A)	117.	(A)
28.	(A)	58.	(D)	88.	(E)	118.	(C)
29.	(E)	59.	(A)	89.	(B)	119.	(A)
30.	(E)	60.	(B)	90.	(B)	120.	(D)

DETAILED EXPLANATIONS OF ANSWERS PRACTICE TEST 1

1. **(B)** Amphibia include cold-blooded (ecothermic) animals with a bony skeleton that usually have four limbs with webbed feet and four toes, a large mouth and small teeth, a three-chambered heart, separate sexes, and fertilize eggs internally or externally (salamanders, frogs, etc.).

2. **(C)** Reptilia have horny epidermal scales, usually with paired limbs that have five toes. They have a bony skeleton and lungs (no gills). Most have a three-chambered heart. They are cold-blooded (ecothermic), have separate sexes, fertilize internally, and lay eggs (snakes, lizards, alligators).

3. **(E)** Chondrichthyes are fish with a cartilaginous endoskeleton, a two-chambered heart, between five and seven gill pairs, no swim bladder or lung, and internal fertilization (sharks, rays, etc.).

4. **(D)** Aves includes warm-blooded (endothermic) birds having a spindle-shaped body (with head, neck, trunk, and tail), a long neck, paired limbs, wings for flying, a four-toed foot, feathers, leg scales, a bony skeleton, bones with air cavities, a beak, no teeth, and a well-developed nervous system. Aves also have a four-chambered heart, lungs with thin air sacs, separate sexes, and lay eggs with a hard calcified shell (birds—ducks, sparrows, etc.).

5. **(A)** Mammalia includes warm-blooded animals with hairy bodies, glands (sweat, scent, sebaceous, mammary), teeth, eyelids, four limbs (usually), external fleshy ears, a four-chambered heart, lungs, a larynx, and a highly developed brain. They fertilize internally, give birth to live young (except monotremes), and produce milk (cows, humans, platypus, apes, etc.).

6. **(E)** Nuclear pores are holes in the nuclear membrane where the double nuclear membrane fuses together, forming a break or hole, allowing the selective intake and excretion of molecules to or from the nucleus. Thus, nuclear pores are the channel of communication between the cytoplasm and the nucleoplasm.

7. **(C)** Microvilli are filaments that extend from the cell membrane, particularly in cells that are involved in absorption (such as in the intestine). These filaments increase the surface area of the cell membrane, thus increasing the area available to absorb nutrients.

8. **(C)** Microvilli also contain enzymes that are involved in digesting certain types of nutrients.

9. **(A)** Secretory vesicles are packets of material packaged by either the Golgi apparatus or the endoplasmic reticulum. The secretory vesicle carries the substance produced within the cell to the cell membrane. The vesicle membrane fuses with the cell membrane, allowing the substance to escape the cell.

10. **(B)** Smooth endoplasmic reticulum is a network of continuous membranous channels that connect the cell membrane with the nuclear membrane and is responsible for the delivery of lipids and proteins to certain areas within the cytoplasm. Smooth endoplasmic reticulum lacks attached ribosomes.

11. **(D)**   Silicon carbide (SiC) is held together with network covalent bonds, which creates a crystal entirely from covalent bonds and confers unusual strength (and a high melting point) upon the crystal.

12. **(E)**   Acetic acid is a molecular compound that is held together with covalent bonds, in which electrons are shared between atoms, so that both atoms in the bond end up having a full octet of electrons.

13. **(C)**   As a metal, copper is held together by metallic bonds, which involve delocalized d-orbital electrons.

14. **(B)**   Nonvascular plants are known as bryophytes (mosses). They lack tissue that will conduct water or food.

15. **(C)**   Angiosperms are those plants that produce flowers as reproductive organs.

16. **(C)**   Angiosperms (flowering plants) have two main systems—the shoot system, which is mainly above ground, and the root system below ground.

17. **(D)**   Gymnosperms produce seeds without flowers.

18. **(D)**   Gymnosperms produce seeds without flowers, which include conifers (cone-bearers) and cycads.

19. **(D)**   Conduction is the transfer of molecules by collisions, passing heat through one material into another.

20. **(B)**   Convection is caused by the flow of heated liquid or gas through a volumetric medium.

21. **(A)**   Radiation is waves traveling through space to transfer heat away from the energy source.

22. **(B)**   The manganese ion in potassium permanganate has a $+5$ oxidation state, and is therefore readily reduced. When it is reduced, it forces another species to be oxidized. Therefore, the permanganate ion is a very strong oxidizing agent.

23. **(C)**   The magnesium atom that is combined with oxygen has a $+2$ oxidation state. Oxygen carries a -2 oxidation state, and the sum of the oxidation states of oxygen and magnesium must total the charge on the compound, which is 0.

24. **(A)**   Hydrogen gas by definition, since it is a standard, has an oxidation potential of 0.

25. **(B)**   One of the modes of population growth is represented by the exponential curve (or J-curve). The rate of growth accelerates over time since there are no limiters of growth.

26. **(C)**   The rate of increase within a population is represented by the birth rate minus the death rate.

27. **(D)**   Mortality is the death rate within a population.

28. **(A)**   Natality is the birth rate within a population.

29. **(E)**   Another mode of population growth is represented by the logistic curve (or S-curve) for populations that encounter limiting factors in which acceleration occurs up to a point and then slows down.

30. **(E)**　The evolution of plant species is considered to have begun with aerobic prokaryotic cells.

31. **(A)**　A sound wave is a compression or longitudinal wave, which means that it compresses and rarefies as it moves through a medium. Transverse waves oscillate up and down as they move through a medium. The other three terms are not commonly used to label sound waves.

32. **(A)**　The desert areas increase evaporation of the water that is present, causing a concentration of salts.

33. **(C)**　The property of an object that determines the object's resistance to motion is its mass. A large watermelon has a far greater mass than the pellet of lead shot, the golf ball, the feather, or the sheet of notebook paper.

34. **(C)**　The placenta is the connection between the mother and embryo; it is the site of transfer for nutrients, water, and waste between them.

35. **(E)**　Gregor Mendel studied the relationships between traits expressed in parents and offspring, and the genes that caused the traits to be expressed.

36. **(B)**　The first cells to evolve were most likely unspecialized. Since Earth's atmosphere was most likely lacking in oxygen, it is presumed that pre-plant cells were also anaerobic. Early cells were also small, aquatic, and prokaryotic.

37. **(D)**　The earliest known hominid fossils were found in Africa in the 1970s. The well-known "Lucy" skeleton was named *Australopithecus afarensis*. The fossilized skull of *Homo erectus*, the oldest known fossil of the human genus, is thought to be about 1.8 million years old. A third fossil, the oldest to be designated *Homo sapiens,* is also called Cro-Magnon man, with a brain size and facial features comparable to modern men. Cro-Magnon *Homo sapiens* are thought to have evolved in Africa and migrated to Europe and Asia approximately 100,000 years ago.

38. **(C)**　Acetylene shows a triple bond between the two carbons, which contains two pi bonds. In multiple bonds, the first bond is a sigma bond, in which electrons are shared along the internuclear axis. Any additional bonding is created by the sideways overlap of unhybridized p-orbitals above and below the internuclear axis. None of the other options for answers contain multiple covalent bonds between any two atoms.

39. **(D)**　Equinoxes are described as the two points on the celestial sphere where the ecliptic crosses the celestial equator. Since the crossing occurs on March 21 in this question, it is the spring equinox. Solstices occur in the summer and winter, and correspond to the ecliptic being farthest from the celestial equator. In general, when this crossing occurs on March 21, the moon is not necessarily aligned with Earth and the sun, so the odds of an eclipse occurring are very low. The autumnal equinox occurs at the other end of the celestial sphere on September 22.

40. **(D)**　The DNA of eukaryotes is organized into chromosomes within the nucleus.

41. **(B)**　Inorganic cofactors are small non-protein molecules that promote proper enzyme catalysis. These molecules may bind to the active site or to the substrate itself. The most common inorganic cofactors are metallic atoms such as iron, copper, and zinc.

42. **(E)** Environmental conditions such as heat or acidity inhibit enzymatic reactions by changing the shape of the active site and rendering the enzyme ineffective. Certain chemicals inhibit enzymatic reactions by changing the shape of the enzyme's active site. If there is a lack of substrate, the enzyme will have no substance to affect. Thus, a large amount of enzyme is the only factor that will not inhibit enzymatic reactions.

43. **(D)** A ketone group has a double bond between oxygen and a carbon atom that is imbedded within a carbon chain.

44. **(A)** An alcohol group has a hydroxide group (OH) with the second bond from oxygen going to a carbon atom.

45. **(C)** An ester group is an ether with an additional double bond to an oxygen from an adjacent carbon.

46. **(B)** An aldehyde group has a double bond between an oxygen atom and a carbon that is one end of a carbon chain, or not otherwise bonded to any other carbons.

47. **(E)** The process of photosynthesis is the crucial reaction that converts the sun's light energy into chemical energy that is usable by living things.

48. **(B)** Entropy is defined as the new state variable that describes the increase of disorder in a system. Stated positively, it describes the amount of increase in the statistical disorder of a physical system.

49. **(C)** The development of photosynthetic cells took place before the development of eukaryotes. The first photosynthetic cells were prokaryotic.

50. **(A)** Energy flows through the entire ecosystem in one direction—from producers to consumers and on to decomposers through the food chain.

51. **(B)** The eclipse must be a solar eclipse because the moon is between Earth and the sun. The solar eclipse is total because the moon's disk covers the sun from our view completely. Parallax has to do with the apparent displacement of a celestial object.

52. **(C)** The celestial poles are extensions of Earth's north and south geographic poles up into the sky. The celestial equator identifies the projection of Earth's equator. The zenith is the point directly overhead above an observer. The ecliptic is the line that describes the sun's orbit across the celestial sphere. The zodiac is the name for the annual cycle of 12 stations along the ecliptic that the sun and planets travel along the celestial sphere.

53. **(D)** Cellular respiration is the process that releases energy for use by the cell. There are several steps involved in cellular respiration; some require oxygen (aerobic) and some do not (anaerobic).

54. **(A)** When tRNA anticodons line up with corresponding mRNA codons, it is the last step in the transcription process before translation begins. Translation begins as a ribosome attaches to the mRNA strand at a particular codon known as the start codon. This codon is only recognized by a particular initiator tRNA. The ribosome continues to add tRNA whose anticodons complement

the next codon on the mRNA string. A third type of RNA is utilized at this point, ribosomal RNA or rRNA. Ribosomal RNA exists in concert with enzymes as a ribosome. In order for the tRNA and mRNA to link up, enzymes connected to rRNA at the ribosome must be utilized. Ribosomal enzymes also are responsible for linking the sequential amino acids into a protein chain. As the protein chain is forming, the rRNA moves along the sequence, adding the amino acids that are designated by the codons on the mRNA. At the end of the translation process, a terminating codon stops the synthesis process, and the protein is released.

55. **(A)** The most likely sequence leading to human evolution begins with coacervates, then eukaryotes, plants, fish, amphibians, mammals, primates, and, finally, man.

56. **(A)** The hydrogen atoms in water molecules have a partial positive charge, while the oxygen atoms in water have a partial negative charge, causing polarity. This polarity allows the oxygen of one water molecule to attract the hydrogen of another. The partial charges attract other opposite partial charges of other water molecules allowing for weak (hydrogen) bonds between the molecules. Inert means non-reactive; it does not explain the attraction between H and O. There are no ionic bonds within water molecules, only covalent bonds. A crystal structure forms in ice because of the attraction of hydrogen bonds; the crystal structure does not cause the attraction. Brownian motion is the random movement of atoms or particles caused by collisions between them; it does not explain attraction between atoms or molecules.

57. **(A)** Using Ohm's law, $V = IR$, we solve for $I = V/R$ with $V = 12$ V and $R = 8$ ohms. $I = 12.0$ V$/8.0$ ohms $= 1.5$ V/ohm $= 1.5$ A. The other answers are results of erroneous calculations or misapplications of Ohm's law.

58. **(D)** Earth is approximately 70% water. Most of the water is in the oceans. Land makes up the remaining 30%.

59. **(A)** Traits, such as height and skin color, are produced from the expression of more than one set of genes and are known as polygenic traits.

60. **(B)** Evolution is driven by the process of natural selection, a feature of population genetics first popularized by Charles Darwin in his book *The Origin of Species* (published in 1859).

61. **(D)** The horn is not a simple machine. Simple machines are mechanical devices that alter the magnitude and direction of a force. They are represented by the following six objects: (1) lever, (2) wheel and axle, (3) pulley, (4) inclined plane, (5) pulley, and (6) screw. On a bike, the tire is a type of wheel. The pedal mechanism is a wheel and axle as well as a gear mechanism (two simple machines). The rear wheel gear mechanism is obviously one of the simple machines. The kickstand is a lever.

62. **(C)** Since nitrogen is in the second row, its highest energy electron is at n = 2, which is the first number. The second number signifies that its outer electron is in a p-orbital. The third number indicates the third p-orbital to receive an electron, since nitrogen is the third element in the p-block in the periodic table. The last number is the magnetic spin quantum number and signifies that the highest energy electron is the only electron in the orbital.

63. **(B)** Although there is a transition from one state of matter to another, there is no term *transition phase* to describe this process. The term *fission* is used in nuclear physics to describe the breaking apart of nuclear particles. It is not used to describe changes of state of matter. Specific heat is the amount of energy in calories required to raise one gram of a substance by 1°C. Equilibrium is the state of a system or body at rest or lacking acceleration which results when all the forces acting upon it are equal to zero and the sum of all of the torques equals zero. In chemistry, it is the state of a reaction when all the products and reactants are balanced.

64. **(E)** A simple cubic crystal is the only unit cell mentioned that has, on average, one atom per unit cell. A simple cubic unit cell has one atom in each of the eight corners of the unit cell, but only one-eighth of each of those atoms is ascribed to that particular unit cell. A face-centered unit cell has four atoms per unit cell, while a body-centered unit cell has two atoms per unit cell.

65. **(E)** The alimentary canal is also known as the gastrointestinal (GI) tract and includes the mouth, pharynx, esophagus, stomach, small intestine, and large intestine.

66. **(D)** Proteins are catalysts in the laboratory, so the formation of proteins in the laboratory under conditions presumed to be representative of early Earth history is key evidence of the evolution of life on Earth. Stanley Miller provided support for the Oparin Hypothesis in experiments in which he succeeded in producing amino acids by exposing simple inorganic molecules to electrical charges similar to lightning. Sidney Fox conducted experiments that proved ultraviolet light may induce the formation of dipeptides from amino acids. He also showed that polyphosphoric acid could increase the yield of these polymers, a process that simulates the modern role of ATP in protein synthesis. Researcher Cyril Ponnamperuma demonstrated that small amounts of guanine formed from the thermal polymerization of amino acids.

67. **(C)** This is known as incomplete dominance. Neither white nor red is dominant over the other.

68. **(B)** *RW* is a symbol for genotype. In this case, the *RW* genotype produces a pink phenotype. *R* and *W* represent the alleles for red and white, respectively.

69. **(B)** Both parents have two alleles that are the same; thus, they have homozygous genotypes for color.

70. **(D)** While (A), (B), and (C) could have been true, a red snapdragon could have been produced by any of those choices. However, a white snapdragon cannot produce a red snapdragon as an offspring even if paired with a red snapdragon.

71. **(E)** If two of the heterozygous offspring of an incomplete dominant trait are bred, the Punnett square would be

	R	*W*
R	*RR*	*RW*
W	*RW*	*WW*

The phenotypic ratio of the offspring then is one-fourth red, one-half pink, and one-fourth white, a 1:2:1 ratio—1 red: 2 pink: 1 white.

72. **(D)** A habitat refers to the physical place where an organism lives. A species' habitat must include all the factors that will support its life and reproduction.

73. **(A)** Nickel has an unpaired electron in its d-orbital, which induces a magnetic field and causes it to be attracted to another magnetic field. Zinc chloride does not have such an unpaired electron and is not attracted to a magnet.

74. **(C)** The heat absorbed by the water equals the mass of the water multiplied by the specific heat of water times the increase in temperature change. The 840 J added to the water is enough heat to raise the temperature of 20 g of water by 10°C.

75. **(B)** A light-year is a distance, not a speed or velocity. It is also not a time measurement. A light-year represents the measurement of the distance to one celestial body from another celestial body, measured as a multiple or fraction of the distance light travels in one year. It is equal to 9.5 trillion kilometers.

76. **(D)** Since the half-life of C-14 is 5,730 years, that means it takes 5,730 years for half the C-14 to decay to C-12. Since the end sample has ¼ C-12, we see that two half-life periods would have occurred. The first would have decayed the sample to half of each type, and the second time period would degrade the half sample to a quarter sample. Two half-life periods is a total of 11,460 years.

77. **(D)** An example of igneous rock is granite. Marble is a metamorphic rock, while limestone, cement, and sandstone are all sedimentary rocks.

78. **(B)** Although it appears that galaxies are moving apart, Hubble's law explains that this apparent motion is the expansion of the space between them, not the motion of the galaxies themselves. Hubble's law states that the redshift in light coming from a distant galaxy is directly and linearly proportional to its distance from Earth.

79. **(D)** There is no epistematic region in plant roots. Roots have four major structural regions that run vertically from bottom to top. The root cap is composed of dead, thick-walled cells and covers the tip of the root, protecting it as the root pushes through soil. The meristematic region is just above the root cap. It consists of undifferentiated cells that undergo mitosis, providing the cells that grow to form the elongation region. In the elongation region, cells differentiate, large vacuoles are formed, and cells grow. As the cells differentiate into various root tissues, they become part of the maturation region.

80. **(B)** Gregor Mendel determined that one gene is sometimes dominant over another gene for the same trait (i.e., it expressed itself over the other). This is known as the law of dominance, Mendel's second law of inheritance.

81. **(B)** Electrons have very small mass, much less than either protons or neutrons. They are found orbiting in a cloud surrounding the nucleus. Electrons are negatively charged. An ion is an atom with a greater or fewer number of electrons than the standard atom for the element, causing a

charge of positive or negative due to the unequal number of protons and electrons. An atom's valence number is the number of electrons in its highest (not lowest) energy level.

82. **(B)** Shortly after the big bang, the universe was as hot and dense as the core of a star undergoing nuclear fusion. However, it wasn't until 300,000 years later that the nuclei could hold on to the electrons, clearing the vast fog. The process then continued to cool, coalesce, and expand through fusion, forming stars and galaxies in the visible universe. Fission does not occur until much later in stellar evolution. Spontaneous generation, disproven by Pasteur, has nothing to do with the evolution of stars. Combustion is common in various exothermic processes in a general way. Stellar explosions indicative of the latter stages of stellar evolution generally occur toward the end of a star's life, not at the origination.

83. **(A)** The answer is that entropy increases as a natural process goes from one equilibrium state to another. This is the only direction that heat flow will go in an irreversible process.

84. **(D)** Using Ohm's law, $V = IR$, solve for $R = V/I$ with $V = 120$ V and $I = 10$ A. $R = 120$ V$/10$ A $= 12$ V/A or 12 ohms. All of the other answers are results of erroneous calculations or misapplications of Ohm's law.

85. **(B)** Stomata are openings in the leaf surface that allow for exchange of water and gases.

86. **(C)** The individual we recognize as an adult fern is actually the mature sporophyte.

87. **(A)** Hydrogen gas is the least polar because it is bonded to itself as a diatomic molecule. Therefore, there is no difference in electronegativity between the two atoms in the bond, and it is entirely nonpolar.

88. **(E)** Both a gas and plasma have no defined shape or volume. A solid has a definite shape and volume. A liquid holds the shape of its container and thus has a definite volume. A plastic is not a state of matter and is confused with the fourth state of matter, plasma.

89. **(B)** Conditions such as temperature, pH, water balance, and sugar levels must be monitored and controlled in order to keep them within the accepted ranges that will not inhibit life. Cells and living organisms have homeostatic mechanisms that serve to keep body conditions within normal ranges.

90. **(B)** The cerebrum controls sensory and motor responses, memory, speech, and intelligence factors. It does not control involuntary muscles.

91. **(C)** Fog consists of a visible collection of minute water droplets suspended in the atmosphere near Earth's surface. It occurs when atmospheric humidity combines with a warm layer of air that is transported over a cold body of water or land surface.

92. **(E)** Due to the high specific heat capacity of water, land surfaces will heat up more rapidly than water surfaces. Since warmer air is less dense than cooler air, this uneven heating along coastal areas causes vertical expansion of the isobaric field over the land and compression of the field over the water. This forms an elevated area of high pressure over the land and an elevated area of low pressure over the water. The pressure gradient force acts on the air and moves it from higher pressure to lower pressure. The net movement of air toward the low pressure aloft induces

an area of high pressure on the water surface, while the net movement of air away from the high pressure aloft induces an area of low pressure on the land surface. The pressure gradient force now begins to move the surface air from the higher pressure on the water surface toward the lower pressure on the land surface. It is this surface flow of air that is the sea (or lake) breeze. The greater the contrast is between water temperature and land temperature, the stronger the breeze. At night, the land will cool faster than the adjacent water, reversing the process and forming a land breeze from the land toward the water.

93. **(D)** The electrical properties of cardiac muscle tissue cause the beating of the heart muscle that results in the pumping of blood through the body.

94. **(C)** Ingested food does not pass through the salivary glands. The saliva secreted from these glands enters the digestive tract and helps digest the food.

95. **(C)** Carrying capacity (designated by K) is the number of organisms that can be supported within a particular ecosystem.

96. **(D)** Quarks, bosons, neutrinos, and positrons are all subatomic particles. An electron is an atomic particle that represents the negatively charged part of an atom.

97. **(A)** Digestive enzymes are released by the pancreas and gallbladder into the small intestine.

98. **(A)** Insects have spiracles that allow for gas exchange.

99. **(A)** Over 70% of Earth's surface is covered by water. The great majority of Earth's photosynthesis takes place near the surface of the oceans with 70% of the entire amount of it taking place in the euphotic zone to a depth of 100 m. Many people mistakenly think that the tropical rain forests and deciduous forests are responsible for most of the production of oxygen during photosynthesis, but this is not so. The tundra and deserts are even more obviously incorrect because the amount of plant life in these biomes is very sparse.

100. **(C)** A replacement reaction occurs when a compound is broken down into its components and recombined with another reactant—as shown by the equation $AB + C \rightarrow AC + B$. The reaction $A + B \rightarrow AB$ represents a combination reaction; $AB \rightarrow A + B$ and $AB + CD \rightarrow A + B + C + D$ are both decomposition reactions; and $A + C \rightarrow AC + B$ is not a possible reaction since it is not consistent with the first law of thermodynamics, which states that matter cannot be created or destroyed in a chemical reaction. Since B was not a reactant, it cannot be a product.

101. **(D)** Ecology is literally "the study of" (*ology*) a "place to live" (*eco*).

102. **(E)** Each species is a distinct group of individuals that are able to mate and produce viable offspring.

103. **(B)** Einstein's energy equation, $E = mc^2$, is based on the premise that the speed of light for all observers is constant, and that energy is directly proportional to mass. As energy increases, so does its mass. The speed of light is considered constant; the mass and energy values must increase or decrease directly and proportionately.

104. **(D)** Plants that produce their own food through photosynthesis are known as autotrophs. (Mushrooms are fungi; they do not produce their own food.)

105. **(A)** The speed of light is the same in all directions. In a vacuum, the speed of light remains constant. The speed of light in a liquid is slower than in air. The speed of light is the same on the moon as it is on Earth.

106. **(B)** The principle of supererogation is completely fictitious, so this is the correct answer. The principle of original horizontality states that if rock layers are not laid horizontally, then something forced the structures to move. The principle of lateral continuity means that sediments are originally deposited in layers that extend laterally in all directions and eventually thin out. The principle of fossil succession says that if rocks are undisturbed, the oldest layers of rock should be on the bottom and will have older fossils in them. The principle of uniformitarianism states that present geological events explain former ones. It is popularly stated as the principle that "the present is the key to the past."

107. **(A)** A redshift in the electromagnetic spectrum of the light from a faraway star means that the star is moving away from the observer. In the 1920s, Edwin Hubble (1889–1953) observed that galaxies around the Milky Way were moving away from us because of this redshift, and those further away are moving away from us even more rapidly; it is not moving toward us. The redshift does not indicate that a star is ready to explode, is a dwarf star, or is a giant nova.

108. **(C)** These eras are parts of the Phanerozoic Eon and represent the past 570 million years. Cenozoic represents "recent life," Mesozoic represents "middle life," and Paleozoic represents "old life." There were complex life-forms during all three of these eras.

109. **(A)** Parasitism is symbiosis in which one species benefits, but the other is harmed.

110. **(B)** An axis is defined as a line connecting two poles. Earth has an axis connecting the North Pole and the South Pole. The other choices are incorrect.

111. **(D)** There are estimated to be about 100 billion stars in the universe.

112. **(B)** The astronaut will feel as if he is being pushed forward toward the front of the spacecraft. The others are incorrect directions of motion. There is a negative acceleration (deceleration) and thus a negative force occurring since the vehicle is slowing down.

113. **(C)** Blue-green algae is a prokaryotic organism in the Kingdom Monera. Prokaryotes have no nucleus- or-membrane-bound organelles.

114. **(B)** The celestial sphere is an imaginary sphere centered on and surrounding Earth upon which the background stars are projected. The sun, moon, planets, and other celestial bodies seem to move relative to this background of fixed stars. It is a model used to describe positions and motions of astronomical bodies. A geodesic dome is not an astronomical tool, but is simply an architectural structure. A stellar ball is a made-up term. The Cartesian coordinate system is a mathematical system used to plot points on an *x-y* graph. The equatorial coordinate system is another mathematical system used to plot specific celestial bodies in the sky using time and angular coordinates of right ascension and declination. It relates the stars to their apparent motion in the sky along the celestial sphere relative to the celestial equator. It is used to make measurements within the celestial sphere, but is not actually the sphere itself.

115. **(B)**   The "greenhouse effect" is the result of radiation being blocked from leaving the atmosphere because of the ozone layer. Depletion of the ozone layer would impact the "greenhouse effect," not cause it. The "greenhouse effect" is also caused mainly by other atmospheric gases such as water vapor and carbon dioxide. This depletion will increase radiation because the hole in the ozone layer will get larger. Acid rain is primarily caused by oxides of sulfur and nitrogen due to pollution. Photochemical reactions involving oxides of nitrogen and chlorofluorocarbons play a major role in ozone destruction. These chemicals react with ozone and lead to a net decrease in ozone concentration in the stratosphere. Since ozone is a strong absorber of incoming ultraviolet (UV) radiation, any decrease in ozone concentration will increase the amount of UV radiation reaching the surface. This will increase the risk of skin cancer from exposure to the sun significantly. With this in mind, it is easy to see why (D) is incorrect. However, the ozone depletion has no impact on global warming directly.

116. **(C)**   The pressure gradient force plays no significant role in vertical air circulations. Since temperature decreases with height, as the valley air warms during the day, it becomes less dense than the air along the adjacent hillsides and begins to flow up the surrounding slopes. At night, air in the hills cools faster than the air in the valleys. Gravity pulls the cooler, denser air down the hillsides into the valleys. It is low pressure near the top of the mountain that forces breezes up from the valley, so (E) is wrong.

117. **(A)**   Only the size of the atom increases as you move down and to the left in the periodic table.

118. **(C)**   The greater the mass of an object, the greater the force necessary to change its state of motion. Newton's first law of motion states that an object in motion will stay in motion and an object at rest will stay at rest until acted upon by an outside force. Since Newton's second law of motion states that Force = (mass)(acceleration), then in order to change its motion, as the object increases in mass, more force will be necessary to alter its acceleration. Its position may be changed slightly with the same amount of force as might be applied to a smaller object, so changing its position is not the correct answer. Greater force may not change its shape at all, and will not change its density.

119. **(A)**   The top of the sine wave is the crest. The bottom is the trough. The amplitude represents the height of the wave. The period is the wave's cycle length. The frequency is the number of cycles per second.

120. **(D)**   The water molecules, which are the medium, are not carried, but the wave peaks do move toward shore. Answer (A) erroneously states the opposite of what is mentioned in the question. Although the ocean is somewhat mixed each day, this mixing is due to turbulence and currents, not waves. Similarly, debris washes ashore by turbulence and currents and not wave action. Waves also do not move swimmers, nor water; the waves travel through the water and the swimmer will bob up and down but will not be carried by the wave. Again, currents and turbulence are responsible for moving both the water and swimmers.

CHAPTER 5

Social Sciences

CLEP SOCIAL SCIENCES AND HISTORY INDEPENDENT STUDY SCHEDULE

The following suggestions provide a framework you can use when preparing for the CLEP Social Sciences exam. As part of your preparation, be sure to set aside time each day to study. This method will work better than trying to review everything at once. No matter which study techniques work best for you, the more time you spend studying, the more prepared and relaxed you will feel.

Step	Activity
1	Take Practice Test 2 for Social Science and History on the CD. This will help you identify areas that you need to practice.
2	Carefully read each topic in the Social Sciences section.
3	In your review, pay particular attention to boldfaced terms and phrases.
4	Use a highlighter or pencil to emphasize items in your text you want to remember.
5	Jot down points of emphasis in a notebook or on index cards as you read.
6	Take Practice Test 3 found on the CD.
7	Review the Detailed Explanations of the answers. These will not only provide the correct answer, but also explain why the other options were incorrect.
8	Note which questions you answered incorrectly on the Practice Test, and focus on these areas during your follow-up review.
9	Read through the Social Sciences section in your book again, paying particular attention to the topics you struggled with while taking the two Practice Tests.
10	Take Practice Test 1 in the book for additional reinforcement.

REVIEW OUTLINE

The following is the order in which the topics are covered in this review:

PASSING THE CLEP SOCIAL SCIENCES AND HISTORY EXAM

ABOUT THIS CHAPTER

This chapter provides you with a targeted review of the CLEP Social Sciences and History exam, as well as test-taking tips and strategies. We also provide a practice test in the book, and two practice tests on the CD. All are based on the official CLEP Social Sciences and History exam and contain every type of question found on the actual exam. Following the practice test is an answer key with detailed explanations designed to help you more completely understand the test material.

FORMAT AND CONTENT OF THE CLEP SOCIAL SCIENCES AND HISTORY EXAM

The CLEP Social Sciences and History exam covers the material one would find in college-level introductory classes in the following disciplines: United States history, western civilization, world history, government/political science, geography, economics, psychology, sociology, and anthropology.

The exam consists of 120 multiple-choice questions, each with five possible answer choices, to be answered in 90 minutes. The approximate breakdown of topics is as follows:

40% History

    17% United States History

    15% Western Civilization

    8%   World History

60% Social Sciences

13%   Government/Political Science

10%   Sociology

10%   Economics

10%   Psychology

11%   Geography

6%   Anthropology

SCORING YOUR PRACTICE TESTS

How do I score my practice tests?

The CLEP Social Sciences and History exam is scored on a scale of 20 to 80. To score your practice test, count the number of correct answers. This is your total raw score. Convert your raw score to a scaled score using the conversion table on the following page. (*Note:* **The conversion table provides only an** *estimate* **of your scaled score. Scaled scores can and do vary over time, and in no case should a sample test be taken as a precise predictor of test performance**).

Practice-Test Raw Score Conversion Table*

Raw Score	Scaled Score	Course Grade	Raw Score	Scaled Score	Course Grade	Raw Score	Scaled Score	Course Grade
120	80	A	103	76	A	86	68	B
119	80	A	102	76	A	85	68	B
118	80	A	101	75	A	84	67	B
117	80	A	100	75	A	83	67	B
116	80	A	99	75	A	82	67	B
115	80	A	98	74	A	81	66	B
114	79	A	97	74	A	80	66	B
113	79	A	96	73	A	79	65	B
112	79	A	95	73	A	78	65	B
111	79	A	94	73	A	77	65	B
110	78	A	93	72	A	76	64	B
109	78	A	92	72	B	75	64	B
108	78	A	91	71	B	74	63	B
107	77	A	90	71	B	73	63	B
106	77	A	89	70	B	72	62	B
105	77	A	88	69	B	71	62	B
104	77	A	87	69	B	70	61	B

(*Continued*)

Practice-Test Raw Score Conversion Table* (*Continued*)

Raw Score	Scaled Score	Course Grade	Raw Score	Scaled Score	Course Grade	Raw Score	Scaled Score	Course Grade
69	61	B	45	48	C	21	33	F
68	60	B	44	47	C	20	32	F
67	59	B	43	47	C	19	32	F
66	59	B	42	47	C	18	31	F
65	58	B	41	47	C	17	31	F
64	57	B	40	46	D	16	30	F
63	57	B	39	46	D	15	29	F
62	56	B	38	45	D	14	28	F
61	56	B	37	45	D	13	28	F
60	55	B	36	44	D	12	27	F
59	54	B	35	44	D	11	27	F
58	54	B	34	43	D	10	26	F
57	53	B	33	43	D	9	25	F
56	53	B	32	42	D	8	24	F
55	52	B	31	41	D	7	23	F
54	52	B	30	40	D	6	22	F
53	51	B	29	39	D	5	21	F
52	51	C	28	38	D	4	20	F
51	50	C	27	37	D	3	20	F
50	50	C	26	36	D	2	20	F
49	50	C	25	35	D	1	20	F
48	49	C	24	34	F	0	20	F
47	49	C	23	34	F			
46	48	C	22	33	F			

* This table is provided for scoring REA practice tests only. The American Council on Education recommends that colleges use a single across-the-board credit-granting score of 50 for all CLEP computer-based exams. Nonetheless, on account of the different skills being measured and the unique content requirements of each test, the actual number of correct answers needed to reach 50 will vary. A "50" is calibrated to equate with performance that would warrant the grade C in the corresponding introductory college course.

INTRODUCTION TO POLITICAL SCIENCE

What Is Political Science?

Political science is the organized study of government and politics. **Political scientists** explore such fundamental questions as: What are the philosophical foundations of modern political systems? What makes a government legitimate? What are the duties and responsibilities of those who govern? Who participates in the political process and why? What is the nature of relations among nations?

Principal Subfields of Political Science

Political theory	An historical exploration of the major contributions to political thought from the ancient Greeks to the contemporary theorists. These theorists raise fundamental questions about the individual's existence and his relationship to the political community.
American government and politics	A survey of the origins and development of the U.S. political system from the colonial days to modern times with an emphasis on the Constitution; various political structures such as the legislative, executive, and judicial branches; the federal system; political parties; voter behavior; and fundamental freedoms.
Comparative government	A systematic study of the structures of two or more political systems (such as those of Britain and the People's Republic of China) to achieve an understanding of how different societies manage the realities of governing, including differences in political processes and behavior and the ideological foundations of various systems.
International relations	A consideration of how nations interact with each other within the frameworks of law, diplomacy, and international organizations such as the United Nations.

The Development of the Discipline of Political Science

1. Early History

Political science developed in the United States and in Western Europe during the nineteenth century as new political institutions evolved. Prior to 1850, during its classical phase, political science relied heavily on philosophy and utilized the deductive method of research.

2. Post-Civil War Period

The faculty at Columbia and Johns Hopkins were deeply influenced by German scholarship on the **nation-state** and the formation of democratic institutions. Emphasis was on constitutional and legal issues, and political institutions were widely regarded as factors in motivating the actions of individuals.

3. Twentieth Century Trends

Political scientists worked to strengthen their research base, to integrate quantitative data, and to incorporate comparative studies of governmental structures in developing countries into the discipline.

4. American Political Science Association (APSA)

The **APSA** was founded in 1903 to promote the organized study of politics and to distinguish it as a field separate from history.

5. The Behavioral Period

From the early 1920s to the present, political science has focused on psychological interpretations and the analysis of the behavior of individuals and groups in a political context. Research has been theory based, values neutral, and concerned with predicting and explaining political behavior.

6. Contemporary Developments

Since the 1960s, interest has focused on such subtopics as African-American politics, public policy, urban and ethnic politics, and women in politics. Influenced by the leadership of Harold Lasswell, political scientists showed greater concern for using their discipline to solve social problems.

The Scientific Method of Research in Political Science

The modern method of scientific inquiry in the field aims to compile a body of data based on direct observation (**empirical knowledge**) that can be utilized both to explain what has been observed and to form valid generalizations. The scientific method in political science has resulted in three types of statements: **observational/evidential**, which describe the principal characteristics of what has been studied; **observational laws**, which are hypotheses based on what has been observed; and **theories**, which analyze the data that have been collected and offer plausible general principles that can be drawn from what has been observed.

1. Examples of Statements Based on the Scientific Method

- **Observational/evidential:** In 1992, 518 out of 535 members of the U.S. Congress were males. In the British Parliament, 550 of the 635 members were males. Eighteen of France's 20 cabinet ministers were males.
- **Observational law (hypothesis):** Legislative and executive bodies in modern democracies tend to be dominated by males.
- **Theory:** Political power in modern democracies is in male hands.

UNITED STATES GOVERNMENT AND POLITICS

Constitutional Foundations

The **Constitution** is a basic plan that outlines the structure and functions of the national government. Clearly rooted in Western political thought, it sets limits on government and protects both property and individual rights.

1. Historical Background

The **Articles of Confederation**, served as the national government from 1781–1787. The consciously weak government under the Articles consisted of a **unicameral** (one-house) legislature that was clearly subordinate to the states. Each state, regardless of size, had one vote in Congress, which could request but not require states to provide financial and military support. **Key weaknesses of the Articles** included its inability to regulate interstate and foreign trade, its lack of a chief executive and a national court system, and its rule that amendments must be approved by unanimous consent.

During the "**critical period**," of the 1780s, the economy deteriorated as individual states printed their own currencies, taxed the products of their neighbors, and ignored foreign trade agreements. The discontent of the agrarian population reached crisis proportions in 1786 in rural Massachusetts when Revolutionary War veteran **Daniel Shays** led a rebellion of farmers against the tax collectors and the banks that were seizing their property. **Shays' Rebellion** symbolized the inability of the government under the Articles to maintain order.

In 1787, the **Constitutional Convention** was convened in **Philadelphia** ostensibly to revise the ineffective Articles. The result was an entirely new plan of government, the Constitution.

2. Philosophy and Ideology of the Founding Fathers

Among the distinguished men assembled at the Constitutional Convention in 1787 were **James Madison**, who recorded the debate proceedings; **George Washington**, president of the body; **Gouverneur Morris**, who wrote the final version of the document; and **Alexander Hamilton**, one of the authors of the *Federalist Papers* (1787–1788). This collection of essays, to which **Madison** and **John Jay** also contributed, expresses the political philosophy of the Founders and was instrumental in bringing about the ratification of the Constitution.

Thomas Jefferson, incorporated John Locke's "social contract" doctrines with respect to equality; government's responsibility to protect the life, liberty, and property of its constituency; and the right of revolution in his **Declaration of Independence** (1776). The Constitution itself includes Montesquieu's separation of powers and checks and balances. British documents, such as the **Magna Carta** (1215), the **Petition of Right** (1628), and the **Bill of Rights** (1689), all promoting the principle of limited government, were influential in shaping the final form of the Constitution.

3. Basic Principles of the Constitution

The **federal system** established by the Founders divides the powers of government between the states and the national government. Local matters are handled on a local level, and those issues that affect the general populace are the responsibility of the federal government. In cases where they conflict, the federal government is supreme. American federalism is defined in the **Tenth Amendment.**

The principle of **separation of powers** is codified in **Articles I**, **II**, and **III** of the main body of the Constitution. The national government is divided into three branches which have separate functions (**legislative**, **executive**, and **judicial**). Not entirely independent, each of these branches can check or limit in some way the power of one or both of the others (**checks and balances**). Following are some examples of checks and balances:

- The legislative branch can check the executive by refusing to confirm appointments.
- The executive can check the legislature by vetoing its bills.
- The judiciary can check both the legislature and the executive by declaring laws unconstitutional.

Additional basic principles embodied in the Constitution include:

- The establishment of a representative government (**republic**).
- **Popular sovereignty** or the idea that government derives its power from the people. This concept is expressed in the **Preamble** which opens with the words, "**We the People**."
- The enforcement of government with limits ("**rule of law**").

Structure and Functions of the National Government

1. The Legislative Branch

Legislative power is vested in a **bicameral** (two-house) Congress. The bicameral structure was the result of a compromise at the Constitutional Convention between the large states, led by Virginia, which presented a plan calling for a strong national government with representation favoring the larger states (**Virginia Plan**), and the smaller states, which countered with the **New Jersey Plan**. The latter would have retained much of the structure of the Articles of Confederation including equal representation of the states in Congress. Connecticut offered a solution in the form of the **Great Compromise**. It called for a two-house legislature with equal representation in the **Senate** and representation in the **House of Representatives** based on population.

The **expressed** or **delegated powers** of Congress are set forth in **Section 8** of **Article I**. **Economic powers** include laying and collecting taxes, borrowing money, regulating foreign and interstate commerce, coining money and regulating its value, and establishing rules concerning bankruptcy.

Judicial powers include establishing courts inferior to the Supreme Court, providing punishment for counterfeiting, and defining and punishing piracies and felonies committed on the high seas.

War powers include declaring war, raising and supporting armies, providing and maintaining a navy, and organizing, arming, and calling forth the militia.

Peace powers include establishing rules on naturalization, establishing post offices and post roads, promoting science and the arts by granting patents and copyrights, and exercising jurisdiction over the seat of the federal government (**District of Columbia**).

The Constitution includes the so-called "**elastic clause**" which grants Congress **implied powers** to implement the delegated powers.

In addition, Congress maintains the power to discipline federal officials through **impeachment** (formal accusation of wrongdoing) and removal from office.

Article V empowers Congress to propose **amendments** (changes or additions) to the Constitution. A two-thirds majority in both houses is necessary for passage. An alternate method is to have amendments proposed by the legislatures of two-thirds of the states. In order for an amendment to become part of the Constitution, it must be **ratified** (formally approved) by three-fourths of the states (through their legislatures or by way of special conventions as in the case of the repeal of Prohibition).

Article I, **Section 9** specifically denies certain powers to the national legislature. Congress is prohibited from suspending the right of **habeas corpus** (writ calling for a party under arrest to be brought before the court where authorities must show cause for detainment) except during war or rebellion. Other prohibitions include: the passage of export taxes, the withdrawal of funds from the treasury without an appropriations law, the passage of **ex post facto** laws (make past actions punishable that were legal when they occurred), and favored treatment of one state over another with respect to commerce.

Congress is organized around a committee system. The **standing committees** are permanent and deal with such matters as agriculture, the armed services, the budget, energy, finance, and foreign policy. Special or **select committees** are established to deal with specific issues and usually have a limited duration. **Conference committees** iron out differences between the House and the Senate versions of a bill before it is sent on to the president.

One committee unique to the House of Representatives is the powerful **Rules Committee,** which acts as a clearinghouse to weed out bills that are unworthy of consideration before the full House. Constitutionally, all revenue-raising bills must originate in the House of Representatives. They are scrutinized by the powerful House **Ways and Means Committee**.

Committee membership is organized on party lines with **seniority** being a key factor. The composition of each committee is largely based on the ratio of each party in the Congress as a whole. The party that has a **majority** is allotted a greater number of members on each committee. The chairmen of the standing committees are selected by the leaders of the majority party.

The legislative process is at once cumbersome and time consuming. A **bill** (proposed law) can be introduced in either house. It is referred to the appropriate **committee** and then to a **subcommittee**, which will hold **hearings** if the members agree that it has merit. The bill is reported back to the **full committee**, which must decide whether or not to send it to the **full chamber** to be debated. If the bill passes in the full chamber, it is then sent to the **other chamber** to begin the process all over again. Any differences between the House and Senate versions of the bill must be resolved in a **conference committee** before it is sent to the **president** for consideration. Most of the thousands of bills introduced in Congress die in committee with only a small percentage becoming law.

Debate on major bills is a key step in the legislative process because of the tradition of attaching **amendments** at this stage. In the House, the rules of debate are designed to enforce limits necessitated by the size of the body (435 members). In the smaller Senate (100 members), unlimited debate (**filibuster**) is allowed. Filibustering is a delaying tactic that can postpone action indefinitely. **Cloture** is a parliamentary procedure that can limit debate and bring a filibuster to an end.

House of Representatives

Constitutional requirements for membership	• At least 25 years of age • U.S. citizen for at least seven years • Resident of state they represent
Number of members in House of Representatives	435
Length of representative's term	2 years
Number of terms a representative can serve	Unlimited
Most powerful member of the House of Representatives	Speaker of the House

Senate

Constitutional requirements for membership	• At least 30 years of age • U.S. citizen for at least nine years • Inhabitant of state they represent
Number of members in Senate	100
Length of senator's term	6 years (one-third of the Senate is elected every two years)
Number of terms a senator can serve	Unlimited
Most powerful member of the Senate	Majority leader

The president of the Senate is the **vice president**. This role is largely symbolic, with the vice president casting a vote only in the case of a tie. There is no position in the Senate comparable to that of the speaker of the house, although the **majority leader** is generally recognized as the most powerful member.

2. The Executive Branch

The **president** is the head of the executive branch of the federal government. **Article II** of the Constitution deals with the powers and duties of the president or chief executive. Following are the president's principal **constitutional responsibilities**:

- serves as **Commander-in-Chief** of the armed forces
- negotiates treaties (with the approval of two-thirds of the Senate)
- appoints ambassadors, judges, and other high officials (with the consent of the Senate)
- grants pardons and reprieves for those convicted of federal crimes (except in impeachment cases)
- seeks counsel of department heads (Cabinet members)
- recommends legislation

- meets with representatives of foreign states
- sees that the laws are faithfully executed

The president remains the most visible and powerful single member of the federal government and the only one (with the exception of the vice president) elected to represent all the people. He shapes foreign policy with his diplomatic and treaty-making powers and largely determines domestic policy. Presidents also possess the power to **veto** legislation. A presidential veto may be overridden by a two-thirds vote in both houses, but such a majority is not easy to build, particularly in the face of the chief executive's opposition. A **pocket veto** occurs when the president neither signs nor rejects a bill, and the Congress adjourns within ten days of his receipt of the legislation.

Although the Constitution makes no mention of a formal **Cabinet,** since the days of George Washington, chief executives have relied on department heads to aid in the decision-making process. Washington's Cabinet was comprised of the secretaries of **state**, **war**, **treasury**, and an **attorney general**. Today there are 15 Cabinet departments, with **Homeland Security** being the most recently created post.

The **White House Staff** manages the president's schedule and is usually headed by a powerful **chief of staff**. Arguably the most critical agency of the Executive Office is the **Office of Management and Budget**, which controls the budget process for the national government. Other key executive agencies include the **Council of Economic Advisors** and the **National Security Council**, which advises the president on matters that threaten the safety of the nation and directs the **Central Intelligence Agency**.

Presidency

Constitutional requirements for presidency	• At least 35 years of age • Natural-born U.S. • Resident of the United States for at least 14 years
Length of president's term	4 years
Number of terms a president can serve	Two

Article II provides for an **Electoral College** to elect the president and vice president. Each state has as many votes in the Electoral College as it has members of Congress, plus three additional electors are appointed from the District of Columbia—making a grand total of 538 electors. The Founding Fathers established the Electoral College to provide an **indirect** method of choosing the chief executive.

The Constitution states that if the president dies or cannot perform his duties, the "powers and duties" of the office shall "devolve" on the vice president. The **Presidential Succession Act** (1947) placed the **speaker of the house** next in line if both the president and the vice president were unable to serve. The **Twenty-Fifth Amendment** (1967) gives the president the power to appoint a new vice president (with the approval of a majority of both houses of Congress). It also provides for the vice president to serve as **acting president** if the chief executive is disabled or otherwise unable to carry out the duties of the office. The **Twenty-Second Amendment** (1951) says "No person shall be elected to the office of the President more than twice. . . ." In addition, anyone who has served more than two years while filling out another person's term may not be elected to the presidency more than once.

3. The Judicial Branch

Article III of the Constitution establishes the **Supreme Court** but does not define the role of this branch as clearly as it does the legislative and executive branches. The most significant piece of legislation with respect to establishing a network of federal courts was the **Judiciary Act of 1789**. This law organized the Supreme Court and set up the 13 **federal district courts**. The district courts have **original jurisdiction** (to hear cases in the first instance) for federal cases involving both civil and criminal law. Federal cases on appeal are heard in the **Courts of Appeal**. The decisions of these courts are final, except for those cases that are accepted for review by the Supreme Court.

The **Supreme Court** today is made up of a **chief justice** and eight **associate justices**. They are appointed for life by the president with the approval of the Senate. In 1803, the process of **judicial review** (power to determine the constitutionality of laws and actions of the legislative and executive branches) was established under **Chief Justice John Marshall** in the case of *Marbury v. Madison*.

The Supreme Court chooses cases for review based on whether or not they address substantial federal issues. If four of the nine justices vote to consider a case, then it will be added to the agenda. In such cases, **writs of certiorari** (orders calling up the records from a lower court) are issued. The justices scrutinize the case with reference to the Constitution and also consider previous decisions in similar cases (**precedent**). When all of the justices agree, the opinion issued is **unanimous**. In the case of a split decision, a **majority opinion** is written by one of the justices in agreement. Sometimes a justice will agree with the majority but for a different principle, in which case he/she can write a **concurring opinion** explaining the different point of view. Justices who do not vote with the majority may choose to write **dissenting opinions** to air their conflicting arguments.

In addition to the Supreme Court, the federal District Courts, and the Courts of Appeal, several special courts at the federal level have been created by Congress. The **U.S. Tax Court** handles conflicts between citizens and the Internal Revenue Service. The **Court of Claims** was designed to hear cases in which citizens bring suit against the U.S. government. Other special courts include the **Court of International Trade**, the **Court of Customs**, and the **Court of Military Appeals**.

4. The Federal Bureaucracy

In addition to the president's Cabinet and the Executive Office, a series of independent agencies makes up the federal bureaucracy, the so-called "**fourth branch**" of the national government. From the time of the establishment of the Interstate Commerce Commission in 1887, these departments have grown in number and influence. Late in the 1970s, the trend began to reverse, as some agencies were cut back and others eliminated altogether.

Among the most important of these powerful agencies are the **regulatory commissions**. The president appoints their administrators with the approval of the Senate. Unlike Cabinet secretaries and other high appointees, they cannot be dismissed by the chief executive. Following are examples of some of the major regulatory agencies and their functions.

Agency	Regulatory Functions
Interstate Commerce Commission	Monitors surface transportation and some pipelines
Federal Reserve Board	Supervises the banking system, sets interest rates, and controls the money supply
Federal Trade Commission	Protects consumers by looking into false advertising and antitrust violations
Federal Communications Commission	Polices the airwaves by licensing radio and television stations and regulating cable and telephone companies
Securities and Exchange Commission	Protects investors by monitoring the sale of stocks and bonds
National Labor Relations Board	Oversees labor and management practices
Consumer Product Safety Commission	Sets standards of safety for manufactured products
Nuclear Regulatory Commission	Licenses and inspects nuclear power plants

Another category of the "fourth branch" of government is made up of the **independent executive agencies**. Some of the key executive agencies created by Congress include the Civil Rights Commission, the Environmental Protection Agency, and the National Aeronautics and Space Administration. The top level executives of these agencies are appointed by the president with the approval of the Senate.

Some of the independent agencies are actually **government corporations** created by Congress. Their roots can be traced back to the **First Bank of the United States** established in 1791 by Secretary of the Treasury **Alexander Hamilton**. The **Federal Deposit Insurance Corporation (FDIC)**, which insures bank deposits, is a more recent example. Under **Franklin Roosevelt's New Deal**, the **Tennessee Valley Authority (TVA)** was authorized to revive a depressed region of the nation. Today it oversees the generation of electric power throughout a vast region and maintains flood control programs as well. The largest of the government corporations and the most familiar to the general public is the **United States Postal Service**. The original Post Office Department was established in 1775 by the Second Continental Congress, and it enjoyed Cabinet status.

Dating back to the administrations of **Andrew Jackson**, the practice of handing out government jobs in return for political favors (**spoils system**) had been the rule. The **Civil Service Act** (the **Pendleton Act**) was passed in 1883 in an attempt to reform the spoils system. Federal workers were to be recruited on the basis of merit determined by a competitive examination. Veterans were given preferential status. The Civil Service system was reorganized in the 1970s with the creation of the **Office of Personnel Management (OPM)**. The OPM is charged with recruiting, training, and promoting government workers. Merit is the stated objective when hiring federal employees. A controversial policy of the OPM is **affirmative action**, a program to help groups discriminated against in the job market to find employment.

Political Beliefs and Characteristics of Citizens

The process by which individuals form their political allegiances is called **political socialization**. Several factors (**cleavages**) are relevant to the formation of political opinions. Following are some generalizations as to the impact of these cleavages on an individual's political identification and activity.

Family—affiliation with a political party is commonly passed from one generation to another.

Race—African Americans tend to be more liberal than whites on economic, social, and public policy issues.

Gender—women tend to be more liberal than men.

Class—citizens from the middle and upper classes tend to be more politically active than those from the lower socioeconomic brackets. Low income voters tend to identify more with the liberal agenda.

Religion—Protestants tend to be more conservative than Catholics and Jews. Evangelical Protestants seem to be most conservative on ethical and moral issues.

Education—graduate-level education seems to have a liberalizing effect that remains potent after schooling is completed.

Region—Southerners tend to be most conservative, midwesterners more liberal, and those living on the East and West coasts the most liberal of all.

Despite the categorization of Americans as either **liberals** or **conservatives**, most studies indicate that they do not follow clearly delineated **ideologies** (firm and consistent beliefs with respect to political, economic, and social issues). Liberals tend to favor change and to view government as a tool for improving the quality of life. Conservatives, on the other hand, are more inclined to view both change and government with suspicion. They emphasize individual initiative and local solutions to problems.

Political Institutions and Special Interests

1. Political Parties

A **political party** is an organization that seeks to influence government by electing candidates to public office. The party provides a label for candidates, recruits and campaigns, and tries to organize and control the legislative and executive branches of government through a set of leaders. The Constitution does not mention political parties, and the Founders in general were opposed to them. Yet they developed simultaneously with the organization of the new government in 1789.

The **Federalist Party** evolved around the policies of Washington's Secretary of the Treasury, **Alexander Hamilton**. He and his supporters favored a "**loose construction**" approach to the interpretation of the Constitution. They advocated a strong federal government with the power to assume any duties and responsibilities not prohibited to it by the text of the document. They generally supported programs designed to benefit banking and commercial interests, and in foreign policy, the Federalists were **pro-British**.

The **Democratic** or **Jeffersonian Republicans** formed in opposition to the Federalists. They rallied around Washington's Secretary of State, **Thomas Jefferson**. The Jeffersonians took a "**strict constructionist**" approach, interpreting the Constitution in a narrow, limited sense. Sympathetic to the needs of the "common man," the Democratic-Republicans were mistrustful of powerful centralized government. In the area of foreign affairs, the Democratic-Republicans were **pro-French**. The present-day Democratic Party traces its roots to the Jeffersonians.

By the 1820s, the Democrats had splintered into factions led by **Andrew Jackson** (the Democrats) and **John Quincy Adams** (National Republicans). The Jacksonians continued with Jefferson's tradition of supporting policies designed to enhance the power of the common man. Their support was largely agrarian. The National Republicans, like their Federalist predecessors, represented the interests of bankers, merchants, and some large planters. Eventually a new party, the **Whigs**, was organized from the remnants of the old Federalists and the National Republicans. The Whigs were prominent during the 1840s but, like their Democratic rivals, they fragmented during the 1850s over the divisive slavery issue. The modern **Republican Party** was born in 1854 as Whigs and anti-slavery Democrats came together to halt the spread of slavery. The Republicans built a constituency around the interests of business, farmers, workers, and the newly emancipated slaves in the post-Civil War era.

Nominating candidates for local, state, and national office is the most visible activity of political parties. At the national level, this function has been diluted somewhat by the popularity of **primary elections** allowing voters to express their preference for candidates. Raucous conventions where party bosses chose obscure **"dark horse"** candidates in "smoke filled rooms" are largely a thing of the past.

At the local level, the fundamental unit of political party organization is the **precinct**. This level features such routine chores as registering voters, distributing party literature, organizing **"grass-roots"** meetings, and getting out the vote on election day.

State central committees are critical to the parties' fundraising activities. They also organize the state party conventions.

In presidential election years, the **national party committees** are most visible. They plan the **national nominating convention**, write the party **platforms** (summaries of positions on major issues), raise money to finance political activities, and carry out the election campaigns. Representatives from each state serve on the national committees, and the **presidential nominee** chooses the individual to serve as the **party chairperson**.

Although the two-party system is firmly established in the United States, over the years "**third parties**" have left their marks. The national nominating conventions were introduced in the 1830s by the **Anti-Masonic Party** and were soon adopted by the Democrats and the Whigs. The **Prohibition Party** opposed the use of alcohol and worked for the adoption of the **Eighteenth Amendment**. In the 1890s, the **Populist Party** championed the causes of the farmers and workers and impacted the mainstream parties with its reform agenda. Among the Populist innovations were the **initiative petition** (a mechanism allowing voters to put proposed legislation on the ballot) and the **referendum** (allowing voters to approve or reject laws passed by their legislatures). The **Progressive** or **Bull Moose Party** was a **splinter party** (one that breaks away from an established party, in this case the Republican Party) built around the personality of Theodore Roosevelt. Another party formed around the personality of a forceful individual was the 1992 **Reform Party** of **H. Ross Perot**. Perot did not capture any electoral votes but garnered 19% of the popular tally.

2. Elections

Elections in the United States are largely regulated by **state law**. The Constitution does assign to Congress the responsibility for determining "the times, places, and manner of holding elections for Senators and Representatives." Article II establishes the Electoral College for presidential elections and specifies that they shall be held on the same day throughout the nation. Several of the Amendments deal with election procedures, voter qualifications, and **suffrage** (the right to vote) for target groups (former slaves, women, and those 18 years of age and older). Nonetheless, the principal responsibility for arranging and supervising elections rests with the states.

The actual election process consists of two phases: nominating the candidates and choosing the final officials. **Primary elections** screen and select the final party candidates. **Closed primaries** allow voters **registered** (legal procedure that must be completed before an individual can vote) in one of the political parties to express their preferences for the final candidate from among the field of hopefuls in that party. **Open primaries** allow voters to select their party affiliations on site. Some states allow "**cross-over**" voting which permits voters registered in one party to vote for candidates in the other party.

In **national elections** (those held in November of each even-numbered year to choose national officeholders), the **campaign** traditionally begins after Labor Day. **Off-year elections** are those in which only members of Congress are chosen and no presidential contest is held. Funding for political campaigns comes from a variety of sources including the candidates' own resources, private supporters, **Political Action Committees (PACs)**, and the federal government. In the election reform drive of the 1970s, the **Federal Election Commission** was created to ensure that laws concerning campaign financing are followed.

The cost of the elections themselves is borne by the state and local governments which must prepare ballots, designate polling places, and pay workers who participate in administering the elections. **Registrars of voters** oversee the preparation of ballots, the establishment of polling places, and the tallying of the votes. In a close election, the loser may request a **recount**. Some states require them in closely contested races.

3. Voter Behavior

There is widespread belief that Americans are dissatisfied with their government and mistrust all elected officials. Therefore, they refuse to participate in the electoral process. Some citizens do not vote in a given election, not because they are "turned-off" to the system, but because they are ill, homeless, away on business, or otherwise preoccupied on election day. College students and others away from their legal residences find registration and the use of **absentee ballots** cumbersome and inconvenient. Efforts have been made in the 1990s to streamline the registration process with such legislation as the **"motor-voter" bill** that makes it possible for citizens to register at their local registries of motor vehicles.

Political participation is not limited to voting in elections. Working for candidates, attending rallies, contacting elected officials and sharing opinions about issues, writing letters to newspapers, marching in protest, and joining in community activities are all forms of political participation. While voter turnout has decreased in recent years, other forms of participation seem to be on the increase.

4. Interest Groups

American officials and political leaders are continually subjected to pressure from a variety of **interest groups** seeking to influence their actions. Interest groups may be loosely organized (**informal**), with no clear structure or regulations. Other interest groups are much more **formal** and permanent in nature. Labor unions, professional and public-interest groups, and single issue organizations fall into this category. The **National Rifle Association** and the **National Right to Life Organization** are examples of **single issue** pressure groups.

Interest groups employ a variety of tactics to accomplish their goals. Most commonly, they **lobby** (influence the passage or defeat of legislation) elected officials, particularly members of Congress. Lobbyists provide legislators with reports and statistics to persuade them of the legitimacy of their respective positions. Lobbyists are required to register in Washington and to make their positions public.

One particularly controversial brand of pressure group is the **Political Action Committee (PAC)**. PACs were formed in the 1970s in an attempt to circumvent legislation limiting contributions to political campaigns.

5. Public Opinion

Public opinion refers to the attitudes and preferences expressed by a significant number of individuals about an issue that involves the government or the society at large.

In today's technological society, the influence of the **mass media** on public opinion cannot be overemphasized. The print and broadcast media can reach large numbers of people cheaply and efficiently, but the electronic media in particular have been criticized for oversimplifying complicated issues and reducing coverage of major events to brief sound bites. **Paid political advertising** is another vehicle for molding public opinion. In this case, objectivity is neither expected nor attempted, as candidates and interest groups employ "hard-sell" techniques to persuade voters to support their causes.

Measuring the effects of the media on public opinion is difficult, as is gauging where the public stands on a given issue at a particular point in time. **Public opinion polls** have been designed to these ends. Pollsters usually address a **random sample** and try to capture a **cross-section** of the population. Results are tabulated and analyzed, and generalizations are presented to the media.

In **exit polls,** interviewers question subjects about their votes as they leave the polling places. These polls may be accurate, but if the media present the results while voting is still in progress, the outcome may be affected.

Civil Rights and Individual Liberties

Civil rights are those legal claims that individuals have to protect themselves from discrimination at the hands of both the government and other citizens. They include the right to vote, equality before the law, and access to public facilities. **Individual** or **civil liberties** protect the sanctity of the person from arbitrary governmental interference and include the fundamental freedoms of speech, religion, press, and rights such as **due process** (government must act fairly and follow established procedures, as in legal proceedings).

When fashioning the Constitution, the Founding Fathers included passages regarding the protection of civil liberties, such as the provision in Article I for maintaining the right of *habeas corpus*. One of the criticisms of the Constitution lodged by its opponents was that it did not go far enough in safeguarding individual rights. During the first session of Congress in 1789, the first ten amendments (the **Bill of Rights**) were adopted and sent to the states for ratification. The Bill of Rights was meant to limit the power of the federal government to restrict the freedom of individual citizens. The **Fourteenth Amendment** of 1868 prohibits **states** from denying civil rights and individual liberties to their residents. The Supreme Court is charged with interpreting the law, particularly as it applies to civil rights and individual liberties cases. Not until the **Gitlow Case** in 1925 did the Supreme Court begin to exercise this function with respect to state enforcement of the Bill of Rights.

The **First Amendment** protects freedom of religion, speech, press, assembly, and petition. The First Amendment sets forth the principle of **separation of Church and State** with its "**free exercise**" and "**establishment**" clauses. These have led the Supreme Court to rule against such practices as school prayer (*Engle v. Vitale,* **1962**) and Bible reading in public schools (*Abington Township v. Schempp,* **1963**).

The **Fourth Amendment**, which outlawed "**unreasonable searches and seizures**," mandates that warrants be granted only "**upon probable cause**," and affirms the "**right of the people to be secure in their persons**," is fundamental to the Court's interpretation of due process and the rights of the accused. The **Fifth Amendment**, which calls for a grand jury, outlawed **double jeopardy** (trying a person who has been acquitted of a charge for a second time), and states that a person may not be compelled to be a witness against himself, is also the basis for Supreme Court rulings that protect the accused. "**Cruel and unusual punishments**" are banned by the **Eighth Amendment**.

When civil rights organizations such as the NAACP brought a series of cases before the courts under the "**equal protection clause**" of the **Fourteenth Amendment**, they began to enjoy some victories. Earlier when the Supreme Court enforced its "**separate but equal**" doctrine in the 1896 case *Plessy v. Ferguson*, it did not apply the equal protection standard and allowed segregation to be maintained. The Court reversed itself in 1954 in the landmark case *Brown v. Board of Education*, which ruled that separate but equal was unconstitutional. This ruling led to an end to most **de jure** (legally enforced) segregation, but **de facto** (exists in fact) segregation persisted, largely due to housing patterns and racial and ethnic enclaves in urban neighborhoods.

1. Landmark Supreme Court Cases

- *Dred Scott v. Sanford* (1857)—ruled that as a slave Scott had no right to sue for his freedom, and further that Congressional prohibitions against slavery in U.S. territories were unlawful.

- *Near v. Minnesota* (1931)—barred states from using the concept of prior restraint (outlawing something before it has taken place) to discourage the publication of objectionable material except during wartime or in the cases of obscenity or incitement to violence.

- *West Virginia Board of Education v. Barnette* (1943)—overturned an earlier decision and ruled that compulsory saluting of the flag was unconstitutional.

- *Korematsu v. United States* (1944)—upheld the legality of the forced evacuation of persons of Japanese ancestry during World War II as a wartime necessity.

- *Mapp v. Ohio* (1961)—extended the Supreme Court's exclusionary rule, which bars the introduction of evidence at trial that has not been legally obtained to states. The Court has modified this ruling, particularly with reference to drug cases, so that evidence that might not initially have been obtained legally, but which would eventually have turned up in lawful procedures, can be introduced.

- *Gideon v. Wainwright* (1963)—ruled that courts must provide legal counsel to poor defendants in all felony cases. A later ruling extended this right to all defendants facing possible prison sentences.

- *Escobedo v. Illinois* (1964)—extended the right to counsel to include consultation prior to interrogation by authorities.

- *Miranda v. Arizona* (1966)—mandated that all suspects be informed of their due process rights before questioning by police.

- *Tinker v. Des Moines School District* (1969)—defined the wearing of black armbands in school in protest against the Vietnam War as "symbolic speech" protected by the First Amendment.

- *New York Times v. United States* (1971)—allowed, under the First Amendment's freedom of the press protection, the publication of the controversial Pentagon Papers during the Vietnam War.

- *Roe v. Wade* (1973)—legalized abortion so long as a fetus is not viable (able to survive outside the womb).

- *Bakke v. Regents of the University of California* (1978)—declared the University's quota system to be unconstitutional while upholding the legitimacy of affirmative action policies in which institutions consider race and gender as factors when determining admissions.

- *Hazelwood School District v. Kuhlmeier* (1988)—ruled that freedom of the press does not extend to student publications that might be construed as sponsored by the school.

COMPARATIVE GOVERNMENT AND POLITICS

Theoretical Frameworks for Government Structures, Functions, and Political Culture

1. Environmental Factors

In order to understand the political institutions and civic life of any nation, several environmental factors need to be considered. Such questions as the **size**, **location**, **geographic features**, **economic strength**, **level of industrialization**, and **cultural diversity** of a society must be explored. Both the **domestic** and **international** contexts need to be examined as well as the level of **dependence** on or **independence** from the world community. Industrialization and economic stability are conditions that are commonly conducive to a highly developed political system.

The **age** and **historical traditions** of a nation have a great impact on its current political culture. **Legitimacy** (acceptance by citizens) is quite another prospect in such places as Somalia and Haiti with their unstable political histories and economic vulnerability.

2. Government Structures and Functions

The **geographic distribution of authority and responsibility** is a key variable. **Confederations** have weak central governments and delegate principal authority to smaller units such as the states.

Federal systems, on the other hand, divide sovereignty between a central government and those of their separate states. Highly centralized, **unitary** forms of government concentrate power and authority at the top.

Separation of governmental powers is another aspect of structure useful in comparing political systems. **Authoritarian** governments center power in a single or collective executive, with the legislative and judicial bodies having little input. The former Soviet Union is an example. Great Britain typifies the **parliamentary** form of government. Here legislative and executive combine, with a prime minister and cabinet selected from within the legislative body. They maintain power only so long as the legislative assembly supports their major policies. The **democratic presidential** system of the United States clearly separates the legislative, executive, and judicial structures.

A third aspect of governmental structure and function involves the **limits** placed on the power to govern. This facet of politics closely reflects the theoretical and ideological roots of a system. **Constitutional** systems limit the powers of government through written and/or unwritten sources. Law, custom, and precedent combine to protect individuals from the unchecked power of a central authority. **Authoritarian** regimes, such as those found in China and the former Soviet Union, do not limit the power of the central authority over the lives of individuals. Those in control impose their values and their will on the society at large regardless of popular sentiments. Authoritarianism is associated with **fascism**, **nazism**, and **totalitarianism** in general.

3. Political Culture, Parties, Participation, and Mechanisms for Change

A nation's **political culture** can be defined as the aggregate values a society shares about how politics and government should operate. Some societies function from a **consensus** framework, while other political cultures are more **conflicted**. The vehicles for transmitting the political culture and the social cleavages that characterize that culture will impact its system of governing and its legitimacy in the minds of its citizenry.

Comparative politics examines questions like: Do elections offer a **choice** between candidates with diverse programs and contrasting agendas, as is often the case in the United States, or do they present citizens the opportunity to show their support for the government in a **one-party** system such as in China? The number, nature, and power of political parties are additional factors for analysis with respect to how the demands and concerns of citizens in various nations are represented and met. Beyond voting in elections and joining and supporting political parties and interest groups, **citizen participation** can take other forms, such as contacting politicians, lobbying for legislation, and demonstrating in the streets.

Comparative politics and government as a field is concerned with **mechanisms for change** in different nations. Can citizens effect reform through ballots, protest, public opinion polls, or revolts? The underlying factors precipitating the need for change are relevant to an understanding of the overall process.

INTERNATIONAL RELATIONS

The Theoretical Framework

The study of how nations interact with one another can be approached from a variety of perspectives including the following:

- A **traditional analysis** uses the descriptive process and focuses on such topics as global issues, international institutions, and the foreign policies of individual nation-states.

- The **strategists' approach** zeroes in on war and deterrence. Scholars in this camp may employ game theory to analyze negotiations, the effectiveness of weapons systems, and the likelihood of limited versus all-out war in a given crisis situation.

- The **middle range theorists** analyze specific components of international relations, such as the politics of arms races, the escalation of international crises, and the role of prejudice and attitudes toward other cultures in precipitating war and peace.

- A **world politics approach** takes into consideration such factors as economics, ethics, law, and trade agreements and stresses the significance of international organizations and the complexities of interactions among nations.

- The **grand theory** of international relations is presented by **Hans J. Morgenthau** in *Politics Among Nations* (1948). He argues for **realism** in the study of interactions on the international stage. Morgenthau suggests that an analysis of relations among nations reveals such recurring themes as "interest defined as power" and striving for equilibrium/balance of power as a means of maintaining peace.

- The **idealists** assume that human nature is essentially good; hence, people and nations are capable of cooperation and avoiding armed conflict. They highlight global organizations, international law, disarmament, and the reform of institutions that lead to war.

An analysis of international politics can be conducted at various levels by looking at the actions of individual statesmen, the interests of individual nations, and/or the mechanics of a whole system of international players. In studying the rise of nazism and its role in precipitating World War II, the **individual** approach would focus on Hitler, the **state** approach would treat the German preoccupation with racial superiority and the need for expansion, and the **systemic** approach would highlight how German military campaigns upset the balance of power and triggered unlikely alliances, such as the linking of the democratic Britain and the United States with the totalitarian Soviet Union in a common effort to restore equilibrium.

Foreign Policy Perspectives

Foreign policy involves the objectives nations seek to gain with reference to other nations and the procedures in which they engage in order to achieve their objectives. The principal foreign policy goals of sovereign states or other political entities may include some or all of the following: independence, national security, economic advancement, encouraging their political values beyond their own borders, gaining respect and prestige, and promoting stability and international peace.

The **foreign policy process** involves the stages a government goes through in formulating policy and arriving at decisions with respect to courses of action. The **primary players** (nations, world organizations, multinational corporations, and non-state ethnic entities such as the Palestine Liberation Organization) are often referred to as **actors**.

The **unitary/rational actor model** assumes that all nations or primary players share similar goals and approach foreign policy issues in like fashion. The actions players take, according to this theory, are influenced by the actions of other players rather than by what may be taking place internally. Maximizing goals and achieving specific objectives motivate the rational actor's course of action.

The **bureaucratic model** assumes that, due to the many large organizations involved in formulating foreign policy, final decisions are the result of struggle among the bureaucratic actors. In the United States, the bureaucratic actors include the **Departments of State and Defense**, as well as the **National Security Council**, the **Central Intelligence Agency**, the **Environmental Protection Agency**, the **Department of Commerce**, and/or any other agencies and departments whose agendas might be impacted by a foreign policy decision. The downside of this model is that inter-agency competition and compromise often drive the final decision.

A third model assumes that foreign policy results from the intermingling of a variety of political factors including national leaders, bureaucratic organizations, legislative bodies, political parties, interest groups, and public opinion.

The **implementation of foreign policy** depends upon the tools a nation or primary player has at its disposal. The major instruments of foreign policy include **diplomacy**, **military strength/actions**, and **economic initiatives**.

Diplomacy involves communicating with other primary players through official representatives. It might include attending conferences and summit meetings, negotiating treaties and settlements, and exchanging official communications.

The extent to which a player may rely on the **military** tool depends upon its technological strength, its readiness, and the support of both its domestic population and the international community. Sometimes the buildup of military capabilities is in itself a powerful foreign policy tool and thus a deterrent to armed conflict—as was the case in the Cold War between the United States and the Soviet Union.

Economic development and the ability to employ economic initiatives to achieve foreign policy objectives are effective means by which a principal player can interact on the international scene. Membership in an economic community such as **OPEC (Organization of Petroleum Exporting Countries)** or the **EC (European Community)** can drive the foreign policy of both member nations and those impacted by their decisions.

The Modern Global System

1. Historical Context of the Modern Global System

The modern global system or network of relationships among nations owes its origins to the emergence of the **nation-state**. It is generally recognized that the **Peace of Westphalia** (1648) gave birth to the concept of the modern nation-state. The old feudal order in Europe that allowed the Holy Roman Emperor to extend his influence over the territories governed by local princes was replaced by a new one in which distinct geographic and political entities interacted under a new set of principles. These allowed the nation-states to conduct business with each other, such as negotiating treaties and settling border disputes, without interference from a higher authority. Hence, the concept of **sovereignty** evolved.

The eighteenth century in Europe was notable for its relatively even distribution of power among the nation-states. With respect to military strength and international prestige, such nations as England, France, Austria, Prussia, and Russia were on the same scale. Some of the former major powers, such as Spain, the Netherlands, and Portugal, occupied a secondary status. Both the major and secondary players created alliances and competed with each other for control of territories beyond their borders. Alignments, based primarily on economic and colonial considerations, shifted without upsetting the global system.

Military conflicts in the eighteenth century tended to be conservative with the concept of the **balance of power** at play. Wiping out the enemy was not the principal goal. Major upheavals were avoided through the formation of alliances and a high regard for the authority of monarchs and the Christian Church. The eighteenth century has been dubbed the "**golden age of diplomacy**" because it was an era of relative stability in which moderation and shared cultural values on the part of the decision-makers were the rule.

The nation-state of the eighteenth century was a relatively new phenomenon. This style of diplomacy was irrevocably altered by the French Revolution and the Napoleonic Wars that saw **nationality** emerge as a rallying point for conducting wars and for raising the citizens' armies necessary to succeed in military conflicts. The twentieth century has seen a particularly impassioned link between nationalism and war.

The scientific and industrial revolutions of the eighteenth century gave rise to advancements in **military technology** in the nineteenth and twentieth centuries that dramatically altered the concept and the conduct of war. Replacing the eighteenth century conservative, play-by-the-rules approach was a new, fiercely violent brand of warfare that increasingly involved civilian casualties and aimed at utter destruction of the enemy. The development of **nuclear weapons** in the mid-twentieth century rendered total war largely unfeasible. Nuclear arms buildups, with the goal of **deterrent capabilities** (the means to retaliate so swiftly and effectively that an enemy will avoid conflict), was viewed by the superpowers as the only safety net.

Another factor molding the structural changes in international relations that surfaced in the nineteenth and twentieth centuries was the **ideological component**. Again the French Revolution, anchored in the ideology of "liberty, equality, and fraternity," is viewed as the harbinger of future trends. Those conservative forces valuing legitimacy and monarchy fought the forces of the Revolution and Napoleon to preserve tradition against the rising tide of republican nationalism. In the twentieth century, with its binding "isms"—**Communism**, **democratic republicanism**, **liberalism**, **Nazism**, **socialism**—competing for dominance, ideological conflicts have become more pronounced.

2. The Contemporary Global System

The values of the contemporary system are rooted in the currents of eighteenth and nineteenth century Europe, transplanted to the rest of the world through colonialism and imperialism. The forces of nationalism, belief in technological progress, and ideological motivations, as well as the desire for international respect and prestige, are evident worldwide.

The contemporary scene in international relations is comprised of a number of entities beyond the nation-state. Contemporary **nation-states** are legal entities occupying well-defined geographic areas and organized under a common set of governmental institutions. They are recognized by other members of the international community as sovereign and independent states.

Non-state actors or **principal players** are movements or parties that function as independent states. They lack sovereignty, but they may actually wield more power than some less developed nation-states. The **Palestine Liberation Organization (PLO)** and the **Irish Republican Army (IRA)** are examples of non-state actors.

Nonterritorial transnational organizations are institutions such as the Catholic Church that conduct activities throughout the world but whose aims are largely nonpolitical. A relatively new nonterritorial transnational organization is the **multi-national corporation (MNC)**, such as General Motors, Hitachi, or British Petroleum. These giant business entities have bases in a number of countries and exist primarily for economic profit.

An **intergovernmental organization**, such as the **United Nations**, **NATO**, or the **European Community (EC)**, is made up of nation-states and can wield significant power on the international scene. While NATO is primarily a military intergovernmental organization and the EC is mainly economic, the UN is really a multipurpose entity. While its primary mission is to promote world peace, the UN engages in a variety of social, cultural, economic, health, and humanitarian activities.

The contemporary global system tends to classify nation-states based on power, wealth, and prestige in the international community. Such labels as **superpower**, **secondary power**, **middle power**, **small power**, and the like tend to be confusing, however, because they are not based on a single set of criteria or a shared set of standards.

The **structure** of the contemporary global system during the Cold War was distinctly **bipolar**, with the United States and the Soviet Union assuming diplomatic, ideological, and military leadership for the international community. When tensions between the United States and the Soviet Union eased, a **multipolar system**, in which new alignments are flexible and more easily drawn, emerged. The **New World Order** involves alliances that transcend the old bipolar scheme with its emphasis on ideology and military superiority and calls for multinational cooperation. It also assumes greater non-military, transnational cooperation in scientific research and humanitarian projects. The multipolar system is less cohesive than the bipolar system of the recent past and the orders of the distant past, such as the **hierarchical system** (one unit dominates) of the Holy Roman Empire or the **diffuse system** (power and influence are distributed among a large number of units) of eighteenth-century Europe.

International Law

The present system of international law is rooted in the fundamental rules of global relations: **territorial integrity**, **sovereignty**, and **legal equality of nation-states**. It embodies a set of basic principles mandating what countries may or may not do and under what conditions the rules should be applied.

1. Historical Context

Contemporary international law emanates from the Western legal traditions of Greece, Rome, and modern Europe. In medieval Europe, the church's emphasis on hierarchical obligations, duty, and obedience to authority helped shape the notion of the "**just war**." **Hugo Grotius** (1583–1645), Dutch scholar and statesman, codified the laws of war and peace and has been called the "**father of international law**."

In 1648, the Peace of Westphalia promulgated the idea of the treaty as the basis of international law. Multilateral treaties dominated the eighteenth century, while Britain, with its unparalleled sea power, established and enforced maritime law. By the nineteenth century, advances in military technology rendered the old standard of the "just war" obsolete. Deterrents, rather than legal and ethical principles, provided the means to a relatively stable world order. The concept of **neutrality** evolved during this period, defining the rights and responsibilities of both warring and neutral nations.

2. Contemporary International Law

In the twentieth century, international law retreated theoretically from the tradition of using force as a legitimate tool for settling international conflicts. The **Covenant of the League of Nations** (1920), the **Kellogg-Briand Pact** (1929), and the **United Nations Charter** (1945) all emphasize peaceful relations among nations, but the use of force continues to be employed to achieve political ends. The **International Court of Justice**, the judicial arm of the United Nations, and its predecessor, the **Permanent Court of International Justice**, represent concerted efforts to replace armed conflict with the rule of law. Unfortunately, the World Court has proven to be an ineffective organization. Nation-states are reluctant to submit vital questions to the Court, and there is a lack of consensus as to the norms to be applied.

The UN Charter seeks to humanize the international scene in its admonition that all member nations assist victims of aggression. Aggressive conflicts can be categorized as crimes against humanity, and individuals may be held personally accountable for launching them.

The concept of international law has been criticized on several fronts. The rise of **multiculturalism**, with its emphasis on multiple perspectives, has called into question the relevance of applying Western legal traditions to the global community. Strong nation-states are in a position to both enforce international law and to violate it without fear of reprisal. These observations have led some to conclude that international law is primarily an instrument to maintain the **status quo**.

International law can be effective if parties involved see some **mutual self-advantage** in compliance. **Fear of reprisal** is another factor influencing nations to observe the tenets of international law. **Diplomatic advantage** and **enhanced global prestige** may follow a nation's decisions to abide by international law. It can be argued that international law is valuable in that it seeks to impose **order** on a potentially chaotic system and sets expectations that, while not always met, are positive and affirming.

SOCIOLOGY

INTRODUCTION TO SOCIOLOGY
What Is Sociology?

Sociology is the science or discipline that studies societies, social groups, and the relationships between people. The field encompasses both the formation and transformation of particular societies and social groups, including their continuation, dissolution, and demise, as well as the origins, structure, and functioning of social groups.

The Unit of Study

Sociologists focus on a number of different levels of analysis in understanding social life. While some study the **social interaction** that occurs within groups (the social processes represented by behavior directed toward, affected by, or inspired by others in the group), other sociologists study the **social structure** of group life. Some are interested in the structure of societies. That is, the organization of populations living in the same area who participate in the same institutions and who share a common culture. Others in the field are concerned with the social system, a social group, or with society conceived as a whole unit distinct from the individuals that make it up.

Others concern themselves with **social relationships**, or relationships between people that are based upon common meaning, or with social action, defined as meaningful behavior that is oriented toward and influenced by others. But no matter what is designated to be the unit of study, the focus of the discipline is on social groups and society as a whole, rather than on the individual, which is the focus of psychology.

The Perspective: Humanistic or Scientific

Some sociologists adopt a **humanistic** approach to their work, which means that they see sociology as a means to advance human welfare. They seek self-realization, the full development of a cultivated personality, or improvement of the human social condition.

On the other hand, some sociologists adopt the **scientific perspective**. They are primarily concerned with acquiring objective **empirical knowledge** (the actual knowledge derived from experience or observation that can be measured or counted) and not with the uses to which such knowledge is put.

The Sociological Imagination

C. Wright Mills proposed a certain quality of mind is required if we are to understand ourselves in relation to society. The **sociological imagination** expresses both an understanding that personal troubles can and often do reflect broader social issues and problems and also faith in the capacity of human beings to alter the course of human history. The sociological imagination, therefore, expresses the humanistic aspect of the sociological perspective.

The Science of Sociology

Unlike the rocks and molecules studied by natural scientists, we are capable of changing our minds and our behavior. Unlike the organisms studied by biologists, we are capable of treating each other as whole and complete beings. Hence, the explanations and predictions offered by sociology cannot be so precise as to express universal laws that are applicable to any thing or event under all circumstances.

The Social Sciences

The **social sciences** are concerned with social life—**psychology**, with its emphasis on individual behavior and mental processes; **economics**, with its emphasis on the production, distribution, and consumption of goods and services; **political science**, with its emphasis on political philosophy and forms of government; and **anthropology**, with its current emphasis on both primitive and modern culture.

THE ORIGINS OF SOCIOLOGY

Compared to other academic disciplines (e.g., history, economics, and physics, in particular), **sociology** is a discipline still in its prime. In 1838 **Auguste Comte** coined the term from *socius* (the Latin word for "companion, with others") and *logos* (the Greek word for "study of") as a means of demarcating the field: its subject matter, society as distinct from the mere sum of individual actions, and its methods, prudent observation and impartial measurement based on the scientific method of comparison.

In the first stage in sociology's development, the **theological stage,** scientists look toward the supernatural realm of ideas for an explanation of what they observed. In the second, or **metaphysical stage**, scientists begin to look to the real world for an explanation of what they have observed. Finally, in the **positive stage**, which is defined as the definitive stage of all knowledge, scientists search for general ideas or laws. With such knowledge of society as how society is held together (social statics) and of how society changes (social dynamics), people can predict and, thereby, control their destiny.

Was Comte's conception of a science of society ahead of its time, or was his conception of a science that would allow human beings control over lives timely? If one considers intellectual history, notwithstanding the accomplishments of Harriet Martineau (1802–1876), who was observing English social patterns at the same time that Comte was laying a foundation for sociology; Karl Marx (1818–1883), "the theoretical giant of communist thought," whose prophecies are still being hotly debated; and Herbert Spencer (1820–1903), whose idea that society follows a natural evolutionary progression toward something better, then Comte was clearly ahead of his time. More than 50 years passed before Emile Durkheim (1858–1917), in his statistical study of suicide, and Max Weber (1864–1920), in a series of studies in which he sought to explain the origins of capitalism, came along and tested Comte's ideas.

Under the influence of Lester Ward (1841–1913) and William Graham Sumner (1840–1910), American sociology experienced a loss of interest in the larger problems of social order and social change and began to concentrate on narrower and more specific social problems. Until 1940 attention in the discipline was focused on the University of Chicago where George Herbert Mead was originating the field of social psychology. Robert Park and Ernest Burgess were concentrating on the city and on such social problems as crime, drug addiction, prostitution, and juvenile delinquency.

By the 1940s, attention began to shift away from reforming society and toward developing abstract theories of how society works and standardizing the research methods that sociologists employ. Talcott Parsons (1902–1979), the famed functionalist, touched a generation of sociologists by advocating **grand theory**. This involved the building of a theory of society based on aspects of the real world and the organization of these concepts to form a conception of society as a stable system of interrelated parts.

Robert Merton (1910–2003) proposed building middle range theories from a limited number of assumptions from which hypotheses are derived. Merton also distinguished between **manifest**, or intended, and **latent**, or unintended, consequences of existing elements of social structure which are either functional or dysfunctional to the system's relative stability.

No single viewpoint or concern has dominated the thinking of sociologists since the 1970s. Sociologists have yet to agree on whether the goals of sociology are description, explanation, prediction, or control.

THE THEORETICAL APPROACH

Sociologists often use a theoretical approach or perspective to guide them in their work. In making certain general assumptions about social life, the perspective provides a point of view toward the study of specific social issues.

The Theory: Inductive or Deductive

A **theory** describes and/or explains the relationship between two or more observations. **Deductive theory** proceeds from general ideas, knowledge, or understanding of the social world from which specific hypotheses are logically deduced and tested. **Inductive theory** proceeds from concrete observations from which general conclusions are inferred through a process of reasoning.

More recent sociology includes three such approaches: **interpretative**, which includes the perspectives of symbolic interaction, dramaturgy, and ethnomethodology; **conflict theory**; and **structural functionalism**.

Interpretative Sociology

Interpretative sociology studies the processes whereby human beings attach meaning to their lives. Derived from the work of Mead and Blumer, **symbolic interaction** is focused on the process of social interaction and on the meanings that are constructed and reconstructed in that process. Human beings are viewed as shaping their actions based upon both the real and anticipated responses of others. Out of the symbolic interactionist school of thought, the social construction of **reality**—the familiar notion that human beings shape their world and are shaped by social interaction—was conceived.

Focused on the details of everyday life, the **dramaturgical approach** of Erving Goffman conceives social interaction as a series of episodes or human dramas in which we are more or less aware of playing roles and, thereby, engaging in impression management. We are actors seeking

(1) to manipulate our audience, or control the reaction of other people in our immediate presence by presenting a certain image of ourselves; (2) to protect or hide our true selves, or who we really are offstage through "onstage," "frontstage," and "backstage" behavior; and (3) to amplify the rules of conduct that circumscribe our daily encounters.

Conflict Theory

The **conflict paradigm** views society as being characterized by conflict and inequality. Sociologists viewing the social world from a conflict perspective question how factors such as race, sex, social class, and age are associated with an unequal distribution of socially valued goods and rewards (i.e., money, education, and power). Generally associated with the work of Coser, Dahrendorf, and Mills, modern conflict theory sees conflict between groups or within social organizations, and not merely class conflict (Marx), as a fact of life of any society.

Structural Functionalism

Inspired by the writings of Emile Durkheim and Herbert Spencer, **functionalism** (or structural functionalism) originally took as its logical starting point a society conceived as a social system of interrelated parts, and therefore analogous to a living organism where each part contributes to the overall stability of the whole. Society, then, is seen as a complex system whose components work with one another.

THE METHODS OF RESEARCH
Defining Research Methods

The term **research methods** refers both to a strategy or plan for carrying out research and the means of carrying out the strategy. Some sociologists favor **quantitative methods**. They make use of statistical and other mathematical techniques of quantification or measurement in their efforts to describe and interpret their observations. Others favor **qualitative methods**, relying on personal observation and description of social life in order to explain behavior. Conceding that their methods entail the loss of precision, they argue that their method achieves a deeper grasp of the texture of social life.

Verstehen, developed by Max Weber, is understanding as a means of characterizing and interpreting or explaining. This is done through applying reason to the external and inner context of specific social situations, such as the origins of Western capitalism.

Survey Research

Sociologists most often use the **survey method** of observation in their research. Subjects are asked about their opinions, beliefs, or behavior in a series of questions. The information is collected directly by means of an **interview**, or indirectly by means of a self-administered **questionnaire** that the respondents fill out themselves. Interviews may be conducted in person, by phone, or even by electronic means of communication.

The interview may be structured where respondents are asked a series of questions in which they are given a limited choice between several possible responses on each question, unstructured where respondents are asked questions to which they can respond freely in their own words, or may involve the use of a combination of both open-ended and close-ended questions.

A survey can be mainly **descriptive** or **explanatory**. In the latter case, researchers may be interested in understanding either causal or correlational relationships between variables. Variables can either be **independent** or **dependent**. An independent variable is one that influences another variable, while the dependent variable is the one being influenced by another variable (the cause and effect, respectively). A **control** is a technique of differentiating between factors that may or may not influence the relationship between variables. Relationships between two variables can either be **correlational** or **causal**. A correlational relationship exists when a change in one variable coincides with, but doesn't cause, a change in another. A causal relationship exists when a change in one variable causes or forces a change in the other.

If the population is relatively large, a sample will be selected for study from the entire population.

Types of Samples

Representative sample	A sample that accurately reflects the population from which it is drawn.
Random sample	A sample where every member of the population has the same chance of being chosen for study.
Systematic sampling	A type of sample in which the *n*th unit in a list is selected for inclusion in the sample. For example, every fiftieth resident listed in a phone book of a given area will be selected.
Stratified sampling	A sample that uses the differences that already exist in a population, such as between males and females, as the basis for selecting a sample. Knowing the percentage of the population that falls into a particular category, the researcher then randomly selects a number of persons to be studied from each category in the same proportion as exists in the population.

Experimentation

In the broadest sense, **experimentation** involves the observation, measurement, or calculation of the consequences of an action. Typically, the social science researcher selects a group of subjects to be studied (the **experimental group**), exposes them to a particular condition, and then measures the results, usually against that of a **control group** (a similar population upon which the action has not been performed). Experiments are used to test theories and the hypotheses drawn from them.

Field experiments are carried out in natural settings. One of the most famous field experiments of social science was conducted in the 1930s at the Hawthorne Plant of the Western Electric Company in Chicago. This research led Elton May to identify what has come to be known as the **Hawthorne effect**, which showed that the mere presence of a researcher affects the subject's behavior.

Observation

Observation is a technique that provides firsthand experience of real situations. **Unobtrusive observation** is observation from a distance, without being involved in the group or activity being studied.

Often referred to as field research, **participant observation** is observation by a researcher who is (or appears to be) a member of the group or a participant in the activity he/she is studying. Participant observers may or may not conceal their identities as researchers.

Secondary Analysis

Secondary analysis refers to the analysis of existing sources of information. In the hope of discovering something new, the researcher examines old records and documents, including archives and official statistics provided by the government.

Content analysis refers to the techniques employed to describe the contents of the materials. They may be quantitative—using such techniques as percentages, rates, or averages to describe how the contents vary (e.g., arithmetic means, modes, or medians), or qualitative—using concepts and employing reason to capture the contents of the materials observed.

The Stages of Research

Research is a process that includes:

1. **Defining the problem**—the questions, issues, or topic with which one is concerned.

2. **Identifying and reviewing the literature or relevant literature bearing upon the problem.**

3. **Formulating a hypothesis**—a tentative statement about what one expects to observe (e.g., the prediction of a relationship between variables or the prediction that a certain relation between people will be obtained).

4. **Selecting and implementing a research design to test one's hypothesis**—the plan for collecting and analyzing information.

5. **Drawing a conclusion**—determining whether or not one's hypothesis is confirmed and presenting one's findings in an organized way that both describes and, wherever possible, explains what one has observed.

Ethical Problems in Conducting Research

Sociologists can and often do encounter ethical problems or dilemmas in conducting research. Some of the following are concerns of sociologists who conduct research:

1. What harm, if any, is the research likely to bring to participants? Does the knowledge gained justify the risks involved?

2. Is the privacy of subjects being invaded, and should the privacy of subjects be maintained under all circumstances?

3. Do subjects have a right to be informed that they are being studied? Is their consent necessary?

4. Does it matter how the research results will or can be applied? Should this affect the research design or the way in which the research is reported?

5. When, if at all, is deception in conducting research or in reporting the research results justified?

SOCIALIZATION

The Process of Socialization and Self-Formation

Socialization is the process through which we learn or are trained to be members of society, to take part in new social situations, or to participate in social groupings. In other words, it is the prescriptive term in sociology for the process of being "social."

Generally, sociologists consider the process of socialization to be based on **social interaction**, the ways in which we behave toward and respond to one another. Sociologists tend to differ in their opinion of what is learned, produced, reproduced, or altered in the process of socialization: (1) in their orientation toward society, social groups, social structure, or man-made culture; and (2) in their conception of the part, if any, human biology and individual psychology play in socialization.

1. Primary and Secondary Forms of Socialization

Sociologists hold the view that the individual cannot develop in the absence of the **social environment**—the groups within which interaction takes place and socialization occurs. Within this context, **primary socialization** refers to the initial socialization that a child receives through which he or she becomes a member of society (i.e., learns and comes to share the social heritage or culture of a society through the groups into which he or she is born). **Secondary socialization** refers to the subsequent experience of socialization into new sectors of society by an already socialized person.

2. Personality

The socialization process is thought to explain both the similarities in personality and social behavior of the members of society and the differences that exist in society between one person and the next. It does not matter then that the two factors of **nature** and **nurture** are intimately related and cannot be separated. Hence, the part that human biology plays in socialization (i.e., of nature in nurture) cannot be accurately measured. Heredity represents a basic potential, the outlines and limits of which are biologically fixed, because the socialization process is thought to be all important to the development of personality.

Instincts (unlearned, inherited behavior patterns that human beings once had) may have been lost in the course of human evolution. There is no human nature outside of what culture makes of us. Hence, the concern that children raised in isolation or in institutions, who have little or no opportunity to develop the sorts of emotional ties with adults that make socialization possible, will be devoid of personality and will lack the social skills necessary to face even the simplest of life's challenges.

The process of becoming human is understood to be the process of socialization. The self at the core of personality, the individual's conscious experience of having a separate unique identity, is thought to be a social product objectively created and transformed throughout a person's life by interaction with others.

Agents of Socialization

1. Family

Generally considered the most basic social institution, the **family** is a union that is sanctioned by the state and often by a religious institution such as a church. As such, the family provides continuity in such areas as language, personality traits, religion, and class. The family is generally believed to be the most important agent of socialization in a child's social world, until schooling begins. Although the school and peer group become central to social experience as the child grows older, the family remains central throughout the entire life course.

2. School

As the social unit devoted to providing an education, the **school** provides continuity both in cognitive skills and in the indoctrination of values. Unlike the family, which is based on personal relationships, in school the child's social experiences broaden to include people of a variety of different social backgrounds. It is here where children learn the importance society gives to race and gender.

3. Peer Groups

As a primary group whose members are roughly equal in status, **peer groups** (such as play groups) provide continuity in lifestyles. Although first peer groups generally consist of a young child's neighborhood playmates, as the child meets new people at school and becomes involved in other activities, his peer group expands. It is in the peer group where the child, free of direct supervision from adults, comes to define him- or herself as independent from his family. During adolescence the peer group becomes particularly important to the child and sometimes proves to be a more influential agent of socialization than the family.

4. Mass Media

Mass media (books, radio, television, the internet, and motion pictures) provides continuity as far as knowledge or public information about the people, the events, and changes occurring in society and the threat they sometimes pose to the existing social order.

Resocialization and the Role of Total Institution

Resocialization refers to the process occurring throughout our lives of discarding behavioral practices and adopting new ones as part of a transition in life. For example, when one becomes a parent for the first time, he or she may have to perform new duties. Resocialization, however, can be a much more dramatic process, especially when it takes place in a **total institution**, such as a place of residence to where persons are confined for a period of time and cut off from the rest of society. Some examples of total institutions include mental hospitals, the military, and prisons.

MAJOR FIGURES IN SOCIOLOGY

Sigmund Freud

An Austrian physician and the founder of psychoanalysis, **Sigmund Freud** (1856–1939) considered biological drives to be the primary source of human activity. Activated by the pleasure principle to demand immediate and complete gratification of biological needs, the id represents these unconscious strivings without specific direction or purpose, which must be repressed and subsequently channeled in socially acceptable directions. Otherwise, the human being would be a violent, amoral, predatory animal, and organized social life would be impossible. According to Freud it is through the processes or mechanisms of identification and repression (the holding back and the hiding of one's own feelings) that the human personality is formed—which is comprised of the **id**, the **ego**, and the **superego**. The ego represents the most conscious aspect of personality. Defining opportunities, the goals one strives toward, and what is "real," the ego controls and checks the id. Operating according to the pleasure principle, the ego deals with the world in terms of what is possible, providing limits and direction.

Charles Horton Cooley

An economist turned social psychologist, **Charles Horton Cooley** (1864–1924) theorized that the self-concept, which is formed in childhood, is reevaluated every time the person enters a new social situation. There are three stages in the process of self-formation, which Cooley referred to as "the **looking-glass self**": (1) we imagine how we appear to others; (2) we wonder whether others see us in the same way as we see ourselves, and in order to find out, we observe how others react to us; and (3) we develop a conception of ourselves that is based on the judgments of others.

George Herbert Mead

An American philosopher and social psychologist, **George Herbert Mead** (1863–1931) is best known for his evolutionary social theory of the genesis of the mind and self. Mead's basic thesis—that a single act can best be understood as a segment of a larger social act or communicative transaction between two or more persons—made social psychology central to his philosophical approach. Mead used several concepts: the "Me" is the image one forms of one's self from the standpoint of a "generalized others" and the "I" is the individual's reaction to a situation as he sees it from his unique standpoint.

Mead pointed out that one outcome of socialization is the ability to anticipate the reactions of others and to adjust our behavior accordingly. We do this, Mead argues, by role taking or learning to model the behavior of significant others, such as our parents. For example, playing "house" allows children to view the world from their parents' perspective.

Erving Goffman

Like other sociologists, **Erving Goffman** (1922–1983) considered the self to be a reflection of others—the cluster of roles or expectations of the people with whom one is involved at that point in the life course. Goffman used the term **role-distance** to describe the gap that exists between who we are and who we portray ourselves to be.

Jean Piaget

Based on experiments with children playing and responding to questions, Swiss psychologist **Jean Piaget** (1896–1980) proposed a theory of **cognitive development** that describes the changes that occur over time in the ways children think, understand, and evaluate a situation. Piaget observed that cognitive development does not occur automatically. A given stage of cognitive development cannot be reached unless the individual is confronted with real life experiences that foster such development. In the **sensorimotor stage**, infants are unable to differentiate themselves from their environment. They are unaware that their actions produce results, and they lack the understanding that objects exist separate from the direct and immediate experience of touching, looking, sucking, and listening.

Through sensory experience and physical contact with their environment, infants begins to experience their surroundings differently. In the **preoperational stage** children begin to use language and other symbols. Not only do children begin to attach meaning to the world, they also are able to differentiate fantasy from reality.

In the **concrete operational stage**, children make great strides in their use of logic to understand the world and how it operates. They begin to think in logical terms, to make the connection between cause and effect, and are capable of attaching meaning or significance to a particular event. During this stage of cognitive development the foundation for engaging in more complex activities with others (such as role taking) is laid. Finally, in the **formal operational stage** children develop the capacity for thinking in highly abstract terms of metaphors and hypotheses which may or may not be based in reality.

Erik Erikson

Departing from Freud's emphasis on childhood and instinct, **Erik Erikson** (1902–1994) delineated eight stages of psychosocial development in which **ego identity** (that sense of continuity and sameness in the conception one has of one's self that does not change over time or situation), **ego development** (the potential for change and growth that exists over the course of a person's life), and the **social environment** are involved. They are:

Stage 1—the nurturing stage, in which one's sense of either basic trust or mistrust is established.

Stage 2—there emerges the feeling of autonomy or feelings of doubt and shame from not being able to handle the situations one encounters in life.

Stage 3—one develops either a sense of initiative and self-confidence or feelings of guilt depending on how successful one is in exploring the environment and in dealing with peers.

Stage 4—the focus shifts from family to school where one develops a conception of being either industrious or inferior.

Stage 5—failure to establish a clear and firm sense of one's self results in the person's becoming confused about his or her identity.

Stage 6—one meets or fails to meet the challenge presented by young adulthood of forming stable relationships, the outcome being "intimacy or isolation and loneliness."

Stage 7—one's contribution to the well-being of others through citizenship, work, and family becomes self-generative, and hence, one's fulfilling of the primary tasks of mature adulthood is complete.

Stage 8—the developmental challenge posed by the knowledge that one is reaching the end is to find a sense of continuity and meaning and hence, to break the sense of isolation and self-absorption that the thought of one's impending death produces, thereby yielding to despair.

Lawrence Kohlberg

Lawrence Kohlberg (1927–1987) concluded that, given the proper experience and stimulation, children go through a sequence of six stages of moral reasoning. At the earliest stage (between ages 4 and 10), a child's sense of good and bad is connected with the fear of being punished for disobeying those in positions of power. During adolescence, a child's conformity to the rules is connected with the belief that the existing social order must ultimately be the right and true order and therefore ought to be followed.

Finally, older children and young adults have reached the highest of two stages of moral development, and are able to consider the welfare of the community, the rights of the individual, and such universal ethical principles as justice, equality, and individual dignity. Kohlberg has been criticized for basing his model of human development on the male experience, having assumed that women and girls are incapable of reaching the higher stages of moral reasoning.

Carol Gilligan

Taking Kohlberg to task on this point, **Carol Gilligan** (b 1936) found that women bring a different set of values to their judgments of right and wrong. In effect, these different approaches to resolving the problem can be explained by the different roles women have in our society as compared with men. Thus, Gilligan concludes there is no essential difference between the inner workings of the psyches of boys and girls.

Major Figures in Sociology

Sigmund Freud	Founder of psychoanalysis, believed biological drives (id, ego, superego) are the primary source of human activity.
Charles Horton Cooley	Postulated the "looking-glass self" in which the self-concept is reevaluated every time a person enters a new social situation.
George Herbert Mead	Best known for his evolutionary theory of the genesis of the mind and self; used the concepts of "me," "generalized others," and "I."
Erving Goffman	Considered the self to be a reflection of others; used the term *role-distance* to describe the gap between who we are and who we portray ourselves to be.

Jean Piaget	Proposed the theory of cognitive development describing the changes one goes through in learning (sensorimotor stage, preoperational stage, concrete operational stage, formal operational stage).
Erik Erikson	Delineated the eight stages of psychosocial development involving ego identity, ego development, and the social environment.
Lawrence Kohlberg	Proposed a sequence of six stages of moral reasoning.
Carol Gilligan	Discovered women bring a different set of values to their judgments of right and wrong compared with men.

SOCIAL INTERACTION

Defining Social Interaction

Consistent with Weber's view of society, every culture has a structure that can be described and analyzed. This structure represents the multitude of shared values, shared beliefs, and common expectations of a particular culture around which people have organized their lives, and leads to a certain degree of predictability in human affairs.

Social Structure, Society, and Social Systems

Social structure is the way in which people's relations in society are arranged to form a relatively organized network. Contrary, then, to the latter definition, *society* here does not represent a whole. The structure is thought to be composed of similar elements of **statuses** (position in a society or in a group), **roles** (the behavior of a person occupying a particular position), **groups** (a number of people interacting with one another in ways that form a pattern and who are united by the feeling of being bound together and by "a consciousness of kind"), and **institutions** (organized systems of social relationships that emerge in response to the basic problems or needs of every society).

The social structure is thought to be composed of multiple systems or institutions—each considered a total system unto itself—in addition to several other types of components. It is argued that certain elements are necessary to both individual and collective survival. When these elements become organized into institutional spheres, they form a society's economic system, political structure, family system, educational processes, and belief system.

Behavior is also thought to be largely determined by the definition of the situation (the process whereby we define, explain, and evaluate the social context of the situation we find ourselves in before deciding the behavior and attitudes that are appropriate).

Status

Status may refer to a position in society and/or in a group. An **ascribed status** is automatically and involuntarily conferred on individuals without any effort or choice made on their part. Being a Native American, a woman, a son, or a widower are examples of ascribed statuses. The opposite status, one that is assumed largely through one's own doings or efforts, is referred to as **achieved status**. Examples of achieved statuses include being a husband, a rock star, an "A" student, and an engineering major. **Master status** is the status with which a person is most identified. It is the most important status that a person holds.

Status set consists of all the statuses that a person occupies. A woman may, simultaneously be a mother to her children, a wife to her husband, a professor to her students, and a colleague to her coworkers.

Roles

Role refers to what a person does (i.e., the part he or she plays or how one is expected to behave) by virtue of occupying a particular status or position.

Every status and role is accompanied by a set of **norms** or **role expectations** describing behavioral expectations, or the limits of what people occupying the position are expected to do and of how they are expected to do it. In effect, group differences and the conflicts they generate are thought to continually transform the system and structure.

Role strain refers to the situation where different and conflicting expectations exist with regard to a particular status. For example, a professor may enjoy his students and may socialize outside of class with them. At the same time, though, he is responsible for ascertaining that their performance is up to par and that they attend class regularly. To achieve this end, he may have to distance himself from his students.

Role conflict occurs when a person occupies multiple statuses that contradict one another. For example, a single mother, who is the primary breadwinner, who plays on her church's softball team, and who is the den mother to her son's Boy Scout troop, may have conflicting roles corresponding to many of these statuses. This single mother may find that her volunteering duties conflict with her parenting and breadwinning duties.

GROUPS AND ORGANIZATIONS

Social Groups and Relationships

Strictly speaking, a **group** is an assembly of people or things. The members of a group are considered united generally through interaction, more specifically by the relationships they share, or in particular by the quality or specific character of the relationship between the individuals of which it is composed.

Associations and Communal Relationships

An **association** is a type of relationship formed on the basis of an accommodation of interests or on the basis of an agreement. A **communal relationship** is one formed on the basis of a subjective feeling of the parties "that they belong together" whether the feeling is personal or is linked with tradition. In practice, however, most actual associations and communities incorporate aspects of both types of relationships.

Social Groups

1. Peer Group

A **peer group** may be defined "as an association of self-selected equals" formed around common interests, sensibilities, preferences, and beliefs. A peer group consists of those whose ages, interests, and social positions or statuses are relatively equivalent and who are closely associated with one another. Peer groups serve to segregate their members from others on the basis of their age, sex, or generation.

2. Family

The conflict between the family and peer group is caused by the widening of the cultural gap that separates different generations who may even speak a different language. For example, **urbanism** (which allowed for sustained contact between age-mates) paved the way not only toward **age-grading** (the sensitivity toward chronological age gradations characteristic of modern culture), but also toward the age-graded sociability that is characteristic of our times.

3. Aggregates and Social Categories

Unlike an **aggregate**, which consists of a number of people who happen to be in the same place at the same time, or a **social category**, which consists of a number of people with certain characteristics in common, a **social group** consists of a collection of people interacting with one another in an orderly fashion.

An interdependence exists among the various members of a social group, which forges a feeling of belonging and a sense that the behavior of each person is relevant to each other. Thus, whether or not the membership of a social group is stable or changing, all such group relationships are thought to have two elements in common: (1) members are mutually aware of one another, and (2) members are mutually responsive to one another, with actions therefore determined by or shaped in the group context.

Social groups have been classified in many different ways—according to the group's size; nature of the interaction or the quality of the relationship that exists; whether or not membership is voluntary; whether or not a person belongs to and identifies with the group; or according to the group's purpose or composition.

4. Primary and Secondary Groups

Charles Horton Cooley (1864–1924) distinguished between primary groups and secondary groups. In a **primary group**, the interaction is direct, the common bonds are close and intimate, and the relationships among members are warm, intimate, and personal. In **secondary groups**, the interaction is anonymous, the bonds are impersonal, the duration of time of the group is short, and the relationships involve few emotional ties.

Characteristics of Groups

1. Gemeinschaft and Gesellschaft

Ferdinand Tönnies (1853–1936) distinguished between *gemeinschaft* (community) and *gesellschaft* (society). By **gemeinschaft**, Tönnies was referring to those small communities characterized by tradition and united by the belief in common ancestry or by geographic proximity in relationships largely of the primary group sort. **Gesellschaft** refers to contractual relationships of a voluntary nature of limited duration and quality, based on rational self-interest, and formed for the explicit purpose of achieving a particular goal.

2. Dyad and Triad

George Simmel (1858–1918) made the distinction between the **dyad** of two people in which either member's departure destroys the group, and the **triad** of three, the addition of a third person sometimes serving as a mediator or nonpartisan party.

3. Group Size and Other General Structural Properties

The smallest group consists of only two persons. Robert Bales developed the technique of **interaction process analysis**, that is, a technique of observing and immediately classifying in predetermined ways the ongoing activity in small groups. Also, J. L. Moreno (1889–1974) developed the technique of **sociometry**, a technique focused on establishing the direction of the interaction in small groups.

In addition to size, some of the other general structural properties and related social processes affecting the functioning of social groups are (1) the extent of association and (2) the social network of persons that together comprises all the relationships in which they are involved and groups to which they belong.

4. Interaction Processes

Also involved in the **interaction processes** (the ways role partners agree on goals, negotiate reaching them, and distribute resources) are such factors as:

1. the differentiation between the characteristics of the role structure with task or instrumental roles. **Instrumental roles** are oriented toward specific goals and expressive roles, which are instrumental in expressing and releasing group tension.

2. **front stage** (public) and **backstage** (free of public scrutiny) behavior.

3. **principles of exchange** (characteristic of market relationships in which people bargain for the goods and services they desire).

4. competition between individuals and groups over scarce resources in which the parties not only agree to adhere to certain rules of the game but also believe they are necessary or fair.

5. **cooperation** (an agreement to share resources for the purpose of achieving a common goal).

6. **compromise** (an agreement to relinquish certain claims in the interest of achieving more modest goals).

7. **conflict** (the attempt by one party to destroy, undermine, or harm another) and such related methods of reducing or temporarily eliminating conflict as **coaptation** (the case of dissenters being absorbed into the dominant group), **mediation** (the effort to resolve a conflict through the use of a third party), and the ritualized release of hostility under carefully controlled circumstances such as the Olympic games.

5. In-Group and Out-Group

Other types of social groups include **in-groups** which, unlike **out-groups** (those groups toward which a person feels a sense of competition or opposition), are those to which "we" belong.

6. Reference Group

Reference groups are social groups that provide the standards in terms of which we evaluate ourselves. For example, if a college student is worried about how her family will react to her grades, she is using her family as a reference group.

7. Group Conformity and Groupthink

Group conformity refers to individuals' compliance with group goals, in spite of the fact that group goals may be in conflict with individual goals. In an attempt to be accepted or "fit in," individuals may engage in behaviors they normally would not.

Groupthink, a related phenomenon, occurs when group members begin to think similarly and conform to one another's views. The danger in this is that decisions may be made from a narrow view.

Group Leadership

Leadership is an element of all groups. A **leader** is a person who initiates the behavior of others by directing, organizing, influencing, or controlling what members do and how they think.

1. Instrumental and Expressive Leaders

Group research has found two different types of leaders: **instrumental** (task-oriented leaders who organize the group in the pursuit of its goals) and **expressive** (social-emotional leaders who achieve harmony and solidarity among group members by offering emotional support).

2. Authoritarian, Democratic, and Laissez-faire Styles of Leadership

The **authoritarian** leader gives orders, the **democratic** leader seeks a consensus on the course of action to be taken, and the **laissez-faire** leader mainly lets the group be—doing little if anything to provide direction or organization.

Organizations

An **organization** represents a specific type of social relationship or arrangement between persons that is either closed to outsiders or that limits their admission. Regulations are enforced by a person or by a number of persons in authority active in enforcing the order governing the organization.

1. Formal Organization

In the latter sense, a **formal organization**, which represents a type of group or structural pattern within which behavior is carried out in a society, is characterized by (1) formality, (2) a hierarchy of ranked positions, (3) large size, (4) a rather complex division of labor, and (5) continuity beyond its membership.

Bureaucracy

1. Weber's Ideal Type

The basic organization of society may be found in its **characteristic institution**. In prehistoric times, the characteristic institution of most societies was the kin, clan, or sib. In modern times, particularly in the West, as cities became urban centers for trade and commerce, the characteristic institution became, and remains today, a bureaucracy.

A **bureaucracy** is a rational system of organization, administration, discipline, and control. Ideally, a bureaucracy has the following characteristics:

1. Paid officials on a fixed salary which is their primary source of income.

2. Officials who are accorded certain rights and privileges as a result of making a career out of holding office.

3. Regular salary increases, seniority rights, and promotions upon passing exams.

4. Officials who qualify to enter the organization by having advanced education or vocational training.

5. The rights, responsibilities, obligations, privileges, and work procedures of these officials are rigidly and formally defined by the organization.

6. Officials are responsible for meeting the obligations of the office and for keeping the funds and files of that office separate from their personal ones.

2. Bureaucracy in Real Life

Weber never meant for his ideal type conception of bureaucracy to be confused with reality. Rather, he intended that it be used as a measuring rod against which to measure empirical reality (as grounded in perceived experience). In so doing Joseph Bensman and Bernard Rosenberg (1976) learned, for instance, that most modern bureaucrats are "people pushing" rather than "pencil pushing" types of white-collar employees. The advancement opportunities for these employees hinge as much on how well they are liked, trusted, and how easy they are to get along with as on how well they objectively qualify for a position.

3. Parkinson's Law

Named after its author, C. Northcote Parkinson, **Parkinson's Law** states that in any bureaucratic organization "work expands to fill the time available for its completion."

4. The Peter Principle

Named after Lawrence Peter, the **Peter Principle** states that "in any hierarchy every employee tends to rise to his level of incompetence."

5. Michels' Iron Law of Oligarchy

Robert Michels had in mind the working-class movements in America and in Europe when he drafted the **Iron Law of Oligarchy**, claiming that a small number of specialists generally hold sway over any organization.

DEVIANCE
Defining Deviance

Strictly speaking, **deviance** represents a departure from a norm. Sociologists have primarily concerned themselves with deviant behavior that violates or is contrary to the rules of acceptable and appropriate behavior of a group or society. Sociologists have tended to differ in their understanding of deviance. The question is whether or not deviance represents more than a violation of a norm and, if so, what this contrary behavior is thought to ultimately represent.

Deviance and Stigma

The one characteristic shared by those with a deviant reputation is stigma. A **stigma** is the mark of social disgrace that sets the deviant apart from other members of society who regard themselves as "normal." In most instances, people escape having their deviant behavior discovered. Because they are not stigmatized or marked deviant, they think of themselves as being relatively normal.

Conformity, Social Order, and Social Control

It is believed that a **social order** depends on its members generally knowing and doing what is expected of them. They have common values and guidelines to which they generally adhere. These norms prescribe the behavior that is appropriate to a situation as it is given or commonly construed at the time. In other words, a social order presumably cannot exist without an effective system of social control. **Social control** is best defined as a series of measures that serve as a general guarantee of people conforming to norms.

When socialization cannot guarantee sufficient conformity through the informal, as well as the formal and organized, ways of rewarding conformity and punishing nonconformity, there becomes a need for negative sanctions. Negative sanctions indicate that social control has failed and that deviance has occurred.

Deviance represents a residual category of behavior unlike that which is generally found. The major function of deviance is to reassure people that the system of social control is working effectively.

Deviance and Social Groups

Consistent with an orientation to social groups and the process through which conformity to **norms** is structured or organized in them, deviance represents an unusual departure from an established group rule of acceptable conduct. These norms denote a negotiated world of meanings; these are rules that shape what individuals perceive and how they behave, thereby eliminating the uncertainty that exists in the absence of such behavior guidelines. The acknowledgment of such a departure assures members that they are "normal." Members can feel that their own behavior falls within the usual parameters of what is and what is not acceptable in the group, while ridiculing those whose observed behavior departs from the expected.

Given the many different groups that make up a society, and the competing values and the diversity of interests they represent, social order is never guaranteed or certain without there being value systems. These **value systems** enjoy such wide acceptance in society that even those groups that represent opposing interests find them to be consistent with, or suited to, their own concerns.

In the competition or struggle between groups, those with the most to lose or gain in terms of immediate self-interest, or those who feel most strongly about their cause, may succeed in defining and shaping the standards of right and wrong that become the group's norms. But they may never succeed in altering the meaning that represents the core values or culture of a society.

"**Deviant**" actions are those that powerful people, those in a position to both define and enforce social norms, find threatening. Because this sector of society agrees with, supports, and serves to define the status quo, anything that threatens this sector is then labeled deviant. In this way, deviance is defined by its opposite rather than any inherent threat it may pose.

Whether or not norms are **proscriptive** ("thou shalt not") or **prescriptive** ("thou shalt"), they all are thought to be relatively arbitrary in principle. Their definition changes over time and from one society to the next but never so much as to be inconsistent with a society's core values.

Functions of Deviance

In terms of the group, deviance serves several functions. Consistent with Durkheim's viewpoint, deviance serves to unify the group by identifying the limits of acceptable behavior and thus identifying who are insiders and who are outsiders. Deviance also serves as a safety valve that allows people to express discontent with existing norms without threatening the social order. Principled challenges to norms are possible.

Social control refers to the ways of getting people to conform to norms. Such techniques, which include persuasion, teaching, and force, may be planned or unplanned, and may be **informal** (involving the approval or disapproval of significant others) or **formal** (involving those in positions responsible for enforcing norms). In this context, **primary deviance** is the term used to refer to behavior violating a norm, while **secondary deviance** refers to the behavior that results from the social response to such deviance.

Biological Explanations of Deviance

In 1875 Cesare Lombroso published the results of his work comparing the body measurements of institutionalized criminals, non-criminals, and primitive human beings. He had concluded that deviant behavior is inherited and that the body measurements of criminals bore a greater resemblance to apes than to non-criminals.

William Sheldon (1941) based his work on the earlier work of Ernst Kretschmer (1925). He concluded that a relationship exists between body type, psychological state, and criminal behavior (with short and fat endomorphs being prone to manic depression and alcoholism; thin and small ectomorphs being prone to schizophrenia; and muscular and large boned mesomorphs being prone to criminal behavior, alcoholism, and manic depression).

More recently efforts have been made to link deviant behavior with an "abnormal" (XYY) chromosomal pattern found among inmates of prisons and mental hospitals. Researchers also have been studying the relationship between the brain and body chemistry, diet, and behavior.

Psychological Explanations of Deviance

Psychologists have attributed antisocial or deviant behavior to the unconscious making itself known to a **superego** that lacks the strength to overcome the id. The **unconscious** is that part of the mind where unpleasant, or perhaps even antisocial, memories of experiences are stored.

Sociological Explanations of Deviance

Sociological explanations of deviance fall into two categories. The first category includes those sociologists who assume that most people conform most of the time as a consequence of adequate socialization. They treat deviance as a special category of behavior and the deviant as deserving of special consideration.

Sociologists also tend to locate the source of deviance outside the individual person. They look within the social structure or in a social process of labeling. **Labeling** focuses on the process through which persons come to be defined as deviant. It also focuses on the means through which deviant behavior is created through the interaction taking place between those committing acts in violation of the group's norms and those responding to such violations.

Robert Merton (1957) expanded upon Durkheim's understanding of deviance as the product of a structural circumstance of disorganization in the individual and in society. Both Merton and Durkheim saw this as a result of weak, inconsistent, or even nonexistent social norms. Merton concluded that in American society, for example, there is a disjunction between means and ends, such as the emphasis on wealth and success without many legitimate means to achieve them. Those individuals without such opportunities attempt to bridge this gap in a number of ways:

- The **"conformist"** seeks to continue the acceptance of the goals and means offered for their attainment.
- The **"innovator"** may continue to accept the goals while seeking new and, in many cases, illegitimate revenues for the attainment of these goals.
- The **"ritualist"** may make the means into an end by rejecting the culturally prescribed goals as being out of his reach. This person is in favor of an overemphasis upon the means of achieving these goals.
- The **"retreater"** rejects both the means and ends offered by society by dropping into drug use, mental illness, alcoholism, and homelessness.
- The **"rebel"** rejects both the means and ends while seeking to replace both with alternatives, thereby changing the way society as a whole is structured.

In his theory of differential association, Edwin Sutherland (1939) states that it is in the primary group where a person acquires knowledge of the techniques used in committing crimes. This primary group also provides reasons for conforming to or violating rules of permissive or not permissive behavior in a given situation, as well as an understanding of what motivates criminal activity.

SOCIAL STRATIFICATION

Defining Social Stratification

All sociologists agree that societies are **stratified**, or arranged along many levels. Where they begin to differ is on the question of what, if anything, the layers represent beyond the distinctions made among differing degrees of power, wealth, and social prestige.

There are some distinctions that always receive differential treatment—as between old and young, or male and female. There are other distinctions that may or may not receive differential treatment depending upon a given society's values. The usual result of a society treating people differently on the basis of their age, sex, race, religion, sexual orientation, or education is social inequality.

Social stratification represents the structured inequality characterized by groups of people with differential access to the rewards of society because of their relative position in the social hierarchy. Thus, a fundamental task of sociology is the determination of why stratified societies are so prevalent.

Life Chances

Sociologists have found that those in the same social stratum generally share the same life chances or opportunities.

Stratification and Social Structure

Consistent with an orientation toward social structure, stratification systems serve to rank some people (whether individuals or groups) as more deserving of power, wealth, and prestige than others.

1. Social Hierarchy

The inevitable result of this stratification is a **social hierarchy** of ranked statuses in which people function. An **ascribed social position** is either received at birth or involuntarily placed upon an individual later in life. An **achieved social position** is usually assumed voluntarily, and generally reflects personal ability or effort. Individuals in a society are treated differently depending on where their social position stands in the overall social hierarchy.

2. Social Mobility

Social mobility refers to the ability of a given individual or group to move through the social strata. Structural mobility refers to factors at the societal level that affect mobility rates.

Social mobility may be either relative or absolute. An example of **relative mobility** would be an entire occupational structure being upgraded so that only the content of the work changes, not relative position in the social hierarchy from one generation to the next. An example of **absolute mobility** would be when a son's education, occupational prestige, and income exceeds that of his father.

Systems of Stratification

A **system of stratification** refers to the institutions and ideas that permit or limit the distribution of prestige, status, and opportunities in life. Stratification may have several sources, including race, ethnicity, gender, age, and sexual orientation—which at times have served as the basis for assigning inferior or superior status to an entire population.

1. Race and Ethnicity

As sociologists use the term, **race** is more than a biologically complex phenomenon in that it involves the attribution of hereditary differences to human populations that are genetically distinct. That we categorize people into "races" is a social phenomenon rather than a biological one. Society, not biology, categorizes people into "races."

Ethnicity refers to a population known and identified on the basis of their common language, national heritage, and/or biological inheritance. Although race primarily refers to differences in physical characteristics, ethnic differences are culturally learned and not genetically inherited.

2. Gender

Gender stratification refers to those differences between men and women that have been acquired or learned and, hence, to the different roles and positions assigned to males and females in a society. Across societies women have been systematically denied certain rights and opportunities based on assumptions regarding their abilities. This inferior status of women has often been legitimized through a **sexist ideology** (a belief system assuming that innate characteristics translate into one gender being superior to another) which is passed on across generations via culture.

3. Age

Age stratification refers to the ways in which people are differentially treated depending on their age. This form of stratification is concerned with the attitudes and behaviors we associate with age, and to the different roles and statuses we assign to people depending upon their age.

4. Sexual Orientation

Stratification on the basis of **sexual orientation** or affection refers to the ways in which individuals are differentially treated on the basis of their sexual preferences. In some societies, the results of this stratification are relatively benign. However, results of this stratification have also taken the form of criminalization of same-sex unions, as well as discrimination in housing, employment, and social status.

Davis and Moore—A Functionalist View of Social Stratification

In their classic presentation of the **functionalist** view of stratification, Kingsley Davis and Wilbert Moore (1945) argue that some stratification is necessary. At any given time, some members of a society will have more of the qualities that are needed and desired than others. Thus, in order to attract the appropriate people with the requisite talents and skills to the more demanding, often stressful, roles, a society must offer greater rewards and higher status. In this way, **inequality** (the unequal distribution of social rewards) is considered functional for society in that it guarantees that those most able will be in the most demanding positions.

Marx, Weber, and Modern Conflict Theory

Marx attributed inequalities of wealth, power, and prestige to the economic situation that class structures present. Thus, the elimination of classes would serve to put an end to inequality, to the exploitation of man by man, and to the basic conflict of interest between the haves and the have nots.

By contrast, Weber distinguished between class, status situation, and parties as a step toward explaining the origins of the different economic, social, political, and religious situations of society that he saw around the world. A status situation consisted of every aspect of a person's situation in life that is caused by a positive or negative social assessment of status.

Focused on the origins of man-made culture, Weber often found such differences to be a source of conflict and change that he could not foresee ending. He discovered various systems of stratification.

Some were modes of organization based on **caste**, where social mobility is not permitted by religious sanctions. Others were based on **class**, including the feudal system of medieval society that was based on vassalage, or reciprocal obligations of loyalty and service between lord and knight or lord and serfs.

Modern conflict theory continues to struggle with the question of the bases of conflict. Believing that Marx placed too much emphasis on class, Ralf Dahrendorf (1959) focused on the struggle among such groups as unions and employers. Randall Collins continues to focus on the way that different groups seek to maintain their social position by acquiring educational credentials that they then use to secure jobs and other advantages. And still others see the conflict over ideological hegemony, including beliefs, attitudes, and ideals, as being the decisive element distinguishing the higher from the lower strata.

ECONOMICS

INTRODUCTION TO ECONOMICS

What Is Economics?

"Economics is what economists do." This statement, attributed to the famous economist Jacob Viner, may in fact be the best description of the discipline available. What it says is that economics cannot be defined by a series of topics that all economists study. **Economics** is the study of making choices, says Saint Michael's College. Consequently, it can be used to study such business-related issues as capital investment, pricing policy, and interest rates, but it can also be used to look at the "bigger" issues of inflation, unemployment, economic growth, and the "non-economic" issues of love, marriage, childbearing, and discrimination, to name but a few.

Macroeconomics is the study of the economy as a whole. Some of the topics considered include inflation, unemployment, and economic growth.

Microeconomics is the study of the individual parts that make up the economy. The parts include households, business firms, and government agencies, and particular emphasis is placed on how these units make decisions and the consequences of these decisions.

Economic Analysis

An **economic theory** is an explanation of why certain economic phenomena occur, such as the rate of inflation, how many hours people choose to work, and the amount of goods and services the United States will import. A **model** is an abstract replica of reality and is the formal statement of a theory. Virtually all economic analysis is done by first constructing a model of the situation the economist wants to analyze. Models, because they avoid many of the messier details of reality, can be comprehended, but good models are always "unrealistic."

Economists do not analyze the economy; they analyze models of the economy. Almost every prediction that an economist makes (e.g., the impact of changes in the money supply on interest rates, the effect of the unemployment rate on the rate of inflation, the effect of increased competition in an industry on profits) is based on a model. Models come in verbal, graphical, or mathematical form.

In **empirical analysis**, economists compare predictions with the actual performance of the economy as measured by economic data. Good empirical analysis often requires mastery of sophisticated statistical and mathematical tools.

Positive economics is the analysis of "what is." For example, positive economics tries to answer such questions as "What will the effect be on the rate of inflation if the rate of growth of the money supply is raised by one percentage point?" Many economists view positive economics as "objective" or "scientific," and believe their special training gives them the expertise to draw conclusions about these types of issues.

Normative economics is the analysis of "what should be." For example, normative economics tries to answer such questions as "What inflation rate should our economy strive for?" Normative economics is clearly a subjective area.

The Economic Way of Thinking

Economics analysis is characterized by an emphasis on certain fundamental concepts.

Scarcity—Human wants and needs (for goods, services, leisure, etc.) exceed the ability of the economy to satisfy those wants and needs.

Opportunity cost—The reality of scarcity implies that individuals, businesses, and governments must make choices, selecting some opportunities while foregoing others. The opportunity cost of a choice is the value of the best alternative choice sacrificed.

Individualism—Economic analysis emphasizes individual action. All groups, such as "society," business firms, or unions, are analyzed as a collection of individuals each acting in a particular way.

Rational behavior—Individuals are assumed to act rationally, meaning that given a person's goals and knowledge, people take actions likely to achieve those goals and avoid actions likely to detract from those goals.

Marginal analysis—Economists assume that people make choices by weighing the costs and benefits of particular actions.

Important Economic Concepts and Terms

Division of labor means that different members of a team of producers are given responsibility for different aspects of a production plan. **Specialization** means that producers become quite apt at those aspects of production they concentrate on. Specialization and division of labor is alleged to lead to efficiency which facilitates economic growth and development.

THE ECONOMIC PROBLEM

Universality of the Problem of Scarcity

Goods and services refer to anything that satisfies human needs, wants, or desires. Goods are tangible items, such as food, cars, and clothing. Services are intangible items, such as education, health care, and leisure.

Resources refer to anything that can be used to produce goods and services. A commonly used classification scheme places all resources into one of six categories:

Land—All natural resources, whether on the land, under the land, in the water, or in the air (e.g., fertile agricultural land, iron ore deposits, tuna fish, corn seeds, and quail).

Labor—The work effort of human beings.

Capital—Productive implements made by human beings (e.g., factories, machinery, and tools).

Entrepreneurship—Creative labor. It refers to the ability to detect new business opportunities and bring them to fruition. Entrepreneurs also manage the other factors of production.

Technology—The practical application of scientific knowledge. Technology is typically combined with the other factors to make them more productive.

Scarcity—Economists assume that human wants and needs are virtually limitless while acknowledging that the resources to satisfy those needs are limited. Consequently, society is never able to produce enough goods and services to satisfy everybody, or most anyone, completely.

Universal Problems Caused by Scarcity

All societies must make three crucial decisions:

1. **What goods and services to produce and in what quantities.**

2. **How to produce the goods and services selected**—what resource combinations and production techniques to use.

3. **How to distribute the goods and services produced among people**—who gets how much of each good and service produced.

Universal Economic Goals

A society achieves **allocative efficiency** if it produces the types and quantities of goods and services that most satisfies its people. A society achieves **technical efficiency** when it is producing the greatest quantity of goods and services possible from its resources.

A society wants the distribution of goods and services to conform with its notions of "**fairness**." Equity is not necessarily synonymous with equality. There is no objective standard of equity, and all societies have different notions of what constitutes equity. Three widely held standards are:

1. **Contributory standard**—Under a contributory standard, people are entitled to a share of goods and services based on what they contribute to society. Those making larger contributions receive correspondingly larger shares.

2. **Needs standard**—Under a needs standard, a person's contribution to society is irrelevant. Goods and services are distributed based on the needs of different households.

3. **Equality standard**—Under an equality standard, every person is entitled to an equal share of goods and services, simply because he or she is a human being.

Economists remain divided over whether the goals of equity and efficiency (allocative and technical) are complementary or in conflict.

Production Possibilities Curve

The **Production Possibilities Curve** is a model of the economy used to illustrate the problems associated with scarcity. It shows the maximum feasible combinations of two goods or services that society can produce, assuming all resources are used in their most productive manner.

Assumptions of the Model

1. Society is only capable of producing two goods (i.e., guns and butter).

2. At a given point in time, society has a fixed quantity of resources.

3. All resources are used in their most productive manner.

The following table shows selected combinations of the two goods that can be produced given the assumptions.

Point	Guns	Butter
A	0	16
B	4	14
C	7	12
D	9	9
E	10	5
F	11	0

The following figure is a graphical depiction of the Production Possibilities Curve (curve FA).

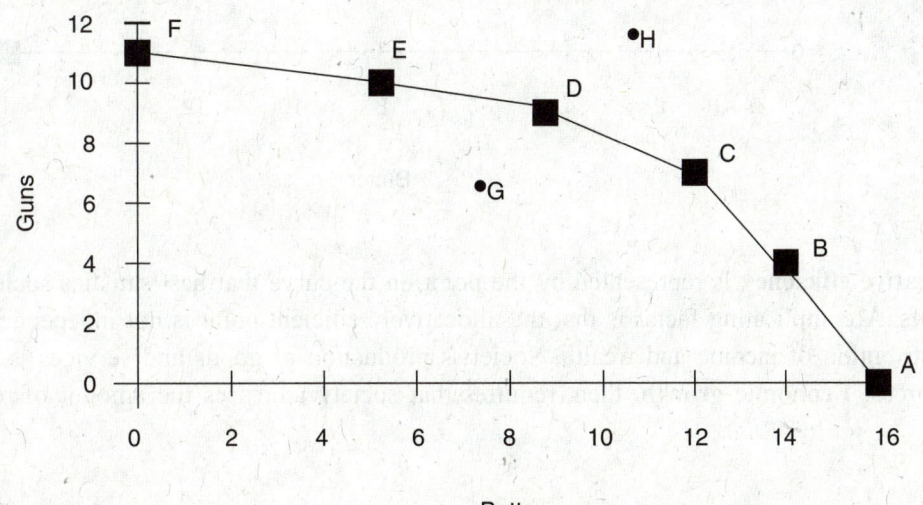

All points on the curve are points of technical efficiency. By definition, **technical efficiency** is achieved when more of one good cannot be produced without producing less of the other good. Find point D on the curve. Any move to a point with more guns (i.e., point E) will necessitate a reduction in butter production. Any move to a point with more butter (such as point C) will necessitate a reduction in guns production. Any point inside the curve (such as point G) represents technical inefficiency. Either inefficient production methods are being used or resources are not fully employed. Points outside the curve (such as H) are technically infeasible given society's current stock of resources and technological knowledge.

Consider a move from D to E. Society gets one more unit of guns, but must sacrifice four units of butter. The four units of butter is the **opportunity cost** of the gun.

The **law of increasing costs** says that as more of a good or service is produced, its opportunity cost will rise. At the commencement of gun production, the resources shifted out of butter will be those least productive in butter (and most productive in guns). Consequently, gun production will rise with little cost in terms of butter. As more resources are diverted, those more productive in butter will be affected, and the opportunity cost will rise. This is what gives the Production Possibilities Curve its characteristic convex shape.

If resources are not specialized in particular uses, opportunity costs will remain constant and the Production Possibilities Curve will be a straight line.

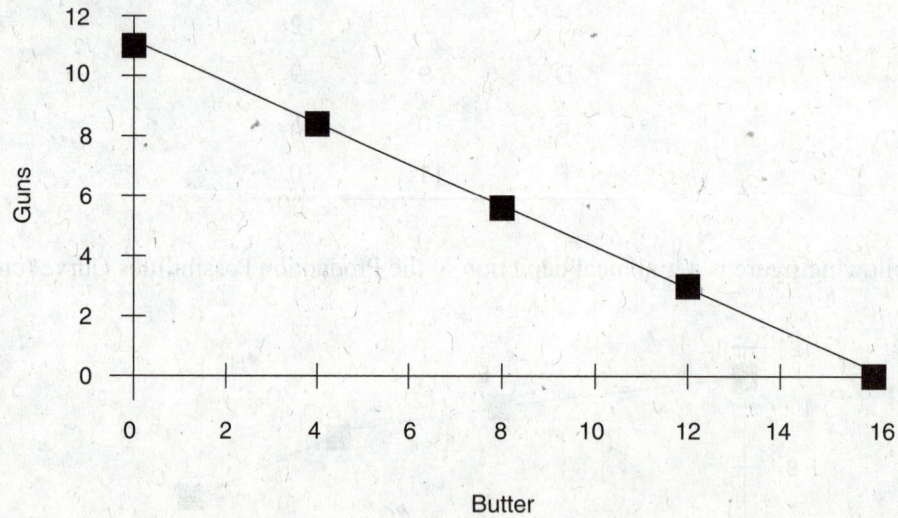

Allocative efficiency is represented by the point on the curve that best satisfies society's needs and wants. A complicating factor is that the allocatively efficient point is not independent of society's distribution of income and wealth. Society's production of goods and services is limited by its resources. **Economic growth**, then, requires that society increases the amount of resources it has or makes those resources more productive through the application of technology. Graphically, economic growth is represented by an outward shift of the curve to IJ.

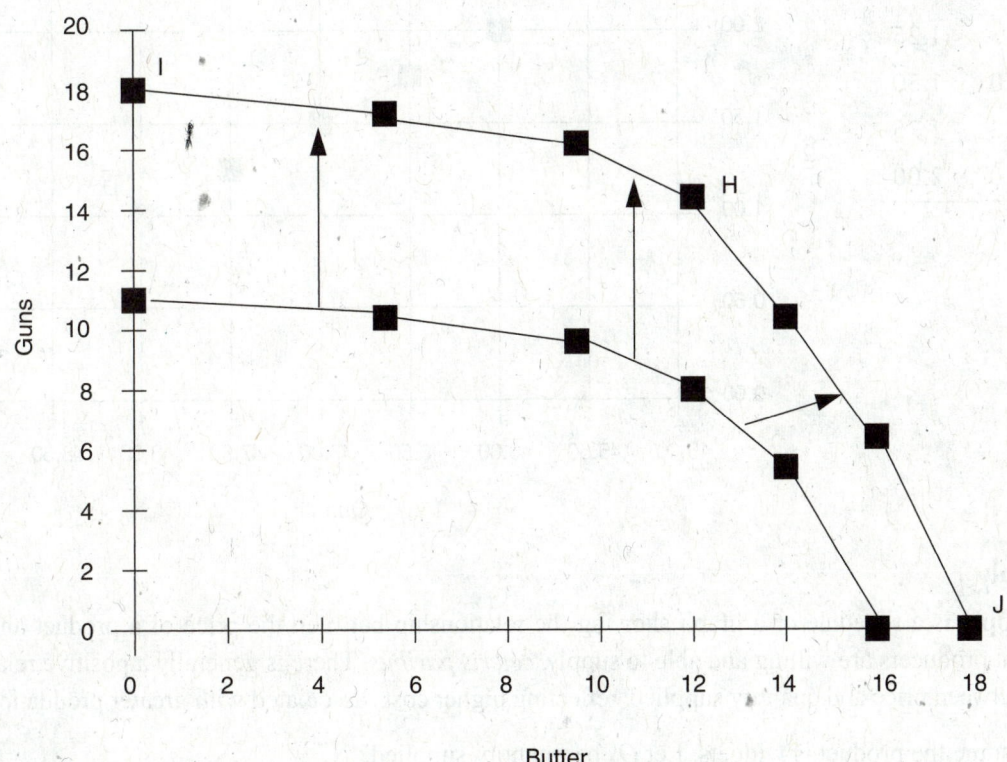

DEMAND AND SUPPLY

Demand

Demand is a schedule or a graph showing the relationship between the price of a product and the amount consumers are willing and able to buy, *ceteris paribus*. The **Law of Demand** says there is an inverse relationship between price and quantity demanded; people will be willing and able to buy more if the product gets cheaper.

1. Ceteris Paribus

All hypothetical relationships between variables in economics include a stated or implied assumption *ceteris paribus*. The term means "all other factors held constant." The demand schedule shows the relationship between price and quantity demanded, holding all the other factors constant. This allows us to investigate the independent effect that price changes have on quantity demanded without worrying about the influence the other factors are having.

Assume the product is widgets. Let Qd be quantity demanded and P be price.

Qd	P
48.0	1.00
47.5	1.25
47.0	1.50
46.5	1.75
46.0	2.00

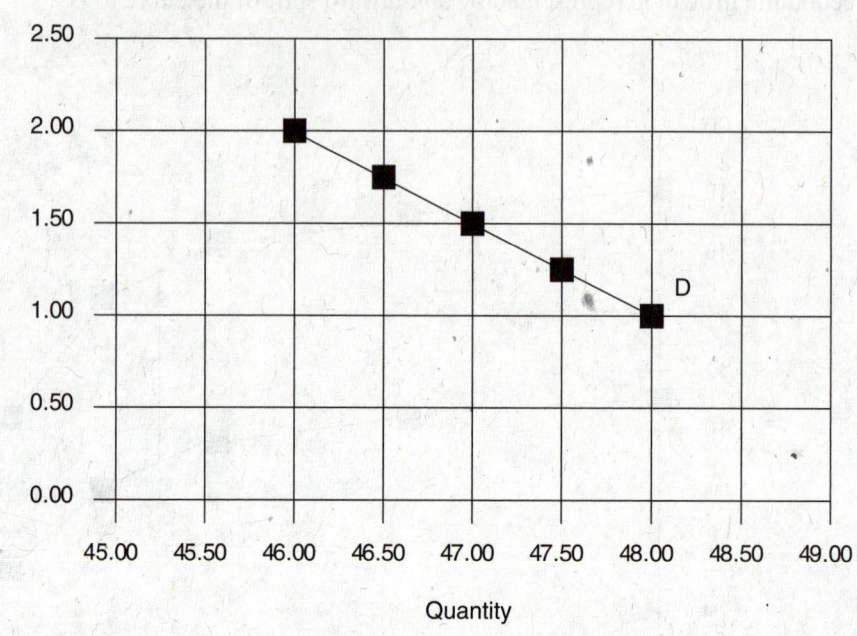

Supply

Supply is a schedule or a graph showing the relationship between the price of a product and the amount producers are willing and able to supply, *ceteris paribus*. There is generally a positive relationship between price and quantity supplied, reflecting higher costs associated with greater production.

Assume the product is widgets. Let Qs be quantity supplied.

Qs	P
46.0	1.00
46.5	1.25
47.0	1.50
47.5	1.75
48.0	2.00

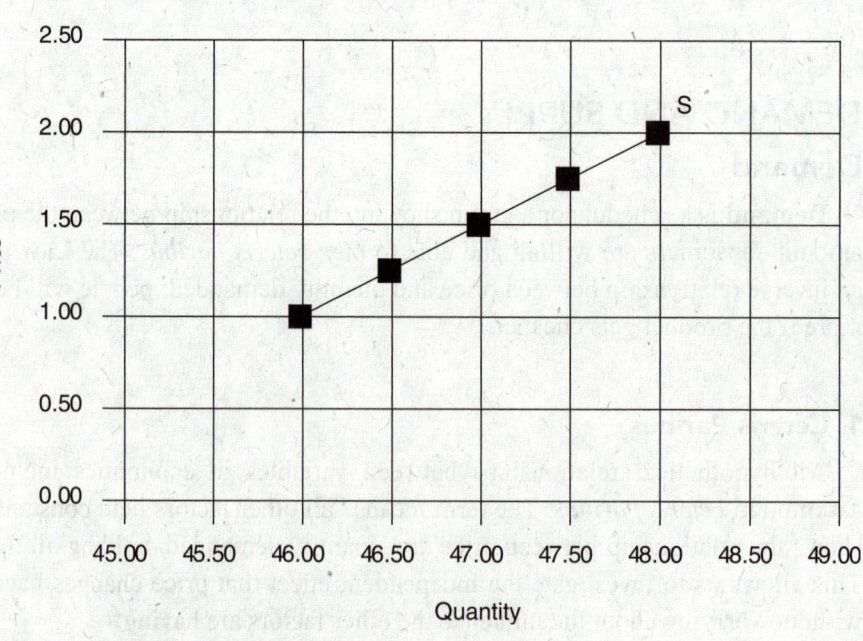

Market Equilibrium

The intersection of the demand and supply curves indicates the equilibrium price and quantity in the market. The word *equilibrium* is synonymous with stable. The price and quantity in a market will frequently not be equal to the equilibrium, but if that is the case then the market will be adjusting, and, hence, not stable.

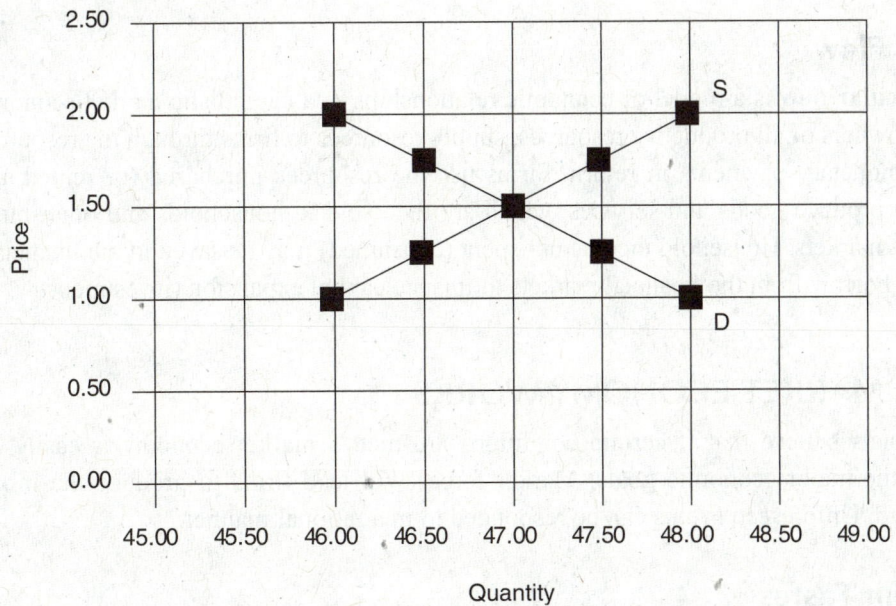

If the price of the product is $1.50, then the quantity demanded (47) is just equal to the quantity supplied (47). Producers can sell all they want. Buyers can buy all they want. Since everyone is satisfied, there is no reason for the price to change. Hence, $1.50 is an equilibrium price and 47 is an equilibrium quantity.

ECONOMIC SYSTEMS

Types of Systems

Traditional systems largely rely on custom to determine production and distribution questions. While not static, traditional systems are slow to change and are not well-equipped to propel a society into sustained growth.

Command economies rely on a central authority to make decisions. The central authority may be a dictator or a democratically constituted government.

In a pure **market system**, there is no central authority and custom plays very little role. Every consumer makes buying decisions based on his or her own needs and desires and income. Every producer decides for him or herself what goods or services to produce, what price to charge, what resources to employ, and what production methods to use. Producers are motivated solely by profit considerations.

A **mixed economy** contains elements of each of the three systems just defined. All real world economies are mixed economies, although the mixture of tradition, command, and market differs greatly.

The key characteristic of a **capitalistic economy** is that productive resources are owned by private individuals. The key characteristic of a **socialist economy**, in contrast, is that productive resources are owned collectively by society. Alternatively, productive resources are under the control of government.

Circular Flow

The **circular flow** is a model of economic relationships in a capitalistic market economy. Households, the owners of all productive resources, supply resources to firms through the resource markets, receiving monetary payments in return. Firms use the resources purchased (or rented, as the case may be) to produce goods and services, which are then sold to households and other businesses in the product markets. Household income not spent (consumed) may be saved in the financial markets. Firms may borrow from the financial markets to finance capital expansion (investment).

HOW A MARKET ECONOMY WORKS

Economists believe that if certain conditions are met, a market economy is easily capable of achieving the major economic goals. Market forces will lead firms to produce the mix of goods most desired. Unforeseen events can be responded to in a rational manner.

Change in Tastes

Assume a change in consumer tastes from beef to chicken. An increase in demand in the chicken market will be accompanied by a decrease in demand in the beef market. The higher price of chicken will attract more resources into the market and lead to an increase in the quantity supplied. The lower price of beef will induce a reduction in the quantity supplied and exit of resources to other industries.

Note that the change in the level of output of both goods occurred because it was in the economic self-interest of firms to do so. Greater demand in the chicken market increased the profitability of chicken; lower demand in the beef market decreased the profitability of beef. Chicken and beef producers responded to society's desires not out of a sense of public spiritedness, but out of self-interest.

Scarcity

An unexpected freeze in Florida will cause a shift in the supply curve of orange juice, driving up its price, and causing consumers to cut back their purchases. The higher price of orange juice will increase the demand for substitute products like apple juice, causing an increase in the quantity supplied of apple juice to take the place of orange juice.

Once again, the reaction of market participants reflects their evaluation of their own self-interest. Consumers reduce their quantity demanded of orange juice because it is now more expensive. Apple juice producers expand production because now it is more profitable.

Consumer sovereignty means that consumers determine what is produced in the economy. In a market economy, business must cater to the whims of consumer tastes or else go out of business.

Market forces will lead firms to produce output in the most efficient manner. The constant struggle for profits will stimulate firms to cut costs. A market economy thrives on competition between firms. In their struggle for survival, firms will be forced to cater to consumer demand (leading to allocative efficiency) and force production costs down as far as possible (leading to technical efficiency).

Full employment of resources is thought to be the normal state of affairs in a market economy. Resource surpluses will force down the resource's price, leading quickly to re-employment. Competition between firms for the consumer's dollar will force a constant search for better products and methods of production. The resulting technological change will lead to optimal growth.

Winners in a market economy are not necessarily the most virtuous of people, just those who sell a better product. While consumer demand determines the pattern of production, those consumers with the most income exert the greatest influence on the pattern.

In order for an economy to operate efficiently, there must be information on what goods and services are in demand, which resources are scarce, and so on. There must also be an incentive to produce the goods and services desired, conserve on scarce resources, and so on. Both information and incentives are provided by prices. High prices indicate goods and services in demand; low prices indicate goods and services that have lost favor. High prices indicate scarce resources; low prices indicate plentiful. Firms responding "properly" to high prices will earn profits; firms responding "properly" to low prices will avoid losses. Firms exploiting cheap resources will earn profits; firms conserving on expensive resources will avoid losses.

Adam Smith and *The Wealth of Nations*

Adam Smith (1723–1790) was a Scottish economist whose writing can be said to have inaugurated the modern era of economic analysis. Published in 1776, *The Wealth of Nations* can be read as an analysis of a market economy. It was Smith's belief that a market economy was a superior form of organization from the standpoint of both economic progress and human liberty. Smith acknowledged that self-interest was a dominant motivating force in a market economy, yet this self-interest was ultimately consistent with the public interest. Market participants were guided by an **invisible hand** to act in ways that promoted the public interest. Firms may only be concerned with profits, but profits are only earned by firms that satisfy consumer demand and keep costs down.

Conditions that Must Be Met for a Market Economy to Achieve Allocative and Technical Efficiency

A market economy will automatically produce the optimum quantity of every good or service at the lowest possible cost if four conditions are met:

1. **Adequate information**—Consumers must be well-enough informed about prices, quality and availability of products, and other matters that they can make intelligent spending decisions. Workers must be well-enough informed about wages and working conditions that they can choose wisely among job opportunities.

2. **Competition**—There must be vigorous competition in every market. Monopolistic elements will reduce output, raise prices, and allow inefficiency in particular markets.

3. **No externalities**—Externalities exist when a transaction between a buyer and seller affects an innocent third party. An example would be if *A* buys a product from *B* that *B* produced under conditions that polluted the air that others breathe.

4. **No public goods**—The market is unlikely to produce the appropriate quantity of public goods.

THE PUBLIC SECTOR IN THE AMERICAN ECONOMY

The **public sector** refers to the activities of government. **Government spending** can be usefully broken down into two categories. One category is **spending on goods and services**. When government buys a battleship, a hammer, or the Space Shuttle, it is acquiring goods. When government pays the salary of a soldier, teacher, or bureaucrat, it is getting a service in return. The second category is **transfer payments**. Transfers are money or in-kind items given to individuals or businesses for which the government receives no equivalent good or service in return. Examples would be social security payments, welfare, or unemployment compensation.

GROSS NATIONAL PRODUCT

Measuring GNP

Gross National Product (or GNP) is a measure of the dollar value of final goods and services produced by the economy over a given period of time, usually one year. It is the most comprehensive indicator of the economy's health available, although it is not a measure of society's overall well-being.

Final goods and services are those sold to their ultimate users. **Intermediate goods and services** are those in an intermediate stage of processing. They are purchased by firms for immediate resale, such as the frozen orange juice a grocery store buys from the processor for resale to consumers, or they are purchased for further processing and then resale, such as the crude oil a refinery buys to refine into gasoline and other petroleum products.

Assume a simple economy composed of three business firms and one household. Firm A manufactures computer chips. It takes silicon from the environment (assumed to be so plentiful as to be a free good) and combines it with resources purchased or rented from the household. The resulting chips are sold to Firm B, a manufacturer of computers. Firm B takes the chips and combines them with the resources purchased from the household to produce computers which it sells to Firm C, a retail computer store. The store uses resources obtained from the household to resell the computers to the household, which is the ultimate user.

The following table traces the transactions that take place in the economy during the course of a year.

Firm	Cost of Intermediate Goods Purchased	Resources Purchased	Cost of Goods Sold	Value-Added
A	0	50	50	50
B	50	75	125	75
C	125	40	165	40

There are three ways to measure GNP.

1. **Expenditures on final goods and services**—In the example, computer chips and wholesale computers are intermediate goods while retail computers are a final good. Since the household spent $165 on retail computers, this is a direct measure of GNP.

2. **Sum of value-added for all firms**—Value-Added (VA) = Cost of Goods Sold − Cost of Intermediate Goods Purchased VA measures the value of the processing and resale activities that the firm performs on the intermediate goods and services it purchases. Adding value-added for all firms in the economy will give GNP.

3. **Gross National Income**—Value-added comes from the services performed by the resources the firms hire. Therefore, value-added for each firm is just equal to the payments made for resources allowing us to total the incomes earned by all households to get GNP. This measure is frequently given the name Gross National Income (or GNI).

MACROECONOMIC PROBLEMS OF THE AMERICAN ECONOMY
The Business Cycle

Business cycles are the alternating periods of prosperity and recession that seem to characterize all market-oriented economies. Every business cycle consists of four phases. The **peak**, the high point of business activity, occurs at a specific point of time. The **contraction**, a period of declining business activity, occurs over a period of time. The **trough**, the low point in business activity, occurs at a specific point in time. The **expansion**, a period of growing business activity, takes place over a period of time.

Although the word *cycle* implies a certain uniformity, that is misleading. Each business cycle differs from every other in terms of duration of contractions and expansions, and height of peak and depth of trough.

Seasonal fluctuations are changes in economic variables that reflect the season of the year. For example, every summer ice cream sales soar. They decrease during winter. Every December, toy sales increase dramatically. They fall back during January.

A **secular trend** is the long run direction of movement of a variable. For example, our economy has become dramatically richer over the past century. We can say that there was a secular upward trend in real GNP. Of course, growth was not steady. There were periods of faster than average followed by slower than average growth, which accounts for business cycles.

MONEY AND BANKING
What Money Is and Does

Money is anything that is generally acceptable in exchange for goods and services and in payment of debts. Money performs four particular functions:

1. **Medium of exchange**—Money is used to facilitate exchanges of goods and services. In a **barter economy** goods and services exchange directly for other goods and services. If you want an axe that someone is selling, you must find an item that person wants to

trade for it. Barter requires a **double coincidence of wants**; each party must want what the other party has. If that condition does not hold, then exchange cannot take place, and valuable resources can be wasted in putting together trades. With money this problem never arises because **everyone always wants money**. Consequently, the resources used to facilitate exchanges can be put to more productive use.

2. **Unit of value**—We use our monetary unit as the standard measure of value. We say a shirt is worth $25.00, not 14 chickens.

3. **Store of value**—Money is one of the forms wealth can be stored in. Alternatives include stocks and bonds, real estate, gold, great paintings, and many others. One advantage of storing wealth in money form is that money is the most liquid of all assets. **Liquidity** refers to the ease with which an asset can be transformed into spendable form. Money is already in spendable form. The disadvantage of holding wealth in money form is that money typically pays a lower return than other assets.

4. **Standard of deferred payment**—Money is used in transactions involving payments to be made at a future date. An example would be building contracts where full payment is made only when the project is completed. This function of money is implicit in the three already discussed.

Virtually anything can and has served as money. Gold, silver, shells, boulders, cheap metal, paper, and electronic impulses stored in computers are examples of the varied forms money has taken. The only requirement is that the item be generally acceptable. Money does **not** have to have intrinsic value.

Typically items that serve as money are durable, divisible, uniform or standardized, portable, relatively stable, and optimally scarce.

Money is valuable if it can be used for or exchanged for something useful. Sellers accept money because they know they can use it anywhere else in the country to buy goods and services and pay off debts. This means that the substance used for money need not be valuable, and that money need not be backed by anything valuable.

The United States' Money Supply

While there are many different definitions of the money supply available, the two most commonly used are M1 and M2.

M1 consists of currency (coins and paper money), demand deposits (checking accounts in commercial banks), other checkable deposits (NOW accounts, ATS accounts), and traveler's checks.

M2 includes all of M1 plus savings deposits, small-denomination time deposits, money-market mutual funds and deposit accounts, overnight repurchase agreements (known as repos), and Eurodollars.

Savings deposits—These are the common passbook savings accounts. They do not provide check-writing privileges.

Small denomination time deposits—Better known as certificates of deposits, or CDs, they typically do not provide check-writing privileges.

Money market mutual funds and deposit accounts—Both mutual funds and deposit accounts are investment funds. Large numbers of people pool their money to allow for diversification and professional investment management. Mutual funds are managed by private financial companies. Deposit accounts are managed by commercial banks. Investors earn a return on their investment and have limited check-writing privileges. Mutual funds are not afforded protection by the government, as is the case with FDIC-insured bank accounts.

Overnight repurchase agreements and eurodollars—Overnight repos essentially are short-term (literally, overnight) loans. A corporation with excess cash may arrange to purchase a security from a bank with the stipulation that the bank will buy the security back the next day at a slightly higher price. The corporation receives a return on its money, and the bank gets access to funds. **Eurodollars** are dollar-denominated demand deposits held in banks outside the United States (not just in Europe). From the standpoint of M2, deposits held in Caribbean branches of Federal Reserve member banks are relevant. These deposits are easily accessed by U.S. residents. While both instruments are important in financial affairs, they are negligible in the totality of M2.

The Financial System

Financial intermediaries are organizations such as commercial banks, savings and loan institutions, credit unions, and insurance companies. They play an important role in facilitating the saving and investment process which helps the economy grow. Through the various types of deposits they offer, financial intermediaries compete for the saved funds. The money so obtained is used to finance borrowing.

Reserves are a bank's money holdings. Most reserves are held in the form of demand deposits at other banks or the Federal Reserve System. The remainder is cash in the bank's vault. Reserves are held to meet the demand for cash on the part of depositors and to honor checks drawn upon the bank. The amount of reserves a bank must hold is based on the **required reserve ratio**. Set by the Federal Reserve System, the required reserve ratio is a number from 0 to 1.00 and determines the level of reserve holdings relative to the bank's deposits.

Required reserves, the amount a bank is legally obligated to hold, are calculated by multiplying the required reserve ratio by the amount of deposits.

$$\text{Required Reserves} = \text{Required Reserve Ratio} \times \text{Deposits}$$

The level of reserves banks are required to hold is probably higher than what they need to be safe. The main purpose of the requirement is to give the Federal Reserve System some control over the banks.

Excess reserves are the difference between the amount of reserves a bank holds and what it is required to hold. All banks hold excess reserves at all times for reasons of financial prudence; however, greater excess reserves will be held during periods of financial uncertainty.

$$\text{Excess Reserves} = \text{Reserves} - \text{Required Reserves}$$

All banks constantly operate with reserve holdings of only a fraction of deposit liabilities. This is known as **fractional reserve banking**. If all depositors tried to withdraw their money simultaneously, banks would not be able to honor the demands. Fortunately, this is unlikely to happen because people like to hold deposits because they are safe and convenient. On a normal business day, some withdrawals are made, but these are counterbalanced by new deposits. Reserve holdings need only be a small fraction of deposits for prudent operation.

MONETARY POLICY

The Federal Reserve System

The **Federal Reserve System** (known as the "Fed") is the central bank of the United States. Its responsibilities are to oversee the stability of the banking system and conduct monetary policy to the end of fighting inflation and unemployment and stimulating economic growth.

The Fed consists of a Board of Governors, 12 regional banks, money subregional banks, and commercial banks that opt for membership in the system. Although it was created by an Act of Congress (in 1913), nominally the Fed is privately owned by the member banks. Members of the **Board of Governors** are appointed by the president and confirmed by the Senate for 14-year terms. The Chair of the Board is appointed by the president and confirmed by the Senate for a four-year term. The Fed's budget is overseen by a committee of Congress, and it must report to Congress about its operations at least twice a year. To a large extent, the Fed can be considered an independent agency of the government.

Is it wise to give the power to influence the state of the economy to an entity that is not directly accountable to the people? The "pro" side claims the Fed's independence puts it "above" politics and leads to decisions more in the "public interest." The "con" side says that in a democracy, the people should be given a voice in all decisions that affect them.

The major functions of the Fed are as follows:

1. **Bank regulation**—The Fed has been given the responsibility of examining member banks to determine if they are financially strong and in conformity with the banking regulations. The Fed also approves mergers.

2. **Clearing interbank payments**—The Fed performs a service for member banks in operating the check clearing function. Banks receiving deposit checks drawn on other banks can present them to the Fed. The Fed will credit the receiving bank's reserve account, reduce the paying bank's reserve account, and send the check back to the paying bank.

3. **Lender of last resort**—One of the original motivations for establishing the Fed was to have a bank that could act as a "lender of last resort."

Bank panics refer to situations where depositors lose faith in their bank and try to withdraw their money. By standing ready to loan reserves to banks experiencing difficulties, the Fed helps reduce the danger of panics.

Federal Deposit Insurance, established during the New Deal era, provides government guarantees for bank deposits should a bank fail. Both commercial banks and savings and loans are insured. Panics were much more common in the days before the Fed and the Federal Deposit Insurance Corporation.

Open market operations refers to the Fed's buying or selling of U.S. Government bonds in the open market. The purpose is to influence the amount of reserves in the banking system, and, consequently, the banking system's ability to extend credit and create money.

Open Market Operations

To expand the economy	The Fed buys bonds in the open market. To induce borrowers, banks are likely to lower interest rates and credit standards. As loans are made, the money supply will expand. The additional credit will stimulate additional spending, primarily for investment goods.
To contract the economy	The Fed sells bonds in the open market. Banks, now deficient in reserves, need to reduce their demand deposit liabilities, and will do so by calling in loans and making new credit more difficult to get. Interest rates will rise, credit requirements will be tightened, and the money supply will fall. Total spending in the economy will be reduced.

Bonds are a financial instrument frequently used by government and business as a way to borrow money. Every bond comes with a **par value** (often $1,000), a **date to maturity** (ranging from 90 days to 30 years), a **coupon** (a promise to pay a certain amount of money each year to the bondholder until maturity), and a promise to repay the par value on the maturity date. The issuing government or business sells the bonds in the bond market for a price determined by supply and demand. The money received from the sale represents the principal of the loan, the annual coupon payment is the interest on the loan, and the principal is repaid at the date of maturity. There is also a secondary market in bonds.

The Fed can set the legal **reserve ratio** for both member and non-member banks. The purpose is to influence the level of excess reserves in the banking system and, consequently, the banking system's ability to extend credit and create money.

Reserve Ratio

To expand the economy	The Fed reduces the reserve requirement. Assume the reserve requirement is 8%, and all banks are "all loaned up." If the Fed reduces the reserve requirement to 6%, required reserves fall to $30 million, and there are immediately $10 million in excess reserves. Banks will lower the interest rates they charge and credit requirements in an attempt to make more loans. As the loans are granted, the economy's money supply and total spending will rise.
To contract the economy	The Fed raises the reserve requirement. Assume the reserve requirement is 8%, and all banks are "all loaned up." If the Fed raises the reserve requirement to 10%, required reserves rise to $50 million, and banks are immediately $10 million deficient in reserves. Banks will raise the interest rates they charge and credit requirements to reduce the amount of money borrowed. They may also call in loans. As the loans are reduced, the economy's money supply and total spending will fall.

One of the Fed's responsibilities is to act as a "lender of last resort." Member banks needing reserves can borrow from the Fed. The interest rate the Fed charges on these loans is called the **discount rate**. By changing the discount rate, the Fed can influence the amount member banks try to borrow, and, consequently, the banking system's ability to extend credit and create money.

Discount Rate

To expand the economy	The Fed lowers the discount rate. Consequently, member banks will be more willing to lend money and hold a low level of excess reserves. A lower discount rate would lead to lower interest rates and credit requirements, a higher money supply, and greater total spending in the economy.
To contract the economy	The Fed raises the discount rate. Consequently, member banks will be less willing to lend money and more likely to hold a high level of excess reserves. A higher discount rate would lead to higher interest rates and more stringent credit requirements, a lower money supply, and lower total spending in the economy.

Monetary Policy Summary Table

Tool	Action	Effect on Interest Rates	Effect on Money Supply	Effect on Total Spending	Effect on GNP
Open Market	buy	lower	raise	raise	raise
Operations	sell	raise	lower	lower	lower
Reserve	raise	raise	lower	lower	lower
Ratio	lower	lower	raise	raise	raise
Discount	raise	raise	lower	lower	lower
Rate	lower	lower	raise	raise	raise

PSYCHOLOGY

INTRODUCTION TO PSYCHOLOGY

What Is Psychology?

Psychology is the science of behavior. Its goal is to measure, predict, and explain behavior. Some psychologists also describe psychology as the study of experience, or an organism's "internal" activities. Other psychologists believe that "experience" cannot be systematically studied.

Psychology was once considered to be the study of the mind. Researchers have come to agree that the mind is neither entirely open to study, nor very well defined. To make the discipline more objective and scientific, psychologists redefined psychology as the study of human behavior.

Behavior refers to any action or reaction of a living organism which can be observed. Some psychologists focus on the biology of behavior, such as the actions of nerve cells, genetics, or sweat glands. Other psychologists study higher level behaviors, such as aggression, prejudice, or problem solving.

The key to the definition of behavior is that behavior is **observable**. Behavior refers to overt movement, activity, or action. Some behaviors are more observable than others. For instance, any bystander can see aggressive behavior on a city street. However, more subtle behavior, such as the change in brain waves during sleep, may require special equipment to be observed.

Psychologists do not want merely to describe behavior: they wish to predict and understand it. To do this, they have set forth four fundamental factors of behavior: the organism, motivation, knowledge, and competence.

The **organism** refers to the biological characteristics of a living biological entity, including the creature's nervous system, endocrine system, biological history, and heredity. **Motivation** entails the states which cause behavior. The term is vague, but motivation generally includes the organism's internal state (e.g., "tired" or "confused") and the behavior related to this state (e.g., searching for a warm den). The term **cognition** refers to "knowledge," that is, what and how the organism thinks, knows, and remembers. **Competence** means the skills and abilities of an organism. How well can it perform a certain task?

Psychology is not as simple as it may first appear. Psychologists today study many other scientific fields such as biology, physics, chemistry, and linguistics, as well as other social sciences like sociology, anthropology, economics, and political science. To evaluate behavior, a psychologist should be familiar with all of these areas.

HISTORY OF PSYCHOLOGY

The science of psychology, began in philosophy. Ancient Greek philosophers first observed and interpreted their environment and organized their findings. Aristotle, in his *Poetics*, discussed the nature of sensory perception; in *The Republic*, Socrates and Plato explored the way government can influence individual behavior. These philosophers were the first Europeans to reason that human beings have, in addition to a physical body, some kind of apparatus used for thinking. They called this thinking apparatus the **psyche**. Over the centuries, this word has meant such things as "soul," "form," and "function." The most popular equivalent evolved into "**mind**." The suffix "-ology" means "the study of." Thus, for many centuries psychology was considered to be the study of the mind.

The French philosopher René Descartes (1596–1650) was very interested in the relationship between the mind and body. He firmly believed in **dualism**, which states that humans have a dual nature—one part mental and the other physical. This is in contrast to "**monism**," which holds that only one type of nature exists.

In the eighteenth century, philosophers described the various functions of the mind as independent faculties. Every mental activity, such as loving, reading, or mathematical long division, was viewed as the work of a particular area of the mind. This approach led to many explanations of behavior.

Certain scientists in the early nineteenth century tried to analyze the mind by examining the shape of the skull, a study called **phrenology**. Lumps in the skull were linked to faculties. For example, if a generous person had a very large lump on her head, that region of the skull would be labelled the "generosity" region of the mind.

By 1850, European laboratories were systematically experimenting with questions of perception, neural conduction, and other aspects of physiological psychology. Gustav Fechner (1801–1887) published a book titled *Elemente der Psychophysik* (Elements of Psychophysics), which detailed the measurement of sensory experiences. In 1879, Wilhelm Wundt (1832–1920) established the first laboratory solely devoted to psychology in Leipzig, Germany; the Johns Hopkins University started the first U.S. psychology lab in 1883.

MAJOR SCHOOLS OF THOUGHT

Structuralism, the first theoretical school in psychology, derived from Wilhelm Wundt's work. Wundt (1832–1920) believed that the science of psychology should study the conscious mind. Influenced by the physical scientists of his time, Wundt embraced the atomic theory of matter. This theory stated that all complex substances could be separated and analyzed into component elements. Wundt wished to divide the mind into **mental elements**. To analyze mental elements, Wundt used an experimental method called **introspection**. Subjects reported the contents of their own minds as objectively as possible, usually in connection with stimuli such as light, sound, or odors. The subjects' verbal reports were analyzed to see the number and types of "mental elements" they contained.

The major drawback of structuralism was that it focused on the internal structure and activity of the mind, rather than overt, objectively observable behavior. Subjective reports of the mind's activities are easily manipulated by both the subject and the experimenter, and they are unreliable.

While structuralist psychologists were busy asking their subjects to describe mental images, **functionalists** were asking what the mind does, and why. Functionalists were inspired by Darwin's theory of evolution; they believed that all behavior and mental processes help organisms to adapt to a changing environment. They expanded their studies beyond perception to include questions of learning, motivation, and problem solving. Functionalist William James (1842–1910) coined the phrase "**stream of consciousness**" to describe the way the mind experiences perception and thought as a constant flow of sensation.

The functionalists' most important contribution to psychology was the introduction of the concept of **learning**, and thus adaptation to the environment, to psychological study. The most influential proponents of functionalism were William James and John Dewey (1859–1952), a philosopher and educator who played a substantial role in the development of educational psychology.

Behaviorism, as developed by John B. Watson (1878–1958), swept the United States at the turn of the century. Watson rejected the idea of the "mind," stating that this structure not only could not be objectively studied, but did not even exist! Instead, Watson presented behavior as consisting of the stimulus, a "**black box**" which processed the stimuli, and the response the "black box" produced. Nothing could be said about the "black box" apart from the behavior it regulated. Watson also disregarded introspection, asserting that only observations of outward behavior could provide valid psychological data. He stated that the major component of psychological study should be the identification of relationships between stimuli (environment) and responses (behavior).

While structuralists believed that the mind could be divided into mental/experiential elements, behaviorists believed that all behavior could be broken down into a collection of conditioned responses. These **conditioned responses (CRs)** were simple learned responses to stimuli. All human behavior was supposed to be the result of learning.

Behaviorists have also studied animal behavior extensively. Many held that there was no difference between human and animal behavior, and several tried to formulate general theories of behavior based on animal experiments. Leaders of this school, prominent in the late 1930s and 1940s, include Edward C. Tolman (1886–1959), Clark L. Hull (1884–1952), and Edwin R. Guthrie (1886–1959).

Gestalt psychology survives only as a name for a collection of theories. It was founded in Germany in 1912 by Max Wertheimer (1880–1943). The word *gestalt* has no exact equivalent in English, but its meaning is similar to "form" or "organization." Gestalt psychologists emphasized the organizational processes in behavior, rather than the content of behavior. Like the structuralists, gestalt psychologists mainly focused on problems of perception.

Unlike the reductionist structuralists and functionalists, gestaltists believed that behavior and experiences consisted of patterns and organized sets. Like many physical scientists, gestalt psychologists believed the whole is more than the sum of its parts.

Gestalt psychologists stressed **phenomenology**, or the study of natural, unanalyzed perception, as the basis for behavior. Wolfgang Kohler (1887–1967) argued that learning and problem solving were organizational processes like perception. He described the "**moment of insight**," when an individual realizes the solution to a problem suddenly crystallizes, as a whole gestalt out of reasoning, intuition, and so on.

Many of the gestaltists' observations about perception are still being explored. Current cognitive psychologists draw heavily on their ideas, particularly when dealing with questions of vision and information processing.

Biological, cognitive, humanistic, and psychoanalytic psychologists are most active today. **Biological psychologists** explore the effect that changes in an organism's physical body or environment have on behavior, and the interaction between behavior and the brain. Biological psychologists concentrate on physical techniques, and hence find physical results.

Major contributors to biological psychology include Ivan Pavlov (1849–1936), who conditioned dogs to salivate when they heard a bell ring; Eric Kandel, (b 1929) who pioneered the use of the sea slug Aplysia to study motor neurons; and Norman Geschwind, (1926–1984) who revolutionized studies of the neural basis of dyslexia.

Cognitive psychology is heir to the early experiential psychologists. It is concerned with the processes of thinking and memory, as well as attention, imagery, creativity, problem solving, and language use. In contrast to the behaviorists, cognitive psychologists discuss the mental processes which determine what humans can perceive, or communicate, as well as how they think.

In the 1950s, psychologists realized that behaviorism, while a useful approach, had taught them nothing about the "black box" of mental processing. Scientists like Norbert Wiener (1894–1964) began work on **cybernetics**, the study of automatic control systems like thermostats and computers, asking, "How does a thinking machine process information?" Noam Chomsky (b 1928) published his theories on language as a system with infinite, non-learned possibilities generated by rules. New technology and logic gave psychologists the power to explore realms that were considered too subjective by the dominant behaviorists.

Humanistic psychology also arose in the 1950s, with a completely different focus. Humanistic psychologists sought to begin a psychology of mental health, not illness, by studying healthy, creative people.

Humanistic psychology grew out of two main influences: **phenomenology**, the idea that behavior is based on subjective perception, and **existentialism**, which states that humans' basic existential anxiety is fear of death. Both approaches concentrated on the individual's point of view. Humanistic psychologists had little use for statistics; the focus was to understand each person's struggle to exist.

Psychoanalytic theories have an important place in psychology. Sigmund Freud (1856–1939), the father of psychoanalysis, is perhaps the most famous psychologist in the world, as well as the most challenged. In the nineteenth century, Freud developed his method of treatment for mental illness and a theory of personality through empirical (observational) and experimental techniques. Freud developed a treatment called **psychoanalysis**, where patients work with a therapist to explore the sources of their illness in their own past, stressing early experience and unconscious, "repressed" memories. Freud's primary tool for investigation was the **case study**, which included both his commentary and a patient's autobiographical material, dream analysis, and free association.

Neo-Freudians revised Freud's theories to provide for more cogent views of women's development, learning throughout life, interpersonal influences on personality, and social interaction. Important writers included Eric Erikson, Karen Horney (1885–1952), Carl Jung (1875–1961), and Alfred Adler (1870–1937).

Though psychoanalytic theory has its limitations, particularly with regard to biologically based illnesses like schizophrenia, it is the most influential of psychological fields to date. Without it, clinical psychology as we know it would not exist.

METHODS OF STUDY
Types of Studies

Naturalistic observation is the systematic observation of an event or phenomenon in the environment as it occurs naturally. The researcher does not manipulate the phenomenon. When psychologists wish to manipulate conditions, they perform experiments. Some event, treatment, or condition is changed, controlled, or recorded by the psychologist: this factor is called the **independent variable**. The change in the organism—behavioral or biological—is recorded by the psychologist. This change is the **dependent variable**. By observing the change in the organism correlated with the change in conditions, the psychologist can infer the change in environment changed the organism's behavior. However, correlation is not causation. A social scientist must beware that the change in the dependent variable, behavior, is truly due to a change in the independent variable and not some other factor.

Surveys are another method of psychological investigation. Individuals are asked to reply to a series of questions or to rate items. The purpose is not to test abilities, but to discover beliefs, opinions, and attitudes. Psychologists may take answers to survey questions and see how they match with respondents' characteristics—age, gender, social class, and so on.

In **longitudinal studies**, psychologists study their subjects over a long period of time to observe changes in their behavior. **Cross-sectional** studies take a group of subjects and examine their behavior at one point in time. **Case studies**, or case histories, are commonly used in clinical psychology and medical research. A single individual is studied intensely to examine a problem or issue relevant to that person.

Reliability and Validity

To be applicable to the general population, any test a psychologist administers must be standardized. The results must be reproducible, and must measure what the psychologist wishes to measure. These concerns are termed **reliability** and **validity**.

In psychology, reliability refers to how consistently individuals score on a test. Reliability measures the extent to which differences between individuals' scores show true difference in characteristics, and not "**error variance**," or the proportion of the score due to errors in test construction.

The question of validity is whether a test measures what the examiner wants it to measure. Specifically, **construct validity** is the extent to which a test measures something—a theoretical construct. **Criterion-related validity** refers to how effective a test is in predicting an individual's behavior in other, specified situations. For example, if a student does well on the SAT, does that student also have high grades now? Criterion contamination occurs when results on a test bias an individual's score on another test.

Ethics in Psychological Research

Since psychological research involves live, fragile humans and animals, psychologists must consider the ethical implications of their research. A careless experimenter can wreak havoc in a trusting subject's life. The U.S. government requires that every institution receiving federal support must set up review boards to decide the ethical implications of all research, and many other professional organizations have also set up ethical guidelines.

In general, experimenters must be honest, practice **informed consent** (telling subjects all features of the experiment prior to the study), allow subjects to leave the experiment at any time, protect subjects from physical and mental harm, and protect all subjects' confidentiality.

Statistical Methods

To scientifically study behavior, psychologists use **statistics**. The **population** is the total set of possible scores, say, the weight of every person in the United States. Most statistics use a **sample** of a total population—the weights of 1,000 U.S. citizens, for example. A **distribution** is simply any set of scores taken from a population or population sample.

Inferential statistics, such as T-tests, chi-squares, and analyses of variance, test the differences between groups. They are used to measure sampling error, draw conclusions from data, and test hypotheses. They answer the question, "What do these data show?"

Descriptive statistics answer the question, "What are the data?" They include measures of **central tendency** (mean, median, and mode), or whether or not the data are clumped in the middle of a graph. Descriptive statistics also include measures of **variability**, or how the data is spread across a graph (i.e., standard deviation, range, and Z-scores), and measures of **correlation**, or the relationship between two sets of scores.

The **mean** is the average of a set of scores. The **median** is the score in the exact middle of the distribution: half the scores fall above the median, half fall below it. The **mode** is the most frequently occurring score. For example, in the series 3, 4, 4, 5, 6, 8, 100, the mode is 4—the number which occurs twice. The median is 5. The mean, though, is 65.

Variability is commonly measured by the **range**, or the distance between the highest and lowest score. In the previous example, the range is $(100 - 3)$, or 97. The **standard deviation** is an index of how much data generally varies from the mean.

To find the standard deviation:

1. Find the mean of the distribution.

2. Subtract each score from the mean.

3. Square each result (these are the deviations).

4. Add the squared deviations from the mean.

5. Divide by the total number of scores (this is the variance).

6. Find the square root of the variance (this is the standard deviation).

Many descriptive statistics involve the **normal distribution**, a bell-shaped curve which can be described completely by the mean and standard deviation. In a normal distribution, about 68% of the scores fall within plus or minus one standard deviation from the mean, 95% fall within plus or minus two standard deviations from the mean, and 99.5% fall within plus or minus three standard deviations from the mean.

Z-scores, or **standard scores**, are a way of expressing a score's distance from the mean in terms of the standard deviation. To find a Z-score for a number in a distribution, subtract the mean from that number and divide the result by the standard deviation. A positive Z-score shows that the number is higher than the mean; a negative Z-score, lower.

Correlations show how closely related two sets of scores are to each other. Possible correlations range between $+1.00$ and -1.00. When a correlation is $+1.00$, high scores on one set are associated with high scores on the second set; in a correlation of -1.00, low scores are associated with high scores. A correlation of 0.00 shows that the two sets are not associated.

These statistics are all usually calculated on **samples**, not total populations. Using the sample, a psychologist can predict the intervals in which the mean and variance of the total population is likely to fall.

CAREERS IN PSYCHOLOGY

In addition to being a science, psychology is also a profession. Psychologists can be either researchers or practitioners.

Careers in Psychology

Experimental psychologists	Conduct experiments in various areas of psychology, such as cognition or sensory perception, to further knowledge of the subject.
Biological psychologists	Study the influence of biological factors on human and animal behavior. These factors include genetics, the nervous system, or the endocrine system.

(Continued)

Careers in Psychology (*Continued*)

Social psychologists	Use scientific research methods to study the behavior of individuals in groups; they are concerned with an organism's interaction with others.
Developmental psychologists	Study individuals' behavioral development from conception through adulthood. They observe the acquisition of skills through the development of cognition, perception, language, motor abilities, and social behavior.
Educational psychologists	Concerned with the process of education. They engage in research to develop new ways of teaching and learning. They also implement new systems of education, including textbooks.
Personality psychologists	Study individuals to discover the development of basic underlying dimensions of personality and how these dimensions or traits affect behavior.
Clinical psychologists	Assess abnormal behavior to diagnose and change it. Psychosis, substance abuse, and reactive depression can be treated by clinical psychologists, though the line between medical and psychological illness grows more blurred each day. Other personnel working in clinical psychology include behavior analysts, psychological nurses, and music therapists.
Counseling psychologists	Usually treat people whose disorders are not so serious. They offer advice on personal, educational, or vocational problems.
Industrial/organizational psychologists	Generally work for public and private businesses or the government. They apply psychological principles to areas such as personnel policies, consumerism, working conditions, production efficiency, and decision making. Two basic fields of industrial psychology are personnel psychology and consumer psychology.

Most researchers and college teachers of psychology have a Ph.D. (Doctor of Philosophy) degree, which requires four to five years of graduate study. Many of the other professions demand a master's degree, which requires one to two years of graduate study.

INTRODUCTION TO SOCIAL PSYCHOLOGY

Social psychology focuses on the psychology of the individual in society. Using the scientific method and objective study, social psychologists have produced a body of knowledge about the underlying psychological processes in social interactions.

Within social psychology, there are two major schools of thought. **Cognitive theorists** concentrate on an individual's internal processes and thoughts. They believe that a human being organizes and processes experience, and that her "world view" greatly influences her social behavior. **Behaviorists**, on the other hand, put more emphasis on external events and tend to believe that people react to events that occur around them.

Attitudes and Attributions

An **attitude** is a person's beliefs about an object or a situation. An attitude both precedes behavior and causes behavior toward an object. A **value**, on the other hand, is a person's enduring belief about how she should act, and what goals are appropriate or desirable. Values direct behavior on a long-term basis. Examples of values (from Rokeach's Value Survey) are pleasure, wisdom, and a sense of accomplishment. A person generally holds many more attitudes than values.

Attitudes are generally formed through imitation, classical conditioning, or operant conditioning. Children often take on their parents' behavior and attitudes. In operant conditioning, a subject emits a behavior. If the behavior is reinforced, it will likely reoccur; if it is punished, it will not recur as often.

An adult's attitudes are quite difficult to trace to their source. This is complicated by the fact that attitudes can change, even quite significantly, in the course of a person's lifetime.

Persuasion

Persuasion refers to a type of social influence that involves attitude change. In general, three factors affect how persuasive a particular communication is: the source of the communication (who says it), the nature of the communication (how it is said), and the characteristics of the audience. All these factors can also be applied to print and broadcast media, not just face-to-face persuasion.

The first aspect of the source that the audience examines is **credibility**. People tend to believe people who appear to be experts or seem trustworthy. Often, visual impressions are the only items a person can base impressions on, and these are what are used to infer credibility. Trustworthiness, on the other hand, can be improved by arguing there is nothing to lose, arguing against one's (apparent) self-interest, and appearing not to be trying to influence people or change their minds.

The concern for the nature of communication is the emotional approach vs. the reasonable (or logical) approach. Research results generally indicate that a shocking (emotional-based) approach is usually more effective in communication and persuasion than the logical approach.

As for the audience, individuals with low self-esteem are quicker to be convinced if the speaker appears credible or takes an emotional approach, while high self-esteem listeners are in higher conflict when presented with less-than-reliable information from a medium-credibility speaker.

The speaker's prior experience with the audience is another crucial factor, as are educational level and previous contact with the issue being discussed.

Prejudice

Prejudice is generally a negative attitude held toward a particular group and any member of that group. Prejudice is translated into behavior through **discrimination**, which refers to any action that results from prejudiced points of view. **Ethnocentrism** is a special form of prejudice where a person holds positive prejudices about her own ethnic group and negative prejudices about all other ethnic groups. It is possible for individuals to be quite prejudiced and still not discriminate. When discrimination decreases and prejudice remains, discrimination may begin to take more subtle forms, such as not being included in informal discussions with other managers at work.

Psychologists hypothesize that there are four basic causes of prejudice. The first cause, **economic and political competition**, states that when any resource is limited, majority groups will vie for resources and thus form prejudices against the competing group for their own personal gain and advantage. Research has demonstrated a clear link between the level of discrimination and prejudice against a certain group in an area and the scarcity of jobs in that area.

The second causal factor of prejudice is **personality needs**. After World War II, researchers began to search for a prejudiced personality type. The major piece of research in this area, by Adorno et al., is titled *The Authoritarian Personality*. Adorno developed the F (fascist) Scale for authoritarianism. These researchers established a relationship between the strictness of parental upbringing and authoritarianism and a correlational relationship between authoritarianism, prejudice, and ethnocentrism. Yet they did not determine what causes prejudice, only what personality traits accompany it.

The third cause of prejudice is the **displacement of aggression**. This is referred to as a "scapegoat" theory of prejudice. Here, aggression that cannot be otherwise expressed is displaced onto socially acceptable victims.

The fourth cause of prejudice is **conformity to preexisting prejudices** within the society or subgroup. Researchers note that while there seems to be a large difference between the amount of anti-black prejudice in the North and the South, neither group is distinguishable on the basis of how they score on the Authoritarian test. The problem appears to be caused by socially acceptable beliefs in each region. As Elliot Aronson (b 1932) has noted, historical events in the South set the stage for greater prejudice against blacks, but it is conformity which keeps it going.

Four other factors contribute to the construction and continuation of prejudice:

1. People need to feel superior to someone.

2. People most strongly feel competition for jobs from the next lower level.

3. People from the lower socio-economic levels are more frustrated and therefore more aggressive.

4. A lack of education increases the likelihood that they will simplify their world by the consistent use of stereotyping.

There are ways of reducing prejudice. If people of different backgrounds are brought together in **equal-status contact**, people tend to change their behavior and their attitudes toward other groups. Finally, one very successful way to reduce prejudice is through **interdependence**, where all participants must work together with a mixed group. Social psychologists are currently trying to apply this method to educational settings.

Attributes and Stereotypes

An **attribute** is a perceived characteristic of some object or person. In attribution, people infer that some individual has certain characteristics. If a person infers that people possess certain characteristics because of their gender, race, or religion, that person is attributing a **stereotype** to that group. Stereotyping is not necessarily an intentional act of insult; very often it is merely used as a means of simplifying the complex world. However, if a stereotype narrows a person's views of actual interpersonal differences, prejudiced attitudes can result.

Attribution theory contends that individuals have a tendency to attribute a cause to any recently viewed behaviors. When viewing an event, the observer uses the information available to her at the time to infer causality. Although there are many factors which affect what inference will be made, the major contributors are a person's beliefs (e.g., stereotypes or prejudices). The process of attribution based on a person's prejudices can be described as a "**vicious circle**."

CONFORMITY AND OBEDIENCE

Conformity is a change in behavior or belief caused by real or imagined social pressure. For example, a student may dress like others in her class. Conformity is generally divided into three subtypes: compliance, identification, and internalization.

Compliance is a change in external behavior, as opposed to a real attitude change, termed "private acceptance." Compliance is generally exhibited by individuals attempting to gain a reward or punishment. This behavior generally ceases once the reward or punishment is either not available or avoidable, respectively.

Identification results from the individual's desire to be like some other person, the person she is identifying with. Such behavior is self-satisfying, and does not require reward or threat of punishment. The individual loosely adopts the beliefs and opinions of the person she identifies with, a fact which differentiates identification from compliance.

Internalization occurs when the individual adopts the group's beliefs as his own. This process is a deeply rooted social response based on the desire to be right. The reward here is intrinsic. Identification is usually the method which introduces a belief to an individual, but once it is internalized it becomes an independent belief, and is highly resistant to change.

The most famous psychological demonstration of conformity was a series of experiments by Solomon Asch. Asch asked subjects to choose which of three lines on a card was the same length as line X, a line on a separate card. Each subject was on a panel with other "subjects" (Asch's confederates) who all initially gave the same wrong answer. Approximately 35% of the real subjects chose to give the obviously incorrect, but conforming, response.

Obedience also involves conforming to others' expectations. Yet in obedience, an authority's demands are clearly expressed; the individual must consciously choose whether or not to obey. The study of obedience became especially important after World War II, when psychologists were eager to investigate just how and why the Nazis committed their death-camp atrocities.

While investigating obedience, Stanley Milgram discovered that the average middle-class American male would, under the direction of a legitimate authority figure, give severe shocks to other people in an experimental setting. Out of the 40 males who took part in the initial experiments, 26 (65%) went all the way to the maximum shock of 450 volts. This alarming finding demonstrates how much ordinary people will comply with the orders of a legitimate authority even to the point of committing cruel and harmful actions.

GROUP DYNAMICS

People tend to act differently when they are in a group. In general, a group's primary purpose is to achieve some definite goal. To accomplish the goal, the group establishes **positions**, or places, where people fit into a group's hierarchy. Individuals themselves choose to fill **roles**, the set of different behaviors an individual displays in connection with a given social position. Most people have many roles which must be filled each day. However, people who occupy the same type of position may play very different roles. Three different roles are possible in any given position in a group. The **task-oriented** role requires that a person be concerned directly with accomplishing the goal of the group. The **maintenance** role requires that the individual playing it be more concerned with the group morale. The final type of role is the **self-oriented** role; the person who takes this role cares mainly for herself, and may even attempt to undermine the group's goals if they interfere with her personal desires or needs.

If a group is large enough—say, the size of New York City—social influence may move the person away from socially acceptable behavior. **Deindividuation** is a state where a person feels a lessened sense of personal identity and a decreased concern about what people think of him. This state, which probably results from feelings of anonymity, lessened responsibility, and arousal, can lead to antisocial behavior. As an example, Philip Zimbardo left a seemingly abandoned car unattended in New York and another in Palo Alto, California. Within 24 hours, the car in New York was completely ransacked, whereas the Palo Alto car remained essentially untouched. The study indicated a person apparently felt less likely to be identified in a city of 8 million (New York) than a city of 100,000.

Groups can also improve performance. In **social facilitation**, the mere presence of other people such as an audience or coworkers can increase individual performance. In the 1890s, Norman Triplett became interested in the fact that cyclists rode faster in groups than alone, while in the 1930s, John Dashiell discovered that though people respond more frequently in the presence of others, their rate of errors also increased. Robert Zajonc (1965) theorized that the presence of other people produces an increase in a person's arousal level and enhances strong responses. However, if responses are poorly learned or weak, responses will suffer.

Altruism and Bystander Intervention

Altruism and the "bystander effect" are two opposite responses to situations where another person needs help. In **altruism**, a person will risk his own health or well-being to help another. Yet if a large group of people witnesses an event where someone desperately needs assistance, each individual person is less likely to intervene than if she were alone. This phenomenon is called the **bystander effect**.

Latane and Darley produced the most famous experiments on bystander intervention. In their study, male subjects heard someone fall, apparently uninjured, in the room next door. Subjects were placed in one of four conditions: alone, with a friend, with another subject who was a stranger, and with a confederate in the experiment who had been instructed to remain passive at the sounds of injury. In the alone situation, subjects responded to the need for help 91% of the time, while with the passive confederate, subjects responded only 7% of the time. With pairs of strangers, at least one of the subjects responded in 40% of the pairs, while in the group of two friends, at least one person intervened in 70% of the pairs. This finding can be explained through **social influence** or **diffusion of responsibility**. The former option suggests that people are susceptible to the apparent reactions of other people present. In diffusion of responsibility, when other people are present, each person's total sense of responsibility (and justification for responding to emergencies) may diminish.

AGGRESSION

In animals, many types of **aggression** are specific to certain species and are clearly controlled by brain structures and hormone levels, such as maternal aggression in rats. In humans, sex steroid hormones called **androgens** have been conclusively linked to an increase in aggressive behavior. However, it is not clear whether high levels of androgens produce aggression, or high levels of aggression result in the production of testosterone; there is evidence for both conclusions. Mazur and Lamb (1980) found that men who lost tennis matches had lower levels of testosterone (an androgen) an hour later, while the men who won had higher levels.

According to social psychologists, three different **distinctions** should be used when discussing aggressive behavior. The first distinction is between **harmful and nonharmful behavior**, which is judged by the outcome of the behavior. The second distinction involves the **intent of the aggressor**, as hitting a person accidentally is not considered aggressive. Finally, there is a distinction between aggression necessary to achieve a goal (as in professional boxing), called **instrumental aggression**, and aggression which is an end in itself (as in common street fighting), called **hostile aggression**. Interpersonal aggression occurs most often between friends, relatives, and acquaintances, and is much less often associated with crime than most people think.

Many social psychologists believe that aggression is a learned behavior, like other behaviors. Albert Bandura's work on modeling, or learning through imitation, was designed to explain aggressive tendencies in children. Aggression, like attitudes, may also be conditioned. The frustration-aggression hypothesis states that frustration toward the accomplishment of some goal produces aggression. If the source of frustration is available and unthreatening, the aggression will be displaced onto that source. Otherwise, the aggression will be displaced onto someone or something else, called a "scapegoat."

However, some psychologists believe that aggression is an inborn tendency. The only reason, according to these theories, that we are not involved in more wars than we currently are is that humans use their intelligence to vent their aggression, and therefore do not always express aggression physically. Konrad Lorenz applied Darwin's "survival of the fittest" theory to aggression, arguing that aggression is necessary for the continued existence of the species. Others, including Freud, believe the catharsis theory. This theory states that aggression is a means of releasing inner tension. If this tension were to remain unreleased, mental illness would result. Research does not support this theory, though, and has actually shown the opposite to be true.

ORGANIZATIONAL PSYCHOLOGY

Organizational psychology studies human behavior in an industrial or organizational environment. It can be divided into two important subfields: **industrial psychology** and **human factors psychology**. Human factors psychology is concerned specifically with how people receive information through their senses, store this information, and process it when making decisions.

The industrial psychologist helps to improve safety programs and works with engineers on the human aspects of equipment design. She assists the office of public relations in its interactions with consumers and the local community. Industrial psychologists also engage in programs dealing with workers' mental health, and assist management in finding ways to reduce absenteeism and grievances.

The role of a human factors engineer, on the other hand, is concerned with contriving, designing, and producing structures and machines useful to humans. He applies his knowledge of the mechanical, electrical, chemical, or other properties of matter to the task of creating all kinds of functional devices—safety pins and automobiles, mousetraps and missiles. The task which confronts the human factors engineer is to describe humans' special abilities and limitations so that design engineers can effectively include the human operator in their man-made system. This requires knowledge about sensation and perception, psychomotor behavior, and cognitive processes as well as knowledge about the properties of the material world.

INTRODUCTION TO GEOGRAPHY

What Is Geography?

Geography is the study of Earth's surface, including such aspects as its climate, topography, vegetation, and population. **Physical geography** is a branch of geography concerned with the natural features of Earth's surface. Physical geography concentrates on such areas as land formation, water, weather, and climate.

Population geography deals with the relationships between geography and population patterns, including birth and death rates. **Political geography** deals with the effect of geography on politics, especially on national boundaries and relations between states. **Economic geography** is a study of the interaction between Earth's landscape and the economic activity of the human population.

UNITED STATES

Many sources of energy in the United States are being developed to lessen the country's dependence on foreign oil. Some of these sources are solar energy, nuclear energy, gasohol, fossil fuels, and others. With the development of these sources of energy, more jobs will be made available and our economy will not be afflicted by adverse situations in oil-rich countries.

The **Middle Atlantic states**, which include New York, West Virginia, Delaware, Maryland, New Jersey, and Pennsylvania, are a hub of activity. This area is highly industrialized and includes a skilled work force. The financial center of the nation is found in New York.

The states of North Dakota, South Dakota, Nebraska, Kansas, Minnesota, Iowa, Missouri, Wisconsin, Illinois, Michigan, Indiana, and Ohio make up the **Plains states**. This area is also referred to as the Midwest Region of the United States. It is known as a great agricultural region. Some of the crops grown are wheat, corn, and oats.

The Plains states are highly industrialized. Their location near waterways and the close proximity to coal and iron deposits have made it relatively easy for industries to develop. Skilled laborers are available and are necessary to work in manufacturing plants.

The **South** includes the following states: Texas, Oklahoma, Louisiana, Arkansas, Mississippi, Alabama, Florida, Georgia, South Carolina, North Carolina, Tennessee, Kentucky, and Virginia. This area is known for its relatively mild weather and good, rich soil. Agriculture and oil are two of the most important industries in the South. Some of the crops grown are cotton, corn, tobacco, peanuts, and rice. Cattle raising is also very important in some of these states.

Texas, the second-largest state in land area, is composed of 267,000 square miles and 254 counties. Texas is, without a doubt, one of the most geographically varied states in the United States.

The **Pacific states** include Washington, Oregon, and California. California has the largest population of any state in the United States. It is known for its agriculture and leads all other states in this regard. Oregon and Washington also are known for farming. All three states also have very developed industries.

Some of the major cities located in the Pacific states are Seattle, Spokane, Portland, Olympia, San Francisco, Los Angeles, Salem, and San Diego. Tourism is a major industry.

The **Mountain states** are Montana, Idaho, Wyoming, Nevada, Utah, Colorado, Arizona, and New Mexico. These states are sparsely populated, even though the combined square mileage is over 800,000. The Rocky Mountains stretch through this area and most people feel they are a beautiful sight to behold.

The **New England states** include Maine, Massachusetts, New Hampshire, Vermont, Rhode Island, and Connecticut. Territorially, this is a very small region. The total size is about 67,000 square miles. The main industries in this area are fishing, shipping, manufacturing, and dairy farming.

MEXICO

Mexico borders the United States on the south and has about 107 million people. The land area is about 762,000 square miles. The capital is Mexico City. Some of the chief crops are coffee, cotton, corn, sugar cane, and rice.

Mexico has an abundance of natural resources, such as oil, gold, silver, and natural gas. Textiles, steel production, tourism, and petroleum are the major industries in Mexico.

CANADA

Canada is the United States' neighbor to the north. It includes the second largest territory in the world. The capital of Canada is Ottawa.

The United States and Canada are two sprawling countries that make up North America. Each country is an industrial giant and provides a very high standard of living for its population. The population of the United States is about nine or ten times larger than that of Canada.

The United States and Canada have large supplies of natural resources. In the United States, the minerals include coal, copper, gold, nickel, silver, zinc, and others. In Canada, the minerals found are nickel, gold, lead, silver, zinc, and others.

SOUTH AND CENTRAL AMERICA

Central America

Central America is the connecting point between North and South America. The countries in Central America have an extremely long coastline. The main industry of this area is agriculture, and most people who live in this area are extremely poor. Bananas, coffee, and corn are some of their chief crops.

The seven nations that make up Central America are Belize, Guatemala, Honduras, El Salvador, Panama, Costa Rica, and Nicaragua.

South America

South America, lying entirely in the Western Hemisphere and mostly south of the equator, has a Pacific shoreline on the west and an Atlantic shoreline east and north. South America connects with Central America and lies to the south and east of the Caribbean Sea and North America. It is the realm closest to Antarctica. The Andes Mountains stretch the length of the west coast while the Amazon Basin covers the north central part of the realm. The remaining parts of the realm consist mainly of plateaus.

Roughly half of the area and half of the population of South America are concentrated in Brazil.

The population of South America resides primarily on the periphery of the continent. The interior is only lightly populated. However, parts of the interior are undergoing extensive development with some population shifts.

South America can be easily divided into four distinct regions: the **North**, the **West**, the **Southern Cone**, and **Brazil**.

The North consists of Colombia, Venezuela, Guyana, French Guiana, and Suriname. Each of the states has a Caribbean orientation both economically and culturally. All the states followed a plantation development model that involved the importation of slaves and contract laborers. Eventually, those immigrants were absorbed into the culture. While Guyana, French Guiana, and Suriname retained the culture from the colonial period, Colombia and Venezuela expanded into farming, ranching, mining, and oil and became much more diversified.

The West includes the Andean states Ecuador, Peru, Bolivia, and Paraguay. In addition to the influence of Andes, these states also share a strong Amerindian heritage.

The South, or Southern Cone, consists of Argentina, Chile, and Uruguay. These states have a strong European influence and little Amerindian influence.

Brazil distinguishes itself in two respects from the rest of South America. First is the influence of Portugal rather than Spain and second is the importance of Africans as opposed to Amerindians in both culture and demography.

Most states exhibit a marked degree of cultural pluralism. While there are a variety of ethnicities that are remnants of the colonial and slave heritage, these groups exist side by side without mixing.

Urban growth throughout the continent continues its rapid rise. Levels of urbanization overall today are equivalent to those in Europe and the United States.

EUROPE

Europe consists of 39 states and approximately 731 million people, according to the United Nations. On the north, west, and south, it has boundaries facing the Atlantic Ocean and the Mediterranean Sea, as well as a large number of other bodies of water. The eastern boundary is somewhat uncertain, with the line of demarcation lying along the border of Russia or along the Ural Mountains.

In the south, the coastal areas have hot dry summers that required the development of specially adapted plants. Lacking the richness of natural resources of other regions, the southern region of Europe has nonetheless achieved a continuity of culture that has continuously depended on the exploitation of agriculture. As a result, the region tends to have a lower standard of living than other parts of Europe with the notable exception of Eastern Europe. While not as urbanized as Northern Europe, Southern Europe is actually more populous than Northern Europe.

Eastern Europe encompasses the largest region in Europe as well as the largest range of physiological, cultural, and political characteristics. This is a region of open plains, major rivers, lowlands, highlands, and mountains and valleys that provide key transit corridors.

Northern or Nordic Europe, one of the largest regions in terms of size, is also one of the most poorly endowed regions in terms of natural resources. Cold climates with poor soil and limited mineral wealth combined with long distances over mountainous, remote terrain result in an isolated region, yet one that has succeeded economically.

The **British Isles**, off the western coast of Europe, consist of two main islands—Ireland and Britain—as well as numerous small islands. While its isolation from continental Europe has protected it from attack, that isolation has led the United Kingdom to look outward to fulfill its economic needs. The United Kingdom had one of the largest empires in history and has become a hub of banking and industry.

Western Europe is at the heart of Europe. It provides the hub of economic power, which has led to its leadership in economic and political union.

The economy of Europe is well developed and depends in large part on manufacturing for its income. While Europe is considered to be overall highly productive and developed, the further east one goes, the lower the level of development.

Being at the western end of the Eurasian landmass, Europe is located in a prime position to facilitate contact with the rest of the world. Location as well as durable power cores provided necessary elements for the creation of wide ranging colonial empires.

Europe has an aging population that enjoys a high standard of living, is highly urbanized, and has a long life expectancy. Immigration is changing the cultural makeup of the states, with some instability resulting.

Unlike most other parts of the world, Europe has made significant progress toward economic integration through the European Union. Political progress, although also a part of the developing and expanding European Union, has come much more slowly.

NORTH AFRICA

Northern Africa is the northernmost part of Africa, separated from Subsaharan Africa by the Sahara Desert. Northern Africa is almost completely surrounded by water in all other directions, with only a small connection to Asia at the Sinai Peninsula of Egypt. Northern Africa is bordered by the Atlantic Ocean to the west, the Red Sea to the east, and the Mediterranean Sea to the north. The states of Algeria, Egypt, Libya, Morocco, Sudan, Tunisia, and Western Sahara make up the region. The **Sahara Desert** covers more than 90% of the region. The other physical feature of note is the Atlas Mountains, which extend across much of Morocco, northern Algeria, and Tunisia. The Atlas Mountains are part of the mountain system, which also runs through much of Southern Europe. The mountains become a steppe landscape as they transition into the Sahara Desert.

Farming has been the traditional economic base of the region, with Atlas Mountain valleys, the Nile Valley and delta, and the Mediterranean coast providing good agricultural land. Cereals, rice, cotton, cedar, and cork are important crops. Olives, figs, dates, and citrus fruits are also grown here. The Nile Valley, being fertile and providing its own source of water, is particularly fertile, while elsewhere irrigation is essential to agricultural production. In the twentieth century, the economies of Algeria and Libya were transformed by the discovery of oil and natural gas. Morocco depends on phosphates, agriculture, and tourism for its economy. Egypt and Tunisia also depend on tourism. Egypt also has a varied industrial base, importing technology to develop its electronics and engineering industries.

The population of North Africa can be divided along the main geographic regions of North Africa: the **Maghreb** (northwest), the **Nile Valley** (northeast), and the **Sahara** (south).

SUBSAHARAN AFRICA

Subsaharan Africa is the whole of the African continent south of the Sahara Desert. It is bordered to the north by the Sahara, the largest desert in the world; the Atlantic Ocean to the west; the Indian Ocean to the east; and the Atlantic and Indian Oceans meeting to border Africa to the south. Despite being geographically part of Subsaharan Africa, the Horn of Africa and large parts of Sudan show a strong Middle Eastern influence.

The landforms of Subsaharan Africa include rain forests, grasslands, and a few mountain ranges. Equatorial Africa, including the **Sahel** (a transitional zone just north of the equator between the Sahara and the tropical savanna), is covered by tropical rain forests while farther south there are grassy flat highlands leading to coastal plains. While Northern Africa has the Atlas Mountains, the Ruwenzri on the Uganda-Zaire border is the main mountain range in the Subsaharan region. Kilimanjaro, part of the Ruwenzri and Africa's highest mountain, is a dormant volcano. Further to the east is the Great Rift Valley, which contains several lakes. In addition to these landforms, Africa has some of the world's longest rivers, including the Nile, Niger, Zaire, and Zambezi. While there are many great lakes and large river systems, Africa has few natural sea harbors.

Subsaharan Africa is culturally rich and diverse with approximately 50 independent states and hundreds of ethnic groups. The large number of states is a legacy of the colonial occupation of Africa by European states. When African states were given their independence, state boundaries were drawn with little thought given to natural geographic boundaries. The result has been great instability that exists to the present day. Governmental fraud, mismanagement, and poor leadership as well as the highest number of refugees and displaced persons in the world compound the instability. In addition to the political instability, health and nutritional conditions in the region are poor. Many diseases remain uncontrolled, malnutrition is rampant, and the AIDS pandemic, which had its genesis in Africa, is a significant health crisis.

Most people in Subsaharan Africa depend on farming to earn a living. States such as Angola and Nigeria have oil reserves, while South Africa is known for diamonds.

RUSSIA

Russia, the largest state in terms of territory, spans most of the northern part of Eurasia. It is almost twice as large as the next biggest state, Canada. Russia's climate is largely continental because of its large size and compactness. Most of its land is more than 200 miles from the sea, and the center is approximately 1,600 miles from the sea.

Despite its large size, comparatively speaking, Russia's population of approximately 143 million people is not very large. Most of that population lives west of the Ural Mountains and is very heterogeneous. Russia is a patchwork of many different ethnic groups, which formed the original basis for the 21 internal republics. As such, Russia is multicultural with a multifaceted political geography.

Despite having 80% of its land mass east of the Ural Mountains, most of the development, population, and infrastructure lie west of the Urals. The largest cities with the attendant industrial and transportation structure as well as the most productive farmland exist on the western 20% of Russia. The **Trans-Siberian Railway** was built to reach one of the few seaports that is usable all year. Despite the fact that Russia is large, it is almost completely encircled by land within Eurasia.

While having extensive industrial development (at least regionally), Russia also holds the greatest mineral resource reserves in the world. It may contain up to half of the world's coal reserves and an even larger percentage of petroleum reserves. While Russia is blessed with plentiful resources, they are located in remote areas with extreme climates, making them difficult to reach and expensive to mine.

Despite the wealth of natural resources, Russia has never been an exporter of manufactured goods, with the exception of weapons. Scarcity and low quality have limited the availability of Russian consumer goods outside of Russia (and, in many cases, inside as well).

SOUTH ASIA

South Asia is a clearly demarcated realm bounded by deserts in the west, the Himalayas to the north, mountains and dense forests to the east, and ocean to the south. Despite containing over 20% of the world's population, South Asia consists of only seven states: Bangladesh, Bhutan, India, the Maldives, Nepal, Pakistan, and Sri Lanka. The realm of South Asia is the most populous and densest in the world. The region has been beset by political instability and is the site of frequent military conflicts including wars between India and Pakistan, both of whom possess nuclear weapons.

The climate varies considerably from area to area. The south is hot in summer and subject to vast quantities of rain during monsoon periods. The north is also hot in summer, but cools during winter. As the elevation increases in mountainous areas, the weather is colder and snow falls at higher altitudes in the Himalayas. However, on the plains at the foot of the Himalayas, the temperatures are much more moderate, as the mountains block the bitter winds that make Siberia so cold.

Despite the temperature variations, the climate of the region is called a **monsoon climate**. The weather is humid during the summer and dry during winter, resulting in two seasons rather than four: wet and dry. In the south, the climate is tropical monsoon while the north has a temperate monsoon climate. The impact of the monsoon climate can be seen on agriculture in the prevalence of jute, tea, rice, and other vegetables being grown in this region.

With more than half its population engaged in subsistence agriculture, it follows that South Asia has a high rate of poverty. Average incomes are low as are levels of education. Moreover, the low income and education levels contribute to poor overall health for the region. All of these factors paint a grim picture of economic prospects.

Sitting on only 3% of the world's land mass, yet possessing over 22% of its population, South Asia has a high population density that will only continue to get worse as it also has one of the highest population growth rates. India, with over 1 billion people, is the world's largest federal republic. Despite having a representative government, economic gains for the majority of the population are limited.

With more than 2,000 ethnic groups, South Asia is one of the most ethnically diverse realms. Ethnic groups range in size from hundreds of millions to small tribal groups. Throughout its history South Asia has been invaded and settled by many ethnic groups. The fusion of the cultures of these different ethnic groups over the centuries has resulted in the creation of a common culture, traditions, and beliefs such as the religions of Hinduism, Jainism, Buddhism, and Sikhism. As a consequence, they share many similar cultural practices, festivals, and traditions.

Religion continues to play a major role in South Asia. Hindus in India, Muslims in Bangladesh and Pakistan, and Buddhists in Sri Lanka display fundamentalist and nationalist tendencies that exacerbate already tendentious religious relationships.

British colonialism created a politically unified South Asia. However, when Britain granted its South Asian colony independence, it split into numerous states along mainly cultural/religious lines. Political friction, particularly between India and Pakistan, remains a constant problem. The cultural and religious differences that contribute to conflict combine with ongoing border disputes between India and Pakistan and India and China to create a potentially disastrous situation, as all three countries possess nuclear weapons.

EAST ASIA

East Asia consists of four states and two other political entities. China, Japan, South Korea, and Mongolia are states, while Taiwan and North Korea cannot be classified as states because they lack general recognition by the states of the world. Taiwan, while considering itself independent, is viewed by the People's Republic of China as a temporarily insubordinate or wayward province. North Korea's political status is uncertain. It is not a full member of the United Nations and there are doubts as to whether the division of Korea into North and South is permanent.

ANTHROPOLOGY

INTRODUCTION TO ANTHROPOLOGY

What Is Anthropology?

Anthropology, the study of human behavior in all places and at all times, is divided into two broad subfields.

Physical anthropology is the study of the biological, physiological, anatomical, and genetic characteristics of both ancient and modern human populations. Physical anthropologists study the evolutionary development of the human species by a comparative analysis of both fossil and living primates.

Cultural anthropology is the study of learned behavior in human societies. Most cultural anthropologists specialize in one or two geographic areas. They may also specialize in selected aspects of culture (e.g., politics, medicine, religion) in the context of the larger social whole. Cultural anthropology is further subdivided as follows:

1. **Archaeology** is the study of the cultures of prehistoric peoples. It also includes the study of modern societies, but from the evidence of their material remains rather than from direct interviews with or observations of the people under study.

2. **Ethnography** is the systematic description of a human society, usually based on firsthand fieldwork. All generalizations about human behavior are based on the descriptive evidence of ethnography.

3. **Ethnology** is the interpretive explanation of human behavior, based on ethnography.

4. **Social anthropology** is the study of human groups, with a particular emphasis on social structure (social relations, family dynamics, social control mechanisms, economic exchange).

5. **Linguistics** is the study of how language works as a medium of communication among humans.

Defining Characteristics of Anthropology

Holism is the belief that the experiences of a human group are unified and patterned. No one aspect of human behavior can be understood in isolation from all the rest.

Culture is the organized sum of everything a people produces, does, and thinks about—all of which they learn as members of a particular social group. A people's culture develops over time as they adapt to their environment.

Comparative method is the belief that generalizations about human behavior can only be made on the basis of data collected from the widest possible range of cultures, both contemporary and historical.

Relativism is the belief that we cannot make value judgments about a culture based on standards appropriate to another culture. When such judgments are made on the basis of one's own culturally derived values, it is said that we are making **ethnocentric** judgments.

Fieldwork is the study of cultures in their natural settings.

Anthropologists attempt to live for an extended period of time among the people they study. They are both **participants** in and **observers** of the culture of the group.

The Development of the Anthropological Perspective

Anthropology is a product of Western civilization, but one that was relatively late to develop. By and large the Greek and Roman philosophers were more concerned with speculations about ideal societies than with descriptions of living ones.

A comparative approach was inaugurated in the Renaissance, with the rediscovery of the past of Western civilization.

Study of contemporary non-Western people began in earnest with the European discovery of the Americas. Aside from the reports of travellers and missionaries, the Age of Exploration resulted in two works of real anthropological interest:

1. **Sahagun**'s study of Aztec beliefs and customs.

2. **Lafitau**'s study of the Iroquois and Huron of western New York.

Scientific anthropology is based on several key assumptions:

1. Cultures evolve through time.

2. Peoples adapted to similar environments in distant parts of the world will establish roughly similar cultures.

3. Human behavior is shaped more by what we learn as members of a social group than by what we inherit genetically.

Evolutionism is the belief that all cultures develop in a uniform and progressive manner. All societies pass through the same stages of development and reach a common end, since the basic problems which all humans have to face are fundamentally similar. This orientation, which is also known as **unilineal evolutionism**, flourished in the late nineteenth century. Key figures in this orientation are Edward B. Tylor and Lewis Henry Morgan.

Diffusionism is the belief that cultures develop not so much by adapting themselves to specific environments as by borrowing traits from other people. This orientation flourished in the early twentieth century. Key figures in this orientation are G. E. Smith, Fritz Graebner, and Clark Wissler.

Historical particularism, stresses the wide range of cultural variability. It is suspicious of "universal laws" of human development and advocates the study of the particular historical development of specific societies as a necessary prerequisite to the formulation of generalizations about cultural evolution. This orientation was founded by Franz Boas early in the twentieth century and dominated anthropology in the United States until the 1960s.

Functionalism, is based on the analysis of specific traits of culture and the ways in which they serve the needs of individuals within the society. This orientation is associated with Bronislaw Malinowski, who influenced anthropology in Britain from the period of World War I through the 1940s.

Structure-functionalism, a variant of Malinowski's functionalism, advocated the analysis of specific traits and the ways in which they serve to maintain the equilibrium of the social structure (rather than the needs of the individuals). This point of view is associated with A. R. Radcliffe-Brown, who was a contemporary of Malinowski.

Psychological anthropology is an attempt to analyze the interaction of cultural and psychological variables in the development of both culture and individual personality. This approach was stimulated by the translation of Freud's work into English in the 1920s. Key figures include Edward Sapir, Margaret Mead, Ruth Benedict, Ralph Linton, Abram Kardiner, and John Whiting.

Neo-evolutionism is the attempt to formulate scientifically testable propositions about cultural evolution, as distinct from the speculative generalizations of the early evolutionists.

Universal evolutionism (general evolutionism) is the concern with the dynamics of culture as a general phenomenon, rather than with specific change within particular cultures. The key figure is Leslie White (1930s–1950s).

Multilineal evolutionism (specific evolutionism) is concerned with patterns of interaction of culture and environment. It is sometimes also known as "cultural ecology." The key figure is Julian Steward (1940s–present).

Structuralism is the analysis of culture as represented in expressions such as art, ritual, and the patterns of daily life. These surface representations are reflections of underlying logical structures of the human mind. The key figure is Claude Levi-Strauss (contemporary).

Ethnoscience is the attempt to derive rules of culturally conditioned behavior by a detailed logical analysis of ethnographic data as seen strictly from the natives' point of view. Key figures include Ward Goodenough and Charles Frake (contemporary).

Sociobiology is the belief that human behavior, including social behavior, is basically the product of genetic and environmental influences. Key figures are Napoleon Chagnon and William Irons (contemporary).

Definitions of –ISMS

Holism	The belief that the experiences of a human group are unified and patterned.
Relativism	The belief that we cannot make value judgments about a culture based on standards appropriate to another culture.
Evolutionism	The belief that all cultures develop in a uniform and progressive manner.
Unilineal evolutionism	The belief that all societies pass through the same stages of development and reach a common end, since the basic problems which all humans have to face are fundamentally the same.
Diffusionism	The belief that cultures develop not so much by adapting themselves to specific environments as by borrowing traits from other people.
Historical particularism	The belief that is suspicious of "universal laws" of human development and advocates the study of the particular historical development of specific societies as a necessary prerequisite to the formulation of generalizations about cultural evolution.
Functionalism	Based on the analysis of specific traits of culture and the ways in which they serve the needs of individuals within the society.
Structure-functionalism	A variant of Malinowski's functionalism that advocated the analysis of specific traits and the ways in which they serve to maintain the equilibrium of the social structure (rather than the needs of the individuals).
Neo-evolutionism	The attempt to formulate scientifically testable propositions about cultural evolution, as distinct from the speculative generalizations of the early evolutionists.
Universal evolutionism (general evolutionism)	The concern with the dynamics of culture as a general phenomenon, rather than with specific change within particular cultures.
Multilineal evolutionism (specific evolutionism)	The belief concerned with patterns of interaction of culture and environment; sometimes known as "cultural ecology."
Structuralism	The analysis of culture as represented in expressions such as art, ritual, and the patterns of daily life. These surface representations are reflections of underlying logical structures of the human mind.

THE FAMILY

When anthropologists study the relationships of marriage and family, they use a shorthand notation system whose symbols allow for the quick diagramming of relationships that would otherwise take extensive narrative description. The following symbols are used in **kinship diagramming**:

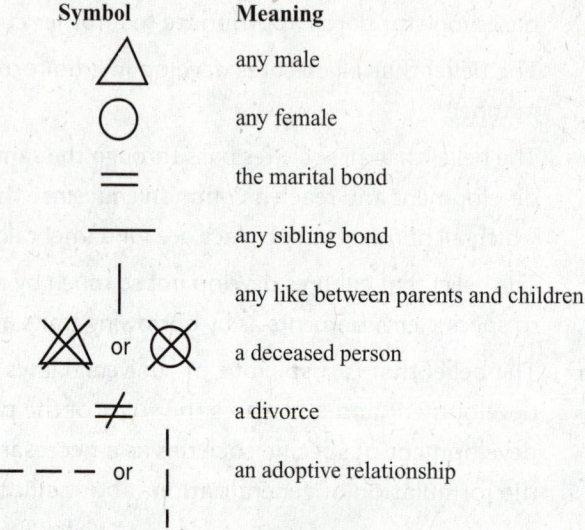

Symbol	Meaning
△	any male
○	any female
=	the marital bond
—	any sibling bond
|	any like between parents and children
⋈ or ⊗	a deceased person
≠	a divorce
– – – or ⋮	an adoptive relationship

All kinship diagrams are drawn from the point of view of a single person at a time. This person, whether a male or a female, is known as **Ego**. Ego is usually shaded or marked in some other way to note his or her special place. All relationships on a kinship diagram are read in relation to Ego. For example,

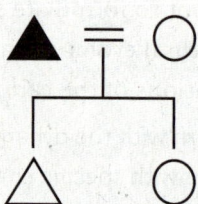

The woman married to Ego is called a "wife" in our kinship system. She is, of course, also a "mother" to the two children shown on the diagram, and she is probably also somebody else's daughter, sister, or aunt. But in terms of this diagram, we identify her relationship to Ego alone.

Marriage establishes the basic unit of family relationship—the nuclear family. The **nuclear family** serves four fundamental functions:

1. to regularize sexual relationships between certain men and women;

2. to bear and nurture new members of the community;

3. to organize and institutionalize a sexual division of labor and to regulate the transfer of property; and

4. to establish the members of the family within a larger network of kin.

Although the role of the family as a social institution has been somewhat de-emphasized in urban, industrial societies, it is still an institution of overwhelming importance.

1. There is no known human society lacking in a family organization.

2. There is no known human society in which the family is not the primary focus of socialization and the model for all later social relationships, no matter how widespread they may become.

Although "the family" is universal, its structure and organization vary widely from culture to culture. There are two types of nuclear family:

1. That into which a person is born is the **nuclear family of orientation**, in which Ego's statuses are those of child and sibling.

2. That which is established upon marriage is the **nuclear family of procreation**, in which Ego's statuses are those of spouse and parent.

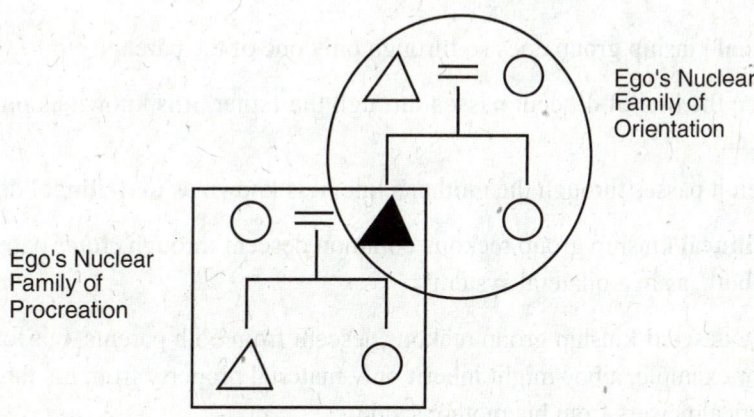

Ego's Nuclear Family of Orientation

Ego's Nuclear Family of Procreation

Our society is quite unusual in its emphasis on the nuclear family. It is much more common for social organization to be based on more extended family groups. One way to extend the family is by extending the marital bond (to create what are called **composite conjugal families**, or **polygamous unions**), which may occur in two ways:

1. **Polygyny**, the simultaneous marriage of one man to two or more women; if the women happen to be sisters, the union is technically called **sororal polygyny**.

2. **Polyandry**, the simultaneous marriage of a woman to two or more men; this is a rare pattern, and only occurs when the men in question are brothers.

A family in which children, upon marriage, bring their spouses to live in the parental households, such that all their children in turn are raised together, is known as a **joint family**.

After marriage, the most important question is where the newly joined couple will live. The decision is rarely allowed to be based on whim. It is, like marriage itself, patterned by rules and expectations:

1. **Virilocal** residence—the couple settles in the vicinity of the husband's kin.

2. **Patrilocal** residence—they settle in the actual household of the husband's father.

3. **Uxorilocal** residence—they settle in the vicinity of the bride's kin.

4. **Matrilocal** residence—they settle in the actual household of the bride's mother.

5. **Ambilocal** residence—they settle in the vicinity of either the husband's or the bride's kin.

6. **Avunculocal** residence—they settle in the household of the groom's mother's brother.

7. **Neolocal** residence—they settle in a new locale, without reference to the location of either family.

KINSHIP-BASED SOCIAL GROUPS

The family may also be extended through the extension of the lines of descent.

1. A **bilateral** kinship group reckons common descent through both parents (as in our system).

2. A **unilineal** kinship group does so through only one of the parents.

   a. When the line of descent passes through the father, it is known as **patrilineal** descent.

   b. When it passes through the mother's line, it is known as **matrilineal** descent.

3. An **ambilineal** kinship group reckons common descent through *either* parental line (but not both, as in a bilateral system).

4. A **double descent** kinship group reckons descent from both parents, but for different purposes; for example, a boy might inherit only material property from his father's side, and only magical powers from his mother's side.

These principles of extended descent create several levels of kin organization:

1. The **kindred** includes all persons to whom one traces a bond, either through "blood" (a **consanguineal** relationship) or marriage (an **affinal** relationship); such persons are known as one's **cognates**. The kindred exists only in societies (such as ours) that practice bilateral descent.

2. The **ramage** includes all persons to whom one is related *either* through the mother or through the father in an ambilineal descent system.

3. The **lineage** includes all persons to whom one is related through the one line prescribed in a unilineal descent system. The vast majority of the world's people live in lineage-based

societies. When the lineage is determined by patrilineal descent, the relatives are known as agnatic kin; when it is determined by matrilineal descent, they are the uterine kin.

A lineage is an extended unilineal kinship group descended from a common, *known* ancestor, going back not more than five or six generations.

4. The **clan** is a group formed when two or more lineages assert a relationship with each other; their common ancestor, however, must have existed so far back in time that he or she is no longer known as a person. Therefore, that ancestor figure is replaced by a mythological figure, often represented by a symbol (such as an animal) known as the clan's **totem**.

5. When two or more clans assert a relationship with each other, the resulting very large groups going back many, many generations in ancestry are known as **moieties** if there are two of them in a society, and as **phratries** if there are three or more.

The most common functions of unilineal descent groups are

1. to broaden the base of the kinship group through mutual aid, protection, and support in disputes; and

2. to regulate and control marriage.

Other functions of unilineal descent groups are

1. to act as a governing or legal body, regulating disputes and setting or enforcing standards of behavior;

2. to administer common economic property; and

3. to regularize religious observances.

Kinship groups are determined by culture, not by biology. In any given kinship system, certain statuses are singled out as being of unique importance; they are given **descriptive** kinship terms—terms that apply to no other category of relative. For example, in our kinship system, mother, father, brother, sister, son, and daughter are all descriptive kin terms because they describe unique relationships.

All other terms, however, are formed by lumping people of various relationships together into a single category, and labelling them with **classificatory** terms. In English, for example, **cousin** is a classificatory term because it lumps people of both sexes, of all generations, and people related either through blood or marriage. Such a term is indicative of the social reality that, for most Americans, relatives outside the nuclear family are remote and do not need to be distinguished by special labels.

Kinship terms therefore designate categories of social status and suggest expected behaviors linking persons. For this reason, anthropologists have spent a great deal of effort in studying systems of **kinship terminology**. Kinship terminology systems are based on one or more of the following principles:

1. differences in generational level (e.g., father/son),

2. differences in age level within the same generation (e.g., elder brother/younger brother),

3. differences between lineal (those in the direct line of descent) and collateral (those outside the direct line of descent) relations (e.g., father/uncle),

4. differences in sex of relations (e.g., brother/sister),

5. differences in sex of the speaker (e.g., male Ego's brother/female Ego's brother),

6. differences in sex of the person through whom relationship is established (e.g., father's brother/mother's brother),

7. differences between "blood" relatives and relatives through marriage (e.g., mother/mother-in-law), and

8. differences in status or life condition of the person through whom the relationship is established (e.g., son of a living sister/son of a deceased sister).

The following kinship terminology systems are based on classification of parental generation:

1. The **lineal system** distinguishes lineal from collateral relations (our system).

2. In the **generational system**, all relatives of the same sex in a given generation are lumped together.

3. In the **bifurcate merging system**, siblings of the same sex are lumped with lineal relatives.

4. The **bifurcate collateral system** is completely descriptive.

WESTERN CIVILIZATION AND WORLD HISTORY

THE ANCIENT AND MEDIEVAL WORLDS

The Appearance of Civilization

Between 6000 and 3000 B.C., humans invented the plow, utilized the wheel, harnessed the wind, discovered how to smelt copper ores, and began to develop accurate solar calendars. The invention of writing in Mesopotamia around 3500 B.C., in combination with heightened refinement in sculpture, architecture, and metal working from about 3000 B.C., marks the beginning of civilization and divides prehistoric from historic times.

Mesopotamia

Sumer (4000 to 2000 B.C.) included the city of Ur. The Sumerians constructed dikes and reservoirs and established a loose confederation of city-states. They probably invented writing (called "cuneiform"). The Amorites, or Old Babylonians (2000 to 1550 B.C.), established a new capital at Babylon, known for its famous Hanging Gardens. King Hammurabi (reigned 1792–1750 B.C.) promulgated a legal code that called for retributive punishment.

The Assyrians (1100–612 B.C.) conquered Syria, Palestine, and much of Mesopotamia. The Chaldeans, or New Babylonians (612–538 B.C.), conquered the Assyrian territory, including Jerusalem. In 538 B.C., Cyrus, king of the southern Persians, defeated the Chaldeans. The Persians created a huge empire and constructed a road network. After 538 B.C., the peoples of Mesopotamia came under the rule of a series of different empires and dynasties.

Egypt

During the end of the Archaic Period (5000–2685 B.C.), Menes, or Narmer, unified Upper and Lower Egypt around 3200 B.C. During the Old Kingdom (2685–2180 B.C.), the pharaohs came to be considered living gods. The capital moved to Memphis during the Third Dynasty (ca. 2650 B.C.). The pyramids at Giza were built during the Fourth Dynasty (ca. 2613–2494 B.C.).

After the Hyksos invasion (1785–1560 B.C.), the New Kingdom (1560–1085 B.C.) expanded into Nubia and invaded Palestine and Syria, enslaving the Jews. King Amenhotep IV or Akhenaton (reigned c. 1372–1362 B.C.) promulgated the idea of a single god, Aton. His successor, Tutankhamen, reestablished pantheism in Egypt.

In the Post-Empire Period (1085–1030 B.C.), Egypt came under the successive control of the Assyrians, the Persians, Alexander the Great, and finally, in 30 B.C., the Roman Empire. The Egyptians developed papyrus.

Palestine and the Hebrews

Phoenicians settled along the present-day coast of Lebanon, established colonies at Carthage and in Spain, and spread Mesopotamian culture through their trade networks.

The Hebrews probably moved to Egypt around 1700 B.C. and were enslaved about 1500 B.C. The Hebrews fled Egypt and, under King David (reigned ca. 1012–972 B.C.), defeated the Philistines and established a capital at Jerusalem. Ultimately, Palestine divided into Israel (10 tribes) and Judah (two tribes). The 10 tribes of Israel—also known as the Lost Tribes—disappeared after Assyria conquered Israel in 722 B.C.

Judah continued until 586 B.C. when the Persians conquered Babylon in 539 B.C., the Jews were allowed to return to Palestine. Alexander the Great conquered Palestine in 325 B.C. The Jews revolted in 70 B.C. and again in 132–135 A.D. The Romans quashed the revolt and ordered the dispersion of the Jews.

Greece

Homer's *Iliad* and *Odyssey* were poems that dramatized ideas like excellence (*arete*), courage, honor, and heroism. Hesiod's *Works and Days* summarized everyday life. His *Theogony* recounted Greek myths.

In the Archaic Period (800–500 B.C.), oligarchs controlled most of the polis (city state) until the end of the sixth century. By the end of the sixth century, democratic governments replaced many tyrants.

Sparta seized control of neighboring Messenia around 750 B.C. Around 640 B.C., Lycurgus promulgated a constitution. Around 540 B.C., Sparta organized the Peloponnesian League.

Draco (ca. 621 B.C.) first codified Athenian law. Solon (ca. 630–560 B.C.) reformed the laws in 594 B.C. He enfranchised the lower classes and gave the state responsibility for administering justice. Peisistratus (ca. 605–527 B.C.) seized control and governed as a tyrant. In 527 B.C., Cleisthenes led a reform movement that established the basis of Athens's democratic government.

1. The Fifth Century (Classical Age)

The fifth century opened with the Persian Wars (490; 480–479 B.C.) after which Athens organized the Delian League. Pericles (ca. 495–429 B.C.) used League money to rebuild Athens, including construction of the Parthenon and other Acropolis buildings.

The Peloponnesian War between Athens and Sparta (431–404 B.C.) ended with Athens's defeat. Sparta fell victim to Thebes, and the other city-states warred amongst themselves until Alexander the Great's conquest unified the Greek city-states in the fourth century B.C., marking the beginning of the Hellenistic Age.

The Sophists emphasized the individual and his/her attainment of excellence through rhetoric, grammar, music, and mathematics. Socrates (ca. 470–399 B.C.) criticized the Sophists' emphasis on rhetoric and emphasized a process of questioning, or dialogues, with his students. Like Socrates, Plato (ca. 428–348 B.C.) emphasized ethics. His *Theory of Ideas or Forms* said that what we see is but a dim shadow of the eternal Forms or Ideas. Plato's *Republic* described an ideal state ruled by a philosopher king.

Aristotle (ca. 384–322 B.C.), Plato's pupil, criticized Plato. He contended that it was necessary to examine four factors in treating any object: its matter, its form, its cause of origin, and its end or purpose.

In architecture, the Greeks developed the Doric and Ionian forms. Euripides (484–406 B.C.) is often considered the most modern tragedian. In comedy, Aristophanes (ca. 450–388 B.C.) used political themes. The New Comedy, exemplified by Menander (ca. 342–292 B.C.), concentrated on domestic and individual themes.

The Greeks were the first to develop the study of history. Herodotus (ca. 484–424 B.C.), called the "father of history," wrote *History of the Persian War*. Thucydides (ca. 460–400 B.C.) wrote *History of the Peloponnesian War*.

2. The Hellenistic Age and Macedonia

The Macedonians were considered semibarbaric by their southern Greek relatives. In 359 B.C. Philip II (382–336 B.C.) became king. To finance his state and secure a seaport, he conquered several city-states. In 338 B.C., Athens fell, and Philip was assassinated two years later.

Philip's son, Alexander the Great (356–323 B.C.), established an empire that included Syria and Persia and extended to the Indus River Valley. Alexander established 70 cities and created a vast trading network. With no succession plan, Alexander's realm was divided among three of his generals. By 30 B.C., all of the successor states had fallen to Rome.

Rome

The traditional founding date for Rome is 753 B.C. Between 800 and 500 B.C., Greek tribes colonized southern Italy, bringing their alphabet and religious practices to Roman tribes. In the sixth and seventh centuries, the Etruscans expanded southward and conquered Rome.

Late in the sixth century (the traditional date is 509 B.C.), the Romans expelled the Etruscans and established an aristocratically based republic. In the early republic, power was in the hands of the patricians (wealthy landowners). Roman executives had great power (the imperium).

Rome's expansion and contact with Greek culture disrupted the traditional agrarian basis of life. Tiberius Gracchus (163–133 B.C.) and Gaius Gracchus (153–121 B.C.) led the People's party (or *Populares*). They called for land reform and lower grain prices to help small farmers. They were opposed by the *Optimates* (best men).

Power passed into the hands of military leaders for the next 80 years. During the 70s and 60s, Pompey (106–48 B.C.) and Julius Caesar (100–44 B.C.) emerged as the most powerful men. In 73 B.C., Spartacus led a slave rebellion, which General Crassus suppressed.

In 60 B.C., Caesar convinced Pompey and Crassus (ca. 115–53 B.C.) to form the First Triumvirate. In 49 B.C., Caesar crossed the Rubicon, and a civil war followed. In 47 B.C., the Senate proclaimed Caesar as dictator, and later named him consul for life. Brutus and Cassius, believing that Caesar had destroyed the Republic, formed a conspiracy and, on March 15, 44 B.C. (the Ides of March), assassinated him in the Roman Forum. His 18-year-old nephew and adopted son, Octavian, succeeded him. Caesar reformed the tax code and eased burdens on debtors. He instituted the Julian calendar, in use until 1582.

Plautus (254–184 B.C.) wrote Greek-style comedy. Terence, a slave (ca. 186–159 B.C.), wrote comedies in the tradition of Menander. Catullus (87–54 B.C.) was the most famous lyric poet. Lucretius's (ca. 94–54 B.C.) *Order of Things* described Epicurean atomic metaphysics, while arguing against the immortality of the soul. Cicero (106–43 B.C.), the great orator and stylist, defended the Stoic concept of natural law. His *Orations* described Roman life.

1. The Roman Empire

Octavian (63 B.C.–14 A.D.) gained absolute control while maintaining the appearance of a republic. When he offered to relinquish his power in 27 B.C., the Senate gave him a vote of confidence and a new title, "Augustus." Augustus ruled for 44 years (31 B.C.–14 A.D.).

The period between 27 B.C. and 14 A.D. is called the **Augustan Age**. Vergil (70–19 B.C.) wrote the *Aeneid*. Horace (65–8 B.C.) wrote the lyric *Odes*. Ovid (43 B.C.–18 A.D.) published the *Ars Amatoria* and the *Metamorphoses*. Livy (57 B.C.–17 A.D.) wrote a narrative history of Rome based on earlier accounts.

The Silver Age lasted from 14–180 A.D. Seneca (5 B.C.–65 A.D.) espoused Stoicism in his tragedies and satires. Juvenal (50–127 A.D.) wrote satire, Plutarch's (46–120 A.D.) *Parallel Lives* portrayed Greek and Roman leaders, and Tacitus (55–120 A.D.) criticized the follies of his era.

Stoicism was the dominant philosophy of the era. Epictetus (ca. 60–120 A.D.), a slave, and Emperor Marcus Aurelius were its chief exponents. Rome distinguished three orders of law: **civil law** (*jus civile*), which applied to Rome's citizens; **law of the people** (*jus gentium*), which merged Roman law with the laws of other peoples of the Empire; and **natural law** (*jus naturale*), governed by reason.

Rome's frontiers were attacked constantly by barbarians. Emperors Diocletian (reigned 285–305 A.D.) and Constantine (reigned 306–337 A.D.) tried to stem Rome's decline. Diocletian divided the Empire into four parts and moved the capital to Nicomedia in Asia Minor. Constantine moved the capital to Constantinople.

Jesus was born around 4 B.C., and began preaching and ministering to the poor and sick at the age of 30. Saul of Tarsus, or Paul (10–67 A.D.), transformed Christianity into a world religion. His *Epistles* (letters to Christian communities) laid the basis for the religion's organization and sacraments.

The **Pax Romana** allowed Christians to move freely through the Empire. Unlike other mystery religions, Christianity included women.

Around 312 A.D., Emperor Constantine converted to Christianity and ordered toleration in the Edict of Milan (ca. 313 A.D.). In 391 A.D., Emperor Theodosius I (reigned 371–395 A.D.) proclaimed Christianity as the Empire's official religion.

The Byzantine Empire

Emperor Theodosius II (reigned 408–450 A.D.) divided his empire between his sons. After the Vandals sacked Rome in 455 A.D., Constantinople was the undisputed leading city of the empire.

In 527 A.D., Justinian I (483–565 A.D.) became emperor in the East and reigned with his wife Theodora until 565 A.D. The Nika revolt in 532 A.D. demolished the city.

In 1204 A.D., Venice contracted to transport the Crusaders to the Near East in return for the Crusaders capturing and looting Constantinople. The Byzantines were defeated in 1204 A.D. In 1453 A.D., Constantinople fell to the Ottoman Turks.

Islamic Civilization in the Middle Ages

Mohammed was born about 570 A.D. and received a revelation from the Angel Gabriel around 610 A.D. In 630 A.D., Mohammed marched into Mecca. The **Sharia** (code of law and theology) outlines five pillars of faith for Muslims to observe. First is that there is one God and that Mohammed is his prophet. The faithful must pray five times a day, perform charitable acts, fast from sunrise to sunset during the holy month of Ramadan, and make a *haj*, or pilgrimage, to Mecca. The Koran, which consists of 114 *suras* (verses), contains Mohammed's teachings. *Mullahs* (teachers) occupy positions of authority.

After Mohammed's death, his father-in-law, Abu Bakr (573–634 A.D.), succeeded as **caliph** (successor to the prophet) and governed until his death in 634 A.D. Omar succeeded him. Between 634 and 642 A.D., Omar established the Islamic Empire.

The Omayyad caliphs, based in Damascus, governed from 661–750 A.D. They called themselves **Shiites** and believed they were Mohammed's true successors. (Most Muslims were **Sunnites**, from *sunna*, oral traditions about the prophet.) They conquered Spain by 730 A.D. and advanced into France until they were stopped by Charles Martel (ca. 688–741 A.D.) in 732 A.D. Muslim armies transformed Damascus into a cultural center and were exposed to Hellenistic culture from the nearby Byzantine Empire.

The Abbasid caliphs ruled from 750–1258 A.D. They moved the capital to Baghdad and treated Arab and non-Arab Muslims as equals. In 1055 A.D., the Seljuk Turks captured Baghdad, allowing the Abbasids to rule as figureheads. Genghis Khan (ca. 1162–1227 A.D.) and his army invaded the Abbasids. In 1258 A.D., they seized Baghdad and murdered the last caliph.

Feudalism in Japan

Feudalism in Japan began with the arrival of mounted nomadic warriors from throughout Asia during the Kofun Era (300–710). During the Heian Era (794–1185), a hereditary military aristocracy arose in the Japanese provinces. By the late Heian Era, many of these nomadic warriors had established themselves as independent land owners, or as managers of landed estates *(shoen)* owned by Kyoto aristocrats. To defend the *shoen,* the warriors organized into small groups called *bushidan.*

After victory in the **Taira-Minamoto War** (1180–1105), Minamoto no Yorimoto forced the emperor to award him the title of *shogun,* which is short for "barbarian subduing generalissimo." He used this power to found the Kamakura Shogunate, under which many vassals were appointed to the position of *jitro* or land steward, or the position of provincial governors *(shugo).*

By the fourteenth century, the *shugo* had augmented their power enough to become a threat to the Kamakura, and in 1333 led a rebellion that overthrew the shogunate. Under the Ashikaga Shogunate, the office of *shogu* was made hereditary, and its powers were greatly extended. These new *shogu* turned their vassals into aggressive local warriors called *kokujin,* or *jizamurai.* The Ashikaga shoguns eventually lost a great deal of their power to political fragmentation, leading to the **Warring States Era** (1467–1568).

Far reaching alliances of *daimyo* (local feudal lords who ruled over autonomous domains) were forged under the Tokugawa Shogunate, the final and most unified of the three shogunates. The warriors were gradually transformed into scholars and bureaucrats under the *bushido,* or code of chivalry, and the principles of Neo-Confucianism. A merchant class, or *chonin,* gained wealth as the samurai class began to lose power, and the feudal system effectively ended when power was returned to the emperor under the Meji Restoration of 1868.

Chinese and Indian Empires

Around 1500 B.C., during the so-called Vedic age, India came to be ruled by the Indo-Aryans, a mainly pastoral people with a speech closely related to the major languages of Europe.

The religion of the Harappan peoples revolved around the god Siva, the belief in reincarnation, in a condition of "liberation" beyond the cycle of birth and death, and in the technique of mental concentration which later came to be called *yoga.* The religion of the Indo-Aryans was based on a pantheon of gods of a rather worldly type. The traditional hymns that accompanied sacrifices were the Vedas, which form the basic scriptures for the religion of Hinduism. Indian society also came to be based on a *caste* system.

In the third century B.C., the Indian kingdoms fell under the Mauryan Empire. The grandson of the founder of this empire, named Asoka, introduced the Buddhist religion. Buddha had disregarded the Vedic gods and the institutions of caste and had preached a relatively simple ethical religion that had two levels of aspiration—a monastic life of renunciation of the world and a high, but not too difficult, morality for the layman. The two religions of Hinduism and Buddhism flourished together for centuries in a tolerant rivalry, and by the thirteenth century A.D. Buddhism virtually disappeared from India.

Chinese civilization originated in the Yellow River Valley and gradually extended to the southern regions. Three dynasties ruled early China: the **Xia** or **Hsia**, the **Shang** (c. 1500–1122 B.C.), and the **Zhou** (c. 1122–211 B.C.). After the Zhous fell, China welcomed the teachings of Confucius. Confucius made the good order of society depend on an ethical ruler, who should be advised by scholar-moralists like Confucius himself.

In contrast to the Confucians, the **Taoists** professed a kind of anarchism. The wise man did not concern himself with political affairs, but by means of mystical contemplation identified himself with the forces of nature.

Sub-Saharan Kingdoms and Cultures

Artifacts indicate that the Nok were peaceful farmers who built small communities in the area now known as Nigeria.

The Ghana people lived about 500 miles from what we now call Ghana. The Ghana offered Berber traders gold from deposits found in the south of their territory. In the 1200s the Mali kingdom conquered Ghana and the civilization mysteriously disappeared.

The Mali lived in a huge kingdom that lay mostly on the savanna bordering the Sahara Desert. Timbuktu, built in the thirteenth century, was a thriving city of culture.

The Songhai lived near the Niger River and gained their independence from the Mali in the early 1400s. The major growth of the empire came after 1464 A.D. under the leadership of Sunni Ali, who devoted his reign to warfare and expansion of the empire.

The Bantu peoples, numbering about 100,000,000, lived across large sections of Africa. Bantu societies lived in tiny chiefdoms, starting in the third millennium B.C., and each group developed its own version of the original Bantu language.

Civilizations of the Americas

Mayan history is divided into three parts, the Old Empire, Middle Period, and the New Empire. By the time the Spanish conquerors arrived, most of the Mayan religious centers had been abandoned and their civilization had deteriorated seriously.

In Mexico, a series of advanced cultures (Zapotecs, Totonacs, Olmecs, and Toltecs) arose that derived much of their substance from the Maya.

The Aztecs then took over Mexican culture. Aztec government was centralized, with an elective king and a large army. Like their predecessors, the Aztecs were skilled builders and engineers, accomplished astronomers and mathematicians.

Andean civilization was characterized by the evolution of beautifully made pottery, intricate fabrics, and flat-topped mounds called *huacas*.

The Incas, a tribe from the interior of South America, controlled an area stretching from Ecuador to central Chile. They were Sun worshippers ("Children of the Sun") and believed themselves to be the vice regent on Earth of the sun god; the Inca were all powerful; every person's place in society was fixed and immutable; the state and the army were supreme.

In the southwestern United States and northern Mexico, meanwhile, two ancient cultures are noteworthy. The **Anasazi** developed adobe architecture, worked the land extensively, had a highly developed system of irrigation, and made cloth and baskets. Their time ran approximately from 100 to 1300 A.D. The **Hohokam**, roughly contemporaneous to the Anasazi, built separate stone and timber houses around central plazas in the desert Southwest.

Europe in Antiquity

Nomadic tribes from the central Asian steppes invaded Europe and pushed Germanic tribes into conflict with the Roman Empire. Ultimately, in 410 A.D., the Visigoths sacked Rome, followed by the Vandals in 455 A.D. In 476 A.D., the Ostrogoth king forced Romulus Augustulus to abdicate, ending the empire in the West.

The Frankish Kingdom was the most important medieval Germanic state. Under Clovis I (reigned 481–511 A.D.), the Franks conquered France and the Gauls in 486 A.D.

Pepin's son, known as Charles the Great or Charlemagne (reigned 768–814 A.D.), founded the Carolingian dynasty. In 800 A.D., Pope Leo III named Charlemagne Emperor of the Holy Roman Empire. In the Treaty of Aix-la-Chapelle (812 A.D.), the Byzantine emperor recognized Charles's authority in the West.

Charles's son, Louis the Pious (reigned 814–840 A.D.), succeeded him. On Louis's death, his three sons vied for control of the Empire. The three eventually signed the Treaty of Verdun in 843 A.D. This gave Charles the Western Kingdom (France), Louis the Eastern Kingdom (Germany), and Lothair the Middle Kingdom.

In the ninth and tenth centuries, Europe was threatened by attacks from the Vikings in the north, the Muslims in the south, and the Magyars in the east. Under the leadership of William the Conqueror (reigned 1066–1087), the Normans conquered England in 1066 A.D. (Battle of Hastings).

Manorialism and feudalism developed in this period. **Manorialism** refers to the economic system in which large estates, granted by the king to nobles, strove for self-sufficiency. Ownership was divided among the lord and his serfs (also called villeins). **Feudalism** describes the decentralized political system of personal ties and obligations that bound vassals to their lords. At its base were serfs—peasants who were bound to the land.

The church was the only institution to survive the Germanic invasions intact. Gregory I (reigned 590–604 A.D.) was the first member of a monastic order to rise to the papacy. He centralized church administration and was the first pope to rule as the secular head of Rome.

The High Middle Ages (1050–1300)

Between 1000 and 1350 A.D., the population of Europe grew from 38 million to 75 million. Agricultural productivity grew, aided by new technologies, such as heavy plows, and a slight temperature rise, which produced a longer growing season.

Enfranchisement, or freeing of serfs, grew in this period, and many other serfs simply fled their manors for the new lands.

The Holy Roman Empire

Charlemagne's grandson, Louis the German, became Holy Roman Emperor under the Treaty of Verdun. After the last Carolingian died in 911 A.D., the German dukes elected the leader of Franconia to lead the German lands. He was replaced in 919 A.D. by the Saxon dynasty, which ruled until 1024 A.D. Otto became Holy Roman Emperor in 962 A.D. His descendants governed the empire until 1024 A.D., when the Franconian dynasty assumed power, reigning until 1125 A.D.

When the Franconian line died out in 1125 A.D., the Hohenstaufen family (Conrad III, reigned 1138–1152 A.D.) won power over a contending family. The Hapsburg line gained control of the empire in 1273 A.D.

Alfred the Great (ca. 849–899 A.D.) defeated the Danes in 878 A.D. In 959 A.D., Edgar the Peacable (reigned 959–975 A.D.) became the first king of all England.

William (reigned 1066–1087 A.D.) stripped the Anglo-Saxon nobility of its privileges and instituted feudalism. He ordered a survey of all property of the realm, which was recorded in the **Domesday Book** (1086 A.D.).

In 1215 A.D., the English barons forced John I to sign the **Magna Carta Libertatum**, acknowledging their "ancient" privileges. The Magna Carta established the principle of a limited English monarchy. Henry III reigned from 1216–1272 A.D. In 1272 A.D., Edward I became king. His need for revenue led him to convene a parliament of English nobles, which would act as a check upon royal power.

In 710 A.D., the Muslims conquered Spain from the Visigoths. Under the Muslims, the caliphate of Córdoba became a center of scientific and intellectual activity. Internal dissent caused the collapse of Córdoba and the division of Spain into more than 20 Muslim states in 1031 A.D.

The **Reconquista** (1085–1340 A.D.) wrested control from the Muslims. Rodrigo Diaz de Bivar, known as El Cid (ca. 1043–1099 A.D.), was the most famous of its knights. The fall of Córdoba in 1234 A.D. completed the Reconquista, except for the small state of Granada.

Poland converted to Christianity in the tenth century, and after 1025 A.D. was dependent on the Holy Roman Empire.

In Russia, Vladimir I converted to Orthodox Christianity in 988 A.D. After 1054 A.D., Russia broke into competing principalities. The Mongols (Tatars) invaded in 1221 A.D., completing their conquest in 1245 A.D.

The Crusades were an attempt to liberate the Holy Land from infidels. There were seven major crusades between 1096 and 1300 A.D. Urban II called Christians to the First Crusade (1096–1099 A.D.) with the promise of a plenary indulgence (exemption from punishment in purgatory). Thousands of Jews and Muslims were massacred as a result of the Crusades, and relations between Europe and the Byzantine Empire collapsed.

Charlemagne mandated that bishops open schools at each cathedral. The expansion of trade and the need for clerks and officials who could read and write spurred an 1179 A.D. requirement that each cathedral set aside enough money to support one teacher.

Scholasticism was an effort to reconcile reason and faith and to instruct Christians on how to make sense of the pagan tradition.

Peter Abelard (ca. 1079–1144 A.D.) was a controversial proponent of Scholasticism. In *Sic et Non* (Yes and No), Abelard collected statements in the Bible and by church leaders that contradicted each other. The church judged his views as heretical.

Thomas Aquinas (ca. 1225–1274 A.D.) believed that there were two orders of truth. The lower, reason, could demonstrate propositions such as the existence of God, but on a higher level, some of God's mysteries (such as the nature of the Trinity) must be accepted on faith.

Although Latin was the language used in universities, the most vibrant works were in the vernacular. The *chansons de geste* were long epic poems composed between 1050 and 1150 A.D. Among the most famous are the *Song of Roland,* the *Song of the Nibelungs,* the Icelandic *Eddas,* and *El Cid.*

The **fabliaux** were short stories, many of which ridiculed the clergy. Boccaccio (1313–1375 A.D.) and Chaucer (ca. 1342–1400 A.D.) belonged to this tradition. The work of Dante (1265–1321 A.D.), the greatest medieval poet, synthesized the pagan and Christian traditions.

In this period, polyphonic (more than one melody at a time) music was introduced. Romanesque architecture (rounded arches, thick stone walls, tiny windows) flourished between 1000 and 1150 A.D. After 1150 A.D., Gothic architecture, which emphasized the use of light, came into vogue.

THE RENAISSANCE, REFORMATION, AND THE WARS OF RELIGION (1300–1648)

The Late Middle Ages

The papacy and monarchs, after exercising much power and influence in the high Middle Ages, were in eclipse after 1300. During the late Middle Ages (1300–1500), all of Europe suffered from the Black Death. While England and France engaged in destructive warfare in northern Europe, in Italy the Renaissance had begun.

Toward the end of the period, monarchs began to assert their power and control. The major struggle, between England and France, was the **Hundred Years' War** (1337–1453). The war was fought in France, though the Scots (with French encouragement) invaded northern England. A few major battles occurred—Crécy (1346), Poitiers (1356), Agincourt (1415)—although the fighting consisted largely of sieges and raids. Eventually the French wore down the English.

Joan of Arc (1412–1431), an illiterate peasant girl who said she heard voices of saints, rallied the French army for several victories. But she was captured by the Burgundians and sold to the English, who tried her for heresy (witchcraft). She was burned at the stake at Rouen.

England lost all of its continental possessions, except Calais. French farmland was devastated, with England and France both expending great sums of money. Population, especially in France, declined. Trade everywhere was disrupted and England's wool trade with the Low Countries slumped badly. To cover these financial burdens, heavy taxation was inflicted on the peasants.

Literature came to express nationalism, as it was written in the language of the people instead of in Latin. Geoffrey Chaucer portrayed a wide spectrum of English life in the *Canterbury Tales*, while François Villon (1431–1463), in his *Grand Testament*, emphasized the ordinary life of the French with humor and emotion.

The New Monarchs

The defeat of the English in the Hundred Years' War and of the duchy of Burgundy in 1477 removed major military threats. Trade was expanded, fostered by the merchant Jacques Coeur (1395–1456). Louis XI (1461–1483) demonstrated ruthlessness in dealing with his nobility as individuals and collectively in the Estates General.

The marriage of Isabella of Castile (reigned 1474–1504) and Ferdinand of Aragon (reigned 1474–1516) created a united Spain. The Muslims were defeated at Granada in 1492. Navarre was conquered in 1512.

The Black Death and Social Problems

The bubonic plague ("Black Death") is a fatal disease affecting the lymph glands. Conditions in Europe encouraged the quick spread of disease. There was no urban sanitation, and streets were filled with refuse, excrement, and dead animals.

Carried by fleas on rats, the plague was brought from Asia by merchants, and arrived in Europe in 1347. The plague affected all of Europe by 1350 and killed perhaps 25% to 40% of the population, with cities suffering more than the countryside.

The Renaissance (1300–1600)

The Renaissance emphasized new learning, including the rediscovery of much classical material, and new art styles. Italian city-states, such as Venice, Milan, Padua, Pisa, and especially Florence, were the home to many Renaissance developments.

Literature, Art, and Scholarship

Humanists, as both orators and poets, were inspired by and imitated works of the classical past. The literature was more secular and wide-ranging than that of the Middle Ages.

Dante (1265–1321) was a Florentine writer whose *Divine Comedy* described a journey through hell, purgatory, and heaven. Petrarch (1304–1374) encouraged the study of ancient Rome, collected and preserved work of ancient writers, and produced much work in the classical literary style. Boccaccio (1313–1375) wrote *The Decameron*, a collection of short stories in Italian, which were meant to amuse, not edify, the reader.

Leonardo da Vinci (1452–1519) produced numerous works, including *The Last Supper* and *Mona Lisa*. Raphael (1483–1520), a master of Renaissance grace and style, theory and technique, represented these skills in *The School of Athens*. Michelangelo (1475–1564) produced masterpieces in architecture, sculpture (*David*), and painting (the Sistine Chapel ceiling). His work was a bridge to a new, non-Renaissance style called Mannerism.

Renaissance scholars were more practical and secular than medieval ones. Leonardo Bruni (1370–1444), a civic humanist, served as chancellor of Florence, where he used his rhetorical skills to rouse the citizens against external enemies. Machiavelli (1469–1527) wrote *The Prince*, which analyzed politics from the standpoint of expedience.

The Reformation

The Reformation destroyed Western Europe's religious unity and introduced new ideas about the relationships between God, the individual, and society. Its course was greatly influenced by politics and led, in most areas, to the subjection of the church to the political rulers.

Martin Luther (1483–1546)

Martin Luther could not reconcile the problem of the sinfulness of the individual with the justice of God. During his studies of the Bible, especially of Romans 1:17, Luther came to believe that personal efforts—good works such as a Christian life and attention to the sacraments of the church—could not "earn" the sinner salvation, but that belief and faith were the only way to obtain grace. By 1515 Luther believed that "justification by faith alone" was the road to salvation.

On October 31, 1517, Luther nailed 95 theses, or statements, about indulgences, the cancellation of a sin in return for money, to the door of the Wittenberg church and challenged the practice of selling them. At this time he was seeking to reform the church, not divide it.

In 1519 Luther presented various criticisms of the church and was driven to say that only the Bible, not religious traditions or papal statements, could determine correct religious practices and beliefs. In 1521 Pope Leo X excommunicated Luther for his beliefs.

In 1521 Luther appeared in the city of Worms before a meeting (Diet) of the important figures of the Holy Roman Empire, including the Emperor, Charles V. He was again condemned. At the Diet of Worms Luther stated; "Here I stand. I can do no other." After this, Luther could not go back; the break with the pope was permanent.

Frederick III of Saxony, the ruler of the territory in which Luther resided, protected Luther in Wartburg Castle for a year although he never accepted Luther's beliefs.

Other Reformers

Anabaptist (derived from a Greek word meaning to baptize again) refers to people who rejected the validity of child baptism and believed that such children had to be rebaptized when they became adults. A prominent leader was Menno Simons (1496–1561). Anabaptists sought to return to the practices of the early Christian church. Anabaptists adopted pacifism and avoided involvement with the state whenever possible.

In 1536 John Calvin (1509–1564), a Frenchman, arrived in Geneva, a Swiss city-state which had adopted an anti-Catholic position. In 1540, Geneva became the center of the Reformation. Calvin's *Institutes of the Christian Religion* (1536), a strictly logical analysis of Christianity, had a universal appeal. Calvin emphasized the doctrine of **predestination** (God knew who would obtain salvation before those people were born) and believed that church and state should be united. Calvinism triumphed as the majority religion in Scotland, under the leadership of John Knox (ca. 1514–1572), and in the United Provinces of the Netherlands. Puritans in England and New England also accepted Calvinism.

Reform in England

In 1533, Henry VIII defied the pope and turned to Archbishop Thomas Cranmer to dissolve his marriage to Catherine of Aragon. Protestant beliefs and practices made little headway during Henry's reign, as he accepted transubstantiation, enforced celibacy among the clergy, and otherwise made the English church conform to most medieval practices.

Under Henry VIII's son, Edward VI (1547–1553), the English church adopted Calvinism. Doctrine included justification by faith, the denial of transubstantiation, and only two sacraments.

Some reformers wanted to purify (hence "Puritans") the church of its remaining Catholic aspects. The resulting church, Protestant in doctrine and practice but retaining most of the physical possessions and many of the powers of the medieval church, was called Anglican.

The Counter Reformation

The Counter Reformation brought changes to the portion of the Western church which retained its allegiance to the pope. Ignatius of Loyola (1491–1556), a former soldier, founded the Society of Jesus in 1540 to lead the attack on Protestantism. Jesuits became the leaders of the Counter Reformation. The Sack of Rome in 1527 was seen by many as a judgment of God against the lives of the Renaissance popes. In 1534 Paul III became pope and attacked abuses while reasserting papal leadership.

The Wars of Religion (1560–1648)

In the latter half of the sixteenth century, fighting occurred along the Atlantic seaboard between Calvinists and Catholics; after 1600 the warfare spread to Germany, where Calvinists, Lutherans, and Catholics fought.

The Catholic Crusade

The territories of Charles V, the Holy Roman Emperor, were divided in 1556 between Ferdinand, Charles's brother, and Philip II (1556–1598), Charles's son. Ferdinand received Austria, Hungary, Bohemia, and the title of Holy Roman Emperor. Philip received Spain, Milan, Naples, the Netherlands, and the New World. Philip, not the pope, led the Catholic attack on Protestants.

Spain dominated the Mediterranean following a series of wars led by Philip's half-brother, Don John, against Moslem (largely Turkish) forces. Don John secured the Mediterranean for Christian merchants with a naval victory over the Turks at Lepanto off the coast of Greece in 1571.

Portugal was annexed by Spain in 1580. This gave Philip the only other large navy of the day as well as Portuguese territories around the globe.

England and Spain

England was ruled by two queens, Mary I (reigned 1553–1558), and then Elizabeth I (reigned 1558–1603), while three successive kings of France from 1559 to 1589 were influenced by their mother, Catherine de' Medici (1519–1589).

Mary I sought to make England Catholic. She executed many Protestants, earning the name "Bloody Mary" from opponents. Mary married Philip II, king of Spain, and organized her foreign policy around Spanish interests. They had no children.

Elizabeth I, a Protestant, achieved a religious settlement between 1559 and 1563 which left England with a church governed by bishops and practicing Catholic rituals, but maintaining a Calvinist doctrine.

Mary, Queen of Scots, fled to England from Scotland in 1568, after alienating the nobles there. In Catholic eyes, she was the legitimate queen of England. Several plots and rebellions to put Mary on the throne led to her execution in 1587. Elizabeth was formally excommunicated by the pope in 1570.

In 1588, as part of his crusade and to stop England from supporting the rebels in the Netherlands, Philip II sent the Armada, a fleet of more than 125 ships, to convey troops from the Netherlands to England as part of a plan to make England Catholic. The Armada was defeated by a combination of superior English naval tactics and a wind which made it impossible for the Spanish to accomplish their goal. A peace treaty between Spain and England was signed in 1604, but England remained an opponent of Spain.

The Thirty Years' War

Calvinism was spreading throughout Germany. The Peace of Augsburg (1555), which settled the disputes between Lutherans and Catholics, had no provision for Calvinists. Lutherans gained more territories through conversions and often took control of previous church-states—a violation of the Peace of Augsburg. A Protestant alliance under the leadership of the Calvinist ruler of the Palatinate opposed a Catholic League led by the ruler of Bavaria. Religious wars were common.

After 1648, warfare, though often containing religious elements, would not be executed primarily for religious goals.

The Catholic crusade to reunite Europe failed, largely due to the efforts of the Calvinists. The religious distribution of Europe has not changed significantly since 1648.

THE GROWTH OF THE STATE AND THE AGE OF EXPLORATION

In the seventeenth century England, the United Provinces, and Sweden moved toward **constitutionalism**, while France was adopting **absolutist** ideas.

England

The English church, a compromise of Catholic practices and Protestant beliefs, was criticized by both groups. The monarchs, after 1620, gave leadership of the church to men with Arminian beliefs, a modified Calvinist creed that deemphasized predestination.

Opponents to this shift in belief were called Puritans. To escape the church in England, many Puritans began moving to the New World, especially Massachusetts.

In financial matters, inflation and Elizabeth's wars left the government short of money. The monarchs lacked any substantial source of income and had to obtain the consent of a Parliament to levy a tax.

Parliament met only when the monarch summoned it. Parliaments consisted of nobles and gentry, and a few merchants and lawyers. The men in a Parliament usually wanted the government to remedy grievances as part of the agreement to a tax.

Charles I inherited both the English and Scottish thrones at the death of his father, James I. He claimed a "divine right" theory of absolute authority for himself as king and sought to rule without Parliament. Charles stumbled into wars with both Spain and France during the late 1620s. In 1628 Parliament passed the Petition of Right, which declared royal actions involving loans and billeting illegal.

In August 1642 Charles abandoned all hope of negotiating with his opponents and instead declared war against them. Charles's supporters were called Royalists or Cavaliers. His opponents were called Parliamentarians or Roundheads, due to many who wore their hair cut short. This struggle is called the Puritan Revolution, the English Civil War, or the Great Rebellion.

Charles was defeated. His opponents had allied with the Scots who still had an army in England. Additionally, the New Model Army, with its general, Oliver Cromwell (1599–1658), was superior to Charles's army, and became a cauldron of radical ideas.

France

Henry IV relied on the Duke of Sully (1560–1641). Sully and Henry increased the involvement of the state in the economy, acting on a theory known as **mercantilism**.

Louis XIII reigned from 1610 to 1643, but Cardinal Richelieu became the real power in France. The unique status of the Huguenots was reduced through warfare and the Peace of Alais (1629), when their separate armed cities were eliminated.

Cardinal Mazarin governed while Louis XIV (reigned 1643–1715) was a minor. During the Fronde, from 1649 to 1652, the nobility controlled Paris, drove Louis XIV and Mazarin from the city, and attempted to run the government. Noble ineffectiveness, the memories of the chaos of the wars of religion, and the overall anarchy convinced most people that a strong king was preferable to a warring nobility. Louis XIV pursued this goal.

Explorations and Conquests

1. Portugal

Prince Henry the Navigator (1394–1460) supported exploration of the African coastline, largely in order to seek gold. Bartholomew Dias (1450–1500) rounded the southern tip of Africa in 1487. Vasco de Gama (1460–1524) reached India in 1498 and, after some fighting, soon established trading ports at Goa and Calicut. Albuquerque (1453–1515) helped establish an empire in the Spice Islands after 1510.

2. Spain

Christopher Columbus (1451–1506), seeking a new route to the (East) Indies, "discovered" the Americas in 1492. Ferdinand Magellan (1480–1521) circumnavigated the globe in 1521–1522. Conquests of the Aztecs by Hernando Cortes (1485–1547), and the Incas by Francisco Pizarro (ca. 1476–1541), enabled the Spanish to send much gold and silver back to Spain.

3. Other Countries

In the 1490s the Cabots, John (1450–1498) and Sebastian (ca. 1483–1557), explored North America, and after 1570, various Englishmen, including Francis Drake (ca. 1540–1596), fought the Spanish around the world. Jacques Cartier (1491–1557) explored parts of North America for France in 1534.

Samuel de Champlain (1567–1635) and the French explored the St. Lawrence River, seeking furs to trade. The Dutch established settlements at New Amsterdam and in the Hudson River Valley. The Dutch founded trading centers in the East Indies, the West Indies, and southern Africa. Swedes settled on the Delaware River in 1638.

BOURBON, BAROQUE, AND THE ENLIGHTENMENT

Through the Treaty of Paris (1763), France lost all possessions in North America to Britain. (In 1762 France had ceded to Spain all French claims west of the Mississippi River and New Orleans.) France entered the French-American Alliance of 1778 in an effort to regain lost prestige in Europe and to weaken her British adversary. In 1779 Spain joined France in the war, hoping to recover Gibraltar and the Floridas.

With the Treaty of Paris (1783) Britain recognized the independence of the United States of America and retroceded the Floridas to Spain. Britain left France no territorial gains by signing a separate and territorially generous treaty with the United States.

Economic Developments

There were several basic assumptions of mercantilism: (1) Wealth is measured in terms of commodities rather than in terms of productivity and income-producing investments; (2) Economic activities should increase the power of the national government in the direction of state controls; (3) Since a favorable balance of trade was important, a nation should purchase as little as possible from nations regarded as enemies; (4) Colonies existed for the benefit of the mother country, not for any mutual benefit that would be gained by economic development.

Thanks to the steam engine, developed by James Watt between 1765 and 1769, it was no longer necessary to locate factories on mountain streams where water wheels were used to supply power. Its portability meant that both steamboats and railroad engines could be built to transport goods across continents. Ocean-going vessels were no longer dependent on winds to power them. At the same time, textile machines revolutionized that industry.

Bourbon France

Louis XIV (reigned 1643–1715) believed in absolute, unquestioned authority. He deliberately chose his chief ministers from the middle class in order to keep the aristocracy out of government. Louis XIV never called the Estates General. His intendants arrested the members of the three provincial estates who criticized royal policy, and the *parlements* were too intimidated by the lack of success of the *Frondes* to offer further resistance.

Control of the peasants, who comprised 95% of the French population, was accomplished by numerous means. Some peasants kept as little as 20% of their cash crops after paying the landlord, the government, and the Church. Peasants also were subject to the *corvée*, a month's forced labor on the roads. People not at work on the farm were conscripted into the French army or put into workhouses. Finally, rebels were hanged or forced to work as galley slaves.

Under Louis XV (reigned 1715–1774) French people of all classes desired greater popular participation in government and resented the special privileges of the aristocracy. The highest offices of government were reserved for aristocrats. Promotions were based on political connections rather than merit.

There was no uniform code of laws and little justice. The king had arbitrary powers of imprisonment. Government bureaucrats were often petty tyrants, many of them merely serving their own interests. Vestiges of the feudal and manorial systems taxed peasants excessively compared to other segments of society. The *philosophes* gave expression to these grievances and discontent grew.

Louis XVI (reigned 1774–1792) married Marie Antoinette (1770). One of his first acts was to restore judicial powers to the French parlements. When he sought to impose new taxes on the undertaxed aristocracy, the parlements refused to register the royal decrees. In 1787 he granted toleration and civil rights to French Huguenots (Protestants).

In 1787 the king summoned the **Assembly of the Notables**, a group of 144 representatives of the nobility and higher clergy. Louis XVI asked them to tax all lands, without regard to privilege of family; to establish provincial assemblies; to allow free trade in grain; and to abolish forced labor on the roads. The Notables refused to accept these reforms and demanded the replacement of certain of the king's ministers. The climax of the crisis came in 1788 when the king was no longer able to achieve either fiscal reform or new loans. By this time one-half of government revenues went to pay interest on the national debt.

For the first time in 175 years, the king called for a meeting of the Estates General (1789). The Estates General formed itself into the National Assembly, and the French Revolution was under way.

England, Scotland, and Ireland

One of the underlying issues in this conflict was whether England was to have a limited constitutional monarchy, or an absolute monarchy as in France and Prussia. The theological issue focused on the form of church government England was to have. The episcopal form meant that the king, the Archbishop of Canterbury, and the bishops of the church would determine policy, theology, and the form of worship and service in the presbyterian form. Each congregation would have a voice in the life of the church, and a regional group of ministers, or "**presbytery**," would attempt to ensure "doctrinal purity." Most Presbyterians, Puritans, and Congregationalists sided with Parliament and most Anglicans and Catholics sided with the king.

The **Petition of Right** in 1628 stipulated that no one should pay any tax, gift, loan, or contribution except as provided by an act of Parliament; no one should be imprisoned or detained without due process of law; all were to have the right to the writ of *habeas corpus;* there should be no forced billeting of soldiers in the homes of private citizens; and martial law was not to be declared in England.

In 1629 Charles I dissolved Parliament—for 11 years. Puritan leaders and leaders of the opposition in the House of Commons were imprisoned by the king, some for several years.

The established Church of England was the only legal church under Charles I. Archbishop of Canterbury William Laud (1573–1645) sought to enforce the king's policies vigorously. Arminian clergymen were to be tolerated, but Puritan clergymen silenced. Criticism was brutally suppressed.

The king, however, had no money, no army, and no popular support. He summoned the Parliament to meet in November 1640. With mobs in the street and rumors of an army en route to London to dissolve Parliament, a bare majority of an underattended House of Commons passed a bill of attainder to execute the Earl of Strafford, one of the king's principal ministers. Strafford was executed in 1641. Archbishop William Laud was also arrested and eventually tried and executed in 1645.

The House of Commons passed a series of laws to strengthen its position and protect civil and religious rights. The **Triennial Act** (1641) provided that no more than three years should pass between Parliaments. Another act provided that the current Parliament should not be dissolved without its own consent. Various hated laws, taxes, and institutions were abolished: the Star Chamber, the High Commission, and power of the Privy Council to deal with property rights.

The king withdrew to Hampton Court and sent the queen to France for safety. In March 1642 Charles II went to York, and the English Civil War began. Charles put together a sizeable force with a strong cavalry and moved on London, winning several skirmishes.

Oliver Cromwell (1599–1658) led the parliamentary troops to victory, first with his cavalry and then as lieutenant general in command of the well-disciplined and well-trained New Model Army. He eventually forced the king to flee.

During the Civil War, under the authority of Parliament, the Westminster Assembly convened to write a statement of faith for the Church of England that was Reformed or Presbyterian in content. Ministers and laymen from both England and Scotland participated for six years and wrote the *Westminster Confession of Faith*, which is still a vital part of Presbyterian theology.

The army tried Charles Stuart, formerly king of England, and sentenced him to death for treason. Parliament then abolished the office of king and the House of Lords. The new form of government was to be a **Commonwealth**, or Free State, governed by the representatives of the people in Parliament. This commonwealth lasted between 1649 and 1653.

Royalists and Presbyterians both opposed Parliament for its lack of broad representation and for regicide. Surrounded by foreign enemies, the Commonwealth became a military state with a standing army of 44,000.

When it became clear that Parliament intended to stay in office permanently, Cromwell agreed to serve as Lord Protector from 1653–1659, with a Council of State and a Parliament. The new government permitted religious liberty, except for Catholics and Anglicans.

The new Parliament restored the monarchy from 1660–1688, but the Puritan Revolution clearly showed that the English constitutional system required a limited monarchy. Two events in 1688 goaded Parliament to action. In May, James reissued the Declaration of Indulgence with the command that it be read on two successive Sundays in every parish church. On June 10, 1688, a son was born to the king and his queen, Mary of Modena.

A group of Whig and Tory leaders, speaking for both houses of Parliament, invited William and Mary to assume the throne of England. On November 5, 1688, William and his army landed at Torbay in Devon. King James finally fled to France. William assumed temporary control of the government and summoned a free Parliament. In February 1689 William and Mary were declared joint sovereigns, with the administration given to William.

The English **Declaration of Rights** (1689) declared the following:

1. The king could not be a Roman Catholic.

2. A standing army in time of peace was illegal without Parliamentary approval.

3. Taxation was illegal without Parliamentary consent.

4. Excessive bail and cruel and unusual punishments were prohibited.

5. Right to trial by jury was guaranteed.

6. Free elections to Parliament would be held.

The **Toleration Act** (1689) granted the right of public worship to Protestant Nonconformists, but did not permit them to hold office. The **Trials for Treason Act** (1696) stated that a person accused of treason should be shown the accusations against him and should have the advice of counsel. Freedom of the press was permitted, but with very strict libel laws.

Control of finances was in the hands of the Commons, including military appropriations. Judges were made independent of the Crown. Thus, England declared itself a limited monarchy and a Protestant nation.

Russia Under the Muscovites and the Romanovs

In 1480, Ivan III (1440–1505), "Ivan the Great," put an end to Mongol domination over Russia. Ivan took the title of Caesar (Tsar) as heir of the Eastern Roman Empire (Byzantine Empire). He encouraged the Eastern Orthodox Church and called Moscow the "Third Rome."

Ivan IV (1530–1584), "Ivan the Terrible," grandson of Ivan III, began westernizing Russia. A contemporary of Queen Elizabeth, he welcomed both the English and Dutch and opened new trade routes to Moscow and the Caspian Sea. English merchant adventurers opened Archangel on the White Sea and provided a link with the outer world free from Polish domination.

After a "Time of Troubles" following Ivan's death in 1584, stability returned to Russia in 1613 when the Zemsky Sobor (Estates General representing the Russian Orthodox church, landed gentry, townspeople, and a few peasants) elected Michael Romanov, who ruled as tsar from 1613 to 1645. Under Michael Romanov, Russia extended its empire to the Pacific. By the end of the seventeenth century, 20,000 Europeans lived in Russia, developing trade and manufacturing, practicing medicine, and smoking tobacco, while Russians began trimming their beards and wearing western clothing.

In 1649 three monks were appointed to translate the Bible for the first time into Russian. The Raskolniki (Old Believers) refused to accept any Western innovations or liturgy in the Russian Orthodox church and were severely persecuted as a result.

Peter I (The Great reigned 1682–1725) was driven to modernize Russia and to compete with the great powers of Europe on equal terms. Peter built up the army through conscription and a 25-year term of enlistment. Artillery was improved and discipline enforced. By the end of his reign, Russia had a standing army of 210,000. The tsar ruled by decree (*ukase*). Government officials and nobles acted under government authority, but there was no representative body.

In return for mandatory government service, landowners received land and serfs to work their fields. Conscription required each village to send recruits for the Russian army. By 1709 Russia manufactured most of its own weapons and had an effective artillery.

After a series of largely ineffective rulers, Catherine II "the Great," (reigned 1762–1796) continued the westernization process begun by Peter the Great. The three partitions of Poland, in 1772, 1793, and 1795, respectively, occurred under Catherine II's rule. Russia also annexed the Crimea and warred with Turkey during her reign.

THE SCIENTIFIC REVOLUTION AND SCIENTIFIC SOCIETIES

Science and religion were not in conflict in the seventeenth and eighteenth centuries. Scientists universally believed they were studying and analyzing God's creation, not an autonomous phenomenon known as "Nature."

The eighteenth century saw the appearance of a secular worldview, known as the **Age of the Enlightenment**. The philosophical starting point for the Enlightenment was the belief in the autonomy of man's intellect apart from God. The most basic assumption was faith in reason rather than faith in revelation.

The Enlightenment believed in the existence of God as a rational explanation of the universe and its form; "God" was a deistic Creator who made the universe and then was no longer involved in its mechanistic operation. That mechanistic operation was governed by "natural law."

Rationalists stressed deductive reasoning or mathematical logic as the basis for their **epistemology** (source of knowledge). They started with "self-evident truths," or postulates, from which they constructed a coherent and logical system of thought. René Descartes (1596–1650) sought a basis for logic and thought he found it in man's ability to think. "I think; therefore, I am" was his most famous statement. Benedict de Spinoza (1632–1677) developed a rational pantheism in which he equated God and nature. He denied all free will and ended up with an impersonal, mechanical universe. Gottfried Wilhelm Leibniz (1646–1716) worked on symbolic logic and calculus, and invented a calculating machine. He, too, had a mechanistic world- and life-view and thought of God as a hypothetical abstraction rather than a persona.

Empiricists stressed inductive observation—the "scientific method"—as the basis for their epistemology. John Locke (1632–1704) pioneered in the empiricist approach to knowledge and stressed the importance of environment in human development. He classified knowledge as (1) according to reason, (2) contrary to reason or, (3) above reason. Locke thought reason and revelation were both complementary and from God. David Hume (1711–1776) was a Scottish historian and philosopher who began by emphasizing the limitations of human reasoning and later became a dogmatic skeptic.

The Enlightenment believed in a closed system of the universe in which the supernatural was not involved in human life. The *Counter-Enlightenment* is a comprehensive term encompassing diverse and disparate groups who disagreed with the fundamental assumptions of the Enlightenment and pointed out its weaknesses.

Roman Catholic Jansenism in France argued against the idea of an uninvolved or impersonal God. Hasidism in Eastern European Jewish communities, especially in the 1730s, stressed a joyous religious fervor in direct communion with God.

Culture of the Baroque and Rococo

The **Baroque** emphasized grandeur, spaciousness, unity, and emotional impact. The splendor of Versailles typifies the Baroque in architecture; gigantic frescoes unified around the emotional impact of a single theme is Baroque art; the glory of Bach's *Christmas Oratorio* expresses the baroque in music. Although the Baroque began in Catholic Counter-Reformation countries to teach in a concrete, emotional way, it soon spread to Protestant nations as well, and some of the greatest Baroque artists and composers were Protestant (e.g., Johann Sebastian Bach and George Frideric Handel).

Characteristics of the Rococo can be found in the compositions of both Franz Josef Haydn (1732–1809) and Wolfgang Amadeus Mozart (1756–1791).

REVOLUTION AND THE NEW WORLD ORDER (1789–1848)
The French Revolution I (1789–1799)

Armed with new scientific knowledge of the physical universe, as well as new views of the human capacity to detect "truth," social critics assailed existing modes of thought governing political, social, religious, and economic life. Ten years of upheaval in France (1789–1799) further shaped modern ideas and practices. Napoleon Bonaparte spread some of the revolutionary ideas about the administration of government as he conquered much of Europe.

1. Influence of the Enlightenment (c. 1700–1800)

France was the center of this intellectual revolution. Voltaire, Denis Diderot, Baron de Montesquieu, and Jean-Jacques Rousseau were among the more famous philosophers.

The major assumptions of the Enlightenment were as follows:

- Human progress was possible through changes in one's environment; in other words: better people, better societies, better standard of living.

- Humans were free to use reason to reform the evils of society.

- Material improvement would lead to moral improvement.

- Natural science and human reason would discover the meaning of life.

- Laws governing human society would be discovered through application of the scientific method of inquiry.

- Inhuman practices and institutions would be removed from society in a spirit of humanitarianism.

- Human liberty would ensue if individuals became free to choose what reason dictated was good.

The Enlightenment's effect on society touched many areas.

Religion. Deism or "natural religion" rejected traditional Christianity by promoting an impersonal God who did not interfere in the daily lives of the people. The continued discussion of the role of God led to a general skepticism associated with Pierre Bayle (1647–1706), a type of religious skepticism pronounced by David Hume (1711–1776), and a theory of atheism or materialism advocated by Baron d'Holbach (1723–1789).

Political Theory.   John Locke (1632–1704) and Jean-Jacques Rousseau (1712–1778) believed that people were capable of governing themselves, either through a political (Locke) or social (Rousseau) contract forming the basis of society. However, most philosophes opposed democracy, preferring a limited monarchy that shared power with the nobility.

Economic Theory.   The physiocrats in France, proposed a "laissez-faire" (nongovernmental interference) attitude toward land usage, and culminated in the theory of economic capitalism associated with Adam Smith (1723–1790) and his slogans of free trade, free enterprise, and the law of supply and demand.

Attempting to break away from the strict control of education by the church and state, Jean-Jacques Rousseau advanced the idea of progressive education, where children learn by doing and where self-expression is encouraged. This idea was carried forward by Johann Pestalozzi, Johann Basedow, and Friedrich Fröbel, and influenced a new view of childhood.

Psychological Theory.   In the *Essay Concerning Human Understanding* (1690), John Locke offered the theory that all human knowledge was the result of sensory experience, without any preconceived notions.

2. Causes of the French Revolution

The clergy (First Estate) and nobility (Second Estate), representing only 2% of the total population of 24 million, were the privileged classes and were essentially tax exempt. The remainder of the population (Third Estate) consisted of the middle class, urban workers, and the mass of peasants, who bore the entire burden of taxation and the imposition of feudal obligations.

Designed to represent the three estates of France, the **Estates General** had only met twice, once at its creation in 1302 and again in 1614. When the French parlements insisted that any new taxes must be approved by this body, King Louis XVI reluctantly ordered it to assemble at Versailles by May 1789. On May 5, 1789, the Estates General met and argued over whether to vote by estate or individual. Each estate was ordered to meet separately and vote as a unit. The Third Estate refused and insisted that the entire assembly stay together.

3. Phases of Revolution

The National Assembly (1789–1791).   After a six-week deadlock over voting methods, representatives of the Third Estate declared themselves the true National Assembly of France (June 17). Defections from the First and Second Estates then caused the king to recognize the National Assembly (June 27) after dissolving the Estates General. At the same time, Louis XVI ordered troops to surround Versailles. Angry because of food shortages, unemployment, high prices, and fear of military repression, the workers and tradespeople began to arm themselves.

The Legislative Assembly (1791–1792).   While the National Assembly had been rather homogeneous in its composition, the new government began to fragment into competing political factions. The most important political clubs were republican groups such as the Jacobins (radical urban) and Girondins (moderate rural), while the *Sans-culottes* (working-class, extremely radical) were a separate faction with an economic agenda.

The National Convention (1792–1795). Meeting for the first time in September 1792, the Convention abolished monarchy and installed republicanism. Louis XVI was charged with treason, found guilty, and executed on January 21, 1793. Later the same year, the queen, Marie Antoinette, met the same fate.

The most notorious event of the French Revolution was the famous **"Reign of Terror"** (1793–1794), the government's campaign against its internal enemies and counterrevolutionaries.

The Directory (1795–1799). The Constitution of 1795 restricted voting and office holding to property owners. The middle class wanted peace in order to gain more wealth and to establish a society in which money and property would become the only requirements for prestige and power. When elections in April 1797 produced a triumph for the royalist right, the results were annulled, and the Directory shed its last pretense of legitimacy. However, the weak and corrupt Directory government managed to hang on for two more years because of great military success. The greatest military victories were won by Napoleon Bonaparte, who drove the Austrians out of northern Italy and forced them to sign the Treaty of Campo Formio (October 1797), in return for which the Directory government agreed to Bonaparte's scheme to conquer Egypt and threaten English interests in the East.

The French Revolution II: The Era of Napoleon (1799–1815)

1. Consulate Period, 1799–1804 (Enlightened Reform)

The new government was installed on December 25, 1799, with a constitution which concentrated supreme power in the hands of Napoleon. Napoleon's domestic reforms and policies affected every aspect of society.

2. Empire Period, 1804–1814 (War and Defeat)

After being made Consul for Life (1801), Napoleon felt that only through an empire could France retain its strong position in Europe. On December 2, 1804, Napoleon crowned himself emperor of France in Notre Dame Cathedral.

3. Militarism and Empire Building

Beginning in 1805 Napoleon engaged in constant warfare that placed French troops in enemy capitals from Lisbon and Madrid to Berlin and Moscow, and temporarily gave Napoleon the largest empire since Roman times. Napoleon's Grand Empire consisted of an enlarged France, satellite kingdoms, and coerced allies.

French-ruled peoples viewed Napoleon as a tyrant who repressed and exploited them for France's glory and advantage. Enlightened reformers believed Napoleon had betrayed the ideals of the Revolution. The downfall of Napoleon resulted from his inability to conquer England, economic distress caused by the Continental System (boycott of British goods), the Peninsular War with Spain, the German War of Liberation, and the invasion of Russia. The actual defeat of Napoleon was the result of the Fourth Coalition and the Battle of Leipzig ("Battle of Nations"). Napoleon was exiled to the island of Elba. After learning of allied disharmony at the Vienna peace talks, Napoleon left Elba and began the Hundred Days by seizing power from the restored French king, Louis XVIII. Napoleon's gamble ended at Waterloo in June 1815. He was exiled as a prisoner of war to the South Atlantic island of St. Helena, where he died in 1821.

The Post-War Settlement: The Congress of Vienna (1814–1815)

The Congress of Vienna met in 1814 and 1815 to redraw the map of Europe after the Napoleonic era, and to provide some way of preserving the future peace of Europe. Europe was spared a general war throughout the remainder of the nineteenth century.

The **Vienna settlement** was the work of the representatives of the four nations that had done the most to defeat Napoleon: England (Lord Castlereagh), Austria (Prince Klemens Von Metternich), Russia (Tsar Alexander I), and Prussia (Karl Von Hardenberg).

Arrangements to guarantee the enforcement of the status quo as defined by the Vienna settlement included two provisions: The "Holy Alliance" of Tsar Alexander I of Russia, an idealistic and unpractical plan, existed only on paper. But the "Quadruple Alliance" of Russia, Prussia, Austria, and England provided for concerted action to arrest any threat to the peace or balance of power through a series of meetings held to monitor and defend the status quo: the Congress of Aix-la-Chapelle (1818), the Congress of Troppau (1820), the Congress of Laibach (1821), and the Congress of Verona (1822).

The Industrial Revolution

Twentieth-century English historian Arnold Toynbee came to refer to the period since 1750 as **the Industrial Revolution**. The term described a time of transition when machines began to significantly displace human and animal power in methods of producing and distributing goods, and an agricultural and commercial society converted into an industrial one. By the middle of the nineteenth century, industrialism had swept across Europe west to east, from England to Eastern Europe.

Roots of the Industrial Revolution could be found in the following: (1) the Commercial Revolution (1500–1700), which spurred the great economic growth of Europe and brought about the Age of Discovery and Exploration; (2) the effect of the Scientific Revolution, which produced the first wave of mechanical inventions and technological advances; (3) the increase in population in Europe from 140 million people in 1750, to 266 million people by the mid-part of the nineteenth century (more producers, more consumers); and (4) the political and social revolutions of the nineteenth century, which began the rise to power of the "middle class," and provided leadership for the economic revolution.

The revolution occurred first in the cotton and metallurgical industries. A series of mechanical inventions (1733–1793) enabled the cotton industry to mass-produce quality goods. The development of steam power allowed the cotton industry to expand and transformed the iron industry. The factory system, which had been created in response to the new energy sources and machinery, was perfected to increase manufactured goods.

A transportation revolution led to the growth of canal systems, the construction of hard-surfaced "macadam" roads, the commercial use of the steamboat (demonstrated by Robert Fulton, 1765–1815), and the railway locomotive (made commercially successful by George Stephenson, 1781–1848).

A subsequent revolution in agriculture made it possible for fewer people to feed the population, thus freeing people to work in factories, or in the new fields of communications, distribution of goods, or services like teaching, medicine, and entertainment.

Until 1850 workers as a whole did not share in the general wealth produced by the Industrial Revolution. Conditions would improve as the century wore on, as union action combined with general prosperity and a developing social conscience to improve the working conditions, wages, and hours first of skilled labor, and later of unskilled labor.

The most important sociological result of industrialism was urbanization. The new factories acted as magnets, pulling people away from their rural roots and beginning the most massive population transfer in history.

Impact of Thought Systems ("Isms") on the European World

Romanticism was a reaction against the rigid classicism, rationalism, and deism of the eighteenth century. English literary Romantics like Wordsworth and Coleridge epitomized the romantic movement. Other romantics included Goethe of Germany, Hugo of France, and Pushkin of Russia. Romanticism also affected music and the visual arts.

Romantic philosophy stimulated an interest in **Idealism**, the belief that reality consists of ideas, as opposed to materialism. This school of thought (**Philosophical Idealism**), founded by Plato, was developed through the writings of Immanuel Kant, Johann Gottlieb Fichte, and Georg Wilhelm Hegel, the greatest exponent of this school of thought. Hegel believed that an impersonal God rules the universe and guides humans along a progressive evolutionary course by means of a process called **dialecticism**; this is a historical process by which one thing is constantly reacting with its opposite (the thesis and antithesis), producing a result (synthesis) that automatically meets another opposite and continues the series of reactions.

Conservatism arose in reaction to liberalism and became a popular alternative for those who were frightened by the violence, terror, and social disorder unleashed by the French Revolution. Early conservatism was allied to the restored monarchical governments of Austria, Russia, France, and England. In essence, conservatives believed in order, society, and the state; faith and tradition.

The theory of **liberalism** was the first major theory in the history of Western thought to teach that the individual is a self-sufficient being whose freedom and well-being are the sole reasons for the existence of society. Liberalism was more closely connected to the spirit and outlook of the Enlightenment than to any of the other "isms" of the early nineteenth century. Liberalism was reformist and political rather than revolutionary in character.

Liberals also advocated economic individualism (i.e., laissez-faire capitalism), heralded by Adam Smith (1723–1790) in his 1776 economic masterpiece, *Wealth of Nations*.

Nationalistic thinkers and writers examined the language, literature, and folkways of their people, thereby stimulating nationalist feelings. Emphasizing the history and culture of the various European peoples reinforced and glorified national sentiment.

Socialism

The Utopian Socialists (from *Utopia*, Saint Thomas More's (1478–1535) book on a fictional ideal society) were the earliest writers to propose an equitable solution to improve the distribution of society's wealth. While they endorsed the productive capacity of industrialism, they denounced its mismanagement. Human society was to be organized as a community rather than a mixture of competing, selfish individuals.

The **Anarchists** rejected industrialism and the dominance of government.

"Scientific" Socialism, or **Marxism**, was the creation of Karl Marx (1818–1883), a German scholar who, with the help of Friedrich Engels (1820–1895), intended to replace utopian hopes and dreams with a militant blueprint for socialist working-class success. The principal works of this revolutionary school of socialism were *The Communist Manifesto* and *Das Kapital*.

The theory of dialectical materialism enabled Marx to explain the history of the world. By borrowing Hegel's dialectic, substituting materialism and realism in place of Hegel's idealism, and inverting the methodological process, Marx was able to justify his theoretical conclusions. Marxism consisted of a number of key propositions: (1) an economic interpretation of history, (i.e., all human history has been determined by economic factors) (2) class struggle; (3) theory of surplus value; and (4) socialism was inevitable; the rich would grow richer and the poor would grow poorer until the gap between each class (proletariat and bourgeoisie) is so great that the working classes would rise up in revolution and overthrow the elite bourgeoisie to install a "dictatorship of the proletariat." As modern capitalism was dismantled, the creation of a classless society guided by the principle "from each according to his abilities, to each according to his needs" would take place.

The Revolutionary Tradition

Generally speaking, the 1848 upheavals shared the strong influences of romanticism, nationalism, and liberalism, as well as a new factor of economic dislocation and instability.

The issues were substantially the same as they had been in 1789. What was new in 1848 was that these demands were far more widespread and irrepressible than ever. Aggravated by rapid population growth and the social disruption caused by industrialism and urbanization, a massive tide of discontent swept across the Western world.

Specifically, a number of similar conditions existed in several countries: (1) severe food shortages caused by poor harvests of grain and potatoes (e.g., Irish potato famine); (2) financial crises caused by a downturn in the commercial and industrial economy; (3) business failures; (4) widespread unemployment; (5) a sense of frustration and discontent among urban artisan and working classes as wages diminished; (6) a system of poor relief which became overburdened; (7) living conditions, which deteriorated in the cities; (8) the power of nationalism in the Germanies, Italies, and in Eastern Europe to inspire the overthrow of existing governments.

In France, working-class discontent and liberals' unhappiness with the corrupt regime of King Louis Philippe (reigned 1830–1848)—especially his minister Guizot (1787–1874)—erupted in street riots in Paris on February 22–23, 1848. With the workers in control of Paris, King Louis Philippe abdicated on February 24, and a provisional government proclaimed the Second French Republic.

The "June Days" revolt was provoked when the government closed the national workshop. This new revolution (June 23–26) marked the inauguration of genuine class warfare; it was a revolt against poverty and a cry for the redistribution of property. The revolt was extinguished after General Cavaignac was given dictatorial powers by the government.

The new Constitution of the Second French Republic provided for a unicameral legislature and executive power vested in a popularly elected president of the Republic. When the election returns were counted, the government's candidate was defeated by a "dark horse" candidate, Prince Louis Napoleon Bonaparte (1808–1873), a nephew of the great emperor. On December 20, 1848, Louis Napoleon was installed as president of the Republic. In December 1852 Louis Napoleon became Emperor Napoleon III (reigned 1852–1870), and France retreated from republicanism again.

Italian nationalists and liberals wanted to end Hapsburg (Austrian), Bourbon (Naples and Sicily), and papal domination and unite these disparate Italian regions into a unified liberal nation. Milan and Venice expelled their Austrian rulers. In March 1848, upon hearing the news of the revolution in Vienna, a fresh outburst of revolution against Austrian rule occurred in Lombardy and Venetia, with Sardinia-Piedmont declaring war on Austria. Simultaneously, Italian patriots attacked the Papal States, forcing the pope, Pius IX (1792–1878), to flee to Naples for refuge.

The temporary nature of these initial successes was illustrated by the speed with which the conservative forces regained control. In the north Austrian Field Marshal Radetzky (1766–1858) swept aside all opposition, regaining Lombardy and Venetia and crushing Sardinia-Piedmont. In the Papal States the establishment of the Roman Republic (February 1849), under the leadership of Giuseppe Mazzini and the protection of Giuseppe Garibaldi (1807–1882), would fail when French troops took Rome in July 1849 after a heroic defense by Garibaldi. Pope Pius IX returned to Rome cured of his liberal leanings.

The immediate effect of the 1848 Revolution in France was a series of liberal and nationalistic demonstrations in the German states (March 1848), with the rulers promising liberal concessions. The liberals' demand for constitutional government was coupled with another demand—some kind of union or federation of the German states.

Great Britain and the Victorian Compromise

The Victorian Age (1837–1901) is associated with the long reign of Queen Victoria, who succeeded her uncle King William IV at the age of 18, and married her cousin, Prince Albert. The early years of her reign coincided with the continuation of liberal reform of the British government, accomplished through an arrangement known as the "**Victorian Compromise.**" The Compromise was a political alliance of the middle class and aristocracy to exclude the working class from political power. The middle class gained control of the House of Commons, while the aristocracy controlled the government, the army, and the Church of England.

Parliamentary reforms continued after passage of the 1832 Reform Bill. Laws were enacted abolishing slavery throughout the empire (1833). The Factory Act (1831) forbade the employment of children under the age of 9. The New Poor Law (1834) required the needy who were able and unemployed to live in workhouses. The Municipal Reform Law (1835) gave control of the cities to the middle class. The last remnants of the mercantilistic age fell with the abolition of the Corn Laws (1846) and repeal of the old navigation acts (1849).

The revolutions of 1848 were spontaneous movements which lost their popular support as people lost their enthusiasm. Initial successes by the revolutionaries were due less to their strength than to the hesitancy of governments to use their superior force. Once this hesitancy was overcome, the revolutions were smashed. The middle class, who led the revolutions, came to fear the radicalism of their working-class allies. Divisions among national groups, and the willingness of one nationality to deny rights to other nationalities, helped to destroy the revolutionary movements in Central Europe.

However, the results of 1848–1849 were not entirely negative. Universal male suffrage was introduced in France; serfdom remained abolished in Austria and the German states; parliaments were established in Prussia and other German states, though dominated by princes and aristocrats; and Prussia and Sardinia-Piedmont emerged with new determination to succeed in their respective unification schemes.

A new age followed the revolutions of 1848–1849, as Otto von Bismarck (1815–1898), one of the dominant political figures of the second half of the nineteenth century, was quick to realize. The period of *Realpolitik*—of realistic, iron-fisted politics and diplomacy—followed.

REALISM AND MATERIALISM (1848–1914)

Realpolitik and the Triumph of Nationalism

After the collapse of the revolutionary movements of 1848, the leadership of Italian nationalism was transferred to Sardinian leaders Victor Emmanuel II (1820–1878), Camillo de Cavour (1810–1861), and Giuseppe Garibaldi (1807–1882). The new leaders were practitioners of the politics of realism, *Realpolitik*.

In 1855, under Cavour's direction, Sardinia joined Britain and France in the Crimean War against Russia. At the Paris Peace Conference (1856), Cavour addressed the delegates on the need to eliminate the foreign (Austrian) presence in the Italian peninsula and attracted the attention and sympathy of the French Emperor, Napoleon III.

After being provoked, the Austrians declared war on Sardinia in 1859. French forces intervened and the Austrians were defeated in the battles of Magenta (June 4) and Solferino (June 24).

Napoleon III, without consulting Cavour, signed a secret peace (The Truce of Villafranca) on July 11, 1859. Sardinia received Lombardy but not Venetia; the other terms indicated that Sardinian influence would be restricted and that Austria would remain a power in Italian politics. The terms of Villafranca were clarified and finalized with the Treaty of Zurich (1859).

In 1860, Cavour arranged the annexation of Parma, Modena, Romagna, and Tuscany into Sardinia. These actions were recognized by the Treaty of Turin between Napoleon III and Victor Emmanuel II; Nice and Savoy were transferred to France.

Giuseppe Garibaldi and his Red Shirts landed in Sicily in May 1860 and extended the nationalist activity to the south. Within three months, Sicily was taken; by September 7, Garibaldi was in Naples and the Kingdom of the Two Sicilies had fallen under Sardinian influence.

In February 1861, in Turin, Victor Emmanuel was declared King of Italy and presided over an Italian Parliament which represented the entire Italian peninsula with the exception of Venetia and the Patrimony of St. Peter (Rome). Cavour died in June 1861.

Venetia was incorporated into the Italian Kingdom in 1866 as a result of an alliance between Bismarck's Prussia and the Kingdom of Italy which preceded the Austro-Prussian War. In return for opening a southern front against Austria, Prussia, upon its victory, arranged for Venetia to be transferred to Italy.

Bismarck was again instrumental in the acquisition of Rome into the Italian Kingdom in 1870. In 1870, the Franco-Prussian War broke out and the French garrison, which had been in Rome providing protection for the Pope, was withdrawn to serve on the front against Prussia. Italian troops seized Rome, and in 1871 Rome became the capital of the Kingdom of Italy.

Bismarck and the Unification of Germany

In the period after 1815, Prussia emerged as an alternative to a Hapsburg-based Germany. Otto von Bismarck (1810–1898) entered the diplomatic service of Wilhelm I as the revolutions of 1848 were being suppressed. By the early 1860s, Bismarck had emerged as the principal adviser and minister to the king.

In 1863, the **Schleswig-Holstein crisis** broke. These provinces, which were occupied by Germans, were under the personal rule of Christian IX (1818–1906) of Denmark. The Danish government advanced a new constitution which specified that Schleswig and Holstein would be annexed into Denmark. German reaction was predictable and Bismarck arranged for joint Austro-Prussian military action. Denmark was defeated and agreed (Treaty of Vienna, 1864) to give up the provinces, and Schleswig and Holstein were to be jointly administered by Austria and Prussia.

In 1870, deteriorating relations between France and Germany collapsed over the **Ems Dispatch**. Wilhelm I was approached by representatives of the French government who requested a Prussian pledge not to interfere on the issue of the vacant Spanish throne. Wilhelm I refused to give such a pledge and informed Bismarck of these developments through a telegram from Ems. Bismarck exploited the situation by initiating a propaganda campaign against the French. Subsequently, the Franco-Prussian War (1870–1871) commenced. Prussian victories at Sedan and Metz proved decisive; Napoleon III and his leading general, Marshal MacMahon, were captured. Paris continued to resist but fell to the Prussians in January 1871. The Treaty of Frankfurt (May 1871) concluded the war and resulted in France ceding Alsace-Lorraine to Germany and a German occupation until an indemnity was paid.

The German Empire was proclaimed on January 18, 1871, with Wilhelm I becoming Emperor. Bismarck became the Imperial Chancellor. Bavaria, Baden, Württemberg, and Saxony were incorporated into the new Germany.

The Crimean War

During the nineteenth century, Palestine was part of the Ottoman Turkish Empire. In 1852, the Turks negotiated an agreement with the French to provide enclaves in the Holy Land to Roman Catholic religious orders; this arrangement appeared to jeopardize already existing agreements which provided access to Greek Orthodox religious orders. Czar Nicholas I (reigned 1825–1855) ordered Russian troops to occupy several Danubian principalities. In October 1853, the Turks demanded that the Russians withdraw from the occupied principalities. The Russians failed to respond, and the Turks declared war. In February 1854, Nicholas advanced a draft for a settlement of the Russo-Turkish War; it was rejected and Great Britain and France joined the Ottoman Turks and declared war on Russia.

The majority of the war was conducted on the Crimean Peninsula in the Black Sea. In September 1854, more than 50,000 British and French troops landed in the Crimea, determined to take the Russian port city of Sebastopol. In December 1854, Austria reluctantly became a co-signatory of the **Four Points of Vienna**, a statement of British and French war aims. In 1855, Piedmont joined Britain and France in the war. In March 1855, Czar Nicholas I died and was succeeded by Alexander II (reigned 1855–1881), who was opposed to continuing the war. In December 1855, the Austrians sent an ultimatum to Russia in which they threatened to renounce their neutrality. In response, Alexander II indicated that he would accept the Four Points.

The resulting Peace of Paris had the following major provisions: Russia had to acknowledge international commissions to regulate maritime traffic on the Danube, recognize Turkish control of the mouth of the Danube, renounce all claims to the Danubian Principalities of Moldavia and Wallachia (which later led to the establishment of Romania), agree not to fortify the Aaland Islands, renounce its previously espoused position of protector of the Greek Orthodox residents of the Ottoman Empire, and return all occupied territories to the Ottoman Empire. The Straits Convention of 1841 was revised by neutralizing the Black Sea. The Declaration of Paris specified rules to regulate commerce during periods of war. Lastly, the independence and integrity of the Ottoman Empire were recognized and guaranteed by the signatories.

The Eastern Question and the Congress of Berlin

In 1876, Turkish forces under the leadership of Osman Pasha soundly defeated Serbian armies. In March 1878, the Russians and the Turks signed the Peace of San Stephano; implementation of its provisions would have resulted in Russian hegemony in the Balkans and dramatically altered the balance of power in the eastern Mediterranean.

Britain, under the leadership of Prime Minister Benjamin Disraeli (1804–1881), denounced the San Stephano Accord, dispatched a naval squadron to Turkish waters, and demanded that the San Stephano agreement be scrapped. The German Chancellor, Otto von Bismarck, intervened and offered his services as mediator.

The delegates of the major powers convened in Berlin in June and July 1878 to negotiate a settlement. Prior to the meeting, Disraeli had concluded a series of secret arrangements with Austria, Russia, and Turkey. The combined impact of these accommodations was to restrict Russian expansion in the region, reaffirm the independence of Turkey, and maintain British control of the Mediterranean.

The Russians, who had won the war against Turkey and had imposed the harsh terms of the San Stephano Treaty, found that they left the conference with very little (Kars, Batum, etc.) for their effort. Although Disraeli was the primary agent of this anti-Russian settlement, the Russians blamed Bismarck for their dismal results. Their hostility toward Germany led Bismarck (1879) to embark upon a new system of alliances which transformed European diplomacy and rendered any additional efforts of the Concert of Europe futile.

Capitalism and the Emergence of the New Left (1848–1914)

The Industrial Revolution, despite its positives, led to a factory system with undesirable working and living conditions and the abuses of child labor. As the century progressed, the inequities of the system became increasingly evident.

During the period from 1815 to 1848, Utopian Socialists such as Robert Owen (1771–1858), Saint Simon, and Charles Fourier advocated the establishment of a political-economic system which was based on romantic concepts of the ideal society. The failure of the Revolutions of 1848 and 1849 discredited the Utopian Socialists, and the new "**Scientific Socialism**" advanced by Karl Marx (1818–1883) became the primary ideology of protest and revolution. Marx stated that the history of humanity was the history of class struggle and that the process of the struggle (the **dialectic**) would continue until a classless society was realized. The industrial working class (proletariat), needed to be educated and led toward a violent revolution which would destroy the institutions which perpetuated the struggle and the suppression of the majority. After the revolution, the people would experience the dictatorship of the proletariat, during which the Communist party would provide leadership. Marx advanced these concepts in a series of tracts and books including *The Communist Manifesto* (1848), *Critique of Political Economy* (1859), and *Capital* (1863–1864).

Britain

In 1865, Palmerston died, and during the next two decades significant domestic developments occurred which expanded democracy in Great Britain. The dominant leaders of this period were William Gladstone (1809–1898) and Benjamin Disraeli (1804–1881). As the leader of the Liberal party (until 1895), Gladstone supported Irish Home Rule, fiscal responsibility, free trade, and the extension of democratic principles. He was opposed to imperialism, the involvement of Britain in European affairs, and the further centralization of the British government. Disraeli argued for an aggressive foreign policy, the expansion of the British Empire, and, after opposing democratic reforms, the extension of the franchise.

The Second French Republic and the Second Empire

Louis Napoleon became the president of the Second French Republic in December 1848. During the three-year life of the Second Republic, Louis Napoleon's deployment of troops in Italy to rescue and restore Pope Pius IX was condemned by the republicans, but strongly supported by the monarchists and moderates.

Louis Napoleon minimized the importance of the Legislative Assembly, capitalized on the developing Napoleonic Legend, and courted the support of the army, the Catholic church, and a range of conservative political groups. The Falloux Law returned control of education to the church. Further, Louis Napoleon was confronted with Article 45 of the constitution, which stipulated that the president was limited to one four-year term; he had no intention of relinquishing power. With the assistance of a core of dedicated supporters, Louis Napoleon arranged for a coup d'état on the night of December 1–2, 1851. The Second Republic fell and was soon replaced by the Second French Empire.

Louis Napoleon drafted a new constitution which resulted in a highly centralized government. On December 2, 1852, he announced that he was Napoleon III, Emperor of the French.

The Second Empire collapsed after the capture of Napoleon III during the Franco-Prussian War (1870–1871). After a regrettable Parisian experience with a communist type of government, the Third French Republic was established; it would survive until 1940.

Imperial Russia

The autocracy of Nicholas I's (reigned 1825–1855) regime was not threatened by the revolutionary movements of 1848. In 1848 and 1849, Russian troops suppressed disorganized Polish attempts to reassert Polish nationalism.

Russian involvement in the Crimean War met with defeat. In 1855 Nicholas I died and was succeeded by Alexander II (reigned 1855–1881).

Alexander II instituted a series of reforms which altered the nature of the social contract in Russia. In 1861, Alexander II declared that serfdom was abolished. Further, he issued the following reforms: (1) The serf (peasant) would no longer be dependent upon the lord; (2) all people were to have freedom of movement and were free to change their means of livelihood; and (3) the serf could enter into contracts and could own property.

As the regime of Alexander II matured, greater importance was placed on traditional values. This attitude developed at the same time that nihilism, which rejected romantic illusions of the past in favor of a rugged realism, was being advanced by such writers as Ivan Turgenev in his *Fathers and Sons*.

The notion of the inevitability and desirability of a social and economic revolution was promoted through the Russian populist movement. Government persecution of the populists resulted in the radicalization of the movement. In the late 1870s and early 1880s, leaders such as Andrei Zheleabov and Sophie Perovsky became obsessed with the need to assassinate Alexander II. In March 1881, the czar was killed in St. Petersburg when his carriage was bombed. He was succeeded by Alexander III (reigned 1881–1894), who advocated a national policy based on "Orthodoxy, Autocracy, and Nationalism." Alexander III died in 1894 and was succeeded by the last of the Romanovs to hold power, Nicholas II (reigned 1894–1917). From his ministers to his wife, Alexandra, to Rasputin (1872–1916), Nicholas was influenced by stronger personalities.

The opposition to the Czarist government became more focused and thus, more threatening, with the emergence of the Russian Social Democrats and the Russian Social Revolutionaries. Both groups were Marxist. Vladimir Ilyich Ulyanov, also known as Lenin, became the leader of the Bolsheviks, a splinter group of the Social Democrats. By winter (1904–1905), the accumulated consequences of inept management of the economy and the prosecution of the Russo-Japanese War reached a critical stage. A group under the leadership of the radical priest Gapon marched on the Winter Palace in St. Petersburg (January 9, 1905) to submit a list of grievances to the czar. Troops fired on the demonstrators and many casualties resulted on this "Bloody Sunday." In June 1905, naval personnel on the battleship *Potemkin* mutinied while the ship was in Odessa. In October 1905, Nicholas II issued the October Manifesto calling for the convocation of a **Duma**, or assembly of state, which would serve as an advisory body to the czar, extending civil liberties to include freedom of speech, assembly, and press, and announcing that Nicholas II would reorganize his government.

The leading revolutionary forces differed in their responses to the manifesto. The Octobrists indicated that they were satisfied with the arrangements; the Constitutional Democrats (Kadets), demanded a more liberal representative system. The Duma convened in 1906 and was paralyzed by factionalism. By 1907, Nicholas II's ministers had recovered the real power of government.

Origins, Motives, and Implications of the New Imperialism (1870–1914)

By the 1870s, the European industrial economies required external markets to distribute their products. Further, excess capital was available and foreign investment, while risky, appeared to offer high returns. Finally, the need for additional sources of raw materials served as a rationale and stimulant for imperialism. European statesmen were also interested in asserting their national power overseas through the acquisition of strategic (and many not so strategic) colonies.

The focus of most of the European imperial activities during the late nineteenth century was Africa. With John Hanning Speke's discovery of Lake Victoria (1858), Livingstone's surveying of the Zambezi, and Stanley's work on the Congo River, Europeans became enraptured with the greatness and novelty of Africa south of the Sahara.

Disraeli was involved in the intrigue which would result in the British acquisition of the Suez Canal (1875), and during the 1870s and 1880s Britain was involved in a Zulu War and announced the annexation of the Transvaal, which the Boers regained after their great victory of Majuba Hill (1881). At about the same time, Belgium established its interest in the Congo; France, in addition to seizing Tunisia, extended its influence into French Equitorial Africa, and Italy established small colonies in East Africa. During the 1880s Germany acquired several African colonies including German East Africa, the Cameroons, Togoland, and German South West Africa. The Berlin Conference

(1884–1885) resulted in an agreement which specified the following: (1) The Congo would be under the control of Belgium through an International Association; (2) More liberal use of the Niger and Congo rivers; and (3) European powers could acquire African territory through first occupation and second notifying the other European states of their occupation and claim.

With the discovery of gold (1882) in the Transvaal, many English Cape settlers moved into the region. The Boers, who had lived in South Africa since the beginning of the nineteenth century, restricted the political and economic rights of the British settlers and developed alternative railroads through Mozambique which would lessen the Boer dependency on the Cape colony. In 1899 until 1902, the British and Boers fought a war which was costly to both sides. Britain prevailed and, by 1909, the Transvaal, Orange Free State, Natal, and the Cape of Good Hope were united into the Union of South Africa.

Another area of increased imperialist activity was the Pacific. In 1890, the American naval officer Captain Alfred Mahan published *The Influence of Sea Power Upon History*; in this book he argued that history demonstrated that nations which controlled the seas prevailed. The United States acquired the Philippines in 1898. Germany gained part of New Guinea, and the Marshall, Caroline, and Mariana island chains. The European powers were also interested in the Asian mainland. Most powers agreed with the American Open Door Policy which recognized the independence and integrity of China and provided economic access for all the powers. Rivalry over China (Manchuria) was a principal cause of the outbreak of the Russo-Japanese War in 1904.

The Age of Bismarck (1871–1890)

From January 1871 to March 1890, Otto von Bismarck dominated European diplomacy and established an integrated political and economic structure for the new German state. During the 1870s and 1880s, Bismarck's domestic policies were directed at the establishment of a strong united German state which would be capable of defending itself from a French war of revenge designed to restore Alsace-Lorraine to France. Laws were enacted which unified the monetary system, established an Imperial Bank and strengthened existing banks, developed universal German civil and criminal codes, and required compulsory military service.

In order to develop public support for the government and to minimize the threat from the left, Bismarck instituted a protective tariff to maintain domestic production and introduced many social and economic laws to provide social security, regulate child labor, and improve working conditions for all Germans.

Bismarck's foreign policy was centered on maintaining the diplomatic isolation of France. In the crisis stemming from the Russo-Turkish War (1877–1878), Bismarck tried to serve as the "Honest Broker" at the Congress of Berlin. Early in the next year, a cholera epidemic affected Russian cattle herds, and Germany placed an embargo on the importation of Russian beef. The Russians were outraged by the German action and launched an anti-German propaganda campaign in the Russian press. Bismarck, desiring to maintain the peace and a predictable diplomatic environment, concluded a secret defensive treaty with Austria-Hungary in 1879. The **Dual Alliance** was very significant because it was the first "hard" diplomatic alliance of the era. A "hard" alliance involved the specific commitment of military support; traditional or "soft" alliances involved pledges of neutrality or to hold military conversations in the event of a war. The Dual Alliance, which had a five-year term and was renewable, directed that one signatory would assist the other in the event that one power was attacked by two or more states.

In 1882, another agreement, the **Triple Alliance**, was signed between Germany, Austria-Hungary, and Italy. In the 1880s, relations between Austria-Hungary and Russia became estranged over Balkan issues. Bismarck, fearing a war, intervened and, by 1887, had negotiated the secret Reinsurance Treaty with Russia. This was a "hard" defensive alliance with a three-year term, which was renewable.

In 1888, Wilhelm I died and was succeeded by his son Friedrich III, who also died within a few months. Friedrich's son, Wilhelm II (reigned 1888–1918), came to power and soon found himself in conflict with Bismarck. Early in 1890, Bismarck evolved a scheme for a fabricated attempted coup by the Social Democratic Party (SDP). Bismarck also intended to renew the Reinsurance Treaty with Russia to maintain his policy of French diplomatic isolation. Wilhelm II opposed both of these plans; in March 1890, Bismarck suggested that he would resign if Wilhelm II would not approve of these actions. Wilhelm II accepted his resignation; in fact, Bismarck was dismissed.

The Movement toward Democracy in Western Europe

Even after the reform measures of 1867 and 1884 to 1885, the movement toward democratic reforms in Great Britain continued unabated.

The most significant political reform of this long-lived liberal government was the **Parliament Act of 1911**, which eliminated the powers of the House of Lords and resulted in the House of Commons becoming the unquestioned center of national power.

The most recurring and serious problem which Great Britain experienced during the period from 1890 to 1914 was the "Irish Question." The Irish situation became more complicated when the Protestant counties of the north started to enjoy remarkable economic growth from the mid-1890s; they were adamant in their rejection of all measures of Irish Home Rule. In 1914, an Irish Home Rule Act was passed by both the Commons and the Lords, but the Protestants refused to accept it. Implementation was deferred until after the war.

The Third French Republic

In the fall of 1870, Napoleon III's Second Empire collapsed when it was defeated by the Prussian armies. Napoleon III and his principal aides were captured; later, he abdicated and fled to England. A National Assembly (1871–1875) was created and Adolphe Thiers was recognized as its chief executive. At the same time, a more radical political entity, the Paris Commune (1870–1871), came into existence and exercised extraordinary power during the siege of Paris. After the siege and the peace agreement with Prussia, the Commune refused to recognize the authority of the National Assembly. Led by radical Marxists, anarchists, and republicans, the Paris Commune repudiated the conservative and monarchist leadership of the National Assembly. From March to May 1871, the Commune fought a bloody struggle with the troops of the National Assembly. France began a program of recovery which led to the formulation of the Third French Republic in 1875. The National Assembly sought to (1) put the French political house in order; (2) establish a new constitutional government; (3) pay off an imposed indemnity and, in doing so, remove German troops from French territory; and (4) restore the honor and glory of France. In 1875 a constitution was adopted which provided for a republican government consisting of a president (with little power), a Senate, and a Chamber of Deputies, which was the center of political power. During the early years of the Republic, Leon Gambetta (1838–1882) led the republicans.

The most serious threat to the Republic came through the **Dreyfus Affair.** In 1894, Captain Alfred Dreyfus (1859–1935) was assigned to the French General Staff. A scandal broke when it was revealed that classified information had been provided to German spies. Dreyfus, a Jew, was charged, tried, and convicted. Later, it was determined that the actual spy was Commandant Marie Charles Esterhazy (1847–1923), who was acquitted in order to save the pride and reputation of the army. In 1906, Dreyfus was declared innocent and returned to the ranks. Rather than lead to the collapse of the Republic, the Dreyfus Affair demonstrated the intensity of anti-Semitism in French society, the level of corruption in the French army, and the willingness of the Catholic church and the monarchists to join in a conspiracy against an innocent man.

International Politics and the Coming of the War (1890–1914)

During the late nineteenth century, the economically motivated "New Imperialism" resulted in further aggravating the relations among the European powers. The Fashoda Crisis (1898–1899), the Moroccan Crisis (1905–1906), the Balkan Crisis (1908), and the Agadir Crisis (1911) demonstrated the impact of imperialism in heightening tensions among European states and in creating an environment in which conflict became more acceptable.

In 1908, the decadent Ottoman Empire was experiencing domestic discord which attracted the attention of both the Austrians and the Russians. These two powers agreed that Austria would annex Bosnia and Herzegovina and Russia would be granted access to the Straits and thus the Mediterranean. Great Britain intervened and demanded that there be no change in the status quo in the Straits. Russia backed down from a confrontation, but Austria proceeded to annex Bosnia and Herzegovina.

WORLD WAR I AND EUROPE IN CRISIS (1914–1935)

The Origins of World War I

The origins of World War I can be traced to numerous factors, beginning with the creation of modern Germany in 1871. From 1871 to 1890, balance of power was maintained through the network of alliances created by the German Chancellor, Otto von Bismarck, and centered around his *Dreikaiserbund* (League of the Three Emperors) that isolated France, and the Dual (Germany, Austria) and Triple (Germany, Austria, Italy) Alliances. Bismarck's fall in 1890 resulted in new policies that saw Germany move closer to Austria, while England and France (Entente Cordiale, 1904), and later Russia (Triple Entente, 1907), drew closer.

Germany's dramatic defeat of France in 1870–1871 coupled with Kaiser William II's decision in 1890 to build up a navy comparable to that of Great Britain created a reactive arms race. This, blended with European efforts to carve out colonial empires in Africa and Asia, helped create an unstable international environment in the years before the outbreak of World War I.

Root Causes of World War I

The Balkans, the area which today comprises the former Yugoslavia, Albania, Greece, Bulgaria, Macedonia, and Romania, were notably unstable. Part of the rapidly decaying Ottoman (Turkish) Empire, it saw two main forces at work: (1) ethnic nationalism among the various small groups who lived there, and (2) an intense rivalry between Austria-Hungary and Russia over spheres of influence. In 1912, with Russia's blessing, the Balkan League (Serbia, Montenegro, Greece, and Bulgaria) went to war with Turkey. Serbia, which sought a port on the Adriatic, was rebuffed when Austria and Italy backed the creation of an independent Albania. Russia, meanwhile, grew increasingly protective of its southern Slavic cousins, supporting Serbia's and Montenegro's claims to Albanian lands.

The Outbreak of the World War

On June 28, 1914, Archduke Franz Ferdinand (1863–1914), heir to the Austrian throne, was assassinated by Gavrilo Princip, a young Serbian nationalist. Austria consulted with the German government on July 6 and received a "blank check" to take any steps necessary to punish Serbia. On July 23, 1914, the Austrian government presented Serbia with a 10-point ultimatum that required Serbia to suppress and punish all forms of anti-Austrian sentiment there with the help of Austrian officials. On July 25, 1914, three hours after mobilizing its army, the Serbians acceded to most of Austria's terms.

Austria immediately broke off official relations with Serbia and mobilized its army. On July 28, 1914, Austria went to war against Serbia, and began to bombard Belgrade the following day. At the same time, Russia gradually prepared for war against Austria and Germany, declaring full mobilization on July 30.

German military strategy, based in part on the plan of the Chief of the General Staff Count Alfred von Schlieffen, viewed Russian mobilization as an act of war. The Schlieffen Plan, based on a two-front war with Russia and France, was predicated on a swift, decisive blow against France while maintaining a defensive position against slowly mobilizing Russia, which would be dealt with after France.

Germany demanded that Russia demobilize in 12 hours and appealed to the Russian ambassador in Berlin. Russia's offer to negotiate the matter was rejected, and Germany declared war on Russia on August 1, 1914. On August 3, Germany declared war on France. On August 4, England declared war on Germany; Belgium followed suit. Between 1914 and 1915, the alliance of the Central Powers (Germany, Austria-Hungary, Bulgaria, and Turkey) faced the Allied Powers of England, France, Russia, Japan, and, in 1917, the United States. A number of smaller countries were also part of the Allied coalition.

The War in 1914

1. The Western Front

After entering Belgium, the Germans attacked France on five fronts in an effort to encircle Paris rapidly. However, the unexpected Russian attack in East Prussia and Galicia from August 17 to 20 forced Germany to transfer important forces eastward to halt the Russian drive.

To halt a further German advance, the French army, aided by Belgian and English forces, counterattacked. In the Battle of the Marne (September 5–9), they stopped the German drive and forced small retreats. Mutual outflanking maneuvers by France and Germany created a battlefront that would determine the demarcation of the Western Front for the next four years. It ran, in uneven fashion, from the North Sea to Belgium and from northern France to Switzerland.

2. The Eastern Front

The Germans retreated after their assault against Warsaw in late September. Hindenburg's attack on Lodz, 10 days after he was appointed Commander-in-Chief of the Eastern Front (November 1), was a more successful venture; by the end of 1914 this important textile center was in German hands.

The War in 1915

1. The Western Front

Wooed by both sides, Italy joined the Allies and declared war on the Central Powers on May 23 after signing the secret Treaty of London (April 26). This treaty gave Italy Austrian provinces in the north and some Turkish territory.

2. The Eastern Front

On January 23, 1915, Austro-German forces began a coordinated offensive in East Russia and in the Carpathians. The two-pronged German assault in the north was stopped on February 27, while Austrian efforts to relieve their besieged defensive network at Przemysl failed when it fell into Russian hands on March 22.

German forces, strengthened by troops from the Western Front under August von Mackensen, began a move on May 2 to strike at the heart of the Russian Front. By August 1915, much of Russian Poland was in German hands.

Germany and Austria invaded Serbia in the early fall, aided by their new ally, Bulgaria. On October 7, the defeated Serbian army retreated to Corfu.

The Eastern Mediterranean

Turkey entered the war on the Central Power side on October 28, 1914, which prevented the shipment of Anglo-French aid to Russians through the Straits.

The War in 1916

1. The Western Front

The Battle for Verdun lasted from February 21 to December 18, 1916. From February until June, German forces assaulted the forts around Verdun. The Germans suffered 281,000 casualties while the French, under Marshal Henri Pétain (1856–1951), lost 315,000 while successfully defending their position.

To take pressure off the French, an Anglo-French force mounted three attacks on the Germans to the left of Verdun in July, September, and November. After the Battle of the Somme (July 1–November 18), German pressure was reduced, but at great loss. Anglo-French casualties totaled 600,000.

2. The Eastern Front

Orchestrated by Aleksei Brusilov (1853–1926), the Brusilov Offensive (June 4–September 20) advanced into Galicia and the Carpathians.

Romania entered the war on the Allied side as a result of Russian successes and the secret Treaty of Bucharest (August 17). The ensuing Romanian thrust into Transylvania was pushed back, and on December 6, a German-Bulgarian army occupied Bucharest as well as the bulk of Romania.

The death of Austrian Emperor Franz Joseph (reigned 1848–1916) on November 21 prompted his successor, Charles I (1887–1922), to discuss the prospect of peace terms with his allies. On December 12, the four Central Powers, strengthened by the fall of Bucharest, offered four separate peace proposals based on their recent military achievements. The Allies rejected them on December 30 because they felt them to be insincere.

By the end of 1914, Allied fleets had gained control of the high seas, which caused Germany to lose control of its colonial empire. German naval leaders began using the submarine as an offensive weapon to weaken the British. Germany, Russia, and Great Britain all had submarines, but the German U-boats were the most effective. On February 4, Germany announced a war zone around the British Isles, and advised neutral powers to sail there at their own risk. On May 7, 1915, a German submarine sank the *Lusitania*, a British passenger vessel, because it was secretly carrying arms.

New Military Technology

By the spring of 1915, British war planners realized that the machine gun had become the mistress of defensive trench warfare. In a search for a weapon to counter trench defenses, the British developed tanks as an armored "land ship," and first used them on September 15, 1916, in the battle of the Somme.

Mid-air struggles using pistols and rifles took place until the Germans devised a synchronized propeller and machine gun on its Fokker aircraft in May 1915. The Allies responded with similar equipment and new squadron tactics and briefly gained control of the skies. They also began to use their aircraft for bombing raids against Zeppelin bases in Germany. Air supremacy shifted to the Germans in 1917.

During the first year of the war, the Germans began to use Zeppelin airships to bomb civilian targets in England. Though their significance was neutralized with the development of the explosive shell in 1916, Zeppelins played an important role as a psychological weapon in the first two years of the war.

In the constant search for methods to counter trench warfare, the Germans and the Allied forces experimented with various forms of internationally outlawed gas. On October 27, 1914, the Germans tried a nose/eye irritant gas at Neuve-Chapelle, and by the spring of 1915 had developed a poison chlorine gas at the Battle of Ypres. That fall, the British countered with a similar chemical at the battles of Champagne and Loos.

The Russian Revolutions of 1917

1. The February Revolution

The government's handling of the war prompted a new wave of civilian unrest. Estimates are that 1,140 riots and strikes swept Russia in January and February 1917. Military and police units ordered to move against the mobs either remained at their posts or joined them.

Though dissolved on March 11, the Duma met in special session on March 13 and created a Provisional Committee of Elders to deal with the civil war. After two days of discussions, it decided that the czar must give up his throne, and on March 15, 1917, President Michael Rodzianko and Aleksandr Ivanovich Guchkov, leader of the Octobrist Party, convinced the czar to abdicate. He agreed, turning over the throne to his brother, the Grand Duke Michael, who himself abdicated the next day.

2. The Bolshevik October Revolution

On October 23–24, Lenin returned from Finland to meet with the party's Central Committee to plan the coup. Though he met with strong resistance, the Committee agreed to create a Political Bureau (Politburo) to oversee the revolution.

Leon Trotsky, head of the Petrograd Soviet and its Military Revolutionary Committee, convinced troops in Petrograd to support Bolshevik moves. While Trotsky gained control of important strategic points around the city, Alexander Kerensky, Prime Minister of the Russian Provisional Government at the time, finally decided on November 6 to move against the plotters. In response, Lenin and Trotsky ordered their supporters to seize the city's transportation and communication centers. The Winter Palace was captured later that evening, along with most of Kerensky's government.

The Second Congress opened at 11 p.m. on November 7, with Lev Kamenev (1883–1936), a member of Lenin's Politburo, as its head. Soon after it opened, many of the moderate socialists walked out in opposition to Lenin's coup, leaving the Bolsheviks and the Left Socialist Revolutionaries in control of the gathering.

The government's new Cabinet, officially called the Council of People's Commissars (Sovnarkom), which was responsible to a Central Executive Committee, would include Lenin as Chairman, Trotsky as Foreign Commissar, and Josef Stalin as Commissar of Nationalities. The Second Congress issued two decrees on peace and land. The first called for immediate peace without any consideration of indemnities or annexations, while the second adopted the Socialist Revolutionary land program that abolished private ownership of land and decreed that a peasant could only have as much land as he could farm.

3. The Constituent Assembly

The **Constituent Assembly** presented serious problems for Lenin, since he knew the Bolsheviks could not win a majority of seats in it. Regardless, Lenin allowed elections to be held on November 25 under universal suffrage. When the Assembly convened on January 18 in the Tauride Palace, it voted down Bolshevik proposals and elected Victor Chernov, a Socialist Revolutionary, as president, and declared the country a democratic federal republic. The Bolsheviks walked out. The next day, troops dissolved the Assembly.

World War I: The Final Phase (1917–1918)

1. Russia Leaves the War

As order collapsed among Russian units along the Eastern Front, the Soviet government began to explore cease fire talks with the Central Powers. Leon Trotsky, the Commissar of Foreign Affairs, offered general negotiations to all sides, and signed an initial armistice as a prelude to peace discussions with Germany at Brest-Litovsk on December 5, 1917.

The Soviets accepted terms that were integrated into the Treaty of Brest-Litovsk of March 3, 1918. According to its terms, in return for peace, Soviet Russia lost its Baltic provinces, the Ukraine, Finland, Byelorussia, and part of Transcaucasia. The area lost totaled 1,300,000 square miles and included 62 million people.

2. The American Presence: Naval and Economic Support

The United States made its naval presence known immediately and helped Great Britain mount an extremely effective blockade of Germany and, through a convoy system, strengthened the shipment of goods across the Atlantic.

The American Expeditionary Force, under General John J. Pershing (1860–1948), arrived in France on June 25, 1917. By the end of April 1918, 300,000 Americans a month were placed as complete divisions alongside British and French units.

Stirred by the successes on the Marne, the Allies began their offensive against the Germans at Amiens on August 8, 1918. By September 3, the Germans retreated to the Hindenburg Line. On September 26, Foch began his final offensive, and took the Hindenburg Line the following day. Two days later, Ludendorff advised his government to seek a peace settlement. Over the next month, the French took St. Quetin (October 1), while the British occupied Cambrai, Le Cateau, and Ostend.

On September 14, Allied forces attacked in the Salonika area of Macedonia and forced Bulgaria to sue for peace on September 29. On September 19, General Allenby began an attack on Turkish forces at Megiddo in Palestine and quickly defeated them. In a rapid collapse of Turkish resistance, the British took Damascus, Aleppo, and finally forced Turkey from the war at the end of October. On October 24, the Italians began an assault against Austria-Hungary at Vitto Veneto and forced Vienna to sign armistice terms on November 3. Kaiser Wilhelm II, pressured to abdicate, fled the country on November 9, and a republic was declared. On November 11, at 11 a.m., the war ended, with Germany accepting a harsh armistice.

The Paris Peace Conference of 1919–1920

1. Preliminary Discussions

The sudden, unexpected end of the war, combined with the growing threat of communist revolution throughout Europe, created an unsettling atmosphere at the Paris Peace Conference. The "Big Four" of Wilson (U.S.), Clemenceau (France), Lloyd-George (England), and Orlando (Italy) took over the peace discussions. The delays caused by uncertainty over direction at the beginning of the conference, Wilson's insistence that the League of Nations be included in the settlement, and fear of European-wide revolution resulted in a hastily prepared, dictated peace settlement.

The Treaty of Versailles

The treaty's war guilt statements were the justification for its harsh penalties. The former German king, Wilhelm II, was accused of crimes against "international morality and the sanctity of treaties," while Germany took responsibility for itself and for its allies for all losses suffered by the Allied Powers.

The Allies presented the treaty to the Germans on May 7, 1919, but the Germans stated that its terms were too much for the German people, and that it violated the spirit of Wilson's Fourteen Points. After some minor changes were made, the Germans were told to sign the document or face an Allied advance into Germany. The treaty was signed on June 28, 1919, at Versailles.

Treaties with Germany's Allies

The Allied treaty with Austria legitimized the breakup of the Austrian Empire in the latter days of the war and saw Austrian territory ceded to Italy and the new states of Czechoslovakia, Poland, and Yugoslavia. The agreement included military restrictions and debt payments.

Weimar Germany (1918–1929)

The dramatic collapse of the German war effort in the second half of 1918 ultimately created a political crisis that forced the abdication of the kaiser and the creation of a German Republic on November 9.

From the outset, the Provisional Government, formed by a coalition of Majority and Independent Social Democratic Socialists, was beset by divisions from within and threats of revolution throughout Germany.

Elections for the new National Constituent Assembly, which was to be based on proportional representation, gave no party a clear majority. A coalition of the Majority Socialists, the Catholic Center party, and the German Democratic party (DDP) dominated the new assembly. On February 11, 1919, the assembly met in the historic town of Weimar and selected Friedrich Ebert President of Germany. Two days later, Phillip Scheidemann (1865–1939) formed the first Weimar Cabinet and became its first chancellor.

On August 11, 1919, a new constitution was promulgated, which provided for a bicameral legislature.

Politics and Problems of the Weimar Republic (1919–1923)

In an effort of good faith based on hopes of future reparation payment reductions, Germany borrowed heavily and made payments in kind to fulfill its early debt obligations. The result was a spiral of inflation. After the Allied Reparations Commission declared Germany in default on its debt, the French and the Belgians occupied the Ruhr on January 11, 1923.

Chancellor Wilhelm Cuno (1876–1933) encouraged the Ruhr's Germans passively to resist the occupation, and printed worthless marks. The occupation ended on September 26, and helped prompt stronger Allied sympathy to Germany's payment difficulties.

1. Weimar Politics (1919–1923)

From February 1919 to August 1923, Germany had six chancellors. Growing right-wing discontent with the Weimar Government resulted in the assassination of the gifted head of the Catholic Center Party, Matthias Erzberger (1875–1921), on August 29, 1921, and the murder of Foreign Minister Walter Rathenau (1867–1922) on June 24, 1922.

Following the death of President Ebert on February 28, 1925, two ballots were held for a new president, since none of the candidates won a majority on the first vote. On the second ballot on April 26, the Reichsblock, a coalition of Conservative parties, was able to get its candidate elected. War hero Paul von Hindenburg was narrowly elected.

The elections of May 20, 1928, saw the Social Democrats get almost one-third of the popular vote which, blended with other moderate groups, created a stable, moderate majority in the Reichstag, which chose Hermann Müller (1876–1931) as chancellor.

Italy (1919–1925)

Benito Mussolini, formed the Fascio Italiano di Combattimento (Union of Combat) in Milan on March 23, 1919. Socialist strikes and unrest enabled him to convince Italians that he alone could bring stability and prosperity to their troubled country.

The resignation of the Bonomi Cabinet on February 9, 1922, underlined the government's inability to maintain stability. In the meantime, the Fascists seized control of Bologna in May, and Milan in August. In response, Socialist leaders called for a nationwide strike on August 1, 1922; it was stopped by Fascist street violence within 24 hours. On October 24, 1922, Mussolini told followers that if he was not given power, he would "March on Rome." Three days later, Fascists began to seize control of other cities, while 26,000 began to move toward the capital. On October 29, the king, Victor Emmanuel III (1869–1947), asked Mussolini to form a new government as Premier of Italy.

Beginning in 1925, Mussolini arrested opponents, closed newspapers, and eliminated civil liberties in a new reign of terror. Throughout 1926, Mussolini intensified his control over the country with legislation that outlawed strikes and created the syndicalist corporate system. A failed assassination attempt prompted the "Law for the Defense of the State" of November 25, 1926, that created a Special Court to deal with political crimes and introduced the death penalty for threats against the king, his family, or the Head of State.

1. Italian Foreign Policy

Because Italy did not receive its desired portions of Dalmatia at the Paris Peace Conference, Italian nationalist Gabriele D'Annunzio seized Fiume on the Adriatic in the fall of 1919. D'Annunzio's daring gesture as well as his deep sense of Italian national pride deeply affected Mussolini. However, in the atmosphere of detente prevalent in Europe at the time, he agreed to settle the dispute with Yugoslavia in a treaty on January 27, 1924, which ceded most of the port to Italy, and the surrounding area to Yugoslavia.

In the fall of 1923, Mussolini used the assassination of Italian officials, who were working to resolve a Greek-Albanian border dispute, to seize the island of Corfu. Within a month, however, the British and the French convinced him to return the island for an indemnity.

Soviet Russia (1922–1932)

On March 1, 1921, a naval rebellion broke out at the Kronstadt naval base. The Soviet leadership sent Trotsky to put down the rebellion, which he did brutally by March 18.

Vladimir Ilyich Lenin, the founder of the Soviet State, suffered a serious stroke on May 26, 1922, and a second in December of that year. Lenin died on January 21, 1924.

Iosef Vissarionovich Dzugashvili (Joseph Stalin, 1879–1953) took over numerous and, in some cases, seemingly unimportant party organizations after the Revolution and transformed them into important bases of power. Among them were **Politburo** (Political Bureau), which ran the country; the **Orgburo** (Organizational Bureau), which Stalin headed, and which appointed people to positions in groups that implemented Politburo decisions; the Inspectorate (Rabkrin, Commissariat of the Workers' and Peasants' Inspectorate) which tried to eliminate party corruption; and the Secretariat, which worked with all party organs and set the Politburo's agenda. Stalin served as the party's General Secretary after 1921.

Lev Davidovich Bronstein (Trotsky, 1879–1940) was Chairman of the Petrograd Soviet, headed the early Brest-Litovsk negotiating team, served as Foreign Commissar, and was father of the Red Army.

In China the Soviets helped found a young Chinese Communist party (CCP) in 1921. When it became apparent that Sun Yat-sen's (1866–1925) revolutionary Kuomintang (KMT) was more mature than the infant CCP, the Soviets encouraged an alliance between its party and this movement. Sun's successor, Chiang Kai-shek (1887–1975), was deeply suspicious of the Communists and made their destruction part of his effort to militarily unite China.

Founded in 1919, the Soviet-controlled **Comintern** (Third International or Communist International) sought to coordinate the revolutionary activities of Communist parties abroad.

Europe in Crisis: Depression and Dictatorship (1929–1935)

In Great Britain in 1929, Ramsay MacDonald formed a minority Labour government that would last until 1931. The most serious problem facing the country was the Depression, which caused unemployment to reach 1,700,000 by 1930 and over 3 million, or 25% of the labor force, by 1932. The government fell on August 24, 1931.

The "National Government" (1931–1935)

The following day, King George VI (1895–1952) helped convince MacDonald to return to office as head of a National Coalition cabinet made up of four Conservatives, four Labourites, and two Liberals. MacDonald's coalition swept the November 1931 general elections, winning 554 of 615 seats.

MacDonald resigned his position in June 1935 because of ill health and was succeeded by Stanley Baldwin, whose conservative coalition won 428 seats in new elections in November.

France: Return of the Cartel des Gauches (1932–1934)

The Socialists in France advocated nationalization of major factories, expanded social reforms, and public works programs for the unemployed, while the Radicals sought a reduction in government spending. The government's inability to deal with the country's economic and political problems saw the emergence of a number of radical groups from across the political spectrum.

Germany: The Depression

The Depression had a dramatic effect on the German economy and politics. The country's national income dropped 20% between 1928 and 1932, while unemployment rose from 1,320,000 in 1929 to 6 million by January 1932. This meant that 43% of the German work force were without jobs (compared to one-quarter of the work force in the United States).

In 1919, Adolf Hitler joined the German Workers party (DAP), which he soon took over and renamed the National Socialist German Workers party (Nazi). In 1920, the party adopted a 25-point program that included treaty revision, anti-Semitism, economic, and other social changes. They also created a defense cadre of the *Sturm-abteilung* (SA)—"Storm Troopers" or "brown shirts"—which was to help the party seize power.

In the midst of the country's severe economic crisis in 1923, the party tried to seize power, first by a march on Berlin, and then on Munich (The Beer Hall Putsch). Though sentenced to five years imprisonment, Hitler was released after eight months. While incarcerated, he dictated *Mein Kampf* to Rudolf Hess.

Hitler's failed coup and imprisonment convinced him to seek power through legitimate political channels, which would require transforming the Nazi party. Hindenburg's seven-year presidential term expired in 1932, and he was convinced to run for reelection to stop Hitler from becoming president in the first ballot of March 13. Hitler got only 30% of the vote (11.3 million) to Hindenburg's 49.45% (18.6 million).

On June 1, Chancellor Bruenig was replaced by Franz von Papen (1879–1969), who formed a government made up of aristocratic conservatives and others that he and Hindenburg hoped would keep Hitler from power. Later in the year, Von Papen convinced Hindenburg to appoint Hitler as chancellor and head of a new coalition cabinet with three seats for the Nazis. Hitler dissolved the Reichstag and called for new elections on March 5. Using presidential decree powers, he initiated a violent anti-Communist campaign that included the lifting of certain press and civil freedoms. On February 27, the Reichstag burned, which enabled Hitler to get Hindenburg to issue the "Ordinances for the Protection of the German State and Nation," that removed all civil and press liberties as part of a "revolution" against communism. In the Reichstag elections of March 5, the Nazis only got 43.9% of the vote and 288 Reichstag seats but, through an alliance with the Nationalists, got majority control of the legislature.

Once Hitler had full legislative power, he began a policy of *Gleichschaltung* (coordination) to bring all independent organizations and agencies throughout Germany under his control. All political parties were outlawed or forced to dissolve, and on July 14, 1933, the Nazi party became the only legal party in Germany. In addition, non-Aryans and Nazi opponents were removed from the civil service, the court system, and higher education. On May 2, 1933, the government declared strikes illegal, abolished labor unions, and later forced all workers to join the German Labor Front (DAF) under Robert Ley. In 1934 the Reichsrat was abolished and a special People's Court was created to handle cases of treason. Finally, the secret police or Gestapo (*Geheime Staatspolizei*) was created on April 24, 1933, under Hermann Göring to deal with opponents and operate concentration camps. The party had its own security branch, the SD (*Sicherheitsdienst*) under Reinhard Heydrich.

From the inception of the Nazi state in 1933, anti-Semitism was a constant theme and practice in all *Gleichschaltung* and nazification efforts. The first wave of anti-Semitic activity culminated with the passage of the Nuremburg Laws on September 15, 1935, that deprived Jews of German citizenship and outlawed sexual or marital relations between Jews and other Germans.

The Reich simultaneously quit the League of Nations. On January 26, 1934, Germany signed a non-aggression pact with Poland, which ended Germany's traditional anti-Polish foreign policy and broke France's encirclement of Germany via the Little Entente. This was followed by the Saarland's overwhelming decision to return to Germany. The culmination of Hitler's foreign policy moves, though, came with his March 15, 1935, announcement that Germany would no longer be bound by the military restrictions of the Treaty of Versailles, that it had already created an air force (Luftwaffe), and that the Reich would institute a draft to create an army of 500,000 men.

Italy (1926–1936)

In 1926, Mussolini's government, through the Lateran Accords of February 11, 1929, recognized the Vatican as an independent state, with the pope as its head, while the papacy recognized Italian independence.

In an effort to counter the significance of France's Little Entente with Czechoslovakia, Yugoslavia, and Romania, Mussolini concluded the Rome Protocols with Austria and Hungary which created a protective bond of friendship between the three countries.

In response to Hitler's announcement of German rearmament in violation of the Treaty of Versailles on March 16, 1935, France, England, and Italy met at Stresa in northern Italy on April 11–14, and concluded agreements that pledged joint military collaboration if Germany moved against Austria or along the Rhine.

Ethiopia (Abyssinia) was slowly brought under Italian control until the Italian defeat at Ethiopian hands at Adowa in 1894. In 1906, the country's autonomy was recognized and in 1923 it joined the League of Nations. Mussolini, established a military base at Wal Wal in Ethiopian territory. Beginning in December 1934, a series of minor conflicts took place between the two countries.

On October 2, 1935, Italy invaded Ethiopia, while the League of Nations finally voted to adopt economic sanctions against Mussolini. Unfortunately, the League failed to stop shipments of oil to Italy and continued to allow it to use the Suez Canal. On May 9, 1936, Italy formally annexed the country and joined it to Somalia and Eritrea, which now became known as Italian East Africa.

Soviet Russia (1933–1938)

The Second Five Year Plan (1933–1937) was adopted by the Seventeenth Party Congress in early 1934. Its economic and production targets were less severe than the First Plan; thus, more was achieved. By the end of the Second Plan, Soviet Russia had emerged as a leading world industrial power, though at great costs.

In the spring of 1935, the recently renamed and organized secret police, the NKVD, oversaw the beginnings of a new, violent purge that eradicated 70% of the 1934 Central Committee, and a large percentage of the upper military ranks. Stalin sent between 8 and 9 million to camps and prisons, and caused untold deaths before the purges ended in 1938.

Stalin remained sensitive to growing aggression and ideological threats abroad such as the Japanese invasion of Manchuria in 1931 and Hitler's appointment as chancellor in 1933. As a result, Russia left its cocoon in 1934, joined the League of Nations, and became an advocate of "collective security" while the Comintern adopted Popular Front tactics, allying with other parties against fascism, to strengthen the U.S.S.R.'s international posture.

International Developments (1918–1935)

Efforts to create an international body to arbitrate international conflicts gained credence with the creation of a Permanent Court of International Justice to handle such matters at the First Hague Conference (1899). But no major efforts toward this goal were initiated until 1915, when pro-League of Nations organizations arose in the United States and Great Britain. Support for such a body grew as the war lengthened, and creation of such an organization became the cornerstone of President Woodrow Wilson's post-war policy, enunciated in his "Fourteen Points" speech before Congress on January 8, 1918.

The Preamble of the League's Covenant defined the League's purposes, which were to work for international friendship, peace, and security. To attain this, its members agreed to avoid war, maintain peaceful relations with other countries, and honor international law and accords.

Headquartered in Geneva, the League came into existence as the result of an Allied resolution on January 25, 1919, and the signing of the Treaty of Versailles on June 28, 1919. The League had the right, according to Article 8 of the League Covenant, to seek ways to reduce arms strength, while Articles 10 through 17 gave it the authority to search for means to stop war.

The Locarno Pact (1925)

Signed on October 16, 1925, by England, France, Italy, Germany, and Belgium, the Locarno Pact guaranteed Germany's western boundaries and accepted the Versailles settlement's demilitarized zones. The Locarno Pact went into force when Germany joined the League on September 10, 1926, acquiring, after some dispute, the U.S.'s permanent seat on the Council.

Germany, also signed arbitration dispute accords that mirrored the Geneva Protocol with France, Belgium, Poland, and Czechoslovakia, and required acceptance of League-determined settlements. Since Germany would only agree to arbitration and not finalize its eastern border, France separately signed guarantees with Poland and Czechoslovakia to defend their frontiers.

The Pact of Paris (Kellogg-Briand Pact)

The "**Era of Locarno**" marked the end of post-war conflict and the beginning of a more normal period of diplomatic friendship and cooperation. It reached its peak with the Franco-American effort in 1928 to seek an international statement to outlaw war. On August 27, 1928, 15 countries, including the United States, Germany, France, Italy, and Japan, signed this accord with some minor limitations, which renounced war as a means of solving differences and as a tool of national policy. Within five years, 50 other countries signed the agreement.

League and Allied Response to Aggression

On September 19, 1931, the Japanese Kwantung Army began the gradual conquest of Manchuria after fabricating an incident at Mukden to justify their actions. Ultimately, they created a puppet state, Manchukuo, under the last Chinese emperor, Henry P'u-i. China's League protest resulted in the creation of an investigatory commission under the Earl of Lytton that criticized Japan's actions and recommended a negotiated settlement that would have allowed Japan to retain most of its conquest. Japan responded by resigning from the League on January 24, 1933.

Hitler's announcement on March 15, 1935, of Germany's decisions to rearm and to introduce conscription in violation of the Treaty of Versailles prompted the leaders of England, France, and Italy to meet in Stresa, Italy (April 11–14). They condemned Germany's actions, underlined their commitment to the Locarno Pact, and re-affirmed the support they collectively gave for Austria's independence in early 1934. Great Britain's decision, however, to separately protect its naval strength vis-à-vis a German buildup in the Anglo-German Naval Treaty of June 18, 1935, effectively compromised the significance of the Stresa Front.

FROM WORLD WAR II TO THE POST-COMMUNIST ERA (1935–1996)

The Course of Events

On March 7, 1936, Hitler repudiated the Locarno agreements and reoccupied the Rhineland (an area demilitarized by the Versailles Treaty). Neither France (which possessed military superiority at the time) nor Britain was willing to oppose these moves.

The Spanish Civil War (1936–1939) is usually seen as a rehearsal for World War II because of outside intervention. Following an election victory by a popular front of republican and radical parties, right-wing generals began a military insurrection. Francisco Franco, stationed at the time in Spanish Morocco, emerged as the leader of this revolt.

The democracies, including the United States, followed a course of neutrality. Nazi Germany, Italy, and the U.S.S.R. did intervene despite non-intervention agreements negotiated by Britain and France. Spain became a battlefield for fascist and anti-fascist forces with Franco winning by 1939 in what was seen as a serious defeat for anti-fascist forces everywhere.

The Spanish Civil War was a factor in bringing together Mussolini and Hitler in a Rome-Berlin Axis. Already Germany and Japan had signed the Anti-Comintern Pact in 1936. Ostensibly directed against international communism, this was the basis for a diplomatic alliance between those countries, and Italy soon adhered to this agreement, becoming Germany's ally in World War II.

In 1938 Hitler pressured the Austrian chancellor to make concessions. When this did not work, German troops annexed Austria (the *Anschluss*). Again Britain and France took no effective action, and about six million Austrians were added to Germany.

Hitler turned next to Czechoslovakia. In 1938, after a series of demands from Hitler, a four-power conference was held in Munich with Hitler, Mussolini, Chamberlain, and Daladier in attendance, at which Hitler's terms were accepted. Hitler signed a treaty agreeing to this settlement as the limit of his ambitions. At the same time the Poles seized control of Teschen, and Hungary (with the support of Italy and Germany and over the protests of the British and French) seized 7,500 square miles of Slovakia.

In March 1939, Hitler annexed most of the Czech state while Hungary conquered Ruthenia. At almost the same time Germany annexed Memel from Lithuania. In April, Mussolini, taking advantage of distractions created by Germany, landed an army in Albania and seized that Balkan state in a campaign lasting about one week.

Disillusioned by these continued aggressions, Britain and France made military preparations. The two democracies also opened negotiations with the U.S.S.R. for an arrangement to obtain that country's aid against further German aggression. Hitler, with Poland next on his timetable, also began a cautious rapprochement with the U.S.S.R. On August 23, 1939, the world was stunned by the announcement of a Nazi-Soviet Treaty of friendship. A secret protocol provided that in the event of a "territorial rearrangement" in Eastern Europe the two powers would divide Poland. In addition, Russia would have the Baltic states (Latvia, Lithuania, and Estonia) and Bessarabia (lost to Romania in 1918) as part of her sphere. Stalin agreed to remain neutral in any German war with Britain or France. World War II began with the German invasion of Poland on September 1, 1939, followed by British and French declarations of war against Germany on September 3.

World War II

The German attack (known as the "blitzkrieg" or "lightning war") overwhelmed the poorly equipped Polish army, which could not resist German tanks and airplanes.

On September 17 the Russian armies attacked the Poles from the east. They met the Germans two days later. Stalin's share of Poland extended approximately to the Curzon Line. Russia also made demands on Finland. Later, in June 1940, while Germany was attacking France, Stalin occupied the Baltic states of Latvia, Lithuania, and Estonia.

On May 10, the main German offensive was launched against France. Belgium and the Netherlands were simultaneously attacked. According to plan, British and French forces advanced to aid the Belgians. At this point the Germans departed from the World War I strategy by launching a surprise armored attack through Luxembourg and the Ardennes Forest. The Dutch could offer no real resistance and collapsed in four days after the May 13 German bombing of Rotterdam.

Paris fell to the Germans in mid-June. The Pétain government quickly made peace with Hitler. The complete collapse of France quickly came as a tremendous shock to the British and Americans.

Mussolini declared war on both France and Britain on June 10. Hitler's forces remained in occupation of the northern part of France, including Paris. He allowed the French to keep their fleet and overseas territories, probably in the hope of making them reliable allies. Pétain and his chief minister Pierre Laval established their capital at Vichy and followed a policy of collaboration with their former enemies. A few Frenchmen, however, joined the Free French movement started in London by the then relatively unknown General Charles de Gaulle (1890–1970).

From the French Defeat to the Invasion of Russia

By mid-summer 1940, Germany, together with its Italian ally, dominated most of Western and Central Europe. Hitler's policy included exploiting areas Germany conquered. Collaborators were used to establish governments subservient to German policy. Germany began the policy of forcibly transporting large numbers of conquered Europeans to work in German war industries. Jews especially were forced into slave labor for the German war effort, and increasingly large numbers were rounded up and sent to concentration camps, where they were systematically murdered as the Nazis carried out Hitler's "final solution" of genocide against European Jewry. Although much was known about this during the war, the full horror of these atrocities was not revealed until Allied troops entered Germany in 1945.

With the fall of France, Britain remained the only power of consequence at war with the Axis. Hitler began preparations for invading Britain ("Operation Sea Lion"). The German Air Force (Luftwaffe) under Herman Göring began its air offensive against the British in the summer of 1940. The Germans concentrated first on British air defenses, then on ports and shipping, and finally in early September they began the attack on London. The Battle of Britain was eventually a defeat for the Germans, who were unable to gain decisive superiority over the British, although they inflicted great damage on both British air defenses and major cities. Despite the damage and loss of life, British morale remained high and necessary war production continued. German losses determined that bombing alone could not defeat Britain.

During the winter of 1940–1941, having given up "Operation Sea Lion," Hitler began to shift his forces to the east for an invasion of Russia ("Operation Bar-barossa"). Russian expansion toward the Balkans dismayed the Germans, who hoped for more influence there themselves.

The German invasion of Russia began June 22, 1941. Along with Finnish, Romanian, Hungarian, and Italian contingents, they surrounded the city of Leningrad (although they never managed to actually capture it) and came within about 25 miles of Moscow. In November the enemy actually entered the suburbs, but then the long supply lines, early winter, and Russian resistance (strong despite heavy losses) brought the invasion to a halt. During the winter a Russian counterattack pushed the Germans back from Moscow and saved the capital.

With the coming of the Great Depression and severe economic difficulties, Japanese militarists gained more and more influence over the civilian government. On September 18, 1931, the Japanese occupied all of Manchuria. On July 7, 1937, a full-scale Sino-Japanese war began with a clash between Japanese and Chinese at the Marco Polo Bridge in Peking (now Beijing). On November 3, 1938, Prince Fumimaro Konoye's (1891–1946) government issued a statement on "A New Order in East Asia." This statement envisaged the integration of Japan, Manchuria (now the puppet state of Manchukuo), and China into one "Greater East Asia Co-Prosperity Sphere" under Japanese leadership. In July 1940, the Konoye government was re-formed with General Hideki Tojo (1884–1948) (Japan's principal leader in World War I) as minister of war.

These events led to worsening relations between Japan, the Soviet Union, and the United States. Despite border clashes with the Russians, Japan avoided any conflict with that state, and Stalin wanted no war with Japan after he became fully occupied with the German invasion. In the few weeks after attacking the United States at Pearl Harbor, Japanese forces were able to occupy strategically important islands (including the Philippines and Dutch East Indies) and territory on the Asian mainland (Malaya, with the British naval base at Singapore, and all of Burma to the border of India).

The Japanese attack brought the United States not only into war in the Pacific, but resulted in German and Italian declarations of war, which meant the total involvement of the United States in World War II.

American involvement in the war was ultimately decisive, for it meant that the greatest industrial power of that time was now arrayed against the Axis powers. The United States became, as President Roosevelt put it, "the arsenal of democracy." American aid was crucial to the immense effort of the Soviet Union. By 1943 supplies and equipment were reaching Russia in considerable quantities.

The German forces launched a second offensive in the summer of 1942. This attack concentrated on the southern part of the front, aiming at the Caucasus and vital oil fields around the Caspian Sea. At Stalingrad on the Volga River the Germans were stopped. With the onset of winter, Hitler refused to allow the strategic retreat urged by his generals. As a result, the Russian forces crossed the river north and south of the city and surrounded 22 German divisions. On January 31, 1943, the German commander Friedrich Paulus (1890–1957) surrendered the remnants of his army.

After entering the war in 1940, the Italians invaded British-held Egypt. In December 1940, the British General Archibald Wavell (1883–1950) launched a surprise attack. The Italian forces were driven back about 500 miles and 130,000 were captured. Then Hitler intervened, sending General Erwin Rommel with a small German force (the Afrika Korps) to reinforce the Italians.

A change in the British high command now placed General Harold Alexander (1891–1969) in charge of Middle Eastern forces, with General Bernard Montgomery (1887–1976) in immediate command of the British Eighth Army. Montgomery attacked at El Alamein, breaking Rommel's lines and starting a British advance which was not stopped until the armies reached the border of Tunisia.

Meanwhile, the British and American leaders decided that they could launch a second offensive in North Africa ("Operation Torch") which would clear the enemy from the entire coast and make the Mediterranean once again safe for Allied shipping. It was only a matter of time before German troops were forced into northern Tunisia and surrendered. The final victory came in May 1943, about the same time as the Russian victory at Stalingrad.

Relatively safe shipping routes across the North Atlantic to Britain were essential to the survival of Britain and absolutely necessary if a force was to be assembled to invade France and strike at Germany proper. New types of aircraft, small aircraft carriers, more numerous and better-equipped escort vessels, new radar and sonar (for underwater detection), extremely efficient radio direction finding, decipherment of German signals, plus the building of more ships, turned the balance against the Germans despite their development of improved submarines by early 1943.

Success in these three campaigns—Stalingrad, North Africa, and the Battle of the Atlantic—made certain that victory was attainable. With the beginning of an Allied offensive in late 1942 in the Solomon Islands against the Japanese, 1943 became the turning point of the war.

At their conference at Casablanca in January 1943, Roosevelt and Churchill developed a detailed strategy for the further conduct of the war. Sicily was to be invaded, then Italy proper. Rome was not captured by the Allied forces until June 4, 1944. With a new Italian government now supporting the

Allied cause, Italian resistance movements in northern Italy became a major force in helping to liberate that area from the Germans.

At the Teheran Conference, held in November 1943 and attended by all three major Allied leaders, Roosevelt and Churchill communicated their plan to invade France to the Russians. Stalin promised to open a simultaneous Russian offensive.

The Normandy invasion ("Operation Overlord") was the largest amphibious operation in history. The landings actually took place beginning June 6, 1944. The first day, 130,000 men were successfully landed. Strong German resistance hemmed in the Allied forces for about a month. Then the Allies, now numbering about 1,000,000, managed a spectacular breakthrough. By the end of 1944, all of France had been seized. A second invasion force landed on the Mediterranean coast in August, freed southern France, and linked up with Eisenhower's forces. By the end of 1944, the Allied armies stood on the borders of Germany ready to invade from both east and west.

Stalin's armies crossed into Poland July 23, 1944. Three days later, the Russian dictator officially recognized a group of Polish Communists (the so-called Lublin Committee) as the government of Poland. As the Russian armies drew near the eastern suburbs of Warsaw, the London Poles, a resistance group, launched an attack. Stalin's forces waited outside the city while the Germans brought in reinforcements and slowly wiped out the Polish underground army in several weeks of heavy street fighting. The offensive then resumed and the city was liberated by the Red Army, but the influence of the London Poles was now virtually nil.

By late summer of 1944, the German position in the Balkans began to collapse. The Red Army crossed the border into Romania, leading King Michael (1921–) to seize the opportunity to take his country out of its alliance with Germany and to open the way to the advancing Russians. German troops were forced to make a hasty retreat. At this point Bulgaria changed sides. The German forces in Greece withdrew in October.

From October 9–18, Winston Churchill visited Moscow to try to work out a political arrangement regarding the Balkans and Eastern Europe. Dealing from a position of weakness, he simply wrote out some figures on a sheet of paper: Russia to have the preponderance of influence in countries like Bulgaria and Romania, Britain to have the major say in Greece, and a fifty-fifty division in Yugoslavia and Hungary. Stalin agreed. The Americans refused to have anything to do with this "spheres of influence" arrangement.

In early spring of 1945 the Allied armies crossed the Rhine. As the Americans, British, and other Allied forces advanced into Germany, the Russians attacked from the east. While the Russian armies were fighting their way into Berlin, Hitler committed suicide in the ruins of the bunker where he had spent the last days of the war. Power was handed over to a government headed by Admiral Karl Dönitz (1891–1980). On May 7, General Alfred Jodl (1890–1946), acting for the German government, made the final unconditional surrender at General Eisenhower's headquarters near Reims.

The future treatment of Germany, and Europe in general, was determined by decisions of the "Big Three" (Churchill, Stalin, and Roosevelt). The first major conference convened at Teheran on November 28, 1943, and lasted until December 1. Here the two Western allies told Stalin of the May 1944 date for the planned invasion of Normandy. In turn, Stalin confirmed a pledge made earlier that Russia would enter the war against Japan after the war with Germany was concluded. The Yalta Conference, the second attended personally by Stalin, Churchill, and Roosevelt, lasted from February 4 to 11, 1945. A plan to divide Germany into zones of occupation, which had been devised in 1943 by a committee under British Deputy Prime Minister Clement Attlee, was formally accepted with the addition of a fourth zone taken from the British and American zones for the French to occupy. Berlin, which lay within the Russian Zone, was also divided into four zones of occupation.

The third summit meeting of the Big Three took place July 17, 1945, at Potsdam outside Berlin after the end of the European war but while the Pacific war was still going on. A Potsdam Declaration, aimed at Japan, called for immediate Japanese surrender and hinted at the consequences that would ensue if it were not forthcoming. While at the conference, American leaders received the news of the successful testing of the first atomic bomb in the New Mexico desert, but the Japanese were given no clear warning.

On August 6, 1945, the bomb was dropped by a single plane on Hiroshima and an entire city disappeared, with the instantaneous loss of 70,000 lives. Since no surrender was received, a second bomb was dropped on Nagasaki, obliterating that city. Even the most fanatical of the Japanese leaders saw what was happening and surrender came quickly. The only departure from unconditional surrender was to allow the Japanese to retain their emperor (Hirohito, 1901–1989), but only with the proviso that he would be subject in every respect to the orders of the occupation commander. The formal surrender took place September 2, 1945, in Tokyo Bay on the deck of the battleship *Missouri*, and the occupation of Japan began under the immediate control of the American commander General Douglas MacArthur (1880–1964).

Europe after World War II: 1945–1953

The Atlantic Charter was a general statement of Anglo-American post-war goals: restoration of the sovereignty and self-government of nations conquered by Hitler, free access to world trade and resources, cooperation to improve living standards and economic security, and a peace that would ensure freedom from fear and want and stop the use of force and aggression as instruments of national policy.

At the Casablanca Conference, the Allies announced the policy of requiring unconditional surrender by the Axis powers. This ensured that at the end of the war, all responsibility for government of the defeated nations would fall on the victors, and they would have a free hand in rebuilding government in those countries.

At Teheran, the Big Three did generally discuss the occupation and demilitarization of Germany. They also laid the foundation for a post-war organization—the United Nations Organization—which, like the earlier League of Nations, was supposed to help regulate international relations, keep the peace, and ensure friendly cooperation between the nations of the world.

In 1946 and 1947 treaties were signed with Italy, Romania, Hungary, Bulgaria, and Finland. These states paid reparations and agreed to some territorial readjustments as a price for peace. No agreement could be reached on Japan or Germany. In 1951, the Western powers led by the United States concluded a treaty with Japan without Russian participation. The latter made their own treaty in 1956. A final meeting of the Council of Foreign Ministers broke up in 1947 over Germany, and no peace treaty was ever signed with that country. The division of Germany for purposes of occupation and military government became permanent, with the three Western zones joining and eventually becoming the Federal Republic of Germany and the Russian zone becoming the German Democratic Republic.

Arrangements for the United Nations were confirmed at the Yalta Conference: the large powers would predominate in a Security Council, where they would have permanent seats together with several other powers elected from time to time from among the other members of the U.N. Consent of all the permanent members was necessary for any action to be taken by the Security Council (thus, giving the large powers a veto). The General Assembly was to include all members.

Eastern Europe: 1945–1953

Much of European Russia had been devastated by the war, and about 25 million people made homeless. In March 1946 a fourth five-year plan was adopted by the Supreme Soviet intended to increase industrial output to a level 50% higher than before the war. At the same time a drastic currency devaluation was put through, which brought immediate hardship to many people but strengthened the Soviet economy in the long run. As a result of these and other forceful and energetic measures, the Soviet Union was able within a few years to make good most of the wartime damage and to surpass pre-war levels of production.

Communization of Eastern Europe and the establishment of regimes in the satellite areas of the Soviet Union occurred in stages over a three-year period following the end of the war.

As relations broke down between the four occupying powers, the Soviet authorities gradually created a Communist state in their zone. On October 7, 1948, a German Democratic Republic was established. In June 1950, an agreement with Poland granted formal recognition of the Oder-Neisse Line as the boundary between the two states. On June 16–17, 1953, riots occurred in East Berlin which were suppressed by Soviet forces using tanks.

In Yugoslavia, Marshal Tito (1892–1980) and his Communist partisan movement emerged from the war in a strong position because of their effective campaign against the German occupation. Tito was able to establish a Communist government in 1945 despite considerable pressure from Stalin.

Western Europe: 1945–1953

The monarchy which had governed Italy since the time of unification in the mid-nineteenth century was now discarded in favor of a republic. King Victor Emmanuel III (1869–1947), compromised by his association with Mussolini, resigned in favor of his son, but a referendum in June 1946 established a republic. In simultaneous elections for a constituent assembly, three parties predominated: the Social Democrats, the Communists, and the Christian Democrats.

In the last two years of the war, France recovered sufficiently under the leadership of General Charles de Gaulle to begin playing a significant military and political role once again. In July 1944, the United States recognized de Gaulle's Committee of National Liberation as the de facto government of areas liberated from the German occupation.

In foreign affairs, France occupied Germany. In addition, the Fourth Republic was faced with two major problems abroad when it attempted to assert its authority over Indochina and Algeria. The Indochina situation resulted in a long and costly war against nationalists and Communists under Ho Chi Minh (1890–1969). French involvement ended with the Geneva Accords of 1954 and French withdrawal. The Algerian struggle reached a crisis in 1958 resulting in General de Gaulle's return to power and the creation of a new Fifth Republic.

In May 1945, when Germany surrendered unconditionally, the country lay in ruins. Economic chaos was the rule, currency was virtually worthless, food was in short supply, and the black market flourished for those who could afford to buy in it. By the Potsdam agreements, Germany lost about one-quarter of its pre-war territory. In addition, some 12 million people of German origin driven from their homes in countries like Poland and Czechoslovakia had to be fed, housed, and clothed along with the indigenous population.

Demilitarization, denazification, and democratization were the initial goals of the occupation forces in Germany. All four wartime allies agreed on the trial of leading Nazis for a variety of war crimes and "crimes against humanity." An International Military Tribunal was established at Nuremburg to try 22 major war criminals, and lesser courts tried many others. Most of the defendants were executed, although a few like Rudolf Hess were given life imprisonment.

In February 1948, a charter granted further powers of government to the Germans in the American and British zones. Later that year, the Russians and East Germans, in an effort to force the Western powers out of their zones in Berlin, began a blockade of the city which was located within the Russian zone. The response was an allied airlift to supply the city; eventually, the blockade was called off.

In 1951 a Conservative majority was returned in Great Britain, and Winston Churchill, who had been defeated in 1945, became prime minister again. In April 1955, Churchill resigned for reasons of age and health and turned over the prime minister's office to Anthony Eden (1897–1977).

The Marshall Plan

European recovery was slow for the first two or three years after 1945. The European Recovery Program (**Marshall Plan**, named after the American secretary of state and World War II army chief of staff) began in 1948 and showed substantial results in all the Western European countries that took part. The most remarkable gains were in West Germany. The Plan aimed to strengthen Western Europe's resistance to communism.

NATO

The United States joined 11 other states in the Atlantic region in a mutual defense pact called the North Atlantic Treaty Organization (NATO) in 1949. NATO was created to counterbalance the Soviet presence in Central and Eastern Europe.

British Overseas Withdrawal

Following World War II, there was a considerable migration of Jews who had survived the Nazi Holocaust to Palestine to join Jews who had settled there earlier. Conflicts broke out with the Arabs. The British occupying forces tried to suppress the violence and to negotiate a settlement between the factions. In 1948, after negotiations failed, the British, announced their withdrawal. Zionist leaders then proclaimed the independent state of Israel and took up arms to fight the armies of Egypt, Syria, and other Arab states which invaded the Jewish-held area.

The Jews of Israel created a modern parliamentary state on the European model with an economy and technology superior to their Arab neighbors. The new state was thought by many Arabs to be simply another manifestation of European imperialism made worse by religious antagonisms.

In 1967, Israel defeated Egypt, Syria, and Jordan in a six-day war, and the Israelis occupied additional territory including the Jordanian sector of the city of Jerusalem. An additional million Arabs came under Israeli rule as a result of this campaign.

Although defeated, the Arabs refused to sign any treaty or to come to terms with Israel. A Palestine Liberation Organization (PLO) was formed to fight for the establishment of an Arab Palestinian state on territory taken from Israel on the west bank of the Jordan River. The PLO resorted to terrorist tactics against both Israel and other states in support of their cause.

In October 1973, the Egyptians and Syrians launched an attack on Israel known as the Yom Kippur War. With some difficulty the attacks were repulsed. A settlement was mediated by American Secretary of State Henry Kissinger. The situation has remained unstable, however, with both sides resorting to border raids and other forms of violence short of full-scale war.

The government under King Farouk I (1920–1965) did little to alleviate the overriding problem of poverty after the war. In 1952, a group of army officers, including Gamal Abdel Nasser (1918–1970) and Anwar Sadat (1918–1981), plotted against the government, and on July 23 the king was overthrown. Colonel Nasser became premier in April 1954. A treaty with Britain later that year resulted in the withdrawal of all British troops from the Canal Zone.

India under Jawaharlal Nehru (1889–1964) and the Congress Party became a parliamentary democracy. The country made economic progress, but gains were largely negated by a population increase to 600 million from 350 million.

The French in Indochina and Algeria

Following World War II, the French returned to Indochina and attempted to restore their rule there. The opposition nationalist movement was led by the veteran Communist Ho Chi Minh. War broke out between the nationalists and the French forces. In 1954 their army was surrounded at Dienbienphu and forced to surrender. This military disaster prompted a change of government in France.

This new government under Premier Pierre Mendès-France (1907–1982) negotiated French withdrawal at a conference held at Geneva, Switzerland, in 1954. Cambodia and Laos became independent and Vietnam was partitioned at the 17th parallel. The North, with its capital at Hanoi, became a Communist state under Ho Chi Minh. The South remained non-Communist. Eventually a second Vietnamese war resulted, with the United States playing the role earlier played by France.

In a referendum, on January 8, 1961, the French people approved of eventual Algerian self-determination. In July 1962 French rule ended in Algeria, followed by a mass exodus of Europeans from Algeria.

The Dutch and Indonesia

During World War II, the Japanese conquered the Dutch East Indies. At the end of the war, they recognized the independence of the area as Indonesia. When the Dutch attempted to return, four years of bloody fighting ensued against the nationalist forces of Achmed Sukarno (1901–1970). In 1949, the Dutch recognized Indonesian independence. In 1954, the Indonesians dissolved all ties with the Netherlands.

The Cold War after the Death of Stalin

Following Stalin's death in 1953, Russian leaders appeared more willing than Stalin to be conciliatory and to consider peaceful coexistence.

In the United States the atmosphere also changed with the election of President Dwight Eisenhower. In 1955 a summit conference of Eisenhower, the British and French leaders, and Khrushchev (1894–1971) met at Geneva in an atmosphere more cordial than any since World War II. The "spirit of Geneva" did not last long, however.

After his return to power in France in 1958, General de Gaulle endeavored to make France a leader in European affairs. Despite his prestige as the last great wartime leader, he did not have great success.

A New Era Begins

Joseph Stalin died in March 1953. Eventually a little-known party functionary, Nikita Khrushchev, became Communist Party General Secretary in 1954. Khrushchev's policy of relaxing the regime of terror and oppression of the Stalin years became known as "The Thaw," after the title of a novel by Ilya Ehrenburg (1891–1967).

Change occurred in foreign affairs also. Khrushchev visited Belgrade and reestablished relations with Tito. He also visited the United States, met with President Eisenhower, and toured the country. Later, relations became more tense after the U-2 spy plane incident.

Following the loss of face sustained by Russia as a result of the Cuban Missile Crisis and the failure of Khrushchev's domestic agricultural policies, he was forced out of the party leadership and lived in retirement in Moscow until his death in 1971.

After Khrushchev's ouster, the leadership in the Central Committee divided power, making Leonid Brezhnev (1906–1982) party secretary and Aleksei Kosygin chairman of the council of ministers, or premier.

Stalin's successors permitted somewhat greater freedom in literary and artistic matters and even allowed some political criticism. Controls were maintained, however, and sometimes were tightened. Anti-Semitism was also still present, and Soviet Jews were long denied permission to emigrate to Israel.

Brezhnev occupied the top position of power until his death in 1982. He was briefly succeeded by Yuri Andropov (1914–1984) (a former secret police chief) and Konstantin Chenenko (1911–1985), then by Mikhail Gorbachev, who carried out a further relaxation of the internal regime. Gorbachev pushed disarmament and detente in foreign relations, and attempted a wide range of internal reforms known as *perestroika* ("restructuring"). Gorbachev resigned in 1991. Boris Yeltsin assumed control over the collapsing Soviet Union, which would later become known as the Commonwealth of Independent States, with Yeltsin as president.

Economic difficulties associated with a transition to a free economy, the mishandled repression of the Chechnya independence movement, and the forceful dispersal of Yeltsin's parliamentary opponents in 1993 gave ammunition to Yeltsin's opponents. In the 1996 elections, Yeltsin retained office as president, but the poor state of his health, despite successful heart bypass surgery in the fall of 1996, eventually made him step down and yield leadership to Vladimir Putin in late 1999.

Change in Eastern Europe

In the 1980s, the trade union movement known as Solidarity and its leader, Lech Walesa, emerged as a political force, organizing mass protests in 1980–1981 and maintaining almost continuous pressure on the government headed by General Wojciech Jaruzelski. In June 1989, after power had passed to the Polish Parliament, a national election gave Solidarity an overwhelming majority, and Walesa assumed the presidency. By 1993–1994, economic problems resulted in a Communist majority and a change of administration, but there was no return to the old Communist dictatorship.

Change in Western Europe

In March 1957, inspired chiefly by Belgian Foreign Minister Paul-Henri Spaak, two treaties were signed in Rome creating a European Atomic Energy Commission (Euratom) and a **European Economic Community** (the Common Market)—which eventually absorbed Euratom. The EEC was to be a customs union creating a free market area with a common external tariff for member nations.

In 1973, the original six were joined by three new members: Britain, Ireland, and Denmark, and the name was changed to "European Community." In 1979, there were three more applicants: Spain, Portugal, and Greece. They were accepted as members in 1986. With the acceptance of the Maastricht treaty in 1993, the group's name became the "European Union."

Relations with Northern Ireland proved a burden to successive British governments. The 1922 settlement had left Northern Ireland as a self-governing part of the United Kingdom. Of 1.5 million inhabitants, one-third were Roman Catholic and two-thirds were Protestant. Catholics claimed they were discriminated against and pressed for annexation by the Republic of Ireland. Activity by the Irish Republican Army brought retaliation by Protestant extremists. From 1969 on, there was considerable violence, causing the British to bring in troops to maintain order.

Under Prime Minister Margaret Thatcher in the 1980s, the British economy improved somewhat. In recent years, an influx of people from former colonies in Asia, Africa, and the West Indies has caused some racial tensions.

Prime Minister Thatcher was a partisan of free enterprise. She fought inflation with austerity and let economic problems spur British employers and unions to change for greater efficiency. She received a boost in popularity when Britain won a brief war with Argentina over the Falkland Islands. She stressed close ties with the Republican administration of Ronald Reagan in the United States. A Conservative victory in the 1987 elections made Thatcher the longest-serving prime minister in modern British history.

In 1990, having lost the support of Conservatives in Parliament, Thatcher resigned and was replaced by Chancellor of the Exchequer John Major. Under Major's leadership, Conservatives had to deal with slow economic growth, unemployment, and racial tensions caused by resentment over the influx of immigrants from other parts of the Commonwealth. And there remains the seemingly intractable religious strife in Northern Ireland, with its Protestant-Catholic animosities. Tony Blair, prime minister from 1997 to 2007, made Northern Ireland peace a priority, with tentative success.

France under de Gaulle saw a new constitution drafted and approved establishing the Fifth Republic with a much strengthened executive in the form of a president with power to dissolve the legislature and call for elections, to submit important questions to popular referendum, and if necessary to assume emergency powers. De Gaulle used all these powers in his 11 years as president.

In domestic politics, de Gaulle strengthened the power of the president by often using the referendum and bypassing the Assembly. De Gaulle was re-elected in 1965, but people became restless with what amounted to a republican monarch. In May 1968, student grievances over conditions in the universities caused hundreds of thousands to revolt. They were soon joined by some 10 million workers, who paralyzed the economy. De Gaulle survived by promising educational reform and wage increases. New elections were held in June 1968, and de Gaulle was returned to power. Promised reforms were begun, but in April 1969, he resigned and died about a year later.

De Gaulle's immediate successors were Georges Pompidou (1969–1974) and Valéry Giscard d'Estaing (1974–1981). Both provided France with firm leadership, and continued to follow an independent foreign policy.

In 1981 François Mitterand inherited a troubled French economy. During his first year Mitterand tried to revitalize economic growth. Loans were made abroad to finance this program. When results were poor, these foreign investors were reluctant to grant more credit. Mitterand then reversed his policy and began to cut taxes and social expenditures.

Mitterand lost his Socialist majority in Parliament in 1986, but regained it in 1988. In 1995, an ailing Mitterand indicated he would retire at the end of his term. He died in January 1996. Out of the election of April 1995 emerged a fractured right-of-center bloc that came to coalesce around Jacques Chirac, the mayor of Paris and former two-time prime minister. Following a second-round runoff, Chirac won 52% of the vote. Chirac won a decisive victory for re-election in 2002.

In Germany in November 1966, the Christian Democrats formed a so-called "great coalition" with the Social Democrats under Willy Brandt. Kurt Georg Kiesinger (1904–1988) became chancellor, and

Brandt the Socialist took over as foreign minister. Brandt announced his intention to work step by step for better relations with East Germany, but found that in a coalition of two very dissimilar parties he could make no substantial progress.

Problems with the economy and the environment brought an end to Kiesinger's chancellorship and the rule of the Socialists in 1982. A loosely organized coalition of environmentalists alienated from society, called the Greens, detracted from Socialist power. In 1982, the German voters turned to the more conservative Christian Democrats again, and Helmut Kohl became chancellor. Kohl served until 1998, when he was replaced by Social Democrat Gerhard Schroeder.

In Italy, the Christian Democrats, who were closely allied with the Roman Catholic Church, dominated the national scene. Their organization, though plagued by corruption, did provide some unity to Italian politics by supplying the prime ministers for numerous coalitions.

Italy advanced economically. Unfortunately, business efficiency found no parallel in the government or civil service. Italy suffered from terrorism, kidnappings, and assassinations by extreme radical groups such as the Red Brigades. These agitators hoped to create conditions favorable to the overthrow of the democratic constitution. The most notorious terrorist act was the 1978 assassination of Aldo Moro (1916–1978), a respected Christian Democratic leader.

In 1983, Bettino Craxi (Socialist) became prime minister at the head of an uneasy coalition that lasted four years—the longest single government in post-war Italian history. By the 1990s Italian industry and its economy had advanced to a point where Italy was a leading center in high-tech industry, fashion, design, and banking, but instability continued to mark Italian politics. In 1993 the electoral system for the Senate was changed from proportional representation to one that gives power to the majority vote-getting party. The 1994 elections for Parliament brought to power the charismatic, conservative Silvio Berlusconi and his *Forzia Italia* ("Let's go, Italy") movement.

In Portugal, Europe's longest right-wing dictatorship came to an end in September 1968, when a stroke incapacitated Antonio Salazar, who died two years later. A former collaborator, Marcelo Caetano (1906–1980), became prime minister, and an era of change began. Censorship was relaxed and some freedom was given to political parties.

In April 1974, the Caetano regime was overthrown and a "junta of national salvation" took over, headed by General Spinola, who later retired and went into exile. Portugal went through a succession of governments. Its African colonies of Mozambique and Angola were finally granted independence in 1975. Portugal joined the Common Market in 1986.

Spain's Francisco Franco, who had been ruler of a fascist regime since the end of the Civil War in 1939, held on until he was close to 70. He then designated the Bourbon prince, Juan Carlos, to be his successor. In 1975, Franco relinquished power and died three weeks later. Juan Carlos proved an able leader and took the country from dictatorship to constitutional monarchy. Basque and Catalan separatist movements, which had caused trouble for so long, were temporarily appeased by the granting of limited local autonomy. Spain also entered the European Community in 1986.

Under the Maastricht Treaties of 1991, all members of the EC began measured steps toward an economic and political union that would ultimately have its own common currency. In 1996, the 12 member nations of the European Union accounted for one-fifth of world trade.

AMERICAN HISTORY: THE COLONIAL PERIOD (1500–1763)

The Age of Exploration

The Treaty of Tordesillas (1494) drew a line dividing the land in the New World between Spain and Portugal. Lands east of the line were Portuguese. Spain administered its new holdings as an autocratic, rigidly controlled empire in which everything was to benefit the parent country. The Spaniards developed a system of large manors or estates (**encomiendas**), with Indian slaves ruthlessly managed for the benefit of the conquistadores (Spanish adventurers). The encomienda system was later replaced by the similar but somewhat milder **hacienda** system. As the Indian population died from overwork and European diseases, Spaniards began importing African slaves to supply their labor needs.

English and French Beginnings

In 1497, the Italian John Cabot (Giovanni Caboto, ca. 1450–1499), sailing under the sponsorship of the king of England in search of a Northwest Passage (a water route to the Orient through or around the North American continent), became the first European since the Vikings to reach the mainland of North America, which he claimed for England. Beginning in 1534, Jacques Cartier (1491–1557), authorized by the king of France, mounted three expeditions to the area of the St. Lawrence River, which he believed might be the hoped for Northwest Passage. He explored up the river as far as the site of Montreal.

The Beginnings of Colonization

Two groups of merchants gained charters from James I, Queen Elizabeth's successor. One group of merchants the Virginia Company of London, received a charter to North America between what are now the Hudson and the Cape Fear rivers. The other, the Virginia Company of Plymouth, was granted the right to colonize in North America from the Potomac to the northern border of present-day Maine.

The Virginia Company of London settled Jamestown in 1607. It became the first permanent English settlement in North America. During the early years of Jamestown, the majority of the settlers died of starvation, various diseases, or hostile actions by Native Americans. In 1624, King James I revoked the London Company's charter and made Virginia a royal colony. This pattern was followed throughout colonial history; both company colonies and proprietary colonies tended eventually to become royal colonies.

The French opened a lucrative trade in fur with the Native Americans. In 1608, Samuel de Champlain established a trading post in Quebec. French exploration and settlement spread through the Great Lakes region and the valleys of the Mississippi and Ohio rivers. French settlements in the Midwest were generally forts and trading posts serving the fur trade.

In 1609, Holland sent an Englishman named Henry Hudson (d. 1611) to search for a Northwest Passage. In this endeavor, Hudson discovered the river that bears his name. In 1624, Dutch trading outposts were established on Manhattan Island (New Amsterdam) and at the site of present-day Albany (Fort Orange).

Many Englishmen came from England for religious reasons. For the most part, these fell into two groups, **Puritans** and **Separatists**. Though similar in many respects to the Puritans, the Separatists believed the Church of England was beyond saving and so felt they must separate from it.

Led by William Bradford (1590–1657), a group of Separatists departed in 1620. Driven by storms, their ship, the *Mayflower*, made landfall at Cape Cod in Massachusetts. Before going ashore, they drew up and signed the **Mayflower Compact**, establishing a foundation for orderly government based on the consent of the governed. After a number of years of hard work, they were able to buy out the investors who had originally financed their voyage, and thus gain greater autonomy.

The Puritans were far more numerous than the Separatists. Charles I determined in 1629 to persecute the Puritans aggressively and to rule without the Puritan-dominated Parliament. In 1629, they chartered a joint-stock company called the Massachusetts Bay Company. The charter neglected to specify where the company's headquarters should be located. Taking advantage of this unusual omission, the Puritans determined to make their headquarters in the colony itself, 3,000 miles from meddlesome royal officials.

Puritans saw their colony not as a place to do whatever might strike one's fancy, but as a place to serve God and build His kingdom. Dissidents would only be tolerated insofar as they did not interfere with the colony's mission. One such dissident was Roger Williams (ca. 1603–1683). He fled to the wilderness around Narragansett Bay, bought land from the Indians, and founded the settlement of Providence (1636). Another dissident was Anne Hutchinson (1591–1643). She also migrated to the area around Narragansett Bay and, with her followers, founded Portsmouth (1638).

In 1663, Charles II, rewarded eight of the noblemen who had helped him regain the crown by granting them a charter for all the lands lying south of Virginia and north of Spanish Florida. The new colony was called Carolina, after the king.

In 1664, Charles gave his brother James, Duke of York, title to all the Dutch lands in America, provided James conquered them first. New Amsterdam fell almost without a shot and became New York.

The Colonial World

New England enjoyed a much more stable and well-ordered society than did the Chesapeake colonies. New England was ahead of the other colonies educationally and enjoyed extremely widespread literacy. The region developed a prosperous economy based on small farming, home industry, fishing, and especially trade and a large shipbuilding industry. Boston became a major international port.

During the first half of the seventeenth century, blacks in the Chesapeake made up only a small percentage of the population, and were treated more or less as indentured servants. Between 1640 and 1670 this gradually changed, and blacks came to be seen and treated as life-long chattel slaves whose status would be inherited by their children. By 1750, they composed 30–40% of the Chesapeake population.

Beginning around 1650, British authorities began to take more interest in regulating American trade. A key idea was the concept of **mercantilism**. Each nation's goal was to export more than it imported (i.e., to have a "favorable balance of trade"). To achieve their goals, mercantilists believed economic activity should be regulated by the government. Parliament passed a series of Navigation Acts (1651, 1660, 1663, and 1673) to help accomplish these goals.

Pennsylvania was founded as a refuge for **Quakers**. One of a number of radical religious sects that had sprung up about the time of the English Civil War, the Quakers believed all persons had an "inner light" which allowed them to commune directly with God, and therefore they placed little importance on the Bible. They were also pacifists and declined to show customary deference to those who were considered to be their social superiors.

Until the American Revolution, Pennsylvania's proprietary governors also functioned as governors of Delaware.

The Eighteenth Century

America's population continued to grow rapidly, both from natural increases due to prosperity and a healthy environment and from large-scale immigration, not only of English but also of other groups such as Scots-Irish and Germans.

In 1732, a group of British philanthropists, led by General James Oglethorpe (1696–1785), obtained a charter for a colony between South Carolina and Florida which was named Georgia.

France was determined to take complete control of the Ohio Valley and western Pennsylvania. British authorities ordered colonial governors to resist this. George Washington (1732–1799), a young major of the Virginia militia, was sent to western Pennsylvania but was forced by superior numbers to fall back and surrender.

While Washington skirmished with the French, delegates of seven colonies met in Albany, New York, to discuss common plans for defense. Delegate Benjamin Franklin proposed a plan for an intercolonial government. While the other colonies showed no support for the idea, it was an important precedent for the concept of uniting in the face of a common enemy.

Between 1756 and 1763 Britain and France fought the Seven Years' War (also known as the French and Indian War). By the Treaty of Paris of 1763, Britain gained all of Canada and all of what is now the United States east of the Mississippi River. France lost all of its North American holdings.

THE AMERICAN REVOLUTION (1763–1787)
The Coming of the American Revolution

In 1763, George Grenville (1712–1770) became prime minister and set out to solve the large national debt incurred in the recent war. In 1764, Grenville pushed through Parliament the **Sugar Act** (also known as the Revenue Act), which aimed at raising revenue by taxing goods imported by the Americans.

The **Stamp Act** (1765) imposed a direct tax on Americans for the first time. It required Americans to purchase revenue stamps on everything from newspapers to legal documents. Americans reacted first with restrained and respectful petitions and pamphlets in which they pointed out that "taxation without representation is tyranny." From there, resistance progressed to stronger protests that eventually became violent.

In October 1765, delegates from nine colonies met as the **Stamp Act Congress**, and passed moderate resolutions against the act, asserting that Americans could not be taxed without the consent of their representatives.

Colonial merchants' boycott of British goods spread throughout the colonies and had a powerful effect on British merchants and manufacturers, who began clamoring for the act's repeal.

Meanwhile, the fickle King George III had dismissed Grenville and replaced him with a cabinet headed by Charles Lord Rockingham (1730–1782). In March 1766 Parliament repealed the Stamp Act. At the same time, however, it passed the Declaratory Act, which claimed the power to tax or make laws for the Americans "in all cases whatsoever."

The Rockingham ministry was replaced with a cabinet dominated by Chancellor of the Exchequer Charles Townshend (1725–1767). In 1766, Parliament passed his program of taxes on items imported into the colonies, known as the **Townshend duties**.

American reaction was at first slow, but the sending of troops aroused them to resistance. Nonimportation was again instituted, and soon British merchants were calling on Parliament to repeal the acts. In March 1770, Parliament, under the new prime minister, Frederick Lord North (1737–1792), repealed all of the taxes except that on tea.

A relative peace was brought to an end by the Tea Act of 1773. In desperate financial condition—partially because the Americans were buying smuggled Dutch tea rather than the taxed British product—the British East India Company sought and obtained from Parliament concessions that allowed it to ship tea directly to the colonies rather than only by way of Britain. The East India Company would be saved, and the Americans would be tacitly accepting Parliament's right to tax them.

The Americans, however, proved resistant to this approach. Various methods, including tar and feathers, were used to prevent the collection of the tax on tea. In most ports, Americans did not allow the tea to be landed.

In Boston, however, pro-British Governor Thomas Hutchinson (1711–1780) forced a confrontation by ordering Royal Navy vessels to prevent the tea ships from leaving the harbor. On December 16, 1773, Bostonians thinly disguised as Native Americans boarded the ships and threw the tea into the harbor. The British responded with four acts collectively titled the **Coercive Acts**. First, the Boston Port Act closed the port of Boston to all trade until local citizens agreed to pay for the lost tea (they would not). Secondly, the Massachusetts Government Act greatly increased the power of Massachusetts's royal governor at the expense of the legislature. Thirdly, the Administration of Justice Act provided that royal officials accused of crimes in Massachusetts could be tried elsewhere, where chances of acquittal might be greater. Finally, a strengthened Quartering Act allowed the new governor, General Thomas Gage (1721–1787), to quarter his troops anywhere, including unoccupied private homes.

The War for Independence

The British government paid little attention to the First Continental Congress. Orders were sent to General Gage to arrest the leaders of the resistance or, failing that, to provoke any sort of confrontation that would allow him to turn British military might loose on the Americans. Seven hundred British troops set out on the night of April 18, 1775, which resulted in skirmishes with the colonists at Lexington and Concord.

Open warfare had begun. Militia came in large numbers from all the New England colonies to join the force besieging Gage and his army in Boston. The following month the Americans tightened the noose around Boston by fortifying Breed's Hill (a spur of Bunker Hill).

The British determined to remove them by a frontal attack. The British finally succeeded when the Americans ran out of ammunition. Over a thousand British soldiers were killed or wounded in what turned out to be the bloodiest battle of the war (June 17, 1775). Meanwhile in May 1775, American forces under Ethan Allen (1738–1789) and Benedict Arnold (1741–1801) took Fort Ticonderoga on Lake Champlain.

While these events were taking place in New England and Canada, the Second Continental Congress met in Philadelphia in May 1775. Congress was divided into two main factions. One was composed mostly of New Englanders and leaned toward declaring independence from Britain. The other drew its strength primarily from the Middle Colonies and was not yet ready to go that far.

The **Declaration of Independence**, primarily the work of Thomas Jefferson (1743–1826) of Virginia, was a restatement of political ideas by then commonplace in America that showed why the former colonists felt justified in separating from Great Britain. It was formally adopted by Congress on July 4, 1776.

The British landed that summer at New York City. Defeated again at the Battle of Washington Heights (August 29–30, 1776) in Manhattan, Washington was forced to retreat across New Jersey with the aggressive British General Lord Charles Cornwallis (1738–1805) in pursuit.

With his victory almost complete, General Howe decided to wait until spring to finish annihilating Washington's army. Scattering his troops in small detachments so as to hold all of New Jersey, he went into winter quarters.

Washington, with his small army melting away as demoralized soldiers deserted, decided on a bold stroke. On Christmas night 1776, his army crossed the Delaware River and struck the Hessians at Trenton, who were easily defeated. A few days later, Washington defeated a British force at Princeton (January 3, 1777). Much of New Jersey was regained, and Washington's army was saved from disintegration.

Hoping to weaken Britain, France began making covert shipments of arms to the Americans early in the war. The American victory at Saratoga convinced the French to join openly in the war against England. Eventually the Spanish (1779) and the Dutch (1780) joined as well.

Howe was replaced by General Henry Clinton (1738–1795), who was ordered to abandon Philadelphia and march to New York. Clinton maintained New York as Britain's main base. In November 1778, the British easily conquered Georgia. Late the following year, Clinton moved on South Carolina and in May 1780 Charleston surrendered. Clinton then returned to New York, leaving Cornwallis to continue the Southern campaign.

In the west, George Rogers Clark (1752–1818) led an expedition down the Ohio River, defeating a British force at Vincennes, Indiana, and securing the area north of the Ohio River for the United States.

On October 7, 1780, a detachment of Cornwallis's force was defeated by American frontiersmen at the Battle of Kings Mountain. Cornwallis unwisely moved north without bothering to secure South Carolina first. The result was that the British would no sooner leave an area than American militia or guerilla bands, such as that under Francis Marion, "the Swamp Fox" (ca. 1732–1795), were once again in control.

American commander Nathaniel Greene's (1742–1786) brilliant southern strategy led to a crushing victory at Cowpens, South Carolina (January 17, 1781). It also led to a near victory at Guilford Court House, North Carolina (March 15, 1781).

The frustrated and impetuous Cornwallis now abandoned the southern strategy and moved north into Virginia, taking a defensive position at Yorktown. With the aid of a French fleet which took control of Chesapeake Bay and a French army which joined him in sealing off the land approaches to Yorktown, Washington succeeded in trapping Cornwallis. After three weeks of siege, Cornwallis surrendered (October 17, 1781).

The final agreement became known as the **Treaty of Paris** of 1783. Its terms stipulated the following: (1) The United States was recognized as an independent nation by the major European powers, including Britain. (2) Its western boundary was set at the Mississippi River. (3) Its southern boundary was set at 31° north latitude (the northern boundary of Florida). (4) Britain retained Canada, but had to surrender Florida to Spain. (5) Private British creditors would be free to collect any debts owed by United States citizens. (6) Congress was to recommend that the states restore confiscated loyalist property.

The Creation of New Governments

By the end of 1777, ten new state constitutions had been formed. Most state constitutions included bills of rights—lists of things the government was not supposed to do to the people.

In the summer of 1776, Congress appointed a committee to begin devising a framework for a national government. The **Articles of Confederation** provided for a unicameral Congress in which each state would have one vote, as had been the case in the Continental Congress. In order to amend the articles, the unanimous consent of all the states was required.

The Articles of Confederation government was empowered to make war, make treaties, determine the amount of troops and money each state should contribute to the war effort, settle disputes between states, admit new states to the Union, and borrow money. But it was not empowered to levy taxes, raise troops, or regulate commerce. Ratification of the Articles of Confederation was delayed by disagreements over the future status of the lands that lay to the west of the original 13 states.

THE UNITED STATES CONSTITUTION (1787–1789)

Development and Ratification

In 1787 a convention of all the states was called to meet in Philadelphia for the purpose of revising the Articles of Confederation. George Washington was unanimously elected to preside, and the enormous respect that he commanded helped hold the convention together through difficult times.

The document that the delegates finally produced contained many checks and balances, designed to prevent the government, or any one branch of the government, from gaining too much power.

Benjamin Franklin played an important role in reconciling the often heated delegates and in making various suggestions that eventually helped the convention arrive at the "**Great Compromise**," proposed by Roger Sherman (1721–1793) and Oliver Ellsworth (1745–1807). The Great (or Connecticut) Compromise provided for a presidency, a Senate with all states represented equally (by two senators each), and a House of Representatives with representation according to population.

Slavery was neither endorsed nor condemned by the Constitution. Each slave was to count as three-fifths of a person for purposes of apportioning representation and direct taxation on the states (the **Three-Fifths Compromise**). The federal government was prohibited from stopping the importation of slaves prior to 1808.

The convention proposed a strong presidency with control of foreign policy and the power to veto Congress's legislation. Should the president commit an actual crime, Congress would have the power to impeach him. Otherwise, the president would serve for a term of four years and be reelectable without limit. As a check to the possible excesses of democracy, the president was to be elected by an **electoral college**, in which each state would have the same number of electors as it did senators and representatives combined. The person with the second highest total in the electoral college would be vice president. If no one gained a majority in the electoral college, the president would be chosen by the House of Representatives.

The new Constitution was to take effect when nine states ratified it. Those favoring the Constitution astutely named themselves Federalists (i.e., advocates of centralized power) and labeled their opponents Antifederalists.

By June 21, 1788, the required nine states had ratified, but New York and Virginia still held out. Ultimately, the promise of the addition of a bill of rights helped win the final states. In March 1789, George Washington was inaugurated as the nation's first president.

THE NEW NATION (1789–1824)

The Federalist Era

George Washington received virtually all the votes of the presidential electors, and John Adams received the next highest number, thus becoming the vice president. Washington was inaugurated in New York City, the temporary seat of government (April 30, 1789).

Ten amendments were ratified by the states by the end of 1791 and became the **Bill of Rights**. The first nine spelled out specific guarantees of personal freedoms, and the Tenth Amendment reserved to the states all those powers not specifically withheld or granted to the federal government.

The Judiciary Act of 1789 provided for a Supreme Court with six justices, and invested it with the power to be the interpreter of the "supreme law of the land." A system of district courts was set up to serve as courts of original jurisdiction, and three courts of appeal were established.

Congress established three departments of the executive branch—state, treasury, and war—as well as the offices of attorney general and postmaster general.

Washington's Administration (1789–1797)

Treasury Secretary Alexander Hamilton, in his "Report on the Public Credit," proposed the funding of the national debt at face value, federal assumption of state debts, and the establishment of a national bank. In his "Report on Manufactures," Hamilton proposed an extensive program for federal stimulation of industrial development through subsidies and tax incentives. The money needed to fund these programs would come from an excise tax on distillers and from tariffs on imports.

Thomas Jefferson, Secretary of State, and others objected to the funding proposal because they believed it would enrich a small elite group at the expense of the more worthy common citizen.

Hamilton interpreted the Constitution as having vested extensive powers in the federal government. This "implied powers" stance claimed that the government was given all powers that were not expressly denied to it. This is the "broad" interpretation. Jefferson and Madison held the view that any action not specifically permitted in the Constitution was thereby prohibited. This is the "strict" interpretation. The Jeffersonian supporters, began to organize political groups in opposition to the Federalist program. They called themselves **Republicans**.

The **Federalists**, as Hamilton's supporters were called, received their strongest support from the business and financial groups in the commercial centers of the Northeast and from the port cities of the South. The strength of the Republicans lay primarily in the rural and frontier areas of the South and West.

Foreign and Frontier Affairs

The United States proclaimed neutrality when France went to war with Europe in 1792. In retaliation, the British began to seize American merchant ships and force their crews into service with the British navy. John Jay negotiated a treaty with the British that attempted to settle the conflict at sea, as well as to curtail English agitation of their Native American allies on the western borders in 1794.

In the **Pinckney Treaty**, ratified by the Senate in 1796, the Spanish opened the Mississippi River to American traffic and recognized the 31st parallel as the northern boundary of Florida.

Internal Problems

In 1794, western farmers refused to pay the excise tax on whiskey. When a group of Pennsylvania farmers terrorized the tax collectors, President Washington sent out a federalized militia force of some 15,000 men and the rebellion evaporated, thus strengthening the credibility of the young government.

John Adams' Administration (1797–1801)

In the Election of 1796 John Adams was the Federalist candidate, and Thomas Jefferson the Republican. Jefferson received the second highest number of electoral votes and became vice president.

Repression and Protest

The elections in 1798 increased the Federalist's majorities in both houses of Congress and they used their "mandate" to enact legislation to stifle foreign influences. The **Alien Act** raised new hurdles in the path of immigrants trying to obtain citizenship, and the **Sedition Act** widened the powers of the Adams administration to muzzle its newspaper critics.

Jefferson and James Madison drew up a series of resolutions which were presented to the Kentucky and Virginia legislatures. They proposed that state bodies could "nullify" federal laws within those states. The principle of states' rights would have great force in later years.

The Revolution of 1800

Thomas Jefferson and Aaron Burr (1756–1836) ran on the Republican ticket against John Adams and Charles Pinckney (1746–1825) for the Federalists. Both Republican candidates received the same number of electoral votes, thus throwing the selection of the president into the House of Representatives. After a lengthy deadlock, Alexander Hamilton threw his support to Jefferson and Burr had to accept the vice presidency. Jefferson appointed James Madison as secretary of state and Albert Gallatin (1761–1849) to the treasury.

The Jeffersonian Era

Thomas Jefferson and his Republican followers envisioned a nation of independent farmers living under a central government that exercised a minimum of control and served merely to protect the individual liberties guaranteed by the Constitution. But Jefferson presided over a nation that was growing more industrialized and urban, and which seemed to need an ever-stronger president.

Domestic Affairs

The Twelfth Amendment was adopted and ratified in 1804, ensuring that a tie vote between candidates of the same party could not again cause the confusion of the Jefferson-Burr affair.

Following the Constitutional mandate, the importation of slaves was stopped by law in 1808.

1. The Louisiana Purchase

An American delegation purchased the trans-Mississippi territory from Napoleon for $15 million in April 1803, even though they had no authority to buy more than the city of New Orleans.

2. Exploring the West

Meriwether Lewis (1774–1809) and William Clark's (1770–1838) group left St. Louis in 1804 and returned two years later with a wealth of scientific and anthropological information. At the same time, Zebulon Pike and others had been traversing the middle parts of Louisiana and mapping the land.

Madison's Administration (1809–1817)

1. The Election of 1808

Republican James Madison won the election over Federalist Charles Pinckney, but the Federalists gained seats in both houses of the Congress.

The Native American tribes of the Northwest and the Mississippi Valley were resentful of the government's policy of pressured removal to the West, and the British authorities in Canada exploited their discontent by encouraging border raids against the American settlements. At the same time, the British interfered with American transatlantic shipping, including impressing sailors and capturing ships.

The Congress in 1811 contained a strong pro-war group called the War Hawks led by Henry Clay (1777–1852) and John C. Calhoun (1782–1850). They gained control of both houses and began agitating for war with the British. On June 1, 1812, President Madison asked for a declaration of war and Congress complied.

After three years of inconclusive war, in 1815 the **Treaty of Ghent** provided for the acceptance of the status quo that had existed at the beginning of hostilities.

The Federalists vehemently opposed the war, and Daniel Webster (1782–1852) and other New England congressmen consistently blocked the Administration's efforts to prosecute the war effort. On December 15, 1814, delegates from the New England states met in Hartford, Connecticut, and drafted a set of resolutions suggesting nullification—and even secession—if their interests were not protected against the growing influence of the South and the West.

Soon after the convention adjourned, the news of Andrew Jackson's victory over the British on January 8, 1815, at New Orleans was announced and their actions were discredited. The Federalist party ceased to be a political force from this point on.

Post-War Developments

The first protective tariff in the nation's history was passed in 1816 to slow the flood of cheap British manufactures into the country. An agreement was reached in 1817 (The Rush-Bagot Treaty) between Britain and the United States to stop maintaining armed fleets on the Great Lakes. Spain had decided to sell the remainder of the Florida territory to the Americans in 1819 before they took it anyway. Under this agreement (The Adams-Onis Treaty), the Spanish surrendered all their claims to Florida.

The Monroe Doctrine

In December 1823, President James Monroe (1758–1831) included in his annual message to Congress a statement that the peoples of the American hemisphere were "henceforth not to be considered as subjects for future colonization by any European powers."

Internal Development (1820–1830)

The years following the War of 1812 featured rapid economic and social development, followed by a severe depression in 1819.

James Monroe, the last of the "Virginia dynasty," was handpicked by the retiring Madison and he was elected with only one electoral vote opposed—a symbol of national unity.

The Marshall Court

John Marshall delivered the majority opinions in a number of critical decisions in these formative years. *Marbury vs. Madison* (1803) established the precedent of the Supreme Court's power to rule on the constitutionality of federal laws. *Gibbons vs. Ogden* (1824) involved competing steamboat companies. Marshall ruled that only Congress has the right to regulate commerce among states. Thus, the state-granted monopoly was voided.

National Expansion

1. The Missouri Compromise (1820)

The Missouri Territory, the first to be organized from the Louisiana Purchase, applied for statehood in 1819. Since the Senate membership was evenly divided between slaveholding and free states at that time, the admission of a new state would give the voting advantage either to the North or to the South. As the debate dragged on, the northern territory of Massachusetts applied for admission as the state of Maine. The two admission bills were combined, with Maine coming in free and Missouri coming in as a slave state.

JACKSONIAN DEMOCRACY AND WESTWARD EXPANSION (1824–1850)

The Election of 1824

Although John Quincy Adams became president in the 1824 election, Andrew Jackson instigated a campaign for the presidency immediately. He won the election of 1828.

Jackson seemed to be the prototype of the self-made westerner: rough-hewn, violent, vindictive, with few ideas but strong convictions. He ignored his appointed cabinet officers and relied instead on the counsel of his "**Kitchen Cabinet**," a group of partisan supporters.

Jackson expressed the conviction that government operations could be performed by untrained, common folk, and he threatened to dismiss large numbers of government employees and replace them with his supporters. He exercised his veto power more than any other president before him.

The War on the Bank of the United States

The Bank of the United States had operated under the direction of Nicholas Biddle (1786–1844) since 1823. His conservative economic policy enforced conservatism among the state and private banks—which many bankers resented. In 1832 Jackson vetoed the Bank's renewal, and it ceased being a federal institution in 1836.

Jackson handpicked his Democratic successor, Martin Van Buren (1782–1862) of New York. The opposition Whig party emerged from the ruins of the National Republicans and other groups who opposed Jackson's policies. Van Buren spent most of his term in office dealing with the financial chaos left by the death of the Second Bank. He eventually persuaded Congress to establish an Independent Treasury to handle government funds, which began functioning in 1840.

The Election of 1840

The Whigs nominated William Henry Harrison, "Old Tippecanoe," a western fighter against the Native Americans. Their choice for vice president was John Tyler (1790–1862), a former Democrat from Virginia. The Democrats put up Van Buren again. Harrison won but died only a month after the inauguration, having served the shortest term in presidential history.

The Meaning of Jacksonian Politics

The Age of Jackson was the beginning of the modern two-party system. The practice of meeting in mass conventions to nominate national candidates for office was established during these years.

The Democrats opposed big government and the requirements of modernization: urbanization and industrialization. Their support came from the working classes, small merchants, and small farmers. In contrast, the Whigs promoted government participation in commercial and industrial development, the encouragement of banking and corporations, and a cautious approach to westward expansion. Their support came largely from northern business and manufacturing interests and large southern planters.

Remaking Society: Organized Reform

The American Colonization Society was organized in 1817, and established the colony of Liberia in 1830. In 1831, William Lloyd Garrison (1805–1879) started his paper, *The Liberator*, and began to advocate total and immediate emancipation. He founded the New England Anti-slavery Society in 1832 and the American Anti-slavery Society in 1833. Theodore Weld (1803–1895) pursued the same goals, but advocated more gradual means.

The movement split into two wings: Garrison's radical followers, and the moderates who favored "moral suasion" and petitions to Congress. In 1840, the Liberty party, the first national anti-slavery party, fielded a presidential candidate on the platform of "free soil" (nonexpansion of slavery into the new western territories).

The Role of Minorities

The women's rights movement focused on social and legal discrimination, and women like Lucretia Mott (1793–1880) and Sojourner Truth (ca. 1797–1883) became well-known figures on the speakers' circuit.

By 1850, 200,000 free blacks lived in the North and West. Their lives were restricted everywhere by prejudice, and **"Jim Crow" laws** separated the races. Black citizens organized separate churches and fraternal orders. Racial violence was a daily threat.

The Growth of Industry

By 1850, the value of industrial output had surpassed that of agricultural production. The Northeast produced more than two-thirds of the manufactured goods. Between 1830 and 1850, the number of patents issued for industrial inventions almost doubled.

The southern states experienced dramatic growth in the second quarter of the nineteenth century. The economy grew more productive and more prosperous, but still was basically agrarian, with few important cities and only scattered industry. The plantation system, with its cash-crop production driven by the use of slave labor, remained the dominant institution.

The most important economic phenomenon of the early decades of the nineteenth century was the shift in population and production from the old "upper South" of Virginia and the Carolinas to the "lower South" of the newly opened Gulf states of Alabama, Mississippi, and Louisiana. In the older Atlantic states, tobacco retained its importance, but shifted westward to the Piedmont. It was replaced in the East by food grains. The southern Atlantic coast continued to produce rice, and southern Louisiana and east Texas retained their emphasis on sugar cane. But the rich black soil of the new Gulf states proved ideal for the production of short-staple cotton, especially after the invention of the "gin." Cotton soon became the center of the southern economy.

Classes in the South

The large plantations growing cotton, sugar, or tobacco used the gang system, in which white overseers directed black drivers who supervised large groups of workers in the fields, all performing the same operation. House servants usually were considered the most favored since they were spared the hardest physical labor and enjoyed the most intimate relationship with the owner's family.

Commerce and Industry

The lack of manufacturing and business development has frequently been blamed for the South's losing its bid for independence in 1861–1865. Actually, the South was highly industrialized for its day and compared favorably with most European nations in the development of manufacturing capacity. However, it trailed far behind the North, so much so that when war erupted in 1861, the northern states owned 81% of the factory capacity in the United States.

Manifest Destiny and Westward Expansion

Although the term "**Manifest Destiny**" was not actually coined until 1844, the belief that the American nation was destined to eventually expand all the way to the Pacific Ocean, and to possibly embrace Canada and Mexico, had been voiced for years by many who believed that American liberty and ideals should be shared with everyone possible, by force if necessary.

The **Adams-Onis Treaty** of 1819 set the northern boundary of Spanish possessions near the present northern border of California. The territory north of that line and west of the vague boundaries of the Louisiana Territory had been claimed over the years by Spain, England, Russia, France, and the United States. By the 1820s, all these claims had been yielded to Britain and the United States. The United States claimed all the way north to the 54°40′ parallel. Unable to settle the dispute, they had agreed on a joint occupation of the disputed land.

In the 1830s, American missionaries followed the traders and trappers to the Oregon country. They began to publicize the richness and beauty of the land. The result was the "**Oregon Fever**" of the 1840s.

Texas had been a state in the Republic of Mexico since 1822, following the Mexican revolution against Spanish control. The new Mexican government invited immigration from the north by offering land grants to Stephen Austin (1793–1836) and other Americans. By 1835, approximately 35,000 "gringos" were homesteading on Texas land.

In 1836, Texas proclaimed independence and established a new republic. The ensuing war was short-lived. The Mexican dictator, Antonio López de Santa Anna (1794–1876), advanced north and annihilated the Texan garrisons at the Alamo and at Goliad. On April 23, 1836, Sam Houston (1793–1863) defeated him at San Jacinto, and the Mexicans were forced to let Texas go its way.

Houston immediately asked the American government for recognition and annexation, but President Andrew Jackson feared the revival of the slavery issue. He also feared war with Mexico and so did nothing. When Van Buren followed suit, the new republic sought foreign recognition and support, which the European nations eagerly provided, hoping thereby to create a counterbalance to rising American power and influence in the Southwest. France and England both quickly concluded trade agreements with the Texans.

The district of New Mexico had, like Texas, encouraged American immigration. Soon that state was more American than Mexican. The Santa Fe Trail, running from Independence, Missouri, to the town of Santa Fe, created a prosperous trade route.

Tyler, Polk, and Continued Westward Expansion

John Tyler, who became president in 1841 upon Harrison's death, rejected the entire Whig program of a national bank, high protective tariffs, and federally funded internal improvements (roads, canals, etc.). In the resulting legislative confrontations, Tyler vetoed a number of Whig-sponsored bills. The Whigs were furious. Rejected by the Whigs and without ties to the Democrats, Tyler was a politician without a party. Hoping to gather a political following of his own, he sought an issue with powerful appeal. Tyler's new secretary of state, John C. Calhoun, negotiated an annexation treaty with Texas. Calhoun's identification with extreme proslavery forces and his insertion in the treaty of proslavery statements caused the treaty's rejection by the Senate (1844).

The Election of 1844

Democratic front-runner Martin Van Buren and Whig front-runner Henry Clay agreed privately that neither would endorse Texas annexation, and that it would not become a campaign issue, but expansionists at the Democratic convention succeeded in dumping Van Buren in favor of James K. Polk (1795–1849). Polk, called "Young Hickory" by his supporters, was a staunch Jacksonian who opposed protective tariffs and a national bank, but favored territorial expansion, including not only annexation of Texas but also occupation of all the Oregon country (up to latitude 54°40′).

The Whigs nominated Clay, who continued to oppose Texas annexation. Later, sensing the mood of the country was against him, he began to equivocate. The antislavery Liberty party nominated James G. Birney. Apparently because of Clay's wavering on the Texas issue, Birney was able to take enough votes away from Clay in New York to give that state, and thus the election, to Polk.

Tyler, as a lame-duck president, made one more attempt to achieve Texas annexation before leaving office. By means of a joint resolution, he was successful in getting the measure through Congress. Texas was finally admitted to the Union in 1845.

As a good Jacksonian, Polk favored a low, revenue-only tariff rather than a high, protective tariff. This he obtained in the **Walker Tariff** (1846). He also opposed a national debt and a national bank and reestablished Van Buren's Independent Sub-Treasury system, which remained in effect until 1920.

By the terms of the **Oregon Treaty** (1846), a compromise with Great Britain was reached. The current United States-Canada boundary east of the Rockies (49°) was extended westward to the Pacific.

Though Mexico broke diplomatic relations with the United States immediately upon Texas's admission to the Union, there was still hope of a peaceful settlement. In the fall of 1845, Polk sent John Slidell (1793–1871) to Mexico City with a proposal for a peaceful settlement. When this proved unsuccessful, Polk sent U.S. troops into the disputed territory in southern Texas. A force under General Zachary Taylor (1784–1850) (who was nicknamed "Old Rough and Ready") took up a position just north of the Rio Grande. Eight days later, (April 5, 1846), Mexican troops attacked an American patrol. When news of the clash reached Washington, Polk sought and received from Congress a declaration of war against Mexico on May 13, 1846.

Americans were sharply divided about the war. Some favored it because they felt Mexico had provoked the war, or because they felt it was the destiny of America to spread the blessings of freedom to oppressed peoples. Others, generally northern abolitionists, saw in the war the work of a vast conspiracy of southern slaveholders greedy for more slave territory.

Negotiated peace finally came about when the State Department clerk Nicholas Trist negotiated and signed the **Treaty of Guadalupe-Hidalgo** (February 2, 1848), ending the Mexican War. Under the terms of the treaty, Mexico ceded to the United States the southwestern territory from Texas to the California coast, increasing the nation's territory by one-third.

SECTIONAL CONFLICT AND THE CAUSES OF THE CIVIL WAR (1850–1860)

The Crisis of 1850 and America at Mid-Century

The Mexican War had no more than started when, on August 8, 1846, freshman Democratic Congressman David Wilmot (1814–1868) of Pennsylvania introduced his **Wilmot Proviso**. It stipulated that "neither slavery nor involuntary servitude shall ever exist" in any territory to be acquired from Mexico. It was passed by the House and, though rejected by the Senate, it was reintroduced again and again amid increasingly acrimonious debate.

John C. Calhoun, now serving as senator from South Carolina, argued that the territories were not the property of the U.S. federal government, but of all the states together. Therefore, Congress had no right to prohibit in any territory any type of "property" (by which he meant slaves) that was legal in any of the states. Antislavery northerners, pointing to the Northwest Ordinance of 1787 and the Missouri Compromise of 1820 as precedents, argued that Congress had the right to make what laws it saw fit for the territories, including, if it so chose, laws prohibiting slavery.

A compromise proposal favored by President Polk and many moderate southerners called for the extension of the 36°30′ line of the Missouri Compromise westward through the Mexican Cession to the Pacific, with territory north of the line to be closed to slavery.

Another compromise solution, favored by northern Democrats such as Lewis Cass (1782–1866) of Michigan and Stephen A. Douglas (1813–1861) of Illinois, was known as "squatter sovereignty" and later as "popular sovereignty." It held that the residents of each territory should be permitted to decide for themselves whether to allow slavery.

Some antislavery northern Whigs and Democrats, disgusted with their parties' failure to take a clear stand against the spread of slavery, deserted the party ranks to form an antislavery third party, called the **Free Soil party**, since it stood for keeping the soil of new western territories free of slavery. Its candidate was Martin Van Buren. The election excited relatively little public interest. Taylor won a narrow victory.

The question of slavery's status in the western territories was made more immediate when, on January 24, 1848, gold was discovered not far from Sacramento, California. The next year, gold seekers from the eastern United States and from many foreign countries swelled California's population from 14,000 to 100,000.

In September, 1849 having more than the requisite population and being in need of better government, California petitioned for admission to the Union as a free state. Southerners were furious. Long outnumbered in the House of Representatives, the South would now find itself, should California be admitted as a free state, also outvoted in the Senate.

At this point, the aged Henry Clay proposed an eight-part package with concessions for both the North and South. President Taylor died on July 9, 1850, and was succeeded by Vice President Millard Fillmore (1800–1874). In Congress, the fight for the Compromise was taken up by Senator Stephen A. Douglas of Illinois who broke Clay's proposal into its component parts so that he could use varying coalitions to push each part through Congress. The Compromise was adopted.

The 1852 Democratic convention deadlocked between Cass and Douglas and so settled on dark horse Franklin Pierce (1804–1869) of New Hampshire. The Whigs chose General Winfield Scott, a war hero with no political background. The result was an easy victory for Pierce.

President Pierce expressed the nation's hope that a new era of sectional peace was beginning. He sought to distract the nation's attention from the slavery issue to an aggressive program of foreign economic and territorial expansion known as "Young America."

In 1853, Commodore Matthew Perry (1794–1858) led a U.S. naval force into Tokyo Bay on a peaceful mission to open Japan—previously closed to the outside world—to American diplomacy and commerce. By means of the Reciprocity Treaty (1854), Pierce succeeded in opening Canada to greater U.S. trade. From Mexico he acquired in 1853 the Gadsden Purchase, a strip of land in what is now southern New Mexico and Arizona along the Gila River.

The chief factor in the economic transformation of America during the 1840s and 1850s was the dynamic rise of the railroads. They helped link the Midwest to the Northeast rather than just the South. The 1850s was the heyday of the steamboat on inland rivers, and the clipper ship on the high seas. The period also saw rapid and sustained industrial growth, especially in the textile industry.

In the North, the main centers of agricultural production shifted from the Mid-Atlantic states to the more fertile lands of the Midwest. Mechanical reapers and threshers came into wide use.

The Whig party was now in the process of complete disintegration. This was partially the result of the slavery issue, which divided the party along North-South lines, and partially the result of the nativist movement. The collapse of a viable two-party system made it much more difficult for the nation's political process to contain the explosive issue of slavery.

The Return of Sectional Conflict

One northerner who was outraged by the Fugitive Slave Act was Harriet Beecher Stowe. She wrote *Uncle Tom's Cabin*, a novel depicting what she perceived as the evils of slavery. Furiously denounced in the South, the book became an overnight bestseller in the North, where it turned many toward active opposition to slavery.

All illusion of sectional peace ended abruptly in 1854 when Senator Stephen A. Douglas of Illinois introduced a bill in Congress to organize the area west of Missouri and Iowa as the territories of Kansas and Nebraska on the basis of popular sovereignty. The Kansas-Nebraska Act aroused a storm of outrage in the North, where its repeal of the Missouri Compromise was seen as the breaking of a solemn agreement. It hastened the disintegration of the Whig party and divided the Democratic party along North-South lines.

In the North, many Democrats left the party and were joined by former Whigs and Know-Nothings in the newly created Republican party. Springing to life almost overnight as a result of northern fury at the Kansas-Nebraska Act, the Republican party included diverse elements whose sole unifying principle was the firm belief that slavery should be banned from all the nation's territories, confined to the states where it already existed, and allowed to spread no further.

In *Dred Scott v. Sanford*, the Supreme Court attempted to finally settle the slavery question. The case involved a Missouri slave, Dred Scott (ca. 1795–1858), who had been encouraged by abolitionists to sue for his freedom on the basis that his owner had taken him for several years to a free state, Illinois, and then to a free territory, Wisconsin. Under the domination of aging pro-southern Chief Justice Roger B. Taney of Maryland, the Court attempted to read the extreme southern position on slavery into the Constitution, ruling not only that Scott had no standing to sue in federal court, but also that temporary residence in a free state, even for several years, did not make a slave free, and that the Missouri Compromise (already a dead letter by that time) had been unconstitutional all along because Congress did not have the authority to exclude slavery from a territory. Nor did territorial governments have the right to prohibit slavery.

The 1858 Illinois senatorial campaign produced a series of debates that got to the heart of the issues that were threatening to divide the nation. Incumbent Democratic senator and front-runner for the 1860 presidential nomination Stephen A. Douglas was opposed by a Springfield lawyer, little known outside the state, by the name of Abraham Lincoln.

Lincoln, in a series of seven debates that the candidates agreed to hold during the course of the campaign, stressed that Douglas's doctrine of popular sovereignty failed to recognize slavery for the moral wrong it was. Douglas, for his part, maintained that his guiding principle was democracy, not any moral standard of right or wrong with respect to slavery.

At the debate held in Freeport, Illinois, Lincoln pressed Douglas to reconcile the principle of popular sovereignty to the Supreme Court's decision in the Dred Scott case. Douglas, in what came to be called his "**Freeport Doctrine**," replied that the people of any territory could exclude slavery simply by declining to pass any of the special laws that slave jurisdictions usually passed for their protection. Douglas's answer was good enough to win him reelection to the Senate, but hurt him in the coming presidential campaign.

The Coming of the Civil War

On the night of October 16, 1859, John Brown, an abolitionist, led 18 followers in seizing the federal arsenal at Harpers Ferry, Virginia, taking hostages, and endeavoring to incite a slave uprising. Quickly cornered by Virginia militia, he was eventually captured by a force under the command of army Colonel Robert E. Lee (1807–1870). Brown was quickly tried, convicted, sentenced, and on December 2, 1859, hanged. Many northerners looked upon Brown as a martyr.

As the 1860 presidential election approached, two Democratic conventions failed to reach consensus, and the sundered halves of the party nominated separate candidates. The southern wing of the party nominated Buchanan's vice president, John C. Breckinridge of Kentucky, on a platform calling for a federal slave code in all the territories. What was left of the national Democratic party nominated Douglas on a platform of popular sovereignty. A third presidential candidate John Bell of Tennessee, was added by the Constitutional Union party.

The Republicans met in Chicago, confident of victory and determined to do nothing to jeopardize their favorable position. Accordingly, they rejected as too radical front-running New York Senator William H. Seward in favor of Illinois' favorite son Abraham Lincoln. The platform called for federal support of a transcontinental railroad and for the containment of slavery.

On election day, the voting went along strictly sectional lines. Breckinridge carried the Deep South; Bell, the border states; and Lincoln, the North. Lincoln led in popular votes, and though he was short of a majority in that category, he did have the needed majority in electoral votes and was elected.

The Secession Crisis

On December 20, 1860, South Carolina, by vote of a special convention, declared itself out of the Union. By February 1, 1861, six more states (Alabama, Georgia, Florida, Mississippi, Louisiana, and Texas) followed suit.

Representatives of the seceded states met in Montgomery, Alabama, in February 1861 and declared themselves to be the Confederate States of America. They elected former Secretary of War and U.S. senator Jefferson Davis of Mississippi as president, and Alexander Stephens (1812–1883) of Georgia as vice president. They also adopted a constitution for the Confederate states which, while similar to the U.S. Constitution in many ways, contained several important differences:

1. Slavery was specifically recognized, and the right to move slaves from one state to another was guaranteed.

2. Protective tariffs were prohibited.

3. The president was to serve for a single nonrenewable six-year term.

4. The president was given the right to veto individual items within an appropriations bill.

5. State sovereignty was specifically recognized.

THE CIVIL WAR AND RECONSTRUCTION (1860–1877)

Hostilities Begin

In his inaugural address, Lincoln urged southerners to reconsider their actions, but warned that the Union was perpetual, that states could not secede, and that he would, therefore, hold the federal forts and installations in the South. Lincoln soon received word from Major Robert Anderson, commander of the small garrison at Sumter, that supplies were running low. Confederate General P. G. T. Beauregard (1818–1893), acting on orders from President Davis, demanded Anderson's surrender. Anderson said he would surrender if not resupplied. Knowing supplies were on the way, the Confederates opened fire at 4:30 a.m. on April 12, 1861. The next day, the fort surrendered. The day following Sumter's surrender, Lincoln declared an insurrection and called for the states to provide 75,000 volunteers to put it down. In response to this, Virginia, Tennessee, North Carolina, and Arkansas declared their secession. The remaining slave states—Delaware, Kentucky, Maryland, and Missouri—wavered, but stayed with the Union.

The North enjoyed at least five major advantages over the South. It had overwhelming preponderance in wealth and was vastly superior in industry. The North also had an advantage of almost three to one in manpower; and over one-third of the South's population was composed of slaves, whom Southerners would not use as soldiers. Unlike the South, the North received large numbers of immigrants during the war. The North retained control of the U.S. Navy, and thus would command the sea and be able to blockade the South. Finally, the North enjoyed a much superior system of railroads.

The South did, however, have several advantages. It was vast in size, making it difficult to conquer. Its troops would be fighting on their own ground, a fact that would give them the advantage of familiarity with the terrain, as well as the added motivation of defending their homes and families. Its armies would often have the opportunity of fighting on the defensive, a major advantage in the warfare of that day.

At a creek called Bull Run near the town of Manassas Junction, Virginia, the Union Army met a Confederate force under generals P. G. T. Beauregard and Joseph E. Johnston on July 21, 1861. In the First Battle of Bull Run (called First Manassas in the South), the Union army was forced to retreat in confusion back to Washington.

The Union Is Preserved

To replace the discredited McDowell, Lincoln chose General George B. McClellan (1826–1885). Lee summoned General Thomas J. "Stonewall" Jackson (1824–1863) and his army from the Shenandoah Valley (where Jackson had just finished defeating several superior federal forces), and with the combined forces attacked McClellan.

After two days of bloody but inconclusive fighting, McClellan lost his nerve and began to retreat. In the remainder of what came to be called the Battle of the Seven Days, Lee continued to attack McClellan, forcing him back to his base. McClellan's army was loaded back onto its ships and taken back to Washington. Before McClellan's army could reach Washington, Lee took the opportunity to thrash Union General John Pope (1822–1892), who was in northern Virginia with another northern army, at the Second Battle of Bull Run.

West of the Appalachian Mountains, matters were proceeding differently. The northern commanders there, Henry W. Halleck (1815–1872) and Don Carlos Buell (1818–1898), were no more enterprising than McClellan, but Halleck's subordinate, Ulysses S. Grant, was. With permission from Halleck, Grant mounted a combined operation—army troops and navy gunboats—against two vital Confederate strongholds, forts Henry and Donelson, which guarded the Tennessee and Cumberland rivers in northern Tennessee. On April 6, 1862, General Albert Sidney Johnston surprised Grant at Pittsburg Landing on the Tennessee River, but in the two-day battle that followed (Shiloh) failed to defeat him. Johnston was among the many killed in what was, up to this point, the bloodiest battle in American history.

Many southerners believed Britain and France would rejoice in seeing a divided and weakened America. They also believed the two countries would likewise be driven by the need of their factories for cotton and thus intervene on the Confederacy's behalf. This view proved mistaken. Britain already had a large supply of cotton. British leaders may also have weighed their country's need to import wheat from the northern United States against its desire for cotton from the southern states. Finally, British public opinion opposed slavery.

Lincoln had the extremely able assistance of Secretary of State William Seward, who took a hard line in warning Europeans not to interfere, and of ambassador to Great Britain Charles Francis Adams (1807–1886). Britain remained neutral, and other European countries, including France, followed its lead.

Congress in 1862 passed two highly important acts dealing with domestic affairs in the North. The **Homestead Act** granted 160 acres of government land free of charge to any person who would farm it for at least five years. The **Morrill Land Grant Act** offered large amounts of the federal government's land to states that would establish "agricultural and mechanical" colleges. Many of the nation's large state universities were later founded under the provisions of this act.

The Emancipation Proclamation

By mid-1862, Lincoln issued the **Emancipation Proclamation**, which declared free all slaves in areas still in rebellion as of January 1, 1863. At Seward's recommendation, Lincoln waited to announce the proclamation until the North won some sort of victory. This was provided by the Battle of Antietam (September 17, 1863).

After his victory at the Second Battle of Bull Run, Lee moved north and crossed into Maryland, where he hoped to win a decisive victory that would force the North to recognize southern independence. The armies finally met along Antietam Creek, just east of the town of Sharpsburg in western Maryland. In a bloody but inconclusive day-long battle, known as Antietam in the North and Sharpsburg in the South, McClellan's timidity led him to miss another excellent chance to destroy Lee's cornered and badly outnumbered army. After the battle, Lee retreated to Virginia, and Lincoln removed McClellan from command. To replace him, Lincoln chose General Ambrose E. Burnside (1824–1881), who promptly demonstrated his unfitness by blundering into a lopsided defeat at Fredericksburg, Virginia (December 13, 1862).

Lincoln then replaced Burnside with General Joseph "Fighting Joe" Hooker (1814–1879). He was soundly beaten at the Battle of Chancellorsville (May 5–6, 1863). At this battle, "Stonewall" Jackson was accidentally shot by his own men and died several days later.

Lee received permission from President Davis to invade Pennsylvania. He was pursued by the Army of the Potomac, now under the command of General George G. Meade (1815–1872), who had replaced the discredited Hooker. They met at Gettysburg in a three-day battle (July 1–3, 1863) that was the bloodiest of the war. Lee, who sorely missed the services of Jackson and whose cavalry leader, the normally reliable J. E. B. Stuart (1833–1864), failed to provide him with timely reconnaissance, was defeated.

Meanwhile, Grant moved on Vicksburg, one of the last two Confederate bastions on the Mississippi River. In a brilliant campaign, he bottled up the Confederate forces of General John C. Pemberton (1814–1881) inside the city and placed them under siege. After six weeks, the defenders surrendered on July 4, 1863. Five days later, Port Hudson surrendered, giving the Union complete control of the Mississippi River.

After Union forces under General William Rosecrans (1819–1898) suffered an embarrassing defeat at the Battle of Chickamauga in northwestern Georgia (September 19–20, 1863), Lincoln named Grant overall commander of Union forces in the West.

Grant went to Chattanooga, Tennessee, where Confederate forces under General Braxton Bragg (1817–1876) were virtually besieging Rosecrans. Gathering Union forces from other portions of the western theater and combining them with reinforcements from the East, Grant won a resounding victory at the Battle of Chattanooga (November 23–25, 1863). This victory put Union forces in position for a drive into Georgia, which began the following spring.

Early in 1864, Lincoln made Grant commander of all Union armies. Grant devised a coordinated plan for constant pressure on the Confederacy. General William T. Sherman would lead a drive toward Atlanta, Georgia, with the goal of destroying the Confederate army under General Joseph E. Johnston (who had replaced Bragg). Grant would accompany Meade and the Army of the Potomac in advancing toward Richmond with the goal of destroying Lee's Confederate army.

In a series of bloody battles (the Wilderness, Spotsylvania, Cold Harbor) in May and June of 1864, Grant drove Lee to the outskirts of Richmond. Still unable to take the city or get Lee at a disadvantage, Grant circled around, attacking Petersburg, Virginia, an important railroad junction just south of Richmond and the key to that city's—and Lee's—supply lines. Once again turned back by entrenched Confederate troops, Grant settled down to besiege Petersburg and Richmond in a stalemate that lasted some nine months.

Sherman had been advancing simultaneously in Georgia. He maneuvered Johnston back to the outskirts of Atlanta with relatively little fighting. At that point, Confederate President Davis lost patience with Johnston and replaced him with the aggressive General John B. Hood (1831–1879). Hood and Sherman fought three fierce but inconclusive battles around Atlanta in late July, and then settled down to a siege of their own during the month of August.

The Election of 1864 and Northern Victory

Lincoln ran on the ticket of the National Union party, essentially the Republican party with loyal or "War" Democrats. His vice presidential candidate was Andrew Johnson (1808–1875), a loyal Democrat from Tennessee.

The Democratic party's presidential candidate was General George B. McClellan, who ran on a platform labeling the war a failure, and calling for a negotiated peace settlement even if that meant southern independence.

In September 1864, word came that Sherman had taken Atlanta. The capture of this vital southern rail and manufacturing center brought an enormous boost to northern morale. Along with other northern victories that summer and fall, it ensured a resounding election victory for Lincoln and the continuation of the war to complete victory for the North. To speed that victory, Sherman marched through Georgia from Atlanta to the sea, arriving at Savannah in December 1864 and turning north into the Carolinas, leaving behind a 60-mile-wide swath of destruction.

Lee abandoned Richmond (April 3, 1865) and attempted to escape with what was left of his army. Pursued by Grant, he was cornered and forced to surrender at Appomattox, Virginia (April 9, 1865). Other Confederate armies still holding out in various parts of the South surrendered over the next few weeks.

Lincoln did not live to receive news of the final surrenders. On April 14, 1865, he was shot in the back of the head while watching a play in Ford's Theater in Washington.

The Ordeal of Reconstruction

Reconstruction began well before the fighting of the Civil War came to an end. Among those who faced adjustments were the recently freed slaves. In 1865, Congress created the **Freedman's Bureau** to provide food, clothing, and education, and generally look after the interests of former slaves.

Tennessee, Arkansas, and Louisiana formed loyal governments under Lincoln's plan, but were refused recognition by a Congress dominated by Radical Republicans. Some, such as Thaddeus Stevens (1792–1868) of Pennsylvania, believed Lincoln's plan did not adequately punish the South, restructure southern society, or boost the political prospects of the Republican party. Instead, the radicals in Congress drew up the more stringent **Wade-Davis Bill**. When Lincoln was assassinated the radicals rejoiced, believing Vice President Andrew Johnson would be less generous to the South.

Congressional Reconstruction

In 1866, the Russian minister approached Seward with an offer to sell Alaska to the United States. In 1867, the sale went through and Alaska was purchased for $7,200,000.

Determined to reconstruct the South as it saw fit, Congress passed a Civil Rights Act and extended the authority of the Freedman's Bureau. Johnson vetoed both bills, claiming they were unconstitutional, but Congress overrode the vetoes. Congress then approved and sent on to the states for ratification (June 1866) the **Fourteenth Amendment**, making constitutional the laws Congress had just passed. The Fourteenth Amendment defined citizenship and forbade states to deny various rights to citizens, reduced the representation in Congress of states that did not allow blacks to vote, forbade the paying of the Confederate debt, and made former Confederates ineligible to hold public office.

To control the president, Congress passed the **Army Act**, reducing the president's control over the army. Congress also passed the **Tenure of Office Act**, forbidding Johnson to dismiss cabinet members without the Senate's permission.

Congress, angry at President Johnson's refusal to cooperate, sought grounds to impeach him. In August 1867, Johnson violated the Tenure of Office Act in order to test its constitutionality. Johnson was impeached by the House of Representatives and came within one vote of being removed by the Senate.

The Election of 1868 and the Fifteenth Amendment

Republican leaders decided that it would be politically expedient to give the vote to all blacks, North as well as South. For this purpose, the Fifteenth Amendment was drawn up and submitted to the states. Ironically, the idea was so unpopular in the North that it won the necessary three-fourths approval only with its ratification by southern states.

Many of the economic difficulties the country faced during President Ulysses S. Grant's administration were caused by the necessary readjustments from a wartime economy back to a peacetime economy. The central economic question was whether to retire the unbacked paper money, greenbacks, printed to meet the wartime emergency, or to print more.

Early in Grant's second term, the country was hit by an economic depression known as the **Panic of 1873**. The Panic was triggered by economic downturns in Europe and, more immediately, by the failure of Jay Cooke and Company, a major American financial firm.

The Panic led to clamor for the printing of more greenbacks. In 1874, Congress authorized a small new issue of greenbacks, but it was vetoed by Grant. Pro-inflation forces were further enraged when Congress in 1873 demonetized silver, going to a straight gold standard. Pro-inflation forces referred to the demonetization of silver as the "Crime of '73."

In the election of 1876, the Democrats campaigned against corruption and nominated New York Governor Samuel J. Tilden (1814–1886), who had broken the Tweed political machine of New York City. The Republicans passed over Grant and turned to Governor Rutherford B. Hayes (1822–1893) of Ohio. Tilden won the popular vote and led in the electoral vote 184 to 165. However, 185 electoral votes were needed for election, and 20 votes, from the three Southern states still occupied by federal troops and run by Republican governments, were disputed. A deal was made whereby those 20 votes went to Hayes in return for removal of federal troops from the South. Reconstruction was over.

INDUSTRIALISM, WAR, AND THE PROGRESSIVE ERA (1877–1912)

Politics of the Period (1877–1882)

The presidencies of Abraham Lincoln and Theodore Roosevelt (1858–1919) mark the boundaries of a half century of relatively weak executive leadership and legislative domination by Congress and the Republican party.

"**Stalwarts**," led by New York senator Roscoe Conkling (1829–1888), favored the old spoils system of political patronage. "**Half-Breeds**," headed by Maine senator James G. Blaine (1830–1893), pushed for civil service reform and merit appointments to government posts.

The Economy (1877–1882)

Between 1860 and 1894, the United States became the world's manufacturing leader through capital accumulation; natural resources, especially in iron, oil, and coal; an abundance of labor helped by massive immigration; railway transportation; and communications and major technical innovations such as the development of the modern steel industry and electrical energy.

Social and Cultural Developments (1877–1882)

In time, advocates of the "social gospel" such as Jane Addams (1860–1939) and Washington Gladden (1836–1918) urged the creation of settlement houses and better health and education services to accommodate the new immigrants. In 1881, Booker T. Washington (1856–1915) became president of Tuskegee Institute in Alabama, a school devoted to teaching and vocational education for African-Americans.

The Economy (1882–1887)

Captains of industry such as John D. Rockefeller in oil, J. P. Morgan (1837–1919) in banking, Gustavus Swift (1839–1903) in meat processing, Andrew Carnegie in steel, and E. H. Harriman (1848–1909) in railroads, put together major industrial empires.

Popular resentment of railroad abuses such as price-fixing, kickbacks, and discriminatory freight rates created demands for state regulation of the railway industry. The **Interstate Commerce Act** (1887) was passed, providing that a commission be established to oversee fair and just railway rates, prohibit rebates, end discriminatory practices, and require annual reports and financial statements.

Samuel Gompers (1850–1924) and Adolph Strasser put together a combination of national craft unions to represent labor's concerns with wages, hours, and safety conditions called the **American Federation of Labor** (1886). Although militant in its use of the strike and in its demand for collective bargaining in labor contracts with large corporations, it did not promote violence or radicalism.

Frederick W. Taylor (1856–1915), an engineer credited as the father of scientific management, introduced modern concepts of industrial engineering, plant management, and time and motion studies. This gave rise to a separate class of managers in industrial manufacturing—efficiency experts.

The Economy (1887–1892)

Although supported by smaller businesses, labor unions, and farm associations, the **Sherman Antitrust Act** of 1890 was in time interpreted by the Supreme Court to apply to labor unions and farmers' cooperatives as much as to large corporate combinations. Monopoly was still dominant over laissez-faire, free-enterprise economics during the 1890s.

Politics of the Period (1892–1897)

The most marked development in American politics was the emergence of a viable third-party movement in the form of the essentially agrarian **Populist party**.

Democrat Grover Cleveland (New York) regained the White House by defeating Republican president Benjamin Harrison (Indiana). The People's party (Populist) nominated James Weaver (Iowa) for president in 1892. The party platform called for the enactment of a program espoused by agrarians, but also for a coalition with urban workers and the middle class.

In the election of 1896, the Republicans nominated William McKinley (Ohio) for president on a platform which promised to maintain the gold standard and protective tariffs. The Democratic party repudiated Cleveland's conservative economics and nominated William Jennings Bryan (1860–1925) (Nebraska) for president on a platform similar to the Populists. Bryan delivered one of the most famous speeches in American history when he declared that the people must not be "crucified upon a cross of gold."

McKinley won a hard-fought election by only about one-half million votes, as Republicans succeeded in creating the fear among business groups and middle-class voters that Bryan represented a revolutionary challenge to the American system.

The Economy (1892–1897)

Iron and steel workers went on strike in Pennsylvania (**Homestead Strike**, 1892) against the Carnegie Steel Company to protest salary reductions.

The primary causes for the depression of 1893 were dramatic growth of the federal deficit, withdrawal of British investments from the American market and the outward transfer of gold, and loss of business confidence. Eventually 20% of the work force was unemployed. The depression would last four years.

The Populist businessman Jacob Coxey (1854–1951) led a march of hundreds of unemployed workers (**March of Unemployed**) on Washington asking for a government work-relief program.

Eugene Debs's (1855–1926) American Railway Union struck the Pullman Palace Car Co. in Chicago over wage cuts and job losses. The **Pullman Strike** (1894) was ended by force.

The **Wilson-Gorman Tariff** (1894) did little to promote overseas trade as a way to ease the depression. The **Dingley Tariff** (1897) raised protection to new highs for certain commodities.

Social and Cultural Developments (1892–1897)

The **Anti-Saloon League** was formed in 1893. Women were especially concerned about the increase of drunkenness during the depression.

Immigration declined by almost 400,000 during the depression. Settlement houses helped poor immigrants. Such institutions also lobbied against sweatshop labor conditions, and for bans on child labor.

Foreign Relations (1892–1897)

The Cuban revolt against Spain in 1895 threatened American business interests in Cuba. Sensational "yellow" journalism, and nationalistic statements from officials such as Assistant Secretary of the Navy Theodore Roosevelt (1858–1919), encouraged popular support for direct American military intervention on behalf of Cuban independence. President McKinley, however, proceeded cautiously through 1897.

The Sino-Japanese War (1894–1895)

Japan's easy victory over China signaled to the United States and other nations trading in Asia that China's weakness might result in its colonization by industrial powers, and thus, in the closing of the China market. This concern led the United States to announce the Open Door policy with China, designed to protect equal opportunity of trade and China's political independence (1899 and 1900).

Foreign Policy (1897–1902)

On March 27, President McKinley asked Spain to call an armistice, accept American mediation to end the war, and end the use of concentration camps in Cuba. Spain refused to comply. On April 21, Congress declared war on Spain with the objective of establishing Cuban independence (**Teller Amendment**). The first U.S. forces landed in Cuba on June 22, 1898, and by July 17 had defeated the Spanish forces.

On May 1, 1898, the Spanish fleet in the Philippines was destroyed, and Manila surrendered on August 13. Spain agreed to a peace conference to be held in Paris in October 1898, where it ceded the Philippines, Puerto Rico, and Guam to the United States, in return for a payment of $20 million to Spain for the Philippines. The Treaty of Paris was ratified by the Senate on February 6, 1900.

Filipino nationalists under Emilio Aguinaldo (1869–1964) rebelled against the United States (February 1899) when they learned the Philippines would not be given independence. The United States used 70,000 men to suppress the revolutionaries by June 1902. A special U.S. commission recommended eventual self-government for the Philippines.

During the war with Spain, the United States annexed Hawaii on July 7, 1898. In 1900, the United States claimed Wake Island, 2,000 miles west of Hawaii.

Although Cuba was granted its independence, the **Platt Amendment** of 1901 guaranteed that it would become a virtual protectorate of the United States. Cuba could not: (1) make a treaty with a foreign state impairing its independence, or (2) contract an excessive public debt. Cuba was required to: (1) allow the United States to preserve order on the island, and (2) lease a naval base for 99 years to the United States at Guantanamo Bay.

Politics of the Period (1900–1902)

The unexpected death of Vice President Garrett Hobart led the Republican party to choose the war hero and reform governor of New York, Theodore Roosevelt, as President William McKinley's vice presidential running mate. The Democrats once again nominated William Jennings Bryan on a platform condemning imperialism and the gold standard. McKinley easily won reelection and the Republicans retained control of both houses of Congress.

President McKinley was shot on September 6 by Leon Czolgosz, an anarchist. The president died on September 14. Theodore Roosevelt became the nation's 25th president, and at age 42, its youngest to date.

Theodore Roosevelt and Progressive Reforms (1902–1907)

The president pledged strict enforcement of the Sherman Antitrust Act (1890), which was designed to break up illegal monopolies and regulate large corporations for the public good.

In the **Hepburn Act (1906)**, membership of the Interstate Commerce Commission was increased from five to seven. The I.C.C. could set its own fair freight rates; had its regulatory power extended over pipelines, bridges, and express companies; and was empowered to require a uniform system of accounting by regulated transportation companies.

The **Pure Food and Drug Act (1906)** prohibited the manufacture, sale, and transportation of adulterated or fraudulently labeled foods and drugs in accordance with consumer demands.

The **Meat Inspection Act (1906)** provided for federal and sanitary regulations and inspections in meat packing facilities.

The Economy (1902–1907)

1. Antitrust Policy (1902)

Attorney General P. C. Knox (1853–1921) first brought suit against the Northern Securities Company, a railroad holding corporation put together by J. P. Morgan (1837–1913), and then moved against Rockefeller's Standard Oil Company. By the time he left office in 1909, Roosevelt had indictments against 25 monopolies.

2. Department of Commerce and Labor (1903)

A new cabinet position was created to address the concerns of business and labor. Within the department, the Bureau of Corporations was empowered to investigate and report on the illegal activities of corporations.

3. Coal Strike (1902)

Roosevelt interceded with government mediation to bring about negotiations between the United Mine Workers union and the anthracite mine owners after a bitter strike over wages, safety conditions, and union recognition. This was the first time that the government intervened in a labor dispute without automatically siding with management.

A brief economic recession and panic occurred in 1907 as a result, in part, of questionable bank speculations, a lack of flexible monetary and credit policies, and a conservative gold standard. This event called attention to the need for banking reform which would lead to the Federal Reserve System in 1913.

Muckrakers (a term coined by Roosevelt) were investigative journalists and authors who were often the publicity agents for reforms.

Foreign Relations (1902–1907)

1. Panama Canal

Roosevelt engineered the separation of Panama from Colombia and the recognition of Panama as an independent country. The **Hay-Bunau-Varilla Treaty of 1903** granted the United States control of the canal zone in Panama for $10 million and an annual fee of $250,000, beginning nine years after ratification of the treaty by both parties. Construction of the canal began in 1904 and was completed in 1914.

2. Roosevelt Corollary to the Monroe Doctrine

The United States reserved the right to intervene in the internal affairs of Latin American nations to keep European powers from using military force to collect debts in the Western Hemisphere. The United States, by 1905, had intervened in the affairs of Venezuela, Haiti, the Dominican Republic, Nicaragua, and Cuba.

3. Taft-Katsura Memo (1905)

The United States and Japan pledged to maintain the Open Door principles in China. Japan recognized American control over the Philippines, and the United States granted a Japanese protectorate over Korea.

4. Gentleman's Agreement with Japan (1907)

After numerous incidents of racial discrimination against Japanese in California, Japan agreed to restrict the emigration of unskilled Japanese workers to the United States.

The Regulatory State and the Ordered Society (1907–1912)

Deciding not to run for reelection, Theodore Roosevelt opened the way for William H. Taft (1857–1930) (Ohio) to run on a Republican platform calling for a continuation of antitrust enforcement, environmental conservation, and a lower tariff policy to promote international trade. The Democrats nominated William Jennings Bryan for a third time on an antimonopoly and low tariff platform. Taft easily won and the Republicans retained control of both houses of Congress. For the first time, the American Federation of Labor entered national politics officially with an endorsement of Bryan. This decision began a long alliance between organized labor and the Democratic party in the twentieth century.

The 1912 election was one of the most dramatic in American history. President Taft's inability to maintain party harmony led Theodore Roosevelt to return to national politics. When denied the Republican nomination, Roosevelt and his supporters formed the Progressive (Bull Moose) party and nominated Roosevelt for president on a political platform nicknamed "The New Nationalism." Roosevelt also called for a Federal Trade Commission to regulate the economy, a stronger executive, and more government planning.

President Taft and Vice President Sherman were nominated by Republicans on a platform of "Quiet Confidence," which called for a continuation of the progressive programs pursued by Taft.

A compromise gave the Democratic nomination to New Jersey Governor Woodrow Wilson. Wilson called his campaign the "New Freedom"; it borrowed pieces from the Progressive and Republican platforms.

The Republican split paved the way for Wilson's victory. Although a minority president, Wilson garnered the largest electoral majority in American history up to that time. Democrats won control of both houses of Congress.

The Wilson Presidency

Before the outbreak of World War I in 1914, President Wilson achieved much of the remaining progressive agenda, including lower tariff reform (**Underwood-Simmons Act**, 1913), the Sixteenth Amendment (graduated income tax, 1913), the Seventeenth Amendment (direct election of senators, 1913), the Federal Reserve banking system (which provided regulation and flexibility to monetary policy, 1913), the Federal Trade Commission (to investigate unfair business practices, 1914), and the Clayton Antitrust Act (improving the old Sherman act and protecting labor unions and farm cooperatives from prosecution, 1914). Other goals such as the protection of children in the work force (**Keating-Owen Act**, 1916), credit reform for agriculture (**Federal Farm Loan Act**, 1916), and an independent tariff commission (1916) came later.

Social and Cultural Developments (1907–1912)

In 1905, the African-American intellectual militant W. E. B. DuBois (1868–1963) founded the **Niagara Movement** which called for federal legislation to protect racial equality and for full rights of citizenship. The **National Association for the Advancement of Colored People (NAACP)** was organized in 1909.

A radical labor organization called the **Industrial Workers of the World** (I.W.W., or Wobblies, 1905–1924) was active in promoting violence and revolution. After the Red Scare of 1919, the government worked to smash the I.W.W. and deported many of its immigrant leaders and members.

Foreign Relations (1907–1915)

President Taft sought to avoid military intervention, especially in Latin America, by replacing "big stick" policies with "dollar diplomacy" in the expectation that American financial investments would encourage economic, social, and political stability. This idea proved an illusion.

Wilson urged Huerta to hold democratic elections and adopt a constitutional government. Huerta refused, and Wilson invaded Mexico with troops at Veracruz in 1914. A second U.S. invasion came in northern Mexico in 1916.

WILSON AND WORLD WAR I (1912–1920)

The Early Years of the Wilson Administration

Wilson was only the second Democrat (Cleveland was the first) elected president since the Civil War. Key appointments to the cabinet were William Jennings Bryan as secretary of state and William Gibbs McAdoo (1863–1941) as secretary of the treasury.

The **Federal Reserve Act of 1913** divided the nation into 12 regions, each with a Federal Reserve bank. Federal Reserve banks loaned money to member banks at interest less than the public paid to the member banks. This allowed the Federal Reserve to control interest rates by raising or lowering the discount rate. The money loaned to the member banks was in the form of a new currency, Federal Reserve notes, which was backed 60% by commercial paper and 40% by gold.

The system was supervised and policy was set by a national Federal Reserve Board composed of the secretary of the treasury, the comptroller of the currency, and five other members appointed by the U.S. president of the United States.

The **Clayton Antitrust Act of 1914** supplemented and interpreted the Sherman Antitrust Act of 1890. Under its provisions, stock ownership by a corporation in a competing corporation was prohibited, and the same persons were prohibited from managing competing corporations. Price discrimination (charging less in some regions than in others to undercut the competition) and exclusive contracts which reduced competition were prohibited.

The Election of 1916

The Democrats, nominated Wilson and adopted his platform calling for continued progressive reforms and neutrality in the European war. The Republican convention bypassed Theodore Roosevelt and chose Charles Evans Hughes (1862–1948), an associate justice of the Supreme Court and formerly a progressive Republican governor of New York. Wilson won the election.

Social Issues in the First Wilson Administration

In 1913, Treasury Secretary William G. McAdoo and Postmaster General Albert S. Burleson segregated workers in some parts of their departments with no objection from Wilson. Many northern blacks and whites protested.

Wilson opposed immigration restrictions and vetoed a literacy test for immigrants in 1915, but in 1917, Congress overrode a similar veto.

Wilson's Foreign Policy and the Road to War

Wilson promised a more moral foreign policy than that of his predecessors, denouncing imperialism and dollar diplomacy, and advocating the advancement of democratic capitalist governments throughout the world.

In 1912, American marines landed in Nicaragua to maintain order. The Wilson administration kept the marines in Nicaragua and negotiated the Bryan-Chamorro Treaty of 1914, which gave the United States an option to build a canal through the country.

Claiming that political anarchy existed in Haiti, Wilson sent marines in 1915 and imposed a treaty making the country a protectorate, with American control of its finances and constabulary. The marines remained until 1934.

Wilson feared in 1915 that Germany might annex Denmark and its Caribbean possession, the Danish West Indies or Virgin Islands. After extended negotiations, the United States purchased the islands from Denmark by treaty on August 4, 1916, for $25 million and took possession of them on March 31, 1917.

In 1913, Wilson refused to recognize the government of Mexican military dictator Victoriano Huerta. When the Huerta government arrested several American seamen in Tampico in April 1914, American forces occupied the port of Veracruz. In July 1914, Huerta abdicated his power to Venustiano Carranza, who was soon opposed by his former general Francisco "Pancho" Villa (1878–1923). Seeking American intervention as a means of undermining Carranza, Villa shot 16 Americans on a train in northern Mexico in January 1916 and burned the border town of Columbus, New Mexico, in March 1916, killing 19 people. A force of about 6,000 army troops under the command of General John J. Pershing crossed the Rio Grande on March 18. The force advanced more than 300 miles into Mexico, failed to capture Villa, and became, in effect, an army of occupation. The Carranza government demanded an American withdrawal, and several clashes with Mexican troops occurred. War threatened, but in January 1917 Wilson removed the American forces.

The Road to War in Europe

When World War I broke out in Europe, Wilson issued a proclamation of American neutrality on August 4, 1914. Nonethess, the United States became a major supplier of Allied munitions, food, and raw materials.

The sinking of the British liner *Lusitania* off the coast of Ireland on May 7, 1915, brought strong protests from Wilson. Secretary of State Bryan, who believed Americans should stay off belligerent ships, resigned rather than insist on questionable neutral rights and was replaced by Robert Lansing.

Early in 1915, Wilson sent his friend and adviser Colonel Edward M. House on an unsuccessful visit to Europe to offer American mediation in the war. Late in the year, House returned to London to propose that Wilson call a peace conference; if Germany refused to attend or was uncooperative at the conference, the United States could enter the war on the Allied side. An agreement to that effect, called the **House-Grey memorandum**, was signed by the British foreign secretary, Sir Edward Grey, on February 22, 1916.

In an address to Congress on January 22, 1917, Wilson made his last offer to serve as a neutral mediator. He proposed a "peace without victory," based not on a "balance of power" but on a "community of power."

Germany announced on January 31, 1917, that it would sink all ships, belligerent or neutral, without warning in a large war zone off the coasts of the Allied nations in the eastern Atlantic and the Mediterranean. Wilson broke diplomatic relations with Germany on February 3. During February and March several American merchant ships were sunk by submarines.

The British intercepted a secret message from the German foreign secretary, Arthur Zimmerman, to the German minister in Mexico, and turned it over to the United States on February 24, 1917. The Germans proposed that, in the event of a war between the United States and Germany, Mexico attack the United States. After the war, the "lost territories" of Texas, New Mexico, and Arizona would be returned to Mexico. When the telegram was released to the press on March 1, many Americans became convinced that war with Germany was necessary. A declaration of war against Germany was signed by Wilson on April 6.

World War I: The Military Campaign

When the Germans mounted a major drive toward Paris in the spring of 1918, the Americans experienced their first important engagements. In June, they prevented the Germans from crossing the Marne at Chateau-Thierry, and cleared the area of Belleau Woods. In July, eight American divisions aided French troops in attacking the German line between Reims and Soissons. The American First Army, with over half a million men under Pershing's immediate command, was assembled in August 1918, and began a major offensive at St. Mihiel on the southern part of the front on September 12. Following the successful operation, Pershing began a drive against the German defenses between Verdun and Sedan, an action called the **Meuse-Argonne offensive**. He reached Sedan on November 7. During the same period the English in the north and the French along the central front also broke through the German lines. The fighting ended with the armistice on November 11, 1918.

Mobilizing the Home Front

The anti-German and antisubversive war hysteria in the United States far exceeded similar public moods in Britain and France during the war. The **Espionage Act of 1917** provided for fines and imprisonment for persons who made false statements which aided the enemy, incited rebellion in the military, or obstructed recruitment or the draft. Printed matter advocating treason or insurrection could be excluded from the mails. The **Sedition Act of May 1918** forbade any criticism of the government, flag, or uniform, even if there were not detrimental consequences. The Espionage Act was upheld by the Supreme Court in the case of *Schenck v. United States* in 1919. The opinion, written by Justice Oliver Wendell Holmes, Jr. (1841–1935), stated that Congress could limit free speech when the words represented a "clear and present danger," and that a person cannot cry "fire" in a crowded theater. The Sedition Act was similarly upheld in *Abrams v. United States* a few months later.

Wartime Social Trends

Large numbers of women, mostly white, were hired by factories and other enterprises in jobs never before open to them. The labor shortage also opened industrial jobs to Mexican-Americans and to African-Americans. About half a million rural southern African-Americans migrated to cities, mainly in the North and Midwest, to obtain employment in war and other industries, especially in steel and meatpacking. In 1917, there were race riots in 26 cities in the North and South, with the worst in East St. Louis, Illinois.

In December 1917, a constitutional amendment to prohibit the manufacture and sale of alcoholic beverages in the United States was passed by Congress and submitted to the states for ratification.

Peacemaking and Domestic Problems (1918–1920)

From the time of the American entry into the war, Wilson insisted that there should be peace without victory, meaning that the victors would not be vindictive toward the losers. In an address to Congress on January 8, 1918, he presented his specific peace plan in the form of the **Fourteen Points**. The first five points called for open rather than secret peace treaties, freedom of the seas, free trade, arms reduction, and a fair adjustment of colonial claims. The next eight points were concerned with the national aspirations of various European peoples and the adjustment of boundaries. The fourteenth point, which he considered the most important and had espoused as early as 1916, called for a "general association of nations" to preserve the peace.

Wilson decided that he would lead the American delegation to the peace conference which opened in Paris on January 12, 1919. In the negotiations, which continued until May 1919, Wilson found it necessary to make many compromises in forging the text of the treaty.

On July 26, 1919, Wilson presented the treaty with the League within it to the Senate for ratification. The main objection centered on Article X of the League Covenant, where the reservationists (those who apposed the treaty but might accept it with changes) wanted it understood that the United States would not go to war to defend a League member without the approval of Congress.

Wilson collapsed after a speech in Pueblo, Colorado, on September 25, and suffered a severe stroke on October 2 which paralyzed his left side. He was seriously ill for several months, and never fully recovered. The treaty failed to get a two-thirds majority either with or without the reservationists.

The Senate took up the treaty again in February 1920, and on March 19 it was again defeated both with and without the reservationists. The United States officially ended the war with Germany by a resolution of Congress signed on July 2, 1921, and a separate peace treaty was ratified on July 25. The United States did not join the League.

Domestic Problems and the End of the Wilson Administration

In January 1919, the Eighteenth Amendment to the Constitution prohibiting the manufacture, sale, transportation, or importation of intoxicating liquors was ratified by the states, and it became effective in January 1920. The Nineteenth Amendment, providing for women's suffrage, was ratified by the states in time for the election of 1920.

Americans feared the spread of the Russian Communist revolution to the United States, and many interpreted the widespread strikes of 1919, spurred by inflation, as Communist-inspired and the beginning of the revolution. The anti-German hysteria of the war years was transformed into the anti-Communist and antiforeign hysteria of 1919 and 1920, and continued in various forms through the 1920s.

In August 1919, Attorney General A. Mitchell Palmer, named J. Edgar Hoover (1895–1972) to head a new Intelligence Division in the Justice Department to collect information about radicals. Palmer announced that huge Communist riots were planned for major cities on May Day (May 1, 1920). When the day passed with no radical activity, Palmer was discredited and the Red Scare subsided.

White hostility based on competition for lower-paying jobs and black encroachment into neighborhoods led to race riots in 25 cities, with hundreds killed or wounded and millions of dollars in property damage.

THE ROARING TWENTIES AND ECONOMIC COLLAPSE (1920–1929)

The Election of 1920

Senator Warren G. Harding (1865–1923) of Ohio was nominated by Republicans as a dark-horse candidate, and Governor Calvin Coolidge (1872–1933) of Massachusetts was chosen as the vice presidential nominee. The platform opposed the League and promised low taxes, high tariffs, immigration restriction, and aid to farmers.

Governor James Cox was nominated by Democrats on the 44th ballot, and Franklin D. Roosevelt (1882–1945), an assistant secretary of the Navy and distant cousin of Theodore, was selected as his running mate. The platform endorsed the League, but left the door open for reservations.

The Twenties: Economic Advances and Social Tensions

The principal driving force of the economy of the 1920s was the automobile. Automobile manufacturing stimulated supporting industries such as steel, rubber, and glass, as well as gasoline refining and highway construction. During the 1920s, the United States became a nation of paved roads. The Federal Highway Act of 1916 started the federal highway system and gave matching funds to the states for construction.

Purchases of "big ticket" items such as automobiles, refrigerators, and furniture were made possible by installment or time payment credit. Consumer interest and demand was spurred by the great increase in professional advertising, which used newspapers, magazines, radio, billboards, and other media.

There was a trend toward corporate consolidation during the 1920s. In the automobile industry, Ford, General Motors, and Chrysler produced 83% of the vehicles in 1929. Government regulatory agencies such as the Federal Trade Commission and the Interstate Commerce Commission were passive and generally controlled by persons from the business world.

There was also a trend toward bank consolidation. Because corporations were raising much of their money through the sale of stocks and bonds, the demand for business loans declined. Commercial banks then put more of their funds into real estate loans, loans to brokers against stocks and bonds, and the purchase of stocks and bonds themselves.

American Society in the 1920s

By 1920 a majority of Americans (51%) lived in an urban area with a population of 2,500 or more. A new phenomenon of the 1920s was the tremendous growth of suburbs and satellite cities. Streetcars, commuter railroads, and automobiles contributed to the process, as well as the easy availability of financing for home construction. The suburbs had once been the domain of the wealthy, but the technology of the 1920s opened them to working-class families.

Traditional American moral standards regarding premarital sex and marital fidelity were widely questioned for the first time during the 1920s. Birth control, though illegal, was promoted by Margaret Sanger (1883–1966) and others and was widely accepted.

Divorce laws were liberalized in many states at the insistence of women. Domestic service was the largest job category. Most other women workers were in traditional female occupations such as secretarial and clerical work, retail sales, teaching, and nursing. Rates of pay were below those for men. Most women still pursued the traditional role of housewife and mother, and society accepted that as the norm.

The migration of southern rural African-Americans to the cities continued. By 1930, about 20% of American blacks lived in the North, with the largest concentrations in New York, Chicago, and Philadelphia. While they were generally better off economically in the cities than they had been as tenant farmers, they generally held low-paying jobs and were confined to segregated areas of the cities.

A native of Jamaica, Marcus Garvey (1887–1940) founded the **Universal Negro Improvement Association**, advocating African-American racial pride and separatism rather than integration, and called for a return of African-Americans to Africa. In 1921, he proclaimed himself the provisional president of an African empire, and sold stock in the Black Star Steamship Line which would take migrants to Africa. The line went bankrupt in 1923, and Garvey was convicted, imprisoned for mail fraud in the sale of the line's stock, and then deported.

Many writers of the 1920s were disgusted with the hypocrisy and materialism of contemporary American society. Often called the "Lost Generation," many of them, such as novelists Ernest Hemingway (1899–1961) and F. Scott Fitzgerald (1896–1940) and poets Ezra Pound (1885–1972) and T. S. Eliot (1888–1965), moved to Europe.

Social Conflicts

The clash of farm values with the values of an industrial society of urban workers was evident. The traditionalist backlash against modern urban industrial society expressed itself primarily through intolerance.

On Thanksgiving Day in 1915, the Knights of the Ku Klux Klan, modeled on the organization of the same name in the 1860s and 1870s, was founded near Atlanta by William J. Simmons. Its purpose was to intimidate African-Americans. By 1923, the Klan had about five million members throughout the nation. The largest concentrations of members were in the South, the Southwest, the Midwest, California, and Oregon.

Labor leaders believed that immigrants depressed wages and impeded unionization. In June 1917, Congress, over Wilson's veto, imposed a literacy test for immigrants and excluded many Asian nationalists. In 1921, Congress passed the Emergency Quota Act. In practice, the law admitted about as many as wanted to come from such nations as Britain, Ireland, and Germany, while severely restricting Italians, Greeks, Poles, and east European Jews. It became effective in 1922 and reduced the number of immigrants annually to about 40% of the 1921 total. Congress then passed the National Origins Act of 1924, which further reduced the number of south and east Europeans, and cut the annual immigration to 20% of the 1921 figure. In 1927, the annual maximum was reduced to 150,000.

Fundamentalist Protestants, under the leadership of William Jennings Bryan, began a campaign in 1921 to prohibit the teaching of evolution in the schools, and thus protect belief in the literal biblical account of creation. The idea was especially well received in the South.

On April 15, 1920, two unidentified gunmen robbed a shoe factory and killed two men in South Braintree, Massachusetts. Nicola Sacco and Bartolomeo Vanzetti, Italian immigrants and admitted anarchists, were tried for the murders. After they were convicted and sentenced to death in July 1921, there was much protest in the United States and in Europe that they had not received a fair trial. After six years of delays, they were executed on August 23, 1927. Fifty years later, on July 19, 1977, the pair were vindicated by Governor Michael Dukakis.

Government and Politics in the 1920s: The Harding Administration

Harding spent much of his life as the publisher of a newspaper in the small city of Marion, Ohio. Harding appointed some outstanding persons to his cabinet, including Secretary of State Charles Evans Hughes, a former Supreme Court justice and presidential candidate; Secretary of the Treasury Andrew Mellon (1855–1937), a Pittsburgh aluminum and banking magnate and reportedly the richest man in America; and Secretary of Commerce Herbert Hoover, a dynamic multimillionaire mine owner famous for his wartime relief efforts. Less impressive was his appointment of his cronies Albert B. Fall as secretary of the interior and Harry M. Daugherty as attorney general.

The **Teapot Dome Scandal** began when Secretary of the Interior Albert B. Fall in 1921 secured the transfer of several naval oil reserves to his jurisdiction. In 1922, he secretly leased reserves at Teapot Dome in Wyoming to Harry F. Sinclair of Monmouth Oil and at Elk Hills in California to

Edward Doheny of Pan-American Petroleum. Sinclair and Doheny were acquitted in 1927 of charges of defrauding the government, but in 1929, Fall was convicted, fined, and imprisoned for bribery.

Vice President Calvin Coolidge became president upon Harding's death in 1923.

The Election of 1924

Calvin Coolidge was nominated by the Republicans. The platform endorsed business development, low taxes, and rigid economy in government. The party stood on its record of economic growth and prosperity since 1922.

Robert M. LaFollette, after failing in a bid for the Republican nomination, formed a new Progressive party, with support from Midwest farm groups, socialists, and the American Federation of Labor. The platform attacked monopolies, and called for the nationalization of railroads, the direct election of the president, and other reforms.

John W. Davis was nominated by the Democrats and presented little contrast with the Republicans.

The Election of 1928

Coolidge did not seek another term, and the Republican convention quickly nominated Herbert Hoover, the secretary of commerce, for president. The platform endorsed the policies of the Harding and Coolidge administrations.

Governor Alfred E. Smith (1873–1944) of New York, a Catholic and an anti-prohibitionist, controlled most of the nonsouthern delegations. Southerners supported his nomination with the understanding that the platform would not advocate repeal of prohibition. The platform differed little from the Republican, except in advocating lower tariffs.

The Great Depression: The Crash

Stock prices increased throughout the decade. The boom in prices and volume of sales was especially active after 1925, and was intensive during 1928–1929. Careful investors, realizing that stocks were overpriced, began to sell to take their profits. During October 1929, prices declined as more stock was sold. On "**Black Thursday**," October 24, 1929, almost 13 million shares were traded, a large number for that time, and prices fell precipitously. Investment banks tried to boost the market by buying, but on October 29, "Black Tuesday," the market fell about 40 points, with 16.5 million shares traded.

THE GREAT DEPRESSION AND THE NEW DEAL (1929–1941)
Reasons for the Depression

A stock-market crash does not mean that a depression must follow. In 1929, a complex interaction of many factors caused the decline of the economy.

Many people had bought stock on a margin of 10%, meaning that they had borrowed 90% of the purchase through a broker's loan and put up the stock as collateral. When the price of a stock fell more than 10%, the lender sold the stock for whatever it would bring and thus further depressed prices. The forced sales brought great losses to the banks and businesses that had financed the broker's loans, as well as to the investors.

There were already signs of recession before the market crash in 1929. The farm economy, which involved almost 25% of the population, had been depressed throughout the decade. Coal, railroads, and New England textiles had not been prosperous. After 1927, new construction declined and auto sales began to sag.

During the early months of the depression, most people thought it was just an adjustment in the business cycle which would soon be over. As time went on, the worst depression in American history set in, reaching its bottom point in early 1932.

Hoover's Depression Policies

Passed in June 1929, before the market crash, **The Agricultural Marketing Act** created the Federal Farm Board. It had a revolving fund of $500 million to lend agricultural cooperatives to buy commodities, such as wheat and cotton, and hold them for higher prices.

The **Hawley-Smoot Tariff**, passed in June 1930, raised duties on both agricultural and manufactured imports.

Chartered by Congress in 1932, the **Reconstruction Finance Corporation (RFC)** loaned money to railroads, banks, and other financial institutions. It prevented the failure of basic firms, on which many other elements of the economy depended, but was criticized by some as relief for the rich.

The **Federal Home Loan Bank Act**, passed in July 1932, created home-loan banks to make loans to building and loan associations, savings banks, and insurance companies to help them avoid foreclosures on homes.

The First New Deal

The Republicans renominated Hoover while the Democrats nominated Franklin D. Roosevelt, governor of New York. Although calling for a cut in spending, Roosevelt communicated optimism and easily defeated Hoover. In February 1933, before Roosevelt took office, Congress passed the Twenty-First Amendment to repeal prohibition.

When Roosevelt was inaugurated on March 4, 1933, the American economic system seemed to be on the verge of collapse. Roosevelt assured the nation that "the only thing we have to fear is fear itself," called for a special session of Congress to convene on March 9, and asked for "broad executive powers to wage war against the emergency." Two days later, he closed all banks and forbade the export of gold or the redemption of currency in gold.

Legislation of the First New Deal

The special session of Congress, from March 9 to June 16, 1933, has been referred to ever since as the "**Hundred Days**." Historians have divided Roosevelt's legislation into the First New Deal (1933–1935) and a new wave of programs beginning in 1935 called the Second New Deal.

The **Emergency Banking Relief Act** provided additional funds for banks from the RFC and the Federal Reserve, allowed the Treasury to open sound banks after 10 days and to merge or liquidate unsound ones, and forbade the hoarding or export of gold. Roosevelt, on March 12, assured the public of the soundness of the banks in the first of many "**fireside chats**," or radio addresses. People believed him, and most banks were soon open with more deposits than withdrawals.

The Banking Act of 1933, or the **Glass-Steagall Act**, established the Federal Deposit Insurance Corporation (FDIC) to insure individual deposits in commercial banks, and separated commercial banking from the more speculative activity of investment banking.

The **Truth-in-Securities Act** required that full information about stocks and bonds be provided by brokers and others to potential purchasers.

The **Home Owners Loan Corporation (HOLC)** had authority to borrow money to refinance home mortgages and thus prevent foreclosures.

The nation went off the gold standard. Eventually, on January 31, 1934, the value of the dollar was set at $35 per ounce of gold, 59% of its former value. The object of the devaluation was to raise prices and help American exports.

The **Securities and Exchange Commission** was created in 1934 to supervise stock exchanges and to punish fraud in securities trading.

The **Federal Housing Administration (FHA)** was created to insure long-term, low-interest mortgages for home construction and repair.

These programs, intended to provide temporary relief for people in need, were to be disbanded when the economy improved.

The **Federal Emergency Relief Act** appropriated $500 million for aid to the poor to be distributed by state and local governments. It also established the Federal Emergency Relief Administration under Harry Hopkins (1890–1946).

The **Civilian Conservation Corps** enrolled 250,000 young men aged 18 to 24 from families on relief to go to camps where they worked on flood control, soil conservation, and forest projects under the direction of the War Department.

The **Public Works Administration**, under Secretary of the Interior Harold Ickes, had $3.3 billion to distribute to state and local governments for building projects such as schools, highways, and hospitals.

In November 1933, Roosevelt established the **Civil Works Administration** to hire four million unemployed workers. The temporary and makeshift nature of the jobs, such as sweeping streets, brought much criticism, and the experiment was terminated in April 1934.

The **Agricultural Adjustment Act of 1933** created the Agricultural Adjustment Administration (AAA). Farmers agreed to reduce production of principal farm commodities and were paid a subsidy in return. Farm prices increased, but tenants and sharecroppers were hurt when owners took land out of cultivation.

The **Federal Farm Loan Act** consolidated all farm credit programs into the Farm Credit Administration to make low-interest loans for farm mortgages and other agricultural purposes.

The **Commodity Credit Corporation** was established in October 1933 by the AAA to make loans to corn and cotton farmers against their crops so that they could hold them for higher prices.

The **Frazier-Lemke Farm Bankruptcy Act of 1934** allowed farmers to defer foreclosure on their land while they obtained new financing, and helped them to recover property already lost through easy financing.

The **National Industrial Recovery Act** was viewed as the cornerstone of the recovery program. It sought to stabilize the economy by preventing extreme competition, labor-management conflicts, and overproduction.

The **TVA**, a public corporation under a three-member board, built 20 dams in an area of 40,000 square miles to stop flooding and soil erosion, improve navigation, and generate hydroelectric power. It also manufactured nitrates for fertilizer, conducted demonstration projects for farmers, engaged in reforestation, and attempted to rehabilitate the whole area.

The economy improved but did not recover. The GNP, money supply, salaries, wages, and farm income rose. Unemployment dropped from about 25% of nonfarm workers in 1933 to about 20.1%, or 10.6 million, in 1935.

The Second New Deal: Opposition

The **Share Our Wealth Society** was founded in 1934 by Senator Huey "The Kingfish" Long (1893–1935) of Louisiana. Long supported Roosevelt in 1932, but then broke with him, calling him a tool of Wall Street for not doing more to combat the depression. His society had more than five million members when he was assassinated on the steps of the Louisiana Capitol on September 8, 1935.

The Second New Deal Begins

The **Works Progress Administration (WPA)** was started in May 1935, following the passage of the Emergency Relief Appropriations Act of April 1935. The WPA employed people from the relief rolls for 30 hours of work a week at pay double the relief payment but less than private employment.

The **National Youth Administration (NYA)** was established as part of the WPA in June 1935, to provide part-time jobs for high school and college students to enable them to stay in school, and to help young adults not in school to find jobs.

The **Rural Electrification Administration (REA)** was created in May 1935 to provide loans and WPA labor to electric cooperatives so they could build lines into rural areas not served by private companies.

The **Social Security Act**, passed in August 1935, established a retirement plan for persons over age 65, which was to be funded by a tax on wages paid equally by employee and employer. The first benefits, ranging from $10 to $85 per month, were paid in 1942.

The **Banking Act of 1935** created a strong central Board of Governors of the Federal Reserve system with broad powers over the operations of the regional banks.

The Election of 1936

Roosevelt had put together a coalition of followers who made the Democratic party the majority party in the nation for the first time since the Civil War. While retaining the Democratic base in the South and among white ethnics in the big cities, Roosevelt also received strong support from mid-western farmers. Two groups that made a dramatic shift into the Democratic ranks were union workers and African-Americans.

The Last Years of the New Deal

Frustrated by a conservative Supreme Court which had overturned much of his New Deal legislation, Roosevelt, in February 1937, proposed to Congress the **Judicial Reorganization Bill**, which would allow the president to name a new federal judge for each judge who did not retire by the age of 70½. The president was astonished by the wave of opposition from Democrats and Republicans alike, but he uncharacteristically refused to compromise. In doing so, he not only lost the bill but control of the Democratic Congress, which he had dominated since 1933. Nonetheless, the Court changed its position, as Chief Justice Charles Evans Hughes and Justice Owen Roberts began to vote with the more liberal members.

Most economic indicators rose sharply between 1935 and 1937. Roosevelt decided that the recovery was sufficient to warrant a reduction in relief programs and a move toward a balanced budget. During the winter of 1937–1938, the economy slipped rapidly and unemployment rose to 12.5%. In July 1938, the economy began to recover, and it regained the 1937 levels in 1939.

Social Dimensions of the New Deal Era

Unemployment for African-Americans was much higher than for the general population, and before 1933 they were often excluded from state and local relief efforts. Roosevelt issued an executive order on June 25, 1941, establishing the Fair Employment Practices Committee to ensure consideration for minorities in defense employment.

John Collier, the commissioner of the Bureau of Indian Affairs, persuaded Congress to repeal the Dawes Act of 1887 by passing the Indian Reorganization Act of 1934. The law restored tribal ownership of lands, recognized tribal constitutions and government, and provided loans to tribes for economic development.

Labor Unions

The National Industrial Recovery Act guaranteed the right to unionize. The passage of the National Labor Relations or Wagner Act in 1935 resulted in a massive growth of union membership. The American Federation of Labor was made up primarily of craft unions. In November 1935, John L. Lewis and others established the Committee for Industrial Organization to unionize basic industries, presumably within the AFL. President William Green of the AFL ordered the CIO to disband in January 1936.

During its organizational period, the CIO sought to initiate several industrial unions, particularly in the steel, auto, rubber, and radio industries. In late 1936 and early 1937, it used a tactic called the **sit-down strike**, with the strikers occupying the workplace to prevent any production. By the end of 1941, the CIO was larger than the AFL.

New Deal Diplomacy and the Road to War

Roosevelt and Secretary of State Cordell Hull endeavored to improve relations with Latin American nations, and formalized their position by calling it the **Good Neighbor Policy**.

At the Montevideo Conference of American Nations in December of 1933, the United States renounced the right of intervention in the internal affairs of Latin American countries. In 1936, in the Buenos Aires Convention, the United States agreed to submit all American disputes to arbitration.

United States Neutrality Legislation

A Gallup poll in April 1937 showed that almost two-thirds of those responding thought that American entry into World War I had been a mistake. The **Johnson Act of 1934** prohibited any nation in default on World War I payments from selling securities to any American citizen or corporation. On outbreak of war between foreign nations, all exports of American arms and munitions to them would be embargoed for six months under the **Neutrality Acts of 1935**.

The **Neutrality Acts of 1936** gave the president authority to determine when a state of war existed, and prohibited any loans or credits to belligerents. The **Neutrality Acts of 1937** gave the president authority to determine if a civil war was a threat to world peace and if it was covered by the Neutrality Acts. It also prohibited all arms sales to belligerents, and allowed the cash-and-carry sale of nonmilitary goods to belligerents.

The American Response to the War in Europe

In August 1939, Roosevelt created the War Resources Board to develop a plan for industrial mobilization in the event of war. The next month, he established the Office of Emergency Management in the White House to centralize mobilization activities.

Roosevelt officially proclaimed the neutrality of the United States on September 5, 1939. A new Neutrality Act in November allowed the cash-and-carry sale of arms and short-term loans to belligerents, but forbade American ships to trade with belligerents or Americans to travel on belligerent ships.

Almost all Americans recognized Germany as a threat. They were divided on whether to aid Britain or to concentrate on the defense of America. The Committee to Defend America by Aiding the Allies was formed in May 1940, and the America First Committee, which opposed involvement, was incorporated in September 1940.

In April 1940, Roosevelt declared that Greenland, a possession of conquered Denmark, was covered by the Monroe Doctrine, and he supplied military assistance to set up a coastal patrol there.

In May 1940, Roosevelt appointed a Council of National Defense, chaired by William S. Knudson (1879–1948), the president of General Motors, to direct defense production and to build 50,000 planes. The **Office of Production Management** was created to allocate scarce materials, and the **Office of Price Administration** was established to prevent inflation and protect consumers.

Congress approved the nation's first peacetime draft, the Selective Service and Training Act, in September 1940.

The Election of 1940

The Republicans nominated Wendell L. Willkie (1892–1944) of Indiana, a dark-horse candidate. The platform supported a strong defense program, but severely criticized New Deal domestic policies.

Roosevelt was nominated for a third term, breaking a tradition which had existed since George Washington. The platform endorsed the foreign and domestic policies of the administration. Roosevelt won by a much narrower margin than in 1936.

American Involvement with the European War

The **Lend-Lease Act** let the United States provide supplies to Britain in exchange for goods and services after the war. It was signed on March 11, 1941.

In April 1941, Roosevelt started the **American Neutrality Patrol**. The American navy would search out but not attack German submarines in the western half of the Atlantic and warn British vessels of their location. Also in April, U.S. forces occupied Greenland, and in May, the president declared a state of unlimited national emergency. American marines occupied Iceland, a Danish possession, in July 1941 to protect it from seizure by Germany.

On August 9, 1941, Roosevelt and Winston Churchill issued the Atlantic Charter.

Germany invaded Russia in June 1941, and in November the United States extended lend-lease assistance to the Russians.

The American destroyer *Greer* was attacked by a German submarine near Iceland on September 4, 1941. The American destroyer *Kearny* was attacked by a submarine on October 16, and the destroyer *Reuben James* was sunk on October 30, with 115 lives lost. In November, Congress authorized the arming of merchant ships.

The Road to Pearl Harbor

In late July 1941, the United States placed an embargo on the export of aviation gasoline, lubricants, and scrap iron and steel to Japan. In December, the embargo was extended to include iron ore and pig iron, some chemicals, machine tools, and other products.

In October 1941, a new military cabinet headed by General Hideki Tojo took control of Japan. A new round of talks followed in Washington, but neither side would make a substantive change in its position, and on November 26, Hull repeated the American demand that the Japanese remove all their forces from China and Indochina immediately. The Japanese gave final approval on December 1 for an attack on the United States.

The Japanese planned a major offensive to take the Dutch East Indies, Malaya, and the Philippines in order to obtain the oil, metals, and other raw materials they needed. At the same time, they would attack Pearl Harbor in Hawaii to destroy the American Pacific fleet to keep it from interfering with their plans.

The United States had broken the Japanese diplomatic codes and knew that trouble was imminent. At 7:55 a.m. on Sunday, December 7, 1941, Japanese carrier-based planes attacked the American fleet in Pearl Harbor. The United States suffered the loss of two battleships sunk, six damaged and out of action, three cruisers and three destroyers sunk or damaged, and a number of lesser vessels destroyed or damaged. All of the 150 aircraft at Pearl Harbor were destroyed on the ground. Worst of all, 2,323 American servicemen were killed and about 1,100 wounded. The Japanese lost 29 planes, five midget submarines, and one fleet submarine.

WORLD WAR II AND THE POST-WAR ERA (1941–1960)

Declared War Begins

On December 8, 1941, Congress declared war on Japan, with one dissenting vote. On December 11, Germany and Italy declared war on the United States. Great Britain and the United States then established the Combined Chiefs of Staff, headquartered in Washington, to direct Anglo-American military operations.

On January 1, 1942, representatives of 26 nations met in Washington, D.C., and signed the Declaration of the United Nations, pledging themselves to the principles of the Atlantic Charter and promising not to make a separate peace with their common enemies.

The Home Front

The **War Production Board** was established in 1942 by President Franklin D. Roosevelt for the purpose of regulating the use of raw materials. In April 1942, the General Maximum Price Regulation Act froze prices and extended rationing. In April 1943, prices, wages, and salaries were frozen.

The **Revenue Act of 1942** extended the income tax to the majority of the population. Payroll deduction for the income tax began in 1944. Passed in 1943, the **Smith-Connolly Antistrike Act** authorized government seizure of a plant or mine idled by a strike if the war effort was impeded. It expired in 1947.

In 1944, the Supreme Court (*Korematsu v. United States*) upheld President Roosevelt's 1942 order that Issei (Japanese-Americans who had emigrated from Japan) and Nisei (native born Japanese-Americans) be relocated to concentration camps. The camps were closed in March 1946.

President Franklin D. Roosevelt, together with new vice-presidential candidate Harry S. Truman (1884–1972) of Missouri, defeated his Republican opponent, Governor Thomas E. Dewey of New York. Roosevelt died on April 12, 1945.

The North African and European Theaters

The Allied army under Dwight D. Eisenhower attacked French North Africa in November 1942. The Vichy French forces surrendered.

In the Battle of Kassarine Pass, North Africa, February 1943, the Allied army met General Erwin Rommel's Africa Korps. Rommel's forces were soon trapped by the British moving in from Egypt. In May 1943, Rommel's Africa Korps surrendered.

Allied armies under George S. Patton (1885–1945) invaded Sicily from Africa in July 1943, and gained control by mid-August. Rome did not fall until June 1944. In March 1944, the Soviet Union began pushing into Eastern Europe.

On "**D-Day**," June 6, 1944, Allied armies under Dwight D. Eisenhower, now commander-in-chief of the Allied Expeditionary Forces, began an invasion of Normandy, France.

Allied armies liberated Paris in August. By mid-September, they had arrived at the Rhine, on the edge of Germany.

Beginning December 16, 1944, at the Battle of the Bulge, the Germans counterattacked, driving the Allies back about 50 miles into Belgium. By January, the Allies were once more advancing toward Germany. The Allies crossed the Rhine in March 1945. In the last week of April, Eisenhower's forces met the Soviet army at the Elbe. On May 7, 1945, Germany surrendered.

The Pacific Theater

The Battle of the Coral Sea, May 7–8, 1942, stopped the Japanese advance on Australia. The Battle of Midway, June 4–7, 1942, proved to be the turning point in the Pacific.

U.S. forces advanced into the Gilberts (November 1943), the Marshalls (January 1944), and the Marianas (June 1944). After the American capture of the Marianas, General Tojo resigned as premier of Japan.

The Battle of Leyte Gulf, October 25, 1944, resulted in Japan's loss of most of its remaining naval power. Forces under General Douglas MacArthur (1880–1964) liberated Manila in March 1945.

Between April and June 1945, in the battle for Okinawa, nearly 50,000 American casualties resulted from the fierce fighting, but the battle virtually destroyed Japan's remaining defenses.

The Atomic Bomb

The Manhattan Engineering District was established by the army engineers in August 1942 for the purpose of developing an atomic bomb (it eventually became known as the **Manhattan Project**). J. Robert Oppenheimer directed the design and construction of a transportable atomic bomb at Los Alamos, New Mexico.

On December 2, 1942, Enrico Fermi (1901–1954) and his colleagues at the University of Chicago produced the first atomic chain reaction. On July 16, 1945, the first atomic bomb was exploded at Alamogordo, New Mexico. The *Enola Gay* dropped an atomic bomb on Hiroshima, Japan, on August 6, 1945, killing about 78,000 persons and injuring 100,000 more. On August 9, a second bomb was dropped on Nagasaki, Japan. On August 8, 1945, the Soviet Union entered the war against Japan. Japan surrendered on August 14, 1945. The formal surrender was signed on September 2.

Diplomacy

At the **Casablanca Conference** on January 14–25, 1943, Franklin D. Roosevelt and Winston Churchill, prime minister of Great Britain, declared a policy of unconditional surrender for "all enemies." At the **Moscow Conference** in October 1943, Secretary of State Cordell Hull obtained Soviet agreement to enter the war against Japan after Germany was defeated, and to participate in a world organization after the war was over.

Issued on December 1, 1943, after Roosevelt met with General Chiang Kai-shek in Cairo from November 22 to 26, the **Declaration of Cairo** called for Japan's unconditional surrender and stated that all Chinese territories occupied by Japan would be returned to China and that Korea would be free and independent.

The Emergence of the Cold War and Containment

In 1947, career diplomat and Soviet expert George F. Kennan wrote an anonymous article for *Foreign Affairs* in which he called for a counterforce to Soviet pressures, for the purpose of "containing" communism.

In February 1947, Great Britain notified the United States that it could no longer aid the Greek government in its war against Communist insurgents. The next month President Harry S. Truman asked Congress for $400 million in military and economic aid for Greece and Turkey. In what became known as the "**Truman Doctrine**," he argued that the United States must support free peoples who were resisting Communist domination.

Secretary of State George C. Marshall (1880–1959) proposed in June 1947 that the United States provide economic aid to help rebuild Europe. The following March, Congress passed the European Recovery Program, popularly known as the **Marshall Plan**, which provided more than $12 billion in aid.

After the United States, France, and Great Britain announced plans to create a West German Republic out of their German zones, the Soviet Union in June 1948 blocked surface access to

Berlin. The United States then instituted an airlift to transport supplies to the city until the Soviets lifted their blockade in May 1949.

NATO

In April 1949, the **North Atlantic Treaty Organization (NATO)** was signed by the United States, Canada, Great Britain, and nine European nations. The signatories pledged that an attack against one would be considered an attack against all. The Soviets formed the Warsaw Treaty Organization in 1955 to counteract NATO.

International Cooperation

From April to June 1945, representatives from 50 countries met in San Francisco to establish the United Nations. The U.N. charter created a General Assembly composed of all member nations which would act as the ultimate policy-making body. A Security Council, made up of 11 members, including the United States, Great Britain, France, the Soviet Union, and China as permanent members and six additional nations elected by the General Assembly for two-year terms, would be responsible for settling disputes among U.N. member nations.

Containment in Asia

General Douglas MacArthur headed a four-power Allied Control Council which governed Japan.

Between 1945 and 1948, the United States gave more than $2 billion in aid to the Nationalist Chinese under Chiang Kai-shek, and sent George C. Marshall to settle the conflict between Chiang's Nationalists and Mao Tse-tung's Communists. In 1949, however, Mao defeated Chiang and forced the Nationalists to flee to Formosa (Taiwan). Mao established the People's Republic of China on the mainland.

Korean War

On June 25, 1950, North Korea invaded South Korea. President Truman committed U.S. forces commanded by General MacArthur, but under United Nations auspices. By October, the U.N. forces (mostly American) had driven north of the 38th parallel, which divided North and South Korea. Chinese troops attacked MacArthur's forces on November 26, pushing them south of the 38th parallel, but by spring 1951, the U.N. forces had recovered their offensive.

In June 1953, an armistice was signed, leaving Korea divided along virtually the same boundary that had existed prior to the war.

Eisenhower-Dulles Foreign Policy

Dwight D. Eisenhower, elected president in 1952, chose John Foster Dulles (1888–1959) as secretary of state. Dulles wished to emphasize nuclear deterrents rather than conventional armed forces.

France, Great Britain, the Soviet Union, and China signed the **Geneva Accords** in July 1954, dividing Vietnam along the 17th parallel. The North would be under Ho Chi Minh and the South under Emperor Bao Dai. Ngo Dinh Diem overthrew Bao Dai and prevented the elections meant to unify the country from taking place.

President Eisenhower announced in January 1957 that the United States was prepared to use armed force in the Middle East against Communist aggression. Under this doctrine, U.S. marines entered Beirut, Lebanon, in July 1958 to promote political stability during a change of governments.

The United States supported the overthrow of President Jacobo Arbenz Guzman of Guatemala in 1954 because he began accepting arms from the Soviet Union.

In January 1959, Fidel Castro overthrew Fulgencio Batista, dictator of Cuba. Castro soon began criticizing the United States and moved closer to the Soviet Union, signing a trade agreement with the Soviets in February 1960. The United States prohibited the importation of Cuban sugar in October 1960, and broke off diplomatic relations in January 1961.

The Politics of Affluence: Demobilization and Domestic Policy

Congress created the **Atomic Energy Commission** in 1946, establishing civilian control over nuclear development and giving the president sole authority over the use of atomic weapons in warfare.

The Republicans, who had gained control of Congress in 1946, sought to control the power of the unions through the **Taft-Hartley Act**. This act made the "closed-shop" illegal; labor unions could no longer force employers to hire only union members. By 1954, 15 states had passed "right to work" laws, forbidding the "union-shop."

In 1948, the president banned racial discrimination in federal government hiring practices and ordered desegregation of the armed forces.

The **Presidential Succession Act** of 1947 placed the Speaker of the House and the president pro tempore of the Senate ahead of the secretary of state and after the vice president in the line of succession. The Twenty-Second Amendment to the Constitution, ratified in 1951, limited the president to election to two terms.

Anticommunism

In 1950, Julius and Ethel Rosenberg and Harry Gold were charged with giving atomic secrets to the Soviet Union. The Rosenbergs were convicted and executed in 1953.

On February 9, 1950, Senator Joseph R. McCarthy (1908–1957) of Wisconsin alleged that he had a list of known Communists who were working in the State Department. He later expanded his attacks. After making unproved charges against the army, he was censured by the Senate in 1954.

Eisenhower's Dynamic Conservatism

The Republicans nominated Dwight D. Eisenhower, most recently NATO commander, for the presidency. The Democrats nominated Governor Adlai E. Stevenson (1900–1965) of Illinois for president. Eisenhower won by a landslide; for the first time since Reconstruction, the Republicans won some southern states.

Eisenhower described his policy as "**dynamic conservatism**," and then as "**progressive moderation**." The administration abolished the Reconstruction Finance Corporation, ended wage and price controls, and reduced farm price supports. Social Security was extended in 1954 and 1956 to an additional 10 million people. The Rural Electrification Administration announced in 1960 that 97% of American farms had electricity.

In 1954, Eisenhower obtained congressional approval for joint Canadian-U.S. construction of the St. Lawrence Seaway, which was to give oceangoing vessels access to the Great Lakes. In 1956, Congress authorized construction of the Interstate Highway System.

The launching of the Soviet space satellite *Sputnik* on October 4, 1957, created fear that America was falling behind technologically. Although the United States launched *Explorer I* on January 31, 1958, the concern continued. In 1958, Congress established the **National Aeronautics and Space Administration (NASA)** to coordinate research and development, and passed the National Defense Education Act to provide grants and loans for education.

On January 3, 1959, Alaska became the 49th state, and on August 21, 1959, Hawaii became the 50th.

Civil Rights

Eisenhower completed the formal integration of the armed forces; desegregated public services in Washington, D.C., naval yards, and veteran's hospitals; and appointed a Civil Rights Commission.

In *Brown v. Board of Education of Topeka* NAACP lawyer Thurgood Marshall challenged the doctrine of "separate but equal" (*Plessy v. Ferguson*, 1896). The Court declared that separate educational facilities were inherently unequal. In 1955, the Court ordered states to integrate "with all deliberate speed."

On December 11, 1955, in Montgomery, Alabama, Rosa Parks, a black woman, refused to give up her seat on a city bus to a white and was arrested. Under the leadership of Martin Luther King (1929–1968), an African-American pastor, African-Americans of Montgomery organized a bus boycott that lasted for a year, until in December 1956, the Supreme Court refused to review a lower court ruling that stated that separate but equal was no longer legal.

On February 1, 1960, upon being denied service, four African-American students staged a sit-in at a Woolworth lunch counter in Greensboro, North Carolina. This inspired sit-ins by thousands elsewhere in the South and led to the formation of the **Student Nonviolent Coordinating Committee**.

The Election of 1960

Vice President Richard M. Nixon won the Republican presidential nomination, and the Democrats nominated Senator John F. Kennedy (1917–1963) for the presidency, with Lyndon B. Johnson (1908–1973), majority leader of the Senate, as his running mate. Kennedy won the election by slightly more than 100,000 popular votes and 94 electoral votes.

THE NEW FRONTIER, VIETNAM, AND SOCIAL UPHEAVAL (1960–1972)

Kennedy's "New Frontier" and the Liberal Revival

Kennedy gained congressional approval for raising the minimum wage from $1.00 to $1.25 an hour and extending it to 3 million more workers.

The 1961 Housing Act provided nearly $5 billion over four years for the preservation of open urban spaces, development of mass transit, and the construction of middle-class housing.

Civil Rights

In May 1961, blacks and whites boarded buses in Washington, D.C., and traveled across the South to New Orleans to test federal enforcement of regulations prohibiting discrimination. They met violence in Alabama but continued to New Orleans.

The Justice Department, under Attorney General Robert F. Kennedy (1925–1968), began to push for civil rights, including desegregation of interstate transportation in the South, integration of schools, and supervision of elections. In the fall of 1962, President Kennedy called the Mississippi National Guard to federal duty to enable an African-American, James Meredith, to enroll at the University of Mississippi.

Kennedy presented a comprehensive civil rights bill to Congress in 1963. With the bill held up in Congress, 200,000 people marched, demonstrating on its behalf on August 28, 1963, in Washington, D.C. Martin Luther King gave his "I Have a Dream" speech.

The Cold War Continues

Under Eisenhower, the Central Intelligence Agency had begun training some 2,000 men for an invasion of Cuba to overthrow Fidel Castro. On April 19, 1961, this force invaded at the Bay of Pigs, but was pinned down and forced to surrender.

In August 1961, Khrushchev closed the border between East and West Berlin and ordered the erection of the Berlin Wall.

The Soviet Union began the testing of nuclear weapons in September 1961. Kennedy then authorized resumption of underground testing by the United States. On October 14, 1962, a U-2 reconnaissance plane brought photographic evidence that missile sites were being built in Cuba.

Kennedy, on October 22, announced a blockade of Cuba and called on Khrushchev to dismantle the missile bases and remove all weapons capable of attacking the United States from Cuba. Six days later, Khrushchev backed down, withdrew the missiles, and Kennedy lifted the blockade. In July 1963, a treaty banning the atmospheric testing of nuclear weapons was signed by all the major powers except France and China.

In 1961, Kennedy announced the **Alliance for Progress**, which would provide $20 million in aid to Latin America.

Johnson and the Great Society

On November 22, 1963, Kennedy was assassinated by Lee Harvey Oswald in Dallas, Texas. Jack Ruby, a nightclub owner, killed Oswald two days later. Lyndon B. Johnson succeeded Kennedy.

The 1964 Civil Rights Act outlawed racial discrimination by employers and unions, created the Equal Employment Opportunity Commission to enforce the law, and eliminated the remaining restrictions on black voting.

Michael Harrington's *The Other America* (1962) showed that 20–25% of American families were living below the governmentally defined poverty line. The **Economic Opportunity Act of 1964** sought to address the problem by establishing a Job Corps, community action programs, educational programs, work-study programs, job training, loans for small businesses and farmers, and Volunteers in Service to America (VISTA), a "domestic peace corps."

In 1964, Lyndon Johnson was nominated for president by the Democrats. The Republicans nominated Senator Barry Goldwater, a conservative from Arizona. Johnson won more than 61% of the popular vote and could now launch his own "Great Society" program.

The Medicare Act of 1965 combined hospital insurance for retired people with a voluntary plan to cover physician's bills. Medicaid provided grants to states to help the poor below retirement age.

Emergence of Black Power

In 1965, Martin Luther King, with help from the federal courts, dramatized his voter registration effort by leading a march from Selma to Montgomery, Alabama, between March 21 and 25. The Voting Rights Act of 1965 authorized the attorney general to appoint officials to register voters.

Around 70% of African-Americans lived in city ghettos. In 1966, New York and Chicago experienced riots, and the following year there were riots in Newark and Detroit. The Kerner Commission, appointed to investigate the riots, concluded that they were directed at a social system that prevented African-Americans from getting good jobs and crowded them into ghettos.

Stokely Carmichael, in 1966, called for the civil rights movements to be "black-staffed, black-controlled, and black-financed." Later, he moved on to the Black Panthers, self-styled urban revolutionaries based in Oakland, California. Other leaders such as H. Rap Brown also called for Black Power.

On April 4, 1968, Martin Luther King was assassinated in Memphis by James Earl Ray. Riots in more than 100 cities followed.

The New Left

Students at the University of California at Berkeley staged sit-ins in 1964 to protest the prohibition of political canvassing on campus. Student protests began focusing on the Vietnam War. In the spring of 1967, 500,000 gathered in Central Park in New York City to protest the war, many burning their draft cards. **Students for a Democratic Society (SDS)** became more militant and willing to use violence. Beginning in 1968, SDS began breaking up into rival factions. By the early 1970s, the New Left had lost political influence, having abandoned its original commitment to democracy and nonviolence.

Women's Liberation

In *The Feminine Mystique* (1963), Betty Friedan argued that middle-class society stifled women and did not allow them to use their individual talents. Friedan and other feminists founded the **National Organization for Women (NOW)** in 1966, calling for equal employment opportunities and equal pay.

Vietnam

After the French defeat in 1954, the United States sent military advisors to South Vietnam to aid the government of Ngo Dinh Diem. The pro-Communist Vietcong forces gradually grew in strength and received support from North Vietnam, the Soviet Union, and China.

In August 1964—after claiming that North Vietnamese gunboats had fired on American destroyers in the Gulf of Tonkin—Lyndon Johnson pushed the Gulf of Tonkin resolution through Congress, authorizing him to use military force in Vietnam. After a February 1965 attack by the Vietcong on Pleiku, Johnson ordered operation "**Rolling Thunder**," the first sustained bombing of North Vietnam. Johnson then sent combat troops to South Vietnam; under the leadership of General William C. Westmoreland, they conducted search and destroy operations. The number of troops increased each year.

Opposition began quickly, with "teach-ins" at the University of Michigan in 1965 and a 1966 congressional investigation led by Senator J. William Fulbright. On January 31, 1968, the first day of the Vietnamese new year (Tet), the Vietcong attacked numerous cities and towns, American bases, and even Saigon. Although they suffered large losses, the Vietcong won a psychological victory, as American opinion began turning against the war.

The Election of 1968

In November 1967, Senator Eugene McCarthy of Minnesota announced his candidacy for the 1968 Democratic presidential nomination, running on the issue of opposition to the war. In February,

McCarthy won 42% of the Democratic vote in the New Hampshire primary, compared with Johnson's 48%. Robert F. Kennedy then announced his candidacy for the Democratic presidential nomination.

Lyndon Johnson withdrew his candidacy on March 31, 1968, and Vice President Hubert H. Humphrey took his place as a candidate for the Democratic nomination.

After winning the California primary over McCarthy, Robert Kennedy was assassinated by Sirhan Sirhan, a young Palestinian. This event assured Humphrey's nomination.

The Republicans nominated Richard M. Nixon. Governor George C. Wallace of Alabama ran for the presidency under the banner of the American Independent party, appealing to fears generated by protestors and big government.

Johnson suspended air attacks on North Vietnam shortly before the election. Nonetheless Nixon, who emphasized stability and order, defeated Humphrey by a margin of 1%. Wallace's 13.5% was the best showing by a third-party candidate since 1924.

The Nixon Conservative Reaction

The Nixon administration sought to block renewal of the Voting Rights Act and delay implementation of court-ordered school desegregation in Mississippi.

In 1969, Nixon appointed Warren E. Burger, a conservative, as chief justice. Although more conservative than the Warren court, the Burger court did declare the death penalty unconstitutional in 1972, and struck down state anti-abortion legislation in 1973.

Vietnamization

The president turned to "**Vietnamization**," the effort to build up South Vietnamese forces while withdrawing American troops. In 1969, Nixon reduced American troop strength by 60,000, but at the same time ordered the bombing of Cambodia, a neutral country.

Protests against escalation of the war were especially strong on college campuses. After several students were killed during protests, several hundred colleges were closed down by student strikes, as moderates joined the radicals. Congress repealed the Gulf of Tonkin Resolution.

The publication in 1971 of classified Defense Department documents, called "**The Pentagon Papers**," revealed that the government had misled the Congress and the American people regarding its intentions in Vietnam during the mid-1960s.

In March 1972, after stepped-up aggression from the North, Nixon ordered the mining of Haiphong and other northern ports.

In the summer of 1972, negotiations between the United States and North Vietnam began in Paris. A few days before the 1972 presidential election, Henry Kissinger, the president's national security advisor, announced that "peace was at hand."

Nixon resumed bombing of North Vietnam in December 1972, claiming that the North Vietnamese were not bargaining in good faith. In January 1973, the opponents reached a settlement in which the North Vietnamese retained control over large areas of the South and agreed to release American prisoners of war within 60 days. Nearly 60,000 Americans had been killed and 300,000 more wounded and the war had cost Americans $109 billion. On March 29, 1973, the last American combat troops left South Vietnam.

Foreign Policy

In February 1972, Nixon and Kissinger went to China to meet with Mao Tse-tung and his associates. The United States agreed to support China's admission to the United Nations and to pursue economic and cultural exchanges. Nixon and Kissinger called their policy *détente*, a French term meaning a relaxation in the tensions between two governments.

WATERGATE, CARTER, THE NEW CONSERVATISM, AND POST–COLD WAR CHALLENGES (1972–2008)

Watergate

Richard M. Nixon, who had been renominated by the Republicans, won a landslide victory over the Democratic nominee, Senator George McGovern. What became known as the **Watergate crisis** began during the 1972 presidential campaign. Early on the morning of June 17, James McCord, a security officer for the Committee to Re-Elect the President, and four other men broke into Democratic headquarters at the Watergate apartment complex in Washington, D.C., and were caught while going through files and installing electronic eavesdropping devices. In March 1974, a grand jury indicted Haldeman, Ehrlichman, former Attorney General John Mitchell, and four other White House aides and named Nixon an unindicted co-conspirator.

Meanwhile, the House Judiciary Committee adopted three articles of impeachment. It charged the president with obstructing justice, misusing presidential power, and failing to obey the committee's subpoenas.

Before the House began to debate impeachment, Nixon announced his resignation on August 8, 1974, to take effect at noon the following day. Gerald Ford then became president. Ford almost immediately encountered controversy when in September 1974 he offered to pardon Nixon. Nixon accepted the offer, although he admitted no wrongdoing and had not yet been charged with a crime.

Vietnam

As North Vietnamese forces pushed back the South Vietnamese, Ford asked Congress to provide more arms for the South. Congress rejected the request, and in April 1975 Saigon fell to the North Vietnamese.

Carter's Moderate Liberalism

Ronald Reagan, a former movie actor and governor of California, opposed Ford for the Republican presidential nomination, but Ford won by a slim margin. The Democrats nominated James Earl Carter, formerly governor of Georgia, who ran on the basis of his integrity and lack of Washington connections. Carter narrowly defeated Ford in the election.

Carter offered amnesty to Americans who had fled the draft and gone to other countries during the Vietnam War. He established the Departments of Energy and Education and placed the civil service on a merit basis. He created a "superfund" for cleanup of chemical waste dumps, established controls over strip mining, and protected 100 million acres of Alaskan wilderness from development.

Carter's Foreign Policy

Carter negotiated a controversial treaty with Panama, affirmed by the Senate in 1978, that provided for the transfer of ownership of the canal to Panama in 1999 and guaranteed its neutrality.

Carter ended official recognition of Taiwan and in 1979 recognized the People's Republic of China.

In 1978, Carter negotiated the Camp David Agreement between Israel and Egypt. Israel promised to return occupied land in the Sinai to Egypt in exchange for Egyptian recognition, a process completed in 1982.

The Iranian Crisis

In 1978, a revolution forced the shah of Iran to flee the country, replacing him with a religious leader, Ayatollah Ruhollah Khomeini. Because the United States had supported the shah with arms and money, the revolutionaries were strongly anti-American, calling the United States the "Great Satan."

After Carter allowed the exiled shah to come to the United States for medical treatment in October 1979, some 400 Iranians broke into the American embassy in Teheran on November 4, taking the occupants captive. They demanded that the shah be returned to Iran for trial and that his wealth be confiscated and given to Iran. Carter rejected these demands; instead, he froze Iranian assets in the United States and established a trade embargo against Iran.

The Election of 1980

Republican Ronald Reagan defeated Carter by a large electoral majority, and the Republicans gained control of the Senate and increased their representation in the House.

After extensive negotiations with Iran, in which Algeria acted as an intermediary, American hostages were freed on January 20, 1981, the day of Reagan's inauguration.

The Reagan Presidency: Attacking Big Government

Ronald Reagan placed priority on cutting taxes. His approach was based on "supply-side" economics, the idea that if government left more money in the hands of the people, they would invest rather than spend the excess on consumer goods. The results would be greater production, more jobs, and greater prosperity, and thus more income for the government despite lower tax rates. Reagan asked for a 30% tax cut, and despite fears of inflation on the part of Congress, in August 1983 obtained a 25% cut, spread over three years.

Congress passed the Budget Reconciliation Act in 1981, cutting $39 billion from domestic programs, including education, food stamps, public housing, and the National Endowments for the Arts and Humanities. While cutting domestic programs, Reagan increased the defense budget by $12 billion. From a deficit of $59 billion in 1980, the federal budget was running $195 billion in the red by 1983.

Because of rising deficits, Reagan and Congress increased taxes in various ways. The 1982 Tax Equity and Fiscal Responsibility Act reversed some concessions made to business in 1981. Social Security benefits became taxable income in 1983. In 1984, the Deficit Reduction Act increased taxes by another $50 billion. But the deficit continued to increase.

Asserting American Power

Reagan took a hard line against the Soviet Union, calling it an "evil empire." He placed new cruise missiles in Europe, despite considerable opposition from Europeans.

Reagan also concentrated on obtaining funding for the development of a computer-controlled strategic defense initiative system (SDI), popularly called "**Star Wars**" after the widely seen movie, that would destroy enemy missiles from outer space.

In Nicaragua, Reagan encouraged the opposition (*contras*) to the leftist Sandinista government with arms, tactical support, and intelligence, and supplied aid to the government of El Salvador in its struggles against left-wing rebels. In October 1983, the president also sent American troops into the Caribbean island of Grenada to overthrow a newly established Cuban-backed regime.

Second-Term Foreign Concerns

Walter Mondale, a former senator from Minnesota and vice president under Carter, won the Democratic nomination. Mondale criticized Reagan for his budget deficits, high unemployment and interest rates, and reduction of spending on social services. However, Reagan was elected to a second term in a landslide.

After Mikhail S. Gorbachev became the premier of the Soviet Union in March 1985 and took a more flexible approach toward both domestic and foreign affairs, Reagan softened his anti-Soviet stance. Reagan and Gorbachev had difficulty in reaching an agreement on arms limitations at summit talks in 1985 and 1986. Finally, in December 1987, they signed an agreement eliminating medium-range missiles from Europe.

Iran-Contra

In 1985 and 1986, several Reagan officials sold arms to the Iranians in hopes of encouraging them to use their influence in getting American hostages in Lebanon released. The profits from these sales were then diverted to the Nicaraguan *contras* in an attempt to get around congressional restrictions on funding the *contras*. The president was forced to appoint a special prosecutor, and Congress held hearings on the affair in May 1987.

Second-Term Domestic Affairs: The Economy

The Tax Reform Act of 1986 lowered tax rates, but also removed many tax shelters and tax credits.

On October 19, 1987, known as "**Black Monday**," the Dow Jones Industrial Average dropped more than 500 points. Between August 25 and October 20, the market lost over a trillion dollars in paper value.

The explosion of the shuttle *Challenger* soon after take-off on January 28, 1986, damaged NASA's credibility and reinforced doubts about the complex technology required for the SDI program.

Reagan reshaped the Supreme Court in 1986, replacing Chief Justice Warren C. Burger with Associate Justice William H. Rehnquist. Reagan appointed other conservatives to the Court: Sandra Day O'Connor, Antonin Scalia, and Anthony Kennedy.

The Election of 1988

Vice President George H. W. Bush won the Republican nomination. Bush easily defeated Michael Dukakis, the Democratic nominee, but the Republicans were unable to make any inroads in Congress.

The Bush Administration

The Bush administration and Congress agreed to increase taxes on gasoline, tobacco, and alcohol; establish an excise tax on luxury items; and raise Medicare taxes. Congress in December transferred the power to decide whether new tax and spending proposals violated the deficit cutting agreement from the White House Office of Management and Budget to the Congressional Budget Office.

With the savings and loan industry in financial trouble in 1989, largely because of bad real-estate loans, Bush signed a bill which created the Resolution Trust Corporation to oversee the closure and merging of savings and loans, and which provided $166 billion over 10 years to cover the bad debts. Estimates of the total costs of the debacle were over $300 billion.

Bush's Activist Foreign Policy

Since coming to office, the Bush administration had been concerned with Panamanian dictator Manuel Noriega because he allegedly served as an important link in the drug traffic between South America and the United States. After economic sanctions, diplomatic efforts, and an October 1989 coup failed to oust Noriega, Bush ordered 12,000 troops into Panama on

December 20. On January 3, 1990, Noriega surrendered to the Americans and was taken to the United States to stand trial on drug trafficking charges; he was convicted and jailed for assisting the Medellín drug cartel.

After years of civil war, Nicaragua held a presidential election in February 1990. Violeta Barrios de Chamorro of the National Opposition Union defeated Daniel Ortega Saavedra of the Sandinistas. The United States lifted its economic sanctions in March and put together an economic aid package for Nicaragua. In September 1991, the Bush administration forgave Nicaragua most of its debt to the United States.

By the middle of May 1989, more than one million people were gathering on Beijing's Tiananmen Square calling for political reform. Martial law was imposed and in early June the army fired on the demonstrators. In July 1989, United States National Security Advisor Brent Scowcroft and Deputy Secretary of State Lawrence Eagleburger secretly met with Chinese leaders. When they again met the Chinese in December and revealed their earlier meeting, the Bush administration faced a storm of criticism for its policy of "constructive engagement" from opponents arguing that sanctions should be imposed. While establishing sanctions in 1991 on Chinese high-technology satellite-part exports, Bush continued to support renewal of Most Favored Nation trading status.

To rescue American citizens threatened by civil war, Bush sent 230 marines into Liberia in August 1990, evacuating 125 people. South Africa in 1990 freed Nelson Mandela, the most famous leader of the African National Congress, after 28 years of imprisonment. South Africa then began moving away from apartheid, and in 1991 Bush lifted economic sanctions imposed five years earlier.

Collapse of East European Communism

In August 1989 Hungary opened its borders with Austria. The following October, the Communists reorganized their party, calling it the Socialist party. Hungary then proclaimed itself a "Free Republic."

With thousands of East Germans passing through Hungary to Austria, Erich Honecker stepped down as head of state in October. On November 1, the government opened the border with Czechoslovakia and eight days later the Berlin Wall fell. On December 6, a non-Communist became head of state, followed on December 11 by large demonstrations demanding German reunification. Reunification took place in October 1990.

On December 8, 1989, the Communists agreed to relinquish power and Parliament elected Václav Havel, a playwright and anti-Communist leader, to the presidency on December 29.

When anti-government demonstrations in Romania were met by force in early December, portions of the military began joining the opposition which captured dictator Nicolae Ceaușescu and his wife, Elena, killing them on December 25, 1989. In May 1990 the National Salvation Front, made up of many former Communists, won the parliamentary elections.

In January 1990 the Bulgarian national assembly repealed the dominant role of the Communist party. A multi-party coalition government was formed the following December.

Amid the collapse of Communism in Eastern Europe, Bush met with Mikhail Gorbachev in Malta from December 1 through December 3, 1989; the two leaders appeared to agree that the Cold War was over. On May 30 and 31, 1990, Bush and Gorbachev met in Washington to discuss the possible reunification of Germany, and signed a trade treaty between the United States and the Soviet Union. At the meeting of the "Group of 7" nations (Canada, France, Germany, Italy, Japan, United Kingdom, and the United States) in July 1991, Gorbachev requested economic aid from the West. A short time later, on July 30 and 31, Bush met Gorbachev in Moscow where they signed the **START treaty**, which cut U.S. and Soviet nuclear arsenals by 30%, and pushed for Middle Eastern talks. With the collapse of the Soviet Union, the United States remained the lone world superpower.

Persian Gulf Crisis

Saddam Hussein of Iraq charged that Kuwait had conspired with the United States to keep oil prices low and began massing troops at the Iraq-Kuwait border.

On August 2, Iraq invaded Kuwait, an act that Bush denounced as "naked aggression." The United States quickly banned most trade with Iraq, froze Iraq's and Kuwait's assets in the United States, and sent aircraft carriers to the Persian Gulf. After the United Nations Security Council condemned the invasion, on August 6 Bush ordered the deployment of air, sea, and land forces to Saudi Arabia, dubbing the operation "Desert Shield."

On October 29, the Security Council warned Saddam Hussein that further actions might be taken if he did not withdraw from Kuwait. On January 9, Iraq's foreign minister, Tariq Aziz, rejected a letter written by Bush to Hussein. On November 29, the United Nations set January 15, 1991, as the deadline for Iraqi withdrawal from Kuwait.

On January 17, an international force including the United States, Great Britain, France, Italy, Saudi Arabia, and Kuwait launched an air and missile attack on Iraq and occupied Kuwait. The United States called the effort "**Operation Desert Storm**." Under the overall command of Army General H. Norman Schwarzkopf, the military effort emphasized high-technology weapons. Beginning on January 17, Iraq fired SCUD missiles into Israel in an effort to draw that country into the war and splinter the U.S.-Arabian coalition. On January 22 and 23, Hussein's forces set Kuwaiti oil fields on fire and spilled oil into the Gulf.

On February 23, the allied ground assault began. Four days later Bush announced that Kuwait was liberated and ordered offensive operations to cease. The United Nations established the terms for the cease-fire: Iraqi annexation of Kuwait to be rescinded, Iraq to accept liability for damages and return Kuwaiti property, Iraq to end all military actions and identify mines and booby traps, and Iraq to release captives. On April 3, the Security Council approved a resolution to establish a permanent cease-fire; Iraq accepted U.N. terms on April 6.

Immediately after cessation of the conflict, Secretary of State James Baker toured the Middle East attempting to promote a conference to address the problems of the region. After several more negotiating sessions, Saudi Arabia, Syria, Jordan, and Lebanon accepted the U.S. proposal for an Arab-Israeli peace conference by the middle of July; Israel conditionally accepted in early August.

Breakup of the Soviet Union

Following the collapse of Communism in Eastern Europe, the Baltic republic of Lithuania, which had been taken over by the Soviet Union in 1939 through an agreement with Adolf Hitler, declared its independence from the Soviet Union.

Two days later, on March 13, the Soviet Union removed the Communist monopoly of political power, allowing non-Communists to run for office. The process of liberalization went haltingly forward in the Soviet Union. Perhaps the most significant event was the election of Boris Yeltsin, who had left the Communist party, as president of the Russian republic on June 12, 1991.

In the aftermath of a coup to overthrow Gorbachev, much of the Communist structure came crashing down, setting the stage for opposition parties to emerge. The remaining Baltic republics of Latvia and Estonia declared their independence. Most of the other Soviet republics then followed suit in declaring their independence.

In September 1991, George Bush announced unilateral removal and destruction of ground-based tactical nuclear weapons in Europe and Asia. Gorbachev responded the next month by announcing the immediate deactivation of intercontinental ballistic missiles covered by START. Gorbachev's hold on the presidency progressively weakened in the final months of 1991, with the reforms he had put in place taking on a life of their own. The dissolution of the U.S.S.R. led to his resignation in December, making way for Boris Yeltsin, who had headed popular resistance. The United States was now the world's only superpower.

The Democrats Reclaim the White House

William Jefferson Clinton, governor of Arkansas, overcame several rivals to win the Democratic presidential nomination in 1992 and with his running mate, Senator Albert Gore of Tennessee, went on to win the White House. During the campaign, Clinton and independent candidate H. Ross Perot, a wealthy Texas businessman, emphasized jobs and the economy while attacking the mounting federal debt. The incumbent, Bush, stressed traditional values and his foreign policy accomplishments. In the 1992 election, Clinton won 43% of the popular vote and 370 electoral votes, defeating Bush and Perot. Perot took 19% of the popular vote, but was unable to garner any electoral votes.

Clinton came to be dogged by a number of controversies, ranging from alleged ill-gotten gains in a complex Arkansas land deal that came to be known as the **Whitewater Affair** to charges of sexual misconduct, brought by a former Arkansas state employee (with whom he would ultimately reach an out-of-court settlement), that dated to an incident she said had occurred when Clinton was governor. In December 1998 Clinton was impeached by the House on charges that stemmed from an adulterous affair with a White House intern, Monica Lewinsky. The impeachment proceedings ended with Clinton's acquittal by the Senate in February 1999.

On the legislative front, Clinton was strongly rebuffed in an attempt during his first term to reform the nation's healthcare system. In the 1994 mid-term elections, the Republicans took both houses of Congress from the Democrats and voted in Newt Gingrich of Georgia as Speaker of the House. Gingrich helped craft the Republican congressional campaign strategy to dramatically shrink the federal government and give more power to the states.

Clinton, however, was not without his successes. He signed legislation establishing a five-day waiting period for handgun purchases as well as a crime bill emphasizing community policing. He signed the Family and Medical Leave Act, which requires large companies to provide up to 12 weeks' unpaid leave to workers for family and medical emergencies. He also championed welfare reform (a central theme of his campaign). In foreign affairs, Clinton signed the **North American Free Trade Agreement (NAFTA)**, which lifted most trade barriers with Mexico and Canada as of 1994. Clinton sought to ease tensions between Israelis and Palestinians, and he helped bring together Itzhak Rabin, prime minister of Israel, and Yasir Arafat, chairman of the Palestine Liberation Organization, for a summit at the White House. Ultimately, the two Middle East leaders signed an accord in 1994 establishing Palestinian self-rule in the Gaza Strip and Jericho. In October 1994 Israel and Jordan signed a treaty to begin the process of establishing full diplomatic relations. Rabin was assassinated a year later by a radical, right-wing Israeli.

Clinton recaptured the Democratic nomination without a serious challenge, while longtime GOP Senator Robert Dole of Kansas earned the Republican mod. In November 1996, with most voters citing a healthy economy and the lack of an enticing alternative in Dole or the Reform Party's Perot, Clinton received 49% of the vote, becoming the first Democrat to be re-elected since FDR. The GOP retained control of both houses of Congress.

Clinton, intent on mirroring the diversity of America in his Cabinet appointments, chose Hispanics, African Americans, and women, including the nation's first woman attorney general, Janet Reno, and Madeleine Albright, the first woman secretary of state in U.S. history.

In 2000, Republican George W. Bush defeated Democrat Al Gore in a close and controversial election with Bush receiving a majority of the electoral votes (after a decision by the Supreme Court to stop a third recount—essentially awarding Florida's electoral votes to him), but Gore receiving a majority of the popular vote. Eight months after being sworn in, the September 11th attacks occurred. In response to the attacks, President Bush declared a **War on Terror**, which led to the creation of a new cabinet level agency, the Department of Homeland Security, an invasion of Afghanistan, and an invasion of Iraq. On the domestic front, President Bush signed into law tax cuts, the No Child Left Behind Act, and Medicare prescription drug benefits for seniors.

After defeating Democrat John Kerry in the 2004 election, President Bush's second term was beset by scandals and criticism related to the War on Terror, Hurricane Katrina, and the perceived failure of the government's response, and an economy that went into recession.

The 2008 presidential election featured two senators, Democrat Barack Obama from Illinois and Republican John McCain from Arizona. Senator Obama won and became the 44th president of the United States and its first African-American president.

Late Twentieth Century Social and Cultural Developments

In 1981 scientists announced the discovery of **Acquired Immune Deficiency Syndrome (AIDS)**, which was especially prevalent among homosexual males and intravenous drug users. Widespread fear resulted, including an upsurge in homophobia. The Centers for Disease Control and Prevention (CDC) and the National Cancer Institute, among others, pursued research on the disease. The Food and Drug Administration responded to calls for fast-tracking evaluation of drugs by approving the drug AZT in February 1991. With the revelation that a Florida dentist had infected three patients, there were calls for mandatory testing of healthcare workers. New drug therapies, meanwhile, were preventing AIDS symptoms from ever appearing, creating the specter of growing numbers of people going unseen by public-health agencies as they spread the virus. These developments came against the backdrop of a marked change in the demographic makeup of the epidemic's victims—from mostly white homosexual males to African-Americans, Hispanics, and women, particularly those who were poor, intravenous drug users, or the sex partners of drug users.

So-called family values became a major theme in presidential politics, powered in part by the publication of leading conservative William J. Bennett's best-selling anthology *The Book of Virtues: A Treasury of Great Moral Stories*. Bennett had served as Bush's secretary of education and, later, as director of the Office of National Drug Control Policy, which the press shortened to "drug czar."

While terrorist attacks continued to be a grim reality overseas through the 1980s and early 1990s, with Americans frequently targeted, such incidents had come to be perceived as something the United States wouldn't have to face on its own soil—until February 26, 1993, when a terrorist bomb ripped through the underground parking garage of the World Trade Center in New York City, killing six people and injuring more than 1,000. The blast shattered America's "myth of invulnerability," wrote foreign policy analyst Jeffrey D. Simon in his book *The Terrorist Trap*. On April 19, 1995, the Oklahoma City federal building was bombed: 168 people were killed and 500 injured. Timothy James McVeigh was convicted and sentenced to death in June 1997. A second defendant, Terry Nichols, was convicted of conspiracy. These attacks, however, were dwarfed by the September 11, 2001, attacks in which terrorists turned hijacked planes into missiles—two destroying the World Trade Center and one damaging the Pentagon. A fourth plane was brought down in Pennsylvania, apparently by passengers who overtook the hijackers. President Bush immediately cast suspicion upon Saudi exile Osama bin Laden and declared a "war on terrorism" that began with a military strike against Afghanistan, bin Laden's alleged base of operations.

In Los Angeles, former pro-football star, broadcaster, and actor O.J. Simpson was tried for the brutal murder in June 1994 of his ex-wife, Nicole Brown Simpson, and her friend Ronald Goldman. The nationally televised trial became a running spectacle for months. Simpson was found not guilty, but later, in a civil trial, would be found responsible for the slaying of Goldman and for committing battery against Nicole.

Between 1987 and 1997, the period spanning the Bush administration and Clinton's first term, the number of Americans in prison doubled, soaring from 800,000 to 1.6 million. Drug abuse continued to be widespread, with cocaine becoming more readily available, particularly in a cheaper, stronger form called "crack."

The U.S. Department of Labor's Bureau of Labor Statistics reported that union membership dropped to 14.5% of wage and salary employment in 1996, down from 14.9% in 1995. In 1983, union members made up 20.1% of the work force.

In a July 1989 decision, *Webster v. Reproductive Health Services*, the U.S. Supreme Court upheld a Missouri law prohibiting public employees from performing abortions, unless the mother's life is threatened. With this decision came a shift in focus on the abortion issue from the courts to the state legislatures. Pro-life (anti-abortion rights) forces moved in several states to restrict the availability of abortions, but their results were mixed. At the national level, Bush in October 1989 vetoed funding for Medicaid abortions. The conflict between pro-choice (pro-abortion) and pro-life forces gained national attention through such events as a pro-life demonstration held in Washington in April 1990, and blockage of access to abortion clinics by Operation Rescue, a militant anti-abortion group, in the summer of 1991. Abortion clinics around the country continued to be the targets of protests and violence through the mid-'90s.

Kevin Phillips's *The Politics of Rich and Poor* (1990) argued that 40 million Americans in the bottom fifth of the population experienced a 1% decline in income between 1973 and 1979 and a 10% decline between 1979 and 1987. Meanwhile, the top fifth saw a rise of 7% and 16% during the same periods. The number of single-parent families living below the poverty line (annual income of $11,611 for a family of four) rose by 46% between 1979 and 1987. Nearly one-quarter of American children under age 6 were counted among the poor, said Phillips.

Senator Jesse Helms of North Carolina proposed that grants for "obscene or indecent" projects, or those derogatory of religion, be cut off. Meanwhile, in March 1990, the Recording Industry Association of America, in a move advocated by, among others, Tipper Gore, wife of Democratic Senator Al Gore of Tennessee (the man who would be elected vice president in 1992), agreed to place new uniform warning labels on recordings that contained potentially offensive language.

The National Commission on Excellence in Education, appointed in 1981, argued in "**A Nation at Risk**" that a "rising tide of mediocrity" characterized the nation's schools. In the wake of the report, many states instituted reforms, including higher teacher salaries, competency tests for teachers, and an increase in required subjects for high school graduation. In September 1989 Bush met with the nation's governors in Charlottesville, Virginia, to work on a plan to improve the schools. The governors issued a call for the establishment of national performance goals to be measured by achievement tests. In February 1990 the National Governors' Association adopted specific performance goals, stating that achievement tests should be administered in grades four, eight, and twelve. As the new millenium approached, however, signs began to emerge that the tide might be turning: a major global comparison found in June 1997 that America's 9- and 10-year-olds were among the world's best in science and also scored well above average in math.

The 1980s and 1990s saw the emergence of writers who concentrated on marginal or regional aspects of national life. William Kennedy wrote a series of novels about Albany, New York, most notably *Ironweed* (1983). The small-town West attracted attention from Larry McMurtry, whose *Lonesome Dove* (1985) used myth to explore the history of the region. The immigrant experience gave rise to Amy Tan's *The Joy-Luck Club* (1989) and Oscar Hijuelos's *The Mambo Kings Play Songs of Love* (1990). Tom Wolfe satirized greed, and class and racial tensions in New York City, in *The Bonfire of the Vanities* (1987). Toni Morrison's *Beloved* (1987) dramatized the African-American slavery experience.

CLEP Social Sciences and History Practice Test 1

(Answer sheets appear in the back of this book)

TIME: *90 Minutes*
Approx. 120 Questions
(10 questions provided for extra practice)

DIRECTIONS: Each of the following questions or incomplete statements is followed by five possible answers or completions. Select the best choice in each case and fill in the corresponding oval on the answer sheet.

1. In 1804, Aaron Burr killed Alexander Hamilton in a duel that was fought because

   (A) Hamilton had formally accused Burr of treason and Burr felt he had to defend his honor.
   (B) Burr blamed his loss of the 1804 election for governor of New York on Hamilton's charges that Burr was dangerous and untrustworthy.
   (C) Hamilton had uncovered Burr's plan to form an independent republic comprised of American territories west of the Appalachians.
   (D) Burr had caught his wife in a sexual liaison with Hamilton and felt that he had to defend his honor.
   (E) Burr believed that Hamilton had financially destroyed him in a real estate deal in which Burr lost nearly all of his wealth.

2. The following cartoon refers to the results of which war?

President McKinley (the tailor) measures Uncle Sam for a new suit to fit the fattening results of his imperial appetite.

(A) War of 1812
(B) Civil War
(C) Spanish-American War
(D) World War I
(E) World War II

3. ". . . There is no place for industry . . . no arts; no letters; no society; and which is the worst of all, continual fear, and danger of violent death; and the life of man, solitary, poor, nasty, brutish, and short." This quotation from Thomas Hobbes' *Leviathan* (1651) described the concept known as

   (A) natural rights.
   (B) state of nature.
   (C) social contract.
   (D) reason of state (raison d'état).
   (E) nationalism.

4. Which one of the following would most likely oppose *laissez-faire* policies in nineteenth-century Europe?

   (A) A factory owner
   (B) A liberal
   (C) A free trader
   (D) A socialist
   (E) A middle-class businessman

5. The first time the Japanese people heard the voice of Emperor Hirohito on the radio was

   (A) during his coronation.
   (B) when he announced his wedding.
   (C) when he announced that Japanese troops were moving into Manchuria.
   (D) when he announced Japan's surrender to the Allied Powers.
   (E) when he declared war on the United States.

6. Which of the following was the first European power to seize control of African territories?

   (A) Portugal
   (B) Belgium
   (C) England
   (D) France
   (E) Germany

7. Sociology is best defined as the scientific study of

   (A) social problems.
   (B) human personality.
   (C) social interaction.
   (D) human development.
   (E) attitudes and values.

8. Sociology developed as a separate discipline in the nineteenth century in response to

   (A) the growth of socialism.
   (B) the spread of colonialism.
   (C) a desire to promote greater equality.
   (D) the growth of industrial society.
   (E) disenchantment with psychology.

9. The German sociologist Max Weber is best known for his study

   (A) *Street Corner Society.*
   (B) *The Division of Labor in Society.*
   (C) *The Human Group.*
   (D) *The Protestant Ethic and the Spirit of Capitalism.*
   (E) *The Theory of the Leisure Class.*

10. In his writing, the French sociologist Emile Durkheim placed great emphasis on the concept of

    (A) class conflict.
    (B) social solidarity.
    (C) rationalization.
    (D) social mobility.
    (E) reference groups.

11. In his theory, Karl Marx explained that conflict between industrial workers and the owners of industry was

    (A) likely to decline in future years.
    (B) usually harmful to social institutions.
    (C) an inevitable consequence of capitalism.
    (D) of little importance to social change.
    (E) a rare occurrence in modern societies.

12. The research method that relies on interviews with a randomly selected sample of people is known as

    (A) survey research.
    (B) participant observation.
    (C) content analysis.
    (D) experimentation.
    (E) exploratory research.

13. Organization theory uses theories of reinforcement to increase worker efficiency and satisfaction. According to reinforcement theory, the best time to reward a worker is

    (A) at the end of the year in the form of a bonus.
    (B) never.
    (C) when he first begins work in the company.
    (D) immediately before a task is performed.
    (E) immediately after a task has been performed.

14. Which of the following is used to effect the release of a person from improper imprisonment?

    (A) A writ of mandamus
    (B) A writ of habeas corpus
    (C) The Fourth Amendment requirement that police have probable cause in order to obtain a search warrant
    (D) The Supreme Court's decision in *Roe v. Wade*
    (E) The constitutional prohibition against *ex post facto* laws

15. When a member of the House of Representatives helps a citizen from his or her district receive some federal aid to which that citizen is entitled, the representative's action is referred to as

(A) casework.
(B) pork barrel legislation.
(C) lobbying.
(D) logrolling.
(E) filibustering.

16. One advantage incumbent members of Congress have over challengers in election campaigns is the use of

(A) unlimited campaign funds.
(B) national party employees as campaign workers.
(C) the franking privilege.
(D) unlimited contributions from "fat cat" supporters.
(E) government-financed air time for commercials.

Questions 17 to 18 refer to the following tables.

Grain Producers				Grain Importers			
Grain	1st	2nd	3rd	Grain	1st	2nd	3rd
Corn	USA	China	Brazil	Corn	CIS	Japan	Spain
Wheat	CIS	USA	China	Wheat	China	CIS	Japan
Rice	China	India	Indonesia	Rice	Indonesia	Iran	CIS

17. Which nation—or group of nations—seems to have the LEAST efficient agricultural system?

(A) Brazil
(B) Indonesia
(C) CIS
(D) India
(E) China

18. Which nation seems to have the MOST self-sufficient agricultural system?

(A) USA
(B) China
(C) Brazil
(D) Indonesia
(E) India

19. Which of the following is NOT a characteristic of American agriculture?

(A) The rich ecosystem of North America
(B) The use of mechanization
(C) The diversity of climate and soil
(D) Total free market capitalism
(E) The trend toward agribusiness

20. All of the following are true of the Confederate war effort during the Civil War EXCEPT

(A) Confederate industry was never able to adequately supply Confederate soldiers with the armaments they needed to successfully fight the war.
(B) Confederate agriculture was never able to adequately supply the people of the South with the food they needed.
(C) inflation became a major problem in the South as the Confederate government was forced to print more paper currency than it could support with gold or other tangible assets.
(D) the inadequate railroad system of the South hindered movement of soldiers, supplies, and food from the places where they were stationed (or produced) to the places where they were most needed.
(E) tremendous resentment at the military draft developed among poor and middle-class Southerners because wealthy Southern males could pay to have a substitute take their place in the army.

21. What was the OVERALL U.S. unemployment rate during the worst periods of the depression?

    (A) 10%
    (B) 25%
    (C) 40%
    (D) 60%
    (E) 90%

Question 22 refers to the following.

22. The painting by François Dubois, an eyewitness, describes the massacre on St. Bartholomew's Day of 1572 of

    (A) Dutch nobility.
    (B) German peasants.
    (C) French Calvinists.
    (D) Spanish Catholics.
    (E) English merchants.

23. Which one of the following was a characteristic of the peace settlements at the end of World War I?

    (A) Division of Germany into two parts
    (B) Expansion of the territory of the Ottoman Empire
    (C) The emergence of the Soviet Union as a significant part of the European diplomatic system
    (D) The long-term stationing of American troops in Europe
    (E) Germany not being required to pay reparations

24. Which of the following has NOT been a leader of an African country?

    (A) Kwame Nkrumah
    (B) Jomo Kenyatta
    (C) Aimé Césaire
    (D) Julius Nyerere
    (E) Patrice Lumumba

25. When Chinese students held a protest in Beijing's Tiananmen Square on May 4, 1989, they were commemorating the May 4 Movement of what year?

    (A) 1919
    (B) 1911
    (C) 1901
    (D) 1895
    (E) 1969

26. "Birth rates are lower in nations with high levels of economic development." This statement is an example of a

    (A) positive correlation.
    (B) spurious correlation.
    (C) circular correlation.
    (D) negative correlation.
    (E) reverse correlation.

27. Which of the following concepts is most clearly at the core of the sociological theory known as functionalism?

    (A) Economic development
    (B) Class conflict
    (C) Human communication
    (D) Intellectual creativity
    (E) Interdependence

28. Which of the following is an example of upward social mobility?

    (A) A farm worker's son becomes president of the United States
    (B) A physician's daughter attends medical school
    (C) A college professor's son works as a truck driver
    (D) The daughter of an army officer joins the navy
    (E) The son of a banker becomes a poet

29. Which of the following is most frequently used by sociologists as a measure of a person's socioeconomic status in industrial societies?

    (A) The prestige of his/her occupation
    (B) The amount of leisure time he/she possesses
    (C) The number of children he/she has
    (D) His/her participation in politics
    (E) His/her religious beliefs

30. For sociologists, the key feature of a middle-class family that distinguishes it from a working-class family is that the

    (A) head of the middle-class family works at more than one job.
    (B) wife of the middle-class family is a full-time homemaker.
    (C) children in the middle-class family attend private schools.
    (D) workers in the middle-class family hold white-collar occupations.
    (E) middle-class family owns more cars and more expensive homes.

31. Sociological research in the United States has found all of the following EXCEPT

    (A) middle-class people attend church more often than lower-class people.
    (B) lower-class people are ill more frequently than middle-class people.
    (C) middle-class parents use physical punishment less often than lower-class parents.
    (D) lower-class people are less involved in politics than middle-class people.
    (E) lower-class families have fewer children than middle-class families.

32. The role of imitation in social learning was first systematically observed by

    (A) Miller and Dollard.
    (B) Bandura and Walters.
    (C) Stanley Milgram.
    (D) B. F. Skinner.
    (E) J. B. Watson.

33. Major differences between procedures in the House of Representatives and the Senate would include:

    I. In the House, time for debate is limited, while in the Senate it is usually unlimited.
    II. In the House, the rules committee is very powerful, while in the Senate it is relatively weak.
    III. In the House, debate must be germane, while in the Senate it need not be.

    (A) I only.
    (B) II only.
    (C) III only.
    (D) I and II only.
    (E) I, II, and III.

34. In the case *McCulloch v. Maryland* (1819), the Supreme Court

    (A) gave a broad interpretation to the First Amendment right of freedom of speech.
    (B) claimed the power of judicial review.
    (C) struck down a law of Congress for the first time.
    (D) gave a broad interpretation to the "necessary and proper clause."
    (E) denied that the president has the right of executive privilege.

35. Which of the following statements about the U.S. president's cabinet is FALSE?

    (A) It includes heads of the 15 executive departments.
    (B) It includes members of the House of Representatives.
    (C) Although not mentioned in the Constitution, the cabinet has been part of American government since the presidency of George Washington.
    (D) Presidents may appoint special advisors to the cabinet.
    (E) Senators may not serve in the cabinet.

Questions 36 and 37 refer to the following graph.

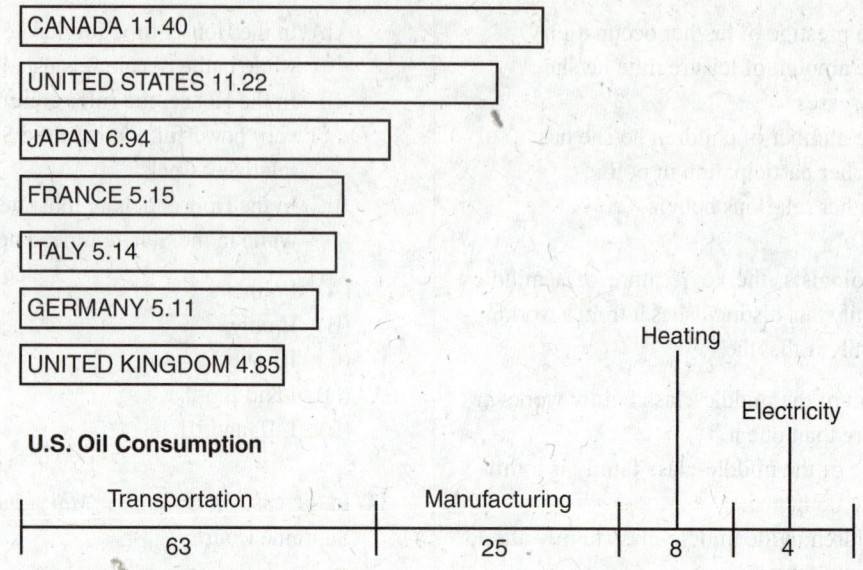

Top Oil Consumers *(in liters per day per person)*

CANADA 11.40

UNITED STATES 11.22

JAPAN 6.94

FRANCE 5.15

ITALY 5.14

GERMANY 5.11

UNITED KINGDOM 4.85

U.S. Oil Consumption

Transportation	Manufacturing	Heating	Electricity
63	25	8	4

36. Which of the following is NOT a conclusion that can be drawn from the graphs?

(A) Transportation takes up too high a portion of U.S. oil usage.
(B) U.S. per capita consumption is over twice that of most European nations.
(C) North American oil demands are the highest.
(D) Manufacturing is a major consumer of oil.
(E) Heating needs take less than 10% of oil use.

37. Which would be LEAST likely to explain the previous statistics?

(A) The area size of a nation has a relationship to oil usage.
(B) The European nations consume large quantities of oil.
(C) The larger the population, the greater the usage.
(D) Japan is the largest industrial power in Asia.
(E) Industrial nations' people have lifestyles that use more oil.

38. Which of the following is NOT true about the petroleum industry?

(A) It is dealing with a nonrenewable resource.
(B) It is essential to the plastics industry.
(C) It reacts quickly to the law of supply and demand.
(D) It is an example of a monopoly.
(E) It is truly a multinational industry.

39. All of the following were main principles of the Navigation Acts EXCEPT

(A) trade in the colonies was limited to only British or colonial merchants.
(B) it prohibited the colonies from issuing their own paper currencies, greatly limiting their trading capabilities.
(C) all foreign goods bound for the colonies had to be shipped through England where they were taxed with British import duties.
(D) the colonists could not build or export products that directly competed with British export products.
(E) colonial enumerated goods could only be sold in England.

40. The reason slavery flourished in the Southern English colonies and not in New England is

(A) most New England farms were too small for slaves to be economically necessary or viable, whereas in the South the cultivation of staple crops such as rice and tobacco on large plantations necessitated the use of large numbers of indentured servants or slaves.

(B) blacks from the tropical climate of Africa could not adapt to the harsh New England winters. Their high death rates made their use as slave laborers unprofitable.

(C) a shortage of females in the Southern English colonies led to many female black Africans being imported as slaves and as potential wives for white planters in the region.

(D) whereas New England religious groups such as the Puritans forbade slavery on moral grounds, the Anglican church, which dominated the Southern English colonies, encouraged the belief that blacks were inferior and thus, not deserving of equal status.

(E) the Stono uprising in 1739 convinced New Englanders that the cost of controlling slaves was not worth their marginal economic benefits.

41. All of the following are characteristics of Renaissance humanism EXCEPT

(A) sanctity of the Latin texts of Scriptures.
(B) belief that ancient Latin and Greek writers were inferior to later authors.
(C) rejection of Christian principles.
(D) functioned as a primary cause of the Reformation.
(E) accomplished scholarship in ancient languages.

42. The October Manifesto of Tsar Nicholas II promised all of the following EXCEPT

(A) a Duma.
(B) political reforms.
(C) a Russian parliament.
(D) a fair, democratic voting system.
(E) full civil liberties.

43. Which independent Asian nation did NOT exist before 1947?

(A) Thailand
(B) Pakistan
(C) India
(D) Korea
(E) Vietnam

44. All of the following were aspects of Britain's policy of indirect rule in colonial Africa EXCEPT

(A) subsidizing primary education for Africans.
(B) the expectation of eventual self-government.
(C) decentralized administration.
(D) uniform government policy throughout the colonized territories.
(E) incorporating traditional rulers into the government structure.

45. The Glorious Revolution of 1688–1689 resulted in all of the following EXCEPT

(A) the flight and abdication of James II.
(B) an agreement that in the event of no heirs, the Hanover house would succeed the Stuarts.
(C) the elevation of William III and Mary as the monarchs.
(D) specification that all future monarchs must be members of the Church of England.
(E) the passage of the Bill of Rights.

46. Many young people around the world now wear American blue jeans and listen to American rock-and-roll music. This is an example of the concept of cultural

(A) decline.
(B) diffusion.
(C) discovery.
(D) innovation.
(E) disintegration.

47. Popular movies frequently portray young African-American men as gang members and drug dealers. This is an example of the sociological process known as

    (A) affirmative action.
    (B) reverse racism.
    (C) stereotyping.
    (D) status inconsistency.
    (E) role conflict.

48. According to the functionalist theory of stratification developed by Kingsley Davis and Wilbert Moore, some occupations are more highly rewarded than others because they

    (A) have been held for a long time.
    (B) are organized into unions.
    (C) require physical labor.
    (D) appeal to widely shared values.
    (E) require long periods of training.

49. Demographers study all of the following aspects of human populations EXCEPT

    (A) growth.
    (B) distribution.
    (C) migration.
    (D) composition.
    (E) socialization.

50. Each of the following is an important agent of socialization EXCEPT

    (A) television.
    (B) bankers.
    (C) parents.
    (D) peers.
    (E) teachers.

51. In our society, money is an example of a

    (A) primary reinforcer.
    (B) secondary (conditioned) reinforcer.
    (C) socio/reinforcer.
    (D) negative reinforcer.
    (E) simple operant.

52. The major responsibility of the Federal Reserve Board is to

    (A) implement monetary policy.
    (B) control government spending.
    (C) regulate commodity prices.
    (D) help the president run the executive branch.
    (E) keep records of troop strength in army reserve units across the country.

53. Which of the following statements most accurately compares political parties in the United States with those in other Western democracies?

    (A) Parties in the United States exert a greater influence over which candidates run for office.
    (B) Parties are much more centralized in the United States.
    (C) There are usually more political parties in other Western democracies.
    (D) Party members in the national legislature are much freer to vote against the party line in other Western democracies.
    (E) Party label is the principal criterion for voting for a candidate in the United States, whereas it is relatively unimportant in other Western democracies.

54. Which of the following is among the differences between a parliamentary and a presidential system?

    I. In a parliamentary system, there is little or no separation of powers as in a presidential system.
    II. In a parliamentary system, the chief executive officer is not chosen by a nationwide vote as in a residential system.
    III. In a presidential system, the chief executive officer may call elections for all members of the legislature at any time, unlike in a parliamentary system.

    (A) I only
    (B) II only
    (C) III only
    (D) I and II only
    (E) I, II, and III

Questions 55 to 57 refer to the following.

- We must develop the vision to see that, in regard to the natural world, private and corporate ownership should be so limited as to preserve the interest of society and the integrity of the environment.

- We need greater awareness of our enormous powers, the fragility of the earth, and the consequent responsibility of men and governments for its preservation.

- We must redefine "progress" toward an emphasis on long-term quality rather than immediate quantity.

"We, therefore, resolve to act. We propose a revolution in conduct toward an environment which is rising in revolt against us. Granted that ideas and institutions long established are not easily changed; yet today is the first day of the rest of our life on this planet. We will begin anew."

55. Which group is NOT called upon to act in the statement?

    (A) Private and corporate ownership
    (B) Government
    (C) Individuals
    (D) Society
    (E) Communities

56. What makes this quote relevant to economics?

    (A) Ethical use of the environment
    (B) Man as a member of the "community of all living things"
    (C) Need for individual responsibility
    (D) References to man's machines and past abuses
    (E) Progress, in terms of quality of life

57. Which of the following is NOT an example of how environmental concerns can become economic priorities?

    (A) Recycling
    (B) Reforestation
    (C) Strip-mining restoration
    (D) Greenhouse effect
    (E) Coal-generated electricity to replace imported oil

58. Which battle was the turning point in the Pacific war between Japan and the United States?

    (A) Leyte Gulf
    (B) Pearl Harbor
    (C) Coral Sea
    (D) Midway
    (E) Guadalcanal

59. The United States Supreme Court case of *Brown v. Board of Education of Topeka* was significant because it

    (A) prohibited prayer in public schools on the grounds of separation of church and state.
    (B) legally upheld the doctrine of "separate but equal" educational facilities for blacks and whites.
    (C) clarified the constitutional rights of minors and restricted the rights of school administrators to set dress codes or otherwise infringe on students' rights.
    (D) upheld school districts' rights to use aptitude and psychological tests to "track" students and segregate them into "college prep" and "vocational" programs.
    (E) ordered the desegregation of public schools, prohibiting the practice of segregation via "separate but equal" schools for blacks and whites.

60. Ferdinand and Isabella's policies of Spanish nationalism led to the expulsion, from Spain, of large numbers of Spanish

    (A) Protestants.
    (B) Catholics.
    (C) Jews.
    (D) Calvinists.
    (E) monks.

61. During the Thirty Years' War, the Lutheran movement was saved from extinction by the military intervention of which foreign monarch?

    (A) The French king, Philip the Fair
    (B) The English king, Henry VIII
    (C) The Swedish king, Gustavus Adolphus
    (D) The Austrian emperor, Charles V
    (E) The Spanish king, Philip II

62. In 1898, the United States took control of the Philippines from which country?

    (A) China
    (B) Japan
    (C) England
    (D) Spain
    (E) Portugal

63. The following pairs of names are the names of African countries before and after achieving independence EXCEPT

    (A) Bechuanaland—Botswana.
    (B) Dahomey—Benin.
    (C) Gold Coast—Ghana.
    (D) Swaziland—Malawi.
    (E) Angola—Angola.

64. Emile Durkheim found that suicide rates were higher for

    (A) women than men.
    (B) young people than old people.
    (C) poor people than wealthy people.
    (D) single people than married people.
    (E) Jews than Protestants.

65. A soldier in combat sacrifices his life so his comrades may survive. This is an example of which of the following types of suicide identified by Durkheim?

    (A) Egoistic
    (B) Altruistic
    (C) Intrinsic
    (D) Anomic
    (E) Euphoric

66. The research method which involves a social scientist living among and interacting with the people being studied is known as

    (A) survey research.
    (B) experimentation.
    (C) content analysis.
    (D) participant observation.
    (E) strategic engagement.

67. "Female college athletes will have higher academic averages than male college athletes." In this hypothesis, which is the independent variable?

    (A) Athletic participation
    (B) College attendance
    (C) Academic achievement
    (D) Gender
    (E) Study habits

68. The concept of culture includes all of the following EXCEPT

    (A) personal values.
    (B) religious beliefs.
    (C) styles of dress.
    (D) family organization.
    (E) individual intelligence.

69. The concept of ethnocentrism refers to the tendency for members of a group to

    (A) speak the same language.
    (B) work for common goals.
    (C) show respect for the elderly.
    (D) teach children to practice religious rituals.
    (E) place a high value on their own culture.

70. An important function of rehearsal in verbal learning is

    (A) mediation.
    (B) transference of material from short-term to long-term memory.
    (C) acclimation to the meaning of the material.
    (D) Both (A) and (B).
    (E) to avoid the loss of the memory.

71. The statement "America has a pluralistic political system" means

(A) there are many subcultures within American society.
(B) political power is divided between national and state governments.
(C) many interest groups compete in the political arena to influence public policy.
(D) rural interests are overrepresented in the national legislature.
(E) candidates for national office are usually elected by plurality vote.

72. Which of the following best describes the relationship between educational background and participation in politics?

(A) The more schooling one has, the more likely one is to vote.
(B) The less schooling one has, the more likely one is to run for public office.
(C) There is no relationship between educational background and participation in politics.

(D) People with a high school education are more likely to vote than either those who did not finish high school or those with a college degree.
(E) Those with no formal schooling have a greater personal interest in politics and tend to vote more often than those with high school diplomas.

73. All of the following are recognized functions of the major political parties EXCEPT

(A) recruiting candidates for public office.
(B) aggregating interests into electoral alliances.
(C) establishing channels of communication between public and government.
(D) providing personnel to staff elections and run the government.
(E) articulating interests.

Questions 74 and 75 refer to the following diagram.

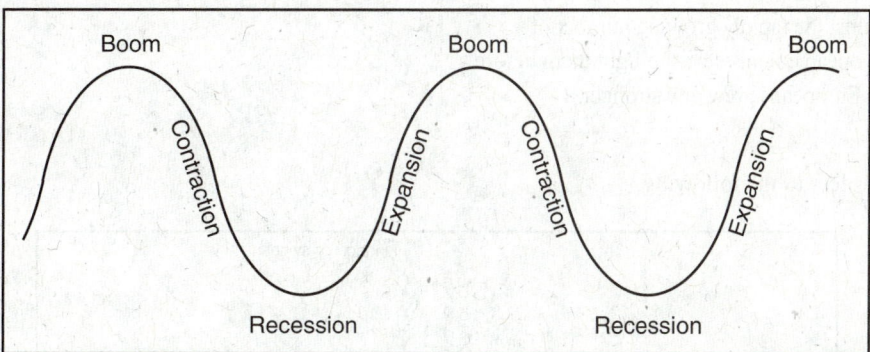

74. Which of the following is the best title for the diagram above?

(A) Boom and Bust
(B) Causes of Economic Change
(C) The Business Cycle
(D) Causes of Recession
(E) The History of Business Activity

75. In referring to the stages of the cycle, which would NOT be a factor considered by economists?

(A) Unemployment figures
(B) Manufacturing production
(C) Income levels
(D) War or peace
(E) Retail sales

76. Which of the following is NOT a method used to encourage expansion during a recession?

(A) Political crisis, such as war
(B) Increased government spending
(C) Increased taxation
(D) Deregulation of industry
(E) Restriction of imports

77. The Great Awakening of the mid-eighteenth century refers to

(A) a series of religious revivals that swept through the English colonies spreading evangelistic fervor and challenging the control of traditional clerics over their congregations.
(B) the intellectual revolution which served as a precursor to the Enlightenment and challenged orthodox religion's claims to knowledge of humankind and the universe.
(C) the beginnings of the Industrial Revolution in England and its New World colonies.
(D) the growing realization among English colonists that independence from England was only a matter of time and was the key to their future success.
(E) the sudden awareness among North American Indians that their only chance for survival against the rapidly growing number of European colonists was to fight them before the Europeans grew any stronger.

78. One of the major effects of the Industrial Revolution of the late nineteenth century in the United States was

(A) an increased emphasis on worker health and safety issues.
(B) an increased emphasis on speed rather than quality of work.
(C) an increased emphasis on high-quality, error-free work.
(D) an increase in the number of small industrial facilities, which could operate more efficiently than larger, more costly industrial plants.
(E) a decrease in worker productivity as a result of continuous clashes between unions and management.

79. All of the following were significant economic trends in Germany during the 1920s EXCEPT

(A) large amounts of money leaving the country to pay reparations.
(B) periods of high inflation.
(C) a very stable currency (the mark).
(D) periods of high unemployment.
(E) the German government placing large amounts of paper money in circulation.

Question 80 refers to the following.

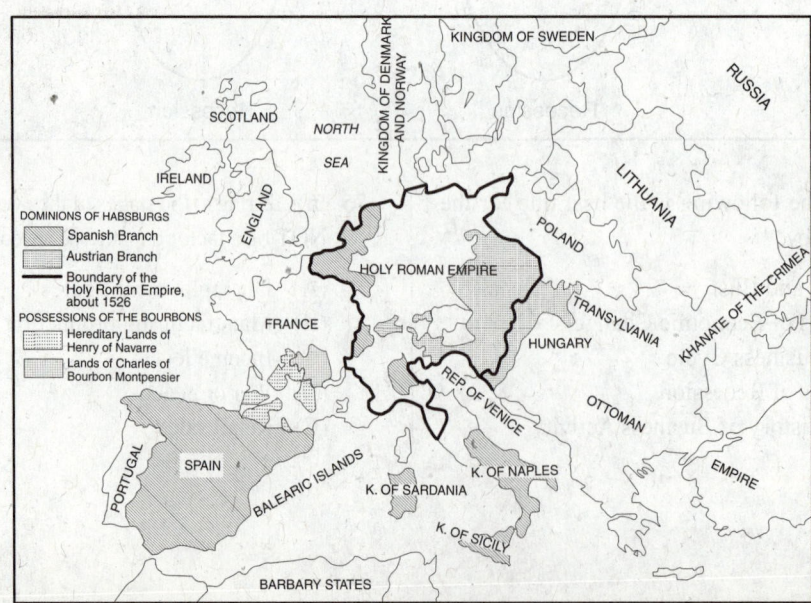

80. The map depicts Europe around

    (A) 1800.
    (B) 1500.
    (C) 1700.
    (D) 1950.
    (E) 1900.

81. By 1914 which of the following countries was still an independent state not under colonial control?

    (A) Algeria
    (B) Congo
    (C) Angola
    (D) Egypt
    (E) Ethiopia

82. Thailand is bordered by which of the following countries?

    I. Myanmar
    II. Laos
    III. Vietnam
    IV. Cambodia

    (A) I, II, and III
    (B) I, II, and IV
    (C) I and II only
    (D) II and III only
    (E) IV only

83. According to sociologists, an important difference between folkways and mores is that

    (A) violation of a folkway leads to severe punishment.
    (B) mores are found among the upper classes only.
    (C) folkways include customary behaviors.
    (D) violations of mores are not considered crimes.
    (E) folkways apply to sexual behavior only.

84. Deviant behavior is the term used by sociologists to describe behaviors which a group defines as

    (A) violating basic norms.
    (B) uncommonly brave or heroic.
    (C) the standard for others to follow.
    (D) very rare or unusual.
    (E) based on personal motives.

85. Which of the following behaviors would NOT be considered an example of deviance in contemporary American society?

    (A) Eating spaghetti with one's fingers
    (B) Running naked down Main Street
    (C) A man regularly dressing in women's clothing
    (D) College students drinking beer on Saturday night
    (E) A person talking to himself in public places

86. According to the symbolic interactionist theory of George Herbert Mead, which of the following processes is central to the development of a self-concept by young children?

    (A) Pretending to be other people
    (B) Memorizing songs and poems
    (C) Learning how to read in school
    (D) Listening to bedtime stories
    (E) Saying prayers in church

87. Studies of children who have been raised with limited contact with other humans during their first years have shown that they

    (A) develop intellectually at a normal rate.
    (B) have better coordination than other children.
    (C) have great difficulty adjusting to society.
    (D) easily learn to distinguish right and wrong.
    (E) often show considerable artistic talent.

88. All of the following are basic assumptions of sociology EXCEPT

    (A) most human behavior follows predictable patterns.
    (B) scientific methods can be used to study human behavior.
    (C) inherited genetic traits shape much human behavior.
    (D) human beliefs and values can be studied objectively.
    (E) human values are acquired through socialization.

89. Stanley Milgram, in his landmark study on obedience to authority, found that when subjects were asked to shock a confederate in increasing amounts in order to teach him a word-matching task,

(A) 65% of the subjects administered shocks throughout the experiment and gave the maximum 450-volt shock.
(B) 75% of the subjects refused to participate in the experiment.
(C) 30% of the subjects administered shocks throughout the experiment and gave the maximum 450-volt shock.
(D) people of low intelligence were more likely to apply the maximum 450-volt shock.
(E) Both (A) and (D).

Question 90 refers to the following.

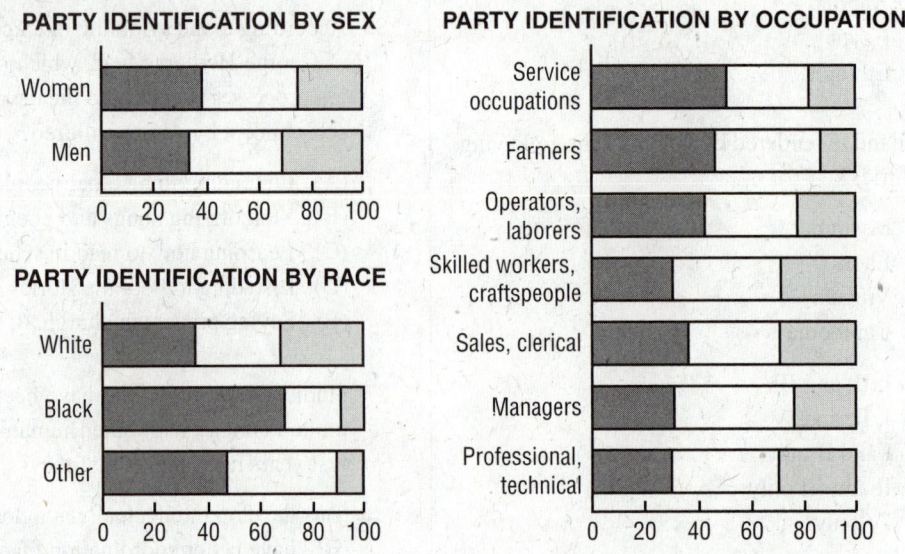

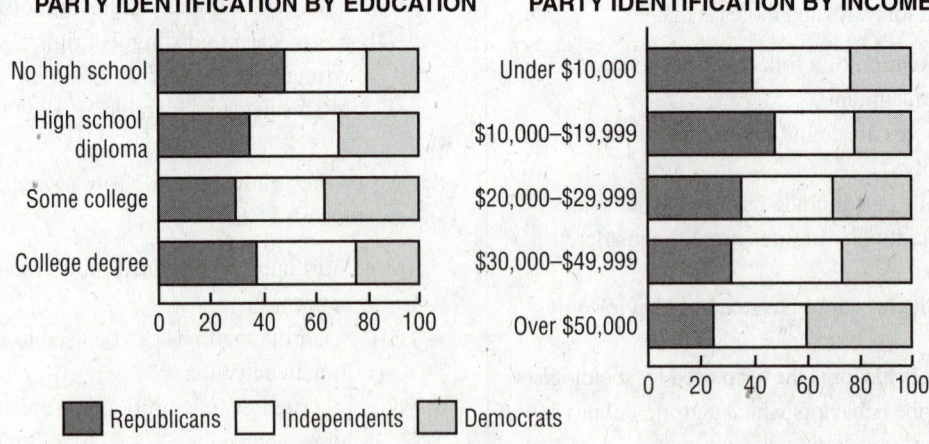

From Janda, Berry, Goldman, *The Challenge of Democracy*, 4th ed., 2001, p. 286.

90. Based on the previous graphs, which of the following were LEAST likely to have voted for Franklin Roosevelt in 1940?

    (A) Southerners
    (B) White northern business leaders
    (C) Blue-collar workers
    (D) Racial minorities
    (E) Union members

91. The federal Constitution guarantees which of the following rights to persons arrested and charged with a serious crime?

    I. To have an attorney appointed for them if they cannot afford to hire one
    II. To remain silent
    III. To compel witnesses in their favor to testify if the case goes to court

    (A) I only
    (B) II only
    (C) III only
    (D) I and II only
    (E) I, II, and III

92. The purpose of grandfather clauses and literacy tests, used in the southern states in the late 1800s and early 1900s, was to

    (A) prevent illiterate whites from voting.
    (B) prevent recent immigrants from voting.
    (C) prevent Hispanics from running for public office.
    (D) prevent blacks from voting.
    (E) prevent "carpetbaggers" from running for public office.

Questions 93 to 95 refer to the following passage.

Business functions by public consent, and its basic purpose is to serve constructively the needs of society—to the satisfaction of society.

"Historically, business has discharged this obligation mainly by supplying the needs and wants of people for goods and services, by providing jobs and purchasing power, and by producing most of the wealth of the nation. This has been what American society required of business, and business on the whole has done its job remarkably well. . . .

"In generating . . . economic growth, American business has provided increasing employment, rising wages and salaries, employee benefit plans, and expanding career opportunities for a labor force. . . .

"Most important, the rising standard of living of the average American family has enabled more and more citizens to develop their lives as they wish with less and less constraint imposed on them by economic need. Thus, most Americans have been able to afford better health, food, clothing, shelter, and education than the citizens of any other nation have ever achieved on such a large scale. . . .

Source: U.S. Government report

93. Which statement BEST summarizes the attitude of the quote?

    (A) Business has successfully met all the needs of society.
    (B) Business has done a good job supplying the economic needs of society.
    (C) Americans are best off with the least government.
    (D) All Americans have benefited from the rising living standard.
    (E) Government and business, in partnership, have created prosperity.

94. Which organization would be most likely to endorse this quote?

    (A) Chamber of Commerce
    (B) Department of Labor
    (C) General Accounting Office
    (D) Socialist Labor party
    (E) AFL/CIO

95. Which of the following economic goals is not addressed by the quote?

    (A) Economic growth
    (B) Economic stability
    (C) Economic security
    (D) Economic justice
    (E) Economic freedom

96. Which of the following is NOT one of the four basic economic activities of capitalism?

    (A) Production
    (B) Distribution
    (C) Manufacturing
    (D) Service
    (E) Labor

97. The key event that guaranteed Lincoln's reelection in 1864 was

    (A) the fall of Vicksburg to General Grant.
    (B) the capture of New Orleans by Admiral Farragut.
    (C) the defeat of Lee's army by General Meade at Gettysburg.
    (D) the fall of Atlanta to General Sherman.
    (E) the successful defense of Nashville by General Thomas against repeated Confederate counterattacks.

98. The American Hostage Crisis in Iran was precipitated by which of the following?

    (A) The American government allowing the deposed Shah of Iran to come to the United States for cancer treatment
    (B) Jimmy Carter's involvement in arranging the Camp David accords between the Egyptians and the Israelis
    (C) American air strikes against Iran's ally, Libya
    (D) American support for Israel's 1980 invasion of southern Lebanon
    (E) American attempts to overthrow the newly emplaced government of Ayatollah Khomeini

99. During the era of European imperialism in Africa, 1870–1914, a "Cape to Cairo railway" was a project envisioned by

    (A) Italy.
    (B) Britain.
    (C) France.
    (D) Germany.
    (E) Spain.

100. Which European nation failed to establish an African colony when its expeditionary force was overwhelmingly defeated by a native force at Adowa, Ethiopia, in 1896?

    (A) Italy
    (B) Belgium
    (C) Portugal
    (D) Britain
    (E) Austria

101. The Himalayan mountain range runs through which of the following Asian countries?

    I. China
    II. Nepal
    III. India
    IV. Bangladesh

    (A) I and II only
    (B) II and III only
    (C) I, II, and III only
    (D) I, III, and IV only
    (E) All of the above

102. Which of the following was the first European country to make the slave trade illegal?

    (A) Holland
    (B) Britain
    (C) France
    (D) Spain
    (E) Portugal

103. "Working-class mothers will place a higher value on obedience in raising their children than will middle-class mothers." In this hypothesis, which is the dependent variable?

    (A) Social class of mothers
    (B) Gender of children
    (C) Value placed on obedience
    (D) Education of parents
    (E) Social status of mothers

104. Which of the following is NOT a method of social control?

    (A) Ridicule
    (B) Insults
    (C) Spanking
    (D) Praise
    (E) Imitation

105. George is a college student. He also works 25 hours a week to support his wife and small child. He is having a hard time pleasing his boss and keeping his grades up. A sociologist would say that George is suffering from

    (A) role ambiguity.
    (B) role conflict.
    (C) role strain.
    (D) role performance.
    (E) role playing.

106. Social mobility refers to the ability to

    (A) gain a college education.
    (B) enter any occupation one chooses.
    (C) travel freely across national borders.
    (D) change one's social class position.
    (E) marry a person of another religion.

107. When sociologists discuss the working class, they are referring to peole who

    (A) work for a living.
    (B) live below the poverty line.
    (C) have not attended college.
    (D) work in blue-collar occupations.
    (E) live near factories.

Questions 108–110 refer to the following passage.

Many psychologists believe that aggression is a behavior which is learned through operant conditioning, in which rewards and punishments shape a person's behavior. Modeling, or vicarious conditioning, is also thought to contribute to the development of aggressive behavior. In contrast with this predominant school of thought is the school that believes that aggression is an inborn tendency, and that because humans use their intelligence to aggress, they have never developed natural controls on aggression against their own species, as have other animals.

108. The belief that aggression is learned is held by

    (A) social learning theorists.
    (B) phenomenological theorists.
    (C) psychodynamic theorists.
    (D) experimental theorists.
    (E) Freudian theorists.

109. Which of the following statements is false?

    (A) If a child is rewarded for random, aggressive behavior, chances are good that the behavior will be repeated.
    (B) If a child is punished for acting aggressively, the likelihood of that behavior recurring is lessened.
    (C) If aggression is reinforced irregularly, the aggressive behavior is gradually discouraged.
    (D) Both (B) and (C).
    (E) Aggression is thought to be an inborn trait.

110. The approach in which it is believed that aggression is an inborn tendency has been most supported by the work of

    (A) Sigmund Freud.
    (B) Konrad Lorenz.
    (C) Carl Rogers.
    (D) Albert Bandura.
    (E) B. F. Skinner.

Question 111 refers to the following excerpt from a Supreme Court decision.

It is emphatically the province and duty of the courts to say what the law is. . . . If two laws conflict with each other, the courts must decide on the operation of each. . . . If, then, the courts are to regard the Constitution, and the Constitution is superior to any ordinary act of the legislature, the Constitution and not such ordinary act, must govern the case to which they both apply.

111. This decision of the Supreme Court upheld the principle that

(A) a law contrary to the Constitution cannot be enforced by the courts.
(B) Congress has the power to pass laws to carry out its constitutional duties.
(C) interpretation of laws is a legislative function.
(D) a law passed by Congress overrides a constitutional provision with which it conflicts.
(E) courts are not equipped to decide questions of constitutional law.

112. "Mark-up sessions," where revisions and additions are made to proposed legislation in Congress, usually occur in which setting?

(A) The majority leader's office
(B) On the floor of the legislative chamber
(C) In party caucuses
(D) In joint conference committees
(E) In committees or subcommittees

113. Which of the following has chief responsibility for assembling and analyzing the figures in the presidential budget submitted to Congress each year?

(A) Department of Commerce
(B) Department of Treasury
(C) Federal Reserve Board
(D) Office of Management and Budget
(E) Cabinet

Questions 114 to 118 refer to the following graphs.

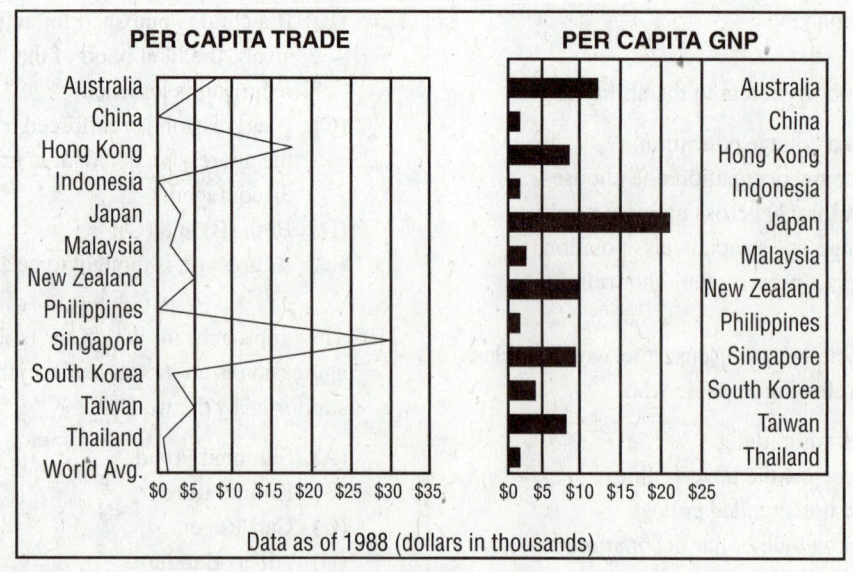

PER CAPITA TRADE — PER CAPITA GNP

Australia, China, Hong Kong, Indonesia, Japan, Malaysia, New Zealand, Philippines, Singapore, South Korea, Taiwan, Thailand, World Avg.

$0 $5 $10 $15 $20 $25 $30 $35 — $0 $5 $10 $15 $20 $25

Data as of 1988 (dollars in thousands)

114. Comparing the two charts, the best conclusion is that

(A) there is a direct relationship between GNP and trade.
(B) the nations all have increased their GNP.
(C) they all exceeded the world average in trade.
(D) Japan is the leader in both GNP and trade.
(E) China ranks lowest in both categories.

115. Which of the following is NOT true about both charts?

(A) Both are figured per person.
(B) Both are in thousands of dollars.
(C) Both compare the same nations.
(D) Both are the same type of graph.
(E) Both use the same year's data.

116. Which economic region of the world is reflected in the graphs?

(A) East Asia
(B) All Asia
(C) Northwest Asia
(D) All Pacific
(E) All ex-British colonies

117. The nation that is increasing its prosperity the most is probably

(A) Australia.
(B) Hong Kong.
(C) Japan.
(D) Singapore.
(E) Taiwan.

118. Which of the following is the best way to describe the GNP?

(A) Total goods and services
(B) Total national production
(C) Greater national production
(D) Government natural production
(E) Gross national resources

119. The Compromise of 1877 resulted in

(A) the ascension of Republican Rutherford B. Hayes to the presidency in return for assurances that what was left of Reconstruction in the South would be ended.
(B) the division of the Dakota Territory into North Dakota and South Dakota.
(C) government financing for a Southern transcontinental railroad route in return for financial grants allowing the completion of the Great Northern Railroad from Minnesota to the Pacific Northwest.
(D) the ascension of Republican Rutherford B. Hayes to the presidency in return for the passage of an Amnesty Act which would pardon former Confederate soldiers, allowing them to regain their voting rights.
(E) the formal separation of Virginia and West Virginia and the official acceptance of statehood for West Virginia.

120. The Albany Congress of 1754 was convened for the major purpose of

(A) adding New York to the Dominion of New England.
(B) getting the colonies to form a "grand council" to coordinate their western expansion and their common defense against Indians.
(C) uniting the colonies under a "grand council" to resist British economic sanctions and coordinate activities against British tax officials.
(D) cooperating with the French in their efforts to rid western New York and southern Canada of raiding Indian tribes.
(E) writing a proclamation to be sent to King George in protest of the Stamp Act.

TEST STOPS HERE. *EXTRA PRACTICE FOLLOWS . . .*

121. "Sturm und Drang" was a significant period in the career of

    (A) Rousseau.
    (B) Goethe.
    (C) Mill.
    (D) Stendahl.
    (E) Kant.

122. All of the following were characteristics of the Positivism of Auguste Comte EXCEPT

    (A) belief in a three-stage view of history.
    (B) belief that all knowledge must be scientifically verified.
    (C) achievement of Progress and Order through a government of major scientists and philosophers.
    (D) a new Religion of Science.
    (E) admiration for science and technology.

123. All of the pairs listed below represent the names of modern African countries and their capitals EXCEPT

    (A) Angola—Luanda.
    (B) Somalia—Mogadishu.
    (C) Nigeria—Abuja.
    (D) Liberia—Monrovia.
    (E) Sierra Leone—Dakar.

124. All of the following countries were colonized by a European power in the nineteenth century EXCEPT

    (A) Cambodia.
    (B) Laos.
    (C) Burma.
    (D) India.
    (E) Thailand.

125. Which of the following is an ascribed status?

    (A) College president
    (B) Nobel prize winner
    (C) Honor student
    (D) White female
    (E) Opera singer

126. Which of the following is an achieved status?

    (A) Television game show host
    (B) Senior citizen
    (C) Japanese-American teenager
    (D) Accident victim
    (E) Seven feet tall

127. If a group is considered a subculture by sociologists, then the people in that group would be most likely to have similar

    (A) values.
    (B) incomes.
    (C) educations.
    (D) ages.
    (E) genders.

128. "Our self-concept is based largely on the ways in which we see other people reacting to us." This statement reflects

    (A) George Herbert Mead's theory of self-development.
    (B) Charles Cooley's theory of the "looking-glass-self."
    (C) Sigmund Freud's theory of ego development.
    (D) Jean Piaget's theory of intellectual development.
    (E) Lawrence Kohlberg's theory of moral development.

129. Sociologists have identified at least five different types of societies based on their level of sociocultural evolution. Hunting and gathering societies differ from other types of societies in that they have

    (A) more rigid social stratification.
    (B) greater occupational specialization.
    (C) extensive inequality of wealth.
    (D) stronger consensus on basic values.
    (E) highly centralized government.

130. Which one of the following statements about poverty in the United States is correct?

    (A) The majority of African-Americans are poor.
    (B) The majority of elderly are poor.
    (C) The majority of the poor are whites.
    (D) The majority of the poor are African-Americans.
    (E) The majority of the poor are single mothers.

CLEP Social Sciences and History Practice Test 1

Answer Key

1.	(B)	34.	(D)	67.	(D)	100.	(A)
2.	(C)	35.	(B)	68.	(E)	101.	(C)
3.	(B)	36.	(A)	69.	(E)	102.	(B)
4.	(D)	37.	(C)	70.	(B)	103.	(C)
5.	(D)	38.	(D)	71.	(C)	104.	(E)
6.	(A)	39.	(B)	72.	(A)	105.	(B)
7.	(C)	40.	(A)	73.	(E)	106.	(D)
8.	(D)	41.	(E)	74.	(C)	107.	(D)
9.	(D)	42.	(D)	75.	(D)	108.	(A)
10.	(B)	43.	(B)	76.	(C)	109.	(C)
11.	(C)	44.	(D)	77.	(A)	110.	(B)
12.	(A)	45.	(B)	78.	(B)	111.	(A)
13.	(E)	46.	(B)	79.	(C)	112.	(E)
14.	(B)	47.	(C)	80.	(B)	113.	(D)
15.	(A)	48.	(E)	81.	(E)	114.	(E)
16.	(C)	49.	(E)	82.	(B)	115.	(D)
17.	(C)	50.	(B)	83.	(C)	116.	(A)
18.	(A)	51.	(B)	84.	(A)	117.	(D)
19.	(D)	52.	(A)	85.	(D)	118.	(A)
20.	(A)	53.	(C)	86.	(A)	119.	(A)
21.	(B)	54.	(D)	87.	(C)	120.	(B)
22.	(C)	55.	(A)	88.	(C)	121.	(B)
23.	(A)	56.	(D)	89.	(A)	122.	(D)
24.	(C)	57.	(E)	90.	(B)	123.	(E)
25.	(A)	58.	(D)	91.	(E)	124.	(E)
26.	(D)	59.	(E)	92.	(D)	125.	(D)
27.	(E)	60.	(C)	93.	(B)	126.	(A)
28.	(A)	61.	(C)	94.	(A)	127.	(A)
29.	(A)	62.	(D)	95.	(D)	128.	(B)
30.	(D)	63.	(D)	96.	(E)	129.	(D)
31.	(E)	64.	(D)	97.	(D)	130.	(C)
32.	(A)	65.	(B)	98.	(A)		
33.	(E)	66.	(D)	99.	(B)		

DETAILED EXPLANATIONS OF ANSWERS
PRACTICE TEST 1

1. **(B)** During the congressional voting to resolve the outcome of the presidential election of 1800, Hamilton made attacks against Burr's personal character. In 1804, as Burr ran for governor of New York, Hamilton repeated and expanded those charges. When Burr lost the election, he blamed Hamilton. Burr demanded "satisfaction" through a duel and Hamilton accepted. Hamilton's death not only deprived the young nation of one of its premier thinkers and statesmen, but it ruined Burr's political career. He was charged with murder and forced to flee to avoid arrest. It was after this disaster that he began formulating his plan for an independent Western empire. Thus, choice (C) is incorrect.

2. **(C)** The question deals with the growth of the United States during President McKinley's tenure. President Madison was in office during the War of 1812. President Lincoln headed the government during the Civil War. President Wilson led the country in World War I. President F. D. Roosevelt was the leader in World War II. Thus, the correct answer is (C).

3. **(B)** Although "quotation" questions may ask the name of the author or the book title, this question requires an ability to recognize the main idea of the passage. Knowledge of the terminology of seventeenth-century writers is also helpful. Hobbes' *Leviathan* described early human society (the "state of nature") as an anarchic "war of all against all." For self-protection, citizens agreed among themselves to form the first government, an agreement termed by Hobbes as the "social contract." It is especially important to read the quotation carefully, since two of the answers, (B) and (C), are from the *Leviathan*; you may be misled into choosing (C) because you have studied the *Leviathan* in a class and the "social contract" sounds familiar. The concept of natural rights, incorporated into the French Declaration of the Rights of Man and the Bill of Rights to the U.S. Constitution, was summarized by John Locke as the idea that human beings are born "free, equal, and independent." "Reason of state" was the justification used by French statesmen such as Cardinal Richelieu to defend measures to create a centralized absolute monarchy in France. Choice (E), nationalism, is not only incorrect but also irrelevant to this question.

4. **(D)** *Laissez-faire* (from the French *laissez-nous faire*, leave us alone) described the economic outlook of nineteenth-century liberals, many of whom were businessmen or industrialists who sought an end to government regulation of business. Proponents of *laissez-faire* envisioned an era of free economic activity in Europe without tariff barriers ("free trade"). Thus factory owners, liberals, and free traders were all supporters of *laissez-faire*. Not so with nineteenth-century socialists, who saw *laissez-faire* as an obstacle to even minimal measures to help the working class, such as government safety inspections of factories.

5. **(D)** On August 15, 1945, traffic came to a halt in Japan, as the nation listened to a prerecorded message in which Emperor Hirohito declared his acceptance of the Potsdam Declaration and Japan's defeat in the Second World War. This was the first time that the country had heard the emperor's voice. In the past, the emperor was considered to hold god-like status, and to

allow his subjects to hear his voice, even for events and announcements like his coronation (A), his wedding (B), and declarations of war (C) and (E), would bring him down to the level of a human being.

6. **(A)** In 1415 the Portuguese captured Ceuta, one of the first of a series of bases they were to take along the African coast. This marks the first incident of European colonial aggression on the African continent. By 1640, when Ceuta passed to the Spanish, other European powers had already entered Africa. While Belgium (B), England (C), France (D), and Germany (E) all eventually had colonial holdings in Africa, the door was opened up by Portugal (A).

7. **(C)** Sociology studies human interaction, both in small groups and in larger settings, and the results of that interaction such as groups, organizations, institutions, and nations. Social problems (A) are only a part of the subject matter of sociology. Human personality (B) and human development (D) are more often studied by psychologists. Attitudes and values (E) are only a part of the subject matter of sociology.

8. **(D)** The Industrial Revolution in Europe brought about the decline of traditional agricultural societies and the rapid growth of cities. The social dislocations that resulted from this change stimulated thinkers to consider the nature of social order and social change, and the outcome was the emergence of sociology as a separate discipline. Socialism (A) was another result of this change, but socialism as a movement for political change was separate from the discipline of sociology. (B) is incorrect because early sociologists were little concerned about the spread of colonialism during this period. While the founders of sociology were interested in the study of social inequality, they did little to promote greater equality; therefore, (C) is incorrect. (E) is incorrect because psychology developed as a separate discipline somewhat later than sociology.

9. **(D)** In *The Protestant Ethic and the Spirit of Capitalism* Weber studied the influence of the religious changes of the Reformation on the growth of capitalism in Europe. *Street Corner Society* (A) is by William F. Whyte. *The Division of Labor in Society* (B) is by Emile Durkheim. *The Human Group* (C) is by George C. Homans. *The Theory of the Leisure Class* (E) is by Thorstein Veblen.

10. **(B)** In his study of suicide, Durkheim explained how the decline of social solidarity in modern society has led to the growth of anomie (normlessness) and associated social problems such as suicide. Class conflict (A) is most closely associated with the work of Karl Marx. Rationalization (C) is most closely associated with the work of Max Weber. (D) is incorrect because Durkheim devoted relatively little attention to social mobility. The theory of reference groups (E) was developed long after Durkheim's death.

11. **(C)** Marx concluded that conflict between workers and owners was an intrinsic feature of capitalist societies. Since Marx saw this conflict as the principal reason for social change, (D) is incorrect. He also believed this conflict would intensify over time and result in a socialist revolution, so (A) is also incorrect. (B) is incorrect because Marx felt this conflict would ultimately benefit society instead of harming it.

12. **(A)** Survey research is based on data gathered by personal interviews or written questionnaires administered to a random sample of a larger population. Participant observation (B) involves

observing people interacting in natural settings. Content analysis (C) involves the analysis of the content of communications such as television, advertising, letters, or textbooks. Experimentation (D) involves manipulation of an experimental stimulus on an experimental group and withholding that stimulus from a control group. Exploratory research (E) employs no specific methodology.

13. **(E)** Reinforcement theory has proven that reinforcement is most effective if it occurs immediately after a task has been performed. End-of-the-year bonuses or quarterly reviews may not be as effective as immediate bonuses. Investigation of optimal schedules of reinforcement is ongoing and diverse; both negative and positive reinforcement schedules have been shown to be quite effective on worker productivity and satisfaction.

14. **(B)** A writ of habeas corpus is a court order which directs an official who is detaining someone to produce the person before the court so that the legality of the detention may be determined. The primary function of the writ is to effect the release of someone who has been imprisoned without due process of law. (A) is incorrect because a writ of mandamus is a court order commanding an official to perform a legal duty of his or her office. The Fourth Amendment requirement that police have probable cause in order to obtain a search warrant regulates police procedure. It is not itself a mechanism for effecting release of a person for improper imprisonment, so (C) is incorrect. Choice (D) is incorrect since the decision in *Roe v. Wade* dealt with a woman's right to have an abortion. Choice (E) is incorrect since the prohibition against *ex post facto* laws is not a mechanism for effecting the release of someone who is improperly imprisoned. Rather, it declares that changing the legal implications of an act, after the act has been committed, is improper.

15. **(A)** is the best answer since the term *casework* is used by political scientists to describe the activities of members of Congress on behalf of individual constituents. These activities might include helping an elderly person secure Social Security benefits, or helping a veteran obtain medical services. Congresspersons supply this type of assistance for the good public relations it provides. Choice (B) fails because pork barrel legislation is rarely, if ever, intended to help individual citizens. Pork barrel legislation authorizes federal spending for special projects, such as airports, roads, or dams, in the home state or district of a congressperson. (C) is not the answer because lobbying is an activity directed toward congresspersons, not one done by congresspersons. A lobbyist attempts to get congressmen to support legislation that will benefit the group which the lobbyist represents. Logrolling (D) is incorrect because it does not refer to congressional service for constituents. It refers instead to the congressional practice of trading votes on different bills. Filibustering (E) is a technique used in the Senate to postpone a vote on a piece of legislation. Senators opposing a bill might get control of the floor and talk until the supporters agree to withdraw the bill from consideration.

16. **(C)** The franking privilege is the right of congressmen to send mail to constituents at public expense. Choice (A) is incorrect since incumbent congresspersons certainly do not have access to unlimited campaign funds. Choice (B) is incorrect because incumbents and challengers may both have access to national party employees as campaign workers. (D) is incorrect because the Federal Election Campaign Act of 1974 placed a limit of $1,000 per election on individual

contributions to political candidates. This put an end to so-called "fat cat" contributors who used to contribute vast sums to candidates. (E) is incorrect because the federal government does not finance any aspect of congressional campaigns.

17. **(C)** is correct. Despite the fact that it comprises leading wheat-producing regions, the former Soviet Union, or CIS, is the only entity that is in the top three in having to *import* extra grain in all three categories, including wheat.

18. **(A)** The United States is the only nation listed that does not import any of the grains but is listed in two categories as a top producer.

19. **(D)** is least correct. The American farmer has traditionally had government assistance available in the form of loan programs, subsidies, price supports, and tariff protection. (A) and (C) are natural assets that American farmers have enjoyed. (B) and (E) have made American farms more efficient and cost effective.

20. **(A)** Contrary to myth, Confederate industry did a masterful job in producing weapons and ammunition for the Confederate military during the war. While it is true that the Confederates never had the abundance of weapons possessed by Union forces, particularly in artillery, it was only near the end of the war, when Union forces had overrun many production centers and totally destroyed the South's transportation network, that severe shortages of ammunition and weapons developed.

21. **(B)** The national unemployment rate soared to approximately 25% of the work force in early 1933. This meant that approximately 13 million workers were unemployed. While 25% was the national unemployment rate, in some cities the number of unemployed approached 90%. Although 25% may not sound catastrophic at first, combined with the collapse of wages and crop prices, as well as the collapse of banks and the sheer amount of time many people were out of work, the nation's economy was close to total collapse.

22. **(C)** The St. Bartholomew's Day Massacre in Paris of French Calvinists, often termed *Huguenots*, led to a civil war in France (the War of the Three Henries) and the first Bourbon monarch (Henry IV). When dealing with questions based on illustrations (paintings or drawings), it is important to look for explicit details or other information in the question and in the illustration itself, since it is usually not possible to arrive at a correct answer by eliminating answers. The clues in this case are in the question rather than in the painting. If the primary clue is not sufficient ("St. Bartholomew's Day"), there is a secondary clue in the obviously French name of the painter. Do not be misled by the use of the term *French Calvinists* instead of the name *Huguenots*, which is the term usually used by textbook writers; the use of the term *French Calvinists* is another detail testing your knowledge and understanding of European history.

23. **(A)** At first glance this question appears to test only the memorization of facts, but another look will show that it also requires understanding of the diplomatic situation in Europe around 1920. The correct answer may require some thought, since there was no political division of Germany into two governments, as happened at the end of World War II. The "division of Germany into two parts" refers to the "Polish Corridor," created by the peacemakers in order to give Poland an "outlet to the sea." The "Polish Corridor," a strip of formerly German land ceded

to Poland in order to provide access to the port city of Danzig, isolated eastern Prussia from the remainder of Germany. It may be possible to arrive at the correct answer by analyzing the other four answers and eliminating them; each is untrue. The end of World War I brought the final collapse of the Ottoman Empire and its reduction to the borders of modern Turkey. The new Communist government of Russia, which came to power in 1917, was ostracized by the other great powers when the war ended. Choice (D) may be tempting because the United States left large numbers of troops in Europe after World War II. This question refers to World War I, however. The United States withdrew from Europe both militarily and diplomatically after that war, preferring to return to "normalcy." Under the terms of the Treaty of Versailles, Germany was required to pay reparations.

24. **(C)**   Aimé Césaire was a poet from Martinique (in the West Indies). Although poetry and political writing have been widely influential for writers and thinkers like Franz Fanon, Cesaire has never been the leader of an African country. (A) Kwame Nkrumah was the prime minister of Ghana, (B) Jomo Kenyatta was president of Kenya, (D) Julius Nyerere was president of Tanzania, and (E) Patrice Lumumba was prime minister of the Congo.

25. **(A)**   When Beijing students chose to hold a protest for the democracy movement in Tiananmen Square, they were making reference to the May 4 Movement of 1919. On this day, students in Beijing demonstrated in Tiananmen Square in protest of the Treaty of Versailles, ending World War I, which denied China all of its demands for return of territory held by foreigners. The demonstrations led to strikes by students and workers; as a result, the Chinese delegation at Versailles refused to sign the treaty.

26. **(D)**   A statistical relationship in which high values in one variable (economic development) are associated with low values in another variable (birth rate) is known as a negative or inverse correlation. Plotting the data points on a graph would produce a line with a downward (negative) slope. A positive correlation (A) is one in which high values in one variable are associated with high values in another variable. A spurious correlation (B) is one in which the apparent relationship between two variables is really due to a third variable. There is no such thing as a circular correlation (C) or a reverse correlation (E).

27. **(E)**   Functionalism stresses the interdependence among parts of a society, pointing out how changes in one part of a social system will have consequences for other parts of that system. Economic development (A), class conflict (B), human communication (C), and intellectual creativity (D) are found in all human societies, but are not especially stressed in functionalist theory.

28. **(A)**   Upward social mobility involves an individual improving his or her social status (i.e., moving from a lower class to a higher class). Going from a farm worker's home to the White House involves considerable upward mobility. The other examples involve children staying at the same status as their parents or, in the case of the professor's son, downward mobility.

29. **(A)**   The prestige of one's occupation is one of the most valid and reliable indicators of a person's status in industrial societies. Of course, there are exceptions (e.g., retired persons). The other answers may have some relation to social status, but none are as consistently or as strongly linked to a person's socioeconomic status.

30. **(D)**   For sociologists, occupation is an essential feature that distinguishes the social classes. Working-class individuals hold blue-collar jobs. Middle-class individuals hold white-collar jobs. The other answers may be true of some middle-class families, but they would not be true of all.

31. **(E)**   Birth rates tend to be higher in lower-class families than in other social classes. All of the other statements are supported by research findings.

32. **(A)**   Experiments with children, in which they were rewarded for imitating a model, formed the basis of Miller and Dollard's conclusions concerning learning from model imitation. They concluded that imitation of social behavior probably derives strength from the fact that conformist behavior is rewarded in many situations, whereas nonconformist behavior often results in punishment.

33. **(E)**   The correct response is (E), since major differences between procedures in the House and Senate include all three of the features mentioned. Because the size of the House is fairly large, with 435 members, time for debate must be limited. If each member was allowed to speak as long as (s)he wanted on every bill, the House could not complete all of its business. Also, debate in the House must be germane. That is, when a member rises to speak, his/her comments must be related to the subject under consideration. This is another time-saving mechanism. The Senate has only 100 members and is not as rushed for time as the House. The Senate has traditionally allowed members to speak as long as they wish and does not force them to confine their remarks to the subject at hand. In the House, the rules committee is very powerful. No bill may get to the House floor without a rule from the rules committee. The rule gives the conditions for debate. The rule sets the time limit for debate and states whether and on what conditions the bill can be amended. The rules committee in the Senate has no such powers.

34. **(D)**   In *McCulloch v. Maryland* (1819), the Supreme Court struck down a Maryland law which levied a tax on the Baltimore branch of the Bank of the United States. The Court's ruling was based on its interpretation of the "necessary and proper clause" of the Constitution. The Court ruled that the necessary and proper clause gives to Congress all powers which make it more convenient for Congress to carry out the enumerated powers of Article I, section 8. (Enumerated powers are those which are specifically mentioned.) The clause is also known as the *elastic clause* since the Court ruled that it gives unspecified powers to Congress. The Court's ruling gave the broadest possible interpretation to the clause, making it possible for Congress to do many things which are not specifically mentioned in the Constitution. (A) is incorrect since *McCulloch v. Maryland* did not deal with freedom of speech. Choice (B) fails because the power of judicial review (the right of the Court to strike down laws of Congress and to review the actions of the executive) was claimed by the Court in *Marbury v. Madison*, 1803. (C) is incorrect since the Court had previously struck down a law of Congress in *Marbury v. Madison*. Finally, (E) is incorrect because *McCulloch v. Maryland* had nothing to do with the question of executive privilege.

35. **(B)**   The question asks which statement about the cabinet is false. Choice (B) is false, and, therefore, the correct answer. The Constitution states in Article I, section 6, that no person holding any office under the United States may be a member of Congress. Since cabinet positions are offices under the United States, cabinet officials may not be members of Congress. Choices (A)

and (D) are true. The cabinet includes the heads of each of the 15 executive departments (State, Treasury, Interior, etc.) as stated in (A). In addition, the president may appoint any other high ranking official whom he wishes to the cabinet, as stated in (D). Choice (C) is true. President Washington was the first to hold cabinet meetings. Every president since Washington has used the cabinet as a tool for managing the federal bureaucracy. So choice (C) is not the correct answer. Choice (E) is not the correct choice. As we saw in the explanation for choice (B), the Constitution states that no one holding office under the United States may be a member of Congress. This means that senators may not be members of the cabinet.

36. **(A)**   is not a proper conclusion because it is an opinion. The facts from the graph may be used to try to prove the need to cut transportation oil consumption, but the graph itself makes no conclusions. (B) is true if the average of Germany, Italy, France, and Great Britain is used. Since the United States and Canada top the chart, (C) is true. (D) is true, with 25%. (E) is true, with about 8%.

37. **(C)**   This cannot be a conclusion from the graphs, which are per person. Also, Canada, ranking second, has the smallest population on the list. (A) This could be a conclusion because the two largest nations are also the top two consumers. (B) Since four of the top seven consumers are European, this is true. (D) Japan is the only Asian nation listed. (E) This is a probable conclusion, especially when the quantity used for manufacturing in the United States is used as an indicator.

38. **(D)**   This is no longer true. Today's industry is divided between many private and nationalized companies. (A) The supply of petroleum is limited and exhaustible. (B) Oil is the key ingredient in plastics. (C) Prices and supply are very sensitive to many conditions. (E) Oil supplies and prices are affected by conditions all over the world with many producers.

39. **(B)**   The Navigation Acts were designed to force the colonies to trade exclusively with England and to give the British government extensive regulatory control over all colonial trade. All of the choices except choice (B) were major principles of these acts. The prohibition of the colonies from issuing paper currencies, while also having a major impact on colonial trade, was the focal point of the Currency Act of 1764 (approximately 100 years later than the Navigation Acts).

40. **(A)**   Slavery never effectively established itself in New England, in large part because the economic system of the New England colonies and the large population of New England, which provided a large pool of workers, rendered the need for large numbers of slaves unnecessary. Most New England farms were relatively small, self-sufficient farms, and the members of farming communities depended on each other to keep their communities economically viable. In the Southern English colonies, there was less community cohesion among the colonists, there were fewer people, and there was a constant demand for laborers to cultivate the cash crops necessary to keep the colonies economically afloat. At first this demand was met by the use of indentured servants, but after the 1660s the supply of potential servants dwindled and the only immediate replacement labor pool was imported slave labor.

41. **(E)**   This question is partly knowledge-based, but it also requires an understanding of the principles of Christian Humanism and an ability to analyze what ideas they would disapprove,

(A) and (C), and approve, (E). Renaissance Humanism, also known as Christian Humanism, combined studies of ancient languages with a zeal to make the Scriptures available in the local languages. Virtually all Christian Humanists translated portions of the Scriptures into European languages, using the Latin text which was the sole version available during the Middle Ages. Very few Christian Humanists were connected with the Reformation; the most famous of them, Erasmus of Rotterdam, criticized laxness within the Catholic church but refused to join with the Protestant reformers.

42. **(D)**   Although the tsar's manifesto succeeded in calming and ending the Revolution of 1905, the document's promises of reforms contained a loophole: no mention was made of election procedures for the promised Duma, or parliament. When Nicholas II called the Duma into session after the Revolution of 1905, he instituted voting procedures which gave considerably heavier representation to the wealthy and to districts around Moscow, which were considered the most loyal to the government.

43. **(B)**   Pakistan, which includes parts of the Punjab, was carved from India in 1947. All of the other choices—Thailand (A), India (C), Korea (D), and Vietnam (E)—existed as independent countries before 1947, though because of the partition, India's borders and political situation changed significantly after 1947. It is worthwhile to note that Pakistan, as created in 1947, was later split apart by the secession of Bangladesh in 1971.

44. **(D)**   The British policy of indirect rule in Africa was designed to reduce tensions and minimize financial costs. It included flexibility and a minimum of direct British intervention. For this reason, the British tried to adapt their colonial policies to fit the wide variety of native systems in and between countries, and they did *not* want a tribal uniform policy (D), which would have been more rigid. Instead, they modified the role of traditional rulers in local areas (E) and relied on a decentralized administration (C). The goal for these colonies was eventual self-rule (B), and for this reason they supported basic primary education for Africans which would equip them for this eventuality (A).

45. **(B)**   The Glorious Revolution of 1688–1689 did not result in an agreement that, in the event of no heirs, the Hanover house would succeed the Stuarts. Such an arrangement was specified in the Act of Succession of 1701, a year before William III's death and the succession of Queen Anne. She outlived all her children. Upon her death in 1714, George I became the first Hanoverian King of England.

46. **(B)**   Cultural diffusion is the spread of an idea, a fashion, or a technology from one culture to another. Blue jeans and rock-and-roll music originated in the United States and have now spread to most other nations of the world. Cultural discovery (C) and cultural innovation (D) imply the appearance of something unique or original. Cultural decline (A) and cultural disintegration (E) imply the destruction of previous cultural traits.

47. **(C)**   A stereotype is a simplified image of personal characteristics (usually negative) which is applied to all members of a group. Affirmative action (A) involves giving preference or special consideration to members of minority groups. Reverse racism (B) involves discrimination against members of dominant or majority groups. Status inconsistency (D) refers to individuals who rank

high in one measure of social status and low in another (e.g., a Ph.D. who drives a taxi). Role conflict (E) refers to individuals who occupy multiple roles with contradictory expectations.

48. **(E)** Davis and Moore hypothesized that high rewards are necessary to motivate individuals to complete the long periods of training required for some occupations, such as physician. This theory does not consider factors such as seniority (A), unionization (B), physical labor (C), or appeal to values (D).

49. **(E)** Demography is the study of the growth (A), composition (D), distribution (B), and migration (C) of human populations. Socialization is not usually studied by demographers.

50. **(B)** Agents of socialization teach social norms and values to children and adults. Parents (C), peers (D), and teachers (E) impart social norms directly to young people. Television (A) is also an important medium for teaching norms and values. Occupations such as banking do not involve the teaching of norms and values as part of their primary responsibilities.

51. **(B)** Conditioned, or secondary, reinforcement occurs when the reinforcing stimulus is not inherently pleasing or reinforcing, but becomes so through association with other pleasant or reinforcing stimuli. Money is an example of a secondary (conditioned) reinforcer. Coins and paper currency are not in themselves pleasing, but the things they buy are pleasing. Therefore, an association is made between money and inherently pleasing primary reinforcers, such as food and drink. Hence, the term *conditioned reinforcer* is used.

52. **(A)** The primary function of the Federal Reserve Board is to implement monetary policy. The Federal Reserve Board has three methods of implementing monetary policy. First, it can change the reserve requirement. Second, the board can change the discount rate, which is the interest rate that member banks must pay to borrow money from a Federal Reserve Bank. Third, the board can buy and sell government securities. To increase the money supply, the board sells securities. To decrease the money supply, the board buys securities. Choice (B) is the most plausible alternative to (A), but fails because controlling government spending is a function of Congress and the president. Choice (C) is incorrect because the Federal Reserve Board has nothing to do with regulating commodity prices. Choice (D) is incorrect because the board does not help the president run the executive branch. Choice (E) is incorrect because the board does not keep records of troop strength in army reserve units.

53. **(C)** The three largest countries of Western Europe—the United Kingdom, France, and the Federal Republic of Germany—have either a multi-party system or a two-plus party system. A multi-party system is one in which three or more major parties compete for seats in the national legislature, while a two-plus party system has two large parties and one or more small parties. The United States has only two parties, which successfully compete on a national basis from one election to the next. These are, of course, the Democrats and the Republicans. Choice (A) is incorrect. In Western European countries, party leaders determine which persons will run for office under the party banner. In the United States, on the other hand, candidates for office are selected by the voters in primary elections. In most Western European countries, political parties are much more centralized than in the United States; therefore, (B) is false. Choice (D) is false. Because the parties are centralized in Western Europe, and because party leaders select

candidates for national office, a party member in the national legislature seldom votes against the party. If one did, party leaders would remove his or her name from the ballot in future elections. Choice (E) is incorrect. Since party members vote the party line almost all of the time in Western Europe, voters tend to not focus on the personalities of candidates, but rather on the party label. In the United States, where legislators vote their personal preference as often as the party line, party label is less important to voters. Voters in the United States tend to focus more on the personalities of candidates than European voters.

54. **(D)**   In a parliamentary system the chief executive, normally called the prime minister, is a member of parliament, the legislative body. The prime minister and cabinet are the highest executive officers of the country and are usually referred to as the government. There is no strict separation of powers, since the executive branch is made up of members of the legislature. In a presidential system, by contrast, the president is not a member of the legislature and is selected by popular, not by legislative, vote. Cabinet members may not sit in the legislature. There is, then, a strict separation of powers, and Statement I is true. In a presidential system, the voters choose the president either by direct popular vote or through an electoral college. In a parliamentary system, the majority party in the lower house of parliament chooses one of its members as prime minister. The general public does not participate in choosing the prime minister. So Statement II is also true. In a parliamentary system the prime minister may call special elections for the lower house of the legislature whenever (s)he wants. In a presidential system the president may not call a special election for members of the legislature, so III is false. The answer, then, is (D), I and II only.

55. **(A)**   Private and corporate ownership is taken to task and it is stated that they should be limited. All other groups are called upon to band together to help the environment.

56. **(D)**   These are obvious references to the past use of the environment for economic purposes rather than environmental concerns. (A) and (B) are moral statements, not economic ones. (C) is a call to action. (E) tries to redefine society's values.

57. **(E)**   This is a political, cost concern. Coal is more polluting than oil. (A) This is now used to sell products and is becoming profitable. (B) This is an attempt to replace trees as a renewable resource. (C) Repair and replacement of topsoil, erosion control, and replanting are attempts to reuse mined areas for agriculture. (D) Concern over this has changed products' chemical contents and created new laws to reduce airborne pollution.

58. **(D)**   In early 1942, the Japanese high command, angered at air raids from American aircraft carriers, decided on an invasion of the American-held island of Midway. It was 1,100 miles northwest of Hawaii. More importantly, it had a seaplane base and an airstrip. If Japan invaded Midway, the Americans would have to send their fleet to defend it or face the loss of Pearl Harbor and Hawaii.

American cryptographers deciphered enough Japanese messages to uncover the plan. In addition, the overconfident Japanese, expecting to surprise a scattered American fleet, didn't concentrate their forces into an overwhelming single attack force. Instead they divided their fleet into four separate attack forces, each of which was vulnerable to American attack if caught off guard. When the Japanese arrived at Midway, a well-prepared, tightly concentrated American fleet was waiting. Despite a series of nearly catastrophic errors, the Americans caught the Japanese by surprise, sinking four of their largest aircraft carriers and killing 600 of Japan's best pilots. Without adequate air protection, the invasion was cancelled and the Japanese fleet returned to base. Midway was saved. At the time, American analysts thought they had just bought the United States some additional time until the Japanese regrouped and attacked again. In reality, the Japanese were so stunned by the defeat that they readjusted their war plans, switching to defensive operations. They never returned to Midway. With the Japanese now on the defensive, the United States was able to seize the initiative at Guadalcanal, beginning an island-hopping campaign that took America to Japan's outer islands. Midway was undoubtedly the turning point, as it marked the first significant American victory over the Japanese and the end of major Japanese offensive operations in the central Pacific.

59. **(E)** *Brown v. Board of Education of Topeka* was the first legal shot in the war to desegregate America's public schools. Up to this time, many school districts, particularly in the South, had segregated schools for black and white school-children under the doctrine of "separate but equal" education. Sadly, most education facilities for black children were anything but equal. Blacks usually got dilapidated facilities, the worst teachers, and an inferior education. Frustrated black parents challenged the "separate but equal" doctrine in several states, and those challenges were consolidated into one case to be presented before the United States Supreme Court in 1954. Up until this case, previous civil rights cases had been heard before conservative Supreme Courts which had upheld the "separate but equal" doctrine. However, by 1954, the Court was a more liberal court, more sensitive to constitutional protections for all people.

60. **(C)** While this question calls for fact retention, it also requires an ability to analyze the implications of their policies—unless the answer is apparent upon first reading. The first monarchs of a united Spain, Ferdinand and Isabella, achieved that unity by gaining control of the remaining Muslim sections of southern Spain. In an effort to promote cultural unity and establish a national identity, they defined Spanish nationalism in terms of their understanding of orthodox Catholicism. Those not fitting their definition of orthodoxy were condemned as disloyal or subversive. Two particular groups, Jews and Muslims who had converted to Christianity but retained Muslim customs or dress, were forced into exile by Spanish authorities.

61. **(C)** The diversity of monarchs listed in the choices should indicate that guessing is a possibility. Two were devout Catholics (D) and (E), while a third (A) predates the Reformation by almost 200 years. During the Thirty Years' War, when Catholic forces from southern Germany and Austria were close to pushing Lutheran forces into the Baltic Sea, the Lutheran convert Gustavus Adolphus intervened in Germany, saving the Lutheran cause. Adolphus was himself killed during a key battle.

62. **(D)** As a result of the Spanish-American War in 1898, the United States gained control of the Philippines from Spain. The Philippines remained a U.S. territory until the Tydings-McDuffie Act of 1934 provided for its independence. This independence was not realized until 1945. Today, however, Spanish influence, mostly in the shape of religion, language, and culture, is still felt, as is America's presence in the form of popular culture.

63. **(D)** Swaziland, a former British colony, has been called Swaziland both before and after its independence. Malawi is a separate independent country, and the other choices—(A), (B), (C), and (E)—are all the former and present names of countries in Africa.

64. **(D)** Durkheim found that people with few social attachments (i.e., single people) tend to commit suicide more frequently. Men (A), old people (B), wealthy people (C), and Protestants (E) all have higher suicide rates.

65. **(B)** Durkheim used the term *altruistic suicide* to refer to people who commit suicide because of their intense sense of loyalty to a group. Egoistic suicide (A) refers to people who kill themselves for selfish, personal reasons. Anomic suicide (D) refers to people killing themselves because they lack clear moral guidelines. *Intrinsic suicide* (C) and *euphoric suicide* (E) are not terms that Durkheim used.

66. **(D)** Participant observation involves a researcher interacting with and observing the personal lives of the research subjects. Survey research (A) gathers data from subjects using questionnaires or interviews. Experimentation (B) involves a researcher manipulating an experimental stimulus, usually in a laboratory setting. Content analysis (C) involves the study of communication products such as books, letters, advertising, or television programs. Strategic engagement (E) is not a method used in social research.

67. **(D)** The independent variable produces an effect or change in the dependent variable. In this case, gender is hypothesized to cause a difference in academic averages. Athletic participation (A) and college attendance (B) are not variables in this hypothesis since they are the same for both groups. Academic achievement (C) is the dependent variable. Study habits (E) may help to explain the difference between men and women, but it has not been stated in this hypothesis.

68. **(E)** Culture consists of the shared products of human interaction, both material and nonmaterial. An individual's intelligence is the result of personal development and genetic inheritance. Because intelligence may vary greatly among individuals, it is not shared among members of a society.

69. **(E)** Ethnocentrism is the practice of placing a high value on one's own culture and demeaning all cultures that differ from it. Shared cultural traits such as language (A) and religion (D) do not constitute ethnocentrism. Working for common goals (B) and showing respect for the elderly (C) also have nothing to do with the concept of ethnocentrism.

70. **(B)** Rehearsal serves two functions. It allows items in short-term memory to be retained. Also, it appears to facilitate material from the short-term to long-term memory. In transference of most contents, rehearsal is necessary for learning.

71. **(C)** Political scientists use the term *pluralistic* to describe a political system in which innumerable groups of people share cultural, economic, religious, or ethnic interests. These groups organize and spend great amounts of time and money competing to influence government policy-making. The pluralistic concept of democracy is in contrast to the elitist model, which states that policy-making is dominated by elites such as wealthy industrialists, military leaders, or organizations such as the Trilateral Commission. Therefore, the answer is (C). Choice (A) fails because pluralism stresses not only cultural groups but economic, religious, and other types of groups. Also important to

pluralism is the idea that the different groups do not merely exist but compete to influence public policy-making. Choice (B) fails because the term to describe a system in which political power is divided between national and state governments is *federalism*. Choice (D) fails because to say that one group is overrepresented is more like an elitist view than a pluralistic view of politics. It is true that candidates for national office are elected by a plurality vote method (E). *Plurality vote* means that the candidate who gets the most votes, even if less than a majority, wins the election. However, the term *pluralism* does not refer to this method of election, so choice (E) is wrong.

72. **(A)** As the following graph shows, there is a direct correlation between voter turnout and educational level. The answer is (A), the more schooling one has, the more likely one is to vote. While it is difficult to find statistics which show the correlation between educational status and running for office, we do know that most people who are completely inactive (that is, do not participate in politics in any way) typically have little education and low incomes and are relatively young. Therefore, it is safe to conclude that the less education one has (B), the LESS likely one is to run for office; so (B) is not the answer. Choice (C) is clearly wrong, since many studies have shown a direct correlation between advanced educational status and political participation by voting. Choice (D) is wrong, as is clear from the following graph. Those with a high school education are NOT more likely to vote than are those with a college degree. Choice (E) is wrong because, as the graph shows, the less education one has, the less likely one is to vote. It is logical to infer from this that those with no formal schooling are less likely to vote than are those with a high school education.

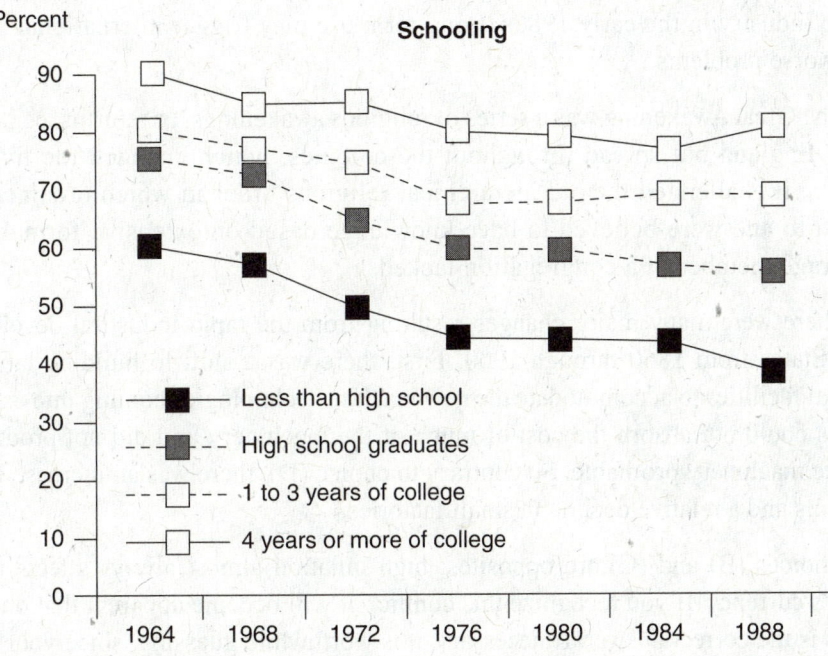

From James Q. Wilson, p. 130, *American Government*

73. **(E)** Articulating interests is generally thought of as the special task of interest groups. Parties, on the other hand, bring together or "aggregate" interests (B) in order to create a working majority to run government. Parties also play a significant role in recruiting candidates (A), serving as channels of communication (C), and staffing elections (D).

74. **(C)** Although the chart can be used for several of the choices, it is a simplified version of the business cycle. (A) The chart does not refer to "bust" or depression. (B) and (D) Changes are shown, but not causes. (E) If you added data, such as dates, it could be used to track historical fluctuations, but doesn't in this form.

75. **(D)** War and peace may influence the other factors, but can have a variety of effects and is not part of the purely economic picture. (A) The number of people employed is used to define whether we are in a recession or not. (B) Obviously directly related to (A), it also shows prosperity, if products are in demand. (C) Personal earnings rise with an economic boom and help sustain it with spending. (E) This is an important indicator of income, production, and consumer confidence in the economy.

76. **(C)** Increased taxation is the most counterproductive to economic growth because it takes money out of spending circulation and reduces sales. (A) War is usually not planned, but has been credited with helping the economy as a side effect because of the increased need for services and products. (B) Keynesian economics calls for "pump-priming" of the economy through government spending to employ people and increase production. (D) Supply-side economics contends that reducing government regulation frees up capital to create products and jobs. (E) This is often used as a short-term solution to help specific industries, such as the auto industry in the early 1980s. Long-term use may trigger international retaliation and create worse problems.

77. **(A)** The Great Awakening was a series of religious awakenings, or rebirths, centered primarily in New England but spread throughout the colonies, which changed the lives of English colonists. It challenged the old hierarchical religious order in which ordained clergy were deferred to and were believed to have knowledge based on extensive formal learning that the average member of a congregation lacked.

78. **(B)** There were many major changes resulting from the rapid industrial development in the United States from 1860 through 1900. First, there was a shift to building larger and larger industrial facilities to accommodate the new machine technologies coming into existence. Small factories could not absorb the cost of much of the machinery and did not produce enough to make the machinery profitable. So contrary to choice (D), there was an increase in large industrial plants and a relative decline in small factories.

79. **(C)** Choices (B) and (C) are opposites; high inflation almost always affects the value of a country's currency. If you recognize this conflict, it will become apparent that one of these two answers is the correct answer. If necessary, it is worthwhile guessing, since your odds are 50% and only 0.25 point is deducted for an incorrect guess.

80. **(B)** On the map, several areas of Europe are depicted with dark shading. These areas are the lands controlled by the Hapsburgs in the sixteenth century. Choice (C) is incorrect, since Spain

was lost by the Hapsburgs in the 1600s. A further clue: The large size of the Ottoman Empire, covering the entire Balkan peninsula, precludes any answer after about 1870.

81. **(E)** In 1914 only Ethiopia, along with Liberia, remained an independent state. Algeria (A) belonged to France; the Congo (B) was Belgian; Angola (C) was occupied by the Portuguese; and Egypt (D) was under British control.

82. **(B)** Thailand is bordered by Myanmar on the northwest, Laos on the north and east, and Cambodia on the southeast. Vietnam borders Laos and Cambodia on the east with China to its north and the South China Sea to its east. The "Golden Triangle," where Myanmar, Laos, and Thailand meet, is a notorious area for the growing and trafficking of drugs.

83. **(C)** Folkways are social norms governing less important areas of behavior such as table manners or proper attire for events. Mores are social norms which concern more serious issues such as laws against murder or incest. (A) is incorrect since violations of folkways usually result in mild reprimands. (D) is incorrect because violations of mores are usually considered crimes and involve more drastic punishments. (B) and (E) are also incorrect because folkways and mores are found among all social groups and cover a wide range of behaviors.

84. **(A)** Deviance refers to those behaviors that a group stigmatizes because they are seen as violating basic norms. Rape, child abuse, and incest are examples of behaviors which are seen as deviant by many groups in the United States. Acts that are rare or unusual (D) are not considered deviant if they involve praiseworthy or inoffensive behaviors.

85. **(D)** In American society, social norms require that people eat spaghetti with a fork (A), wear gender-appropriate clothing in public (B), and not talk to oneself (E). Beer drinking (D), however, is a normal activity among many American college students.

86. **(A)** Mead's theory of social development emphasizes the importance of children's play. He maintains that they develop their self-concepts by imagining themselves in the roles of other people. "Taking the role of the other" is central to his theory.

87. **(C)** Children who have been isolated from human contact do not learn basic social skills and values and, even with special help, have considerable difficulty functioning in society. Their intellectual (A) and moral development (D) lags behind other children of the same age. Unusual coordination (B) or artistic talents (E) have not been reported for these children.

88. **(C)** Sociologists believe that social conditions and processes such as socialization (E), rather than genetic factors, are the basic explanatory variables in human behavior. They also assume human behavior follows predictable patterns (A) and that scientific methods (B) can be used to study these behaviors objectively (D).

89. **(A)** In spite of the confederate's "desperate" screams and complaints of a heart condition, most of the subjects reluctantly complied with the orders of the experimenter—a "legitimate authority"—and eventually applied the maximum shock. Although intelligence of the subject had no effect on compliance, the status of the experimenter showed a strong effect. From this experiment, Milgram concluded that Nazi Germany could have occurred anywhere, even in small-town America, because of people's tendency to obey authority.

90. **(B)**   The answer is (B), northern business leaders, since most of these voters supported the Republicans in each of the years Roosevelt ran for president (1932, 1936, 1940, and 1944). Choice (A) is wrong because most southerners, white and black alike, voted for Roosevelt each time he ran for president. Choice (C) is wrong because blue-collar workers heavily supported Roosevelt in each of his elections. Choice (D) is wrong because blacks and Jews, two prominent racial minorities, voted for Roosevelt. Choice (E) is false because union members, who were mostly blue-collar workers, heavily supported Roosevelt.

91. **(E)**   The Fifth Amendment to the U.S. Constitution states "No person shall be compelled in any criminal case to be a witness against himself. . . ." The Supreme Court held in *Miranda v. Arizona*, 1966, that "In order to . . . permit a full opportunity to exercise the privilege against self-incrimination, the accused must be adequately and effectively apprised of his rights and the exercise of those rights must be fully honored." This means that when police apprehend a suspect in a criminal case they must immediately tell the person that (s)he has a right to remain silent. The Sixth Amendment to the U.S. Constitution states "In all criminal prosecutions, the accused shall enjoy the right . . . to have compulsory process for obtaining witnesses in his favor, and to have Assistance of Counsel for his defense. The compulsory process clause means that the accused can subpoena witnesses in his/her favor to appear in court to testify for the defense. (A subpoena is a court order which commands a person to appear at a certain time and place to give testimony upon a certain matter.) The Assistance of Counsel clause of the Sixth Amendment was interpreted by the Supreme Court in *Argersinger v. Hamlin*, 1972, to mean that if the accused cannot afford an attorney, (s)he is entitled to have one appointed at government expense, in any felony or misdemeanor criminal case in which, if the accused is found guilty, (s)he may be sentenced to jail. It is clear from the above that the rights mentioned in statements I, II, and III are all guaranteed by the Constitution. Therefore, choice (E) is correct.

92. **(D)**   During the 1870s the Supreme Court held that the Fifteenth Amendment did not automatically confer the right to vote on anybody. States could not pass laws to prevent anyone from voting on the basis of race, but they could restrict persons from voting on other grounds. This interpretation of the Fifteenth Amendment allowed southern states to use several techniques to effectively exclude blacks from voting. Since most former slaves were illiterate, prospective voters were often required to pass literacy tests. Poll taxes were also levied, which kept blacks, who were mostly poor, from voting. Since many whites were also poor and illiterate, grandfather clauses were enacted to allow them to bypass the legal restrictions on voting. Grandfather clauses stated that if you or your ancestors had voted before 1867, you could vote without paying a poll tax or passing a literacy test. Choice (D) is correct because the purpose of grandfather clauses and literacy tests was to keep blacks from voting. Choice (A) is wrong because the purpose of the grandfather clause was to allow poor and illiterate whites to escape voting restrictions. Choice (B) is wrong because the intent of the restrictions was to prevent blacks, not immigrants, from voting. In addition, there was little immigration into the South during the time in question. Choices (C) and (E) are wrong because the measures were restrictions on the right to vote, not on the right to run for office.

93. **(B)**   is the most specific statement because, although the first paragraph refers to the "needs of society," those needs are specified as economic in the rest of the quote. (A) Many of

society's needs—legal rights, social needs, poverty—are not addressed. (C) This is not discussed. (D) The terms *average*, *more* and *more*, and *most* are used, not *all*. (E) The government role is not discussed.

94. **(A)** The Chamber of Commerce represents U.S. businesspeople and this is definitely a pro-business statement. (B) The federal Department of Labor is not anti-business, but it is not its major concern to advocate pro-business stands. (C) The GAO is the auditing branch of the government and doesn't take a stand on pro- or anti-business statements. (D) The Socialist belief would probably be the opposite of the quote. (E) The union position would probably credit workers more and business less.

95. **(D)** Justice means fair treatment for all, sometimes enforced by government regulation. (A) This is specifically referred to in relation to employment, wages, and so on. (B) This is indirectly referred to through rising living standards and growth which also provides security (C). (E) This is implied throughout and referred to as "less constraint."

96. **(E)** Labor is a factor in creating all of the others, which are the basic activities.

97. **(D)** In the autumn of 1864, a war-weary North faced a presidential election that offered them a clear choice. Abraham Lincoln ran on a platform of continuing the Civil War until the South was totally defeated. His opponent, former general George McClellan, ran on a platform calling for an armistice and recognition of the South as a separate nation. Lincoln realized he needed a decisive victory before the election, pointing to a rapid defeat of the Confederacy, if he was to win. That victory occurred in September 1864 when Union forces under the command of William T. Sherman occupied Atlanta and followed up on this victory with his infamous "march to the sea." This victory pointed to the imminent destruction of the Confederacy. Finally, people could see a "light at the end of the tunnel" and desire to completely defeat the Confederates rose again in the North. The capture of Atlanta guaranteed Lincoln's reelection and sealed the fate of the Confederate States of America.

98. **(A)** After he was overthrown by revolutionary forces in 1978, the Shah of Iran asked for permission to enter the United States to receive cancer treatment. President Carter was warned that admitting the Shah to the United States, for any reason, would look to the Iranians like America still supported the Shah's regime and would lead to trouble. However, other advisors told Carter that the United States owed the Shah a large debt of gratitude for the favors he had done for America and also for the lack of decisive support from the United States when his government was overthrown. Carter had previously refused to grant the Shah exile in the United States, but when he was told of the Shah's need for cancer treatment, he decided to allow the Shah to enter the United States on humanitarian grounds. As predicted, the Iranians were infuriated by this. On November 4, 1979, young Iranian males, backed by their government and claiming to be students, seized the American embassy compound and took 76 hostages, 62 of whom were held for more than a year. It was the beginning of one of the worst nightmares in American foreign policy, and it helped ruin Carter's presidency.

99. **(B)** Here is a question that may be answered correctly even if, upon first reading, you are tempted to pass it by. The correct answer must be a country which had some degree of control

over land in both Egypt and South Africa. If no answer comes to mind, you still may be able to remember the fact that the British had the largest colonial empire. After wrestling control of the Suez Canal in Egypt from its French builders and the Egyptian Khedive, the British government planned construction of a rail line linking Egypt with its recent acquisition of largely Dutch-settled land in South Africa. Typically, other European nations successfully moved to block the railroad by making claims to central African land along the route.

100. **(A)** The mention of Ethiopia may bring Italy to mind. If not, a possible guess is indicated if you are able to remember Mussolini's invasion of Ethiopia during the 1930s. The sole European nation to have its plans to establish an African colony in the late nineteenth century blocked by a native African force, Italy for some time regarded the incident a national humiliation. The incident was one of several reasons the Italian dictator Mussolini gave for his successful military takeover of Ethiopia in 1935.

101. **(C)** The Himalayan mountain range, the highest in the world, runs 1,500 miles from the northernmost tip of India, through Nepal, and along the southwest border of China. The Himalayas include Mt. Everest (Qomolongma), the tallest mountain in the world, and India's tallest mountain, Nanda Devi, which rises 25,645 feet. Bangladesh is almost completely surrounded by the northeastern border of India, facing the Bay of Bengal. It does have a small border with Burma on its southeast side.

102. **(B)** When Britain, bowing to internal abolitionist pressure, declared the slave trade illegal for its people in 1807, only Denmark, which made illegal the slave trade in 1805, had already outlawed the practice. The next to follow suit was Holland (A) in 1814, France (C) in 1818, and Spain (D) and Portugal (E) which restricted their slave trade to the seas south of the equator in 1815 and 1817, respectively.

103. **(C)** The dependent variable (value placed on obedience) may be influenced by the independent variable—social class of mothers (E). Gender of children (B) and education of parents (D) are not mentioned in this hypothesis. Social class (A) is the independent variable in this hypothesis.

104. **(E)** Verbal and physical rewards (D) and punishments such as ridicule (A), insults (B), and spanking (C) are commonly used methods for enforcing conformity to social norms. (E) Imitation is not used to control the behavior of others.

105. **(B)** Role conflict is a situation where the multiple roles which an individual occupies place competing, and often contradictory, demands on his or her time and energy. Role ambiguity (A) implies that role expectations are not clearly understood. Role strain (C) refers to the excessive demands of a single role. Role performance (D) and role playing (E) refer to the process of carrying out the expectations of a role.

106. **(D)** Social mobility is movement to a higher (upward) or lower (downward) social status. Societies differ in the amount of social mobility that is possible for their members. The ability to gain an education (A) or enter an occupation (B) does not always lead to a change in status. Social mobility should not be confused with geographic mobility (C), moving across borders. It also has nothing to do with marriage to a person of another religion (E).

107. **(D)** The working class consists of people who hold manual, blue-collar jobs. Some may be highly skilled, such as electricians or tool makers, while others are unskilled laborers. Working-class status is not based on one's education (C), residence (E), or income level (B).

108. **(A)** The social learning theory of aggression holds that most aggression is learned through operant conditioning. Therefore, aggression results only after certain actions are reinforced by rewards and discouraged by punishments. Modeling is another form of social learning that contributes to the development of aggressive behavior.

109. **(C)** According to the social learning theory of aggression, if a child is rewarded for random aggressive behavior, it is highly probable that the behavior will occur again. On the other hand, if a child is punished for acting aggressively, the likelihood of that behavior occurring again is reduced. It has been found that the schedule of reinforcement is particularly important in the learning of aggressive responses. For example, if aggression is reinforced irregularly, the aggressive behavior will tend to last longer than if the reinforcement is continuous.

110. **(B)** The belief that aggression is an inborn tendency in all animals, including man, has been most supported by the work of Konrad Lorenz.

111. **(A)** The passage is taken from the landmark case *Marbury v. Madison,* 1803. What the passage means, in everyday language, is:

   1. Interpreting laws is a judicial function. 2. When two laws conflict, the courts must decide which will be enforced. 3. The Constitution is superior to laws passed by Congress or state legislatures (called statutory law). 4. Therefore, if a statute conflicts with the Constitution, the statute cannot be enforced by the courts.

   Choice (B) is incorrect because the passage says nothing about Congress's right to pass laws to carry out its duties. Rather, the passage deals with a conflict between statutory and Constitutional law. Choice (C) is incorrect because it contradicts the main thesis of the passage. The passage clearly says that it is the duty of *courts*, not legislatures, to "say what the law is," which means the same as "interpretation of laws." Choice (D) is incorrect because the passage says when an act of the legislature and the Constitution conflict, the Constitution governs the case. Choice (E) is incorrect because the passage states specifically that if two laws conflict, the courts must decide the operation of each. It then posits a case where the two laws in conflict are an act of the legislature and the Constitution. The clear implication is that, in such a case, the courts must decide on the operation of the Constitution, which means deciding questions of Constitutional law.

112. **(E)** After a bill is introduced into either house of Congress, it is referred to the appropriate committee. The bill will then usually be referred by the committee to a subcommittee. After holding a hearing on the bill, the subcommittee will then have a mark-up session where revisions and additions are made to the bill. The bill is then referred back to the full committee, which may also hold a hearing and have a mark-up session. Choices (A), (B), and (C) are incorrect because mark-up sessions do not occur in the majority leader's office, on the floor of the legislative chambers, or in party caucuses. Choice (D) is the most plausible alternative to (E), because a joint conference committee is, after all, a committee. However, proposed legislation goes

to a joint conference committee only after it has passed both houses of Congress. The Constitution requires that before a piece of legislation can become law, it must pass both houses in identical form. The purpose of the joint conference committee is to iron out differences in a bill that has passed one house in a different form than in the other. It is true that changes are made to such a bill in a joint conference committee, to satisfy members of both houses. However, the term *mark-up session* refers only to the activity of standing committees and subcommittees in Congress, not to joint conference committees.

113. **(D)** The Office of Management and Budget is the chief presidential staff agency. Its primary responsibility is to put together the budget that the president submits to Congress. Each agency and office of the executive branch must have its budget requests cleared by OMB before it gets into the president's budget. The OMB also studies the organization and operations of the executive branch, to ensure that each office and agency is carrying out its appropriate duty, as assigned by law. Choice (A) is incorrect because the Department of Commerce does not help the president to draw up his annual budget. The Department of Commerce was created in 1903 to protect the interests of businesspeople at home and abroad. Choice (B) is incorrect because the Department of Treasury is not involved in drawing up the president's budget. The functions of the Treasury Department include collecting taxes through the Internal Revenue Service, an administrative unit of the department, administering the public debt, and coining money. Choice (C) is incorrect because the main responsibility of the Federal Reserve Board is the implementation of monetary policy. It has nothing to do with drawing up the president's annual budget. Choice (E) is incorrect because the cabinet does not help the president draw up his budget. It advises the president on the administration of the executive departments.

114. **(E)** is correct. (A) is not correct, because there are some variances between nations high in GNP while not so high in trade. (B) is incorrect because there is no data comparing previous years. (C) is incorrect. Thailand, the Philippines, and Indonesia did not exceed the world average in trade. (D) is incorrect; Japan was not the leader in trade.

115. **(D)** is not true. The trade graph is a line graph, and the GNP is a bar graph. All the others are true. (A) Per capita means per person.

116. **(A)** is most accurate; all are on the eastern edge of Asia. (B) is incorrect because all of Asia is not represented, for example, India or the Persian Gulf. (C) is wrong; northwest Asia would be either the Persian Gulf area or Asian USSR. (D) is incorrect; Malaysia and Thailand are as close to the Indian Ocean as to the Pacific. (E) is wrong; only Australia, Hong Kong, Malaysia, New Zealand, and Singapore were ever British colonies. Japan and Thailand were never colonized by foreigners.

117. **(D)** Singapore shows the greatest growth rate because its per capita trade is not only highest but exceeds its GNP, which means its people are producing exportable products which bring money back into the nation. Hong Kong is second.

118. **(A)** GNP is the gross national product and is defined as the total goods and services produced by the nation in a given year. (B) is only partially correct because services are not specified. The others are not correct.

119. **(A)**   In the presidential election of 1876, Samuel Tilden defeated his Republican opponent, Rutherford B. Hayes, in the popular vote by 250,000 votes. However, there were 20 contested votes in the electoral college. If Hayes received all the contested electoral votes, he would win the election by one vote in the Electoral College and he would gain the presidency. The matter was turned over to Congress, where a Republican-dominated commission awarded the disputed electoral votes to Hayes. The Senate ratified the commission's decision, but the Democrats in the House threatened to use political means to gain Tilden's victory through a House vote. Republicans negotiated the issue and the Compromise of 1877 was the result. Hayes got the presidency. Democrats received assurances that federal soldiers would be withdrawn from Southern states (effectively ending Reconstruction) and that blanket federal government support for Republicans in the South would end. This opened the door for Democrats to regain control in all the Southern states (they had already effectively regained control in all but three). None of the other choices listed in the question were in any way involved in the Compromise of 1877.

120. **(B)**   Benjamin Franklin perceived that united action by the colonies was the only hope of providing for their security. He called together the Albany Congress to discuss plans to enlist the aid of the various Iroquois tribes in colonial defense and to coordinate defense plans between the English colonies. It also called for the establishment of a "grand council" with representatives from each of the colonies to enact taxes and coordinate colonial economic activity. The plan is notable because it was the first plan calling for the individual colonies to act as a single, united entity.

121. **(B)**   Knowledge-based questions such as this are not usually susceptible to successful guessing, since the other choices cannot be eliminated unless you know as least two or three of them well. As a young man, the German poet Goethe anticipated elements of Romanticism, and his youthful writings, such as *The Sorrows of the Young Werther* (1774), exhibited some Romantic characteristics. This period is often termed his "Sturm und Drang" (storm and stress) period.

122. **(D)**   Comte, an early nineteenth-century writer, based his system of Positivism on the belief that history was entering a third, scientifically oriented stage. In this new era, only statements that might be scientifically verified were to be considered knowledge. A committee of scientists and philosophers would govern, creating "Progress and Order." Religion would be considered outdated.

123. **(E)**   The capital of Sierra Leone is Freetown, not Dakar, which is the capital of Senegal. All of the other capital cities in choices (A), (B), (C), and (D) correspond correctly to the country with which they are paired.

124. **(E)**   In the nineteenth century, France and Britain were moving into most countries in South and Southeast Asia. In order to prevent them from taking control of Thailand (or Siam, as it was known then), King Mongkut (Rama IV) signed trade agreements with the two countries, granting them extraterritorial rights. Elsewhere in the region, the French, who were occupying southern Vietnam, made Cambodia (A) a protectorate in 1863 and Laos (B) a protectorate in the 1880s, ruling it as part of Indochina. By 1886 the British had made all of Burma (C) a province of India (D), which they had been occupying in various forms since the 1600s.

125. **(D)** An ascribed status is one which an individual gains through no effort on his or her part. Often one is born into an ascribed status. Becoming a college president (A), a Nobel prize winner (B), an honor student (C), or an opera singer (E) all require considerable effort by an individual. Being a white female is a condition over which one has no control.

126. **(A)** An achieved status is one which an individual receives through his or her own efforts. Categories based on age (B) or ethnic group (C) are ascribed, not achieved. Similarly, one has no control over one's height (E) or being an accident victim (D).

127. **(A)** A subculture is a distinctive lifestyle that exists within a larger culture. Members of the subculture share some values with the larger culture, but have other values that are unique to their group. People of the same income (B), education (C), age (D), or gender (E) do not necessarily share the same values.

128. **(B)** Cooley's theory of the "looking-glass-self" maintains that our perceptions of others' actions toward us are a key factor in developing our self-concepts. Mead (A), Freud (C), Piaget (D), and Kohlberg (E) do not place similar emphasis on the individual's perceptions of others' reactions.

129. **(D)** Hunting and gathering societies are characterized by small size, low level technology, equal status among adults, lack of strong authority figures, and consensus on values. There is little difference in wealth (C) or occupation (B) and there is no centralized government (E).

130. **(C)** While a higher percentage of African-Americans live in poverty, the largest number of poor people are white. While many single mothers (E) are poor, they are not a majority of poor Americans. The poverty rate for the elderly (B) is about the same as the national average—13%.

ANSWER SHEETS

PRACTICE TEST 1: College Composition Answer Sheet

CONVENTIONS OF STANDARD WRITTEN ENGLISH

1. Ⓐ Ⓑ Ⓒ Ⓓ Ⓔ 4. Ⓐ Ⓑ Ⓒ Ⓓ Ⓔ

2. Ⓐ Ⓑ Ⓒ Ⓓ Ⓔ 5. Ⓐ Ⓑ Ⓒ Ⓓ Ⓔ

3. Ⓐ Ⓑ Ⓒ Ⓓ Ⓔ

REVISION SKILLS

1. Ⓐ Ⓑ Ⓒ Ⓓ Ⓔ 6. Ⓐ Ⓑ Ⓒ Ⓓ Ⓔ 11. Ⓐ Ⓑ Ⓒ Ⓓ Ⓔ 16. Ⓐ Ⓑ Ⓒ Ⓓ Ⓔ

2. Ⓐ Ⓑ Ⓒ Ⓓ Ⓔ 7. Ⓐ Ⓑ Ⓒ Ⓓ Ⓔ 12. Ⓐ Ⓑ Ⓒ Ⓓ Ⓔ 17. Ⓐ Ⓑ Ⓒ Ⓓ Ⓔ

3. Ⓐ Ⓑ Ⓒ Ⓓ Ⓔ 8. Ⓐ Ⓑ Ⓒ Ⓓ Ⓔ 13. Ⓐ Ⓑ Ⓒ Ⓓ Ⓔ 18. Ⓐ Ⓑ Ⓒ Ⓓ Ⓔ

4. Ⓐ Ⓑ Ⓒ Ⓓ Ⓔ 9. Ⓐ Ⓑ Ⓒ Ⓓ Ⓔ 14. Ⓐ Ⓑ Ⓒ Ⓓ Ⓔ 19. Ⓐ Ⓑ Ⓒ Ⓓ Ⓔ

5. Ⓐ Ⓑ Ⓒ Ⓓ Ⓔ 10. Ⓐ Ⓑ Ⓒ Ⓓ Ⓔ 15. Ⓐ Ⓑ Ⓒ Ⓓ Ⓔ 20. Ⓐ Ⓑ Ⓒ Ⓓ Ⓔ

ABILITY TO USE SOURCE MATERIALS

1. Ⓐ Ⓑ Ⓒ Ⓓ Ⓔ 4. Ⓐ Ⓑ Ⓒ Ⓓ Ⓔ 7. Ⓐ Ⓑ Ⓒ Ⓓ Ⓔ 10. Ⓐ Ⓑ Ⓒ Ⓓ Ⓔ

2. Ⓐ Ⓑ Ⓒ Ⓓ Ⓔ 5. Ⓐ Ⓑ Ⓒ Ⓓ Ⓔ 8. Ⓐ Ⓑ Ⓒ Ⓓ Ⓔ 11. Ⓐ Ⓑ Ⓒ Ⓓ Ⓔ

3. Ⓐ Ⓑ Ⓒ Ⓓ Ⓔ 6. Ⓐ Ⓑ Ⓒ Ⓓ Ⓔ 9. Ⓐ Ⓑ Ⓒ Ⓓ Ⓔ 12. Ⓐ Ⓑ Ⓒ Ⓓ Ⓔ

RHETORICAL ANALYSIS

1. Ⓐ Ⓑ Ⓒ Ⓓ Ⓔ 6. Ⓐ Ⓑ Ⓒ Ⓓ Ⓔ 11. Ⓐ Ⓑ Ⓒ Ⓓ Ⓔ

2. Ⓐ Ⓑ Ⓒ Ⓓ Ⓔ 7. Ⓐ Ⓑ Ⓒ Ⓓ Ⓔ 12. Ⓐ Ⓑ Ⓒ Ⓓ Ⓔ

3. Ⓐ Ⓑ Ⓒ Ⓓ Ⓔ 8. Ⓐ Ⓑ Ⓒ Ⓓ Ⓔ 13. Ⓐ Ⓑ Ⓒ Ⓓ Ⓔ

4. Ⓐ Ⓑ Ⓒ Ⓓ Ⓔ 9. Ⓐ Ⓑ Ⓒ Ⓓ Ⓔ

5. Ⓐ Ⓑ Ⓒ Ⓓ Ⓔ 10. Ⓐ Ⓑ Ⓒ Ⓓ Ⓔ

PRACTICE TEST 1: College Composition Modular Answer Sheet

CONVENTIONS OF STANDARD WRITTEN ENGLISH

1. (A) (B) (C) (D) (E)   4. (A) (B) (C) (D) (E)   7. (A) (B) (C) (D) (E)
2. (A) (B) (C) (D) (E)   5. (A) (B) (C) (D) (E)   8. (A) (B) (C) (D) (E)
3. (A) (B) (C) (D) (E)   6. (A) (B) (C) (D) (E)   9. (A) (B) (C) (D) (E)

REVISION SKILLS

1. (A) (B) (C) (D) (E)   10. (A) (B) (C) (D) (E)   19. (A) (B) (C) (D) (E)   28. (A) (B) (C) (D) (E)
2. (A) (B) (C) (D) (E)   11. (A) (B) (C) (D) (E)   20. (A) (B) (C) (D) (E)   29. (A) (B) (C) (D) (E)
3. (A) (B) (C) (D) (E)   12. (A) (B) (C) (D) (E)   21. (A) (B) (C) (D) (E)   30. (A) (B) (C) (D) (E)
4. (A) (B) (C) (D) (E)   13. (A) (B) (C) (D) (E)   22. (A) (B) (C) (D) (E)   31. (A) (B) (C) (D) (E)
5. (A) (B) (C) (D) (E)   14. (A) (B) (C) (D) (E)   23. (A) (B) (C) (D) (E)   32. (A) (B) (C) (D) (E)
6. (A) (B) (C) (D) (E)   15. (A) (B) (C) (D) (E)   24. (A) (B) (C) (D) (E)   33. (A) (B) (C) (D) (E)
7. (A) (B) (C) (D) (E)   16. (A) (B) (C) (D) (E)   25. (A) (B) (C) (D) (E)   34. (A) (B) (C) (D) (E)
8. (A) (B) (C) (D) (E)   17. (A) (B) (C) (D) (E)   26. (A) (B) (C) (D) (E)   35. (A) (B) (C) (D) (E)
9. (A) (B) (C) (D) (E)   18. (A) (B) (C) (D) (E)   27. (A) (B) (C) (D) (E)   36. (A) (B) (C) (D) (E)

ABILITY TO USE SOURCE MATERIALS

1. (A) (B) (C) (D) (E)   7. (A) (B) (C) (D) (E)   13. (A) (B) (C) (D) (E)   19. (A) (B) (C) (D) (E)
2. (A) (B) (C) (D) (E)   8. (A) (B) (C) (D) (E)   14. (A) (B) (C) (D) (E)   20. (A) (B) (C) (D) (E)
3. (A) (B) (C) (D) (E)   9. (A) (B) (C) (D) (E)   15. (A) (B) (C) (D) (E)   21. (A) (B) (C) (D) (E)
4. (A) (B) (C) (D) (E)   10. (A) (B) (C) (D) (E)   16. (A) (B) (C) (D) (E)   22. (A) (B) (C) (D) (E)
5. (A) (B) (C) (D) (E)   11. (A) (B) (C) (D) (E)   17. (A) (B) (C) (D) (E)
6. (A) (B) (C) (D) (E)   12. (A) (B) (C) (D) (E)   18. (A) (B) (C) (D) (E)

RHETORICAL ANALYSIS

1. Ⓐ Ⓑ Ⓒ Ⓓ Ⓔ   7. Ⓐ Ⓑ Ⓒ Ⓓ Ⓔ   13. Ⓐ Ⓑ Ⓒ Ⓓ Ⓔ   19. Ⓐ Ⓑ Ⓒ Ⓓ Ⓔ

2. Ⓐ Ⓑ Ⓒ Ⓓ Ⓔ   8. Ⓐ Ⓑ Ⓒ Ⓓ Ⓔ   14. Ⓐ Ⓑ Ⓒ Ⓓ Ⓔ   20. Ⓐ Ⓑ Ⓒ Ⓓ Ⓔ

3. Ⓐ Ⓑ Ⓒ Ⓓ Ⓔ   9. Ⓐ Ⓑ Ⓒ Ⓓ Ⓔ   15. Ⓐ Ⓑ Ⓒ Ⓓ Ⓔ   21. Ⓐ Ⓑ Ⓒ Ⓓ Ⓔ

4. Ⓐ Ⓑ Ⓒ Ⓓ Ⓔ   10. Ⓐ Ⓑ Ⓒ Ⓓ Ⓔ   16. Ⓐ Ⓑ Ⓒ Ⓓ Ⓔ   22. Ⓐ Ⓑ Ⓒ Ⓓ Ⓔ

5. Ⓐ Ⓑ Ⓒ Ⓓ Ⓔ   11. Ⓐ Ⓑ Ⓒ Ⓓ Ⓔ   17. Ⓐ Ⓑ Ⓒ Ⓓ Ⓔ   23. Ⓐ Ⓑ Ⓒ Ⓓ Ⓔ

6. Ⓐ Ⓑ Ⓒ Ⓓ Ⓔ   12. Ⓐ Ⓑ Ⓒ Ⓓ Ⓔ   18. Ⓐ Ⓑ Ⓒ Ⓓ Ⓔ

PRACTICE TEST 1: Humanities Answer Sheet

1. Ⓐ Ⓑ Ⓒ Ⓓ Ⓔ
2. Ⓐ Ⓑ Ⓒ Ⓓ Ⓔ
3. Ⓐ Ⓑ Ⓒ Ⓓ Ⓔ
4. Ⓐ Ⓑ Ⓒ Ⓓ Ⓔ
5. Ⓐ Ⓑ Ⓒ Ⓓ Ⓔ
6. Ⓐ Ⓑ Ⓒ Ⓓ Ⓔ
7. Ⓐ Ⓑ Ⓒ Ⓓ Ⓔ
8. Ⓐ Ⓑ Ⓒ Ⓓ Ⓔ
9. Ⓐ Ⓑ Ⓒ Ⓓ Ⓔ
10. Ⓐ Ⓑ Ⓒ Ⓓ Ⓔ
11. Ⓐ Ⓑ Ⓒ Ⓓ Ⓔ
12. Ⓐ Ⓑ Ⓒ Ⓓ Ⓔ
13. Ⓐ Ⓑ Ⓒ Ⓓ Ⓔ
14. Ⓐ Ⓑ Ⓒ Ⓓ Ⓔ
15. Ⓐ Ⓑ Ⓒ Ⓓ Ⓔ
16. Ⓐ Ⓑ Ⓒ Ⓓ Ⓔ
17. Ⓐ Ⓑ Ⓒ Ⓓ Ⓔ
18. Ⓐ Ⓑ Ⓒ Ⓓ Ⓔ
19. Ⓐ Ⓑ Ⓒ Ⓓ Ⓔ
20. Ⓐ Ⓑ Ⓒ Ⓓ Ⓔ
21. Ⓐ Ⓑ Ⓒ Ⓓ Ⓔ
22. Ⓐ Ⓑ Ⓒ Ⓓ Ⓔ
23. Ⓐ Ⓑ Ⓒ Ⓓ Ⓔ
24. Ⓐ Ⓑ Ⓒ Ⓓ Ⓔ
25. Ⓐ Ⓑ Ⓒ Ⓓ Ⓔ

26. Ⓐ Ⓑ Ⓒ Ⓓ Ⓔ
27. Ⓐ Ⓑ Ⓒ Ⓓ Ⓔ
28. Ⓐ Ⓑ Ⓒ Ⓓ Ⓔ
29. Ⓐ Ⓑ Ⓒ Ⓓ Ⓔ
30. Ⓐ Ⓑ Ⓒ Ⓓ Ⓔ
31. Ⓐ Ⓑ Ⓒ Ⓓ Ⓔ
32. Ⓐ Ⓑ Ⓒ Ⓓ Ⓔ
33. Ⓐ Ⓑ Ⓒ Ⓓ Ⓔ
34. Ⓐ Ⓑ Ⓒ Ⓓ Ⓔ
35. Ⓐ Ⓑ Ⓒ Ⓓ Ⓔ
36. Ⓐ Ⓑ Ⓒ Ⓓ Ⓔ
37. Ⓐ Ⓑ Ⓒ Ⓓ Ⓔ
38. Ⓐ Ⓑ Ⓒ Ⓓ Ⓔ
39. Ⓐ Ⓑ Ⓒ Ⓓ Ⓔ
40. Ⓐ Ⓑ Ⓒ Ⓓ Ⓔ
41. Ⓐ Ⓑ Ⓒ Ⓓ Ⓔ
42. Ⓐ Ⓑ Ⓒ Ⓓ Ⓔ
43. Ⓐ Ⓑ Ⓒ Ⓓ Ⓔ
44. Ⓐ Ⓑ Ⓒ Ⓓ Ⓔ
45. Ⓐ Ⓑ Ⓒ Ⓓ Ⓔ
46. Ⓐ Ⓑ Ⓒ Ⓓ Ⓔ
47. Ⓐ Ⓑ Ⓒ Ⓓ Ⓔ
48. Ⓐ Ⓑ Ⓒ Ⓓ Ⓔ
49. Ⓐ Ⓑ Ⓒ Ⓓ Ⓔ
50. Ⓐ Ⓑ Ⓒ Ⓓ Ⓔ

51. Ⓐ Ⓑ Ⓒ Ⓓ Ⓔ
52. Ⓐ Ⓑ Ⓒ Ⓓ Ⓔ
53. Ⓐ Ⓑ Ⓒ Ⓓ Ⓔ
54. Ⓐ Ⓑ Ⓒ Ⓓ Ⓔ
55. Ⓐ Ⓑ Ⓒ Ⓓ Ⓔ
56. Ⓐ Ⓑ Ⓒ Ⓓ Ⓔ
57. Ⓐ Ⓑ Ⓒ Ⓓ Ⓔ
58. Ⓐ Ⓑ Ⓒ Ⓓ Ⓔ
59. Ⓐ Ⓑ Ⓒ Ⓓ Ⓔ
60. Ⓐ Ⓑ Ⓒ Ⓓ Ⓔ
61. Ⓐ Ⓑ Ⓒ Ⓓ Ⓔ
62. Ⓐ Ⓑ Ⓒ Ⓓ Ⓔ
63. Ⓐ Ⓑ Ⓒ Ⓓ Ⓔ
64. Ⓐ Ⓑ Ⓒ Ⓓ Ⓔ
65. Ⓐ Ⓑ Ⓒ Ⓓ Ⓔ
66. Ⓐ Ⓑ Ⓒ Ⓓ Ⓔ
67. Ⓐ Ⓑ Ⓒ Ⓓ Ⓔ
68. Ⓐ Ⓑ Ⓒ Ⓓ Ⓔ
69. Ⓐ Ⓑ Ⓒ Ⓓ Ⓔ
70. Ⓐ Ⓑ Ⓒ Ⓓ Ⓔ
71. Ⓐ Ⓑ Ⓒ Ⓓ Ⓔ
72. Ⓐ Ⓑ Ⓒ Ⓓ Ⓔ
73. Ⓐ Ⓑ Ⓒ Ⓓ Ⓔ
74. Ⓐ Ⓑ Ⓒ Ⓓ Ⓔ
75. Ⓐ Ⓑ Ⓒ Ⓓ Ⓔ

76. Ⓐ Ⓑ Ⓒ Ⓓ Ⓔ
77. Ⓐ Ⓑ Ⓒ Ⓓ Ⓔ
78. Ⓐ Ⓑ Ⓒ Ⓓ Ⓔ
79. Ⓐ Ⓑ Ⓒ Ⓓ Ⓔ
80. Ⓐ Ⓑ Ⓒ Ⓓ Ⓔ
81. Ⓐ Ⓑ Ⓒ Ⓓ Ⓔ
82. Ⓐ Ⓑ Ⓒ Ⓓ Ⓔ
83. Ⓐ Ⓑ Ⓒ Ⓓ Ⓔ
84. Ⓐ Ⓑ Ⓒ Ⓓ Ⓔ
85. Ⓐ Ⓑ Ⓒ Ⓓ Ⓔ
86. Ⓐ Ⓑ Ⓒ Ⓓ Ⓔ
87. Ⓐ Ⓑ Ⓒ Ⓓ Ⓔ
88. Ⓐ Ⓑ Ⓒ Ⓓ Ⓔ
89. Ⓐ Ⓑ Ⓒ Ⓓ Ⓔ
90. Ⓐ Ⓑ Ⓒ Ⓓ Ⓔ
91. Ⓐ Ⓑ Ⓒ Ⓓ Ⓔ
92. Ⓐ Ⓑ Ⓒ Ⓓ Ⓔ
93. Ⓐ Ⓑ Ⓒ Ⓓ Ⓔ
94. Ⓐ Ⓑ Ⓒ Ⓓ Ⓔ
95. Ⓐ Ⓑ Ⓒ Ⓓ Ⓔ
96. Ⓐ Ⓑ Ⓒ Ⓓ Ⓔ
97. Ⓐ Ⓑ Ⓒ Ⓓ Ⓔ
98. Ⓐ Ⓑ Ⓒ Ⓓ Ⓔ
99. Ⓐ Ⓑ Ⓒ Ⓓ Ⓔ
100. Ⓐ Ⓑ Ⓒ Ⓓ Ⓔ

101. Ⓐ Ⓑ Ⓒ Ⓓ Ⓔ   111. Ⓐ Ⓑ Ⓒ Ⓓ Ⓔ   121. Ⓐ Ⓑ Ⓒ Ⓓ Ⓔ   131. Ⓐ Ⓑ Ⓒ Ⓓ Ⓔ

102. Ⓐ Ⓑ Ⓒ Ⓓ Ⓔ   112. Ⓐ Ⓑ Ⓒ Ⓓ Ⓔ   122. Ⓐ Ⓑ Ⓒ Ⓓ Ⓔ   132. Ⓐ Ⓑ Ⓒ Ⓓ Ⓔ

103. Ⓐ Ⓑ Ⓒ Ⓓ Ⓔ   113. Ⓐ Ⓑ Ⓒ Ⓓ Ⓔ   123. Ⓐ Ⓑ Ⓒ Ⓓ Ⓔ   133. Ⓐ Ⓑ Ⓒ Ⓓ Ⓔ

104. Ⓐ Ⓑ Ⓒ Ⓓ Ⓔ   114. Ⓐ Ⓑ Ⓒ Ⓓ Ⓔ   124. Ⓐ Ⓑ Ⓒ Ⓓ Ⓔ   134. Ⓐ Ⓑ Ⓒ Ⓓ Ⓔ

105. Ⓐ Ⓑ Ⓒ Ⓓ Ⓔ   115. Ⓐ Ⓑ Ⓒ Ⓓ Ⓔ   125. Ⓐ Ⓑ Ⓒ Ⓓ Ⓔ   135. Ⓐ Ⓑ Ⓒ Ⓓ Ⓔ

106. Ⓐ Ⓑ Ⓒ Ⓓ Ⓔ   116. Ⓐ Ⓑ Ⓒ Ⓓ Ⓔ   126. Ⓐ Ⓑ Ⓒ Ⓓ Ⓔ   136. Ⓐ Ⓑ Ⓒ Ⓓ Ⓔ

107. Ⓐ Ⓑ Ⓒ Ⓓ Ⓔ   117. Ⓐ Ⓑ Ⓒ Ⓓ Ⓔ   127. Ⓐ Ⓑ Ⓒ Ⓓ Ⓔ   137. Ⓐ Ⓑ Ⓒ Ⓓ Ⓔ

108. Ⓐ Ⓑ Ⓒ Ⓓ Ⓔ   118. Ⓐ Ⓑ Ⓒ Ⓓ Ⓔ   128. Ⓐ Ⓑ Ⓒ Ⓓ Ⓔ   138. Ⓐ Ⓑ Ⓒ Ⓓ Ⓔ

109. Ⓐ Ⓑ Ⓒ Ⓓ Ⓔ   119. Ⓐ Ⓑ Ⓒ Ⓓ Ⓔ   129. Ⓐ Ⓑ Ⓒ Ⓓ Ⓔ   139. Ⓐ Ⓑ Ⓒ Ⓓ Ⓔ

110. Ⓐ Ⓑ Ⓒ Ⓓ Ⓔ   120. Ⓐ Ⓑ Ⓒ Ⓓ Ⓔ   130. Ⓐ Ⓑ Ⓒ Ⓓ Ⓔ   140. Ⓐ Ⓑ Ⓒ Ⓓ Ⓔ

PRACTICE TEST 1: Mathematics
Answer Sheet

1. Ⓐ Ⓑ Ⓒ Ⓓ
2. Ⓐ Ⓑ Ⓒ Ⓓ
3. Ⓐ Ⓑ Ⓒ Ⓓ
4. [   ]
5. Ⓐ Ⓑ Ⓒ Ⓓ
6. Ⓐ Ⓑ Ⓒ Ⓓ
7. Ⓐ Ⓑ Ⓒ Ⓓ
8. Ⓐ Ⓑ Ⓒ Ⓓ
9. Ⓐ Ⓑ Ⓒ Ⓓ
10. Ⓐ Ⓑ Ⓒ Ⓓ
11. [   ]
12. Ⓐ Ⓑ Ⓒ Ⓓ
13. Ⓐ Ⓑ Ⓒ Ⓓ
14. Ⓐ Ⓑ Ⓒ Ⓓ
15. Ⓐ Ⓑ Ⓒ Ⓓ

16. [   ]
17. Ⓐ Ⓑ Ⓒ Ⓓ
18. [   ]
19. Ⓐ Ⓑ Ⓒ Ⓓ
20. Ⓐ Ⓑ Ⓒ Ⓓ
21. Ⓐ Ⓑ Ⓒ Ⓓ
22. Ⓐ Ⓑ Ⓒ Ⓓ
23. Ⓐ Ⓑ Ⓒ Ⓓ
24. Ⓐ Ⓑ Ⓒ Ⓓ
25. Ⓐ Ⓑ Ⓒ Ⓓ
26. Ⓐ Ⓑ Ⓒ Ⓓ
27. Ⓐ Ⓑ Ⓒ Ⓓ
28. Ⓐ Ⓑ Ⓒ Ⓓ
29. Ⓐ Ⓑ Ⓒ Ⓓ
30. [   ]

31. Ⓐ Ⓑ Ⓒ Ⓓ
32. Ⓐ Ⓑ Ⓒ Ⓓ
33. Ⓐ Ⓑ Ⓒ Ⓓ
34. Ⓐ Ⓑ Ⓒ Ⓓ
35. Ⓐ Ⓑ Ⓒ Ⓓ
36. Ⓐ Ⓑ Ⓒ Ⓓ
37. Ⓐ Ⓑ Ⓒ Ⓓ
38. Ⓐ Ⓑ Ⓒ Ⓓ
39. Ⓐ Ⓑ Ⓒ Ⓓ
40. Ⓐ Ⓑ Ⓒ Ⓓ
41. [   ]
42. Ⓐ Ⓑ Ⓒ Ⓓ
43. Ⓐ Ⓑ Ⓒ Ⓓ
44. Ⓐ Ⓑ Ⓒ Ⓓ
45. Ⓐ Ⓑ Ⓒ Ⓓ

46. Ⓐ Ⓑ Ⓒ Ⓓ
47. Ⓐ Ⓑ Ⓒ Ⓓ
48. Ⓐ Ⓑ Ⓒ Ⓓ
49. Ⓐ Ⓑ Ⓒ Ⓓ
50. Ⓐ Ⓑ Ⓒ Ⓓ
51. Ⓐ Ⓑ Ⓒ Ⓓ
52. [   ]
53. Ⓐ Ⓑ Ⓒ Ⓓ
54. Ⓐ Ⓑ Ⓒ Ⓓ
55. Ⓐ Ⓑ Ⓒ Ⓓ
56. Ⓐ Ⓑ Ⓒ Ⓓ
57. [   ]
58. Ⓐ Ⓑ Ⓒ Ⓓ
59. [   ]
60. Ⓐ Ⓑ Ⓒ Ⓓ

PRACTICE TEST 1: Natural Sciences
Answer Sheet

1. Ⓐ Ⓑ Ⓒ Ⓓ Ⓔ
2. Ⓐ Ⓑ Ⓒ Ⓓ Ⓔ
3. Ⓐ Ⓑ Ⓒ Ⓓ Ⓔ
4. Ⓐ Ⓑ Ⓒ Ⓓ Ⓔ
5. Ⓐ Ⓑ Ⓒ Ⓓ Ⓔ
6. Ⓐ Ⓑ Ⓒ Ⓓ Ⓔ
7. Ⓐ Ⓑ Ⓒ Ⓓ Ⓔ
8. Ⓐ Ⓑ Ⓒ Ⓓ Ⓔ
9. Ⓐ Ⓑ Ⓒ Ⓓ Ⓔ
10. Ⓐ Ⓑ Ⓒ Ⓓ Ⓔ
11. Ⓐ Ⓑ Ⓒ Ⓓ Ⓔ
12. Ⓐ Ⓑ Ⓒ Ⓓ Ⓔ
13. Ⓐ Ⓑ Ⓒ Ⓓ Ⓔ
14. Ⓐ Ⓑ Ⓒ Ⓓ Ⓔ
15. Ⓐ Ⓑ Ⓒ Ⓓ Ⓔ
16. Ⓐ Ⓑ Ⓒ Ⓓ Ⓔ
17. Ⓐ Ⓑ Ⓒ Ⓓ Ⓔ
18. Ⓐ Ⓑ Ⓒ Ⓓ Ⓔ
19. Ⓐ Ⓑ Ⓒ Ⓓ Ⓔ
20. Ⓐ Ⓑ Ⓒ Ⓓ Ⓔ
21. Ⓐ Ⓑ Ⓒ Ⓓ Ⓔ
22. Ⓐ Ⓑ Ⓒ Ⓓ Ⓔ
23. Ⓐ Ⓑ Ⓒ Ⓓ Ⓔ
24. Ⓐ Ⓑ Ⓒ Ⓓ Ⓔ
25. Ⓐ Ⓑ Ⓒ Ⓓ Ⓔ

26. Ⓐ Ⓑ Ⓒ Ⓓ Ⓔ
27. Ⓐ Ⓑ Ⓒ Ⓓ Ⓔ
28. Ⓐ Ⓑ Ⓒ Ⓓ Ⓔ
29. Ⓐ Ⓑ Ⓒ Ⓓ Ⓔ
30. Ⓐ Ⓑ Ⓒ Ⓓ Ⓔ
31. Ⓐ Ⓑ Ⓒ Ⓓ Ⓔ
32. Ⓐ Ⓑ Ⓒ Ⓓ Ⓔ
33. Ⓐ Ⓑ Ⓒ Ⓓ Ⓔ
34. Ⓐ Ⓑ Ⓒ Ⓓ Ⓔ
35. Ⓐ Ⓑ Ⓒ Ⓓ Ⓔ
36. Ⓐ Ⓑ Ⓒ Ⓓ Ⓔ
37. Ⓐ Ⓑ Ⓒ Ⓓ Ⓔ
38. Ⓐ Ⓑ Ⓒ Ⓓ Ⓔ
39. Ⓐ Ⓑ Ⓒ Ⓓ Ⓔ
40. Ⓐ Ⓑ Ⓒ Ⓓ Ⓔ
41. Ⓐ Ⓑ Ⓒ Ⓓ Ⓔ
42. Ⓐ Ⓑ Ⓒ Ⓓ Ⓔ
43. Ⓐ Ⓑ Ⓒ Ⓓ Ⓔ
44. Ⓐ Ⓑ Ⓒ Ⓓ Ⓔ
45. Ⓐ Ⓑ Ⓒ Ⓓ Ⓔ
46. Ⓐ Ⓑ Ⓒ Ⓓ Ⓔ
47. Ⓐ Ⓑ Ⓒ Ⓓ Ⓔ
48. Ⓐ Ⓑ Ⓒ Ⓓ Ⓔ
49. Ⓐ Ⓑ Ⓒ Ⓓ Ⓔ
50. Ⓐ Ⓑ Ⓒ Ⓓ Ⓔ

51. Ⓐ Ⓑ Ⓒ Ⓓ Ⓔ
52. Ⓐ Ⓑ Ⓒ Ⓓ Ⓔ
53. Ⓐ Ⓑ Ⓒ Ⓓ Ⓔ
54. Ⓐ Ⓑ Ⓒ Ⓓ Ⓔ
55. Ⓐ Ⓑ Ⓒ Ⓓ Ⓔ
56. Ⓐ Ⓑ Ⓒ Ⓓ Ⓔ
57. Ⓐ Ⓑ Ⓒ Ⓓ Ⓔ
58. Ⓐ Ⓑ Ⓒ Ⓓ Ⓔ
59. Ⓐ Ⓑ Ⓒ Ⓓ Ⓔ
60. Ⓐ Ⓑ Ⓒ Ⓓ Ⓔ
61. Ⓐ Ⓑ Ⓒ Ⓓ Ⓔ
62. Ⓐ Ⓑ Ⓒ Ⓓ Ⓔ
63. Ⓐ Ⓑ Ⓒ Ⓓ Ⓔ
64. Ⓐ Ⓑ Ⓒ Ⓓ Ⓔ
65. Ⓐ Ⓑ Ⓒ Ⓓ Ⓔ
66. Ⓐ Ⓑ Ⓒ Ⓓ Ⓔ
67. Ⓐ Ⓑ Ⓒ Ⓓ Ⓔ
68. Ⓐ Ⓑ Ⓒ Ⓓ Ⓔ
69. Ⓐ Ⓑ Ⓒ Ⓓ Ⓔ
70. Ⓐ Ⓑ Ⓒ Ⓓ Ⓔ
71. Ⓐ Ⓑ Ⓒ Ⓓ Ⓔ
72. Ⓐ Ⓑ Ⓒ Ⓓ Ⓔ
73. Ⓐ Ⓑ Ⓒ Ⓓ Ⓔ
74. Ⓐ Ⓑ Ⓒ Ⓓ Ⓔ
75. Ⓐ Ⓑ Ⓒ Ⓓ Ⓔ

76. Ⓐ Ⓑ Ⓒ Ⓓ Ⓔ
77. Ⓐ Ⓑ Ⓒ Ⓓ Ⓔ
78. Ⓐ Ⓑ Ⓒ Ⓓ Ⓔ
79. Ⓐ Ⓑ Ⓒ Ⓓ Ⓔ
80. Ⓐ Ⓑ Ⓒ Ⓓ Ⓔ
81. Ⓐ Ⓑ Ⓒ Ⓓ Ⓔ
82. Ⓐ Ⓑ Ⓒ Ⓓ Ⓔ
83. Ⓐ Ⓑ Ⓒ Ⓓ Ⓔ
84. Ⓐ Ⓑ Ⓒ Ⓓ Ⓔ
85. Ⓐ Ⓑ Ⓒ Ⓓ Ⓔ
86. Ⓐ Ⓑ Ⓒ Ⓓ Ⓔ
87. Ⓐ Ⓑ Ⓒ Ⓓ Ⓔ
88. Ⓐ Ⓑ Ⓒ Ⓓ Ⓔ
89. Ⓐ Ⓑ Ⓒ Ⓓ Ⓔ
90. Ⓐ Ⓑ Ⓒ Ⓓ Ⓔ
91. Ⓐ Ⓑ Ⓒ Ⓓ Ⓔ
92. Ⓐ Ⓑ Ⓒ Ⓓ Ⓔ
93. Ⓐ Ⓑ Ⓒ Ⓓ Ⓔ
94. Ⓐ Ⓑ Ⓒ Ⓓ Ⓔ
95. Ⓐ Ⓑ Ⓒ Ⓓ Ⓔ
96. Ⓐ Ⓑ Ⓒ Ⓓ Ⓔ
97. Ⓐ Ⓑ Ⓒ Ⓓ Ⓔ
98. Ⓐ Ⓑ Ⓒ Ⓓ Ⓔ
99. Ⓐ Ⓑ Ⓒ Ⓓ Ⓔ
100. Ⓐ Ⓑ Ⓒ Ⓓ Ⓔ

101. Ⓐ Ⓑ Ⓒ Ⓓ Ⓔ	106. Ⓐ Ⓑ Ⓒ Ⓓ Ⓔ	111. Ⓐ Ⓑ Ⓒ Ⓓ Ⓔ	116. Ⓐ Ⓑ Ⓒ Ⓓ Ⓔ
102. Ⓐ Ⓑ Ⓒ Ⓓ Ⓔ	107. Ⓐ Ⓑ Ⓒ Ⓓ Ⓔ	112. Ⓐ Ⓑ Ⓒ Ⓓ Ⓔ	117. Ⓐ Ⓑ Ⓒ Ⓓ Ⓔ
103. Ⓐ Ⓑ Ⓒ Ⓓ Ⓔ	108. Ⓐ Ⓑ Ⓒ Ⓓ Ⓔ	113. Ⓐ Ⓑ Ⓒ Ⓓ Ⓔ	118. Ⓐ Ⓑ Ⓒ Ⓓ Ⓔ
104. Ⓐ Ⓑ Ⓒ Ⓓ Ⓔ	109. Ⓐ Ⓑ Ⓒ Ⓓ Ⓔ	114. Ⓐ Ⓑ Ⓒ Ⓓ Ⓔ	119. Ⓐ Ⓑ Ⓒ Ⓓ Ⓔ
105. Ⓐ Ⓑ Ⓒ Ⓓ Ⓔ	110. Ⓐ Ⓑ Ⓒ Ⓓ Ⓔ	115. Ⓐ Ⓑ Ⓒ Ⓓ Ⓔ	120. Ⓐ Ⓑ Ⓒ Ⓓ Ⓔ

PRACTICE TEST 1: Social Sciences
Answer Sheet

1. Ⓐ Ⓑ Ⓒ Ⓓ Ⓔ
2. Ⓐ Ⓑ Ⓒ Ⓓ Ⓔ
3. Ⓐ Ⓑ Ⓒ Ⓓ Ⓔ
4. Ⓐ Ⓑ Ⓒ Ⓓ Ⓔ
5. Ⓐ Ⓑ Ⓒ Ⓓ Ⓔ
6. Ⓐ Ⓑ Ⓒ Ⓓ Ⓔ
7. Ⓐ Ⓑ Ⓒ Ⓓ Ⓔ
8. Ⓐ Ⓑ Ⓒ Ⓓ Ⓔ
9. Ⓐ Ⓑ Ⓒ Ⓓ Ⓔ
10. Ⓐ Ⓑ Ⓒ Ⓓ Ⓔ
11. Ⓐ Ⓑ Ⓒ Ⓓ Ⓔ
12. Ⓐ Ⓑ Ⓒ Ⓓ Ⓔ
13. Ⓐ Ⓑ Ⓒ Ⓓ Ⓔ
14. Ⓐ Ⓑ Ⓒ Ⓓ Ⓔ
15. Ⓐ Ⓑ Ⓒ Ⓓ Ⓔ
16. Ⓐ Ⓑ Ⓒ Ⓓ Ⓔ
17. Ⓐ Ⓑ Ⓒ Ⓓ Ⓔ
18. Ⓐ Ⓑ Ⓒ Ⓓ Ⓔ
19. Ⓐ Ⓑ Ⓒ Ⓓ Ⓔ
20. Ⓐ Ⓑ Ⓒ Ⓓ Ⓔ
21. Ⓐ Ⓑ Ⓒ Ⓓ Ⓔ
22. Ⓐ Ⓑ Ⓒ Ⓓ Ⓔ
23. Ⓐ Ⓑ Ⓒ Ⓓ Ⓔ
24. Ⓐ Ⓑ Ⓒ Ⓓ Ⓔ
25. Ⓐ Ⓑ Ⓒ Ⓓ Ⓔ

26. Ⓐ Ⓑ Ⓒ Ⓓ Ⓔ
27. Ⓐ Ⓑ Ⓒ Ⓓ Ⓔ
28. Ⓐ Ⓑ Ⓒ Ⓓ Ⓔ
29. Ⓐ Ⓑ Ⓒ Ⓓ Ⓔ
30. Ⓐ Ⓑ Ⓒ Ⓓ Ⓔ
31. Ⓐ Ⓑ Ⓒ Ⓓ Ⓔ
32. Ⓐ Ⓑ Ⓒ Ⓓ Ⓔ
33. Ⓐ Ⓑ Ⓒ Ⓓ Ⓔ
34. Ⓐ Ⓑ Ⓒ Ⓓ Ⓔ
35. Ⓐ Ⓑ Ⓒ Ⓓ Ⓔ
36. Ⓐ Ⓑ Ⓒ Ⓓ Ⓔ
37. Ⓐ Ⓑ Ⓒ Ⓓ Ⓔ
38. Ⓐ Ⓑ Ⓒ Ⓓ Ⓔ
39. Ⓐ Ⓑ Ⓒ Ⓓ Ⓔ
40. Ⓐ Ⓑ Ⓒ Ⓓ Ⓔ
41. Ⓐ Ⓑ Ⓒ Ⓓ Ⓔ
42. Ⓐ Ⓑ Ⓒ Ⓓ Ⓔ
43. Ⓐ Ⓑ Ⓒ Ⓓ Ⓔ
44. Ⓐ Ⓑ Ⓒ Ⓓ Ⓔ
45. Ⓐ Ⓑ Ⓒ Ⓓ Ⓔ
46. Ⓐ Ⓑ Ⓒ Ⓓ Ⓔ
47. Ⓐ Ⓑ Ⓒ Ⓓ Ⓔ
48. Ⓐ Ⓑ Ⓒ Ⓓ Ⓔ
49. Ⓐ Ⓑ Ⓒ Ⓓ Ⓔ
50. Ⓐ Ⓑ Ⓒ Ⓓ Ⓔ

51. Ⓐ Ⓑ Ⓒ Ⓓ Ⓔ
52. Ⓐ Ⓑ Ⓒ Ⓓ Ⓔ
53. Ⓐ Ⓑ Ⓒ Ⓓ Ⓔ
54. Ⓐ Ⓑ Ⓒ Ⓓ Ⓔ
55. Ⓐ Ⓑ Ⓒ Ⓓ Ⓔ
56. Ⓐ Ⓑ Ⓒ Ⓓ Ⓔ
57. Ⓐ Ⓑ Ⓒ Ⓓ Ⓔ
58. Ⓐ Ⓑ Ⓒ Ⓓ Ⓔ
59. Ⓐ Ⓑ Ⓒ Ⓓ Ⓔ
60. Ⓐ Ⓑ Ⓒ Ⓓ Ⓔ
61. Ⓐ Ⓑ Ⓒ Ⓓ Ⓔ
62. Ⓐ Ⓑ Ⓒ Ⓓ Ⓔ
63. Ⓐ Ⓑ Ⓒ Ⓓ Ⓔ
64. Ⓐ Ⓑ Ⓒ Ⓓ Ⓔ
65. Ⓐ Ⓑ Ⓒ Ⓓ Ⓔ
66. Ⓐ Ⓑ Ⓒ Ⓓ Ⓔ
67. Ⓐ Ⓑ Ⓒ Ⓓ Ⓔ
68. Ⓐ Ⓑ Ⓒ Ⓓ Ⓔ
69. Ⓐ Ⓑ Ⓒ Ⓓ Ⓔ
70. Ⓐ Ⓑ Ⓒ Ⓓ Ⓔ
71. Ⓐ Ⓑ Ⓒ Ⓓ Ⓔ
72. Ⓐ Ⓑ Ⓒ Ⓓ Ⓔ
73. Ⓐ Ⓑ Ⓒ Ⓓ Ⓔ
74. Ⓐ Ⓑ Ⓒ Ⓓ Ⓔ
75. Ⓐ Ⓑ Ⓒ Ⓓ Ⓔ

76. Ⓐ Ⓑ Ⓒ Ⓓ Ⓔ
77. Ⓐ Ⓑ Ⓒ Ⓓ Ⓔ
78. Ⓐ Ⓑ Ⓒ Ⓓ Ⓔ
79. Ⓐ Ⓑ Ⓒ Ⓓ Ⓔ
80. Ⓐ Ⓑ Ⓒ Ⓓ Ⓔ
81. Ⓐ Ⓑ Ⓒ Ⓓ Ⓔ
82. Ⓐ Ⓑ Ⓒ Ⓓ Ⓔ
83. Ⓐ Ⓑ Ⓒ Ⓓ Ⓔ
84. Ⓐ Ⓑ Ⓒ Ⓓ Ⓔ
85. Ⓐ Ⓑ Ⓒ Ⓓ Ⓔ
86. Ⓐ Ⓑ Ⓒ Ⓓ Ⓔ
87. Ⓐ Ⓑ Ⓒ Ⓓ Ⓔ
88. Ⓐ Ⓑ Ⓒ Ⓓ Ⓔ
89. Ⓐ Ⓑ Ⓒ Ⓓ Ⓔ
90. Ⓐ Ⓑ Ⓒ Ⓓ Ⓔ
91. Ⓐ Ⓑ Ⓒ Ⓓ Ⓔ
92. Ⓐ Ⓑ Ⓒ Ⓓ Ⓔ
93. Ⓐ Ⓑ Ⓒ Ⓓ Ⓔ
94. Ⓐ Ⓑ Ⓒ Ⓓ Ⓔ
95. Ⓐ Ⓑ Ⓒ Ⓓ Ⓔ
96. Ⓐ Ⓑ Ⓒ Ⓓ Ⓔ
97. Ⓐ Ⓑ Ⓒ Ⓓ Ⓔ
98. Ⓐ Ⓑ Ⓒ Ⓓ Ⓔ
99. Ⓐ Ⓑ Ⓒ Ⓓ Ⓔ
100. Ⓐ Ⓑ Ⓒ Ⓓ Ⓔ

101. Ⓐ Ⓑ Ⓒ Ⓓ Ⓔ   106. Ⓐ Ⓑ Ⓒ Ⓓ Ⓔ   111. Ⓐ Ⓑ Ⓒ Ⓓ Ⓔ   116. Ⓐ Ⓑ Ⓒ Ⓓ Ⓔ

102. Ⓐ Ⓑ Ⓒ Ⓓ Ⓔ   107. Ⓐ Ⓑ Ⓒ Ⓓ Ⓔ   112. Ⓐ Ⓑ Ⓒ Ⓓ Ⓔ   117. Ⓐ Ⓑ Ⓒ Ⓓ Ⓔ

103. Ⓐ Ⓑ Ⓒ Ⓓ Ⓔ   108. Ⓐ Ⓑ Ⓒ Ⓓ Ⓔ   113. Ⓐ Ⓑ Ⓒ Ⓓ Ⓔ   118. Ⓐ Ⓑ Ⓒ Ⓓ Ⓔ

104. Ⓐ Ⓑ Ⓒ Ⓓ Ⓔ   109. Ⓐ Ⓑ Ⓒ Ⓓ Ⓔ   114. Ⓐ Ⓑ Ⓒ Ⓓ Ⓔ   119. Ⓐ Ⓑ Ⓒ Ⓓ Ⓔ

105. Ⓐ Ⓑ Ⓒ Ⓓ Ⓔ   110. Ⓐ Ⓑ Ⓒ Ⓓ Ⓔ   115. Ⓐ Ⓑ Ⓒ Ⓓ Ⓔ   120. Ⓐ Ⓑ Ⓒ Ⓓ Ⓔ

EXTRA PRACTICE

121. Ⓐ Ⓑ Ⓒ Ⓓ Ⓔ   124. Ⓐ Ⓑ Ⓒ Ⓓ Ⓔ   127. Ⓐ Ⓑ Ⓒ Ⓓ Ⓔ   129. Ⓐ Ⓑ Ⓒ Ⓓ Ⓔ

122. Ⓐ Ⓑ Ⓒ Ⓓ Ⓔ   125. Ⓐ Ⓑ Ⓒ Ⓓ Ⓔ   128. Ⓐ Ⓑ Ⓒ Ⓓ Ⓔ   130. Ⓐ Ⓑ Ⓒ Ⓓ Ⓔ

123. Ⓐ Ⓑ Ⓒ Ⓓ Ⓔ   126. Ⓐ Ⓑ Ⓒ Ⓓ Ⓔ

NOTES

NOTES

NOTES

NOTES

NOTES

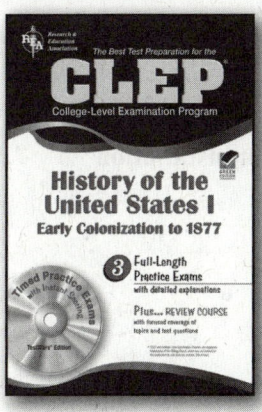

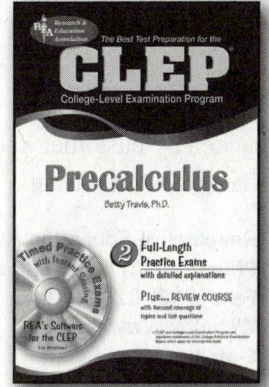

INSTALLING REA's TestWare®

SYSTEM REQUIREMENTS

Pentium 75 MHz (300 MHz recommended) or a higher or compatible process. Microsoft Windows 98 or later; 64 MB Available RAM; Internet Explorer 5.5 or higher.

INSTALLATION

1. Insert the CLEP TestWare® CD-ROM into the CD-ROM drive.

2. If the installation doesn't begin automatically from the Start Menu choose the RUN command. When the Run dialog box appears, type d:\setup (where d is the letter of your CD-ROM drive) at the prompt and click OK.

3. The installation process will begin. A dialog box proposing the directory "Program Files\ REA\CLEP" will appear. If the name and location are suitable, click OK. If you wish to specify a different name or location, type it in and click OK.

4. Start the CLEP TestWare® application by double-clicking on the icon.

REA's CLEP TestWare® is EASY TO LEARN AND USE. To achieve maximum benefits, we recommend that you take a few minutes to go through the on-screen tutorial on your computer.

SSD ACCOMMODATIONS FOR STUDENTS WITH DISABILITIES

Many students qualify for extra time to take CLEP exams, and our TestWare® can be adapted to accommodate your extension. This allows you to practice under the same extended-time accommodations that you will receive on the actual test day. To customize your TestWare® to suit the most common extensions, visit our website at *www.rea.com/ssd*.

TECHNICAL SUPPORT

REA's TestWare® is backed by customer and technical support. For questions about **installation or operation of your software**, contact us at:

Research & Education Association
Phone: (732) 819-8880 (9 a.m. to 5 p.m. ET, Monday–Friday)
Fax: (732) 819-8808
Website: www.rea.com
E-mail: info@rea.com

Note to Windows XP Users: In order for the TestWare® to function properly, please install and run the application under the same computer administrator-level user account. Installing the TestWare® as one user and running it as another could cause file-access path conflicts.